INTERNATIONAL BIBLIOGRAPHY OF THEATRE: 1983

Sponsored by   The American Society for Theatre Research, and

The International Association of Libraries and Museums
of the Performing Arts

In cooperation with The International Federation for Theatre Research

International Bibliography of Theatre: 1983

Published by the Theatre Research Data Center, Brooklyn College, City University of New York, NY 11210

Distributed by the Publishing Center for Cultural Resources, 625 Broadway, New York, NY 10012

© Theatre Research Data Center, 1986: ISSN 0882-9446; ISBN 0-89062-219-1. All rights reserved.

The paper used in this book complies with the Permanent Paper Standard issued by the National Information Standards Organization (Z39.48-1984).

This publication was made possible in part by grants from the National Endowment for the Humanities, the American Society for Theatre Research, and in-kind support and services provided by Brooklyn College of the City University of New York.

INTERNATIONAL BIBLIOGRAPHY OF THEATRE: 1983

Benito Ortolani, Editor

BIBLIOGRAPHY PROJECT STAFF

Associate Editor: Margaret Loftus Ranald   **Assistant Editor:** Aviv Orani

Technical Editor: Jeff Reynolds

THEATRE RESEARCH DATA CENTER

Director: Irving M. Brown   **Systems Analyst:** Rosabel A. Wang

Staff: Vanessa Christman, Catherine Hilton, Hélène Kuttner, Donna Mehle, Richard Ruskell

INTERNATIONAL BIBLIOGRAPHY OF THEATRE: 1983

TABLE OF CONTENTS

PREFACE

IBT:1983 represents a substantial advance over last year's pilot volume, *IBT:1982*, which was a first step toward the establishment of a functional, computerized classification system for the total field of theatre and toward the development of a long-needed comprehensive tool of research. The pilot volume was expected to elicit corrective comments, since it was a venture into virgin territory. We were not disappointed. Colleagues have responded generously both with data and critical analysis.

As a result, this present volume, *IBT:1983*, incorporates recommendations received from a number of national and international authorities, particularly the members of the International Bibliography Commission of SIBMAS. The changes affect three main areas: coverage, classification systems, and indexes.

COVERAGE.   *IBT:1983* includes citations from theatre periodicals in Catalan, English, French, German, Italian, Polish, Russian, Scandinavian languages and Spanish, as well as books published in Austria, Canada, England, France, East and West Germany, Italy, Poland, the Soviet Union, Spain, and the United States. The 1982 volume relied heavily on scholars from its country of origin, the United States of America, who furnished data from materials readily available to them. As a result there was a significantly smaller coverage of European scholarship. Now, through the efforts of SIBMAS and many individual foreign colleagues *IBT:1983* provides a much more comprehensive picture of the international contribution to theatre scholarship. With this increasing scholarly support we anticipate that the next bibliography will include extensive listings for a number of nations which are still under-represented, such as Hungary, India, Israel, Japan, Poland, Yugoslavia, and the Soviet Union.

CLASSIFICATION SYSTEMS.   Changes in the taxonomy have been designed to simplify the basic classification scheme, while maintaining a consistent logic.

Classed entries are now organized into three columns. Column One and its subset Column Two reflect a specific form or genre of the performance medium. Column Three further defines the specific field or nature of the research demonstrated in the cited document.

Changes from *IBT:1982:*

> Column One of the 1983 taxonomy includes only the major categories of theatrical performance.

> The heterogeneous categories of Reference Materials, Basic Theatrical Documents and Individuals have been transferred to other parts of the Bibliography. Reference Materials and Basic Theatrical Documents have been moved to Column Three to indicate the specific aspect of the particular theatre type, which itself is classified in accordance with the categories of Column One and its subset Column Two.

> Individuals, including the names of listed production personnel, theorists, playwrights, composers, philosophers, etc., are now to be found in the Subject Index.

> Column Four in the *IBT:1982* taxonomy no longer exists as a separate entity, but its headings appear as lead entries in the Subject Index. This change was made in order to eliminate the splintering of Classed Entries into many blocks too small for general comprehension. Column Five in the *IBT:1982* taxonomy does not print as a separate entity. Its material appears in the abstract accompanying each entry and is used as a definition of the primary purpose and scope of each citation.

INDEXES. A major overhaul of the Indexes was undertaken with the aim of facilitating direct and comprehensive access to all entries.

The Subject Index is no longer a supplement to the process of finding an entry but a basic mode of access to all materials contained in the Classed Entries. For instance, every entry related to a person, without consideration of importance or number of citations, is now found under the name of the individual in the Subject Index. Further to facilitate access, the Subject Index also prints the subdivisional category of Column Three for every subject heading included in the Index. All of the categories of Columns Three and Four in the *IBT:1982* taxonomy are also to be found as subject headings in the Subject Index. The categories of Column Two are incorporated into the Subject Index with "SEE ALSO" references.

A new Geographical-Chronological Index replaces the Document Content Geography Index of *IBT:1982*. Now the entire body of the entries is arranged first by the country of the subject or topic treated, then subdivided chronologically, with a Column Three category listed for each citation.

The Document Authors Index, which provides access to every entry through an alphabetical listing by the last name of the author of the referenced material, remains unchanged. A Guide for Users, together with the modified Taxonomy, appears in the introductory pages following the acknowledgments.

We look forward to the development of a stable, universally effective taxonomy through this series of bibliographies, appreciating the need for regular evaluation of our annual efforts. From these evaluations we will be able to respond more fully to the requirements and wishes of the scholarly community with each succeeding issue of the International Bibliography of Theatre.

ACKNOWLEDGMENTS

We express our gratitude to the many institutions and individuals who made this volume possible, particularly:

The members and the leaders of ASTR, especially President Kalman Burnim and past President Joseph Donohue, the Executive Committees and the Committee on Research;

President Robert Hess and the Theatre Department of Brooklyn College, City University of New York;

President Harald Zielske of SIBMAS;

The Republic of Austria, Ministry of Science and Research;

President William Green and the University Commission of FIRT;

Dr. Heinrich Heusmann, Deutsches Theatermuseum, Munich;

Prof. Wolfgang Greisenegger, Institut für Theaterwissenschaft, University of Vienna;

Dr. Alessandro Tinterri, Museo Biblioteca dell'Attore di Genova;

Charles Boeheim and Betsey Jackson, SPIRES Consortium, Stanford University;

Benjamin S. Klein, Pat Reber, and Dominick Sciusco of the CUNY/University Computer Center;

Pat Shadle, Program Specialist, Division of Research Programs, National Endowment for the Humanities.

Prof. William Gargan, Library, Brooklyn College, City University of New York

Prof. Barbara Sheeran. Librarty, Brooklyn College, City University of New York

ACKNOWLEDGMENTS—Cont'd

Special thanks to those who generously offered suggestions:

Gertrud Dolata and Dr. Werner Meder of the Gesellschaft für Information und Dokumentation MBH, Frankfurt am Main;

Dr. Gabriele Fischborn, Theaterhochschule "Hans Otto," Leipzig;

SIBMAS (Britain), especially Ian Herbert and Dr. Lindsay Newman;

SIBMAS (International Bibliography Commission), especially Dr. Otto Schindler, Chair, and:
    Annie Bethery, École Nationale Supérieure de Bibliothécaires, Paris;
    Magnus Blomkvist, Stockholms Universitets Bibliotek;
    Marie-Françoise Christout, Bibliothèque Nationale, Paris;
    Paul Emond, Archives et Musée de la Litterature A.S.B.L., Brussels;
    Cécile Giteau, Bibliothèque Nationale, Paris;
    Dr. Rainer Maria-Köppl, University of Vienna;
    Pirkko Koski, Teatterimuseo, Helsinki;
    Silvia Maurer, Schweizerische Theatersammlung, Bern;
    Prof. André Veinstein, Bibliothèque Nationale, Paris;
    Dr. Zbigniew Wilski, Polska Akademia Nauk Instytut Sztuki, Warsaw;

Prof. Felicia Londré, University of Missouri–Kansas City;

Prof. Thomas Postlewait, University of Georgia;

Dorothy Swerdlove, The Billy Rose Theatre Collection of the New York Public Library;

Prof. Barry Brook, RILM, Graduate Center of the City University of New York; and

Prof. Hélène Volat-Shapiro, State University of New York, Stonybrook.

Finally, we thank our hard working field bibliographers whose contributions have made this work a reality. Their names follow,

Arnold Aronson	University of Delaware
Patrick Atkinson	University of Missouri
Laura Barbieri	Museo Biblioteca dell'Attore, Genoa
Sri Ram V. Bakshi	State University of New York, Brockport
Jerry Bangham	Alcorn State University
Dan Barto	New York, NY
Will Bellman	California State University, Northridge
Thomas L. Berger	St. Lawrence University
Maurizio Bosco	Museo Biblioteca dell'Attore, Genoa
Jane Brittain	Leicester Polytechnic
John W. Brokaw	University of Texas, Austin
Monica Burdex	California State University, Northridge
Marvin Carlson	Graduate Center, City University of New York
David Cheshire	Middlesex Polytechnic
Oh-kon Cho	State University of New York, Brockport
VèVè Clark	Tufts University
Johnnye L. Cope	North Texas State University, Denton
Moisés Pérez Coterillo	Centro Nacional de Documentacion Teatral, Madrid
Barry Daniels	Kent State University
Angela Douglas	Central School of Speech and Drama
Weldon B. Durham	University of Missouri
Dorothy Faulkner	Dartington College of Arts
Mari Kathleen Fielder	Santa Monica, CA
Linda Fitzsimmons	University College of North Wales
Kathy Foley	University of California, Santa Cruz
Marian J. Fordom	Royal Scottish Academy of Music and Drama

Liz Fugate	University of Washington, Seattle
Paul J. Gaffney	University of Texas, Austin
Steven H. Gale	Missouri Southern State College
Arturo García Giménez	Institut del Teatre, Barcelona
Guillem-Jori Graells	Museu de les Arts de l'Espectacle, Barcelona
Constance F. Gremore	College of St. Thomas
Ian Herbert	London Theatre Record
Frank S. Hook	Lehigh University
Frederick J. Hunter	University of Texas, Austin
Stephen Johnson	University of Guelph
Gerhard Knewitz	University of Vienna
Christine King	State University of New York, Stony Brook
Ann Marie Koller	Palo Alto, CA
Pirkko Koski	Teatterimuseo, Helsinki
Rainer-Maria Köppl	University of Vienna
Werner Kropik	University of Vienna
Ludmila Lévina	State Central Theatre Library, Moscow
Julia Martin	Liverpool Institute of Higher Education
Jack W. McCullough	Trenton State College
Barbara Mittman	University of Illinois, Chicago
William Nelson	Carnegie-Mellon University
Lindsay M. Newman	University of Lancaster
Richard Plant	Queens University, Kingston
Renata Quartini	Museo Biblioteca dell'Attore, Genoa
Nicholas F. Radel	St. Lawrence University
Margaret Loftus Ranald	Queens College, City University of New York
Maarten A. Reilingh	New York, NY
John W. Robinson	University of Nebraska, Lincoln
Bari Rolfe	Oakland, CA
Patricia Sandback	San Diego State University
Otto G. Schindler	University of Vienna
Linda Schroeder	La Mesa, CA
Freda Scott	City College, City University of New York
Eleanor Silvis-Milton	University of Pittsburgh, Greensburg
Susan Tuck	Sherbourne, MA
Ronald W. Vince	McMaster University
Paul D. Voelker	University of Wisconsin Center, Richland
Hélène Volat-Shapiro	State University of New York, Stony Brook
Carla Waal	University of Missouri
Richard Wall	Queens College, City University of New York
Lisa C. Warren	Roanoke College
Daniel Watermeier	University of Toledo
Harold A. Waters	University of Rhode Island
Margaret Watson	Sunderland Polytechnic
Margaret B. Wilkerson	University of California, Berkeley
Zbigniew Wilski	Polska Akademia Nauk Instytut Sztuki

A GUIDE FOR USERS

SCOPE

The *International Bibliography of Theatre: 1983* contains entries for books, book articles, dissertations, journal articles, and miscellaneous theatre documents published during 1982 (which were not included in the *IBT:1982*) and 1983. The Bibliography includes all aspects of theatre significant to research, without historic, cultural, or geographic limitations. Published works (with the exceptions noted below) are included without restriction on the internal organization, format, or purpose of those works. Entries evolve from materials that include theatre histories, essays, studies, surveys, conference papers and proceedings, catalogues of theatrical holdings of any type, portfolios, handbooks and guides, dictionaries, bibliographies, thesauruses and other reference works, records and production documents. The term "production documents" should be taken to include non-verbal theatrical artifacts such as scene and costume designs, lighting plots, and materials relating to production and design disseminated through the agency of media other than print.

Generally, only newly published documents are included, though revised editions of previously published works are considered new works. Reprints of previously published works are usually excluded unless they represent significant documents which have been unavailable. Literary studies, textual studies, and dissertations are selectively represented, and then only when they contain significant components that examine or reflect on theatrical performance. Purely literary scholarship is excluded since it is already listed in established bibliographical instruments. Playtexts are included when they are particularly important for theatre research, as when the playtext is published with extensive or especially noteworthy introductory material, or when it is the first translation or adaptation of a classic into a major language from an especially rare language. Book reviews and reviews of performances are not included, except for those reviews of sufficient scope to constitute a review article. There is no restriction upon the language in which the data appear. English is the primary vehicle for compiling the materials. The Subject Index, however, gives primary importance to titles in their original language. Original language titles also appear (at least once) in items of the Classed Entries that involve plays in translation.

CLASSED ENTRIES

The Classed Entries section contains one entry for each document analyzed in this edition of the Bibliography. It differs from the Subject Index in which an item description appears as many times as it has subject headings. Items are arranged sequentially, with numbers attached, based on an item's classification according to the Taxonomy (see Basic Classification Systems, next page). Within each category they are also arranged alphabetically according to the content geographical designation. Entries with no country appear first.

The Classed Entries section provides the user with complete information on all material indexed in this volume. It is the only place where publication citations may be found, and where detailed abstracts may be furnished. Users are advised to familiarize themselves with the workings of the Taxonomy, to simplify the process of locating items indexed in the Classed Entries section. When in doubt concerning the appropriate category for a search, the user should refer to the Subject Index for direction. The Classed Entries section does not duplicate the Subject Index. On the contrary, the Subject Index provides additional points of access to the Classed Entries section.

The Taxonomy (See next page)

Column One classifies theatre into eleven categories, beginning with Theatre in General and ranging alphabetically from "Dance" to "Ritual-Ceremony." Column Two divides each of the eleven categories into a number of smaller components. Column Three headings relate each of the previously selected fields to specific areas of the theatre. The forth column, Subject Headings, is a list of possibilities for the Subject Index.

THE TWO BASIC CLASSIFICATION SYSTEMS

THE TAXONOMY OF THEATRE
(organizing structure for the Classed Entries)

Column One	Column Two	Column Three
THEATRE IN GENERAL	Comprehensive	Administration
	Multiple application	
DANCE	General	
	Ballet	
	Ethnic dance	
	Modern dance	
DANCE-DRAMA	General	Audience
	Kabuki	
	Kathakali	
	Nō	
		Basic theatrical documents
DRAMA	General	
	Comedy	
	Experimental forms	
	Tragedy	
MEDIA	General	Design/technology
	Audio forms	
	Film	
	Video forms	
MIME	General	
	Pantomime	
MIXED PERFORMANCES	General	
	Court Masque	
	Performance art	
MUSIC-DRAMA	General	Institutions
	Musical theatre	
	Opera	
	Operetta	
POPULAR ENTERTAINMENT	General	Performance/production
	Cabaret	
	Carnival	
	Circus	
	Commedia dell'arte	
	Pageants/parades	
	Variety acts	

THE SUBJECT INDEX
(the alphabetical list of subject headings)

Related Subject Headings

Agents
Financial operations
Fundraising
Legal aspects
Personnel
Planning/organization
Public relations

Audience composition
Audience/performer relationship
Audience reactions/comments

Choreographies
Film treatments/scores
Librettos
Miscellaneous texts
Playtexts
Scores
Promptbooks

Camera work/projection
Costuming
Equipment
Lighting
Make-up
Masks
Properties
Puppets
Scenery
Sound
Technicians/crews
Wigs

Institutions, associations
  producing
  research
  service
  social
  special
  training

Acting
Choreography
Dance
Music
Performance management
Puppeteers
Singing
Staging

Column One	Column Two	Column Three
	Performance spaces	Amphitheatres/arenas
		Found spaces
		Halls
		Religious structures
		Show boats
		Theatres
	Plays/librettos/scripts	Adaptations
		Characters/roles
		Dramatizations
		Dramatic structure
		Editions
		Language
		Plot/subject/theme
	Reference materials	Bibliographies
		Catalogues
		Collected materials
		Databanks
		Descriptions of resources
		Dictionaries
		Discographies
		Encyclopedias
		Glossaries
		Guides
		Iconographies
		Indexes
		Lists
		Videographies
		Yearbooks
	Relation to other fields	Anthropology
		Economics
		Education
		Ethics
		Literature
		Figurative arts
		Philosophy
		Politics
		Psychology
		Religion
		Sociology
	Research/historiography	Methodology
		Research tools
	Theory/criticism	Aesthetics
		Deconstruction
		Dialectics
		Phenomenology
		Semiotics
		Semantics
	Training	Apprenticeship
		Teaching methods
PUPPETRY	General	
	Bunraku	
	Marionettes	
	Shadow puppets	
RITUAL-CEREMONY	General	
	Civic	
	Religious	

—NOTE—

1) Column Two divisions are the subsets of the related Column One entries

2) Column Three divisions are the subsets of any Column Two category

3) The above items print in the CLASSED ENTRIES.

4) The Related Subject Headings-a small fraction of the total subject headings actually used-are organized in small groups representing a further subdivision of the related Column Three headings at their left. They print only in the SUBJECT INDEX.

Arrangement of Entries

Items classified under the Column One heading "Theatre in General" appear first before those classified under Column One heading "Dance," etc.

Items classified under the Column Two heading of "Music-drama: Musical theatre" appear before those classified under the Column Two heading of "Music-drama: Opera, etc."

Items further classified under the Column Three heading of "Administration" appear before those classified under "Design/technology," etc.

Each group of items under any of the divisions of the Classed Entries is printed according to the alphabetic order of their content geography: e.g., all items with geography primarily related to Japan in the section classified under "Drama: General," and subdivided into "Plays/librettos/scripts" are printed together, after items related to Italy and before those related to Malaysia.

Description of Taxonomy Terms

The following descriptions have been established to clarify the terminology used in classifying data via the Taxonomy. These descriptions reflect the understanding of the IBT editorial staff for this edition, and are not meant to serve as definitions of the terms involved. Their appearance here is for purposes of clarification only, as a searching tool for users of the Bibliography. In cases where clarification has been deemed unnecessary (as in the case of "Ballet," "*Kabuki*," "Film," etc.) no further description appears below. Throughout the Classed Entries, the term "General" distinguishes miscellaneous items that cannot be more specifically classified by the remaining terms in the Column Two category.

> **THEATRE IN GENERAL:** Only for items which cannot be properly classified by categories "Dance" through "Ritual-Ceremony." Such items are related either to all ten theatrical categories, or to more than one.

>> **Comprehensive:** Items encompassing all or most areas of theatre. Under "Comprehensive" are to be found all items belonging to the category of "Theatre in General" with Column Three classification of "Basic theatrical documents," "Reference materials," "Relation to other fields," "Research/historiography," and "Theory/criticism."

>> **Multiple Application:** Items focusing on one particular element of theatre which can be applied to two or more of the categories "Dance" through "Ritual-Ceremony." Under "Multiple application" are to be found all items belonging to the category of "Theatre in General" with Column Three classification of "Administration," "Audience," "Design/technology," "Institutions," "Performance/production," "Performance spaces," "Plays/librettos/scripts," and "Training." Examples of the kinds of materials indexed here are:

>> (a) Administration: a document concerning business operation of theatre.
>> (b) Audience: a document concerning the composition of audiences.
>> (c) Design/technology: a document concerning the design or technical aspect of production.
>> (d) Institutions: a document concerning the activity of one or more theatrical companies.
>> (e) Performance/production: a study of an actor or other theatre professional who was active in more than one theatrical category: drama, music-drama, media, etc.
>> (f) Performance spaces: a document concerning a space used in more than one kind of theatrical performance.
>> (g) Training: a document concerning a school training performers, technicians, etc. for work in more than one theatrical mode.

> **DANCE:** Items pertaining to dance as a separate form of theatre. Only those documents with relevance to theatre as a phenomenon are indexed.

> **DANCE-DRAMA:** Items related to theatrical genres where dance is traditionally considered the dominant element. Used primarily for specific forms of non- Western theatre.

> **DRAMA:** Items related to playtexts and performances of them where the spoken word is traditionally considered the dominant element. (i.e., all Western dramatic literature and all spoken drama everywhere.) An article on acting as a discipline will also fall into this category, as well as books about directing, unless these endeavors are more closely related to musical theatre forms or other genres. Playtexts, when included, will be indexed under "Basic Theatrical Documents:"

A GUIDE FOR USERS—Cont'd

General: Items that cannot be more specifically categorized by the terms listed below. Because of the great variety of meanings given to such terms as melodrama, tragicomedy, domestic drama, etc., the term "General" is used in this area whenever "Comedy," "Experimental forms," or "Tragedy" do not obviously apply.

Comedy: Items related to plays that are traditionally and commonly called "comedies," including farce, and other humorous plays with a happy ending. When the issue of classification in this category is disputable, the term "General" is used.

Experimental forms: Items related to forms that are commonly called "experimental," both in the past (such as Futuristic or Dadaist performances), or in the present (such as the work of Grotowski, or the Japanese *angura* performances).

Tragedy: Items related to plays that are traditionally and commonly called "tragedies." When the issue of classification in this category is disputable, the category "General" is used.

MEDIA: Items related to performances of a theatrical nature conveyed through media.

MIME: Items related to performances where mime is the dominant element. This category comprises all forms of mime from every epoch and/or country.

Pantomime: Performance form epitomized in modern times by Etienne Decroux and Marcel Marceau. Roman pantomime is indexed here. Eighteenth century English pantomime is indexed under "Popular Entertainment/General."

MIXED PERFORMANCES: Items related to performances consisting of a variety of elements, among which none is considered dominant.

Court Masque: Items related to seventeenth century performances that used music, dance, and other dramatic forms in the context of court pageantry.

Performance art: Items related to a hybrid form of performance which combines visual arts, theatre, dance, music, poetry and ritual, and is usually presented outside traditional theatre venues.

MUSIC DRAMA: Items related to theatrical genres where the element of music is traditionally considered dominant.

Musical theatre: Items related to musical comedies and similar performances. Revues, variété, floor shows etc. are indexed under "Popular Entertainment."

Opera: Items related to opera in its various forms, including opera buffa, opera da camera, etc.

Operetta: Items primarily related to operetta, a lighter entertainment falling somewhere between opera and musical comedy. Includes Hungarian and Viennese forms known by this name, as well as the Spanish Zarzuela.

POPULAR ENTERTAINMENT: Items related to performances where the element of spectacle and the function of broad audience appeal are dominant. Because of the great variety of terminology in different circumstances, times, and countries for similar types of spectacle, such items as café-chantant, café-concert, quadrille réaliste, one-man-shows, night club acts, pleasure gardens, tavern concerts, night cellars, saloons, Spezialitätentheater, storytelling, divertissement, rivistina, etc. are classified under "General," "Variety acts," or "Cabaret," etc. depending on time period, circumstances, and/or country. Sufficient subject headings enable users to locate the item regardless of how it is indexed here.

Variety acts: Items related to variety entertainment of mostly unconnected "numbers," including some forms of vaudeville, revue, petite revue, intimate revue, burlesque, etc.

PUPPETRY: Items related to all kinds of puppets, marionettes, and mechanically operated figures.

RITUAL-CEREMONY: Items related to the theatrical aspects of religious and/or civic ceremonies.

Notice that entries related to individuals are classified according to the Column Three category describing their primary field of activity: e.g., a manager under "Administration," a set designer under "Design/technology," an actor under "Performance/production," a playwright under "Plays/librettos/scripts," a teacher under "Training," etc.

A GUIDE FOR USERS—Cont'd

Citation

Each citation includes the standard bibliographical information: author(s), title, publisher, pages, and notes, preface, appendixes, etc., when appropriate. Journal titles are usually in the form of an acronym, for which see the List of Periodicals. Pertinent additional information is provided in square brackets.

When the title is not in English, a translation in parentheses follows the original title. Established English translations of play titles or names of institutions are used when they exist. Geographical names are given in standard English form as defined by *Webster's New Geographical Dictionary* (1984). Names of institutions, companies, buildings, etc., unless an English version is in common use, are as a rule left untranslated.

An indication of the time and place to which a document pertains is included wherever appropriate and possible. The geographical information refers usually to a country, sometimes to a larger region such as the Middle East or English-speaking countries. The geographical information is relative to the time of the content: Russia is used before 1917; East and West Germany after 1945; Roman Empire until its official demise, Italy thereafter. When appropriate, a precise date related to the content of the item is given. Otherwise the decade(s) or the century(ies) are indicated.

Unless the content of a document is sufficiently clear from the title, the classed entry provides a brief abstract. Titles of plays not in English are given in English translation in the abstract, except for most operas and titles that are widely know in their original language. If the original title does not appear in the document title, it is provided in the abstract, in parentheses following the English title. English form is used for transliterated personal names. In the subject index, each English spelling refers the user to the international spelling, under which all relevant entries are listed.

Affiliation with a group or movement and influence by or on individuals or groups is indicated only when the document itself suggests such information. When a document belongs to more than one Column 1 category of the taxonomy, the entry may be cross-referenced to the other applicable Column 1 category.

Here follows an example (in this case a book article) of a Classed Entries item with explanation of its elements:

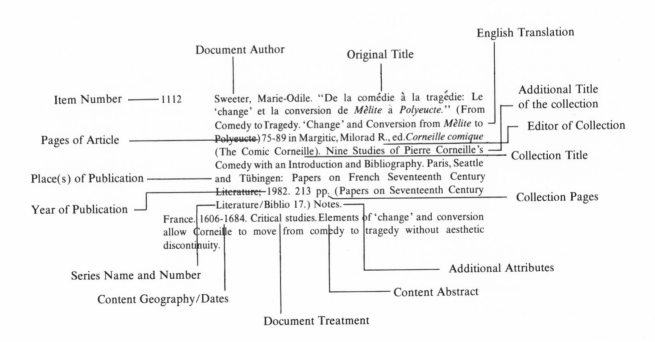

A GUIDE FOR USERS—Cont'd

"Document treatment" indicates the type of scholarly approach used in the writing of the document. The following terms are used in the present bibliography:

Bibliographical studies treat as their primary object bibliographic material.
Biographical studies are articles on part of the subject's life.
Biographies are in most cases a book-length treatment of an entire life.
Critical studies present an evaluation resulting from the application of criteria.
Empirical research designates studies that incorporate as part of their design an experiment or series of experiments.
Historical studies are brief treatments of one or a few events.
Histories-general cover the whole spectrum of theatre—or most of it—over a period of time and typically appear in one or several volumes.
Histories-specific cover a particular genre, institution, or component of theatre.
Histories-sources treat source documents that are not primarily critical or historiographical in nature.
Histories-reconstruction attempt to reconstruct some aspect of the theatre.
Instructional materials include textbooks, manuals, guides or any other publication to be used as a pedagogical device.
Linguistic studies deal with issues pertaining to the meaning or value of the language itself, not to textual accuracy.
Technical studies examine theatre from the point of view of the applied sciences or discuss particular theatrical techniques.
Textual studies examine the texts themselves for origins, accuracy, and the like, not evaluation.

SUBJECT INDEX

The Subject Index is an additional means of access to all materials contained in the Classed Entries section. In many cases it will guide the user to the appropriate section of the bibliography.

The Subject Index contains names of persons, names of institutions, forms and genres of theatre, and terms from the taxonomy other than those used to classify the document in the Classed Entries section. At the end of each short abstract a number is given to direct the researcher to the relevant citation in the Classed Entries section.

NOTE: To locate the complete data relevant to areas of interest, both the Subject Index and the Classed Entries should be consulted.

Names of persons, including titles of address, are listed alphabetically by last name, according to the standard established in *Anglo-American Cataloguing Rules* (Library of Congress, 2nd edition, 1978). Names from Greek and Roman Antiquity follow the standard established by Sir William Smith, *Classical Dictionary* (1958). All terms originating in non-Roman alphabets, including Russian, Greek, Chinese and Japanese have been transliterated. Geographical names are spelled according to *Webster's New Geographical Dictionary* (1984). "See" references direct users from common English spelling to names or terms indexed in a less familiar manner.

> **Example:** Chekhov, see Čechov.

Individuals are listed in the Subject Index when:

    (a) they are the primary or secondary focus of the document;
    (b) when the document addresses aspects of their life and/or work in a primary or supporting manner;
    (c) when he or she is the author of the document, but only when his or her life and/or work is also the document's primary focus;
    (d) when his or her life has influenced (or has been influenced by) the primary subject of the document, or the writing of it, as evidenced by explicit statement.

This index is particularly useful when a listed individual is the subject of numerous citations. In such cases a search should not be limited only to the main subject heading (e.g. Shakespeare). A more specific one (e.g. Hamlet) could bring quicker and better results.

A GUIDE FOR USERS—Cont'd

SUBJECT INDEX, cont.

Institutions, groups, and social or theatrical movements appear as subject headings, following the above criteria. Names of theatre companies, theatre buildings, etc. are given in their original languages, or transliterated. "See" references are provided only when an English term for them is in current and general use:

> **Example:** "Moscow Art Theatre" directs users to the company's title of origin:
> "Moskovskij Chudožestvennyj Akademičeskij Teat'r."
> No commonly used English term exists for "Comédie-Française," and it therefore appears under its title of origin.

Play titles appear in their original languages, with "see" references next to their English translations. Subject headings of plays in a third language may exist if the translation of the play in that third language is of primary importance to the finding of it in the Subject Index. Opera titles are not translated.

Subject headings such as "Politics" and "Political theatre" are neither synonymous nor mutually exclusive. They aim to differentiate between a phenomenon and a theatrical genre. Likewise, such terms as "Feminism" refer to social and cultural movements and are not intended to be synonomous with "Women in theatre." The term "Ethnic theatre" is used to classify any type of theatrical literature or performance where the ethnicity of those concerned is of primary importance. Because of the number of items, and for reasons of accessibility, "Black theatre," "Native American theatre" and the theatre of certain other ethnic groups are given separate subject headings.

Generic subject headings such as "Victorian theatre," "Expressionism" etc. are only complementary to other more specific groupings and do not list all items in the bibliography related to that period or generic subject: e.g. the subject heading "Elizabethan theatre" does not list a duplicate of all items related to Shakespeare, which are to be found under "Shakespeare," but lists materials explicitly related to the actual physical conditions or style of presentation typical of the Elizabethan theatre. For a complete search according to periods, use the Geographical-Chronological Index, searching by country and by the years related to the period.

The short abstracts under each subject heading are arranged sequentially according to the item number they refer to in the Classed Entries. This will enable the frequent user to recognize immediately the location and classification of the entry. When you do not find a subject heading you think should be there, try a related term: e.g. for Church dramas, see Religious theatre. In some cases, a see reference is provided. A thesaurus of related terms is in the making, but not yet available.

Notice that in each group under each subject heading the short abstracts are ordered according to the number of the related Classed Entries items. This will enable the frequent user to recognize immediately the location and classification of the entry.

Here follows an example of a subject heading with explanation of its elements:

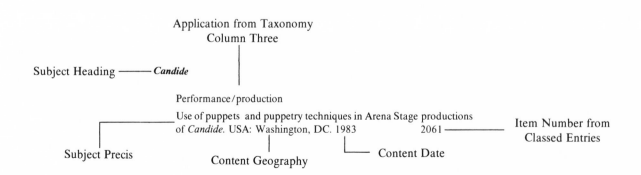

A GUIDE FOR USERS—Cont'd

GEOGRAPHICAL-CHRONOLOGICAL INDEX

The Geographical-Chronological index is arranged first by the country relevant to the subject or topic treated and then subdivided by date, with a Column Three category listed for each citation. A series of numbers is given to direct the researcher to the full citation in the Classed Entries section:

Example: For material on Drama in Italy between World Wars I and II, look under Italy, 1918-1939

Dates as a rule reflect the content period covered by the item and not the publication year. However, the publication year is used for theoretical writings and for present assessments about old traditions, problems etc.

When precise dates cannot be established, the decade (e.g. 1970-1979) or the century (e.g. 1800-1899) is given.

In the case of biographies of people who are still alive the year of birth of the biographee and the year of publication of the biography are given. The same criterion is followed for histories of institutions such as theatres or companies which are still in existence. The date of beginning of such institutions and the date of publication of the entry are given—unless the entry explicitly covers only a specific period of the history of the institution.

No dates are given when the content is either theoretical or not meaningfully definable in time. Entries without date print first.

DOCUMENT AUTHORS INDEX

The term Document Author means the author of the scholarly work cited, **not** the author of the dramatic artifact or topic under discussion.

The Document Authors Index gives in one alphabetical list the author of each document cited in the Bibliography. The names are listed in the Roman alphabet, with cross references when an unfamiliar English-language form is used. Numbers are given with each entry to direct the researcher to the full citation in the Classed Entries section.

N.B. Users are urged to familiarize themselves with the taxonomy and all the indexes provided. The four-way access possible through consultation of the Classed Entries section, the Subject Index, the Geographical-Chronological Index, and the Document Authors Index should be sufficient to locate even the most highly specialized material.

CLASSED ENTRIES

THEATRE IN GENERAL
Comprehensive

1   Wilson, Edwin; Goldfarb, Alvin. *Living Theater: An Introduction to Theater History.* New York: McGraw-Hill; 1983. xii, 482 pp. Biblio. Illus.: Photo.

2   Allen, John Piers. *A History of the Theatre in Europe.* London and Totowa, NJ: Heinemann Educational Books and Barnes & Noble; 1983. 314 pp. Biblio. Index. Illus.: Photo.
Europe. Histories-general.

3   Molinari, Cesare. *Storia universale del teatro.* (Universal History of the Theatre.) Milan: Mondadori; 1983. 358 pp. (Libri illustrati Mondadori.) Index. Biblio. Tables. Illus.: Photo. B&W. Color. [New augmented and revised edition of *Il Teatro.*]
Europe. North America. Asia. Histories-general. ■General history of the theatre.

4   Diederichsen, Diedrich. "Das babylonische Theater." (Babylonian Theatre.) *MuK.* 1983; 29: 221-241. Notes.
Germany, West. 1962-1980. Historical studies. ■Main trends in and problems of theatrical culture in the 60's and 70's.

5   Chatterjee, Sekhar. "The Colonial Theatre in India." *ThR.* 1983 Autumn; 8(3): 233-234.
India. 1750-1983. Historical studies. ■Modern theatre in India still remains largely a foreign art form.

6   Maurer, Roland. *Die Schweizer Theaterszene.* (The Swiss Stage.) Zurich: Edition Pro Helvetia; 1983. 86 pp. (Information, Theater, DI.) Biblio. Illus.: Photo. ■Swiss theatre history in the twentieth century.
Switzerland. 1900-1983. Histories-general. ■Swiss theatre history in the twentieth century.

7   Anon. "Index 1976: 1 — 1983: 2." *REEDN.* 1983; 8(2): 1-3.
UK. 1976-1983. Bibliographical studies. ■Index to the contents of *Records of Early English Drama,* the first eight volumes.

8   Goldie, Terry. "Australia: The Gentrification of the Alternative." *CTR.* 1983 Fall; 38: 119-122. Illus.: Photo. Print. B&W. 1: 2 in. x 2 in.
Australia. Canada. 1970-1983. Historical studies. ■Comparative study of Australian and Canadian theatre, stressing cultural similarities.

9   Mackerras, Colin, ed. *Chinese Theater: From Its Origins to the Present Day.* Honolulu: Univ. of Hawaii P; 1983. viii, 220 pp. Biblio. Index.
China. 206 B.C.-1983 A.D. Histories-general. ■Articles by William Dolby, John Hu, Colin Mackerras, A.C. Scott and Elizabeth Wichmann on aspects of Chinese theatre from early plays to contemporary practice.

10   Carvajal, Christa. "German-American Theatre." 175-189 in Seller, Maxine Schwartz, ed. *Ethnic Theatre in the United States.* Westport, CT: Greenwood P; 1983. viii, 606 pp. Notes. Biblio.

USA. 1830-1939. Historical studies. ■History of German immigrants' theatre.

Reference materials

11   Edwards, Christopher, ed. *The World Guide to Performing Arts Periodicals.* London: International Theatre Institute; 1982. 66 pp.
1982. ■Over 600 statistical entries organized by country.

12   Hartnoll, Phyllis, ed. *The Oxford Companion to the Theatre.* Oxford: Oxford UP; 1983. x, 934 pp. Pref. Biblio. Illus.: Graphs. Photo. B&W. [4th Edition.]
■Generic guide to theatre terms, institutions and personalities.

13   Sarkissian, Adele, ed. *Contemporary Authors.* Volume 107. Detroit, MI: Gale Research Co.; 1983. 273 pp.
1983. Biographies. ■Over 1400 biographical entries including playwrights and screenwriters. Related to Media.

14   Goertz, Harald. *Musikhandbuch für Österreich.* (Music Guide for Austria.) Vienna and Munich: Doeblinger; 1983. 157 pp. Biblio. Index.
Austria. 1983. ■2500 entries on Austrian music with names, addresses and other information.

15   Brown, Mary M.; Rewa, Natalie. "Ottawa Calendar of Performance in the 1870's." *THC.* 1983 Fall; 4(2): 134-191. Tables.
Canada. 1870-1879. Historical studies. ■Advertised and reviewed performances of professional troupes.

16   Ibbotson, Anthony. "The Stage Design Collection of the National Arts Centre, Ottawa, Canada." 10-13 in Cocuzza, Ginnine, ed.; . Cohen-Stratyner, Barbara Naomi, ed. *Stage Design: Papers from the 15th International Congress of SIBMAS (Societé Internationale des Bibliothèques et Musées des Arts de Spectacle.* New York: Theatre Library Association; 1983. (Performing Arts Resources 8.) Illus.
Canada. 1969-1982. ■Subject collection described.

17   Nadvornikova, Marie. *Postavy ceskeho divadla: vyberova bibliograife kniznich publikaci a clanku z divadelniho tisku 1945-1980.* (Productions of the Czech Theatre: Selected Bibliography of Books on Theatrical Activities, 1945-1980.) Olomouc: Statni vedecke knihovny v Olomouci; 1983. 85 pp. (Publikace Statni vedecke knihovny v Olomouci 4.) Index.
Czechoslovakia. 1945-1980.

18   Awad, Ramsis. *Mawsu'at al-masrah al-Misri al-bibliyujrafi-yah, 1900-1930.* (Who's Who in Egypt: Bibliography, 1900-1930.) Cairo: al-Hay'ah al-Misriyah al-'Ammah lil-Kitab; 1983. 902 pp.
Egypt. 1900-1930. ■Bibliography of Arabic theatre.

19   Highfill, Philip H., Jr., ed.; Burnim, Kalman, A., ed.; Langhans, Edward A., ed. *A Biographical Dictionary: 1660-1800 in London.* Carbondale, IL: Southern Illinois UP; 1982.

THEATRE IN GENERAL: Comprehensive—Reference Materials

England. 1660-1800. ■Information about various theatre personalities.

20 Milhous, Judith, ed.; Hume, Robert D., ed. *Vice Chamberlain Coke's Theatrical Papers 1706-1715*. Carbondale, IL: Southern Illinois UP; 1982. xliii, 274 pp.
England. 1706-1715. ■Licensing papers related to managerial and repertorial changes at London theatres.

21 Price, Jocelyn. "Theatrical Vocabulary in Old English: A Preliminary Survey (1)." *MET*. 1983; 5(1): 58-71. Notes.
England. ■Lists alphabetically all Latin theatrical terms for which there exist Old English translations, equivalents or glosses. Grp/movt: Medieval theatre.

22 Anon. "Festspiele 1983." (Festivals 1983.) *TH*. 1983; 5: 59-63.
Europe. 1983. ■European music and theatre festivals in 1983: cities, productions and dates. Related to Music-Drama: Opera.

23 Tainio, Ilona, ed. *Suomen teatterit ja teatterintekijät 1983 (Yhteisö- ja henkilöhakemisto)*. (Finnish Theatres and Theatre Professionals 1983: Guide to Organizations and Individuals.) Helsinki: Tammi; 1983. 487 pp. (Suomen Teatterijärjestöjen Keskusliiton julkaisu.) Pref. Illus.: Photo. B&W. 5.
Finland. 1983. ■Includes review of theatres and organizations and register of professionals.

24 Giteau, Cécile. "Models of Scenery and Costumes in the Performing Arts Department of the Bibliothèque Nationale, Paris." 55-58 in Cocuzza, Ginnine, ed.; . Cohen-Stratyner, Barbara Naomi, ed. *Stage Design: Papers from the 15th International Congress of SIBMAS (Société Internationale des Bibliothèques et Musees des Arts du Spectacle)*. New York: Theatre Library Association; 1983. (Performing Arts Resources 8.)
France. 1982. ■Collection described, as well as criteria for selecting items to include in the collection.

25 Scherer, Colette. "Recherche théâtre et documentation." (Theatre Research and Documentation.) *RHT*. 1983; 35(4): 470-479.
France. 1981-1983. ■List of theses at the Gaston Baty library of the University of Paris III.

26 *Il Patalogo 4: Annuario 1982 dello spettacolo*. (The Patalogo 4: Annals of Theatre.) Milan: Ubulibri; 1982. v. 1: 284 pp./v. 2: 268 pp. Biblio. Illus.: Photo. B&W.
Italy. 1982. Histories-sources. ■List of dramatic, cinematographic and television productions with short critical notes on the most important ones.

27 Gavazza, Ezia; Sborgi, Franco; Croce, Franco. *Maria Antonietta Gambaro*. Rome: De Luca; 1983. 158 pp. Notes. Biblio. Tables. Illus.: Photo. B&W. Color.
Italy. 1951-1980. Histories-sources. ■Catalogue of the exhibition (Genoa, 1983) of M.A. Gambaro's paintings and scene designs. Related to Music-Drama: Opera.

28 Mazzochi Doglio, Mariangela; Tintori, Giampiero; Padovan, Maurizio; Tiella, Marco. *Leonardo e gli spettacoli del suo tempo*. (Leonardo and Theatre Productions of His Time.) Milan: Electa; 1983. 116 pp. Pref. Notes. Tables. Illus.: Photo. B&W. Color.
Italy. 1484-1500. ■Catalogue of the exhibition dealing with Leonardo da Vinci's activity as a costume and scene designer and inventor of machinery for Sforza's festivals.

29 Quadri, Franco, ed.; Ponte di Pino, Oliviero, ed.; Buttafava, Giovanni, ed.; Grasso, Aldo, ed. *Il Patalogo 5/6 — Annuario 1983 dello spettacolo*. (The Patalogo 5/6 — 1983 Theatre Yearbook.) Milan: Ubulibri; 1983. v. 1: 291 pp./vo. 2: 306 pp. Biblio. Tables. Illus.: Photo. B&W. [Two volumes.]
Italy. 1983. Histories-sources. ■Yearbook of theatre, television and cinema, with brief critical notations and statistical data. Related to Media.

30 Savarese, Nicola, ed. *Anatomia del teatro: Un dizionario di antropologia teatrale*. (Anatomy of the Theatre: A Dictionary of Theatrical Anthropology.) From the International School of Theatre Anthropology, Eugenio Barba, director. Florence: Casa Usher; 1983. 231 pp. Biblio. Illus.: Photo. B&W. Color.
Italy. 1981. Technical studies. ■Compilation of entries focusing on most important concepts and techniques studied at the International School of Theatre Anthropology. Related to Dance-Drama.

31 U.S. Institute for Theatre Technology. *Theatre Words*. New York: U.S. Institute for Theatre Technology; 1983. 156 pp.
North America. Europe. 1983. ■Dictionary of international theatre terms in nine languages, with illustrations.

32 Moger, Art. *Hello! My Real Name Is — *. Secaucus, NJ: Citadel P; 1983. 159 pp. Illus.: Photo.
North America. Europe. ■Pseudonyms of entertainers, with portraits.

33 "Bibliografia teatral catalana, 1980-1981." (Theatre Bibliography in Catalan Language, 1980-1981.) *EECIT*. 1983 June; 23 : 135-140.
Spain. 1980-1981. ■Theatre bibliography in Catalan language, including original Catalan texts, translation of foreign playtexts into Catalan, theatre essays and theatre histories.

34 Pérez de Olaguer, Gonzalo, ed. *Documents del Centre Dramàtic, 1*. (Documents of the Dramatic Center, 1.) Barcelona: Centre Dramàtic de la Generalitat de Catalunya; 1983. 52 pp. Pref. Index. Illus.: Design. Photo. Print. B&W. 83: 19 cm. x 26 cm.
Spain. 1982-1983. Reviews of performances. ■Annals of theatre productions in Catalonia for the 1982-1983 season.

35 Mullin, Donald C., ed. *Victorian Actors and Actresses in Review: A Dictionary of Contemporary Views of Representative British and American Actors and Actresses, 1837-1901*. Westport, CT: Greenwood P; 1983. xxxvi, 571 pp. Biblio. Illus.: Photo.
UK. USA. 1837-1901.

36 Barclay, Michael. "Edward Gordon Craig Exhibition." *TN*. 1983; 37(3): 121-123. Notes. Illus.: Dwg. 1: 3 in. x 6 in.
UK-England. 1900-1935. ■Description of Edward Gordon Craig designs, bas-relief figures, black figure prints, autograph manuscripts, books, periodicals, woodblocks, woodcuts, wood engravings and photographs on display at Gillian Jason Gallery, London, 1982.

37 Great Lakes Arts Alliance. *Resource Directory, Presenting Organizations, 1983-84*. Cleveland, OH: Great Lakes Arts Alliance; 1983. iv, 147 pp.
USA. 1983.

38 Association for Communication Administration; University and College Theatre Association Chief Administrators Program. *Directory of Theatre Programs*. Annandale, VA: ACA; 1983. vi, 81 pp.
USA. 1983.

39 American Theatre Association. "1983 ATA Election Provides New Leaders." *ThNe*. 1983 Summer; 15(6): 3.
USA. 1983. ■Slate of new officers for national, divisional and regional offices.

40 Beaufort, John. *Five Hundred Five Theatre Questions Your Friends Can't Answer*. New York: Walker; 1983. vii, 136 pp.
USA. Instructional materials. ■Theatre trivia.

41 Conboy, Neil; Hatch, James V. "An Index of Proper Nouns for *The Place of the Negro in the Evolution of the American Theatre, 1767 to 1940*." *BALF*. 1983 Spring; 17: 38-48. [From a dissertation by Fannin Saffore Belcher, Yale University, 1945.]
USA. 1767-1940. ■Proper noun index from the first major study of the history of Black American theatre.

42 Demo, Mary Penasack. "Creative Activity in the Classroom." *ChTR*. 1983 Feb.; 32(1): 27-30.
USA. 1976-1982. ■Recently published Education Resources Information Center documents relating to creativity and dramatic activities in the elementary classroom.

CLASSED ENTRIES

THEATRE IN GENERAL: Comprehensive—Reference Materials

43   Greenberg, Jan W. *Theater Careers: A Comprehensive Guide to Non-Acting Careers in the Theater.* New York: Holt, Rinehart, and Winston; 1983. viii, 206 pp. Index.
USA. 1983. ■Various careers in management, design, music, public relations, etc. Interviews with individuals in various fields. Intended for children.

44   Headley, Robert. "Theatre Preservation Bibliography." *M.* 1983 Fourth Quarter; 15(4): 39-40.
USA. 1935-1983. ■List of books related to the restoration of historic theatres.

45   Loney, Glenn. *Twentieth Century Theatre: Premieres, Personalities and Events in the Theatre.* New York, NY: Facts On File Publications; 1983. v. 1: xiii, 256 pp./v. 2: 264 pp. Pref. Index. Biblio. Illus.: Photo. B&W. [In two volumes.]
USA. UK. Canada. 1900-1979. ■Chronological guide to premieres, revivals, personalities and events.

46   Rice, Ryan, comp. *The Entertainment Yellow Pages.* Los Angeles: Creative Actors' Association; 1983. 170 pp. Illus.: Photo. [Spine title: *New York to LA.*]
USA. 1980-1983. Instructional materials. ■Guide to training in acting and theatre.

47   Seligman, Kevin. "Bibliography of Flat Pattern Sources." *TD&T.* 1983 Spring; 19(1): 32-36. Biblio.
USA. 1900-1983. ■Bibliography of flat pattern sources. Addendum to the articles from *Theatre Design & Technology*, Fall and Winter 1983 issues.

48   Swenson, Janet. "From the Archives Almanac." *CueM.* 1983 Spring-Summer; 61(2): 10.
USA. 1900-1983. ■Brief summary of the theatre, film and television holdings in the archives at Brigham Young University: set and costume renderings for Cecil B. DeMille's *The Ten Commandments*, Max Steiner's original scores for *Gone with the Wind, Casablanca* and *The Three Musketeers* and personal papers of Dean Jagger and Howard Hawks. Related to Media: Film.

49   Willis, John, ed. *Theatre World, 1981-1982.* New York: Crown; 1983. 255 pp.
USA. 1981-1982. ■Annual record of Broadway and Off Broadway theatre season.

50   Woll, Allen. *Dictionary of the Black Theatre: Broadway, Off-Broadway, and Selected Harlem Theatre.* Westport, CT: Greenwood P; 1983. xvi, 359 pp. Biblio. Index.
USA. 1983.

51   Voskanian, E.A., comp.; Iordanskaja, I.D., comp.; Morinova, L.K., comp. *Teat'r, annotirovannyj ukazatel' spravočnych i bibliografičeskich izdanii na russkom i inostrannych jazykach, XIX-XX vv.* (Theatre: Annotated Index of Reference and Bibliographic Publications in Russian and Foreign Languages, 19th-20th Centuries.) Moscow: V.I. Lenin State Library; 1983. 66 pp. [Teat'r spravočnye i bibliografičeskije izdanija.]
USSR. Europe. North America. 1800-1983. Bibliographical studies.

Relation to other fields

52   Böhm, Gotthard. "Die Menschen wollen wieder erhoben werden." (People Again Want to Be Exalted.) *Buhne.* 1983 May: 8-14. Illus.: Photo. Color.
Austria. 1983. Historical studies. ■Revival of religious and metaphysical theatre, church operas and mystery plays.

53   Thompson, David W., ed. *Performance of Literature in Historical Perspective.* Lanham, MD: UP of America; 1983. xiv, 728 pp.
Europe. North America. 499 B.C.-1980 A.D. Historical studies. ■Essays on five main concerns of oral interpretation: language, culture, teaching, theory and entertainment.

54   Murray, Timothy. "Theatrical Legitimation: Forms of French Patronage and Portraiture." *PMLA.* 1983; 98(2): 170-182. Notes. Biblio.
France. 1610-1643. Historical studies. ■Political ramifications of the theatrical patronage of Louis XIII and Cardinal de Richelieu.

55   Valentin, Karl. "Tvångsföreställningar." (Mandatory Performances.) *Entre.* 1983; 10(2): 27.
Germany. 1882-1948. Critical studies. ■Humorous proposal of the late Karl Valentin that all citizens be required to attend theatre daily for the benefit of individuals and society.

56   Hofmann, Jürgen. "Theater-Tabus: Roundtable-Gespräch über die ungelösten Probleme einer Klassenkultur." (Theatre-Taboos: Round-table Discussion on the Unsolved Problems of a Class-culture.) *Tzs.* 1983 Fall; 5: 99-121. [Kultur im Widerspruch (IV) (Culture in Contradiction, Part 4).]
Germany, West. 1983. Histories-sources. ■Critics, researchers and politicians discuss theatre for the elite and theatre for the working class.

57   Clark, VèVè A. "Contemporary Forms of Popular Theatre in Haiti." *Ufa.* 1983; 12(2): 93-100. Pref. Notes.
Haiti. 1956-1976. Historical studies. ■Relationship of contemporary popular theatre methods to forms of folk performance in work, religion and festivals.

58   Bharucha, Rustom. *Rehearsals of Revolution: The Political Theater of Bengal.* Honolulu: Univ. of Hawaii P; 1983. 276 pp. Biblio. Index.
India. 1757-1983. Historical studies. ■Interrelationship of Bengali political theatre with historical events.

59   Pietzsch, Ingeborg. "Theatererfahrungen in der Dritten Welt: Gespräch mit Fritz Bennewitz." (Theatre Experiences in the Third World: Interview with Fritz Bennewitz.) *TZ.* 1983; 38(5): 42-46. Illus.: Photo. B&W. 6.
India. Venezuela. Sri Lanka. 1970-1983. Histories-sources. ■Report on theatre work in the Third World and its political and social importance.

60   Varadpande, Manohar Laxman. *Religion and Theatre.* New Delhi: Abhinav; 1983. 148 pp. Index. Illus.: Photo. 12.
India. 1983. Critical studies. ■Role of religion in Indian theatre.

61   "Le visioni del teatro nel *Fuoco* di D'Annunzio." (Theatre Visions in *The Fire* by D'Annunzio.) *QT.* 1982 May; 4(16): 102-111.
Italy. 1900. Critical studies. ■Gabriele D'Annunzio's aesthetic vision of theatre in his novel *The Fire.*

62   Cruciani, Fabrizio. *Teatro nel Rinascimento: Roma 1450-1550.* (Theatre During the Renaissance: Rome, 1450-1550.) Rome: Bulzoni; 1983. 719 pp. (Europa delle Corti: Centro studi sulle società di antico regime — Biblioteca del Cinquecento 22.) Biblio. Index.
Italy. Vatican. 1450-1550. Histories-specific. ■Papal cultural policy and organization of various public festivities.

63   Mele, Rino. *Scena oscena: Rappresentazione e spettacolo.* (Obscene Scene: Representation and Performance.) Rome: Officina; 1983. 110 pp. (Saggi/Documenti 14.) Notes. Tables. Illus.: Photo. B&W.
Italy. 1983. Critical studies. ■Psychological implications of theatrical performance.

64   Plassard, Didier. "Il Teatro nella società dello spettacolo." (The Theatre among the Show Business Community.) *TeatroC.* 1982 Oct.-1983 Jan.; 1(2): 129-142.
Italy. 1982. Critical studies. ■Main subject of the 3rd seminar of the International Centre of Aesthetic Studies in Palermo: theatre in relation to other performing arts and its future goals.

65   Seragnoli, Daniele. "Le storie nella storia." (Histories within History.) *QT.* 1982 May; 4(16): 84-91. Notes.
Italy. 1851. Historical studies. ■Teatro di Cittadella fire in Reggio Emilia in 1851: theatre as a social mirror of the town.

66   Smith, Alex. "PETA: Theatre of Conscience." *Tk.* 1983 Mar.-Apr.; 3(3): 55-60. Illus.: Dwg. B&W. 1: 5 in. x 5 in.
Philippines. 1983. Histories-sources. ■Interview with Gardy Labad concerning theatre in the Philippines: emphasis on work of the PETA (Philippine Educational Theatre Association).

67   Szydlowski, Roman. "Poland: Theatre under Martial Law." *CTR.* 1983 Spring; 37: 118-120. Illus.: Photo. Print. B&W. 1: 3 in. x 5 in.
Poland. 1981-1982. Historical studies. ■Review of the 1981-1982 season, revealing the role of theatre and its survival under martial law.

THEATRE IN GENERAL: Comprehensive—Relation to other fields

68   Marranca, Bonnie. "Kärnvapenteater." (Nuclear Theatre.) *Entre.* 1982; 9(4): 8-9. [Translation of 'Nuclear Theatre' from *Village Voice*, June 29, 1982.]
Sweden. 1982. Critical studies. ▪Danger of using theatrical metaphors to discuss nuclear arms race.

69   Meisel, Martin. *Realizations: Narrative, Pictorial, and Theatrical Arts in Nineteenth-Century England.* Princeton, NJ: Princeton UP; 1983. xix, 471.
UK-England. 1805-1902. Critical studies. ▪Narrative/pictorial modes of representation in theatre, painting and literature.

70   Schino, Mirella. "L'incendio del teatro." (Fire of Theatre.) *QT.* 1982 May; 4(16): 177-184. Notes.
UK-England. France. 1853. Critical studies. ▪Theatrical vision and the portrait of the great French actress Rachel in Charlotte Brontë's *Villette*.

71   American Theatre Association. "Drama and Theatre in Elementary Education: An ATA Statement of Policy." *ThNe.* 1983 Jan.-Feb.; 15(1): 1-2. Illus.: Photo. B&W. 1: 6 in. x 5 in. [First of two statements issued by American Theatre Association.]
USA. 1983. Histories-sources. ▪'Creative drama' and 'play production' are defined as essential tools for children's education, artists' training and teacher preparation.

72   Anon. "Arts Are a Counterpoint to Technology." *ThNe.* 1983 Jan.-Feb.; 15(1): 1-3. [Excerpt from keynote address to the 2nd Annual Maryland Alliance for Arts Education Conference.]
USA. 1983. Critical studies. ▪Contrasts role of technology and arts, emphasizing importance of arts, especially theatre, for rounded education.

73   Demo, Mary Penasack. "Ten Theatre Resources." *ChTR.* 1983 July; 32(3): 18-20. Biblio.
USA. 1983. Bibliographical studies. ▪Annotated list of documents related to educational theatre available from Education Resources Information Center.

74   Fink, Guido. "Il salotto del diavolo e la casa del vicino." (Devil's Drawing-room and Neighbour's House.) *QT.* 1982 May; 4(16): 129-143. Notes.
USA. 1700-1982. Critical studies. ▪Perception of theatre in American novel.

75   Ritch, Pamela. "A Good Substitute for Recess in Winter: Some Elementary Classroom Teacher's Perceptions about Creative Drama, an Informal Report." *ChTR.* 1983 Oct.; 32(4): 3-8. Notes.
USA. 1983. Critical studies. ▪Examines elementary teachers' attitudes toward creative drama and classroom practices.

76   Rosenblatt, Bernard S. "New President Affirms: 'ATA's Members Should Wield Impact on Public Policy'." *ThNe.* 1983 Dec.; 15(9): 3, 12. Illus.: Photo. B&W. 1: 4 in. x 5 in. [Inaugural address of American Theatre Association's new president at the 1983 convention.]
USA. 1983. Histories-sources. ▪Mentions specific areas for attention.

77   Snyder-Greco, Teresa. "The Effects of Creative Dramatic Techniques on Selected Language Functions of Language Disordered Children." *ChTR.* 1983 Apr.; 32(2): 9-13. Biblio. Tables.
USA. 1983. Empirical research. ▪Empirical evidence supporting hypothesis that creative drama activities have a significant impact on specific language functions, number of words spoken and facilitating interaction of children with language disorders.

78   Plassard, Didier. "Il teatro sovietico di Agit-prop." (Soviet Agit-prop Theatre.) *TeatrC.* 1983-1984 Oct.-Jan.; 3(5): 145-158.
USSR. 1919-1934. Historical studies. ▪History, function and methods of Soviet agitprop theatre.

Research/historiography

79   Cohen, Robert; Von Szeliski, John, illus. *Theatre: Brief Edition.* Palo Alto, CA: Mayfield; 1983. xii, 239 pp. Biblio. Index.

Instructional materials. ▪Concise version of a theatre textbook.

80   Vince, R.W. "Comparative Theatre Historiography." *ET.* 1983 May; 1(2): 64-72. Notes.
Canada. 1983. Critical studies. ▪Five propositions for the construction and evaluation of models of historical research.

81   Doglio, Federico. *Teatro in Europa.* (Theatre in Europe.) Milan: Garzanti; 1982. 568 pp. (Strumenti di studio 1.) Pref. Notes. Biblio. Illus.: Photo. B&W.
Europe. 534 B.C.-1499 A.D. Histories-general. ▪First volume of a general history of theatre in Europe, accompanied by documents.

82   Stryz, Jan A. "Newsletter." *NCTR.* 1983 Winter; 11(2): 118-120.
Europe. North America. 1800-1899. Bibliographical studies. ▪Notes on recent publications, works in progress, forthcoming conferences and queries concerning 19th century theatre.

83   Veinstein, André. "Elements of a Method for Using Models of Scenery or of Scenery Arrangements as Study Documents." 59-62 in Cocuzza, Ginnine, ed.; . Cohen-Stratyner, Barbara Naomi, ed. *Stage Design: Papers from the 15th International Congress of SIBMAS (Société Internationale des Bibliothèques et Musées des Arts du Spectacle).* New York: Theatre Library Association; 1983. (Performing Arts Resources 8.)
Europe. North America. 1982. Instructional materials. ▪Typology of models and method to be used to describe and evaluate each type of model, by editor of *Performing Arts Libraries and Museums of the World.*

84   Zörner, Wolfgang. "Möglichkeiten der Zusammenarbeit von Theaterwissenschaft und Theaterpraxis." (Possibilities of Cooperation between Theatre Research and Theatre Practice.) 59-70 in Lüthi, Hans Jürg. *Dramatisches Werk und Theaterwirklichkeit.* Bern: Haupt; 1983. 72 pp. (Berner Universitätsschriften 28.)
Europe. 1983. Critical studies. ▪Relation of theatre research to theatre practice.

85   Swaminathan, Saraswati. "Performing Arts: Documentation, Preservation, Retrieval." *SNJPA.* 1983 Oct.-Dec.; 70: 32-37.
India. 1983. Bibliographical studies. ▪Methods for collection, documentation and retrieval used at the performing arts archives.

86   Borzacchini, Dario. "L'universo del teatro: la prima storia." (Theatre Universe: The First History.) *QT.* 1982 May; 4 (16): 74-83. Notes.
Italy. 1777. Historical studies. ▪Study of historian Pietro Napoli Signorelli's *Storia critica de' teatri antichi e moderni.*

87   Dietrich, Margret. "Theaterwissenschaft und Theaterpraxis." (Theatre Research and Theatre Practice.) 45-58 in Lüthi, Hans Jürg. *Dramatisches Werk und Theaterwirklichkeit.* Bern: Haupt; 1983. 72 pp. (Berner Universitätsschriften 28.)
Switzerland. 1983. Critical studies. ▪Relationship of theatre research, criticism and practice.

88   McCarthy, Willard. "A New Typesetting System for REED." *REEDN.* 1983; 8(2): 19-24. Notes.
UK. 1983. Histories-sources. ▪Description of the new computer typesetting and editing system to be used by the REED project.

89   Nelson, Alan H. "Computer Texts for REED." *REEDN.* 1983; 8(2): 11-19.
UK. 1983. Critical studies. ▪Advantages and methods of transcribing theatrical documents directly into a computer file. Grp/movt: Medieval theatre.

90   McNamara, Brooks. "TDR: Memoirs of the Mouthpiece, 1955-1983." *TDR.* 1983; 27(4): 3-21.
USA. 1955-1983. Historical studies. ▪History of *The Drama Review* on the occasion of its 100th issue.

91   Rosenberg, Helen S.; Pinciotti, Patricia; Smith, Jeffrey K. "On Quantifying Dramatic Behavior." *ChTR.* 1983 Apr.; 32(2): 3-8. Notes. Biblio. Tables. Illus.: Graphs.
USA. 1980. Empirical research. ▪Discusses validity and reliability of the *Inventory of Dramatic Behavior Adapted for Group Observation.*

THEATRE IN GENERAL: Comprehensive

Theory/criticism

92   Wagner, Anton. "Dr. Lawrence Mason, Music and Drama Critic, 1924-1939." *THC.* 1983 Spring; 4(1): 3-14. Notes. Illus.: Photo. Neg. B&W. 1: 5 in. x 7 in.
Canada. 1924-1939. Historical studies. ■Dr. Lawrence Mason: an overview of his career as music critic for *Toronto Globe*, with emphasis upon need for indigenous Canadian theatre.

93   Tatlow, Anthony. "Social Space and Aesthetic Time, East Asian Theatre: Transcultural Challenge." *ThR.* 1983 Autumn; 8(3): 207-219. Notes.
China. Japan. 1900-1983. Historical studies. ■Various Eastern theatre artists have absorbed and transformed Western techniques and in turn inspired Western artists to reevaluate and transform Western aesthetics. Related to Music-Drama: Beijing Opera.

94   Dürrenmatt, Friedrich; Baunibusch, Brigitte, transl.; Ciabatti, Gianfranco, transl. *Lo scrittore nel tempo: Scritti su letteratura, teatro e cinema.* (The Writer in His Time: Writings about Literature, Theatre and Cinema.) Turin: Einaudi; 1983. viii, 225 pp. [Translation from German.]
Europe. 1921. Histories-sources. ■Italian translation of *Theater-Schriften und Reden, Dramaturgisches und Kritisches, Der Mitmacher*. Related to Media: Film.

95   Erbe, Berit. "Theatrical Codes." *MuK.* 1983; 29: 307-310. Notes.
Europe. 1983. Critical studies. ■Performance and communication: problems of semiotic approach.

96   Fiebach, Joachim. "Mobility and Profanation of the Theatrical Mode of Expression and Communication in the Seventies: Specificity and Emancipators' Implications of the Theatre." *MuK.* 1983; 29: 212-220. Notes.
Europe. 1970-1980. Historical studies. ■Main trends in contemporary theatrical cultures. Changes concerning performance spaces, environment, modes of expression and attitudes toward audience.

97   Kamerman, Jack B., ed.; Martorella, Rosanne, ed. *Performers and Performances: The Social Organization of Artistic Work.* South Hadley, MA: J.F. Bergin; 1983. vi, 303 pp.
Europe. North America. 1983. Critical studies. ■Collection of essays by scholars and professionals in the performing arts including Dmitri Shostakovich: analysis of performing arts from sociological perspective.

98   Otto, Werner, comp. "Theatergeschichte(n): Theaterreformen um 1900." (Theatre History(ies): Theatre Reforms around 1900.) *TZ.* 1983; 38(4): 33-36. Illus.: Photo. Plan. Dwg. B&W. 3. [12th and last installment.]
Europe. 1870-1910. Histories-sources. ■Reformers on their theories.

99   Pavis, Patrice. *Languages of the Stage: Essays in the Semiology of the Theatre.* New York: Performing Arts Journal Publications; 1982. 206 pp.
France. 1982. Critical studies. ■Essays on various critical aspects and approaches to theatre within a sophisticated system of the author's aesthetic theories. Spectator is seen at the center of this semiological network. Grp/movt: Post-structuralism.

100   Souriau, Paul; Souriau, Manon, transl., ed. *The Aesthetics of Movement.* Amherst, MA: Univ. of Massachusetts P; 1983. xxi, 159 pp. Pref. Notes. Index. Illus.: Dwg. Photo. B&W. 38. [English translation of *L'esthétique du mouvement* (1889).]
France. 1889. Critical studies. ■Physical experience and aesthetic perception of body movement.

101   Pfützner, Klaus. "Theatererbe in umfassender Gestalt." (Theatre Heritage in a Comprehensive Frame.) *TZ.* 1982 Apr.; 37: 7-8. [Monthly column.]
Germany, East. 1982. Critical studies. ■Communist interpretation of theatrical tradition: function, purpose, philosophy and sociology.

102   Fischer-Lichte, Erika. *Semiotik des Theaters: eine Einführung.* (Semiotics of the Theatre: An Introduction.) Tuebingen: G. Narr Verlag; 1983. Vo. 1: 266 pp./vo. 2: 211 pp./vo. 3: 220 pp. Biblio. [Volume 1: *Das System der theatralischen Zeichen* (The System of Theatrical Signs)/ Volume 2: *Vom 'künstlichen' zum 'natürlichen' Zeichen — Theater des Barocks und der Aufklärung* (From 'Artistic' to 'Natural' Signs — Theatre of Baroque and of Enlightenment)/Volume 3: *Die Auffürung als Text* (The Performance as Text).]
Germany, West. 1983. Critical studies.

103   Girshausen, Theo. "Der anmutige Herr der Aggression: Der 'unvermutete Zusammenhang von Theater und Krieg' in der 'Philosophie' Erik Grawert-Mays." (The Graceful Master of Aggression: The 'Unexpected Connection between Theatre and War' in the 'Philosophy' of Erik Grawert-May.) *Tzs.* 1983 Spring; 3: 50-58. Notes.
Germany, West. 1982. ■Evaluation of Erik Grawert-May's study 'Theatre Nuclear Forces' and his view of the relation between theatre and war.

104   Oberer, Walter. "Theater — gestern, heute und morgen." (Theatre — Yesterday, Today and Tomorrow.) 9-20 in Lüthi, Hans Jürg, ed. *Dramatisches Werk und Theaterwirklichkeit.* Bern: Haupt; 1983. 72 pp. (Berner Universitätsschriften 28.)
Germany, West. Switzerland. 1983. Critical studies. ■Development and function of theatre in our time, mainly in German Federal Republic and Switzerland.

105   Forlani, Mimma; Rovetta, Angelo. *La critica teatrale militante in Italia — Aspetti storici, Aspetti teoretici.* (Militant Theatrical Criticism in Italy — Historical Aspects, Theatrical Aspects.) Milan: I.S.U. — Università del Sacro Cuore; 1983. 200 pp. Pref. Notes. Biblio. Append.
Italy. 1900-1980. Critical studies. ■Historical study of Italian theatrical criticism. Some criteria are suggested for the objective evaluation of the field.

106   Eichbaum, Julius. "Editorial." *Scenaria.* 1983 Jan. 28; 35: 1.
South Africa, Republic of. 1983. Critical studies. ■Examination of dearth of critical work by newspapers, and the responsibilities of the critic.

107   Abellan, Joan. *La representació teatral: Introducció als llenguatges del teatre actual.* (The Theatre Performance: Introduction to the Languages of the Actual Theatre.) Barcelona: Institut del Teatre; 1983. 156 pp. (Monografies de Teatre 13.) Notes. Index. Biblio. Tables. Illus.: Photo. Print. B&W. 49: 14 cm. x 11 cm.
Spain. 1983. Critical studies. ■Comprehensive discussion of theatre. Includes: fiction and real world, the performance and the audience, spatial relationship, staging, role playing, time of performance.

108   Fàbregas, Xavier. "Futur de l'espectador davant l'espectacle." (Future of the Audience's Relation to the Performance.) *EECIT.* 1983 June; 23: 117-134. Tables.
Spain. 1983. Critical studies. ■Semiotic study of the specific nature of theatre in relation to other arts and audience interaction with it. Related to Media: Video forms.

109   Ödeen, Mats. "Kritikerna och den nya publiken." (The Critics and the New Audience.) *Entre.* 1983; 10(1): 14-16.
Sweden. 1960-1983. Critical studies. ■Theatre criticism in Sweden said to have become subjective, journalistic and politicized. Theatres and critics function as ideological avant-garde of a new social class created by bureaucratization and economic stagnation.

110   Balint, Steve. "A Dream, a Proposal, a Manifesto." *TDR.* 1983; 27(4): 22-25.
USA. 1983. Histories-sources. ■Expressionistic proposal for the future of theatre by a founding member of Squat Theatre. Grp/movt: Expressionism.

111   Bogart, Anne. "Stepping Out of Inertia." *TDR.* 1983; 27(4): 26-27.
USA. 1983. Critical studies. ■Lack of socio-political engagement in contemporary performance.

112   Chekhov, Michael. "The Theatre of the Future." *TDR.* 1983; 27(4): 29-31. [Transcribed from a lecture, 1942.]
USA. 1942. Histories-sources. ■Need to change the focus and operating structures of theatre to make it relevant.

THEATRE IN GENERAL: Comprehensive—Theory/criticism

113 Huerta, Jorge A. *Chicano Theater: Themes and Forms.* Ypsilanti, MI: Bilingual P./Editorial Bilingüe; 1982. xiv, 274 pp.
USA. 1965-1982. ■History and philosophy of Chicano theatre movement.

114 Malpede, Karen, ed. *Women in Theatre: Compassion & Hope.* New York: Drama Book Publishers; 1983. xvi, 281 pp.
USA. UK. 1850-1983. Histories-sources. ■Collected writings on theory and criticism by female performers of the nineteenth and twentieth centuries. Also essays on feminist theatre. Grp/movt: Feminism.

115 Miller, Tice L. "George Jean Nathan and the 'New Criticism'." *THSt.* 1983; 3: 99-107. Notes.
USA. 1909-1922. Historical studies. ■Development of George Jean Nathan's critical approach and his impact on the theatre of his time.

Multiple application

Administration

116 Guimaraes, Carmelinda. "Kritik och censur i brasiliansk teater." (Criticism and Censorship in Brazilian Theatre.) *Entre.* 1983; 10(4): 7-9.
Brazil. 1557-1983. Historical studies. ■History of censorship of Brazilian theatre from a Church ban ca. 1570 to economic pressure to produce only Broadway hits.

117 Fulks, Wayne. "Albert Tavernier and the Guelph Royal Opera House." *THC.* 1983 Spring; 4(1): 41-56. Append. Notes. Tables. Illus.: Photo. Print. B&W. 3: 3 in. x 4 in., 2 in. x 2 in.
Canada. 1893-1895. Historical studies. ■History of construction of Royal Opera House and its management under Albert Tavernier.

118 Green, Joseph G. "That Is Not What I Meant at All." *CTR.* 1983 Spring; 37: 9-13. Illus.: Photo. Neg. Print. B&W. 1: 4 in. x 5 in.
Canada. 1976-1983. Critical studies. ■Critique of recommendations made by Canadian Federal Cultural Policy Review Committee of 1982, with specific attention to visual arts.

119 Mallet, Gina. "The St. Lawrence Centre: Toronto's Persistent Problem." *CTR.* 1983 Fall; 38: 25-32. Illus.: Diagram. Photo. Neg. B&W. Grd.Plan. 5.
Canada. 1983. Historical studies. ■Disappointments and mismanagement at Toronto's Centre Stage, in the St. Lawrence Centre.

120 Wallace, Robert. "Theatre and Community: An Introduction." *CTR.* 1983 Spring; 37: 7-8.
Canada. 1983. Historical studies. ■Discussion of symbiotic relationship between theatre and community.

121 George, David; Ory, Monica. "Six Payments to Players and Entertainers in Seventeenth-Century Warwick." *REEDN.* 1983; 8(1): 8-12. Notes.
England. 1601-1637. Histories-sources. ■Six payments to traveling entertainers from two hitherto unpublished documents in Warwick County Records Office. Grp/movt: Elizabethan theatre.

122 Greenfield, Peter H. "Entertainments of Henry, Lord Berkeley, 1593-4 and 1600-5." *REEDN.* 1983; 8(1): 12-24. Notes.
England. 1593-1605. Histories-sources. ■New records of nearly 100 payments to travelling players, musicians, fools, bearwards and morris dancers who performed before Lord Berkeley. Grp/movt: Elizabethan theatre.

123 *Teattereiden valtionosuustyöryhmä: Ehdotus esitykseksi valtionosuuksista ja -avustuksista.* (The Working Group on Government Grants for Theatres: A Suggestion for the Bill on State Aid for Theatres.) Helsinki: Ministry of Education; 1983. 33 pp. (Memorials of the working groups of the Ministry of Education.) Pref. Append. Tables.
Finland. 1980-1983. Histories-sources. ■Suggestions on government funding of theatres in Finland, by a working group of the Ministry of Education.

124 Macnaughton, Peter. "Carte Blanche: France, Theatre under the Socialists." *CTR.* 1983 Spring; 37: 113-117. Illus.: Photo. Neg. B&W. 1: 2 in. x 3 in.
France. 1982-1983. Historical studies. ■Analysis of efforts of Minister of Culture Jack Lang to encourage French theatre to decentralize and attract wider range of audiences, writers and directors.

125 Shorter, Eric. "French Cultural Imperatives." *Drama.* 1983 Autumn; 149: 33-34.
France. 1900-1983. Critical studies. ■Success of French cultural policy in subsidizing theatre, reviews of some productions.

126 Gerhards, Fritzdieter. "Rettet die Kunst — spart an der Technik." (Rescue Art — Reduce Technology.) *BtR.* 1983; 76(5): 14. [Report of Oberhausen's manager on the occasion of the 43rd Conference of Theatre Technology.]
Germany, West. 1983. Histories-sources. ■Economical and financial problems facing today's theatres.

127 Mayer, Gerhard. "Muss das so nackt sein?" (Does It Have to Be So Naked?) *Buhne.* 1983 May: 33-34.
Germany, West. 1983. Critical studies. ■Private ownership — a solution for the economic crisis of the government-funded theatre.

128 Merschmeier, Michael. "Kühn oder tollkühn? Heribert Sasse, der Aufsteiger des Jahres." (Bold or Foolhardy? Heribert Sasse, the Newcomer of the Year.) *TH.* 1983(8): 1-3. Illus.: Photo.
Germany, West. 1983. Histories-sources. ■Heribert Sasse succeeds Boy Gobert as manager at Staatliche Schauspielbühnen Berlin.

129 Nestler, Peter; Grosser, Helmut. "Rettet die Kunst — spart an der Technik." (Rescue Art — Reduce Technology.) *BtR.* 1983; 76(4): 11-15. Illus.: Photo. B&W. 3. [Speeches at the 43rd Conference for Theatre Technology.]
Germany, West. 1983. Histories-sources. ■Economic organization of and financial problems faced by today's theatres.

130 Rosenke, Manfred. "Ein brisantes Thema: Schusswaffen im Theater." (A High-explosive Theme: Firearms in the Theatre.) *BtR.* 1983; 76(3): 22-23.
Germany, West. 1983. Technical studies. ■Firearm laws as they relate to theatre.

131 Schäfer-Rose, Helmut. "Mut zur Provinz: Würzburger Theater im Rhythmus der Region." (Courage to Be Province: Würzburg Theatres in the Rhythm of the Region.) *BGs.* 1983 Mar.; 35(3): 12-15. Illus.: Photo.
Germany, West. 1945-1983. Historical studies. ■Political and cultural background of Würzburg theatres and their financial operations.

132 Siede, Claudia. "Vom Mitbestimmungskasper zum Sparkommissar: Krise oder Tendenzwende des öffentlichen Theaters?" (From Collective Decision Taking to the Rule of the Commissar in Theatre Economics: Crisis or New Trends in Public Theatre?) *Tzs.* 1983 Summer; 4: 91-97. Notes.
Germany, West. 1982. Critical studies. ■Administrative apparatus and theatre management: focus on financial and political situation.

133 Siede, Horst. "Theater im Aufbruch: Modelle zur Überwindung der gegenwärtigen Krise am deutschen Theater." (A New Start for Theatre: Models to Overcome the Present Crisis in the German Theatre.) *TH.* 1983; 9: 46-47.
Germany, West. 1983. Critical studies. ■Plans to overcome financial crisis in German theatre.

134 Windrich, Hermann. "In Schönheit sterben: Wird das Stadttheater zu Tode gespart?" (To Die in Beauty: Will the Municipal Theatre Be Spared?) *Tzs.* 1983 Spring; 3: 113-121.
Germany, West. 1982. Critical studies. ■Financial situation of municipal theatres.

135 Zimmermann, Jörg. "Rettet die Kunst — spart an der Technik." (Rescue Art — Reduce Technology.) *BtR.* 1983; 76(5): 15. [Report on the occasion of the 43rd Conference for Theatre Technology.]
Germany, West. 1983. Histories-sources. ■Financial problems facing scene designers.

136 Cesari, Maurizio. *La censura in Italia oggi: 1944-1980.* (Censorship in Italy Today: 1944-1980.) Naples: Liguori;

THEATRE IN GENERAL: Multiple application—Administration

1982. 205 pp. (Le istituzioni culturali 7.) Notes. Tables. Illus.: Photo. B&W.
Italy. 1944-1980. Histories-specific. ■History of censorship in journals, theatre, cinema, radio and television. Related to Media.

137 Grieco, Bruno. *Entrare nell'immagine: Per una politica dello spettacolo.* (Entering a Vision: On Theatre Policy.) Florence: Casa Usher; 1983. 113 pp. (Quaderni 1983.)
Italy. 1983. Critical studies. ■Suggestions for government theatre funding policy.

138 Jarach, Giorgio. *Manuale del diritto d'autore.* (Handbook of Copyrights.) Milan: Mursia; 1983. 475 pp. (Il Bivio, Guide e Manuali, Serie libri completi.) Notes. Index. Append. [New, augmented and up-to-date edition.]
Italy. 1983. Instructional materials.

139 Pranteddu, Francesco. *L'attivitá lavorativa nello spettacolo: elementi di diritto del lavoro di legislazione sociale e indicazioni amministrative.* (Work in Theatre: Elements of Labor and Social Legislation and Administrative Information.) Milan: Unicopli; 1983. 207 pp. Pref. Append.
Italy. 1983. Technical studies. ■Laws, provisions and contracts regulating conditions of employment in different fields of theatre.

140 Quargnolo, Mario. *La censura ieri e oggi nel cinema e nel teatro.* (Censorship Yesterday and Today in Cinema and Theatre.) Milan: Pan; 1982. 198 pp. (Il timone 123.) Append. Index. Biblio.
Italy. 1924-1982. Histories-sources. ■Intervention of Italian censorship in cinema, radio and theatre. Appendix of letters and documents is included. Related to Media.

141 Teixidor, Jordi, ed. "Una Frustració: La Proposició de Llei de Teatre." (A Frustration: The Bill on Theatre.) *EECIT.* 1983 June; 23: 19-48.
Spain. 1982. Histories-sources. ■Legislation on theatre presented to the Parliament of Catalonia by the PSUC (Socialist Party): included is editor's introduction, summary of the parliamentary debate and evaluation.

142 Englund, Claes. "En framtida teater." (A Future Theatre.) *Entre.* 1983; 10(2): 3.
Sweden. Denmark. 1970-1983. Critical studies. ■Editorial on the need for a new cultural policy and innovative theatrical organizations in Scandinavia. Includes discussion of the ideas of Henrik Bering Liisberg on possible cooperation between amateur and professional theatre.

143 Englund, Claes. "Teater och 'sponsring'." (Theatre and 'Sponsorship'.) *Entre.* 1983; 10(5): 2.
Sweden. 1983. Critical studies. ■Call for theatres to refuse offers of sponsorship from business and industry in favor of greater reliance on government subsidy in order to preserve freedom of expression.

144 Gillham, Geoff. "Truth Is No Defence: An Examination of the Theatres Act (1968)." *SCYPT.* 1983; 11: 49-56.
UK. 1968-1986. Historical studies. ■Reasons for the private prosecution of Michael Bogdanov's production of *The Romans in Britain* as related to the Theatres Act.

145 Watson, Ian. "The Death of the British Theatre." *E&AM.* 1983 Oct.; 7-9. Illus.: Photo. Print. B&W. 2.
UK. 1983. Critical studies. ■Objections to the phenomenon of ad-hoc theatre companies and temporary writers-in-residence.

146 Stanback, Thurman W. "The Black Presence in London Theatre, 1974-1979." *WJBS.* 1983 Summer; 7(2): 83-93. Notes. Illus.: Photo. 1: 2 in. x 2 in.
UK-England. 1974-1979. Historical studies. ■The problem of severe unemployment among Black performers, playwrights and directors in London's West End, National Theatres and Fringe — even in Black roles, plays and companies — is delineated and discussed.

147 Boyd, Eddie. "Don't Say You Care — I Can't Afford It." *STN.* 1983 Apr.; 26: 26-29. Illus.: Sketches. B&W. 1.
UK-Scotland. 1980-1983. Critical studies. ■Critical discussion of the Scottish Arts Council's policy of funding community theatre.

148 Gallacher, Tom. "Fakes and Ladders." *STN.* 1983 Jan.; 23: 11-14. Illus.: Sketches. B&W. 1.
UK-Scotland. 1983. Critical studies. ■Discussion of Scottish Arts Council's policy of funding theatre.

149 American Theatre Association Board of Directors. "Board Resolution Sets ATA 'Billing' Guidelines." *ThNe.* 1983 Summer; 15(6): 3.
USA. 1983. Histories-sources. ■Full text of the resolution, concerning billing guidelines of ATA.

150 Anon. "ATA By-law Changes Will Be Voted at Convention." *ThNe.* 1983 May; 15(5): 10.
USA. 1983. Histories-sources. ■Amendments to the By-laws of the American Theatre Association to be voted on by general membership at the 1983 convention.

151 Anon. "Additional By-Law Changes." *ThNe.* 1983 Summer; 15(6): 14.
USA. 1983. Histories-sources. ■Two additional proposed changes in the by-laws of the American Theatre Association.

152 Anon. "'Mutual Needs, Mutual Action' Focus of New York Theatre Meeting." *ThNe.* 1983 Summer; 15(6): 1, 4. Illus.: Photo. B&W. 1: 3 in. x 4 in.
USA. 1983. Histories-sources. ■Officers of the American Theatre Association and representatives of six other organizations meet to discuss four major areas of concern: legislative planning, advocacy, audience development and cooperative support. Includes lengthy list of those present.

153 Bailey, A. Peter. "AUDELCO, An Organization of True Believers." *BlC.* 1983 Feb.-Mar.; 13(4): 140. Illus.: Photo. B&W. 1: 2 in. x 3 in.
USA. 1983. Histories-sources. ■Description of the activities of a community organization dedicated to audience development for Black theatres.

154 Benjamin, Patricia J. "Managing Historic Theatres for the Performing Arts." *M.* 1983 Fourth Quarter; 15(4): 33-37. Illus.: Photo. B&W. 3.
USA. 1981-1983. Instructional material. ■Discussion and guidelines for the use of historic theatres as performing arts centers based on a Purdue University study of fifty-five such theatres.

155 Engle, Ron. "Theatrical Contracts and Letterheads." *THSt.* 1983; 3: 121-135. Illus.: Photo. B&W. 12: 5 in. x 6 in.
USA. 1890-1899. Histories-sources. ■Various letters and contracts concerning performances at the Metropolitan Opera House in Grand Forks, ND, in the 1890's. Includes one letter concerning management of the Grand Opera House in Crookston, MN.

156 Hewitt, Ken. "Regional Section Programming Arts Administration." *USITT.* 1983 Spring; 22(6): 9-10.
USA. 1983. Instructional materials. ■How to locate free or low-cost professional assistance in law, insurance, finance, accounting, marketing, human resources management and information systems.

157 Larson, Gary O. *The Reluctant Patron.* Philadelphia: Univ. of Pennsylvania P; 1983. xvi, 314 pp.
USA. 1943-1965. Historical studies. ■History of the debate over federal involvement in the arts, including the use of art as a weapon in the Cold War, by the National Council Coordinator of the National Endowment for the Arts (NEA).

158 Martorella, Rosanne. "Rationality in the Artistic Management of Performing Arts Organizations." 95-107 in Kamerman, Jack B.; . Martorella, Rosanne. *Performers and Performances: The Social Organization of Artistic Work.* South Hadley, MA: J.F. Bergin; 1983. xiii, 303 pp.
USA. 1982. Historical studies. ■Trend toward decreased artistic control over arts organizations in favor of rationalization of production under the control of administrators.

159 Martorella, Rosanne. "Art and Public Policy: Ideologies for Aesthetic Welfare." 281-288 in Kamerman, Jack B.; . Martorella, Rosanne. *Performers and Performances: The Social Organization of Artistic Work.* South Hadley, MA: J.F. Bergin; 1983. xiii, 303 pp.
USA. 1965-1982. Critical studies. ■Impact of government funding on the arts, resulting in their being seen as a service and the artist as accountable to the public.

160 Melillo, Joseph R. *Market the Arts!* New York: FEDAPT; 1983. 287 pp.

THEATRE IN GENERAL: Multiple application—Administration

USA. 1983. Technical studies. ■Overall plans for promotional campaigns for arts organizations.

161 Selznick, Irene Mayer. *A Private View*. New York: Knopf; 1983. 384 pp. Illus.: Photo. 32.

USA. 1910-1983. Biographies. ■Autobiography of Broadway producer Irene Mayer Selznick.

162 Webster, Jean. "Taxes and You." *USITT*. 1983 Winter; 22(5): 5.

USA. 1983. Instructional materials. ■Recent tax law changes regarding office space, second incomes and educational expenses.

163 Zolberg, Vera L. "Changing Patterns of Patronage in the Arts." 251-268 in Kamerman, Jack B.; . Martorella, Rosanne. *Performers and Performances: The Social Organization of Artistic Work*. South Hadley, MA: J.F. Bergin; 1983. xiii, 303 pp.

USA. 1950-1982. Critical studies. ■Effect of different kinds of financial support on artists. Concentrates on constraints imposed by corporate and government involvement.

Audience

164 Gourdon, Anne-Marie. *Théâtre, Public, Perception*. Paris: Editions du CNRS; 1982. 253 pp.

1982. Critical studies. ■Study of public perception of theatrical performances.

165 Institute for Empirical Social Research. "Josefstadt: Innige Freundschaft." (Josefstadt: Close Friendship.) *Buhne*. 1983 Jan.: 8-9.

Austria. 1982. Empirical research. ■Poll on the ethnic background, average age and education of the audience attending Theater in der Josefstadt in Vienna.

166 Engel, Ann Mari. "Internationellt teatermöte i Havana." (International Theatre Meeting in Havana.) *Entre*. 1983; 10 (2): 33. Illus.: Photo. B&W.

Cuba. 1983. ■Seminar on new methods and theatre's relationships to audience held by the New Theatre Committee of the International Theatre Institute (ITI).

167 Krug, Hartmut. "Zielgruppentheater in der BRD: Eine Entwicklungsgeschichte: Vorüberlegungen zu (k)einer eigenständigen Theater-reform." (Target-group Theatre in FRG: History of Its Development.) *Tzs*. 1983 Summer; 4: 6-20. Notes.

Germany, West. 1960-1983. Historical studies. ■History, aims and methods of 'target-group theatre' activities: political theatre for special audiences with common characteristics such as age, socio-economic class and ethnic background.

168 De Marinis, Marco; Covi, Giovanna, transl. "Theatrical Comprehension: A Socio-Semiotic Approach." *ThM*. 1983 Winter; 15 (1): 12-17. Notes. Biblio.

Italy. 1983. Critical studies. ■Process by which the audience assigns meaning to a performance.

169 Slate, Libby. "California Youth Theatre: An Investment in the Future." *PArts*. 1983 July; 17(7): 38. Illus.: Photo.

UK-England. USA. 1980. Historical studies. ■Audience development program founded by Jack Nakano whereby young people are exposed to theatre as performers, technical and creative personnel, and viewers.

170 Research Division, National Endowment for the Arts. "Audience Development in Four Southern Cities." 227-240 in Kamerman, Jack B.; Martorella, Rosanne. *Performers and Performances: The Social Organization of Artistic Work*. South Hadley, MA: J.F. Bergin; 1983. xiii, 303 pp.

USA. 1983. Empirical research. ■Use of a questionnaire to determine audience composition for arts events in an attempt to use life-style information in the creation of arts marketing strategies.

171 Burstyn, Ellen. " 'Striking an Arc' between Actor and Audience: Vital Exchange Defines the Theatre Experience." *ThNe*. 1983 Nov.; 15(8): 2-3, 10. [Edited version of 'New Allies', the closing address of the American Theatre Association 1983 convention.]

USA. 1983. Critical studies. ■Interaction among playwright, actor and audience is needed for vital theatre.

172 Davis, Ken. " 'Playgrounding': Theatres Discover New Horizons in Audience Education." *ThNe*. 1983 Election Issue; 15(2): 1, 16. Illus.: Diagram. [Part One. Second part, entitled 'Playgrounding: A New Model for Audience Education', appears in *ThNe*, 1983 Nov., pages 2-3 and 10.]

USA. 1983. Technical studies. ■Techniques and activities for educating the playgoer, from children to adults, and the accruing benefits.

173 DiMaggio, Paul; Useem, Michael. "Cultural Democracy in a Period of Cultural Expansion: The Social Composition of Arts Audiences in the United States." 199-225 in Kamerman, Jack B., ed.; . Martorella, Rosanne, ed. *Performers and Performances: The Social Organization of Artistic Work*. South Hadley, MA: J.F. Bergin; 1983. xiii, 303 pp.

USA. 1830-1982. Critical studies. ■Sociological studies of contemporary audience suggest that democratization of the arts, predicted by Tocqueville, has not taken place.

174 Stell, W. Joseph. "Extraversion, Neuroticism and Cognitive Complexity as Factors Affecting Responses to Set Designs." *ERT*. 1983 Aug.; 9: 21-46. Notes. [Second report.]

USA. 1974. Empirical research. ■Experiments with 123 undergraduates. Extraversion measured by Eysenck Personality Inventory, and cognitive complexity by Bierri Role Concept Repertory as modified by Gourd. Subjects evaluated scenery using author-designed semantic differential of 15 bi-polar adjective scales. Scores compared and interpreted.

Design/technology

175 Anon. "A Bakst Galaxy." *Apollo*. 1983 July; 118(257): 92-93. Illus.: Design. Color.

1911-1923. Histories-sources. ■Reproduction of three costume designs and two set designs (*Phèdre*, 1923, and *Sleeping Beauty*, Act IV, 1911) from collection of Baron Thyssen-Bornemisza.

176 Wilcox, Ruth Turner. *The Mode in Costume*. 2nd edition, revised and expanded. New York: Charles Scribner's Sons; 1983. xxviii, 477 pp. Biblio. Index. Illus.: Dwg. B&W. [Reissue of 1958 edition.]

3000 B.C.-1983 A.D. Histories-sources. ■Guide to costume design, including prevailing period fashions and origins, dates, fabrics, colors and accessories.

177 Adedeji, Cecilia Folasade. "African Stage Design: Problems of Collecting, Cataloguing and Conserving Documents." 6-9 in Cocuzza, Ginnine, ed.; . Cohen-Stratyner, Barbara Naomi, ed. *Stage Design: Papers from the 15th International Congress of SIBMAS (Société Internationale des Bibliothèques et Musées des Arts du Spectacle)*. New York: Theatre Library Association; 1983. (Performing Arts Resources 8.) Biblio.

Africa. 1982. Technical studies. ■Problems of collecting and preserving documents of African stage design.

178 Schneider-Siemssen, Günther. "Tätigkeitsbericht der Gesellschaft für zukunftsorientierte Bühnengestaltung." (Progress Report of the Society for Future-Oriented Stage Design.) *BtR*. 1983; 76(1): 20.

Austria. 1948-1985. Technical studies. ■Work on future plans with an emphasis on holographic research project. Related to Puppetry: Marionettes.

179 Pietzsch, Ingeborg. "Quadriennale mit Fragezeichen: V. Weltausstellung des Bühnenbildes und der Theaterarchitektur in Prag." (Quadriennale with a Question Mark: 5th International Exhibition of Scenery and Theatre Architecture in Prague.) *TZ*. 1983; 38(10): 48-53. Illus.: Photo. B&W. 9.

Czechoslovakia. 1983. Histories-sources. ■Report on the exhibition.

180 Vychodil, Ladislav. "Szenografie international (10): Ladislav Vychodil, Tendenzen im Bühnenbild der ČSSR." (Scenery International (10): Ladislav Vychodil, Tendencies in ČSSR Scenery.) *TZ*. 1983; 38(12): 39-42. Illus.: Photo. B&W. 8.

Czechoslovakia. 1983. Historical studies. ■Tendencies in Czechoslovakian scene design.

THEATRE IN GENERAL: Multiple application—Design/technology

181 Visser, Colin. *"The Descent of Orpheus* at the Cockpit, Drury Lane."* *ThS.* 1983; 24(1-2): 35-53. Notes. Illus.: Design. Dwg. Architec. 6: 3 in. x 5 in.
England. France. Belgium. 1640-1661. Historical studies. ■Description of the settings and machines based upon contemporary accounts of related productions in London, Paris and Brussels.

182 Ashelford, James. *A Visual History of Costume: The Sixteenth Century.* London and New York: B.T. Batsford and Drama Book Publishers; 1983. 144 pp. (A Visual History of Costume.) Pref. Biblio. Gloss. Index. Illus.: Pntg. Photo. Sketches. Color. B&W. 157.
Europe. 1500-1599. Histories-sources. ■Illustrations of sixteenth century costume.

183 Cocuzza, Ginnine, ed.; Cohen-Stratyner, Barbara Naomi, ed. *Performing Arts Resources, Volume 8 (Stage Design: Papers from the 15th International Congress of SIBMAS).* New York: Theatre Library Association; 1983. xix, 94 pp.
Europe. North America. 1982. Critical studies. ■Thirteen papers dealing primarily with particular collections of designs and of scenography itself: The National Arts Centre in Ottawa, designs by Motley, models at the Bibliothèque Nationale in Paris and collections of historical decor at Drottningholm, Gripsholm and Ludwigsburg.

184 Kaiser, Gunter. "'Mitarbeiter' – Publikum: Zu Problemen der Szenografie des Schauspieltheaters." ('Cooperation' – Audience: On Problems of the Scenography of the Legitimate Theatre.) *BtR.* 1983; 76(1): 18-19. [From *Theater der Zeit* April, 1980.]
Europe. 1970-1983. Technical studies. ■Problems of the formation of performance spaces and the character and effect of scenography on the audience.

185 Laver, James; Probert, Christine. *Costume and Fashion: A Concise History.* New edition with concluding chapter by C. Probert. New York and Toronto: Oxford UP; 1983. 288 pp. (The World of Art.) Biblio. Index. [First published 1969 as *A Concise History of Costume.*]
Europe. North America. 999 B.C.–1969 A.D. Histories-specific. ■Underlying motives of fashion related to social changes and shifting cultural patterns with respect to the three functions of clothing: protection, expression of personality and attractiveness to others.

186 Maeder, Edward, ed. *An Elegant Art: Fashion and Fantasy in the Eighteenth Century.* New York: Harry N. Abrams; 1983. 256 pp. Illus.: Dwg. Photo. Color. [Accompanies exhibition at the Los Angeles County Museum of Art.]
Europe. 1700-1800. Historical studies. ■Photographs of exhibit and essays on aspects of dress in the eighteenth century, including textiles and movement.

187 Marly, Diana de. *Costume on the Stage 1600-1940.* Totowa, NJ: Barnes & Noble; 1982. 167 pp. Illus.: Dwg.
Europe. North America. 1600-1940. Historical studies. ■History of costuming.

188 Ribeiro, Aileen. *A Visual History of Costume: The Eighteenth Century.* London and New York: B.T. Batsford and Drama Book Publishers; 1983. 144 pp. (A Visual History of Costume.) Pref. Biblio. Gloss. Index. Illus.: Pntg. Photo. Sketches. Color. B&W. 156.
Europe. 1700-1799. Histories-sources. ■Illustrations of eighteenth century costume.

189 Russell, Douglas A. *Costume History and Style.* Englewood Cliffs, NJ: Prentice-Hall; 1983. xiv, 544 pp. Illus.: Photo. Dwg. 250.
Europe. North America. 499 B.C.-1983 A.D. Instructional materials. ■Costume history textbook including discussion of social, cultural and artistic characteristics of each period.

190 Tarrant, Naomi E.A. *Collecting Costume: The Care and Display of Clothes and Accessories.* London and Boston: George Allen & Unwin; 1983. xiii, 146 pp. Pref. Index. Biblio. Illus.: Diagram. Photo. B&W. 40.
Europe. North America. 1750-1983. Instructional materials. ■Procedures for collecting costumes, identifying and dating, repairing, preserving and displaying the collections. Includes list of museums, libraries, archives and societies.

191 Corvin, Michel. "Espace urbain et théâtre occidental." (Urban Space and Western Theatre.) *RHT.* 1983; 35(2): 222-232. Notes. Illus.: Pntg. Photo. Print. B&W. 5.
France. 1500-1750. Critical studies. ■Open and closed urban structures in relation to Renaissance and neoclassical perspective scenery.

192 Daniels, Barry V. "A Footnote to Daguerre's Career as a Stage Designer." *ThS.* 1983; 24(1-2): 134-137. Notes. Illus.: Dwg. 2: 2 in. x 2 in.
France. 1815-1822. Historical studies. ■As scene designer, Daguerre was also responsible for refurbishing auditorium and painting the house curtain. Descriptions and drawings from Théâtre Favart, Ambigu-Comique and Odéon.

193 Daniels, Barry V. "L.J.M. Daguerre: A Catalogue of His Stage Designs for the Ambigu-Comique Theatre." *TheatreS.* 1981-1982, 1982-1983; 28-29: 5-40. Notes. Append. Illus.: Design. Plan. B&W. Architec. Fr.Elev. 7.
France. 1709-1850. Historical studies. ■Innovations in stage design by Louis-Jacques Daguerre, including a catalogue of his designs.

194 Kalman, Jean; Banu, Georges, ed. "La llum al teatre." (Light in Theatre.) *EECIT.* 1983 Mar.; 22(22): 87-125. Illus.: Dwg. Print. B&W. Schematic. 4: 11 cm. x 11 cm. [Catalan translation by Maite Labourdette of articles published in *Travail Théâtral*, June 31, 1978.]
France. 1978. Technical studies. ■Three interviews with French lighting designers — Pierre Savron, André Diot and Pierre Trottier, and a short description of lighting design materials by Jean Kalman.

195 Marceillac, Laurence. "Cubisme et théâtre — les réalisations de Valmier pour Art et Action." (Cubisim and Theatre: Valmier's Productions for Art and Action.) *RHT.* 1983; 35(3): 338-347. Notes. Illus.: Design. Photo. Print. B&W. 12.
France. 1922-1926. Historical studies. ■Study of sets and costume designs for Théâtre de l'Art et Action by painter Valmier. Grp/movt: Cubism; Futurism.

196 Kämpfe, Gottfried. "Die elektrotechnischen Anlagen im Neuen Gewandhaus zu Leipzig." (The New Electro-Technical Systems of the Neues Gewandhaus in Leipzig.) *BtR.* 1983; 76(4): 18-20. Illus.: Photo. B&W. 1.
Germany, East. 1781-1983. Technical studies. ■Short history and description of the electro-technical system in the Neues Gewandhaus, Leipzig.

197 Pietzsch, Ingeborg. "Szenografie national (9): Otto Kähler." (Scenography National (9): Otto Kähler.) *TZ.* 1983; 38(6): 44-47. Illus.: Dwg. Photo. Poster. B&W. 11.
Germany, East. 1969-1983. Historical studies. ■Portrait of Otto Kähler and his work.

198 "43. Bühnentechnische Tagung." (43rd Conference for Theatre Technology.) *BtR.* 1983; 76(4): 10.
Germany, West. 1983. Histories-sources. ■Report on the conference and welcoming speech given by Helmut Grosser, president of the Deutsche Theatertechnische Gesellschaft.

199 Behne, D.; Dewidowicz, A.; Delion, R. "Elektronische Tonregie- und Akustik-einrichtungen im Nationaltheater München." (Electronic Equipment for Sound and Acoustics in Munich's National Theatre.) *BtR.* 1983; 76(2): 20-22. Illus.: Photo. Diagram. B&W. Schematic. 2.
Germany, West. 1983. Technical studies. ■Construction and operating procedures of new sound system.

200 Bergfeld, Wolfgang. "Szenische Lichtregieanlagen als Instrumente für Komposition und Nachschöpfung in der Bühnenbeleuchtung." (Scenic Lighting Control-Systems as Instruments of Composition and Creation in Stage Lighting.) *BtR.* 1983 ; 76(5): 16-19. Illus.: Plan. Schematic. 4. [Report on the symposium 'Models of the Future' at Salzburg, 25-27 May, 1983.]
Germany, West. 1983. Technical studies. ■Composition of artistic stage lighting is compared to that of a piece of music.

THEATRE IN GENERAL: Multiple application—Design/technology

201 Butzmann, Volker; Seeger, Martin; Walz, Ruth, photo. "Die erste Spielzeit der Schaubühne am Lehniner Platz." (First Season of the Schaubühne am Lehniner Platz.) *BtR*. 1983; 76(1): 10-14. Illus.: Photo. Plan. B&W. Grd.Plan. 10.
Germany, West. 1962-1982. Technical studies. ▪Description of new theatre building and technical equipment used in performances since 1981.

202 Grosser, Helmut. "Berufsaus- und Weiterbildung in den Theatern." (Career Training in the Theatre.) *BtR*. 1983; 76(3): 15.
Germany, West. 1983. Technical studies. ▪Training of the non-artistic staff within the existing wage and contract situation.

203 Haas, Hanns-Joachim. "Neue Lichtregieanlagen in den Württembergischen Staatstheatern." (New Equipment for Lighting-Control at the State Theatre, Württemberg.) *BtR*. 1983; 76(1): 21-23. Illus.: Design. Photo. Color. 5.
Germany, West. 1964-1983. Technical studies. ▪Description of lightboard by the firm Rank Strand and the electronic system Galaxy. Cooperation of the eventual user during planning and installation of the equipment is very important.

204 Keller, Werner. "Tontechnische Impressionen bei der BTT-Heilbronn." (Technological Tone — Impressions at the BTT-Heilbronn.) *BtR*. 1983; 76(5): 13. [BTT = Bühnentechnische Tagung (Conference for Theatre Technology).]
Germany, West. 1983. Critical studies. ▪Critical look at the work of the Sound Technology Commission at the 43rd Conference of Theatre Technology.

205 Mittmann, Otfried. "Reserve — oder Havarieteil für computergesteuerte Lichtstellsysteme." (Reserve or Spare Component for Computer-Controlled Lighting Systems.) *BtR*. 1983; 76(2): 22-23. Illus.: Photo. Diagram. B&W. Schematic. 2.
Germany, West. 1983. Technical studies. ▪Variant to counter the risk of computer malfunctions in modern lighting control systems.

206 Mittmann, Otfried. "Technologie des Datolux-Systems." (Technology of the Datolux-System.) *BtR*. 1983; 76(4): 20-22. Illus.: Photo. B&W. 2.
Germany, West. 1983. Technical studies. ▪Technical construction and areas of application.

207 Pietzsch, Ingeborg. "Theaterkritik und Bühnenbild." (Theatre Criticism and Stage Scenery.) *BtR*. 1982 Feb.; 1: 18.
Germany, West. 1980-1982. Critical studies. ▪Theatre critics and their problems in discussing design.

208 Schneider, Horst. "Verwendung gefährlicher Arbeitsstoffe im Theaterbetrieb." (The Use of Dangerous Materials in the Theatre.) *BtR*. 1983; 76(3): 23-24. Illus.: Design. 3.
Germany, West. 1983. Technical studies. ▪Risks involved in technical workshops.

209 Schwarz, Othmar; Schmitsberger, Gottfried, photo. "Der malerische Veloureffekt im Bühnenbild." (The Pictorial Effect of Velvet in Scenery.) *BtR*. 1983; 76(4): 22-23. Illus.: Photo. B&W. 3.
Germany, West. 1983. Technical studies. ▪Explanation of a system for electrostatically covering objects with fibers and thereby obtaining an effect similar to velvet or velour.

210 Zwingmann, Ruth; Schubert, Karl-Heinz. "Brandschutzeinrichtungen im Gebäude." (Fire-Prevention Equipment in Building.) *BtR*. 1983; 76(5): 20-23.
Germany, West. 1973-1983. Technical studies. ▪Various functions of fire prevention equipment, which must be included in the planning of theatres.

211 Anderson, Dave. "Spartan Masks." *TheatreS*. 1981-1982, 1982-1983; 28-29: 59-72. Notes. Illus.: Photo. B&W. PR. 1: 4 in. x 5 in.
Greece. 999-560 B.C. Historical studies. ▪Study of terracotta masks excavated from 1906 to 1909 at the sanctuary of Artemis Orthia in ancient Sparta. Grp/movt: Ancient Greek theatre.

212 Adams, Patricia B. "Interpreting Renaissance Costume Design: A Proposed Methodology." *TheatreS*. 1981-1982,
1982-1983; 28-29: 85-100. Notes. Illus.: Sketches. Pntg. B&W. PR. 2: 4 in. x 4 in.
Italy. 1539. Critical studies. ▪Costumes of the Muses designed by Tribolo (Niccolò dei Pericoli) are compared with the painting *The Parnassus* (1497) by Mantegna and drawings by Cyriacus to formulate methodology for the interpretation of symbolism in Renaissance costume.

213 Belli, Carlo. "Il teatro di Depero." (Depero's Theatre.) *TeatrC*. 1982-1983 Oct.-Jan.; 1(2): 143-157.
Italy. 1916-1924. Historical studies. ▪Survey of Fortunato Depero's activities as a designer.

214 Borisch, Frank. "Szenografie international: 9 Emanuele Luzzati." (Scenery International: 9 Emanuele Luzzati.) *TZ*. 1983; 38(3): 60-63. Illus.: Photo. B&W. 6.
Italy. 1921-1983. Biographical studies. ▪Portrait of the scene and costume designer and description of his work on the occasion of an exhibition in Magdeburg.

215 Dalla Palma, Diego. *Il Make-up, professionale, teatrale e cinetelevisivo.* (Professional Make-up for Theatre, Cinema and Television.) Milan: 1982. 165 pp. (Il Bivio — Guide e manuali.) Biblio. Illus.: Dwg. B&W.
Italy. 1982. Instructional materials. ▪Practical and theoretical handbook for aspiring make-up artists.

216 Dottori, Gerardo. "Cenni sul rinnovamento della scenotecnica." (Brief Account on Renovating Scenery.) *TeatrC*. 1983-1984 Oct.-Jan.; 3(5): 281-284.
Italy. 1906-1930. Histories-sources. ▪Short notes written by Gerardo Dottori in 1930 on the Renaissance of scene design. Grp/movt: Futurism.

217 Fagone, Vittorio. *Baldessari: Progetti e scenografie.* (Baldessari: Plans and Scenery.) Milan: Electa; 1983. 207 pp. Notes. Biblio. Tables. Illus.: Photo. B&W. Color.
Italy. 1923-1972. Historical studies. ▪Luciano Baldessari's architectural and theatrical works.

218 Manzella, Myriam, ed. *Duilio Cambelloti: Pitture, sculture, opere grafiche, vetrate, scenografie.* (Duilio Cambellotti: Paintings, Sculptures, Graphic Works, Stained-glass Windows and Scenery.) Rome: Quasar; 1982. 85 pp. Biblio. Tables. Illus.: Photo. B&W.
Italy. 1876-1960. Histories-sources. ▪Catalogue of exhibition (Rome, 1982) of work of Duilio Cambelloti.

219 Weil, Mark S. *Baroque Theatre and Stage Design.* St. Louis: Washington Univ.; 1983. 40 pp. Biblio. Illus.: Photo. [Accompanies exhibit at Washington Univ. Gallery of Art, St. Louis, MO, February 24-April 10, 1983.]
Italy. 1600. Historical studies. ▪Supplementary materials to exhibit of Baroque theatre and stage design. Grp/movt: Baroque theatre. Related to Music-Drama: Opera.

220 North, John. "Sound Out Master Sheets." *ThCr*. 1983 Jan.; 17(1): 30-31. Illus.: Diagram. 2: 16 in. x 4 in.
North America. 1983. Technical studies. ▪Report of sound design with emphasis on notation of sound effects in relationship to other cues.

221 Król-Kaczorowska, Barbara. "Architekt i razem malarz, Wloch Maraino." (The Italian Architect and Painter, Innocente Maraino.) *PaT*. 1983; 32(1): 80-88. Notes.
Poland. 1767-1799. Biographical studies. ▪Biography of Innocente Maraino who worked in Poland as stage designer and architect, and who constructed an open amphitheatre in Lwów.

222 Stribolt, Barbro. "Eighteenth-Century Stage Settings at the Court Theatres of Drottningholm and Gripsholm." 83-89 in Cocuzza, Ginnine, ed; . Cohen-Stratyner, Barbara Naomi, ed. *Stage Design: Papers from the 15th International Congress of SIBMAS (Societé Internationale des Bibliothèques et Musées des Arts du Spectacle).* New York: Theatre Library Association; 1983. (Performing Arts Resources 8.) Illus.
Sweden. 1766-1800. Bibliographical studies. ▪Description by curator of Drottningholm Theatre Museum (Sweden) of cataloguing work done since 1975.

THEATRE IN GENERAL: Multiple application—Design/technology

223   Weiss, David W. "Nordisk TeaterTeknik 83: A Report." *TD&T*. 1983 Fall; 29(3): 33.
Sweden. 1983. Histories-sources. ■Report of Scandinavian conference where theatre architects, designers and technicians met to share ideas and information.

224   Schulthess, Ernst. "Ergebnisse der Diskussionen über die UVV-Schweiz." (Results of Discussions Concerning the Swiss UVV.) *BtR*. 1983; 76(6): 21-22.
Switzerland. 1983. Technical studies. ■Safety and accident-prevention.

225   Bottle, Ted. "Surviving Theatre Grooves." *TN*. 1983; 37(1): 24-26.
UK. 1850-1983. Technical studies. ■Surviving upper-wing groove mechanisms in five provincial theatres.

226   Burian, Jarka M. "Contemporary British Stage Design: Three Representative Scenographers." *TJ*. 1983 May; 35(2): 213-234. Notes.
UK. 1958-1983. Historical studies. ■Designers Jocelyn Herbert, Ralph Koltai and John Napier have influenced contemporary English staging.

227   Burian, Jarka M. "Contemporary British Scenography." *TD&T*. 1983 Spring; 19(1): 4-12. Notes. Illus.: Photo. B&W. 17: 4 in. x 5 in.
UK. 1960-1983. Histories-sources. ■Description of current scenographic practices by British designers Chris Dyer, Maria Bjornson, Hayden Griffin, Jocelyn Herbert, John Gunter, John Napier and William Dudley.

228   Burian, Jarka M. "Contemporary British Scenography." *TD&T*. 1983 Fall; 19(3): 4-13. Notes. Illus.: Photo. B&W. 17: 4 in. x 5 in.
UK. 1960-1983. Historical studies. ■Description of current scenographic practices by British designers Patrick Robertson, John Bury, Timothy O'Brien, Ralph Koltai and Abd 'Elkader Farrah.

229   Friedman, Martin. *Hockney Paints the Stage*. With contributions by John Cox and others. Minneapolis & New York: Walter Art Center & Abbeville P; 1983. 227 pp. Biblio. Illus.: Photo. [Accompanies an exhibit organized by Walker Art Center on designer David Hockney.]
UK-England. USA. 1937. Historical studies. ■Essays by director John Cox and others on the designer David Hockney.

230   Levene, Ellen. "Ultz: Britain's Renaissance Designer." *TrCr*. 1983 Aug.-Sep.; 17(7): 37-84. Illus.: Photo. Print. B&W. 8.
UK-England. USA. 1983. Biographical studies. ■Review of Ultz's career as scene and costume designer in London and New York.

231   Pinkham, Roger, ed. *Oliver Messel*. London: Victoria and Albert Museum; 1983. 200 pp. Biblio. Index. Illus.: Photo. [Accompanies an exhibition held at the Theatre Museum, Victoria and Albert Museum, 22 June-30 October, 1983.]
UK-England. 1904-1978. Historical studies. ■Articles on designer Oliver Messel, including contributions by Cecil Beaton and others.

232   Robertson, Bryan. "A New Safety Curtain for Covent Garden." *BM*. 1983; 125: 422-425. Illus.: Design. Color. 1: 7 in. x 10 in.
UK-England. 1983. Historical studies. ■Describes and reproduces the design for a new safety curtain at Covent Garden. The curtain was designed by Christopher LeBrun and installed in autumn 1983. Related to Music-Drama: Opera.

233   Hewlett Gallery. *Jo Mielziner, Theatrical Designer: Selected Works 1928-1960, from the Collection of Jules Fischer*. Pittsburgh, PA: Hewlett Gallery; 1983. 29 pp.
USA. 1928-1960. Histories-sources. ■Supplementary materials to Mielziner exhibit in Hewlett Gallery, February 11-March 9, 1983.

234   Anon. "Polish Designer Discovers US Theatre Scene." *ThNe*. 1983 May; 15(5): 4. Illus.: Photo. B&W. 1: 2 in. x 2 in. [News note under 'Callboard,' a regular feature.]
USA. Poland. 1983. Historical studies. ■Marek Dobrowolski, a Polish scene designer based at New York's Studio and Forum of Stage Design, contrasts the role of lighting designers in Poland and in the USA.

235   Arnink, Donna. "Color Theory in Makeup." *ThCr*. 1983 Jan.; 17(1): 24-25, 49-54. Illus.

USA. 1983. Technical studies. ■Use of color theory in designing makeup.

236   Aronson, Arnold, ed. "New Products." *TD&T*. 1983 Winter; 19(4): 28. Illus.: Photo. B&W. 3: 2 in. x 3 in.
USA. 1900-1983. Instructional materials. ■Descriptions and photographs of new products of interest to theatre designers and technicians.

237   Atkinson, Patrick, ed. *USITT Newsletter*. Volume 23, 1,2,3,4. New York: USITT; 1983.
USA. 1983. Histories-sources. ■Newsletter for members of United States Institute for Theatre Technology (USITT).

238   Bailey, A. Peter. "The Magic of Technical Theatre." *BlC*. 1983 Sep.-Oct.; 14(1): 75-76. Illus.: Photo. Print. B&W. 1: 2 in. x 3 in.
USA. 1983. Historical studies. ■Discussion of the functions of stage designers and technicians, with a special focus on Roger Furman and information on technical theatre training programs.

239   Bay, Howard. "Keynote Address." 3-5 in Cocuzza, Ginnine, ed.; . Cohen-Stratyner, Barbara Naomi, ed. *Stage Design: Papers from the 15th International Congress of SIBMAS (Société Internationale des Bibliothèques et Musées des Arts du Spectacle)*. New York: Theatre Library Association; 1983. (Performing Arts Resources 8.)
USA. 1982. Critical studies. ■Keynote address calling for the accumulation of records to preserve theatre history.

240   Baygan, Lee. *Techniques of Three-Dimension Makeup*. New York: Watson-Guptill Publications; 1982. 183 pp.
USA. 1982. Instructional materials.

241   Bellman, Willard F. *Scene Design, Stage Lighting, Sound, Costume & Makeup: A Scenographic Approach*. New York: Harper & Row; 1983. xiv, 474 pp. Biblio. Illus.: Photo. [Revised edition of *Scenography and Stage Technology*, 1977.]
USA. 1977. Instructional materials. ■Study of scenography and stage technology.

242   Benson, Robert. "Maintaining Lighting Equipment." *ThCr*. 1983 Jan.; 17(1): 67-72.
USA. 1983. Instructional materials. ■Practical comments on care of lighting equipment.

243   Blom, Patricia VandenBerg. *Tanya Moiseiwitsch, Costume Designer: The Creative Process*. Ann Arbor: Univ. of Michigan; 1982. 201 pp. [Diss.: University Microfilms order no. DA8214965.]
USA. UK. 1914-1982. Critical studies. ■Creative process of the costume design: case study of the work of Tanya Moiseiwitsch based on theoretical model of A.F. Osborn.

244   Brook, Rollins. "Sound." *TD&T*. 1983 Spring; 29(1): 13, 39. Append.
USA. 1983. Technical studies. ■Published material available to anyone working with performance sound systems.

245   Brook, Rollins. "Fundamentals of Loudspeakers." *TD&T*. 1983 Summer; 19(2): 4-11, 21. Illus.: Diagram. Graphs. B&W. Detail. 17: 2 in. x 5 in.
USA. 1945-1983. Instructional materials. ■Guidelines to selection of loudspeakers limited to general principles and their application to professional theatre equipment. Discussion of specific applications and positions for best results.

246   Brook, Rollins. "Sound Systems for the Hearing Impaired." *TD&T*. 1983 Summer; 19(2): 22-25. Append. Illus.: Graphs. B&W. 1: 5 in. x 5 in.
USA. 1960-1983. Technical studies. ■Description of systems developed to aid hearing impaired in their enjoyment of theatre. Includes a directory of manufacturers.

247   Cain, Melissa; Mullin, Michael. "Design by Motley: A Theatre and Costume Arts Collection." 14-21 in Cocuzza, Ginnine, ed.; . Cohen-Stratyner, Barbara Naomi, ed. *Stage Design: Papers from the 15th International Congress of SIBMAS (Société Internationale des Bibliothèques et Musées des Arts du Spectacle)*. New York: Theatre Library Association; 1983. (Performing Arts Resources 8.) Illus.

THEATRE IN GENERAL: Multiple application—Design/technology

USA. 1982. Technical studies. ■Overview of the designers' contribution to theatre history, an account of how the designs came to be at Illinois and a description of their processing by the University Library.

248 Callahan, Michael. "Bright New World? Tour Systems Design for the 1980s." *LDM.* 1983 Apr.-May; 7(2): 27-39. Illus.: Graphs. Diagram. PD. 5. [Part 2 of 'Bright New World' series on equipment controls for concert tours. Part 3 appears in *LDM*, 1983 June, pages 35-42.]
USA. 1979-1983. Technical studies. ■Lighting design for touring concerts.

249 Chapman, J.M. "GOBOs for Performance Lighting." *TD&T.* 1983 Fall; 19(3): 24-25.
USA. 1900-1983. Technical studies. ■Properties of and hints for the correct use of GOBOs in stage lighting.

250 Chase, Ronald. "Cinematic Approaches to Theatre." *ThCr.* 1983 Aug.-Sep.; 17(7): 32-76. Illus.: Photo. Diagram. Print. B&W. Grd.Plan. 5.
USA. 1983. Technical studies. ■Summary of projection techniques for live theatre using film and/or still projection.

251 Davidson, Randall W.A. "Chemical Hazard Identification and Safety Practices." *USITT.* 1983 Fall; 23(4): 1.
USA. 1983. Instructional materials. ■Listing of precautions for safe use of chemical substances in the workplace.

252 Fielding, Eric. "Contemporary American Designers: Robin Wagner." *TD&T.* 1983 Winter; 29(4): 4-10. Append. Illus.: Plan. Photo. B&W. Grd.Plan. 10: 3 in. x 5 in.
USA. 1957-1983. Biographical studies. ■Biographical information, personal views and a production chronology of scenic design work of Robin Wagner.

253 File, William Daniel; Joy, Kenneth I. "The Computer as an Aid in Scenic Design." *TD&T.* 1983 Spring; 19(1): 18-19. Illus.: Dwg. B&W. 1: 5 in. x 7 in.
USA. 1980-1983. Technical studies. ■Description of a computer system developed to aid designers with perspective drawings.

254 Folke, Ann, ed.; Wells, Terry H., ed. "New Products." *TD&T.* 1983 Summer; 19(2): 32-33. Illus.: Photo. B&W. 6: 2 in. x 2 in.
USA. 1983. Instructional materials. ■Regular feature with photos and descriptions of new products of interest to designers and theatre technicians.

255 Foreman, Chris. "Automatic Microphone Mixing." *TD&T.* 1983 Summer; 19(2): 16-20. Illus.: Diagram. B&W. Schematic. 1: 4 in. x 5 in.
USA. 1945-1983. Technical studies. ■Definition and use of automatic microphone mixers in the theatre and description of brand-name mixers. Although automatic mixers were not developed for theatre use, they can be useful to sound operators.

256 Frezza, Christine Anne. *Music as an Integral Design Element of Theatrical Production.* Pittsburgh: Univ. of Pittsburgh; 1982. 256 pp. [Diss.: University Microfilms order no. DA8222787.]
USA. 1982. Critical studies. ■Model for music design training through analysis of function of music in theatrical productions.

257 Golding, Alfred S. "Problems and Observations Concerning the Translation of Scenographic Terms from French to English." 36-40 in Cocuzza, Ginnine, ed.; . Cohen-Stratyner, Barbara Naomi, ed. *Stage Design: Papers from the 15th International Congress of SIBMAS (Société Internationale des Bibliothèques et Musées des Arts du Spectacle).* New York: Theatre Library Association; 1983. (Performing Arts Resources 8.)
USA. France. 1982. Linguistic studies. ■Experience gained in preparing the English text for the Third Edition of *Performing Arts Libraries and Museums of the World.*

258 Halttunen, Karen. *Confidence Men and Painted Women.* New Haven, CT: Yale UP; 1982. 262 pp. (Yale Historical Publications.) Biblio. Index. Illus.: Photo. B&W.
USA. 1830-1870. Historical studies. ■Study of middle class culture, morality, social values and hypocrisy as evidenced by dress.

259 Hillyard, Sylvia J. "Theatre Design Research Is Active and Varied." *ThNe.* 1983 Election Issue; 15(2): 6, 14.
USA. 1981-1983. Studies of research/researchers. ■Scope of research among theatrical designers, is explored on the basis of three examples: a new book, the annual costume research panel and a historic exhibit.

260 Hirsch, John E. "Costumes of a Gilded Age: 'La Belle Epoque'." *USITT.* 1983 Summer; 23(3): 7.
USA. 1870-1910. Histories-sources. ■The costume exhibition 'La Belle Epoque' at The Costume Institute of The Metropolitan Museum of Art shows an era both elegant and formal to a fault, decadent, dangerous and exotic.

261 Ingham, Rosemary; Covey, Liz. *The Costume Designer's Handbook: A Complete Guide for Amateur and Professional Costume Designers.* Englewood Cliffs, NJ: Prentice-Hall; 1983. viii, 264 pp. Biblio. Index. Illus.: Photo. Color. B&W.
USA. 1983. Instructional materials. ■Guide to the techniques of costume design. Includes lists of booksellers, costume organizations, selected painters for costume design research, shopping guides for Boston, Chicago, Los Angeles, San Francisco and other areas.

262 King, Keith, ed.; Wallberg, Mark, ed. "Children's Touring Shows Reap Adult Costume Ideas." *USITT.* 1983 Spring; 22(6): 10.
USA. 1983. Instructional materials. ■Notes, reminders and suggestions regarding children's productions and costuming.

263 Koenig, Bruce A. "Technical Report: Cab-O-Sil in Scene Paint." *TD&T.* 1983 Summer; 19(2): 26-27, 36. Tables.
USA. 1983. Technical studies. ■Cab-O-Sil (silicon dioxide powder) makes an excellent filler and thickening agent in dry pigment scene paint, increasing its viscosity and bonding properties.

264 Nebozenko, Jan. "Sound Systems for Broadway." *TD&T.* 1983 Summer; 19(2): 12-15. Illus.: Diagram. B&W. Detail. Schematic. 3: 4 in. x 5 in.
USA. 1945-1983. Instructional materials. ■Description of sound systems and techniques for controlling sound in Broadway productions.

265 North, John. "Sounding Out Master Sheets." *ThCr.* 1983 Jan.; 17(1): 30-31. Illus.
USA. 1983. Instructional materials. ■Master sheet format for sound plots.

266 O'Donnol, Shirley Miles. *American Costume: 1915-1970. A Sourcebook for the Stage Costumer.* Bloomington, IN: Indiana UP; 1982. xiv, 270 pp. Illus.: Photo. Dwg. B&W.
USA. 1915-1970. Instructional materials. ■Style of American clothing in the twentieth century.

267 Rubin, Joel. "Stage Lighting and the State of the Art: in Twenty Years." *LDM.* 1983 Mar.; 7(1): 52-60. Illus.: Sketches. B&W. 4: 3 in. x 3 in.
USA. 1983. Critical studies. ■Changes in the lighting industry and its output in the next twenty years.

268 Seligman, Kevin L. "Costume Pattern Drafts: Women's Sleeves – 1930's." *TD&T.* 1983 Fall; 19(3): 22-23. Illus.: Sketches. B&W. 6: 4 in. x 5 in.
USA. 1930-1939. Technical studies. ■How to cut and assemble women's sleeves from patterns published in the 1930's.

269 Seligman, Kevin L. "Costume Pattern Drafts." *TD&T.* 1983 Winter; 19(4): 26-27. Illus.: Diagram. Sketches. B&W. Detail. 2: 3 in. x 5 in.
USA. 1900-1983. Technical studies. ■Article on how to cut and assemble an apron consisting of a wide skirt and bib.

270 Sellman, Hunton D.; Lessley, Merrill. *Essentials of Stage Lighting.* Englewood Cliffs, NJ: Prentice-Hall; 1982. xvii, 199 pp.
USA. 1982. Instructional materials. ■Introductory textbook.

271 Stell, W. Joseph. "Increasing the Density and Breadth of Theatrical Communication through Projections." *TD&T.* 1983 Fall ; 19(3): 14-18. Notes. Illus.: Photo. B&W. 7: 3 in. x 5 in.
USA. 1945-1983. Technical studies. ■Projections may be used to concentrate stimuli into a brief span of time and expand the parameters of a production by supplying visual images otherwise only suggested through the subtext. Related to Media: Video forms.

THEATRE IN GENERAL: Multiple application—Design/technology

272 Sweet, Harvey. "Education Activities." *USITT*. 1983 Summer; 23(3): 6.
USA. 1900-1983. Instructional materials. ■Listing of projects and materials for the education of theatre technicians. Sponsored by the Education Commission of the United States Institute for Theatre Technology.

273 Vagenas, Peter T. "Conserving Theatre Designs for the Record and for Exhibition: A Designer's Views." 43-48 in Cocuzza, Ginnine, ed.; . Cohen-Stratyner, Barbara Naomi, ed. *Stage Design: Papers from the 15th International Congress of SIBMAS (Société Internationale des Bibliothèques et Musées des Arts du Spectacle)*. New York: Theatre Library Association; 1983. (Performing Arts Resources 8.)
USA. 1982. Technical studies. ■Why collecting, maintaining and exhibiting designers' work is problematical.

274 Watson, Lee. "T.O.L.D. II." *TD&T*. 1983 Summer; 19(2): 31. [Training of Lighting Designers.]
USA. 1983. Histories-sources. ■Report on lighting World II Conference, New York, April 1983.

275 Whaley, Frank D., Jr. "Property Master's Notebook, 'So let it be written...'." *ThCr*. 1983 Jan.; 17(1): 33-35, 66.
USA. 1900. Instructional materials. ■Brief history of written materials to aid the property master.

276 Woods, Alan. "The McDowell Research Classification System for the Cataloguing of Scene and Costume Designs." 30-35 in Cocuzza, Ginnine, ed.; . Cohen-Stratyner, Barbara Naomi, ed. *Stage Design: Papers from the 15th International Congress of SIBMAS (Société Internationale des Bibliothèques et Musées des Arts du Spectacle)*. New York: Theatre Library Association; 1983. (Performing Arts Resources 8.) Illus.
USA. 1982. Bibliographical studies. ■Theatre collection taxonomy based on an iconographic approach.

277 Aronson, Arnold. "Some Recent Soviet and East German Designs." *TD&T*. 1983 Spring; 19(1): 20-21. Illus.: Plan. Photo. B&W. Grd.Plan. 8: 3 in. x 5 in.
USSR. Germany, East. 1970-1983. Historical studies. ■Examination of recent scenic designs by Sergei Barkhin of the USSR and Jochen Finke of East Germany.

278 Lodder, Christina. *Russian Constructivism*. New Haven, CT: Yale UP; 1983. viii, 328 pp. Index. Illus.: Photo. B&W. Color.
USSR. 1917-1940. Historical studies. ■Comprehensive study of the Russian constructivists with emphasis on stage design in the context of October Revolution ideology. Includes biographical appendix. Grp/movt: Constructivism.

279 Milanovic, Olga. "Some Experience in Collection of Documents on Theatre Scenery from the Past." 41-42 in Cocuzza, Ginnine, ed.; . Cohen-Stratyner, Barbara Naomi, ed. *Stage Design: Papers from the 15th International Congress of SIBMAS (Société Internationale des Bibliothèques et Musées des Arts du Spectacle)*. New York: Theatre Library Association; 1983. (Performing Arts Resources 8.) Illus.
Yugoslavia. 1982. Technical studies. ■Remarks by the scientific advisor to the Serbian Museum of Theatrical Art on collection of documents.

280 Nadežda, Mosusova. "Influence of Stage Design on Music/Drama." 49-54 in Cocuzza, Ginnine, ed.; . Cohen-Stratyner, Barbara Naomi, ed. *Stage Design: Papers from the 15th International Congress of SIBMAS (Société Internationale des Bibliothèques et Musées des Arts du Spectacle)*. New York: Theatre Library Association; 1983. (Performing Arts Resources 8.)
Yugoslavia. 1980. Historical studies. ■Consideration of the kind and amount of influence possible and analysis of an example. Related to Music-Drama: Music theatre.

Institutions

281 Dragún, Osvaldo. "Den Öppna Teatern." (The Open Theatre.) *Entre*. 1983; 10(4): 14-15.
Argentina. 1981-1983. Historical studies. ■Study of Teatro Abierto, founded in 1981 in defiance of the military dictatorship, which started a broad social movement.

282 Foley, Kathy; Scott, Trudy, ed. "Convention Program Report." *ThNe*. 1983 Mar.; 15(3): 7-8. [Second in a series of articles reprinted from *Asian Theatre Bulletin*.]
Asia. USA. 1983. Histories-sources. ■Brief notes on various programs and activities of the New York ATA convention program on Asian theatre.

283 Carinthischer Sommer. *Carinthischer Sommer: Ossiach/Villach*. (Carinthian Summer: Ossiach/Villach.) Klagenfurt: Carinthischer Sommer; 1983. 120 pp. Illus.: Photo. B&W.
Austria. 1983. Histories-sources. ■Detailed description about the whole program of the Carinthian Summer 1983.

284 Österreichischer Bundestheaterverband. *Österreichischer Bundestheaterverband: Bericht, 1982/83*. (Austrian Federal Theatres: Report, 1982-83.) Vienna: Österreichischer Bundestheaterverband; 1983. 456 pp. Pref. Tables. Append. Illus.: Photo. B&W. Grd.Plan.
Austria. 1982-1983. Histories-sources. ■Report on Burgtheater, Staatsoper and Volksoper. Texts of agreements, listing of radio and television broadcasts, guest performances abroad and in provinces, listing of new productions and casts, statistics on plays, authors, composers and spectators.

285 Cziep, Norbert; Mayer, Gerhard; Gottfried, Böhm. "Festspiele in Österreich." (Festivals in Austria.) *Buhne*. 1983 Sep.: 26-32.
Austria. 1983. Reviews of performances. ■Reviews of Steirischer Herbst, Bregenz Festival, Porcia, Carinthischer Sommer and other festivals.

286 Schindler, Otto G. "Die Fachbibliothek für Theaterwissenschaft an der Universität Wien: Probleme und Perspektiven." (The Theatre Research Library at the University of Vienna: Problems and Prospects.) *MdVO*. 1983; 36(4): 38-56.
Austria. 1983. Bibliographical studies.

287 Stöger, Gabi; Karolyi, Claudia; Weinberger, Christian. "Anpassung oder Emanzipation? 'Animazione' als Zielgruppenkonzept in Österreich." (Conformity or Emancipation? 'Animazione' as Target-group Concept in Austria.) *Tzs*. 1983 Summer; 4: 46-59. Notes.
Austria. 1972-1983. Critical studies. ■Structure, aims and methods of animation by Dramatisches Zentrum (Vienna).

288 Stremitzer, Reinald. *Karlsplatz: Wiener Festwochen 1983*. (Karlsplatz: Vienna Festival Weeks.) Vienna: Vorwärts; 1983. 72 pp. Illus.: Photo. Poster. Color. B&W.
Austria. 1983. Histories-sources. ■Documentation pertaining to the Karlsplatz festival, a division of the Wiener Festwochen.

289 Bains, Yashdip Singh. "Frederick Brown and Montreal's Doomed Theatre Royal, 1825-26." *ThS*. 1983; 24(1-2): 65-75. Notes.
Canada. 1825-1826. Historical studies. ■Trustees and manager of Theatre Royal failed to recognize the difficulties of operating a theatre in a country without common culture or concentrated population.

290 Bessai, Diane. "Responding to the Region: The Little Company with the Big Name." *CTR*. 1983 Spring; 37: 55-58. Illus.: Photo. Print. B&W. 1: 4 in. x 6 in.
Canada. 1976-1983. Historical studies. ■History of the Great Canadian Theatre Company and its devotion to cultural and political nationalism.

291 Brown, Mary M. "'Pepper's Ghost Is Tearing Its Hair': Ottawa Theatre in the 1870's." *THC*. 1983 Fall; 4(2): 121-133. Notes.
Canada. 1870-1879. Historical studies. ■Performance calendar of shows at Her Majesty's Theatre, the Rink Music Hall and Gowan's Opera House reveals Ottawa's prominence in the South-Eastern Ontario touring circuit.

292 Dafoe, Christopher. "The Manitoba Theatre Centre: Reaffirming Community." *CTR*. 1983 Spring; 37: 127-130. Illus.: Photo. Print. B&W. 1: 1 in. x 3 in.

CLASSED ENTRIES

THEATRE IN GENERAL: Multiple application—Institutions

Canada. 1958-1983. Historical studies. ■Richard Ouzounian attempts to restore community interest and excitement to Manitoba Theatre Centre.

293 Doolittle, Joyce. "The West Coast's Hardy Perennial: Green Thumb." *CTR.* 1983 Spring; 37: 59-65. Illus.: Photo. Neg. B&W. 2: 5 in. x 6 in., 6 in. x 6 in.
Canada. 1975-1983. Historical studies. ■History of Green Thumb Theatre, examining works, themes and concerns of the company and its continuing development.

294 Milliken, Paul. "PACT: Networking the National Community." *CTR.* 1983 Spring; 37: 34-38. Illus.: Photo. Print. B&W. 1: 2 in. x 3 in.
Canada. 1983. Historical studies. ■Analysis of operation and effectiveness of Professional Association of Canadian Theatres under direction of Curtis Barlow.

295 Rubin, Don. "The Toronto Movement." *CTR.* 1983 Fall; 38: 8-17. Notes. Illus.: Photo. Neg. 3: 4 in. x 5 in., 5 in. x 6 in.
Canada. 1973-1983. Historical studies. ■Movement of Toronto theatres from inspiring, challenging social activities to 'respectable' conservatism.

296 Smith, Patricia Keeney. "Living with Risk: Toronto's New Alternate Theatre." *CTR.* 1983 Fall; 38: 33-43. Illus.: Photo. Print. B&W. 9.
Canada. 1979-1983. Historical studies. ■Examination of intention, motivation and success of alternative theatres in Toronto, focusing on Theatre Centre, Buddies in Bad Times, A.K.A. Performance Interfaces, Nightwood Theatre, Autumn Angel Repertory Company, Actor's Lab, Triple Action Theatre, Passe Muraille and Mercury Theatre.

297 Århus teater akademi. *Århus teater akademi: en status sommeren 1983.* (Århus Theatre Academy: Status Report 1983.) Arhus: Institut for dramaturgi; 1983. 40 pp. (Aktuelle teaterproblemer 9.)
Denmark. 1983. Histories-sources.

298 Andreasen, John; Langsted, Jörn; Bohn, Rainer, transl. "Frieden auf der Strasse: Über Strassentheater." (Peace on the Street: Street Theater.) *Tzs.* 1983 Winter; 6: 90-101. Illus.: Photo.
Denmark. 1982. Historical studies. ■Peace-theatre workshop and their street theatre production in collaboration with the Århus theater akademi, Johnny Melville and the Swedish group Jordcirkus.

299 "Finnish Theatre Abroad." *NFT.* 1983; 35: 12-13. Illus.: Photo. B&W. [Also in French as Le théâtre finlandais à l'étranger.]
Finland. Sweden. 1982-1983. Historical studies. ■Individual Finnish artists who have directed and designed productions abroad. Theatre groups who have made guest appearances in Sweden, Tenerife, USSR and USA.

300 Haapanen, Marjatta. "Amateur Theatre Training." *NFT.* 1983; 36: 26-27. [Also in French as 'La formation dans le domaine du théâtre d'amateurs'.]
Finland. 1983. Historical studies. ■Finnish amateur associations form a joint committee, whose Training Council runs courses on acting, directing, dramaturgy and design. Other courses stress creative drama, children's theatre, church drama, voice and movement.

301 Mäkelä, Heikki. "Any Age Learns." *NFT.* 1983; 36: 14-19. Illus.: Photo. B&W. [Also in French as 'Il n'est jamais trop tard pour apprendre'.]
Finland. 1973-1983. Historical studies. ■Over 200 professional theatre artists have participated in courses for renewal and increased competence administered by the Theatre Academy of Finland.

302 Viherjuuri, Mikko. "Actor Training at Tampere University." *NFT.* 1983; 36: 25-26. Illus.: Photo. B&W. [Also in French as 'La formation des acteurs à l'université de Tampere'.]
Finland. 1967-1983. Historical studies. ■Eino Salemelainen and Matti Tapio established actor training program at Tampere University in 1967. The program stresses individuality, independence and originality.

303 Vuori, Jyrki. "Turku City Theatre." *NFT.* 1983; 35: 2-3, 18. Illus.: Photo. B&W. [Also in French as 'Théâtre municipal de Turku'.]

Finland. 1946-1983. Historical studies. ■Taisto-Bertil Orsmaa manages the Turku Municipal Theatre (founded 1946). Productions in Finnish are presented on two stages built in 1962. The city's theatre history has 16th century origins.

304 Anglès, Auguste. "Jacques Copeau co-fondateur, collaborateur et directeur de *La Nouvelle Revue Française.*" (Jacques Copeau: Cofounder, Collaborator and Director of the *Nouvelle Revue Française.*) *RHT.* 1983; 35(1): 29-41.
France. 1909-1914. Historical studies. ■Founding of the periodical *Nouvelle Revue Française* by Copeau, André Ruyters and Jean Schlumberger.

305 Porrmann, Maria. "Theater als Waffengattung oder: Der Etappenhase im Einsatz." (Theatre as a Type of Weapon.) *Tzs.* 1983 Spring; 3: 59-70. Illus.: Photo.
Germany. 1914-1945. Critical studies. ■Theatre on the battle-front during World Wars I and II: its function as entertainment and political instrument.

306 Ahrens, Ursula. "Tiyatro: Von den Versuchen, in Berlin türkisches Theater unter die Leute zu Bringen." (*Tiyatro*: Attempts to Establish Turkish Theatre in Berlin.) *Tzs.* 1983 Summer; 4: 34-45.
Germany, West. 1982. Histories-sources. ■Theatre-activities of Turkish immigrant workers.

307 Hofmann, Jürgen. "Dortmunder Unionen oder: 1100 Jahre Kultur sind genug." (Dortmund Unions or: 1100 Years of Culture are Enough.) *Tzs.* 1983 Summer; 4: 98-113. [Kultur im Widerspruch (III) (Culture in Contradiction, Part III).]
Germany, West. 1972-1982. Critical studies. ■Theatre and cultural work in the Ruhr-District: social, political and financial circumstances.

308 Jahnke, Manfred. "Erkundungen in der Provinz: Zum Beispiel Ulm." (Investigations in the Provinces: Ulm for Example.) *Tzs.* 1983 Winter; 6: 6-20. Notes.
Germany, West. 1983. Critical studies. ■Theatre in Ulm as an example for the conditions and problems of regional theatre.

309 Kahle, Ulrike. "Für jede Frau und jedermann: Zwischen Zirkuszelt und Eisenbahndepot — Deutsche und französische Frauen machen Theater." (For Every Woman and Every Man: Between a Circus Tent and a Railway Station — German and French Women Make Theatre.) *TH.* 1983(7): 1-6. Illus.: Photo.
Germany, West. 1983. Historical studies. ■Report on Theatre Festival Munich, including brief survey of productions.

310 Klunker, Heinz; Schulze-Reimpell, Werner; Unger, Wilhelm; Iversen, Fritz; Kraus, Friederich; Naumann-Will, Cornelia. "Erstickungszustände und Innovationen: Ein Gespräch mit drei Theaterkritikern über 'Provinztheater'." (Suffocation and Innovation: A Discussion with Three Drama Critics on 'Provincial Theatre'.) *Tzs.* 1983 Winter; 6: 74-89.
Germany, West. 1983. Critical studies. ■Drama critics and members of the *Theaterzeitschrift* editorial staff talk about regional theatre.

311 Krauss, Gisela. "...und nebenbei noch Theater: Zur Kulturarbeit in kleinen Städten." (...and Theatre Besides: On Cultural Work in Small Towns.) *Tzs.* 1983 Winter; 6: 34-44.
Germany, West. 1976-1982. Histories-sources. ■Conditions for the problems of cultural work in small towns, specifically in theatre.

312 Manthey, Brigitta. "Theater als (Über-)Lebenskunst: Motivationen der neuen freien Gruppen in Berlin." (Theatre to Live — Theatre to Survive: Motivations of the New Free Groups in Berlin.) *Tzs.* 1983 Fall; 5: 39-50.
Germany, West. 1982. Historical studies. ■Motivation and goals of the increasing number of free theatre groups in Berlin.

313 Praml, Willy. "Zwangsvorstellungen? oder: Wie das Theater zum Dorf kommt." (Obsessions? or: How Theatre Comes to the Village.) *Tzs.* 1983 Winter; 6: 45-63. Notes.
Germany, West. 1979-1982. Histories-sources. ■Project to intensify cultural work in the village of Niederbrechen, subsidized by the Ministry for Youth, Health and Family.

314 Seiler, Manfred. "Zwischen Spielen Und Sparen: Kulturpolitik und Kulturproduktion in einer 'Provinz' — Metropole."

THEATRE IN GENERAL: Multiple application—Institutions

(Between Playing and Saving: Cultural Politics and Productions in a 'Province' — Metropole.) *TH*. 1983 Apr.; 23: 48-52.
Germany, West. 1983. Historical studies. ▪Brief survey of productions and financial situation of a theatre in Nuremberg.

315 Susen, Gerd; Wack, Edith. "Provinztheater — provinziell? Nicht-All-tägliches aus Moers." (Theatre in the Country — Provincial? Moers Is an Exception.) *Tzs*. 1983 Winter; 6: 21-33. Notes.
Germany, West. 1975-1983. Historical studies. ▪History, financial situation and productions of the Schlosstheater.

316 Sircar, Badal. "Our Street Theatre." *SNJPA*. 1983 July-Sep.; 69: 18-23. Illus.: Photo. B&W. 8.
India. 1983. Historical studies. ▪Description of street theatre performances whose purpose is social change.

317 Sezione Problemi dello Spettacolo — Dipartimento Culturale Partito Comunista Italiano. *La formazione teatrale.* (Theatre Training.) Rome: Partito Comunista Italiano; 1983. 106 pp. (Materiali di lavoro e documentazione 6.) [Proceedings of meeting — Frattocchie (Roma), February 6-7, 1982.]
Italy. 1982. Critical studies. ▪State of theatre schools in Italy and suggestions for their improvement.

318 Cappello, Salvato, ed. *Cronache di cent'anni.* (Chronicles of a Hundred Years.) Rome: Società Italiana degli Autori e Editori; 1983. 346 pp. Tables. Illus.: Diagram. Graphs. Photo. B&W. Color.
Italy. 1882-1982. Histories-specific. ▪History of the Società Italiana degli Autori ed Editori published in celebration of its first centenary.

319 Catalano, Ettore. *Il contesto teatrale: Ricerche sulla condizione teatrale meridionale.* (Theatrical Context: Inquiries about the Theatrical Situation in Southern Italy.) Bari: Levante; 1982. 142 pp. Notes. Tables. Illus.: Diagram.
Italy. 1982. Critical studies. ▪State of theatre in Southern Italy.

320 Rood, Arnold. "E. Gordon Craig, Director, School of the Art of the Theatre." *ThR*. 1983 Spring; 8(1): 1-17. Notes. Illus.: Photo. B&W. 27.
Italy. UK-England. 1900-1917. Historical studies. ▪Plans and efforts of Craig to establish his School for the Art of Theatre in Florence. He considered it more as a place for theatrical experimentation than for training.

321 Haerdter, Michael. "Theater in den Niederlanden: Nachricht von einer geglückten Erneuerung." (Theatre in the Netherlands: News of a Successful Renewal.) *Tzs*. 1983 Winter; 6: 107-120.
Netherlands. 1945-1983. Historical studies. ▪Efforts to establish 'modern' theatre.

322 Epskamp, Kees P. "Training Popular Theatre Trainers: A Case Study of Nigeria." *MuK*. 1983; 29: 272-281. Notes.
Nigeria. 1981-1982. Historical studies. ▪First Benue International Popular Theatre Workshop for Development, organized by the Benue Council for Arts and Culture.

323 Anon. "Le Langage Universel du Théâtre: Entretien avec le Professeur Bohdan Korzeniewski." (The Universal Language of Theatre: An Interview with Professor Bohdan Korzeniewski.) *TP*. 1983; 294-296: 8-10. [In French and English.]
Poland. 1900-1983. Historical studies. ▪How the International Theatre Institute (ITI) has expanded the universal character of theatre.

324 Grodzicki, August. "Le Théâtre en Pologne a Vingt-Cinq Ans." (Twenty-Fifth Anniversary of Theatre in Poland.) *TP*. 1983; 294-296: 11-14. [In French and English.]
Poland. 1958-1982. Historical studies. ▪History of the Polish International Theatre Institute (ITI) Centre.

325 Sieroszewski, Andrzej. "Polak Węgier dwa bratanki. Węgierski bestseller 1981." (Pole and Hungarian — Two First Cousins. Hungarian Bestseller 1981.) *PaT*. 1983; 32(1): 31-38. Notes. Illus.: Photo. B&W. 3: 7 cm. x 9 cm., 12 cm. x 17 cm. [Title is Polish proverb.]

Poland. Russia. Hungary. 1815-1829. Critical studies. ▪Review essay on György Spiró's novel *Az Ikszek* about the Polish theatre in Warsaw under Russian rule and its relation to political life.

326 Rodriguez, Orlando. "Latinamerikansk teater idag: En översikt." (Latin American Theatre Today: An Overview.) *Entre*. 1983; 10(4): 3-5.
South America. North America. 1950-1983. Historical studies. ▪Diversity of Latin American theatre, due to social change and foreign influence, reflected in political drama, light entertainment, collectives, amateur groups and ensembles in exile.

327 Coca, Jordi. "Hermann Bonin: Cristal i marbre." (Hermann Bonin: Glass and Marble.) *SdO*. 1983 Jan.; 280: 35-40. Print. B&W. 10: 9 cm. x 12 cm.
Spain. 1945-1982. Histories-sources. ▪Interview with the director of the Centre Dramàtic de la Generalitat on his relation with different theatrical institutions. Bonin was also director of the Institut del Teatre de Barcelona.

328 Nordlund, Gunilla. "Den undersökande skådespelaren eller Modet att skapa." (The Investigative Actor, or, The Courage to Create.) *Entre*. 1983; 10(3): 14-19.
Sweden. 1970-1983. Critical studies. ▪Effect of the women's movement on experimental theatre groups such as Fågel Blå and Unga Klara, led by Suzanne Osten. Grp/movt: Feminism.

329 Öhrn, Anders. "White Out! — för en breddning av begreppet teater." (White Out! For a Broadening of the Concept of the Theatre.) *Entre*. 1983; 10(1): 4-7.
Sweden. 1983. Historical studies. ▪Acrobatic, multimedia performances of experimental group theatres such as Sargasso, Fjärde teatern and Remote Control. Related to Mixed Performances.

330 Hyde, Phil. "Hyping the Avant Garde." *PM*. 1983 Oct.-Nov.; 26: 17-26. Illus.: Photo. Print. B&W.
UK-England. 1983. Historical studies. ▪Festivals with an international scope (Avignon, LIFT and WOMAD) are examined, as is the festival concept itself.

331 Pick, John. "Mismanagement and Snobbery." *E&AM*. 1983 Nov.: 17-20. Illus.: Photo. Print. B&W. 2.
UK-England. 1942-1960. Critical studies. ▪West End theatre failing as popular art due to practices and policies adopted by theatre managers.

332 McIvor, Peter. "Forrest Reid, *Uladh*, and the Ulster Literary Theatre." *Éire*. 1982 Summer; 17(2): 134-140. Notes.
UK-Ireland. 1902-1905. Historical studies. ▪Foundations of Ulster Literary Theatre and relationship of critic Forrest Reid to the theatre's literary magazine, *Uladh*.

333 Campbell, Donald. *A Brighter Sunshine: A Hundred Years of the Edinburgh Royal Lyceum Theatre.* Edinburgh: Polygon Books; 1983. 223 pp. Index. Illus.: Photo. Color. B&W.
UK-Scotland. 1883-1983. Histories-specific. ▪History of the Edinburgh Royal Lyceum Theatre.

334 Anon. "Mid-America Theatre Conference Theatre History Symposium 1983." *THSt*. 1983; 3: 139-140.
USA. 1983. Histories-sources. ▪Brief description of the 1983 symposium with a listing of all papers presented.

335 Anon. "Diversity and Theatre Achievement Mark New ATA Fellows." *ThNe*. 1983 Nov.; 15(8): 7, 12. Illus.: Photo. B&W. 4: 3 in. x 3 in.
USA. 1983. Histories-sources. ▪Four new members inducted into the American Theatre Association's College of Fellows: Howard Bay, Orlin Corey, Ann Shaw, Sam M. Smiley.

336 Anon. "Theatre Programs Serve Needs of Military Audiences." *ThNe*. 1983 Summer; 15(6): 15.
USA. 1960-1983. Histories-sources. ▪Organization, people and theatres involved in the Army Theatre Arts Association of the American Theatre Association.

337 Anon. "Waterloo Playhouse Honored by State." *ThNe*. 1983 Fall; 15(7): 12. Illus.: Photo. B&W. 1: 5 in. x 5 in.
USA. 1983. Histories-sources. ▪Waterloo Community Playhouse receives 1983 Iowa Award for Distinguished Service to the Arts for providing professional level theatre to the Midwest.

THEATRE IN GENERAL: Multiple application—Institutions

338 Anon. "An ATA Position Paper on the Status of a National Theatre in the United States." *ThNe.* 1983 Mar.; 15(3): 2. [Formulated by the American Theatre Association's Commission on Theatre Development.]
USA. 1983. Histories-sources. ■Reasons why the Commission feels no real need for an institutionalized national theatre.

339 Anon. "It's Papp Versus Stevens on National Theatre." *ThNe.* 1983 Nov.; 15(8): 3. Illus.: Photo. B&W. 2: 2 in. x 2 in.
USA. 1983. Histories-sources. ■Influential producers outline two different plans for a national theatre.

340 Bailey, A. Peter. "A Look at Contemporary Black Theatre Movement." *BALF.* 1983 Spring; 17: 19-21.
USA. 1982. Historical studies. ■Overview of Black theatre groups and performances during the 1982 season as well as comment on the political and economic aspects of the theatres and their producers.

341 Boston, Taquiena; Katz, Vera. "Witnesses to a Possibility: The Black Theatre Movement in Washington, DC, 1968-1976." *BALF.* 1983 Spring; 17: 22-26. Illus.: Photo. 1: 8 in. x 10 in.
USA. 1968-1976. Historical studies. ■Overview of the production history of university, community and professional groups in the nation's capital over a decade, with editorial comment.

342 Dasgupta, Gautam. "Squat: Nature Theatre of New York." *PerAJ.* 1983; 7(1): 7-20. Illus.: Photo.
USA. Hungary. 1975-1977. Critical studies. ■Description of Squat performances in Budapest in 1975 and New York in 1977, explaining the theatrical, theoretical and metaphysical importance of the troupe's work.

343 Dorsey, Francis E. "African Community Theatre Development: Consciousness, Communication, and Culture." *WJBS.* 1983 Summer; 7(2): 78-82. Notes. Illus.: Plan. Photo. Print. B&W. Grd.Plan. 5: 2 in. x 2 in., 3 in. x 5 in.
USA. 1972-1983. Histories-sources. ■Brief history and description of the growth and development of a community theatre program under the auspices of Kent State University.

344 Fallon, Richard G. "State of the American Theatre Association Address: Future Challenges Will Demand Increased Strength and Support." *ThNe.* 1983 Fall; 15(7): 2, 14.
USA. 1983. Histories-sources. ■President of the American Theatre Association in his address to the 1983 annual business meeting discusses nine priorities for the Association.

345 Fox, Ted. *Showtime at the Apollo.* New York: Holt, Rinehart, and Winston; 1983. xii, 322 pp. Index. Illus.: Photo.
USA. 1930-1983. Histories-specific. ■History of the Apollo Theatre and those who performed there. Related to Popular Entertainment.

346 Hild, Stephen. "Costume Training Programs." *TD&T.* 1983 Spring; 19(1): 28-29. Notes. Illus.: Dwg. B&W. 1: 2 in. x 3 in.
USA. 1979-1983. Histories-sources. ■Statistical summary of a four-year study to investigate and list current faculty positions, course work, facilities and basic philosophies of colleges and universities in the areas of costume design, construction and history.

347 Hughes, Anna May. "News from the Secondary School Theatre Association: Divisional Awards Honor Educators." *ThNe.* 1983 Nov.; 15(8): 8.
USA. 1983. Histories-sources. ■Three awards — the first John C. Barner Memorial Award, the Secondary School Theatre Association (SSTA) Founders Award, and the Walter Peck Award — are presented for 1983.

348 Koenig, Linda Lee. *The Vagabonds: America's Oldest Little Theater.* Rutherford, NJ and London: Fairleigh Dickinson UP and Associated UP; 1983. 166 pp. Biblio. Index. Illus.: Photo.
USA. 1916. Historical studies.

349 Lee, Maryat. "To Will One Thing." *TDR.* 1983; 27(4): 47-53.
USA. 1975. Historical studies. ■Origin and work of Eco Theatre in West Virginia.

350 Lynn, Margaret. "ATA Exploring New Publications Outlets with National Publisher." *ThNe.* 1983 Summer; 15(6): 2, 14. [ATA: American Theatre Association.]
USA. 1983. Histories-sources. ■Seven benefits of a proposed co-publishing program with University Press of America.

351 Meserve, Walter J. "ATA Helped Realize Institute's 'Long-held Dream'." *ThNe.* 1983 Summer; 15(6): 6. [ATA: American Theatre Association.]
USA. 1983-1984. Historical studies. ■Organization, objectives and long-range projects of the recently established Institute for American Theatre Studies (IATS) at Indiana University in Bloomington.

352 Ramirez, Elizabeth C. "A History of Mexican American Professional Theatre in Texas Prior to 1900." *ThS.* 1983; 24(1-2): 99-116. Notes. Tables.
USA. Mexico. 1848-1900. Historical studies. ■Brief survey of Spanish language repertory theatre troupe activities in Texas: tours, performances, performers, practices, spaces, repertory and audiences.

353 Regan, F. Scott. "A Preliminary Investigation of Current Practices in American Youth Theatres." *ChTR.* 1983 July; 32(3): 13-15.
USA. 1983. Historical studies. ■Profile of American youth theatres, including information on goals, courses offered, organization, funding and needs.

354 Wright, Lin. "Play Citation, Bell Award Join List of Children's Theatre Honors." *ThNe.* 1983 Nov.; 15(8): 6.
USA. 1983. Histories-sources. ■Two new awards — The Distinguished Play Award and the Campton Bell Award — are added to the annual Jennie Heiden Award in honoring individuals and organizations serving the children's theatre profession.

355 Ateneo de Caracas; Presidencia de la República. *Quinto Festival Internacional de Teatro, Caracas '81, Ateneo de Caracas, 50 aniversario.* (Fifth International Festival of Theatre, Caracas '81: 50th Anniversary of the Ateneo de Caracas.) Caracas: Gobernación del Distrito Federal; 1983. 248 pp.
Venezuela. 1981. Histories-sources.

Performance spaces

356 Thorne, Ross. "Australian Theatre Historical Society." *M.* 1983 Third Quarter; 15(3): 7-8. Illus.: Photo. B&W. 2.
Australia. 1982-1983. Histories-sources. ■Brief description of the Australian Theatre Historical Society, their 1983 convention and the theatres toured during that meeting.

357 Böhm, Gotthard. "Rückkehr zu den Wurzeln." (Back to the Roots.) *Buhne.* 1983 June: 11-12. Illus.: Photo. Color.
Austria. 1983. Historical studies. ■Use of churches as performance spaces: revival of religious themes and church opera.

358 Keil-Budischowsky, Verena. *Die Theater Wiens.* (The Theatres of Vienna.) Vienna: Zsolnay; 1983. 410 pp. (Wiener Geschichtsbücher 30/31/32.) Notes.
Austria. 1300-1983. Histories-specific. ■Concise history of theatre buildings in Vienna.

359 Budnick, Carol. "Theatre on the Frontier: Winnipeg in the 1800's." *THC.* 1983 Spring; 4(1): 25-40. Notes. Illus.: Dwg. Photo. Print. B&W. 4: 3 in. x 4 in., 2 in. x 2 in.
Canada. 1882-1892. Historical studies. ■Influence of frontier environment on theatres in Winnipeg, suppression of variety theatres and Princess Opera House.

360 Stuart, Ross. "A Circle without a Centre: The Predicament of Toronto's Theatre Space." *CTR.* 1983 Fall; 38: 18-24. Illus.: Photo. Neg. B&W. 4.
Canada. 1983. Historical studies. ■Building, restoration and revitalization of theatres in Toronto.

361 Astington, John H. "The Site of the Show for Queen Elizabeth at Greenwich." *REEDN.* 1982; 2: 8-14. Notes.
England. 1500. Historical studies. ■Location of the turret in Greenwich Park. Grp/movt: Elizabethan theatre.

362 Barlow, Graham. "Hampton Court Theatre, 1718." *TN.* 1983; 37(2): 54-63. Notes. Illus.: Plan. Architec. Grd.Plan. 3.

THEATRE IN GENERAL: Multiple application—Performance spaces

England. 1718-1798. Histories-reconstruction. ■Conjectural reconstruction of the theatre in the Great Hall of Hampton Court Palace, based on a floorplan by the architect, and contemporary records and accounts.

363   Barlow, Graham. "Gibbon's Tennis Court: Hollar v. Wilkinson." *ThR.* 1983 Summer; 8(2): 130-146. Notes. Illus.: Diagram. Dwg. Maps. Plan. Photo. 20.

England. 1636-1660. Historical studies. ■Based upon contemporary graphic representations and civic records, the probable dimensions, orientation and dates are established for theatre at Gibbon's court at Lincoln's Inn Fields.

364   George, David. "Jacobean Actors and the Great Hall at Gawthorpe, Lancashire." *TN.* 1983; 37(3): 109-121. Notes.

England. 1600-1618. Historical studies. ■Although modified slightly, the Great Hall at Gawthorpe is one of the few remaining spaces where plays were presented in Shakespeare's lifetime. Financial accounts provide information on the activities of various Jacobean traveling companies.

365   Limon, Henryck; Limon, Jerzy. "An Interpretation of De Witt's Drawing on the Methodological Ground of Perspective Restitution." *CompD.* 1983 Fall; 17(3): 233-242. Notes. Illus.: Diagram. Schematic. 2: 3 in. x 5 in.

England. 1596. Critical studies. ■De Witt's drawing of the Swan theatre is interpreted using 'the scientific methods of theoretical and artistic perspective restitution'. Grp/movt: Elizabethan theatre.

366   Pilkington, Mark C. "The Playhouse in Winestreet, Bristol." *TN.* 1983; 37(1): 14-21. Notes.

England. 1580-1630. Historical studies. ■Evidence pertaining to leases for properties in the area and dating of the playhouse operations.

367   Visser, Colin. "Information on the Cockpit-in-Court from the Diplomatic Correspondence of Isaac Bartet, 1660." *TN.* 1983 ; 37(3): 99-101. Notes.

England. 1660. Historical studies. ■Correspondence of Bartet to Mazarin, now in the archives of the Ministry of Foreign Affairs in Paris, reveals some architectural details of Whitehall in the areas adjacent to the Cockpit Theatre.

368   Norri, Marja-Riitta. "Taiteen ja tilan ristiriita." (The Conflict of the Art with the Space.) *Ark.* 1983; 80(5-6): 30-33.

Finland. 1983. Critical studies. ■Interview with director Ralf Långbacka about performance spaces.

369   Rittaud-Hutinet, Jacques; Besançon. *La Vision d'un futur: Ledoux et ses théâtres.* (Vision of a Future: Ledoux and His Theatres.) Lyon: UP de Lyon; 1982. 198 pp. Illus.: Photo.

France. 1736-1806. Critical studies. ■Analysis of the relation between architectural structure and the social function of the theatre through the example of Claude-Nicolas Ledoux's main architectural project: Theatre of Besançon.

370   Kähler, Otto; Steinfeldt, Maria, photo. "Ein ungewöhnliches Theater: Theater im Palast der Republik (TIP)." (An Uncommon Theatre: Theatre at the Palast der Republik (TIP).) *BtR.* 1983; 76(1): 15. Illus.: Plan. Photo. B&W. Schematic.

Germany, East. 1983. Technical studies. ■Typical architecture of Palast der Republik influences the relationship between the performers and the audience.

371   Skoda, Rudolf; Sieg, Volker. "Messepalast in Prag vor dem Wiederaufbau." (Exhibition Hall in Prague before the Reconstruction.) *BK.* 1982; 1: 5-13. Illus.: Photo. Plan. 11.

Germany, East. 1982. Histories-sources. ■Description of a full surround-style concert hall. Considerable physical detail, written by project architect.

372   Biste, Rudolf; Kirsch, Eberhard; Gerling, Kurt; Ziller, Alexander. "Theaterneubau Heilbronn." (A New Theatre Building in Heilbronn.) *BtR.* 1983; 76(4): 16-18. Illus.: Photo. FL. B&W. Grd.Plan. Fr.Elev. 6. [Part Two.]

Germany, West. 1961-1983. Technical studies. ■Construction and technical equipment of a new theatre building.

373   Bredenbeck, Günther. "Zugerscheinungen im Theater: Ursachen und Möglichkeiten zu deren Beseitigung." (Drafts in Theatres: Causes and Possibilities for Removing

Them.) *BtR.* 1983; 76(4): 24. [From *Bauten der Kultur*, 2/81.]

Germany, West. 1983. Technical studies. ■Problem of drafts in theatres and ways to eliminate them.

374   Fiebelkorn, Jan. "1970-1980: Das junge Theater erobert sich neue, offene Spielräume." (1970-1980: The Young Theatre Conquers New Open Performance Spaces.) *BtR.* 1983 Special; 76: 24-31. Illus.: Design. Photo. Plan. B&W. Grd.Plan. Schematic. 38.

Germany, West. 1962-1980. Technical studies. ■New aesthetical forms of staging, new formations of performance spaces at the Concordia Theater (Bremen), Ballhof Hanover, Bo-Fabrik of the Bochumer Schauspiel and the Schaubühne am Halleschen Ufer.

375   Lotz, Walter. "Mobilität des Kleinen Hauses Gelsenkirchen." (Mobility of the Small House of Gelsenkirchen.) *BtR.* 1983; 76: 12-13. Illus.: Photo. Plan. B&W. Grd.Plan. 7.

Germany, West. 1962-1983. Technical studies. ■Design, construction and partitions of the Musiktheater in Revier.

376   Maier, Hanns; Lorenz, Werner. "Das 'entfesselte' neue Theater in Mannheim und eine vertane Chance: Herausforderung, Wirkung, Grenzen und Erfahrung in Neubau." (The Restored New Theatre in Mannheim and a Squandered Chance: Challenge, Effect, Limits and Experience in the New Building.) *BtR.* 1983; 76: 10-11. Illus.: Photo. Plan. B&W. Schematic. 7.

Germany, West. 1777-1983. Technical studies. ■Design and history of the Nationaltheater Mannheim.

377   Tschermak, Martin. "Theater in den Hallen: Das Deutsche Schauspielhaus Hamburg in der Kampnagelfabrik." (Theatre in Industrial Works: Hamburg's Deutsches Schauspielhaus in the Kampnagelfabrik.) *BtR.* 1983; 76(2): 15-18. Illus.: Plan. Photo. B&W. Grd.Plan. 24.

Germany, West. 1980-1983. Technical studies. ■Technical problems and artistic challenges of performing at a former factory, during the renovations of the theatre building of the Deutsches Schauspielhaus (Hamburg).

378   *L'Accademia Filarmonica di Verona e il suo teatro.* (The Accademia Filarmonica in Verona and Its Theatre.) Verona: Accademia Filarmonica; 1982. 303 pp. Append. Notes. Index. Tables. Illus.: Photo. B&W. Color. [250th anniversary of the inauguration of Teatro Filarmonico.]

Italy. 1732-1978. Historical studies. ■History of Teatro Filarmonico in Verona and productions mounted there. Related to Music-Drama: Opera.

379   Ente Manifestazioni Mantovane, ed.. *Il teatro di Antonio Bibiena in Mantova e il Palazzo accademico.* (Antonio Bibiena's Theatre in Mantua and the Palazzo Accademico.) Mantua: Citem/Emm; 1982. 48 pp. Biblio. Tables. Illus.: Plan. Photo. B&W. Color. [2nd revised edition.]

Italy. 1767-1982. Historical studies. ■History and architecture of Teatro Scientifico and Palazzo Accademico of Mantua. Includes a chapter on Mozart's concert in 1770.

380   Gori, Maria Cristina. *Il Teatro Comunale di Forlimpopoli.* (Municipal Theatre of Forlimpopoli.) Florence: Alinea; 1982. 91 pp. (Saggi e documenti 32.) Pref. Notes. Index. Biblio. Illus.: Photo. B&W.

Italy. 1600-1982. Historical studies. ■Architecture of Municipal Theatre at Forlimpopoli.

381   Isgrò, Giovanni. *Teatro del 500 a Palermo.* (Sixteenth Century Theatre in Palermo.) Palermo: Flaccovio; 1983. 193 pp. (Quaderni per l'immaginario 3.) Append. Notes. Biblio. Tables. Illus.: Photo.

Italy. 1500-1600. Historical studies. ■Use of urban areas to mount theatre spectacles between Renaissance and Baroque periods. Appendix contains contemporary public records and fragments of staging notes. Grp/movt: Renaissance theatre; Baroque theatre.

382   Kronberg, Karl. "Historische Theater — moderne Technik?" (Historic Theatres and Modern Technology?) *BtR.* 1983; 76(2): 10-14. Illus.: Design. Photo. Plan. Sketches.

CLASSED ENTRIES

B&W. Grd.Plan. 20. [Congress in Reggio Emilia in November, 1982.]
Italy. 1588-1985. Technical studies. ■Construction, renovation and technical equipment of historic theatre buildings.

383 Lanzellotto, Girolamo, ed. *Locali di pubblico spettacolo: Norme di sicurezza.* (Performance Halls: Security Measures.) Naples: Simone; 1983. 240 pp. (Pubblicazioni giuridiche 80.)
Italy. 1983. Histories-sources. ■Security measures and regulations in Italian theatres.

384 Picchi, Arnaldo, ed. *La città viva: Materiali sulla teatralizzazione dello spazio urbano.* (The Living City: Materials on the Theatricalization of the Urban Space.) Bologna: Clueb; 1983. 280 pp. Pref. Append. [Second series.]
Italy. 1983. ■Proposals and experiences by theatrical operators to utilize the urban space for performances.

385 Rotondi, Sergio. *L'architettura teatrale a Roma: Il teatro Quirino.* (Theatrical Architecture in Rome: Teatro Quirino.) Rome: Kappa; 1983. 65 pp. Pref. Notes. Biblio. Tables. Illus.: Photo. B&W.
Italy. 1870-1954. Technical studies. ■Architecture and restorations of Teatro Quirino in Rome.

386 Bojar, Jerzy. "150 Jahre Wielki-Theater Warschau." (150 Years of Teatr Wielki in Warsaw.) *BtR.* 1983; 76(5): 10-13. Illus.: Photo. Plan. B&W. Grd.Plan. 5.
Poland. 1779-1983. Technical studies. ■History, external and internal design of one of the world's largest theatres.

387 Manodori, Alberto. *Anfiteatri, circhi e stadi di Roma.* (Amphitheatres, Circuses and Stadiums of Rome.) Rome: New Compton; 1982. 254 pp. (Quest'Italia 26.) Pref. Append. Index. Biblio. Tables. Illus.: Photo. B&W.
Roman Republic. Roman Empire. 616 B.C.-523 A.D. Histories-specific. ■*Naumachiae*, gladiatorial contests, circus races and other acts in ancient Rome. Related to Popular Entertainment.

388 Allen, John J. *The Reconstruction of a Spanish Golden Age Playhouse: El Corral del Príncipe.* Gainesville, FL: UP of Florida; 1983. xii, 129 pp. Biblio. Index. Illus.: Dwg. 42.
Spain. 1583-1744. Historical studies. ■Describes attempts to reconstruct complex and irregular theatre of the Siglo de Oro. Includes comparison with English playhouses of the period.

389 González Hurtado de Mendoza, María Francisca; Martín de la Torre, Mercedes. *Historia y reconstrucción del teatro romano de Málaga.* (History and Reconstruction of Málaga Roman Amphitheatre.) Malaga: Universidad de Málaga; 1983. 132 pp. Biblio. Illus.: Plan. Photo.
Spain. Roman Empire. 200. Historical studies. ■Town-planning and reconstruction of Roman amphitheatre in Málaga.

390 Pla Dalmau, Joaquim, ed.; Codina, Pere. *Estampes populars gironines, Tercera Sèrie: Teatre Municipal de Girona.* (Popular Imprints of Girona, Third Series: Municipal Theatre of Girona.) Girona: Llibreria Pla i Dalmau; 1983. (Estampes populars gironines 3.) Pref. Illus.: Design. Print. Color. 6: 29 cm. x 40 cm.
Spain. 1769-1860. Histories-sources. ■Series of six engravings of cutting, numbered from 21 to 26, representing different perspectives of Municipal Theatre House of Girona, with brief history of the house by Pere Codina.

391 Sirera, Josep-Lluis. "Els primers cent cinquanta anys d'un teatre: el Principal de València." (The First 150 Years of a Theatre: The Principal de València.) *SdO.* 1983 Feb.; 281: 49-52. Notes. Illus.: Design. Poster. Photo. Print. B&W. 6: 12 cm. x 8 cm.
Spain. 1823-1979. Historical studies. ■History of the Principal de València Theatre: political changes and its relocation into a new building.

392 Koenig, Bruce A. "Where Was Garrick's Prompter?" *TN.* 1983; 37(1): 9-14. Notes. Illus.: Plan. 3: 4 in. x 7 in.
UK-England. 1747-1776. Historical studies. ■Placement of the prompter's and royal boxes at Drury Lane by David Garrick.

393 Aronson, Arnold, ed. "Theatre Architecture." *TD&T.* 1983 Spring; 19(1): 22-27, 43. Illus.: Design. Dwg. Plan. Photo. B&W. Architec. Grd.Plan. 15: 4 in. x 5 in., 5: 3 in. x 5 in.. [Other parts in: Fall 19: 26-29 and Winter 19: 22-23.]
USA. Canada. 1972-1980. Histories-sources. ■On-going series of reproductions of panels displayed at the United States Institute for Theatre Technology conferences showing examples of contemporary theatre architecture.

394 Bhavnani, Ashok M. "Rebuilding the Paper Mill Playhouse: Architect's Description." *TD&T.* 1983 Winter; 19(4): 16-19. Illus.: Plan. Photo. B&W. Grd.Plan. 7: 5 in. x 3 in., 2 in. x 7 in.
USA. 1980-1982. Histories-sources. ■History and description of the Paper Mill Playhouse and plans showing its features after reconstruction following a fire in 1980.

395 Chavanne, J. Paul. "The Columbia Theatre in the South End of Boston." *M.* 1983 Third Quarter; 15(3): 3-6. Illus.: Photo. B&W. 3.
USA. 1881-1957. Historical studies. ■Historical survey of Columbia Theatre built in 1881 and used both as a legitimate playhouse and for burlesque and vaudeville. The theatre was remodeled several times before its demolition in 1957. Related to Popular Entertainment: Burlesque.

396 George, Peter J. "Getting a Theatre Project off Square One." *M.* 1983 Fourth Quarter; 15(4): 4-6. Tables. Illus.: Photo. Diagram. B&W. Chart. 1.
USA. 1983. Instructional materials. ■Steps required to restore a historic theatre including organization, planning and developing a feasibility study.

397 Gruenke, Bernard E., Jr. "The Decorator's View." *M.* 1983 Fourth Quarter; 15(4): 23. Illus.: Photo. B&W. 2.
USA. 1983. Technical studies. ■One of the owners of the Conrad Schmitt Studios, a firm involved in the restoration of theatres, comments on the restoration process.

398 Hays, Michael. "Lincoln Center and Some Other Cultural Paradigms." *ThM.* 1983 Winter; 15(1): 25-30. Notes. Illus.: Photo. Print. B&W. 4.
USA. France. 1967. Critical studies. ■Socio-semiotic analysis of performance spaces, with discussion of the Metropolitan Opera House, Lincoln Center and the Paris Opera. Related to Music-Drama.

399 Kinkaid, Frank. "News from: Eugene, Oregon." *OpN.* 1983 Sep.; 48(3): 48-49. Illus.: Photo. B&W. 1.
USA. 1982. Historical studies. ■History of the Hult Center for the Performing Arts, a multi-purpose space.

400 Knapp, Margaret Mary. *A Historical Study of the Legitimate Playhouses on West Forty-Second Street between Seventh and Eighth Avenues in New York City.* New York: City Univ. of New York; 1982. 493 pp. [Diss.: University Microfilms order number DA8212198.]
USA. 1893-1944. Histories-specific. ■History of the 'theatre block' from the early nineteenth century to the present, with emphasis on the period of growth and decline. Related to Music-Drama.

401 Madison, Gordon. "Restoration of the Capitol Theatre, Chambersburg, Pennsylvania." *M.* 1983 Fourth Quarter; 15(4): 14-15 . Illus.: Photo. B&W. 3.
USA. 1926-1983. Histories-sources. ■Discussion of how a commercial operator has renovated a 1926 movie theatre for both film and community theatre use.

402 Margolis, Tina, ed. "Houston Approves Design Concept for Wortham Theater Center." *USITT.* 1983 Fall; 23(4): 11.
USA. 1983. Histories-sources. ■Design for the 400,000 square foot Wortham Theater Center to be built in Houston, Texas, is outlined.

403 Matthews, Marianne. "The Rialto, Joliet, Illinois: Preservation and Restoration." *M.* 1983 Fourth Quarter; 15(4): 18-22. Biblio. Illus.: Photo. B&W. 4.
USA. 1926-1983. Historical studies. ■Description of the Rialto Square Theatre: some notes on its history and on its 1981 restoration as a performing arts center.

THEATRE IN GENERAL: Multiple application—Performance spaces

404 Meyer, Patricia A.; Bosner, Leo. "Saving the Tivoli Theatre: A Case Study in Organi Historical Preservation." *M.* 1983 Fourth Quarter; 15(4): 10-13. Illus.: Photo. B&W. 3.
USA. 1980-1983. Instructional materials. ■Discussion of the steps taken to save a specific theatre followed by some generalizations on how to save historic theatres.

405 Panzer, James; Christianson, Carl; Kahn, David. "Theatrical and Acoustical Systems for the Renovated Historic Theatre." *M.* 1983 Fourth Quarter; 15(4): 7-9. Illus.: Photo. B&W. 1.
USA. 1983. Technical studies. ■Aspects of restoring historic theatres including modifications to the stage, house and various support systems.

406 Peterson, Richard S. "From Ballets to Ballots and Back." *TD&T.* 1983 Fall; 19(3): 19-21. Illus.: Plan. Photo. B&W. 4: 3 in. x 4 in.
USA. 1982-1983. Historical studies. ■Description of the process of converting the Crouse-Hinds Concert Theatre for the Democratic Party 1982 Convention. Related to Dance: Ballet.

407 Sterling, Wallace. "Cleveland Play House Unveils New Theatre Complex." *ThNe.* 1983 Dec.; 15(9): 1, 12. Illus.: Dwg. B&W. 1: 4 in. x 10 in.
USA. 1915-1983. Histories-sources. ■Philip Johnson's design for Cleveland Play House complex which includes the new Kenyon C. Bolton Theatre, with a brief history of the Cleveland Play House performance spaces.

408 Uzzle, Ted. "Acoustical Considerations in Theatre Preservation." *M.* 1983 Fourth Quarter; 15(4): 25-26. Biblio.
USA. 1983. Technical studies. ■Discussion of theatre acoustics and sound reinforcement with special reference to the problems encountered in theatre renovation.

409 Waldo, William S. "Theatre Chair Restoration." *M.* 1983 Fourth Quarter; 15(4): 38. Illus.: Photo. B&W. 1.
USA. 1983. Technical studies. ■Restoration of old theatre chairs, written by an officer of Country Roads Inc., a company that restores old theatre chairs.

410 Goodwin, Noël. "News from Caracas." *OpN.* 1983 Dec. 10; 48(6): 62, 66-67. Illus.: Photo. B&W. 1.
Venezuela. 1983. Historical studies. ■Opening of the Teresa Carreño Arts Center in Caracas.

411 Brehms, Joan. "Das älteste 'Städtische Theater' Europas auf der Insel Hvar." (Europe's Oldest 'Municipal Theatre' on the Isle of Hvar.) *BtR.* 1983; 76(3): 19-20. Illus.: Photo. B&W. 2.
Yugoslavia. 1612-1983. Historical studies. ■Cultural history and architectural design.

Performance/production

412 Wilson, Edwin; Goldfarb, Alvin. *Living Theatre.* New York: McGraw-Hill; 1983. xii, 482 pp.
499 B.C.-1983 A.D. Histories-general. ■Survey of world theatre history presented conceptually, including structural and cultural context.

413 Germain, Jean-Claude; Rouyer, Philippe, trans.; Rubin, Don, trans. "Quebec: Beginning the Dialogue." *CTR.* 1982 Spring; 34: 28-33.
Canada. 1982. Histories-sources. ■Leading Montreal director suggests avenues for communication between Quebec theatre and the rest of Canada.

414 Scott, A.C. *Actors Are Madmen: Notebook of a Theatregoer in China.* Madison, WI: Univ. of Wisconsin P; 1982. xii, 225 pp.
China, People's Republic of. 1949-1956. Histories-sources. ■Author's experience of Chinese theatre both before and after Mao Tse-tung's rise to power and its relation to other political events taking place in the country.

415 Dijk, Maarten van. "The Kembles and Vocal Technique." *ThR.* 1983 Spring; 8(1): 23-42. Notes.
England. 1780-1817. Historical studies. ■Descriptions of John Philip Kemble's vocal technique are compared to the contemporary theories of elocution.

416 Ingram, William. "Arthur Savill, Stage Player." *TN.* 1983; 37(1): 21-22.
England. 1616-1640. Historical studies. ■Other trades plied by English actors: e.g. briefly explores the notion that Savill was an apprentice to the actor and goldsmith, Andrew Cane. Grp/movt: Elizabethan theatre.

417 Milhous, Judith. "David Garrick and the Dancing Master's Apprentice." *ET.* 1983 Nov.; 2(1): 19-29. Notes. Illus.: Photo. B&W. 2: 5 in. x 7 in.
England. 1747-1757. Historical studies. ■Records of a lawsuit in Chancery provide the details in a sketch of the early career of dancer John Dennison as well as an episode in the life of David Garrick.

418 Scouten, Arthur; Hume, Robert D. "Additional Players Lists in the Lord Chamberlain's Register, 1708-10." *TN.* 1983; 37(2): 77-79. Notes.
England. 1708-1710. Historical studies. ■Two newly discovered 'Players Lists' in the Lord Chamberlain's Registers (PRO LC 5/166), provide information on performers active at the time.

419 Visser, Colin. "The Comte de Gisors In London, 1754." *TN.* 1983; 37(2): 51-54. Notes.
England. 1754. Historical studies. ■Impressions of a French visitor to various masquerades, balls and theatre performances recorded in his diary. Related to Popular Entertainment.

420 Dresen, Adolf; Sandig, Holger; Drewitz, Ingeborg; Greiff, Ulrich; Schwab, Lothar; Langsted, Jörn; Spielhoff, Alfons; Reinshagen, Gerlind; Kofler, Leo; Karsunke, Jaak; Lubda, Ulrich; Schnetz, Wolf Peter. "Chances des Theaters." (Chances of the Theatre.) *Tzs.* 1983; 5: 5-12, 31-38, 51-58.
Europe. 1982. Histories-sources. ■Twelve statements concerning the relationship between theatre and mass media in a world where mass media take a dominant position. Theatre's survival in the 'global village'. Related to Media.

421 Glover, J. Garrett. *The Cubist Theatre.* Ann Arbor, MI: UMI Research P; xvii, 154 pp. (Studies in the Fine Arts: The Avant-garde 38.) Biblio. Illus.: Photo.
Europe. 1900. Historical studies. ■Study of the influence of Cubism on staging and scene design. Grp/movt: Cubism.

422 Marker, Frederick J. "An Actor Prepares: The Prenaturalistic Alternative." *ET.* 1983 May; 1(2): 119-125. Notes.
Europe. North America. 1781-1873. Historical studies. ■Independent status of virtuoso actors suggests need for reassessment of their rehearsal practices.

423 Seppälä, Riitta, ed.; Lukjanov, Marianna, ed.; Westman, Pirjo, ed.; Khasanov, Valery, ed.; Teryoshin, Sergey, ed.; Shvydkoy, Michael, ed. *Neuvostoliitto ja Suomi teatteriyhteistyössä.* (USSR-Finland: Theatre Cooperation.) Helsinki: The Soviet and Finnish National Centres of the International Theatre Institute (ITI); 1983. 114 pp. Pref.
Finland. USSR. 1981. Critical studies. ■Papers presented in a series of seminars on Finnish-Soviet theatrical contacts.

424 Moureau, François. "Du côté cour: la Princesse Palatine et le théâtre." (From the Court's Point of View: Princess Palatine and the Theatre.) *RHT.* 1983; 35(1): 275-286. Notes.
France. 1671-1722. Histories-sources. ■Reaction of Louis XIV's sister-in-law to French theatre in the late 17th and early 18th centuries. Details from her correspondence.

425 "Dangers of the New Sensibilities in Eighteenth Century German Acting." *ThR.* 1983 Summer; 8(2): 95-109. Notes.
Germany. 1700-1800. Historical studies. ■Examination of German eighteenth-century perceptions, theories and attitudes in relation to psychological involvement or emotionalism in acting.

426 Rüedi, Peter. "Imitation of Life: Die langen Abschiede des Douglas Sirk." (Imitation of Life: The Long Goodbyes of Douglas Sirk.) *TH.* 1983; 6: 1-8.
Germany. Switzerland. USA. 1933-1983. Histories-sources. ■Portrait of and interview with Douglas Sirk (Detlef Sierck), director of the premiere of *Silbersee (Silverlake)*, Leipzig 1933, by Georg Kaiser and Kurt Weill.

CLASSED ENTRIES

THEATRE IN GENERAL: Multiple application—Performance/production

427 Otte, Eva-Maria. "Garderobengespräch mit Heinrich Schmidt." (Dressing Room Interview with Heinrich Schmidt.) *TZ*. 1983; 38(12): 51-55. Illus.: Photo. B&W. 12.
Germany, East. 1922-1983. Histories-sources. ■Actor's portrait.

428 Pietzsch, Ingeborg. "Für unsere Haltung leben!" (Living for Our Attitude!)*TZ*. 1983; 38(11): 6-10. Illus.: Photo. B&W. 8. [Eight actors on their responsibilities.]
Germany, East. 1983. Histories-sources. ■Eight actors take positions on their political and social responsibilities.

429 Lokko, Sophia D. "Plays and Players — A Means of Transmission and Dissemination of Ghanian Culture." *MuK*. 1983; 29: 261-271. Notes.
Ghana. 1983. Historical studies. ■Present situation of theatre in Ghana. Includes lists of plays, players, promoters and halls.

430 Choudhuri, Indra Nath. "Traditional Indian Theatre and Kabuki: A Passage toward a Total Theatre." *SNJPA*. 1983 Oct.-Dec. ; 70: 38-48. Notes.
India. Japan. 1600-1980. Critical studies. ■Comparison of Indian traditional theatre and *kabuki* in aspects of stylization, participation, and total theatre. Related to Dance-Drama: *Kabuki*.

431 Wade, Bonnie C., ed. *Performing Arts in India: Essays on Music, Dance, and Drama*. Berkeley, CA and Lanham, MD: Center for South and Southeast Asia Studies, Univ. of California, Berkeley and UP of America; 1983. 270 pp. (University of California Center for South and Southeast Asia Studies Monograph Series 21.) Biblio. Index.
India. Historical studies.

432 Mammun, Parvis. "*Taglid* — das politische Improvisationstheater in Persien." (*Taglid* — Political Improvisation Theatre in Persia.) *MuK*. 1983; 29: 293-300.
Iran. 1600-1980. Historical studies. ■History and forms of political improvisational theatre in Iran. Related to Popular Entertainment.

433 Flaiano, Ennio; Cattaneo, Giulio, ed.; Pautasso, Sergio, ed. *Lo spettatore addormentato*. (The Sleeping Spectator.) Milan: Rizzoli; 1983. 391 pp. (Opere di Ennio Flaiano.) Index.
Italy. 1939-1967. Reviews of performances. ■Anthology of performance reviews.

434 Magni, Laura. *Il teatro: Come nasce, come si fa, come si può fare*. (The Theatre: How It Is Born, How It Is Done, How It Can Be Done.) Milan: Signorelli; 1983. 141 pp. Tables. Illus.: Dwg. Photo. B&W. Color.
Italy. 1983. Instructional materials. ■What the theatre is: a short guide for primary school children.

435 Hamilton, Isaac Bile. "Rituels et Théâtre en Côte d'Ivoire." (Ritual and Theatre in Ivory Coast.) *MuK*. 1983 ; 29: 282-291. Notes. Biblio.
Ivory Coast. 1800-1983. Historical studies. Related to Ritual-Ceremony.

436 Chong, Chin-su. "Drama in the First Half of 1982." *KoJ*. 1983 Oct.; 22: 65-67, 70.
Korea. 1982. Critical studies. ■Short review of contemporary trends of Korean theatre in 1982.

437 Kim, Bang-ock. "Review of Theatrical Activities in 1982." *KoJ*. 1983 Mar.; 23: 62-65. Illus.: Photo. B&W. 2: 4 in. x 3 in.
Korea. 1982. Reviews of performances.

438 Mendoza López, Margarita. "Españoles en el teatro mexicano." (Spanish Exiles in the Mexican Theatre.) *PrAc*. 1983 Nov.-Dec.; 201: 15-22.
Mexico. Spain. 1939-1983. Historical studies.

439 Rodriguez, Orlando B. "Teatern i Panama, Costa Rica, Guatemala." (Theatre in Panama, Costa Rica and Guatemala.) *Entre*. 1983; 10(4): 29-31.
Panama. Costa Rica. Guatemala. 1954-1983. Historical studies. ■History of Central American theatre.

440 Bharucha, Rustom; Paran, Janice; Shyer, Laurence; Schechter, Joel. "Directors, Dramaturgs and War in Poland: An Interview with Jan Kott." *ThM*. 1983 Spring; 14(2): 27-31. Illus.: Photo. 1: 4 in. x 5 in.

Poland. Austria. 1957-1981. Histories-sources. ■Excerpts from an interview in Manhattan, October 1982, embracing Kott's relations with Peter Brook, Giorgio Strehler, the Burgtheater, Vienna, 1976, as well as Kott's observations on Grotowski, Polish theatre and Poland after December 1981.

441 "El exilio español en México." (The Spanish Exile in Mexico.) *PrAc*. 1983 Nov.-Dec.; 201: 2-77.
Spain. Mexico. 1939-1983. Historical studies. ■Article and interviews about the exhibition and performances in Madrid on the theme of The Spanish Theatre in Mexican Exile.

442 Santa Cruz, Lola. "Esperanza Roy: Retrato intermitente." (Esperanza Roy: An Intermittent Portrait.) *ElPu*. 1983 Nov.: 16-17.
Spain. 1936-1983. Histories-sources. ■Interview with theatre and music hall actress Esperanza Roy. Related to Popular Entertainment: Variety acts.

443 Nordlund, Gunilla. "Konstens innersta väsen ar kärleken." (The Innermost Quality of Art Is Love.) *Entre*. 1983; 10(6): 36-38.
Sweden. 1983. Critical studies. ■Importance of the male and female principles, myths and archetypes in stimulating creativity of acting.

444 Mayer, Gerhard. "Ausstellungen: Der Traum vom neuen Menschen." (Exhibitions: The Dream of the New Man.) *Buhne*. 1983 Sep.: 12-14. Illus.: Photo. Color.
Switzerland. Austria. 1983. Histories-sources. ■Exhibition about the tendency toward the *Gesamtkunstwerk*.

445 Ullrich, Peter. "Zwischen Damaskus und Palmyra: Streiflichter vom syrischen Theater." (Between Damascus and Palmyra: Sidelights of Syrian Theatre.) *TZ*. 1983; 38(10): 40-43. Illus.: Photo. B&W. 3.
Syria. 1983. Histories-sources. ■State of Theatre in Syria.

446 Booth, Michael R. "The Pip Simmons Company." *MuK*. 1983; 29: 206-211. Notes.
UK. 1968-1980. Histories-specific. ■Cruelty, nudity and involvement of audience as elements of the avant-garde presentational style.

447 Happé, Peter; Carpenter, Sarah; Twycross-Martin, Henrietta; Wyatt, Diana; Heap, Carl. "Thoughts on 'Transvestism'." *MET*. 1983; 5(2): 110-122. Notes. Illus.: Photo.
UK-England. 1980. Critical studies. ■Observations on the effects of men playing female parts, based on modern revivals. Grp/movt: Medieval theatre.

448 Langhans, Edward A. "An Edinburgh Promptbook from 1679-80." *TN*. 1983; 37(3): 101-104. Notes.
UK-Scotland. 1678-1680. Historical studies. ■Promptbook used in production of Etherege's *The Man of Mode* provides information on the activities of players who left the King's Company, and some details on staging.

449 Aleandri, Emelise; Seller, Maxine Schwartz, ed. "Italian-American Theatre." 237-276 in Seller, Maxine Schwartz, ed. *Ethnic Theatre in the United States*. Westport, CT: Greenwood P; 1983. viii, 606 pp. Notes. Biblio.
USA. 1871-1970. Historical studies. ■History of Italian immigrant theatre.

450 Allain, Mathé; St. Martin, Adele Cornay. "French Theatre in Louisiana." 139-174 in Seller, Maxine Schwartz, ed. *Ethnic Theatre in the United States*. Westport, CT: Greenwood P; 1983. viii, 606 pp. Notes. Biblio. Illus.: Photo. B&W. 1.
USA. 1764-1902. Historical studies. ■French theatre in New Orleans.

451 Becker, Barbara. "An Interview with Charlton Heston." *LPer*. 1983 Apr.; 3(2): 67-80. Illus.: Photo.
USA. 1956-1976. Histories-sources. ■Charlton Heston talks about his training and performance history, as well as the role of arts in society.

452 Brokaw, John W. "Mexican-American Theatre." 335-353 in Seller, Maxine Schwartz, ed. *Ethnic Theatre in the United States*. Westport, CT: Greenwood P; 1983. viii, 606 pp. Notes. Biblio.
USA. 1845-1980. Historical studies. ■History of Spanish language theatre in the southwestern United States.

THEATRE IN GENERAL: Multiple application—Performance/production

453 Carballido, Emilio. "I Mexikos hjarta." (In the Heart of Mexico.) *Entre.* 1983; 10(4): 36-37.
USA. Mexico. 1965-1983. Historical studies. ■History of Chicano theatre from its beginnings in strikes in California.

454 Čistjakova, V.V., ed. *Problemy zarubežnoj teatralnoj kritiki.* (Problems of Foreign Theatrical Criticism.) Leningrad: State Institute of Theatre, Music and Cinema; 1983. [Collection of scholarly articles.]
USA. Europe. 1800-1970. Critical studies. ■Essays dealing with various aspects of the development of European and American theatre: critical thought, staging, acting and design.

455 Crawford, Jerry L.; Pryce-Jones, Ellis M., illus. *Acting, In Person and In Style.* Dubuque, IA: W.C. Brown; 1983. xv, 323 pp. Index. Biblio. [Third edition.]
USA. 1983. Instructional materials. ■Study of acting styles and techniques.

456 Dietrich, John E.; Duckwall, Ralph W. *Play Direction.* Englewood Cliffs, NJ: Prentice-Hall; 1983. xvi, 334 pp. Biblio. Index. Illus.: Photo.
USA. 1983. Instructional materials.

457 Evans, Chad. *Frontier Theatre: A History of Nineteenth-Century Theatrical Entertainment in the Canadian Far West and Alaska.* Victoria, BC: Sono Nis P; 1983. 326 pp. Biblio. Index. Illus.: Photo. 40.
USA. Canada. 1800-1899. Histories-specific.

458 Fabre, Geneviève; Dixon, Melvin, transl. *Drumbeats, Masks, and Metaphor: Contemporary Afro-American Theatre.* Cambridge, MA: Harvard UP; 1983. 274 pp. Biblio. Index. Illus.: Photo. 12. [English translation of *Le théâtre noir aux Etats-Unis.*]
USA. 1983. Historical studies. Related to Ritual-Ceremony.

459 Feldman, Ellen. "The Radio City Music Hall Archives." *Brs.* 1982 Summer; 10(1): 3.
USA. 1933-1979. Histories-sources. ■Account of the holdings of Radio City Music Hall Archives: inlcuding photographs, cast lists and fabric swatches.

460 Funk, Joel. "On Writing Songs for Children's Theatre." *ChTR.* 1983 July; 32(3): 17.
USA. 1983. Technical studies. ■Seven basic rules for writing songs for children's theatre.

461 Gorelik, Mordecai. "Professional Profiles: The Divided Actor." *CueM.* 1983 Spring-Summer; 61(2): 7-8.
USA. 1983. Critical studies. ■Discussion of stage fright, and the dual nature of the actor, who must assume another identity on stage. Representational acting is seen as superior to presentational acting.

462 Harvey, Anne-Charlotte Hanes. "Swedish-American Theatre." 491-524 in Seller, Maxine Schwartz, ed. *Ethnic Theatre in the United States.* Westport, CT: Greenwood P; 1983. viii, 606 pp. Notes. Biblio. Append. Illus.: Photo. B&W. 3.
USA. 1860-1925. Historical studies. ■History of Swedish language theatre in America.

463 Huntsman, Jeffrey F. "Native American Theatre." 355-385 in Seller, Maxine Schwartz, ed. *Ethnic Theatre in the United States.* Westport, CT: Greenwood P; 1983. viii, 606 pp. Notes. Biblio.
USA. 1850-1980. Historical studies. ■Survey of types of Native American dramatic rituals, current Native American dramatists and their plays.

464 Hyde, Clinton M. "Danish-American Theatre." 101-118 in Seller, Maxine Schwartz, ed. *Ethnic Theatre in the United States.* Westport, CT: Greenwood P; 1983. viii, 606 pp. Notes. Biblio. Illus.: Diagram.
USA. 1900-1961. Historical studies. ■History of Danish immigrant theatre in various Midwestern and Western cities.

465 Johnson, Claudia D., comp.; Johnson, Vernon E., comp. *Nineteenth-Century Theatrical Memoirs.* Westport, CT: Greenwood P; 1983. xvii, 269 pp. Biblio. Index.

USA. UK. 1800-1899. Histories-sources.

466 Kezer, Claude D. *Principles of Stage Combat.* Schulenberg, TX: I.E. Clark; 1983. viii, 54 pp. Illus.: Photo.
USA. 1983. Instructional materials.

467 Kipel, Vitalit; Kipel, Zora. "Byelorussian-American Theatre." 67-100 in Seller, Maxine Schwartz, ed. *Ethnic Theatre in the United States.* Westport, CT: Greenwood P; 1983. viii, 606 pp. Notes. Biblio.
USA. 1920-1975. Historical studies. ■History of Byelorussian immigrant theatre in various industrial cities.

468 LaTempa, Susan. "Critical Encounters." *PArts.* 1983 Apr.; 17(4): 17. Illus.: Photo.
USA. 1983. Histories-sources. ■Conversations with four 'first string' California newspaper theatre critics: Bernard Weiner — *San Francisco Chronicle,* Dan Sullivan — *Los Angeles Times,* Jack Viertel — *Los Angeles Herald Examiner* and Welton Jones — *San Diego Union.*

469 Lifson, David. "Yiddish Theatre." 549-587 in Seller, Maxine Schwartz, ed. *Ethnic Theatre in the United States.* Westport, CT: Greenwood P; 1983. viii, 606 pp. Notes. Biblio.
USA. Europe. 1876-1960. Historical studies. ■Origins of Yiddish theatre in Europe and its arrival and history in America.

470 Maguire, Matthew. "The Site of Language." *TDR.* 1983; 27(4): 54-69. Illus.: Photo.
USA. 1970-1983. Critical studies. ■Analysis and critique of avant-garde trends in theatre.

471 Márquez, Rosa Luisa; Fiet, Lowell A. "Puerto Rican Theatre on the Mainland." 419-446 in Seller, Maxine Schwartz, ed. *Ethnic Theatre in the United States.* Westport, CT: Greenwood P; 1983. viii, 606 pp. Notes. Biblio.
USA. 1800-1983. Historical studies. ■History of Puerto Rican theatre in America.

472 Murphy, Maureen. "Irish-American Theatre." 221-235 in Seller, Maxine Schwartz, ed. *Ethnic Theatre in the United States.* Westport, CT: Greenwood P; 1983. viii, 606 pp. Notes. Biblio.
USA. 1830-1974. Historical studies. ■History of the Irish immigrant theatre.

473 Onyshkevych, Larissa. "Ukrainian-American Theatre." 525-548 in Seller, Maxine Schwartz, ed. *Ethnic Theatre in the United States.* Westport, CT: Greenwood P; 1983. viii, 606 pp. Notes. Biblio. Append.
USA. 1900-1979. Historical studies. ■Ukrainian language theatre from its inception in the U.S. to 1979.

474 Parlakian, Nishan. "Armenian-American Theatre." 19-35 in Seller, Maxine Schwartz, ed. *Ethnic Theatre in the United States.* Westport, CT: Greenwood P; 1983. viii, 606 pp. Notes. Biblio.
USA. 1903-1979. Historical studies. ■Armenian immigrant theatre since its inception.

475 Riippa, Timo R.; Karni, Michael G. "Finnish-American Theatre." 119-138 in Seller, Maxine Schwartz, ed. *Ethnic Theatre in the United States.* Westport, CT: Greenwood P; 1983. viii, 606 pp. Notes. Biblio.
USA. 1880-1939. Historical studies. ■History of the Finnish immigrant theatre.

476 Seller, Maxine Schwarz, ed. *Ethnic Theatre in the United States.* Westport, CT: Greenwood P; 1983. viii, 606 pp. Biblio. Index. Illus.: Photo.
USA. 1983. Critical studies. ■Brief histories of theatres associated with and catering to several ethnic groups.

477 Smith, Edward G. "Black Theatre." 37-66 in Seller, Maxine Schwartz, ed. *Ethnic Theatre in the United States.* Westport, CT: Greenwood P; 1983. viii, 606 pp. Notes. Biblio.
USA. 1795-1975. Historical studies. ■History of Black theatre with emphasis on actors and dramatists.

478 Straumanis, Alfreds. "Latvian-American Theatre." 277-318 in Seller, Maxine Schwartz, ed. *Ethnic Theatre in the United*

THEATRE IN GENERAL: Multiple application—Performance/production

States. Westport, CT: Greenwood P; 1983. viii, 606 pp. Notes. Biblio. Illus.: Photo. B&W. 1.
USA. 1888-1976. Historical studies. ■History of Latvian language theatre.

479 Szendrey, Thomas. "Hungarian-American Theatre." 191-220 in Seller, Maxine Schwartz, ed. *Ethnic Theatre in the United States.* Westport, CT: Greenwood P; 1983. viii, 606 pp. Notes. Biblio.
USA. 1870-1979. Historical studies. ■History of the Hungarian immigrants' theatre.

480 Triplett, Robert; Corb, Cea, illus. *Stage Fright: Letting It Work for You.* Chicago: Nelson-Hall; 1983. vi, 200 pp. Biblio. Illus.: Dwg.
USA. 1983. Instructional materials.

481 Tybor, M. Martina. "Slovak-American Theatre." 447-490 in Seller, Maxine Schwartz, ed. *Ethnic Theatre in the United States.* Westport, CT: Greenwood P; 1983. viii, 606 pp. Notes. Biblio. Append.
USA. Slovakia. 1890-1919. Historical studies. ■Slovak language theatre in Europe and America.

482 Vaškelis, Bronius. "Lithuanian-American Theatre." 319-333 in Seller, Maxine Schwartz, ed. *Ethnic Theatre in the United States.* Westport, CT: Greenwood P; 1983. viii, 606 pp. Notes. Biblio. Illus.: Photo. B&W. 2.
USA. 1885-1970. Historical studies. ■History of Lithuanian language theatre.

483 Waldo, Arthur Leonard. "Polish-American Theatre." 387-417 in Seller, Maxine Schwartz, ed. *Ethnic Theatre in the United States.* Westport, CT: Greenwood P; 1983. viii, 606 pp. Notes. Biblio. Illus.: Photo. B&W. 1.
USA. 1850-1940. Historical studies. ■History of Polish language theatre.

484 Whitaker Long, Beverly; Hopkins, Mary Frances. *Performing Literature: An Introduction to Oral Interpretation.* Englewood Cliffs, NJ: Prentice-Hall; 1982. xviii, 474 pp. Biblio. Append. Filmography.
USA. 1982. Instructional materials. ■Practical suggestions and theoretical concepts essential for oral interpretation of literature that is fundamentally treated as a dramatic form.

485 Ančipolovskij, Z. *Liudi russkovo teat'ra.* (Russian Theatre Personalities.) Vorone*07z: Central'noje-Černozemnoje knižnoje izd-vo; 1983. 213 pp. Biblio. Index. Illus.: Photo.
USSR. 1918-1983. Histories-general. ■Theatre history of the Voronež region.

486 Carner-Ribalta, J. "Un nou teatre en somni." (A New Theatre in Dreams.) *EE.* 1983 June; 23: 7-15.
USSR. Spain. 1936-1937. Historical studies. ■Deficiencies of the Catalonian theatre during the Spanish Civil War, as compared to the contemporary theatrical activities in USSR and other European countries.

487 Maronek, James. "Show Business Soviet Style." *TD&T.* 1983 Spring; 19(1): 14-17, 40-41. Illus.: Photo. B&W. 2: 5 in. x 7 in.
USSR. 1981. Histories-sources. ■Tour of Soviet theatres by a delegation of American union representatives gives a view of relations between Soviet workers and their institutions as well as a look backstage at various productions.

489 Vlahov, Riccardo. *La scatola ottica – Fotografia di un teatro.* (The Optic Box – Photographs of a Theatre.) Bologna: CLUEB; 1982. n.p. Illus.: Photo. B&W.
Italy. 1982. Histories-sources. ■Catalogue of photographic exhibition of the Teatro Comunale di Ferrara.

Plays/librettos/scripts

488 Johnson, Robert K. *Neil Simon.* Boston: G.K. Hall; 1983. 154 pp.
USA. 1927-1981. Critical studies. ■Comprehensive study of Neil Simon's plays, screenplays and musical comedies. Related to Media: Film.

Relation to other fields

490 Östensson, Lena. "Kvinnor och män – kult och drama." (Women and Men, Cult and Drama.) *Entre.* 1983; 10(5): 13-15 .
Critical studies. ■Argument against application of Jungian ideas to theatre and the position of women in theatre.

491 Schleuning, Neala. "A Look Back: The U.S. Cultural Policy Debate." *Tk.* 1983 May-June; 3(4): 53-58. Notes. Illus.: Photo. B&W. 6.
USA. 1800-1983. Historical studies. ■Some specific historical occasions on which cultural policy issues were debated.

Training

492 Lessac, Arthur. *Body Wisdom: The Use and Training of the Human Body.* New York: Drama Book Specialists; 1982. vii, 278 pp.
1982. Instructional materials. ■Training manual for performers. Related to Mime.

493 Coblenzer, Horst; Muhar, Franz. *Atem und Stimme: Anleitung zum guten Sprechen.* (Breathing and Voice: Introduction to Correct Speech.) Vienna: Österreichischer Bundesverlag; 1983. 119 pp. Index. Illus.: Dwg. B&W.
Austria. 1983. Instructional materials. ■Guide to conscious breathing, speaking and dealing with partners, with 71 exercises.

494 Berry, Herbert. "The Player's Apprentice." *ET.* 1983 May; 1(2): 73-80. Notes.
England. 1597-1599. Historical studies. ■Implications for the history of apprenticeship conditions in the Elizabethan acting companies based on two newly discovered allusions in public records of Bridgewater, Somersetshire. Grp/movt: Elizabethan theatre.

495 Hotinen, Juha-Pekka. "Theatre Academy of Finland – a Theatre Among Others." *NFT.* 1983; 36: 8-11. Illus.: Photo. B&W. [Also in French 'L'école supérieure d'art dramatique, un théâtre parmi les autres'.]
Finland. 1983. Historical studies. ■Theatre Academy of Finland has a flexible program focussing on productions directed by teachers and students, in cooperation with programs in music, film and television. Related to Media: Video forms.

496 Kanto, Anneli. "Theatre Academy of Body-Builders Heroes of Our Time." *NFT.* 1983; 36: 2-6. Illus.: Photo. B&W. [Also in French as 'Les futurs héros de nos jours font du culturisme à l'école d'art dramatique'.]
Finland. 1982-1983. Historical studies. ■Demanding physical training is an integral part of the program of the Theatre Academy of Finland, where Jouko Turkka organizes the work into projects leading to productions in various spaces.

497 Zilliacus, Clas; Suur-Kujala, Anneli, transl. "Turkan aihetehdas." (The Teaching Methods of Jouko Turkka.) *Teat.* 1983; 38(10): 12-13. Illus.: Photo. B&W. 8. [Originally published in Swedish in *Nya Argus* 11-12, 1983.]
Finland. 1983. Critical studies. ■Review of teaching methods and theories of acting of Jouko Turkka, principal of Theatre Academy of Finland.

498 Maier, Scotch; Jörg, Hans. "Lehrlingstheater – ein Nachruf?" (Theatre for Apprentices – An Obituary?)*Tzs.* 1983 Summer; 4: 21-33.
Germany, West. 1971-1983. Historical studies. ■Workshops and theatre productions by and for apprentices, organized by two educational institutions: Hessische Jugendbildungsanstalt (Dietzenbach) and Wannseeheim für Jugendarbeit (West Berlin).

499 Prosperi, Mario. "Lo psicodramma e l'attore." (Psychodrama and the Actor.) *AdP.* 1983; 8(1): 121-124. Illus.: Photo.
Italy. 1960. Critical studies. ■Ideological and cultural reasons for the hostility to psychodrama within academic circles as a method of actor training.

500 Alexander, Robert; Haynes, Wendy, ed. *Improvisational Theatre for the Classroom: A Curriculum Guide for Training Regular and Special Education Teachers in the Art of*

THEATRE IN GENERAL: Multiple application—Training

Improvisational Theatre. Washington, DC: R. Alexander; 1983. iii, 84 pp. Biblio.
USA. 1983. Instructional materials.

501 Appel, Libby. *Mask Characterization: An Acting Process.* Carbondale, IL: Southern Illinois UP; 1982. xv, 120 pp. Illus.: Photo.
USA. 1982. Instructional materials. ■Actor training program using character masks.

502 Fichandler, Zelda. "Keynote address for the League of Professional Theatre Training Programs." *PerAJ.* 1983; 7(2): 88-99 . [1983 Design Portfolio Review held at The Juilliard School.]
USA. 1983. Critical studies. ■Plea for humanistic training of theatre professionals.

503 Jacobi, Henry N. *Building Your Best Voice.* A Leading Voice Teacher Shows You How to Develop Your Speaking or Singing Voice to Its Fullest Potential. Englewood Cliffs, NJ: Prentice-Hall; 1982. 271 pp.
USA. 1982. Instructional materials.

504 King, Keith, ed.; Wallberg, Mark, ed. "TDTICH Project." *USITT.* 1983 Winter; 22(5): 11.
USA. 1983. Histories-sources. ■Theatre Design and Technology Internship Clearinghouse project provides detailed information concerning experiences offered by a theatre or firm on request.

505 Sabatine, Jean; Hodge, David. *The Actor's Image: Movement Training for Stage and Screen.* A Spectrum Book. Englewood Cliffs, NJ: Prentice-Hall; 1983. x, 246 pp. Biblio.
USA. 1983. Instructional materials.

506 Sacheli, Robert. "Zelda Fichandler: From Arena to Academe." *ThNe.* 1983 Nov.; 15(8): 1, 12. Illus.: Photo. B&W. 1: 7 in. x 4 in.
USA. 1950-1983. Histories-sources. ■Artistic director and cofounder of Arena Stage, now chairman of the acting and directing department of New York University's Tisch School of the Arts, expresses her philosophy of theatre education with special emphasis on actors' training.

507 Saint-Denis, Michel; Saint-Denis, Suria, ed. *Training for the Theatre: Premises and Promises.* New York: Theatre Arts Books; 1982. 243 pp.
USA. 1897-1971. Instructional materials. ■Theory and practice of actor training.

508 Work, William. "The ERIC Connection Offers Access to Research Tools." *ThNe.* 1983 Dec.; 15(9): 10.
USA. 1983. Technical studies. ■Includes among other academic areas, documents dealing with theatre instruction or research plus directions on how to submit one's own educational materials for possible inclusion.

509 Wright, Lin; Willenbrink, Rosemarie. "Child Drama 1982: A Survey of College and University Programs in the U.S." *ChTR.* 1983 Feb.; 32(1): 3-18. Tables.
USA. 1950-1982. Histories-sources. ■Results of 1982 survey of college courses, programs and productions in children's theatre and creative drama, comparing data to that compiled in 1950, 1953, 1957 and 1963.

510 Yowell, Robert. "Are We Content with a 'No Risk' Choice? Questions on Constructing a Valid Theatre Curriculum." *ThNe.* 1983 Election Issue; 15(2): 15.
USA. 1983. Critical studies. ■Four basic questions a theatre curriculum should address.

Other entries with significant content related to Theatre In General: 1821, 1968.

DANCE

General

Performance/production

511 Kaila, Katariina. "Tanssi on muuttunut synnistä taiteeksi." (The Dance Has Changed from a Sin to an Art.) *SuK.* 1983;

25: 64-68. Illus.: Photo.
Finland. 1983. Reviews of performances. ■Discussion of Kuopio Dance Festival.

512 Wendland, Jens. "Eine Kultur ohne Fundament – oder: Das westdeutsche Tanztheater hat seine Geschichte nicht begriffen." (A Culture without Foundation – or: West German Dance-Theatre Does not Understand Its Own History.) *TH.* 1983 Mar.; 3: 40-44.
Germany, West. 1983. Historical studies. ■Analysis of the situation and brief survey of the productions of the German dance theatre.

513 Fàbregas, Xavier. "Comedians: demonios mediterraneos." (The Comedians: Mediterranean Devils.) *ElPu.* 1983 Oct.: 5-7.
Spain. 1983. Historical studies. ■Analysis of dramatic works presented by Catalan group Els Comediants, their techniques and influence by other movements: Bread and Puppet Theatre, Odin Teatret, etc.

514 Kirstein, Lincoln. "A Memoir: The Education." *Raritan.* 1983 Winter; 2(3): 27-65.
USA. India. Europe. 1916-1949. Biographical studies. ■Author's brief association with George Ivanovitch Gurdjieff and its influence on him. Description of schools attended, literature read, and persons who influence the author's life.

515 Saunder, Charles L. "Debbie Allen." *Ebony.* 1983 Mar.; 38(5): 74-76, 78, 80, 84. Illus.: Photo. Print. B&W. Color. 9.
USA. 1983. Biographical studies. ■Debbie Allen discusses her struggle for success and her relationship with her family. Related to Media: Video forms.

Ballet

Institutions

516 Suhonen, Tiina. "Art of Dance Department in Theatre Academy." *NFT.* 1983; 36: 13. [Also in French as 'Un institut d'art choréographique créé à l'école supérieure d'art dramatique'.]
Finland. 1910-1983. Historical studies. ■Four-year program in dance, teaching and choreography, previously offered at the Opera, is now conducted by the Dance Department of the Theatre Academy of Finland.

Performance/production

517 Crabb, Michael. "Evelyn Hart's Giselle." *Dm.* 1983 Apr.; 57(4): 60-67. Illus.: Photo. B&W. Color. 8.
Canada. 1966-1982. Historical studies. ■Evelyn Hart's debut as Giselle with the Royal Winnipeg Ballet.

518 Chazin-Bennahum, Judith. "Cahusac, Diderot, and Noverre: Three Revolutionary French Writers on the Eighteenth Century Dance." *TJ.* 1983 May; 35(2): 149-167. Notes.
France. 1752-1781. Historical studies. ■Comparison of the writers, showing that all three attempted to break the grip of conventions in the static French theatre concerning the dance of that period.

519 Como, William. "In Search of the Red Shoes." *Dm.* 1983 Sep.; 57(9): 58-65. Illus.: Photo. B&W. Color. 16.
Monaco. 1948-1983. Historical studies. ■Ballet in Monte Carlo. Emphasis on the filming of *The Red Shoes.* Also discussion of ballet teacher for the Académie de Danse Classique Princesse Grace, Marika Besobrasova. Related to Media: Film.

520 Federico, Ronald. "The Decision to End a Performing Career in Ballet." 57-69 in Kamerman, Jack B.; . Martorella, Rosanne. *Performers and Performances: The Social Organization of Artistic Work.* South Hadley, MA: J.F. Bergin; 1983. xiii, 303 pp.
USA. 1982. Critical studies. ■Sociological and psychological implications of the career change dancers must face when they stop performing.

Plays/librettos/scripts

521 Whitney, Mary. "John Neumeier's *Passion.*" *Dm.* 1983 Mar.; 57(3): 50-54. Illus.: Photo. B&W. 6.

DANCE: Ballet—Plays/librettos/scripts

Germany, West. USA. 1982-1983. Historical studies. ■Analysis and review of John Neumeier's (Hamburg Ballet) four-hour dance epic *St. Matthew Passion* set to Bach's score.

522 Au, Susan. "*Apollo*: The Transformation of a Myth." *CORD*. 1983; 1: 50-63. Notes. Biblio.

USA. 1927-1979. Critical studies. ■Stravinsky's selections of dramatic elements from the Apollo myth for his ballet *Apollon Musagete* and the changes in dramatic emphasis with sets, costumes and choreography in its major performances.

Training

523 Fritzsche, Dietmar. "Die Menschen bewegen: Gespräch mit den Choreographen Hermann Rudolph, Tom Schilling, Dietmar Seyffert, Harald Wandtke über Fragen des Ballettschaffens in der DDR." (Agitating People: Interview with the Choreographers Hermann Rudolpf, Tom Schilling, Dietmar Seyffert and Harald Wandtke on Questions of Ballet Work in East Germany.) *TZ*. 1983; 38(6): 48-51. Illus.: Photo. B&W. 4.

Germany, East. 1981-1983. Histories-sources. ■Conditions of ballet work and training at important opera houses in East Germany.

Modern dance

Institutions

524 Lindblom, Mårten. "Danskontens vara." (Product of the Art of Dance.) *Entre*. 1983; 10(5): 22-25.

Sweden. USA. 1636-1983. Historical studies. ■Dance group L'Étoile du Nord, featuring experiments, strong personalities and flexible staging, is part of the international dance scene in which Merce Cunningham and Pina Bausch are prominent.

Performance/production

525 Ferrari, Curzia. *La 'divina' Isadora Duncan*. (The 'Divine' Isadora Duncan.) Milan: Sungarco; 1983. 327 pp. Tables. Index. Illus.: Photo.

Europe. USA. 1878-1927. Biographies. ■Biography of Isadora Duncan.

526 Booth, Laure. "Illegitimate Movement." *AnSt*. 1983 Autumn: 16-17. Illus.: Photo. B&W. 1.

UK. 1978-1983. Histories-sources. ■Laurie Booth describes his working practice in the light of contemporary attitudes toward dance.

527 Banes, Sally, ed. *Democracy's Body: Judson Dance Theater 1962-64*. Ann Arbor, MI: UMI Research P; 1983. xviii, 270 pp. IN. Biblio. Illus.: Photo. 9.

USA. 1962-1964. Historical studies. ■Documents dances, dancers and choreographers of group associated with genesis of post-modern dance. Grp/movt: Postmodernism.

528 Oswald, Genevieve. "Myth and Legend in Martha Graham's *Night Journey*." *CORD*. 1983; 1: 42-49. Notes. Biblio.

USA. 1947. Historical studies. ■Graham's view of man and recurring symbolism from Greek myth are examined through the choreography and scene design of Isamu Noguchi for *Night Journey*.

Other entries with significant content related to Dance: 406, 749, 889, 1735, 1787, 1803, 1991, 2028.

DANCE-DRAMA

General

Design/technology

529 Khaznadar, Cherif. "Korea's Masked Dances." *TDR*. 1982 Winter; 26(4): 64-65.

Korea. 1600-1899. Historical studies. ■Brief description of traditional Korean ritualistic masked dances and the design and use of masks. Related to Ritual-Ceremony.

530 Chatel, Françoise; Khaznadar, Cherif; Donne, John. "Masks in Tibet, India, Bhutan and Sri Lanka." *TDR*. 1982 Winter; 26(4): 73-78.

Tibet. Sri Lanka. India. Historical studies. ■Brief descriptions of the designs and uses of masks in various sacred dances in Tibet, India, Bhutan and Sri Lanka. Related to Ritual-Ceremony: Religious.

Performance/production

531 Snow, Stephen. "Rangda: Archetype in Action in Balinese Dance-Drama." *TID*. 1983; 5: 273-291. Illus.: Photo. B&W. 8: 3 in. x 3 in.

Bali. 1983. Critical studies. ■Analysis of Balinese dance-drama and interpretation of the character of Rangda as the archetypal image of the devouring mother. Related to Ritual-Ceremony: Religion.

532 Kothari, Sunil. "The Kuchipudi Dance-Drama Tradition." *CORD*. 1983; 1: 120-125. Notes. Biblio.

India. 200 B.C.-1983 A.D. Critical studies. ■Origins and evolution of dance-drama in India: stories, characters and music in the *Kuchipudi* repertoire, and the staging traditions which integrate music, speech, dance and stylized acting.

533 Foley, Kathy; Conaway, Lin, ed. "Playing the Demon and the Divine: The Physically Based Theatre of Indonesia." *ThNe*. 1983 Mar.; 15(3): 8-9. [Third in a series of articles.]

Indonesia. 1977-1980. Historical studies. ■Stylized system of movements is used to convey a story and to portray character in the Indonesian theatre.

534 Marek, Jan. "Tanz: Auf Leben und Tod." (Dance: A Matter of Life and Death.) *Buhne*. 1983 May: 25-27. Illus.: Photo. Color.

Japan. Austria. 1983. Reviews of performances. ■Guest production of Japanese Butō-company Ariadone at Serapionstheater, Vienna.

535 Cho, Oh-kon. "The Mask-dance Theatre from Hwanghae Province." *KoJ*. 1982 May; 22: 36-71. Notes. Illus.: Photo. 8: 3 in. x 4 in. [Continued in June issue, pp. 42-59.]

Korea. 1700-1983. Historical studies. ■Comprehensive essay on almost every aspect of mask-dance theatre, including an annotated translation of *Pongsan T'alch'um*, a regional dance-drama by an unknown author.

536 Chong, Pyong-ho. "Revival and Significance of the 'Madang nori'." *KoJ*. 1982 Sep.; 22: 50-52, 54.

Korea. 1982. Critical studies. ■Critical review of recent performances of *madang nori* (yard play), allegedly originating in the heaven worship festival of primitive society. Related to Ritual-Ceremony: Religious.

Plays/librettos/scripts

537 Marie Chee, Wai-ling. "References to Dance in the Shih Ching and Other Early Chinese Texts." *CORD*. 1983; 1: 126-143. Notes. Biblio. Illus.: Photo. Print. B&W. 6: 7 in x 9 in., 3 in. x 4 in.

China. 1099-600 B.C. Critical studies. ■Plot analysis of Chinese song poems for references to dance and for elements which appear thematically or symbolically in dance, such as war images, birds and social rituals.

538 Strauss, G.B. "The Tradition of Warrior Heroines in Chinese Myth, Dance, and Drama." *CORD*. 1983; 1: 16-31. Notes. Append. Biblio.

China. 500 B.C.-1978 A.D. Historical studies. ■Tradition of warrior heroines in Chinese drama and dance, and the origins of movements requiring skill with sword, spear, rifle, etc.

539 Jones, Betty True. "Mythological Themes in Classical Indian Dance." *CORD*. 1983; 1: 64-79. Biblio. Illus.: Photo. Print. B&W. 7: 5 in. x 8 in., 5 in. x 7 in., 3 in. x 4 in.

India. 800-1800. Critical studies. ■Epic texts form the basis of Indian dance-drama's themes of heroism, hierarchical structure of society, love and devotion.

540 Ranganathan, Edwina. "*Terukkuttu*: A Street Play from Tamil Nadu." *SNJPA*. 1983 Jan.-Mar.; 67: 5-16. Illus.: Photo. B&W. 6.

India. 1980. Historical studies. ■Description of *Terukkuttu*, which developed as a dance-drama with a Bhagavatar leading the performance.

DANCE-DRAMA: General—Plays/librettos/scripts

541   Olsin-Windecker, Hilary. "Characterization in Classical Yogyanese Dance." *CORD*. 1983; 1: 185-193. Notes. Append. Biblio.
Java. 1755-1980. Critical studies. ■Symbolic aspect of the system of characterization in Yogyanese classical dance: character as inner disposition, character as role portrayal and the five basic movement motifs utilized to develop the characters.

Relation to other fields

542   Varadpande, Manohar Laxman. *Krishna Theatre in India.* Atlantic Highlands, NJ: Humanities P; 1982. xii, 145 pp.
India. 1982. Critical studies.

543   Dunn, Charles. "Religion and Japanese Drama." *TID*. 1983; 5: 225-237. Notes.
Japan. 1300-1800. Historical studies. ■Historical consideration of the many forms of Japanese drama in terms of religious origins and aspects. Related to Puppetry.

Kabuki

Performance/production

544   Kōzō, Yamaji; Hoff, Frank, transl. "Early Kabuki Dance." *CORD*. 1983; 1: 105-112. Biblio.
Japan. 900-1900. Critical studies. ■Typical movement, music, costumes, performers and historic influences in *odori* and *mai* dance.

Plays/librettos/scripts

545   Hoff, Frank. "*Dōjōji: A Woman and a Bell.*" *CORD*. 1983; 1: 32-41. Biblio. Append.
Japan. 1041-1800. Historical studies. ■Traces the narrative theme of *Dōjōji (A Woman and a Bell)* from origins in 1041 AD and earliest *kabuki* dance on this theme in 1670, to the *nō* and *kabuki* treatments in 18th century Japan.

Kathakali

546   Namboodiri, M.P. Sankaran. "Bhāva as Expressed through the Presentational Techniques of Kathakali." *CORD*. 1983; 1: 194-209. Notes. Biblio. Illus.: Photo. Print. B&W. 8: 6 in. x 9 in.
India. 1600-1983. Critical studies. ■Stylized gestures, sound qualities of the song texts and music interrelate to create the *bhāvas* (feelings, moods, ideas, characters), in a principal dance-drama of India, *kathakali*.

Nō

Performance/production

547   Shigeyama, Sengorō. *Sengorō kyōgen-banashi.* (The Sengorō Kyōgen Story.) Tokyo: Kodansha; 1983. 235 pp.
Japan. 1919-1983. Biographies. ■Autobiography of *kyōgen* actor Sengorō Shigeyama.

Theory/criticism

548   Ishii, Tatsurō. "Zeami on Performance." *ThR*. 1983 Autumn; 8(3): 190-206. Tables.
Japan. 1363-1443. Critical studies. ■Descriptive account of principal themes in Zeami's various treatises on the art of *nō* performance.

549   Komparu, Kunio; Corddry, Jane, transl.; Comee, Stephen, transl. *The Noh Theater: Principles and Perspectives.* New York: Weatherhill/Tankosha; 1983. xxiv, 376 pp. Index. Illus.: Photo. [Revised and expanded English translation of *Nō e no izanai.*]
Japan. 1300-1980. Histories-specific. ■Theoretical and practical analysis of the *nō* theatre. Elements of *nō* aesthetics, architecture, plays, music, costumes and masks. The *nō* actor and the process of performance. Many illustrations. Appendices on Zeami, the current *nō* repertory and a practical guide to *nō* theatres in Japan.

550   Ortolani, Benito. "Spirituality for the Dancer-Actor in Zeami's and Zenchiku's Writings on the Nō." *CORD*. 1983; 1 : 147-158. Notes. Biblio.
Japan. 1363-1470. Historical studies. ■Roots and purposes of a genuine spirituality for the *nō* master: the dancer-actor's training process, trials

and achievements are compared to those of a monk in the quest for enlightenment.

551   Zeami, Motokiyo; Rimer, J. Thomas, transl.; Yamazaki, Masakazu, transl. *On the Art of the Nō Drama: The Major Treatises of Zeami.* Princeton, NJ: Princeton UP; 1983. liv, 298 pp. Biblio. Gloss. B&W. Color.
Japan. 1402-1430. Histories-sources. ■Annotated translation of nine treatises by fifteenth-century actor-playwright Zeami on the art of the playwright, the development of the *nō* master's art and the relationship between performer and audience. With essays by J. Thomas Rimer and Masakazu Yamazaki, glossaries and illustrations.

Other entries with significant content related to Dance-Drama: 30, 430, 1195, 1196, 1364, 1583, 2073, 2104.

DRAMA

General

Administration

552   Godin, Jean-Cléo. "Julien Daoust, Dramaturge 1866-1943." *THC*. 1983 Fall; 4(2): 113-120. Notes. Illus.: Photo. Print. B&W. 2: 5 in. x 4 in., 2 in. x 2 in.
Canada. 1866-1943. Biographical studies. ■Biography and legacy of dramaturg Julien Daoust.

553   Wallace, Robert; Zimmerman, Cynthia. "The Audience and the Season: Four Artistic Directors in Search of a Community." *CTR*. Spring; 37: 14-33. Illus.: Photo. Neg. B&W. 6: 2 in. x 3 in., 3: 3 in. x 5 in., 4 in. x 5 in., 5 in. x 6 in., 3 in. x 3 in.
Canada. 1983. Histories-sources. ■Four Artistic directors express concern of theatre relationship with community: Bill Millerd talks about the Arts Club, Ken Kramer about The Globe, Urjo Kareda about Tarragon Theatre and Rick McNair about Theatre Calgary.

554   McDonald, Arthur W. "The Season of 1782 on the Yorkshire Circuit." *TN*. 1983; 37(3): 104-109. Notes.
England. 1781-1784. Historical studies. ■Surviving expense account books reveal sound financial condition and practices of Tate Wilkinson's productions on the Yorkshire circuit.

555   Baricchi, Walter, ed. *La rete teatrale nella provincia di Reggio Emilia.* (Theatre Network in the District of Reggio Emilia.) Preface by Ludovico Zorzi. Reggio Emilia: Tecnostampa; 1982. 35 pp. Pref. Biblio. Illus.: Maps. 1: 59 cm x 84 cm.
Italy. 1981. Historical studies. ■Theatre network developed to rotate productions among several principal theatres, thus allowing season's repertory to be subscribed by the population of the entire region.

556   Cowan, David. "Andy Arnold: An Interview." *STN*. 1983 Sep.; 31: 13-14. Illus.: Photo. B&W. 1.
UK-Scotland. 1983. Histories-sources. ■Discussion with Andy Arnold on his work with Theatre Workshop in Edinburgh.

557   Hart, Charles. "Why Is Theatre Given Such a Low Priority?" *STN*. 1983 Aug.; 30: 2-5. Illus.: Sketches. B&W. 1. [Charles Hart spoke to Alex Clark, Scottish Secretary of British Actors Equity Association, about funding support for drama in Scotland.]
UK-Scotland. 1922-1983. Critical studies. ■Funding of theatre in Scotland and discussion of theatrical activity there, particularly Mayfest.

558   Hutchison, David. "The Responsibility to New Writing." *STN*. 1983 Mar.; 25: 10-13. Illus.: Sketches. B&W. 1.
UK-Scotland. 1982. Critical studies. ■Relationship between funding, repertoire and the commissioning of new works.

559   McMillan, Joyce. "Faynia Williams and Richard Crane." *STN*. 1983 July; 29: 7-11.
UK-Scotland. 1973-1983. Histories-sources. ■Interview with the new artistic director and literary advisor for the Iron Theatre (Glasgow).

560   Barrett, Daniel. "Freedom of Memory v. Copyright Law: The American Premiere of *Caste*." *ThR*. 1983 Spring; 8(1): 43-52. Notes.

DRAMA: General—Administration

USA. UK-England. 1866-1891. Historical studies. ■Legal wrangling and publicity surrounding the American premiere of *Caste* contributed to a shifting perception of dramatists' rights and stipulated passage of the 1891 American Copyright Act.

561   LaTempa, Susan. "The Literary Manager." *PArts.* 1983 Jan.; 17(1): 6. Illus.: Photo.

USA. 1980. Histories-sources. ■Definition and duties of literary managers in regional theatres in California.

562   Leverett, James, ed. "Working Friendships: A Round Table with Two Playwrights and Their Agents." 89-103 in Leverett, James. *Dramatists Sourcebook.* 1983-1984 Edition. New York: Theatre Communications Group, Inc.; 1983. 196 pp.

USA. 1983. Histories-sources. ■Round table discussion with two playwrights — A.R. Gurney, Jr. and Mary Gallagher — and their agents — Gilbert Parker and Mary Harden.

563   Marowitz, Charles. "Director and Playwright." *DGQ.* 1983 Winter; 19(4): 28-31.

USA. 1983. Critical studies. ■In some instances a stage director's contribution to the production is equal to or greater than that of the playwright. The director should be allowed to copyright these original ideas.

564   Rogoff, Gordon. "Distinctions." *VV.* 1982 May 11; 27(19): 91.

USA. 1941-1949. Critical studies. ■Censorship on the American stage, particularly of Bertolt Brecht.

565   Trauth, Suzanne. "One on the Aisle: Broadway's Best." *CueM.* 1983 Spring-Summer; 61(2): 5.

USA. 1982-1983. Historical studies. ■Difficulties of getting some plays to Broadway.

Audience

566   Scott, Michael. *Renaissance Drama and a Modern Audience.* Atlantic Highlands, NJ: Humanities P; 1982. xii, 127 pp.

Europe. 1982. Critical studies.

567   Eskola, Katarina. *Teatterin matka Martinlaaksoon (Tutkimus teatterialan lähiökulttuuritoiminnasta ja sen eräistä historiallis-sosiaalisista ehdoista.* (The Theatre Comes to Martinlaakso: A Study of the Theatre as Part of the Cultural Activity of a Housing Estate and Some of the Sociohistorical Preconditions.) Helsinki: European Council CCC, Finnish Project; 1983. (European Council CCC, Finnish project 7.) Pref. Biblio. Tables. [Summary in Swedish and English.]

Finland. 1979-1981. Historical studies. ■Effects of theatre on a suburban audience.

568   Niemi, Irmeli. *Pääosassa katsoja (Teatteriesityksen vastaanotosta).* (The Role of the Spectator.) Helsinki: Tammi; 1983. 128 pp. (FORUM-library.) Pref. Biblio.

Finland. 1979. Histories-sources. ■Reception of a performance by a small audience in a village regularly visited by the regional theatre.

569   Millard, David Eugene. *The Nature and Origin of the Dramatic Spectator's Knowledge.* Seattle: Univ. of Washington; 1982. 220 pp. [Diss.: University Microfilms order number DA8212590.]

USA. 1982. Critical studies. ■Speculative argument for adopting a rationalist account for spectator knowledge based on Stanislavskij's treatment of the question.

Basic theatrical documents

570   Meredith, Peter, ed.; Tailby, John E., ed. *The Staging of Religious Drama in Europe in the Later Middle Ages.* Kalamazoo, MI: Medieval Institute Publications; 1982. 301 pp. (Early Drama, Art, and Music Monograph Series 4.) Illus.: Dwg.

Europe. 1300-1600. ■Texts and descriptions of all aspects of the production of medieval religious plays.

571   Institut d'Experimentació Teatral. *Urfaust (Faust primigeni).* (Ur-Faust — First Faust.) Barcelona: Publicacions i edicions de la Universitat de Barcelona; 1983. 138 pp. Pref. Illus.: Dwg. Sketches. Pntg. Photo. Print. B&W. 12: 12 cm. x 18 cm.

Germany. Spain. 1887-1983. Critical studies. ■Published to commemorate the 150th anniversary of Goethe's death. The book contains translation of playtext, and several articles on *Ur-Faust* and its stage production by Company Andrià Gual.

572   Verdone, Mario, ed. "Il teatro visionico." (Visionary Theatre.) *TeatroC.* 1982 May-Sep.; 1(1): 73-120.

Italy. 1920. Histories-sources. ■Playtext and manifesto of the Teatro Visionico and example of visionary performance: *Tocca a me (It's My Turn)* by Pino Masnata.

573   Verga, Giovanni; Nardecchia, Simonetta, ed. *Verga e il teatro inedito: Divagazioni tra la prima e l'ultima opera.* (Verga and the Unpublished Drama: Discrepancies between the First and the Last Plays.) Rome: Manzella — Edizioni scientifiche e letterarie; 1982. 127 pp. Pref. Notes. [2nd edition, revised and corrected.]

Italy. 1865-1908. Histories-sources. ■Annotated texts of Giovanni Verga's plays: *L'onore (The Honour), Le farfalle (The Butterflies), Il Mistero (The Mystery).* Editor's critical/historical essays included.

574   Arn, Mary Jo. "A Little-Known Fragment of a Dutch Abraham-and-Sara Play." *CompD.* 1983-1984 Winter; 17(4): 318-326. Notes.

Netherlands. 1400-1499. ■Discussion of prints and translation of the *fragmenten verzameling* 3-8 found in Zutphen Archive. Grp/movt: Medieval theatre.

575   Colum, Pádraic; Christopher, Murray, ed. "*The Princess and the Jester.* A Play in Two Acts." *IUR.* 1983 Autumn; 13 (2): 149-167.

UK-Ireland. 1900. ■Publication of a lost play by Pádraic Colum.

Design/technology

577   Banu, Georges. "Un été de bois et de cendres." (A Summer of Wood and Ashes.) *CF.* 1983 July; 120: 11-14. Illus.: Photo.

France. 1983. Histories-sources. ■Interview with Yannis Kokkos, designer of Comédie-Française production of Gorky's *Dačniki (Summer Folk)* [*Les estivants*].

578   DeShong, Andrew. *The Theatrical Designs of George Grosz.* Ann Arbor, MI: UMI Research P; 1982. xiv, 182 pp. Biblio. Index. Illus.: Dwg. Design. 45.

Germany. 1926. Historical studies. ■George Grosz's work with Erwin Piscator and Bertolt Brecht.

579   Ceccarelli, Patrizia. "*La Rappresentazione di Sant'Orsola*: testimonianze testuali e figurative." (*The Representation of Saint Ursula*: Textual and Figurative Testimonies.) *QT.* 1983 Aug.-Nov.; 6(21-22): 125-167. Notes. Tables. Illus.: Photo. B&W.

Italy. 1400-1599. Histories-sources. ■Textual analysis and wood engravings are used as the basis for the description of the scenery for the first staging of *La Rappresentazione di Sant'Orsola*, by Castellano de' Castellani. Grp/movt: Medieval theatre.

580   Lathe, Carla. "Edvard Munch's Dramatic Images 1892-1909." *JWCI.* 1983; 46: 191-206. Notes. Illus.

Norway. 1892-1909. Historical studies. ■Response of Edvard Munch to Scandinavian dramatists, especially Ibsen, reveals dramatically inspired 'images of psychological tension and atmospheric vibration.' Demonstrated in sets for *Gengangere (Ghosts)* (1906) and *Hedda Gabler* (1906-07) and in illustrations of scenes from Ibsen's plays.

581   Shafer, Yvonne. "Costuming Ibsen: An interview with Jane Greenwood." *INC.* 1982; 3: 10-12. Illus.: Design. Photo. B&W. 2.

USA. 1980-1981. Histories-sources. ■Interview with Jane Greenwood on her experiences in costuming Ibsen, particularly *Hedda Gabler.*

582   Shafer, Yvonne. "Designing *Enemy* and *Ghosts.* An Interview with Douglas Schmidt." *INC.* 1983; 4: 28-31. Illus.: Photo. B&W. 2. [Interview held June 30, 1982.]

USA. 1964-1982. Histories-sources. ■Designer Douglas Schmidt discusses his art and career.

DRAMA: General

Institutions

583 Wipplinger, Erna; Roessler, Peter. "Gegen die Verdrängung: Interview mit Reinhold Auer vom Jura Soyfer Theater am Spittelberg in Wien." (Against Suppression: Interview with Reinhold Auer from the Jura Soyfer Theater am Spittelberg in Vienna.) *Tzs.* 1983; 5: 130-137.
Austria. 1980-1983. Histories-sources. ■Interview with Reinhold Auer, dramatic adviser at Jura Soyfer Theater am Spittelberg, Vienna.

584 Beaulne, Guy. "Un demi-siècle de théâtre de langue française dans la région Ottawa-Hull." (A Half-Century of French Language Theatre in the Ottawa-Hull Region.) *THC.* 1983 Spring; 4(1): 100-110. [Paper originally presented in English to Association for Canadian Theatre History in Ottawa, June 1982.]
Canada. 1900-1950. Historical studies. ■Author describes 50 years of French-language theatre in Ottawa-Hull region.

585 Page, Malcolm. "Vancouver: Roger Hodgman and the Playhouse: Where Was the Audience?" *CTR.* 1983 Spring; 37: 124-127. Illus.: Photo. Neg. B&W. 1: 4 in. x 6 in.
Canada. 1979-1983. Historical studies. ■Discussion of events leading to Roger Hodgman's resignation as Artistic Director of Vancouver Playhouse.

586 Usmiani, Renate. "The Classical Tradition in Contemporary Québecois Theatre: Patterns of Ambivalence." *MD.* 1983 Sep.; 26(3): 368-381. Notes.
Canada. 1960-1979. Historical studies. ■Study of classical and anti-classical traditions in contemporary Québecois theatre, specifically the battles over dramatic idiom, proper role and function of theatre in society and theatrical form.

587 Hurtago, Maria de la Luz. "Teatersituationen i Chile." (The Theatre Situation in Chile.) *Entre.* 1983; 10(4): 26-28.
Chile. 1970-1983. Historical studies. ■Effects of political instability and materialism on Chilean theatre: structural changes, artistic experiments and formation of provincial ensembles.

588 Hellberg, Hans. "Escambray." *Entre.* 1983; 10(4): 10-15. [In Swedish.]
Cuba. Nicaragua. 1961-1983. Historical studies. ■Teatro Escambray, directed by Sergio Corieri, produces plays and films reflecting developments in Cuban society.

589 "Teater i svenska Österbotten." (Theatre in Swedish East Bothnia.) *Horis.* 1983; 30(2): 1-6.
Finland. 1983. Historical studies. ■Discussion of theatre in the Swedish-speaking areas of East Bothnia.

590 Häkkänen, Juha; Kemppainen, Tiina; Viinikainen, Kaija; Torvinen, Oskari. "Kajaanin kaupunginteatteri: Pohjoan villi länsi." (Kajaani City Theatre.) *Teat.* 1983; 38(7): 9-17. Illus.: Photo. 17. [A series of articles on Theatre in Finland.]
Finland. 1983. Historical studies. ■Articles on Kajaani City Theatre, which also tours the province of Oulu.

591 Kanto, Anneli. "Vaasan kaupunginteatteri." (Vaasa City Theatre.) *Teat.* 1983; 38(9): 4-7. Illus.: Photo. B&W. 5. [Ninth in a series on Theatre in Finland.]
Finland. 1983. Historical studies. ■Vaasa City Theatre's season in review.

592 Lehtonen, Soila. "Lahden kaupunginteatteri: menninkäisiä, kuninkaita, betonia." (Lahti City Theatre.) *Teat.* 1983; 38(10): 8-11. Illus.: Photo. 4. [Fourth in a series on Theatre in Finland.]
Finland. 1983. Critical studies. ■Building of and performances at Lahti City Theatre.

593 Tähti-Wahl, Pirjo-Riitta. "Imatran teatteri: kunnalliskamppi ja sodanpelko." (Imatra Theatre.) *Teat.* 1983; 38(10): 6-7. Illus.: Photo. B&W. 4. [Fifth in a series on Theatre in Finland.]
Finland. 1983. Critical studies. ■Review of Imatra theatre's 1983-1984 season.

594 Tiihonen, Matii. "Jyväskylän kaupunginteatteri: heikot sortui farssin tiellä." (Jyväskylä City Theatre.) *Teat.* 1983; 38(10): 4-5. Illus.: Photo. 2. [Second in a series on Theatre in Finland.]

Finland. 1983. Critical studies. ■Review of Jyväskylä City Theatre's 1983-1984 season.

595 Gershman, Judith. "Revealing the Spirit of History: The National Theatre of Strasbourg." *TDR.* 1983 Spring; 27(1): 17-24. Illus.: Photo.
France. 1975-1980. Historical studies. ■Description of the productions at the Théâtre National of Strasbourg, focusing on the evolution of new scripts and the treatment of classics.

596 Mayer, Gerhard. "Paris: Treffpunkt für Brüderlichkeit." (Paris: Meeting Point for Brotherhood.) *Buhne.* 1983 Nov.: 34-35.
France. 1983. Historical studies. ■Concepts of and preparations for Théâtre de l'Europe, managed by Giorgio Strehler.

597 Toja, Jacques. "Le Bicentenaire de l'Odéon." (The Bicentenary of the Odéon.) *RHT.* 1983; 35(2): 267-268.
France. 1982-1983. Historical studies. ■Notes on the bicentenary celebration of the Odéon Theatre, Paris, 1982-1983.

598 Bab, Julius; Kuschnia, Michael; Funke, Christoph. *Hundert Jahre Deutsches Theater Berlin 1883-1983.* (One Hundred Years of Deutsches Theater Berlin, 1883-1983.) Berlin: Henschelverlag Kunst und Gesellschaft; 1983. 517 pp. Biblio. Illus.: Photo. Print. Color. B&W. 841.
Germany. 1883-1983. Histories-specific. ■History of Deutsches Theatre Berlin.

599 Kuschnia, Michael, ed. *100 Jahre Deutsches Theater Berlin, 1883-1983.* (100 Years of Deutsches Theater Berlin, 1883-1983.) Berlin: Henschel; 1983. 517 pp. Index. Biblio. [Publication of the Deutsches Theater Berlin in celebration of its centennial.]
Germany, East. 1883-1983. Histories-sources. ■Textual and pictorial documentation of 100 years of Deutsches Theater Berlin, including materials on managers, directors, designers, actors and complete list of productions from 1945-1982.

600 Pietzsch, Ingeborg; Brendal, Silvia. "Streit — ein Lernprozess: IV Werkstatt-Tage des Kinder- und Jugendtheaters der DDR." (Quarrel — A Learning Process: IVth Workshop of East Germany's Children's and Youth Theatre.) *TZ.* 1983; 38(4): 21-25. Illus.: Photo. B&W. 6.
Germany, East. 1983. Historical studies. ■Review of the festival under the general theme of ideology and its relation to reality in new pieces and performances of the children's and youth theatre.

601 Rischbieter, Henning. "Serie: Deutsches Theater nach 1945 V — Brechts Wiederkehr." (Series: German Theatre after 1945 V — Brecht's Comeback.) *TH.* 1983; 10: 12-20. [Fifth in a series of articles.]
Germany, East. 1949. Historical studies. ■Brecht's comeback at Deutsches Theater Berlin, a production of *Mutter Courage (Mother Courage)* and the founding of the Berliner Ensemble.

602 Schrader, Willi. "Theater und *kein* Ende." (Theater and *No* End.) *SJW.* 1983; 119: 80-85. Notes. [Contribution to a colloquium held at the Shakespeare Conference, Weimar, April 25, 1982.]
Germany, East. 1982. Historical studies. ■Overview of the Conference of the German Shakespeare Society, with a list of proposals for future conferences.

603 Becker, Peter von. "Die republikanischen Masken oder deutsches Theater im Januar." (The Republican Masks, or German Theatre in January.) *TH.* 1983 Mar.; 3: 11-24.
Germany, West. 1983. Reviews of performances. ■Brief survey of productions at German theatres in January 1983.

604 Hofmann, Jürgen. "Dortmunder Unionen oder: 1100 Jahre Kultur sind genug." (Dortmund Unions, or 1100 Years of Culture Are Enough.) *Tzs.* 1983 Spring; 3: 124-145. Notes. Illus.: Photo. [Part 3 of 'Kultur in Widerspruch' ('Culture in Contradiction').]
Germany, West. 1970-1982. Critical studies. ■Financial situation of Städtische Bühnen Dortmund and its relations to cultural policy in the Ruhr district.

605 Jahnke, Manfred. "'O Herr, schmeiss Hirn vom Himmel': Eine notwendige Polemik zum Jugendtheater." ('Oh God,

DRAMA: General—Institutions

Let Brains Rain': A Necessary Polemic Concerning Theatre for Young People.) *Tzs.* 1983 Summer; 4: 60-70. Notes.
Germany, West. 1980-1983. Critical studies. ■State of school-theatre and theatre for young people.

606 John, Hans-Rainer. "Zwischen Reeperbahn und Kampnagelfabrik: Eine Woche am Deutschen Schauspielhaus Hamburg." (Between *Reeperbahn* and *Kampnagelfabrik*: One Week at Deutsches Schauspielhaus Hamburg.) *TZ.* 1983; 38(3): 56-60. Illus.: Photo. B&W. 5.
Germany, West. 1893. Reviews of performances. ■Intentions and working methods of the Deutsches Schauspielhaus, reviews of various performances.

607 Schäfer-Rose, Helmut. "Freiburger Bühnen: Prüflabor und Musterwerkstatt." (Theatres of Freiburg: Testing Laboratory and Model Factory.) *BGs.* 1983 Jan.; 35(1): 15-17. Illus.: Photo.
Germany, West. 1911-1983. Histories-sources. ■Interviews with the manager Manfred Beilharz and dramaturgs Rainer Mennicken, Dieter Neuhaus and Frider Weber about their work in obtaining subsidies for Freiburg theatres.

608 Schlaffer, Hannelore. "Von der Strasse auf die Bühne: Zwei Jahre 'Jugendclub Kritisches Theater' in Stuttgart." (From the Street to the Stage: Two Years of the Youth Club Critic's Theatre in Stuttgart.) *TH.* 1983(7): 49-50.
Germany, West. 1981-1983. Histories-sources. ■Note on the Jugendclub Kritisches Theater and on two of its productions: Edward Bond's *Saved (Gerettet)* and Shakespeare's *Troilus and Cressida.*

609 Koh, Myung-shik. "The Seventh Drama Festival." *KoJ.* 1983 Dec.; 23: 67-70. Illus.: Photo. B&W. 4: 5 in. x 3 in.
Korea. 1983. Reviews of performances.

610 Fjelde, Rolf. "A Knife in the Ground." *INC.* 1982; 3: 18-19. [Toward an Ibsen Theater: Three Views, Part II.]
Norway. USA. 1906-1982. Critical studies. ■New American Ibsen Theatre Movement, characteristics and future trends. Part of colloquium held at the Spring 1981 meeting of the Ibsen Society of America.

611 Anon. "La Pologne au Théâtre des Nations." (Poland in the Theatre of Nations.) *TP.* 1983; 294-296: 43-49. Illus.: Photo. Print. B&W. 7. [In French and English.]
Poland. France. 1954-1982. Historical studies. ■Chronological survey of presentations by Polish theatre companies at the festival of Théâtre des Nations.

612 Got, Jerzy. "Wiadomość z Krakowa, 1781." (News from Cracow, 1781.) *PaT.* 1983; 32(1): 57-58. Notes.
Poland. 1781. Histories-sources. ■Polish translation of a correspondence printed in 1781 in *Theater-Journal für Deutschland* concerning the foundation of Polish theatre in Cracow.

613 Grodzicki, August. "Arnold Szyfman (1882-1967)." *TP.* 1983; 294-296: 50-53. [In French and English.]
Poland. 1882-1967. Biographical studies. ■Career of Arnold Szyfman and establishment of the Teatr Polski.

614 Limon, Jerzy. "George Jolly w Gdańsku." (George Jolly in Gdansk.) *PaT.* 1983; 32(2): 254-261. Notes. [Text in Polish, original documents in German.]
Poland. England. Germany. 1649-1650. Histories-sources. ■Letters signed by George Jolly concerning the visit of his troupe to Gdańsk in August, 1650.

615 Michalik, Jan. "Czytelnia Teatru Miejskiego w Krakowie." (Reading-room of the Municipal Theatre in Cracow.) *PaT.* 1983; 32(2): 262-267. Notes.
Poland. Austro-Hungarian Empire. 1902-1912. Historical studies. ■Reading-room was a first association of Polish actors having the educational puposese but also defending the professional interests.

616 Sobańska, Anna. "Le Théâtre Juif de Varsovie." (The Jewish Theatre in Warsaw.) *TP.* 1983; 302-303: 18-23. Illus.: Photo. Print. B&W. 5. [In French and English.]
Poland. 1876-1983. Historical studies.

617 González, José Emilio. "Samtida dramatik i Puerto Rico." (Contemporary Drama in Puerto Rico.) *Entre.* 1983; 10 (4): 39-41.

Puerto Rico. 1811-1970. Historical studies. ■History of Puerto Rican theatre, including the renaissance of the 1930s-1970s and treatment of national problems using avant-garde techniques.

618 Radillo, Carlos Miguel Suárez. "Kort panorama over den hispanoamerikanska teatern." (Short Panorama of Spanish-American Theatre.) *Entre.* 1983; 10(4): 6-7.
South America. North America. 1800-1983. Historical studies. ■Traveling Spanish troupes, folklife drama and superficial realism have been replaced in Latin America by artistic experiments, nationalistic movements and groups including university and prison ensembles.

619 Rosenberg, Helen. "Vad ar 'reading'?" (The Meaning of 'Reading'?)*Entre.* 1983; 10(3): 20-22.
Sweden. Denmark. 1969-1983. Historical studies. ■Limited success of the concept of staged readings as performed by FTV (Uppsala) and The O'Neill Center.

620 Sander, Anki. "Barnkultur i praktik och teori." (Children's Culture in Theory and Practice.) *Entre.* 1983; 10(2): 34-35.
Sweden. 1983. Critical studies. ■Call for children's theatre to consider children's need for mythology, as film *E.T.* has done, in coping with the nuclear threat and computer technology.

621 Taviani, Ferdinando. "Epíleg a *Les illes flotants*, d'Eugenio Barba." (Epilogue to *The Floating Islands*, by Eugenio Barba.) 205-248 in Barba, Eugenio. *Les illes flotants.* Barcelona: Institut del Teatre; 1983. 256 pp. (Monografies de teatre 12.) [Catalan translation by Montserrat Ingla from French.]
Sweden. 1964-1979. Historical studies. ■Evolution of the Odin Teatret, its theories, training system, influence and tours.

622 Stumm, Reinhardt. "Betrieb gibt's eine ganze Menge!" (A Lot of Things Happening!)*TH.* 1983 Jan.; 23(1): 13-16.
Switzerland. 1983. Histories-sources. ■Brief survey of the new season's productions at the Basel Stadttheater, plays by Schiller, Kafka, Ionesco, Pasolini and Jürgen Laederach.

623 Mazer, Cary M. "Treasons, Stratagems, and Spoils: Edwardian Actor-Managers and the Shakespeare Memorial National Theatre." *ThS.* 1983; 24(1-2): 1-34. Notes.
UK. 1905-1915. Historical studies. ■Records of the Executive Committee of the Shakespeare Memorial National Theatre indicate that several participating actor-managers had a self-serving vision of the form and purpose of the SMNT.

624 Beauman, Sally. *The Royal Shakespeare Company: A History of Ten Decades.* Oxford: Oxford UP; 1982. 388 pp. Notes. Index.
UK-England. 1864-1981. Histories-specific. ■History of the Royal Shakespeare Company with emphasis on financial and aesthetic problems as well as personal rivalries and political conflicts.

625 Bryden, Bill. "The Cottesloe Company on the Cottesloe Company Directed and Written by Bill Bryden." *Drama.* 1983 Winter; 150: 13-14.
UK-England. 1900-1983. Critical studies. ■Review of successes in Cottesloe Company by the company members.

626 Chambers, Colin; Brown, John Russell. "Literary Policy and Repertoire." *Drama.* 1983 Winter; 150: 15-18.
UK-England. 1900-1983. Critical studies. ■Balance of classics against modern plays at the National Theatre and the Royal Shakespeare Company, encouragement of new writers, process of selection.

627 Coveney, M. "The NT and the RSC." *Drama.* 1983 Winter; 150: 4-8. Illus.: Dwg. Photo. B&W. 5.
UK-England. 1960. Historical studies. ■Comparison of the National Theatre and Royal Shakespeare Company: policies, productions and funding, directors and actors.

628 Croft, Michael. "The Story of the Youth Theatre." *Drama.* 1983 Spring; 147: 16-18. Illus.: Photo. B&W. 2: 2 in. x 3 in.
UK-England. 1956. Historical studies. ■History of the National Youth Theatre.

629 Elliot, Vivian. "Genius Loci: The Malvern Festival Tradition." 191-218 in Leary, Daniel. *Shaw's Plays in Performance.* University Park, PA and London: Pennsylvania State UP; 1983. vi, 262 pp. (Shaw: The Annual of Bernard Shaw Studies 3.) Notes. Illus.: Photo. B&W.

CLASSED ENTRIES

DRAMA: General—Institutions

UK-England. 1929-1977. Historical studies. ∎Brief history of Malvern Festival from its inception to its close.

630 Elyot, Kevin; Gems, Jonathan; Byrne, John. "The Bush Theatre." *Drama*. 1983 Autumn; 149: 13-14. Illus.: Photo. 1: 2 in. x 3 in.
UK-England. 1983. Historical studies. ∎Writers, actors, directors, designers and technicians co-operate to produce new plays.

631 Hay, Malcolm. "The Black Theatre Co-operative." *Drama*. 1983 Autumn; 149: 11-12. Illus.: Photo. B&W. 1: 3 in. x 4 in.
UK-England. 1979. Historical studies. ∎Organization and development of Black Theatre Co-operative, including plays written and produced for the company and Arts Council support.

632 Lichtenfels, Peter. "The Traverse." *Drama*. 1983 Autumn; 149: 19-20. Illus.: Photo. B&W. 1: 3 in. x 3 in.
UK-England. 1963. Historical studies. ∎First studio theatre in Great Britain: artistic directors, policy, development and funding.

633 Rees, Roland. "Foco Novo." *Drama*. 1983 Autumn; 149: 15-16. Illus.: Photo. B&W. 1: 3 in. x 4 in.
UK-England. 1972. Historical studies. ∎Development and funding of company, its policies and its changing company of actors.

634 Retallack, John; Russell, John; Tighe, C. "Touring Theatre." *Drama*. 1983 Summer; 148: 15-20. Histories-sources. ∎Accounts of the Actors Touring Company, 7:84 Theatre Company's tour of USSR, and Cardiff Laboratory Theatre.
UK-England. UK-Wales. UK-Scotland. USSR. 1983.

635 Woddis, Carole. "Joint Stock." *Drama*. 1983 Autumn; 149: 17-18. Illus.: Photo. B&W. 1: 2 in. x 6 in.
UK-England. 1974. Historical studies. ∎Collective theatre company with emphasis on rehearsal workshops, range and style of performance.

636 Woddis, Carole. "Sir Peter Hall Interviewed by Carole Woddis." *Drama*. 1983 Winter; 150: 9-10. Illus.: Photo. B&W. 2: 2 in. x 4 in., 3 in. x 2 in.
UK-England. 1973-1983. Historical studies. ∎Peter Hall's role as artistic director of the National Theatre, including devising the repertory and obtaining funds.

637 FitzGerald, Mary. "How the Abbey Said No: Readers' Reports and the Rejection of *The Silver Tassie*." *OCA*. 1982; 1: 73-87. Notes.
UK-Ireland. 1928. Historical studies. ∎Rejection of O'Casey's play *The Silver Tassie* by the Abbey Theatre and the subsequent furor.

638 Johns, Christina Jacqueline. "TAG: Alive and Fresh." *STN*. 1983 Jan.; 23: 6-10. Illus.: Photo. B&W. 4.
UK-Scotland. 1967-1983. Historical studies. ∎History and study of the work of TAG (Theatre About Glasgow).

639 MacKenney, Linda. "Glasgow Unity Theatre: The Post-War Years." *STN*. 1983 July; 29: 2-6. Illus.: Photo. B&W. 3.
UK-Scotland. 1945-1959. Critical studies. ∎Historical overview of the Glasgow Unity Theatre.

640 MacKenney, Linda. "Legends." *STN*. 1983 Feb.; 24: 4-8. Illus.: Photo. B&W. 2.
UK-Scotland. 1930-1963. Historical studies. ∎History of the Glasgow Jewish Institute Players.

641 MacKenney, Linda. "Legends." *STN*. 1983 Apr.; 26: 11-14. Illus.: Photo. B&W. 1.
UK-Scotland. 1920-1940. Historical studies. ∎Report on Glasgow's popular theatre companies of the 1920s and 30s.

642 McGowan, Moray. "Report: Glasgows Citizens' Theatre — Die Kultur blüht in der Wüste." (Report: Glasgow's Citizens' Theatre — Culture Flourishes in the Desert.) *TH*. 1983 Aug.; 8: 32-36.
UK-Scotland. 1983. Histories-sources. ∎Report on the Glasgow Citizens' Theatre and brief survey of repertory: Brecht, Goethe, Shakespeare and Coward.

643 Oliver, Cordelia. "7:84 in the USSR." *STN*. 1983 May; 27: 5-10. Illus.: Photo. B&W. 1.
UK-Scotland. USSR. 1982. Historical studies. ∎Description of 7:84 Theatre Company (Scotland)'s tour of the USSR.

644 Paterson, Tony. "Early Years of the Close." *STN*. 1983 June; 28: 5-8. Illus.: Photo. B&W. 1.
UK-Scotland. 1964-1969. Historical studies. ∎Early years of Glasgow's Close Theatre Club.

645 Koene, Jane. "No Escape in the Welsh Valleys — A Discussion on Spectacle Theatre's Community Play *All's Fair*." *SCYPT*. 1983 Sep.; 11: 39-48. Illus.: Photo. B&W. 3.
UK-Wales. 1983. Histories-sources. ∎Play synopsis (set in 1942). Actors discuss script, production, role of women, audience creation in Welsh valleys and the success/failure thereof.

646 "Minoritets teater i USA." (Minority Theatre in the United States.) *Entre*. 1983; 10(4): 38-39.
USA. 1981-1983. Critical studies. ∎Minority theatre groups united by an interest in internationalism, the wish to preserve their cultural heritage and participation in political activism.

647 Abookire, Noerena. *Children's Theatre Activities at Karamu House in Cleveland, Ohio 1915-1975*. New York: New York Univ.; 1982. 375 pp. [Diss.: University Microfilms order no. DA8214861.]
USA. 1915-1975. Histories-specific. ∎History of Karamu Children's Theatre, which developed from a settlement house day care program to an internationally recognized children's theatre organization.

648 Barth, Diana. "The Irish Rebel Theatre: The First Ten Years." *AG*. 1983 Feb.; 1(2): 5-12. Illus.: Photo. Print. B&W. 6.
USA. 1973-1983. Historical studies. ∎History of the Irish Rebel Theatre: plays produced, personnel, audiences, purposes, financial support, organizational mode and public relations.

649 Duffy, Susan; Duffy, Bernard K. "Watchdogs of the American Theatre, 1910-1940." *JAC*. 1983 Spring; 6(1): 52-59. Notes.
USA. 1910-1940. Historical studies. ∎Activities of the church and theatre associations to promote 'decent' dramaturgy.

650 Harris, Dale. "NY Report: Children First." *PArts*. 1982 July; 16(7): 20. Illus.: Photo.
USA. 1982. Historical studies. ∎Review of the First All Children's Theatre (First ACT) production of *Nightingale*, and of Meridee Stein, founder of First ACT.

651 Lieberman, Susan. "The League of Chicago Theatres: Strength in Numbers." *TrCr*. 1983 Feb.; 17(2): 20-34. Illus.: Dwg. Print. B&W. 1: 14 in. x 12 in.
USA. 1970-1983. Historical studies. ∎Survey and recent history of the League and how it benefits its members.

652 McClave, Nancy R. *The American Repertory Theatre, Inc.: A Case Study*. Kent, OH: Kent State Univ.; 1982. 299 pp. [Diss.: University Microfilms order no. DA8216948.]
USA. 1945-1947. Critical studies. ∎Determines cause of failure of American Repertory Theatre in the contradiction of its commercial structure and its artistic goals.

653 Monroe, John G. "The Harlem Little Theatre Movement, 1920-1929." *JAC*. 1983 Winter; 6(4): 63-70. Notes.
USA. 1915-1934. Historical studies. ∎Black theatre groups started in Harlem to produce plays by, with, for and about Blacks.

654 Nelson, Richard. "Non-Profit Theatre in America: Where We Are." *PerAJ*. 1983; 7(1): 87-93.
USA. 1960-1983. Historical studies. ∎Article laments the loss of conscious artistic platforms, political engagement and other ideals in non-profit theatre, which concerns itself now with buildings and grants, and not with building creative artists.

655 Shafer, Yvonne. "The Guthrie Revisited: Minneapolis Celebrates 20 Years of Theatre Achievement." *ThNe*. 1983 Summer; 15 (6): 8-9. Illus.: Photo. B&W. 3.
USA. 1963-1983. Historical studies. ∎The Guthrie's architectural features, directors and productions, with special emphasis on Artistic Director Liviu Ciulei's production of Rolfe Fjelde's translation of Ibsen's *Peer Gynt*.

656 Sigel, David Leo. *The Masterworks Laboratory Theatre: A Historical and Critical Study*. New York: City Univ. of New York; 1982. 187 pp. [Diss.: University Microfilms order number DA8212215.]

DRAMA: General—Institutions

USA. 1965-1980. Histories-specific. ■Study of Masterworks Laboratory Theater, which produces non-contemporary drama according to the Stanislavskij System under the artistic direction of Walt Witcover.

657 Akuratere, Livija. *Rižskij teat'r russkoj dramy, 1940-1983: očerk istorii.* (Russian Drama Theatre of Riga, 1940-1983: Historical Survey.) Riga: Zinatne; 1983. 357 pp. Index. Biblio. Illus.: Photo. 80.
USSR. 1940-1983. Historical studies.

Performance/production

658 Beck, Roy A. *Play Production Today.* Skokie, IL: National Textbook Co.; 1983. 309 pp.
1983. Instructional materials. ■Teacher's manual.

659 Brockett, Oscar G. *Modern Theatre: Realism and Naturalism to the Present.* Boston: Allyn and Bacon; 1982. 200 pp.
1850-1982. Histories-general. ■Historical overview of modern theatre from realism and naturalism onward. Grp/movt: Realism; Naturalism.

660 Cohen, Robert. *Theatre: Brief Edition.* Palo Alto, CA: Mayfield Publishing Co; 1983. xii, 239 pp.
Instructional materials. ■Brief, historical introductory survey of theatre.

661 Gillibert, Jean. *Les illusiades: essai sur le théâtre de l'acteur.* (The Illusionists: An Essay on Actors' Theatre.) Paris: Éditions Clancier-Guenaud; 1983. 333 pp. (Bibliothèque des signes.)
Critical studies. ■Psychological aspects of acting.

662 Mitchell, Lee. *Staging Premodern Drama: A Guide to Production Problems.* Westport, CT: Greenwood P; 1983. xiv, 236 pp. Biblio. Index.
1983. Technical studies.

663 Oz, Avraham. "Transformations of Authenticity: *The Merchant of Venice* in Israel 1936-1980." *JDSh.* 1983: 165-177. Notes.
1936-1980. Critical studies. ■Concept of Shakespearean antisemitism in staging *The Merchant of Venice* in Israel.

664 Marga, Iris. *El teatro, mi verdad.* (The Theatre: My Truth.) Buenos Aires: Ediciones Tres Tiempos; 1983. xxii, 386 pp. Illus.: Photo.
Argentina. 1945. Biographies. ■Autobiography of actress Iris Marga.

665 Tatlow, Antony; Tak-Wai, Wong. *Brecht and East Asian Theatre.* Hong Kong: Hong Kong UP; 1982. 227 pp. Gloss. Index. Illus.: Photo. 11. [Papers of International Brecht Seminar, Hong Kong, 1981.]
Asia. Germany. 1925-1981. Historical studies. ■Papers on the influence of *Nō* and Chinese Opera on Brecht, performance of Brecht's plays in Asia and the relationship of these productions to the political and cultural climate of both East and West.

666 Anon. "Im Spiegel der Kritik." (Performance in Review.) *Buhne.* 1983 Jan.-Dec.. Illus.: Photo. Color. [Monthly series.]
Austria. 1983. Reviews of performances. ■Monthly report about main productions at Viennese theatres.

667 Böhm, Gotthard. "Reinhardts *Faust*: Zeugnisse einer Legende." (Reinhardt's *Faust*: Documents of a Legend.) *Buhne.* 1983 Oct.: 28-29. Illus.: Photo.
Austria. 1933-1937. Histories-sources. ■Documents of Max Reinhardt's production of Goethe's *Faust I* in Salzburg, 1933. Report on an exhibition of Salzburger Max-Reinhardt- Forschungsstätte.

668 Böhm, Gotthard. "Vienna's English Theatre: Unikum auf dem Kontinent." (Vienna's English Theatre: Unique on the Continent.) *Buhne.* 1983 Nov.: 11-12. Illus.: Photo.
Austria. 1963. Historical studies. ■Vienna's English Theatre celebrates its 20th anniversary with G.B. Shaw's *Candida*.

669 Böhm, Gotthard. "Komisch ist man nur im Zusammenhang." (You Are Comic Only in Context.) *Buhne.* 1983 Apr.: 10-11.
Austria. 1900-1983. Biographical studies. ■Career of actress Lotte Lang and her forthcoming roles at Theater in der Josefstadt.

670 Forester, Horst. *Der Turmbau von Babel.* (The Tower of Babel.) Vienna: Dramatisches Zentrum; 1983. 48 pp. (Texte zur Theaterarbeit 7.) Illus.: Photo. Poster. B&W.

Austria. 1980-1983. Histories-sources. ■Ruben Fraga's concept for the production of *Der Turmbau von Babel (The Tower of Babel)*, with notes on acting.

671 Friedl, Peter. "Eckermanns Leiden: Martin Walsers *In Goethes Hand* am Wiener Akademietheater uraufgeführt." (Eckermann's Suffering: World Premiere of Martin Walser's *In Goethe's Hand* at the Akademietheater in Vienna.) *TH.* 1983 Feb.; 2: 28.
Austria. 1983. Reviews of performances. ■World premiere of Martin Walser's *In Goethe's Hand* at Vienna's Akademietheater, directed by Karl Fruchtmann.

672 Fuhrich, Edda; Prossnitz, Gisela. *Max Reinhardt: 'Ein Theater, das den Menschen wieder Freude gibt'.* (Max Reinhardt: 'A Theatre That Makes People Happy Again'.) Salzburg: Max Reinhardt-Forschungsstätte, Salzburg; 112 pp. Append. Illus.: Photo. Plan. B&W.
Austria. 1893-1943. Historical studies. ■Exhibition on Max Reinhardt's theatre with emphasis on the variety of genres and performance spaces used by the director.

673 Kruntorad, Paul. "Ein Zyniker als Jedermann: Ingmar Bergman inszeniert Molières *Dom Juan* für die Salzburger Festspiele." (A Cynic as *Everyman*: Ingmar Bergman Stages Molière's *Dom Juan* for the Salzburg Festival.) *TH.* 1983(9): 14-16. Illus.: Photo.
Austria. 1983. Reviews of performances.

674 Löbl, Hermi. "Kein Rastelli der Verwandlung: über Michael Heltau." (No Rastelli of Transformation: On Michael Heltau.) *Buhne.* 1983 Jan.: 16-18. Illus.: Photo.
Austria. 1983. Histories-sources. ■Interview with actor Michael Heltau about his career and forthcoming roles at the Burgtheater.

675 Löbl, Hermi; Brandauer, Klaus Maria. "Klaus Maria Brandauer: 'Ich bin für Weltmeister'." (Klaus Maria Brandauer: 'I Root for World Champions'.) *Buhne.* 1983 June: 13-15. Illus.: Photo. Color.
Austria. 1983. Histories-sources. ■Interview with the actor Klaus Maria Brandauer about his career and forthcoming roles.

676 Löbl, Hermi. "Josef Meinrad." *Buhne.* 1983 Apr.: 17-20.
Austria. 1983. Biographical studies. ■Portrait of the actor Josef Meinrad.

677 Styan, J.L. *Max Reinhardt.* Cambridge and New York: Cambridge UP; 1982. 206 pp. Biblio. Index. Illus.: Photo. 33.
Austria. 1873-1943. Critical studies. ■Survey of director Max Reinhardt's career, including discussion of his various styles and his productions of works by Ibsen, Strindberg, Molière, Shakespeare and others.

678 Warren, John. "Max Reinhardt and the Viennese Theatre of the Interwar Years." *MuK.* 1983; 29: 123-136. Notes.
Austria. 1924-1937. Historical studies. ■Max Reinhardt's activities in Vienna, especially at the Theater in der Josefstadt.

679 Vander Motten, J.P. "*The Merchant of Venice, Rosamond* and Other English Plays Performed on the Continent in 1703." *THR.* 1981-1982 Winter; 7(1): 54-58. Notes.
Belgium. 1703. Historical studies. ■Questionable production chronology results from performances by English officers.

680 Dinev, Christo Christov. *Putešestvije po suša i voda.* (A Trip by Land and Sea.) Varna: Kn-vo Georgi Bakalov; 1983. 381 pp.
Bulgaria. 1900-1977. Biographical studies. ■Autobiography of Bulgarian actor Christo Dinev.

681 Gorina, E. "Ruskaja klasičeskaja dramaturgija na bolgarskoj scene." (Russian Classical Drama on the Bulgarian Stage.) 50-61 in Jakubovsky, A.A., ed. *Russian Classics and the World Theatre.* Moscow: State Institute of Theatrical Arts; 1983. 183 pp. Biblio.
Bulgaria. 1960-1970. Historical studies. ■Production study of plays by Suhovo-Kobilin, Anton Chekhov (Čechov) and Aleksand'r Ostrovskij as they were staged by Bulgarian directors.

682 Solnzeva, L. "Ruskaja dramaturgija i formirovanije sceničeskoj kultury stran vostočnoj jevropy." (Russian

DRAMA: General—Performance/production

Dramaturgy and Shaping of Theatre in East European Countries.) 17-30 in Jakubovsky, A.A., ed. *Russian Classics and the World Theatre.* Moscow: State Institute of the Theatrical Arts; 1983. 183 pp.
Bulgaria. Yugoslavia. Czechoslovakia. 1850-1914. Historical studies. ■Productions of Russian classical drama in the repertories of Bulgarian, Serbian, Croatian, Slovene and Czech theatres.

683 Adams, Rose. "Halifax: Reclaiming Popular Theatre." *CTR.* 1983 Fall; 38: 128-131. Notes. Illus.: Photo. Print. B&W. 1: 6 in. x 4 in.
Canada. 1982. Reviews of performances. ■Production of *Eight Men Speak* by Popular Projects Society, Halifax.

684 Clopper, Lawrence M. "The Chester Plays at Toronto." *RORD.* 1983; 26: 109-116.
Canada. 1983. Reviews of performances. ■Review of a contemporary three-day performance of Chester plays. Grp/movt: Medieval theatre. Related to Popular Entertainment: Pageants/parades.

685 Knowles, Richard Paul. "Responding to the Region: Co-operative Theatre on Mulgrave Road." *CTR.* 1983 Spring; 37: 51-54. Illus.: Photo. Neg. B&W. 1: 4 in. x 5 in.
Canada. 1981-1983. Historical studies. ■Alistair MacLeod's production of *The Lost Salt Gift of Blood*, in Nova Scotia's Mulgrave Road Co-op Theatre Company.

686 Lynde, Denyse. "Sir Peters and Lady Teazles of Montreal's Theatre Royal, 1829-1839." *THC.* 1983 Spring; 4(1): 57-72. Notes.
Canada. 1829-1839. Historical studies. ■Examines productions of *The School for Scandal* performed at Montreal's Theatre Royal, tracing changing acting styles and growing audience sophistication.

687 Mills, David. "The Chester Cycle of Mystery Plays PLS Toronto: 21-23 May 1983." *MET.* 1983; 5(1): 44-51. Illus.: Photo.
Canada. 1983. Critical studies. ■Adverse criticism of a production for addressing itself too much to a modern audience. Grp/movt: Medieval theatre. Related to Popular Entertainment: Pageants/parades.

688 Neilson, Patrick G. "Charles Burket Rittenhouse: Theatrical Avocations and Affiliations 1925-1976." *THC.* 1983 Spring; 4(1): 73-92. Notes. Append. Print. B&W. 6.
Canada. 1925-1976. Biographical studies. ■Chronology of Charles Burket Rittenhouse's work in Montreal as actor, playwright, director, administrator and educator.

689 Ryan, Toby. *Stage Left: Canadian Theatre in the Thirties.* Downsview, ON: Canadian Theatre Review Publications; 1982. 239 pp.
Canada. 1930-1939. Critical studies. ■Overview of Canadian theatrical productions and their relation to politics.

690 Miller, Arthur. *Salesman* in Beijing. New York: Viking P; 1983. xvi, 254 pp. Illus.: Photo. 37.
China, People's Republic of. 1983. Histories-sources. ■Arthur Miller's journal, kept while directing his *Death of a Salesman*, focuses on the problems of staging the play in Chinese and effects of the Cultural Revolution.

691 Bablet, Denis, ed. *Krejča et Brook.* (Krejča and Brook.) Paris: Editions du CNRS; 1982. 307 pp. (Les Voies de la Création Théâtrale 10.) Pref. Index. Illus.: Photo. B&W. 115.
Czechoslovakia. UK-England. 1921-1982. Critical studies. ■Primary source analysis regarding the work of directors Otomar Krejča and Peter Brook, who in spite of their differences share common aspirations.

692 Mellgren, Thomas. "Otomar Krejca." *Entre.* 1983; 10(6): 3-9. [In Swedish.]
Czechoslovakia. 1898-1983. Critical studies. ■Career of director Otomar Krejča, his interpretation of works of Shakespeare and Chekhov (Čechov), and his concept of the roles of actor and director.

693 Nawrat, Elżbieta. "Występ Osterwy w Pradze." (Osterwa's Appearances in Prague.) *PaT.* 1983; 32(1): 115-117. Illus.: Poster. B&W. 1: 11 cm. x 17 cm.
Czechoslovakia. Poland. 1920-1935. Historical studies. ■Guest performance in Prague of eminent Polish actors Juliusz Osterwa and Stanisława Lubicz-Sarnowska from Warsaw.

694 Svehla, Jaroslav. *Stary komediant: o ceskem herci Janu Kaskovi.* (An Old Comedian: Czech Actor Jan Kaska.) Prague: Melantrich; 1983. 237 pp. Illus.: Photo. 16.
Czechoslovakia. 1810-1869. Biographies. ■Biography of Czech actor Jan Kaska.

695 Astington, John H. "Gallows Scenes on the Elizabethan Stage." *TN.* 1983; 37(1): 3-9. Notes.
England. 1560-1600. Historical studies. ■Gallows scenes in the Elizabethan playhouses were managed by methods which had been long established in the provincial cycle plays. Grp/movt: Elizabethan theatre.

696 Cohen, Walter. "The Artisan Theatres of Renaissance by England and Spain." *TJ.* 1983 Dec.; 35(4): 499-518. Notes.
England. Spain. 1576-1635. Historical studies. ■Marxist theory of capitalism is applied to qualify public theatres in England and Spain. In both cases concern with actors, dramatists, audience and theatrical structures reveals profoundly popular nature of theatre. The difference is seen in the patronage and the role of monarchy. Grp/movt: Elizabethan theatre.

697 Cohen, Walter. "Calderón in England: A Social Theory of Production and Consumption." *BCom.* 1983 Summer; 35(1): 69-77. Notes.
England. 1660-1983. Historical studies. ■Influence of Calderón on the English stage from the Restoration to contemporary Marxist interpretations.

698 Gillispie, Norman. "Henry Carey's 'Missing' Music to *Hamlet*, 1736." *TN.* 1983; 37(3): 124-127. Notes.
England. 1736. Historical studies. ■Evidence suggests that Henry Carey composed both words and music for a 'lying-in-state' tableau inspired by the death and funeral services for the Duke of Buckingham.

699 Manogue, Ralph Anthony. "Robert Southey's *Wat Tyler.*" *TN.* 1983; 37(1): 22-24. Notes. Illus.: Handbill. 1: 3 in. x 7 in.
England. 1817. Historical studies. ■Documentation of the performance of Robert Southey's play *Wat Tyler* (1794) at Whittington Theatre.

700 Rose, Martial. "*The Magi*: The Litter and the Wristed Crown." *MET.* 1983; 5(1): 72-76. Notes. Illus.: Dwg.
England. 1200. Histories-reconstruction. ■Possible dramatic convention used in the medieval performance of the *Adoration of the Magi* plays. Grp/movt: Medieval theatre.

701 Salmon, Eric. *Granville Barker: A Secret Life.* Exeter, NH: Heinemann Educational Books; 1983. xxii, 354 pp. Index. Biblio. Illus.: Photo.
England. 1877-1946. Biographies. ■Study of writer, producer and director Harley Granville-Barker.

702 Twycross, Meg. "'Transvestism' in the Mystery Plays." *MET.* 1983; 5(2): 123-180. Notes. Illus.: Photo.
England. 1300-1550. Historical studies. ■Evidence and theatrical style implications of men playing women's parts in the middle ages, based on revivals of various plays, especially the Chester *Purification.* Grp/movt: Medieval theatre. Related to Popular Entertainment: Pageants/parades.

703 Twycross, Meg; Meredith, Peter. "The Chester Plays at Chester: 26th June 1983." *MET.* 1983; 5(1): 36-44. Illus.: Maps. Photo.
England. 1983. Reviews of performances. ■Review of 'a mini-Cycle of eight plays' performed for one day only. Grp/movt: Medieval theatre. Related to Popular Entertainment: Pageants/parades.

704 Tydeman, Bill. "Stanislavski in the Garden of Gethsemane: An Interlude." *MET.* 1983; 5(1): 53-57.
England. 1900-1983. Historical studies. ■Acting of medieval plays in a simulated session with Stanislavskij's methods of acting. Grp/movt: Medieval theatre. Related to Popular Entertainment.

705 White, Eileen. "The Girdlers' Pageant House in York." *REEDN.* 1983; 8(1): 1-8. Notes.
England. 1548-1554. Historical studies. ■New information from York about problems with the Girdlers' pageant wagon and their play, *The Slaughter of the Innocents.* Grp/movt: Medieval theatre.

706 Williams, Simon. "Lost Vitality: A Review Essay." *ET.* 1983 Nov.; 2(1): 56-61.

DRAMA: General—Performance/production

England. Germany. 1500-1939. Reviews of publications. ■Three books in Routledge and Kegan Paul's *Theatre Production Series* define the peculiar strengths needed for theatre reform. Grp/movt: Elizabethan theatre; Victorian theatre; Expressionism.

707 Wolf, William D. "Lord and Lady Northampton and Queen Henrietta's Men: An Approach to the Castle Ashby Plays." *ThR.* 1983 Spring; 8(1): 17-22. Notes.

England. 1637-1659. Historical studies. ■New evidence pertaining to actors' living arrangements suggests that the Castle Ashby plays were performed at Canonbury House.

708 Braun, Edward. *The Director and the Stage: From Naturalism to Grotowski.* London: Methuen; 1982. 218 pp. Index. Illus.: Photo. 16.

Europe. 1882-1982. Histories-specific. ■History of directing during the last one hundred years.

709 Cima, Gay Gibson. "Discovering Signs: The Emergence of the Critical Actor in Ibsen." *TJ.* 1983 Mar.; 35(1): 5-22. Notes.

Europe. North America. 1875-1983. Historical studies. ■Change of acting technique from type playing to psychological and critical interpretation required for an Ibsen performer. Instead of elocutionary gesture, the performer must develop introspective or 'autistic' movement.

710 Elliott, John R., Jr. "Census of Medieval Drama Productions." *RORD.* 1983; 26: 117-123.

Europe. 1982-1983. Historical studies. ■Census, with brief reviews, of performances of medieval drama. Grp/movt: Medieval theatre.

711 Good, Graham. "Early Productions of Oscar Wilde's *Salome.*" *NCTR.* 1983 Winter; 11(2): 78-92. Notes.

Europe. USA. 1892-1917. Historical studies. ■Critical reaction to early productions of Wilde's *Salome*, including productions in Paris (1896), Berlin (1902, 1903), London (1905, 1906, 1911), Moscow (1917) and New York (1905).

712 Groppali, Enrico. "Spettacolarità della morte." (Theatricality of Death.) *QT.* 1983 May; 5(20): 31-38.

Europe. North America. 1983. Critical studies. ■Effectiveness of death in modern theatre productions.

713 Halstead, William Perdue, ed. *Statistical History of Acting Editions of Shakespeare.* Co-published with American Theatre Association. Washington, DC: UP of America; 1983. 618 pp. (Statistical history of acting editions of Shakespeare.) [Volume 13.]

Europe. North America. 1590. Histories-sources.

714 Jakubovsky, A.A., ed. *Ruskaja klassika i mirovoj teatralnyj proces.* (The Russian Classics and the World Theatre.) Moscow: State Institute of Theatrical Arts; 1983. 183 pp. Pref. [Materials for instruction at institutions of higher education.]

Europe. USA. 1850-1979. Historical studies. ■Influence of Russian drama and Stanislavskij's system on European and American theatre.

715 Jomaron, Jacqueline. *La mise en scène contemporaine, II, 1914-1940.* (Contemporary Staging, II: 1914-1940.) Brussels: La Renaissance du Livre; 1982. 126 pp.

Europe. 1914-1940. Histories-specific. ■Movements and individuals that shaped modern directing: theatre of revolution in Russia, Expressionism, Bauhaus, Piscator and Brecht in Germany, Futurism in Italy and Copeau, Artaud and others in France. Grp/movt: Futurism; Expressionism.

716 Neuss, Paula. "God and Embarassment." *TID.* 1983; 5: 241-253. Illus.: Photo. B&W. 3: 3 in. x 3 in.

Europe. North America. 1965-1978. Reviews of performances. ■Survey of modern productions of over twenty cycle plays. Grp/movt: Medieval theatre.

717 Salvat, Ricard. *El teatro como texto, como espectáculo.* (The Theatre as Text, as Entertainment.) Barcelona: Montesinos Editor, S.A; 1983. 152 pp. (Biblioteca de Divulgación Temática 17.) Biblio. Illus.: Photo. Print. B&W. 14: 9 cm. x 11 cm.

Europe. 600 B.C.-1982 A.D. Histories-general. ■History of theatre performance and drama.

718 Taviani, Ferdinando. "Alcuni suggerimenti per lo studio della poesia degli artisti nell'Ottocento." (Some Suggestions for the Study of Artists' Poetry in the Nineteenth Century.) *QT.* 1983 Aug.-Nov.; 6(21-22): 69-95. Notes.

Europe. 1800-1899. Textual studies. ■Period accounts provide the basis for the present critical study of the 19th century acting tradition.

719 Kanto, Anneli. "Kaisa Korhonen." *NFT.* 1983; 35: 6-7, 19. Illus.: Photo. B&W.

Finland. 1965-1983. Historical studies. ■Former singer-actress, Kaisa Korhonen, the leader of political theatre, now manages Helsinki's Swedish-language Lilla Teatern and directs Finnish and foreign scripts with merciless honesty.

720 Kyrö, Pekka; Hotinen, Jukka-Pekka. "Tampereen teatterikesä." (Tampere Theatre Summer Festival.) *Teat.* 1983; 38 (7): 4-7. Illus.: Photo. 4.

Finland. Japan. 1983. Reviews of performances. ■Discussion of performances at Tampere summer theatre festival.

721 Räty-Hämäläinen, Aino. *Esiripun takaa: Mitä on olla näytelijä sumoalaisessa teatterissa.* (From Behind the Curtain: What It Is to Be an Actor in the Finnish Theatre.) Helsinki: Tammi; 1982. 191 pp. Illus.: Photo. 32.

Finland. 1872-1980. Histories-specific. ■Status and work of actors since the beginning of professional theatre in Finland.

722 Steinbock, Dan. "Moderning teatterin haasteet." (Challenge of the Modern Theatre.) *Teat.* 1983; 38(8): 10-11, 91. Illus.: Photo. 3.

Finland. Europe. 1983. Critical studies. ■Study of Finnish conception of modern theatre compared to that of other European countries.

723 Taivalsaari, Eero. "Jouko Turkan teollinen maailma." (The Industrial World of Jouko Turkka.) *Näköpiiri.* 1983; 6 (7): 11-13.

Finland. 1983. Histories-sources. ■Interview with director and head of Theatre Academy of Finland on his views of art and society.

724 Bing, Bernard. "Le souvenir de Suzanne Bing." (Recollections of Suzanne Bing.) *RHT.* 1983; 35(1): 17-21.

France. 1913-1948. Biographical studies. ■Son of actress Suzanne Bing recalls her memories of Jacques Copeau.

725 Copeau, Pascal. "Jacques Copeau, le père." (Jacques Copeau, My Father.) *RHT.* 1983; 35(1): 9-16. Illus.: Photo. B&W. 4: 6 in. x 9 in.

France. USA. 1910-1949. Biographical studies. ■Pascal Copeau's biographical memoirs of his father, Jacques Copeau, director of the Théâtre du Vieux Colombier.

726 Cruciani, Fabrizio. "Il buco nel sipario: Frammenti del teatro del Novecento." (The Hole in the Curtain: Fragments of the Twentieth Century Theatre.) *QT.* 1982 May; 4(16): 12-19. Biblio.

France. USSR. Germany. 1900-1956. Historical studies. ■Actor-audience relationship in productions by Copeau, Brecht and Russian directors.

727 Dasté, Catherine. "Catherine Dasté parle de son grand-père." (Catherine Dasté Talks about Her Grandfather.) *RHT.* 1983; 35(1): 22-23.

France. 1940-1949. Biographical studies. ■Actress Catherine Dasté talks about her memories of her grandfather Jacques Copeau rehearsing his play *Le miracle du pain doré (The Miracle of the Glazed Bread)*.

728 Didier, Béatrice. "Rétif de la Bretonne et le jeu de l'acteur." (Restif de la Bretonne and Acting.) *RHT.* 1983; 35(3): 324-328. Notes.

France. 1700-1799. Critical studies. ■Move toward realism in acting in the novels and plays of Nicolas-Edme Restif de la Bretonne.

729 Durant, Philippe. *Gérard Philippe.* Paris: Editions PAC; 1983. 234 pp. Biblio. Illus.: Photo. 88.

France. 1922-1959. Biographies. ■Biography of actor Gérard Philippe.

730 Gillespie, John K. "Interior Action: The Impact of Noh on Jean-Louis Barrault." *CompD.* 1982-1983 Winter; 16(4): 325-344. Notes.

France. 1935. Critical studies. ■Influenced by *nō*, Jean-Louis Barrault's productions meld Eastern and Western techniques.

DRAMA: General—Performance/production

731 Guibert, Noëlle. "La création de *La vie est un songe* chez Dullin." (Dullin's Production of *Life Is a Dream.*) *CF.* 1983; 115: 13-16. Notes.
France. 1922. Historical studies. ■Success of Charles Dullin's innovative presentation of Calderón's play.

732 Huet, Marie-Hélène; Hurley, Robert, transl. *Rehearsing the Revolution: The Staging of Marat's Death, 1793-1797.* Berkeley and Los Angeles: Univ. of California P; 1983. 116 pp.
France. 1793-1797. Critical studies. ■Plays about Marat's death and their relationship to contemporary events.

733 Korzeniewski, Bohdan. "Wizyta u Craiga." (Visit with Craig.) *PaT.* 1983; 32(2): 155-166. Illus.: Photo. B&W. 3: 12 cm. x 17 cm., 10 cm. x 10 cm.
France. 1957. Histories-sources. ■Reminiscence of the visit paid by the Polish director and historian of theatre to Edward Craig.

734 Mann, Thomas; Bloch, Ernst; Héliot, Armelle; Raoul-Davis, Michèle. "*Marie Stuart.*" *CF.* 1983 Nov.-Dec.; 123-124: 58-69.
France. 1800. Histories-sources. ■Short articles and illustrations pertainig to various aspects of Schiller's *Maria Stuart*, performed at the Comédie-Française.

735 McCormick, John. *Melodrama Theatres of the French Boulevard.* In association with the Consortium for Drama and Media in Higher Education. Cambridge, England: Chadwyck-Healey; 1982. 78 pp. Illus.: Photo. B&W.
France. 1800-1900. Historical studies. ■Collection of illustrations of melodramas in performance.

736 Merschmeier, Michael. "Im eiskalten Dschungel: Patrice Chéreau inszeniert Bernard-Marie Koltès *Kampf des Negers und der Hunde* mit Michel Piccoli und Philippe Léotard." (In the Icy Cold Jungle: Patrice Chéreau Directs Bernard-Marie Koltès' *Fight of the Negro and the Dogs.*) *TH.* 1983(7): 7-14, 16-27. Illus.: Photo.
France. 1982. Historical studies. ■Patrice Chéreau directs Bernard-Marie Koltès' play *Combat du nègre et des chiens (Fight of the Negro and the Dogs)* at Théâtre des Amandiers, starring Michel Piccoli and Philippe Léotard. Includes interview with Koltès and German translation of the playtext.

737 Phillips, J.H. "Le Théâtre scolaire dans la querelle du théâtre au XVIIe siècle." (The Involvement of School Theatre in the Theatrical Debate of the Seventeenth Century.) *RHT.* 1983; 35(2): 190-221. Notes.
France. 1600-1699. Historical studies. ■Involvement of the school theatre in the debate between the Church and the public theatre.

738 Reliquet, Philippe. "*Les Estivants,* de Gorki: Un entretien avec Jacques Lassalle." (Gorky's *Summer Folk*: A Conversation with Jacques Lassalle.) *CF.* 1983; 119: 3-6.
France. Russia. 1904-1983. Critical studies. ■Director Jacques Lassalle discusses interpretation of Gorky's *Dačniki (Summer Folk)* for performance at the Comédie-Française.

739 Vincent, Jean-Pierre; Roudaut, Jean; Didi-Huberman, Georges; Macé, Gérard; Avila, Alin-Alexis. "*Félicité.*" *CF.* 1983 Nov.-Dec.; 123-124: 11-35. Illus.: Photo. [In French.]
France. 1983. Histories-sources. ■Articles and photos pertaining to various aspects of Jean Audureau's play as performed at the Comédie-Française.

740 Jauslin, Christian. "Bühnenbericht 1981-82." (Stage Report 1981-82.) *JDSh.* 1983: 200-214.
German-speaking countries. 1977-1982. Reviews of performances. ■Emphasizes Shakespearean productions of the 1981-1982 season.

741 Braun, Matthias. "Die Briefschreiberin Helene Weigel: Anmerkungen zu einer Korrespondenz." (Helene Weigel as a Letter Writer: Notes to a Correspondence.) *NIMBZ.* 1983 Sep.; 6(5): 13-15. Notes. Illus.: Photo.
Germany. 1900-1971. Critical studies. ■Notes on Helene Weigel's letters as resources for theatre history.

742 Kröplin, Wolfgang. "Wagner und die Theaterreformatoren des 20 Jahrhunderts: Versuch einer auswählenden Darstellung (I): Appia, Wyspiański, Brecht." (Wagner and the Reformers of the 20th Century Theatre (Part I): A Representative Selection: Appia, Wyspiański, Brecht.) *TZ.* 1983; 38(2): 21-23. Notes. Illus.: Dwg. 1.
Germany. Poland. Switzerland. 1813-1983. Critical studies. ■Wagner's influence on modern theatrical conceptions.

743 Tehranchian, Hassan. *Agitprop Theatre: Germany and the Soviet Union.* New York: New York Univ.; 1982. 230 pp. [Diss.: University Microfilms order no. DA8214848.]
Germany. USSR. 1848-1930. Historical studies. ■History of German political theatre and its importation into the post-revolutionary Soviet Union.

744 Adling, Wilfried. "Shakespeare und das Sozialistische Amateurtheater." (Shakespeare and the Socialist Amateur Theatre.) *SJW.* 1983; 119: 75-79. Notes. [Contribution to a colloquium held at the Shakespeare Conference, Weimar, April 24, 1982.]
Germany, East. 1982. Critical studies. ■Purposes, goals and rewards of performing Shakespeare on amateur stages. Grp/movt: Social realism.

745 Funke, Christoph. "Gastspiel zu den Brecht-Tagen 1983: 'Baal' aux Erfurt: Gespräch der Aufführung." (Starring at the Brecht Days 1983: *Baal* from Erfurt: Post-Performance Interview.) 353-358 in Brecht-Zentrum, DDR. *Brecht und Marxismus: Dokumentation: Protokoll der Brecht-Tage 1983* (Brecht and Marxism: Documentation: Proceedings of the Brecht-Days, 1983). East Berlin: Brecht-Zentrum der DDR; 1983. 405 pp. (Brecht 83.) Illus.: Photo.
Germany, East. 1983. Histories-sources. ■Interview with director Solter on his staging of *Baal* and a review of this production.

746 Gleiss, Jochen. "Ablass vom Möglichen: Zur Problematik von Shakespeare-Inszenierungen in Meiningen, Zwickau, Leipzig und Dresden-Radebeul." (Indulgence in Possibilities: On Problems of Shakespeare Productions in Meiningen, Zwickau, Leipzig und Dresden-Radebeul.) *TZ.* 1983; 38(4): 7-12. Illus.: Photo. B&W. 4.
Germany, East. 1983. Reviews of performances. ■Review essay of four Shakespeare productions.

747 Hecht, Werner. "Blick auf Brecht nach vorn: Werk und Wirkung zum 85 Geburtstag." (Look to Brecht: His Work and Influence on the Occasion of His 85th Birthday.) *TZ.* 1983; 38(2): 7-12. Notes. Illus.: Photo. B&W. 12.
Germany, East. USSR. Italy. 1956-1983. Critical studies. ■Brecht's influence today is shown by means of various productions. Also discusses tendencies of actual interpretations.

748 Kuckhoff, Armin-Gerd. "Anlässe, Shakespeare zu Spielen." (Occasions for Playing Shakespeare.) *SJW.* 1983; 119: 9-30. Notes. [Expanded version of a lecture given at the Shakespeare Conference, Weimar, April 23, 1982.]
Germany, East. 1982. Critical studies. ■Relations among author, actor and public with special emphasis on Marxist orientation in Shakespearean productions.

749 Kuckhoff, Armin-Gerd, ed.; Schlösser, Anselm, ed. "Shakespeare auf den Bühnen der DDR im Jahre 1981." (Shakespeare on the Stages of the German Democratic Republic in 1981.) *SJW.* 1983; 119: 137-153. Notes. Illus.: Photo.
Germany, East. 1981. Reviews of performances. ■List and short reviews of Shakespearean productions listed according to city with four pages of photographs. Related to Dance: Ballet.

750 Kunick, Klaus. "Zur Arbeit mit Amateurspielern." (On Working with Amateur Actors.) *SJW.* 1983; 119: 154-158. Notes. [Contribution to a colloquium at the Shakespeare Conference, Weimar, April 22, 1982.]
Germany, East. 1981. Critical studies. ■Staging Shakespeare with amateur actors.

751 Lysell, Roland. "Bernhard Minetti." *Entre.* 1983; 10(1): 27-30. [In Swedish.]
Germany, East. 1982-1983. Histories-sources. ■Interview with actor Bernhard Minetti about his emphasis on language, movement and textual concreteness, and his performance in Klaus Michael Grüber's production of Goethe's *Faust.*

DRAMA: General—Performance/production

752 Pietzsch, Ingeborg. "...fliegen zu können: Porträt-Versuch über den Schauspieler Christian Grashof." (...To Be Able to Fly: Attempt at a Portrait of the Actor Christian Grashof.) *TŽ.* 1983; 38(9): 24-27. Illus.: Photo. B&W. 4.
Germany, East. 1975-1983. Biographical studies. ■Portrait of the actor.

753 Pietzsch, Ingeborg. "Für ein komödiantisches Theater: Gespräch mit dem Regisseur Alexander Lang." (For a Comedians' Theatre: Interview with Director Alexander Lang.) *TŽ.* 1983; 38(5): 21-24. Illus.: Photo. B&W. 6.
Germany, East. 1983. Histories-sources. ■Interview with director Lang, a former actor, who argues for ensemble productions.

754 Pietzsch, Ingeborg. "Regisseure über ihren Umgang mit Brecht." (Directors on Their Association with Brecht.) *TŽ.* 1983; 38(2): 13-16. Illus.: Photo. B&W. 2.
Germany, East. 1983. Critical studies. ■Literally applying Brecht's theories to production.

755 Pietzsch, Ingeborg; Weigel, Alexander. "Dieter Franke: Fragmentarische Erinnerungen an das noch nicht geschriebene Porträt eines Schauspielers." (Dieter Franke: Fragmentary Remembrances about the Not Yet Written Portrait of an Actor.) *TŽ.* 1983; 38(1): 29-32. Illus.: Photo. B&W. 8.
Germany, East. 1964-1982. Biographical studies. ■Obituary portrait of Dieter Franke.

756 Rischbieter, Henning. "Serie: Deutsche Theatergeschichte nach 1945 I: *Nathan* – als Märchen." (Series: German History of Theatre After 1945 #I: *Nathan* – As a Fairytale.) *TH.* 1983 Mar.; 3: 24-29.
Germany, East. 1945. Historical studies. ■Gotthold Ephraim Lessing's *Nathan the Wise* at Deutsches Theater Berlin, directed by Fritz Wisten.

757 Rossmann, Andreas. "Bilder ferner Hoffnung: Über einen DDR-Regisseur, den (fast) niemand kennt." (Pictures of a Far Hope: An East German Director (Almost) Nobody Knows.) *TH.* 1983 Jan.; 23(1): 8-11.
Germany, East. 1973-1983. Historical studies. ■Portrait of the stage director Herbert König.

758 Weigel, Alexander. "Das Erbe und das Theater der Schauspieler von Heute." (The Inheritance and the Theater of Today's Actors.) *SJW.* 1983; 119: 66-71. Notes. [Reworked contribution to a colloquium held at the Shakespeare Conference, Weimar, April 23, 1982.]
Germany, East. 1982. Critical studies. ■Problems for the actor in interpreting texts in the light of traditional theatre and some suggested solutions.

759 Anon. "The Plays of Thomas Bernhard: A Photo Portfolio." *ThM.* 1983 Winter; 15(1): 52-57. Illus.: Photo. Print. B&W. 9: 9 in. x 13 in.
Germany, West. 1970-1979. Histories-sources. ■Photo portfolio of plays of Thomas Bernhard.

760 Becker, Peter von. "Tod eines Komödianten: Rollenporträt: Branko Samarovski spielt in Bochum Molières *Eingebildeten Kranken*." (Death of a Comedian, Portrait of a Role: Branko Samarovksi Plays in Bochum Molière's *The Imaginary Invalid*.) *TH.* 1983; 12: 4-9.
Germany, West. 1983. Histories-sources. ■Portrait of the actor Branko Samarovski. Focus on Samarovski in the role of Argan in Molière's *The Imaginary Invalid (Le malade imaginaire)*, directed in Bochum by Alfred Kirchner.

761 Becker, Peter von. "Hanne Hiob – Ein Porträt: 'Ich muss über meine Sachen am meisten lachen': Begegnungen mit der Tochter Brechts." (Hanne Hiob – a Portrait: 'I Must Laugh Most at Things That Concern Me': Meeting Brecht's Daughter.) *TH.* 1983; 4: 8-13. Illus.: Photo.
Germany, West. 1923-1983. Biographical studies. ■Portrait of the actress Hanne Hiob.

762 Becker, Peter von. "Bruno Ganz: nach fast sieben Jahren wieder auf der Bühne: 'Im Grunde bin ich ein Kurzstreckenläufer'." (Bruno Ganz: After Seven Years, Back on Stage: 'After All, I'm a Short Distance-Runner'.) *TH.* 1983(2): 14-19. Illus.: Photo.

Germany, West. 1965-1983. Histories-sources. ■Portrait of and interview with the actor Bruno Ganz.

763 Becker, Peter von. "Das Portrait: Cornelia Froboess – 'Ich habe lernen müssen, nein zu sagen'." (The Portrait: Cornelia Froboess – 'I Had to Learn to Say No'.) *TH.* 1983; 8: 4-11.
Germany, West. 1951-1983. Histories-sources. ■Portrait and interview with the actress Cornelia Froboess.

764 Becker, Peter von; Kaiser, Joachim; Iden, Peter; Krieger, Hans; Ignée, Wolfgang. "An den Münchner Kammerspielen: Bond und Bondys *Sommer* – ein Höhepunkt der Spielzeit." (At the Münchner Kammerspiele: Bond and Bondy's *Summer* – A Highlight of the Season.) *TH.* 1983; 4: 14-33. Illus.: Photo.
Germany, West. 1983. Reviews of performances. ■First night of Edward Bond's *Summer* at Münchener Kammerspiele, directed by Luc Bondy. Includes German translation of the playtext by Christian Enzensberger.

765 Becker, Peter von. "Heinar Kipphardts letztes Stück: ein fataler Text: Kein *Bruder Eichmann*!" (Heinar Kipphardt's Last Play: An Awkward Text – No *Brother Eichmann*!) *TH.* 1983; 3: 1-3. Illus.: Photo.
Germany, West. 1983. Critical studies. ■Analysis of problems concerning the staging of Kipphardt's *Brother Eichmann*.

766 Cruse, Axel; Roth, Friedhelm. "*Unternehmen Arche Noah*: Eine Produktion des Lichterloh Theaters: Logbuchnotizen einer 'Kreozfahrt auf den Spuren der ersten Überlebenskünstler'." (*Noah's Ark Enterprise*: A Production of Lichterloh Theatre: Logbook Notes from a 'Cruise on the Track of the First Survival-Artists'.) *Tzs.* 1983 Spring; 3: 11-27. Notes. Illus.: Photo.
Germany, West. 1981. Histories-sources. ■Notes on the preparation of a production on civil defense, survival strategies and the peace movement.

767 Erdmann, Michael. "Theatralische Texttransport-Maschine: Zur Uraufführung von Heiner Müller's *Medeamaterial* in Bochum." (Theatrical Machine for Text-transportation: On the Premiere of Heiner Müller's *Medeamaterial* in Bochum.) *TH.* 1983 ; 6: 36-43.
Germany, West. 1983. Reviews of performances. ■Premiere of Heiner Müller's *Verkommenes Ufer Medeamaterial Landschaft Mit Argonauten (Wrecked Shore Medeamaterial Landscape with Argonauts)* directed by Manfred Karge. Includes playtext.

768 Holkenbrink, Jörg. "Das *Weber*-Projekt: Anmerkungen zur Inszenierung einer Zielgruppe." (The *Weavers* Project: Remarks on the Production of a Target Group.) *Tzs.* 1983; 4: 71-80.
Germany, West. 1979. Histories-sources. ■Report on a project organized by Westfälisches Landestheater and Kommunale Informationsstelle für Weiterbildung von Erwerbslosen. Production of a topical version of Gerhart Hauptmann's *The Weavers* in collaboration with and especially for the residents of working-class district Recklinghausen-Süd.

769 John, Hans-Rainer. "Stagnation, dämmernde Krise?: Zum Westberliner Theatertreffen 1982." (Stagnation: Threatening Crisis?: On the Theatre Meeting in West Berlin 1982.) *TŽ.* 1982; 37(8): 51-54.
Germany, West. 1982. Critical studies. ■Commentary on productions selected for the 19th Theatre Festival of West Berlin on the theme of social contradictions.

770 Kage, Hedda. "Friedensoffensive im Theater: Ein Rückblick auf die Friedenswoche im Schauspiel der Württembergischen Staatstheater, 18-24 März 1982." (Offensive of Peace: A Retrospect on the Peace-Week at Schauspiel der Württembergischen Staatstheater, March 18-24, 1982.) *Tzs.* 1983 Spring; 3: 28-38.
Germany, West. 1982. Histories-sources. ■Productions at the Württembergisches Staatstheater (Stuttgart) on the occasion of the 'Peace Offensive at Theatre' and political reactions.

DRAMA: General—Performance/production

771 Merschmeier, Michael. "Komik und Katastrophe: Friedrich Dürrenmatts *Achterloo* in Zürich/ Michel Vinavers *Flug in die Anden* in München." (Comic and Catastrophe: Friedrich Dürrenmatt's *Achterloo* in Zurich — Michel Vinaver's *Flight in the Andes* in Munich.) *TH*. 1983; 11: 19-24.
Germany, West. Switzerland. 1983. Reviews of performances. ▪Opening night of Friedrich Dürrenmatt's *Achterloo* in Zürich, directed by Gerd Heinz. Opening night of Michel Vinaver's *Flight in the Andes* in Munich, directed by Arie Zinger.

772 Merschmeier, Michael. "*Baumeister Solness* am Münchener Residenztheater: Himmelhoch jauchzend zu Tode gestürzt." (*The Master Builder* at Residenztheater, Munich: from the Heights of Ecstasy to the Depths of Despair.) *TH*. 1983; 6: 9-18.
Germany, West. 1983. Reviews of performances. ▪Ibsen's *Bygmester Solness (The Master Builder)* starring Barbara Sukowa and Michael Rehberg at Residenztheater Munich, directed by Peter Zadek.

773 Merschmeier, Michael. "Erfahrungen eines Zuschauers, der das Entstehen einer Inszenierung miterlebt hat: Theaterillusionen, Theaterwirklichkeit." (Experiences of a Spectator Watching the Development of a Production: Theater Illusion, Theater Reality.) *TH*. 1983; 5: 3-5, 8-12. Illus.: Photo.
Germany, West. 1983. Reviews of performances. ▪Jean Genet's *Le Balcon (The Balcony)* at Schillertheater Berlin, directed by Hans Neuenfels.

774 Merschmeier, Michael. "Verlorene Liebesmüh: Shakespeares *Komödie der Irrungen* an der Berliner Freie Volksbühne." (Love's Labour's Lost: Shakespeare's *Comedy of Errors* at the Freie Volksbühne Berlin.) *TH*. 1983; 10: 5-6.
Germany, West. 1983. Reviews of performances. ▪*The Comedy of Errors* at Freie Volksbühne, directed by Werner Schroeter.

775 Merschmeier, Michael. "Viktoria, Victoria? Caryl Churchills *Cloud Nine (Der Siebte Himmel)* am Berliner Schlossparktheater erstaufgeführt — Siegt die Prüderie über Britanniens Lüste?" (Viktoria, Victoria? Caryl Churchill's *Cloud Nine* Produced at the Berliner Schlossparktheater — Does Prudery Win out over Britain's Lust?) *TH*. 1983 Jan.; 23 (1): 32-33.
Germany, West. 1983. Reviews of performances. ▪First German production of Caryl Churchill's *Cloud Nine* at Berliner Schlossparktheater, directed by Harald Clemens.

776 Merschmeier, Michael. "Entertaining Professor Halder: Cecil P. Taylors *So gut, so schlecht* in Düsseldorf erstaufgeführt — Eine normale Nazi-Biographie mit Musik." (Entertaining Professor Halder: Cecil P. Taylor's *Good* First Produced in Düsseldorf — A Normal Nazi-Biography with Music.) *TH*. 1983 Jan.; 23(1): 35-37.
Germany, West. 1982. Reviews of performances. ▪Cecil P. Taylor's *Good* at Kleines Haus, directed by Thomas Schulte-Michels.

777 Müller, Christoph. "Das Mannheimer Nationaltheater hat Erfolg — aber: Wer geht nach Mannheim?" (The Mannheimer Nationaltheater Is Successful, But Who Goes to Mannheim?) *TH*. 1983; 6: 44-47. Illus.: Photo.
Germany, West. 1983. Critical studies. ▪Chekhov's (Čechov's) *Diadia Vania (Uncle Vanya)* [*Onkel Wanja*], directed by Harald Clemens. Interview with Jürgen Bosse, manager of Nationaltheater.

778 Rischbieter, Henning. "Deutsche Theatergeschichte nach 1945 III: Draussen vor der Tür." (German History of Theatre after 1945 III: The Man Outside.) *TH*. 1983 May: 46-51. [Third in a series of articles.]
Germany, West. 1947-1948. Historical studies. ▪Wolfgang Borchert's *Draussen vor der Tür (The Man Outside)* at Hamburg, directed by Wolfgang Liebeneiner and at Berlin, directed by Rudolf Noelte.

779 Rischbieter, Henning. "Serie: Deutsche Theatergeschichte nach 1945 II: Davongekommen?" (Series: German History of Theatre after 1945 Part II: Escaped?) *TH*. 1983 Mar.; 23: 37-43. [Second in a series of articles.]

Germany, West. 1946. Historical studies. ▪Thornton Wilder's *The Skin of Our Teeth* at Hebbeltheater Berlin, directed by Karlheinz Stroux. Included is dramaturg Heinrich Goertz' discussion of theatre.

780 Rossmann, Andreas. "Die Unfähigkeit zu träumen: Jürgen Gosch inszeniert Shakespeares *Sommernachtstraum* in Köln." (Not Able to Dream: Jürgen Gosch Directs Shakespeare's *A Midsummer Night's Dream* in Cologne.) *TH*. 1983(7): 35-36 . Illus.: Photo.
Germany, West. 1983. Reviews of performances. ▪Shakespeare's *A Midsummer Night's Dream (Ein Sommernachtstraum)* at Schauspielhaus, directed by Jürgen Gosch.

781 Rühle, Günther. "Was wird wohl sein am Ende? Gerhart Hauptmanns *Michael Kramer*, am Hamburger Thalia-Theater inszeniert." (What Will Be at the End? Gerhart Hauptmann's *Michael Kramer* Directed by Rudolf Noelte at the Thalia-Theater in Hamburg.) *TH*. 1983; 11: 13-15.
Germany, West. 1983. Reviews of performances. ▪Rudolf Noelte directs Gerhart Hauptmann's *Michael Kramer* at Thalia Theater, Hamburg.

782 Simon, Heide. "Fassbinder, das geniale Monster: Er hat das Theater verraten, seine erste Liebe — und das Theater hat ihn verraten." (Fassbinder, the Genial Monster: He Has Betrayed the Theatre, His First Love — and Theatre Has Betrayed Him.) *TH*. 1983 ; 6: 26-33.
Germany, West. 1966-1981. Biographical studies. ▪Portrait of the actor and director Rainer Werner Fassbinder. Related to Media: Film.

783 Sondermann, Marliese. "Alle Menschen wollen Frieden: Erfahrungen des Berliner Zan Pollo Theaters mit der Inszenierung des Friedensstücks *Wiespätissn*." ('All People Want Peace': Experiences of the Berlin Zan Pollo Theater with the Production of the Peace Play *Wiespätissn*.) *Tzs*. 1983 Spring; 3: 4-10. Illus.: Photo.
Germany, West. 1982. Histories-sources. ▪Report on the production of the play *Wiespätissn* by the free theatre group Zan Pollo (West Berlin), a critical treatment of the peace movement. Includes audience comments.

784 Stadelmeier, Gerhard. "Wahn-Reise und Kegelausflug: Claus Peymann inszeniert Shakespeares *Winter Märchen* in Bochum." (False-Journey and Skittles-Trip: Claus Peymann Directs Shakespeare's *A Winter's Tale* in Bochum.) *TH*. 1983(7): 33-35. Illus.: Photo.
Germany, West. 1983. Reviews of performances.

785 Steiner, Peter; Rischbieter, Henning. "Deutsche Theatergeschichte nach 1945 IV: Sartres *Fliegen* — Freiheit oder Reue." (German History of Theatre after 1945 IV: Sartre's *The Flies* — Liberty or Compunction.) *TH*. 1983; 7: 37-43. [Fourth in a series of articles.]
Germany, West. 1947-1948. Historical studies. ▪Jean Paul Sartre's *Les mouches (The Flies)* at Düsseldorfer Schauspielhaus, directed by Gustaf Gründgens and at Hebbeltheater, Berlin, directed by Jürgen Fehling.

786 Volz, Ruprecht. "Strindbergpremieren in Deutschland 1982." (Strindberg Premieres in Germany 1982.) *MfS*. 1983 Apr.: 67: 30-32.
Germany, West. 1981-1982. Reviews of performances. ▪Productions of *Fröken Julie (Miss Julie)* and *Dödsdansen (The Dance of Death)* emphasized Strindberg's revolutionary dramatic form and the dialectics of comedy and tragedy.

787 Wirth, Andrzej. "'Doesn't Matter': Zum zwanzigsten Berliner Theatertreffen." ('Doesn't Matter': On the Twentieth Berlin Theatre Conference.) *TH*. 1983(7): 44-48. Illus.: Photo.
Germany, West. 1983. Histories-sources. ▪Brief survey of productions.

788 Zander, Horst. "Die Darstellung Richmonds auf der westdeutschen Bühne." (The Performance of the Role of Richmond on the West German Stage.) *JDSh*. 1983: 111-124. Notes.
Germany, West. UK-England. 1945. Critical studies. ▪Tillyard's interpretation of Richmond in *Richard III* and the interpretation of this role on the German stage.

DRAMA: General—Performance/production

789 Zerull, Ludwig. "Dichter inszenieren ihre Stücke: Vom treuen Eckermann bis zum blutigen Scheramkeks." (Authors Direct Their Own Plays: From the Faithful Eckermann to the Bloody Joker.) *TH.* 1983; 5: 18-23.
Germany, West. 1983. Reviews of performances. ■Playwrights Martin Walser, Hartmut Lange, Dieter Kühn and Rolf Hochhuth as directors of their own plays.

790 Lanza, Diego. "L'attore." (The Actor.) 127-139 in Vegetti, Mario. *Oralità scrittura spettacolo (Oral Tradition, Writting, Performance).* Turin: Boringhieri; 1983. 226 pp. (Introduzione alla culture antiche 1.) Biblio.
Greece. Roman Empire. 600-1 B.C. Historical studies. ■Actor's role in theatre and social status in ancient Greece and Rome. Grp/movt: Ancient Greek theatre; Roman theatre.

791 Hecht, Werner. "'Eine Erneuerung Brechts kann nur von genauer Kenntnis ausgehen': Werner Hecht sprach mit dem Regisseur und Schauspieler Tamás Major über die Brecht-Rezeption in Ungarn." ('A Brecht Renewal Can Only Proceed from Detailed Knowledge': Werner Hecht Spoke with the Director and Actor Tamás Major about the Brecht Reception in Hungary.) *NIMBZ.* 1983 Feb.; 6(1): 6-7. Illus.: Photo.
Hungary. 1962-1982. Histories-sources. ■Interview about the staging of Brecht's plays in Hungary and the influence of Giorgio Strehler and Juri Ljubimov.

792 Haery, Mahmoud M. *Ru-howzi: The Iranian Traditional Improvisational Theatre.* New York: New York Univ.; 1982. 178 pp. [Diss.: University Microfilms order no. DA8214803.]
Iran. 1780-1950. Histories-reconstruction. ■Analysis of satirical improvisational plays that flourished in the mid-nineteenth century and are now chiefly rural. Includes a reconstruction of a *Ru-howzi* performance.

793 "Modena rivisto." (Modena Reviewed.) *QT.* 1983 Aug.-Nov.; 6(21-22): 16-27. Notes.
Italy. 1832-1861. Critical studies. ■Critical re-examination of the *mattatore* (actor-manager) Gustavo Modena by the author of the book *Profilo di Gustavo Modena (A Profile of Gustavo Modena),* published in 1971.

794 *La mantellina di Santuzza: Teatro siciliano tra Ottocento e Novecento.* (Santuzza's Cape: Sicilian Theatre between the Nineteenth and Twentieth Centuries.) Rome: Bulzoni; 1983. 334 pp. (Culture regionali d'Italia — Saggi e testi 4.) Pref. Notes. Index. Tables. Illus.: Photo. B&W.
Italy. 1800-1950. Histories-general. ■Survey of theatre institutions, repertory and actors of the Sicilian theatre. Special emphasis is placed on relationship between Luigi Pirandello and Nino Martoglio.

795 Allegri, Luigi. *Tre Shakespeare della Compagnia del Collettivo/teatro Due:* Amleto, Macbeth, Enrico IV. (Three Works by Shakespeare Performed by the Compagnia del Collettivo/Teatro Due: *Hamlet, Macbeth, Henry IV.*) Photographs by Maurizio Buscarino. Florence: Liberoscambio; 1983. 145 pp. (Quaderni di analisi dello spettacolo 6.) Tables. Illus.: Photo. B&W.
Italy. 1980-1983. Histories-specific. ■Compagnia del Collettivo productions of three plays by Shakespeare dialectically examine society through the relationship between the actor and his actions.

796 Bajma Griga, Stefano, ed. *Scena disgusto e clandestinità: Due allestimenti di Mario Missiroli — Les bonnes di Genet e Musik di Wedekind.* (Scenes of Disgust and Clandestiny: Two Productions by Mario Missiroli — *The Maids* by Genet and *Music* by Wedekind.) Photographs by Maurizio Buscarino. Florence: Liberoscambio; 1983. 124 pp. (Quaderni di analisi dello spettacolo 5.) Notes. Tables. Illus.: Photo. Maps. B&W.
Italy. 1980. Historical studies. ■Analysis of Missiroli's productions of Genet's *The Maids* and Wedekind's *Music.*

797 Bartalotta, Gianfranco. "L'*Amleto* di Andrzej Wajda." (The *Hamlet* of Andrzej Wajda.) *TeatrC.* 1983 June-Sep.; 2(4): 127-138. Notes.

Italy. Poland. 1982. Historical studies. ■Wajda's staging of *Hamlet* at Teatro Argentina in Rome.

798 Bušujeva, S.K. *Ital'janskij sovremenny teat'r.* (Contemporary Italian Theatre.) State Institute of Theatre, Music and Cinema. Leningrad: Iskusstvo; 1983. 176 pp. Notes. Biblio. Index. Illus.: Photo. B&W. 24.
Italy. 1945-1975. Historical studies. ■Study of productions by the leading post-World War II Italian directors.

799 Castriota, Emanuela. "Il viaggio come forma delle *memorie.*" (The Journey as the Form of *Memoires.*) *QT.* 1982 May; 4(16): 112-119. Notes.
Italy. 1800-1899. Critical studies. ■Theatrical tours in the memoirs of the *mattatori* — actor-managers.

800 Cirio, Rita. *Serata d'onore: Diletto e castigo a teatro.* (Gala Performance: Pleasure and Punishment at the Theatre.) Milano: Bompiani; 1983. 317 pp. (Saggi Bompiani.) Index.
Italy. 1976-1982. Reviews of performances. ■Collection of performance reviews.

801 Di Franco, Fiorenza. *Eduardo da scugnizzo a senatore.* (Eduardo from *scugnizzo* to Senator.) Rome — Bari: Laterza; 1983. 178 pp. (I Robinson.) Notes. Index. Biblio.
Italy. 1900-1983. Biographies. ■Biography of actor/playwright Eduardo De Filippo.

802 Geraci, Stefano. "La vanificazione del teatro e il materializzarsi dell'attore nel metodo storiografico di Mario Apollonio." (As the Theatre Vanishes the Actor Emerges According to the Historiographic Method of Mario Apollonio.) *QT.* 1982 May; 4(16): 168-176.
Italy. 1781-1841. Historical studies. ■Study of the Italian actor Luigi Vestri applying Mario Apollonio's historiographic methodology.

803 Geraci, Stefano. "Per uno studio dei fondamenti dell'aneddotica." (Towards a Study of Fundamentals of Theatrical Anecdotage.) *QT.* 1983 Aug.-Nov.; 6(21-22): 51-59. Notes.
Italy. 1891-1965. Historical studies. ■Tradition of theatrical anecdotes as it is reported in *Il libro degli aneddoti (Book of Anecdotes)* by Luigi Rasi, *Storie di palcoscenico (Stories of the Stage)* by Marco Praga, *Il teatro e la sua gente (Theatre and Its People)* by Arturo Falconi and *Il teatro all'antica italiana (Theatre Old Italian Style)* by Sergio Tofano.

804 Groppali, Enrico. "La Duse e Shakespeare: una Cleopatra smarrita tra Boito e D'Annunzio." (Duse and Shakespeare: Cleopatra Lost between Boito and D'Annunzio.) *QT.* 1983 Feb.; 5(19): 189-196.
Italy. 1873-1924. Historical studies. ■Eleonora Duse's interpretation of Cleopatra in the play translated by Boito and staged by D'Annunzio.

805 Hofmannsthal, Hugo von; Ritter Santini, Lea, ed.; Keller, Marta, transl. *Saggi italiani.* (Italian Essays.) Milan: Mondadori; 1983. 135 pp. (Oscar saggi 85.) Pref. Append. [Translated from German.]
Italy. Austria. 1892-1927. Critical studies. ■Italian translation of some of Hofmannsthal's essays on Italian culture and Eleonora Duse in particular. Includes an editor's essay on Hofmannsthal.

806 Hofmannsthal, Hugo von; Mazzarella, Arturo, ed.; Lindlar, Marion, transl. *Gabriele D'Annunzio e Eleonora Duse.* (Gabriele D'Annunzio and Eleonora Duse.) Brescia: Shakespeare and Company; 1983. 106 pp. Pref. Notes. [Translated from German.]
Italy. 1892-1903. Critical studies. ■Italian translation of Hugo von Hofmannsthal's essays on Gabriele D'Annunzio and Eleonora Duse.

807 Iden, Peter. "Hier, jenseits der Trauer: Giulia Lazzarini in *Glückliche Tage,* Giorgio Strehlers Beckett-Inszenierung am Mailänder Piccolo Teatro." (Here, on the Other Side of Affliction: Giulia Lazzarini in *Happy Days,* Giorgio Strehler's Beckett Production Staged at the Piccolo Teatro of Milan.) *TH.* 1983 Feb.; 2: 20-24.
Italy. 1983. Histories-sources. ■Beckett's *Happy Days* at Piccolo Teatro di Milano, directed by Giorgio Strehler. Interview with Strehler about Beckett.

808 Lucignani, Luciano, ed. *Giorgio Albertazzi.* Rome: Armando Curcio; 1983. 149 pp. Filmography. Tables. Illus.: Photo. B&W. [Armando Curcio Award for Theatre, 1982.]

DRAMA: General—Performance/production

Italy. 1949-1982. Historical studies. ▪Articles on theatrical career of actor Giorgio Albertazzi.

809 Pontiero, Giovanni, ed. *Duse on Tour: Guido Noccioli's Diaries, 1906-07.* Amherst, MA: Univ. of Massachusetts P; 1982. x, 178 pp.

Italy. 1906-1907. Histories-sources. ▪Playwright Guido Noccioli's account of Eleonora Duse's tour.

810 Rischbieter, Henning. "Reise zu Shakespeare." (Travel to Shakespeare.) *TH.* 1983 Feb.; 2: 2-12.

Italy. Germany, West. 1983. Reviews of performances. ▪Shakespearean productions by Compagnia del Collettivo/Teatro Due, Theater an der Ruhr (Hamburg) and Schaubühne (West Berlin).

811 Ruffini, Franco. "Piccolo glossario teatrale di Gustavo Modena." (Gustavo Modena's Little Theatrical Glossary.) *QT.* 1983 Aug.-Nov.; 6(21-22): 28-36. Notes.

Italy. 1829-1861. Linguistic studies. ▪Study of particular terms used by the *mattatore* (actor-manager) Gustavo Modena in his letters with reference to theatre life.

812 Savinio, Alberto; Tinterri, Alessandro, ed. *Palchetti romani.* (Roman Boxes.) Milan: Adelphi; 1982. 442 pp. (Biblioteca 119.) Pref. Notes. Index. Illus.: Photo. B&W.

Italy. France. 1937-1939. Reviews of performances. ▪Collection of performance reviews written by Alberto Savinio for the weekly magazine *Omnibus*, provides a survey of theatrical life in Rome.

813 Schino, Mirella. "Il primo libro su Eleonora Duse." (The First Book on Eleonora Duse.) *QT.* 1983 Aug.-Nov.; 6(21-22): 37-50. Notes.

Italy. 1859-1901. Reviews of publications. ▪Review of Luigi Rasi's book *La Duse*, which was edited in 1901, and provided the first biography of the noted actress.

814 Sogliuzzo, A. Richard. *Luigi Pirandello, Director: The Playwright in the Theatre.* London and Metuchen, NJ: Scarecrow P; 1982. xxix, 274 pp.

Italy. 1867-1936. Biographies. ▪Pirandello's career as director: his contribution to the promotion of the art of directing, the resident theatres, his theory of acting and scenography.

815 Solaris, Claudia. "Fulvia Giuliani da attrice futurista ad 'astro indipendente'." (Fulvia Giuliani, from Futurist Actress to a 'Singular Celebrity'.) *TeatrC.* 1983 Feb.-May; 2(3): 285-293. Notes. Tables. Illus.: Photo. B&W.

Italy. 1900-1983. Biographical studies. ▪Short biographical notes on the actress Fulvia Giuliani. Grp/movt: Futurism.

816 Valenti, Cristina. "Reperti del grande attore." (Great Actors' Exhibits.) *QT.* 1983 Aug.-Nov.; 6(21-22): 7-15.

Italy. 1850-1899. Historical studies. ▪Outline notes on theatre life in Italy from the seminar held in Bologna from February-March 1982.

817 Valli, Romolo; Bonino, Guido Davico, ed. *Ritratto d'attore.* (Actor's Portrait.) Milan: Il Saggiatore; 1983. 233 pp. (Politeama 7.) Tables. Illus.: Photo. B&W.

Italy. 1942-1980. Histories-sources. ▪Collection of Romolo Valli's writings and interviews.

818 De Luca Ferrero, Maria Costanza. "*Edipo* in Giappone." (*Oedipus* in Japan.) 65-78 in De Luca Ferrero, Maria Costanza. *Studi giapponesi di letteratura e teatro (Japanese Studies in Literature and Theatre).* Filelfo; 1983. 81 pp. (Docet 3.) Notes.

Japan. 1922-1978. Critical studies. ▪Japanese adaptations and productions of Sophocles' *Oedipus*.

819 Kim, Bang-ock. "Drama in the First Half of 1983." *Koj.* 1983 July; 23: 58-61. Illus.: Photo. B&W. 2: 3 in. x 5 in.

Korea. 1983. Historical studies. ▪Review of the theatrical performances of the first half of 1983 in Korean theatres.

820 Miras, Antonio Joven-Domingo. "Dos exiliados en casa." (Two Exiles at Home.) *PrAc.* 1983 Nov.-Dec.; 201: 23-34.

Mexico. Spain. 1939-1983. Histories-sources. ▪Interview with actor Augusto Benedico and director Alvaro Custodio, Spanish exiles in Mexico.

821 Schindlbeck, Michael. "Botho Strauss meets Dario Fo: Die Gruppe 'Baal' spielt *Kalldewey, Farce* am Amsterdamer

Theater Frascati." (Botho Strauss Meets Dario Fo: The Theatre Group 'Baal' plays *Kalldewey, Farce* at Theater Frascati, Amsterdam.) *TH.* 1983; 3: 34-35. Illus.: Photo.

Netherlands. 1983. Reviews of performances. ▪Botho Strauss' *Kalldewey, Farce* played by the theatre group Baal at Theater Frascati.

822 Howard, Tony. "Census of Renaissance Drama Productions 1982-83." *RORD.* 1983; 26: 73-97.

North America. Europe. 1982-1983. Reviews of performances. ▪List of productions of English Renaissance drama with brief reviews.

823 Nygaard, Knut. "Peer Gynt's scenehistorie: Hans Midbøes trilogi: *Peer Gynt*, Teatret og tident: En presentasjon." (The Stage History of *Peer Gynt*: Hans Midbøes' Trilogy: *Peer Gynt*, The Theatre and the Times: A Presentation.) *IA.* 1981-1982: 108-114.

Norway. 1976-1980. Critical studies. ▪Discussion of productions by Hans Midbøes.

824 Diaz, Grégor. "Tretio års dramatik i Peru." (Thirty Years of Drama in Peru.) *Entre.* 1983; 10(4): 31-34.

Peru. 1950-1983. Historical studies. ▪Development of acting from declamatory style to physical expressiveness and adoption of the Stanislavskij system. Includes discussion of playwright Sebastián Salazar Bondy.

825 Korzeniewski, Bohdan. "Leon Schiller." *PaT.* 1983; 32(1): 3-7. Illus.: Photo. B&W. 1: 7 cm. x 10 cm.

Poland. 1918-1954. Biographical studies. ▪Speech during the ceremony of unveiling the monument of leading Polish director Leon Schiller.

826 Kuchtówna, Lidia, ed. "Lwowskie wywiady Wilama Horzycy." (Wilam Horzyca's Interviews in Lwów.) *PaT.* 1983; 32(2): 213-253. Pref.

Poland. 1931-1936. Histories-sources. ▪25 interviews with Wilam Horzyca as manager of Municipal Theatre in Lwów, published in various periodicals.

827 Lachmann, Peter. "Das Leiden — Ein Traum: Zum Tod des Polnischen Dramatikers und Regisseurs Helmut Kajzar (1941-1982)." (The Suffering — A Dream: On Occasion of the Death of Polish Dramatist and Director Helmut Kajzar (1941-1982).) *TH.* 1983 Jan.; 23 (1): 17-26.

Poland. 1941-1982. Historical studies. ▪Work of Polish dramatist and director Helmut Kajzar. Theatre in the first years of martial law.

828 Małkowska, Hanna. "'Zły to teatr, który każdego widza przeobrazić w poetę nie umie'." ('Theatre that Cannot Transform Every Spectator into a Poet Is Bad'.) *PaT.* 1983; 32(1): 8-10. Illus.: Photo. B&W. 1: 10 cm. x 13 cm.

Poland. 1922-1923. Biographical studies. ▪Reminiscence of Leon Schiller's directing in Reduta Theatre in Warsaw delivered during the ceremony of unveiling his monument in Łódź.

829 Terlecki, Tymon. "Horzyca — człowiek teatru." (Horzyca - Man of Theatre.) *PaT.* 1983; 32(2): 201-212. Illus.: Photo. B&W. 1: 12 cm. x 17 cm.

Poland. 1889-1959. Biographical studies. ▪Essay on the artistic activity of Wilam Horzyca, Polish director and stage mananger.

830 Altšuller, A.J. "J.M. Jurjev i V.E. Mejerchol'd." (J.M. Jurjev and V.E. Meyerhold.) 4-31 in Altšuller, A.J., ed.; . Zajcev, N.V., ed. *Mastery of Acting at the Academic Drama Theatre of A.S. Pushkin.* Leningrad: State Institute of Theatre, Music and Cinema; 1983. 139 pp. Biblio.

Russia. USSR. 1910-1938. Historical studies. ▪Study of Juriev's character portrayals and Mejerchol'd's staging techniques at the Aleksandrinskij Theatre (now the Academic Drama Theatre of A.S. Pushkin).

831 Worthen, William B. "Stanislavsky: The Ethos of Acting." *TJ.* 1983 Mar.; 35(1): 32-40. Notes.

Russia. USSR. 1904-1983. Critical studies. ▪Modern analyses of Stanislavskij showing the relationship between the original theories of the Russian director and those who wrote about him in terms of naturalism and his efforts to theatricalize theatre.

832 Anon. "*Virginia: Scenaria* Interviews Sandra Duncan." *Scenaria.* 1983 Jan. 28; 35: 9-11. Illus.

South Africa, Republic of. 1983. Histories-sources. ▪Interview with English actress Sandra Duncan about her career, working in South Africa and the play *Virginia*.

DRAMA: General—Performance/production

833 "José María Rodero. Los silencios de un actor." (José María Rodero. The Silence of an Actor.) *ElPu.* 1983 Dec.: 9-10.
Spain. 1943-1983. Histories-sources. ■Interview with actor José María Rodero.

834 Benach, Joan Anton. "*Glups*, o la higiene mental." (*Glups*, or The Intellectual Hygiene.) *ElPu.* 1983 Dec.: 12-13.
Spain. 1973-1983. Historical studies. ■Ten years in the life of Dagoll-Dagom Company and their new play *Glups.*

835 Cabal, Fermín. "Con Angel Facio: Escarbando las raíces." (Interview with Angel Facio: In Search of Roots.) *PrAc.* 1983 Mar.-Apr.; 198: 2-12.
Spain. 1966-1983. Histories-sources. ■Interview with director Angel Facio.

836 Ebersole, Alva V. "A Production of *La Vida es Sueño* at Madrid's Teatro Español." *BCom.* 1982 Summer; 34(1): 123-124.
Spain. 1636. 1981. Reviews of performances. ■Review of the production of *La Vida es sueño (Life Is a Dream)* at Teatro Español.

837 Hermangildo, Alfredo. "Del icono visual al símbolo textual: el *Auto de la Pasión* de Lucas Fernández." (From Visual Icon to Textual Symbol: The *Auto de la Pasión* of Lucas Fernández.) *BCom.* 1983 Summer; 35(1): 31-49. Notes.
Spain. 1514. Historical studies. ■Evidence from explicit and implicit stage directions suggests that the *Pasión* was not performed by ecclesiastics in church for general public but for aristocrat amateurs at the court.

838 Salvat, Ricard. *El teatro: Como texto, como espectáculo.* (The Theatre: As a Text and As a Production.) Barcelona: Montesinos Editor, S.A.; 1983. 152 pp. Biblio.
Spain. 1983. Technical studies. ■Analysis of some production elements: staging, mime, acting, playwriting, design and technology. Related to Mime.

839 Fern, Peter. "Finn Poulsen." *Entre.* 1983; 10(5): 8-12. [In Swedish.]
Sweden. 1969-1983. Critical studies. ■Rehearsal method of Danish director Finn Poulsen, which includes the actor as creative artist, emphasizing wholeness, storytelling, naiveté, emotions and realism.

840 Firdén, Ann. "'He Shall Live a Man Forbid': Ingmar Bergman's *Macbeth.*" *ShS.* 1983; 36: 65-72. Notes. Illus.: Photo. Print. B&W. 2: 3 in. x 5 in.
Sweden. 1940-1948. Historical studies. ■Discussion of Ingmar Bergman's three productions of *Macbeth*: a student production in Stockholm (1940), an anti-Nazi production in Helsingborg (1944) and a philosophical treatment in Gothenborg (1948).

841 Hägglund, Kent. "Sommarteatern i Södertälje." (Summer Theatre in Södertälje.) *Entre.* 1983; 10(5): 3-7.
Sweden. 1981-1983. Historical studies. ■Reviews of summer productions of Shakespeare's *Romeo and Juliet* and *The Tempest* and an adaptation of Molière's plays, stressing high artistic standards and cooperation between professionals and amateurs.

842 Janzon, Leif. "Ingmar Bergman." *Entre.* 1983; 10(3): 7-13, 44. [In Swedish.]
Sweden. Germany. 1930-1983. Biographical studies. ■Ingmar Bergman's emotional/theoretical approach to directing, characterized by painstaking preparation and respect for his actors, is influenced by Swedish tradition of great directors.

843 Livingston, Paisley. *Ingmar Bergman and the Rituals of Art.* Ithaca, NY: Cornell UP; 1982. 291 pp. Illus.: Photo. B&W. 27.
Sweden. 1918-1982. Critical studies. ■Draws on the director's films, early stage productions, untranslated essays, interviews and scripts to elucidate Bergman's cinematic art.

844 Marker, Frederick J., ed.; Marker, Lise-Lone, ed. *Ingmar Bergman: A Project for the Theatre.* New York: Frederick Ungar; 1983. 215 pp.
Sweden. Germany, West. 1981. Historical studies. ■Documents Bergman's trilogy production consisting of his own adaptation of *Miss Julie (Julie)*, *A Doll's House (Nora)* and *Scenes from a Marriage* at the Munich Residenztheater. Includes annotated translation of the three scripts.

845 Marker, Lise-Lone. "The Magic Triangle: Ingmar Bergman's Implied Philosophy of Theatrical Communication." *MD.* 1983 Sep. ; 26(3): 251-261. Notes.
Sweden. Germany, West. 1944. Critical studies. ■Study of Ingmar Bergman's use of text, stage and audience (the major triangle) as dynamically interrelated components of theatrical communication.

846 Ödeen, Mats. "Teatern som spelautomat." (Theatre as Pinball Machine.) *Entre.* 1983; 10(5): 18-21.
Sweden. 1983. Critical studies. ■Theatre scholars said to lose sight of drama and focus exclusively on directors.

847 Ollén, Gunnar. "Strindbergspremiärer 1982." (Strindberg Premieres 1982.) *MfS.* 1983 Apr.; 67: 13-23.
Sweden. Italy. USA. 1982. Critical studies. ■Discussion of Strindberg productions in eleven countries, with emphasis on Peter Oskarsson's *Ett drömspel (A Dream Play)* in Seattle, some productions by Gruppo Abeliano and Ingmar Bergman's *Fröken Julie (Miss Julie).*

848 Strindberg, August; D'Agostini, Maria Pia, ed. "Un *memorandum* di Strindberg." (A Strindberg Memorandum.) *TeatrC.* 1982 Oct.-1983 Jan.; 1(2): 203-237.
Sweden. 1907-1920. Histories-sources. ■August Strindberg's advice for the actors of Intima Theatre.

849 Rischbieter, Henning. "Hallo, Iwanow! Arie Zinger inszeniert Tschechows zweites Stück am Züricher Schauspielhaus." (Hello, Ivanov! Arie Zinger Directs Čechov's Second play at Züricher Schauspielhaus.) *TH.* 1983; 2: 44-47.
Switzerland. 1983. Reviews of performances. ■Chekhov's (Čechov's) *Ivanov* at Züricher Schauspielhaus, directed by Arie Zinger. New German translation by Thomas Brasch.

850 Barkworth, Peter. *First Houses.* London: Secker & Warburg; 1983. 132 pp. Index. Illus.: Photo. 16.
UK. 1929-1983. Biographical studies. ■Autobiography of Peter Barkworth.

851 Carpenter, Sarah. "The Chester Cycle at Leeds: 30th April-2nd May 1983." *MET.* 1983; 5(1): 29-35. Illus.: Photo.
UK. England. 1550-1983. Histories-reconstruction. ■Performance review of the entire Chester cycle, in a 1550's design. Grp/movt: Medieval theatre. Related to Popular Entertainment: Pageants/parades.

852 Gill, Richard. "'When the Angel Appeared I Thought I Was in Heaven': Theatre for the Under 13's." *Drama.* 1983 Spring; 147: 21-22. Illus.: Photo. B&W. 2: 3 in. x 4 in., 2 in. x 3 in.
UK. 1983. Histories-sources. ■Director of Polka Children's Theatre discusses children's attitude to plays and puppets, and difficulty of staging productions. Related to Puppetry.

853 Lanchester, Elsa. *Elsa Lanchester, Herself.* New York: St. Martin's P; 1983. 327 pp. Index. Illus.: Photo. 32.
UK. 1902-1983. Biographies. ■Autobiography of actress Elsa Lanchester.

854 MacDonald, Eric. "Kay Gallie." *STN.* 1983 Mar.; 25: 2-5. Illus.: Photo. Sketches. B&W. 2.
UK. 1983. Histories-sources. ■Interview with actress Kay Gallie about her life and career.

855 Redgrave, Michael. *In My Mind's I: An Actor's Autobiography.* New York: Viking P; 1983. vi, 256 pp. Index. Illus.: Photo. 24.
UK. 1908-1983. Biographies.

856 Shaw, George Bernard. "Less Scenery Would Mean Better Drama." 25-27 in Leary, Daniel, ed. *Shaw's Plays in Performance.* University Park, and London: Pennsylvania State UP; 1983. vi, 262 pp. (SHAW: The Annual of Bernard Shaw Studies 3.)
UK. 1909. Histories-sources. ■George Bernard Shaw's remarks on desirability of multiple staging.

DRAMA: General—Performance/production

857 Sherrin, Ned. *A Small Thing — Like an Earthquake.* London: Weidenfeld and Nicolson; 1983. xii, 268 pp. Index. Illus.: Photo. 8.
UK. 1931-1983. Biographical studies. ■Memoirs of director Ned Sherrin.

858 Simmons, Dawn Langley. *Margaret Rutherford: A Blithe Spirit.* New York: McGraw-Hill; 1983. xxiii, 208 pp. Biblio. Illus.: Photo. 8.
UK. 1892-1972. Biographies. ■Biography of actress Margaret Rutherford.

859 Wapshott, Nicholas. *Peter O'Toole: A Biography.* Sevenoaks, Kent: New English Library; 1983. 239 pp. Index. Illus.: Photo. 32.
UK. 1932-1983. Biographies.

860 "The Marriage of True Minds: The Bartons and *Hamlet,* 1980-81." *JDSh.* 1983: 151-163. Notes.
UK-England. 1961-1980. Critical studies. ■John Barton's staging of *Hamlet* at the Royal Shakespeare Theatre influenced by the dissertation of his later wife, Anne Righter.

861 Anderson, Miles. "One Actor's Diary." *Drama.* 1983 Winter; 150: 26-27. Illus.: Photo. B&W. 2: 4 in. x 3 in., 3 in. x 3 in.
UK-England. 1900-1983. Biographical studies. ■Miles Anderson describes his life as a member of the Royal Shakespeare Company in London and Stratford, and his wife Lesley Duff who also works with the RSC.

862 Bachalise, T.I.; Zingerman, B.I., ed. *Šekspir i Kreg.* (Shakespeare and Craig.) All-Union Scientific Research Institute under the USSR Ministry of Culture. Moscow: Nauka; 1983. 352 pp. Notes. Append. Illus.: Dwg. B&W.
UK-England. Europe. 1872-1940. Historical studies. ■Edward Gordon Craig's productions of and theories on Shakespeare.

863 Berry, Ralph. "Beerbohm Tree As Director: Three Shakespearean Productions." *ET.* 1983 May; 1(2): 81-100. Notes. Illus.: Photo. Print. B&W. 4: 5 in. x 7 in.
UK-England. 1905-1911. Historical studies. ■Shift from the role of an 'actor-manager' to that of a 'director' in Beerbohm Tree's conceptual approach to staging and casting his productions of *Much Ado About Nothing* (1905), *Antony and Cleopatra* (1906) and *Macbeth* (1911).

864 Berry, Ralph. "Komisarjevsky at Stratford-upon-Avon." *ShS.* 1983; 36: 73-84. Notes. Illus.: Photo. B&W. 2: 3 in. x 5 in.
UK-England. 1932-1939. Historical studies. ■Theodore Komisarjevsky's Stratford-upon-Avon productions of *The Merchant of Venice* (1932), *Macbeth* (1932), *The Merry Wives of Windsor* (1935), *King Lear* (1936, 1937), *Antony and Cleopatra* (1936), *The Comedy of Errors* (1938, 1939) and *The Taming of the Shrew* (1939).

865 Bertolini, John A. "Imagining *Saint Joan.*" 149-161 in Leary, Daniel. *Shaw's Plays in Performance.* University Park: Pennsylvania State UP; 1983. vi, 262 pp. (SHAW: The Annual of Bernard Shaw Studies 3.) Notes.
UK-England. 1923. Critical studies. ■Use of properties, lighting, business and dialogue to develop Joan as a symbol of imagination.

866 Bloom, Claire. *Limelight and After: The Education of an Actress.* London: Penguin; 1982. 187 pp. Illus.: Photo.
UK-England. 1931-1982. Biographies. ■Autobiography of actress Claire Bloom with some discussion of acting techniques.

867 Candy, Edward. "The Coming of Age of Peter Pan." *Drama.* 1983 Spring; 147: 9-10.
UK-England. 1902-1983. Critical studies. ■Importance of a boy actor playing the title role in *Peter Pan.*

868 Cobin, Martin. "Text, Subtext, Antitext: The Relation of Verbal and Nonverbal Communication in the Production of Shakespeare." *MuK.* 1983; 29: 153-160.
UK-England. 1980. Critical studies. ■Relationship between nonverbal behavior and written text in productions of Shakespeare's *Macbeth, Othello* and *Julius Caesar.*

869 Cowhig, Ruth. "Northcote's Portrait of a Black Actor." *BM.* 1983; 125: 741-742, 744. Notes. Illus.: Pntg. B&W. 1: 4 in. x 5 in.
UK-England. USA. 1826. Historical studies. ■Ira Aldridge as Othello is identified in James Northcote's painting in the Manchester City Art Gallery.

870 Craig, Edward Gordon; Walton, J. Michael, ed. *Craig on Theatre.* London: Methuen; 1983. 192 pp. Illus.: Photo.
UK-England. 1872-1966. Histories-sources. ■Edward Gordon Craig's theoretical writings on theatre.

871 Crane, Gladys M. "Directing Early Shaw: Acting and Meaning in *Mrs. Warren's Profession.*" 29-39 in Leary, Daniel. *Shaw's Plays in Performance.* University Park: Pennsylvania State UP; 1983. vi, 262 pp. (SHAW: The Annual of Bernard Shaw Studies 3.)
UK-England. 1923. Critical studies. ■Director's analysis of characterization techniques makes clear the development of the conventional/unconventional theme.

872 DeLong, Kenneth; Salter, Denis. "C.V. Stanford's Incidental Music to Henry Irving's Production of Tennyson's *Becket.*" *THSt.* 1983; 3: 69-86. Notes. Illus.: Dwg. B&W. 5.
UK-England. 1893. Critical studies. ■Analysis of Stanford's musical score for Irving's production of *Becket* which was composed to enhance the play's dramatic conception. Authors consider it one of the finest examples of Victorian theatre music.

873 Dessen, Alan C. "Shakespeare's Scripts and the Modern Director." *ShS.* 1983; 36: 57-64. Notes.
UK-England. USA. Canada. 1975-1982. Critical studies. ■Discusses modern productions of Shakespeare, with emphasis on cutting, shifting, reshaping and reconceptualizing lines, characters and scenes.

874 Dowling, Ellen. "Christopher Sly on the Stage." *THSt.* 1983; 3: 87-98. Notes. Tables.
UK-England. USA. 1844-1978. Historical studies. ■Why modern directors choose to stage the induction scene in *The Taming of the Shrew.* Table lists treatment of Sly in many English language productions.

875 Emeljanow, Victor. "Komisarjevsky Directs Chekhov in England." *TN.* 1983; 37(2): 66-77. Notes.
UK-England. 1926-1936. Historical studies. ■Descriptive account of Komisarjevsky's productions of *Diadia Vania (Uncle Vanya), Višněvy Sad (The Cherry Orchard), Čaika (The Seagull)* and *Tri Sestry (Three Sisters).*

876 Evans, T.F. "*Man and Superman,* Notes for a Stage History." 79-101 in Leary, Daniel. *Shaw's Plays in Performance.* University Park, PA and London: Pennsylvania State UP; 1983. vi, 262 pp. (Shaw: The Annual of Bernard Shaw Studies 3.)
UK-England. 1903-1982. Historical studies. ■Survey of stage history based on reviews and author's personal recollections.

877 Furnas, J.C. *Fanny Kemble: Leading Lady of the Nineteenth-Century Stage.* New York: Dial P; 1982. xiv, 494 pp.
UK-England. USA. 1809-1893. Biographies. ■Biography of actress Fanny Kemble.

878 Gielgud, John. "Waiting in the Wings." *Drama.* 1983 Summer; 148: 5-6.
UK-England. 1983. Histories-sources. ■Nervous tension in actors and actresses.

879 Gordon, Giles. "Emrys James, Classical Actor." *Drama.* 1983 Winter; 150: 24-25. Illus.: Photo. B&W. 1: 4 in. x 2 in.
UK-England. 1900-1983. Biographical studies. ■Emrys James discusses his work in theatre, especially with the Royal Shakespeare Company.

880 Hall, Peter; Goodwin, John, ed. *Peter Hall's Diaries: The Story of a Dramatic Battle.* London: H. Hamilton; 1983. xiii, 507 pp. Illus.: Photo. 32.
UK-England. 1930. Histories-sources. ■Peter Hall's diaries regarding his productions.

881 Hickman, Christie. "Stephen Rea, Fringe Actor Par Excellence." *Drama.* 1983 Autumn; 149: 23-25. Illus.: Photo. B&W. 1: 3 in. x 4 in.
UK-England. UK-Ireland. 1900-1983. Biographical studies. ■Critical review of career of actor Stephen Rea and his work with Field Day Theatre Company.

DRANMA: General—Performance/production

882 Hickman, Christie. "Geraldine McEwan." *Drama.* 1983 Winter; 150: 19-20. Illus.: Photo. B&W. 1: 3 in. x 2 in.
UK-England. 1900-1983. Biographical studies. ■Career of an actress associated with the National Theatre.

883 Innes, Christopher D. *Edward Gordon Craig.* New York & Cambridge, England: Cambridge UP; 1983. xiv, 240 pp. (Directors in Perspective.) Biblio. Index. Illus.: Photo.
UK-England. 1872-1966. Historical studies. ■Study of director Edward Gordon Craig.

884 Leary, Daniel. *Shaw's Plays in Performance.* University Park: Pennsylvania State Univ.; 1983. 262 pp. Biblio.
UK-England. 1856-1950. Histories-sources. ■Collection of Shaw's addresses and essays concerning his plays in performance.

885 Leary, Daniel, ed. *Shaw's Plays in Performance.* University Park: Pennsylvania State UP; 1983. vi, 262 pp. (SHAW: The Annual of Bernard Shaw Studies 3.) Notes. Illus.: Photo. B&W.
UK-England. 1892. Critical studies. ■Collection of articles and reviews dealing with directing and acting Shaw's plays, including 'A Continuing Checklist of Shaviana'.

886 McCarthy, Lillah. "How Bernard Shaw Produces Plays: As Told by Lillah McCarthy." 163-168 in Leary, Daniel. *Shaw's Plays in Performance.* University Park: Pennsylvania State UP; 1983. vi, 262 pp. (SHAW: The Annual of Bernard Shaw Studies 3.)
UK-England. 1927. Histories-sources. ■Reprint of an interview (revised by Shaw and published in 1927) in which Lillah McCarthy comments on Shaw's aims, mode of working and methods as a director.

887 McGowan, Moray. "Erwachen aus dem Totenreich: Verlässt Harold Pinter sein *Niemandsland*?" (Awakening from the Realm of Death: Does Harold Pinter Leave His *No Man's Land*?) *TH.* 1983; 3: 30-33. Illus.: Photo.
UK-England. 1983. Reviews of Performances. ■Tom Stoppard's *The Real Thing* at Strand Theatre, directed by Peter Wood. Harold Pinter's *Other Places* at National Theatre, directed by Peter Hall.

888 McGowan, Moray. "Der Gipfel der Geliebten: Robert David MacDonalds Nazipsychothriller *Summit Conference* im Londoner Westend: Hitlers und Mussolinis Mätressen im Theater — Glenda Jackson als Eva Braun." (The Summit of the Sweethearts: Robert David Macdonald's Nazi Psychothriller *Summit Conference* in London's West End — Hitler's and Mussolini's Mistresses on the Stage — Glenda Jackson as Eva Braun.) *TH.* 1983(1): 34-35.
UK-England. 1982. Reviews of performances. ■Robert David MacDonald's Nazi psychothriller *Summit Conference* at Lyric Theatre, directed by Philip Prowse.

889 Meredith, Peter. "The Killing of the Children at Winchester Cathedral: 26-28 May 1983." *MET.* 1983; 5(1): 51-52.
UK-England. 1983. Reviews of performances. ■John Marshall production of the Digby plays at Winchester Cathedral places particular emphasis on dance. Grp/movt: Medieval theatre. Related to Dance.

890 Meyer, Michael. "Strindberg Productions in Great Britain, 1982." *MfS.* 1983 Apr.; 67: 33-34.
UK-England. 1982-1983. Reviews of performances. ■Michael Meacham's *The Dance of Death*, a radio production of *A Dream Play* and *Miss Julie* on a bill with Harold Pinter's *The Lover* were among the most interesting Strindberg productions of 1982.

891 Olivier, Laurence. *Confessions of an Actor: An Autobiography.* Published in large print. Boston: G.K. Hall; 1983. 510 pp. [Also published (1983) in Italian as *Confessioni di un peccatore.*]
UK-England. 1907-1983. Biographies.

892 Olivier, Laurence; Caminoli, Francesca transl. *Confessioni di un peccatore.* (Confessions of an Actor.) Milan: Rizzoli; 1983. 292 pp. (Miti d'oggi.) Notes. Index. [Translated from English.]
UK-England. 1907-1983. Biographies. ■Italian translation of Laurence Olivier's autobiography *Confessions of an Actor.*

893 Pinkston, C. Alex, Jr. "Richard Mansfield's Production of *Richard III*: The Brave Finale to a Disappointing London

Venture." *THSt.* 1983; 3: 3-27. Notes. Illus.: Dwg. Handbill. Photo. B&W. 12.
UK-England. USA. 1889. Histories-reconstruction. ■Account and reconstruction of Mansfield's production of *Richard III* at the Globe Theatre in London in 1889. Author considers it a signal example of Mansfield's artistry as an actor-manager.

894 Rjapolova, V. "O prošlom, nastojaščem i buduščem." (About the Past, Present and Future.) 316-343 in *Theatrical Dilemmas — 82.* All-Union Scientific Research Institute of Art Education under the USSR Ministry of Culture. Moscow: All-Russian Theatrical Society; 1983. 383 pp. [Political Performances on the Modern English Stage.]
UK-England. 1970-1979. Histories-specific. ■Discussion of political theatre in England.

895 Salenius, Elmer W. *Harley Granville-Barker.* Boston: Twayne; 1982. 167 pp.
UK-England. 1877-1946. Biographies. ■Study of career of director Harley Granville-Barker.

896 Small, Barbara J. "On Speaking Shaw: An Interview with Ann Casson." 169-179 in Leary, Daniel, ed. *Shaw's Plays in Performance.* University Park, and London: Pennsylvania State UP; 1983. vi, 262 pp. (SHAW: The Annual of Bernard Shaw Studies 3.) Notes.
UK-England. 1945-1981. Histories sources. ■Ann Casson discusses vocal technique in performing Shaw, with specific anecdotes related to *Saint Joan.*

897 Weintraub, Stanley. "Music Criticism for Deaf Stockbrokers." 235-245 in Leary, Daniel, ed. *Shaw's Plays in Performance.* University Park, and London: Pennsylvania State UP; 1983. vi, 262 pp. (SHAW: The Annual of Bernard Shaw Studies 3.)
UK-England. 1876-1897. Historical studies. ■Review of *Shaw's Music: The Complete Musical Criticism* (1981) discusses Shaw's career as critic.

898 Williams, Arthur E. "Charles Kean the Director." *TheatreS.* 1981-1982, 1982-1983; 28-29: 73-84. Notes.
UK-England. 1850-1859. Historical studies. ■Study of Charles Kean's directing methods as an actor-manager at the Princess Theatre.

899 Falletti, Clelia. "Yeats e l'attore di cultura poetica." (Yeats and the Actor with Poetic Sensitivity.) *QT.* 1982 May; 4 (16): 92-101. Notes.
UK-Ireland. 1904-1939. Historical studies. ■Yeats's theories on acting and the Abbey Theatre.

900 Murray, Christopher. "*Richelieu* at the Theatre Royal, Dublin, 1839." *TN.* 1983; 37(3): 128-131. Notes.
UK-Ireland. 1839. Historical studies. ■Edward Bulwer-Lytton's response to theatre manager John William Calcraft's staging of *Richelieu* describes production standards at a provincial theatre and indicates interest in unified staging. Grp/movt: Realism.

901 McDonald, J. "The Citizens' Theatre, Glasgow, 1969-1979 — A house of illusions." *MuK.* 1983; 29: 196-205.
UK-Scotland. 1969-1979. Critical studies. ■Fusion of visual and verbal elements creates a style of voluptuous theatricality.

902 Thorn, Fritz. "Edinburgh: Wien in Schottland." (Edinburgh: Vienna in Scotland.) *Buhne.* 1983 Oct.: 36-37. Illus.: Photo. Color.
UK-Scotland. 1983. Reviews of performances. ■Productions at Edinburgh Festival devoted to Vienna of 1900: Karl Kraus' *Die letzten Tage der Menschheit* (The Last Days of Mankind) and Jehoshua Sobol's *The Soul of a Jew.*

903 Whitebrook, Peter. "Edinburgh." *STN.* 1983 Aug.; 30: 9-13. Illus.: Photo. B&W.
UK-Scotland. 1983. Reviews of performances. ■Changes of directors in the Lyceum Theatre and the Edinburgh Festival as well as reviews of various companies and performances.

904 "Shylock, Kate, and Annie Oakley in Focus: Observations on Ethics and Theatre." *ThNe.* 1983 Dec.; 15(9): 2. [From 'Arts View,' a regular column.]
USA. 1980-1983. Critical studies. ■Directorial choices made in staging plays with inherent moral and ethic values, even when the sexist and

DRAMA: General—Performance/production

racist remarks contradict style in which the characters are played. Related to Music-Drama: Musical theatre.

905 Allensworth, Carl; Allensworth, Dorothy; Rawson, Clayton. *The Complete Play Production Handbook.* New York: Harper and Row; 1982. xi, 384 pp.
USA. 1982. Instructional materials. ■Guide to play production.

906 Anderson, Deborah Dorothy. *Story Theatre: Its Development, Implementation and Significance as a Theatrical Art Form and a Performance Technique.* Minneapolis: Univ. of Minnesota; 1982. 256 pp. [Diss.: University Microfilms order number DA8213593.]
USA. 1968-1980. Critical studies. ■Definition of story theatre, which uses both enactment and narration, and is particularly appropriate to dramatization of folklore.

907 Anon. *"Ett drömspel på Seattle-Intiman."* (*A Dream Play* at Seattle-Intiman.) *MfS.* 1983 Apr.; 67: 24-29.
USA. 1982. Critical studies. ■Peter Oskarsson's production of Strindberg's *A Dream Play* in universal and modern form, stressing philosophical questions and ensemble playing and avoiding biographical allusions to the playwright's life. Compared and contrasted to a production by Ingmar Bergman.

908 Anon. "Reinterpreting *Macbeth* through the Director's Employment of Non-verbal Devices." *MuK.* 1983; 29: 161-167.
USA. Canada. 1971-1973. Critical studies. ■Two radically unconventional productions of *Macbeth*, directed by Peter Gill and Michael Kahn.

909 Barnes, Clive; Rich, Frank; Beaufort, John; O'Haire, Patricia; Cohen, Ron. "Win/Lose/Draw." *NYTCR Off Broadway Supplement II.* 1983 June 13; 44(10): 222-225.
USA. 1983. Reviews of performances. ■Five critics review Mary Gallagher's *Win/Lose/Draw*, directed by Amy Saltz at the Provincetown Playhouse.

910 Beaufort, John; Rich, Frank; Kissel, Howard; Wilson, Edwin; Watt, Douglas; Corliss, Richard; Barnes, Clive; Kroll, Jack; Siegel, Joel; Cunningham, Dennis. "Heartbreak House." *NYTCR.* 1983 Dec. 5; 44(17): 90-95.
USA. 1983. Reviews of performances. ■Ten critics review Anthony Page's production of G.B. Shaw's *Heartbreak House*, presented at Circle in the Square.

911 Becker, Peter von. "Manhattan Momente: Neues von Burton und Taylor, Fierstein und Foreman." (Manhattan Moments: News about Burton and Taylor, Fierstein and Foreman.) *TH.* 1983(7): 60. Illus.: Photo.
USA. 1983. Reviews of performances. ■Productions of Noel Coward's *Private Lives* with Richard Burton and Elizabeth Taylor, Harvey Fierstein's *Torch Song Trilogy* and Richard Foreman's *Egyptology*.

912 Beckerman, Bernard. "Acts of Truth and Wonder." *MuK.* 1983; 29: 179-188.
USA. 1969-1980. Critical studies. ■Innovations in actor's relationship to audiences in contemporary American Theatre. Physical intimacy and direct contact.

913 Breneman, Lucille; Breneman, Brian. *Once upon a Time: A Storytelling Handbook.* Chicago: Nelson Hall; 1983. xi, 192 pp.
USA. 1983. Technical studies. ■Study of storytelling techniques. Related to Popular Entertainment.

914 Bruce, Shelley. *Tomorrow is Today.* Indianapolis: Bobbs-Merrill; 1983. 207 pp. Illus.: Photo.
USA. 1964. Biographies. ■Actress' personal experience with childhood leukemia. Related to Music-Drama: Musical theatre.

915 Carey, Gary. *Katharine Hepburn: A Hollywood Yankee.* Revised and updated version of *Katharine Hepburn*, 1975. Thorndike, ME: Thorndike P; 1983. n.p. [Large print edition.]
USA. 1909-1983. Biographies. Related to Media: film.

916 Cavett, Dick; Porterfield, Christopher. *Eye on Cavett.* New York: Arbor House; 1983. 250 pp. Illus.: Photo. 12.
USA. 1936-1983. Biographies. ■Biography of actor and television personality Dick Cavett. Related to Media: Video forms.

917 Clarke, Janis Dawn. *The Influence of the Delsarte System of Expression on American Acting 1871-1970.* Seattle: Washington State Univ.; 1982. 79 pp. [Diss.: University Microfilms order no. DA8215128.]
USA. 1871-1970. Historical studies. ■Growth of the Delsarte System and persistence of many of its elements to the present day despite widespread rejection of the system itself.

918 Clevinger, Donna L.; Powers, William G. "Cognitive Complexity and Cast Performance: A Research Note." *ERT.* 1983 Aug.; 9: 3-8. Notes.
USA. 1981. Empirical research. ■Analysis showing how administering the Hale and Delia Role Category Questionnaire to cast of *When You Coming Back, Red Ryder?* at North Texas State University, both before and during rehearsal period, affected selection and training of the cast.

919 Cunningham, Dennis; Siegel, Joel; Rich, Frank; Watt, Douglas; Barnes, Clive; Sharp, Christopher; Beaufort, John; Wilson, Edwin; Kalem, T.E.; Kroll, Jack. "Passion." *NYTCR.* 1983 May 30; 44(9): 233-238.
USA. 1983. Reviews of performances. ■Ten critics review Peter Nichols' *Passion*, directed by Marshall Mason. Presented at the Longacre Theatre.

920 Dietrich, John E.; Duckwall, Ralph W. *Play Direction.* Englewood Cliffs, NJ: Prentice-Hall; 1982. xvi, 334 pp.
USA. 1982. Instructional materials. ■Textbook for introductory directing course.

921 Fehl, Fred. *Stars of the Broadway Stage.* New York: Dover P; 1983. 122 pp. Pref. Illus.: Photo. B&W.
USA. 1940-1967. Historical studies. ■Collection of photographs of Broadway productions with emphasis on actors.

922 Fjelde, Rolf. "A Conversation with Francis Fergusson." *INC.* 1982; 3: 1, 18-22. Illus.: Photo. B&W. 1. [Interview held August 26, 1982.]
USA. 1945-1982. Histories-sources. ■Francis Fergusson talks about his involvement with Ibsen productions.

923 Gladiševa, K. "Sistema Stanislavskova i formirovanije nacionalnoj aktërskoj školy v SŠA." (The Stanislavsky System and the Formation of the National Acting School in the USA.) 163-173 in Jakubovsky, A.A., ed. *The Russian Classics and the World Theatre.* Moscow: State Institute of Theatrical Arts; 1983. 183 pp. Biblio.
USA. USSR. 1910-1959. Historical studies. ■Tour by the Moscow Art Theatre in USA and its effect on the formation of the small experimental theatre groups: Group Theatre, Actors' Laboratory Theatre and Actor's Studio. Study of Stanislavskij's system in America.

924 Gray, Beverly. "A Conversation with Tom Moore." *PArts.* 1983 June; 17(6): 8. Illus.: Photo.
USA. 1983. Histories-sources. ■Interview with director Tom Moore.

925 Gussow, Mel; Zakariasen, Bill; Stasio, Marilyn; Sterritt, David; Kroll, Jack. "Cold Harbor." *NYTCR Off Broadway Supplement I.* 1983 Apr. 18; 44(6): 299-301.
USA. 1983. Reviews of performances. ■Five critics review Bill Raymond and Dale Worsley's production of *Cold Harbor*, by Dale Worsley. Presented at the Public Theatre.

926 Gussow, Mel; Kissel, Howard; Watt, Douglas; Barnes, Clive; Corliss, Richard. "Isn't It Romantic." *NYTCR Off Broadway Supplement IV.* 1983 Dec. 12; 44(18): 68-70.
USA. 1983. Reviews of performances. ■Five critics review Wendy Wasserstein's *Isn't It Romantic*, directed by Gerald Gutierrez at Playwrights' Horizons.

927 Gussow, Mel; Nelson, Don; Kissel, Howard; Barnes, Clive; Beaufort, John. "A Private View." *NYTCR Off Broadway Supplement IV.* 1983 Dec. 12; 44(18): 71-74.
USA. 1983. Reviews of performances. ■Five critics review Vaclav Havel's *A Private View*, translated by Vera Blackwell and directed by Lee Grant at the Public Theater.

928 Gussow, Mel; Sharp, Christopher; Watt, Douglas; Barnes, Clive. "Ohio Impromptu, Catastrophe, and What Where." *NYTCR Off Broadway Supplement III.* 1983 Sep. 5; 44(13): 171-174.

DRAMA: General—Performance/production

USA. 1983. Reviews of performances. ■Four critics review three plays by Samuel Beckett, directed by Alan Schneider at the Harold Clurman Theatre.

929 Gussow, Mel; Watt, Douglas; Barnes, Clive. "*The Guys in the Truck.*" *NYTCR.* 1983 July 11; 44(11): 203-205.

USA. 1983. Reviews of performances. ■Three critics review Howard Reifsnyder's *The Guys in the Truck*, directed by David Black at the New Apollo Theatre.

930 Gussow, Mel; Barnes, Clive; Nelsen, Don; Beaufort, John; Kissel, Howard; Siegel, Joel; Cunningham, Dennis. "*The Corn is Green.*" *NYTCR.* 1983 Aug. 22; 44(12): 182-186.

USA. 1983. Reviews of performances. ■Seven critics review *The Corn is Green*, written by Emlyn Williams and directed by Vivian Matalon at the Lunt-Fontanne Theatre.

931 Gussow, Mel; Nelson, Don; Cohen, Ron; Beaufort, John; Barnes, Clive. "*Do Lord Remember Me.*" *NYTCR.* 1983 Feb. 14; 44 (2): 382-384.

USA. 1983. Reviews of performances. ■Five critics review Regge Life's production of *Do Lord Remember Me* by James de Jongh, presented at Town Hall.

932 Hagen, Uta. *Sources: A Memoir.* New York: Performing Arts Journal; 1983. 135 pp. Illus.: Photo. Dwg.

USA. Germany. 1919-1983. Biographies. ■Uta Hagen's lyrical autobiography, with frequent references to her love for nature.

933 Harris, Laurilyn J. "'In Truth, She Has Good Cause for Spleen': Madame Vestris' American Tour." *TheatreS.* 1981-1982, 1982-1983; 28-29: 41-52. Notes.

USA. UK-England. 1838. Historical studies. ■Reasons for adverse reception of Madame Vestris and Charles Mathews on their tour to USA in 1838.

934 Houseman, John. *Final Dress.* New York: Simon and Schuster; 1983. 559 pp. Index. Illus.: Photo. [Continuation of *Front and Center.*]

USA. 1983. Critical studies. ■Actor John Houseman comments on theatrical producers and directors.

935 Kahan, Gerald. "Fanny Kemble Reads Shakespeare: Her First American Tour, 1849-50." *ThS.* 1983; 24(1-2): 77-98. Notes. Illus.: Dwg. Photo. 3.

USA. 1849-1850. Historical studies. ■Description of performances, editing techniques and audience response. Related to Popular Entertainment: Monodrama.

936 Kilker, Marie J. "Mordecai Gorelik: 'Altogether' Theatre Man." *CueM.* 1983 Spring-Summer; 61(2): 9, 20.

USA. 1899-1983. Biographical studies. ■Tribute to Mordecai Gorelik: scenic designer, theorist, teacher, director and playwright.

937 Klett, Renate. "Die Sprache der Kämpferinnen: *Talking With* von Jane Martin — ein Grosses neues drama aus den USA: Elf Frauen in elf ungewöhnlichen Szenen." (The Language of the Female Fighters: *Talking With* by Jane Martin — One of the Most Important New American Plays: Eleven Women in Eleven Unusual Scenes.) *TH.* 1983 Jan.; 23(1): 30-32.

USA. 1982. Reviews of performances. ■Jane Martin's *Talking With* at Manhattan Theatre Club, directed by Jon Jory.

938 Kolin, Philip C., ed. *Shakespeare in the South: Essays on Performance.* Jackson, MI: UP of Mississippi; 1983. 297 pp.

USA. 1751-1980. Historical studies. ■Essays by Arnold Aronson, Larry S. Champion, Earl L. Dachslager, Woodrow L. Holbein, Patricia A. Madden, Waldo F. McNeir, Sara Nalley, Stuart E. Omans, Linwood E. Orange, Joseph Patrick Roppolo, Christopher J. Thaiss and Mary Duggar Toulmin on aspects of Shakespearean productions in the American South from colonial times to the present.

939 Koon, Helene Wickham. *Twentieth Century Interpretations of* Death of a Salesman. Englewood Cliffs, NJ: Prentice-Hall; 1983. 115 pp.

USA. 1949-1983. Critical studies. ■Collection of critical essays.

940 Korf, Jean Prinz. "Louisville Fest Is Marathon Theatre Experience." *ThNe.* 1983 Summer; 15(6): 13. Illus.: Photo. B&W. 1: 5 in. x 5 in.

USA. 1983. Histories-sources. ■Thirteen plays presented at the Humana Festival of New American Plays, a feature of the Actors' Theatre of Louisville.

941 Larsen, June Bennett. *Margo Jones: A Life in the Theatre.* New York: City Univ. of New York; 1982. 299 pp. Pref. Append. Illus.: Photo. [Diss.: University Microfilms order no. DA8222956.]

USA. 1913-1955. Biographies. ■Study of director Margo Jones' early life to determine the factors contributing to her success.

942 Long, Linda Sue. *The Art of Beatrice Herford, Cissie Loftus, and Dorothy Sands within the Tradition of Solo Performance.* Austin: Univ. of Texas; 1982. 346 pp. [Diss.: University Microfilms order no. DA8217900.]

USA. 1900-1920. Biographies. ■Careers of three early twentieth-century solo performers and their influence on later monodrama. Includes performance reconstructions.

943 MacLaine, Shirley. *Out on a Limb.* Toronto: Bantam; 1983. 372 pp.

USA. 1934-1983. Biographies. ■Autobiography of actress Shirley MacLaine. Related to Media: Film.

944 McNally, Terence, moderator; Anderson, Robert; Kazan, Elia. "Landmark Symposium: *Tea and Sympathy.*" *DGQ.* 1983 Winter; 19(4): 11-27.

USA. 1953. Histories-sources. ■Playwright Robert Anderson and director Elia Kazan discuss the creation of the drama *Tea and Sympathy.*

945 Nelsen, Don; Cohen, Ron; Kroll, Jack; Beaufort, John; Stasio, Marilyn; Rich, Frank; Kalem, T.E.; Gussow, Mel. "*Poppie Nongena.*" *NYTCR Off Broadway Supplement I.* 1983 Apr. 18; 44(6): 302-305.

USA. 1983. Reviews of performances. ■Eight critics review Hilary Blecher's production of *Poppie Nongena*, by Elsa Joubert and Sandra Kotze. Presented at the Douglas Fairbanks Theatre.

946 Nelson, Don; Beaufort, John; Shepard, Richard F.; Stasio, Marilyn; Kissel, Howard; Kanfer, Stefan; Treen, Joseph. "*Jeeves Takes Charge.*" *NYTCR Off Broadway Supplement II.* 1983 June 13; 44(10): 216-219.

USA. 1983. Reviews of performances. ■Seven critics review Edward Duke's adaptation of P.G. Wodehouse's *Jeeves Takes Charge*, directed by Gillian Lynne at the Space at City Center.

947 Novick, Julius. "On Directing Shaw: An Interview with Stephen Porter." 181-189 in Leary, Daniel, ed. *Shaw's Plays in Performance.* University Park, and London: Pennsylvania State UP; 1983. vi, 262 pp. (SHAW: The Annual of Bernard Shaw Studies 3.)

USA. 1964-1982. Critical studies. ■Director of successful American productions of Shaw comments on Shaw as dramatist and thinker and his place in current repertory.

948 Patch, Jerry; Alper, Jonathan; McKenney, Kerry; Vandenbroucke, Russell; Jenner, C. Lee; Passannante, Jean. "Playwrights' Little Crimes: Things Six Literary Managers Wish You Wouldn't Do When You Submit Scripts." 1-8 in *Dramatists Sourcebook.* New York: Theatre Communications Group, Inc.; 1983. 1-196 pp.

USA. 1983. Instructional materials. ■Six literary managers of regional theatres provide lists of recommendations for writers submitting new plays.

949 Pauly, Thomas H. *An American Odyssey: Elia Kazan and American Culture.* Philadelphia: Temple UP; 1983. viii, 282 pp.

USA. 1909-1965. Biographies. ■Kazan's career interpreted as a function of shifting social and political forces in American society.

950 Plummer, Rick James. *Revivifying America's Historical Figures: Acting Problems in Creating a Role for One-Performer Biography-Drama.* Carbondale, IL: Southern Illinois Univ.; 1982. 269 pp. [Diss.: University Microfilms order no. DA8215821.]

USA. 1982. Historical studies. ■History of monodrama traces its roots to vaudeville. Characters often representative of national character. Acting problems similar to those of multi-character drama but more intense.

DRAMA: General—Performance/production

951   Rich, Frank; Watt, Douglas; Barnes, Clive; Kissel, Howard; Cunningham, Dennis. *"Total Abandon." NYTCR*. 1983 May 2; 44(7): 275-278.

USA. 1983. Reviews of performances. ■Five critics review Larry Atlas' *Total Abandon*, directed by Jack Hofsiss. Presented at the Booth Theatre.

952   Rich, Frank; Watt, Douglas; Kissel, Howard; Beaufort, John; Kalem, T.E.; Kroll, Jack; Barnes, Clive; Wilson, Edwin. *"Angels Fall." NYTCR*. 1983 Jan. 1; 44(1): 390-394.

USA. 1983. Reviews of performances. ■Eight critics review Lanford Wilson's *Angels Fall*, directed by Marshall Mason. Presented at the Circle Repertory.

953   Rich, Frank; Kalem, T.E.; Beaufort, John; Wilson, Edwin; Watt, Douglas; Barnes, Clive; Kroll, Jack; Kissel, Howard. *"Plenty." NYTCR*. 1983 Jan. 1; 44(1): 394-399.

USA. 1983. Reviews of performances. ■Eight critics review David Hare's *Plenty*, directed by the author. Presented at the Newman Theatre.

954   Rich, Frank; Barnes, Clive; Watt, Douglas; Cunningham, Dennis; Kissel, Howard. *"Teaneck Tanzi: The Venus Flytrap." NYTCR*. 1983 May 2; 44(7): 278-281.

USA. 1983. Reviews of performances. ■Five critics review Claire Luckham's *Teaneck Tanzi: The Venus Flytrap*, directed by Chris Bond. Presented at the Nederlander Theatre.

955   Rich, Frank; Kissel, Howard; Watt, Douglas; Siegel, Joel; Beaufort, John; Barnes, Clive; Wilson, Edwin. *"The Caine Mutiny Court-Martial." NYTCR*. 1983 May 16; 44(8): 258-261.

USA. 1983. Reviews of performances. ■Seven critics review Herman Wouk's *The Caine Mutiny Court-Martial*, directed by Arthur Sherman. Presented at Circle in the Square presented at Circle in the Square.

956   Rich, Frank; Watt, Douglas; Kissel, Howard; Barnes, Clive; Beaufort, John; Kroll, Jack; Siegel, Joel; Cunningham, Dennis. *"The Man Who Had Three Arms." NYTCR*. 1983 Apr. 4; 44(5): 322-326.

USA. 1983. Reviews of performances. ■Eight critics review Edward Albee's production of his play *The Man Who Had Three Arms*. Presented at the Lyceum Theatre.

957   Rich, Frank; Nelsen, Don; Kissel, Howard; Barnes, Clive; Beaufort, John; Swan, Christopher; Kroll, Jack; Kalem, T.E. *"Quartermaine's Terms." NYTCR Off Broadway Supplement I*. 1983 Apr. 18; 44(6): 294-299.

USA. 1983. Reviews of performances. ■Eight critics review Kenneth Frankel's production of *Quartermaine's Terms*, by Simon Gray. Presented at Playhouse 91.

958   Rich, Frank; Beaufort, John; Barnes, Clive; Kalem, T.E.; Cohen, Ron; Watt, Douglas; Kroll, Jack; Wilson, Edwin. *"Top Girls." NYTCR Off Broadway Supplement I*. 1983 Apr. 18; 44(6): 305-309.

USA. 1983. Reviews of performances. ■Eight critics review Caryl Churchill's *Top Girls*, directed by Max Stafford-Clark. Presented at the Public Theatre.

959   Rich, Frank; Watt, Douglas; Barnes, Clive; Kissel, Howard; Kalem, T.E. *"Painting Churches." NYTCR Off Broadway Supplement IV*. 1983 Dec. 12; 44(18): 74-77.

USA. 1983. Reviews of performances. ■Five critics review Tina Howe's *Painting Churches*, directed by Carole Rothman at Lambs' Theatre.

960   Rich, Frank; Kissel, Howard; Barnes, Clive; Beaufort, John; Watt, Douglas; Cunningham, Dennis. *"American Buffalo." NYTCR*. 1983 Oct. 3; 44(14): 142-145.

USA. 1983. Reviews of performances. ■Six critics review David Mamet's *American Buffalo*, directed by Arvin Brown at the Booth Theatre.

961   Rich, Frank; Watt, Douglas; Kissel, Howard; Barnes, Clive; Beaufort, John; Wilson, Edwin. *"And a Nightingale Sang." NYTCR*. 1983 Nov. 14; 44(16): 108-111.

USA. 1983. Reviews of performances. ■Six critics review C.P. Taylor's *And a Nightingale Sang*, directed by Terry Kinney at Lincoln Center.

962   Rich, Frank; Kissel, Howard; Watt, Douglas; Barnes, Clive; Beaufort, John. *"Winners." NYTCR Off Broadway Supplement II*. 1983 June 13; 44(10): 225-227.

USA. 1983. Reviews of performances. ■Five critics review Brian Friel's *Winners*, directed by Nye Heron at the Susan Bloch Theatre.

963   Rich, Frank; Watt, Douglas; Barnes, Clive; Sharp, Christopher; Beaufort, John; Kalem, T.E.; Kroll, Jack. *"Fool for Love." NYTCR Off Broadway Supplement II*. 1983 June 13; 44(10): 212-216.

USA. 1983. Reviews of performances. ■Seven critics review Sam Shepard's *Fool for Love*, directed by the author at the Circle Repertory Company.

964   Rich, Frank; Watt, Douglas; Barnes, Clive; Beaufort, John; Gold, Sylviane; Kalem, T.E. *"Fen." NYTCR Off Broadway Supplement II*. 1983 June 13; 44(10): 208-212.

USA. 1983. Reviews of performances. ■Six critics review Caryl Churchill's *Fen*, directed by Les Waters at the Public Theater.

965   Rich, Frank; Watt, Douglas; Kissel, Howard; Corliss, Richard; Cunningham, Dennis; Barnes, Clive; Wilson, Edwin; Beaufort, John; McGuigan, Cathleen; Behr, Edward. *"Edmund Kean." NYTCR*. 1983 Aug. 22; 44(12): 176-182.

USA. 1983. Reviews of performances. ■Eight critics review *Edmund Kean*, written by Raymund FitzSimons and directed by Alison Sutcliffe. Presented at the Brooks Atkinson Theater, includes two reviews of London production.

966   Rich, Frank; Watt, Douglas; Barnes, Clive; Cohen, Ron; Beaufort, John. *"Big Maggie." NYTCR Off-Broadway Supplement III*. 1983 Sep. 5; 44(13): 154-157.

USA. 1983. Reviews of performances. ■Five critics review John B. Keane's *Big Maggie*, directed by Donal Donnelly at the Douglas Fairbanks Theatre.

967   Rich, Frank; O'Haire, Patricia; Kissel, Howard; Stasio, Marilyn; Beaufort, John; Kroll, Jack. *"Uncle Vanya." NYTCR Off-Broadway Supplement III*. 1983 Sep. 5; 44(13): 157-160.

USA. 1982. Reviews of performances. ■Six critics review Anton Chekhov's (Čechov's) *Uncle Vanya*, directed by Andre Serban at La Mama.

968   Rich, Frank; Sharp, Christopher; Watt, Douglas; Barnes, Clive; Siegel, Joel; Cunningham, Dennis. *"Moose Murders." NYCTR*. 1983 Feb. 14; 44(2): 368-370.

USA. 1983. Reviews of performances. ■Six critics review John Roach's production of Arthur Bicknell's play *Moose Murders* at the Eugene O'Neill Theatre.

969   Rich, Frank; Barnes, Clive; Watt, Douglas; Kalem, T.E.; Kissel, Howard; Beaufort, John; Cunningham, Dennis; Siegel, Joel; Wilson, Edwin. *"A View from the Bridge." NYTCR*. 1983 Feb. 14; 44(2): 377-382.

USA. 1983. Reviews of performances. ■Nine critics review Arvin Brown's production of Arthur Miller's *A View from the Bridge*.

970   Rich, Frank; Watt, Douglas; Barnes, Clive; Kissel, Howard; Henry, William A., III; Siegel, Joel. *"Slab Boys." NYTCR*. 1983 Mar. 7; 44(3): 356-359.

USA. 1983. Reviews of performances. ■Six critics review Robert Allan Ackerman's production of John Byrne's *Slab Boys* at the Playhouse Theatre.

971   Rich, Frank; Watt, Douglas; Wilson, Edwin; Barnes, Clive; Kissel, Howard; Henry, William A., III; Siegel, Joel; Cunningham, Dennis. *"'Night, Mother." NYTCR*. 1983 Mar. 21; 44(4): 333-337.

USA. 1983. Reviews of performances. ■Eight critics review Tom Moore's production of Marsha Norman's play *'Night, Mother*. Presented at the Golden Theatre.

972   Rich, Frank; Watt, Douglas; Kissel, Howard; Barnes, Clive; Beaufort, John; Kalem, T.E.; Siegel, Joel; Cunningham, Dennis. *"You Can't Take It with You." NYTCR*. 1983 Mar. 21; 44(4): 328-332.

DRAMA: General—Performance/production

USA. 1983. Reviews of performances. ■Eight critics review Ellis Rabb's production of *You Can't Take It with You* by George S. Kaufman and Moss Hart, presented at the Plymouth Theatre.

973 Roose-Evans, James. "*84 Charing Cross Road — The Most Sought After Address on Broadway.*" *Drama.* 1983 Summer; 148: 9-11. Illus.: Dwg. Photo. B&W. 3: 2 in. x 6 in., 3 in. x 4 in.

USA. 1982. Histories-sources. ■Extracts from the New York journal of James Roose-Evans, director of the play.

974 Rosenberg, Helane S.; Pinciotti, Patricia A.; Smith, Jeffrey K. "Stability and Growth in Dramatic Behavior." *ERT.* 1983 Aug.; 9: 9-19. Notes.

USA. 1980-1983. Empirical research. ■Analysis of usefulness of Inventory of Dramatic Behavior, modified for administering to groups, in measuring identifiable, observable and quantifiable qualities in creative drama.

975 Samples, Gordon. *Lust for Fame: The Stage Career of John Wilkes Booth.* Jefferson, NC: McFarland; 1982. xii, 238 pp. Append.

USA. 1855-1865. Biographies. ■Study of John Wilkes Booth, the actor-manager who killed Lincoln.

976 Smirnov, B. "Vlijanije ruskovo klasičeskovo iskusstva na amerikanskuju scenu dvacatova veka." (Influence of the Russian Classical Art on the Twentieth Century American Theatre.) 152-162 in Jakubovsky, A.A. *Russian Classics and the World Theatre.* Moscow: State Institute of Theatrical Arts; 1983. 183 pp.

USA. Russia. 1905-1979. Historical studies. ■Tours and activities of Russian actors and directors in America. Influence of Stanislavskij, Tolstoj, Gorky, Čechov and Dostoevskij on American theatre and drama.

977 Stasio, Marilyn; Rich, Frank; Watt, Douglas; Beaufort, John; Kissel, Howard. "*A Weekend Near Madison.*" *NYTCR Off-Broadway Supplement III.* 1983 Sep. 5; 44(13): 160-163.

USA. 1983. Reviews of performances. ■Five critics review Kathleen Tolan's *A Weekend Near Madison*, directed by Emily Mann at the Astor Place Theater.

978 Vallillo, Stephen M. "The Shakespeare Productions of the Federal Theatre Project." *THSt.* 1983; 3: 29-53. Notes. Illus.: Dwg. Photo. B&W. 18.

USA. 1930-1939. Historical studies. ■Account of the Federal Theatre Project's often innovative approach to performing, staging and interpreting Shakespeare's plays.

979 Walker, Ethel Pitts; Walker, Phillip E. "Can I Speak for You Brother?" *WJBS.* 1983 Winter; 7: 214-215. Illus.: Photo. Print. B&W. 4: 2 in. x 2 in., 4 in. x 6 in.

USA. 1976-1983. Historical studies. ■Brief history of a production by the African American Drama Company of California which dramatizes the contributions of nine Black leaders from Frederick Douglass to Martin Luther King, Jr.

980 Watt, Douglas; Rich, Frank; Barnes, Clive; Kalem, T.E.; Beaufort, John; Kissel, Howard; Kroll, Jack. "*Extremities.*" *NYTCR Off Broadway Supplement I.* 1983 Apr. 18; 44(6): 310-313.

USA. 1983. Reviews of performances. ■Seven critics review William Mastrosimone's *Extremities*, directed by Robert Allan Ackerman. Presented at the Cheryl Crawford Theatre.

981 Watt, Douglas; Rich, Frank; Barnes, Clive; Wilson, Edwin; Kissel, Howard; Beaufort, John; Corliss, Richard; Kroll, Jack; Siegel, Joel; Cunningham, Dennis. "*The Glass Menagerie.*" *NYTCR.* 1983 Nov. 14; 44(16): 102-108.

USA. 1983. Reviews of performances. ■Ten critics review Tennessee Williams' *The Glass Menagerie*, directed by John Dexter at the Eugene O'Neill Theatre.

982 Watt, Douglas; Beaufort, John; Kissel, Howard; Barnes, Clive; Rich, Frank. "*Buried Inside Extra.*" *NYTCR Off Broadway Supplement II.* 1983 June 13; 44(10): 220-222.

USA. 1983. Reviews of performances. ■Five critics review Thomas Babe's *Buried Inside Extra*, directed by Joseph Papp at the Public Theater.

983 Williams, Grayling. "Black Image in Cinema and Theatre in America." *Ufa.* 1983; 12(2): 102-115. Notes. Biblio.

USA. 1890-1930. Historical studies. ■Authentic expression in Black films and Harlem theatre is contrasted with stereotypical images in Black minstrelsy, musical comedies and dramas white authors. Related to Music-Drama: Musical theatre.

984 Wilson, Edwin; Watt, Douglas; Beaufort, John; Rich, Frank; Cunningham, Dennis; Siegel, Joel; Kroll, Jack; Kissel, Howard; Barnes, Clive; Kalem, T.E.; Meyers, Patrick; Schreiber, Terry. "*K2.*" *NYTCR.* 1983 Mar. 21; 44(4): 338-343.

USA. 1983. Reviews of performances. ■Ten critics review Patrick Meyers' *K2*, directed by Terry Schreiber. Presented at the Brooks Atkinson Theatre.

985 Wilson, Edwin; Rich, Frank; Kissel, Howard; Watt, Douglas; Cunningham, Dennis; Barnes, Clive; Siegel, Joel. "*Brothers.*" *NYTCR.* 1983 Nov. 7; 44(15): 135-140.

USA. 1983. Reviews of performances. ■Seven critics review George Sibbald's *Brothers*, directed by Carroll O'Connor at the Music Box Theatre.

986 Akuratere, Livija. *Aktiermaksla latviesu teatri.* (The Art of Acting in Latvian Theatre.) Riga: Zinatne; 1983. 295 pp. Biblio. Illus.: Photo. 32.

USSR. 1945. Histories-specific.

987 Altšuller, A.J., ed.; Zajcev, N.V., ed. *Aktërskoje masterstvo akademičeskovo teatra dramy imini A.S. Puškina.* (Mastery of Acting at the Academic Drama Theatre of A.S. Pushkin.) Leningrad: State Institute of Theatre, Music and Cinema; 1983. 139 pp. [Collection of scholarly articles.]

USSR. 1910-1970. Historical studies. ■Collection of articles discussing the work of the young generation of actors as well as the great masters of the Soviet stage.

988 Benedetti, Jean. *Stanislavski: An Introduction.* New York: Theatre Arts Books; 1982. xii, 81 pp.

USSR. Russia. 1863-1938. Historical studies. ■Overview of the Stanislavskij system.

989 Frolov, V.V., ed. *Voprosy teatra — 82.* (Theatrical Dilemmas — 82.) All-Union Scientific Research Institute of Art Education under the USSR Ministry of Culture. Moscow: All-Russian Theatrical Society; 1983. 383 pp. [Collection of scholarly articles and other materials.]

USSR. UK-England. 1930-1979. Historical studies. ■Articles dealing with theory and practice in Soviet and foreign theatres.

990 Girdžijanskaitė, Audronė. *Kazimiera Kymantaitė.* Vilnius: Mintis; 1983. 133 pp. Illus.: Photo. 16.

USSR. 1909-1983. Biographies. ■Biography of the Lithuanian stage director Kazimiera Kymantaitė.

991 Kröplin, Wolfgang. "Wagner und die Theaterreformatoren des 20. Jahrhunderts: Versuch einer auswählenden Darstellung (II): Meyerhold, Wachtangow, Grotowski." (Wagner and the Reformers of the 20th Century Theatre: A Representative Selection (Part II): Mejerchol'd, Vachtangov, Grotowski.) *TZ.* 1983; 38(3): 18-20. Notes.

USSR. Poland. Germany. 1813-1983. Critical studies. ■Wagner's influence on modern theatrical conceptions.

992 Markov, P.A.; Feldman, O.M., ed.; Udalcova, Z.G., comp. *Kniga vospominanij.* (Memoirs.) Moscow: Iskusstvo; 1983. 608 pp. Pref. Index. Illus.: Photo. B&W. 24.

USSR. 1910-1930. Critical studies. ■Recollections of the noted Soviet theatre critic Markov, including diaries of his youth and several articles and reviews of performances.

993 Mironova, V.M., comp.; Zolotnickij, D.I., ed. *Studinyje tečenija v soveckoj režisure 1920-1930ych godov.* (Soviet Directors of the 1920-1930s and the Phenomena of the Studio Theatre.) Leningrad: State Institute of Theatre, Music and Cinema; 1983. 134 pp. Pref. Index. [Collection of articles.]

DRAMA: General—Performance/production

USSR. 1920-1939. Historical studies. ■Role studios played in the formation of the Soviet theatre. Study discusses productions mounted at the experimental studios associated with Mejerchol'd and those of the Moscow Art Theatre and the Malyj Theatre.

994 Ribnik, A.M., ed. *Oktiab'rskaja revoliucija i uzbekskij teat'r.* (October Revolution and the Uzbek Theatre.) Tashkent State Institute of Theatre Art. Tashkent: FAN; 1983. 192 pp.

USSR. 1917-1930. Historical studies. ■Theatre in Uzbekistan and the October Revolution: emergence and development of the social criticism in drama and performance.

995 Shostakovich, Dmitri. "Politics and Artistic Interpretation." 183-186 in Kamerman, Jack B.; . Martorella, Rosanne. *Performers and Performances: The Social Organization of Artistic Work.* South Hadley, MA: J.F. Bergin; 1983. xiii, 303 pp.

USSR. 1930. Historical studies. ■Noted composer's memoirs of productions of *Hamlet*, including one that was personally cancelled in rehearsal by Stalin, another, directed by Mikhail Chekhov, that was set in Purgatory, and a third, directed by Nikolai Akimov, as a comedy in which Boris Shchukin played Polonius by imitating Stanislavskij.

996 Tumanišvili, M. *Režiser uchodit iz teatra.* (Director Leaves Theatre.) Moscow: Iskusstvo; 1983. 277 pp. Illus.: Photo. 32.

USSR. 1905-1983. Biographical studies. ■Autobiography of Georgian director M. Tumanišvili.

997 Verdone, Mario. "La cineficazione del teatro di Mejerchol'd." ('Cinematization' of Mejerchol'd's Theatre.) *TeatrC.* 1983 Feb.-May; 2(3): 355-359.

USSR. 1915-1927. Historical studies. ■Interweaving of theatrical and cinematographic techniques in Mejerchol'd's staging. Related to Media: Film.

998 Zorkaja, N. *Aleksej Popov.* Moscow: Iskusstvo; 1983. 303 pp. (The Life in Art.) Notes. Illus.: Photo. B&W. 24.

USSR. 1900-1958. Biographies. ■Study of Aleksej Popov's acting and directing methods, theories of the theatre and teaching techniques.

Plays/librettos/scripts

999 Dragún, Osvaldo. "Teatern i Argentina." (Theatre in Argentina.) *Entre.* 1983; 10(4): 12-14.

Argentina. 1900-1983. Critical studies. ■Effects of foreign invasion and political instability on Argentine theatre, including the grotesque, fragmentation, myths, storytelling and questions about the future.

1000 Fitzsimmons, Brian Arthur. *The Place of David Williamson in the History of Australian Drama: A Provisional Perspective.* Boulder, CO: Univ. of Colorado; 1982. 364 pp. [Diss.: University Microfilms order no. DA8221075.]

Australia. 1969-1980. Histories-specific. ■History of contemporary Australian drama with emphasis on popular playwright David Williamson.

1001 Got, Jerzy. "Das Jahr 1683 im Drama und auf der Bühne." (The Year 1683 in Drama and on the Stage.) *MuK.* 1983; 29: 1-97. [First Part: Austria.]

Austria. 1683-1983. Historical studies. ■Turkish siege and the relief of Vienna in 1683 as a subject of drama and theatre. Includes a chronological list of productions from 1720 to 1983, and passages of playtexts.

1002 Honegger, Gitta. "Wittgenstein's Children: The Writings of Thomas Bernhard." *ThM.* 1983 Winter; 15(1): 58-62. Notes. Illus.: Photo. Print. B&W. 1: 4 in. x 4 in.

Austria. 1970-1982. Critical studies. ■Playwright Thomas Bernhard's affinity with philosophy of Ludwig Joseph Johan Wittgenstein.

1003 Palm, Kurt. *Vom Boykott zur Anerkennung: Brecht und Österreich.* (From Boycott to Appreciation: Brecht and Austria.) Vienna and Munich: Löcker; 1983. 318 pp. Pref. Index. Notes. Biblio. Append. Illus.: Photo. B&W.

Austria. 1922-1982. Biographies. ■Bertolt Brecht's efforts to obtain Austrian citizenship.

1004 Scheibelreiter, Georg. "Franz Grillparzer und Bischof Gregor von Tours." *JGG.* 1983; 3(15): 65-78. Notes.

Austria. 1838. Critical studies. ■Franz Grillparzer's play *Weh'dem, der lügt! (Thou Shalt Not Lie)*, as influenced by Grégoire de Tours' *Historia Francorum*: treatment of truth, barbarism and civilization. Grp/movt: Vormärz.

1005 Schnitzler, Arthur. *Arthur Schnitzler: Tagebuch 1913-1916.* (Arthur Schnitzler: Diary, 1913-1916.) Vienna: Österreichischer Akademie der Wissenschaften; 1983. 432 pp. Index. Tables.

Austria. 1913-1916. Histories-sources. ■Austrian dramatist discusses his plays, his private life and theatre in general.

1006 Škreb, Zdenko. "Die Idee des Rechtes bei Grillparzer." (The Idea of Justice in Grillparzer.) *JGG.* 1983; 3(15): 37-49. Notes.

Austria. 1791-1872. Critical studies. ■Treatment of justice and order in plays by Franz Grillparzer.

1007 Sliziński, Jerzy. "Grillparzer in polnischen Enzyklopädien des XIX. und XX. Jahrunderts." (Grillparzer in Polish Encyclopedias of the 19th and 20th Centuries.) *JGG.* 1983; 15(3): 113-116. Notes.

Austria. Poland. 1800-1983. Critical studies. ■Treatment of Franz Grillparzer in Polish encyclopedias.

1008 Torresani, Sergio. "Appunti per una lettura del teatro di Elias Canetti." (Notes to a Reading of Elias Canetti's Plays.) *TeatrC.* 1983 June-Sep.; 2(4): 1-14. Notes.

Austria. 1932-1964. Critical studies. ■Critical analysis of Canetti's plays *Hochzeit (Wedding)*, *Komödie der Eitelkeit (Comedy of Vanity)* and *Die Befristeten (The Limited)*.

1009 Nicoletti, Gianni. "Fonctions du 'poème en prose' dans la dramaturgie ghelderodienne." (Functions of the 'Prose Poem' in Ghelderode's Dramaturgy.) 19-23 in Trousson, Raymond. *Michel de Ghelderode, dramaturge et conteur.* Brussels: Editions de l'Université de Bruxelles; 1983. 175 pp.

Belgium. 1918-1962. Critical studies. ■Importance of poetry in the theatre of Ghelderode.

1010 Otten, Michel. "Le rite sacrificiel dans *Barabbas*." (Sacrificial Rite in *Barabbas*.) 67-77 in Trousson, Raymond. *Michel de Ghelderode, dramaturge et conteur.* Brussels: Editions de l'Université de Bruxelles; 1983. 175 pp. Notes.

Belgium. 1929. Critical studies. ■Structural role of rite in Ghelderode's theatre reflects the playwright's denunciation of collective violence.

1011 Salvat, Ricard. "A l'entorn de Michel de Ghelderode i de Joan Argenté." (About Michel de Ghelderode and Joan Argenté.) 5-9 in *La Balada del Gran Macabre.* Barcelona: Institut del Teatre; 1983. 198 pp. (Biblioteca Teatral 13.) [Prologue to Michel de Ghelderode's *La balade du Grande Macabre.*]

Belgium. 1919-1962. Critical studies. ■Influence on Ghelderode's work of his national culture, particularly its paintings, and also of Bertolt Brecht.

1012 Simon, John. "Behind a Veil of Tears." *OpN.* 1983 Jan. 15; 47(9): 9-10, 32, 34. Illus.: Photo. B&W. 1: 11 in. x 11 in.

Belgium. 1900-1983. Critical studies. ■Comparative study of the symbolist dramas by Maurice Maeterlinck, including *Pelléas et Mélisande*, and the opera by Claude Debussy. Grp/movt: Symbolism. Related to Music-Drama: Opera.

1013 Stolarek, Zbigniew. "Vivre avec Ghelderode en Pologne." (Living with Ghelderode in Poland.) 91-98 in Trousson, Raymond. *Michel de Ghelderode, dramaturge et conteur.* Brussels: Editions de l'Université de Bruxelles; 1983. 175 pp.

Belgium. 1918-1973. Linguistic studies. ■Translating Ghelderode into Polish.

1014 Soria, Mario T. "Tre stadier i Bolivias teaterhistoria." (Three Stages of Bolivian Theatre History.) *Entre.* 1983; 10(4): 15-17.

Bolivia. 1944-1983. Critical studies. ■Three phases of Bolivian drama: social protest, political/historical theatre and universality.

DRAMA: General—Plays/librettos/scripts

1015   Lawrence, Robert G. "*The Land of Promise*: Canada, As Somerset Maugham Saw It in 1914." *THC*. 1983 Spring; 4(1): 15-24. Notes. Illus.: Photo. Print. B&W. 3: 4 in. x 4 in.
Canada. USA. UK-England. 1914. Historical studies. ■Cancellation of Canadian tour of *The Land of Promise* and contemporary indignation at its depiction of Canadians and women.

1016   Leeper, Muriel. "Linda Griffiths: The Actress As Playwright." *CTR*. 1983 Fall; 38: 110-113. Illus.: Photo. Print. B&W. 2: 2 in. x 2 in., 6 in. x 4 in.
Canada. 1983. Histories-sources. ■Interview with Linda Griffiths about her career as actress and playwright.

1017   Rubin, Don. "Celebrating the Nation: History and the Canadian Theatre." *CTR*. 1982 Spring; 34: 12-22. Notes.
Canada. 1867-1982. Historical studies. ■Canadian theatre and history as subject in Canadian drama.

1018   Wylie, Betty Jane. "Betty Jane Wylie: The Playwright as Participant." *CTR*. 1983 Fall; 38: 114-118. Illus.: Photo. Neg. B&W. 2: 2 in. x 4 in., 2 in. x 3 in. [Excerpts from journal.]
Canada. 1976. Histories-sources. ■Excerpts from journal of Betty Jane Wylie chronicling her work in a collective theatre project with Theatre Passe Muraille.

1019   Lu, Gu-Sun. "*Hamlet* across Space and Time." *ShS*. 1983; 36: 53-56. Notes.
China. 1903-1983. Critical studies. ■Reception of *Hamlet* in China. Problems in its translation and interpretation.

1020   Rong, Cheng; Graschy, Anneliese, transl., adap.; Siegert, Wolf, transl., adap. "'Der Held ist das Volk': Zu einer Aufführung von *Leben des Galilei* in Peking." ('The Hero Is the People': On a Performance of *Galileo* in Peking.) *NIMBZ*. 1983 May; 6(3): 8-10. Illus.: Photo. B&W. 3: 8 cm. x 14 cm., 7 cm. x 10 cm.
China, People's Republic of. 1979. Histories-sources. ■Adaptation of *Galileo* for Chinese stage.

1021   Wei, Qixuan; Zhen, Shen, transl. "*Li Shimin, Prince Qin of Tang*: A New Historical Drama and Its Author." *ChinL*. 1983 Feb.; 2: 130-132. Illus.: Photo.
China, People's Republic of. 1979-1982. Historical studies. ■Research, writing and first performance of historical drama by Yan Haiping on the subject of Chinese Emperor Li Shimin.

1022   Bravo-Elizondo, Pedro. "Politiskt-dokumentär teater i Latinamerika." (Political Documentary Theatre in Latin America.) *Entre*. 1983; 10(4): 21-26.
Costa Rica. Argentina. Peru. 1588-1983. Historical studies. ■Significant theatre work in Latin America builds on the history of colonialism, current anti-establishment politics and sociological research. Collective creativity and contact with audience are emphasized.

1023   Rodriguez, Orlando B. "Den kubanska dramatiken och revolutionen." (Cuban Drama and the Revolution.) *Entre*. 1983; 10(4): 42-44.
Cuba. 1850-1983. Historical studies. ■Cuban theatre as reflective of political climate: formerly a product of colonialism and dictatorship, today it reflects the revolutionary process and is influenced by Brecht. Playwriting contests and serious criticism encourage innovation.

1024   Vapenik, Rudolf. "'Brecht in ernster Gefahr, ersucht um kurzfristigen Pass': Zu Brechts Prag-Aufenthalten und ČSR-Reisepapieren." ('Brecht in Grave Danger, Applies for a Short-Term Passport': Brecht in Prague and his Czechoslovakian Travel Papers.) *NIMBZ*. 1983 Nov.; 6(6): 14-15. Illus.: Photo.
Czechoslovakia. USA. 1943-1949. Biographical studies. ■On Brecht's efforts to get a Czechoslovakian passport, the circumstances of his leaving the USA and his stay in Prague.

1025   Griffin, Cynthia. "The Language of My Dreams: A Profile of the Playwright Antoine O'Flatharta." *AG*. 1983 Winter; 2(1): 8-10. Illus.: Photo. Print. B&W. 1: 4 in. x 5 in.
Eire. 1981. Historical studies. ■Profile derived from an interview with young bilingual Irish playwright Antoine O'Flatharta whose *Gaeilgeoiri* was a highly acclaimed production of the Abbey Theatre in 1981.

1026   Rollins, Ronald G. "Enigmatic Ghosts of Swift in Yeats and Johnston." *Éire*. 1983 Summer; 18(2): 103-115. Notes.
Eire. 1928-1960. Critical studies. ■Examines the assessments of both the person and philosophy of Anglo-Irish satirist and clergyman Jonathan Swift presented in William Butler Yeats's *The Words upon the Window-pane* and Denis Johnston's *The Dreaming Dust*.

1027   Andrews, Michael Cameron. "The Stamp of One Defect." *SQ*. 1983 Summer; 34(2): 217-218. Notes. [Note.]
England. 1600-1601. Critical studies. ■Hamlet's criticism of his countrymen (I.iv. 13-38: Arden 1982) is not a gloss on Aristotelian *hamartia*, but expression of his contempt for human incapacity to judge intelligently.

1028   Bamber, Linda. *Comic Women, Tragic Men: A Study of Gender and Genre in Shakespeare*. Stanford, CA: Stanford UP; 1982. 211 pp.
England. 1595-1615. Critical studies. ■Feminist analysis of sex roles in Shakespeare.

1029   Bates, Paul A. "Elements of Folklore and Humanism in *Pericles*." *SJW*. 1983; 119: 112-114. Notes. [Remarks made in an exchange of ideas with director Heinz-Uwe Haus during the preparation of the Weimar, DDR premiere of *Pericles* in March 1978.]
England. 1608-1609. Critical studies. ■Examples of folklore and humanistic philosophy in *Pericles*. Grp/movt: Humanism.

1030   Braunmuller, A.R. "How to Do Things with the Dekker Commentary." *RORD*. 1983; 26: 13-21. Notes.
England. 1597-1630. Critical studies. ■Cyrus Hoy's commentaries on Thomas Dekker (1980) will be useful in reassessing aspects of Dekker's work, including themes, relationships with plays of other dramatists, language and dates.

1031   Broich, Ulrich. "Shakespeares Historien und das Geschichtsbewusstsein ihres Publikums." (Shakespeare's Historical Plays and Their Audience's Consciousness of History.) *JDSh*. 1983: 41-60. Notes.
England. 1590-1613. Critical studies. ■Relationship between the historical plays and history: knowledge of history by the audience and the actuality of the plays. Grp/movt: Elizabethan theatre.

1032   Carpenter, Sarah. "Morality Play Characters." *MET*. 1983; 5(1): 18-28. Notes.
England. 1300-1550. Critical studies. ■Determining factor of the demonstrative mode of morality play characters. Grp/movt: Medieval theatre. Related to Popular Entertainment: Pageants/parades.

1033   Cartelli, Thomas. "*Bartholomew Fair* as Urban Arcadia: Jonson Responds to Shakespeare." 155-174 in Barkan, Leonard. *Renaissance Drama, New Series XIV: Relations and Influences*. Evanston, IL: Northwestern UP; 1983. x, 196 pp.
England. 1614. Critical studies. ■Pastoralism in Jonson reflects Shakespearean influence.

1034   Cartelli, Thomas. "Banquo's Ghost: The Shared Vision." *TJ*. 1983 Oct.; 35(3): 389-405.
England. 1605-1606. Critical studies. ■Appearance of Banquo's ghost clarifies the relation of the audience to the play.

1035   Cary, Cecile Williamson; Limouze, Henry S., ed. *Shakespeare and the Arts: A Collection of Essays from the Ohio Shakespeare Conference, 1981, Wright State University, Dayton, Ohio*. Washington, DC: UP of America; 1982. viii, 247 pp. Illus.: Photo. 11.
England. USA. 1590-1981. Critical studies. ■Interdisciplinary studies on effect of music, painting, film and television on productions of Shakespeare from the Elizabethan period to the present. Grp/movt: Mannerism.

1036   Cheney, Patrick. "Jonson's *The New Inn* and Plato's Myth of the Hermaphrodite." 175-196 in Barkan, Leonard. *Renaissance Drama, New Series XIV: Relations and Influences*. Evanston, IL: Northwestern UP; 1983. x, 196 pp.
England. 1629. Critical studies. ■Androgyny in Jonson and Plato: *The New Inn* as a 'humours romance'.

1037   Clopper, Lawrence M. "Arneway, Higden and the Origin of the Chester Plays." *REEDN*. ; 8(2): 4-11. Notes.

DRAMA: General—Plays/librettos/scripts

England. 1268-1375. Historical studies. ■False association of Mayor John Arneway and monk Ranulf Higden with the Chester mystery plays, and the possible authorship by Henry Francis of a lost Chester Corpus Christi play. Related to Popular Entertainment: Pageants/parades.

1038 Daley, A. Stuart. "Where Are the Woods in *As You Like It*?" *SQ.* 1983 Summer; 34(2): 172-180. Notes.
England. 1599-1600. Linguistic studies. ■Pastoral scenes do not all take place in the woods. Shakespeare understands word 'forest' to refer not simply to woods but to pastures and wastes as well.

1039 Davis, Bertram H. *Thomas Otway.* Boston: Twayne; 1982. vi, 162 pp.
England. 1652-1685. Critical studies. ■Biography, bibliography and textual analysis of Thomas Otway's plays.

1040 Davis, Nicholas, ec. "Allusions to Medieval Drama in Britain: A Findings List (3)." *MET.* 1983; 5(2): 83-86.
England. 1200. Histories-sources. ■Six recently discovered contemporary allusions to the medieval drama — part of an ongoing collection of such allusions. Grp/movt: Medieval theatre.

1041 Draudt, Manfred. "Another Senecan Echo in *Hamlet.*" *SQ.* 1983 Summer; 34(2): 216-217. Notes. [Note.]
England. 1600-1601. Critical studies. ■Echo of Seneca's Epistle 24, *On Despising Death,* suggests fusion of Christian and Stoic concepts in *Hamlet.*

1042 Dutton, Richard. *Ben Jonson: To the First Folio.* Cambridge, England: Cambridge UP; 1983. xii, 188 pp. (British and Irish Authors: Introductory Critical Studies.)
England. 1598-1614. Critical studies. ■Involvement of the audience in Ben Jonson's work as satirist and playwright. Includes *Bartholomew Fair* as well as First Folio plays.

1043 Elton, G.R. "Kann man sich auf Shakespeare verlassen?: Das 15. Jahrhundert bei Shakespeare und in der Wirklichkeit." (Can We Trust Shakespeare?: 15th Century According to Shakespeare and in Reality.) *SHJ.* 1983: 27-39.
England. 1590-1616. Critical studies. ■Shakespeare's use of sources.

1044 Gaskell, Ian Douglas Peter. *The Ironic Perspective in Christopher Marlowe's Plays.* Toronto: Univ. of Toronto; 1982. [Dissertation.]
England. 1564-1593. Critical studies. ■Analysis of irony in Marlowe's plays, which are all found to be metatheatrical.

1045 Gregson, J.M. *Public and Private Man in Shakespeare.* London/Totowa, NJ: Croom Helm/Barnes & Noble; 1983. 255 pp.
England. 1590-1612. Critical studies. ■Contrast between public and private life in Shakespeare's history plays.

1046 Hume, Robert D.; Scouten, Arthur M., collaborator. *The Rakish Stage: Studies in English Drama, 1660-1800.* Carbondale, IL: Southern Illinois UP; 1983. xvi, 382 pp. [Collection of 10 articles, including previously unpublished 'Content and Meaning in the Drama', 'The London Theatre from *The Beggar's Opera* to the Licensing Act' and 'Restoration Comedy' (in collaboration with Arthur H. Scouten).]
England. 1660-1800. Historical studies. ■Essays discussing various aspects of Restoration theatre, with an emphasis on drama (criteria and methods of evaluation), audience and ramifications of the Licensing Act on theatrical activities in London between 1727 to 1737.

1047 Hutchings, Geoffrey. "Hutchings, G.A. — Fool!" *Drama.* 1983 Spring; 147: 14-15. Illus.: Photo. B&W. 1: 3 in. x 4 in.
England. 1590-1613. Critical studies. ■Analysis of roles of clowns and fools in Shakespeare.

1048 Jaech, Sharon L. Janson. "Political Prophecy and Macbeth's 'Sweet Bodements'." *SQ.* 1983 Autumn; 34(3): 290-297. Notes.
England. 1605-1606. Critical studies. ■Example of 16th century political prophecy is found in *Macbeth* IV.i, in the appearance of the armed head, bloody child and crowned child.

1049 Jardine, Lisa. *Still Harping on Daughters: Women and Drama in the Age of Shakespeare.* Sussex, England and Totowa, NJ: Harvester P. and Barnes & Noble; 1983. iv, 202 pp.

England. 1590-1613. Critical studies. ■Status of women in Elizabethan society as reflected in Shakespeare's plays.

1050 Kaston, David Scott. "'To Set a Form upon That Indigest': Shakespeare's Fictions of History." *CompD.* 1983 Spring; 17(1): 1-16. Notes.
England. 1590-1599. Critical studies. ■Finds analogy in Shakespeare's history plays between 'the art of rule' and the 'rule of art'. Both kingship and historical drama impose form on chaotic human action.

1051 Kay, Carol McGinnis. "Othello's Need for Mirrors." *SQ.* 1983 Autumn; 34(3): 261-270. Notes.
England. 1604-1605. Critical studies. ■Othello's search for self in relation to others — most notably Desdemona and Iago — suggests that he suffers from what psychologists call 'an immature ego'.

1052 Kerins, Frank. "The Crafty Enchanter: Ironic Satires and Jonson's *Every Man Out of His Humour.*" 135-154 in Barkan, Leonard. *Renaissance Drama, New Series XIV: Relations and Influences.* Evanston, IL: Northwestern UP; 1983. x, 196.
England. 1599. Critical studies. ■Action of the play as dramatic representation of ironic satires of Marston and Guilpin.

1053 Lawry, J.S. "Imitations and Creation in *Measure for Measure.*" 217-229 in Carey, Cecile Williamson; . Limouze, Henry S. *Shakespeare and the Arts: A Collection of Essays from the Ohio Shakespeare Conference, 1981, Wright State University, Dayton, Ohio.* Washington, DC: UP of America; 1982. viii, 247 pp. Notes.
England. 1604-1605. Critical studies. ■Themes of imitation, creation and recreation in *Measure for Measure.*

1054 Macdonald, Virginia L. "The Complex Moral View of Robert Greene's *A Disputation.*" *SJW.* 1983; 119: 122-136. Notes.
England. 1581-1592. Historical studies. ■Discussion of one of playwright Greene's 'rogue' pamphlets as personal document of repentance and confession.

1055 May, Stephen. "Good Kings and Tyrants: A Re-assessment of the Regal Figure on the Medieval Stage." *MET.* 1983; 5(2): 87-102. Notes.
England. 1264-1560. Critical studies. ■Sympathetic portrayals of splendid monarchs are rare in the Corpus Christi cycles. Grp/movt: Medieval theatre. Related to Popular Entertainment: Pageants/parades.

1056 Merghelani, Abdul-Rahman Amin. *Saracenism on the British Stage 1580-1642: A Formula for Distance.* Boulder, CO: Univ. of Colorado; 1982. 284 pp. [Diss.: University Microfilms order no. DA8221102.]
England. 1580-1642. Critical studies. ■Drama about 'Saracens' enjoyed comparative freedom from censorship due to the remoteness of the subject, but owed its popularity to the topicality concealed by this remoteness.

1057 Mills, David. "Characterization in the English Mystery Cycles: A Critical Prologue." *MET.* 1983; 5(1): 5-17. Notes.
England. 1200-1550. Critical studies. ■Possible meanings of characterization in the mystery plays. Grp/movt: Medieval theatre. Related to Popular Entertainment: Pageants/parades.

1058 Morse, Ruth. "Unfit for Human Consumption: Shakespeare's Unnatural Food." *JDSh.* 1983: 125-149. Notes.
England. 1590-1613. Critical studies. ■Animal nature of some characters in Shakespeare's plays and their animal-like eating habits.

1059 Müller, Wolfgang G. "Politische Probleme in Shakespeares Königsdramen." (Political Problems in Shakespeare's History Plays.) *JDSh.* 1983: 99-109. Notes.
England. 1591-1595. Critical studies. ■Delineation of struggle for power in Shakespeare's history plays.

1060 Mullini, Roberta. *Corruttore di parole: Il fool nel teatro di Shakespeare.* (Corrupter of Words: The Fool in Shakespeare's Plays.) Bologna: Clueb; 1983. 188 pp. (Testi e discorsi 1.) Notes. Index. Biblio.
England. 1592-1605. Critical studies. ■Analysis of the fool's rhetorical technique of speech in Shakespeare's plays.

DRAMA: General—Plays/librettos/scripts

1061 Oakes, Elizabeth Thompson. "Killing the Calf in *Hamlet*." *SQ*. 1983 Summer; 34(2): 215-216. Notes. [Note.]
England. 1600-1601. Historical studies. ∎Contemporary folk entertainment, *Killing the Calf*, lies behind Hamlet's reference to Polonius as 'calf', especially at the old advisor's death. Related to Popular Entertainment.

1062 Pfister, Manfred. "'Proportion Kept': Zum dramatischen Rythmus in *Richard II*." ('Proportion Kept': On Dramatic Rhythm in *Richard II*.) *JDSh*. 1983: 61-72. Notes.
England. 1595-1596. Critical studies. ∎Study of recurring themes and dramatic structure of *Richard II*.

1063 Reynolds, J.A. *Repentance and Retribution in Early English Drama*. Salzburg and Atlantic Highlands, NJ: Institut für Anglistik und Amerikanistik, Universität Salzburg and Humanities P; 1982. viii, 116 pp.
England. 1500-1600. Critical studies.

1064 Richek, Roslyn G. *Thomas Randolph (1605-1635): Christian Humanist, Academic and London Theater Playwright*. Norman, OK: Univ. of Oklahoma; 1982. 307 pp. [Diss.: University Microfilms order no. DA8215916.]
England. 1605-1635. Biographies. ∎Study of academic theatre of Thomas Randolph, who apparently became company playwright to a London theatre for a year before returning to Trinity College, Cambridge.

1065 Roberts, Jeanne Addison. "Horses and Hermaphrodites: Metamorphoses in *The Taming of the Shrew*." *SQ*. 1983 Summer; 34 (2): 159-171. Notes. B&W. 5: 3 in. x 3 in.
England. 1592-1603. Critical studies. ∎Use and variation of Ovidian metamorphosis creates a romantic subtext in *The Taming of the Shrew*, a play generally regarded as realistic.

1066 Rudnytsky, Peter L. "*A Woman Killed with Kindness* as Subtext for *Othello*." 104-134 in Barkan, Leonard. *Renaissance Drama, New Series XIV: Relations and Influences*. Evanston, IL: Northwestern UP; 1983. x, 196 pp.
England. 1604. Critical studies. ∎Heywood's play as a source for Shakespeare.

1067 Schlösser, Julia. "Überlegungen zur Interpretation *Westward Ho!*." (Considerations in the Interpretation of *Westward Ho!*.) *SJW*. 1983; 119: 115-121. Notes.
England. 1570-1637. Critical studies. ∎Authorship, censorship and thematic analysis of *Westward Ho!*.

1068 Schuman, Samuel. *The Theatre of Fine Devices: The Visual Drama of John Webster*. Atlantic Highlands, NJ: Humanities P; 1982. 165 pp.
England. 1580-1634. Critical studies.

1069 Scouten, Arthur H. "Designation of Locale in Shakespeare Texts." *ET*. 1983 Nov.; 2(1): 41-55. Notes.
England. 1605-1606. Critical studies. ∎Inconsistent, inaccurate, gratuitous and impossible designations of locale in *King Lear*. Sketch history of editorial designation of place in Shakespeare's plays included.

1070 Sen, S.K. "When Malone Nods." *SQ*. 1983 Summer; 34(2): 212-214. Notes.
England. 1790-1821. Historical studies. ∎Consistent misquotation of Shakespeare in notes to Edmond Malone's edition of Shakespeare (1790) suggests that editor cited bard from memory, without reference to the original text.

1071 Sharma, Kavita A. *Byron's Plays: A Reassessment*. Atlantic Highlands, NJ: Humanities P; 1982. iv, 222 pp.
England. 1788-1824. Critical studies. ∎Reevaluation of Byron's plays, only one of which was produced during his lifetime.

1072 Siegel, Paul. "Historical Ironies in *The Tempest*." *SJW*. 1983; 119: 101-111. Notes.
England. North America. South America. 1611-1612. Historical studies. ∎Ironic parallels between events on the enchanted island in *The Tempest*, the discovery of the new world and the political situation in Elizabethan England and the Americas.

1073 Slater, Ann Pasternak. *Shakespeare the Director*. Brighton and Totowa, NJ: Harvester P. and Barnes & Noble; 1982. ix, 244 pp.

England. 1590-1612. Textual studies. ∎Examination of stage directions in the early printed texts of Shakespeare's plays to reconstruct Elizabethan staging practice. Grp/movt: Elizabethan theatre.

1074 Snyder, Richard C. "Discovering 'A Dramaturgy of Human Relationships' in Shakespearean Metadrama: *Troilus and Cressida*." 199-216 in Carey, Cecile Williamson; . Limouze, Henry S. *Shakespeare and the Arts: A Collection of Essays from the Ohio Shakespeare Conference, 1981, Wright State University, Dayton, Ohio*. Washington, DC: UP of America; 1982. viii, 247 pp. Notes.
England. 1601-1602. Critical studies. ∎Metadramatic (self-reflexive) scenes, characters and themes in *Troilus and Cressida*.

1075 Soyinka, Wole. "Shakespeare and the Living Dramatist." *ShS*. 1983; 36: 1-10. Notes.
England. Arabia. 1606-1981. Critical studies. ∎Discussion of Shakespeare's knowledge of the Arab world, especially in *Antony and Cleopatra*, and his influence on Arab and North African writers.

1076 Spiel, Hilde. "Shakespeare der Fürstendiener." (Shakespeare the Sovereign Servant.) *JDSh*. 1983: 9-25.
England. 1592-1593. Historical studies. ∎Sources used by Shakespeare for his play *Richard III*, and changes made to cater to his sovereign's political beliefs.

1077 Stamm, Rudolf. "Die theatralische Physiognomie der Haupt- und Nebenszenen in Shakespeares *Richard II*." (The Theatrical Physiognomy of the Main and Secondary Scenes in Shakespeare's *Richard II*.) *JDSh*. 1983: 89-98. Notes.
England. 1595. Critical studies. ∎Semiotic analysis of scenes in *Richard II* by distinguishing functional, conventional and innovational signs.

1078 Suerbaum, Ulrich. "'This Royal Throne of Kings, This Sceptred Isle — ': Struktur und Wirkungsweise von Gaunts England-Variationen." ('This Royal Throne of Kings, This Sceptred Isle — ': Structure and Mode of Action of Gaunt's England-Variations.) *JDSh*. 1983: 73-88. Notes.
England. 1595-1596. Critical studies. ∎Structural analysis of Gaunt's last speech in Shakespeare's *Richard II*.

1079 Thomson, Peter; Sundelson, David. *Shakespeare's Restorations of the Father*. New Brunswick, NJ: Rutgers UP; 1983. vii, 152 pp.
England. 1595-1615. Critical studies. ∎Patterns of concern with and conflict over paternal authority and sex roles in Shakespeare's plays.

1080 Weis, René J.A. "Caesar's Revenge: A Neglected Elizabethan Source of *Antony and Cleopatra*." *JDSh*. 1983: 178-186. Notes.
England. 1606-1607. Critical studies. ∎Parallels between *Caesar's Revenge* and *Antony and Cleopatra*.

1081 White, Eileen. "The Disappearance of the York Play Texts: New Evidence for the Creed Play." *MET*. 1983; 5(2): 103-109. Notes.
England. 1420-1580. Historical studies. ∎York Creed plays may not have been confiscated by the ecclesiastical authorities. Grp/movt: Medieval theatre. Related to Popular Entertainment: Pageants/parades.

1082 Winton, Calhoun. "Authorship of *The Fatal Extravagance*." *ThS*. 1983; 24(1-2): 130-134. Notes.
England. 1721-1760. Historical studies. ∎Authorship of the acted version of *The Fatal Extravagance* is ascribed to Aaron Hill, and not to Joseph Mitchell. Argument based on contemporary testimonies.

1083 Wright, George T. "The Play of Phrase and Line in Shakespeare's Iambic Pentameter." *SQ*. 1983 Summer; 34(2): 147-158. Notes.
England. 1559-1603. Linguistic studies. ∎Elizabethan experimentation with the placement of the caesura leads Shakespeare to explore various relationships between the poetic line and the syntax of his phrases and sentences.

1084 Wright, Stephen K. "The Durham Play of Mary and the Poor Knight: Sources and Analogues of a Lost English Miracle Play." *CompD*. 1983 Fall; 17(3): 254-265. Notes.

DRAMA: General—Plays/librettos/scripts

England. 1200-1500. Historical studies. ■*Dialogus miraculorum* by Caesarius of Heisterbach (c. 1223) is seen as a source for 36-line 'Durham prologue'. Grp/movt: Medieval theatre.

1085 Barkan, Leonard, ed. *Renaissance Drama, New Series XIV: Relations and Influences.* Evanston, IL: Northwestern UP; 1983. x, 196 pp.
Europe. 1513-1616. Critical studies. ■Essays on plays from Machiavelli to Jonson.

1086 Belsey, Catherine. "Literature, History, Politics." *L&H.* 1983 Spring; 9(1): 17-27. Notes.
Europe. 1605-1606. Critical studies. ■Analysis and production of texts about the past place the present in a perspective of relativity and have the effect of demonstrating the possibility of dialogue. References to *Macbeth.*

1087 Benjamin, Walter; Cetti Marinoni, Bianca, transl.; Carchia, Giovanni, transl.; Marietti Solmi, Anna, transl.; Bertolini, Marisa, transl. *Strada a senso unico: Scritti vari 1926-1927.* (One-way Street: Writings 1926-1927.) Turin: Einaudi; 1983. xiv, 299 pp. (Einaudi Letteratura 78, Opere di Walter Benjamin 4.) Notes. Index. [Translated from German.]
Europe. 1926-1927. Histories-sources. ■Among Benjamin's articles and aphorisms, some notes on theatrical events.

1088 Egri, Peter. "Beneath *The Calms of Capricorn*: O'Neill's Adaptation and Naturalization of European Models." *EON.* 1983; 7(2): 6-17. Notes.
Europe. USA. 1953. Critical studies. ■Dramatic ancestry of *The Calms of Capricorn* shows influence of numerous playwrights (Shakespeare, Strindberg, Čechov, Ibsen, Wilde, Shaw, Maeterlinck, Yeats), and several dramatic types among them, including melodrama, farce, symbolism, expressionism and absurdist drama. Grp/movt: Symbolism; Expressionism; Absurdism.

1089 Jones, Joseph R. "The *Song of Songs* as a Drama in the Commentators from Origen to the Twelfth Century." *CompD.* 1983 Spring; 17(1): 17-39. Notes. Append.
Europe. 1400-1499. Critical studies. ■Interpretations of *Song of Songs* as documented medieval drama. Grp/movt: Medieval theatre.

1090 Lenssen, Claudia; Nusser, Peter; Klar, Burkhard; Gruber, Birgit; Bohn, Rainer. "Die Faszination der Brutalität: Gewaltdarstellung im Medienvergleich." (Fascination with Brutality: Presentation of Violence in the Media.) *Tzs.* 1983 Spring; 3: 39-49. Illus.: Photo.
Europe. 1983. Critical studies. ■Treatment of violence and its aesthetics in theatre, film and literature. Related to Media: Film.

1091 Lindner, Ines. "*Kalldewey:* Dionysos: Geschichte als Wiederholungszwang — Über Mythenzitate in *Kalldewey, Farce.*" (*Kalldewey:* Dionysos: History as Repetitive Cycles — about Quotes of Myths in *Kalldewey, Farce.*) *TH.* 1983; 10: 58-61. Notes. Illus.: Photo.
Europe. 1964. Critical studies. ■Analysis of Botho Strauss' *Kalldewey, Farce.*

1092 Mairbäurl, Gunda. *Die Familie als Werkstatt der Erziehung: Rollenbilder des Kindertheaters und soziale Realität im späten 18. Jahrhundert.* (The Family As an Instrument of Education: Roles of Children's Theatre and Social Reality in the Late Eighteenth Century.) Vienna: Verlag für Geschichte und Politik; 1983. 210 pp. Notes. Biblio. Tables. Append. Illus.: Dwg. B&W.
Europe. 1770-1800. Historical studies. ■Study of the bourgeois way of life through children's plays.

1093 Perloff, Eveline; Clergé, Claude. "Théâtre et folie." (Theatre and Madness.) *CF.* 1982 Apr.; 108: 22-27.
Europe. 1664-1936. Critical studies. ■Aspects of madness in theatre. Focuses on Jean Racine, Heinrich von Kleist and Luigi Pirandello.

1094 Schiff, Ellen. *From Stereotype to Metaphor: The Jew in Contemporary Drama.* Albany: State Univ. of New York P; 1982. xiii, 276 pp.
Europe. North America. 1982. Critical studies. ■Jews as stereotyped characters in contemporary drama.

1095 Worthen, William B. "Beckett's Actor." *MD.* 1983 Dec.; 26(4): 415-424. Notes.
Europe. 1957. Critical studies. ■Actor's role as an essential element in plays of Samuel Beckett.

1096 Järvinen, Pentti. "Ilpo Tuomarila, Profession: Playwright." *NFT.* 1983; 35: 8-9. Illus.: Photo. B&W.
Finland. 1972-1983. Critical studies. ■Ilpo Tuomarila's plays and scripts for radio, television and film, are concerned with alienation, power conflicts and deep moral questions. Related to Media: Multi-media.

1097 Niemi, Irmeli. "Uuden suomalaisen näytelmän pääsuuntaviivoja — yhteiskunnallisia ja moraalisia aspekteja." (The Main Features of the New Finnish Drama, Its Social and Moral Aspects.) 26-30, 60-64, 103-106 in Westman, Pirjo; . Khasanov, Valery; . Teryoshin, Sergey; . Shvydkov, Michael. *Neuvostoliitto ja Suomi teatteriyhteisyössä (USSR-Finland: Theatre Cooperation).* Helsinki: The Soviet and Finnish National Centers of the International Theatre Institute (ITI); 1983. 114 pp. Pref. [In Finnish, Russian and English.]
Finland. 1981. Critical studies. ■Brief study of moral and social themes of contemporary Finnish drama.

1098 Steinbock, Dan. "'Suomalainen' Brecht." ('Finnish' Brecht.) *Teat.* 1983; 38(9): 21-24. Illus.: Photo. 3.
Finland. 1930-1969. Critical studies. ■Brecht's influence on Finnish theatre.

1099 Angelini, Franca. "Il Teatro di sole e acciaio: Mishima, Genet (e Fassbinder)." (Theatre of Sun and Steel: Mishima, Genet (and Fassbinder).) *QT.* 1983 Feb.; 5(19): 126-133. Notes.
France. Japan. 1947-1983. Critical studies. ■Cult of manhood in Mishima and Genet.

1100 Bonvalet-Mallet, Nicole. "Marcel Achard adapteur de Ben Jonson." (Marcel Achard, Adaptor of Ben Jonson.) *RHT.* 1983; 35 (3): 348-363.
France. 1926. Critical studies. ■Achard's adaptation of Jonson's *Epicoene, or The Silent Women* directed by Charles Dullin.

1101 Bourgeault, Cynthia. "Liturgical Dramaturgy." *CompD.* 1983 Summer; 17(2): 124-140. Notes.
France. 1100-1200. Critical studies. ■Based on Fleury Playbook, (Beauvais' *Daniel* and *Peregrinus*, and Rouen's *Officium Pastorum*), liturgical drama rests on theatre, music and liturgy in a fluid state between ritual and theatre. Grp/movt: Medieval theatre. Related to Ritual-Ceremony.

1102 Cardwell, Douglas. "The Well-Made Play of Eugène Scribe." *FR.* 1983 May; 56(6): 876-884. Notes. [Article also appears in French.]
France. 1830-1840. Critical studies. ■Analysis of the well-made play structure of Scribe and his influence on later drama.

1103 Cooper, Barbara T. "Canvas Walls and Cardboard Fortresses: Representations of Place in the National Historical Dramas of Early Nineteenth-Century France." *CompD.* 1983-1984 Winter; 17(4): 327-347. Notes.
France. 1806-1827. Critical studies. ■Metaphorical nature of decor implied in playtexts.

1104 Forestier, Georges. "Le Théâtre dans le Théâtre ou la Conjonction de deux dramaturgies à la fin de la Renaissance." (Theatre within Theatre, or the Conjunction of Two Dramaturgies at the End of the Renaissance.) *RHT.* 1983; 35(2): 162-173. Notes.
France. 1500-1599. Critical studies. ■Play-within-a-play as a device of Renaissance drama. Grp/movt: Renaissance theatre.

1105 Garapon, Robert. *Le premier Corneille: De Mélite à L'illusion comique.* (The Early Corneille: From *Mélite* to *The Comic Illusion.*) Paris: Société d'Edition d'Enseignement Supérieur; 1983. 168 pp. Biblio.
France. 1629-1640. Critical studies. ■Themes of love and freedom and emergence of the generous hero in Corneille's early plays.

1106 Knight, Alan E. "The Condemnation of Pleasure in Late Medieval French Morality Plays." *FR.* 1983 Oct.; 57(1): 1-9. Notes.

DRAMA: General—Plays/librettos/scripts

France. 1400-1499. Critical studies. ■Two sins of the flesh — gluttony and lust — dominate the condemnation of pleasure in morality plays where one temptation leads to another, especially among the wealthy. Grp/movt: Medieval theatre.

1107   Memola, Massimo Marino. "Per una intepretazione materialistica dell'opera di Samuel Beckett." (Materialistic Interpretation of Samuel Beckett's Work.) *QT.* 1983; 5(20): 39-73. Notes.
France. 1938. Critical studies. ■Negation of divinity in Beckett's drama and re-evaluation of the plays applying materialistic dialectics.

1108   Payen, J.-C. "Théâtre médiéval et culture urbaine." (Medieval Theatre and Urban Culture.) *RHT.* 1983; 35 (2): 233-250. Notes.
France. 1200. Historical studies. ■Necessity of an urban middle class to the development of drama in the Middle Ages. Grp/movt: Medieval theatre.

1109   Scherer, Colette. *Comédie et société sous Louis XIII.* (Drama and Society in the Reign of Louis XIII.) Paris: A.G. Nizet; 1983. x, 254 pp.
France. 1610-1643. Critical studies. ■Comparative sociological study of the French theatre.

1110   Stoltzfus, B.F. "Caligula's Mirrors: Camus' Reflexive Dramatization of Play." *FrF.* 1983 Jan.; 8(1): 75-86. Notes. [Article also appears in French.]
France. 1945. Critical studies. ■Themes of freedom, death and suicide in *Caligula* and their implications on the notion of 'play'. Grp/movt: Existentialism; Absurdism.

1111   Street, J.S. *French Sacred Drama from Bèze to Corneille: Dramatic Forms and Their Purpose in the Early Modern Theatre.* Cambridge: Cambridge UP; 1983. 344 pp. Pref. Index. Notes. Biblio. Illus.: Dwg. B&W. 32.
France. 1550-1650. Critical studies. ■Typology of sacred drama from Théodore de Bèze to Pierre Corneille with a detailed analysis of one hundred little known texts.

1112   Sweeter, Marie-Odile. "De la comédie à la tragédie: Le 'change' et la conversion de *Mélite* à *Polyeucte*." (From Comedy to Tragedy: 'Change' and Conversion from *Mélite* to *Polyeucte*.) 75-89 in Margitic, Milorad R., ed. *Corneille comique* (The Comic Corneille). Nine Studies of Pierre Corneille's Comedy with an Introduction and Bibliography. Paris, Seattle and Tubingen: Papers on French Seventeenth Century Literature; 1982. 213 pp. (Papers on Seventeenth Century Literature/Biblio 17.) Notes.
France. 1606-1684. Critical studies. ■Elements of 'change' and conversion allow Corneille to move from comedy to tragedy without aesthetic discontinuity.

1113   Takvorian, Richard; Spingler, Michael. "Sounding Ionesco: Problems in Translating *La Leçon* and *Jacques ou La Soumission*." *CompD.* 1983 Spring; 17(1): 40-54. Notes.
France. 1950-1970. Linguistic studies. ■Translation of Ionesco must take into account 'vocal gesture and sonic event,' go beyond semantic correctness and reflect the nature of the original sound.

1114   Vinaver, Michel; Henry, Michelle, ed. *Ecrits sur le théâtre.* (Writings on Theatre.) Lausanne: Editions de l'Aire; 1982. 328 pp. (Collection l'Aire théâtrale.) Pref. Append. Illus.: Photo. 16.
France. 1954-1980. Critical studies. ■Essays on theatre in general with emphasis on the plays of Michel Vinaver.

1115   Midiohouan, Guy Ossito. "Le théâtre négro-africain d'expression française depuis 1960." (Black African Theatre in French Since 1960.) *Pnpa.* 1983 Jan.-Feb.; 31: 54-78. Notes.
French-speaking countries. 1937-1980. Historical studies. ■Folklore spectacles and 'safe' subjects have replaced political drama and set contemporary theatre in a comatose state.

1116   Aliverti, Maria Ines. "Quelle Pupille tenere..." (Those Tender Eyes...) *QT.* 1982 May; 4(16): 52-63. Notes.
Germany. 1777-1785. Critical studies. ■Bourgeois interests in *Wilhelm Meisters Theatralische Sendung* by Goethe.

1117   Bogdal, Klaus Michael; Fadini, Ubaldo transl. "Il teatro naturalista e la guerra." (The Naturalist Theatre and the War.) *QT.* 1983 Feb.; 5(19): 53-61. Notes. [Translated from German.]
Germany. 1896. Critical studies. ■Italian translation of Bogdal's essay on Gerhart Hauptmann's *Florian Geyer*. Grp/movt: Naturalism.

1118   Bondavalli, Leila. "Guerra e utopia nel teatro di Toller." (War and Utopia in Toller's Drama.) *QT.* 1983 Feb.; 5(19): 69-76.
Germany. 1918-1927. Critical studies. ■Toller's attitude towards war based on the study of his plays.

1119   Chiarini, Paolo. "Dialektik, Realismus und Wandlungen des Tragischen bei Brecht." (Dialetics, Realism and Changes in the Tragic in Brecht.) 139-147, 376-377 in Brecht-Zentrum, DDR. *Brecht und Marxismus: Dokumentation: Protokoll der Brecht-Tage 1983* (Brecht and Marxism: Documentation: Proceedings of the Brecht-Days, 1983). East Berlin: Brecht-Zentrum der DDR; 1983. 405 pp. (Brecht 83.)
Germany. 1918-1956. Critical studies. ■The tendency of Brecht's plays to promote social change is seen as a barrier to their universal value.

1120   Cometa, Michele. "Alfred Döblin e la follia delle cose." (Alfred Döblin and the Madness of Things.) *TeatrC.* 1982-1983 Oct.-Jan.; 1(2): 195-202. Notes.
Germany. 1906. Critical studies. ■Linguistic analysis of *Lydia und Mäxchen* by Alfred Döblin.

1121   Engler, Wolfgang. "Brechts Stellungnahme zur philosophischen Kontroverse um die Krise der bürgerlichen Vernunft in den zwanziger Jahren." (Brecht's Comments on the Philosophical Controversy Regarding the Crisis of Civic Sense in the 1920s.) 70-81, 370-371 in Brecht-Zentrum, DDR. *Brecht und Marxismus: Dokumentation: Protokoll der Brecht-Tage 1983* (Brecht and Marxism: Documentation: Proceedings of the Brecht Days, 1983). East Berlin: Brecht-Zentrum der DDR; 1983. 405 pp. (Brecht 83.) Notes.
Germany. 1918-1956. Critical studies. ■Divergence between theoreticians and pragmatists in late capitalistic era and Brecht's discussion of this problem in his plays.

1122   Goldhann, Johannes. "Zur Dialektik von Weltbild und Methode in Brechts Parabel *Der Gute Mensch von Sezuan*." (On the Dialectic of World View and Method in Brecht's Parable *The Good Woman of Sezuan*.) 298-304, 386-388 in Brecht-Zentrum, DDR. *Brecht und Marxismus: Dokumentation: Protokoll der Brecht-Tage 1983* (Brecht and Marxism: Documentation: Proceedings of the Brecht-Days, 1983). East Berlin: Brecht-Zentrum der DDR; 1983. 405 pp. (Brecht 83.) Notes.
Germany. 1938-1941. Critical studies. ■Contradiction of good and evil in capitalist society as seen in *Der gute Mensch von Sezuan*.

1123   Hayman, Ronald. *Brecht.* New York: Oxford UP; 1983. xxiv, 423 pp.
Germany. 1898-1956. Biographies. ■Biography of playwright Bertolt Brecht.

1124   Heine, Thomas. "The Force of Gestures: A New Approach to the Problem of Communication in Hofmannsthal's *Der Schwierige*." *GQ.* 1983 May; 56(3): 408-418. Notes.
Germany. 1921. Critical studies. ■Older assessment of elusive meaning and a clearer understanding of the non-verbal communication in the gestures of Hans Karl as a newly intelligible character.

1125   Henning, Hans. "Goethes Shakespeare-Rezeption, Namentlich in *Faust*." (Goethe's Perception of Shakespeare As Indicated in *Faust*.) *SJW.* 1983; 119: 49-65. Notes. [Contribution to a colloquium held at the Shakespeare Conference, Weimar, April 23, 1982.]
Germany. 1770-1832. Critical studies. ■Goethe's regard for Shakespeare and influences observed in *Faust*.

1126   Hermand, Jost. "Schweyk oder Hörderlein? Brechts und Bechers Ostfrontdramen." (Schweyk or Hörderlein? The Eastern Front Plays of Brecht and Becher.) *Tzs.* 1983 Spring; 3: 92-96, 108-112. Notes. Illus.: Photo.

DRAMA: General—Plays/librettos/scripts

Germany. 1942-1943. Critical studies. ■Analysis of Brecht's *Schweyk im Zweiten Weltkrieg (Schweik in World War II)* and Johannes R. Becher's *Schlacht um Moskau (Battle of Moscow)*, two anti-war plays on the German invasion of the Soviet Union.

1127 Hozier, Anthony. "Brecht's Epic Form: The Actor as Narrator." *RLtrs.* 1982-1983 Winter; 14: 24-38. Notes. Illus.: Sketches. B&W. 1. [Sequel to 'Empathy and Dialectics' in *RLtrs* 13.]

Germany. UK. 1920-1983. Critical studies. ■Brecht's method of play construction and its significance for contemporary British playwriting and acting.

1128 Jost, Roland. "Brecht und Lenin." (Brecht and Lenin.) 82-90, 371-372 in Brecht-Zentrum, DDR. *Brecht und Marxismus: Dokumentation: Protokoll der Brecht-Tage 1983* (Brecht and Marxism: Documentation: Proceedings of the Brecht-Days, 1983). East Berlin: Brecht-Zentrum der DDR; 1983. 405 pp. (Brecht 83.) Notes.

Germany. 1930. Critical studies. ■Lenin's writings as source for Brecht's plays, especially *Die Massnahme (The Measures Taken)* and *Die Tage der Kommune (The Days of the Commune)*.

1129 Klenner, Hermann. "Widerspruch und Rechtsbruch bei Brecht." (Contradiction and Infringement of the Law in Brecht.) in Brecht-Zentrum, DDR. *Brecht und Marxismus: Dokumentation: Protokoll der Brecht-Tage 1983* (Brecht and Marxism: Documentation: Proceedings of the Brecht-Days, 1983). East Berlin: Brecht-Zentrum der DDR; 1983. 405 pp. (Brecht 83.) Notes.

Germany. 1918-1956. Critical studies. ■Brecht's theory of the social basis for personal contradictions.

1130 Knopf, Jan. "Zur theoretischen Begründung der 'Grossen Methode' bei Brecht." (On the Theoretical Motivation of Brecht's 'Great Method'.) 45-51, 368 in Brecht-Zentrum, DDR. *Brecht und Marxismus: Dokumentation: Protokoll der Brecht-Tage 1983* (Brecht and Marxism: Documentation: Proceedings of the Brecht-Days, 1983). East Berlin: Brecht-Zentrum der DDR; 1983. 405 pp. (Brecht 83.) Notes.

Germany. 1918-1956. Critical studies. ■Brecht's 'Great Method' to describe social process and its influence on his works.

1131 Lamport, F.J. *Lessing and Drama.* New York: Oxford UP; 1982. 247 pp.

Germany. 1729-1781. Critical studies. ■Study of plays and criticism of Gotthold Lessing.

1132 Marxhausen, Thomas. "Wie tief sind 'acht Schuh'?: Zum *Kapital*-Studium Bertolt Brechts." (How Deep Are 'Eight Feet'?: On Bertolt Brecht's Study of *Capital*.) *NIMBZ.* 1983 Feb.; 6(1): 10-13. Notes. [Reprint of an article appearing in *Brecht und Marxismus: Dokumentation: Protokoll der Brecht-Tage 1983 (Brecht and Marxism: Documentation: Protocol of the Brecht Days 1983)*.]

Germany. 1926-1934. Historical studies. ■Brecht's study of writings by Marx and Lenin and their influence on his dramas and other works.

1133 Masini, Ferruccio. "Dalla guerra alla rivoluzione: la scena come epifania dell'umano." (From War to Revolution: Stage as Human Epiphany.) *QT.* 1983 Feb.; 5(19): 3-10. Notes.

Germany. 1914-1919. Critical studies. ■Theme of war in German expressionist drama. Grp/movt: Expressionism.

1134 Mauceri, Maria Cristina. "*Der 24 Februar* di Zacharias Werner." (*The 24th of February* by Zacharias Werner.) *QT.* 1982 Feb.; 4(15): 172-184. Notes.

Germany. 1809-1814. Critical studies. ■Catholic interpretation of *Der 24 Februar* by Zacharias Werner.

1135 Roetzer, Hans Gerd; Segarra, Marta, transl.; Gabriel, Asunción, transl. "Goethe i Calderón." (Goethe and Calderón.) 39-47 in Teatral, Institut d'Experimentació. *Ur-Faust (Faust primigeni).* Barcelona: Publicacions i edicions de la Universitat de Barcelona; 1983. 138 pp.

Germany. Spain. 1765-1832. Historical studies. ■Analysis of the influence and impact of Spanish Baroque theatre on German pre-romantic theatre: specifically Calderón on Herder, the *Sturm und Drang* and Goethe. Grp/movt: Pre-romanticism; *Sturm und Drang*; Baroque theatre.

1136 Rouse, John. "Shakespeare and Brecht: The Perils and Pleasures of Inheritance." *CompD.* 1983 Fall; 17(3): 266-280. Notes.

Germany. 1920-1930. Critical studies. ■Brecht's directorial approach to Shakespeare: particularly the adaptations of *Coriolanus, Macbeth* and *King Lear.*

1137 Salvat, Ricard. "Consideracions sobre l'*Urfaust* i la seva posta en escena." (Considerations on the *Ur-Faust* and Its Staging.) 55-65 in Teatral, Institut d'Experimentació. *Ur-Faust (Faust primigeni).* Barcelona: Publicacions i edicions de la Universitat de Barcelona; 1983. 138 pp. Notes.

Germany. 1775-1832. Historical studies. ■Compostion, thematic and character analysis of *Ur-Faust.* Goethe's personal involvement in staging the play and influence of Calderón and Shakespeare. Grp/movt: *Sturm und Drang*; Pre-romanticism.

1138 Sanna, Simonetta. Minna von Barnhelm *di G.E. Lessing: Analisi del testo teatrale.* (G.E. Lessing's *Minna of Barnhelm:* Analysis of the Playtext.) Pisa: Pacini; 1983. 296 pp. Append. Notes. Biblio.

Germany. 1767. Critical studies. ■Dramatic structure of Lessing's *Minna of Barnhelm* represents cultural atmosphere of the time.

1139 Schebera, Jürgen. "*Die Massnahme* — 'Geschmeidigkeitsübung für gute Dialektiker'?" (*The Measures Taken*: 'An Exercise in Flexibility for Good Dialecticians'?) 91-102, 372-374 in Brecht-Zentrum, DDR. *Brecht und Marxismus: Dokumentation: Protokoll der Brecht-Tage 1983* (Brecht and Marxism: Documentation: Proceedings of the Brecht-Days, 1983). East Berlin: Brecht-Zentrum der DDR; 1983. 405 pp. (Brecht 83.)

Germany. 1930. Historical studies. ■Marxist philosophy in Brecht's play *Die Massnahme (The Measures Taken)*, written in collaboration with Hanns Eisler.

1140 Speirs, Ronald. *Brecht's Early Plays.* Atlantic Highlands, NJ: Humanities P; 1982. xi, 224.

Germany. 1925. Critical studies.

1141 Valverde, José; Villanueva, M., transl. "Introducció a *Faust*." (Introduction to *Faust*.) 9-25 in Teatral, Institut d'Experimentació. *Ur-faust (Faust primigeni).* Barcelona: Publicacions i edicions de la Universitat de Barcelona; 1983. 138 pp. [Originally published as introduction to Goethe's *Works* in 1963.]

Germany. 1480-1832. Textual studies. ■Analysis of the genesis of *Faust* and its characters, with the discussion of later playtexts and changes introduced thereafter. Grp/movt: *Sturm und Drang*.

1142 Walch, Günter. "*Ein Sommernachtstraum:* Komödienform und Rezeptionslenkung." (*A Midsummer Night's Dream:* Form and Reception.) *SJW.* 1983; 119: 31-48. Notes. [An expanded version of a contribution to a colloquium held at the Shakespeare Conference, Weimar, April 23, 1982.]

Germany. 1700-1982. Critical studies. ■Discussion of Shakespeare's *A Midsummer Night's Dream* touching on form, critical history and interpretation.

1143 Wandruszka, Marie Luise. "Kleist e la metafora della guerra." (Kleist and the Metaphor of War.) *QT.* 1982 Feb.; 5(19): 42-52. Notes.

Germany. 1808. Critical studies. ■Study of Hermann's character in Kleist's *Hermannschlacht (The Battle of Arminius).*

1144 Case, Sue-Ellen. "From Bertolt Brecht to Heiner Müller." *PerAJ.* 1983; 7(1): 94-102.

Germany, East. 1960-1982. Critical studies. ■Discussion of the way Heiner Müller has inherited and developed the Brechtian tradition. Müller's works are metaphorically ambiguous and episodic, as befits contemporary political understanding.

CLASSED ENTRIES

DRAMA: General—Plays/librettos/scripts

1145 Funke, Christoph. "Jürgen Gross: Keine Schwierigkeiten mit Brecht." (Jürgen Gross: No Difficulties with Brecht.) *NIMBZ*. 1983 Sep.; 6(5): 6-7. Illus.: Photo.
Germany, East. 1980. Histories-sources. ■The *Mutter Courage (Mother Courage)* of Bertolt Brecht is contrasted with the Mother Courage appearing in Jürgen Gross' play *Denkmal (Memorial)*.

1146 Kuczynski, Jürgen. "Brecht und die Macht der Arbeiterklasse." (Brecht and the Power of the Working Class.) 246-254, 383 in Brecht-Zentrum, DDR. *Brecht und Marxismus: Dokumentation: Protokoll der Brecht-Tage 1983* (Brecht and Marxism: Documentation: Proceedings of the Brecht-Days, 1983). East Berlin: Brecht-Zentrum der DDR; 1983. 405 pp. (Brecht 83.) Notes.
Germany, East. Germany, West. 1953. Critical studies. ■Brecht's adaptation of *Coriolanus* compared to Günter Grass's *Die Plebejer proben den Aufstand (The Plebeians Test the Revolt)* in view of the events of June 17, 1953.

1147 Müller-Waldeck, Gunnar. "Ein marxistischer Grundkurs sozialen Verhaltens: Zu Brechts 'Eulenspiegel'-Projekt." (A Marxist Head-On Course of Social Behavior: On Brecht's 'Owl-Glass' Project.) 255-267, 383-384 in Brecht-Zentrum, DDR. *Brecht und Marxismus: Dokumentation: Protokoll der Brecht-Tage 1983* (Brecht and Marxism: Documentation: Proceedings of the Brecht-Days, 1983). East Berlin: Brecht-Zentrum der DDR; 1983. 405 pp. (Brecht 83.) Notes.
Germany, East. 1954-1956. Historical studies. ■Bertolt Brecht's experiments in audience education through his plays in order to change society.

1148 Honegger, Gitta. "Acts of Translation." *PerAJ*. 1983; 7(1): 21-26.
Germany, West. USA. 1900-1983. Linguistic studies. ■Discussion of the intimate relationship between language and culture, and the difficulty of translation without caricature. Examples include Tom Stoppard's *On the Razzle*, Cecil Philip Taylor's *Good* and Richard Foreman's *Three Acts of Recognition*.

1149 Less, Avner; Strittmatter, Thomas; Kruntorad, Paul; Laube, Horst; Schütz, Johannes. "Der Streit um Kipphardts *Bruder Eichmann*: Dubios, Brisant und Spielbar — oder was?" (The Dispute about Kipphardt's *Brother Eichmann*: Dubious, Explositve and Playable — or What?) *TH*. 1983; 4: 67-70.
Germany, West. 1983. Critical studies. ■Brief comments on Heinar Kipphardt's play *Brother Eichmann*.

1150 Merschmeier, Michael. "Canettis Todesfuge — Fürs Theater? Der Theaterautor Elias Canetti und *Die Befristeten* in Stuttgart." (Canetti's Death-fugue — for Theatre? Playwright Elias Canetti and *The Limited* in Stuttgart.) *TH*. 1983; 4: 34-36. Illus.: Photo.
Germany, West. 1983. Critical studies. ■Problems in stage adaptation of Canetti's *Die Befristeten (The Limited)*, directed by Hans Hollmann.

1151 Merschmeier, Michael. "Der eingebildete Menschenfeind: Molières *Misanthrope* in Köln und Bonn." (The Imaginary Misanthrope: Molière's *Misanthrope* in Cologne and Bonn.) *TH*. 1983 Jan.; 23(1): 3-7.
Germany, West. 1982. Reviews of performances. ■Molière's *Le Misanthrope* at Cologne and Bonn: comparison of adaptations to determine the genre of the play as comedy or as tragedy.

1152 Ponzi, Mauro. "Il teatro e la guerra fredda." (The Theatre and the Cold War.) *QT*. 1983 Feb.; 5(19): 111-125. Notes.
Germany, West. 1945-1966. Critical studies. ■Problem of German responsibility in World War II in period plays and documentary theatre written during the period of the cold war.

1153 Rischbieter, Henning. "Dies muss veröffentlicht werden." (This Must Be Published.) *TH*. 1983 Jan.; 23(1): 1.
Germany, West. 1982. Histories-sources. ■German Fascism as main theme in Heiner Kipphardt's work, particularly his last play *Bruder Eichmann (Brother Eichmann)*.

1154 Stadelmaier, Gerhard. "Theater und Macht: Anlässlich der Karlsruher Uraufführung von Volker Brauns *Dmitri*."

(Theater and Authority: On Occasion of the Karlsruhe Production of Volker Braun's *Dmitri*.) *TH*. 1983 Feb.; 2: 29-33.
Germany, West. 1983. Critical studies. ■Volker Braun's *Dmitri*: treatment of power by German authors including Dürrenmatt, Thomas Bernhard and Heinar Müller.

1155 Konstan, David. "A Dramatic History of Misanthropes." *CompD*. 1983 Summer; 17(2): 97-123. Notes.
Greece. England. France. 317 B.C.-1666 A.D. Critical studies. ■Compares the treatment of the misanthrope in Menander's *Dýskolos (The Grouch)*, Shakespeare's *Timon of Athens*, and Molière's *Le Misanthrope*.

1156 Platt, Michael. "Shakespeare's Apology for Poetic Wisdom." 231-244 in Carey, Cecile Williamson; . Limouze, Henry S. *Shakespeare and the Arts: A Collection of Essays from the Ohio Shakespeare Conference, 1981, Wright State University, Dayton, Ohio*. Washington, DC: UP of America; 1982. viii, 247 pp. Notes.
Greece. England. 400 B.C.-1613 A.D. Critical studies. ■Contrasts Shakespeare's and Plato's conceptions of the wise man using *The Tempest* and Plato's *Laws*.

1157 Lai, Jane. "What Do We Put Centre Stage?" *ThR*. 1983 Autumn; 8(3): 246-251.
Hong Kong. 1950-1982. Historical studies. ■Brief survey of themes and techniques employed by dramatists and performing groups.

1158 Alatri, Paolo. *Gabriele D'Annunzio*. Turin: Unione Tipografica Editrice Torinese; 1983. xii, 669 pp. (La vita sociale della nuova Italia 31.) Notes. Biblio. Index. Tables. Illus.: Photo. B&W.
Italy. 1863-1938. Biographies. ■General biography of Gabriele D'Annunzio.

1159 Anglani, Bartolo. *Goldoni: il mercato, la scena, l'utopia*. (Goldoni: The Market, the Theatre, the Utopia.) Napoli: Liguori; 1983. 252 pp. (Letterature 1.) Pref. Notes.
Italy. 1734-1793. Critical studies. ■Relationship between mercantile society and playwright's creation in Goldoni's plays.

1160 Anon. *Vitaliano Brancati fra scena e schermo*. (Vitaliano Brancati between Stage and Screen.) Catania: Tipo-lito 'La Celere'; 1983. 135 pp. Biblio. Filmography. [Proceedings of the meeting — Catania 8-12 October — organized by Associazione Nazionale dei Critici di Teatro and by Teatro Stabile di Catania.]
Italy. 1924-1954. Critical studies. ■Essays on Brancati's plays and motion picture scripts. Related to Media: Film.

1161 Antonucci, Giovanni, ed. *Mario Federici*. Rome: Bulzoni; 1983. xiii, 157 pp. (Quaderni dell'Istituto di Studi Pirandelliani 6.) Pref. Tables. Illus.: Photo. B&W.
Italy. 1900-1975. Critical studies. ■Most important themes, political influences and fortune of Mario Federici's theatre. Includes biographical notes and some unpublished writings.

1162 Bisicchia, Andrea. *Invito alla lettura di Eduardo De Filippo*. (Invitation to the Reading of Eduardo De Filippo.) Milan: Mursia; 1982. 156 pp. (Invito alla lettura — Sezione italiana 73.) Notes. Index. Biblio.
Italy. 1900-1982. Critical studies. ■Critical analysis of the most significant themes in Eduardo De Filippo's plays and phases of his acting career. Biographic sketch is included.

1163 Bonanni, Francesca. "Sul teatro di Bruno Corra." (On Bruno Corra's Theatre.) *TeatrC*. 1983-1984 Oct.-Jan.; 3(5): 189-200 . Notes. Biblio.
Italy. 1915-1940. Critical studies. ■Modification of themes of Corra's plays from Futurism to bourgeois tradition. Also discussed is Corra's review of the first Milanese performance of Pirandello's *Così è (se vi pare) (Right You Are If You Think You Are)*. Grp/movt: Futurism.

1164 Borsellino, Nino. *Ritratto di Pirandello*. (Portrait of Pirandello.) Rome, Bari: Laterza; 1983. 206 pp. (Universale Laterza 619.) Notes. Index.
Italy. 1889-1934. Biographies. ■Luigi Pirandello's artistic biography.

1165 Borsellino, Nino. *Storia di Verga*. (Verga's Story.) Bari: Laterza; 1982. 149 pp. (UL 610.) Pref. Notes. Index.

DRAMA: General—Plays/librettos/scripts

Italy. 1840-1922. Histories-specific. ■Biography of Giovanni Verga with an analysis of his plays and views on art and other matters.

1166 Bucciolini, Giulio; Personé, Luigi Maria, ed. *Cronache del teatro fiorentino.* (Chronicles of Florentine Theatre.) Florence: Olschki; 1982. 409 pp. Pref. Index. Biblio. Illus.: Photo. B&W.
Italy. 1524-1964. Histories-sources. ■Chronicle of theatre activities, accompanied by a note on Giulio Bucciolini's life and works.

1167 Cappa, Marina; Nepoti, Roberto. *Dario Fo.* Rome: Gremese; 1982. 140 pp. (Teatro Italiano 3.) Biblio. Illus.: Photo. B&W.
Italy. 1926-1982. Historical studies. ■Biographical note, chronology and a brief analysis of Dario Fo's plays in performance.

1168 Cappello, Giovanni. *Giovanni Testori.* Florence: La Nuova Italia; 1983. 166 pp. (Il Castoro 193.) Biblio.
Italy. 1940-1982. Critical studies. ■Critical study of Testori's narrative, theatrical and poetical works.

1169 Carotenuto, Aldo. "La personalità e lo psicodramma." (Personality and Psychodrama.) *AdP.* 1983; 8(1): 76-80. Illus.: Photo.
Italy. 1916-1936. Critical studies. ■Jungian point of view on personality in Pirandello's work.

1170 Cascetta, Annamaria. *Invito alla lettura di Testori.* (Invitation to Read Testori.) Milan: Mursia; 1983. 200 pp. (Invito alla lettura – Sezione italiana 76.) Index. Biblio.
Italy. 1923-1981. Critical studies. ■Critical trends and thematic analysis of Giovanni Testori's works, with a biographical sketch of the playwright.

1171 Corra, Bruno. "La commedia, o dell'artificio." (The Play, or about the Craft.) *TeatrC.* 1983-1984 Oct.-Jan.; 3(5): 257-279.
Italy. 1983. Textbooks/manuals/guides. ■Bruno Corra's practical suggestions are drawn from his book *How to Become a Successful Writer* dedicated to young playwrights.

1172 Finocchiaro Chimirri, Giovanna. *Per una lettura analitica di Brancati: Caterina Leher, governante.* (An Analytic Reading of Brancati: Caterina Leher, Housekeeper.) Rome: Bulzoni; 1983. 79 pp. (Biblioteca di cultura 246.) Pref. Notes. Biblio.
Italy. 1952. Critical studies. ■Freudian analysis of the character of Caterina Leher in Brancati's play *La governante (The Housekeeper).*

1173 Fontanelli, Giorgio. "Mussolini – Forzano, 1983: Un centenario (e altro) in comune." (Mussolini – Forzano, 1983: A Centenary (and Other Things) in Common.) *QT.* 1983 Feb.; 5(19): 160-166.
Italy. 1939. Critical studies. ■Giovacchino Forzano's play *Cesare* written following Benito Mussolini's advice. Grp/movt: Fascism.

1174 Frascani, Federico. *Eduardo segreto.* (Secret Eduardo.) Naples: Edizioni del Delfino; 1982. 161 pp. Notes. Index.
Italy. 1926-1982. Histories-specific. ■Biographic and cultural sources of Eduardo De Filippo's plays. Included is a chapter on his cinematographic activity. Related to Media: film.

1175 Giammattei, Emma. *Eduardo De Filippo.* 105 pp. Florence: La Nuova Italia; 1983. (Il Castoro 187 and 188.) Biblio.
Italy. 1905-1981. Critical studies. ■Criticism of Eduardo De Filippo's plays and analysis of the principal concepts of his dramaturgy: 'theatre-within-the-theatre', 'closed scene' and moralism.

1176 Gimmi, Annalisa. "Teatro 'da leggere' o teatro 'da rappresentare?' Le *Proposte* di Renzo Ricchi." (Drama 'to Read' or Drama 'to Perform?' The *Proposal* by Renzo Ricchi.) *QT.* 1983 Aug.-Nov.; 6(21-22): 113-123.
Italy. 1973-1983. Reviews of publications. ■Critical notes on the collected edition of Renzo Ricchi's plays entitled *Proposte di teatro (Theatrical Suggestions).*

1177 Gioanola, Elio. *Pirandello la follia.* (Pirandello the Madness.) Genoa: Il Melangolo; 1983. 286 pp. (Università, serie letteraria 6.) Index. Biblio.
Italy. 1894-1936. Critical studies. ■Psychological motivations in thematic and formal choices of Pirandello's work.

1178 Kärnell, Karl-Åke. "Strindbergsmanifestation i Italien." (Strindberg Event in Italy.) *MfS.* 1983 Apr.; 67: 35-36 .
Italy. 1982. Critical studies. ■Report on a major Strindberg conference in which the playwright's relationship to modern culture, painting, photography and theatrical productions were discussed.

1179 Kunin, Mireya. "Ribellione e creatività." (Rebellion and Creativity.) *AdP.* 1983; 8(1): 26-28.
Italy. 1930. Critical studies. ■'Rebellion of the actors against the stage director in *Tonight We Improvise* is seen as an expression of the dialectic life and form used by Pirandello'.

1180 Lauretta, Enzo. "Del primer teatre pirandellià a *Così è, se vi pare.*" (From the First Pirandello Theatre to *Right You Are If You Think You Are.*) 5-7 in *És aixi, si us ho sembla.* Translated by Bonaventura Vallespinosa. Barcelona: Institut del Teatre; 1983. 80 pp. (Biblioteca Teatral 11.)
Italy. 1898-1917. Critical studies. ■Productions of Pirandello's early work from *La Morsa (The Morse)* to the writing of *Così è (se vi pare) (Right You Are If You Think You Are)* are contrasted with *Liolà* and *Berretto a sonagli (The Bell Cap).*

1181 Mangini, Nicola. "Evolution of the Theatre in Dialect in Twentieth Century Italy." *MuK.* 1983; 29: 254-260. Biblio.
Italy. 1863-1980. Historical studies. ■Problems leading to gradual disappearance of the dialect theatre.

1182 Marranca, Bonnie. "Pirandello: A Work in Progress." *PerAJ.* 1983; 7(2): 7-28.
Italy. 1916-1936. Critical studies. ■Pirandello's concept of the relationships of character, society and reality.

1183 Martinez, Ronald L. "The Pharmacy of Machiavelli: Roman Lucretia in *Mandragola.*" 3-41 in Barkan, Leonard. *Renaissance Drama, New Series XIV: Relations and Influences.* Evanston, IL: Northwestern UP; 1983. x, 196 pp.
Italy. 1513-1520. Critical studies. ■Comparison of Machiavelli's and Livy's history of Lucretia.

1184 Norén, Kjerstin. "Det omvända eller det annorlunda?" (Reversed or Different?)*Entre.* 1983; 10(2): 22-26. Illus.: Photo. B&W.
Italy. Sweden. Norway. 1983. Critical studies. ■Dario Fo's farce *The Kidnapping* reflects the terrorism and chaos in Italian society. Though Fo is said to be isolated intellectually, his plays are well performed in Scandinavia for artistic rather than political reasons.

1185 Pieri, Marzia. *La scena boschereccia nel Rinascimento italiano.* (Pastoral Scenes in Italian Renaissance.) Padua: Liviana; 1983. x, 269 pp. (Biblioteca di cultura, sezione letteraria.) Notes. Tables. Index. Illus.: Photo. B&W.
Italy. 1400-1599. Histories-specific. ■Pastoral as dramatic genre and its literary and scenic derivations. Grp/movt: Renaissance theatre.

1186 Poli, Gianni. "La bocca del lupo — Teatralità del romanzo di Remigio Zena." (*The Wolf's Mouth* — Theatricality of Remigio Zena's Novel.) *TeatrC.* 1982 Oct.-1983 Jan.; 1(2): 239-253. Notes. Biblio.
Italy. 1980. Critical studies. ■Dramatization of Remigio Zena's novel *The Wolf's Mouth* by Teatro Stabile.

1187 Puppa, Paolo. "Arditi, cocottes, professori nel teatro della guerra futurista." (Storm Troops, Cocottes, Professors in the Futurist Theatre of Futurist War.) *QT.* 1983 Feb.; 5(19): 83-100. Notes.
Italy. 1909-1931. Critical studies. ■Principal themes of the Italian Futurist theatre. Grp/movt: Futurism.

1188 Ravasi Bellocchio, Lella. "Appunti di lettura del profondo su *La figlia di Jorio.*" (Short Notes on Comprehensive Reading of *Jorio's Daughter.*) *QT.* 1983 Feb.; 5(10): 167-175.
Italy. 1904. Critical studies. ■Psychoanalytical interpretation of principal characters in Gabriele D'Annunzio's *Jorio's Daughter.*

1189 Roda, Frederic. "Ritorno a Pirandello." (Return to Pirandello.) 5-8 in *Els gegants de la muntanya.* Barcelona: Edicions Robrenyo; 1983. 80 pp. (Teatre de tots els temps 24.) [Prologue to Luigi Pirandello's *I giganti della montagna.*]

DRAMA: General—Plays/librettos/scripts

Italy. 1921-1937. Textual studies. ■Evaluation of Pirandello's tetralogy: *Six Characters in Search of an Author (Sei personaggi in cerca d'autore), Henry IV (Enrico Quarto), Tonight We Improvise (Questa sera si recita a soggeto)* and the epilogue *The Giants of the Mountain (I giganti della montagna)*.

1190 Verdone, Mario. "Teatro pirandelliano e Futurismo." (Pirandellian Theatre and Futurism.) *TeatrC.* 1983 June-Sep.; 2(4): 113-125. Notes.
Italy. 1915-1936. Critical studies. ■Elements of futurist dramaturgy in Pirandello's theatre. Grp/movt: Futurism.

1191 Viziano, Teresa. *Paolo Giacometti, Adelaide Ristori: diritto d'autore, diritto d'attrice.* (Paolo Giacometti, Adelaide Ristori: Author's Rights Versus Interpreter's Rights.) Novi Ligure: Arti Grafiche Novesi; 1982. 64 pp. Illus.: Photo. B&W.
Italy. 1836-1882. Histories-reconstruction. ■Catalogue of the exhibition (Novi Ligure, September/October 1982) reconstructs the debate between playwright Paolo Giacometti and Adelaide Ristori regarding the original playtexts and their free stage adaptations by the noted actress.

1192 Zappulla Muscarà, Sarah. *Pirandello in guanti gialli.* (Pirandello in Yellow Gloves.) Rome: Sciascia; 1983. 357 pp. (Viaggi e studi 25.) Notes. Biblio. Index.
Italy. 1884-1935. Historical studies. ■Some lesser known facts about Pirandello's productions, poems, essays on dialect and newspaper articles. Included is the text of author's novel *I muriccioli, un fico, un uccellino (The Low Walls, a Fig-tree, a Birdie)*.

1193 Zorzi, Ludovico; Innamorati, Giuliano; Ferrone, Siro, ed. *Il teatro del Cinquecento — I luoghi, i testi, gli attori.* (Theatre of 16th Century — Places, Texts and Actors.) Florence: Sansoni; 1982. 107 pp. Pref. Notes. Index. Biblio. Illus.: Photo. B&W.
Italy. 1845-1982. Critical studies. ■Theatres, actors and drama of the Renaissance in the work of the modern directors. Proceedings of the two day study at Teatro Metastasio (Prato, April 1982), with commentary by Gianfranco De Bosio, Roberto Guicciardini, and Aldo Trionfo. Grp/movt: Renaissance theatre.

1194 Ojo, S. Ade. "L'Ecrivain africain et ses publics: Le cas de Bernard Dadié." (The African Writer and His Audience: The Case of Bernard Dadié.) *Pnpa.* 1983 Mar.-Apr.; 32: 63-99. Notes. Biblio.
Ivory Coast. 1933-1973. Critical studies. ■Dadié's theatre work is primarily devoted to African audiences, leaving Europeans bewildered by his dramas. Grp/movt: Négritude.

1195 Durnell, Hazel B. *Japanese Cultural Influences on American Poetry and Drama.* Tokyo: Hokuseido P; 1983. xix, 305 pp.
Japan. USA. 1900-1980. Critical studies. ■Influence of *nō* and *kabuki* on American theatre. Related to Dance-Drama.

1196 Gillespie, John K. "The Impact of Noh on Paul Claudel's Style of Playwriting." *TJ.* 1983 Mar.; 35(1): 58-73. Notes.
Japan. France. 1921-1927. Critical studies. ■After outlining the nature of *nō* and showing the importance of dreams, Gillespie analyzes the role of the principal character and the uses of retrospect in both bodies of drama. Related to Dance-Drama.

1197 Yang, Margaret. "Malaysian Drama in English: Is There a Case for a Post-Mortem?" *ThR.* 1983 Autumn; 8(3): 234-246. Notes.
Malaysia. 1957-1982. Historical studies. ■Without institutional support or professional productions a small group of writers continues to experiment with themes and techniques in English-language drama.

1198 Obregón, Claudio. "Mexiko: det prekolombianska arvet." (Mexico: The Pre-Columbian Heritage.) *Entre.* 1983; 10(4): 36-37.
Mexico. 1910-1983. Critical studies. ■Views of playwright Rodolfo Usigli and director Julio Castillo on the possibilities of incorporating pre-colonial material into modern drama.

1199 Bolt, Alan; Prego, José Daniel. "Den aktuella teatern i Nicaragua." (Current Theatre in Nicaragua.) *Entre.* 1983; 10 (4): 41-42.

Nicaragua. 1980-1983. Historical studies. ■Collective creativity and peasant theatre in Nicaragua. Drama reflects revolutionary struggle and folk tradition.

1200 Rosen, Carol. *Plays of Impasse: Contemporary Drama Set in Confining Institutions.* Princeton, NJ: Princeton UP; 1983. 325 pp.
North America. Europe. 1900-1983. Critical studies. ■Discussion of plays set in hospitals, asylums, prisons and barracks.

1201 Alonge, Roberto. *Epopea borghese nel teatro di Ibsen.* (Epic of the Bourgeoisie in Ibsen's Drama.) Naples: Guida; 1983. 342 pp. (Tascabili 82.) Notes. Index.
Norway. 1867-1899. Critical studies. ■Contrary to general belief, Ibsen is viewed as bard of the bourgeois mythology and not as critic of the middle class.

1202 Alonge, Roberto. "Lettura di *Spettri*." (Reading of *Ghosts*.) *QT.* 1983 May; 5(20): 5-30. Notes.
Norway. 1881. Critical studies. ■Analysis of Ibsen's *Gengangere (Ghosts)* with particular attention to dramatis personae.

1203 Berlin, Jeffrey B. "The Concept of Truth in Ibsen's *An Enemy of the People*." *IA.* 1981-1982: 8-22. Notes.
Norway. 1882. Critical studies. ■Theme of truth is examined through Stockmann's relationship to the community.

1204 Durback, Errol. *Ibsen the Romantic: Analogues of Paradise in the Later Plays.* Athens, GA: Univ. of Georgia P; 1982. vii, 213 pp.
Norway. 1828-1906. Critical studies. ■Romantic aspects of Ibsen's plays.

1205 Haakonsen, Daniel. "*Vildanden* og fir russik romaner." (*The Wild Duck* and Four Russian Novels.) *IY.* 1981-1982: 93-107. Notes.
Norway. 1884. Critical studies. ■Literary influences on *The Wild Duck*, mainly Turgenev's *Fathers and Sons*, Flaubert's *Madame Bovary* and the novels of Georg Brandes. Grp/movt: Romanticism.

1206 Hiorth, Ingunn. "Ibsens retrospektive tekknikk tolket av Ingunn Hiorth: Et resymé." (Ibsen's Retrospective Technique Interpreted by Ingunn Hiorth: A Summary.) *IY.* 1981-1982: 86-92.
Norway. 1881. Critical studies. ■Discussion of Ibsen's retrospective technique, including comments on exposition, using *Ghosts (Gengangere)* as a study model.

1207 Hornby, Richard. "Deconstructing Realism in Ibsen's *The Master Builder*." *ET.* 1983 Nov.; 2(1): 34-40. Illus.: Photo. B&W. 2: 5 in. x 7 in.
Norway. 1892. Critical studies. ■Ibsen creates apparently realistic characters in a realistic situation, then, anticipating much of Freud's theory of psychopathology, dramatizes the hero's unconscious desires. Grp/movt: Realism.

1208 Johnston, Brian. "The Psychologistic Fallacy in Ibsen Interpretation." *INC.* 1983; 4: 32-34.
Norway. 1850-1906. Critical studies. ■Claims that Ibsen characters do not have psychological complexity.

1209 Nettum, Rolf N. "Den åpne og den lukkede verden: En kommentar til noen av Henrik Ibsens samtidsskuespill." (The Open and Closed World: A Commentary on Some of Ibsen's Plays of Contemporary Life.) *IY.* 1981-1982: 47-72. Notes.
Norway. 1850-1906. Critical studies. ■Commentary on themes of contemporary life in Henrik Ibsen's plays.

1210 Polesso, Paola. "Tragicità di Nora Helmer." (Tragic Nature of Nora Helmer.) *QT.* 1982 Nov.; 5(18): 121-128. Notes.
Norway. 1879. Critical studies. ■Tragic view of the world in Ibsen's play *Et Dukkehjem (A Doll's House)* is particularly evident in Nora Helmer's character.

1211 Puppa, Paolo. *La figlia di Ibsen — Lettura di* Hedda Gabler. (Ibsen's Daughter — A Reading of *Hedda Gabler*.) Bologna: Patron; 1982. 183 pp. (Collana di teatro e regia teatrale 7.) Notes. Index.
Norway. 1890. Critical studies. ■Thematic analysis of the play, focusing on father-child relationship and other psychological matters synthesized in title character.

DRAMA: General—Plays/librettos/scripts

1212   Van Laan, Thomas F. "The Ending of *A Doll's House* and Augier's *Maître Guérin*." *CompD*. 1983-1984 Winter; 17 (4): 297-317. Notes.
Norway. France. 1864-1879. Critical studies. ■Émile Augier's *Maître Guérin* is seen as the most likely source for the ending of *Et Dukkehjem (A Doll's House)*.

1213   Bardijewska, Slawa. "Portraits d'Auteurs Dramatiques Polonais: Le Moralisme Pervers d'Ireneusz Iredyński." (Portraits of Polish Playwrights: The Perverse Moralism of Ireneusz Iredyński.) *TP*. 1983; 297: 3-12. Illus.: Photo. Print. B&W. 4. [In French and English.]
Poland. 1962-1982. Critical studies. ■Description and analysis of Ireneusz Iredyński's plays.

1214   Bardijewska, Slawa. "Portraits d'Auteurs Dramatiques Polonais: Helmut Kajzar (1941-1982)." (Profiles of Polish Playwrights: Helmut Kajzar (1941-1982).) *TP*. 1983; 299-300: 30-37. Illus.: Photo. Print. B&W. 4. [In French and English.]
Poland. 1969-1981. Historical studies. ■Description and analysis of Helmut Kajzar's plays.

1215   Bardijewska, Slawa. "Portraits d'Auteurs Dramatiques Polonais: Discours de Krysztof Choiński sur Notre Epoque." (Profiles of Polish Playwrights: Krysztof Choiński's Discourse on Topicality.) *TP*. 1983; 302-303: 32-37. Illus.: Photo. Print. B&W. 2. [In French and English.]
Poland. 1961-1983. Critical studies. ■Analysis of Krysztof Choiński's plays.

1216   Majcherek, Janusz. "Gombrowicz a teatr." (Gombrowicz and Theatre.) *PaT*. 1983; 32(2): 187-200. Notes. Illus.: Photo. B&W. 1: 9 cm. x 12 cm.
Poland. 1904-1969. Critical studies. ■Witold Gombrowicz's experiences with theatre and his ambivalent attitude toward it.

1217   Malinowski, Jerzy. "Jerzy Hulewicz, Melchior Wańkowicz i cenzura krakowska." *PaT*. 1983; 32(2): 268-272. Illus.: Poster. B&W. 1: 12 cm. x 17 cm.
Poland. 1925. Historical studies. ■Conflict between the Municipal Theatre in Cracow and local censorship concerning the production of the expressionist play *Aruna*, written by Jerzy Hulewicz.

1218   Poulet, Jacques. "*Yvonne Princesse de Bourgogne* de Gombrowicz: Rencontre avec l'homme qui a rencontré l'auteur." (*Yvonne, Princess of Bourgogne* by Gombrowicz: Conversation with the Man Who Knew the Author.) *CF*. 1982 Apr.; 108: 28-30.
Poland. France. 1969-1982. Histories-sources. ■Jacques Rosner, director of the Witold Gombrowicz play at the Odéon Theatre, recalls a 1969 visit with the playwright shortly before his death.

1219   Mimoso-Ruiz, Duarte. "Deux figures de navigateurs portugais: Camoẽs, Fernão Mendes Pintoty et la dramaturgie contemporaine de Helda Costa." (Two Types of Portuguese Navigators: Camoẽs, Fernão Mendes Pinto and the Contemporary Dramaturgy of Helda Costa.) *RHT*. 1983; 35(1): 293-310. Notes. Tables.
Portugal. 1981-1982. Critical studies. ■Analysis of Helda Costa's plays *A Viagem (The Journey)* and *Fernão Mendes Pinto*.

1220   Eisen, Donald Gilbert. *The Art of Anton Chekhov: Principles of Technique in His Drama and Fiction*. Pittsburgh: Univ. of Pittsburgh; 1982. 720 pp. Biblio. Gloss. Index. [Diss.: University Microfilms order no. DA8222786.]
Russia. 1860-1904. Critical studies. ■Traces Čechov's techniques of objectivity, tension, absence and orchestration from his early fiction through the major plays.

1221   Gottlieb, Vera. *Chekhov and the Vaudeville: A Study of Chekhov's One-Act Plays*. New York: Cambridge UP; 1982. xii, 224 pp.
Russia. 1884-1892. Critical studies. ■Study of Čechov's ten early plays, showing the development of his art on the foundation of vaudeville conventions.

1222   Master, Carol Tendler. *The Development of the Chekhovian Scene: A Study in Dramatic Structure*. New York: Columbia Univ.; 1982. 229 pp. [Diss.: University Microfilms order no. DA8222445.]
Russia. 1860-1904. Critical studies. ■Application of Bernard Beckerman's method of segmental analysis to Čechov's plays to determine that he focused on small segments rather than on large actions.

1223   Collins, Michael J. "The Sabotage of Love: Athol Fugard's Recent Plays." *WLT*. 1983 Summer; 57(3): 369-371. Notes.
South Africa, Republic of. USA. 1979-1983. Critical studies. ■Universal themes in Fugard's *A Lesson from Aloes* and *Master Harold and the Boys* overshadow autobiographical references.

1224   "Några vägra för realismen i Latinamerikas teater." (Some Paths for Realism in Latin American Theatre.) *Entre*. 1983; 10(4): 9-11.
South America. North America. 1955-1983. Critical studies. ■Ibsen's influence on plays of psychological, poetic and critical realism. Also: influence of Cuban revolution and Brecht. Grp/movt: Realism; Absurdism.

1225   "*La gallina ciega* de Max Aub: Una emocion permanente." (*Blindman's Buff* of Max Aub: A Permanent Emotion.) *PrAc*. 1983 Nov.-Dec.; 201: 43-45.
Spain. 1970-1983. Historical studies. ■Two reports about Max Aub's play *Blindman's Buff*.

1226   Alonso de Santos, José Luis. "Taibo: sobre su obra: Paco Ignacio Taibo: Canto al exilio en una crónica representable." (Taibo: About His Work: Paco Ignacio Taibo: Singing in Exile: Chronicle to Be Performed.) *PrAc*. 1983 Nov.-Dec.; 201: 47-49.
Spain. Mexico. 1958-1973. Historical studies. ■Two reports about playwright Paco Ignacio Taibo and his play *Morir del todo*.

1227   Alonso de Santos, José Luis. "León Felipe, un juglar desterrado de su patria." (León Felipe. The Banished Juggler.) *PrAc*. 1983 Nov.-Dec.; 201: 44.
Spain. Mexico. 1939-1983. Historical studies. ■Report concerning poet León Felipe and his play *El Juglarón*.

1228   Alvaro, Francisco. *El Espectador y la Critica*. (The Spectator and the Critic.) Valladolid: Francisco Alvaro; 1983. 323 pp. Pref. Notes. Illus.: Photo.
Spain. 1983. Critical studies. ■Critical report on new plays in Spanish theatre.

1229   Beaumud, Anna M. "*Las Hilanderas*, the Theatre, and a *Comedia* by Calderón." *BCom*. 1982 Summer; 34(1): 37-44. Notes.
Spain. 1625-1651. Critical studies. ■Diego Velázquez's painting *Las Hilanderas* is compared to Calderón de la Barca's play *Darlo todo y no dar nada (To Give It All and Nothing)* via spatial analogies and narrative.

1230   Benet i Jornet, Josep M. "Notes d'urgència al mage d'una adaptació." (Pertinent Notes Written in the Margins of an Adaptation.) 5-11 in Benet i Jornet, Josep M. *Maria Rosa*. Barcelona: Centre Dramàtic de la Generalitat – Edhasa; 1983. 100 pp. (Els Textos del Centre Dramàtic 2.) [Prologue to Angel Guimerà's *Maria Rosa*.]
Spain. 1894. Textual studies. ■Evaluation of the language, stage notations and symbolism of the playtext and the evolution of the critical point of view on it.

1231   Cascardi, A.J. "Sobre La Fecha de *Los Hechos de Garcilaso* de Lope de Vega." (Dating *The Deeds of Garcilaso* by Lope de Vega.) *BCom*. 1982 Summer; 34: 51-61. Notes. Biblio.
Spain. 1573. Historical studies. ■Menéndez y Pelayo dated *Los hechos de Garcilaso* (composed 1573-1574) as the oldest play by Lope de Vega. This contention is questioned by disputing the authorship and suggesting that the play could not have been written until later, whether by Lope de Vega or Lucas Rodriguez.

1232   Dietz, Donald T. "Theology and the Stage: The God Figure in Calderón's *Autos Sacramentales*." *BCom*. 1982 Summer; 34(1): 97-105. Notes.

DRAMA: General—Plays/librettos/scripts

Spain. 1626. Critical studies. ■Portrayal of Catholic dogma and virtues of God and the Trinity in Calderón's *autos sacramentales.*

1233   Dille, Glen F. "The Tragedy of Don Pedro: Old and New Christian Conflict in *El valiente Campuzano.*" *BCom.* 1983 Summer ; 35(1): 97-109. Notes.

Spain. 1649. Critical studies. ■Indictment of Christian notion of honor, bigotry and injustice in Antonio Gómez' play *El Valiente Campuzano (The Valiant Campuzano).*

1234   Dowling, John. "Moratin's Creation of the Comic Role for the Older Actress." *ThS.* 1983; 24(1-2): 55-63. Notes. Illus.: Dwg. 2: 2 in. x 3 in.

Spain. 1780-1825. Historical studies. ■Combining the neoclassical principle of verisimilitude and the talents of older, unemployed actress Leandro Fernández de Moratín pioneered development of the older, comic woman character type in Spanish drama of this type.

1235   Fischer, Susan L. "The Psychological Stages of Feminine Development in *La Hija del Aire*: A Jungian Point of View." *BCom.* 1982 Winter; 34(2): 137-158. Notes.

Spain. 1600-1699. Critical studies. ■Demonstration of Calderón's psychological insight via dramatic and psychological analysis of Semiramis from *La hija del aire (Daughter of the Air).*

1236   Formosa, Feliu. "Joan Oliver o el *Realisme.*" (Joan Oliver or *Realism.*) *EE.* 1983 Mar.; 22: 5-20.

Spain. 1899-1983. Histories-sources. ■Joan Oliver talks about his work and other questions of Catalan theatre. Grp/movt: Realism.

1237   Fornasa, Giuliano Mario. *Sociedad español y cambio social en el teatro de Galdós.* (Spanish Society and Social Change in the Plays of Galdós.) Washington, DC: George Washington Univ.; 1982. 277 pp. [Diss.: University Microfilms order no. DA8217575.]

Spain. 1843-1920. Critical studies. ■Chronological study of Benito Pérez Galdós' plays, which are said to have established the basis for drama of social concern in nineteenth century Spain.

1238   Friedman, Edward H. "Toward a More Perfect Union: Art and Craft in Calderón's *Saber del mal y del bien* and *¿Quál es mayor perfección?.*" *BCom.* 1983 Summer; 35(1): 51-67. Notes.

Spain. 1608-1681. Critical studies. ■Application of recent Lope de Vega criticism to two Calderón plays. Metacritical analysis.

1239   Gitlitz, David M. "The New Christian Dilemma in Two Plays by Lope de Vega." *BCom.* 1982 Summer; 34(1): 63-81. Notes. Biblio.

Spain. 1600. Critical studies. ■In *El galón de la Mambrilla* and in *La pobreza estimada,* Lope de Vega articulates concern for the Christian minority.

1240   Goldberg, Alice. "Felipe Godínez' Queen Esther Play." *BCom.* 1983 Summer; 35(1): 47-49. Notes.

Spain. 1624. Critical studies. ■Theological content of Felipe Godínez's play *La Obra de la reina Esther (The Queen Esther Play),* may have been responsible for his Inquisition trial.

1241   Heiple, Daniel L. "Tirso's *Esto si que es negociar* and the Marriage Negotiations of 1623." *BCom.* 1982 Winter; 34(2): 189-199. Notes.

Spain. 1623. ■New information from original text of *Esto sí que es negociar (This Is Business)* establishes authorship, date of composition and chronology of for the play, as well as for *El Melancólico (The Melancholic).*

1242   Jones, Harold. "The First Edition of Antonio de Solís' *Triunfos de amor y Fortuna.*" *BCom.* 1982 Summer; 34(1): 117-121 . Notes. Biblio.

Spain. Vatican. 1658. Histories-sources. ■Additional notes and bibliographical descriptions of the Vatican edition of Antonio de Solís y Rivadeneyra's *Triunfos de amor y fortuna (Triumph of Love and Fortune).*

1243   Londré, Felicia Hardison. "Lorca in Metamorphosis: His Posthumous Plays." *TJ.* 1983 Mar.; 35(1): 102-108. Notes.

Spain. English-speaking countries. North America. 1930-1978. Critical studies. ■Transforming themes in Lorca's plays *El Publico (The Public)* and *Comedia sin titulo (Untitled Comedy)* teach a difference between theatre as a lie and reality as a truth.

1244   McGaha, Michael D. "Sobre La Fecha de Composition de *La Fábula de Perseo* de Lope." (On the Date of the Composition of *The Fable of Perseus* by Lope de Vega.) *BCom.* 1982 Winter; 34(2): 209-216. Notes. Biblio.

Spain. 1604-1635. Historical studies. ■Dating of Lope de Vega's *The Fable of Perseus.*

1245   Monleón, José. "Bergamín: Un dramaturgo sin Público." (Bergamín: A Playwright without a Public.) *PrAc.* 1983 Mar.-Apr.; 198: 41-47.

Spain. 1925-1980. Histories-sources. ■Interview with playwright José Bergamín.

1246   Penalva, Gonzalo. "José Bergamín y el lenguaje de la Máscara." (José Bergamín and the Language of Masks.) *PrAc.* 1983 Mar.-Apr.; 198: 33-40.

Spain. 1925-1980. Critical studies. ■Analysis of José Bergamín's plays.

1247   Pérez Stansfield, Maria Pilar. *Direcciones de Teatro Español de Posguerra.* (Trends of Spanish Postwar Theatre.) Madrid: José Porrúa Turanzas; 1983. 361 pp. Biblio.

Spain. 1939-1980. Critical studies. ■Study of playwrights, forms and styles in the Spanish theatre.

1248   Randel, Mary Gaylord. "The Order in the Court: Cervantes' *Entremés del Juez de los Divorcios.*" *BCom.* 1982 Summer; 34(1): 83-95. Notes.

Spain. 1547-1616. Critical studies. ■Discussion of *Entremés del Juez de los Divorcios (The Farce of the Divorce Judge)* in view of Aristotle's *mimesis.*

1249   Rogers, Elizabeth S. "Role Constraints Versus Self-Identity in *La tejedora de sueños* and *Anillos para una dama.*" *MD.* 1983 Sep.; 26(3): 310-319. Notes.

Spain. 1949. Critical studies. ■Conflict between position and desire in Antonio Buero Vallejo's *La Tejedora de sueños (The Knitter of Dreams)* and Antonio Gala's *Anillos para una dama (Rings for a Lady).*

1250   Ruano De la Haz, José M. "An Early Rehash of Lope's *Peribáñez.*" *BCom.* 1983 Summer; 35(1): 5-29. Notes.

Spain. 1607. Critical studies. ■Comparative analysis of miscellaneous adaptations of Lope de Vega's *Peribáñez* intended for less sophisticated rural audiences.The original is frequently censored and simplified.

1251   Rubia Barcia, José. *Mascarón de proa.* (Figurehead.) Sada (La Coruna): Edición Castro; 1983. 358 pp. Notes. Illus.: Pntg. Photo.

Spain. 1866-1936. Histories-specific. ■Work and life of the playwright and novelist Ramón María del Valle-Inclán.

1252   Sherr, Richard. "A Note on the Biography of Juan de la Encina." *BCom.* 1982 Winter; 34(2): 159-172. Biblio.

Spain. Vatican. 1469-1529. Histories-sources. ■Reprint and discussion of the new documents from the Vatican Archives, regarding Encina's political and ecclesiastical appointments.

1253   Sirera, Jóse Luis. "La Evolucion del Espectaculo Dramático en Los Autores Valencianos del XVI, Desde el Punto de Vista de la Técnica Teatral." (The Evolution of Dramatic Performances among Valencia Playwrights of the 16th Century: Discussion from the Perspective of Theatrical Technology.) *BCom.* 1982 Winter; 34(2): 173-187. Notes. Biblio.

Spain. 1500-1699. Historical studies. ■Studies conducted at University of Valencia on the forerunners and contemporaries of Lope de Vega and the staging and scenic practices of the period.

1254   Smyth, Philip. "*El Lacayo Fingido*: New Evidence Against Lope's Authorship." *BCom.* 1982 Summer; 34(1): 44-50. Notes.

Spain. 1609-1635. Critical studies. ■Examination of Lope de Vega's forty extant texts to determine authorship of *El lacayo fingido (The False Lackey).*

1255   Soufas, Teresa Scott. "Caldefon's Joyless Jester: The Humanization of a Stock Character." *BCom.* 1982 Winter; 34(2): 201-208. Notes.

Spain. 1626-1681. Critical studies. ■Calderón's departure from standardized character portrayals is best seen in the fool, or *gracioso.*

1256   Stern, Charlotte. "Lope de Vega, Propagandist?" *BCom.* 1982 Summer; 34(1): 1-36. Notes.

DRAMA: General—Plays/librettos/scripts

Spain. 1573-1635. Critical studies. ■Sociological approach to Lope de Vega points out shortcomings of Maravall-Diez Borque study of *comedia*. Questions degree of the playwright's compatibility with ideology of the period in promoting social change and the function of defining the literary genre.

1257 Zatlin-Boring, Phyllis. "Expressionism in the Contemporary Spanish Theatre." *MD*. 1983 Dec.; 26(4): 555-569. Notes.

Spain. 1920-1980. Critical studies. ■Expressionism in contemporary Spanish theatre: psychological depth in the development of character, vision of contemporary reality and innovative staging techniques. Grp/movt: Expressionism.

1258 Barba, Eugenio. *Les illes flotants.* (The Floating Islands.) Barcelona: Institut del Teatre; 1983. 256 pp. (Monografies de Teatre 12.) Append. Filmography. Biblio. Illus.: Design. Photo. 93: 13 cm. x 21 cm. [Catalan translation by Montserrat Ingla from French.]

Sweden. 1964-1979. Histories-sources. ■Collected materials on theory and development of Eugenio Barba's work at Odin Teatret, including letters, interviews, theoretical texts and plots of his plays.

1259 Bennett, Benjamin K. "Strindberg and Ibsen: Toward a Cubism of Time in Drama." *MD*. 1983 Sep.; 26(3): 262-281.

Sweden. Norway. 1828-1912. Critical studies. ■Comparison of the use of time in the works of Strindberg and Ibsen. Relates cubism in art (space) with cubism in drama (time). Grp/movt: Cubism.

1260 D'Agostini, Maria Pia. "*Teatro-verità:* Un dramma su August Strindberg di Per Olov Enquist." (*Theatre-Truth:* A Play about August Strindberg by Per Olov Enquist.) *TeatrC.* 1983 Feb.-May; 2(3): 295-313. Notes.

Sweden. 1974. Critical studies. ■Exposition of the plot of Enquist's *Tribadernasnatt (Theatre-Truth)* and critical notes on the play.

1261 Englund, Claes. "Dramatiken i sköra trådar." (Drama in Fragile Threads.) *Entre.* 1983; 10(1): 2-3.

Sweden. 1983. Historical studies. ■Complaints of Swedish dramatists that their works are not sufficiently produced or reviewed: lack of opportunities in television, function of dramaturgs and the responsibility of the press.

1262 Gillespie, Diane Filby. "Strindberg's *To Damascus:* Archetypal Autobiography." *MD*. 1983 Sep.; 26(3): 290-304. Notes.

Sweden. 1898. Critical studies. ■Analysis of Strindberg's To Damascus, an archetypal autobiography in which he draws attention to the elements in his personal life as fundamental patterns of human experience as a whole.

1263 Mellgren, Thomas. "Arne Andersson." *Entre.* 1983; 10(2): 10-15. Illus.: Photo. B&W. [In Swedish.]

Sweden. 1970-1983. Historical studies. ■Profile of Arne Andersson, who organized a play about a Norberg strike and thus started the trend of local history plays.

1264 Napieralski, Edmund A. "*Miss Julie:* Strindberg's Tragic Fairy Tale." *MD*. 1983 Sep.; 26(3): 282-289. Notes.

Sweden. 1870-1908. Critical studies. ■Fairy-tale elements in August Strindberg's *Miss Julie (Fröken Julie)* function as structural components to intensify the power of the play as tragedy.

1265 Ödeen, Mats. "Dumheter, Willmar Sauter!" (Stupidities, Willmar Sauter!)*Entre.* 1983; 10(1): 13.

Sweden. Historical studies. ■Debate between playwright/theorist Ödeen and historian Willmar Sauter on the issue of folk vs. literary theatre. Criticism of Brecht's epic theatre, Stanislavskij's emphasis on subtext and Willmar's scholarship.

1266 Sprinchorn, Evert. *Strindberg as Dramatist.* New Haven, CT: Yale UP; 1982. xi, 332 pp.

Sweden. 1849-1912. Critical studies. ■Argues that Strindberg's plays represent different phases of his ideological development.

1267 Steene, Birgitta. *August Strindberg.* Atlantic Highlands, NJ: Humanities P; 1982. ix, 178 pp.

Sweden. 1849-1912. Critical studies. ■Strindberg's life and works.

1268 Tornqvist, Egil. *Strindbergian Drama.* Atlantic Highlands, NJ: Humanities P; 1982. 259 pp.

Sweden. 1849-1912. Critical studies. ■Analysis of August Strindberg's plays.

1269 Tucker, Peter. "I hyacintrummet finns de unga: Om Strindberg och *Spöksonaten* för var tid." (In the Hyacinth Room Are the Young: On Strindberg and *The Ghost Sonata* for Our Time.) *Entre.* 1983; 10(1): 8-11. Illus.: Photo. B&W.

Sweden. 1907-1983. Critical studies. ■Interpretation of the 'spiritual socialism' and ecological ideals of Strindberg's *The Ghost Sonata* as a vision of the future for today's youth.

1270 Usselmann, Henri. "Strindberg et l'impressionisme." (Strindberg and Impressionism.) *GdBA.* 1982 Apr.; 99(4): 153-162. Notes.

Sweden. 1874-1884. Critical studies. ■Strindberg's attitude toward and use of impressionism. Focuses on art criticism published in *Dagens Nyheter*, and finds little effect beyond decor of *Fröken Julie (Miss Julie)*. Grp/movt: Impressionism.

1271 Kässens, Wend. "Montagsszenen aus einem Büro: Gerlind Reinshagens *Eisenherz* in Bochum und Zürich uraufgeführt." (Monday at the Office: Gerlind Reinshagen's *Ironheart* Produced in Bochum and Zurich.) *TH.* 1983; 1: 38-51.

Switzerland. Germany, West. 1983. Histories-sources. ■Interview with Gerlind Reinshagen and review of his play *Eisenherz.*

1272 Gibbs, A.M. *The Art and Mind of Shaw: Essays in Criticism.* New York: St. Martin's P; 1983. ix, 224 pp.

UK. 1856-1950. Critical studies. ■Criticism of George Bernard Shaw's plays from the standpoint of twentieth century critical methodology.

1273 Gilbert, Elliot L. "'Tumult of Images': Wilde, Beardsley and *Salome.*" *VS.* 1983 Winter; 26(2): 133-159. Notes. Illus.: Dwg. B&W. 6.

UK. 1894-1900. Critical studies. ■Coherence of playwright Oscar Wilde's and artist Aubrey Beardsley's work and revolutionary vision of their collaborative project.

1274 Hornby, Richard. "Beyond the Verbal in *Pygmalion.*" 122-127 in Leary, Daniel, ed. *Shaw's Plays in Performance.* University Park, and London: Pennsylvania State UP; 1983. vi, 262 pp. (SHAW: The Annual of Bernard Shaw Studies 3.) Notes.

UK. 1916. Critical studies. ■Semiology of setting, costume, properties. Metalinguistic and metatheatrical elements in *Pygmalion.*

1275 Knotts, Robert Marvin. *The Use of Epic Structure in Contemporary British Leftist Drama.* Columbus, OH: Ohio State Univ.; 1982. 605 pp. [Diss.: University Microfilms order no. DA8222114.]

UK. 1968-1981. Critical studies. ■Epic structure, as an alternative to traditional Aristotelian structure, used extensively in the twentieth century by leftist dramatists since Brecht. Infl. by Bertolt Brecht.

1276 McMillan, Joyce. "The Nerve and the Energy to Dream." *STN.* 1983 Feb.; 24: 9-13. Illus.: Sketches. B&W. 1.

UK. 1941-1983. Histories-sources. ■Interview with the playwright Stewart Parker and discussion of his life and works.

1277 Weintraub, Stanley. *The Unexpected Shaw: Biographical Approaches to G.B.S. and His Work.* New York: Frederick Ungar; 1982. 254 pp.

UK. 1856-1950. ■Essays on various aspects of George Bernard Shaw's life and work.

1278 Adler, Doris. "Thomas Dekker and Bibliography." *RORD.* 1983; 26: 3-12. Notes.

UK-England. 1808-1983. Bibliographical studies. ■Dekker materials offer an object study in methods of analytical bibliography.

1279 Almansi, Guido; Henderson, Simon. *Harold Pinter.* London, New York: Methuen; 1983. 111 pp.

UK-England. 1930-1983. Critical studies. ■Failing to find meaning in Pinter's plays, the authors concentrate on what they call 'language games'.

1280 Barrett, Daniel. "T.W. Robertson's Early Contempt for the Theatre: A Newly Discovered Letter." *THSt.* 1983; 3: 108-110.

UK-England. 1862. Historical studies. ■Description of a significant letter by playwright T.W. Robertson in the Stanford University Library.

DRAMA: General—Plays/librettos/scripts

1281 Berst, Charles. "The Action of Shaw's Settings and Props." 41-65 in Leary, Daniel, ed. *Shaw's Plays in Performance.* University Park PA, and London: Pennsylvania State UP; 1983. vi, 262 pp. (SHAW: The Annual of Bernard Shaw Studies 3.) Notes.
UK-England. 1894-1907. Critical studies. ■Props and settings function in relation to action and meaning: *Arms and the Man, Candida, Caesar and Cleopatra* and *Man and Superman.*

1282 Brown, Barbara. "Bernard Shaw's 'Unreasonable Man'." *MD.* 1983 Mar.; 26(1): 75-84. Notes.
UK-England. 1885-1950. Critical studies. ■Study of the qualities which distinguish and define Bernard Shaw's 'Unreasonable Man' and the effects such men have on society.

1283 Charles, Timothy. "Willy Russell — The First Ten Years." *Drama.* 1983 Summer; 148: 20-21. Illus.: Photo. B&W. 1: 3 in. x 4 in.
UK-England. 1970-1983. Critical studies. ■Review of plays with discussion of playwright's social and political commitment.

1284 Dukore, Bernard F. "The Director As Interpreter: Shaw's *Pygmalion.*" 129-147 in Leary, Daniel. *Shaw's Plays in Performance.* University Park, PA and London: Pennsylvania State UP; 1983. vi, 262 pp. (Shaw: The Annual of Bernard Shaw Studies 3.) Notes.
UK-England. 1914. Critical studies. ■Bernard Shaw's rehearsal notes for staging *Pygmalion* discuss production details later incorporated in printed versions of the play.

1285 Edwards, Philip. "Tragic Balance in *Hamlet.*" *ShS.* 1983; 36: 43-52. Notes.
UK-England. USA. 1864-1983. Critical studies. ■20th century criticism of *Hamlet* upsets the balance between the Apollonian and Dionysian elements of the play.

1286 Eichbaum, Julius. "Ronald Harwood: Divine Sarah." *Scenaria.* 1983 Jan. 28; 35: 18-19. Illus.
UK-England. 1983. Histories-sources. ■Ronald Harwood discusses two of his plays: *The Dresser* and *After the Lions,* based on the life of Sarah Bernhardt.

1287 Everding, Robert G. "Fusion of Character and Setting: Artistic Strategy in *Major Barbara.*" 103-116 in Leary, Daniel. *Shaw's Plays in Performance.* University Park: Pennsylvania State UP; 1983. vi, 262 pp. (SHAW: The Annual of Bernard Shaw Studies 3.) Notes.
UK-England. 1907. Critical studies. ■Use of characterization and setting to challenge audiences' conventional views and convert them to a readiness to accept new ideas.

1288 Forsas-Scott, Helena. "Life and Love and *Serjeant Musgrave*: An Approach to Arden's Play." *MD.* 1983 Mar.; 26(1): 1-11. Notes.
UK-England. 1959. Critical studies. ■Investigates the action of John Arden's *Serjeant Musgrave's Dance* and demonstrates how Arden uses a given plot structure as a means of making a statement in artistic terms.

1289 Gale, Steven H. "The Significance of Orson Welles in Harold Pinter's *Old Times.*" *NConL.* 1983 Mar.; 13(2): 11-12.
UK-England. USA. 1942-1971. Critical studies. ■Deeley's calling himself Orson Welles in *Old Times* suggests that no statements in the play are to be taken at face value and relates to the theme of recreating the past by recalling the film *The Magnificent Ambersons.* Related to Media: Film.

1290 Gianakaris, C.J. "Shaffer's Revision in *Amadeus.*" *TJ.* 1983 Mar.; 35(1): 88-101. Notes.
UK-England. USA. 1979-1980. Critical studies. ■Circumstances under which Peter Shaffer revised *Amadeus* and concentrated on Salieri's motivations as a surrogate father to Mozart.

1291 Goldstone, Herbert. *Coping with Vulnerability: The Achievement of John Osborne.* Lanham, MD: UP of America; 1982. vii, 265 pp.
UK-England. 1929-1982. Critical studies. ■Analysis of plays by John Osborne.

1292 Hauger, George. "Ghelderode en Grande-Bretagne — Hélas!" (Ghelderode in Great Britain — Alas!)85-89 in Trousson, Raymond. *Michel de Ghelderode dramaturge et conteur.* Brussels: Editions de l'Université de Bruxelles; 1983. 175 pp.
UK-England. Belgium. 1957-1982. Critical studies. ■Lack of familiarity in Britain with the work of Michel de Ghelderode.

1293 Hubert, Judd. "Upstaging in *The Devil's Disciple.*" *TJ.* 1983 Mar.; 35(1): 51-57. Notes.
UK-England. USA. 1897-1983. Critical studies. ■Mrs. Dudgeon, Richard and Judith upstage the other characters and thus reveal melodramatic and comedic elements in G.B. Shaw's *The Devil's Disciple.*

1294 Hunter, Jim. *Tom Stoppard's Plays.* New York: Grove P; 1982. viii, 250 pp.
UK-England. 1937-1982. Critical studies.

1295 Jackson, Russell. "Horrible Flesh and Blood — A Rejoinder." *TN.* 1983; 37(1): 29-31.
UK-England. 1880-1900. Textual studies. ■Oscar Wilde's stage directions in various editions of *An Ideal Husband* and other plays.

1296 Jarvis, Janice; Chamberlain, Roger. "Acting in Theatre in Education — A Discussion between Janice Jarvis and Roger Chamberlain." *SCYPT.* 1983 Sep.; 11: 14-25. Illus.: Photo. B&W. 2.
UK-England. 1970-1983. Instructional materials. ■Director and actor/teacher discuss ways of working and approaches to scripts and characters including feelings, characterisation, improvisation and audience participation (young people).

1297 Jones, Mervyn. "Peter Nichols, the Playwright Who Has Had Enough." *Drama.* 1983 Summer; 148: 7-8. Illus.: Photo. B&W. 1: 2 in. x 2 in.
UK-England. 1967-1983. Histories-sources. ■Peter Nichols, after fifteen successful years in the theatre, has decided to give up writing plays. Analysis of his work and reasons for doing so.

1298 Lahr, John. *Coward: The Playwright.* London, New York: Methuen; 1983. 178 pp.
UK-England. 1899-1973. Critical studies.

1299 Lambert, J.W. "Peter Terson, a Mighty Reservoir for Boys and Girls." *Drama.* 1983 Spring; 147: 11-13.
UK-England. 1960-1983. Historical studies. ■Review of Terson's work in British theatre, especially his association with the National Youth Theatre.

1300 Larson, Janet L. "*The Elephant Man* as Dramatic Parable." *MD.* 1983 Sep.; 26(3): 335-356. Notes.
UK-England. 1978. Critical studies. ■Study of Bernard Pomerance's dramatic parable, *The Elephant Man*: its broad thematic range and construction.

1301 Leary, Daniel. "From Page to Stage to Audience in Shaw." 1-23 in Leary, Daniel, ed. *Shaw's Plays in Performance.* University Park, and London: Pennsylvania State UP; 1983. vi, 262 pp. (SHAW: The Annual of Bernard Shaw Studies 3.) Notes.
UK-England. 1914. Critical studies. ■*Pygmalion* demonstrates use of universal myths and realism to encourage audience to break from settled beliefs.

1302 Levenson, Jill L. "*Hamlet* Andante/*Hamlet* Allegro: Tom Stoppard's Two Versions." *ShS.* 1983; 36: 21-28.
UK-England. 1963-1979. Critical studies. ■Influence of Shakespeare's *Hamlet,* Beckett's *Waiting for Godot* and Wittgenstein's *Investigations* on Stoppard's *Rosencrantz and Guildenstern Are Dead, Dogg's Hamlet* and *Cahoot's Macbeth.*

1303 Malani, Hiran K.S. *D.H. Lawrence: A Study of His Plays.* Atlantic Highlands, NJ: Humanities P; 1982. 181 pp.
UK-England. 1885-1930. Critical studies. ■D.H. Lawrence as dramatist.

1304 Myerson, Jonathan. "David Hare: Fringe Graduate." *Drama.* 1983 Autumn; 149: 26-28. Illus.: Photo. B&W. 1: 2 in. x 3 in.
UK-England. 1947-1983. Critical studies. ■Hare's interest in Fringe theatre, his work as writer and director and his interest in film and television. Related to Media.

DRAMA: General—Plays/librettos/scripts

1305 Nath, Suresh. *D.H. Lawrence the Dramatist.* Atlantic Highlands, NJ: Humanities P; 1982. ix, 183 pp.
UK-England. 1885-1930. Critical studies. ■Analysis of the novelist's eight plays.

1306 Page, Malcolm. "The Serious Side of Alan Ayckbourn." *MD.* 1983 Mar.; 26(1): 36-46. Notes.
UK-England. 1970-1979. Critical studies. ■Analysis of the depth and seriousness of some of Alan Ayckbourn's plays, particularly those between 1974 and 1978, often obscured by his early comedies.

1307 Potter, Rosanne G. "The Rhetoric of a Shavian Exposition: Act I of *Major Barbara.*" *MD.* 1983 Mar.; 26(1): 62-74. Notes.
UK-England. 1907. Critical studies. ■Examination of the first act of George Bernard Shaw's *Major Barbara* shows how his representation of the expository facts controls the audience's reaction to characters and plot.

1308 Roberts, Philip. "Edward Bond's *Summer:* 'A Voice from the Working Class'." *MD.* 1983 June; 26(2): 127-138. Notes.
UK-England. 1980-1983. Critical studies. ■Examination of the evolution of Edward Bond's *Summer,* showing why and how the play took final shape as it did.

1309 Rod, David K. "Carr's Views on Art and Politics in Tom Stoppard's *Travesties.*" *MD.* 1983 Dec.; 26(4): 536-542. Notes.
UK-England. 1974. Critical studies. ■Examination of the scenes in which the views of Henry Carr are in conflict with those of Tzara, Joyce and Lenin revealing both Carr's centrality to the aesthetic-political debate and a clearer picture of the position he espouses.

1310 Rump, Eric. "London: Politics on the Upswing." *CTR.* 1983 Fall; 38: 123-127. Illus.: Photo. Neg. B&W. 2: 6 in. x 4 in.
UK-England. 1983. Reviews of performances. ■Examination of political London-based plays: *Trafford Tanzi, Another Country* and *The Real Thing.*

1311 Ruskin, Phyllis; Lutterbie, John H. "Balancing the Equation." *MD.* 1983 Dec.; 26(4): 543-554. Notes.
UK-England. 1967-1983. Critical studies. ■Analysis of Tom Stoppard's plays in which he integrates three primary factors: theatricality, pragmatism and abstract concepts.

1312 Shewan, Rodney. "Oscar Wilde and *A Wife's Tragedy:* Facts and Conjectures." *ThR.* 1983 Summer; 8(2): 83-94. Notes.
UK-England. 1882-1900. Historical studies. ■Based on literary and biographical evidence, Oscar Wilde's *A Wife's Tragedy* is dated prior to *Lady Windermere's Fan.*

1313 Stedman, Jane W. "The Victorian After-Image of Samuel Johnson." *NCTR.* 1983 Summer; 11(1): 13-27. Notes.
UK-England. 1862-1893. Critical studies. ■Examination of Johnson as a character and the influence of his point of view in William Brough's *Rasselas, Prince of Abyssinia* and in W.S. Gilbert's *Utopia Unlimited.* Grp/movt: Victorian theatre.

1314 Tyson, Brian. *The Story of Shaw's Saint Joan.* Toronto: McGill-Queen's UP; 1982. viii, 142 pp.
UK-England. 1923. Historical studies. ■Composition and production of George Bernard Shaw's *Saint Joan.*

1315 Whitman, Robert F. "Shaw Listens to the Actors: The Completion of *The Devil's Disciple.*" 67-78 pp in Leary, Daniel. *Shaw's Plays in Performance.* University Park: Pennsylvania State UP; 1983. vi, 262 pp. (SHAW: The Annual of Bernard Shaw Studies 3.) Notes.
UK-England. 1897. Historical studies. ■Shaw's difficulty with finding satisfactory theatrical endings illustrated through manuscript revisions, some evidently based on suggestions from actors in the original production of *The Devil's Disciple.*

1316 Young, B.A. "The Plays of Christopher Hampton." *Drama.* 1983 Winter; 150: 21-23. Illus.: Photo. B&W. 2: 2 in. x 3 in., 3 in. x 6 in.
UK-England. 1900-1983. Critical studies. ■Critical account of Christopher Hampton's work.

1317 Zeifman, Hersh. "Comedy of Ambush: Tom Stoppard's *The Real Thing.*" *MD.* 1983 June; 26(2): 139-149. Notes.
UK-England. 1982. Critical studies. ■Analysis of Tom Stoppard's *The Real Thing,* which contrasts the artificial and the real, specifically in relation to the theme of love.

1318 Benstock, Bernard. "Sean O'Casey's Little Cloud." *OCA.* 1982; 1: 64-72.
UK-Ireland. 1923-1946. Critical studies. ■Role of poetry in O'Casey's plays, especially as influenced by Percy Bysshe Shelley.

1319 Callan, Patrick. "The Political War Ballads of Sean O'Casey, 1916-1918." *IUR.* 1983 Autumn; 13(2): 68-179. Notes.
UK-Ireland. 1916-1918. Critical studies. ■O'Casey's anti-war stance in his ballads critical and the growth of Irish cynicism toward the war in the wake of post-1916 nationalism. Background of O'Casey's dramatic themes.

1320 Daniels, William. "Thoreau and Synge: The Cape and the Islands." *Éire.* 1983 Winter; 18(4): 57-71. Notes.
UK-Ireland. USA. 1898-1907. Critical studies. ■Compares and contrasts Irish playwright John Millington Synge's writings about the remote Aran Islands with philosopher and essayist Henry David Thoreau's writings about Cape Cod, Massachusetts.

1321 Doherty, Francis. "*Krapp's Last Tape:* The Artistry of the Last." *IUR.* 1982 Autumn; 12(2): 191-204. Notes.
UK-Ireland. 1957. Critical studies. ■Samuel Beckett's *Krapp's Last Tape* as a parody of performance as well as a parody of themes in Samuel Johnson and Percy Bysshe Shelley.

1322 Foster, John Wilson. "Yeats and the Folklore of the Irish Revival." *Éire.* 1982 Summer; 17(2): 6-18. Notes.
UK-Ireland. 1888-1920. Critical studies. ■Focusing on Yeats and Lady Gregory, an assessment of the role of folklore in Irish Literary Revival works and centers on authenticity and impact on theme and structure. Grp/movt: Irish Literary Revival.

1323 Gontarski, S.E. "The Anatomy of Beckett's *Eh Joe.*" *MD.* 1983 Dec.; 26(4): 425-434. Notes.
UK-Ireland. France. 1958. Textual studies. ■Analysis of Samuel Beckett's *Eh Joe* from the earliest typescript to rewriting as *Ghost Trio* and comparison with *Krapp's Last Tape* and *Film.*

1324 Grene, Nicholas, ed.; Saddlemyer, Ann, ed. "Stephen McKenna on Synge: A Lost Memoir." *IUR.* 1982 Autumn; 12(2): 141-151. Notes.
UK-Ireland. France. 1895-1902. Historical studies. ■Publication of the memoirs of Irish journalist Stephen McKenna regarding the apprentice days of playwright John Millington Synge in Paris.

1325 Hamburger, Mark. "Anti-Illusionism and the Use of Song in the Early Plays of Sean O'Casey." *OCA.* 1983; 2: 3-26.
UK-Ireland. 1923-1926. Critical studies. ■Role of song in O'Casey's early plays to overcome the boundaries of illusionist drama.

1326 Hirsch, Edward. "The Gallous Story and the Dirty Deed: The Two *Playboys.*" *MD.* 1983 Mar.; 26(1): 85-102. Notes.
UK-Ireland. 1907. Critical studies. ■Representational and modernist comedic aspects of J.M. Synge's *The Playboy of the Western World.*

1327 Knowland, A.S. *W.B. Yeats, Dramatist of Vision.* Totowa, NJ: Barnes & Noble; 1983. 272 pp.
UK-Ireland. 1865-1939. Critical studies.

1328 Kosok, Heinz. "The Three Versions of *Red Roses for Me.*" *OCA.* 1982; 1: 141-147. Notes.
UK-Ireland. 1942-1956. Historical studies. ■Changes made in the three different versions of the play by Sean O'Casey.

1329 Lawley, Paul. "Counterpoint, Absence and the Medium in Beckett's *Not I.*" *MD.* 1983 Dec.; 26(4): 407-414. Notes.
UK-Ireland. France. 1971. Critical studies. ■Study of Beckett's *Not I,* demonstrates that a part of a human body yields more dramatic interest than the whole body ordinarily does.

1330 Lowery, Robert G. *Sean O'Casey's Autobiographies: An Annotated Index.* Westport, CT: Greenwood P; 1983. xxxi, 487 pp.

DRAMA: General—Plays/librettos/scripts

UK-Ireland. 1880-1964. Biographical studies. ▪Includes information on theatres and personalities of the period, especially those involved with production and film adaptation of O'Casey's plays.

1331 Maroldo, William J. "Insurrection as Enthymeme in O'Casey's Dublin Trilogy." *OCA*. 1983; 2: 88-113. Notes.
UK-Ireland. 1923-1926. Critical studies. ▪Analysis of themes in Sean O'Casey's three Dublin plays.

1332 O'Valle, Violet. "Bird Imagery and Bird Lore Motifs in *The Shadow of a Gunman*." *OCA*. 1983; 2: 114-148. Notes.
UK-Ireland. 1923. Critical studies. ▪Influence of Shakespeare and Shelley on bird lore in Sean O'Casey's play.

1333 O'Valle, Violet M. "Melville, O'Casey, and *Cock-a-Doodle Dandy*." *OCA*. 1982; 1: 167-179. Notes.
UK-Ireland. USA. 1949. Critical studies. ▪American influence of Melville's short story *Cock-A-Doodle Doo!* on O'Casey's play.

1334 Putzel, Steven D. "The Black Pig: Yeats's Early Apocalyptic Beast." *Éire*. 1982 Fall; 17(3): 86-102. Notes.
UK-Ireland. 1880-1910. Historical studies. ▪Irish folkloric, general anthropological and psychological connnections of the 'black pig' image which William Butler Yeats fashioned into a primary symbol of the apocalypse in his poetry and drama.

1335 Simone, R. Thomas. "'Faint, though by no means invisible': A Commentary on Beckett's *Footfalls*." *MD*. 1983 Dec.; 26(4) : 435-446. Notes.
UK-Ireland. France. 1957. Critical studies. ▪Analysis of the sources of power in Samuel Beckett's *Footfalls* and its significance in his career.

1336 Smith, Peter Alderson. "*The Countess Cathleen* and the Otherworld." *Éire*. 1982 Summer; 17(2): 141-146. Notes.
UK-Ireland. 1890. Critical studies. ▪Imagery in William Butler Yeat's *The Countess Cathleen* related to the traditional Gaelic concept of fairies and fairyland.

1337 Steinman, Michael A. "Yeats's Parnell: Sources of His Myth." *Éire*. 1983 Spring; 18(1): 46-60. Notes.
UK-Ireland. 1891-1936. Critical studies. ▪William Butler Yeats's reading of and about Anglo-Irish patriot Charles Stewart Parnell and the effect on his writing, notably *On Baile's Strand*. Contrasts this work with Lady Gregory's *The Deliverer*, Lennox Robinson's *The Lost Leader* and W.R. Fearon's *Parnell of Avondale*.

1338 Watt, Stephen M. "Boucicault and Whitbread: The Dublin Stage at the End of the Nineteenth Century." *Éire*. 1983 Fall; 18(3): 23-53. Notes.
UK-Ireland. 1860-1905. Critical studies. ▪Interpretation of Irish comic melodrama, exemplified by Dion Boucicault's plays, and historical melodrama, exemplified by J.W. Whitbread's dramas, in light of late 19th century historical and political developments. Suggests influence on Sean O'Casey and George Bernard Shaw.

1339 Lannon, Tom. "Child of the Dead End, or – How I Became a Playwright." *STN*. 1983 Mar.; 25: 20-22. Illus.: Photo. B&W. 1.
UK-Scotland. 1983. Histories-sources. ▪Tom Lannon discusses background of his play *Children of the Dead End*.

1340 MacKenney, Linda. "Legends." *STN*. 1983 Jan.; 23: 16-20. Illus.: Photo. B&W. 1.
UK-Scotland. 1894-1968. Biographical studies. ▪Discussion of the life and works of Joe Corrie.

1341 McMillan, Joyce. "Stanley Eveling: Joyce McMillan Talks to the Playwright Stanley Eveling, Author of *The Bugler Boy*." *STN*. 1983 Sep.; 31: 19-23. Illus.: Photo. B&W. 1.
UK-Scotland. 1930-1983. Histories-sources. ▪Biographical interview with Stanley Eveling which also discusses his career in philosophy and its effects on his playwriting.

1342 "Tennessee Williams: 'Wenn ich von meinen Dämonen loskäme, würde ich auch meine Engel, alle guten Geister, verlieren'." (Tennessee Williams: 'Getting Rid of My Demons Would Be Losing My Angels, All Good Spirits, Too'.) *TH*. 1983; 4: 1-3. Illus.: Photo.
USA. 1911-1983. Histories-sources. ▪Brief comments on Tennessee Williams by Marlon Brando, Arthur Miller, Douglas Sirk, Rolf Boysen, Marianne Hoppe, Adolf Dresen, Werner Düggelin and Grete Mosheim.

1343 Anderman, Gunilla. "*True West*: Sam Shepards syn på Amerika." (*True West*: Sam Shepard's View of America.) *Entre*. 1983; 10(6): 20-24.
USA. 1943-1983. Critical studies. ▪Themes of Sam Shepard's plays, including the myth of the Old West in modern culture, the world of jazz and rock music and the dissolution of family life.

1344 Anon. "Tennessee Williams Leaves a Playwright's Legacy to Texas Theatre Scholars." *ThNe*. 1983 Mar.; 15(3): 15.
USA. 1962-1971. Histories-sources. ▪Extensive collection of materials relating to Tennessee Williams left to Humanities Research Center at the University of Texas at Austin, including manuscripts for most of his major works, screenplays, short stories, essays, letters and programs.

1345 Arkatov, Janice. "If You Liked the Play..." *PArts*. 1983 Mar.; 17(3): 6. Illus.: Photo.
USA. 1974. Critical studies. ▪Problems and failures in adapting plays to movies: *Equus, When You Coming Back, Red Ryder?, On Golden Pond, Children of a Lesser God* and *Amadeus*. Related to Media: Film.

1346 Bank, Rosemarie K. "Theatre and Narrative Fiction in the Work of the Nineteenth-Century American Playwright Louisa Medina." *THSt*. 1983; 3: 55-67. Notes. Tables. Illus.: Dwg. B&W. 3.
USA. 1833-1838. Critical studies. ▪Study of Louisa Medina's popular dramatic adaptations of Edward Bulwer-Lytton's *Last Days of Pompeii* and Ernest Maltravers and Robert Montgomery Bird's *Nick of the Woods*.

1347 Ben-Zvi, Linda. "Eugene O'Neill and Film." *EON*. 1983; 7(1): 3-10. Notes.
USA. 1916. Critical studies. ▪O'Neill's plays that have been made into films, with special emphasis on *The Emperor Jones* and *Before Breakfast*. Related to Media: Film.

1348 Bentley, Eric. "The Brecht Memoir." *ThM*. 1983 Spring; 14(2): 4-26. Pref. Notes. Illus.: Photo. 11.
USA. Germany, East. 1942-1956. Histories-sources. ▪From Bentley's first meeting with Brecht in Santa Monica, California in 1942, to his last in Berlin in 1956, a view of the German dramatist.

1349 Berlin, Normand. *Eugene O'Neill*. New York: Grove P; 1982. xii, 178 pp.
USA. 1888-1953. Critical studies. ▪Eugene O'Neill's life and work.

1350 Ceynowa, Andrzej. "The Dramatic Structure of *Dutchman*." *BALF*. 1983 Spring; 17: 15-18. Illus.: Handbill.
USA. 1964. Critical studies. ▪Close examination of the play *The Dutchman* by Imamu Amiri Baraka, showing its similarities to *Zoo Story* by Edward Albee and refuting popular interpretation of the play's racial roles.

1351 Clark, Annabel B. "The Image of Old Age As Reflected on the Current American Stage." *ChTR*. 1983 July; 32(3): 7-11. Notes. Biblio. Tables.
USA. 1980. Historical studies. ▪Older adults in the recent New York productions are no longer stereotyped as negative characters.

1352 Cless, Downing. "Alienation and Contradiction in *Camino Real*: A Convergence of Williams and Brecht." *TJ*. 1983 Mar.; 35(1): 41-50. Notes.
USA. Germany, East. 1941-1953. Critical studies. ▪Brecht's theory of alienation is related to irony and contradiction of the characters and situations in Tennesse Williams' *Camino Real*.

1353 Cohen, Sarah Blacher. *From Hester Street to Hollywood: The Jewish-American Stage and Screen*. Bloomington, IN: Indiana UP; 1983. viii, 278 pp.
USA. 1900-1983. Historical studies. ▪Essays on Jewish-American performers and writers including Woody Allen, Saul Bellow, Mel Brooks, Paddy Chayefsky, Lillian Hellman, Arthur Miller, Clifford Odets, Elmer Rice, I.B. Singer and Neil Simon, as well as Yiddish theatre.

1354 Debusscher, Gilbert. "'Minting their Separate Wills': Tennessee Williams and Hart Crane." *MD*. 1983 Dec.; 26(4): 455-476. Notes.
USA. 1938-1980. Critical studies. ▪Evidence analysis of the influences of Hart Crane in the works of Tennessee Williams: *The Glass Menagerie, Suddenly Last Summer* and *Steps Must Be Gentle: A Dramatic Reading for Two Performers*.

DRAMA: General—Plays/librettos/scripts

1355 Fark, William E. "Greasepaint Politics." *PArts.* 1982 Oct.; 16(10): 26. Illus.: Photo.
USA. 1900-1982. Historical studies. ■Survey of the political play in America.

1356 Fink, Guido. "'La porta non è mai chiusa': Broadway e la seconda guerra mondiale." ('The Front Door Is Never Closed': Broadway and World War II.) *QT.* 1983 Feb.; 5(19): 101-110. Notes.
USA. 1936-1943. Critical studies. ■Treatment of the theme of war in American drama.

1357 Soon 3. "Manifesto." *TDR.* 1983; 27(4): 40-42. Illus.: Diagram.
USA. 1983. Instructional materials. ■Conceptual statement on how to write a play.

1358 Gordon, Alvin J. "Meeting Eugene O'Neill." *EON.* 1983; 7(1): 14-15.
USA. 1937. Histories-sources. ■Author's meeting with O'Neill at the dramatist's home.

1359 Greenbaum, Everett. "A Day in the Life of George S. Kaufman." *PArts.* 1982 Apr.; 16(4): 58. Illus.: Photo.
USA. 1922-1961. Biographical studies. ■Writer Greenbaum tells of his first meeting with George S. Kaufman.

1360 Grimm, Reinhold. "A Note on O'Neill, Nietzsche, and Naturalism: *Long Day's Journey into Night* in European Perspective." *MD.* 1983 Sep.; 26(3): 331-334. Notes.
USA. 1940. Critical studies. ■Eugene O'Neill's *Long Day's Journey into Night* constitutes a unique combination of acceptance, rejection and reevaluation of Nietzsche and Naturalism. Grp/movt: Naturalism.

1361 Hay, Peter. "American Dramaturgy: A Critical Re-Appraisal." *PerAJ.* 1983; 7(3): 7-24. Notes.
USA. 1983. Critical studies. ■Assessment of dramaturgy as practiced in English-speaking theatre.

1362 Kanellos, Nicolás, ed. *Mexican American Theatre: Then and Now.* Houston: Arte Público P; 1983. 120 pp.
USA. Mexico. 1983. Historical studies. ■Collection of vaudeville sketches in Spanish, historical and theatrical articles in English and Spanish and interviews in English. Related to Popular Entertainment.

1363 Kramer, Aaron. "Remembering Owen Dodson." *Fds.* 1983; 23(4): 258-268.
USA. 1983. Biographical studies. ■Tribute to playwright Owen Dodson.

1364 Lai, Sheng-chuan. "Mysticism and Noh in O'Neill." *TJ.* 1983 Mar.; 35(1): 74-87. Notes.
USA. Japan. 1915-1956. Critical studies. ■Sheng-chuan Lai traces O'Neill's mysticism to his possession of the book *Light on the Path* by Mabel Collins and shows how the mysticism of his earlier plays is transcended in his last four. Related to Dance-Drama.

1365 Levett, Karl. "A.R. Gurney, Jr.: American Original." *Drama.* 1983 Autumn; 149: 6-7. Illus.: Photo. B&W. 1: 3 in. x 4 in.
USA. 1983. Critical studies. ■World-wide response to upper middle class New England drama.

1366 Londré, Felicia Hardison. *Tennessee Williams.* New York: Frederick Ungar; 1983. vi, 213 pp.
USA. 1914-1983. Critical studies. ■Life and works of Tennessee Williams.

1367 Loney, Glenn. "Tennessee Williams: The Catastrophe of Success." *PerAJ.* 1983; 7(2): 73-87. Illus.: Photo. B&W. 4: 4 in. x 6 in., 2 in. x 3 in.
USA. 1965-1983. Critical studies. ■Assessment of the apparent artistic decline in Tennessee Williams' later writings.

1368 Marranca, Bonnie; Dasgupta, Gautam. "The Drama in American Letters." *PerAJ.* 1983; 7(1): 4-6. [Editorial.]
USA. 1900-1983. Critical studies. ■Plea to have plays considered as literature and thus be treated with seriousness by institutions such as colleges, newspapers and periodicals.

1369 McCaslin, Nellie. "'Over the Hill' to the Playhouse: Children's Theatre Must Take a New Look at Old Age." *ThNe.* 1983 Nov.; 15(8): 1, 10.

USA. 1983. Critical studies. ■Stereotypes of old age in children's drama, and some examples that break it.

1370 Motley, Warren. "Hamlin Garland's *Under the Wheel*: Regionalism Unmasking America." *MD.* 1983 Dec.; 26(4): 477-485. Notes.
USA. 1890. Critical studies. ■Study of Hamlin Garland's regional social drama, *Under the Wheel*, in which he challenges the audience's vision of American society, and contributes to realism in drama.

1371 Murphy, Brenda. "O'Neill's Realism: A Structural Approach." *EON.* 1983; 7(2): 3-6. Notes.
USA. 1940-1949. Critical studies. ■Realistic structure of *The Iceman Cometh* is used by O'Neill to deflate dramatic tension. Each of the four acts focuses on conflict, only to have that tension dispelled by Hickey's confessions. Grp/movt: Realism.

1372 Murray, Timothy. "Patriarchal Panopticism, or the Seduction of a Bad Joke: *Getting Out* in Theory." *TJ.* 1983 Oct.; 35(3): 376-388. Notes.
USA. 1981. Critical studies. ■Sociology of the main character and her relationship to the audience. Grp/movt: Absurdism.

1373 Nash, Thomas. "Sam Shepard's *Buried Child*: The Ironic Use of Folklore." *MD.* 1983 Dec.; 26(4): 486-491. Notes.
USA. 1978. Critical studies. ■Study of the ironic use of folklore — the death and rebirth of the Corn King — in Sam Shepard's *Buried Child*.

1374 O'Brien, Susan. "The Image of Woman in Tony-Award-Winning Plays, 1960-1979." *JAC.* 1983 Fall; 6(3): 45-49. Notes.
USA. UK-England. 1960-1979. Critical studies. ■Tennessee Williams' *The Night of the Iguana*, Lillian Hellman's *Toys in the Attic* and Harold Pinter's *The Homecoming* are the only three Tony-Award-winning plays that reflect the striving of women for liberation. Grp/movt: Feminism.

1375 Richards, Sandra L. "Negative Forces and Positive Non-Entities: Images of Women in the Dramas of Amiri Baraka." *TJ.* 1982 May; 34(2): 233-240. Notes.
USA. 1964-1978. Critical studies. ■Examination of two principal female archetypes of Baraka's drama: evil white women and neurotic, self-destructive Black women. By moderating a positive Black woman, Baraka creates a sexless character.

1376 Riley, Clayton. "To Liberate Black Actors." *Fds.* 1983 Fourth Quarter; 23(4): 236-239.
USA. 1980. Critical studies. ■Implications of Black and non-Black theatre segregation, noting that Black playwrights are expected to write about Black life.

1377 Robinson, James. *Eugene O'Neill and Oriental Thought: A Divided Vision.* Carbondale, IL: Southern Illinois UP; 1982. 201 pp.
USA. 1888-1953. Critical studies. ■Role of Oriental philosophy in O'Neill's work: tension between Orientalism and Catholicism.

1378 Schäfer, Jürgen. *Geschichte des amerikanischen Dramas im 20. Jahrhundert.* (History of American Drama in the Twentieth Century.) Stuttgart: Verlag W. Kohlhammer; 1982. 206 pp.
USA. 1900-1982. Histories-general.

1379 Schlueter, June; Forsyth, Elizabeth. "America as Junkshop: The Business Ethic in David Mamet's *American Buffalo*." *MD.* 1983 Dec.; 26(4): 492-500. Notes.
USA. 1977. Critical studies. ■Study of David Mamet's *American Buffalo* in which the junkshop is the image for an America in which the business ethic with its values of power and greed has replaced traditional human values.

1380 Schuttler, Georg W. "William Gillette: Marathon Actor and Playwright." *JPC.* 1983 Winter; 17(3): 115-129. Notes.
USA. 1873-1936. Biographical studies. ■Sixty-three year career of William Gillette as actor and playwright.

1381 Scudder, Janice Pryor. *The Dramatic Potential in the Adaptations of the Short Stories of Flannery O'Connor for Readers Theatre: A Case Study.* Kent, OH: Kent State Univ.; 1982. 179 pp. [Diss.: University Microfilms order no. DA8216953.]

DRAMA: General—Plays/librettos/scripts

USA. 1982. Critical studies. ■Characterization and themes make Flannery O'Connor's stories appropriate to readers theatre.

1382 Sheaffer, Louis. "Correcting Some Errors in Annals of O'Neill." *EON.* 1983; 7(3): 13-25. Notes. [Part I. Article also published in *CompD,* 17 (Fall 1983), 201-232.]
USA. 1888-1953. Biographical studies. ■Well-known O'Neill critic points out errors in O'Neill biographies by such writers as Doris Alexander, Barrett Clark and Arthur and Barbara Gelb.

1383 Sipple, William L. "From Stage to Screen: *The Long Voyage Home* and *Long Day's Journey into Night.*" *EON.* 1983; 7(1): 10-14. Notes.
USA. 1940-1962. Critical studies. ■John Ford's *The Long Voyage Home* (1940) and Sidney Lumet's *Long Day's Journey into Night* (1962) effectively transfer O'Neill's plays to the screen. Article argues that film can convey essence and spirit of original stage drama. Related to Media: Film.

1384 Swortzell, Lowell. "The Young Playwrights Festival — 1982." *ChTR.* 1983 Feb.; 32(1): 25-26. Illus.: Photo.
USA. 1982. Historical studies. ■Plays and productions offered at the Young Playwrights Festival of 1982 sponsored by the Dramatists Guild.

1385 Terruso, Gene; Fjelde, Rolf. "Lee Strasberg on Ibsen and *Peer Gynt.*" *INC.* 1982; 3: 6-9. [Interview held October 13, 1981.]
USA. 1906-1982. Critical studies. ■Interview with Lee Strasberg of the Actors' Studio.

1386 Weiss, William. "Drama Views: Hypernaturalism, The Theatre of the 70's." *CDr.* 1983 Fall; 9(2): 507-511.
USA. Europe. 1970-1983. Critical studies. ■Definition of a contemporary dramatic genre in which characters lose all idealism and optimistic rebelliousness, and function by rules in which they no longer believe. Grp/movt: Hypernaturalism.

1387 Wilkerson, Margaret B. "The Sighted Eyes and Feeling Heart of Lorraine Hansberry." *BALF.* 1983 Spring; 17: 8-13.
USA. 1960-1979. Critical studies. ■Through a critical discussion of her major works, Hansberry is viewed as a literary catalyst for the Black and American drama of the 60's and 70's.

1388 Williams, Dakin; Mead, Shepherd. *Tennessee Williams: An Intimate Biography.* New York: Arbor House; 1983. 352 pp.
USA. 1911-1983. Biographies. ■Unauthorized biography co-authored by Williams' brother.

1389 Zelenak, Michael. "Philandering with Shaw: GBS 'Made in America'." *ThM.* 1983 Summer-Fall; 14(3): 72-77. Illus.: Photo. Print. B&W. 3.
USA. 1982. Histories-sources. ■Interview with David Hammond, director of Yale Rep production of Shaw's *The Philanderer* and performers Christopher Walken, Tandy Cronyn and Brooke Adams.

1390 Kovalëvskaja, Evgenija Grigor'evna, ed.; Kulivova, I.S., ed.; Ponomarenko, T.G., ed. *Aspekty i priemy analiza teksta chudožestvennovo proizvedenija: mežvuzovskij sbornik naučnych trudov.* (Aspects and Methods of Textual Analysis for Artistic Compositions: Textbook of Scholarly Articles for Institutions of Higher Education.) Leningrad: A.I. Gercen State Pedagogical Institute; 1983. 146 pp. Biblio.
USSR. 1983. Instructional materials.

1391 Vasilinina, I.A. *Teat'r Arbuzova.* (Theatre of Arbuzov.) Moscow: Iskusstvo; 1983. 264 pp.
USSR. 1930-1970. Critical studies. ■Stage incarnations of Arbuzov's characters.

1392 Giménez, Leonardo Azparren. "Teatern i Venezuela." (The Theatre in Venezuela.) *Entre.* 1983; 10(4): 18-21.
Venezuela. 1945-1983. Historical studies. ■Discussion of Venezuelan playwrights of the 'generation of 1958,' the Rajatabla ensemble and the effects of national and international politics on the future of the theatre.

1393 Klunker, Heinz. "Die *Taubenschlucht* öffnet sich: Wie sich Vergangenheit und Gegenwart Jugoslawiens in neuen Stücken darstellen." (The *Pigeon-cleft* Opens: The Past and Present of Yugoslavia as Shown in New Plays.) *TH.* 1983; 9: 18-23 . Illus.: Photo.

Yugoslavia. 1983. Critical studies. ■Contemporary drama and theatre in Yugoslavia, including Jean Radulović's *The Pigeon-cleft (Golubnajača),* Slobodan Šnajder's *Croatian Faust* and other plays.

1394 Koruza, Jože. "Il cosmopolitismo del teatro di Slavko Grum." (Cosmopolitan Nature of Slavko Grum's Theatre.) *TeatrC.* 1983 June-Sep.; 2(4): 105-112.
Yugoslavia. 1920-1929. Critical studies. ■Influence of European avant-garde on Grum's drama.

1395 Vagapova, N.M.; Bromley, U.V., ed. *Formirovanije realizma v sceničeskom iskusstve Jugoslavii.* (The Shaping of Realism in the Yugoslav Theatre.) All-Union Scientific Research Institute of Art-Education under the USSR Ministry of Culture. Moscow: Nauka; 1983. 222 pp. Illus.: Photo. B&W. [The Twenties and Thirties of the Twentieth century.]
Yugoslavia. 1920-1930. Histories-specific. ■Spread of realism in all aspects of the Yugoslav theatre, including drama, staging, acting and design. Grp/movt: Realism.

Reference materials

1396 Hochman, Stanley, ed. *Encyclopedia of World Drama.* New York: McGraw-Hill; 1983. [Five volumes.]
499 B.C.-1983 A.D.

1397 Waters, Harold A. "Black French Theatre Update." *WLT.* 1983 Winter; 57(1): 43-48. Biblio.
Africa. 1977-1983. ■Twenty-two plays from nine countries, with plots and an overview of Black French theatre. Sequel to 1978 and 1981 bio-bibliographies by the same author.

1398 Hebbel-Gesellschaft; Österreich-Haus/Palais Palffy. *Friedrich Hebbel in Wien 1845-1863.* (Friedrich Hebbel in Vienna 1845-1863.) Vienna: Österreich Haus/Palais Palffy; 1983. 47 pp. Illus.: Photo. Dwg. B&W.
Austria. 1845-1863. ■Illustrated documentation of Friedrich Hebbel's stay in Vienna, his dramatic contribution and his novel *Anna.*

1399 Brown, J. Frederick. "The Charlottetown Festival in Review." *CDr.* 1983 Fall; 9(2): 227-368.
Canada. 1965-1982. ■Collection of cast lists, production information and reviews for 19 productions of the annual festival. Related to Music-Drama.

1400 Brock, D. Heyward. *A Ben Jonson Companion.* Bloomington, IN: Indiana UP; 1983. xii, 307 pp.
England. 1572-1637. ■Guide to the life and work of Ben Jonson.

1401 Carnegie, David. "A Preliminary Checklist of Professional Productions of the Plays of John Webster." *RORD.* 1983; 26: 55-63. Notes.
England. USA. 1614-1983. ■Chronological listing with actors, designers, directors and companies of all of Webster's plays.

1402 Carpenter, Charles A. "Modern Drama Studies: An Annual Bibliography." *MD.* 1983 June; 26(2): 150-233.
Europe. North America. South America. 1979-1982. ■Current scholarship, criticism and commentary on areas and topics of modern world drama.

1403 Molinari, Cesare, ed. *Il Teatro — Repertorio dalle origini ad oggi.* (The Theatre — Repertory from the Origins until Today.) Milan: Mondadori; 1982. 894 pp. Illus.: Photo. B&W. Color.
Europe. North America. 672 B.C.-1982 A.D. Histories-sources. ■Comprehensive listing of the dramatic repertory, with a note on important productions.

1404 Saunders, J.W. *A Biographical Dictionary of Renaissance Poets and Dramatists.* Totowa, NJ: Barnes & Noble; 1983. xxxiv, 216 pp.
Europe. 1400-1600. ■Biographies of Renaissance playwrights.

1405 Schlösser, Anselm, ed.; Kuckhoff, Armin-Gerd, ed. "Bibliographie." (Bibliography.) *SJW.* 1983; 119: 207-286.
Europe. North America. France. 1980. ■1779 items of published Shakespearean materials in English, German, French and other languages listed according to plays, critical studies, performances, etc., followed by list of contributors.

1406 Bajh, Enrico, ed.; Accame, Vincenzo, ed.; Eruli, Brunella, ed. *Jarry e la Patafisica: Arte, Letteratura, Spettacolo.*

DRAMA: General—Reference materials

(Jarry and Pataphysics: Art, Literature, Performance.) Milan: Gruppo Editoriale Fabbri; 1983. 175 pp. Pref. Index. Tables. Illus.: Photo. B&W. Color.
France. 1873-1907. Histories-sources. ■Catalogue of exhibition on pataphysics in figurative arts, theatre and cinema.

1407 Felkay, Nicole. "Dans les coulisses du théâtre romantique." (In the Wings of the Romantic Theatre.) *RHT*. 1983; 35(4): 442-453. Notes. Illus.: Photo. Print. B&W. 4.
France. 1825-1845. ■Publication of all references to theatre preserved in the 'Registres d'actes sous seing privé' in the Archives de Paris. Grp/movt: Romanticism.

1408 Siegel, Patricia Jean. *Alfred de Musset: A Reference Guide.* Boston: G.K. Hall; 1982. xxv, 439 pp. (Reference Guide to Literature Series.) Index.
France. 1830-1980. ■Chronological reference guide to works in French, English, German, Spanish and Italian on and about Musset, and productions of his plays.

1409 Webb, Richard C.; Webb, Suzanne A. *Jean Genet and His Critics: An Annotated Bibliography 1943-1980.* Metuchen, NJ: Scarecrow P; 1982. xii, 600 pp.
France. 1943-1980. ■Bibliography of critical studies of the plays of Jean Genet.

1410 Boltz, Ingeborg. "Shakespeare auf der Bühne: Spielzeit 1981/1982." (Shakespeare on Stage: Season 1981/1982.) *JDSh*. 1983: 269-295.
German-speaking countries. 1981-1982. ■Bibliography of research on Shakespearean productions in German-speaking countries.

1411 Valentin, Jean-Marie. *Le Théâtre des Jésuites dans les pays de langue allemande: répertoire chronologique des pièces représentées et des documents conservés (1555-1773).* (The Jesuit Theatre in German-Speaking Countries: Chronological Repertory of Plays Produced and Documents Preserved (1555-1773).) Part 1: 1555-1728. Stuttgart: Hiersemann; 1983. xiv, 612 pp. (Hiersemanns bibliographische Handbücher 3.) Pref.
German-speaking countries. 1555-1728. ■Listing of performances of Jesuit drama in German-speaking countries: bibliography of preserved plays.

1412 Anon. *Petrolini.* Rome: De Luca; 1982. n.p. (Associazione Culturale Witz Ologramma 2.) Pref. Biblio. Illus.: Photo. B&W.
Italy. 1982. Histories-sources. ■Illustrated catalogue of the exposition at the Palazzo Braschi in Rome — dedicated to the actor Ettore Petrolini.

1413 Falvey, Kathleen C. "Italian Vernacular Religious Drama of the 14th through the 16th Centuries: A Selected Bibliography on the *Lauda Drammatica* and the *Sacra Rappresentazione*." *RORD*. 1983; 26: 125-144. Biblio.
Italy. 1300-1983. ■List with brief introductory commentary of 94 works written between 1960 and 1983 dealing with Italian sacred drama. Grp/movt: Medieval theatre. Related to Popular Entertainment.

1414 Maier, Bruno. "Note sul teatro di Italo Svevo e sulla sua cronologia." (Notes on Italo Svevo's Theatre and Its Chronology.) *TeatrC*. 1983 Feb.-May; 2(3): 265-272. Notes.
Italy. 1885-1928. Histories-sources. ■Chronology of composition for Italo Svevo's plays.

1415 Niccodemi, Dario. *Niobe: Storia vera di un amore.* (Niobe: The True Story of a Love.) Milan: Artemide Editrice; 1982. 363 pp. Pref. Notes. Illus.: Photo. B&W.
Italy. 1921-1927. Histories-sources. ■Playwright Dario Niccodemi's letters to actress Niobe Sanguinetti.

1416 Zappulla, Enzo, ed.; Zappulla, Sarah, ed. *Sicilia: dialetto e teatro — Materiali per una storia del teatro dialettale siciliano.* (Sicily: Dialect and Theatre — Materials on a History of Sicilian Dialect Theatre.) Agrigento: Edizioni del Centro Nazionale di Studi Pirandelliani; 1982. xciii, 264 pp. (Collana di studi e documentazione 3.) Biblio. Illus.: Photo. B&W.
Italy. 1902-1937. Histories-sources. ■Illustrated catalogue of an exhibition on Sicilian dialect theatre.

1417 *We Are Strong: A Guide to the Work of Popular Theatres across the Americas, Volume 1.* Mankato, MN: Institute for Cultural Policy Studies; 1983. xv, 244 pp. Append. Illus.: Photo. B&W. 99. [A publication of *Theaterwork Magazine*.]
North America. South America. 1980-1983. ■Work of 63 theatres of social relevance. Description of work. Appendix lists classes offered and scripts developed.

1418 Gershator, David, ed. *Federico García Lorca: Selected Letters.* New York: New Directions; 1983. xiv, 172 pp.
Spain. 1918-1936. Collected materials. ■Translated letters of the Spanish playwright.

1419 Williamson, Vern G.; Reynolds, John T. "Bibliography of Publications on the *Comedia*." *BCom*. 1982 Winter; 34(2): 233-284. Index. Biblio.
Spain. 1580-1650. ■Bibliography of Spanish and English publications on *comedias* and their playwrights.

1420 Brown, John Russell. *A Short Guide to Modern British Drama.* Totowa, NJ: Barnes & Noble; 1983. viii, 101 pp.
UK. 1945-1983. ■Brief survey of post-war theatre with 25 play synopses.

1421 Laurence, Dan H. *Bernard Shaw: A Bibliography.* New York: Oxford UP; 1983. xxiii, 1058 pp. (The Soho Bibliographies, 22.) [2 vols.]
UK. 1856-1983. ■Exhaustive bibliography of writings by and about George Bernard Shaw.

1422 Nightingale, Benedict. *A Reader's Guide to Fifty Modern British Plays.* Totowa, NJ: Barnes & Noble; 1983. 479 pp.
UK. 1902-1975. ■Historical and critical survey of 34 modern British plays.

1423 Weintraub, Stanley, ed. *British Dramatists Since World War II.* Detroit: Gale Research P; 1982. xiv, 657 pp.
UK. 1945-1983. Biographical studies. ■Biographical essays on major and minor dramatists of stage, screen and radio, with a review essay by Tom Stoppard.

1424 Barrett, Daniel. "T.W. Robertson's Plays: Revisions to Nicoll's Handlist." *NCTR*. 1983 Winter; 11(2): 93. Notes.
UK-England. 1849-1866. ■Revision of the handlist of Robertson's plays in Allardyce Nicoll's *History of English Drama 1660-1900, V* (Cambridge, 1959), pp 546-547.

1425 Herbert, Ian, ed. *London Theatre Index 1982.* London: London Theatre Record; 1983. 48 pp.
UK-England. 1982. ■Listing of 333 London productions mounted in 1983 with an index to actors, production personnel and reviewers.

1426 Klein, Dennis A. *Peter and Anthony Shaffer: A Reference Guide.* Boston: G.K. Hall; 1982. xii, 110 pp.
UK-England. USA. 1926-1982. ■Reference guide to playwrights Peter and Anthony Shaffer.

1427 Mello, Frank E. "A Bibliography of Laurence Olivier's Life and Stage Career." *TN*. 1983; 37(1-2): 26-29, 80-84.
UK-England. 1907-1983. ■Contains 95 entries of books, 22 articles and 5 miscellaneous documents.

1428 Wearing, J.P. *The London Stage 1910-1919: A Calendar of Plays and Players.* Metuchen, NJ: Scarecrow P; 1982. xvi, 1369 pp. [Two volumes.]
UK-England. 1910-1919.

1429 White, Katherine. "Edward Gordon Craig Documents." *USITT*. 1983 Summer; 23(3): 8.
UK-England. USA. 1872-1966. ■Arnold Rood's 3,000 item collection of historical materials relating to Edward Gordon Craig is available to designers and researchers.

1430 Mikhail, E.H. "Sean O'Casey: An Annual Bibliography." *OCA*. 1982; 1: 180-192. [Continued in OCA 1983: 2: 166-171.]
UK-Ireland. 1923-1982. ■Bibliography of bibliographies, criticism, reviews and works by Sean O'Casey.

1431 Saddlemyer, Ann, ed. *John Millington Synge: Collected Letters I.* Oxford: Oxford UP; 1983. 416 pp.
UK-Ireland. 1871-1909. ■Letters of playwright John Millington Synge.

1432 Saddlemyer, Ann, ed. *Theatre Business, The Correspondence of the First Abbey Directors: William Butler Yeats,*

DRAMA: General—Reference materials

Lady Gregory and J.M. Synge. University Park, PA: Pennsylvania State UP; 1982. 330 pp.
UK-Ireland. 1904-1909. ■Correspondence relating mainly to administrative concerns of the Abbey Theatre.

1433 Anon. "Career Opportunities." 104-169 in *Dramatists Sourcebook.* New York: Theatre Communications Group, Inc.; 1983. 196 pp.
USA. 1983. Instructional materials. ■Career opportunities for playwrights: agents, fellowships and grants, emergency funds, state arts councils, university programs, service organizations, artist colonies and media.

1434 Anon. "Script Opportunities." 9-86 in *Dramatists Sourcebook.* New York: Theatre Communication Group, Inc.; 1983. 196 pp.
USA. 1983. Instructional materials. ■Script opportunities for the playwright: production, prizes, publication and development.

1435 Archer, Stephen M., ed. *American Actors and Actresses: A Guide to Information Sources.* Detroit: Gale Research P; 1983. xxii, 710 pp. (Performing Arts Information Guide Series, 8.) Index.
USA. 1700-1950. ■3263 annotated entries of books and articles about 226 American actors of the legitimate stage.

1436 Harris, Andrew B. "The Brander Matthews Collection at Columbia." *ASTRN.* 1983 Fall; 12(1): 1-3. Illus.: Design. B&W. 3.
USA. 1891-1929. ■Account of drama materials, particularly set designs and model theatres in the Brander Matthews Collection.

1437 Leaming, Gregory, ed. *TCG Theatre Directory 1983-84.* New York: Theatre Communications Group; 1983. 59 pp.
USA. 1983-1984. ■Directory of Theatre Communications Group members in the U.S.

1438 Leonard, William Torbert. *Broadway Bound: A Guide to Shows that Died Aborning.* Metuchen, NJ: Scarecrow P; 1983. x, 618 pp.
USA. 1900-1982. Related to Music-Drama: Musical theatre.

1439 Osborn, M. Elizabeth, ed. *Dramatists Sourcebook.* New York: Theatre Communications Group; 1983. 193 pp.
USA. 1983. ■Listing of theatre companies, playwriting awards and grants.

1440 Woll, Allen. *Dictionary of the Black Theatre.* Westport, CT: Greenwood P; 1983. xvi, 351 pp.
USA. 1983. ■Includes Broadway, Off Broadway and selected Harlem theatres.

Relation to other fields

1441 Hecht, Werner. "Beiträge zur demokratischen Öffnung: Brecht in Argentinien." (Contributions to the Democratic Opening: Brecht in Argentina.) *NIMBZ.* 1983 Nov.; 6(6): 12-13. Illus.: Photo.
Argentina. 1980-1983. Historical studies. ■Brecht reception in Argentina vis-à-vis political situation in the country.

1442 Schvey, Henry I. *Oskar Kokoschka: The Painter as Playwright.* Detroit: Wayne State UP; 1982. 168 pp.
Austria. 1917. Historical studies. Grp/movt: Dadaism.

1443 Got, Jerzy. "Wilhelm Tell i sprawa polska." (Wilhelm Tell and the Polish Question.) *PaT.* 1983; 32(1): 29-56. Pref. Notes.
Austro-Hungarian Empire. Poland. 1863-1865. Historical studies. ■German theatre in Cracow and its relationship to Polish people during the uprising against Russia.

1444 Schlenker, Wolfram. "Modern Chinese Drama: Characteristics — Problems — Perspectives." *ThR.* 1983 Autumn; 8(3): 220-232. Notes.
China. 1900-1983. Historical studies. ■Discussion of current dramatic themes and forms in relation to historical development, cultural policy and theatre practice.

1445 Greenblatt, Stephen. "China: Visiting Rites." *Raritan.* 1983 Spring; 2(4): 1-23. Illus.: Photo. B&W. 7: 3 in. x 4 in.
China, People's Republic of. 1920-1982. Critical studies. ■English professor's six-week stay in Beijing while delivering four lectures on

Shakespeare and two on contemporary American literature: reactions to the Cultural Revolution and intellectual freedom by Chinese intellectuals.

1446 Hazard, Mary E. "Shakespeare's 'Living Art': A Live Issue from *Love's Labour's Lost.*" 181-198 in Carey, Cecile Williamson; . Limouze, Henry S. *Shakespeare and the Arts: A Collection of Essays from the Ohio Shakespeare Conference, 1981, Wright State University, Dayton, Ohio.* Washington, DC: UP of America; 1982. viii, 247 pp. Notes.
England. 1594-1595. Critical studies. ■Shakespeare's rhetoric in *Love's Labour's Lost* expresses commonplace figures also to be found in pictorial art of the period.

1447 Wentersdorf, Karl P. "Animal Symbolism in Shakespeare's *Hamlet:* The Imagery of Sex Nausea." *CompD.* 1983-1984 Winter; 17(4): 348-382. Notes. Illus.: Photo. Sketches. B&W. 12.
England. 1600-1601. Critical studies. ■Twenty-eight misericords in Holy Trinity Church link imagery of *Hamlet* to Medieval and Renaissance decorative art. Grp/movt: Medieval art; Renaissance art.

1448 Hays, Michael. "Theatrical Texts and Social Context." *ThM.* 1983 Winter; 15(1): 5-7. Notes. Biblio.
Europe. North America. 1983. Critical studies. ■Introduction to essay collection *The Sociology of Theater,* a coherent sociological method of reading texts and their contexts.

1449 McCabe, William H., S.J.; Oldani, Louis J., S.J., ed. *An Introduction to the Jesuit Theatre.* St. Louis, MO: Institute of Jesuit Sources; 1983. xiv, 346 pp.
Europe. Japan. 1550-1773. Histories-specific. ■Jesuit theatre as an effort to combine the ideas of an omnipotent deity and the implications of free will with classical tragic theory.

1450 Bourgeon, L. "L'âme chrétienne de Jacques Copeau." (Jacques Copeau's Christian Soul.) *RHT.* 1983; 35(1): 24-28.
France. 1940-1944. Biographical studies. ■Jacques Copeau's attendance at Mass during the Occupation and his reading of his play *Le Petit pauvre (The Little Pauper)* to the monks at Cîteaux in 1943.

1451 Meller, Stefan. "Teatr francuski podczas Rewolucji." (French Theatre During the Revolution.) *PaT.* 1983; 32(1): 13-30. Biblio. Illus.: Dwg. B&W. 8.
France. 1789-1794. Politics. ■Relations between theatre and politics during the French Revolution.

1452 Skeg, Miriam Anne. "The Iconography of Herod in the Fleury Playbook and the Visual Arts." *CompD.* 1983 Spring; 17(1): 55-78. Notes.
France. England. 1100-1200. Historical studies. ■Representation of Herod in two Fleury plays dealing with the feast of the Epiphany and the Holy Innocents illustrated in contemporary English and French icons. Grp/movt: Medieval theatre.

1453 Schirmer, Lothar. "Wider den Krieg: Die Darstellung des Kriegs in Theater und Film zum Ende der Weimarer Republik — Beispiele und Reaktionen." (Against War: The Presentation of War in Theatre and Film at the End of the Weimar Republic.) *Tzs.* 1983 Spring; 3: 71-91. Illus.: Photo.
Germany. 1930. Historical studies. ■Political reactions to anti-war plays and films. Related to Media: Film.

1454 Schölzel, Arnold. "Korsch, Brecht und die Negation der Philosophie." (Korsch, Brecht and the Negation of Philosophy.) 32-44 in Brecht-Zentrum, DDR. *Brecht und Marxismus: Dokumentation: Protokoll der Brecht-Tage 1983* (Brecht and Marxism — Documentation: Proceedings of the Brecht Days 1983). East Berlin: Henschel; 1983. 408 pp. (Brecht 83.) Illus.: Photo.
Germany. Hungary. 1898-1971. Studies of theories/theorists. ■Difference in dialectics and philosophy in writings by Karl Korsch, Bertolt Brecht and György Lukács.

1455 Lanza, Diego. "Lo spettacolo." (The Production.) 107-126 in Vegetti, Mario. *Oralità, scrittura, spettacolo (Oral Tradition, Writing, Performance).* Turin: Boringhieri; 1983. 226 pp. (Introduzione alle culture antiche 1.) Biblio.

DRABA: General—Relation to other fields

Greece. Roman Empire. 600-1 B.C. Historical studies. ■Different social functions of the dramatic theatre in Greece and Rome and their modifications. Grp/movt: Ancient Greek theatre; Roman theatre.

1456 Warner, Keith Q. "Culture and Politics: The Tragedies of Césaire's Christophe and 'Mr. West Indian Politician'." *JCSt*. 1983 Winter; 3(3): 314-323. Notes.
Haiti. Trinidad and Tobago. Martinique. 1962-1979. Critical studies. ■Relationship between politics and the heroic tradition of Caribbean drama.

1457 Anon. "Intervista sull'attore e lo psicanalista." (Interview on the Actor and the Psychoanalist.) *AdP*. 1983; 8(1): 33-42. Illus.: Photo.
Italy. 1960. Histories-sources. ■Cesare Musatti recalls his experience with psychodrama and portrayal of a psychoanalyst.

1458 Bigari, Ivana. "'Non è poco, ma basterà così'." ('It Isn't Little, but It'll Do'.) *AdP*. 1983; 8(1): 24-26.
Italy. 1930. Historical studies. ■Playbill used by Pirandello introduced his play *Questa sera si recita a soggetto (Tonight We Improvise)* as though it were an improvised performance rather than an ordinary play.

1459 Gibbs, James. "Tear the Painted Masks, Join the Poison Stains: A Preliminary Study of Wole Soyinka's Writings for the Nigerian Press." *RAL*. 1983 Spring; 14(1): 3-44. Notes.
Nigeria. 1962-1982. Critical studies. ■Soyinka's journalism is important for its quality, its involvement and for the light it sheds on some of his poems and plays.

1460 Haakonsen, Daniel. "Ibsen som statue — bundet og fri." (Ibsen as Statue: Bound and Free.) *IY*. 1981-1982: 77-79. Illus.: Photo.
Norway. 1828-1906. Critical studies. ■Discussion of Ibsen statue in Oslo.

1461 Targosz, Karolina. "Wyspiański i Lajkonik." (Wyspiański and Lajkonik.) *PaT*. 1983; 32(1): 89-114. Notes. Illus.: Design. Photo. B&W. 5.
Poland. Austria. 1901-1907. Historical studies. ■Relations between eminent Polish dramatist and painter Stanisław Wyspiański and an old folk tradition popular in Cracow until today of the man in Tartar costume with a wooden horse. Wyspiański painted a costume for Lajkonik and used this figure in his plays. Related to Ritual-Ceremony.

1462 Willett, John. "'Reagan und Thatcher haben Brecht wieder jung gemacht': Anmerkungen zur Brecht-Rezeption in Grossbritannien." ('Reagan and Thatcher Have Rejuvenated Brecht': Notes on Brecht Reception in Great Britain.) *NIMBZ*. 1983 July; 6(4): 5-6. Illus.: Photo.
UK. 1980-1983. Historical studies. ■Renewed interest in Brecht stimulated by political situations.

1463 Pyle, Hilary. "Many Ferries: Jack B. Yeats and J.M. Synge." *Éire*. 1983 Summer; 18(2): 17-35. Notes. Illus.: Pntg. Sketches. Dwg. Print. B&W. 3: 5 in. x 7 in.
UK-Ireland. 1896-1948. Critical studies. ■Biographical bases of and association between J.M. Synge's plays and essays and Jack B. Yeats' sketches, drawings and paintings of the Aran Islands and Western Ireland.

1464 Ardizzone, Mario. "Nuova lettura di Moreno." (Moreno: A New Interpretation.) *AdP*. 1983; 8(1): 64-70. Notes. Illus.: Design.
USA. 1917-1983. Critical studies. ■Zerka Moreno's work placed in coherent, logical perspective to explain the dialectics of human interaction.

1465 Greenfield, Thomas Allen. *Work and the Work Ethic in American Drama, 1920-1970*. Columbia, MO: Univ. of Missouri; 1982. x, 187 pp. Index. Biblio.
USA. 1920-1969. Critical studies. ■Thematic study of work ethic in American drama in general and in the plays of Elmer Rice and Arthur Miller in particular.

1466 Hairston, Andrea. "If You Just Change the Key, It's Still the Same Old Song." *BALF*. 1983 Spring; 17: 36-37.
USA. 1983. Critical studies. ■Criticism of racial stereotypes in American theatre.

1467 Harris, Lee Franklin; Rosenberg, Helen S. "Creative Drama and Affective Response to Literature." *ChTR*. 1983 Apr.; 32(2): 21-25. Notes. Tables.
USA. 1983. Critical studies. ■Comparison of the relative effectiveness of using lecture/discussion, creative drama and small group study methods in teaching literature.

1468 Magli, Adriano. "Moreno e il teatro: spontaneità e mediazione simbolica." (Moreno and Theatre: Spontaneity and Symbolic Mediation.) *AdP*. 1983; 8(1): 87-99. Illus.: Photo.
USA. Italy. 1916-1983. Technical studies. ■Techniques of spontaneity are applied by Zerka Moreno in a form of symbolical mediation that can be compared to Pirandello's drama.

1469 Matassarin, Kat. "Jane Addams of Hull House: Creative Drama at the Turn of the Century." *ChTR*. 1983 Oct.; 32(4): 13-15. Notes.
USA. 1889-1910. Historical studies. ■Describes Jane Addams' creative drama activities at Hull House.

1470 McNeece, Lucy Stone. "The Uses of Improvisation: Drama in the Foreign Language Classroom." *FR*. 1983 May; 56(6): 829-839. Notes.
USA. 1983. Linguistic studies. ■Uses of improvisation in teaching foreign languages, and shows attitudes and feelings expressed through movement in language exercises.

1471 Vitz, Kathie. "A Review of Empirical Research in Drama and Language." *ChTR*. 1983 Oct.; 32(4): 17-25. Biblio. Tables.
USA. 1983. Empirical research. ■Results of 32 studies on the effects of creative drama on the development of language skills.

1472 Wilkins, Frederick C. "Lawson & Cole Revisited." *EON*. 1983; 7(2): 17-23. Notes.
USA. 1954. Historical studies. ■Articles written in the early fifties by playwright John Howard Lawson and film writer and dramatist Lester Cole in response to the death of Eugene O'Neill express mixed feelings toward O'Neill in the 'progressive' segment of society.

Research/historiography

1473 Bank, Rosemarie K. "Shaping the Script: Commission Produces a Bibliography of Dramaturgy." *ThNe*. 1983 Jan.-Feb.; 15(1): 6. Illus.: Design. B&W. 1: 6 in. x 5 in. [Project of Commission of Theatre Research (COTR).]
USA. 1980-1983. Bibliographical studies. ■Sample bibliography of 34 items — 24 of which were compiled and annotated by Laurence Shyer in *Theatre*, Fall 1978 — illustrates how a dramaturg provides resources for performance. Notes six areas needing scholarly attention.

1474 Goldberg, Patricia D. "Development of a Category System for the Analysis of the Response of the Young Theatre Audience." *ChTR*. 1983 Apr.; 32(2): 27-32. Biblio. Tables.
USA. 1983. Empirical research. ■Fifteen categories were devised to measure children's responses to theatre productions. The categorization was based on the results of a study involving 188 subjects, ranging in age between 4th and 10th grade.

1475 Morrison, Jack; Page, Anita. "Insights and Viewpoints." *ChTR*. 1983 Oct.; 32(4): 27.
USA. 1900-1983. Empirical research. ■Views on the relative values and pitfalls of descriptive and empirical research in children's drama.

1476 Wilkinson, Joyce A. "On Evaluation of Involvement in Developmental Drama and Its Relationship to Self-Monitoring and Hemisphericity." *ChTR*. 1983 Apr.; 32(2): 15-19. Biblio.
USA. 1983. Empirical research. ■Developmental Drama Scale is used to characterize subjects who are highly involved in drama activities as right brained with high monitoring and acting skills.

Theory/criticism

1477 Schechner, Richard. *Performative Circumstances from the Avant-Garde to Ramila*. Calcutta: Seagull Books; 1983. xii, 337. Index. Illus.: Photo. Dwg. 37.
1976-1983. Critical studies. ■Collection of Richard Schechner's journal articles on performance theories.

DRAMA: General—Theory/criticism

1478 Natev, Atanas. *Teatralna ideografiia: iavleniia, problemy, nasoki v dneshniia chuzhdestranen teatur.* (Theatre Ideology: Phenomena, Problems and Questions of the Artistic Nature of Theatre.) Sofia: Partizdat; 1983. 338 pp. (Poreditsa Epokha i Kultura.)
Bulgaria. 1900-1983. Histories-general. ■History and criticism of twentieth-century theatre.

1479 Rina, Juan Andrés. "Problem och begränsninger för kritiken i Chile och Latinamerika." (Problems and Limitations of Criticism in Chile and Latin America.) *Entre.* 1983; 10(4): 28-29.
Chile. North America. 1960-1983. Critical studies. ■Because of inadequate training and uncritical attitudes toward culture, Latin American critics fail to provide the serious criticism needed by theatre artists and audiences.

1480 Hardison, O.B., Jr. "Speaking the Speech." *SQ.* 1983 Summer; 34(2): 133-146. Notes.
England. 1559-1603. Critical studies. ■Renaissance ideal of dramatic language was not that it was related to poetry, but to action. Poetry arises from and is validated by actions.

1481 Calendoli, Giovanni. *Il grido di Laoconte: Tre saggi sul teatro.* (Laocoon's Scream: Three essays on Theatre.) Fossalta di Piave (Venice): Rebellato; 1982. 157 pp. (Parola, immagine e società.) Notes.
Europe. 1700-1982. Critical studies. ■Birth of modern drama in 18th century theatre. Pirandello's concept of theatre within theatre is seen as matrix of theatrical avant-garde.

1482 Piccioli, Gianandrea, ed. "Teatro." (Theatre.*) 431-502 in Bottero, Bianca, ed.; . Negri, Antonello, ed.; . Fofi, Goffredo, ed.; . Piccioli, Gianandrea, ed.; . Pitazzi, Paolo, ed.; . Santi, Piero, ed. La cultura del 900 (The Culture of the Twentieth Century).* Milan: Mondadori; 1982. 650 pp. (Oscar Studio 87.)
Europe. North America. 1900-1982. Critical studies. ■Dramatic theories of the 20th century reflect a complex relationship between plays, designs, staging and acting.

1483 Scrivano, Riccardo, ed. *Letteratura e teatro.* (Literature and Theatre.) Bologna: Zanichelli; 1983. Pref. Notes. Biblio.
Europe. 384 B.C.-1983 A.D. Histories-sources. ■Anthology of theory and criticism regarding the relationship of playtext and production.

1484 Styan, J.L. *Modern Drama in Theory and Practice.* Cambridge, England: Cambridge UP; 1982. v. 1: 181 pp./v. 2: 198 pp./v. 3: 222 pp. Pref. Biblio. Index. [3 Volumes.]
Europe. North America. 1900-1980. Critical studies. ■Study of realism, naturalism, symbolism, surrealism, expressionism and epic theatre. Grp/movt: Realism; Naturalism; Symbolism; Surrealism; Expressionism; Dialectics.

1485 Watson, G.J. *Drama: An Introduction.* New York: St. Martin's Press; 1983. x, 219 pp.
Europe. North America. 499 B.C.-1983 A.D. Critical studies. ■Critical analysis of dramatic methods from Sophocles to Harold Pinter.

1486 Wilshire, Bruce. *Role Playing and Identity: The Limits of Theatre as Metaphor.* Bloomington, IN: Indiana UP; 1982. xvii, 301 pp.
Europe. North America. 1982. Critical studies.

1487 Daniels, Barry V. *Revolution in the Theatre: French Romantic Theories of Drama.* Westport, CT: Greenwood P; 1983. xii, 249 pp.
France. 1800-1850. Critical studies. Grp/movt: Romanticism.

1488 Marty, Robert. "Fenomenologia i semiòtica del teatre." (Phenomenology and Semiotics of Theatre.) *EECIT.* 1983 June; 23: 95-115. Notes. Biblio. Tables. Illus.: Diagram. Print. B&W. Schematic. 4: 12 cm. x 3 cm. [Translation from the French and notes by Montserrat Ingla.]
France. Italy. 1980. Critical studies. ■Essentially triadic nature of Frank Pierce's phenomenology and semiotics is applied to the theory of drama.

1489 Pavis, Patrice; Knode, Helen. "Socio-Criticism." *ThM.* 1983 Winter; 15(1): 8-11. Notes. Biblio. Illus.: Photo. Print. B&W. 3.

France. 1971-1980. Critical studies. ■Schematic approach to examining the rapport between the dramatic text and its social setting.

1490 Szondi, Peter; Pavis, Patrice, transl. *Théorie du drame moderne 1880-1950.* (Modern Dramatic Theory, 1880-1950.) Lausanne: Editions l'âge d'homme; 1983. 144 pp.
France. 1880-1950. Critical studies. ■Translation from Szondi's original German *Theorie des Modernen Dramas* (1956).

1491 Anikst, A.A.; Ziss, A.J., ed. *Teorija dramy ot Gegelia do Marksa.* (Theories of Drama from Hegel to Marx.) History of the Theories of Drama. Moscow: Nauka; 1983. 288 pp. Pref. Biblio.
Germany. 1770-1883. Histories-specific. ■Theories of drama by German philosophers.

1492 Chiarini, Gioachino. *Lessing e Plauto.* (Lessing and Plautus.) Naples: Liguori; 1983. 168 pp. (Forme materiali e ideologie del mondo antico 22.) Notes. Index.
Germany. 1747-1755. Critical studies. ■Lessing's imitation of contemporary criticism of Plautus in his 'Contributions to History and Theatre Revival' ('Beyträge zur Historie und Aufnahme des Theaters').

1493 Chiarini, Paolo. *Brecht, Lukács e il realismo.* (Brecht, Lukács and Realism.) Rome, Bari: Latina; 1983. 186 pp. (Universale Laterza 141.) Append. Notes. Index.
Germany. Hungary. 1918-1956. Critical studies. ■Brecht's theatrical poetics and polemic with Lukács on realism. Grp/movt: Realism.

1494 Franz, Michael. "Die Krise des 'Werk'-Begriffs." (The Crisis of the Term 'Work'.) 212-221, 382 in Brecht-Zentrum, DDR. *Brecht und Marxismus: Dokumentation: Protokoll der Brecht-Tage 1983* (Brecht and Marxism: Documentation: Proceedings of the Brecht-Days, 1983). East Berlin: Brecht-Zentrum der DDR; 1983. 405 pp. (Brecht 83.) Notes.
Germany. 1898-1956. Critical studies. ■Brecht's civic perception of arts as an expression of socio-cultural coherence and consequences.

1495 Görner, Rüdiger. "Über die 'Trennung der Elemente': Das Gesamtkunstwerk — ein Steinbruch der Moderne?" (On the 'Separation of the Elements': The *Gesamtkunstwerk* — A Quarry for Modern Theatre?)*MuK.* 1983; 29: 98-122. Notes.
Germany. 1849-1977. Historical studies. ■Influence of Richard Wagner's *Gesamtkunstwerk* on modern theatre. Reception of Wagner's theories by Bertolt Brecht, Ernst Toller and Max Frisch. Related to Music-Drama: Opera.

1496 Hahn, Karl-Claus; Krebs, Dieter; Eichler, Rolf-Dieter. "Brecht-Tage 1983: Brechts Verhältnis zum Marxismus." (Brecht Days 1983: Brecht's Relation to Marxism.) *NIMBZ.* 1983 Mar.; 6(2): 6-9. Illus.: Photo.
Germany. 1922-1956. Critical studies. ■Marxist philosophy in Brecht's work: dialectics of his thinking, his theory of realism and his political aesthetics. Grp/movt: Social realism.

1497 Heise, Wolfgang. "Theater und Spiel — ein Bewegungsferment des Sozialismus: Zum Lehrstück Brechts." (Theatre and Play — A Ferment of Socialism: On the Didactic Plays of Brecht.) *NIMBZ.* 1983 Sep.; 6(5): 8-9. Illus.: Photo.
Germany. 1922-1956. Critical studies. ■Brecht's theory of didactic functions in the development of socialism.

1498 Irrlitz, Gerd. "Philosophiegeschichtliche Quellen Brechts: Brechtsches im Lichte der Philosophiegeschichte: Brecht — Schiller: Einsatz von Philosophie." (Historical Sources of Brecht's Philosophy: Brechtian Positions in the Light of the History of Ideas: Brecht — Schiller: Philosophical Context.) 148-167 in DDR, Brecht-Zentrum der. *Brecht und Marxismus: Dokumentation: Protokoll der Brecht-Tage 1983 (Brecht and Marxism: Documentation: Proceedings of the Brecht-Days, 1983).* East Berlin: Brecht-Zentrum der DDR; 1983. 405 pp. (Brecht 83.) Notes.
Germany. 1848-1956. Historical studies. ■Schiller's influence on Brecht, and Brecht's view of Bacon, Descartes, Socrates, Hegel and the philosophy of the Enlightenment. Grp/movt: Enlightenment.

DRAMA: General—Theory/criticism

1499 Jones, Michael T. "From History to Aesthetics: Schiller's Early Jena Years." *GerSR*. 1983 May; 6(2): 195-213. Notes.
Germany. 1789-1791. Historical studies. ■Schiller's philosophy of history.

1500 Klatt, Gudrun. "Realismus in der Diskussion: Neue Fragen bei der Durchsicht der Debatten der dreissiger Jahre." (Realism in Discussion: New Questions upon Examining Debates of the 1930s.) 128-138, 374-376 in Brecht-Zentrum, DDR. *Brecht und Marxismus: Dokumentation: Protokoll der Brecht-Tage 1983* (Brecht and Marxism: Documentation: Proceedings of the Brecht-Days, 1983). East Berlin: Brecht-Zentrum der DDR; 1983. 405 pp. (Brecht 83.) Notes.
Germany. Hungary. 1900-1956. Critical studies. ■Brecht's and Lukács' debate on realism initiated by Claude Prévost. Grp/movt: Realism.

1501 Lukeš, Milan. "Dialektischer Widerspruch in Brechts Theorie des Theaters." (Dialectic Contradiction in Brecht's Theory of Theatre.) 174-179, 379 in Brecht-Zentrum, DDR. *Brecht und Marxismus: Dokumentation: Protokoll der Brecht-Tage 1983* (Brecht and Marxism: Documentation: Proceedings of the Brecht-Days, 1983). East Berlin: Brecht-Zentrum der DDR; 1983. 405 pp. (Brecht 83.) Notes.
Germany. 1898-1956. Critical studies. ■Dialectic and discontinuity as main principles of Brecht's work.

1502 Schumacher, Ernst. "Brecht und der Frieden." (Brecht and Peace.) 311-332, 389-391 in Brecht-Zentrum, DDr. *Brecht und Marxismus: Dokumentation: Protokoll der Brecht-Tage 1983* (Brecht and Marxism: Documentation: Proceedings of the Brecht-Days, 1983). East Berlin: Brecht-Zentrum der DDR; 1983. 405 pp. (Brecht 83.) Notes. Illus.: Photo.
Germany. 1898-1956. Historical studies. ■Brecht's work for peace and view that all wars are caused by contradictions in society.

1503 Trost, Karl Heinz; Estelrich, Pilar, transl. "El concepte goethiá de Literatura Universal." (Goethe's Idea of Universal Literature.) 27-37 in Teatral, Institut d'Experimentació. *Ur-Faust (Faust primigeni)*. Barcelona: Publicacions i edicions de la Universitat de Barcelona; 1983. 138 pp.
Germany. 1766-1832. Historical studies. ■Analysis of Goethe's views on German literature of his time and its role in relation to the literature of other nations.

1504 Heinitz, Werner. "Heiner Müller: Man muss nach der Methode fragen." (Heiner Müller: One Must Inquire about the Method.) *NIMBZ*. 1983 Sep.; 6(5): 3-5. Illus.: Photo.
Germany, East. 1983. Histories-sources. ■Interview with the playwright Heiner Müller about Brecht's methodology and its application for today's theatre.

1505 Schumacher, Ernst. "Entfaltete Schauspielkunst — Kollektive Produktionsweise." (Developed Dramatic Art — Collective Production Methods.) *TZ*. 1982 Apr.; 37: 6-8.
Germany, East. 1982. Critical studies. ■Marxist criteria for theatre criticism.

1506 Lyotard, Jean-Francois; Lydon, Mary, transl. "Fiscourse Digure: The Utopia Behind the Scenes of the Phantasy." *TJ*. 1983 Oct.; 35(3): 333-357. Notes. [Translated from German: *Discours, Figure*, (Paris: Editions Klincksieck, 1974) 327-355.]
Germany, West. France. USA. 1974-1983. Critical studies. ■Freudian analysis is used to divide fantasy into three phases from genital-masochism to anal-sadism: 'The drive is the author, the representative is the actor, the object is the play's reference'.

1507 De Marinis, Marco. *Semiotica del teatro — L'analisi testuale dello spettacolo.* (Theatre Semiotics — Textual Analysis of the Production.) Milano: Bompiani; 1982. 330 pp. (Studi Bompiani, Il campo semiotico.) Notes. Biblio. Index.
Italy. 1982. Critical studies. ■Production text is viewed as interlacing of different expressive components that require from the spectator certain cultural backgrounds and experiences.

1508 Gozzi, Carlo; Beniscelli, Alberto, ed. *Il ragionamento ingenuo.* (The Naive Reasoning.) Genoa: Costa e Nolan; 1983. 149 pp. (Testi della cultura italiana 4.) Pref. Notes.
Italy. 1772-1773. Histories-sources. ■New edition of Carlo Gozzi's *The Naive Reasoning* with an appendix on theories of drama used as a preface to Gozzi's plays.

1509 Selvaggi, Caterina. "La grammatica di un onirodramma dedicato a Pirandello." (The Grammar of a Pirandellian Dream Play.) *AdP*. 1983; 8(1): 59-63. Illus.: Design. Photo.
Italy. 1983. Critical studies. ■Theatrical dream phenomenon is compared to theory of roles in psychodrama, then linguistically and semantically analyzed according to the canons of the Pirandellian 'play within a play'.

1510 Salvat, Ricard. *El teatro, como texto, como espectaculo.* (Theatre as Text and Performance.) Barcelona: Montesinos; 1983. 152 pp. (Biblioteca de divulgación temática.) Biblio. Illus.: Photo.
Spain. 1983. Critical studies.

1511 Snyder, Susan. "Auden, Shakespeare, and the Defence of Poetry." *ShS*. 1983; 36: 29-37. Notes.
UK-England. 1939-1962. Critical studies. ■Auden's use of Shakespeare, especially *The Tempest*, in his poetic meditation on art's relation to life, *The Sea and the Mirror*, answering the Kierkegaardian Christianity charge of that art is not serious.

1512 Tiusanen, Timo. "Shaw ja teatteri." (Shaw and the Theatre.) *Kanava*. 1983; 11(5): 326-335.
UK-England. 1880-1950. Historical studies. ■Review of Shaw's work as a theatre critic.

1513 Walton, J. Michael, ed. *Craig on Theatre.* London and New York: Methuen; 1983. 192 pp. Biblio. Append. Illus.: Dwg. 24.
UK-England. 1907-1957. Critical studies. ■Collection of writings by director and designer Edward Gordon Craig on various aspects of theatrical theory and practice.

1514 Bensman, Joseph. "The Phenomenology and Sociology of the Performing Arts." 1-37 in Kamerman, Jack B.; . Martorella, Rosanne. *Performers and Performances: The Social Organization of Artistic Work.* South Hadley, MA: J.F. Bergin; 1983. xiii, 303 pp.
USA. 1982. Historical studies. ■Introductory essay develops a phenomenology and sociological theory of performing arts.

1515 Blau, Herbert. "Ideology and Performance." *TJ*. 1983 Dec.; 35(4): 441-460. Notes.
USA. Europe. 1850-1956. Critical studies. ■Semiological links in drama among the work of Artaud, Brecht, Pinter, Hebdige, Barthes, Marx and 'Lacanian Freud' and their influence by Nietzsche.

1516 Freydberg, Elizabeth Hadley. "The Concealed Dependence upon White Culture in Baraka's 1969 Aesthetic." *BALF*. 1983 Spring; 17: 27-29.
USA. 1969. Critical studies. ■Attempt to show that Baraka's nationalist Black philosophy and aesthetic is based on traditional white Western aesthetics.

1517 Gaylord, Karen. "Theatrical Performances: Structure and Process, Tradition and Revolt." 135-149 in Kamerman, Jack B.; . Martorella, Rosanne. *Performers and Performances: The Social Organization of Artistic Work.* South Hadley, MA: J.F. Bergin; 1983. xiii, 303 pp.
USA. Greece. 499 B.C.-1983 A.D. Critical studies. ■Performance styles and conventions as reflective of contemporary current social conditions. Major examples taken from ancient Greek theatre. Grp/movt: Naturalism.

1518 Kateb, George. "Hannah Arendt: Alienation and America." *Raritan*. 1983 Summer; 3(1): 4-34.
USA. Europe. 1900-1983. Critical studies. ■Criticism of antimodernist Hannah Arendt's work, with reference to Lessing, Brecht, Kafka and Isak Dinesen. Grp/movt: Antimodernism.

1519 Moore, John Joseph. *A Phenomenological Approach to the Aesthetic Receptivity of a Dramatic Art Work.* Buffalo: State Univ. of New York at Buffalo; 1982. 95 pp. [Diss.: University Microfilms order no. DA8223997.]

DRAMA: General—Theory/criticism

USA. 1982. Critical studies. ■Application of Roman Ingarden's phenomenological approach to receptivity to audiences of three productions of Sam Shepard's *Curse of the Starving Class*.

1520 Showalter, Elaine. "Critical Cross-Dressing: Male Feminists and The Woman of the Year." *Raritan*. 1983 Fall; 3(2): 130-149.

USA. France. UK-England. 1983. Critical studies. ■Significance of gender in feminist criticism with reference to historical materialism, deconstruction and phenomenon of cross-dressing in theatre. Grp/movt: Feminism.

1521 Smith, James F. "Blacks and Blues: Amiri Baraka's Esthetics." *JAC*. 1983 Spring; 6(1): 76-83. Notes.

USA. 1963-1967. Critical studies. ■Baraka's aesthetics found in the Blues, are used in *Blues People: Negro Music in America, The Dutchman* and *The Screamers*, as means of coping.

Training

1522 "Dramaturgy is an Art, Not a Science." *NFT*. 1983; 36: 12-13. Illus.: Photo. B&W. [Also in French as 'La dramaturgie est un art, non une science'.]

Finland. 1965-1983. Historical studies. ■Dramaturgy, as taught by Ritva Holmberg at the Theatre Academy of Finland, stresses artistic creativity. Dramaturgs learn to write scripts and to work with directors in rehearsal.

1523 Gontard, Denis. "Jacques Copeau et les problèmes d'école." (Jacques Copeau and School Problems.) *RHT*. 1983; 35(1): 110-116. Notes.

France. 1913-1930. Historical studies. ■Concept of school in Jacques Copeau's work.

1524 Sacchetti, Luciana. "Entrare con la gamba destra dalla quinta sinistra." (To Enter with the Right Foot from the Left Wing.) *QT*. 1983; 5(20): 156-162.

Italy. 1981-1983. Historical studies. ■Interview with Jeray Sthur and Marisa Fabbri about research project entitled 'Theatre's Heresy: Stanislavskij'.

Comedy

Performance/production

1525 Schrickx, Willem. "'Pickleherring' and English Actors in Germany." *ShS*. 1983; 36: 135-147. Notes.

Germany. England. 1590-1620. Historical studies. ■Account of English actors Robert Browne, John Green, Robert Reynolds, George Vincent and Richard Jones on the continent, with special attention to Germany. Comic character types of John Posset, Stockfish and Pickleherring discussed.

1526 Fritzsche, Dietmar. "Umkehr von Aufwand und Wirkung." (A Turning Away from Display and Effect.) *TZ*. 1982 Jan.; 37: 11-12. Illus.: Photo.

Germany, East. 1975-1982. Reviews of performances. ■Premiere of Shakespeare's *A Midsummer Night's Dream* at the Berlin Metropol Theater and a revival of the 1975 production of the same play staged by Georg Kreisler. Grp/movt: Social realism.

1527 Michaelis, Rolf. "Schweigesprache, Schweigelüge." (Language of Silence, Language of Lies.) *TH*. 1983 May: 13-15.

Germany, West. 1983. Histories-sources. ■Report on director Ernst Wendt's work on Heinrich von Kleist's *Der zerbrochene Krug (The Broken Jug)* at Deutsches Schauspielhaus, Hamburg.

1528 Passow, Wilfred. "Ein Requisit zum Sprechen bringen: Die vielfältige Verwendung einer Holzperlenkette als Requisit in Einer Inszenierung von Niccolò Machiavellis Komödie *Mandragola* am Institut für Theaterwissenschaft der Universität München." (To Make a Property Talk: The Manifold Use of a String of Wooden Pearls As a Property in a Production of Niccolò Machiavelli's Comedy *Mandragola* at the Institut für Theaterwissenschaft, University of Munich.) *MuK*. 1983; 29: 189-195. Notes. Biblio.

Germany, West. 1979-1980. Critical studies. ■Methods of communication involving a string of wooden pearls used by the actor playing the role of Ligurio.

1529 De Luigi, Gianni. "Il reduce ovvero l'eroismo della vigliaccheria." (The 'War Horse', or the Heroism of Cowardice.)

Italy. 1983. Histories-sources. ■Director Gianni De Luigi explains his ideas of interpretation and staging of Ruzante's *Il reduce (Ruzante Returns from the Wars)*.

1530 Paladini Volterra, Angela. "Verso una moderna produzione teatrale." (Towards a Modern Theatrical Production.) *QT*. 1983; 5(20): 87-144. Notes. Append.

Italy. 1770-1797. Historical studies. ■Success of bourgeois comedy over *commedia dell'arte*.

1531 Benach, Joan Anton. "El Teatre Lliure en el misterio de Shakespeare." (Teatre Lliure and the Shakespeare Mystery.) *ElPu*. 1983 Dec.: 14-15.

Spain. 1983. Historical studies. ■Catalan version of Shakespeare's *As You Like It* by Teatre Lliure.

1532 Melendres, Jaume. "Escenificar Labiche, elogi de l'apart." (Staging Labiche, Tribute to the Aside.) *EECIT*. 1983 June; 23: 49-67. Notes. Illus.: Plan. Print. B&W. Grd.Plan. 4: 12 cm. x 6 cm.

Spain. France. 1967-1982. Technical studies. ■Importance of the aside technique and relation between the form and the content in staging Eugène Labiche plays *Mon Ismen (My Ismenia)* and *Le plus heureux des trois (The Happiest of the Three)*.

1533 Edwards, Christopher. "Sheridan's *The Rivals* at the National." *Drama*. 1983 Autumn; 149: 4-5. Illus.: Design. B&W. 4: 3 in. x 5 in.

UK-England. 1983. Reviews of performances. ■Review of production at the National Theatre: rare revival of eighteenth century comedy.

1534 Hickman, Christie. "Beryl Reid, Comedy Actress." *Drama*. 1983 Summer; 148: 12-14. Illus.: Photo. B&W. 1: 3 in. x 4 in.

UK-England. 1920-1983. Critical studies. ■Critical account of Beryl Reid's work as a comedy actress.

1535 Cunningham, Dennis; Rich, Frank; Barnes, Clive; Wilson, Edwin; Watt, Douglas; Siegel, Joel; Kissel, Howard; Kalem, T.E.; Kroll, Jack; Beaufort, John. "*Brighton Beach Memoirs*." *NYTCR*. 1983 Mar. 21; 44(4): 344-349.

USA. 1983. Reviews of performances. ■Ten critics review Neil Simon's *Brighton Beach Memoirs*, directed by Gene Saks. Presented at the Alvin Theatre.

1536 Gussow, Mel; Stasio, Marilyn; Clarke, Gerald; Kroll, Jack; Barnes, Clive; Wilson, Edwin; Nelson, Don. "*Torch Song Trilogy*." *NYTCR*. 1983 May 30; 44(9): 242-246.

USA. 1983. Reviews of performances. ■Seven critics review Harvey Fierstein's *Torch Song Trilogy*, directed by Peter Pope. Presented at the Little Theatre.

1537 Kalb, Jonathan. "Building the Better *Benno Blimpie*." *ThM*. 1983 Winter; 15(1): 73-78. Illus.: Photo. Print. B&W. 3.

USA. 1973-1983. Reviews of performances. ■New production of revised play, directed by author Albert Innaurato, at Playwrights Horizons, 'solves many of the problems that the play has had in the past'.

1538 Kissel, Howard; Beaufort, John; Watt, Douglas; Rich, Frank; Cunningham, Dennis; Siegel, Joel; Barnes, Clive; Corliss, Richard; Kroll, Jack. "*All's Well That Ends Well*." *NYTCR*. 1983 May 2; 44(7): 281-288.

USA. 1983. Reviews of performances. ■Nine critics review Shakespeare's *All's Well That Ends Well*, directed by Trevor Nunn. Presented at the Martin Beck Theatre.

1539 Rheuban, Joyce. *Harry Langdon: The Comedian as Metteur-en-Scène*. Rutherford, NJ: Fairleigh Dickinson UP; 1983. 244 pp. Biblio. Index. Filmography.

USA. 1884-1944. Historical studies. Related to Media: Film.

1540 Rich, Frank; Schickel, Richard; Barnes, Clive; Watt, Douglas; Beaufort, John; Cohen, Ron. "*Breakfast with Les and Bess*." *NYTCR*. 1983 May 30; 44(9): 230-233.

USA. 1983. Reviews of performances. ■Six critics review Lee Kalcheim's *Breakfast with Les and Bess*, directed by Barnet Kellerman. Presented at the Hudson Guild.

DRAMA: Comedy—Performance/production

1541 Rich, Frank; Watt, Douglas; Wilson, Edwin; Kroll, Jack; Barnes, Clive; Kissel, Howard; Beaufort, John; Siegel, Joel; Cunningham, Dennis; Worrell, Denise. "*Noises Off.*" *NYTCR.* 1983 Dec. 31; 44(19): 61-66.
USA. 1983. Reviews of performances. ■Ten critics review Michael Blakemore's production of *Noises Off*, by Michael Frayn. Presented at the Brooks Atkinson Theatre.

1542 Rich, Frank; Watt, Douglas; Kissel, Howard; Barnes, Clive; Beaufort, John; Kalem, T.E.; Kroll, Jack. "*The Middle Ages.*" *NYTCR Off Broadway Supplement I.* 1983 Apr. 18; 44(6): 290-293.
USA. 1983. Reviews of performances. ■Seven critics review David Trainer's production of *The Middle Ages*, by A.R. Gurney, Jr. presented at the Theatre at St. Peter's.

1543 Watt, Douglas; Rich, Frank; Barnes, Clive; Kissel, Howard; Beaufort, John; Cunningham, Dennis; Siegel, Joel. "*The Misanthrope.*" *NYTCR.* 1983 Jan. 1; 44(1): 386-389.
USA. 1983. Reviews of performances. ■Seven critics review Molière's *The Misanthrope*, translated by Richard Wilbur and directed by Stephen Porter at Circle in the Square.

1544 Watt, Douglas; Cohen, Ron; Gold, Sylviane; Barnes, Clive; Rich, Frank. "*Baby with the Bathwater.*" *NYTCR Off Broadway Supplement IV.* 1983 Dec. 12; 44(18): 78-81.
USA. 1983. Reviews of performances. ■Five critics review Christopher Durang's *Baby with the Bathwater*, directed by Jerry Zaks at Playwrights Horizons.

1545 Wilson, Edwin; Rich, Frank; Watt, Douglas; Barnes, Clive; Siegel, Joel; Kissel, Howard; Kalem, T.E.; Kroll, Jack; Cunningham, Dennis. "*Private Lives.*" *NYTCR.* 1983 May 16; 44(8): 252-257.
USA. 1983. Reviews of performances. ■Nine critics review Noel Coward's *Private Lives*, directed by Milton Katselas. Presented at the Lunt-Fontanne Theatre.

Plays/librettos/scripts

1546 Hein, Jürgen. "Themen und Formen der Parodie in Nestroys Theaterliedern." (Themes and Forms of Parody in Nestroy's Theatre Songs.) *Ns.* 1983-1984; 5(3-4): 62-65. Biblio.
Austria. 1833-1862. Critical studies. ■Relation between couplet and parody as exemplified in Johann Nestroy's songs.

1547 Hüttner, Johann. "Die Parodie auf dem Wiener Volkstheater vor Johann Nestroy." (The Parody on the Stage of Viennese Popular Theatre before Johann Nestroy.) *Ns.* 1983-1984; 5(3-4): 59-61.
Austria. 1801-1861. Critical studies. ■Parody as a tradition of a popular theatre.

1548 Mautner, Franz H. "*Die verhängnisvolle Faschingsnacht:* Eine 'Parodie?'." (*The Fateful Carnival Night:* A Parody?) *Ns.* 1983-1984; 5(3-4): 41-48. Illus.: Photo.
Austria. 1839. Critical studies. ■Genre-analysis and comparison of Nestroy's play *Die verhängnisvolle Faschingsnacht* with Karl von Holtei's *Ein Trauerspiel in Berlin* (A Tragedy in Berlin).

1549 Obermaier, Walter. "Johann Nestroys *Häuptling Abendwind*: Offenbachrezeption und satirisches Element." (Johann Nestroy's *Häuptling Abendwind*: Reception of Offenbach and Satirical Elements.) *Ns.* 1983-1984; 5(3-4): 49-58.
Austria. 1833. Critical studies. ■Role of censorship in Nestroy's *Häuptling Abendwind* as an adaptation of Jacques Offenbach's *Vent de soir*.

1550 Pausch, Oskar. "Unbekannte Nestroyana in der Theatersammlung der Österreichische Nationalbibliothek: 2. Bericht." (Unknown Nestroyana in the Theatre Collection of the Austrian National Library: 2nd Report.) *Ns.* 1983-1984; 5(1-2): 16-20. Notes. Illus.: Photo.
Austria. 1801-1862. Historical studies. ■Report on recently discovered materials on Johann Nestroy in the Theatre Collection of the Austrian National Library.

1551 Walla, Friedrich. "*Prinz Friedrich* und kein Ende." (*Prince Friedrich* and No End.) *Ns.* 1983-1984; 4(1-2): 12-15.
Austria. 1833. Textual studies. ■Recently discovered manuscript of Nestroy's play.

1552 Walla, Friedrich. "Parodie, Parodistisches Seitenstück, Singspiel?" (Parody, Parodic Sideshow, or Operetta?)*Ns.* 1983-1984; 5(3-4): 66-74. Notes.
Austria. 1833-1862. Critical studies. ■Genre classification of parody and related forms in Johann Nestroy's plays.

1553 Yates, W. Edgar. "Kriterien der Nestroy-Rezeption, 1837-1838." (Criteria of Nestroy-Reception, 1837-1838.) *Ns.* 1983-1984; 5(1-2): 3-11. Notes.
Austria. 1837-1838. Historical studies. ■Critical reception of performances of Johann Nestroy's plays.

1554 Argetsinger, Gerald S. *Ludvig Holberg's Comedies.* Carbondale, IL: Southern Illinois UP; 1983. xxxvi, 175 pp.
Denmark. 1684-1754. Critical studies. ■Study of Holberg's plays and their original productions, with historical and biographical information.

1555 Krause, David. *The Profane Book of Irish Comedy.* Ithaca, NY: Cornell UP; 1982. 337 pp. Pref. Notes. Index.
Eire. UK-Ireland. 1840-1965. Critical studies. ■Irreverent aspects of Irish comedy seen through the works of 14 Irish dramatists. Includes discussions of barbarous comedy, manners and morality.

1556 Bednarz, James P. "Imitations of Spenser in *A Midsummer Night's Dream.*" 81-103 in Barkan, Leonard. *Renaissance Drama, New Series XIV: Relations and Influences.* Evanston, IL: Northwestern UP; 1983. x, 196 pp.
England. 1595. Critical studies. ■*A Midsummer Night's Dream* as a parody of Spenser's *The Teares of the Muses*.

1557 Campbell, Thomas J. "Richard Cumberland's *The Wheel of Fortune:* An Unpublished Scene." *NCTR.* 1983 Summer; 11(1): 1-11. Notes. Illus.: Handbill. B&W. 2: 5 in. x 6 in.
England. 1795. Textual studies. ■Description and transcription of an hitherto unpublished scene from Cumberland's *The Wheel of Fortune*.

1558 Hume, Robert D. "'The Change in Comedy': Cynical Versus Exemplary Comedy on the London Stage, 1678-1698." *ET.* 1983 May; 1(2): 101-118. Notes.
England. 1678-1693. Historical studies. ■New evaluation of the change from Restoration to sentimental comedy prescribes new definition of cynical comedy and redates its decline.

1559 Norland, Howard B. "Formalizing English Farce: *Johan Johan* and Its French Connection." *CompD.* 1983 Summer; 17(2): 141-152. Notes.
England. France. 1520-1533. Critical studies. ■*Johan Johan* is considered an English cultural and dramatic adaptation from the French *Farce nouvelle très bonne et fort joyeuse du Pasté*.

1560 Robinson, J.W. "The Art and Meaning of *Gammer Gurton's Needle.*" 42-80 in Barkan, Leonard. *Renaissance Drama, New Series XIV: Relations and Influences.* Evanston, IL: Northwestern UP; 1983. x, 196 pp.
England. 1530-1555. Critical studies. ■Comparison of *Gammer Gurton's Needle* with *Ralph Roister Doister, Jack Juggler, The Two Angry Women of Abingdon* and others.

1561 Singh, Sarup. *Family Relationships in Shakespeare and the Restoration Comedy of Manners.* Delhi: Oxford UP; 1983. x, 233 pp.
England. 1595-1699. Critical studies. ■Examination of Shakespeare's concern with family relationships by using socio-political writing from the sixteenth and seventeenth centuries.

1562 Teatro Stabile di Torino. *A teatro con Scapino.* (At the Theatre with Scapino.) Turin: Comune di Torino; 1983. 37 pp. (Quaderni di ricerca). Tables. Illus.: Photo. B&W.
France. Italy. 1671-1983. Instructional materials. ■Discussion of *The Tricks of Scapin* (Les Fourberies de Scapin), addressed to teachers and children of primary schools, designed to enhance their appreciation of the production mounted by Teatro Stabile di Torino.

1563 Albanese, Ralph, Jr. "Modes de théâtralité dans *L'Illusion comique.*" (Theatrical Modes in *The Comic Illusion*.) 129-149 in Margitic, Milorad R. *Corneille comique (The Comic Corneille)*. Nine Studies of Pierre Corneille's Comedy with

DRAMA: Comedy—Plays/librettos/scripts

an Introduction and Bibliography. Paris, Seattle and Tuebingen: Papers on French Seventeenth Century Literature; 1982. 213 pp. (Papers on Seventeenth Century Literature/Biblio 17.) Notes.
France. 1606-1684. Critical studies. ∎*L'Illusion comique* as a meditation on problems of theatricality, including the powers and limits of illusions, the dynamic relationship among dramatist, actor and spectator, distantiation and catharsis.

1564 Allentuch, Harriet R. "Corneille, *Mélite*, and the Comedy of Narcissism." 91-105 in Margitic, Milorad R. *Corneille comique (The Comic Corneille)*. Nine Studies of Pierre Corneille's Comedy with an Introduction and Bibliography. Paris, Seattle and Tuebingen: Papers on French Seventeenth Century Literature; 1982. 213 pp. (Papers on Seventeenth Century Literature/Biblio 17.) Notes.
France. 1606-1684. Critical studies. ∎Pscychological foundations of Corneille's *oeuvre* laid in *Mélite*. Analysis of the concept of narcissism in three young protagonists.

1565 Blanc, André. "L'image de la Cour dans le théâtre comique sous le règne de Louis XIV." (The Image of the Court in Comic Theatre During the Reign of Louis XIV.) *RHT*. 1983; 35(4): 402-412. Notes.
France. 1650-1715. Critical studies. ∎Representation of court manners in seventeenth century French comedy, including plays by Gabriel Gilbert, Molière and Boursault.

1566 Formosa, Feliu. "Próleg a *Ubú, rei*, d'Alfred Jarry." (Prologue to Alfred Jarry's *Ubu Roi*.) 5-13 in *Ub7, rei*. Translated from the French by Joan Oliver. Barcelona: Institut del Teatre; 1983. 80 pp. (Biblioteca Teatral 22.)
France. 1896-1907. Critical studies. ∎Analysis of the *Ubu* Cycle with an emphasis on its protagonist. Study of the public reaction at the first performance and the social implication of the play.

1567 Grivelet, Michel. "Jacques Copeau, traducteur de Shakespeare." (Jacques Copeau, Translator of Shakespeare.) *RHT*. 1983; 35(1): 71-81. Notes.
France. 1914. Textual studies. ∎Compares the Suzanne Bing and Jacques Copeau translations of *Twelfth Night* with the Théodore Lascarais version published as part of the repertory of the Vieux Colombier.

1568 Guichemerre, Roger. "Le personnage du rival perfide dans les premières comédies de Pierre Corneille." (The Treacherous Rival in Pierre Corneille's Early Comedies.) 55-74 in Margitic, Milorad R., ed. *Corneille comique (The Comic Corneille)*. Nine Studies of Pierre Corneille's Comedy with an Introduction and Bibliography. Paris, Seattle and Tuebingen: Papers on French Seventeenth Century Literature; 1982. 213 pp. (Papers on Seventeenth Century Literature/Biblio 17.) Notes.
France. 1606-1684. Critical studies. ∎Role of the unhappy rival in Corneille's early comedies.

1569 Kerr, Cynthia B. "Corneille, Molière et le comique de l'amour absolu." (Corneille, Molière and the Comedy of Absolute Love.) 107-128 in Margitic, Milorad R., ed. *Corneille comique (The Comic Corneille)*. Nine Studies of Pierre Corneille's Comedy with an Introduction and Bibliography. Paris, Seattle and Tuebingen: Papers on French Seventeenth Century Literature; 1982. 213 pp. (Papers on Seventeenth Century Literature/Biblio 17.) Notes.
France. 1606-1684. Critical studies. ∎Affinities of style and content between Corneille's *La Place Royale (The Royal Square)* and Molière's *Le Misanthrope*.

1570 Knutson, Harold C. "Corneille's Early Comedies: Variations in Comic Form." 35-54 in Margitic, Milorad R., ed. *Corneille comique (The Comic Corneille)*. Nine Studies of Pierre Corneille's Comedy with an Introduction and Bibliography. Paris, Seattle and Tuebingen: Papers on French Seventeenth Century Literature; 1982. 213 pp. (Papers on Seventeenth Century Literature/Biblio 17.) Notes.
France. 1606-1684. Critical studies. ∎Corneille's early comedies as a series of variations in comic form.

1571 Lyons, John D. "Discourse and Authority in *Le Menteur*." 151-168 in Margitic, Milorad R., ed. *Corneille comique (The Comic Corneille)*. Nine Studies of Pierre Corneille's Comedy with an Introduction and Bibliography. Paris, Seattle and Tuebingen: Papers on French Seventeenth Century Literature; 1982. 213 pp. (Papers on Seventeenth Century Literature/Biblio 17.) Notes.
France. 1606-1684. Critical studies. ∎Four principal types of discursive authority in *Le Menteur (The Liar)*: textuality, empiricism, nobility and urbanity.

1572 Margitic, Milorad R., ed. *Corneille comique*. (The Comic Corneille.) Nine Studies of Pierre Corneille's Comedy with an Introduction and Bibliography. Paris, Seattle and Tuebingen: Papers on French Seventeenth Century Literature; 1982. 213 pp. (Papers on Seventeenth Century Literature/Biblio 17.) Pref. Biblio. Illus.: Dwg. 2.
France. 1606-1684. Critical studies. ∎Collections of essays dealing with aesthetics, psychology, sociology and ideology in Corneille's work, including four general studies, five studies of individual plays and a bibliographical guide.

1573 Miller, Judith G. "The Theatrics of Triangular Trysts, or Variations on a Form: Labiche, Vitrac, Beckett." *MD*. 1983 Dec.; 26(4): 447-454. Notes.
France. 1870-1983. Critical studies. ∎Bedroom farce as a genre in Roger Vitrac's *Entrée Libre (Free Admission)*, Samuel Beckett's *Comédie et actes divers (Play and Various Acts)*, and Eugène Labiche's *Le plus heureux des trois (The Happiest of the Three)*.

1574 Planson, Claude. "*Amphitryon ou le mythe ressuscité*." (*Amphitryon* or Myth Revived.) *CF*. 1983 July; 120: 16-17. Illus.: Photo.
France. 1668-1980. Critical studies. ∎Reasons for different responses to the Amphitryon myth between the 17th and 20th century audiences.

1575 Pronko, Leonard C. *Eugène Labiche and Georges Feydeau*. New York: Grove P; 1982. ix, 181 pp.
France. 1815-1921. Critical studies. ∎Analysis of farces by Eugène Labiche and Georges Feydeau.

1576 Reliquet, Philippe. "Molière et la normalité absolue." (Molière and Absolute Normality.) *CF*. 1983 July; 120 : 18-21. Illus.: Photo.
France. 1642-1673. Critical studies. ∎Molière is sometimes accused of anti-feminism, but his satire is directed at both sexes equally.

1577 Scherer, Jacques. "Le sens des *Femmes savantes*." (The Meaning of *The Learned Ladies*.) *CF*. 1982 Apr.; 108: 11-13.
France. 1672. Critical studies. ∎Analysis of Molière's intended meaning of the play.

1578 Sellstrom, Donald A. "Comedy in *Theodore* and Beyond." 169-183 in Margitic, Milorad R., ed. *Corneille comique (The Comic Corneille)*. Nine Studies of Pierre Corneille's Comedy with an Introduction and Bibliography. Paris, Seattle and Tuebingen: Papers on French Seventeenth Century Literature; 1982. 213 pp. (Papers on Seventeenth Century Literature/Biblio 17.) Notes.
France. 1606-1684. Critical studies. ∎The main interest of *Théodore* today is not the subject of prostitution, but Corneille's handling of it: he avoids scandalizing the audience, but creates an aesthetic imbalance.

1579 Verhoeff, Han. "Le don chez Corneille." (The Gift in Corneille.) 15-34 in Margitic, Milorad R., ed. *Corneille comique (The Comic Corneille)*. Nine Studies of Pierre Corneille's Comedy with an Introduction and Bibliography. Paris, Seattle and Tuebingen: Papers on French Seventeenth Century Literature/Biblio 17.) Biblio.
France. 1606-1684. Critical studies. ∎Gift-giving is a constant and important factor of which women are always the object.

1580 Aikin, Judith P. "Practical Uses of Comedy at a Seventeenth Century Court: The Polemic in Caspar Stieler's *Der Vermeinte Printz*." *TJ*. 1983 Dec.; 35(4): 519-532. Notes.

DRAMA: Comedy—Plays/librettos/scripts

Germany. 1600-1699. Critical studies. ■Revised view of Stieler's comedies in terms of their political meaning (female inheritance) places Stieler in the mainstream of the best European comedic writers.

1581 Parente, James A., Jr. "Baroque Comedy and the Stability of the State." *GQ*. 1983 May; 56(3): 419-430.

Germany. 1618-1685. Critical studies. ■Examination of Baroque themes and writers. Grp/movt: Baroque theatre.

1582 Goldberg, Sander M. "Terence and the Death of Comedy." *CompD*. 1982-1983 Winter; 16(4): 312-324. Notes.

Greece. Roman Empire. 343 B.C.-1400 A.D. Critical studies. ■Comparison of the structure of Greek and Roman comedy through the works of Menander and Terence. Discusses the subsequent death of the genre in the second century BC and its revival by Italian humanists in the 14th century.

1583 Chaitanya, Krishna. "The Thullal of Kerala." *SNJPA*. 1983 July-Sep.; 69: 24-30. Illus.: Photo. B&W. 4.

India. 1700-1799. Critical studies. ■Description of *thullal*, a form of comedy, created by Kunchan Nambiar, and performed by a single actor. The subject matter is taken from Puranas but social evils are satirized during the performances. Related to Dance-Drama.

1584 Guidotti, Angela. *Il modello e la trasgressione: commedie del primo '500*. (Model and Transgression: Comedies of the Early Sixteenth Century.) Rome: Bulzoni; 1983. 165 pp. (Strumenti di ricerca 37.) Notes. Index.

Italy. Roman Empire. 1508-1533. Critical studies. ■Usage of vernacular in Ariosto's, Machiavelli's and Ruzante's comedies, as compared with Roman drama.

1585 Fujii, Takeo. *Humor and Satire in Early English Comedy and Japanese* Kyōgen *Drama: A Cross-Cultural Study in Dramatic Arts*. Tokyo: KUFS Publication; 1983. xii, 195 pp.

Japan. England. 1400. Historical studies. ■Comparison of sources of humor in *kyōgen* and early English comedy: includes development of *kyōgen* and its relation to ritual.

1586 Chiarini, Gioachino; Tessari, Roberto. *Teatro del corpo, teatro della parola — Due saggi sul 'comico'*. (Theatre of the Body, Theatre of the Word — Two Essays on Comedy.) Pisa: ETS; 1983. vi, 168 pp. (Caverna e skene — Gli archetipi e le forme dello spettacolo 1.) Notes. Biblio. Tables. Illus.: Photo. B&W.

Roman Republic. 254-184 B.C. Critical studies. ■Comic mechanism in Plautus' *Amphitruo* and *Casina*. Grp/movt: Roman theatre.

1587 Konstan, David. *Roman Comedy*. Ithaca, NY: Cornell UP; 1983. 182 pp.

Roman Republic. 254-159 B.C. Critical studies. ■Literary analysis of the plays of Plautus and Terence as they relate to Roman society. Grp/movt: Roman theatre.

1588 Porrúa, del Carmen. *La Galicia decimonónica en las Comedias Bárbaras de Valle-Inclán*. (The Nineteenth Century Galicia in Valle-Inclán's Comedias Bárbaras.) Sada (La Coruna): Edición Castro; 1983. 288 pp. Notes. Biblio.

Spain. 1866-1936. Critical studies. ■Analysis of forms, styles, characters and influences in Valle-Inclán's *comedias bárbaras*.

1589 Blistein, Elmer M. "Alan Ayckbourn: Few Jokes, Much Comedy." *MD*. 1983 Mar.; 26(1): 26-35. Notes.

UK-England. 1974. Critical studies. ■Study of Alan Ayckbourn's comedy, particularly *The Norman Conquests*, which depends on adroit juxtaposition of episodes, the clever manipulation of time and the dexterous use of props.

1590 Ellis, James. "The Counterfeit Presentment: Nineteenth Century Burlesques of *Hamlet*." *NCTR*. 1983 Summer; 11(1): 29-50 . Notes.

UK-England. USA. 1810-1888. Reviews of publications. ■Review essay of several *Hamlet* parodies published in Stanley Wells' *Nineteenth-Century Shakespeare Burlesques*, (Wilmington, DE: Michael Glazier, Inc., 1978) 5 vols.

1591 Hendrickx, Johan R. "Pinero's Court Farces: A Reevaluation." *MD*. 1983 Mar.; 26(1): 54-61. Notes.

UK-England. 1890-1899. Critical studies. ■Study of Arthur Wing Pinero's court farces, (which have been critically neglected) showing a new formula for farce — possible people doing improbable things.

1592 Whitaker, Tom. *Tom Stoppard*. New York: Grove P; 1983. xiii, 177 pp.

UK-England. 1937-1983. Critical studies. ■Playfulness in Tom Stoppard's comedies.

1593 Krause, David. "The Ironic Victory of Defeat in Irish Comedy." *OCA*. 1982; 1: 33-63. Notes.

UK-Ireland. Eire. 1900-1940. Critical studies. ■Role of comic irony and anti-heroes in Irish comedy and its influence on Pinter, Beckett and Stoppard.

1594 Gray, Beverly. "A Conversation with Beth Henley." *PArts*. 1983 Apr.; 17(4): 30. Illus.: Photo. [1983 interview in West Hollywood, CA.]

USA. 1983. Histories-sources. ■Interview with playwright Beth Henley.

1595 Kleb, William. "Sam Shepard's Free-For-All: *Fool for Love* at the Magic Theatre." *ThM*. 1983 Summer-Fall; 14(3): 77-82. Illus.: Photo. Print. B&W. 2.

USA. 1983. Critical studies. ■Throughout his work, Shepard insists on the blood-bond as a powerful, primal connective force.

1596 Powers, Kim. "Fragments of a Trilogy: Harvey Fierstein's *Torch Song*." *ThM*. 1983 Spring; 14(2): 63-67. Illus.: Photo. 3.

USA. 1983. Critical studies. ■In *Torch Song Trilogy*, Harvey Fierstein has translated his specific masculine/feminine concerns into a universal statement about acceptance.

1597 Worth, Katherine. "Farce and Michael Frayn." *MD*. 1983 Mar.; 26(1): 47-53.

USA. 1983. Critical studies. ■Michael Frayn's *Noises Off* is critiqued as a farce in the true sense even though social and moral structures, the launching pad for the farces of the past, have been loosened.

Reference materials

1598 Margitic, Milorad R. "*Corneille Comique*: A Bibliographical Guide." 185-213 in Margitic, Milorad R., ed. *Corneille comique (The Comic Corneille)*. Nine Studies of Pierre Corneille's Comedy with an Introduction and Bibliography. Paris, Seattle and Tuebingen: Papers on French Seventeenth Century Literature; 1982. 213 pp. (Papers on Seventeenth Century Literature/Biblio 17.)

France. 1633-1980. ■Bibliography of Corneille criticism with indexes to authors and subjects, and a chronological index.

Theory/criticism

1599 Harwood, John T. *Critics, Values, and Restoration Comedy*. Carbondale, IL: Southern Illinois UP; 1982. xvii, 177 pp.

England. 1670-1700. Critical studies. ■Restoration critical polemic on morality in drama. Implications of the raised issues are also seen in the modern perspective, applying government-sponsored *Report of the Commission on Obscenity and Pornography* (1970) as a criterion.

1600 Bermel, Albert. *Farce: A History from Aristophanes to Woody Allen*. New York: Simon & Schuster; 1982. 464 pp.

Europe. USA. 425 B.C.-1982 A.D. Critical studies. ■Nature and history of farce in theatre, film and media, with a division into four types: realism, fantasy, theatricalism and the well-made play. Grp/movt: Realism; Theatricalism; Well-made Play.

1601 Grawe, Paul H. *Comedy in Space, Time, and the Imagination*. Chicago: Nelson-Hall; 1983. vi, 362 pp.

Europe. North America. 499 B.C.-1980 A.D. Critical studies. ■Author's definition of the comedy genre eliminates any Aristotelian or psychological notions. The origin of comedy is seen in biblical literature.

1602 Wade, Gerald E. "Concerning a Recent Interpretation of Calderonian Comedy." *BCom*. 1982 Summer; 34(1): 125-129. Notes.

Spain. 1600-1681. Critical studies. ■Calderón's plays and theory of comedy as set forth in Robert Ter Horst's 'The Origin and Meaning of Comedy' from *Studies in Honor of Everett W. Hesse*, published in 1981.

Training

1603 Abraham, Lee. "Comedy Acting: Jokes Are a Serious Business." *ThNe*. 1983 May; 15(5): 9, 16.

DRAMA

USA. 1980-1983. Instructional materials. ■Seven suggestions for providing young actors a coherent approach to the problems of comic acting.

Experimental forms

Audience

1604 Brooks, Chris. "Seize the Day: The Mummers' *Gros Mourn.*" *CTR.* 1983 Spring; 37: 38-50. Illus.: Photo. Neg. B&W. 4. [Excerpt from *None of That Artsy-Fartsy Stuff: A History of the Newfoundland Mummers Troupe, 1972-1982.*]
Canada. 1973. Historical studies. ■Evolution of *Gros Mourn,* a collective creation about a community crisis encountered by mummers in Gros Morne area of Newfoundland.

Basic theatrical documents

1605 Lombardi, Sandro; D'Amburgo, Marion; Tiezzi, Federico. Sulla strada *dei Magazzini Criminali.* (*On the Road* by Magazzini Criminali.) Milan: Ubulibri; 1983. 166 pp. (Photographs by Maurizio Buscarino.) Pref. Append. Filmography. Biblio. Tables. Illus.: Photo. B&W. Color.
Italy. 1982. Histories-sources. ■Playtext of the Magazzini Criminali's production of *Sulla strada (On the Road)* including some writings of the authors which explain their theory of theatre.

Institutions

1606 Smith, Patricia Keeney. "Canada: Steven Rumbelow and the Triple Action Theatre." *CTR.* 1983 Spring; 37: 121-123. Print. B&W. 1: 4 in. x 5 in.
Canada. 1980-1983. Historical studies. ■Description of Steven Rumbelow and work of Triple Action Theatre.

1607 Bianchi, Ruggero. "A Process of Transformation: Falso Movimento." *TDR.* 1983 Spring; 27(1): 40-53. Illus.: Photo.
Italy. 1977-1983. Historical studies. ■History and analysis of the avant-garde theatre Falso Movimento and descriptions of three productions. Related to Media: Mixed media.

1608 Donker, Janny. "Hauser Orkater and Its Offspring: The Herd and the Mexican Hound." *TDR.* 1983 Spring; 27(1): 25-39. Illus.: Photo.
Netherlands. 1971-1983. Historical studies. ■History of the Hauser Orkater theatre company and two groups that emerged from it: De Mexicaanse Hond (The Mexican Hound) and De Horde (The Herd).

1609 John, Hans-Rainer. "Vielfältiges Nebeneinander: Theater in der Niederlanden." (Multifarious Coexistence: Theatre in the Netherlands.) *TZ.* 1983; 38(1): 33-37. Illus.: Photo. B&W. 10.
Netherlands. 1963-1983. Historical studies. ■Free operating groups and institutionalized theatre in the Netherlands.

1610 Moreno, Fernando. "Towards a New Latin American Theater." *Tk.* 1983 May-June; 3(4): 34-39. Illus.: Dwg. B&W. 4.
North America. South America. 1983. Historical studies. ■Discussion of the Latin American popular theatre workshops, organized by International Theatre Institute with participation of 25 countries.

1611 Bablet, Denis. "Tadeusz Kantor et le Théâtre Cricot 2." (Tadeusz Kantor and Cricot 2 Theatre.) 17-53 in Bablet, Denis. *Tadeusz Kantor.* Le Théâtre Cricot 2: La classe morte — Wielopole-Wielepole. Paris: Editions du CNRS; 1983. v, 288 pp. (Les Voies de la Création Théâtrale 11.) Illus.: Photo. Sketches. 34.
Poland. 1955-1983. Critical studies. ■History of the Cricot 2 Theatre, seen as an alternative form to official Polish theatrical life.

1612 Khan, Naseem. "The Fringe." *Drama.* 1983 Autumn; 149: 8-10.
UK. 1983. Historical studies. ■Growth of alternative theatre and its influence on traditional theatre productions.

1613 Coco, William. "The Open Theatre (1963-1973): Looking Back." *PerAJ.* 1983; 7(3): 25-48. Illus.: Photo. B&W. 13.

USA. 1963-1973. Critical studies. ■Reflections on the significance of The Open Theatre by several of its performers, writers and critical advisers.

Performance/production

1614 Friedlander, Mira. "Survivor: George Luscombe at Toronto Workshop Productions." *CTR.* 1983 Fall; 38: 44-52. Neg. Print. B&W. 4.
Canada. 1983. Historical studies. ■Analysis of artistic style and theory of George Luscombe at Toronto Workshop Productions.

1615 Quadri, Franco. *Il teatro degli anni Settanta: Tradizione e ricerca — Stein, Chéreau, Ronconi, Mnouchkine, Grüber, Bene.* (Theatre of the Seventies: Tradition and Research — Stein, Chéreau, Ronconi, Mnouchkine, Grüber, Bene.) Turin: Einaudi; 1982. 371 pp. (La ricerca critica 13.) Biblio. Illus.: Photo. B&W.
Europe. 1960-1980. Histories-sources. ■Six essays on the productions and artistic views held by leading European directors. Also included: interviews, bibliographies and productions for each director.

1616 Steinbock, Dan. "Nuoren teatterin kriisistä." (On the 'Young Finnish Theatre'.) *Teat.* 1983; 39(5): 12-14. Illus.: Photo. B&W. 2.
Finland. 1978-1983. Critical studies. ■'Young theatre,' by which the author refers primarily to Helsinki avant-garde group theatre and student theatre and indeed as self-reflexive.

1617 Bartram, Graham, ed.; Waine, Anthony, ed. *Brecht in Perspective.* New York: Longman Group; 1982. xv, 231 pp.
Germany. 1925-1956. Critical studies. ■Thirteen essays on Brecht's practical and literary theatre work, including contemporary influences, styles and theory.

1618 Anon. "Revival futurista." (Futurist Revival.) *TeatrC.* 1983-1984 Oct.-Jan.; 3(5): 285-301.
Italy. 1983. Reviews of performances. ■Review of Futurist theatrical and musical performances during Roman Summer festival. Grp/movt: Futurism. Related to Music-Drama: Musical theatre.

1619 Bartalotta, Gianfranco. "L'*Amleto* di Carmelo Bene." (Carmelo Bene's *Hamlet.*) *TeatrC.* 1983 Feb.-May; 2(3): 361-392. Notes. Tables. Illus.: Photo. B&W.
Italy. 1961-1975. Critical studies. ■Critical analysis of Carmelo Bene's rewritten version of *Hamlet.*

1620 Bene, Carmelo. *Sono apparso alla Madonna — Vie d'(H)eros(es).* (I Appeared to the Madonna — Ways of (H)eros(es).) Milan: Longanesi; 1983. 215 pp. (La gaia scienza 69.)
Italy. 1959-1983. Histories-sources. ■Carmelo Bene's autobiography.

1621 Bene, Carmelo; Colomba, Sergio, ed. *La voce di Narciso.* (Narcissus' Voice.) Milan: Il Saggiatore; 1982. 173 pp. (Politeama 3.) Pref.
Italy. 1960-1982. Critical studies. ■Short essays and other writings on theory of acting and theatre in general.

1622 De Marinis, Marco. *Al limite del teatro — Utopie, progetti e aporie nella ricerca teatrale degli anni sessanta e settanta.* (At the Border of Theatre — Utopias, Projects and Doubts in the Theatrical Research of the Sixties and Seventies.) Florence: Casa Usher; 1983. 273 pp. (Saggi 14.) Notes. Index. Tables. Illus.: Photo. B&W.
Italy. 1968-1977. Historical studies. ■Experimental theatre in Italy in the 1960s and 1970s and role of the actor in it.

1623 Grant, Steve; Mitchell, Tony. "An Interview with Dario Fo and Franca Rame." *ThM.* 1983 Summer-Fall; 14(3): 43-49. Illus.: Photo. Print. B&W. 6.
Italy. 1982. Histories-sources. ■Interview with Dario Fo and his wife, actress Franca Rame, on feminism, English production of *Medea,* Italian social and political concerns as well as Fo and Rame's collaboration.

1624 Nava, Piergiulia. *Invenzione e 'stravolgimento' scenico nel teatro di Ezio Maria Caserta.* (Creativity and Scenic Disarray in Ezio Maria Caserta's Theatre.) Negrar: Il Segno; 1983. 211 pp. Notes. Biblio. Tables. Illus.: Photo. B&W.

DRAMA: Experimental forms—Performance/production

Italy. 1983-1975. Historical studies. ■Ezio Maria Caserta's theories and practice of theatre.

1625 Tessari, Roberto. Pinocchio: Summa atheologica di Carmelo Bene. (Pinocchio: Carmelo Bene's Summa atheologica.) Florence: Liberoscambio; 1982. 121 pp. (Quaderni di analisi dello spettacolo 4.) Notes. Biblio. Tables. Illus.: Plan. Photo. B&W.

Italy. 1981. Critical studies. ■Analysis of Carmelo Bene's avant-garde adaptation and staging of Collodi's tale. Interview with the playwright.

1626 Bablet, Denis, ed. T. Kantor. (Tadeusz Kantor.) Paris: Editions du CNRS; 1983. 287 pp. (Les Voies de la Création Théâtrale.) Biblio. Filmography. Illus.: Photo. Dwg.

Poland. 1975-1980. Critical studies. ■Analysis of the recent productions by Tadeusz Kantor.

1627 Filipowicz, Halina. "Expedition into Culture: The Gardzienice." TDR. 1983 Spring; 27(1): 54-71. Illus.: Photo.

Poland. 1968-1983. Historical studies. ■Description of group that performs with and for remote and rural areas.

1628 Gieraczynski, Bogdan. "From The Dead Class to Wielopole, Wielopole: An Interview with Tadeusz Kantor." ThM. 1983 Summer-Fall; 14(3): 59-62. Notes. Illus.: Photo. Print. B&W. 3.

Poland. 1982. History-sources. ■An interview with playwright-director Tadeusz Kantor. After creating The Dead Class (Umarla klasa) with his Polish avant-garde troupe, Cricot 2, Kantor staged a new production called Wielopole, Wielopole, a theatrical evocation of people of the past and their affairs in the village of Wielopole, Kantor's birthplace.

1629 Rzepz, Joanna. Tadeusz Kantor und sein Theater Cricot 2. (Tadeusz Kantor and His Theatre Cricot 2.) Dissertation. Vienna: Univ. of Vienna; 1983. 198 pp.

Poland. 1943-1975. Histories-specific. ■Application of Stanislaw Witkiewicz's philosophy in the productions of Cricot 2 and Tadeusz Kantor's theory of art and theatre. Included are interviews and manifestos.

1630 Auerback, Doris. Shepard, Kopit and Off-Broadway. Boston: Twayne; 1983. vi, 145 pp.

USA. 1957-1983. Critical studies. ■Overview of production of plays by Sam Shepard and Arthur Kopit.

1631 Beck, Julian; Malina, Judith; Quadri, Franco, ed. Il lavoro del Living Theatre (Materiali 1952-1962). (The Work of the Living Theatre — Materials 1952-1962.) Milan: Ubulibri; 1982. 341 pp. Illus.: Photo. B&W.

USA. Europe. 1952-1962. Histories-sources. ■Collection of writings by Julian Beck and Judith Malina accompanied by many pictures. Includes extracts from Judith Malina's diary.

1632 Kott, Jan; Kott, Michael, transl.; Firincioglu, Deniz, transl. "The Theatre of Essence: Kantor and Brook." ThM. 1983 Summer-Fall; 14(3): 55-58. Illus.: Photo. Print. B&W. 4.

USA. France. Poland. 1982. Historical studies. ■Comments on La Mama Theatre production of Tadeusz Kantor's The Dead Class, Kantor's Wielopole, Wielopole and on Peter Brook's Carmen at Bouffes du Nord, Paris. Related to Music-Drama: Opera.

1633 Pivano, Fernanda. "Nuovo teatro d'America e psicodramma." (The New American Theater and Psychodrama.) AdP. 1983; 8(1): 114-120. Illus.: Photo.

USA. 1945-1983. Historical studies. ■New forms of expression (mixed media, happenings, events, etc.) of the post-World War II period mark a decisive break with intimist, neo-realist and expressionist forms of theatre. Grp/movt: Expressionism; Neo-realism.

Plays/librettos/scripts

1634 Verdone, Mario. "Due agitka dell'armeno Egische Ciarenz." (Two Agitkas by the Armenian Egische Ciarenz.) TeatrC. 1983-1984 Oct.-Jan.; 3(5): 209-225. Notes.

Armenia. 1923. Critical studies. ■Egische Ciarenz's plays, particularly Kafkaz, are placed between Futurism and agitprop theatre. Grp/movt: Futurism.

1635 Knapp, Bettina. "Oskar Kokoschka's Murderer Hope of Womankind: An Apocalyptic Experience." TJ. 1983 May; 35(2): 179-194. Notes.

Austria. 1904-1912. Critical studies. ■Kokoschka reveals his rejection of the status quo and of conventions by use of violent language, stage directions and illustrations. His characters show hostility, antagonism and primitivism.

1636 Kokoschka, Oskar; Benincasa, Carmine, ed.; Shanzer, Andrea, transl. La mia vita. (My Life.) Venice: Marsilio; 1982. 216 pp. (Saggi 105 — Frammenti sull'arte 2.) Pref. Tables. Illus.: Photo. B&W. [Translated from German.]

Austria. 1886-1970. Biographies. ■Italian translation of Kokoschka's autobiography Mein Leben, with editorial essay.

1637 Beja, Morris, ed.; Gontarski, S.E., ed.; Astier, Pierre, ed. Samuel Beckett: Humanistic Perspectives. Columbus, OH: Ohio State UP; 1983. x, 217 pp.

Europe. 1906-1983. Critical studies. ■Humanist examination of Samuel Beckett's plays. Grp/movt: Absurdism.

1638 Cascetta, Annamaria. "La sfida del corpo sulla scena teatrale." (Distrust of the Body on the Theatre Stage.) 138-193 in Melchiorre, Virgilio; . Cascetta, Annamaria. Il corpo in scena (The Body Onstage). Milan: Vita e pensiero; 1983. 290 pp. Pref. Notes. Tables. Illus.: Photo. B&W.

Europe. 1930-1980. Critical studies. ■Use of body language in the theatre by Beckett, Artaud, Decroux and Grotowski.

1639 Gelderman, Carol. "Hyperrealism in Contemporary Drama: Retrogressive or Avant-Garde?" MD. 1983 Sep.; 26(3): 357-367. Notes.

Europe. North America. 1970. Historical studies. ■'New' realism (hyperrealism) is a major innovative impulse in the theatre today: realism now, sharp-focus realism, photographic realism, hyperrealism, the realist revival and radical realism.

1640 Lyons, Charles R. Samuel Beckett. New York: Grove P; 1983. 199 pp. (Modern Dramatists Series.)

Europe. 1906-1983. Critical studies. ■Beckett's plays dramatize an epistemological paradox. Grp/movt: Absurdism.

1641 Hervic, Elizabeth. "L'espace des Paravents, espace d'un mystère." (The Space of The Screens: Space of a Mystery Play.) RHT. 1983; 35(2): 251-266. Notes. Tables.

France. 1961. Critical studies. ■Similarities between the structural elements of Genet's Les Paravents and medieval dramaturgy.

1642 Lagrave, Henri. "L'espace théâtral de Jean Tardieu." (Jean Tardieu's Theatrical Space.) MuK. 1983; 29: 242-253.

France. 1947-1980. Critical studies. ■Study of Jean Tardieu's plays. Grp/movt: Absurdism.

1643 Memola, Massimo Marino. "Il teatro del negativo: Beckett e Artaud." (The Negative Theatre: Beckett and Artaud.) QT. 1983 Aug.-Nov.; 6(21-22): 97-104. Notes.

France. Italy. 1925-1960. Critical studies. ■Negation of theatre in plays by Samuel Beckett and Antonin Artaud, and in productions by Carmelo Bene.

1644 Norrish, Peter. "Farce and Ritual: Arrabal's Contribution to Modern Tragic Farce." MD. 1983 Sep.; 26(3): 320-330. Notes.

France. 1932. Critical studies. ■Study of Fernando Arrabal's techniques combining tragic farce and ceremonial ritual both to attack and to liberate himself from the people who controlled his childhood and youth. Related to Ritual-Ceremony: Civic.

1645 Podol, Peter. "Contradictions and Dualities in Artaud and Artaudian Theatre: The Conquest of Mexico and the Conquest of Peru." MD. 1983 Dec.; 26(4): 518-527. Notes.

France. 1921-1948. Critical studies. ■Discussion of Antonin Artaud's use of contradiction, a central mode in his personal and artistic life, and his fascination with the dualities in himself, in life, in his ideal theatre and in the interrelationship of the three.

1646 Poli, Gianni. "I poemi della voce di Antonin Artaud." (Antonin Artaud's Poems of Voice.) TeatrC. 1983 June-Sep.; 2(4): 15-34. Notes.

France. 1938-1948. Textual studies. ■Graphic and linguistic structure of Antonin Artaud's last writings.

DRAMA: Experimental forms—Plays/librettos/scripts

1647 Warner, Keith Q. "*Les Nègres:* A Look at Genet's Excursion into Black Consciousness." *CLAJ.* 1983 June; 26(4): 397-414. Notes.
France. 1948-1968. Textual studies. ■Comparison of Genet's ritual happening to Négritude poetry and Existential philosophy in the context of Theatre of the Absurd and Total Theatre. Grp/movt: Négritude; Existentialism; Absurdism.

1648 Barsotti, Anna. "L'angoscia del macchinismo futurista nel teatro di Ruggero Vasari." (Anguish of *Macchinismo* in Ruggero Vasari's Futurist Theatre.) *TeatrC.* 1983 June-Sep.; 2(4): 65-104. Notes. [Part 1.]
Italy. 1923-1932. Critical studies. ■Part one of an essay on Ruggero Vasari's *macchinismo* as a theme of the Futurist theatre. Grp/movt: Futurism.

1649 Barsotti, Anna. "L'angoscia del macchinismo futurista nel teatro di Ruggero Vasari." (Anguish of Futurist Machinery in Ruggero Vasari's Theatre.) *TeatrC.* 1983-1984 Oct.-Jan.; 3(5): 149-188. Notes. [Part 2.]
Italy. 1923-1932. Critical studies. ■Part two of an essay on Ruggero Vasari's plays and machinery as a theme of the Futurist theatre. Grp/movt: Futurism.

1650 Fo, Dario; Mitchell, Tony, transl. "Popular Culture." *ThM.* 14(3): 50-54. Notes. Append.
Italy. 1974. Histories-sources. ■Text of a speech about the playwright's involvement in revolutionary theatre.

1651 Plassard, Didier. "Le techniche di disumanizzazione nel teatro futurista italiano." (Techniques of Dehumanization in Italian Futurist Theatre.) *TeatrC.* 1983 June-Sep.; 2(4): 35-64. Notes.
Italy. 1909-1931. Historical studies. ■Techniques of character dehumanization and linguistic usage in Italian Futurist theatre. Grp/movt: Futurism.

1652 Sekoni, 'Ropo. "Metaphor As a Basis of Form in Soyinka's Drama." *RAL.* 1983 Spring; 14(1): 45-57. Notes.
Nigeria. 1956-1982. Critical studies. ■Soyinka's plays abound with incremental repetition and are characterized by a web-like interrelationship drawn from Obatala drama. These features attract critics to the world behind the plays more than to their raw action.

1653 Libucha, Iwona. "Le Théâtre à Part de Miron Bialaszewski." (Miron Bialaszewski's Separate Theatre.) *TP.* 1983; 304: 12-16. Illus.: Photo. Print. B&W. 4. [In French and English.]
Poland. 1955-1983. Critical studies. ■Analysis of Bialaszewski's experiments in producing his own work.

1654 Dieckman, Suzanne Burgoyne; Brayshaw, Richard. "*Wings,* Watchers, and Windows: Imprisonment in the Plays of Arthur Kopit." *TJ.* 1983 May; 35(2): 195-211. Notes.
USA. 1965-1982. Critical studies. ■Prior to *Wings,* Kopit keeps his characters imprisoned through their fear of being watched. A sense of freedom characterizes the plays which follow.

1655 Edgerton, Gary. "*Wings:* Radio Play Adapted to Experimental Stage." *JPC.* 1983 Spring; 16(4): 152-158. Notes.
USA. 1978-1979. Critical studies. ■Comparison and contrast of radio and stage presentations of Arthur Kopit's play *Wings.* Related to Media.

1656 Marranca, Bonnie, interviewer; McAnnus, Des; Epstein, Martin; Jones, Jeffrey; Willman, John. "The American Playwright: Insider or Outsider?" *PerAJ.* 1983; 7(2): 36-47. Illus.: Photo. B&W. 5.
USA. 1983. Critical studies. ■Problems of reconciling experimentation and acceptance are discussed by four new playwrights.

1657 Shank, Theodore. *American Alternative Theatre.* New York: St. Martin's P; 1983. 224 pp. (Modern Dramatists.) Biblio.
USA. 1945. Historical studies.

Relation to other fields

1658 Croce, Elena B. "La sublimazione possibile alternativa tra inibizione e acting out." (Sublimation: A Possible Alternative between Inhibition and Acting Out.) *AdP.* 1983; 8(1): 152-165. Illus.: Photo.
Italy. 1983. Critical studies. ■Analytical psychodramatic treatment of a young artist who is seriously inhibited in her activity by social erotic behavior.

1659 Dimartino, Tania. "Contrario dello psicodramma." (The Opposite of Psychodrama.) *AdP.* 1983; 8(1): 19-24. Illus.: Photo.
Italy. 1980. Technical studies. ■Mounting neurotic conflict experienced by the psychologist while collaborating on psychodrama directed by Zerka Moreno, which began with staging of Pirandello's *Tonight We Improvise (Questa sera si recita a soggetto).*

1660 Fersen, Alessandro. "Psicodramma e Mnemodramma." (Psychodrama and Mnemodrama.) *AdP.* 1983; 8(1): 81-86. Illus.: Photo.
Italy. 1983. Historical studies. ■Founder of 'mnemodrama,' a drama of the memory, recalls the genesis of his research work with the actor.

1661 Gerbaudo, Renato. "I numeri e il corpo." (The Numbers and the Body.) *AdP.* 1983; 8(1): 166-176. Notes. Illus.: Photo.
Italy. 1983. Technical studies. ■Description of a series of psychodrama sessions with a young boy.

1662 Miglietta, Donato. "Essere parlante o essere parlato." (Acting Out or Acting Through.) *AdP.* 1983; 8(1): 177-184. Illus.: Photo.
Italy. 1983. Technical studies. ■Special difficulties faced by a psychodrama group with a paranoid patient, in view of Melanie Klein's theories.

1663 Papa, Santuzza. "Questa sera parla il soggetto." (Tonight the Subject Speaks.) *AdP.* 1983; 8(1): 104-113. Illus.: Photo.
Italy. 1960. Histories-sources. ■Author talks about her transition from Freudian psychodrama to a Jungian conception.

1664 Scabia, Giuliano. "Rappresentare un'azione (drama) può portare a trovare l'anima." (Performing as Soul-finding.) *AdP.* 1983; 8(1): 149-151. Illus.: Photo.
Italy. 1983. Histories-sources. ■First hand experience of portraying primitive and wild characters of mythical plays in open air settings.

1665 Muronda, Elfigio Freeborn. "Drama in the Political Struggle in South Africa." *Ufa.* 1983; 12(2): 78-92. Notes.
South Africa, Republic of. 1955-1980. Historical studies. ■Plays by exiled dramatist Athol Fugard are compared to contemporary Bantustan agitprop and historical dramas performed in a climate of censorship.

1666 Bartolucci, Giuseppe. "Dal teatro della spontaneità al teatro del volo." (From the Theater of Spontaneity to the Theater of Flight.) *AdP.* 1983; 8(1): 71-76. Illus.: Photo.
USA. Italy. 1960-1983. Critical studies. ■Author recalls his meeting with Zerka Moreno, the destiny of his first Italian translation of *Theatre of Spontaneity* and discusses Moreno's psychodrama held at the Teatro Flaiano in connection with the new cultural situation in Italy.

1667 Vicentini, Claudio. "Il teatro di guerriglia: Proposta di una revisione critica." (Guerrilla Theatre: Suggestion for a Critical Revision.) *QT.* 1983 Feb.; 5(19): 141-149. Notes.
USA. 1965-1966. Critical studies. ■History, motivations and methods of North American guerrilla theatre.

1668 Schechter, Joel. "Brecht, Lazarenko & Mayakovsky: Jesters to His Majesty the People." *Tk.* 1983 May-June; 3(4): 18-23. Illus.: Photo. B&W. 6.
USSR. Germany. Italy. 1914-1930. Historical studies. ■Discussion of the clown Vitalij Lazarenko, his political circus routines and his collaboration with Vladimir Majakovskij. Influence and comparative study of Majakovskij's satiric spectacles (which incorporated circus acts as a staging device) on Bertolt Brecht and Dario Fo. Grp/movt: Futurism. Related to Popular Entertainment: Circus.

DRAMA: Experimental forms

Theory/criticism

1669 Finter, Helga; Walker, E.A., transl.; Grardal, Kathryn, transl. "Experimental Theatre and Semiology of Theatre: The Theatricalization of Voice." *MD*. 1983 Dec.; 26(4): 501-517. Notes.
Canada. 1970-1979. Critical studies. ■Analysis of semiology as a theory of the signifying process showing what experimental theatre teaches about the conditions and modalities of vocal emission.

1670 Ebstein, Jonny, ed.; Ivernel, Philippe, ed. *Le Théâtre d'intervention depuis 1968.* (The Theatre of Intervention Since 1968.) Lausanne: Editions l'âge d'homme; 1983. [2 vols.]
Europe. 1968-1983. Critical studies. ■Collected essays on theoretical and practical aspects of theatre.

1671 Casali, Renzo. *Antropologia dell'attore.* (Actor's Anthropology.) Milan: Jaca Book; 1983. 216 pp. (Di fronte e attraverso 107.) Index.
Italy. 1983. Critical studies. ■Renzo Casali, director and founder of Comuna Baires, expounds his theory on actors and acting.

1672 Taylor, Thomas J. "Terminal: The Text as History." *MD*. 1983 Mar.; 26(1): 12-25. Notes.
North America. 1983. Critical studies. ■Possibilities for description and clarification of the postscriptive performance text, especially in regard to experimental theatre groups that proceed without a prescriptive text.

1673 Tomaselli, Keyan G. "The Semiotics of Alternative Theatre in South Africa." *Tk.* 1983 July-Aug.; 3(5): 25-39. Notes.
South Africa, Republic of. 1981-1983. Critical studies. ■Genesis, development and consequences of plays performed by Black workers. Detailed analysis of *Ilanga Le So Phonela Abasebenzi* reveals structural components stimulating strong interaction between audience and performers, as well as between 'theatre-as-drama' and the actual sociopolitical events concerning the community. Related to Ritual-Ceremony: Civic.

1674 Kowsar, Mohammad. "Althusser on Theatre." *TJ*. 1983 Dec.; 35(4): 461-474. Notes.
USA. France. Italy. 1962-1985. Critical studies. ■Essay in Louis Althusser's book *For Marx* undermines his own Marxist philosophy, discussed in his review of Strehler's production of *El Nost Milan*, a play by Carlo Bertoluzzi staged at Piccolo Teatro di Milano.

Tragedy

Design/technology

1675 Young, Peter B. "Mannerism in *Hamlet* Scene Designs." 95-107 in Carey, Cecile Williamson, ed.; . Limouze, Henry S., ed. *Shakespeare and the Arts: A Collection of Essays from the Ohio Shakespeare Conference, 1981, Wright State University, Dayton, Ohio.* Washington, DC: UP of America; 1982. viii, 247 pp. Notes. Illus.: Photo. B&W. 2.
UK-England. 1948-1976. Critical studies. ■Comparison of designs for productions of *Hamlet* at the Royal Shakespeare Company and the National Theatre: those using 'Mannerist' elements are found more appropriate to the style and tone of the play. Grp/movt: Mannerism.

Performance/production

1676 Good, Maurice; Ustinov, Peter, intro. *Every Inch a Lear: A Rehearsal Journal of* King Lear *with Peter Ustinov and the Stratford Festival Company Directed by Robin Phillips.* Victoria, BC: Sono Nis P; 1982. 242 pp. Illus.: Dwg.
Canada. 1979. Histories-sources. ■Production journal by well-known Canadian actor, understudy to Peter Ustinov.

1677 Anon. "Episodes in the History of the Stage Business of Shakespeare's *King Lear*." *MuK.* 1983; 29: 168-178. Notes.
England. 1605-1983. Historical studies. ■Interdependent evolution of text and staging: changes in the complex relationship between the actor and the text.

1678 Anon. "*Macbeth* in der Diskussion." (*Macbeth* in Discussion.) *TZ.* 1983; 38(1): 11-19. Illus.: Photo. B&W. 2. [Round-table discourse on Heiner Müller's production at the Volksbühne Berlin.]
Germany, East. 1971-1982. Reviews of performances. ■Dispute on the controversial adaptation and its staging and importance for socialist theatre.

1679 Michaelis, Rolf. "Schlaf der Welt, Halbschlaf des Theaters: Ernst Wendt inszeniert *Gyges und sein Ring* in Hamburg." (Sleep of the World, Doze of the Theatre: Ernst Wendt Directs *Gyges and His Ring* in Hamburg.) *TH.* 1983; 2: 47-49. Illus.: Photo.
Germany, West. 1983. Reviews of performances. ■Ernst Wendt directs Friedrich Hebbel's tragedy *Gyges and His Ring*.

1680 Stadelmaier, Gerhard. "Wehrmachtsmädel weinen nicht: Hansgünther Heyme eröffnet in Stuttgart das Neue Kammertheater furios mit Aischylos' *Persern*." (Girls from the Army Don't Cry: Hansgünther Heyme Opens in Stuttgart at the Neues Kammertheater with Aeschylus' *The Persians*.) *TH.* 1983; 11: 15-19.
Germany, West. 1983. Reviews of performances. ■The Neues Kammertheater Stuttgart opens with Aeschylus' *The Persians*, directed by Hansgünther Heyme.

1681 Monleón, José; Ruiz Ramón, Francisco; Pérez Pisonero, Arturo; Reid, Walker M.; Dietz, Donald M. "El Paso, 1983." *PrAc.* 1983 Mar.-Apr.; 198: 82-94.
Mexico. USA. Spain. 1983. Historical studies. ■Repertory of the Golden Age of Spanish theatre at the El Paso (Texas) Festival.

1682 Senelick, Laurence. *Gordon Craig's Moscow* Hamlet: *A Reconstruction.* Westport, CT: Greenwood P; 1982. xviii, 234 pp.
Russia. 1908-1912. Histories-reconstruction. ■Production history of Edward Gordon Craig's collaboration with Stanislavsky at Moscow Art Theatre. Includes comprehensive, detailed study of primary sources (both English and Russian), with closing critical remarks.

1683 Pérez Coterillo, Moisés. "Mérida recuerda a Margarita Xirgu." (Mérida Remembers Margarita Xirgu.) *ElPu.* 1983 Summer: 16-17.
Spain. 1932-1933. Histories-sources. ■Memorial exhibition to commemorate fifty years since the first performance of *Medea* by Margarita Xirgu at the Mérida Roman Theatre.

1684 Rich, Frank; Watt, Douglas; Beaufort, John; Kalem, T.E.; Kissel, Howard; Barnes, Clive. "*Richard III*." *NYTCR Off Broadway Supplement III.* 1983 Sep. 5; 44(13): 166-170.
USA. 1983. Reviews of performances. ■Six critics review Shakespeare's *Richard III*, directed by Jane Howell at the Delacorte Theatre.

1685 Abellan, Joan; Melendres, Jaume. "El quadern de dericció d'*Otello*, de Shakespeare establert per Konstantin Stanislavskij." (The Prompt-book for Shakespeare's *Otello*, written by Konstantin Stanislavskij.) *EECIT.* 1983; 22: 59-86. Notes. [Proceedings of a seminar organized by the Department of Theatre Sciences of the ITB in 1978.]
USSR. 1929-1930. Critical studies. ■Stanislavskij's stage adaptation of the play to suit his system and stimulate actor's internal energy control. Grp/movt: Realism.

Plays/librettos/scripts

1686 Bliss, Lee. *The World's Perspective: John Webster and the Jacobean Drama.* New Brunswick, NJ: Rutgers UP; 1983. 246 pp. Biblio. Index.
England. 1603-1640. Critical studies. ■Study of Webster's drama with emphasis on form, style and theme.

1687 Calderwood, James L. *To Be and Not To Be: Negation and Metadrama in* Hamlet. New York: Columbia UP; 1983. xvi, 222 pp.
England. 1600-1601. Critical studies. ■Metadramatic analysis of *Hamlet* play as a metaphorical reflection of its dramatic art.

1688 Danson, Lawrence N., ed. *On King Lear.* Princeton, NJ: Princeton UP; 1982. 185 pp.
England. 1605. Critical studies. ■Critical essays.

1689 Leggatt, Alexander. "*Arden of Faversham*." *ShS.* 1983; 36: 121-133. Notes.
England. 1588-1593. Critical studies. ■*Arden* playwright opens 'a vein of realism in Elizabethan drama to run beside and later enrich the

DRAMA: Tragedy—Plays/librettos/scripts

heroics of tragedy and the romantic fantasy of comedy. It is a realism that consists of a hard, tough appraisal of things as they are, and a resistance to conventional formulae'.

1690 Lombardo, Agostino. *Lettura del* Macbeth. (Reading of Macbeth.) Vicenza: Neri Pozza; 1983. 302 pp. (Nuova biblioteca di cultura 32.) Pref. Notes. Index.
England. 1605-1606. Linguistic studies. ■Linguistic analysis of *Macbeth*.

1691 Sutherland, Sarah P. *Masques in Jacobean Tragedy*. New York: AMS Press; 1983. xv, 148 pp.
England. 1600-1625. Critical studies. ■Organic relationship between tragedies and interpolated masques. Related to Mixed Performances: Court masques.

1692 Taylor, Gary. "The Folio Copy for *Hamlet, King Lear*, and *Othello*." *SQ*. 1983; 34(1): 44-61. Notes. Tables.
England. 1558-1621. Textual studies. ■Editorial problems in the first folio of *Hamlet, Othello* and *King Lear*.

1693 Gethner, Perry J. "Poetic Justice in the Plays and Critical Writings of Pierre Corneille." *FrF*. 1983 May; 8(2): 109-121. Notes.
France. 1630-1639. Critical studies. ■Principle of 'poetic justice' as related to the denouement in the major works of Corneille.

1694 Arnott, Peter. "Some Costume Conventions in Greek Tragedy." *ET*. 1983 Nov.; 2(1): 3-18. Notes. Illus.: Photo. B&W. 1: 5 in. x 7 in.
Greece. 405 B.C. Critical studies. ■Conventions of the Greek drama, specifically Euripides' *The Bacchae*, are explored in terms of the change of costume, which reflects upon the characters' fate.

1695 Bain, David. *Masters, Servants and Orders in Greek Tragedy*. Dover, NH: Manchester UP; 1983. 73 pp.
Greece. 523-406 B.C. Critical studies. ■Mutes in Greek tragedy.

1696 Lesky, Albin; Dillon, Mathew, transl. *Greek Tragic Poetry*. New Haven, CT & London: Yale UP; 1983. xii, 503 pp. Biblio. [Translation of German *Die tragische Dichtung der Hellenen* (3rd edition), 1972.]
Greece. 499-400 B.C. Critical studies. ■English translation of the standard work on Greek tragedy. Although the emphasis is placed on the lives and work of Aeschylus, Sophocles and Euripides, the author also traces some data on the origins and decline of the form.

1697 Paduano, Guido. "La scena di Dioniso non è il fronte: Conflitto drammatico e conflitto militare nella tragedia greca." (The Stage of Dionysus Is Not a Battle Front: Dramatic Conflict and Military Conflict in Greek Tragedy.) *QT*. 1983 Feb.; 5 (19): 31-41.
Greece. 484-415 B.C. Critical studies. ■Necessity of war in Aeschylus' *The Persians* and in Euripides' *Hecuba* and *The Trojan Women*.

1698 Anon. *Studi sul teatro classico italiano tra Manierismo ed età dell'Arcadia*. (Studies of Italian Classical Theatre between Mannerism and the Age of Arcadia.) Univ. of Trieste. Rome: Ateneo; 1982. 117 pp. (NS 4.) Notes.
Italy. 1627-1713. Critical studies. ■Analysis of three tragedies: *Ester* by Federico Della Valle, *Aristodemo* by Carlo Dottori and *Merope* by Scipione Maffei. Grp/movt: Mannerism; Arcadia.

1699 Bishop, Norma. "A Nigerian Version of a Greek Classic: Soyinka's Transformation of *The Bacchae*." *RAL*. 1983 Spring; 14 (1): 68-80. Notes.
Nigeria. 1973. Critical studies. ■Wole Soyinka, while occasionally borrowing from Murray and Arrowsmith, has very ably transferred the ambience of Greece and Dionysus to Yorubaland and Ogun.

1700 Brockbank, Philip. "Blood and Wine: Tragic Ritual from Aeschylus to Soyinka." *ShS*. 1983; 36: 11-19. Notes.
Nigeria. Greece. UK-England. 1980. Critical studies. ■Discusses Wole Soyinka's plays *The Strong Breed* and *The Death of the King's Horseman* as they echo themes of Aeschylus, Euripides and Shakespeare. Ancient, Renaissance and modern blend in Soyinka's translation of *The Bacchae* for a 1972 National Theatre (London) production.

1701 Pérez Coterillo, Moisés. "*Absalón*: Lectura contemporánea de una tragedia barroca." (*Absalón*: A Contemporary Version of a Baroque Tragedy.) *ElPu*. 1983 Dec.: 4-5.
Spain. 1983. Critical studies. ■New José Luis Gómez version of Calderón's tragedy, *Absalón*.

1702 O'Brien, Ellen J. "Ophelia's Mad Scene and the Stage Tradition." 109-125 in Carey, Cecile Williamson, ed.; . Limouze, Henry S., ed. *Shakespeare and the Arts: A Collection of Essays from the Ohio Shakespeare Conference, 1981, Wright State University, Dayton, Ohio*. Washington, DC: UP of America; 1982. viii, 247 pp. Notes.
UK-England. 1980. Critical studies. ■Ways in which performance tradition can clarify difficult scenes in Shakespeare: Ophelia's mad scene in *Hamlet* from John Barton's 1980 Royal Shakespeare Company production is used as an example.

Theory/criticism

1703 Anon. "Pirandello e Jaspers." (Pirandello and Jaspers.) *AdP*. 1983; 8(1): 43-46. Illus.: Photo.
Italy. 1916-1936. Critical studies. ■Pirandello's philosophy is compared with the conception of tragedy as multiplicity of truths as defined by Karl Jaspers in the essay *Von der Warheit*.

———

Other entries with significant content related to Drama: 1711, 1940, 1953, 1978, 2007, 2100.

MEDIA

General

Administration

1704 Internationale Gesellschaft für Urheberrecht. *Jahrbuch-Revue Annuelle-Yearbook-Annuario-1983*. Vienna: Manz; 1983. 409 pp. Biblio. Illus.: Photo. B&W. [Volume 5 in English, French, German and Spanish.]
Austria. Italy. North America. 1976-1981. Histories-sources. ■International exchange of experiences about problems of copyrights in the field of communication technologies.

Design/technology

1705 Christout, Marie Françoise. "Audio-Visual Techniques Used in Exhibits: Various Procedures." 79-82 in Cocuzza, Ginnine, ed.; . Cohen-Stratyner, Barbara Naomi, ed. *Stage Design: Papers from the 15th International Congress of SIBMAS (Société Internationale des Bibliothèques et Musées des Arts du Spectacle)*. New York: Theatre Library Association; 1983. (Performing Arts Resources 8.)
France. 1982. Instructional materials. ■Theoretical and practical problems in choosing the best type of audio-visual material in support of an exhibit by member of Department of Performing Arts of the Bibliothèque Nationale in Paris.

1706 English, Sherri. "Oh, No! It's Devo." *LDM*. 1983 Apr.-May; 7(2): 42-49. Illus.: Photo. Print. Color. Grd.Plan. 5.
USA. 1983. Reviews of performances. ■Combination of film and theatrical techniques to produce unusual effects for rock concert.

Theory/criticism

1707 Sauerbier, S.D. "Die Medien und das ästhetische Handeln: Aspekte der ästhetischen Realisation in den technischen Reproduktionsmitteln." (Media and Aesthetic Treatment: Aspects of the Aesthetic Perception in the Technical Reproduction by Media.) *Tzs*. 1983 Fall; 5: 13-30.
Europe. USA. 1983. Critical studies. ■Media as subject (theme) and object (medium to transport the message) of aesthetic treatment.

Audio forms

Design/technology

1708 Martin, George. "Live from the Met — 1910." *OpN*. 1983 Dec. 10; 48(6): 36, 38, 84. Illus.: Photo. B&W. 1.
USA. 1910. Historical studies. ■Account of the first live broadcast of a complete opera performance from the Metropolitan Opera House, January 13, 1910. Related to Music-Drama: Opera.

MEDIA: Audio forms

Plays/librettos/scripts

1709 Pavelich, Joan E. "*Nazaire et Barnabé:* Learning to Live in an Americanized World." *CDr*. 1983 Spring; 9(1): 16-22. Notes.
Canada. 1939-1958. Critical studies. ∎Semiotic analysis of popular radio comedy.

1710 Vigouroux-Frey, N. "Le théâtre radiophonique de la B.B.C.: tribune sociale et politique? (1970-1980)." (B.B.C. Radio Drama: A Social and Political Tribune? (1970-1980).) *RHT*. 1983; 35(3): 311-323. Notes. Biblio. Tables.
UK-England. 1970-1980. Critical studies. ∎Study of predominant themes in B.B.C. radio drama.

Film

Performance/production

1711 Berthold, Margot, ed. *Max Reinhardts Theater im Film: Materialien.* (Max Reinhardt's Theatre in Film: Materials.) Munich: Münchner Filmzentrum; 1983. (Film 1983/1.) Notes. Biblio. Illus.: Photo.
Europe. North America. 1910-1943. Historical studies. ∎Max Reinhardt's film adaptations of his theatre productions. Some reviews included. Related to Drama.

1712 Swindell, Larry. *Charles Boyer: The Reluctant Lover.* Garden City, NY: Doubleday; 1983. viii, 280 pp. Index. Filmography. Illus.: Photo. 12.
France. USA. 1899-1978. Biographies.

1713 Taylor, John Russell. *Ingrid Bergman.* Photographs from the Kobal Collection. New York: St. Martin's P; 1983. 127 pp. Illus.: Photo. 9. [First U.S. edition.]
Sweden. USA. 1915-1983. Biographies.

1714 Gehring, Wes D. *Charlie Chaplin: A Bio-Bibliography.* Westport, CT: Greenwood P; 1983. xv, 227 pp. (Popular Culture Bio-Bibliographies.) Filmography. Pref. Append. Index. Filmography. Biblio. Illus.: Dwg. Photo. B&W. 18.
USA. 1889-1977. Biographies. ∎Research guide to Chaplin as a performer, with annotated bibliography, filmography, discography and list of musical compositions. Related to Popular Entertainment.

1715 Lenburg, Jeff. *Dustin Hoffman, Hollywood's Anti-Hero.* New York: St. Martin's P; 1983. 172 pp.
USA. 1937-1983. Biographical studies.

1716 Resnick, Sylvia. *Burt Reynolds: An Unauthorized Biography.* New York: St. Martin's P; 1983. 224 pp.
USA. 1936-1983. Biographies.

1717 Sabatine, Jean; Hodge, David. *The Actor's Image: Movement Training for Stage and Screen.* Englewood Cliffs, NJ: Prentice-Hall; 1983. x, 246 pp. Pref. Append. Biblio. Illus.: Photo. B&W. 152.
USA. 1983. Instructional materials. ∎Unites the three primary disciplines of acting: acting, voice and movement.

Plays/librettos/scripts

1718 Nelson, Roy Jay. "Reflections in a Broken Mirror: Varda's *Cleo de 5 à 7.*" *FR*. 1983 Apr.; 56(5): 735-743. Notes.
France. 1900-1983. Critical studies. ∎Uses of dramatic structures in making films and the need for specific film techniques to reveal the drama.

1719 Kliman, Bernice W. "A Palimpsest for Olivier's *Hamlet.*" *CompD*. 1983 Fall; 17(3): 243-253. Notes.
UK-England. 1948. Textual studies. ∎By examining the preproduction script of Olivier's *Hamlet* (1948), author discloses the 'shaping intentions' behind the finished film.

Reference materials

1720 King, Keith, ed.; Wallberg, Mark, ed. "University of Texas at Austin Acquires Gloria Swanson Archive." *USITT*. 1983 Winter; 22(5): 7-8.
USA. 1913-1983. Histories-sources. ∎Announcement of acquisition of 100,000-item silent film archive from film star Gloria Swanson by the Humanities Research Center at the University of Texas.

1721 Margolis, Tina, ed. "*Gone with the Wind* Exhibition." *USITT*. 1983 Fall; 23(4): 8.
USA. 1939-1983. Historical studies. ∎The exhibition '*Gone with the Wind:* A Legend Endures' displays over 500 items from the David O. Selznick collection including photos, costumes, letters, film clips and memorabilia.

Video forms

Institutions

1722 McMillan, Joyce. "Rod Graham: Joyce McMillan Talks to Rod Graham about His Work As Head of BBC Scotland's Television Drama Department, and as Chairman of the Scottish Arts Council Drama Committee." *STN*. 1983 Dec.; 33: 5-9. Illus.: Photo. Print. B&W. 1: 17 cm. x 13 cm.
UK-Scotland. 1946-1983. Histories-sources. ∎Interview with Rod Graham, head of BBC Scotland's television drama department and chairman of the Scottish Arts Council's drama committee.

Performance/production

1723 Sturken, Marita. "Video As a Performance Medium." *Sis*. 1983 Spring; 16(3): 19-21. Illus.: Photo. B&W. 1: 5 in. x 4 in.
USA. 1980. Critical studies. ∎Performance video, work designed specifically for the architectural space defined by a video camera, brings viewers into more intimate relationship with performers than does theatre. Comic skits, dance and 'video opera' are briefly discussed. Related to Music-Drama: Video opera.

Relation to other fields

1724 Toor, David. "Shakespeare's Life and Times." *SFN*. 1983 Apr.; 7(2): 1, 4.
USA. 1973-1983. Instructional materials. ∎Creation of seven videotape programs for instructional use, including: *The Globe Playhouse* and *Shakespeare on Stage.* Grp/movt: Elizabethan theatre.

Other entries with significant content related to Media: 13, 29, 48, 94, 108, 136, 140, 271, 420, 488, 495, 515, 519, 782, 915, 916, 943, 997, 1090, 1096, 1160, 1174, 1289, 1304, 1345, 1347, 1383, 1453, 1539, 1607, 1655, 1729, 1746, 1769, 1777, 1788, 1790, 1885, 1888, 1912, 1995, 2059, 2064, 2082.

MIME

General

Institutions

1725 Skotnicki, Jan. "Les Vingt-Cinq Ans de la Pantomime des Sourds d'Olsztyn." (Twenty-Five Years of Olsztyn Mime of the Deaf.) *TP*. 1983; 294-296: 75-79. Illus.: Photo. Print. B&W. 4. [In French and English.]
Poland. 1958-1983. Historical studies. ∎History of the Olsztyn Mime of the Deaf theatre company.

Performance/production

1726 Decroux, Etienne; Magli, Valeria, ed.; Caronia, Maria, transl.; Poli, Giovanna, transl. *Parole sul mimo.* (Words on Mime.) Milan: Edizioni del corpo; 1983. 182 pp. Pref. Notes. Tables. Illus.: Photo. B&W. [Translated from French.]
France. 1935. Histories-sources. ∎Italian translation of Decroux's *Paroles sur le mime.*

1727 "Parque antropológico: La rara especie del hombre urbano." (Anthropological Gardens: The Rare Species of the Urban Man.) *ElPu*. 1983 Nov.: 7-9.
Spain. 1983. Histories-sources. ∎*El hombre urbano:* Original vision of the man in the street by mime Albert Vidal.

1728 Badiou, Maryse. "Albert Vidal 'Yo quería ser clown'." (Albert Vidal 'I Wanted to Be a Clown'.) *ElPu*. 1983 Nov.: 10-12.

MIME: General—Performance/production

Spain. 1983. Histories-sources. ■Interview with the mime Albert Vidal.

1729   Melendres, Jaume. "*Mary d'Ous*, un punt d'inflexió." (*Mary d'Ous*, a Point of Inflection.) *EECIT*. 1983 Mar.; 22: 39-57. Illus.: Photo. Print. B&W. 23: 12 cm. x 12 cm. [Results of a seminar conducted by the Department of Theatre Sciences of the ITB.]

Spain. 1972. Critical studies. ■Semiotic analysis of Els Joglars' production of *Mary d'Ous* recorded on video. Related to Media: Video forms.

1730   Gussow, Mel; Nelson, Don; Stasio, Marilyn; Mazo, Joseph H.; Henry, William A., III; Siegel, Joel; Beaufort, John. "*Marcel Marceau on Broadway*." *NYTCR*. 1983 Mar. 7; 44(3): 352-355.

USA. 1983. Reviews of performances. ■Seven critics review *Marcel Marceau on Broadway* at the Belasco Theatre.

Relation to other fields

1731   Puchner, Walter. "Byzantinischer Mimos, Pantomimos und Mummenschanz im Spiegel der Griechischen Patristik und Ekklesiastischer Synodalverordnungen: Quellenkritische Anmerkungen aus theaterwissenschaftlicher Sicht." (Byzantine Mime, Pantomime and Masquerade as Reflected by the Greek Patristic and Ecclesiastical Synod Decrees: Critical Remarks on the Sources from the Point of View of a Theatre Historian.) *MuK*. 1983; 29: 311-317. Notes.

Byzantine Empire. Asia. 691-1200. Critical studies. ■Byzantine theatrical culture as a possible link between antiquity and the Middle Ages. Related to Popular Entertainment: Carnival.

Pantomime

Performance/production

1732   Weiler, Christel; Becker, Ulrich; Führner, Ruth. "Das stumme Spiel geht weiter." (The Dumb Show Goes On.) *TH*. 1983; 12: 38-45.

Europe. Yugoslavia. 1983. Historical studies. ■Survey of the international pantomime scene.

1733   Requeno, Vincenzo; Ricci, Giovanni R., ed. *L'arte di gestire con le mani*. (The Art of Hand Gestures.) Palermo: Sellerio; 1982. 99 pp. (Prisma 43.) Pref. Notes. Illus.: Photo. B&W.

Italy. 1982. Instructional materials. ■Instructional material on the art of gesture accompanied with a biographic and bibliographic note on the author and an introduction on sources of the work.

Reference materials

1734   Ruston, Alan. "Richard Nelson Lee and the Victorian Pantomime in Great Britain." *NCTR*. 1983 Winter; 11(2): 106-117. Notes.

UK-England. 1830-1872. ■Biographical sketch of Richard Lee with a list of his pantomimes and non-pantomimic works, totaling 132 entries. Grp/movt: Victorian theatre.

———

Other entries with significant content related to Mime: 492, 838.

MIXED PERFORMANCES

General

Performance/production

1735   Watanabe-O'Kelly, Helen. "The Equestrian Ballet in Seventeenth-Century Europe: Origin, Description, Development." *GL&L*. 1983; 36(1): 198-212. Notes. Illus.: Photo. B&W. 12.

Europe. 1559-1854. Historical studies. ■Development of equestrian ballet from martial and sporting contests to formal ballet. Related to Dance: Ballet.

Reference materials

1736   *Fochi d'allegrezza a Roma dal Cinquecento all'Ottocento*. (Fireworks of Joy in Rome from the Sixteenth to the Nineteenth Centuries.) Rome: Edizioni Quasar; 1982. 126 pp. Pref. Index. Biblio. Illus.: Photo. B&W.

Italy. 1500-1899. Histories-sources. ■Short essays about firework displays and a catalogue of the exhibition held at Palazzo Braschi, 15th September-31 October, 1982.

Court Masque

Administration

1737   Streitberger, W.R. "Court Festivities of Henry VII: 1485-1491, 1502-1505." *RORD*. 1983; 26: 31-54. Notes.

England. 1485-1505. Histories-sources. ■Reprints, with brief introduction, of records from miscellaneous account books during the reign of Henry VII.

Performance art

Audience

1738   Iles, Chrissie. "Performance Nightlife." *PM*. 1983 Feb.-Mar.; 22: 34-35. Illus.: Photo. B&W. 1.

UK-England. 1983. Histories-sources. ■Performance artist and audience relationship in night clubs.

Institutions

1739   Anon. "Jack Helen Brut: matkalla ihmisen hämärään." (Jack Helen Brut: Approaching the Mystery of Man.) *SuK*. 1983; 8: 74-77. Illus.: Photo.

Finland. 1983. Critical studies. ■Discussion of performance group Jack Helen Brut consisting of fifteen art students, artists and dancers.

1740   Keskimäki, Ilpo. "Jack Helen Brut." *Teat*. 1983; 39(5): 16-17. Illus.: Photo. 5. [In Finnish.]

Finland. 1981-1983. Historical studies. ■History and nature of performance group Jack Helen Brut.

1741   Hall, Sheila. "Bloodgroup." *PM*. 1983 Feb.-Mar.; 22: 8-11. Illus.: Photo. Print. B&W.

UK. 1983. Histories-sources. ■Profile of the women's company Bloodgroup, illustrating their awareness of the need for researched women's performance, especially on a non-textual basis. Grp/movt: Feminism.

1742   Hyde, Phil. "Welfare State." *PM*. 1983 Apr.-May; 23: 4-7. Illus.: Photo. Print. B&W. 4.

UK-England. 1983. Histories-sources. ■Profile of the innovative projects of the Welfare State Company, demonstrating that art within a broad setting benefits both community and artist.

1743   Shank, Theodore. "Paintings You Can See Into: Hesitate and Demonstrate." *TDR*. 1983 Spring; 27(1): 3-16. Illus.: Diagram. Photo.

UK-England. Netherlands. 1972-1983. Historical studies. ■History and analysis of Hesitate and Demonstrate, an English group that creates surrealistic performances based on juxtaposition of images. Grp/movt: Surrealism.

Performance/production

1744   Künstlerhaus Bethanien. *Performance — Another Dimension*. Berlin: Frölich & Kaufmann; 1983. 223 pp.

Europe. USA. 1983. Histories-sources. ■Interviews in German and English with American and European performance artists.

1745   La Franais, Rob. "Kazuko Hohki." *PM*. 1983 June-July; 24: 6-9. Illus.: Photo. Print. B&W. 3.

Japan. UK-England. 1983. Histories-sources. ■Kazuko Hohki, responsible for the Japanese-American Toy Theatre of London and performance and music groups, is asked about her work and the nature of Japanese society.

1746   Elwes, Kate. "Interview — Nan Hoover." *PM*. 1983 Apr.-May; 23: 8-10. Illus.: Photo. Print. B&W. 3.

UK-England. 1900-1983. Histories-sources. ■Aspects of the work of video performance artist Nan Hoover and her concerns with redefining images of women, relating the body to landscape and timelessness. Grp/movt: Feminism. Related to Media: Video forms.

MIXED PERFORMANCES: Performance art—Performance/production

1747   Godfrey, Peter; Powell, Helen. "Performance and the Third Dimension — Rational Theatre: ABDC Workshop." *PM.* 1983 Dec.-Jan.; 20-21: 24-29. Illus.: Photo. Print. B&W. 6.
UK-England. UK-Scotland. 1983. Histories-sources. ■Philosophy behind the work of Rational Theatre is holistic, not rationalistic. Intentions behind ABDC Workshop's Edinburgh project.

1748   La Franais, Rob. "Basement Group, Newcastle." *PM.* 1983 Feb.-Mar.; 22: 12-13. Illus.: Photo. Print. B&W. 4.
UK-England. 1983. Histories-sources. ■Performance work and organization of events staged by The Basement Group.

1749   Millar, Chris. "A Portentous Event within Earshot of Braying Donkeys." *PM.* 1983 Dec.-Jan.; 20-21: 5-8. Illus.: Photo. Print. B&W. 4.
UK-England. 1970-1980. Biographical studies. ■Author's personal record of the ideas and work of Anne Bean: involving performance art and the rock and entertainment world. Related to Popular Entertainment.

1750   Rogers, Steve. "Impact Theatre." *PM.* 1983 Feb.-Mar.; 22: 5-8. Illus.: Photo. Print. B&W. 4.
UK-England. 1983. Histories-sources. ■Profile of the work of the Impact Theatre Co-operative, focusing on its political and theatrical radicalism.

1751   Antin, Eleanor. *Being Antinova.* Los Angeles: Astro Arts; 1983. 86 pp. Illus.: Photo. Dwg. 50.
USA. 1980. Biographical studies. ■Actress's journal of the creation of the persona of a retired Black ballerina of Diaghilev's Ballet Russe.

1752   Carroll, Noel. "A Select View of Earthlings: Ping Chong." *TDR.* 1983 Spring; 27(1): 72-81. Illus.: Photo.
USA. 1972-1983. Critical studies. ■Description and analysis of Ping Chong's work.

1753   Chin, Daryl. "An Anti-Manifesto." *TDR.* 1983; 27(4): 32-37.
USA. 1976. Histories-sources. ■Author's theories and analysis of his own work.

1754   Hardman, Chris. "Walkmanology." *TDR.* 1983; 27(4): 43-46.
USA. 1980. Historical studies. ■Description of three theatre events in which the audience participated by following instructions on Walkman cassettes.

1755   Kalb, Jonathan. "Ping Chong: From *Lazarus* to *Anna into Nightlight.*" *ThM.* 1983 Spring; 14(2): 68-75. Illus.: Diagram. Photo. Print. B&W. 4.
USA. 1972-1982. Biographical studies. ■Retrospective account of Ping Chong and his career as performance artist.

1756   Klett, Renate. "United States." *TH.* 1983; 6: 34-35.
USA. 1983. Biographical studies. ■Portrait of the performance artist Laurie Anderson.

1757   Roth, Moira, ed.; Burdick, Janet; Dubiel, Alice; Jacobs, Mary Jane. *The Amazing Decade, Woman and Performance Art in America 1970-1980.* Los Angeles: Astro Arts; 1983. 163 pp. Biblio. Illus.: Photo. 75.
USA. 1970-1980. Histories-sources. ■Source book of information on women's involvement in performance art. Includes an essay on the history and character of women's performance art, individual profiles of 37 artists and collectives and a chronology setting the art in the context of U.S. history and the women's movement.

Other entries with significant content related to Mixed Performances: 329, 1691.

MUSIC-DRAMA

General

Administration

1758   Kohl, Helen. "Floyd Chalmers." *OC.* 1983 Winter; 24(4): 14-15, 41, 44.
Canada. 1898-1983. Biographical studies. ■Profile of Canadian philanthropist and patron of the arts, on his 85th birthday.

1759   Trezzini, Lamberto; Curtolo, Angelo. *Oltre le quinte: Idee, cultura e organizzazione del teatro musicale in Italia.* (Behind the Scenes: Ideas, Culture and Organization of the Music Theatre in Italy.) Venice: Marsilio; 1983. ix, 215 pp. (Materiali marsilio 39.) Pref. Biblio. Append.
Italy. 1920-1981. Histories-specific. ■Brief history of the organization and legislation of musical theatre.

Performance spaces

1760   Morrison, William. "Oscar Hammerstein I: The Man Who Invented Times Square." *M.* 1983 First Quarter; 15(1): 3-15. Biblio. Illus.: Photo. B&W. 13.
USA. 1889-1904. Historical studies. ■Oscar Hammerstein's managerial career and the theatres he built for plays, operas and vaudeville. The article describes the theatres and traces their use under later management.

Performance/production

1761   Löbl, Hermi. "Mein Herz gehört den Sängern." (My Heart Belongs to the Singers.) *Buhne.* 1983 Dec.: 6-9.
Austria. 1915-1983. Historical studies. ■Career of Karl Dönch, opera singer and manager of Vienna's Volksoper.

1762   Jarman, Douglas. *Kurt Weill: An Illustrated Biography.* Bloomington: Indiana UP; 1982. 160 pp. Illus.: Photo.
Germany. USA. 1900-1950. Biographies. ■Kurt Weill biography with emphasis on the activities of the German artists between the two wars and critical assessment of Weill's music.

1763   Erdmann, Michael. "'Was der Ohr noch aufregt': Ein Gespräch mit dem (Theater-)Musiker Heiner Goebbels." ('Things Still Exciting the Ear': An Interview with Theatre-Composer Heiner Goebbels.) *TH.* 1983; 7: 28-31.
Germany, West. 1983. Histories-sources. ■Portrait and interview with composer for the theatre Heiner Goebbels.

1764   Bussotti, Sylvano. *I miei teatri: Diario segreto, diario pubblico, alcuni saggi.* (My Theatres: Secret Diary, Public Diary, Some Essays.) Palermo: Novecento; 1982. 392 pp. (Narciso di Novecento 2.) Pref. Tables. Illus.: Photo. B&W.
Italy. 1978-1981. Histories-sources. ■Passages from Bussotti's personal and artistic diary. Essays on musical theatre.

Reference materials

1765   *Giuseppe Sarti: Musicista del '700 (1729-1802).* (Giuseppe Sarti: Musician of the Eighteenth Century — 1729-1802.) Faenza: Tipografia faentina; 1983. 133 pp. Pref. Index. Tables. Illus.: Photo. B&W.
Italy. 1729-1802. Histories-sources. ■Catalogue of the exhibition on Giuseppe Sarti, composer and man of the theatre.

Musical theatre

Administration

1766   Böhm, Gotthard. "Rolf Kutschera: 'Ich war eine Notlösung'." (Rolf Kutschera: 'I Was an Expedient'.) *Buhne.* 1983 July/Aug.: 16-17. Illus.: Photo. Color.
Austria. 1961-1983. Histories- sources. ■Portrait of Rolf Kutschera, manager of Theater an der Wien.

1767   Löbl, Hermi. "Peter Weck: 'Unmögliches möglich machen'." (Peter Weck: 'To Make the Impossible Possible'.) *Buhne.* 1983 Sep.: 4-6. Illus.: Photo.
Austria. 1983. Historical studies. ■Portrait of Peter Weck, new manager of Theater an der Wien, and its first production in German of Andrew Lloyd Webber's *Cats.*

Design/technology

1768   Anon. *Cats* — A Superlative Spectacle." *LDM.* 1983 Mar.; 7(1): 26-33. Tables. Illus.: Plan. Photo. 9: 3 in. x 4 in., 3 in. x 3 in.
USA. 1982. Critical studies. ■*Cats:* its mood and style, followed by detailed exposition of the lighting with emphasis on director and lighting designer interaction.

MUSIC-DRAMA: Musical theatre—Design/technology

1769 Newberger, Marcia. "Vincente Minnelli: The Broadway Years." *PArts.* 1983 Feb.; 17(2): 6. Illus.: Photo.
USA. 1931-1939. Historical studies. ■Pre-Hollywood years of the director Vincente Minnelli, in the capacity of a set and costume designer of Broadway revues and shows. Related to Media: Film.

1770 Smith, Ronn. "*Cats*, a Tail of Two Cities." *ThCr.* 1983 Jan.; 17(1): 17-21, 38-44. Illus.: Photo. B&W. 10.
USA. UK-England. 1983. Histories-sources. ■Interviews with John Napier and David Hersey on *Cats*, concerning costumes, sets, lighting and production details. Comparison of English and American productions.

1771 Smith, Ronn. "*La Cage aux Folles:* It Is What It Is — a Hit!" *TrCr.* 1983 Nov.-Dec.; 17(9): 17-64. Illus.: Photo. Print. Color. B&W. 8.
USA. 1983. Technical studies. ■Survey of New York production including set, costumes, make-up and lighting.

Institutions

1772 Dugan, Gene. "Nebraska Community Theatre Troupe Wins International." *ThNe.* 1983 Dec.; 15(8): 1, 12. Illus.: Photo. B&W. 1: 4 in. x 2 in.
Japan. USA. 1983. Histories-sources. ■Center Stage of Omaha won first place in the Toyama International Amateur Theatre Festival 1983 with Fats Waller musical *Ain't Misbehavin'*, directed by Bill Davis.

Performance spaces

1773 Koger, Alicia Kae. "Harrigan's Theatre." *M.* 1983 First Quarter; 15(1): 16-18. Biblio. Illus.: Dwg. 3.
USA. 1890-1932. Historical studies. ■Construction of Harrigan's Theatre, designed by Francis Hatch Kimball. First used for Harrigan's musical comedies — later renamed the Garrick and used for legitimate productions.

1774 Lazzara, Robert L. "Orpheum Theatre, San Francisco, California." *M.* 1983 Fourth Quarter; 15(4): 16-17. Illus.: Photo. B&W. 1.
USA. 1981-1983. Technical studies. ■Modification of acoustical systems in the Orpheum Theatre to make it acceptable for touring Broadway musicals.

Performance/production

1775 Abellan, Joan. "Mestres Quadreny, un compositor per als confins teatrals de la Música." (Mestres Quadreny, a Composer of Music for Theatre.) *EECIT.* 1983 Mar.; 22: 21-38. [From 'Ixart 15,' organized by the CEDAEC of the ITB, October 21, 1977.]
Spain. 1945-1955. Histories-sources. ■Interview with Mestres Quadreny, a postmodern composer, on his musical training, influence by Anton Webern and other Catalan artists. Grp/movt: Postmodernism.

1776 Green, Jeffrey P. "*In Dahomey* in London in 1903." *BPM.* 1983 Fall; 11: 23-40. Notes.
UK-England. 1903-1904. Historical studies. ■Account of the successful 1903 London production of *In Dahomey*, written by Bert Williams, George Walker, Will Marion Cook and Paul Laurence Dunbar.

1777 Windeler, Robert. *Julie Andrews: A Biography.* Ann Arbor, MI: UMI Research P; 1983. 223 pp. Index. Filmography. Illus.: Photo. [First U.S. edition.]
UK-England. USA. 1935-1983. Biographies. Related to Media: Film.

1778 Anon. "The Dream Guys of *Dreamgirls*." *Ebony.* 1983 Apr.; 38(6): 74-76, 78, 80. Illus.: Photo. Print. B&W. Color. 13.
USA. 1983. Histories-sources. ■Interview with Ben Harney, Clevant Derricks and Obba Babutunde, who star in Broadway musical *Dreamgirls*, about families and friends.

1779 Beaufort, John; Barnes, Clive; Gussow, Mel; Cohen, Ron; Watt, Douglas. "*Preppies*." *NYTCR Off Broadway Supplement III.* 1983 Sep. 5; 44(13): 163-166.
USA. 1983. Reviews of performances. ■Five critics review Tony Tanner's production of *Preppies*, with book by David Taylor and Carlos Davis, music and lyrics by Gary Portnoy and Judy Hart Angelo. Presented at the Promenade Theatre.

1780 Bordman, Gerald. *Days to Be Happy, Years to Be Sad: The Life and Music of Vincent Youmans.* New York: Oxford UP; 1982. vii, 266 pp.
USA. 1898-1946. Biographies. ■Biography of songwriter who produced hit songs for musical comedies.

1781 Cunningham, Dennis; Rich, Frank; Watt, Douglas; Kissel, Howard; Siegel, Joel; Corliss, Richard; Kroll, Jack; Beaufort, John; Barnes, Clive. "*The Tap Dance Kid*." *NYTCR.* 1983 Dec. 31; 44(19): 52-57.
USA. 1983. Reviews of performances. ■Nine critics review *The Tap Dance Kid*. Book by Charles Blackwell, music by Henry Krieger and lyrics by Robert Lorick. Directed by Vivian Matalon at the Broadhurst Theatre.

1782 Gruen, John. "Reviving *On Your Toes*." *Dm.* 1983 Mar.; 57(3): 60-67. Illus.: Photo. B&W. Color. 12.
USA. 1982. Historical studies. ■Discussion of 1982 production of musical *On Your Toes*. Emphasis placed on George Balanchine's choreography and dancers in lead roles: Natalia Makarova, Starr Danias, Valentina Kozlov and Leonid Kozlov.

1783 Gussow, Mel; Beaufort, John; Kissel, Howard; Barnes, Clive; Watt, Douglas. "*Five-Six-Seven-Eight...Dance!*" *NYTCR.* 1983 July 11; 44(11): 199-203.
USA. 1983. Reviews of performances. ■Five critics review *Five-Six-Seven-Eight...Dance!*, directed by Ron Field at Radio City Music Hall.

1784 King, Larry L. *The Whorehouse Papers.* New York: Viking P; 1982. xiii, 283 pp.
USA. 1974-1982. Historical studies. ■Chronicle of inception and production of *The Best Little Whorehouse in Texas* from Broadway musical to bowdlerized Hollywood film, by the author of the show.

1785 Kiziuk, Len. "The New Musical." *ThNe.* 1982 Jan.; 14(1): 2-3.
USA. 1982. Critical studies. ■Changes needed in production and direction of musical theatre.

1786 Lamont, Rosette C. "Le Théâtre à New York: triomphe d'Off-Broadway." (Theatre in New York: Triumph of Off-Broadway.) *CRB.* 1983; 106: 104-116.
USA. 1983. Critical studies. ■Shift from Broadway to Off Broadway is attributed to the new rise in consciousness by the American public looking for less trivial and more honest forms of expression.

1787 Loney, Glenn. "Balanchine on Broadway." *Dm.* 1983 July; 57(7): 90-93. Illus.: Photo. B&W. 5.
USA. 1929-1962. Biographical studies. ■George Balanchine's role in the development of dance in musical theatre. Related to Dance: Ballet.

1788 Loney, Glenn. "The Legacy of Jack Cole." *Dm.* 1983 Jan.; 57(1): 40-46. Illus.: Photo. B&W. 8. [13 part series, published monthly January 1983 through March 1984: Part 2 (Feb): 38-43, Part 3 (Mar): 78-80, Part 4 (Apr): 79-81, Part 5 (May): 123-129, Part 6 (June): 62-64, Part 7 (Aug): 82-85, Part 8 (Sep): 45-48, Part 9 (Nov): 76-80, Part 10 (Dec): 54-58.]
USA. 1933-1974. Biographical studies. ■Overview of Jack Cole's career as dancer, teacher and choreographer including his work in film, nightclubs and musical theatre. Related to Media: Film.

1789 Mordden, Ethan. *Broadway Babies: The People who Made the American Musical.* New York: Oxford UP; 1983. 244 pp.
USA. 1800-1983. Histories-specific. ■Brief overview of Broadway musical theatre with an extensive annotated discography.

1790 Petrucelli, Alan W. *Liza! Liza! An Unauthorized Biography of Liza Minnelli.* New York: Karz-Cohl; 1983. xii, 174 pp. Biblio. Index. Filmography. Illus.: Photo.
USA. 1946-1983. Biographies. Related to Media: Film.

1791 Pikula, Joan. "Kickin' the Clouds Away." *Dm.* 1983 Sep.; 57(9): 66-73. Illus.: Photo. Color. 6.
USA. 1971-1983. Critical studies. ■Discussion of production and casting, and review of the musical comedy *My One and Only*. Emphasis on choreographer-performer Tommy Tune, performer Twiggy and choreographer Thommie Walsh.

1792 Rich, Frank; Sharp, Christopher; Beaufort, John; Barnes, Clive; Watt, Douglas; Siegel, Joel; Cunningham, Dennis.

MUSIC-DRAMA: Musical theatre—Performance/production

"Marilyn: An American Fable." NYTCR. 1983 Nov. 14; 44(16): 118-122.
USA. 1983. Reviews of performances. ■Seven critics review Kenny Ortega's production of *Marilyn: An American Fable*, with music and lyrics by Jeanne Napoli, Doug Frank, Gary Portnoy, Beth Lawrence, Norman Thalheimer and others, and libretto by Patricia Michaels. Presented at the Minskoff Theatre.

1793 Rich, Frank; Watt, Douglas; Barnes, Clive; Kissel, Howard; Siegel, Joel; Cunningham, Dennis. *"Dance a Little Closer."* NYTCR. 1983 May 16; 44(8): 248-251.
USA. 1983. Reviews of performances. ■Six critics review *Dance a Little Closer*, with book and lyrics by Alan Jay Lerner and music by Charles Strouse. Directed by Lerner. Presented at the Minskoff Theatre.

1794 Rich, Frank; Barnes, Clive; Kissel, Howard; Watt, Douglas; Cunningham, Dennis; Siegel, Joel. "Peg." NYTCR. 1983 Dec. 31; 44(19): 57-60.
USA. 1983. Reviews of performances. ■Six critics review Robert Drivas' production of *Peg*, by Peggy Lee. Presented at the Lunt-Fontanne Theatre.

1795 Rich, Frank; Watt, Douglas; Barnes, Clive; Kissel, Howard; Kalem, T.E.; Walsh, Michael; Cunningham, Dennis; Eckert, Thor, Jr.; Siegel, Joel. *"Porgy and Bess."* NYTCR. 1983 Apr. 4; 44(5): 316-321.
USA. 1983. Reviews of performances. ■Nine critics review Jack O'Brien's production of *Porgy and Bess*. Composed by George Gershwin, with lyrics by DuBose Heyward and Ira Gershwin and libretto by Heyward. Presented at Radio City Music Hall.

1796 Rich, Frank; Beaufort, John; Watt, Douglas; Cohen, Ron; Barnes, Clive. *"Tallulah."* NYTCR Off Broadway Supplement IV. 1983 Dec. 12; 44(18): 82-84.
USA. 1983. Reviews of performances. ■Five critics review Tony Lang's *Tallulah*, with music by Arthur Siegel and lyrics by Mae Richard. Directed by David Holdgrive at the Cheryl Crawford Theatre.

1797 Rich, Frank; Cohen, Ron; O'Haire, Patricia; Barnes, Clive; Corliss, Richard; Sterritt, David. *"Galas."* NYTCR Off Broadway Supplement IV. 1983 Dec. 12; 44(18): 85-88.
USA. 1983. Reviews of performances. ■Six critics review Charles Ludlam's *Galas*, directed by the author at the Ridiculous Theatrical Company.

1798 Rich, Frank; Watt, Douglas; Kissel, Howard; Barnes, Clive; Beaufort, John; Wilson, Edwin; Kroll, Jack; Cunningham, Dennis; Siegel, Joel. *"Zorba."* NYTCR. 1983 Oct. 3; 44(14): 146-152.
USA. 1983. Reviews of performances. ■Nine critics review Michael Cacoyannis' production of *Zorba*, with lyrics by Fred Ebb, music by John Kander and book by Joseph Stein. Presented at the Broadway Theatre.

1799 Rich, Frank; Sharp, Christopher; Watt, Douglas; Corliss, Richard; Kroll, Jack; Beaufort, John; Barnes, Clive; Cunningham, Dennis; Siegel, Joel. *"Doonesbury."* NYTCR. 1983 Nov. 14; 44(16): 112-117.
USA. 1983. Reviews of performances. ■Nine critics review Jacques Levy's production of *Doonesbury*, with book and lyrics by Garry Trudeau and music by Elizabeth Swados. Presented at the Biltmore Theatre.

1800 Rich, Frank; Cunningham, Dennis; Watt, Douglas; Siegel, Joel; Barnes, Clive; Sharp, Christopher; Beaufort, John; Wilson, Edwin. *"Amen Corner."* NYTCR. 1983 Nov. 7; 44(15): 132-136.
USA. 1983. Reviews of performances. ■Eight critics review Philip Rose's production of the musical *Amen Corner*, with music by Garry Sherman and book and lyrics by Peter Udell and Philip Rose, presented at the Nederlander Theatre.

1801 Rich, Frank; Beaufort, John; Kissel, Howard; Watt, Douglas; Cunningham, Dennis; Barnes, Clive. *"Mame."* NYTCR. 1983 July 11; 44(11): 196-199.
USA. 1983. Reviews of performances. ■Six critics review John Bowab's production of *Mame*, book by Jerome Laurence and Robert E. Lee, with music and lyrics by Jerry Herman at the Gershwin Theatre.

1802 Rich, Frank; Watt, Douglas; Barnes, Clive; Kissel, Howard; Wilson, Edwin; Beaufort, John; Kanfer, Stefan; Siegel, Joel. *"Merlin."* NYTCR. 1983 Feb. 14; 44(2): 370-377.
USA. 1983. Reviews of performances. ■Eight critics review Ivan Reitman's production of the musical *Merlin* by Richard Levinson, William Link, Elmer Bernstein and Don Black at the Mark Hellinger Theatre.

1803 Rich, Frank; Watt, Douglas; Beaufort, John; Barnes, Clive; Stasio, Marilyn; Wilson, Edwin; Kroll, Kissel; Mazo, Joseph H. *"On Your Toes."* NYTCR. 1983 Mar. 7; 44(3): 359-366.
USA. 1983. Reviews of performances. ■Six critics review George Abbott's production of *On Your Toes* by Richard Rodgers and Lorenz Hart, presented at the Virginia Theatre. Related to Dance.

1804 Rinaldi, Nicholas George. *Music as Mediator: A Description of the Process of Concept Development in the Musical, Cabaret.* Columbus: Ohio State Univ.; 1982. 225 pp. [Diss.: University Microfilms order no. DA8214132.]
USA. 1966. Historical studies. ■Descriptive study of the original Broadway production of *Cabaret*. Documents evolution of director Harold Prince's concept of the production.

1805 Siegel, Joel; Watt, Douglas; Kissel, Howard; Schickel, Richard; Kroll, Jack; Cunningham, Dennis; Rich, Frank; Beaufort, John; Barnes, Clive; Wilson, Edwin. *"Baby."* NYTCR. 1983 Dec. 5; 44(17): 96-100.
USA. 1983. Reviews of performances. ■Ten critics review *Baby*, with lyrics by Richard Maltby Jr., music by David Shire and book by Sybille Pearson. Directed by the lyricist at the Ethel Barrymore Theatre.

1806 Siegel, Joel; Rich, Frank; Watt, Douglas; Barnes, Clive; Kissel, Howard; Wilson, Edwin; Beaufort, John; Kroll, Jack; Clarke, Gerald; Cunningham, Dennis. *"La Cage aux Folles."* NYTCR. 1983 July 11; 44(11): 188-195.
USA. 1983. Reviews of performances. ■Ten critics review Arthur Laurent's production of *La Cage aux Folles*, book by Harvey Fierstein and music and lyrics by Jerry Herman at the Palace Theatre.

1807 Watt, Douglas; Rich, Frank; Barnes, Clive; Kissel, Howard; Beaufort, John; Wilson, Edwin; Kroll, Jack; Cunningham, Dennis. *"Show Boat."* NYTCR. 1983 May 2; 44(7): 270-275.
USA. 1983. Reviews of performances. ■Eight critics review Jerome Kern and Oscar Hammerstein's *Show Boat*, directed by Michael Kahn. Presented at the Uris Theatre.

1808 Watt, Douglas; Kissel, Howard; Beaufort, John; Rich, Frank; Siegel, Joel; Barnes, Clive; Kroll, Jack; Wilson, Edwin; Kalem, T.E.; Cunningham, Dennis. *"My One and Only."* NYTCR. 1983 May 16; 44(8): 261-267.
USA. 1983. Reviews of performances. ■Ten critics review *My One and Only*, music by George Gershwin, lyrics by Ira Gershwin and book by Peter Stone and Timothy S. Mayer. Staged by Tommy Tune and Thommie Walsh. Presented at the St. James Theatre.

Plays/librettos/scripts

1809 Loney, Glenn. "Broadway Nora: The Musical, *A Doll's Life.*" INC. 1983; 4: 14-18. Illus.: Photo. B&W. 2.
USA. 1983. Historical studies. ■Musical adaptation of Henrik Ibsen's *A Doll's House (Et Dukkehjem)*.

Opera

Administration

1810 Gelatt, Roland. "An American in Vienna." OpN. 1983 Sep.; 48(3): 26-30. Illus.: Photo. B&W. Color. 2.
Austria. USA. 1983. Historical studies. ■American conductor Lorin Maazel as intendant of the Vienna Staatsoper.

1811 Kutschera, Edda. "Das unsichtbare Puzzle." (The Invisible Puzzle.) Buhne. 1983 Nov.: 28-30.
Austria. 1983. Historical studies. ■Administration in the making of a production at Vienna's Staatsoper.

1812 Seefehlner, Egon. *Die Musik meines Lebens: Vom Rechtspraktikanten zum Opernchef in Berlin und Wien.* (The Music of My Life: From Practicing Law to Manager of the

MUSIC-DRAMA: Opera—Administration

Opera House in Berlin and Vienna.) Vienna: Paul Neff; 1983. 277 pp. Index. Append. Illus.: Photo. B&W.
Austria. Germany, West. 1912-1983. Biographies. ■Life and career of opera manager Egon Seefehlner.

1813 Karpf, Deborah. "Terry McEwen." *OC.* 1983 June; 24(2): 18-19, 41-42.
Canada. USA. 1983. Histories-sources. ■Interview with general director of San Francisco War Memorial Opera House.

1814 Milhous, Judith; Hume, Robert D. "New Light on Handel and the Royal Academy of Music in 1720." *TJ.* 1983 May; 35(2): 149-167. Notes.
England. 1719-1721. Historical studies. ■Discussion of financial arrangements and management organization at the Royal Academy of Music. Included are box-office estimates, members, salaries and other expenses.

1815 St. Clair, F.B. "Wizard of the West." *OpN.* 1983 Sep.; 48(3): 22, 24. Illus.: Photo. B&W. 1.
USA. 1964-1983. Historical studies. ■Account and evaluation of the tenure of Glynn Ross as founding general director of the Seattle Opera.

Audience

1816 Heymont, George. "Singing Opera, Signing Opera." *PArts.* 1982 Sep.; 16(9): 8. Illus.: Photo.
USA. 1979. Histories-sources. ■Mainstreaming hearing impaired at the New York City Opera through the use of the sign interpreters.

Design/technology

1817 Apponius, Harald. "Eine Plattform für den *Ring* 1983 im Festspielhaus Bayreuth." (A Platform for the 1983 *Ring* in the Festspielhaus Bayreuth.) *BtR.* 1983; 76(6): 19-21. Illus.: Design. Plan. Fr.Elev. Schematic. Grd.Plan. 3.
Germany, West. 1983. Technical studies. ■Technical realization of the main platform for the sets.

1818 Huneke, Walter. "Bühnentechnik in der Bayreuther *Ring* — Neuinszenierung 1983." (Stage Technology of the New Bayreuth *Ring* — Production 1983.) *BtR.* 1983; 76(6): 17-18. Illus.: Photo. Plan. B&W. Fr.Elev. 8.
Germany, West. 1983. Technical studies. ■Various safety requirements for the construction of the platform.

1819 Fagone, Vittorio; La Torre, Anna Maria; Mateldi, Brunetta; Pasi, Mario; Siribaldi Suso, Giorgio. *La danza, il canto, l'abito: Costumi del Teatro alla Scala, 1947-1982.* (Dancing, Singing, Clothing: Costumes of Teatro alla Scala, 1947-1982.) Cinesello Balsamo (Milan): Silvana Editoriale; 1982. 159 pp. Pref. Tables. Illus.: Photo. B&W. Color.
Italy. 1947-1982. Histories-sources. ■Importance of costume in musical theatre. Included are photographs of costumes of Teatro alla Scala and chronology of costumers.

1820 Steinbrink, Mark. "Stroke of Genius." *OpN.* 1983 Dec. 10; 48(6): 54, 56. Illus.: Photo. B&W. 1.
Italy. USA. 1954-1983. Historical studies. ■Discussion of Pier Luigi Samaritani and his work in scene design.

1821 Viale Ferrero, Mercedes. *La scenografia della Scala in età neoclassica.* (Scenery at Teatro alla Scala in the Neoclassic Period.) Milan: Il Polifilo; 1983. 168 pp. (La Scala nell'età neoclassica.) Notes. Biblio. Tables. Illus.: Sketches. B&W. Color.
Italy. 1778-1832. Historical studies. ■Scene designers and scenery at Teatro alla Scala in Neoclassic period. Grp/movt: Neoclassicism. Related to Theatre in General.

1822 Bravo, Isidre. "L'escenografia wagneriana a Catalunya." (The Wagnerian Scenography in Catalonia.) *SdO.* 1983 Feb.; 281: 15-22. Notes. Illus.: Design. Pntg. Print. B&W. 24: 23 cm. x 14 cm. [Included in a dossier entitled *Wagner's Presence (1883-1983)*.]
Spain. 1882-1960. Historical studies. ■Development of Wagnerian stage design is divided into three categories: naturalism (promoted by Soler i Rovirosa group), symbolism (Oleguer Junyent) and avant-garde (by Batlle i Gordó group). Grp/movt: Symbolism; Naturalism.

1823 Burian, Jarka M. *Svoboda Wagner: Josef Svoboda's Scenography for Richard Wagner's Operas.* Middletown, CT: Wesleyan UP; 1983. 144 pp.
Switzerland. UK-England. Czechoslovakia. 1948-1983. Historical studies. ■Development of Svoboda's scenographic theory and practice with an emphasis on his productions of *Der Ring des Nibelungen* (1974, 1975, 1976) and *Die Meistersinger* (1978).

1824 Loney, Glenn. "It's All in the Plot: Tom Munn of the San Francisco Opera." *ThCr.* 1983 Nov.-Dec.; 17(9): 20-69. Illus.: Photo. Plan. Print. B&W. Grd.Plan. 5.
USA. 1975-1983. Biographical studies. ■Methodology and design history of Tom Munn, lighting director of the San Francisco Opera Company.

1825 Margolis, Tina, ed. "Opera Scene Designs and Manuscripts on View at Morgan Library." *USITT.* 1983 Fall; 23(4): 10.
USA. 1583-1983. History-sources. ■Exhibition 'Four Centuries of Opera' illustrates the history of opera with operatic stage designs, music manuscripts and rare printed editions of scores and librettos.

1826 Nadelson, Regina. "Youngest Old Man." *OpN.* 1983 Oct.; 48(4): 82, 84-86, 88, 90. Illus.: Photo. B&W. 1.
USA. 1930-1983. Historical studies. ■Career of Metropolitan Opera wigmaker Adolf Senz.

Institutions

1827 Mujica Lainez, Manuel; Franze, Juan Pedro; Sessa, Aldo, photo. *Vida y gloria del Teatro Colón.* (The Glorious Life of the Colón Theatre.) Buenos Aires: Ediciones Cosmogonias; 1983. 190 pp. Illus.: Photo. Print. Color. B&W. [In Spanish with English, French, Italian and German translations.]
Argentina. 1857-1983. Histories-specific. ■History of Teatro Colón in essays and photographs.

1828 Paavolainen, Paula; Kulovaara, Leena. "Suomen Kansallisooppera." (The Finnish National Opera.) *Teat.* 1983; 39(9): 8-11. Illus.: Photo. 4. [Series of articles.]
Finland. 1983. Historical studies. ■Management and artistic goals of the Finnish National Opera. Trend towards theatricality and composition of original Finnish operas.

1829 Boland, Maura. "The Total Picture." *OpN.* 1983 Nov.; 48(5): 16-18, 19. Illus.: Photo. 1.
USA. 1934-1983. Histories-sources. ■An account of the performances and training at the Academy of Vocal Arts.

1830 Giffen, Glenn. "Ring Around the Opera." *OpN.* 1983 July; 48(1): 14-17. Illus.: Photo. B&W. 6.
USA. 1981-1983. Histories-sources. ■Account of the 1983 season of Opera Colorado.

1831 Kolodin, Irving. "Good Neighbors." *OpN.* 1983 Nov.; 48(5): 32-34. Illus.: Photo. B&W. 3.
USA. 1919-1983. Historical studies. ■Account of the relationship between the Juilliard School and the Metropolitan Opera.

1832 Waleson, Heidi. "Eye to the Future." *OpN.* 1983 Feb. 12; 47(11): 13-14, 44, 46. Illus.: Photo. B&W. 4.
USA. 1980-1983. Histories-sources. ■Account of the Metropolitan Opera Company's Young Artist Development Program.

Performance spaces

1833 Armenian, Raffi. "A New Ring for Kitchener." *OC.* 1983 Fall; 24(3): 22-23, 42.
Canada. 1983. Histories-sources. ■Music director of the Kitchener-Waterloo Symphony on the influence of Bayreuth in Kitchener's new facility and on plans for a Wagnerian production.

1834 Bornemann, Fritz. "Projekt 'Opern-Werkstatt-Studio' für die Deutsche Oper Berlin." ('Opera-Workshop-Studio' Project for the Deutsche Oper Berlin.) *BtR.* 1983; 76(3): 20-21. Illus.: Photo. Plan. B&W. Grd.Plan. Schematic. 9.
Germany, West. 1983. Technical studies. ■Project for the new studio to optimize communication between the general public and the theatrical event.

1835 Mezzanotte, Gianni. *L'architettura della Scala in età neoclassica.* (Architecture of Teatro alla Scala in the Neoclassical Period.) Milan: Il Polifilo; 1982. 164 pp. (La Scala

MUSIC-DRAMA: Opera—Performance spaces

nell'età neoclassica.) Notes. Index. Biblio. Tables. Illus.: Design. B&W.

Italy. 1776-1830. Histories-specific. ■Giuseppe Piermarini built Teatro alla Scala in accordance with architectural theories of his time. Grp/movt: Neoclassicism.

1836 Gelatt, Roland. "Crown Jewel." *OpN.* 1983 June; 47(17): 16-22. Illus.: Handbill. Photo. B&W. 6.

UK-England. 1732-1983. Historical studies. ■Account of the Royal Opera House, Covent Garden.

1837 Yant, Gwen Sommers. "Small Town Theatre Revitalization: The Case of the Hayesville Opera House." *M.* 1983 Fourth Quarter ; 15(4): 27-32. Biblio. Illus.: Photo. B&W. 7.

USA. 1886-1983. Technical studies. ■Case-study of the renovation of a small-town opera house with recommendations for ways such a renovation should be undertaken.

Performance/production

1838 Bachmann, Robert C. *Karajan: Anmerkungen zu einer Karriere.* (Karajan: Notes on a Career.) Vienna and Duesseldorf: Econ; 1983. 399 pp. Notes. Index. Tables. Illus.: Photo. B&W.

Austria. Germany. 1908-1982. Biographies. ■Biography of conductor Herbert von Karajan, including his theories on opera and music in general.

1839 Böhm, Gotthard. "Vom Musical zur Opera." (From Musical to Opera.) *Buhne.* 1983 June: 16-17.

Austria. 1983. Histories-sources. ■Harold Prince leaves Broadway for opera and directs Puccini's *Turandot* at Vienna's Staatsoper, conducted by Lorin Maazel.

1840 Kutschera, Edda. "Keine 'Wunder' ohne Arbeit." (No 'Miracles' without Work.) *Buhne.* 1983 Dec.: 28-30.

Austria. 1983. Historical studies. ■Making of a production at Vienna's Staatsoper: rehearsals.

1841 Löbl, Hermi. "Ich will kein altes Hausmöbel sein: Über Walter Berry und sein Falstaff-Debüt an der Wiener Staatsoper." (I Don't Want to Be Old Stuff: on Walter Berry and His *Falstaff* Debut at the Vienna Staatsoper.) *Buhne.* 1983 Feb.: 8-9. Illus.: Photo.

Austria. 1983. Biographical studies. ■Bass Walter Berry's career and debut in *Falstaff* at the Vienna Staatsoper.

1842 Mayer, Gerhard. "Zemlinsky-Renaissance: Eine Fussnote macht Furore." (Zemlinsky-Renaissance: A Footnote Makes a Splash.) *Buhne.* 1983 Nov.: 32-33. Illus.: Photo. Color.

Austria. 1983. Historical studies. ■Recent productions of operas by Alexander von Zemlinsky.

1843 Sandor, Peter E. "Mozart's Favorite Ladies." *OC.* 1983 June; 24(2): 15-17, 44.

Austria. 1777-1791. Historical studies. ■Survey of the women who created the best known roles in Mozart's operas.

1844 Anon. "Spotlight: Steven Thomas." *OC.* 1983 Fall; 24(3): 12-13.

Canada. 1983. Histories-sources. ■Interview with and profile of artistic director of Opera Hamilton.

1845 Anon. "Spotlight: Lynn Blaser." *OC.* 1983 Winter; 24(4): 12-13.

Canada. 1983. Histories-sources. ■Interview with Canadian Opera Company soprano Lynn Blaser.

1846 Berges, Ruth. "Canada's Ermanno Mauro." *OC.* 1983 Fall; 24(3): 18-21.

Canada. USA. 1958-1983. Histories-sources. ■Interview with and profile of Metropolitan Opera tenor who settled in Canada.

1847 Giannini, Vera. "Anna Russell." *OC.* 1983 Mar.; 24(1): 18-19, 46.

Canada. 1912-1983. Histories-sources. ■Interview with concert singer and comedienne Anna Russell.

1848 Michaud, Marie-Andrée; Tourigny, Maurice. "Louis Quilico." *OC.* 1983 Mar.; 24(1): 20-23.

Canada. USA. 1983. Histories-sources. ■Interview with and profile of Metropolitan Opera baritone Louis Quilico.

1849 Stearns, David Patric. "Revisionist." *OpN.* 1983 Aug.; 48(2): 30-31. Illus.: Photo. B&W. 1.

England. 1597-1759. Historical studies. ■English conductor John Eliot Gardiner discusses baroque opera, with emphasis on the contributions of Handel. Grp/movt: Baroque theatre.

1850 Arrau, Claudio. "Of Songs and Singers." *OpN.* 1983 Apr. 9; 47(15): 14-15, 61-62. Illus.: Photo. 1.

Europe. USA. 1903-1983. Histories-sources. ■Pianist Claudio Arrau recalls operas and singers he has heard.

1851 Bauer, Oswald Georg. *Richard Wagner: The Stage Designs and Productions from the Premieres to the Present.* New York: Rizzoli International Publications; 1873. 288 pp. Illus.: Sketches. Dwg. Photo. B&W. Color. 300.

Europe. USA. Canada. 1832-1983. Histories specific. ■Comprehensive production history of all of Wagner's operas. Included are circumstances of composition, relevant biographical information and critical commentary.

1852 Herrero, Fernando. *La ópera y su estética.* (Opera and Aesthetics.) Madrid: Dirección General Música y Teatro (Ministerio de Cultura); 1983. 293 pp. Biblio. Illus.: Photo.

Europe. 1597-1982. Historical studies. ■History of opera staging. Analysis of the composition and specific aesthetics of the genre.

1853 Jacobson, Robert; Steiner, Christian, photo.; Scott, Michael. *Opera People.* New York: Vendome P; 1983. 112 pp. Illus.: Photo. Color. 75.

Europe. North America. 1945-1983. Biographical studies. ■Illustrated biographical survey of 37 opera stars with a brief essay on opera history. Authors suggest that these singers and conductors have replaced the composers in sustaining cultural value of opera.

1854 Lanier, Thomas P. "Viva Cossotto." *OpN.* 1983 Jan. 1; 47(8): 8-11, 42. Illus.: Photo. B&W. Color. 3.

Europe. USA. 1957-1983. Biographical studies. ■Mezzosoprano Fiorenza Cossotto speaks about her career and art.

1855 Löbl, Hermi. "Luciano Pavarotti: 'Einer muss der Erste sein.'" (Luciano Pavarotti: 'One Must Be the First.') *Buhne.* 1983 July-Aug.: 4-6.

Europe. North America. 1983. Histories-sources. ■Interview with tenor Luciano Pavarotti about his career and forthcoming roles.

1856 Lossmann, Hans. "Savonlinna: Bemerkenswerte Lebenszeichen." (Savonlinna: Remarkable Zest for Life.) *Buhne.* 1983 Sep.: 44-45. Illus.: Photo. Color.

Finland. 1983. Historical studies. ■Bass Martti Talvela produces Finnish opera at the Opera-festival at Savonlinna Castle.

1857 Ashbrook, Jon. "Perspectives on an Aria." *OpN.* 1983 Jan. 29; 47(10): 28, 42. Illus.: Photo. B&W. 1.

France. USA. 1911-1983. Critical studies. ■Comparison of performances of tenor aria 'O Dieu de quelle ivresse' by Jacques Offenbach.

1858 De La Gorce, Jérôme. "Documents de critique musicale et théâtrale: dix lettres extraites de la correspondance entre Ladvocat et l'Abbé Dubos (1694-1696)." (Documents of Musical and Theatrical Criticism: Ten Letters from the Correspondence of Ladvocat and Abbé Dubos (1694-1696).) *DSS.* 1983 Apr.-June; 39(2): 267-282.

France. 1694-1696. Histories-sources. ■Critical commentary by two prominent figures of the time about several operas being performed in Paris.

1859 Kahane, Martine; Wild, Nicole. *Wagner et la France.* (Wagner and France.) Paris: Bibliothèque Nationale and Théâtre National de l'Opéra de Paris; 1983. 175 pp. Biblio. Illus.: Photo. [Accompanies exhibit organized by the Bibliothèque Nationale and the Théâtre National de l'Opéra de Paris.]

France. 1841-1983. Historical studies. ■Studies Wagner's works, reception and influence in France. Includes chronology of Wagnerian works produced in France.

1860 La Gorce, Jérôme de. "L'Opéra français à la Cour de Louis XIV." (French Opera at the Court of Louis XIV.) *RHT.* 1983; 35(4): 387-401. Notes. Illus.: Photo. Print. B&W. 2.

MUSIC-DRAMA: Opera—Performance/production

France. 1671-1704. Historical studies. ■Repertory and history of opera performances at the French court with emphasis on the work of scene designer Carlo Vigarani.

1861   Loney, Glenn. "The *Carmen* Connection." *OpN.* 1983 Sep.; 48(3): 10-14. Illus.: Photo. Color. 5.

France. 1981. Historical studies. ■The Paris Opera staging of Georges Bizet's *La Tragédie de Carmen* adapted by Peter Brook at the Bouffes du Nord.

1862   Stearns, David Patrick. "Fête Fantastique." (Fantastic Festival.) *OpN.* 1983 May; 47(16): 30, 32-33. Illus.: Photo. B&W. 1.

France. 1960-1983. Histories-sources. ■Account of the Hector Berlioz festival, and Serge Baudo, director.

1863   Zucker, Stefan. "Seismic Shocker." *OpN.* 1983 Jan. 1; 47(8): 12-14, 44. Illus.: Dwg. B&W. 1.

France. 1806-1896. Historical studies. ■The high 'C' from the chest, now standard practice among tenors, was popularized by Gilbert-Louis Duprez.

1864   Hamilton, David. "More Echoes from the Shrine." *OpN.* 1983 Aug.; 48(2): 22-25, 46. Illus.: Photo. B&W. 6.

Germany. 1882-1982. Histories-sources. ■Discussion of one hundred years of *Parsifal* performances at Bayreuth and on records.

1865   Osborne, Charles. *The World Theatre of Wagner: A Celebration of 150 Years of Wagner Productions.* New York: Macmillan; 1982. 244 pp. Illus.: Photo. Dwg.

Germany. USA. 1832-1982. Histories specific. ■Critical re-examination of the genesis of Wagner's operas, with emphasis on the production history of his operas. The most successful productions said to be faithful to the composer's intent.

1866   "*Siegfried.*" *OpN.* 1983 Apr. 9; 47(15): 44-45. Illus.: Photo. Color. 4.

Germany, West. 1980. Histories-sources. ■Stills from April 16, 1983 telecast of 1980 Bayreuth Festival production of *Siegfried* by Richard Wagner. Directed by Patrice Chéreau. List of principals, conductor, production staff included.

1867   "*Götterdämmerung.*" *OpN.* 1983 June; 47(17): 32-33. Illus.: Photo. Color. 6.

Germany, West. 1980. Histories-sources. ■Stills from the June 6, 13, 1983 telecasts of the 1980 Bayreuth Festival production of *Götterdämmerung*, directed by Patrice Chéreau. List of principals, conductor, production staff included.

1868   Buchau, Stephanie von. "Tales of Hofman." *OpN.* 1983 Aug.; 48(2): 16-20. Illus.: Photo. B&W. Color. 5.

Germany, West. 1983. Histories-sources. ■German tenor Peter Hofman speaks of his career and art which encompass Wagner and rock music.

1869   Chéreau, Patrice. "*Der Ring des Nibelungen: Die Walküre.*" *OpN.* 1983 Feb. 26; 47(12): 32-33. [Telecast, 1980 Bayreuth Festival production, February 21 and 28, 1983.]

Germany, West. 1980. Histories-sources. ■Stills from the 1980 Bayreuth Festival production of *Die Walküre* by Richard Wagner. List of principals, conductor, production staff and synopsis included.

1870   Geleng, Ingvelde. "Vom Endspiel zurück zum Märchen: *Der Ring des Nibelungen* 1983 in Bayreuth." (From Endgame Back to Fairytale: *The Ring of the Nibelungen* 1983 at Bayreuth.) *BtR.* 1983; 76(6): 10-16. Illus.: Photo. B&W. 19.

Germany, West. 1983. Reviews of performances. ■Stage design and description of the new production of Wagner's *Ring* as an illusionary fairytale marked by technical sophistication.

1871   Geleng, Ingvelde. "Wiederbelebungsversuch an Korngolds *Die tote Stadt* in Berlin." (Attempt to Restore Life in Korngold's *The Dead City* in Berlin.) *BtR.* 1983; 76(3): 16-18. Illus.: Plan. Photo. B&W. Grd.Plan. 7.

Germany, West. 1855. 1983. Reviews of performances. ■Gustav Mahler's and Richard Strauss' influence on Korngold's *Die tote Stadt.* Technical and artistic treatment of the opera staged at the Deutsche Oper Berlin. Grp/movt: Expressionism.

1872   Jacobson, Robert. "State of Ecstasy." *OpN.* 1983 Aug.; 48(2): 8-12, 14. Illus.: Photo. Color. 4.

Germany, West. 1981. Histories-sources. ■American conductor Leonard Bernstein and a discussion of his multimedia *Tristan und Isolde*, by Richard Wagner.

1873   Jacobson, Robert. "Bayreuth Diary, 1983." *OpN.* 1983 Nov.; 48(5): 10-14, 60-63. Illus.: Photo. B&W. 8.

Germany, West. 1983. Historical studies. ■1983 Bayreuth *Der Ring des Nibelungen*, directed by Peter Hall, conducted by Georg Solti.

1874   Lipton, Gary D. "Having Fun." *OpN.* 1983 Mar. 12; 47(13): 30-31. Illus.: Photo. B&W. 2. [Interview with bass Kurt Moll.]

Germany, West. 1950-1983. Histories-sources. ■German bass Kurt Moll speaks about his art and career, particularly his role as Baron Ochs in *Der Rosenkavalier* by Richard Strauss.

1875   Loney, Glenn. "The Perfect Wagnerite." *OpN.* 1983 Jan. 1; 47(8): 32-37. Illus.: Photo. B&W. Color. 5.

Germany, West. 1976. Histories-sources. ■Patrice Chéreau talks about his controversial Bayreuth production of *Der Ring des Nibelungen* by Richard Wagner.

1876   Loney, Glenn. "Götz Friedrich." *OpN.* 1983 May; 47(16): 17-19, 42. Illus.: Photo. B&W. 3. [Great Directors VIII.]

Germany, West. 1982. Histories-sources. ■Discussion of centennial Bayreuth production of *Parsifal* directed by Götz Friedrich.

1877   Seabury, Deborah. "Seizing the Moment." *OpN.* 1983 May; 47(16): 25-26, 28, 43. Illus.: Photo. B&W. Color. 2.

Germany, West. 1940-1983. Histories—sources. ■American baritone David Holloway of Deutsche Oper am Rhein speaks of his art and career.

1878   Lanier, Thomas P. "Having It All." *OpN.* 1983 Feb. 12; 47(11): 9-11, 46. Illus.: Photo. Color. 1.

Hungary. USA. 1968-1983. Histories-sources. ■Eva Marton, Hungarian dramatic soprano, speaks of her art and career.

1879   Bufalino, Gesualdo. "'U' teatru' intervista sul melodramma in Sicilia." ('U' teatru': Interview about Opera in Sicily.) *AdP.* 1983; 8(1): 47-51. Illus.: Photo.

Italy. 1907-1983. Histories-sources. ■Theatrical spontaneity, informal role-playing and appreciation for improvisation are still alive in the bourgeois clubs as depicted in Vitaliano Brancati's novels.

1880   Del Monaco, Mario. *La mia vita e i miei successi.* (My Life and My Successes.) Milan: Rusconi; 1982. 137 pp. (Gente nel tempo.) Index. Tables. Illus.: Photo. B&W.

Italy. 1915-1975. Biographies. ■Autobiography of tenor Mario Del Monaco.

1881   Fabbri, Paolo, ed.; Pompilio, Angelo, ed. *Il corago o vero Alcune annotazioni per mettere bene in scena le composizioni drammatiche.* (The *Corago*, or Some Notes for The Staging of Dramatic Compositions.) Florence: Olschki; 1983. 128 pp. (Studi e testi per la storia della musica 4.) Pref. Notes.

Italy. 1597-1699. Instructional materials. ■Reprint of a production manuscript for all aspects of staging an opera, with editorial essay on original manuscript.

1882   Friedl, Peter. "Wer sich erinnert, lebt: Eine Theaterreise ins 19. Jahrhundert: Klaus Michael Grübers *Tannhäuser* in Florenz." (Those Who Remember, Live: Theatrical Journey into the 19th Century: Klaus Michael Grüber's *Tannhäuser* in Florence.) *TH.* 1983; 8: 37-38. Illus.: Photo.

Italy. 1983. Historical studies. ■Klaus Michael Grüber directs Wagner's *Tannhäuser* at Teatro Comunale, Florence.

1883   Paoletti, Pier Maria. *Quella sera alla Scala.* (That Evening at La Scala.) Milan: Rusconi; 1983. 224 pp. Index. Tables. Illus.: Photo. B&W.

Italy. 1958-1982. Historical studies. ■Collection of interviews, reviews of performances and other writings on the most famous opera singers and directors.

1884   Pintorno, Giuseppe. *Le prime.* (Opening Nights.) With collaboration of Ente Autonomo Teatro alla Scala. Gorle (Bergamo): Grafica Gutenberg; 1982. 304 pp. (Duecento anni di Teatro alla Scala.) Notes. Index. Tables. Illus.: Photo. B&W.

Italy. 1778-1977. Histories-specific. ■History of opening nights at Teatro alla Scala is conveyed through newspaper reviews.

MUSIC-DRAMA: Opera—Performance/production

1885 Rasponi, Lanfranco. "Dream Traviata." *OpN.* 1983 Mar. 12; 47(13): 8-14. Illus.: Photo. Color. 8. [Discussion of the Franco Zeffirelli film *La Traviata.*]
Italy. 1981-1983. Historical studies. ■Making of the Franco Zeffirelli film of *La Traviata* by Giuseppe Verdi, with Teresa Stratas, Placido Domingo and Cornell MacNeil. Related to Media: Film.

1886 Albet, Montserrat. "Els primers anys wagnerians." (The First Wagnerian Years.) *SdO.* 1983 Feb.; 281: 9-10. Illus.: Photo. Print. B&W. 3: 6 cm. x 8 cm. [Included in a dossier entitled *Wagner's Presence (1883-1983).*]
Spain. 1862-1901. Historical studies. ■First performance of Wagner's *Lohengrin* promoted by Josep-Anselm Clavé and Felip Pedrell. Also discussed is the initial controversy between Wagner's followers and Verdi's followers.

1887 Marfany, Joan-Lluis. "El wagnerisme a Catalunya." (Wagnerism in Catalonia.) *SdO.* 1983 Feb.; 281: 10-14. Illus.: Design. Pntg. Photo. Print. B&W. 7: 9 cm. x 12 cm. [Included in a dossier entitled *Wagner's Presence (1883-1983).*]
Spain. 1878-1926. Historical studies. ■History of Wagnerian study and performance. Grp/movt: Modernism.

1888 Geis, Darlene. *The Gilbert and Sullivan Operas.* New York: Harry N. Abrams; 1983. 240 pp. Illus.: Photo. Color. B&W. 270.
UK-England. 1867-1983. Histories-sources. ■Largely pictorial work containing historical material about Gilbert and Sullivan, the D'Oyly Carte Opera Company, plot summaries, excerpts from the operas, and production information from a British television series of Gilbert and Sullivan operas. Related to Media: Video forms.

1889 Jacobson, Robert. "Dame Kiri." *OpN.* 1983 Feb. 26; 47(12): 8-14, 46. Illus.: Photo. Color. 2.
UK-England. USA. New Zealand. 1945-1983. Histories-sources. ■Kiri Te Kanawa, New Zealand soprano, speaks about her career and art.

1890 Anon. "Happy Hundred!" *OpN.* 1983 Dec. 24; 48(7): 6-10. Illus.: Photo. B&W. Color. 20.
USA. 1983. Histories-sources. ■Photographs of gala centennial concert at the Metropolitan Opera House.

1891 Bergman, Beth. "*Boris Godunov.*" *OpN.* 1983 Jan. 29; 47(10): 20-22. Illus.: Photo. B&W. 7.
USA. 1983. Histories-sources. ■Photographs of Metropolitan Opera production of *Boris Godunov* by Modeste Moussorgsky. List of principals, conductor, designer, production staff, discography and synopsis included.

1892 Bergman, Beth. "*Parsifal.*" *OpN.* 1983 Apr. 9; 47(15): 36-38. Illus.: Photo. B&W. 9. [Metropolitan Opera broadcast of April 16, 1983.]
USA. 1983. Histories-sources. ■Photographs of the Metropolitan Opera production of *Parsifal* by Richard Wagner. List of principals, conductor, design and production staff, discography and synopsis included.

1893 Bergman, Beth. "*Lucia di Lammermoor.*" *OpN.* 1983 Sep.; 48(3): 42. Illus.: Photo. Color. 3.
USA. 1983. Histories—sources. ■Stills from the Metropolitan Opera telecast of September 28, 1983, videotaped November 12, 1982. List of principals, conductor, design and production staff, discography and synopsis included.

1894 Bergman, Beth. "*Arabella.*" *OpN.* 1983 Feb. 26; 47(12): 24-26. Illus.: Design. B&W. Color. 7. [Metropolitan Opera broadcast of March 5, 1983.]
USA. 1983. Histories-sources. ■Set designs by Günther Schneider-Siemssen for the Metropolitan Opera production of *Arabella* by Richard Strauss. List of principals, conductor, production staff, discography and synopsis included.

1895 Bergman, Beth. "*Il Trovatore.*" *OpN.* 1983 Jan. 1; 47(8): 26-28. Illus.: Photo. B&W. 7. [Metropolitan Opera broadcast of January 8, 1983.]
USA. 1983. Histories-sources. ■Photographs of Metropolitan Opera performance of *Il Trovatore* by Giuseppe Verdi. List of principals, conductor, designer, production staff, discography and synopsis included.

1896 Bergman, Beth. "*Tannhaüser.*" *OpN.* 1983 Jan. 1; 47(8): 20-23. Illus.: Photo. B&W. 6. [Metropolitan Opera broadcast of January 1, 1983.]
USA. 1983. Histories-sources. ■Photographs of Metropolitan Opera performance of *Tannhaüser* by Richard Wagner. List of principals, conductor, designer, production staff, discography and synopsis included.

1897 Bergman, Beth. "*Adriana Lecouvreur.*" *OpN.* 1983 Feb. 26; 47(12): 20-22. Illus.: Photo. B&W. 5. [Metropolitan Opera broadcast of February 26, 1983.]
USA. 1983. Histories-sources. ■Photographs of the Metropolitan Opera production of *Adriana Lecouvreur* by Francesco Cilèa. List of principals, conductor, designer, production staff, discography and synopsis included.

1898 Bergman, Beth. "*La Gioconda.*" *OpN.* 1983 Feb. 12; 47(11): 24-27. Illus.: Photo. B&W. 8. [Metropolitan Opera broadcast of February 12, 1983.]
USA. 1983. Histories-sources. ■Photographs of the Metropolitan Opera production of *La Gioconda* by Amilcare Ponchielli. List of principals, conductor, designer, production staff, discography and synopsis included.

1899 Bergman, Beth. "*Un Ballo in Maschera.*" *OpN.* 1983 Feb. 12; 47(11): 28-30. Illus.: Photo. B&W. 6. [Metropolitan Opera broadcast of February 19, 1983.]
USA. 1983. Histories-sources. ■Photographs of Metropolitan Opera production of *Un Ballo in Maschera* by Giuseppe Verdi. List of principals, conductor, designer, production staff, discography and synopsis included.

1900 Bergman, Beth. "*Les Contes d'Hoffman.*" *OpN.* 1983 Jan. 29; 47(10): 24-26. Illus.: Photo. B&W. 7. [Metropolitan Opera broadcast of February 5, 1983.]
USA. 1983. Histories-sources. ■Photographs of Metropolitan Opera production of *Les Contes d'Hoffman* by Jacques Offenbach. List of principals, conductor, designer, production staff, discography and synopsis included.

1901 Bergman, Beth. "*Pelléas et Mélisande.*" *OpN.* 1983 Jan. 15; 47(9): 28-30. Illus.: Photo. B&W. 5.
USA. 1983. Histories-sources. ■Photographs of Metropolitan Opera performance of *Pelléas et Mélisande* by Claude Debussy. List of principals, conductor, designer, production staff, discography and synopsis included.

1902 Bergman, Beth. "*Il Barbiere di Siviglia.*" *OpN.* 1983 Apr.9; 47(15): 26-28. Illus.: Photo. B&W. 10. [Metropolitan Opera broadcast of April 9, 1983.]
USA. 1983. Histories-sources. ■Photographs of Metropolitan Opera production of *Il Barbiere di Siviglia* by Gioacchino Rossini. List of principals, conductor, design and production staff, synopsis and discography included.

1903 Bergman, Beth. "*Die Walküre.*" *OpN.* 1983 Mar. 26; 47(14): 24-26. Illus.: Photo. B&W. 9. [Metropolitan Opera broadcast of April 2, 1983.]
USA. 1983. Histories-sources. ■Photographs of Metropolitan Opera production of *Die Walküre* by Richard Wagner. List of principals, conductor, design/production staff, discography and synopsis included.

1904 Bergman, Beth. "*Don Carlo.*" *OpN.* 1983 Mar. 26; 47(14): 20-21. Illus.: Photo. B&W. 7. [Metropolitan Opera broadcast of March 26, 1983.]
USA. 1983. Histories-sources. ■Photographs of Metropolitan Opera production of *Don Carlo* by Giuseppe Verdi. List of principals, conductor, design, production staff, discography and synopsis included.

1905 Bergman, Beth. "*La Bohème.*" *OpN.* 1983 Mar. 12; 47(13): 20-22. Illus.: Photo. B&W. 6. [Metropolitan Opera broadcast, March 12, 1983.]
USA. 1983. Histories-sources. ■Photographs of Metropolitan Opera production of *La Bohème* by Giacomo Puccini. List of principals, conductor, designer, production staff, discography and synopsis included.

1906 Bergman, Beth. "*Der Rosenkavalier.*" *OpN.* 1983 Mar. 12; 47(13): 26-28. Illus.: Photo. B&W. 9. [Metropolitan Opera broadcast, March 19, 1983.]

MUSIC-DRAMA: Opera—Performance/production

USA. 1983. Histories-sources. ■Photographs of the Metropolitan Opera production of *Der Rosenkavalier* by Richard Strauss. List of principals, conductor, designer, production staff, discography and synopsis included.

1907 Bergman, Beth. "*Les Dialogues des Carmélites.*" *OpN.* 1983 Dec. 10; 48(6): 46-48. Illus.: Photo. B&W. 7. [Metropolitan Opera broadcast of December 10, 1983.]

USA. 1983. Histories-sources. ■Photographs of the Metropolitan Opera production of *Les Dialogues des Carmélites* by Francis Poulenc. List of principals, conductor, production staff, discography and synopsis included.

1908 Bergman, Beth. "*Ernani.*" *OpN.* 1983 Dec. 10; 48(6): 50-53. Illus.: Photo. Color. Architec. 4. [Metropolitan Opera broadcast of December 17, 1983.]

USA. 1983. Histories-sources. ■Photographs of the Metropolitan Opera Broadcast performance, December 17, 1983 of *Ernani* by Giuseppe Verdi. List of principals, conductor, design/ production staff, discography and synopsis included.

1909 Bergman, Beth. "*Tristan und Isolde.*" *OpN.* 1983 Dec. 24; 48(7): 22-24. Illus.: Photo. B&W. 7. [Metropolitan Opera broadcast of December 24, 1983.]

USA. 1983. Histories-sources. ■Photographs of the Metropolitan Opera production of *Tristan und Isolde* by Richard Wagner. List of principals, conductor, design and production staff, discography and synopsis included.

1910 Bergman, Beth. "*Hänsel und Gretel.*" *OpN.* 1983 Dec. 24; 48(7): 26-29. Illus.: Photo. B&W. 5. [Metropolitan Opera broadcast of December 21, 1983.]

USA. 1983. Histories-sources. ■Photographs of the Metropolitan Opera production of *Hänsel und Gretel* by Engelbert Humperdinck. List of principals, conductor, design and production staff, discography and synopsis included.

1911 Chatfield-Taylor, Joan; Nowinski, Ira, photo,. *Backstage at the Opera.* San Francisco: Chronicle Books; 1983. 132 pp. Illus.: Photo. B&W. 129.

USA. 1970-1982. Histories-sources. ■Backstage look at San Francisco Opera with candid photos of various aspects in mounting opera production, including choir rehearsals, ballet, make-up, etc.

1912 Collier, Aldore. "Leona Mitchell, an All-American Opera Star." *Ebony.* 1983 Sep.; 38(11): 37-38, 40, 42. Illus.: Photo. B&W. Color. 9.

USA. 1983. Biographical studies. ■Soprano Leona Mitchell's career at the Metropolitan Opera and roles in *Madama Butterfly, Carmen, La Forza del Destino* and the film *Yes, Giorgio.* Related to Media: Film.

1913 Crutchfield, Will. "Grooves of Academe." *OpN.* 1983 Aug.; 48(2): 26-29. Illus.: Photo. B&W. 1.

USA. 1983. Histories-sources. ■Descriptive account of Laurence Witten's collection of historic sound recordings at Yale University.

1914 Cunningham, Dennis; Rich, Frank; Watt, Douglas; Barnes, Clive; Kissel, Howard; Wilson, Edwin; Beaufort, John; Rich, Alan; Porterfield, Christopher; Siegel, Joel. "*La Tragédie de Carmen.*" *NYTCR.* 1983 Nov. 7; 44(15): 124-131.

USA. 1983. Reviews of performances. ■Ten critics review Jean-Claude Carrière and Marius Constant's adaptation of the Georges Bizet opera *La Tragédie de Carmen,* directed by Peter Brook at the Vivian Beaumont Theatre.

1915 Eaton, Quaintance. "Prima Donna Americana." *OpN.* 1983 Oct.; 48(4): 32, 34-35. Illus.: Photo. B&W. 1.

USA. 1848-1925. Biographical studies. ■Life and career of soprano Alwina Valleria, the Metropolitan Opera's first American-born diva.

1916 Freeman, John W. "Flight of the Eagle: *From the House of the Dead.*" *OpN.* 1983 Mar. 26; 47(14): 34-35. Illus.: Photo. B&W. 1.

USA. Czechoslovakia. 1930-1983. Histories-sources. ■Background of the U.S. premiere of *From the House of the Dead,* by Leos Janáček.

1917 Gordon, Eric. "The Met's First Hänsel." *OpN.* 1983 Dec. 24; 48(7): 30-31.

USA. Germany. 1905-1963. Biographical studies. ■Life and career of Lina Abarbanell, the first Hänsel at the Metropolitan Opera House.

1918 Hamilton, Donald. "For the Record." *OpN.* 1983 Oct.; 48(4): 45-46, 48. Illus.: Photo. B&W. 2.

USA. 1902-1983. Historical studies. ■Relationship between the phonograph and the Metropolitan Opera: recordings of its productions and artists.

1919 Jacobson, Robert. "The Gift to Be Simple." *OpN.* 1983 June; 47(17): 8-12, 59-60. Illus.: Photo. B&W. Color. 4.

USA. 1925-1983. Histories-sources. ■American baritone Thomas Stewart speaks of his career and art.

1920 Kozlowski, Marc. "*Idomeneo.*" *OpN.* 1983 Jan. 15; 47(9): 15-22. Illus.: Design. Photo. B&W. Color. 13. [Metropolitan Opera broadcast of January 15, 1983.]

USA. 1983. Histories-sources. ■Photographs of Metropolitan Opera production of *Idomeneo* by Wolfgang Amadeus Mozart. Produced by Jean-Pierre Ponelle. List of principals, conductor, designer, production staff, discography and synopsis included.

1921 Lanier, Thomas P. "Practical Lady." *OpN.* 1983 Dec. 24; 48(7): 18-19, 46. Illus.: Photo. B&W. 2.

USA. 1944-1983. Histories-sources. ■American mezzo-soprano Blanche Thebom reminisces about her career and art.

1922 Lipton, Gary D. "Like Father Like Son." *OpN.* 1983 Mar. 26; 47(14): 28-29, 44, 46. Illus.: Photo. B&W. 1.

USA. Canada. 1960-1983. Biographical studies. ■Life and art of the Canadian father-son baritones Louis and Gino Quilico.

1923 Porter, Andrew. "Alfano Resurrected." *OpN.* 1983 June; 47(17): 24, 26-28. Illus.: Photo. B&W. 2.

USA. 1904-1983. Historical studies. ■*Risurrezione* of Franco Alfano to be performed by the Cincinnati Summer Opera, director James de Blasis. An account of earlier performances.

1924 Rasponi, Lanfranco. "Czar Boris." *OpN.* 1983 Jan. 29; 47(10): 11-13. Illus.: Photo. B&W. 4.

USA. 1947-1983. Histories-sources. ■Boris Christoff, bass, speaks of his career and art.

1925 Rothmann, Robert. "Backstage Boss." *OpN.* 1983 Oct.; 48(4): 50-52. Illus.: Photo. B&W. 1.

USA. 1949-1982. Historical studies. ■Career of Stanley Levine, stage manager of the Metropolitan Opera. ■

1926 Tassel, Janet. "A Real Thoroughbred." *OpN.* 1983 Apr. 9; 47(15): 16, 20, 40. Illus.: Photo. B&W. Color. 3.

USA. 1945-1983. Histories-sources. ■American lyric mezzo soprano Frederica von Stade interviewed about her career and art.

1927 Van Buchau, Stephanie. "Keeping the Faith." *OpN.* 1983 Mar. 26; 47(14): 17-19. Illus.: Photo. B&W. Color. 3.

USA. Europe. 1939-1983. Histories-sources. ■Simon Estes, American baritone, speaks of his life and career as a Black artist.

1928 Waleson, Heidi. "Beard on Opera." *OpN.* 1983 July; 48(1): 26-28, 43. Illus.: Photo. Color. 1.

USA. 1983. Histories-sources. ■James Beard, American cooking expert, recalls opera performances he has seen.

1929 Cannon, Robert. "Stanislavski and the Opera — In Production." *Opera.* 1983; 34(7): 714-720.

USSR. 1918-1935. Historical studies. ■Stanislavskij's training of opera singers, with special reference to *Boris Gudunov* and *La Bohème.*

1930 Čepalov, A. "Forreger v muzykalnom teatre." (Forreger at the Musical Theatre.) 254-269 in *Theatrical Dilemmas — 82.* All-Union Scientific Research Institute of Art Education under the USSR Ministry of Culture. Moscow: All-Russian Theatrical Society; 1983. 383 pp.

USSR. 1929-1939. Histories-specific. ■Work of director/choreographer N.M. Forreger in the musical theatre.

1931 Robinson, Harlow. "Letter from Moscow." *OpN.* 1983 Jan. 29; 47(10): 14-15, 46. Illus.: Photo. B&W. 1: 3 in. x 5 in.

USSR. 1982-1983. Critical studies. ■State of opera in Moscow.

Plays/librettos/scripts

1932 Davis, Peter G. "At the Top of the Steps." *OpN.* 1983 Feb. 26; 47(12): 28-30. Illus.: Photo. B&W. 1.

MUSIC-DRAMA: Opera—Plays/librettos/scripts

Austria. 1927-1929. Critical studies. ∎In *Arabella*, Richard Strauss develops psychologically and emotionally viable characters through his musical vocabulary.

1933   Phillips, Steven. "Coming of Age." *OpN.* 1983 Jan. 15; 47(9): 12-14. Illus.: Photo. B&W. 1.

Austria. 1780-1781. Critical studies. ∎Evaluation of *Idomeneo*, the first mature opera masterpiece of Wolfgang Amadeus Mozart.

1934   Simon, John. "The Right One." *OpN.* 1983 Feb. 26; 47(12): 16-19, 30. Illus.: Photo. B&W. 1.

Austria. 1920-1929. Historical studies. ∎Work of librettist Hugo von Hofmannsthal on *Arabella* by Richard Strauss is the culmination of their long collaboration.

1935   Kolodin, Irving. "Wagner and Weber — Legend and Lore." 75-92 in Osterfestspiel-Gesellschaft. *Osterfestspiele Salzburg: Grosses Festspielhaus (Salzburg Easter Festival: Grosses Festspielhaus).* Salzburg: Osterfestspiel-Gesellschaft; 1983. 132 pp. Illus.: Photo. B&W. [Text in English, French and German.]

Europe. 1822-1844. Biographical studies. ∎Carl Maria von Weber's influence on Wagner, particularly his *Der Freischütz* and *Euryanthe.*

1936   Pestalozza, Luigi. "La musica, la guerra e la lotta di classe." (Music, War and Class Struggle.) *QT.* 1983 Feb.; 5(19): 11-22. Notes.

Europe. 1597-1983. Critical studies. ∎Theme of war in European opera.

1937   Berges, Ruth. "Bizet — and His Gounod Connection." *OC.* 1983 Winter; 24(4): 20-23.

France. 1856-1875. Historical studies. ∎Personal and professional relationship of Georges Bizet and Charles Gounod.

1938   Gerbod, Paul. "L'histoire sur la scène lyrique parisienne dans la deuxième moitié du XIXe siècle." (History on the Lyric Stage in Paris in the Second Half of the Nineteenth Century.) *RHT.* 1983; 35(4): 413-429. Notes.

France. 1850-1900. Critical studies. ∎Subjects from history found in a significant portion of the lyric repertory.

1939   Join-Diéterle, Catherine. "La monarchie, source d'inspiration de l'Opéra à l'époque romantique." (Monarchy: A Source of Inspiration for Opera During the Romantic Period.) *RHT.* 1983; 35(4): 430-441. Notes.

France. 1814-1850. Historical studies. ∎Treatment of monarchy in operas during the Romantic period in France and its effect on scenery. Grp/movt: Romanticism.

1940   Marek, George. "Behold the Lion!" *OpN.* 1983 Dec. 10; 48(6): 22, 24, 26, 83. Illus.: Photo. B&W. 2.

France. 1830. Historical studies. ∎Victor Hugo and the original plot for the opera *Ernani* by Giuseppe Verdi. Related to Drama.

1941   Morey, Carl; Maheu, Renée. "Rameau, and the French Lyric Theatre." *OC.* 1983 Autumn; 24(3): 14-17, 40-41. [In English and French.]

France. 1683-1764. Historical studies. ∎Life of Jean-Philippe Rameau and his contribution to the development of lyric theatre.

1942   Münch, Stefan. "Co to jest Grand Opera." (What Is Grand Opera?)*PaT.* 1983; 32(2): 167-186. Notes. Illus.: Pntg. Dwg. B&W. 11.

France. 1828-1865. Historical studies. ∎Analysis of the phenomenon of Grand Opera in France taking into consideration music and librettos as well as mise en scène.

1943   Simon, John. "Poulenc's Inner Dialogue." *OpN.* 1983 Dec. 10; 48(6): 32-34, 83. Illus.: Photo. B&W. 1.

France. 1931-1983. Critical studies. ∎Composer Francis Poulenc, author Georges Bernanos and composition of the opera *Les Dialogues des Carmélites.*

1944   Tubeuf, André. "The Adventures of a Dutchman in Paris." 93-106 in Osterfestspiel-Gesellschaft. *Osterfestspiele Salzburg: Grosses Festspielhaus (Salzburg Easter Festival: Grosses Festspielhaus).* Salzburg: Osterfestspiel-Gesellschaft; 1983. 132 pp. [Text in English, French and German.]

France. 1830-1897. Biographical studies. ∎Richard Wagner's life in Paris, where his work was rejected.

1945   "Brünnhilde's Choice." *OpN.* 1983 Mar. 26; 47(14): 8-11. Print. Color. 2.

Germany. 1840-1860. Critical studies. ∎'What is human?' is central to *Der Ring des Nibelungen* of Richard Wagner.

1946   Janés, Alfonsina. "Wagner, avui." (Wagner, Today.) *SdO.* 1983 Feb.; 281: 23-24. Illus.: Photo. Print. B&W. 4: 6 cm. x 8 cm. [Included in a dossier entitled *Wagner's Presence (1883-1983).*]

Germany. 1845-1951. Critical studies. ∎Pertinence of the human characterizations in Wagner's operas: *Tannhäuser, Die Meistersinger von Nürnberg, Der Ring des Nibelungen* and *Parsifal.*

1947   Kestner, Joseph. "Romantic Rebel." *OpN.* 1983 Jan. 1; 47(8): 16-19. Illus.: Pntg. B&W. 2.

Germany. 1842-1845. Historical studies. ∎Account of the sources and quasi-autobiographical material Richard Wagner adapted for his opera *Tannhäuser.*

1948   Marek, George. "Danse Macabre." *OpN.* 1983 Jan. 29; 47(10): 30-32. Illus.: Pntg. Photo. B&W. 1: 11 in. x 8 in.

Germany. 1776-1822. Historical studies. ∎Identity and personality of the real E.T.A. Hoffman.

1949   Marek, George. "Wagner Today." *OpN.* 1983 Jan. 1; 47(8): 29-31. Illus.: Photo. B&W. 1.

Germany. 1833-1983. Critical studies. ∎Evaluation of the place of Richard Wagner in opera today.

1950   Sandow, Gregory. "Uninterrupted Flow." *OpN.* 1983 Mar. 26; 47(14): 12, 14.

Germany. 1852. Critical studies. ∎Discussion of the seamless transitions in Act III of *Die Walküre* by Richard Wagner.

1951   Singer, Irving. "Night's Wonder World." *OpN.* 1983 Dec. 24; 48(7): 10-12, 14-17. Illus.: Dwg. 3.

Germany. 1854-1983. Critical studies. ∎In *Tristan und Isolde*, Wagner explores the world of darkness outside reality.

1952   Steinberg, Michael. "Portrait of the Artist." *OpN.* 1983 Apr.9; 47(15): 22-24, 40. Illus.: Photo. B&W. 1.

Germany. 1870-1900. Critical studies. ∎Discussion of character development of Wotan in *Parsifal* by Richard Wagner.

1953   Marker, Frederick J.; Marker, Lise-Lone. "Words to Music: *Peer Gynt* and *Lear* at the Munich Opera Festival." *ThM.* 1983 Spring; 14(2): 55-62. Illus.: Photo. Print. B&W. 7.

Germany, West. 1982. Critical studies. ∎Werner Egk's *Peer Gynt* and Aribert Reimann's *Lear* shed new light on the inner essence of Ibsen and of Shakespeare without diminishing the theatrical effect of the plays. Related to Drama.

1954   Wanderer, Emmerich. *Im Zeichen des Ringes: Richard Wagner's Tetralogie — Vision und Prophetie.* (In the Sign of the Ring: Richard Wagner's Tetralogy — Vision and Prophecy.) Vienna: Österreichische Verlagsanstalt; 1983. 205 pp. Pref.

Germany, West. 1853-1874. Critical studies. ∎Analysis and interpretation of Richard Wagner's librettos for the Ring Tetralogy.

1955   Ashbrook, William. "Verismo." *OC.* 1983 Mar.; 24(1): 14-17, 45. [In English.]

Italy. 1879-1926. Critical studies. ∎Naturalism in the works of Pietro Mascagni and Giacomo Puccini. Grp/movt: Verismo.

1956   Conrad, Peter. "Sea and Sky." *OpN.* 1983 Feb. 12; 47(11): 17-18. Illus.: Photo. Color. 1.

Italy. 1862-1900. Critical studies. ∎Shakespeare's influence on Arrigo Boito's libretto for the opera *La Gioconda* by Amilcare Ponchielli. Grp/movt: Romanticism.

1957   Gronda, Giovanna. "Una scena, una 'pièce': ambiguità comica nel *Don Giovanni* dapontiano." (A Scene, a 'Pièce': Comic Ambiguity in Da Ponte's *Don Giovanni.*) 117-134 in Ferroni, Giulio, ed. *Ambiguità del comico* (Ambiguity of the Comic). Palermo: Sellerio; 1983. 173 pp. (Prisma 47.) Notes.

Italy. 1787. Critical studies. ∎Leporello is seen as an alter ego of the protagonist in Da Ponte's libretto for Mozart's *Don Giovanni.*

1958   Jacobson, Robert. "Personaggio." *OpN.* 1983 Dec. 10; 48(6): 16-17, 67. Illus.: Photo. Color. 1. [In English]

MUSIC-DRAMA: Opera—Plays/librettos/scripts

Italy. 1983. Histories-sources. ■Italian tenor Luciano Pavarotti discusses the title role of *Ernani* by Giuseppe Verdi.

1959 Parsons, James. "Made to Measure." *OpN.* 1983 Dec. 10; 48(6): 19-20. Illus.: Photo. B&W. 1.

Italy. Russia. 1844. Historical studies. ■Account of the way Giuseppe Verdi wrote the title role of *Ernani* for Russian tenor Nicolai Ivanoff.

1960 Salla Di Felice, Elena. *Metastasio: Ideologia, drammaturgia, spettacolo.* (Metastasio: Ideology, Dramaturgy, Performance.) Milan: Franco Angeli; 1983. 238 pp. (Il Settecento 1.) Notes. Append. Index.

Italy. 1698-1782. Critical studies. ■Precise scenery and gesture notations in Metastasio's libretti suggest the important role librettists played in opera.

1961 Ujetti, Ugo; Weaver, William, trans. "Glimpses of Puccini." *OpN.* 1983 July; 48(1): 18-20. Illus.: Photo. B&W. Color. 2.

Italy. 1913. Histories-sources. ■Interview with Giacomo Puccini.

1962 Lerín, Miquel; Millet, Lluis; Maragall, Joan; Pedrell, Felip; Pena, Joaquim; Domènec, Espanyol Miguel; Gual, Adriá; Viura, Xavier; Pujols, Francesc; Llongueras, Joan; Vives, Amadeu; Sagarra, J.M. de; Alavedra, Joan; Pahissa, Jaume; Pla, Josep; Cirici, Alexandre; Tharrats, Joan-Josep. *Wagner i Catalunya: Antologia de textos i Gràfics sobre la influència wagneriana a la nostra cultura.* (Wagner and Catalonia: Anthology of Texts and Graphics about Wagner's Influence on Our Culture.) Barcelona: Edicions del Cotal; 1983. 288 pp. (L'autor i l'obra 10.) Biblio. Index. Illus.: Design. Pntg. Photo. Print. B&W. 64: 10 cm. x 16 cm. [In Catalan and Spanish.]

Spain. 1868-1983. Historical studies. ■Anthology of essays on Wagner's influence on Catalonian culture, including graphic materials.

1963 Shyer, Laurence. "Robert Wilson: Current Projects." *ThM.* 1983 Summer-Fall; 14(3): 83-98. Notes. Illus.: Sketches. Photo. Print. B&W. 39.

USA. 1983. Histories-sources. ■In an interview, Robert Wilson discusses *Great Day in the Morning*, an evening of Black spirituals staged in Paris, and reveals plans for staging a Civil War opera, a play based on fables (*The Golden Windows*) and an adaptation of *Medea*.

Reference materials

1964 Osterfestspiel-Gesellschaft, ed. *Osterfestspiele Salzburg: Grosses Festspielhaus.* (Easter Festival Salzburg: Grosses Festspielhaus.) Salzburg: Osterfestspiel-Gesellschaft; 1983. 132 pp. Illus.: Photo. Dwg. Color. B&W. [Offizielles Programm der Osterfestspiele Salzburg 1983, in French, English and German.]

Austria. France. 1983. ■Program of the Easter Festival Salzburg 1983 including essays on Richard Wagner and Johannes Brahms.

1965 Lanza Tomasi, Gioacchino, ed. *Guida all'opera da Monteverdi a Henze.* (Guide to Opera from Monteverdi to Henze.) Milan: Mondadori; 1983. 839 pp. (Studio 110.)

Europe. 1567-1983. ■Short essays, in alphabetical order, on the most important composers and their best known operas. Discography included.

1966 Zelinsky, Hartmut. *Richard Wagner — ein deutsches Thema: Eine Dokumentation zur Wirkungsgeschichte Richard Wagners 1876-1976.* (Richard Wagner — A German Theme: Documentation on the History of Richard Wagner's Influence, 1876-1976.) Vienna and Berlin: Medusa; 1983. 292 pp. Pref. Index. Notes. Illus.: Photo. Dwg. Poster. B&W.

Germany. Austria. USA. 1869-1976. ■Wagner's influence on theatre and art: collection of source materials. Grp/movt: Fascism.

1967 Civico Museo Teatrale Carlo Schmidl; Associazione Culturale 'L'Officina'. *Toti Dal Monte — Enzo De Muro Lomanto — Due voci nel mondo: documenti, immagini, suoni.* (Toti Dal Monte — Enzo De Muro Lomanto — Two Voices in the World: Documents, Images, Sounds.) Trieste: Direzione Civico Museo Teatrale Carlo Schmidl; 1983. 32 pp. Tables. Illus.: Photo. B&W.

Italy. 1893-1975. Histories-sources. ■Catalogue of the exhibition held in Trieste, October 1983.

1968 Ministero per i Beni Culturali e Ambientali — Centro socioculturale. *'Sogni e favole io fingo': Teatro pubblico e melodramma a Roma all'epoca di Metastasio.* ('Visualized Dreams and Tales': Public Theatre and Opera in Metastasio's Rome.) Rome: Tipografia Editrice Romana; 1983. 124 pp. Notes. Biblio. Tables. Illus.: Photo. B&W.

Italy. 1698-1782. Histories-sources. ■Catalogue of the exhibition (Rome: December, 1983-February, 1984) on scenery, architecture, dance, opera and public theatres. Related to Theatre in General: Multiple application.

1969 Angrisani, Simonetta, ed. *I Galliari, primi scenografi della Scala.* (The Galliari, First Scenographers of the Teatro alla Scala.) Milan: Alinari; 1983. n.p. Pref. Biblio. Tables. Illus.: Photo. B&W. Color.

Italy. 1778-1823. ■Catalogue of Galliari's scene designs owned by Museo Teatrale alla Scala.

1970 Conati, Marcello. *La bottega della musica: Verdi e la Fenice.* (The Music Shop: Verdi and La Fenice.) Milan: Il Saggiatore; 1983. 452 pp. (Opere e libri.) Pref. Notes. Index. Tables. Illus.: Photo. B&W. Color.

Italy. 1844-1852. Histories-sources. ■Letters and documents placed in archives concerning Verdi's operas *Ernani*, *Attila*, *Rigoletto*, *La Traviata*, *Simon Boccanegra* performed at Teatro La Fenice.

1971 Tuggle, Robert. "Encore!" *Con.* 1983 Oct.; 213(860): 114-119. Illus.: Photo. B&W. 6.

USA. 1910-1932. Histories-sources. ■Annotated selection of photographs by Herman Mishkin of Enrico Caruso, Claudia Muzio, Feodor Chaliapin, Rosa Ponselle and Olive Fremstad at the Metropolitan Opera House.

Research/historiography

1972 De Angelis, Marcello, ed. *Le cifre del melodramma.* (Figures of Opera.) Florence: Giunta Regionale Toscana, La nuova Italia; 1982. v. 1: xxvi, 342 pp./v. 2: 384 pp. (Inventari e cataloghi toscani 10-11.) Pref. Notes. Index. Tables. Append. Illus.: Photo. B&W. Color. [Manager Alessandro Lanari's unpublished archives in Biblioteca Nazionale Centrale in Florence 1815-1870.]

Italy. 1815-1870. Bibliographical studies. ■Classification system used by Alessandro Lanari at the Biblioteca Nazionale Centrale.

Training

1973 Seabury, Deborah. "Old Master." *OpN.* 1983 June; 47(17): 30.

Italy. 1920-1983. Biographical studies. ■Biographical sketch of Italian voice coach Luigi Ricci.

Operetta

Institutions

1974 Zamponi, Linda. "Noch einmal ins Maxim." (Once Again at Maxim.) *Buhne.* 1983 Oct.: 12-13.

Austria. 1893-1983. Historical studies. ■Brief history of Raimundtheater.

Plays/librettos/scripts

1975 Gómez Labac, José María. *El Madrid de la Zarzuela.* (Madrid of the *Zarzuela*.) Madrid: Juan Piñero García; 1983. 529 pp. Index. Biblio. Illus.: Photo.

Spain. 1850-1935. Historical studies. ■Manners and customs of old Madrid in the Spanish light opera *Zarzuela*.

Reference materials

1976 Traubner, Richard. *Operetta: A Theatrical History.* Garden City: Doubleday; 1983. xvii, 461 pp. Biblio. Illus.: Photo.

Europe. USA. 1600-1983. ■Guide to operetta terms and personalities, organized chronologically by composer.

Other entries with significant content related to Music-Drama: 22, 27, 93, 219, 232, 280, 378, 398, 400, 904, 914, 983, 1012, 1399, 1438, 1495, 1618, 1632, 1708, 1723, 1982, 1993, 2079.

POPULAR ENTERTAINMENT

General

Design/technology

1977 Mitzner, Piotr. "Fajerwerki." (Fireworks.) *PaT*. 1983; 32(1): 59-79. Append. Illus.: Dwg. B&W. 9. [In appendix: fragments of text about fireworks by Michał Kado, Ernst Theodor, Amadeus Hoffmann, Adam Naruszewicz, Cyprian Norwid.]

Poland. 1500-1983. Historical studies. ▪Fireworks used during performances and different public festivities.

Institutions

1978 Böhm, Gotthard. "Das Lachen eines Sommerabends." (The Laughter of a Summer Evening.) *Buhne*. 1983 July-Aug.: 28-31. Illus.: Photo.

Austria. 1938-1983. Historical studies. ▪Report on Tschauner-Theatre, Vienna's only surviving improvisation company. Related to Drama: Comedy.

1979 Spaziani, Marcello. *Gli Italiani alla Foire: Quattro studi con due appendici.* (The Italians at the Foire: Four Essays with Two Appendixes.) Rome: Edizioni di Storia e Letteratura; 1982. xii, 221 pp se Quaderni di cultura francese 20. Pref. Notes. Append. Index.

France. 1679-1721. Historical studies. ▪Théâtre de la Foire and its initial repertory, partially derived from the Théâtre Italien. Appendix includes a calendar of performances from 1700 to 1721 and text of *Powers of Love and Magic (Les forces de l'Amour et de la Magie).*

1980 Marzán, Julio. "Dramatic Revolutions: The Latin American Popular Theatre Festival." *VV*. 1982 Oct. 12; 27(41): 89, 101. Illus.: Photo.

USA. 1982. Critical studies. ▪Description of third Latin American Popular Theatre Festival at New York Shakespeare Festival as a cultural and political event.

Performance spaces

1981 LaLanne, Bruce. "Hippodrome Memories." *M*. 1983 Third Quarter; 15(3): 14-15. Illus.: Photo. B&W. 1.

USA. 1911-1940. Historical studies. ▪Childhood recollections of the Adolphus vaudeville theatre and a brief history of its existence.

1982 Morrison, A. Craig; Wheeler, Lucy Pope; Myers, Denys Peter. "Keith Memorial Theatre — Boston, Massachusetts." *M*. 1983 Second Quarter; 15(2): 1-32. Biblio. Illus.: Photo. Plan. B&W. Grd.Plan. 19.

USA. 1925-1980. Historical studies. ▪Description of the Keith Memorial Theatre, built by Edward Franklin Albee and designed by Thomas W. Lamb. The theatre now houses the Opera Company of Boston. Related to Music-Drama: Opera.

1983 Robinson, Jack. "Fourteenth Street: Cradle of American Vaudeville." *M*. 1983 First Quarter; 15(1): 19-20.

USA. 1881-1940. Historical studies. ▪Survey of the vaudeville houses in the Fourteenth Street area.

Performance/production

1984 O'Neill, Patrick B. "The Canadian Concert Party in France." *THC*. 1983 Fall; 4(2): 192-208. Notes. Illus.: Photo. Neg. B&W. 8.

Canada. UK. France. 1914-1918. Historical studies. ▪Description of various actors and companies providing diversion to Canadian troops in WW I, traces growth and history of concert parties.

1985 Cerny, Frantisek; Kolarova, Eva. *Sto let Narodniho divadla.* (One Hundred Years of Popular Theatre.) Prague: Albatros; 1983. 199 pp. Illus.: Photo. B&W. Color. 48.

Czechoslovakia. 1883-1983. Histories-specific.

1986 Salmen, Walter. *Der Spielmann im Mittelalter.* (The Minstrel in the Middle Ages.) Innsbruck: Edition Helbling; 1983. 238 pp. (Innsbrucker Beiträge zur Musikwissenschaft 8.) Pref. Notes. Biblio. Illus.: Photo. Diagram.

Europe. 1100-1500. Historical studies. ▪Social status and role of minstrels, with emphasis on musical aspects.

1987 Gerould, Daniel, ed. *Gallant and Libertine.* New York: Performing Arts Journal Publications; 1983. 151 pp.

France. 1700-1799. Historical studies. ▪Historical overview and English translation of ten divertissement-parades.

1988 Vila, Pep; Bruguet, Montserrat. *Festes Públiques i Teatre a Girona: Segles XIV-XVIII (Notícies i documents).* (Public Festivities and Theatre at Girona: from XIVth to XVIIIth Centuries (Notices and Documents).) Girona: Ajuntament de Girona; 1983. 232 pp. Pref. Append. Notes. Biblio. Illus.: Design. Dwg. Pntg. Photo. Print. B&W. 5: 10 cm. x 15 cm.

Spain. 1300-1799. Historical studies. ▪Description of the popular (religious and civil) festivities with six documented appendixes of specific entertainment.

1989 Hyde, Phil. "Horse and Bamboo." *PM*. 1983 Dec.-Jan.; 20-21: 9-12. Illus.: Photo. Print. B&W. 5.

UK-England. 1983. Histories-sources. ▪Horse and Bamboo, a collaborative company of performers, musicians and artists with a policy of touring by horse and cart.

1990 Ashby, Clifford; May, Suzanne DePauw. *Trouping through Texas: Harley Sadler and His Tent Show.* Bowling Green, OH: Bowling Green Univ. Popular P; 1982. 188 pp. . Illus.: Photo.

USA. 1912-1950. Historical studies. ▪History of a small tent show and its surprising success in a rural, Christian fundamentalist area.

1991 Dixon-Stowell, Brenda. "Dancing in the Dark: The Life and Times of Margot Webb in Afroamerican Vaudeville of the Swing Era." *BALF*. 1983; 17(1): 3-7. Illus.: Photo. Print. B&W. 1: 3 in. x 5 in.

USA. 1933-1947. Biographical studies. ▪Survey of the career of Margot Webb and the ballroom dance team of Norton and Webb. Related to Dance: Ballroom dance.

1992 Hanners, John. "'It Was Play or Starve': John Banvard's Account of Early Showboats." *ThR*. 1983 Spring; 8(1): 53-64. Notes. Illus.: Dwg. 2: 4 in. x 6 in.

USA. 1833-1836. Historical studies. ▪Excerpts from the unpublished autobiography of adventurer, painter, poet and theatre manager reveal harsh conditions endured by players on showboats on the Western frontier.

1993 Johnson, Herschel. "Cab Calloway: After 50 Years in Show Business the Hi-De-Ho Man Is Still Going Strong." *Ebony*. 1983 Feb.; 37(4): 66-67, 70. Illus.: Photo. Print. B&W. Color. 9.

USA. 1930-1983. Biographical studies. ▪Brief discussion of Cab Calloway's fifty years in show business and his ability to remain active despite advancing years. Related to Music-Drama: Musical theatre.

1994 Lindfors, Bernth. "Circus Africans." *JAC*. 1983 Summer; 6(2): 9-14. Notes.

USA. UK. 1800-1899. Critical studies. ▪Attitude of Western audiences to the performances of native Africans in various settings.

1995 Toll, Robert C. *The Entertainment Machine: American Show Business in the Twentieth Century.* New York: Oxford UP; 1982. ix, 284 pp.

USA. 1900-1982. Histories-specific. ▪Interaction of technology and popular entertainment. Related to Media.

1996 Turner, Mason. *Rx, Applause: Biography of a Blind Performer.* Brookline Village, MA: Branden P; 1983. 151 pp. Illus.: Photo.

USA. 1914-1983. Biographies. ▪Biography of blind entertainer Sylvester Meinert.

Reference materials

1997 Greco, Franco Carmelo, ed. *La tradizione del comico a Napoli dal XVIII secolo ad oggi.* (Tradition of Comedians in Naples from 18th Century to the Present.) Naples: Guida; 1982. 92 pp. (La scrittura e il gesto — Itinerari del teatro napoletano dal '500 ad oggi 4.) Tables. Illus.: Photo. B&W.

Italy. 1799-1982. Histories-sources. ▪Catalogue of exhibition (September-October, 1982): comedians provide a true historical bond to all forms of Neapolitan theatre.

CLASSED ENTRIES

POPULAR ENTERTAINMENT: General—Reference materials

1998 Wilmeth, Don B. *Variety Entertainment and Outdoor Amusements: A Reference Guide.* London and Westport, CT: Greenwood P; 1982. xii, 242 pp.
USA. 1840. ■Historical essays, literature survey and bibliography of a variety of genres of popular entertainment.

Relation to other fields

1999 Ozouf, Mona; Cataldi Villari, Fausta, transl. *La festa rivoluzionaria 1789-1799.* (Revolutionary Festivity 1789-1799.) Bologna: Patron; 1982. 468 pp. (Collana di teatro e regia teatrale 4.) Pref. Notes. Index. Illus.: Photo. B&W. [Translated from French.]
France. 1789-1799. Histories-reconstruction. ■Italian translation of 'La fête revolutionnaire'.

Cabaret

Performance/production

2000 Böhm, Maxi; Markus, Georg, ed. *Bei uns in Reichenberg: Unvollendete Memoiren.* (With Us at Liberec: Unfinished Memoirs.) Vienna and Munich: Amalthea; 1983. 320 pp. Pref. Index. Append. Illus.: Photo. B&W.
Austria. 1916-1982. Biographies. ■Cabaret comedian's anecdotal reminiscences. Includes comic songs by Maxi Böhm, and a list of his roles on stage and in radio and television serials.

2001 Hill, Murray. "Karl Valentin in the Third Reich: No Laughing Matter." *GL&L.* 1983; 37(1): 41-56. Notes.
Germany. 1933-1945. Historical studies. ■Decline of Karl Valentin's popularity under the Nazi regime.

2002 Naumann, Uwe. "Satire im Aufwind: Das 'neue' deutsche Kabarett — am Beispiel Hamburg." (Satire Flourishes: Hamburg as an Example for the 'New' German Cabaret.) *Tzs.* 1983 Winter; 6: 121-125.
Germany, West. 1982. Historical studies. ■State of political cabaret.

2003 Nico, Franco, ed.; Cipriani, Pina, ed. *Il Sancarluccio: 10 anni di teatro.* (Sancarluccio: 10 Years of Theatre.) Naples: Società Editrice Napoletana; 1982. 119 pp. Tables. Illus.: Photo. B&W.
Italy. 1972-1982. Review of performances. ■Collection of reviews of performances at Teatro Sancarluccio in Naples, published by Neapolitan journals.

2004 Serra, Michele. *Giorgio Gaber — La canzone a teatro.* (Giorgio Gaber — The Song at the Theatre.) Milan: Saggiatore; 1982. 94 pp. (Politeama 2.) Tables. Illus.: Photo. B&W.
Italy. 1959-1981. Critical studies. ■Artistic career of the singer Giorgio Gaber: his recordings and performances, that combined songs and monologues.

Plays/librettos/scripts

2005 Melendres, Jaume. "Traduir explosius." (Translating Explosives.) 5-6 in Monterde, Pau, ed. *Teatre de Cabaret: Peces de Karl Valentin de l'espectacle Tafalitats.* Barcelona: Institut del Teatre; 1983. 90 pp. (Biblioteca Teatral 16.) [Prologue to Karl Valentin's *Anthology*.]
Germany. 1882-1948. Critical studies. ■Difficulty of translating Karl Valentin's scripts, with an emphasis on his originality and personality influence on Brecht.

Carnival

Performance/production

2006 Colangeli, Mario; Fraschetti, Anna. *Carnevale: i luoghi, le maschere, i riti e i protagonisti di una pazza, inquietante festa popolare.* (Carnival: Places, Masks, Rites and Protagonists of a Mad and Riotous Popular Festivity.) Rome: Lato Side Editori; 1982. 184 pp. (Cultura popolare 1.) Illus.: Photo. B&W.
Europe. North America. South America. 1900-1982. Historical studies. ■Review of the most interesting modern Carnival festivities.

2007 Mazouer, Charles. "Théâtre et Carnaval en France jusqu'à la fin du XVIe siècle." (Theatre and Carnival in France to the End of the Sixteenth Century.) *RHT.* 1983; 35(2): 147-161. Notes.
France. 1200-1599. Historical studies. ■Links between popular forms of medieval drama and theatrical presentations during the carnival period. Grp/movt: Medieval theatre. Related to Drama.

Relation to other fields

2008 Bernardi, Claudio. "Il corpo in festa: il carnevale." (Festive Body: Carnival.) 277-290 in Melchiorre, Virgilio; . Cascetta, Annamaria. *Il corpo in scena (The Body on Stage).* Milan: Vita e pensiero; 1983. 290 pp. Notes.
Europe. 1400-1983. Critical studies. ■Bodily rituals of carnival tradition. Related to Ritual-Ceremony: Civic.

Circus

Performance/production

2009 Amiard-Chevrel, Claudine, ed. *Du cirque au théâtre.* (From Circus to Theatre.) Paris: L'âge d'homme; 1983. 238 pp. (CNRS Collection Théâtre des années vingt 27.) Illus.: Photo. B&W.
France. 1920-1929. Historical studies. ■Development of theatre from circus acts.

2010 Bromley, Bob. "Hector and the Little Ballerina." *PuJ.* 1983 Sep.; 35(1): 15-17. Illus.: Dwg.
France. 1980. Historical studies. ■Story of a live horse and a marionette ballerina act at the Circus Medrano. Related to Puppetry.

2011 Hadjipantazis, Theodore. "A Footnote to the Memoirs of Leonora Whiteley." *TN.* 1983; 37(3): 131-137. Notes.
Greece. 1880-1899. Historical studies. ■Memoirs of circus acrobat Leonora Whiteley are supplemented and contradicted by the record established in various press accounts.

2012 Vinyes i Sabatés, Josep. *Charlie Rivel.* Barcelona: Edicions de Nou Art Thor; 1983. 32 pp. (Gent Nostra 25.) Biblio. Filmography. Tables. Illus.: Poster. Photo. Print. B&W. 62: 12 cm. x 18 cm.
Spain. 1896-1983. Biographical studies. ■Biography of the clown Charlie Rivel (Josep Andreu i Lasserre), his training and his international success.

2013 Jenkins, Ron. "Dan Rice." *ThM.* 1983 Spring; 14(2): 86-92. Biblio. Illus.: Dwg. Poster. Photo. 4. ['Great Satirists', Number Three in a Series.]
USA. 1823-1900. Biographical studies. ■Dan Rice, an American clown who transformed his circus tent into a forum for political and cultural debate.

2014 Lindfors, Bernth. "Circus Africans." *JAC.* 1983 Summer; 6(2): 9-14. Notes.
USA. 1810-1926. Historical studies. ■Importation of African Blacks for exhibition as 'exotics' and evolution of this practice into a circus sideshow. The most famous of such performers, Zip, was introduced by P.T. Barnum.

2015 Rich, Frank; Nelson, Don; Beaufort, John; Kissel, Howard; Barnes, Clive; Siegel, Joel; Cunningham, Dennis. "The Flying Karamozov Brothers." *NYTCR.* 1983 May 30; 44(9): 239-242.
USA. 1983. Reviews of performances. ■Seven critics review *The Flying Karamozov Brothers.* Presented at the Ritz Theatre.

Reference materials

2016 Saxon, A.H., ed. *Selected Letters of P.T. Barnum.* New York: Colombia UP; 1983. xxxv, 351 pp.
USA. 1832-1891. ■Letters of circus entrepreneur P.T. Barnum.

Commedia dell'arte

Basic theatrical documents

2017 Leabo, Karl B., ed. *The Tragical Comedy, or Comical Tragedy of Punch and Judy.* New York: Theatre Arts Books; 1983. 37 pp. Pref. Notes. Illus.: Dwg. B&W. 31.
UK-England. 1873-1983. ■Revised from the 1873 edition. Illustrations by Cruikshank.

POPULAR ENTERTAINMENT: *Commedia dell'arte*

Performance/production

2018 Gordon, Mel, ed. *Lazzi: The Comic Routines of the Commedia dell'Arte.* New York: Performing Arts Journal Publications; 1983. vi, 92 pp.
Italy. 1734. Histories-sources. ▪Translations of 207 *commedia* bits, including acrobatic, mimic, violence, food and illogical lazzi. Includes two complete scenarios: *Pulcinella, the False Prince* and *Pulcinella the Physician.*

2019 Taviani, Ferdinando; Schino, Mirella. *Il segreto della Commedia dell'Arte — La memoria delle compagnie italiane del XVI, XVII e XVIII secolo.* (The Secret of the Commedia dell'arte — Legacy of the Italian Companies of the 16th, 17th and 18th Centuries.) Florence: La Casa Usher; 1982. 529 pp. (Oggi, del teatro 4.) Notes. Biblio. Index. Illus.: Photo. B&W.
Italy. 1550-1750. Histories-specific. ▪History of *commedia dell'arte* and companies of comedians.

2020 Uribe, María de la Luz. *La Comedia del Arte.* (The Commedia Dell'Arte.) Barcelona: Ediciones Destino; 1983. 139 pp. Notes. Biblio. Illus.: Photo.
Italy. 1500-1750. Historical studies. ▪Historical influences that shaped the *commedia dell'arte.*

Reference materials

2021 Mancini, Franco, ed.; Greco, Franco Carmelo, ed. *La Commedia dell'Arte e il teatro erudito.* (*Commedia dell'arte* and Erudite Theatre.) Naples: Guida; 1982. 71 pp. (La scrittura e il gesto — itinerari del teatro napoletano dal 1500 ad oggi 1.) Biblio. Tables. Illus.: Photo. B&W.
Italy. 1550-1750. Histories-sources. ▪Catalogue of exhibition in Naples, September-October 1982 with a list of plays by Southern authors.

Relation to other fields

2022 Berardi, Enza. *Le maschere.* (The Masks.) Turin: Paravia; 1982. 63 pp. (Ideechiave 64.) Biblio. Gloss. Tables. Illus.: Photo. B&W.
Italy. 1550-1750. Instructional materials. ▪Short introduction, for children of primary school, to *commedia dell'arte* and to the role of masks. Grp/movt: Renaissance theatre.

2023 Mignatti, Alessandra. "Zanni, la fame e il diavolo." (Zanni, Hunger and the Devil.) *QT.* 1982 Aug.; 5(17): 30-55. Notes.
Italy. Germany. 1300-1599. Historical studies. ▪Research on the origin and meaning of Zanni's names and masks. Grp/movt: Renaissance theatre.

Pageants/parades

Institutions

2024 Cummings, Scott T. "The First Annual Mermaid Parade." *ThM.* 1983 Winter; 15(1): 87-91. Illus.: Poster. Photo. Print. B&W. 11.
USA. 1983. Histories-sources. ▪Coney Island, USA, a non-profit organization, inaugurates annual 'Mermaid Parade' in effort to revive Coney Island.

Performance/production

2025 Lapointe, Gilles. "*Vie et mort du Roi Boiteux* de Jean-Pierre Ronfard." (*Life and Death of King Boiteux* by Jean-Pierre Ronfard.) *CDr.* 1983 Fall; 9(2): 220-225. Notes.
Canada. 1982. Historical studies. ▪Description of a spectacle devised by Jean-Pierre Ronfard for the Nouveau Théâtre Expérimental de Montréal, with approximately 15 hours of historical pageants.

Variety acts

Institutions

2026 Moy, James S. "The Folies Bergère in New York City in 1911." *ThR.* 1983 Summer; 8(2): 146-156. Notes. Illus.: Handbill. Photo. Print. B&W. 6.
USA. 1911. Historical studies. ▪One-year tenure of the Folies-Bergère at the theatre later renamed the Helen Hayes Theatre 'contributed to the early development of the dinner theatre and night club industry in America'.

Performance/production

2027 Heller, André. *Die Trilogie der möglichen Wunder: Roncalli — Flic Flac — Theater des Feuers.* (The Trilogy of Possible Miracles: *Roncalli, Flic Flac* and *Theater of Fire.*) Vienna and Berlin: Medusa; 1983. 177 pp. Pref. Biblio. Illus.: Photo. Plan. Dwg. Color. B&W. Grd.Plan.
Austria. Germany, West. Portugal. 1975-1983. Histories-sources. ▪André Heller's résumé of his Circus *Roncalli,* his poetic variété *Flic Flac* and his pyrotechnic display *Theater des Feuers.* Includes photos and interviews with performers, spectators and critics.

2028 Lotz, Ranier E. "The 'Louisiana Troupes' in Europe." *BPM.* 1983 Fall; 11: 133-142. Illus.: Poster. Photo. Print. B&W. 3: 3 in. x 4 in., 4 in. x 6 in.
Europe. 1901-1916. Historical studies. ▪Several troupes of Black entertainers had the word 'Louisiana' in their titles. A chronology of those troupes which toured Eastern and Western Europe between 1901 and 1916. Related to Dance: Popular dance.

2029 MacMathuna, Ciaran. "Who Wrote That?" *IW.* 1983 Nov.-Dec.; 32(6): 32-34. Notes. [Popular song lyrics condensed.]
USA. UK. 1800-1899. Historical studies. ▪Information on the composers of the popular 19th century Irish songs *The Irish Emigrant, Kathleen Mavoureen, Bantry Bay* and *Killarney* which often comprised part of theatrical or variety performances, especially the vocal performances of John McCormack.

2030 McCullough, Jack W. *Living Pictures on the New York Stage.* Ann Arbor, MI: UMI Research Press; 1983. ix, 202 pp. (TDS 13.) Notes. Index. Append. Biblio. Append. Illus.: Design. Dwg. Handbill. Poster. Pntg. Photo.
USA. 1831-1899. Historical studies. ▪History of *tableaux vivants* on the New York stage with special emphasis on the work of Edward Kilanyi.

2031 McCullough, Jack W. "Model Artists Versus the Law: The First American Encounter." *JAC.* 1983 Summer; 6(2): 3-8. Notes.
USA. 1800-1899. Historical studies. ▪Evolution of tableaux vivants into displays of nudity which were eventually suppressed.

2032 Plotkins, Marilyn Jane. *Irving Berlin, George Gershwin, Cole Porter and the Spectacular Revue: The Theoretical Context of Revue Songs from 1910 to 1937.* Medford, MA: Tufts Univ.; 1982. 227 pp. [Diss.: University Microfilms order no. DA8217374.]
USA. 1910-1937. Historical studies. ▪Study of revue songs in theatrical contexts.

2033 Zeif, Sasha. "My Night at the Palace." *ThM.* 1983 Spring; 14(2): 48-54. Illus.: Diagram. Photo. Print. B&W. 5.
USA. 1980. Historical studies. ▪New vaudevillians such as The Flying Karamazov Brothers and Bill Irwin have chosen music hall comedic forms to express their unique theoretical concerns and incorporate their wide range of talents.

Other entries with significant content related to Popular Entertainment: 345, 387, 395, 419, 432, 442, 684, 687, 702, 703, 704, 851, 913, 935, 1032, 1037, 1055, 1057, 1061, 1081, 1362, 1413, 1668, 1714, 1731, 1749, 2095.

PUPPETRY

General

Audience

2034 Dundee, Daren. "Kids Are Different." *PuJ.* 1983 Mar.; 34(3): 20.
USA. 1983. Critical studies. ▪Characteristics of a typical children's audience.

PUPPETRY : General

Design/technology

2035 Anon. "Children's Classic at Kennedy Center." *PuJ.* 1983 June; 34(4): 11. Biblio. Illus.: Photo.
USA. 1983. Historical studies. ■Puppets and performance techniques used in Kennedy Center production of *The Tale of Peter Rabbit*.

2036 Anon. "Puppet Spectacle of Neiman-Marcus." *PuJ.* 1983 June; 34(4): 13-14. Illus.: Photo.
USA. 1983. Histories-sources. ■Exhibit of 50 puppets owned by Tom Maud at Neiman Marcus.

2037 Buck, Gary. "Balloon Blowing Clown Marionette." *PuJ.* 1983 Dec.; 35(2): 19-20. Illus.: Dwg.
USA. 1983. Instructional materials. ■Technique for creating a self-contained balloon-blowing puppet.

2038 Conover, Virginia. "Puppetry in Education: The Spelling Monsters." *PuJ.* 1983 June; 34(4): 18. Illus.: Dwg.
USA. 1980. Instructional materials. ■Construction and use of monster puppets for teaching spelling.

2039 Danner, Howard. "Puppetry and a Medieval Mystery Play." *PuJ.* 1983 Dec.; 35(2): 15, 31. Illus.: Photo.
USA. 1983. Histories-sources. ■Puppets and design concept of author's production of *The Second Shepherds Play*.

2040 Sander, Nancy H. "Eureka!" *PuJ.* 1983 Mar.; 34(3): 21-22. Illus.: Dwg.
USA. 1983. Instructional materials. ■Hints on construction of puppets and properties and lighting techniques.

2041 Sander, Nancy H. "Eureka!" *PuJ.* 1983 Sep.; 35(1): 27-28. Illus.: Dwg.
USA. 1983. Instructional materials. ■Suggestions for puppet construction and producing and marketing puppet shows.

2042 Sandler, Nancy H. "Eureka!" *PuJ.* 1983 June; 34(4): 19-20. Illus.: Dwg.
USA. 1983. Instructional materials. ■Suggestions for materials, construction and production techniques for puppeteers.

Institutions

2043 Francis, Penny. "The Intriplicate Mime Company." *Anim.* 1983; 6(4): 15-16. Illus.: Photo. B&W. 5.
UK. 1977-1983. Historical studies. ■Educational project of Intriplicate Mime Company using puppets.

2044 Comesford, Millie. "Twenty-first Anniversary of DaSilva Puppets." *Anim.* 1983; 7: 15-16. Illus.: Photo. B&W. 6.
UK-England. 1962-1983. Historical studies. ■Development of a puppet theatre troupe and the setting up of a permanent base for performance.

2045 Francis, Penny. "Pulling the Right Strings: The Work of Puppet Centre Trust." *E&AM.* 1983 Mar.: 23-25. Illus.: Photo. B&W. 2.
UK-England. 1983. Histories-sources. ■Support, information, publicity, study facilities, fundraising advice, etc., offered by the Puppet Centre Trust.

2046 Anon. "Forty-Fourth Festival Follow-Up." *PuJ.* 1983 Sep.; 35(1): 21-22. Illus.: Photo.
USA. 1983. Histories-sources. ■Highlights of the 1983 festival of the Puppeteers of America.

2047 Kurten, Allelu. "A History of UNIMA – U.S.A." *PuJ.* 1983 Mar.; 34(3): 4.
USA. 1929-1983. Historical studies. ■Brief history of the U.S. branch of the Union Internationale de la Marionette.

2048 Sager, J. Gregory. "From the Heart." *PuJ.* 1983 Dec.; 35(2): 9-10, 27-28. Illus.: Photo.
USA. 1983. Histories-sources. ■Description of *Circle of Waters Circus*, a travelling puppet pageant using 150 puppets and 30 performers.

Performance/production

2049 Magnin, Charles. *Histoire des marionettes en Europe depuis l'antiquité jusqu'à nos jours.* (History of Puppets in Europe from Antiquity to the Present.) Sala Bolognese: Arnaldo Forni; 1983. 356 pp. Notes. [Anastatic reprint of 1863 edition.]
Europe. 600 B.C.-1863 A.D. Histories-general. ■Comprehensive history of puppetry.

2050 Regan, F. Scott. "'Round As a Cube': La Compagnie Philippe Gentry." *PuJ.* 1983 Mar.; 34(3): 9-10. Illus.: Photo.
France. 1980. Reviews of performances. ■Recent production by puppeteer Philippe Gentry's company.

2051 Colla, Gianni; Colla, Cosetta; Minoli, Chiara, ed. *Il popolo di legno.* (The Wood-people.) Milan: Imago, s.r.l.; 1982. 57 pp. (Mirabilia 1.) Pref. Append. Tables. Illus.: Photo. B&W. Color.
Italy. 1946-1981. Biographies. ■Autobiography of Gianni Colla, heir to a family of puppet-masters. List of performances is included.

2052 Olson, Barbara; Pasqualino, Fortunato. *L'arte dei Pupi: Teatro popolare siciliano.* (The Art of the *Pupi*: Sicilian Popular Theatre.) Milan: Rusconi; 1983. 191 pp. (Rusconi immagini/Lunaria.) Tables. Illus.: Photo. B&W. Color.
Italy. 1800-1983. Histories-specific. ■Extensively illustrated study of the most famous form of Sicilian popular puppet theatre.

2053 Pandolfini Barberi, Antonio. *Burattini e burattinai bolognesi.* (Puppets and Puppet-masters of Bologna.) With appendix by Oreste Trebbi. Sala Bolognese: Arnaldo Forni; 1983. 184 pp. Tables. Append. Illus.: Dwg. Photo. B&W. [Anastatic reprint of 1923 edition.]
Italy. 1800-1923. Histories-specific. ■History of puppets and puppet-masters, in particular of Filippo and Angelo Cuccoli. Includes *canovacci* of comedies and the text of *Il muto di Saint Malo (The Mute of Saint Malo)* by Augusto Galli.

2054 Bäcklin, Jan. "Totems 8:e internationella dockteaterfestival." (Totem's Eighth International Puppet Theatre Festival.) *Entre.* 1983; 10(6): 25-27.
Sweden. 1983. Critical studies. ■Review of Totem theatre festival, which hosted fourteen puppet theatre groups.

2055 Anon. "*Alice in Wonderland*." *PuJ.* 1983 June; 34(4): 5-6. Biblio. Illus.: Photo.
USA. 1982. Histories-sources. ■Work of The Puppet People on Broadway production of *Alice in Wonderland*.

2056 Anon. "Professional Puppetry." *PuJ.* 1983 June; 34(4): 18.
USA. 1983. Histories-sources. ■Children's Theatre Association of America standards for productions for young audiences.

2057 Anon. "Heigh-Ho, Come to the Fest." *PuJ.* 1983 June; 34(4): 35-39. Illus.: Dwg. Photo.
USA. 1983. Histories-sources. ■Events and exhibits of Puppeteers of America Festival.

2058 Jones, Kenneth Lee. "Showcase 1983." *PuJ.* 1983 June; 34(4): 9-10. Illus.: Photo.
USA. 1983. Reviews of performances. ■Performances by Ragabush Puppet Theatre and Lampoon Puppet Theatre at Children's Theatre Association of America sponsored 'Showcase 1983' with a chronology of previous Showcase puppet shows.

2059 Latshaw, Patricia H. "Refractions form the *Dark Crystal*." *PuJ.* 1983 Mar.; 34(3): 11-12, 31. Illus.: Photo.
USA. 1980-1983. Critical studies. ■Contributions made to puppetry by Jim Henson's *Dark Crystal*. Related to Media: Film.

2060 Malkin, Michael R. "Interview: Bruce D. Schwartz." *PuJ.* 1983 Dec.; 35(2): 6-8. Illus.: Photo.
USA. 1983. Histories-sources. ■Bruce Schwartz' work and plans for new shows.

2061 Rooney, Lynn Brice. "*Candide* at Arena Stage." *PuJ.* 1983 Sep.; 35(1): 13-14. Biblio. Illus.: Photo.
USA. 1983. Histories-sources. ■Use of puppets and techniques borrowed from puppet theatre in an Arena Stage production of *Candide*.

2062 Salter, Ted. "Personality Profile: Sylvia Meredith." *PuJ.* 1983 Mar.; 34(3): 13-14. Illus.: Dwg.
USA. 1938-1983. Histories-sources. ■Sylvia Meredith discusses her work as an actress and puppeteer.

2063 Salter, Ted. "Personality Profile: Molly Jameson." *PuJ.* 1983 June; 34(4): 15-16. Illus.: Dwg.
USA. 1983. Histories-sources. ■Interview with puppeteer Molly Jameson.

PUPPETRY: General—Performance/production

2064   Sears, David. "Creation at La Mama." *PuJ.* 1983 Sep.; 35(1): 11-12. Illus.: Photo.
USA. 1983. Reviews of performances. ■Experimental multi-media presentation of Biblical creation story by Esteban Fernandez Sanchez at La Mama Experimental Theatre Club. Related to Media: Mixed media.

2065   Staub, Nancy L. "Words about Burr Tillstrom." *PuJ.* 1983 Dec.; 34(2): 5, 28. Illus.: Photo.
USA. 1983. Historical studies. ■Artistry of Burr Tillstrom and his Kuklapolitan Players.

Plays/librettos/scripts

2066   Bäcklin, Jan. "Dockteater som allra bäst." (Puppet Theatre at Its Best.) *Entre.* 1983; 10(6): 28-29.
USA. Sweden. 1970-1983. Historical studies. ■Review of Eric Bass's puppet plays for adults, presented at the Uppsala Festival and incorporating folk tales on the theme of death.

Relation to other fields

2067   Riggs, Rosee; Festenstein, Richard. "Puppets in Zaria." *Anim.* 1983; 6(4): 12-13. Illus.: Photo. B&W. 4.
Nigeria. 1983. Critical studies. ■Workshop at Ahmadu Bello University investigating the use of puppets in education and therapy.

2068   Combs, Ellen; Hagey, Grace. "Partners with Puppets." *PuJ.* 1983 Sep.; 35(1): 25-26. Illus.: Photo.
USA. 1983. Histories-sources. ■Educational project in which senior citizens used puppets to teach handicapped children.

2069   Condon, Camy. "Multi-Cultural Puppetry." *PuJ.* 1983 Dec.; 35(2): 16. Illus.: Photo.
USA. 1983. Instructional materials. ■Use of puppets to teach international culture and English as a second language.

2070   Conover, Virginia. "Puppetry in Language Arts: Junior High School." *PuJ.* 1983 Mar.; 34(3): 15. Illus.: Dwg. Photo.
USA. 1983. Instructional materials. ■Construction and use of a puppet to teach basic grammar.

Research/historiography

2071   Anon. "Puppetry in Libraries: Sources and Searches." *PuJ.* 1983 Mar.; 34(3): 20. Biblio.
USA. 1983. Technical studies. ■Ways that library research can help puppeteers.

Theory/criticism

2072   Phillips, John. "Toward an Aesthetic of Puppet Theatre." *Anim.* 1983; 7(1): 3-4. Illus.: Photo. B&W. 4.
Europe. 1907-1983. Historical studies. ■Overview of early aesthetic theory of puppetry which extends to an examination of contemporary examples of its primal nature.

Bunraku

Performance/production

2073   Leith, Christopher. "Bunraku: The Classical Puppet Theatre of Japan." *Anim.* 1983; 6(5): 15-16. Illus.: Photo. B&W. 3.
Japan. 1600-1983. Historical studies. ■History and development of *bunraku* as theatre, alongside *kabuki*. Related to Dance-Drama: Kabuki.

2074   Drummond, Andrew. "Bunraku at Japan House." *PuJ.* 1983 June; 34(4): 7-8. Illus.: Photo.
USA. 1983. Reviews of performances. ■Bunraku performances of the Bunrakuza (Osaka Bunraku Theatre) at New York's Japan House.

Plays/librettos/scripts

2075   Sorgenfrei, Carol; Sturtz, Lisa A. "Puppetry at UCLA: Experiment in East-West Fusion." *PuJ.* 1983 Dec.; 35(2): 17-18. Illus.: Photo.
USA. 1983. Historical studies. ■Description of a *bunraku* version of John Ford's *'Tis Pity She's a Whore* at University of California Los Angeles.

Relation to other fields

2076   Dasgupta, Gautam. "Bunraku Miniatures." *PerAJ.* 1983; 7(2): 29-35. Illus.: Photo. B&W. 4: 6 in. x 5 in., 6 in. x 4 in.
Japan. 1983. Critical studies. ■*Bunraku* is seen as Japanese miniaturization of social concepts.

Marionettes

Design/technology

2077   Phillips, Sandra S. "Marionette Photographs by André Kertész." *PerAJ.* 1983; 7(3): 115-120. Illus.: Photo. B&W. 4: 4 in. x 5 in., 4 in. x 3 in.
Belgium. 1925-1929. Historical studies. ■Photographs by Kertész document surrealist fascination with marionettes as metaphors of human reality. Grp/movt: Surrealism.

2078   Speaight, George. "Wires or Strings." *TN.* 1983; 37(2): 63-66. Notes.
UK-England. 1796-1852. Historical studies. ■All-string-controlled marionettes introduced by Samuel Seward.

2079   Mikotowicz, Tom. "Robert Edmond Jones' Eight Foot Marionettes for *Oedipus Rex*." *PuJ.* 1983 Dec.; 35(2): 11-12, 29-30. Illus.: Photo.
USA. 1931. Histories-sources. ■Description of marionettes Robert Edmond Jones designed for 1931 Metropolitan Opera production of *Oedipus Rex*, suggesting influences of *bunraku* and Edward Gordon Craig. Related to Music-Drama: Opera.

2080   Solomon, Alisa. "Reminiscences of Meyer Levin's Marionette Studio Theatre: From an Interview with Lou Bunin." *PerAJ.* 1983; 7(3): 109-114. Illus.: Photo. B&W. 4.
USA. 1925-1930. Histories-sources. ■Puppet creation as 'ideal type casting' to provide character abstractions for experimental plays. Grp/movt: Expressionism.

2081   Solomon, Alisa. "The Marionette Theatre of Meyer Levin." *PerAJ.* 1983; 7(3): 103-108. Illus.: Photo. B&W. 3: 4 in. x 5 in., 3 in. x 4 in.
USA. 1926-1930. Historical studies. ■Levin's marionettes as abstract visual images for experimental plays and dramatized Hasidic tales. Influence by Gordon Craig and Fernand Léger. Grp/movt: Expressionism.

Institutions

2082   Hogarth, Ann. "The London Marionette Theatre: A Personal Impression." *Anim.* 1983; 6(5): 7. Illus.: Photo. B&W. 2.
UK-England. 1927-1935. Historical studies. ■Foundation and history of the theatre and its decline with the advent of television. Related to Media: Video forms.

Performance/production

2083   Raitmayr, Babette. "Salzburger Marionetten: Zukunft auf Draht." (Salzburger Marionettes: Future on Wire.) *Buhne.* 1983 Oct.: 8-10. Illus.: Photo. Color.
Austria. 1983. Historical studies. ■Salzburger Marionettentheater celebrates its 70th birthday with Mozart's *Figaro*. First attempts with holography on stage.

2084   Hogarth, Ann. "Walter Wilkinson, 1889-1970." *Anim.* 1983; 6(3): 3-4. Illus.: Photo. Dwg. B&W. 3. [From notes by Winifred Wilkinson.]
UK-England. 1889-1970. Biographical studies. ■Life of writer and promoter of puppet theatre.

2085   Salter, Ted. "Personality Profile: Rod Young." *PuJ.* 1983 Sep.; 35(1): 18-20, 29. Illus.: Dwg.
USA. 1937-1983. Histories-sources. ■Interview with Rod Young on his life and work with marionettes.

Reference materials

2086   *Fra marionette e burattini: Itinerario magico nella civiltà veneta.* (Amid Marionettes and Puppets: Magic Tour of Venetian Civilization.) Verona: Cassa di Risparmio di Verona, Vicenza e Belluno; 1983. 36 pp. (Le mostre della Cassa di Risparmio 34.) Tables. Illus.: Photo. B&W. Color.

PUPPETRY: Marionettes

Italy. 1700-1899. ∎Catalogue for the exhibition of Venetian marionettes and puppets held in Verona, May 8 – June 13, 1983.

Theory/criticism

2087 Lixl, Andreas. "Utopie in der Miniatur: Heinrich von Kleists Aufsatz 'Über das Marionettentheater'." (Utopia in Miniature: Heinrich von Kleist's Essay 'On the Marionette Theatre'.) *GQ.* 1983 Mar.; 56(2): 257-270. Notes.
Germany. 1810. Critical studies. ∎Because the gesture of the marionette reflects human dancing, it also shows the hopes and memories in man's desire for utopia and paradise. This extends beyond Kleist's criticism which unmasked the mendacity and social misery of his time.

Shadow puppets

Performance/production

2088 Verdone, Mario. "Teatro e arte delle ombre." (Theatre and the Art of Shadows.) *TeatrC.* 1982 Oct.-1983 Jan.; 1(2): 175-194. Illus.: Photo. B&W.
Europe. Asia. North America. 1500-1982. Historical studies. ∎Brief history of shadow theatre.

2089 Polus, Betty. "Contemporary Shadow Puppets in France." *PuJ.* 1983 Mar.; 34(3): 7-8. Illus.: Photo.
France. 1979. Reviews of performances. ∎Performances of shadow puppet theatres at the 1979 French Festival of Traditional Arts.

2090 Pallottino, Paolo, ed. *Il libro delle ombre.* (The Book of Shadows.) Milan: Longanesi; 1983. 156 pp. (I tascabili del bibliofilo 21.) Pref. Notes. Tables. Illus.: Dwg. B&W.
Italy. Germany. UK-England. 1850-1899. Histories-sources. ∎Reissue of some passages and drawings from books on hand shadow puppets.

2091 Meschke, Michael. "The Dying Art of Thai Puppetry." *Anim.* 1983; 6(5): 6. Illus.: Photo. B&W. 1.
Thailand. 1983. Critical studies. ∎Swedish cultural delegation comments on the poor state of puppetry in Thailand.

Other entries with significant content related to Puppetry: 178, 543, 852, 2010.

RITUAL-CEREMONY

General

Design/technology

2092 Brunet, Jacques. "Masks of Southeast Asia." *TDR.* 1982 Winter; 26(4): 66-69.
Asia. 1982. Historical studies. ∎Brief account of ritual masks in Southeast Asia.

2093 Revel-Macdonald, Nicole. "Dayak and Kalimantan Masks." *TDR.* 1982 Winter; 26(4): 70-72.
Borneo. 1982. Historical studies. ∎Brief description of traditional ritual masks in the Kalimantan Timur province of Borneo.

2094 Monod-Becquelin, A. "Masks in South America." *TDR.* 1982 Winter; 26(4): 10-12.
Colombia. 1982. Historical studies. ∎Brief description of South American Indian masks, with emphasis on their function and design.

2095 Glotz, Samuel. "European Masks." *TDR.* 1982 Winter; 26(4): 14-18.
Europe. 1982. Historical studies. ∎Summary of traditional European masks and their uses in historical pageants and masquerades. Related to Popular Entertainment: Pageants/parades.

2096 Steinlen, Jean Marie. "Winter Customs in Eastern European Countries." *TDR.* 1982 Winter; 26(4): 19-24.
Europe. 1982. Historical studies. ∎Brief account of the design and use of masks in traditional Eastern European ceremonies and festivals.

2097 Levi-Strauss, Claude. "North American Masks." *TDR.* 1982 Winter; 26(4): 4-8.

North America. Historical studies. ∎Brief assessment of North American Indian ritual masks — their uses and designs — concentrating on Iroquois, Pacific Northwest and American Southwest tribes.

Performance/production

2098 Fulchignoni, Enrico. "Forme possessive e liberatorie nel teatro contemporaneo." (Possessive and Liberating Forms in the Contemporary Theatre.) *TeatrC.* 1982 Oct.-1983 Jan.; 1(2): 159-174.
North America. Europe. 1700-1982. Historical studies. ∎Possession, ecstasy and dionysiac practices applied by avant-garde theatre groups.

Relation to other fields

2099 Thomsen, Christian W. *Menschenfresser in der Kunst und Literatur, in fernen Ländern, Mythen, Märchen und Satiren, in Dramen, Liedern, Epen und Romanen.* (Man-Eaters in Art and Literature in Distant Countries: Myths, Tales and Satires in Drama, Song, Epic and the Novel.) Vienna: Christian Brandstätter; 1983. 223 pp. Pref. Index. Biblio. Illus.: Photo. Graphs. Sketches. Poster. B&W.
Europe. Africa. North America. Critical studies. ∎Collection of essays on cannibalism in myth, religion, fairy-tales, ethnology, science fiction, psychology, philosophy, eroticism, drama and art.

2100 Walker, Ethel Pitts. "Traditional African Theatre." *BALF.* 1983 Spring; 17: 14.
Senegal. USA. 1976. Historical studies. ∎Description of *Bandia Woli*, a traditional folk drama (part of an initiation ceremony) performed in Senegal, with emphasis on ties to Black American church ritual. Related to Drama: Folk drama.

Civic

Performance/production

2101 Obregon, Osvaldo; Brody, Jean E., transl. "The University Clasico in Chile." *ThM.* 1983 Winter; 15(1): 18-24. Notes. Illus.: Photo. Print. B&W. 3.
Chile. 1938-1980. Critical studies. ∎Theatrical spectacles traditionally presented twice yearly from 1938 to 1973 are considered a vehicle for transmission and celebration of national values.

2102 Hill, Anthony D. "Rituals at the New Lafayette Theatre." *BALF.* 1983 Spring; 17: 31-35.
USA. 1969-1972. Histories-sources. ∎Robert Macbeth, founder-director of the Harlem New Lafayette Theatre, describes the purpose and style of the rituals written and performed there over 3 years.

Religious

Design/technology

2103 Nadir, Chems. "Masks and Non-masks in Islam." *TDR.* 1982 Winter; 26(4): 79-81.
Asia. Africa. 1982. Historical studies. ∎Account of Islamic masks and veils.

2104 Amankulor, J. N. Ndukaku. "*Odo:* The Mass Return of the Masked Dead among the Nsukka-Igbo." *TDR.* 1982 Winter; 26(4): 46-58.
Nigeria. 1982. Historical studies. ∎Staging of the Odo Festival — the traditional return of the dead — and its use of masks and dance. Related to Dance-Drama.

Performance/production

2105 King, Eleanor. "Dionysus in Seoul: Notes from the Field on a Shaman Ritual in Korea." *CORD.* 1983; 1: 213-223. Biblio.
Korea. 1977. Critical studies. ∎Religious elements of the Korean shamanistic ritual (*kut*) are applied to a ceremony witnessed by the author. Detailed description of the costume, movements, symbolic implications and plot and resulting emotional impact.

Plays/librettos/scripts

2106 James, Mervyn. "Ritual, Drama and Social Body in the Late Medieval English Town." *Pa&Pr.* 1983 Feb.; 98: 3-29. Notes.

RITUAL-CEREMONY: Religious

England. 1300-1499. Historical studies. ■Religious rites and ideology of medieval urban societies reflected in Corpus Christi plays.

Relation to other fields

2107 Badowy, Alexander. "Astronomy and Architecture in Ancient Egypt." *GdBA*. 1983 Sep.; 102: 47-59. Notes. IL.
Egypt. 1000-500 B.C. Historical studies. ■Links religious beliefs and ritual performance to astronomy and architecture: a 'recurring theophany'.

2108 Ashley, Wayne. "From Ritual to Theatre in Kerala: Creativity and Flexibility in Performance Systems in South India." *ThNe*. 1983 Mar.; 15(3): 7. Illus.: Photo. B&W. 2:8 in. x 5 in., 4 in. x 8 in. [First in a series of articles.]
India. 1982. Historical studies. ■Study of the transformations, adaptations and reworkings of Teyyam, a festival of a religious cult, into new forms.

2109 Noguera, Elma. "Notiser om den prekolumbianska teatern." (Notes on the Pre-Columbian Theatre.) *Entre*. 1983; 10(4): 34-35.
North America. South America. 1200-1533. Historical studies. ■Dramatic religious rituals in pre-Hispanic Latin America, including sacrifices to Tláloc, the rain god.

Theory/criticism

2110 Friedrich, Rainer. "Drama and Ritual." *TID*. 1983; 5: 159-223. Notes.
USA. Africa. 1983. Critical studies. ■Theory of ritual is used to clarify the relationship between ritual and drama.

———

Other entries with significant content related to Ritual-Ceremony: 435, 458, 529, 530, 531, 536, 1101, 1461, 1644, 1673, 2008.

SUBJECT INDEX

Aaron, Joyce

Institutions

Reflections on the significance of The Open Theatre by several of its performers, writers and critical advisers. USA: New York, NY. 1963-1973. 1613

Abarbanell, Lina

Performance/production

The life and career of Lina Abarbanell, the first Hänsel at the Metropolitan Opera House. USA: New York, NY. Germany: Berlin. 1905-1963. 1917

Abbey Theatre (Dublin)

Institutions

Rejection of O'Casey's play *The Silver Tassie* by the Abbey Theatre and the subsequent furor. UK-Ireland: Dublin. 1928. 637

Performance/production

Yeats's theories on acting and the Abbey Theatre. UK-Ireland: Dublin. 1904-1939. 899

Plays/librettos/scripts

Profile of bilingual playwright Antoine O'Flatharta. Eire. 1981. 1025

Reference materials

Correspondence relating to administrative concerns at the Abbey Theatre between William Butler Yeats, Lady Gregory and John Millington Synge. UK-Ireland: Dublin. 1904-1909. 1432

Abbott, George

Performance/production

Nine critics review George Abbott's production of the musical *On Your Toes*. USA: New York, NY. 1983. 1803

ABDC Workshop (Edinburgh)

Philosophy and intentions of Rational Theatre and ABDC Workshop's Edinburgh project. UK-England. UK-Scotland: Edinburgh. 1983. 1747

About Face SEE: ***Clacson, Trombette e Pernacchi***

Abraham and Isaac

Basic theatrical documents

Discussion of prints and translation of the *fragmenten verzameling* 3-8 found in Zutphen Archive. Netherlands. 1400-1499. 574

Absalón

Plays/librettos/scripts

New José Luis Gómez version of Calderón de la Barca's tragedy, *Absalón*. Spain. 1983. 1701

Absurdism

Performance/production

Samuel Beckett's *Happy Days* with Giulia Lazzarini at Piccolo

Teatro di Milano, directed by Giorgio Strehler. Italy: Milan. 1983. 807

Plays/librettos/scripts

Playwrights and dramatic forms influencing Eugene O'Neill's *The Calms of Capricorn*. Europe. USA. 1953. 1088

The themes of freedom, death and suicide in Albert Camus' *Caligula*. France. 1945. 1110

Some paths for realism in Latin American theatre. South America. North America. 1955-1983. 1224

The character of Arlene in Marsha Norman's play *Getting Out*, and her effect on the audience. USA. 1981. 1372

Humanist examination of Samuel Beckett's plays. Europe. 1906-1983. 1637

Epistemological paradox in Samuel Beckett's plays. Europe. 1906-1983. 1640

Study of Jean Tardieu's plays. France. 1947-1980. 1642

Jean Genet's *The Blacks* and his theory of ritual in context of Theatre of the Absurd and Total Theatre. France: Paris. 1948-1968. 1647

Academic Drama Theatre of A.S. Pushkin SEE: **Akademičeskij Teat'r Dramy imeni A.S. Puškina**

Académie de Danse Classique Princesse Grace (Monte Carlo)

Performance/production

Discussion of ballet in Monte Carlo. Monaco. 1948-1983. 519

Academy of Vocal Arts (Philadelphia, PA)

Institutions

Performances and training at Academy of Vocal Arts. USA: Philadelphia, PA. 1934-1983. 1829

Accademia dei Rozzi

Plays/librettos/scripts

Pastoral as dramatic genre and its literary and scenic derivations. Italy. 1400-1599. 1185

Accademia Filarmonica (Verona)

Performance spaces

History of Teatro Filarmonico in Verona and productions mounted there. Italy: Verona. 1732-1978. 378

Accounting

Administration

Resolution concerning billing guidelines of American Theatre Association. USA. 1983. 149

Achard, Marcel

Plays/librettos/scripts

Adaptation of Ben Jonson's *Epicoene* by Marcel Achard, directed by Charles Dullin. France: Paris. 1926. 1100

Acting — cont'd

Acting — cont'd

Biography of actor Peter O'Toole. UK. 1932-1983.   859

Actor Miles Anderson, his wife Lesley Duff, and their work with the Royal Shakespeare Company. UK-England. 1900-1983.   861

Autobiography of actress Claire Bloom. UK-England. 1931-1982.   866

Importance of boy actor playing the title role in *Peter Pan*. UK-England. 1902-1983.   867

Relationship between verbal and nonverbal communication in productions of *Macbeth, Othello* and *Julius Caesar*. UK-England. 1980.   868

Portrait of Ira Aldridge as Othello in painting by James Northcote. UK-England: Manchester. USA. 1826.   869

Director's analysis of Shaw's *Mrs. Warren's Profession*. UK-England. 1923.   871

Biography of actress Fanny Kemble. UK-England. USA. 1809-1893.   877

John Gielgud discusses nervous tension in actors. UK-England. 1983.   878

Actor Emrys James discusses his work, especially with the Royal Shakespeare Company. UK-England. 1900-1983.   879

Career of actor Stephen Rea. UK-England. UK-Ireland. 1900-1983.   881

Career of National Theatre actress Geraldine McEwan. UK-England. 1900-1983.   882

Collection of materials dealing with directing and acting Shavian drama. UK-England. 1892.   885

Philip Prowse's production of Robert MacDonald's Nazi psychothriller *Summit Conference*. UK-England: London. 1982.   888

Actor Laurence Olivier's autobiography. UK-England. 1907-1983.   891

Italian translation of Laurence Olivier's autobiography *Confessions of an Actor*. UK-England. 1907-1983.   892

Importance of vocal techniques for Shavian drama. UK-England. 1945-1981.   896

Yeats's theories on acting and the Abbey Theatre. UK-Ireland: Dublin. 1904-1939.   899

Changes of directors and reviews of performances at the Edinburgh Festival and Lyceum Theatre. UK-Scotland: Edinburgh. 1983.   903

Notes on three Broadway productions. USA: New York, NY. 1983.   911

Physical intimacy and direct contact with the audiences in contemporary American theatre. USA. 1969-1980.   912

Study of storytelling techniques. USA. 1983.   913

Actress Shelley Bruce's struggle with childhood leukemia. USA. 1964.   914

Biography of actress Katharine Hepburn. USA. 1909-1983.   915

Biography of actor and television personality Dick Cavett. USA. 1936-1983.   916

Persistence of Delsartian methodology in modern acting technique. USA. 1871-1970.   917

Use of cognitive complexity questionnaire in selecting and training cast. USA: Denton, TX. 1981.   918

Collection of photographs of Broadway productions and actors. USA: New York, NY. 1940-1967.   921

Stanislavskij's system in the USA and the tour by the Moscow Art Theatre. USA. USSR. 1910-1959.   923

Memoirs of the noted actress and theorist Uta Hagen. USA. Germany. 1919-1983.   932

Adverse reception of Madame Vestris and Charles Mathews on tour in USA. USA: New York, NY, Philadelphia, PA. UK-England: London. 1838.   933

Actor John Houseman comments on producers and directors. USA. 1983.   934

Performances, editing and audience response to Fanny Kemble's first American tour. USA: Boston, MA, New York, NY, Philadelphia, PA. 1849-1850.   935

Shakespearean productions and festivals in the American South. USA. 1751-1980.   938

Careers of solo performers Beatrice Herford, Cissie Loftus and Dorothy Sands. USA. 1900-1920.   942

Autobiography of actress Shirley MacLaine. USA. 1934-1983.   943

History and problems of monodrama. USA. 1982.   950

Use of Inventory of Dramatic Behavior in actor training. USA. 1980-1983.   974

Career of actor-manager John Wilkes Booth. USA. 1855-1865.   975

Federal Theatre Project's often innovative approach to staging Shakespeare's plays. USA. 1930-1939.   978

History of a production about nine Black leaders by the African American Drama Company. USA. 1976-1983.   979

Authentic expression in Black theatre and film is contrasted with stereotypical Black portrayals by white authors and performers. USA: New York, NY. 1890-1930.   983

History of Latvian actors and theatre. USSR. 1945.   986

Articles discussing the work of individual actors at the Academic Drama Theatre of A.S. Puškin. USSR: Leningrad. 1910-1970.   987

Overview of the Konstantin Stanislavskij system. USSR. Russia. 1863-1938.   988

Recollections of theatre critic P.A. Markov, including reviews of performances. USSR: Moscow. 1910-1930.   992

Study of A.D. Popov's acting and directing methods, theories of the theatre and teaching techniques. USSR: Moscow. 1900-1958.   998

English actors' work in Germany, with mention of stock comic characters. Germany. England: London. 1590-1620.   1525

Critical account of Beryl Reid's work as a comedy actress. UK-England. 1920-1983.   1534

Comedian Harry Langdon as a stage director. USA. 1884-1944.   1539

Director, actor and playwright Carmelo Bene's autobiography. Italy. 1959-1983.   1620

Theories of acting and theatre by controversial director Carmelo Bene. Italy. 1960-1982.   1621

Role of the actor in experimental theatre. Italy. 1968-1977.   1622

Interview with playwright Dario Fo and his actress-wife and collaborator Franca Rame. Italy: Milan. 1982.   1623

Analysis of Carmelo Bene's avant-garde adaptation and staging of *Pinocchio*. Italy. 1981.   1625

Description of group that performs with and for remote and rural areas. Poland: Gardzienice. 1968-1983.   1627

Writings by the founders of the Living Theatre. USA. Europe. 1952-1962.   1631

Post-World War II forms of American theatre. USA. 1945-1983.   1633

Production journal of *King Lear*. Canada: Stratford, ON. 1979.   1676

Evolution of the text of *King Lear* through performance. England. 1605-1983.   1677

Exhibit to commemorate Margarita Xirgu's debut as Medea. Spain: Mérida. 1932-1933.   1683

Konstantin Stanislavskij's stage adaptation of Shakespeare's *Othello* for the Moscow Art Theatre. USSR: Moscow. 1929-1930.   1685

Biography of actor Charles Boyer, including filmography of his work. France. USA. 1899-1978.   1712

Biography of actress Ingrid Bergman with photographs. Sweden. USA. 1915-1983.   1713

Biography and all-inclusive reference materials to Charlie Chaplin. USA. 1889-1977.   1714

Actor Dustin Hoffman as an anti-hero. USA. 1937-1983.   1715

Biography of actor Burt Reynolds. USA. 1936-1983.   1716

Voice and movement for film acting. USA. 1983.   1717

Intimate relationship with the audience in the work designed for performance video. USA. 1980.   1723

Interviews with American and European performance artists. Europe. USA. 1983.   1744

Creation of the character of a Black ballerina in Diaghilev's Ballet Russe. USA: New York, NY. 1980.   1751

Description and analysis of Ping Chong's work. USA. 1972-1983.   1752

Biography of singer-actress Julie Andrews. UK-England. USA. 1935-1983.   1777

Interview with principal male stars of *Dreamgirls*. USA: New York, NY. 1983.   1778

History of Broadway musical theatre with an extensive annotated discography. USA: New York, NY. 1800-1983.   1789

Biography of Liza Minnelli. USA. 1946-1983.   1790

Acting — cont'd

Acting — cont'd

Training

Training manual for performers. 1982.   492

Manual on voice and respiration, with exercises. Austria. 1983.   493

Conditions of apprenticeship in Elizabethan acting companies. England: Bridgewater. 1597-1599.   494

Improvisational theatre as a tool for special education teachers. USA. 1983.   500

Actor training program using character masks. USA. 1982.   501

Vocal training manual. USA. 1982.   503

Zelda Fichandler expresses her philosophy of theatre education. USA: New York, NY, Washington, DC. 1950-1983.   506

Theory and practice of actor training by director, Michel Saint-Denis. USA. 1897-1971.   507

Concept of school in Jacques Copeau's work. France: Paris. 1913-1930.   1523

Research project in theatre heresy and Stanislavskij. Italy: Pontedera. 1981-1983.   1524

Actor behavior SEE: Behavior/psychology, actor

Actor psychology SEE: Behavior/psychology, actor

Actor training SEE: Training, actor

Actor-managers

Administration

Sound financial practices of the productions mounted by the actor-manager Tate Wilkinson. England. 1781-1784.   554

Institutions

Letters signed by George Jolly concerning the visit of his troupe to Gdansk in August, 1650. Poland: Gdańsk. England. Germany. 1649-1650.   614

Actor-managers with self-serving interests at Shakespeare Memorial National Theatre. UK. 1905-1915.   623

Performance/production

Critical re-examination of the monograph on the actor Gustavo Modena. Italy. 1832-1861.   793

Theatrical tours in the memoirs of the *mattatori* — actor-managers. Italy. 1800-1899.   799

Playwright Guido Noccioli's account of Eleonora Duse's tour. Italy. 1906-1907.   809

Linguistic study of the letters written by the actor-manager Gustavo Modena. Italy. 1829-1861.   811

Beerbohm Tree's conceptual and directorial approach to staging Shakespeare. UK-England: London. 1905-1911.   863

Reconstruction of Richard Mansfield's production of *Richard III*. UK-England: London. USA. 1889.   893

Charles Kean's staging methods and the influences on them. UK-England: London. 1850-1859.   898

Shakespearean productions and festivals in the American South. USA. 1751-1980.   938

Career of actor-manager John Wilkes Booth. USA. 1855-1865.   975

Plays/librettos/scripts

Catalogue of the exhibition on the copyright debate between playwright Paolo Giacometti and actress Adelaide Ristori. Italy. 1836-1882.   1191

Actor's Lab (Toronto, ON)

Institutions

Survey of alternative theatres. Canada: Toronto, ON. 1979-1983. 296

Actors Equity Association, Britain

Administration

Funding and theatre activity, particularly Mayfest. UK-Scotland. 1922-1983.   557

Actors SEE: Acting and Performance/production

Actors Touring Company (England)

Institutions

Touring accounts of Actors Touring Company, 7:84 Theatre Company and Cardiff Laboratory Theatre. UK-England. UK-Wales. UK-Scotland. USSR. 1983.   634

Actors' Laboratory Theatre (New York, NY)

Performance/production

Stanislavskij's system in the USA and the tour by the Moscow Art Theatre. USA. USSR. 1910-1959.   923

Actors' Studio (New York, NY)

Stanislavskij's system in the USA and the tour by the Moscow Art Theatre. USA. USSR. 1910-1959.   923

Plays/librettos/scripts

Lee Strasberg on Ibsen and *Peer Gynt*. USA: New York, NY. 1906-1982.   1385

Actors' Theatre of Louisville

Performance/production

Description of plays presented at Humana Festival of New American Plays. USA: Louisville, KY. 1983.   940

Adams, Brooke

Plays/librettos/scripts

Interview with director and cast of Yale Repertory's production of G.B. Shaw's *The Philanderer*. USA: New Haven, CT. 1982.   1389

Adaptations

Performance/production

Production of *Eight Men Speak* by Popular Projects Society. Canada: Halifax, NS. 1982.   683

Marxist orientation in Shakespearean plays on German stage. Germany, East. 1982.   748

Japanese adaptations and productions of Sophocles' *Oedipus*. Japan. 1922-1978.   818

Critical examination of modern interpretations of Shakespeare's plays. UK-England: London. USA. Canada: Stratford, ON. 1975-1982.   873

Albert Innaurato directs production of his revision of *Benno Blimpie*. USA: New York, NY. 1973-1983.   1537

Critical analysis of Carmelo Bene's rewritten version of *Hamlet*. Italy. 1961-1975.   1619

Analysis of Carmelo Bene's avant-garde adaptation and staging of *Pinocchio*. Italy. 1981.   1625

Ten critics review Peter Brook's production of *La Tragédie de Carmen* at the Vivian Beaumont Theatre. USA: New York, NY. 1983.   1914

Plays/librettos/scripts

Terukkuttu, a street theatre piece developed from traditional dance-drama. India: Tamil Nadu. 1980.   540

Adaptation of *Galileo* for Chinese stage. China, People's Republic of: Peking. 1979.   1020

Playwrights and dramatic forms influencing Eugene O'Neill's *The Calms of Capricorn*. Europe. USA. 1953.   1088

Influence of Bertolt Brecht on Finnish theatre. Finland. 1930-1969.   1098

Adaptation of Ben Jonson's *Epicoene* by Marcel Achard, directed by Charles Dullin. France: Paris. 1926.   1100

Brecht's directorial approach to staging Shakespeare's *Coriolanus*, *Macbeth* and *King Lear*. Germany. 1920-1930.   1136

Problems in stage adaptation of Elias Canetti's *The Limited*. Germany, West: Stuttgart. 1983.   1150

Comparison of two German adaptations of Molière's *The Misanthrope* to determine the genre of the play. Germany, West: Cologne. 1982.   1151

Catalogue of the exhibition on the copyright debate between playwright Paolo Giacometti and actress Adelaide Ristori. Italy. 1836-1882.   1191

Adaptation of the Angel Guimerà play *Maria Rosa*. Spain. 1894.   1230

Comparative analysis of miscellaneous adaptations of Lope de Vega's *Peribáñez*. Spain. 1607.   1250

Adaptations — cont'd

Examination of plays adapted for movies. USA. 1974. 1345

Louisa Medina's popular dramatic adaptations of the works of Edward Bulwer-Lytton, Ernest Maltravers and Robert Bird. USA. 1833-1838. 1346

Eugene O'Neill plays that have been made into films. USA. 1916. 1347

The Long Voyage Home and *Long Day's Journey into Night* successfully transferred to film. USA. 1940-1962. 1383

Role of censorship in Johann Nestroy's *Häuptling Abendwind* as an adaptation of Jacques Offenbach's *Vent de soir*. Austria. 1833. 1549

A Midsummer Night's Dream as a parody of Edmund Spenser's *The Teares of the Muses*. England. 1595. 1556

Adaptation of a French farce into *Johan Johan*. England. France. 1520-1533. 1559

Review essay of *Hamlet* burlesques from a collection of Shakespeare parodies. UK-England. USA. 1810-1888. 1590

Comparison and contrast of radio and stage presentations of Arthur Kopit's play *Wings*. USA. 1978-1979. 1655

Wole Soyinka's adaptation of Euripides' *The Bacchae*. Nigeria. 1973. 1699

New José Luis Gómez version of Calderón de la Barca's tragedy, *Absalón*. Spain. 1983. 1701

Musical adaptation of *A Doll's House*. USA: New York, NY. 1983. 1809

Theatrical effect preserved in operatic adaptations of Werner Egk's *Peer Gynt* and Aribert Reimann's *King Lear* at the Münchener Festspiele. Germany, West: Munich. 1982. 1953

Robert Wilson discusses current and forthcoming projects. USA: New York, NY. 1983. 1963

Addams, Jane

Relation to other fields

Description of Jane Addams' creative drama activities at Hull House. USA: Chicago, IL. 1889-1910. 1469

Addison, Joseph

Performance/production

Questionable chronology results from performances by English officers. Belgium: Maastricht. 1703. 679

Administration

Administration

Sound financial practices of the productions mounted by the actor-manager Tate Wilkinson. England. 1781-1784. 554

Audience

Audience development survey. USA: Atlanta, GA, Baton Rouge, LA, Columbia, SC, Memphis, TN. 1983. 170

Institutions

Annual report of the Austrian Federal Theatres. Austria: Vienna. 1982-1983. 284

History and concerns of Green Thumb Theatre. Canada. 1975-1983. 293

Curtis Barlow as director of Professional Association of Canadian Theatres. Canada. 1983. 294

State of theatre in Ruhr-District. Germany, West: Dortmund. 1972-1982. 307

Brief survey of productions and financial situation of a local theatre. Germany, West: Nürnberg. 1983. 314

History, financial situation and productions of the Schlosstheater. Germany, West: Moers. 1975-1983. 315

First hundred years of the Società Italiana degli Autori ed Editori published in celebration of its centenary. Italy. 1882-1982. 318

Economic and political aspects of several Black theatre groups. USA: New York, NY, Chicago, IL. 1982. 340

Interview with Reinhold Auer, dramatic advisor of Jura Soyfer Theater am Spittelberg, Vienna. Austria: Vienna. 1980-1983. 583

Events leading to Roger Hodgman's resignation as Artistic Director of Vancouver Playhouse. Canada: Vancouver, BC. 1979-1983. 585

Financial situation of Städtische Bühnen Dortmund. Germany, West: Dortmund. 1970-1982. 604

Interviews with personnel of Freiburg theatres on obtaining subsidies and other aspects of administration. Germany, West: Freiburg. 1911-1983. 607

History of Royal Shakespeare Company with emphasis on financial and aesthetic aspects and internal politics. UK-England: London. 1864-1981. 624

Aspects of the National Theatre and the Royal Shakespeare Company are compared. UK-England. 1960. 627

Organization and productions of Black Theatre Co-operative. UK-England. 1979. 631

Artistic directors, policy, development and funding of The Traverse studio theatre. UK-England. 1963. 632

Development and funding of Foco Novo, Fringe theatre company. UK-England. 1972. 633

Peter Hall's role as artistic director of the National Theatre, including devising the repertory and obtaining funds. UK-England: London. 1973-1983. 636

History and organization of the Irish Rebel Theatre. USA: New York, NY. 1973-1983. 648

Activities of church and theatre associations to promote 'decent' dramaturgy. USA: New York, NY, Chicago, IL. 1910-1940. 649

History of League of Chicago Theatres. USA: Chicago, IL. 1970-1983. 651

History of American Repertory Theatre. USA. 1945-1947. 652

Critical examination of lack of idealism among non-profit theatres. USA. 1960-1983. 654

Administration and repertory of Finnish National Opera. Finland: Helsinki. 1983. 1828

Support, information, publicity, study facilities, fundraising advice, etc., offered by the Puppet Centre Trust. UK-England: London. 1983. 2045

Performance spaces

Great Hall at Gawthorpe and financial accounts provide information on the activities of Jacobean traveling companies. England. 1600-1618. 364

Proposals and experiences by theatrical operators to utilize the urban space for performances. Italy. 1983. 384

Steps involved in restoring historic theatres. USA. 1983. 396

Career of Oscar Hammerstein I and the theatres he built. USA: New York, NY. 1889-1904. 1760

Influence of Bayreuth Festival on architecture of Kitchener-Waterloo Symphony Hall. Canada: Kitchener, ON. 1983. 1833

Performance/production

Current state of Syrian theatre. Syria: Damascus, Aleppo, Basra. 1983. 445

Sociological and psychological implications faced by dancers at end of their performing careers. USA. 1982. 520

Charles Burket Rittenhouse as actor, playwright, director, administrator and educator. Canada: Montreal, PQ. 1925-1976. 688

Changes of directors and reviews of performances at the Edinburgh Festival and Lyceum Theatre. UK-Scotland: Edinburgh. 1983. 903

Political censorship and Soviet productions of *Hamlet*. USSR. 1930. 995

Performance art and organization of events staged by The Basement Group. UK-England: Newcastle upon Tyne. 1983. 1748

Interview with Steven Thomas, artistic director of Opera Hamilton. Canada: Hamilton, ON. 1983. 1844

Evolution of *tableaux vivants* into displays of nudity which were eventually suppressed. USA: New York, NY. 1800-1899. 2031

Plays/librettos/scripts

Essays on Restoration theatre and drama, with devised criteria for evaluation. England. 1660-1800. 1046

Catalogue of the exhibition on the copyright debate between playwright Paolo Giacometti and actress Adelaide Ristori. Italy. 1836-1882. 1191

Censorship involving Jerzy Hulewicz' play *Aruna*, produced at Municipal Theatre of Cracow. Poland: Kraków. 1925. 1217

Reference materials

Bibliography of performing arts periodicals. 1982. 11

Music guide for Austria with names, addresses and other information. Austria. 1983. 14

Administration — cont'd

Licensing papers related to managerial and repertorial changes at London theatres. England: London. 1706-1715.   20

Guide to theatre organizations and professionals. Finland. 1983.   23

Directory of resources for presenters of performing arts. USA. 1983.   37

Vocational guidance directed at young people for non-acting careers in theatre. USA. 1983.   43

Correspondence relating to administrative concerns at the Abbey Theatre between William Butler Yeats, Lady Gregory and John Millington Synge. UK-Ireland: Dublin. 1904-1909.   1432

List of theatre companies, playwriting awards and grants. USA. 1983.   1439

Administration SEE ALSO: Classed Entries 116-163, 552-565, 1704, 1737, 1758, 1759, 1766, 1767, 1810-1815.

Adolphus Theatre (Los Angeles, CA)

Performance spaces

Recollections of the Hippodrome, formerly the Adolphus Theatre. USA: Los Angeles, CA. 1911-1940.   1981

Adoration of the Magi

Performance/production

Possible dramatic convention used in the medieval performance of the *Adoration of the Magi* plays. England. 1200.   700

Adriana Lecouvreur

Photographs, cast lists, synopsis and discography of Metropolitan Opera production of *Adriana Lecouvreur*. USA: New York, NY. 1983.   1897

Aeschylus

Hansgünther Heyme's production of *The Persians*. Germany, West: Stuttgart. 1983.   1680

Plays/librettos/scripts

Mutes in Greek tragedy. Greece. 523-406 B.C.   1695

English translation of Albin Lesky's standard work on Greek tragedy. Greece. 499-400 B.C.   1696

Dramatic and military conflict in Greek tragedy. Greece. 484-415 B.C.   1697

Wole Soyinka's plays echo themes of Aeschylus, Euripides and Shakespeare. Nigeria. Greece: Athens. UK-England: London. 1980.   1700

Theory/criticism

Effect of social conditions on performance styles. USA. Greece. 499 B.C.-1983 A.D.   1517

Aesthetics

Institutions

History of Royal Shakespeare Company with emphasis on financial and aesthetic aspects and internal politics. UK-England: London. 1864-1981.   624

Performance/production

Autobiographical survey by choreographer Lincoln Kirstein. USA. India: Marrakesh. Europe. 1916-1949.   514

Women's involvement in performance art in the context of feminism. USA. 1970-1980.   1757

History of opera staging and its aesthetics. Europe. 1597-1982. 1852

Plays/librettos/scripts

Treatment of violence and its aesthetics in theatre, film and literature. Europe. 1983.   1090

Aesthetic continuity in Pierre Corneille's movement from comedy to tragedy. France. 1606-1684.   1112

Metacritical analysis of Calderón's plays applying criteria devised for Lope de Vega. Spain. 1608-1681.   1238

Aesthetic imbalance resulting from Pierre Corneille's concern for propriety in *Théodore*. France. 1606-1684.   1578

Relation to other fields

Gabriele D'Annunzio's aesthetic vision of theatre in his novel *The Fire*. Italy. 1900.   61

Theory/criticism

Intermingling of Eastern and Western performance aesthetics. China. Japan. 1900-1983.   93

Physical experience and aesthetic perception of body movement. France. 1889.   100

Principal themes in Zeami's treatises on *nō* performance. Japan. 1363-1443.   548

Nature and history of *nō* theatre. Japan. 1300-1980.   549

Zeami's dramatic theory of *nō*. Japan. 1402-1430.   551

Marxist philosophy in Bertolt Brecht's work. Germany. 1922-1956.   1496

Schiller's philosophy of history. Germany: Jena. 1789-1791.   1499

Bertolt Brecht's and György Lukács' debate on realism. Germany. Hungary. 1900-1956.   1500

Wystan Hugh Auden's poetic meditation on art as related to Shakespeare's *The Tempest* and Kierkegaardian thought. UK-England. 1939-1962.   1511

Imamu Amiri Baraka's links to aesthetically white culture. USA. 1969.   1516

Phenomenology of audience reception of Sam Shepard's *Curse of the Starving Class*. USA: New York, NY, Buffalo, NY, Tempe, AZ. 1982.   1519

Imamu Amiri Baraka's aesthetics find their origins in Blues music. USA. 1963-1967.   1521

Media as subject (theme) and object (medium to transport the message) of aesthetic treatment. Europe. USA. 1983.   1707

Overview of early aesthetic theory of puppetry. Europe. 1907-1983.   2072

Heinrich von Kleist's perception of marionettes reveals man's desire for utopia and paradise. Germany. 1810.   2087

African American Drama Company (California)

Performance/production

History of a production about nine Black leaders by the African American Drama Company. USA. 1976-1983.   979

After the Lions

Plays/librettos/scripts

Ronald Harwood discusses his plays *The Dresser* and *After the Lions*, the latter play based on the life of Sarah Bernhardt. UK-England: London. 1983.   1286

Agathon

English translation of Albin Lesky's standard work on Greek tragedy. Greece. 499-400 B.C.   1696

Agents

Administration

Round table discussion between playwrights and their agents. USA. 1983.   562

Agitprop theatre

Performance/production

History of Agitprop theatre. Germany. USSR. 1848-1930.   743

Plays/librettos/scripts

Egische Ciarenz's plays, particularly *Kafkaz*, are placed between Futurism and agitprop theatre. Armenia. 1923.   1634

Relation to other fields

History, function and methods of Soviet agitprop theatre. USSR. 1919-1934.   78

Athol Fugard's plays are compared to Bantustan agitprop and historical drama. South Africa, Republic of. 1955-1980.   1665

Ain't Misbehavin'

Institutions

Center Stage wins top honor in Toyama International Amateur Theatre Festival with *Ain't Misbehavin'*. Japan: Toyama. USA: Omaha, NE. 1983.   1772

Aischylos SEE: Aeschylus

AKA Performance Interfaces (Toronto, ON)

Institutions

Survey of alternative theatres. Canada: Toronto, ON. 1979-1983. 296

Akademičeskij Teat'r Dramy imeni A.S. Puškina (Leningrad)

Performance/production

Actor Juri Jurjev and director Vsevolod Mejerchol'd at the Aleksandrinskij Theatre (now Academic Drama Theatre of A.S. Pushkin). Russia: St. Petersburg. USSR: Leningrad. 1910-1938. 830

Articles discussing the work of individual actors at the Academic Drama Theatre of A.S. Puškin. USSR: Leningrad. 1910-1970. 987

Akademietheater (Vienna)

World premiere of Martin Walser's *In Goethe's Hand* at Vienna's Akademietheater, directed by Karl Fruchtmann. Austria: Vienna. 1983. 671

Akimov, Nikolai Pavlovič

Political censorship and Soviet productions of *Hamlet*. USSR. 1930. 995

Albee, Edward

Performance spaces

History of the Keith Memorial Theatre. USA: Boston, MA. 1925-1980. 1982

Performance/production

Eight critics review Edward Albee's production of his play *The Man Who Had Three Arms*. USA: New York, NY. 1983. 956

Plays/librettos/scripts

Similarities between the plays *The Dutchman* and *Zoo Story*. USA: New York, NY. 1964. 1350

Albertazzi, Giorgio

Performance/production

Articles on theatrical career of Giorgio Albertazzi, recipient of Armando Curzio award. Italy. 1949-1982. 808

Aldridge, Ira

Portrait of Ira Aldridge as Othello in painting by James Northcote. UK-England: Manchester. USA. 1826. 869

Aleksandrinskij Theatre SEE: Akademičeskij Teat'r Dramy imeni A.S. Puškina

Alekseev, Konstantin Sergeevič SEE: Stanislavskij, Konstantin Sergeevič

Alexander, Doris

Plays/librettos/scripts

Errors in various Eugene O'Neill biographies. USA. 1888-1953. 1382

Alfano, Franco

Performance/production

Account of *Risurrezione*, to be performed by Cincinnati Summer Opera. USA: Cincinnati, OH. 1904-1983. 1923

Alguilar, Gaspar

Plays/librettos/scripts

Staging and scenic practices in the plays of Lope de Vega's forerunners and contemporaries. Spain: Valencia. 1500-1699. 1253

Alice in Wonderland

Performance/production

Work of The Puppet People on Broadway production of *Alice in Wonderland*. USA: New York, NY. 1982. 2055

Alienation effect SEE: *Verfremdungseffekt*

All's Fair

Institutions

Collaborative effort in Welsh community results in play *All's Fair*. UK-Wales: Mid Glamorgan. 1983. 645

All's Well That Ends Well

Administration

Difficulties of getting some plays on Broadway. USA: New York, NY. 1982-1983. 565

Performance/production

Nine critics review Trevor Nunn's production of *All's Well That Ends Well*. USA: New York, NY. 1983. 1538

Allard, Charles

Institutions

History of Théâtre de la Foire. France: Paris. 1679-1721. 1979

Allen, Debbie

Performance/production

Debbie Allen discusses her struggle for success and her relationship with her family. USA. 1983. 515

Allen, Woody

Plays/librettos/scripts

Essays on the trends of the Jewish-American theatre and its personalities. USA. 1900-1983. 1353

Alternative theatre

Institutions

Change in idealism among alternative theatres. Canada: Toronto, ON. 1973-1983. 295

Survey of alternative theatres. Canada: Toronto, ON. 1979-1983. 296

Althusser, Louis

Theory/criticism

Louis Althusser's Marxist philosophy is contrasted with his review of Carlo Bertolazzi's play staged by Giorgio Strehler. USA. France. Italy. 1962-1985. 1674

Amadeus

Plays/librettos/scripts

Peter Shaffer's revision of *Amadeus*. UK-England: London. USA: New York, NY. 1979-1980. 1290

Examination of plays adapted for movies. USA. 1974. 1345

AMAM

Performance/production

Description and analysis of Ping Chong's work. USA. 1972-1983. 1752

Amateur theatre

Administration

Need for new cultural policy and cooperation between amateur and professional theatre. Sweden. Denmark. 1970-1983. 142

Institutions

Formation of joint committee by amateur theatres and its Training Council. Finland. 1983. 300

Theatre-activities of Turkish immigrant workers. Germany, West: West Berlin. 1982. 306

Motivation and goals of free theatre groups. Germany, West: West Berlin. 1982. 312

Project to intensify cultural work in the village of Niederbrechen, subsidized by the Ministry for Youth, Health and Family. Germany, West: Niederbrechen. 1979-1982. 313

Diversity of Latin American theatre. South America. North America. 1950-1983. 326

Center Stage wins top honor in Toyama International Amateur Theatre Festival with *Ain't Misbehavin'*. Japan: Toyama. USA: Omaha, NE. 1983. 1772

Performance/production

Purposes, goals and rewards of performing Shakespeare on socialist amateur stages. Germany, East. 1982. 744

Staging Shakespeare with amateur actors. Germany, East. 1981. 750

Indications of audience and actor composition of a performance of Lucas Fernández' *Auto de la Pasión*. Spain. 1514. 837

Summer productions of Shakespeare and Molière involving professional and amateur actors. Sweden: Södertälje. 1981-1983. 841

Amateur theatre – cont'd

Plays/librettos/scripts

Arne Andersson, creator of local history plays. Sweden: Härnösand, Norberg, Sundsvall. 1970-1983.   1263

Ambigu-Comique, Théâtre de l' (Paris)

Design/technology

Additional duties of scene designer Louis-Jacques Daguerre. France: Paris. 1815-1822.   192

Innovations in stage design by Louis-Jacques Daguerre, including a catalogue of his designs. France. 1709-1850.   193

Amen Corner

Performance/production

Eight critics review Philip Rose's production of the musical *Amen Corner*. USA: New York, NY. 1983.   1800

American Buffalo

Six critics review Arvin Brown's production of David Mamet's play *American Buffalo*. USA: New York, NY. 1983.   960

Plays/librettos/scripts

Study of David Mamet's *American Buffalo*. USA. 1977.   1379

American Indian theatre SEE: Native American theatre

American Repertory Theatre (New York, NY)

Institutions

History of American Repertory Theatre. USA. 1945-1947.   652

American Theatre Association (ATA)

Administration

Resolution concerning billing guidelines of American Theatre Association. USA. 1983.   149

Proposed amendments to by-laws of the American Theatre Association. USA: Minneapolis, MN. 1983.   150

Two additional proposed changes in the by-laws of the American Theatre Association. USA. 1983.   151

Legislative planning, advocacy, audience development and support discussed by American Theatre Association officers. USA: New York, NY. 1983.   152

Design/technology

Report of research among theatrical designers. USA. 1981-1983.   259

Institutions

Activities of the New York ATA convention program on Asian theatre. Asia. USA: New York, NY. 1983.   282

Annual symposium of Mid-America Theatre Conference. USA: Iowa City, IA. 1983.   334

Four new members inducted into American Theatre Association's College of Fellows. USA. 1983.   335

Organization, people and theatres involved in the Army Theatre Arts Association. USA: Fort Polk, LA. 1960-1983.   336

ATA commission opposes creation of a national theatre. USA. 1983.   338

American Theatre Association President's address to 1983 annual business meeting. USA: Minneapolis, MN. 1983.   344

Three awards presented by American Theatre Association. USA. 1983.   347

Seven benefits of a proposed co-publishing program between the University Press of America and the American Theatre Association. USA. 1983.   350

Activities of church and theatre associations to promote 'decent' dramaturgy. USA: New York, NY, Chicago, IL. 1910-1940.   649

Reference materials

New officers of American Theatre Association. USA. 1983.   39

Relation to other fields

American Theatre Association statement of policy on theatre in elementary education. USA. 1983.   71

Inaugural address of American Theatre Association president Bernard S. Rosenblatt calling for support in creating public policy. USA: Minneapolis, MN. 1983.   76

Amphitheatres/arenas

Design/technology

Career of Italian designer and architect Innocente Maraino. Poland: Warsaw, Lvov, Slonim. 1767-1799.   221

Performance spaces

Location of the turret in Greenwich Park. England: London. 1500.   361

Naumachiae, gladiatorial contests, circus races and other acts in ancient Rome. Roman Republic. Roman Empire. 616 B.C.-523 A.D.   387

Town-planning and reconstruction of Roman amphitheatre in Málaga. Spain: Málaga. Roman Empire. 200.   389

Performance/production

Current state of Syrian theatre. Syria: Damascus, Aleppo, Basra. 1983.   445

Amphitruo

Plays/librettos/scripts

Comic mechanism in Plautus' *Amphitruo* and *Casina*. Roman Republic. 254-184 B.C.   1586

Amphitryon

Reasons for different responses to the Amphitryon myth between the 17th and 20th century audiences. France. 1668-1980.   1574

Ancient Greek theatre

Design/technology

Terracotta masks from the sanctuary of Artemis Orthia. Greece: Sparta. 999-560 B.C.   211

Performance/production

Actor's role in theatre and social status in ancient Greece and Rome. Greece. Roman Empire. 600-1 B.C.   790

Relation to other fields

Different social functions of the dramatic theatre in Greece and Rome and their modifications. Greece. Roman Empire. 600-1 B.C.   1455

Ancient Greek theatre SEE ALSO: Geographical-Chronological Index under Greece 600 BC-100 AD

And a Nightingale Sang

Performance/production

Six critics review Terry Kinney's production of C.P. Taylor's play *And a Nightingale Sang*. USA: New York, NY. 1983.   961

And They Put Handcuffs on the Flowers SEE: *Et ils passèrent des menottes aux fleurs*

Anderson, Laurie

Performance/production

Portrait of the performance artist Laurie Anderson. USA: New York, NY. 1983.   1756

Anderson, Miles

Actor Miles Anderson, his wife Lesley Duff, and their work with the Royal Shakespeare Company. UK-England. 1900-1983.   861

Anderson, Robert

Playwright Robert Anderson and director Elia Kazan discuss the creation of *Tea and Sympathy*. USA. 1953.   944

Andersson, Arne

Plays/librettos/scripts

Arne Andersson, creator of local history plays. Sweden: Härnösand, Norberg, Sundsvall. 1970-1983.   1263

Andrews, Julie

Performance/production

Biography of singer-actress Julie Andrews. UK-England. USA. 1935-1983.   1777

Architecture — cont'd

Survey of vaudeville houses in the Fourteenth Street area. USA: New York, NY. 1881-1940. 1983

Plays/librettos/scripts

Comparison between a painting by Diego Velázquez and a play by Calderón de la Barca. Spain. 1625-1651. 1229

Reference materials

List of books related to the restoration of historic theatres. USA. 1935-1983. 44

Description of the Brander Matthews Collection of theatre materials. USA: New York, NY. 1891-1929. 1436

Catalogue of the exhibition on scenery, architecture, dance, opera and public theatres during Pietro Metastasio's life. Italy: Rome. 1698-1782. 1968

Relation to other fields

Religious belief and ritual performance as related to astronomy and architecture. Egypt. 1000-500 B.C. 2107

Theory/criticism

Nature and history of *nō* theatre. Japan. 1300-1980. 549

Archives/libraries

Basic theatrical documents

Discussion of prints and translation of the *fragmenten verzameling* 3-8 found in Zutphen Archive. Netherlands. 1400-1499. 574

Design/technology

SIBMAS papers on collections of designs and scenography. Europe. North America. 1982. 183

History and description of the Motley Theatre and Costume Arts Collection. Discussed at SIBMAS. USA: Urbana, IL. 1982. 247

Institutions

Problems and prospects of the theatre research library at the University of Vienna. Austria: Vienna. 1983. 286

Performance/production

Holdings of the Radio City Music Hall Archives. USA: New York, NY. 1933-1979. 459

Plays/librettos/scripts

Tennessee Williams collection at the University of Texas at Austin. USA: Austin, TX. 1962-1971. 1344

Reference materials

Description of the Stage Design Collection of National Arts Center. Canada: Ottawa, ON. 1969-1982. 16

Description of archive holdings at Brigham Young University including personal papers of Howard Hawks and Dean Jagger. USA: Provo, UT. 1900-1983. 48

References to theatre preserved in the Archives de Paris. France: Paris. 1825-1845. 1407

Collection of Edward Gordon Craig materials available to researchers. UK-England. USA. 1872-1966. 1429

Description of the Brander Matthews Collection of theatre materials. USA: New York, NY. 1891-1929. 1436

Acquisition of Gloria Swanson's silent film archive by University of Texas, Austin. USA: Austin, TX. 1913-1983. 1720

Letters and documents placed in archives concerning Verdi's operas at Teatro La Fenice. Italy: Venice. 1844-1852. 1970

Research/historiography

Methods for collection, documentation and retrieval used at the performing arts archives. India. 1983. 85

Classification system of Biblioteca Nazionale Centrale used by Alessandro Lanari. Italy: Florence. 1815-1870. 1972

Ways that library research can help puppeteers. USA. 1983. 2071

Arden of Faversham

Performance/production

List of productions of plays from English Renaissance drama with brief reviews. North America. Europe. 1982-1983. 822

Plays/librettos/scripts

Realism in *Arden of Faversham*. England: London. 1588-1593. 1689

Arden, John

Plot, structure and action in John Arden's *Serjeant Musgrave's Dance*. UK-England. 1959. 1288

Arena Stage (Washington, DC)

Performance/production

Use of puppets and puppetry techniques in Arena Stage production of *Candide*. USA: Washington, DC. 1983. 2061

Training

Zelda Fichandler expresses her philosophy of theatre education. USA: New York, NY, Washington, DC. 1950-1983. 506

Arendt, Hannah

Theory/criticism

Hannah Arendt's theoretical work with reference to Gotthold Lessing, Bertolt Brecht, Franz Kafka and Isak Dinesen. USA. Europe. 1900-1983. 1518

Århus teater akademi (Århus Theatre Academy)

Institutions

Status report of the Århus Theatre Academy. Denmark: Århus. 1983. 297

Street theatre production of Århus theater akademi in collaboration with Jordcirkus and Johnny Melville. Denmark: Århus. 1982. 298

Ariadone (Japan)

Performance/production

Guest production of Japanese Butō-company Ariadone at Serapionstheater, Vienna. Japan. Austria: Vienna. 1983. 534

Ariosto, Lodovico

Plays/librettos/scripts

Use of vernacular in Ariosto's, Machiavelli's and Ruzante's comedies, as compared with Roman drama. Italy. Roman Empire. 1508-1533. 1584

Aristodemo

Analysis of three tragedies written between Mannerism and the Age of Arcadia. Italy. 1627-1713. 1698

Aristophanes

Theory/criticism

Effect of social conditions on performance styles. USA. Greece. 499 B.C.-1983 A.D. 1517

Aristoteles

Plays/librettos/scripts

Examination of *Hamlet*, I.iv. 13-38 applying Aristotelian criteria. England: London. 1600-1601. 1027

Discussion of Miguel de Cervantes' *The Farce of the Divorce Judge* in view of Aristotelian *mimesis*. Spain. 1547-1616. 1248

Theory/criticism

Dramatic language related to action. England. 1559-1603. 1480

Theory and definition of the comedy genre. Europe. North America. 499 B.C.-1980 A.D. 1601

Arkhurst, Sandy

Relation to other fields

Workshop on the use of puppets in education and therapy. Nigeria: Zaria. 1983. 2067

Arlt, Roberto

Plays/librettos/scripts

Effects of foreign invasion and political instability on theatre. Argentina. 1900-1983. 999

Arms and the Man

Function of props and settings in plays by George Bernard Shaw. UK-England. 1894-1907. 1281

Army Theatre Arts Association (ATAA)

Institutions

Organization, people and theatres involved in the Army Theatre Arts Association. USA: Fort Polk, LA. 1960-1983. 336

Arneway, John

Plays/librettos/scripts

Possible authorship of a lost Chester Corpus Christi play. England: Chester. 1268-1375. 1037

Arnold, Andy

Administration

Andy Arnold on his work with Theatre Workshop in Edinburgh. UK-Scotland. 1983. 556

Arrabal, Fernando

Plays/librettos/scripts

Study of Fernando Arrabal's playwriting technique. France. 1932. 1644

Arrau, Claudio

Performance/production

Pianist Claudio Arrau recalls operas and singers he has heard. Europe. USA. 1903-1983. 1850

Arrom, José

Institutions

Development of nationalistic and experimental theatre in Latin America. South America. North America. 1800-1983. 618

Artaud, Antonin

Performance/production

History of directing. Europe. 1882-1982. 708

Artistic movements and critical thought that shaped modern directing. Europe. 1914-1940. 715

Plays/librettos/scripts

Use of body language in the theatre by Samuel Beckett, Antonin Artaud, Etienne Decroux and Jerzy Grotowski. Europe. 1930-1980. 1638

Negation of the theatre by Samuel Beckett, Antonin Artaud and Carmelo Bene. France. Italy. 1925-1960. 1643

Contradiction in personal and artistic life of Antonin Artaud. France. 1921-1948. 1645

Graphic and linguistic structure of Antonin Artaud's last writings. France. 1938-1948. 1646

Theory/criticism

Vocal emission as a mode of theatricalization in experimental theatre. Canada. 1970-1979. 1669

Artieda, Andrés Rey de

Plays/librettos/scripts

Staging and scenic practices in the plays of Lope de Vega's forerunners and contemporaries. Spain: Valencia. 1500-1699. 1253

Artistic directors

Administration

Four artistic directors discuss theatre relationship with community. Canada: Regina, SK, Vancouver, BC, Toronto, ON, Calgary, AB. 1983. 553

Interview with the new artistic director and literary advisor for the Iron Theatre (Glasgow). UK-Scotland. 1973-1983. 559

Institutions

Events leading to Roger Hodgman's resignation as Artistic Director of Vancouver Playhouse. Canada: Vancouver, BC. 1979-1983. 585

Concepts of and preparations for Théâtre de l'Europe, managed by Giorgio Strehler. France: Paris. 1983. 596

Peter Hall's role as artistic director of the National Theatre, including devising the repertory and obtaining funds. UK-England: London. 1973-1983. 636

Performance/production

Interview with Steven Thomas, artistic director of Opera Hamilton. Canada: Hamilton, ON. 1983. 1844

Account of the Hector Berlioz festival, and Serge Baudo, director. France: Lyons. 1960-1983. 1862

Arts Club, The (Vancouver, BC)

Administration

Four artistic directors discuss theatre relationship with community. Canada: Regina, SK, Vancouver, BC, Toronto, ON, Calgary, AB. 1983. 553

ARTS SEE: Arts Recognition and Talent Search

Aruna

Plays/librettos/scripts

Censorship involving Jerzy Hulewicz' play *Aruna*, produced at Municipal Theatre of Cracow. Poland: Kraków. 1925. 1217

As You Like It

Performance/production

Catalan version of Shakespeare's *As You Like It* by Teatre Lliure. Spain. 1983. 1531

Plays/librettos/scripts

Interpretations of locale of scenes in *As You Like It*. England. 1599-1600. 1038

Animal nature and eating habits of characters in Shakespeare's plays. England. 1590-1613. 1058

Ashes

Epic structure in contemporary drama. UK. 1968-1981. 1275

Associació Wagneriana (Wagnerian Association)

Performance/production

First performance of Richard Wagner's *Lohengrin* and the debate generated with followers of Giuseppe Verdi. Spain. 1862-1901. 1886

History of Wagnerian study and performance. Spain. 1878-1926. 1887

Associations SEE: Institutions, associations

Associazione Nazionale dei Critici di Teatro

Plays/librettos/scripts

Essays on Vitaliano Brancati's plays and motion picture scripts. Italy: Catania. 1924-1954. 1160

Associazione Teatri Emilia-Romagna (ATER)

Administration

Network of subscription among several theatres. Italy. 1981. 555

Astronomy

Relation to other fields

Religious belief and ritual performance as related to astronomy and architecture. Egypt. 1000-500 B.C. 2107

ATAA SEE: Army Theatre Arts Association

Atakschiew, Hussein

Performance/production

Tendencies of Bertolt Brecht stage interpretations. Germany, East. USSR. Italy. 1956-1983. 747

Atcher, William

Theory/criticism

Morality of Restoration comedy. England. 1670-1700. 1599

ATER SEE: Associazione Teatri Emilia-Romagna

Atlas, Larry

Performance/production

Five critics review Jack Hofsiss' production of Larry Atlas' play *Total Abandon*. USA: New York, NY: cd. 1983. 951

Attila

Reference materials

Letters and documents placed in archives concerning Verdi's operas at Teatro La Fenice. Italy: Venice. 1844-1852. 1970

SUBJECT INDEX

Aub, Max

Plays/librettos/scripts

Two reports about Max Aub's play *Blindman's Buff*. Spain. 1970-1983. 1225

Auber, Daniel François

Phenomenon of Grand Opera is examined in view of its music, librettos and staging. France. 1828-1865. 1942

Auden, Wystan Hugh

Theory/criticism

Wystan Hugh Auden's poetic meditation on art as related to Shakespeare's *The Tempest* and Kierkegaardian thought. UK-England. 1939-1962. 1511

Audience

Administration

Discussion of symbiotic relationship between theatre and community. Canada. 1983. 120

Efforts of Jack Lang, Minister of Culture, to decentralize theatre. France. 1982-1983. 124

Legislative planning, advocacy, audience development and support discussed by American Theatre Association officers. USA: New York, NY. 1983. 152

Four artistic directors discuss theatre relationship with community. Canada: Regina, SK, Vancouver, BC, Toronto, ON, Calgary, AB. 1983. 553

Design/technology

Performance spaces and effect of scenery on the audience. Europe. 1970-1983. 184

Institutions

Annual report of the Austrian Federal Theatres. Austria: Vienna. 1982-1983. 284

Richard Ouzounian attempts to restore community interest in Manitoba Theatre Centre. Canada: Winnipeg, MB. 1958-1983. 292

History of Spanish-language repertory troupe activities in Texas. USA. Mexico. 1848-1900. 352

Performance/production

Changes in acting and audiences at Theatre Royal. Canada: Montreal, PQ. 1829-1839. 686

Marxist theory applied in comparison of public theatres in England and Spain. England. Spain. 1576-1635. 696

Ingmar Bergman's use of text, stage and audience. Sweden. Germany, West. 1944. 845

Intimate relationship with the audience in the work designed for performance video. USA. 1980. 1723

Children's Theatre Association of America standards for productions for young audiences. USA. 1983. 2056

Plays/librettos/scripts

Appearance of Banquo's ghost in *Macbeth* clarifies the relation of the audience to the play. England. 1605-1606. 1034

Essays on Restoration theatre and drama, with devised criteria for evaluation. England. 1660-1800. 1046

Characterization and setting used to challenge audience views in George Bernard Shaw's *Major Barbara*. UK-England. 1907. 1287

Universal myths in *Pygmalion* as encouragement for the audience to break from settled beliefs. UK-England. 1914. 1301

Shaw's manipulation of audience reaction in *Major Barbara*. UK-England. 1907. 1307

The character of Arlene in Marsha Norman's play *Getting Out*, and her effect on the audience. USA. 1981. 1372

Relation to other fields

Introduction of Luigi Pirandello's play *Tonight We Improvise*. Italy. 1930. 1458

Theory/criticism

Spectator at the center of semiological network of theoretical approaches to theatre. France. 1982. 99

Comprehensive discussion of theatre performance. Spain. 1983. 107

Audience SEE ALSO: Classed Entries 164-174, 566-569, 1604, 1738, 1816, 2034.

Audience areas

Design/technology

Additional duties of scene designer Louis-Jacques Daguerre. France: Paris. 1815-1822. 192

Performance spaces

Placement of the prompter's and royal boxes at Drury Lane by David Garrick. UK-England: London. 1747-1776. 392

Restoration of theatre chairs. USA. 1983. 409

Audience behavior SEE: Behavior/psychology, audience

Audience composition

Audience

Political theatre for audiences of common age, economic and ethnic background. Germany, West. 1960-1983. 167

Audience development survey. USA: Atlanta, GA, Baton Rouge, LA, Columbia, SC, Memphis, TN. 1983. 170

Sociological studies suggest that democratization of the arts has not taken place. USA. 1830-1982. 173

Sign interpretation at the New York City Opera. USA: New York, NY. 1979. 1816

Characteristics of a typical children's audience. USA. 1983. 2034

Institutions

Structure, aims and methods of animation by Dramatisches Zentrum (Vienna). Austria: Vienna. 1972-1983. 287

Performance/production

Topical production of Gerhart Hauptmann's *The Weavers* in working class neighborhood. Germany, West: Recklinghausen. 1979. 768

Indications of audience and actor composition of a performance of Lucas Fernández' *Auto de la Pasión*. Spain. 1514. 837

Relation to other fields

Class-conscious approach to theatre. Germany, West. 1983. 56

Theory/criticism

Political stagnation and bureaucratization of theatre critics. Sweden. 1960-1983. 109

Audience Development Committee (AUDELCO)

Administration

Activities of the Audience Development Committee. USA: New York, NY. 1983. 153

Audience psychology SEE: Behavior/psychology, audience

Audience reactions/comments

Audience

Process by which audience assigns meaning to a performance. Italy. 1983. 168

Testing undergraduates' reactions to set designs. USA: Athens, GA. 1974. 174

Modern productions of Renaissance drama. Europe. 1982. 566

Study of a small rural audience of regional theatre. Finland: Joensuu. 1979. 568

Speculative argument for adopting a rationalist account for spectator knowledge, based on Konstantin Stanislavskij's treatment of the question. USA. 1982. 569

Institutions

Innovative projects of Welfare State Company, and community benefits. UK-England. 1983. 1742

Performance/production

Production of *Wiespätissn*, a peace play, and audience reactions. Germany, West: West Berlin. 1982. 783

Performances, editing and audience response to Fanny Kemble's first American tour. USA: Boston, MA, New York, NY, Philadelphia, PA. 1849-1850. 935

Audience reactions/comments — cont'd

Shift of public interest from Broadway to Off Broadway. USA: New York, NY. 1983. 1786

First performance of Richard Wagner's *Lohengrin* and the debate generated with followers of Giuseppe Verdi. Spain. 1862-1901. 1886

History of Wagnerian study and performance. Spain. 1878-1926. 1887

Religious and civil popular entertainment, with documented appendixes. Spain: Girona. 1300-1799. 1988

Attitude of Western audiences to the performances of native Africans in various settings. USA. UK. 1800-1899. 1994

Plays/librettos/scripts

Audience reaction and cancellation of tour of Somerset Maugham's *The Land of Promise*. Canada. USA. UK-England. 1914. 1015

Reception of *Hamlet* in China and problems in production. China. 1903-1983. 1019

Shakespeare's historical plays and the reaction of the Elizabethan audience. England. 1590-1613. 1031

Bertolt Brecht's experiments in audience education through his plays. Germany, East. 1954-1956. 1147

Bernard Dadié's plays intended for African audiences, bewilder Europeans. Ivory Coast. 1933-1973. 1194

Lack of familiarity in Britain with the work of Michel de Ghelderode. UK-England. Belgium. 1957-1982. 1292

Assessment of dramaturgy in English-speaking theatre. USA. 1983. 1361

World-wide response to A.R. Gurney Jr.'s dramas of New England life. USA. 1983. 1365

Reasons for different responses to the Amphitryon myth between the 17th and 20th century audiences. France. 1668-1980. 1574

Aesthetic imbalance resulting from Pierre Corneille's concern for propriety in *Théodore*. France. 1606-1684. 1578

Richard Wagner's life and work in Paris. France: Paris. 1830-1897. 1944

Research/historiography

Categories devised to measure young people's responses to children's theatre productions. USA. 1983. 1474

Theory/criticism

Physical experience and aesthetic perception of body movement. France. 1889. 100

Flaws in Latin American theatre criticism. Chile. North America. 1960-1983. 1479

Phenomenology of audience reception of Sam Shepard's *Curse of the Starving Class*. USA: New York, NY, Buffalo, NY, Tempe, AZ. 1982. 1519

Audience/performer relationship

Audience

International Theatre Institute seminar on theatre's relation to audience. Cuba: Havana. 1983. 166

Interaction needed among playwright, audience and actors. USA. 1983. 171

Study of a small rural audience of regional theatre. Finland: Joensuu. 1979. 568

Evolution of *Gros Mourn* by Newfoundland Mummers Troupe. Canada. 1973. 1604

Performance artist and audience relationship in night clubs. UK-England: London. 1983. 1738

Performance spaces

Foyer of the Palast der Republik used as performance space. Germany, East: East Berlin. 1983. 370

Project for a new studio to optimize the audience/performer relationship. Germany, West: West Berlin. 1983. 1834

Performance/production

Actor-audience relationship in productions by Jacques Copeau, Bertolt Brecht and Russian directors. France. USSR. Germany. 1900-1956. 726

Marxist orientation in Shakespearean plays on German stage. Germany, East. 1982. 748

Indications of audience and actor composition of a performance of Lucas Fernández' *Auto de la Pasión*. Spain. 1514. 837

Director of Polka Children's Theatre discusses children's attitude to plays and puppets. UK. 1983. 852

Physical intimacy and direct contact with the audiences in contemporary American theatre. USA. 1969-1980. 912

Plays/librettos/scripts

Approaches to drama for young people. UK-England. 1970-1983. 1296

Relation to other fields

Political ramifications of the theatrical patronage of Louis XIII and Cardinal de Richelieu. France. 1610-1643. 54

Theory/criticism

Performance and communication: problems of semiotic approach. Europe. 1983. 95

Trend toward mobility and profanation in contemporary theatre. Europe. 1970-1980. 96

Comprehensive discussion of theatre performance. Spain. 1983. 107

Semiotic study of the specific nature of theatre in relation to other arts and audience interaction with it. Spain. 1983. 108

Study of genesis, development, structural components and consequences of theatre-drama performed by the Black workers. South Africa, Republic of. 1981-1983. 1673

Audio forms

Performance/production

Interaction of technology and popular entertainment. USA. 1900-1982. 1995

Audio forms SEE ALSO: Classed Entries: MEDIA — Audio forms

Audio-visual aids

Design/technology

Choosing audio-visual materials for exhibits. Discussed at SIBMAS. France: Paris. 1982. 1705

Audio-visual SEE ALSO: Classed Entries: MEDIA

Audureau, Jean

Performance/production

Aspects of Jean Audureau's *Happiness* produced at the Comédie-Française. France: Paris. 1983. 739

Auerbach, Nina

Theory/criticism

Significance of gender in feminist criticism with reference to historical materialism, deconstruction and phenomenon of cross-dressing in theatre. USA. France. UK-England. 1983. 1520

Aufstieg und Fall der Stadt Mahoganny (Rise and Fall of the City of Mahoganny)

Relation to other fields

Circus as a staging device for a political satire. USSR. Germany. Italy. 1914-1930. 1668

Augier, Émile

Plays/librettos/scripts

Émile Augier's *Maître Guérin* is seen as the most likely source for the ending of *A Doll's House*. Norway. France. 1864-1879. 1212

Austin, Gilbert

Performance/production

Examination of John Philip Kemble's vocal technique. England. 1780-1817. 415

Australian Theatre Historical Society

Performance spaces

Tour of theatres by the Australian Theatre Historical Society. Australia: Melbourne. 1982-1983. 356

Auto de la Pasión

Performance/production

Indications of audience and actor composition of a performance of Lucas Fernández' *Auto de la Pasión*. Spain. 1514. 837

Autos sacramentales

Marxist theory applied in comparison of public theatres in England and Spain. England. Spain. 1576-1635. 696

Indications of audience and actor composition of a performance of Lucas Fernández' *Auto de la Pasión*. Spain. 1514. 837

Plays/librettos/scripts

Portrayal of Catholic dogma and virtues of God and the Trinity in Calderón de la Barca's *autos sacramentales*. Spain. 1626. 1232

Autumn Angel Repertory Company (Toronto, ON)

Institutions

Survey of alternative theatres. Canada: Toronto, ON. 1979-1983. 296

Avant-garde theatre

Study of the nature and the international scope of theatre festivals. UK-England: London. 1983. 330

History of Puerto Rican avant-garde theatre. Puerto Rico. 1811-1970. 617

History and analysis of three productions by the avant-garde theatre group Falso Movimento. Italy. 1977-1983. 1607

Performance/production

Influence of Cubism on staging and scenery. Europe. 1900. 421

Productions and presentational style of the Pip Simmons avant-garde theatre company. UK. 1968-1980. 446

Mordecai Gorelik discusses stage fright and compares acting styles. USA. 1983. 461

Analysis and critique of avant-garde trends in theatre. USA. 1970-1983. 470

Six essays on the productions and artistic views held by leading European directors. Europe. 1960-1980. 1615

Self-reflexivity of Helsinki avant-garde theatre. Finland: Helsinki. 1978-1983. 1616

Comprehensive study of productions by Tadeusz Kantor's experimental theatre group Cricot 2 and Kantor's philosophy. Poland. 1975-1980. 1626

Interview with playwright-director Tadeusz Kantor about *Wielopole, Wielopole*. Poland: Wielopole. 1982. 1628

Production styles of directors Peter Brook and Tadeusz Kantor. USA: New York, NY. France: Paris. Poland: Wielopole. 1982. 1632

Possession, ecstasy and dionysiac practices applied by avant-garde theatre groups. North America. Europe. 1700-1982. 2098

Plays/librettos/scripts

New forms of realism. Europe. North America. 1970. 1639

Theory/criticism

Political stagnation and bureaucratization of theatre critics. Sweden. 1960-1983. 109

Articles on performance theory and practice. 1976-1983. 1477

Theoretical and practical aspects of theatre of invention. Europe. 1968-1983. 1670

Media as subject (theme) and object (medium to transport the message) of aesthetic treatment. Europe. USA. 1983. 1707

Averulino SEE: Filarete, Il

Avignon Festival

Institutions

Study of the nature and the international scope of theatre festivals. UK-England: London. 1983. 330

Awards

Distinguished Service award presented to Waterloo Community Playhouse. USA: Waterloo, IA. 1983. 337

Three awards presented by American Theatre Association. USA. 1983. 347

New awards — Distinguished Play Award and Campton Bell Award — honor those serving children's theatre. USA. 1983. 354

Center Stage wins top honor in Toyama International Amateur Theatre Festival with *Ain't Misbehavin'*. Japan: Toyama. USA: Omaha, NE. 1983. 1772

Performance/production

Articles on theatrical career of Giorgio Albertazzi, recipient of Armando Curzio award. Italy. 1949-1982. 808

Reference materials

List of theatre companies, playwriting awards and grants. USA. 1983. 1439

Awards, Tony

Plays/librettos/scripts

Only three Tony-Award-winning plays reflect feminist ideology. USA: New York, NY. UK-England. 1960-1979. 1374

Ayckbourn, Alan

Alan Ayckbourn's plays: their seriousness. UK-England. 1970-1979. 1306

Comic techniques in Alan Ayckbourn's *The Norman Conquests*. UK-England. 1974. 1589

Az Ikszek

Institutions

Polish theatre under Russian rule as reflected in György Spiró's novel *Az Ikszek*. Poland: Warsaw. Russia. Hungary. 1815-1829. 325

Azarjan, K.

Performance/production

Productions of Russian classics by Bulgarian directors. Bulgaria: Sofia. 1960-1970. 681

Ba-Kathir, Ahmad

Plays/librettos/scripts

Shakespeare's knowledge of Arab world and influence on later regional writers. England. Arabia. 1606-1981. 1075

Baal

Performance/production

Solter's concept for staging Bertolt Brecht's *Baal*. Germany, East. 1983. 745

Directors on Bertolt Brecht's dramas. Germany, East: Schwerin, Erfurt, East Berlin. 1983. 754

Babe, Thomas

Five critics review Joseph Papp's production of Thomas Babe's play *Buried Inside Extra*. USA: New York, NY. 1983. 982

Babutunde, Obba

Interview with principal male stars of *Dreamgirls*. USA: New York, NY. 1983. 1778

Baby

Ten critics review Richard Maltby's production of *Baby*. USA: New York, NY. 1983. 1805

Baby with the Bathwater

Five critics review Jerry Zak's production of Christopher Durang's play *Baby with the Bathwater*. USA: New York, NY. 1983. 1544

Bacchae, The

Plays/librettos/scripts

Relationship between costume changes and change in wearer's fate. Greece. 405 B.C. 1694

Wole Soyinka's adaptation of Euripides' *The Bacchae*. Nigeria. 1973. 1699

Wole Soyinka's plays echo themes of Aeschylus, Euripides and Shakespeare. Nigeria. Greece: Athens. UK-England: London. 1980. 1700

Bach, Johann Sebastian

Analysis of John Neumeier's production of *St. Matthew Passion*. Germany, West: Hamburg. USA: New York, NY. 1982-1983. 521

Bacon, Francis

'Great Method' used by Bertolt Brecht in his plays, and influences from others. Germany. 1918-1956. 1130

Bacon, Francis — cont'd

Theory/criticism

Bertolt Brecht's perception of the philosophy of the Enlightenment. Germany. 1848-1956.   1498

Bahr, Hermann

Reformers on their theories. Europe. 1870-1910.   98

Bakst, Leon

Design/technology

Three costume and two set designs by Leon Bakst for ballet. 1911-1923.   175

Balade du Grand Macabre, La (Ballad of the Grand Macabre, The)

Plays/librettos/scripts

Influences on Michel de Ghelderode from his national culture and Bertolt Brecht. Belgium. 1919-1962.   1011

Balanchine, George

Performance/production

Autobiographical survey by choreographer Lincoln Kirstein. USA. India: Marrakesh. Europe. 1916-1949.   514

Production elements and choreography of *On Your Toes*. USA. 1982.   1782

George Balanchine's contribution to dance in musical theatre. USA: New York, NY. 1929-1962.   1787

Plays/librettos/scripts

Shift in dramatic emphasis in Igor Strawinsky's *Apollon Musagete* due to sets, costumes and choreography. USA: Washington, DC, New York, NY. 1927-1979.   522

Balcon, Le (Balcony, The)

Performance/production

Jean Genet's *The Balcony* at Schillertheater Berlin, directed by Hans Neuenfels. Germany, West: West Berlin. 1983.   773

Baldessari, Luciano

Design/technology

Luciano Baldessari's architectural and theatrical works. Italy. 1923-1972.   217

Ballester, Manuel Méndeo

Institutions

History of Puerto Rican avant-garde theatre. Puerto Rico. 1811-1970.   617

Ballet

Design/technology

Three costume and two set designs by Leon Bakst for ballet. 1911-1923.   175

Costumes of Teatro alla Scala and chronology of its costumers. Italy: Milan. 1947-1982.   1819

Institutions

Dance training at Theatre Academy of Finland. Finland: Helsinki. 1910-1983.   516

Performance/production

Contributors to dance reform in French theatre. France: Paris. 1752-1781.   518

History of equestrian ballet with an emphasis on 17th century. Europe. 1559-1854.   1735

Work of the director/choreographer N.M. Forreger in the musical theatre. USSR. 1929-1939.   1930

Theory/criticism

Collected theory and criticism by women in theatre on women in theatre. USA. UK. 1850-1983.   114

Ballet SEE ALSO: Classed Entries: DANCE — Ballet

Ballet training SEE: Training, ballet

Ballhof Hanover

Performance spaces

New aesthetic forms of staging. Germany, West: Bremen, Bochum, Hanover. 1962-1980.   374

Ballo in Maschera, Un

Performance/production

Photographs, cast lists, synopsis and discography of Metropolitan Opera production of *Un Ballo in Maschera*. USA: New York, NY. 1983.   1899

Bandia Woli

Relation to other fields

Description of *Bandia Woli*, a traditional folk drama. Senegal. USA. 1976.   2100

Bania (Bath House)

Circus as a staging device for a political satire. USSR. Germany. Italy. 1914-1930.   1668

Banvard, John

Performance/production

John Banvard's autobiography reveals harsh conditions endured by showboat performers. USA. 1833-1836.   1992

Barabbas

Plays/librettos/scripts

Denunciation of collective violence reflected in the role of sacrifice in Michel de Ghelderode's *Barabbas*. Belgium. 1929.   1010

Baraka, Imamu Amiri (Jones, LeRoi)

Similarities between the plays *The Dutchman* and *Zoo Story*. USA: New York, NY. 1964.   1350

Two principal female archetypes of Imamu Amiri Baraka's drama. USA. 1964-1978.   1375

Theory/criticism

Imamu Amiri Baraka's links to aesthetically white culture. USA. 1969.   1516

Imamu Amiri Baraka's aesthetics find their origins in Blues music. USA. 1963-1967.   1521

Barba, Eugenio

Institutions

Evolution and theories of Odin Teatret. Sweden. 1964-1979.   621

Plays/librettos/scripts

Collected materials on Eugenio Barba and Odin Teatret. Sweden. 1964-1979.   1258

Barbiere di Siviglia, Il

Performance/production

Photographs, cast lists, synopsis and discography of Metropolitan Opera production of *The Barber of Seville*. USA: New York, NY. 1983.   1902

Barish, Jonas

Modern analyses of Konstantin Stanislavskij's acting theory. Russia. USSR. 1904-1983.   831

Barkhin, Sergei

Design/technology

Recent scene designs by Jochen Finke and Sergei Barkhin. USSR. Germany, East. 1970-1983.   277

Barkworth, Peter

Performance/production

Autobiography of actor Peter Barkworth. UK. 1929-1983.   850

Barletta, Leónidas

Institutions

Development of nationalistic and experimental theatre in Latin America. South America. North America. 1800-1983.   618

Barlow, Curtis

Curtis Barlow as director of Professional Association of Canadian Theatres. Canada. 1983. 294

Barnum, Phineas Taylor (P.T.)

Performance/production

Importation of African Blacks for exhibition as 'exotics' and evolution of this practice into a circus side-show. USA. 1810-1926. 2014

Reference materials

Letters of circus entrepreneur P.T. Barnum. USA. 1832-1891. 2016

Baroque theatre

Design/technology

Supplementary materials to exhibit of Baroque theatre and stage design. Italy. 1600. 219

Performance spaces

Use of urban areas to mount theatre spectacles. Italy: Palermo. 1500-1600. 381

Performance/production

Conductor John Eliot Gardiner discusses baroque opera. England. 1597-1759. 1849

Plays/librettos/scripts

Influence of Siglo de Oro on German pre-romantic theatre. Germany. Spain. 1765-1832. 1135

Examination of Baroque themes and writers. Germany. 1618-1685. 1581

Barrault, Jean-Louis

Performance/production

Eastern and Western techniques in productions by Jean-Louis Barrault. France. 1935. 730

Barrie, James M.

Importance of boy actor playing the title role in *Peter Pan*. UK-England. 1902-1983. 867

Bartet, Isaac

Performance spaces

New documents on Cockpit-in-Court. England: London. 1660. 367

Barthes, Roland

Theory/criticism

Spectator at the center of semiological network of theoretical approaches to theatre. France. 1982. 99

Semiotic comparison of dramatic theory, philosophy and performance. USA. Europe. 1850-1956. 1515

Bartholomew Fair

Plays/librettos/scripts

Shakespearean influence on Ben Jonson's *Bartholomew Fair*. England. 1614. 1033

Bartolucci, Giuseppe

Relation to other fields

Zerka Moreno's psychodrama in Italy. USA: New York, NY. Italy: Rome. 1960-1983. 1666

Barton, John

Performance/production

John Barton's staging of *Hamlet* influenced by Anne Righter. UK-England. 1961-1980. 860

Plays/librettos/scripts

Traditional approaches to acting and staging as clarifying methods for complex Shakespeare scenes. UK-England: Stratford-upon-Avon. 1980. 1702

Basel Stadttheater

Institutions

New season's productions at the Basel Stadttheater. Switzerland: Basel. 1983. 622

Basement Group, The (Newcastle)

Performance/production

Performance art and organization of events staged by The Basement Group. UK-England: Newcastle upon Tyne. 1983. 1748

Basic theatrical documents

Administration

Intervention of censorship in cinema, radio and theatre. Italy. 1924-1982. 140

Letters and documents concerning performances at local opera houses. USA: Grand Forks, ND, Crookston, MN. 1890-1899. 155

Design/technology

Three costume and two set designs by Leon Bakst for ballet. 1911-1923. 175

Performance/production

Two newly discovered 'Players Lists' in the Lord Chamberlain's Registers. England. 1708-1710. 418

Impressions of theatre and popular entertainment by a French visitor. England: London. 1754. 419

Activities of King's Company and their staging of George Etherege's *The Man of Mode*. UK-Scotland: Edinburgh. 1678-1680. 448

Aspects of Korean mask-dance theatre, including an annotated translation of *Pongsan T'alch'um*. Korea. 1700-1983. 535

Documents of Max Reinhardt's production of Goethe's *Faust*. Austria: Salzburg. 1933-1937. 667

Documentation on Ruben Fraga's production of *The Tower of Babel* by the Dramatic Center Vienna. Austria: Vienna. 1980-1983. 670

Notes on Helene Weigel's letters as resources for theatre history. Germany. 1900-1971. 741

Brief comments on and German translation of Edward Bond's *Summer*. Germany, West: Munich. 1983. 764

Documentation of Ingmar Bergman's tripartite theatre project. Sweden. Germany, West: Munich. 1981. 844

Peter Hall's diaries regarding his productions. UK-England. 1930. 880

Writings by the founders of the Living Theatre. USA. Europe. 1952-1962. 1631

Production journal of *King Lear*. Canada: Stratford, ON. 1979. 1676

Opera production textbook. Italy. 1597-1699. 1881

English translations of *commedia dell'arte* lazzi and two complete scenarios. Italy. 1734. 2018

Plays/librettos/scripts

Involvement of the audience in Ben Jonson's work as satirist and playwright, with some playtexts from the First Folio. England. 1598-1614. 1042

Collected materials on Eugenio Barba and Odin Teatret. Sweden. 1964-1979. 1258

Description of a letter by playwright T.W. Robertson. UK-England: London. 1862. 1280

Tennessee Williams collection at the University of Texas at Austin. USA: Austin, TX. 1962-1971. 1344

Unpublished scene from Richard Cumberland's *The Wheel of Fortune*. England: London. 1795. 1557

Research/historiography

First volume of a general history of theatre in Europe, accompanied by documents. Europe. 534 B.C.-1499 A.D. 81

Basic theatrical documents SEE ALSO: Classed Entries 570-575, 1605, 2017.

Basic Training of Pavlo Hummel, The

Plays/librettos/scripts

Modern plays set in confining institutions. North America. Europe. 1900-1983. 1200

Basoches

Performance/production

Links between popular forms of medieval drama and theatrical presentations during the carnival period. France. 1200-1599. 2007

Bass, Eric

Plays/librettos/scripts

Review of puppet plays for adults by Eric Bass presented at the Uppsala Festival. USA: New York, NY. Sweden: Uppsala. 1970-1983. 2066

Bath House SEE: *Bania*

Batlle i Gordó

Design/technology

Development of Wagnerian stage design and groups and movements involved in its production. Spain. 1882-1960. 1822

Battle of Arminius, The SEE: *Hermannschlacht*

Baty, Gaston

Plays/librettos/scripts

Italian translation of Walter Benjamin's articles, aphorisms and other notes on theatrical events. Europe. 1926-1927. 1087

Baudo, Serge

Performance/production

Account of the Hector Berlioz festival, and Serge Baudo, director. France: Lyons. 1960-1983. 1862

Bauhaus

Artistic movements and critical thought that shaped modern directing. Europe. 1914-1940. 715

Bausch, Pina

Institutions

History of dance group L'Étoile du Nord. Sweden. USA. 1636-1983. 524

Bay, Howard

Four new members inducted into American Theatre Association's College of Fellows. USA. 1983. 335

Bayreuth Festspiele

Design/technology

Technical realization of the main platform for the sets of *Der Ring des Nibelungen*. Germany, West: Bayreuth. 1983. 1817

Various safety requirements for the construction of the platform for the production of *Der Ring des Nibelungen*. Germany, West: Bayreuth. 1983. 1818

Performance spaces

Influence of Bayreuth Festival on architecture of Kitchener-Waterloo Symphony Hall. Canada: Kitchener, ON. 1983. 1833

Performance/production

One hundred years of recordings and Bayreuth Festival performances of Wagner's *Parsifal*. Germany: Bayreuth. 1882-1982. 1864

Photographs and personnel of Bayreuth Festival production of *Siegfried*. Germany, West: Bayreuth. 1980. 1866

Photographs and personnel of Bayreuth Festival production of *Götterdämmerung*. Germany, West: Bayreuth. 1980. 1867

Photographs and personnel of Bayreuth Festival production of *Die Walküre*. Germany, West: Bayreuth. 1980. 1869

Peter Hall's production of Richard Wagner's *Ring* at Bayreuth Festspielhaus. Germany, West: Bayreuth. 1983. 1870

1983 Bayreuth *Der Ring des Nibelungen*, directed by Peter Hall, conducted by Georg Solti. Germany, West: Bayreuth. 1983. 1873

Reference materials

Source materials on Richard Wagner's influence on theatre. Germany. Austria. USA. 1869-1976. 1966

Bayrische Staatsoper (Munich)

Design/technology

Construction and operating procedures of new sound systems at the München Nationaltheater. Germany, West: Munich. 1983. 199

BBC Scotland

Institutions

Interview with Rod Graham, head of BBC Scotland's television drama department. UK-Scotland. 1946-1983. 1722

Bean, Anne

Performance/production

Mixing popular entertaining, particularly rock music, with performance art. UK-England. 1970-1980. 1749

Beard, James

James Beard, American cooking expert, recalls opera performances he has seen. USA: New York, NY. 1983. 1928

Beardsley, Aubrey Vincent

Plays/librettos/scripts

Revolutionary vision of collaborative effort between Oscar Wilde and illustrator Aubrey Beardsley. UK. 1894-1900. 1273

Bearwards

Administration

Accounts of payment to assorted entertainers performing for Lord Berkeley. England: Coventry. 1593-1605. 122

Beaumont, Francis

Plays/librettos/scripts

Relationship between Jacobean tragedy and interpolated masque. England. 1600-1625. 1691

Becher, Johannes R.

Anti-war plays by Bertolt Brecht and Johannes R. Becher on German invasion of the Soviet Union. Germany. 1942-1943. 1126

Beck, Julian

Institutions

Reflections on the significance of The Open Theatre by several of its performers, writers and critical advisers. USA: New York, NY. 1963-1973. 1613

Performance/production

Writings by the founders of the Living Theatre. USA. Europe. 1952-1962. 1631

Beckerman, Bernard

Plays/librettos/scripts

Segmental analysis of Anton Čechov's plays. Russia. 1860-1904. 1222

Becket

Performance/production

Analysis of C.V. Stanford's incidental music for *Becket*. UK-England: London. 1893. 872

Beckett, Samuel

Interview with and influences on actor Bernhard Minetti, including production of *Faust*. Germany, East: East Berlin. 1982-1983. 751

Samuel Beckett's *Happy Days* with Giulia Lazzarini at Piccolo Teatro di Milano, directed by Giorgio Strehler. Italy: Milan. 1983. 807

Four critics review Alan Schneider's production of three Samuel Beckett plays. USA: New York, NY. 1983. 928

Plays/librettos/scripts

Actor's role in plays of Samuel Beckett. Europe. 1957. 1095

Materialistic reading of Samuel Beckett's work. France. 1938. 1107

Influence of Shakespeare, Beckett and Wittgenstein on the plays of Tom Stoppard. UK-England. 1963-1979. 1302

Krapp's Last Tape by Samuel Beckett as a parody of both performance and themes in poetry. UK-Ireland. 1957. 1321

Analysis of Samuel Beckett's earliest typescript of *Eh Joe* to revision as *Ghost Trio*. UK-Ireland. France. 1958. 1323

Analysis of Samuel Beckett's *Not I*. UK-Ireland. France. 1971. 1329

Themes of and influences on Sam Shepard's plays. USA. 1943-1983. 1343

Beckett, Samuel — cont'd

Irreverent aspects of Irish comedy seen through the works of 14 playwrights. Eire. UK-Ireland. 1840-1965.　　　1555

Variations on the bedroom farce form in the works of Eugène Labiche, Roger Vitrac and Samuel Beckett. France. 1870-1983.　1573

Comic irony and anti-heroes in Irish comedy and influence on Harold Pinter, Samuel Beckett and Tom Stoppard. UK-Ireland. Eire. 1900-1940.　　　1593

Humanist examination of Samuel Beckett's plays. Europe. 1906-1983.　　　1637

Use of body language in the theatre by Samuel Beckett, Antonin Artaud, Etienne Decroux and Jerzy Grotowski. Europe. 1930-1980.　　　1638

Epistemological paradox in Samuel Beckett's plays. Europe. 1906-1983.　　　1640

Negation of the theatre by Samuel Beckett, Antonin Artaud and Carmelo Bene. France. Italy. 1925-1960.　　　1643

Before Breakfast

Eugene O'Neill plays that have been made into films. USA. 1916.　　　1347

Befristeten, Die (Limited, The)

Critical analysis of three of Elias Canetti's plays. Austria. 1932-1964.　　　1008

Problems in stage adaptation of Elias Canetti's The Limited. Germany, West: Stuttgart. 1983.　　　1150

Beggar's Opera, The

Essays on Restoration theatre and drama, with devised criteria for evaluation. England. 1660-1800.　　　1046

Behan, Brendan

Modern plays set in confining institutions. North America. Europe. 1900-1983.　　　1200

Irreverent aspects of Irish comedy seen through the works of 14 playwrights. Eire. UK-Ireland. 1840-1965.　　　1555

Behavior/psychology

Research/historiography

Discussion of the Inventory of Dramatic Behavior Adapted for Group Observation. USA. 1980.　　　91

Results of a study which measures acting and monitoring skills in children. USA. 1983.　　　1476

Behavior/psychology, actor

Performance/production

Psychological aspects of acting.　　　661

Theory/criticism

Articles on performance theory and practice. 1976-1983.　　　1477

Behavior/psychology, audience

Audience

Study of public perception of theatrical performances. 1982.　164

Sociological studies suggest that democratization of the arts has not taken place. USA. 1830-1982.　　　173

Testing undergraduates' reactions to set designs. USA: Athens, GA. 1974.　　　174

Modern productions of Renaissance drama. Europe. 1982.　566

Institutions

State of theatre in Southern Italy. Italy. 1982.　　　319

Performance/production

Actor-audience relationship in productions by Jacques Copeau, Bertolt Brecht and Russian directors. France. USSR. Germany. 1900-1956.　　　726

Description of three theatre events in which the audience participated by following instructions on Walkman cassettes. USA. 1980.　　　1754

Plays/librettos/scripts

Involvement of the audience in Ben Jonson's work as satirist and playwright, with some playtexts from the First Folio. England. 1598-1614.　　　1042

Relation to other fields

Introduction of Luigi Pirandello's play Tonight We Improvise. Italy. 1930.　　　1458

Theory/criticism

Articles on performance theory and practice. 1976-1983.　1477

Effect of social conditions on performance styles. USA. Greece. 499 B.C.-1983 A.D.　　　1517

Behavior/psychology, ballet

Performance/production

Sociological and psychological implications faced by dancers at end of their performing careers. USA. 1982.　　　520

Behrens, Peter

Theory/criticism

Reformers on their theories. Europe. 1870-1910.　　　98

Beilharz, Manfred

Institutions

Interviews with personnel of Freiburg theatres on obtaining subsidies and other aspects of administration. Germany, West: Freiburg. 1911-1983.　　　607

Belavel, Emilio S.

History of Puerto Rican avant-garde theatre. Puerto Rico. 1811-1970.　　　617

Belcher, Fannin Saffore

Reference materials

Proper noun index from Fannin Saffore Belcher's history of Black theatre. USA. 1767-1940.　　　41

Belle Epoque, La

Design/technology

Costumes of 'La Belle Epoque' at the Metropolitan Museum of Art. USA: New York, NY. 1870-1910.　　　260

Bellow, Saul

Plays/librettos/scripts

Essays on the trends of the Jewish-American theatre and its personalities. USA. 1900-1983.　　　1353

Bene, Carmelo

Performance/production

Six essays on the productions and artistic views held by leading European directors. Europe. 1960-1980.　　　1615

Critical analysis of Carmelo Bene's rewritten version of Hamlet. Italy. 1961-1975.　　　1619

Director, actor and playwright Carmelo Bene's autobiography. Italy. 1959-1983.　　　1620

Theories of acting and theatre by controversial director Carmelo Bene. Italy. 1960-1982.　　　1621

Analysis of Carmelo Bene's avant-garde adaptation and staging of Pinocchio. Italy. 1981.　　　1625

Plays/librettos/scripts

Negation of the theatre by Samuel Beckett, Antonin Artaud and Carmelo Bene. France. Italy. 1925-1960.　　　1643

Benedico, Augusto

Performance/production

Interview with actor Augusto Benedico and director Alvaro Custodio, Spanish exiles in Mexico. Mexico. Spain. 1939-1983.　　　820

Beneyto, Miguel

Plays/librettos/scripts

Staging and scenic practices in the plays of Lope de Vega's forerunners and contemporaries. Spain: Valencia. 1500-1699.　1253

Benjamin, Walter

Italian translation of Walter Benjamin's articles, aphorisms and other notes on theatrical events. Europe. 1926-1927.　　　1087

Bennewitz, Fritz

Relation to other fields

Interview with Fritz Bennewitz on theatre work in the Third World. India. Venezuela. Sri Lanka. 1970-1983.   59

Benno Blimpie SEE: *Transfiguration of Benno Blimpie, The*

Benue International Popular Theatre Workshop for Development (Gboko)

Institutions

Popular theatre workshop for training theatre educators. Nigeria: Gboko. 1981-1982.   322

Beolco, Angelo SEE: Ruzante

Bergamín, José

Plays/librettos/scripts

Interview with playwright José Bergamín. Spain. 1925-1980.   1245

Bergman, Ingmar

Performance/production

Ingmar Bergman directs Molière's *Dom Juan* at Salzburg Festival. Austria: Salzburg. 1983.   673

Three productions of *Macbeth* by director Ingmar Bergman. Sweden: Stockholm, Hälsingborg, Göteburg. 1940-1948.   840

Study of Ingmar Bergman's approach to directing, and the influences on it. Sweden. Germany. 1930-1983.   842

Analysis of Ingmar Bergman's stage and film direction. Sweden. 1918-1982.   843

Documentation of Ingmar Bergman's tripartite theatre project. Sweden. Germany, West: Munich. 1981.   844

Ingmar Bergman's use of text, stage and audience. Sweden. Germany, West. 1944.   845

August Strindberg productions in eleven countries. Sweden. Italy. USA. 1982.   847

Comparative study of Peter Oskarsson's production of August Strindberg's *A Dream Play* with that of Ingmar Bergman. USA: Seattle, WA. 1982.   907

Bergman, Ingrid

Biography of actress Ingrid Bergman with photographs. Sweden. USA. 1915-1983.   1713

Berkeley, Henry, Lord

Administration

Accounts of payment to assorted entertainers performing for Lord Berkeley. England: Coventry. 1593-1605.   122

Berlin, Irving

Performance/production

Study of revue songs by Irving Berlin, George Gershwin and Cole Porter in their theatrical contexts. USA: New York, NY. 1910-1937.   2032

Berliner Ensemble (East Berlin)

Institutions

History of Deutsches Theater Berlin. Germany: Berlin. 1883-1983.   598

Bertolt Brecht's return to Deutsches Theater and production of *Mother Courage* with Berliner Ensemble. Germany, East: East Berlin. 1949.   601

Berliner Staatsoper SEE: Staatsoper (East Berlin)

Berliner Theatertreffen

Performance/production

Brief survey of productions at the 20th Berlin Theatre Conference festival. Germany, West: West Berlin. 1983.   787

Berlioz, Hector

Account of the Hector Berlioz festival, and Serge Baudo, director. France: Lyons. 1960-1983.   1862

Bernanos, Georges

Plays/librettos/scripts

Composition of the opera *Les Dialogues des Carmélites*. France. 1931-1983.   1943

Bernhard, Thomas

Performance/production

Photo portfolio of plays of Thomas Bernhard. Germany, West. 1970-1979.   759

Plays/librettos/scripts

Playwright Thomas Bernhard's affinity with philosophy of Ludwig Josef Johan Wittgenstein. Austria. 1970-1982.   1002

Treatment of power by German playwrights and Volker Braun's *Dmitri*. Germany, West: Karlsruhe. 1983.   1154

Bernhardt, Sarah

Ronald Harwood discusses his plays *The Dresser* and *After the Lions*, the latter play based on the life of Sarah Bernhardt. UK-England: London. 1983.   1286

Bernstein, Elmer

Performance/production

Eight critics review Ivan Reitman's production of the musical *Merlin*. USA: New York, NY. 1983.   1802

Bernstein, Leonard

Discussion of Leonard Bernstein's production of Wagner's *Tristan und Isolde*. Germany, West: Munich. 1981.   1872

Berretto a sonagli (Bell Cap, The)

Plays/librettos/scripts

Productions of Luigi Pirandello's early work contrasted with later ones. Italy. 1898-1917.   1180

Berry, Walter

Performance/production

Bass Walter Berry's debut in *Falstaff* at the Vienna Staatsoper. Austria: Vienna. 1983.   1841

Bersenev, Ivan Nikolajevič

Role experimental studios played in the formation of the Soviet theatre. USSR: Moscow, Leningrad. 1920-1939.   993

Bertolazzi, Carlo

Theory/criticism

Louis Althusser's Marxist philosophy is contrasted with his review of Carlo Bertolazzi's play staged by Giorgio Strehler. USA. France. Italy. 1962-1985.   1674

Besobrasova, Marika

Performance/production

Discussion of ballet in Monte Carlo. Monaco. 1948-1983.   519

Best Little Whorehouse in Texas, The

Production history of *The Best Little Whorehouse in Texas*. USA: New York, NY. 1974-1982.   1784

Bèze, Théodore de

Plays/librettos/scripts

Typology and analysis of French sacred drama. France. 1550-1650.   1111

Bharnani, Ashok M.

Performance spaces

History and reconstruction of Paper Mill Playhouse. USA: Millburn, NJ. 1980-1982.   394

Bhavas

Plays/librettos/scripts

Bhāva (mood) as expressed through the presentational techniques of *kathakali*. India. 1600-1983.   546

Bialaszewski, Miron

Miron Bialaszewski's experiments in producing his own work. Poland. 1955-1983.   1653

SUBJECT INDEX

Bibliographies

Design/technology

Published materials for sound technicians. USA. 1983.   244

Performance/production

Biography and all-inclusive reference materials to Charlie Chaplin. USA. 1889-1977.   1714

Plays/librettos/scripts

Uses of Thomas Dekker materials in analytical bibliography. UK-England: London. 1808-1983.   1278

Essays on and a bibliographical guide to Pierre Corneille's comedies. France. 1606-1684.   1572

Reference materials

Bibliography of performing arts periodicals. 1982.   11

Selected bibliography of Czechoslovakian theatre. Czechoslovakia. 1945-1980.   17

Bibliography of Arabic theatre. Egypt. 1900-1930.   18

List of theses at Gaston Baty library of the University of Paris III. France: Paris. 1981-1983.   25

General theatre bibliography of works in Catalan language. Spain. 1980-1981.   33

Bibliography of education resources on creativity and dramatic activities in elementary schools. USA. 1976-1982.   42

List of books related to the restoration of historic theatres. USA. 1935-1983.   44

Bibliography of flat pattern sources continued from *Theatre Design & Technology*, Winter 1983. USA. 1900-1983.   47

Index to reference works in Russian and other languages. USSR. Europe. North America. 1800-1983.   51

Current scholarship, criticism and commentary on areas and topics of modern world drama. Europe. North America. South America. 1979-1982.   1402

Annotated Shakespearean bibliography. Europe. North America. France. 1980.   1405

Bibliography of Jean Genet criticism. France. 1943-1980.   1409

Bibliography of research on Shakespearean productions in German-speaking countries. German-speaking countries. 1981-1982.   1410

Listing of the preserved Jesuit plays and their performances. German-speaking countries. 1555-1728.   1411

Bibliography of Spanish and English publications on *comedias* and their playwrights. Spain. 1580-1650.   1419

George Bernard Shaw bibliography. UK. 1856-1983.   1421

Bibliography of Laurence Olivier. UK-England. 1907-1983.   1427

Sean O'Casey bibliography. UK-Ireland. 1923-1982.   1430

Annotated bibliography of actors. USA. 1700-1950.   1435

Bibliography of Pierre Corneille criticism. France. 1633-1980.   1598

Biblioteca Nazionale Centrale (Florence)

Research/historiography

Classification system of Biblioteca Nazionale Centrale used by Alessandro Lanari. Italy: Florence. 1815-1870.   1972

Bibliothèque Nationale (Paris)

Design/technology

SIBMAS papers on collections of designs and scenography. Europe. North America. 1982.   183

Choosing audio-visual materials for exhibits. Discussed at SIBMAS. France: Paris. 1982.   1705

Reference materials

Models of scenery and costumes in the Bibliothèque Nationale. France: Paris. 1982.   24

Bicknell, Arthur

Performance/production

Six critics review John Roach's production of Arthur Bicknell's play *Moose Murders*. USA: New York, NY. 1983.   968

Bie, Oskar

Theory/criticism

Reformers on their theories. Europe. 1870-1910.   98

Bierri Role Concept Repertory

Audience

Testing undergraduates' reactions to set designs. USA: Athens, GA. 1974.   174

Big Maggie

Performance/production

Five critics review Donal Donnelly's production of John B. Keane's play *Big Maggie*. USA: New York, NY. 1983.   966

Bignall, John

Shakespearean productions and festivals in the American South. USA. 1751-1980.   938

Bing, Suzanne

Son of actress Suzanne Bing recalls her memories of Jacques Copeau. France: Paris. 1913-1948.   724

Plays/librettos/scripts

Comparison of two French translations of *Twelfth Night*, by Jacques Copeau/Théodore Lascarais and Suzanne Bing. France: Paris. 1914.   1567

Bird, Robert Montgomery

Louisa Medina's popular dramatic adaptations of the works of Edward Bulwer-Lytton, Ernest Maltravers and Robert Bird. USA. 1833-1838.   1346

Bizet, Georges

Performance/production

The Paris Opera production of Peter Brook's *La Tragédie de Carmen*. France: Paris. 1981.   1861

Career of soprano Leona Mitchell at the Metropolitan Opera. USA. 1983.   1912

Ten critics review Peter Brook's production of *La Tragédie de Carmen* at the Vivian Beaumont Theatre. USA: New York, NY. 1983.   1914

Plays/librettos/scripts

Personal and professional relationship of Georges Bizet and Charles Gounod. France: Paris. 1856-1875.   1937

Bjornson, Maria

Design/technology

Scenic practices of various designers. UK. 1960-1983.   227

Black cinema

Performance/production

Authentic expression in Black theatre and film is contrasted with stereotypical Black portrayals by white authors and performers. USA: New York, NY. 1890-1930.   983

Black theatre

Administration

Unemployment among Black theatre professionals. UK-England: London. 1974-1979.   146

Activities of the Audience Development Committee. USA: New York, NY. 1983.   153

Design/technology

Functions and training of theatre designers and technicians. USA: New York, NY. 1983.   238

Institutions

Economic and political aspects of several Black theatre groups. USA: New York, NY, Chicago, IL. 1982.   340

Production histories of various groups. USA: Washington, DC. 1968-1976.   341

Development of a community theatre under the auspices of Kent State University. USA: Akron, OH. 1972-1983.   343

History of the Apollo Theatre. USA: New York, NY. 1930-1983.   345

Organization and productions of Black Theatre Co-operative. UK-England. 1979.   631

Activism, internationalism and preservation in minority theatre groups. USA. 1981-1983.   646

Black theatre — cont'd

Harlem Little Theatre movement started to produce plays by, with, for and about Blacks. USA: New York, NY. 1915-1934.　653

Performance/production

Ritual, masks and metaphors of Black theatre. USA. 1983.　458

History of Black theatre with emphasis on actors and dramatists. USA. 1795-1975.　477

Debbie Allen discusses her struggle for success and her relationship with her family. USA. 1983.　515

History of a production about nine Black leaders by the African American Drama Company. USA. 1976-1983.　979

Authentic expression in Black theatre and film is contrasted with stereotypical Black portrayals by white authors and performers. USA: New York, NY. 1890-1930.　983

Creation of the character of a Black ballerina in Diaghilev's Ballet Russe. USA: New York, NY. 1980.　1751

Account of the musical *In Dahomey*. UK-England: London. 1903-1904.　1776

Interview with principal male stars of *Dreamgirls*. USA: New York, NY. 1983.　1778

Career of soprano Leona Mitchell at the Metropolitan Opera. USA. 1983.　1912

Simon Estes, American baritone, speaks of his life and career as a Black artist. USA. Europe. 1939-1983.　1927

Career of dancer Margot Webb. USA. 1933-1947.　1991

Brief biography and interview with Cab Calloway. USA: White Plains, NY, Hollywood, CA. 1930-1983.　1993

Importation of African Blacks for exhibition as 'exotics' and evolution of this practice into a circus side-show. USA. 1810-1926.　2014

Chronology of Black entertainers associated with 'Louisiana troupes'. Europe. 1901-1916.　2028

Founder-director of New Lafayette Theatre discusses purpose and style of rituals. USA: New York, NY. 1969-1972.　2102

Plays/librettos/scripts

Similarities between the plays *The Dutchman* and *Zoo Story*. USA: New York, NY. 1964.　1350

Tribute to playwright Owen Dodson. USA. 1983.　1363

Implications of Black and non-Black theatre segregation, noting that Black playwrights are expected to write about life. USA. 1980.　1376

Critical examination of Lorraine Hansberry's influence on drama. USA. 1960-1979.　1387

Reference materials

Proper noun index from Fannin Saffore Belcher's history of Black theatre. USA. 1767-1940.　41

Dictionary of Black theatre. USA: New York, NY. 1983.　50

Bibliography of Black French theatre in Africa. Africa. 1977-1983.　1397

Relation to other fields

Racial stereotypes in American theatre. USA. 1983.　1466

Athol Fugard's plays are compared to Bantustan agitprop and historical drama. South Africa, Republic of. 1955-1980.　1665

Description of *Bandia Woli*, a traditional folk drama. Senegal. USA. 1976.　2100

Theory/criticism

Collected theory and criticism by women in theatre on women in theatre. USA. UK. 1850-1983.　114

Imamu Amiri Baraka's links to aesthetically white culture. USA. 1969.　1516

Imamu Amiri Baraka's aesthetics find their origins in Blues music. USA. 1963-1967.　1521

Study of genesis, development, structural components and consequences of theatre-drama performed by the Black workers. South Africa, Republic of. 1981-1983.　1673

Black Theatre Co-operative (England)

Institutions

Organization and productions of Black Theatre Co-operative. UK-England. 1979.　631

Black, David

Performance/production

Three critics review Howard Reifsnyder's *The Guys in the Truck* directed by David Black. USA: New York, NY. 1983.　929

Black, Don

Eight critics review Ivan Reitman's production of the musical *Merlin*. USA: New York, NY. 1983.　1802

Blacks, The* SEE: *Nègres, Les

Blackwell, Charles

Performance/production

Nine critics review Vivian Matalon's production of the musical *The Tap Dance Kid*. USA: New York, NY. 1983.　1781

Blackwell, Vera

Five critics review Lee Grant's production of Vaclav Havel's play *A Private View* translated by Vera Blackwell. USA: New York, NY. 1983.　927

Blakemore, Michael

Ten critics review Michael Blakemore's production of Michael Frayn's play *Noises Off*. USA: New York, NY. 1983.　1541

Blaser, Lynn

Interview with soprano Lynn Blaser. Canada. 1983.　1845

Blasis, James de

Account of *Risurrezione*, to be performed by Cincinnati Summer Opera. USA: Cincinnati, OH. 1904-1983.　1923

Blecher, Hilary

Eight critics review Hilary Blecher's production of *Poppie Nongena*. USA: New York, NY. 1983.　945

Bloodgroup (UK)

Institutions

Profile of the women's company Bloodgroup. UK. 1983.　1741

Bloom, Claire

Performance/production

Autobiography of actress Claire Bloom. UK-England. 1931-1982.　866

Blues Music

Theory/criticism

Imamu Amiri Baraka's aesthetics find their origins in Blues music. USA. 1963-1967.　1521

Blues People: Negro Music in America

Imamu Amiri Baraka's aesthetics find their origins in Blues music. USA. 1963-1967.　1521

Blum, Friedrich

Relation to other fields

German theatre in Cracow and its relationship to Polish people during the uprising against Russia. Austro-Hungarian Empire: Cracow. Poland. 1863-1865.　1443

Bo-Fabrik (Bochumer Schauspiel)

Performance spaces

New aesthetic forms of staging. Germany, West: Bremen, Bochum, Hanover. 1962-1980.　374

Bocca del Lupo, La (Wolf's Mouth, The)

Plays/librettos/scripts

Dramatization of Remigio Zena's novel *The Wolf's Mouth* by Teatro Stabile di Genova. Italy: Genoa. 1980.　1186

Bodenstedt, Frederick von

Performance/production

Charles Kean's staging methods and the influences on them. UK-England: London. 1850-1859.　898

Bogdanov, Michael

Administration

Private prosecution of Michael Bogdanov's production of Howard Brenton's *The Romans in Britain*. UK. 1968-1986.   144

Bogusławski, Wojcieck

Institutions

Polish theatre under Russian rule as reflected in György Spirò's novel *Az Ikszek*. Poland: Warsaw. Russia. Hungary. 1815-1829.   325

Bohème, La

Performance/production

Photographs, cast lists, synopsis and discography of Metropolitan Opera production of *La Bohème*. USA: New York, NY. 1983.   1905

Konstantin Stanislavskij's training of opera singers. USSR. 1918-1935.   1929

Böhm, Maxi

Unfinished memoirs of the cabaret comedian Maxi Böhm. Austria. 1916-1982.   2000

Boito, Arrigo

Eleonora Duse's portrayal of Cleopatra in the Boito/D'Annunzio production. Italy. 1873-1924.   804

Photographs, cast lists, synopsis and discography of Metropolitan Opera production of *La Gioconda*. USA: New York, NY. 1983.   1898

Plays/librettos/scripts

Shakespeare's influence on Arrigo Boito's libretto for *La Gioconda*, based on Victor Hugo's play. Italy. 1862-1900.   1956

Bol'šoj Teat'r Opery i Baleta Sojuza SSR (Moscow)

Performance/production

Current state of Bolshoi opera performance. USSR: Moscow. 1982-1983.   1931

Bond, Chris

Five critics review Chris Bond's production of Clair Luckham's play *Teaneck Tanzi: The Venus Flytrap*. USA: New York, NY. 1983.   954

Bond, Edward

Institutions

Edward Bond's *Saved* and Shakespeare's *Troilus and Cressida* at the Jugendclub Kritisches Theater. Germany, West: Stuttgart. 1981-1983.   608

Performance/production

Brief comments on and German translation of Edward Bond's *Summer*. Germany, West: Munich. 1983.   764

Plays/librettos/scripts

Epic structure in contemporary drama. UK. 1968-1981.   1275

Evolution of Edward Bond's *Summer*. UK-England. 1980-1983.   1308

Bondy, Luc

Performance/production

Brief comments on and German translation of Edward Bond's *Summer*. Germany, West: Munich. 1983.   764

Bondy, Sebastián Salazar

Development of acting from declamatory style to physical expressiveness. Peru. 1950-1983.   824

Bonin, Hermann

Institutions

Interview with the director of the Centre Dramàtic de la Generalitat. Spain. 1945-1982.   327

Bonnes, Les (Maids, The)

Performance/production

Analysis of Mario Missiroli's productions of Jean Genet's *The Maids* and Frank Wedekind's *Music*. Italy. 1980.   796

Booker, Margaret

Comparative study of Peter Oskarsson's production of August

Strindberg's *A Dream Play* with that of Ingmar Bergman. USA: Seattle, WA. 1982.   907

Boone, Colonel Daniel (lion tamer)

Circus life and performance based on the memoirs of acrobat Leonora Whiteley. Greece: Athens. 1880-1899.   2011

Booth, Edwin

Reconstruction of Richard Mansfield's production of *Richard III*. UK-England: London. USA. 1889.   893

Shakespearean productions and festivals in the American South. USA. 1751-1980.   938

Booth, John Wilkes

Career of actor-manager John Wilkes Booth. USA. 1855-1865.   975

Booth, Junius Brutus

Shakespearean productions and festivals in the American South. USA. 1751-1980.   938

Booth, Laurie

Working practice of Laurie Booth in light of contemporary attitudes toward dance. UK. 1978-1983.   526

Borchert, Wolfgang

Productions of Wolfgang Borchert's play *The Man Outside* in Hamburg and Berlin. Germany, West: West Berlin, Hamburg. 1947-1948.   778

Boris Godunov

Photographs, cast lists, synopsis and discography of Metropolitan Opera production of *Boris Godunov*. USA: New York, NY. 1983.   1891

Boris Christoff, bass, speaks of his career and art. USA: New York, NY. 1947-1983.   1924

Konstantin Stanislavskij's training of opera singers. USSR. 1918-1935.   1929

Borisov, A.F.

Articles discussing the work of individual actors at the Academic Drama Theatre of A.S. Puškin. USSR: Leningrad. 1910-1970.   987

Borque, Maravall-Diez

Plays/librettos/scripts

Sociological approach to Lope de Vega's drama. Spain. 1573-1635.   1256

Bosse, Jürgen

Performance/production

Harald Clemens' production of Anton Čechov's *Uncle Vanya* at Nationaltheater. Germany, West: Mannheim. 1983.   777

Boston Opera Company

Performance spaces

History of the Keith Memorial Theatre. USA: Boston, MA. 1925-1980.   1982

Boucicault, Dion

Plays/librettos/scripts

Developments of Irish melodrama and its influence on later writers. UK-Ireland: Dublin. 1860-1905.   1338

Irreverent aspects of Irish comedy seen through the works of 14 playwrights. Eire. UK-Ireland. 1840-1965.   1555

Bouffes du Nord (Paris)

Performance/production

Production styles of directors Peter Brook and Tadeusz Kantor. USA: New York, NY. France: Paris. Poland: Wielopole. 1982.   1632

The Paris Opera production of Peter Brook's *La Tragédie de Carmen*. France: Paris. 1981.   1861

Boulevard theatre

Collection of illustrations of melodramas in performance. France: Paris. 1800-1900.   735

Bourgeois theatre

Success of bourgeois comedy over *commedia dell'arte*. Italy: Venice. 1770-1797.   1530

Bourgeois theatre — cont'd

Plays/librettos/scripts

Bourgeois interests in *Wilhelm Meister's Theatrical Mission* by Goethe. Germany. 1777-1785. 1116

Modification of themes of Corra's plays from Futurism to bourgeois tradition. Italy. 1915-1940. 1163

Relation to other fields

Circus as a staging device for a political satire. USSR. Germany. Italy. 1914-1930. 1668

Theory/criticism

Study of genesis, development, structural components and consequences of theatre-drama performed by the Black workers. South Africa, Republic of. 1981-1983. 1673

Boursault, Edmé

Plays/librettos/scripts

Representation of court manners in comedy. France: Paris. 1650-1715. 1565

Bowab, John

Performance/production

Six critics review John Bowab's production of the musical *Mame*. USA: New York, NY. 1983. 1801

Bowery Theatre (New York, NY)

Plays/librettos/scripts

Louisa Medina's popular dramatic adaptations of the works of Edward Bulwer-Lytton, Ernest Maltravers and Robert Bird. USA. 1833-1838. 1346

Boyer, Charles

Performance/production

Biography of actor Charles Boyer, including filmography of his work. France. USA. 1899-1978. 1712

Boyl, Carlos

Plays/librettos/scripts

Staging and scenic practices in the plays of Lope de Vega's forerunners and contemporaries. Spain: Valencia. 1500-1699. 1253

Boyle, 'Captain Jack' (William)

Irreverent aspects of Irish comedy seen through the works of 14 playwrights. Eire. UK-Ireland. 1840-1965. 1555

Boysen, Rolf

Compilation of comments by various artists on Tennessee Williams. USA. 1911-1983. 1342

Brahm, Otto

Theory/criticism

Reformers on their theories. Europe. 1870-1910. 98

Brahms, Johannes

Reference materials

Program of Easter Festival Salzburg, including essays on Richard Wagner and Johannes Brahms. Austria: Salzburg. France: Paris. 1983. 1964

Brancati, Vitaliano

Performance/production

Theatrical spontaneity, role-playing and improvisation in Sicilian opera. Italy. 1907-1983. 1879

Plays/librettos/scripts

Essays on Vitaliano Brancati's plays and motion picture scripts. Italy: Catania. 1924-1954. 1160

Freudian analysis of the character of Caterina Leher in *The Housekeeper* by Vitaliano Brancati. Italy. 1952. 1172

Brandes, Georg

Literary influences on Henrik Ibsen's *Vildanden (The Wild Duck)*. Norway. 1884. 1205

Brando, Marlon

Compilation of comments by various artists on Tennessee Williams. USA. 1911-1983. 1342

Brasch, Thomas

Performance/production

Arie Zinger's production of Čechov's *Ivanov* at Züricher Schauspielhaus. Switzerland: Zürich. 1983. 849

Braun, Volker

Plays/librettos/scripts

Treatment of power by German playwrights and Volker Braun's *Dmitri*. Germany, West: Karlsruhe. 1983. 1154

Bread and Puppet Theatre (New York, NY)

Performance/production

Productions by Els Comediants and influence on them by other groups. Spain: Catalonia. 1983. 513

Breakfast with Les and Bess

Six critics review Barnet Kellerman's production of Lee Kalcheim's play *Breakfast with Les and Bess*. USA: New York, NY. 1983. 1540

Brecht, Bertolt

Administration

Censorship on the American stage, particularly of Bertolt Brecht. USA. 1941-1949. 564

Design/technology

Designer George Grosz's collaborations with Bertolt Brecht and Erwin Piscator. Germany. 1926. 578

Institutions

History of Deutsches Theater Berlin. Germany: Berlin. 1883-1983. 598

Evolution and theories of Odin Teatret. Sweden. 1964-1979. 621

Repertory and workings of Glasgow Citizens' Theatre. UK-Scotland: Glasgow. 1983. 642

Performance/production

Relationship between Bertolt Brecht and Asian theatre. Asia. Germany. 1925-1981. 665

History of directing. Europe. 1882-1982. 708

Artistic movements and critical thought that shaped modern directing. Europe. 1914-1940. 715

Actor-audience relationship in productions by Jacques Copeau, Bertolt Brecht and Russian directors. France. USSR. Germany. 1900-1956. 726

Notes on Helene Weigel's letters as resources for theatre history. Germany. 1900-1971. 741

Richard Wagner's influence on modern theatrical conceptions, including those of Adolphe Appia, Stanisław Wyspiański and Bertolt Brecht. Germany. Poland. Switzerland. 1813-1983. 742

Solter's concept for staging Bertolt Brecht's *Baal*. Germany, East. 1983. 745

Interview with and influences on actor Bernhard Minetti, including production of *Faust*. Germany, East: East Berlin. 1982-1983. 751

Directors on Bertolt Brecht's dramas. Germany, East: Schwerin, Erfurt, East Berlin. 1983. 754

Portrait of the actress (and daughter of Bertolt Brecht) Hanne Hiob. Germany, West. 1923-1983. 761

Interview with actor-director Tamás Major on staging plays by Bertolt Brecht. Hungary. 1962-1982. 791

Essays on Bertolt Brecht's practical and literary theatre work. Germany. 1925-1956. 1617

Plays/librettos/scripts

Bertolt Brecht's efforts to obtain Austrian citizenship. Austria. 1922-1982. 1003

Influences on Michel de Ghelderode from his national culture and Bertolt Brecht. Belgium. 1919-1962. 1011

Adaptation of *Galileo* for Chinese stage. China, People's Republic of: Peking. 1979. 1020

Modern Cuban theatre, influenced by Bertolt Brecht, reflects the revolutionary process. Cuba. 1850-1983. 1023

Bertolt Brecht's efforts to stay in Czechoslovakia. Czechoslovakia: Prague. USA. 1943-1949. 1024

Determining factor of the demonstrative mode of Morality play characters. England. 1300-1550. 1032

Brecht, Bertolt — cont'd

Possible meanings of characterization in the Mystery plays. England. 1200-1550.   1057

Influence of Bertolt Brecht on Finnish theatre. Finland. 1930-1969.
                                                                      1098

Tendency of Bertolt Brecht's plays to promote social change as barrier to their universal value. Germany. 1918-1956.   1119

Divergence of theoretical and practical concerns in Bertolt Brecht's plays. Germany. 1918-1956.   1121

Contradiction between good and evil in capitalist society as reflected in Bertolt Brecht's *The Good Woman of Sezuan*. Germany. 1938-1941.   1122

Biography of playwright Bertolt Brecht. Germany. 1898-1956.   1123

Anti-war plays by Bertolt Brecht and Johannes R. Becher on German invasion of the Soviet Union. Germany. 1942-1943.   1126

Brechtian play construction in contemporary theatrical practice. Germany. UK. 1920-1983.   1127

Influence of Lenin's writings on Bertolt Brecht's plays. Germany. 1930.   1128

Bertolt Brecht's theory of social basis of personal contradictions. Germany. 1918-1956.   1129

'Great Method' used by Bertolt Brecht in his plays, and influences from others. Germany. 1918-1956.   1130

Influence of Marxist and Leninist ideology on Bertolt Brecht's plays. Germany. 1926-1934.   1132

Brecht's directorial approach to staging Shakespeare's *Coriolanus*, *Macbeth* and *King Lear*. Germany. 1920-1930.   1136

The Measures Taken as Bertolt Brecht's first Marxist play. Germany. 1930.   1139

Analysis of the early plays of Bertolt Brecht. Germany. 1925.   1140

Heiner Müller continues the Brechtian tradition in political drama. Germany, East. 1960-1982.   1144

Title character of *Mother Courage* is contrasted with similar figure in Jürgen Gross' drama *Memorial*. Germany, East. 1980.   1145

Two versions of *Coriolanus* by Bertolt Brecht and Günter Grass in view of events of June 17, 1953. Germany, East: East Berlin. Germany, West. 1953.   1146

Bertolt Brecht's experiments in audience education through his plays. Germany, East. 1954-1956.   1147

Some paths for realism in Latin American theatre. South America. North America. 1955-1983.   1224

Collected materials on Eugenio Barba and Odin Teatret. Sweden. 1964-1979.   1258

Debate on folk and literary theatre. Sweden.   1265

Epic structure in contemporary drama. UK. 1968-1981.   1275

Influence on Brecht of Sean O'Casey's use of songs to overcome the boundaries of illusion in his drama. UK-Ireland: Dublin. 1923-1926.
                                                                      1325

Eric Bentley's meetings with Bertolt Brecht. USA: Santa Monica, CA. Germany, East: East Berlin. 1942-1956.   1348

Bertolt Brecht's theory of alienation applied to characters and situations in Tennessee Williams' *Camino Real*. USA. Germany, East. 1941-1953.   1352

Difficulty of translating Karl Valentin's scripts. Germany. 1882-1948.
                                                                      2005

Relation to other fields

Interview with Fritz Bennewitz on theatre work in the Third World. India. Venezuela. Sri Lanka. 1970-1983.   59

Reception of Bertolt Brecht in Argentina vis-à-vis political situation in the country. Argentina. 1980-1983.   1441

Difference in dialectics and philosophy in writings by Karl Korsch, Bertolt Brecht and György Lukács. Germany. Hungary. 1898-1971.
                                                                      1454

Renewed interest in Bertolt Brecht stimulated by political situations. UK. 1980-1983.   1462

Circus as a staging device for a political satire. USSR. Germany. Italy. 1914-1930.   1668

Theory/criticism

Intermingling of Eastern and Western performance aesthetics. China. Japan. 1900-1983.   93

Bertolt Brecht's theatrical poetics and polemic with György Lukács on realism. Germany. Hungary. 1918-1956.   1493

Bertolt Brecht's idea of art as a socio-cultural coherence. Germany. 1898-1956.   1494

Influence of Richard Wagner's *Gesamtkunstwerk* on modern theatre. Germany. 1849-1977.   1495

Marxist philosophy in Bertolt Brecht's work. Germany. 1922-1956.
                                                                      1496

Bertolt Brecht's didactic plays function in the development of Socialism. Germany. 1922-1956.   1497

Bertolt Brecht's and György Lukács' debate on realism. Germany. Hungary. 1900-1956.   1500

Dialectic contradiction in Bertolt Brecht's theory of theatre. Germany. 1898-1956.   1501

Bertolt Brecht's view that all wars stem from social conflict. Germany. 1898-1956.   1502

Influence of Bertolt Brecht's methods on playwright Heiner Müller and concept of today's theatre. Germany, East. 1983.   1504

Semiotic comparison of dramatic theory, philosophy and performance. USA. Europe. 1850-1956.   1515

Effect of social conditions on performance styles. USA. Greece. 499 B.C.-1983 A.D.   1517

Hannah Arendt's theoretical work with reference to Gotthold Lessing, Bertolt Brecht, Franz Kafka and Isak Dinesen. USA. Europe. 1900-1983.   1518

Significance of gender in feminist criticism with reference to historical materialism, deconstruction and phenomenon of cross-dressing in theatre. USA. France. UK-England. 1983.   1520

Louis Althusser's Marxist philosophy is contrasted with his review of Carlo Bertolazzi's play staged by Giorgio Strehler. USA. France. Italy. 1962-1985.   1674

Bregenz Festival

Institutions

Review of Austrian summer festivals. Austria. 1983.   285

Brenton, Howard

Administration

Private prosecution of Michael Bogdanov's production of Howard Brenton's *The Romans in Britain*. UK. 1968-1986.   144

Plays/librettos/scripts

Epic structure in contemporary drama. UK. 1968-1981.   1275

Brig, The

Modern plays set in confining institutions. North America. Europe. 1900-1983.   1200

Brigham Young University

Reference materials

Description of archive holdings at Brigham Young University including personal papers of Howard Hawks and Dean Jagger. USA: Provo, UT. 1900-1983.   48

Brighton Beach Memoirs

Performance/production

Ten critics review Gene Saks' production of Neil Simon's play *Brighton Beach Memoirs*. USA: New York, NY. 1983.   1535

Brinkmann, Ruth

Vienna's English Theatre's 20th anniversary production of G.B. Shaw's *Candida*. Austria: Vienna. 1963.   668

British Broadcasting Corporation

Plays/librettos/scripts

Themes of British Broadcasting Corporation radio drama. UK-England: London. 1970-1980.   1710

Broadway theatre

Administration

Censorship of Brazilian theatre, causing only Broadway hits to be produced. Brazil. 1557-1983.   116

Autobiography of Broadway producer Irene Mayer Selznick. USA. 1910-1983.   161

Difficulties of getting some plays on Broadway. USA: New York, NY. 1982-1983.   565

Broadway theatre — cont'd

Design/technology

Sound systems and techniques for controlling sound. USA: New York, NY. 1945-1983. 264

Close collaboration between director and lighting designer in *Cats*. USA: New York, NY. 1982. 1768

Vincente Minnelli's pre-Hollywood years as Broadway designer. USA: Hollywood, CA, New York, NY. 1931-1939. 1769

Interviews with the designers of *Cats*. USA: New York, NY. UK-England: London. 1983. 1770

Technical aspects of Broadway production of *La Cage aux Folles*. USA: New York, NY. 1983. 1771

Performance spaces

History of West 42nd Street theatres. USA: New York, NY. 1893-1944. 400

Acoustical modifications at the Orpheum Theatre made to accommodate Broadway musicals. USA: San Francisco, CA. 1981-1983. 1774

Performance/production

Notes on three Broadway productions. USA: New York, NY. 1983. 911

Actress Shelley Bruce's struggle with childhood leukemia. USA: 1964. 914

Ten critics review Marshall Mason's production of Peter Nichols' play *Passion*. USA: New York, NY. 1983. 919

Collection of photographs of Broadway productions and actors. USA: New York, NY. 1940-1967. 921

Seven critics review *The Corn Is Green*. USA: New York, NY. 1983. 930

Five critics review Jack Hofsiss' production of Larry Atlas' play *Total Abandon*. USA: New York, NY: cd. 1983. 951

Eight critics review David Hare's production of his play *Plenty*. USA: New York, NY. 1983. 953

Five critics review Chris Bond's production of Clair Luckham's play *Teaneck Tanzi: The Venus Flytrap*. USA: New York, NY. 1983. 954

Eight critics review Edward Albee's production of his play *The Man Who Had Three Arms*. USA: New York, NY. 1983. 956

Six critics review Arvin Brown's production of David Mamet's play *American Buffalo*. USA: New York, NY. 1983. 960

Eight critics review Alison Sutcliffe's production of Raymund FitzSimons' play *Edmund Kean*. USA: New York, NY. 1983. 965

Six critics review John Roach's production of Arthur Bicknell's play *Moose Murders*. USA: New York, NY. 1983. 968

Nine critics review Arvin Brown's production of Arthur Miller's play *A View from the Bridge*. USA: New York, NY. 1983. 969

Eight critics review Tom Moore's production of Marsha Norman's play *'Night Mother*. USA: New York, NY. 1983. 971

Eight critics review Ellis Rabb's production of George S. Kaufman's and Moss Hart's play *You Can't Take It with You*. USA: New York, NY. 1983. 972

Extracts from journal of James Roose-Evans, director of *84 Charing Cross Road*. USA: New York, NY. 1982. 973

Ten critics review John Dexter's production of *The Glass Menagerie*, by Tennessee Williams. USA: New York, NY. 1983. 981

Seven critics review Carroll O'Connor's production of George Sibbald's play *Brothers*. USA: New York, NY. 1983. 985

Ten critics review Gene Saks' production of Neil Simon's play *Brighton Beach Memoirs*. USA: New York, NY. 1983. 1535

Six critics review Peter Pope's production of Harvey Fierstein's play *Torch Song Trilogy*. USA: New York, NY. 1983. 1536

Six critics review Barnet Kellerman's production of Lee Kalcheim's play *Breakfast with Les and Bess*. USA: New York, NY. 1983. 1540

Ten critics review Michael Blakemore's production of Michael Frayn's play *Noises Off*. USA: New York, NY. 1983. 1541

Nine critics review Milton Katselas' production of Noel Coward's play *Private Lives*. USA: New York, NY. 1983. 1545

Seven critics review *Marcel Marceau on Broadway*. USA: New York, NY. 1983. 1730

Interview with principal male stars of *Dreamgirls*. USA: New York, NY. 1983. 1778

Biography of Broadway and film songwriter Vincent Youmans. USA. 1898-1946. 1780

Nine critics review Vivian Matalon's production of the musical *The Tap Dance Kid*. USA: New York, NY. 1983. 1781

Production elements and choreography of *On Your Toes*. USA. 1982. 1782

Production history of *The Best Little Whorehouse in Texas*. USA: New York, NY. 1974-1982. 1784

Shift of public interest from Broadway to Off Broadway. USA: New York, NY. 1983. 1786

George Balanchine's contribution to dance in musical theatre. USA: New York, NY. 1929-1962. 1787

Overview of Jack Cole's career as dancer, teacher and choreographer. USA. 1933-1974. 1788

History of Broadway musical theatre with an extensive annotated discography. USA: New York, NY. 1800-1983. 1789

Production, casts and review of musical *My One and Only*. USA: New York, NY. 1971-1983. 1791

Seven critics review Kenny Ortega's production of the musical *Marilyn: An American Fable*. USA: New York, NY. 1983. 1792

Six critics review Alan Jay Lerner's production of the musical *Dance a Little Closer*. USA: New York, NY. 1983. 1793

Six critics review Robert Drivas' production of Peggy Lee's play *Peg*. USA: New York, NY. 1983. 1794

Nine critics review Jack O'Brien's production of *Porgy and Bess*. USA: New York, NY. 1983. 1795

Nine critics review Michael Cacoyannis' production of the musical *Zorba*. USA: New York, NY. 1983. 1798

Nine critics review Jacques Levy's production of the musical *Doonesbury*. USA: New York, NY. 1983. 1799

Eight critics review Philip Rose's production of the musical *Amen Corner*. USA: New York, NY. 1983. 1800

Six critics review John Bowab's production of the musical *Mame*. USA: New York, NY. 1983. 1801

Eight critics review Ivan Reitman's production of the musical *Merlin*. USA: New York, NY. 1983. 1802

Nine critics review George Abbott's production of the musical *On Your Toes*. USA: New York, NY. 1983. 1803

Evolution of director Harold Prince's concept for the Broadway musical *Cabaret*. USA: New York, NY. 1966. 1804

Ten critics review Richard Maltby's production of *Baby*. USA: New York, NY. 1983. 1805

Ten critics review *La Cage aux Folles*. USA: New York, NY. 1983. 1806

Eight critics review Michael Kahn's production of *Show Boat*. USA: New York, NY. 1983. 1807

Ten critics review *My One and Only*, staged by Thommie Walsh and Tommy Tune. USA: New York, NY. 1983. 1808

Ten critics review Peter Brook's production of *La Tragédie de Carmen* at the Vivian Beaumont Theatre. USA: New York, NY. 1983. 1914

Seven critics review *The Flying Karamozov Brothers*. USA: New York, NY. 1983. 2015

Study of revue songs by Irving Berlin, George Gershwin and Cole Porter in their theatrical contexts. USA: New York, NY. 1910-1937. 2032

Work of The Puppet People on Broadway production of *Alice in Wonderland*. USA: New York, NY. 1982. 2055

Plays/librettos/scripts

Treatment of the war in American dramaturgy. USA. 1936-1943. 1356

Memoir of meeting with playwright George S. Kaufman. USA. 1922-1961. 1359

Examination of Harvey Fierstein's *Torch Song Trilogy*. USA: New York, NY. 1983. 1596

Musical adaptation of *A Doll's House*. USA: New York, NY. 1983. 1809

Reference materials

Chronological guide to premieres, revivals, personalities and events. USA. UK. Canada. 1900-1979. 45

Annual record of Broadway and Off Broadway season. USA: New York, NY. 1981-1982. 49

Dictionary of Black theatre. USA: New York, NY. 1983. 50

Broadway theatre — cont'd

Guide to shows that closed before coming to Broadway. USA. 1900-1982. 1438

Broken Jug, The SEE: ***Zerbrochene Krug, Der***

Brontë, Charlotte

Relation to other fields

Theatrical vision and the portrait of the great French actress Rachel in Charlotte Brontë's *Villette*. UK-England. France. 1853. 70

Brook, Peter

Performance/production

Memoirs of dramaturg Jan Kott. Poland. Austria: Vienna. 1957-1981. 440

Comparative study of directors Otomar Krjča and Peter Brook. Czechoslovakia. UK-England. 1921-1982. 691

Modern analyses of Konstantin Stanislavskij's acting theory. Russia. USSR. 1904-1983. 831

Production styles of directors Peter Brook and Tadeusz Kantor. USA: New York, NY. France: Paris. Poland: Wielopole. 1982. 1632

The Paris Opera production of Peter Brook's *La Tragédie de Carmen*. France: Paris. 1981. 1861

Ten critics review Peter Brook's production of *La Tragédie de Carmen* at the Vivian Beaumont Theatre. USA: New York, NY. 1983. 1914

Brooks, Mel

Plays/librettos/scripts

Essays on the trends of the Jewish-American theatre and its personalities. USA. 1900-1983. 1353

Brossa, Joan

Performance/production

Interview with and influences on postmodern composer Mestres Quaderny. Spain. 1945-1955. 1775

Brothers

Seven critics review Carroll O'Connor's production of George Sibbald's play *Brothers*. USA: New York, NY. 1983. 985

Brough, William

Plays/librettos/scripts

Examination of Samuel Johnson as a character in plays by William Brough and W.S. Gilbert. UK-England: London. 1862-1893. 1313

Brown, Arvin

Performance/production

Six critics review Arvin Brown's production of David Mamet's play *American Buffalo*. USA: New York, NY. 1983. 960

Nine critics review Arvin Brown's production of Arthur Miller's play *A View from the Bridge*. USA: New York, NY. 1983. 969

Brown, Frederick

Institutions

Frederick Brown and Montreal's doomed Theatre Royal. Canada: Montreal, PQ. 1825-1826. 289

Brown, Kenneth

Plays/librettos/scripts

Modern plays set in confining institutions. North America. Europe. 1900-1983. 1200

Browne, Robert

Performance/production

English actors' work in Germany, with mention of stock comic characters. Germany. England: London. 1590-1620. 1525

Bruce, Shelley

Actress Shelley Bruce's struggle with childhood leukemia. USA. 1964. 914

Bruder Eichmann (Brother Eichmann)

Analysis of problems concerning the staging of Heinar Kipphardt's *Brother Eichmann*. Germany, West: Munich. 1983. 765

Plays/librettos/scripts

Brief comments on Heinar Kippardt's play *Brother Eichmann*. Germany, West. 1983. 1149

German Fascism as the main theme of Heinar Kipphardt's plays. Germany, West. 1982. 1153

Bruun-Rasmussen, Ole

Performance/production

Review of international puppet theatre festival. Sweden: Uppsala. 1983. 2054

Bryden, Bill

Institutions

Company members review successes of Cottesloe Company. UK-England: London. 1900-1983. 625

Bucciolini, Giulio

Plays/librettos/scripts

Chronicle of theatre activities, accompanied by a note on Giulio Bucciolini's life and works. Italy: Florence. 1524-1964. 1166

Buckingham, Duke of

Performance/production

Henry Carey's missing music for *tableaux vivant* in the production of *Hamlet* inspired by funeral services for the Duke of Buckingham. England: London. 1736. 698

Buddies in Bad Times (Toronto, ON)

Institutions

Survey of alternative theatres. Canada: Toronto, ON. 1979-1983. 296

Buenaventura, Enrique

Plays/librettos/scripts

Latin American theatre and progressive social movements. Costa Rica. Argentina. Peru. 1588-1983. 1022

Bugler Boy, The

Career of playwright Stanley Eveling. UK-Scotland. 1930-1983. 1341

Bullins, Ed

Performance/production

Founder-director of New Lafayette Theatre discusses purpose and style of rituals. USA: New York, NY. 1969-1972. 2102

Bulwer-Lytton, Edward

Edward Bulwer-Lytton's theory of the need for unified approach to productions, in response to John Calcraft's staging of *Richelieu*. UK-Ireland: Dublin. 1839. 900

Plays/librettos/scripts

Louisa Medina's popular dramatic adaptations of the works of Edward Bulwer-Lytton, Ernest Maltravers and Robert Bird. USA. 1833-1838. 1346

Bundle, The

Epic structure in contemporary drama. UK. 1968-1981. 1275

Bunin, Louis

Design/technology

Lou Bunin memoirs of Meyer Levin's marionettes as ideally cast abstract visual images. USA: Chicago, IL. 1925-1930. 2080

Meyer Levin's marionettes as abstract visual images, influenced by Gordon Craig and Fernand Léger. USA. 1926-1930. 2081

Bunraku

Marionettes designed by Robert Edmond Jones for Metropolitan Opera production of *Oedipus Rex*, under the influence of Gordon Craig and *bunraku*. USA: New York, NY. 1931. 2079

Relation to other fields

Historical consideration of the many forms of Japanese drama in terms or religious origins and aspects. Japan. 1300-1800. 543

Bunraku SEE ALSO: Classed Entries: PUPPETRY — ***Bunraku***

Bunrakuza (Osaka Bunraku Theatre)

Performance/production

Bunraku performances of the Osaka Bunraku Theatre at New York's Japan House. USA: New York, NY. 1983. 2074

Relation to other fields

Bunraku is seen as Japanese miniaturization of social concepts. Japan: Osaka. 1983. 2076

Burbage, James

Performance/production

Marxist theory applied in comparison of public theatres in England and Spain. England. Spain. 1576-1635. 696

Burgtheater (Vienna)

Institutions

Annual report of the Austrian Federal Theatres. Austria: Vienna. 1982-1983. 284

Performance spaces

Concise history of theatre buildings in Vienna. Austria: Vienna. 1300-1983. 358

Performance/production

Memoirs of dramaturg Jan Kott. Poland. Austria: Vienna. 1957-1981. 440

Interview with actor Michael Heltau about his career and forthcoming roles at the Burgtheater. Austria: Vienna. 1983. 674

Portrait of actor Josef Meinrad. Austria: Vienna. 1983. 676

Plays/librettos/scripts

Bertolt Brecht's efforts to obtain Austrian citizenship. Austria. 1922-1982. 1003

Reference materials

Illustrated documentation of Friedrich Hebbel's stay in Vienna. Austria: Vienna. 1845-1863. 1398

Buried Child

Plays/librettos/scripts

Ironic use of folklore in Sam Shepard's *Buried Child*. USA. 1978. 1373

Buried Inside Extra

Performance/production

Five critics review Joseph Papp's production of Thomas Babe's play *Buried Inside Extra*. USA: New York, NY. 1983. 982

Burlesque

Interview with concert singer and comedienne Anna Russell. Canada: Toronto, ON. 1912-1983. 1847

Evolution of *tableaux vivants* into displays of nudity which were eventually suppressed. USA: New York, NY. 1800-1899. 2031

Plays/librettos/scripts

Review essay of *Hamlet* burlesques from a collection of Shakespeare parodies. UK-England. USA. 1810-1888. 1590

Reference materials

Reference guide to popular entertainments. USA: 1840. 1998

Burlesque SEE ALSO: Classed Entries: POPULAR ENTERTAINMENT — Variety acts

Burnaby, William

Performance/production

Questionable chronology results from performances by English officers. Belgium: Maastricht. 1703. 679

Burton, Richard

Notes on three Broadway productions. USA: New York, NY. 1983. 911

Bury, John

Design/technology

Trends in scenic practices by British designers. UK. 1960-1983. 228

Bush Theatre (England)

Institutions

Collaborative production efforts of Bush Theatre. UK-England. 1983. 630

Business is Business* SEE: *Affaires sont les Affaires, Les

Bussotti, Sylvano

Performance/production

Composer Sylvano Bussotti's memoirs and essays on musical theatre. Italy. 1978-1981. 1764

Butō

Guest production of Japanese Butō-company Ariadone at Serapionstheater, Vienna. Japan. Austria: Vienna. 1983. 534

Butterflies, The* SEE: *Farfalle, Le

Bygmester Solness (Master Builder, The)

Performance/production

Peter Zadek's production of *The Master Builder* at the Residenztheater. Germany, West: Munich. 1983. 772

Plays/librettos/scripts

Ibsen's creation of realistic characters displaying unconscious desires. Norway. 1892. 1207

Byrne, John

Performance/production

Six critics review Robert Allan Ackerman's production of John Byrne's play *Slab Boys*. USA: New York, NY. 1983. 970

Byron, George Gordon, Lord

Plays/librettos/scripts

Reevaluation of Lord Byron's plays. England. 1788-1824. 1071

Cab-O-Sil

Design/technology

Use of Cab-O-Sil (silicon dioxide powder) in scene paint. USA. 1983. 263

Cabaret

Performance/production

Evolution of director Harold Prince's concept for the Broadway musical *Cabaret*. USA: New York, NY. 1966. 1804

Cabaret

Relation to other fields

Karl Valentin's humorous proposal that theatre be mandatory for purposes of educating and improving society. Germany. 1882-1948. 55

Cabaret SEE ALSO: Classed Entries: POPULAR ENTERTAINMENT — Cabaret

Cabaret Simpl

Performance/production

Unfinished memoirs of the cabaret comedian Maxi Böhm. Austria. 1916-1982. 2000

Cable

Administration

Yearbook of the international society for copyright. Austria. Italy. North America. 1976-1981. 1704

Cabrujas, José Ignacio

Plays/librettos/scripts

Effects of national and international politics on playwrights of the 'generation of 1958'. Venezuela. 1945-1983. 1392

Canadian Federal Cultural Policy Review Committee

Administration

Critique of recommendations made by Canadian Federal Cultural Policy Review Committee. Canada. 1976-1983.   118

Canadian Opera Company

Performance/production

Interview with soprano Lynn Blaser. Canada. 1983.   1845

Candida

Vienna's English Theatre's 20th anniversary production of G.B. Shaw's *Candida*. Austria: Vienna. 1963.   668

Plays/librettos/scripts

Function of props and settings in plays by George Bernard Shaw. UK-England. 1894-1907.   1281

Candide

Performance/production

Use of puppets and puppetry techniques in Arena Stage production of *Candide*. USA: Washington, DC. 1983.   2061

Cane, Andrew

Other trades plied by English actors. England: London. 1616-1640.
                    416

Canetti, Elias

Plays/librettos/scripts

Critical analysis of three of Elias Canetti's plays. Austria. 1932-1964.
                    1008

Problems in stage adaptation of Elias Canetti's *The Limited*. Germany, West: Stuttgart. 1983.   1150

Canna, Pasquale

Design/technology

Scene designers and scenery at Teatro alla Scala in Neoclassic period. Italy: Milan. 1778-1832.   1821

Cannibalism

Relation to other fields

Cannibalism in drama, art and religion. Europe. Africa. North America.   2099

Canonbury House (London)

Performance/production

New evidence suggests that Castle Ashby plays were performed at Canonbury House. England: London. 1637-1659.   707

Canovacci SEE: *Scenari*

Čapek, Karel

Plays/librettos/scripts

Part one of an essay on Ruggero Vasari's *macchinismo* as a theme of the Futurist theatre. Italy. 1923-1932.   1648

Part two of an essay on Ruggero Vasari's plays and machinery as a theme of the Futurist theatre. Italy. 1923-1932.   1649

Capitol Theatre (Chambersburg, PA)

Performance spaces

Renovation of theatre now used for community theatre and film. USA: Chambersburg, PA. 1926-1983.   401

Car Cemetery SEE: *Cimetière des Voitures, Le*

Cardiff Laboratory Theatre (Wales)

Institutions

Touring accounts of Actors Touring Company, 7:84 Theatre Company and Cardiff Laboratory Theatre. UK-England. UK-Wales. UK-Scotland. USSR. 1983.   634

Carey, Henry

Performance/production

Henry Carey's missing music for *tableaux vivant* in the production

of *Hamlet* inspired by funeral services for the Duke of Buckingham. England: London. 1736.   698

Carinthischer Sommer (Austria)

Institutions

Review of Austrian summer festivals. Austria. 1983.   285

Carmen

Performance/production

Production styles of directors Peter Brook and Tadeusz Kantor. USA: New York, NY. France: Paris. Poland: Wielopole. 1982. 1632

The Paris Opera production of Peter Brook's *La Tragédie de Carmen*. France: Paris. 1981.   1861

Career of soprano Leona Mitchell at the Metropolitan Opera. USA. 1983.   1912

Ten critics review Peter Brook's production of *La Tragédie de Carmen* at the Vivian Beaumont Theatre. USA: New York, NY. 1983.   1914

Carnival

Design/technology

Traditional masks in pageants and masquerades. Europe. 1982. 2095

Performance/production

Impressions of theatre and popular entertainment by a French visitor. England: London. 1754.   419

Relation to other fields

Papal cultural policy and organization of various public festivities. Italy: Rome. Vatican. 1450-1550.   62

Legislative documents related to Byzantine mime, pantomime and masquerade. Byzantine Empire. Asia. 691-1200.   1731

Carnival SEE ALSO: Classed Entries: POPULAR ENTERTAINMENT − Carnival

Carrière, Jean-Claude

Performance/production

Ten critics review Peter Brook's production of *La Tragédie de Carmen* at the Vivian Beaumont Theatre. USA: New York, NY. 1983.   1914

Carroll, Paul Vincent

Plays/librettos/scripts

Irreverent aspects of Irish comedy seen through the works of 14 playwrights. Eire. UK-Ireland. 1840-1965.   1555

Caruso, Enrico

Reference materials

Annotated selections of photographs taken by Herman Mishkin of Metropolitan Opera singers. USA: New York, NY. 1910-1932. 1971

Casablanca

Description of archive holdings at Brigham Young University including personal papers of Howard Hawks and Dean Jagger. USA: Provo, UT. 1900-1983.   48

Casali, Renzo

Theory/criticism

Renzo Casali's theory of acting. Italy. 1983.   1671

Caserta, Ezio Maria

Performance/production

Ezio Maria Caserta's theories and practice of theatre. Italy. 1983-1975.   1624

Casina

Plays/librettos/scripts

Comic mechanism in Plautus' *Amphitruo* and *Casina*. Roman Republic. 254-184 B.C.   1586

Casson, Ann

Performance/production

Importance of vocal techniques for Shavian drama. UK-England. 1945-1981.   896

Casson, Lewis

Importance of vocal techniques for Shavian drama. UK-England. 1945-1981.   896

Caste

Administration

Premiere of *Caste* contributed to passage of American Copyright Act. USA: New York, NY. UK-England: London. 1866-1891.   560

Castellani, Castellano de'

Design/technology

Scenery for the first performance of *Representation of Saint Ursula*. Italy. 1400-1599.   579

Castillo, Julio

Plays/librettos/scripts

Pre-colonial material in modern Mexican drama. Mexico. 1910-1983.   1198

Casting

Administration

Unemployment among Black theatre professionals. UK-England: London. 1974-1979.   146

Performance/production

Production, casts and review of musical *My One and Only*. USA: New York, NY. 1971-1983.   1791

Castle Ashby plays

New evidence suggests that Castle Ashby plays were performed at Canonbury House. England: London. 1637-1659.   707

Castro, Guillén

Plays/librettos/scripts

Staging and scenic practices in the plays of Lope de Vega's forerunners and contemporaries. Spain: Valencia. 1500-1699.   1253

Catalogues

Design/technology

Supplemental materials to costume exhibit. Europe. 1700-1800.   186

Innovations in stage design by Louis-Jacques Daguerre, including a catalogue of his designs. France. 1709-1850.   193

Illustrated catalogue of work of designer Duilio Cambelloti. Italy. 1876-1960.   218

Supplementary materials to exhibit of Baroque theatre and stage design. Italy. 1600.   219

Essays and supplemental materials to exhibition of David Hockney designs, with plates. UK-England. USA. 1937.   229

Articles on designer Oliver Messel. UK-England. 1904-1978.   231

Supplementary materials to exhibit of Jo Mielziner's works. USA. 1928-1960.   233

New products of interest to designers and technicians. USA. 1900-1983.   236

New products for technical theatre use. USA. 1983.   254

Performance/production

Catalogue of exhibition on Max Reinhardt's use of genres and performance spaces. Austria. 1893-1943.   672

Richard Wagner's works, reception and influence. France. 1841-1983.   1859

Plays/librettos/scripts

Catalogue of the exhibition on the copyright debate between playwright Paolo Giacometti and actress Adelaide Ristori. Italy. 1836-1882.   1191

Reference materials

Catalogue of the exhibition of Maria Antonietta Gambaro's paintings and scene designs. Italy. 1951-1980.   27

Catalogue of the exhibition dealing with Leonardo da Vinci's activity as costume and scene designer and inventor of machinery for Sforza's festivals. Italy: Milan. 1484-1500.   28

Catalogue of photographic exhibition of the Teatro Comunale di Ferrara. Italy: Ferrara. 1982.   489

Illustrated documentation of Friedrich Hebbel's stay in Vienna. Austria: Vienna. 1845-1863.   1398

Catalogue of exhibition on pataphysics in figurative arts, theatre and cinema. France. 1873-1907.   1406

Illustrated catalogue of the exposition at the Palazzo Braschi in Rome — dedicated to the actor Ettore Petrolini. Italy. 1982.   1412

Illustrated catalogue of an exhibition on Sicilian dialect theatre. Italy. 1902-1937.   1416

Short essays and a catalogue of an exhibit on fireworks. Italy: Rome. 1500-1899.   1736

Catalogue of exhibition on Giuseppe Sarti, composer and man of the theatre. Italy. 1729-1802.   1765

Catalogue of the exhibition on soprano Toti Dal Monte and tenor Enzo De Muro Lomanto. Italy: Trieste. 1893-1975.   1967

Catalogue of the exhibition on scenery, architecture, dance, opera and public theatres during Pietro Metastasio's life. Italy: Rome. 1698-1782.   1968

Catalogue of Galliari's scene designs owned by Museo Teatrale alla Scala. Italy: Milan. 1778-1823.   1969

Catalogue of an exhibition dealing with Neapolitan comedians. Italy: Naples. 1799-1982.   1997

Catalogue of exhibition on *Commedia dell'arte* and erudite drama with a list of plays by Southern authors. Italy. 1550-1750.   2021

Catalogue for an exhibition of Venetian marionettes and puppets. Italy: Venice. 1700-1899.   2086

Catastrophe

Performance/production

Four critics review Alan Schneider's production of three Samuel Beckett plays. USA: New York, NY. 1983.   928

Cats

Administration

Peter Weck, new manager of Theater an der Wien plans to produce first German language production of Andrew Lloyd Webber's *Cats*. Austria: Vienna. 1983.   1767

Design/technology

Close collaboration between director and lighting designer in *Cats*. USA: New York, NY. 1982.   1768

Caucasian Chalk Circle, The SEE: *Kaukasische Kreidekreis, Der*

Cavett, Dick

Performance/production

Biography of actor and television personality Dick Cavett. USA. 1936-1983.   916

Čechov, Anton Pavlovič

Productions of Russian classics by Bulgarian directors. Bulgaria: Sofia. 1960-1970.   681

Production of Russian classical plays at Eastern European theatres. Bulgaria. Yugoslavia. Czechoslovakia. 1850-1914.   682

Career of director Otomar Krejča, and his interpretations of major playwrights. Czechoslovakia. 1898-1983.   692

Harald Clemens' production of Anton Čechov's *Uncle Vanya* at Nationaltheater. Germany, West: Mannheim. 1983.   777

Arie Zinger's production of Čechov's *Ivanov* at Züricher Schauspielhaus. Switzerland: Zürich. 1983.   849

Descriptive account of Theodore Komisarjevsky's productions of Anton Čechov's plays. UK-England: London. 1926-1936.   875

Six critics review Čechov's *Uncle Vanya* directed by Andre Serban at La Mama. USA: New York, NY. 1982.   967

Influence of Russian playwrights, directors and actors on American theatre. USA. Russia. 1905-1979.   976

Plays/librettos/scripts

Playwrights and dramatic forms influencing Eugene O'Neill's *The Calms of Capricorn*. Europe. USA. 1953.   1088

Continuity of technique throughout Anton Čechov's career. Russia. 1860-1904.   1220

Conventions of vaudeville in Anton Čechov's one-act plays. Russia. 1884-1892.   1221

Segmental analysis of Anton Čechov's plays. Russia. 1860-1904.   1222

Čempionat vsemirnoj klassovoj b'rby (Championship of the Universal Class Struggle, The)

Relation to other fields

Circus as a staging device for a political satire. USSR. Germany. Italy. 1914-1930.   1668

Censorship

Administration

Censorship of Brazilian theatre, causing only Broadway hits to be produced. Brazil. 1557-1983.   116

History of censorship in journals, theatre, cinema, radio and television. Italy. 1944-1980.   136

Intervention of censorship in cinema, radio and theatre. Italy. 1924-1982.   140

Effect of corporate sponsorship on freedom of expression in theatre. Sweden. 1983.   143

Private prosecution of Michael Bogdanov's production of Howard Brenton's *The Romans in Britain*. UK. 1968-1986.   144

Effect of different kinds of financial support on artists. USA. 1950-1982.   163

Censorship on the American stage, particularly of Bertolt Brecht. USA. 1941-1949.   564

Institutions

Activities of church and theatre associations to promote 'decent' dramaturgy. USA: New York, NY, Chicago, IL. 1910-1940.   649

Performance/production

Political censorship and Soviet productions of *Hamlet*. USSR. 1930.   995

Evolution of *tableaux vivants* into displays of nudity which were eventually suppressed. USA: New York, NY. 1800-1899.   2031

Plays/librettos/scripts

Essays on Restoration theatre and drama, with devised criteria for evaluation. England. 1660-1800.   1046

Hidden topicality of 'Saracen' drama. England: London. 1580-1642.   1056

Authorship, censorship and thematic analysis of *Westward Ho!*. England. 1570-1637.   1067

York Creed plays may not have been confiscated by the ecclesiastical authorities. England: York. 1420-1580.   1081

Comparative sociological study of French theatre. France. 1610-1643.   1109

Censorship involving Jerzy Hulewicz' play *Aruna*, produced at Municipal Theatre of Cracow. Poland: Kraków. 1925.   1217

Role of censorship in Johann Nestroy's *Häuptling Abendwind* as an adaptation of Jacques Offenbach's *Vent de soir*. Austria. 1833.   1549

Reference materials

Licensing papers related to managerial and repertorial changes at London theatres. England: London. 1706-1715.   20

Relation to other fields

Athol Fugard's plays are compared to Bantustan agitprop and historical drama. South Africa, Republic of. 1955-1980.   1665

Center Stage of Omaha

Institutions

Center Stage wins top honor in Toyama International Amateur Theatre Festival with *Ain't Misbehavin'*. Japan: Toyama. USA: Omaha, NE. 1983.   1772

Central Red Army Theatre SEE: Centralnyj Teat'r Soveckoj Armii

Central Soviet Army Theatre SEE: Centralnyj Teat'r Soveckoj Armii

Centralnyj Teat'r Soveckoj Armii (Moscow)

Performance/production

Study of A.D. Popov's acting and directing methods, theories of the theatre and teaching techniques. USSR: Moscow. 1900-1958.   998

Centre Dramàtic de la Generalitat (Barcelona)

Institutions

Interview with the director of the Centre Dramàtic de la Generalitat. Spain. 1945-1982.   327

Centre Stage (Toronto, ON)

Administration

Disappointments and mismanagement at Centre Stage. Canada: Toronto, ON. 1983.   119

Centro internazionale di studi estetici (International Centre of Aesthetic Studies)

Relation to other fields

Theatre in relation to other performing arts at the seminar of the International Centre of Aesthetic Studies. Italy. 1982.   64

Čerkasov, N.K.

Performance/production

Articles discussing the work of individual actors at the Academic Drama Theatre of A.S. Puškin. USSR: Leningrad. 1910-1970.   987

Cervantes Saavedra, Miguel de

Plays/librettos/scripts

Discussion of Miguel de Cervantes' *The Farce of the Divorce Judge* in view of Aristotelian *mimesis*. Spain. 1547-1616.   1248

Césaire, Aimé

Jean Genet's *The Blacks* and his theory of ritual in context of Theatre of the Absurd and Total Theatre. France: Paris. 1948-1968.   1647

Relation to other fields

Relationship between politics and the heroic tradition of Caribbean drama. Haiti. Trinidad and Tobago. Martinique. 1962-1979.   1456

Cesare

Plays/librettos/scripts

Analysis of Giovacchino Forzano's play *Cesare*. Italy. 1939.   1173

Ch'eng, Yen-ch'iu

Performance/production

Theatre before and after Mao Tse-tung. China, People's Republic of. 1949-1956.   414

Chaikin, Joseph

Institutions

Reflections on the significance of The Open Theatre by several of its performers, writers and critical advisers. USA: New York, NY. 1963-1973.   1613

Chaliapin, Feodor

Reference materials

Annotated selections of photographs taken by Herman Mishkin of Metropolitan Opera singers. USA: New York, NY. 1910-1932.   1971

Chalmers, Floyd

Administration

Profile of Floyd Chalmers, patron of the arts. Canada. 1898-1983.   1758

Championship of the Universal Class Struggle, The SEE: *Čempionat vsemirnoj klassovoj b'rby*

Changeling, The

Plays/librettos/scripts

Relationship between Jacobean tragedy and interpolated masque. England. 1600-1625.   1691

Chaplin, Charlie

Performance/production

Biography and all-inclusive reference materials to Charlie Chaplin. USA. 1889-1977.   1714

Biography of the clown Charlie Rivel and influence of Charlie Chaplin. Spain. 1896-1983.   2012

Chaplin, Charlie — cont'd

Relation to other fields

Circus as a staging device for a political satire. USSR. Germany. Italy. 1914-1930.   1668

Chapman, George

Plays/librettos/scripts

Authorship, censorship and thematic analysis of *Westward Ho!*. England. 1570-1637.   1067

Chapman, William

Performance/production

John Banvard's autobiography reveals harsh conditions endured by showboat performers. USA. 1833-1836.   1992

Chapman's Ark

John Banvard's autobiography reveals harsh conditions endured by showboat performers. USA. 1833-1836.   1992

Characters/roles

Character of Rangda in Balinese dance-drama. Bali. 1983.   531

Stylized system of movements is used to convey a story and to portray character in the Indonesian theatre. Indonesia. 1977-1980.   533

Contemporary events reflected in staging plays about Jean-Paul Marat's death. France. 1793-1797.   732

Actor Branko Samarovski as Argan in Alfred Kirchner's production of *The Imaginary Invalid*. Germany, West: Bochum. 1983.   760

Various treatments of the induction scene with Christopher Sly in *The Taming of the Shrew*, including lists. UK-England. USA. 1844-1978.   874

Originators of female roles in operas by Wolfgang Amadeus Mozart. Austria. 1777-1791.   1843

Plays/librettos/scripts

Tradition of warrior heroines in Chinese dance and myth. China. 500 B.C.-1978 A.D.   538

Characterization in classical Yogyanese dance. Java. 1755-1980.   541

Bhāva (mood) as expressed through the presentational techniques of *kathakali*. India. 1600-1983.   546

Feminist analysis of sex roles in Shakespeare. England. 1595-1615.   1028

Determining factor of the demonstrative mode of Morality play characters. England. 1300-1550.   1032

Appearance of Banquo's ghost in *Macbeth* clarifies the relation of the audience to the play. England. 1605-1606.   1034

Contrast between public and private life in Shakespeare's history plays. England. 1590-1612.   1045

Analysis of clowns and fools in plays by Shakespeare. England. 1590-1613.   1047

Status of women in Elizabethan society as reflected in Shakespeare's plays. England. 1590-1613.   1049

Psychological examination of title character in *Othello*. England: London. 1604-1605.   1051

Sympathetic portrayals of splendid monarchs are rare in the Corpus Christi cycles. England. 1264-1560.   1055

Possible meanings of characterization in the Mystery plays. England. 1200-1550.   1057

Animal nature and eating habits of characters in Shakespeare's plays. England. 1590-1613.   1058

Analysis of the fool's rhetorical technique of speech in Shakespeare's plays. England. 1592-1605.   1060

Metadramatic elements in Shakespeare's *Troilus and Cressida*. England. 1601-1602.   1074

Sources used by Shakespeare for his play *Richard III*, and changes made to cater to his sovereign's political beliefs. England. 1592-1593.   1076

Paternal authority and sex roles in Shakespeare's plays. England. 1595-1615.   1079

Jewish stereotypes in contemporary drama. Europe. North America. 1982.   1094

Actor's role in plays of Samuel Beckett. Europe. 1957.   1095

Love, freedom and the emergence of the generous hero in Pierre Corneille's early plays. France. 1629-1640.   1105

Italian translation of Bogdal's essay on Gerhart Hauptmann's *Florian Geyer*. Germany. 1896.   1117

Elusive meaning and non-verbal communication in Hofmannsthal's *The Difficult Man*. Germany. 1921.   1124

Genesis of Goethe's *Faust* and changes introduced in the play thereafter. Germany. 1480-1832.   1141

Study of Hermann's character in Heinrich von Kleist's *The Battle of Arminius*. Germany. 1808.   1143

Title character of *Mother Courage* is contrasted with similar figure in Jürgen Gross' drama *Memorial*. Germany, East. 1980.   1145

Comparison of the misanthrope in *Dýskolos*, *Timon of Athens* and *Le Misanthrope*. Greece. England. France. 317 B.C.-1666 A.D.   1155

Relationship between mercantile society and playwright's creation in Carlo Goldoni's plays. Italy: Venice. 1734-1793.   1159

Freudian analysis of the character of Caterina Leher in *The Housekeeper* by Vitaliano Brancati. Italy. 1952.   1172

Productions of Luigi Pirandello's early work contrasted with later ones. Italy. 1898-1917.   1180

Views on Lucretia held by Titus Livius and Niccolò Machiavelli. Italy. 1513-1520.   1183

Psychoanalysis of the protagonists in Gabriele D'Annunzio's *Jorio's Daughter*. Italy. 1904.   1188

Luigi Pirandello's earlier plays are considered prologues to *The Giants of the Mountain*. Italy. 1921-1937.   1189

Analysis of Henrik Ibsen's *Ghosts*. Norway. 1881.   1202

Examination of Stockmann's relationship to the community in *An Enemy of the People*. Norway. 1882.   1203

Ibsen's creation of realistic characters displaying unconscious desires. Norway. 1892.   1207

Examination of psychological complexity of Ibsen characters. Norway. 1850-1906.   1208

Tragic view of the world in Ibsen's plays. Norway. 1879.   1210

Thematic analysis of Ibsen's *Hedda Gabler*. Norway. 1890.   1211

Analysis of Helda Costa's plays about Portuguese Renaissance navigators. Portugal. 1981-1982.   1219

Development of older, comic woman as character type. Spain: Madrid. 1780-1825.   1234

Psychological analysis of Semiramis character from Calderón's *Daughter of the Air*. Spain. 1600-1699.   1235

Work and life of the playwright and novelist Ramón María del Valle-Inclán. Spain: Galicia. 1866-1936.   1251

Calderón's departure from the stock types in the character of the fool, or *gracioso*. Spain. 1626-1681.   1255

Study of George Bernard Shaw's 'Unreasonable Man'. UK-England. 1885-1950.   1282

Characterization and setting used to challenge audience views in George Bernard Shaw's *Major Barbara*. UK-England. 1907.   1287

Reasons for Deeley's calling himself Orson Welles in *Old Times* are based on film *The Magnificent Ambersons*. UK-England. USA. 1942-1971.   1289

Peter Shaffer's revision of *Amadeus*. UK-England: London. USA: New York, NY. 1979-1980.   1290

Analysis of character and structure in G.B. Shaw's *The Devil's Disciple*. UK-England. USA. 1897-1983.   1293

Approaches to drama for young people. UK-England. 1970-1983.   1296

Character analysis of Carr in *Travesties*, by Tom Stoppard. UK-England. 1974.   1309

Examination of Samuel Johnson as a character in plays by William Brough and W.S. Gilbert. UK-England: London. 1862-1893.   1313

Patriot Charles Stewart Parnell's influence on Irish drama. UK-Ireland. 1891-1936.   1337

Decrease in stereotypes of older adults in children's theatre. USA: New York, NY. 1980.   1351

Bertolt Brecht's theory of alienation applied to characters and situations in Tennessee Williams' *Camino Real*. USA. Germany, East. 1941-1953.   1352

Stereotypes of old age in children's plays, and some examples that break it. USA. 1983.   1369

The character of Arlene in Marsha Norman's play *Getting Out*, and her effect on the audience. USA. 1981.   1372

Characters/roles — cont'd

Only three Tony-Award-winning plays reflect feminist ideology. USA: New York, NY. UK-England. 1960-1979.   1374

Two principal female archetypes of Imamu Amiri Baraka's drama. USA. 1964-1978.   1375

Stage incarnations of the characters in Aleksej Nikolajevič Arbuzov's plays. USSR. 1930-1970.   1391

Realism in drama, acting, staging and design. Yugoslavia. 1920-1930.   1395

Alfred Jarry's *Ubu* Cycle with an emphasis on its protagonist. France. 1896-1907.   1566

Unhappy rival in Pierre Corneille's early comedies. France. 1606-1684.   1568

Satire addressed against both sexes in Molière's comedies. France. 1642-1673.   1576

Analysis of forms, styles, characters and influences in Valle-Inclán's *comedias bárbaras*. Spain: Galicia. 1866-1936.   1588

Comic irony and anti-heroes in Irish comedy and influence on Harold Pinter, Samuel Beckett and Tom Stoppard. UK-Ireland. Eire. 1900-1940.   1593

Techniques of dehumanization and linguistic usage in Futurist theatre. Italy. 1909-1931.   1651

Critical essays on *King Lear*. England. 1605.   1688

Relationship between costume changes and change in wearer's fate. Greece. 405 B.C.   1694

Mutes in Greek tragedy. Greece. 523-406 B.C.   1695

Characterization through music in Richard Strauss' *Arabella*. Austria: Vienna. 1927-1929.   1932

Pertinence of human characterizations in Wagner's operas. Germany. 1845-1951.   1946

Identity and personality of the real E.T.A. Hoffman. Germany: Königsberg. 1776-1822.   1948

Discussion of character development of Wotan in *Parsifal* by Richard Wagner. Germany. 1870-1900.   1952

Leporello as alter ego of protagonist in *Don Giovanni*. Italy. 1787.   1957

Italian tenor Luciano Pavarotti discusses the title role of *Ernani* by Giuseppe Verdi. Italy. 1983.   1958

Creation of the title role in *Ernani* for tenor Nicolai Ivanoff. Italy. Russia. 1844.   1959

Relation to other fields

Dramatist Stanisław Wyspiański's painting of a Tartar costume, based on a folk tradition stock type — Lajkonik. Poland: Kraków. Austria. 1901-1907.   1461

First hand experience of performing mythical plays in country fields. Italy. 1983.   1664

Theory/criticism

Issues of role playing and identity in theatre. Europe. North America. 1982.   1486

Charlottetown Festival (Charlottetown, PE)

Reference materials

Cast listings and other information on 19 productions mounted at Charlottetown Festival. Canada: Charlottetown, PE. 1965-1982. 1399

Chatterjee, Sekhar

Performance/production

Relationship between Bertolt Brecht and Asian theatre. Asia. Germany. 1925-1981.   665

Chayefsky, Paddy

Plays/librettos/scripts

Essays on the trends of the Jewish-American theatre and its personalities. USA. 1900-1983.   1353

Cheadle, Halton

Theory/criticism

Study of genesis, development, structural components and consequences of theatre-drama performed by the Black workers. South Africa, Republic of. 1981-1983.   1673

Chekhov, Anton SEE: Čechov, Anton Pavlovič

Chekhov, Michael

Performance/production

History of directing. Europe. 1882-1982.   708

Political censorship and Soviet productions of *Hamlet*. USSR. 1930.   995

Theory/criticism

Michael Chekhov's lecture on changing the focus and operating structure of theatre to make it relevant. USA. 1942.   112

Chéreau, Patrice

Performance/production

Patrice Chéreau directs Bernard-Marie Koltès' *Fight of the Negro and the Dogs* at Théâtre des Amandiers. France: Nanterre. 1982.   736

Six essays on the productions and artistic views held by leading European directors. Europe. 1960-1980.   1615

History and production history of Wagnerian opera. Germany. USA. 1832-1982.   1865

Photographs and personnel of Bayreuth Festival production of *Siegfried*. Germany, West: Bayreuth. 1980.   1866

Photographs and personnel of Bayreuth Festival production of *Götterdämmerung*. Germany, West: Bayreuth. 1980.   1867

Photographs and personnel of Bayreuth Festival production of *Die Walküre*. Germany, West: Bayreuth. 1980.   1869

Patrice Chéreau talks about his production of Richard Wagner's *Der Ring des Nibelungen*. Germany, West: Bayreuth. 1976.   1875

Cherry Orchard, The SEE: *Višněvy Sad*

Chesnaye, Nicolas de la

Plays/librettos/scripts

The condemnation of pleasure dominated by lust and gluttony in morality plays. France. 1400-1499.   1106

Chester cycle

Performance/production

Review of contemporary three-day performance of the Chester plays. Canada: Toronto, ON. 1983.   684

Review of the Chester cycle performed in Toronto, May 1983. Canada: Toronto, ON. 1983.   687

Men acting in women's roles, particularly in the Chester cycle's *Purification*. England: Chester. 1300-1550.   702

Review of the Chester plays performed in Chester, June 1983. England: Chester. 1983.   703

Census, with brief reviews, of performances of medieval drama. Europe. 1982-1983.   710

Review of the Chester cycle performed in a 1550's design. UK: Leeds. England: Chester. 1550-1983.   851

Plays/librettos/scripts

Possible authorship of a lost Chester Corpus Christi play. England: Chester. 1268-1375.   1037

Chestnut Street Theatre (Philadelphia, PA)

Performance/production

Adverse reception of Madame Vestris and Charles Mathews on tour in USA. USA: New York, NY, Philadelphia, PA. UK-England: London. 1838.   933

Chicano theatre SEE: Ethnic theatre

Chikamatsu, Monzaemon

Relation to other fields

Bunraku is seen as Japanese miniaturization of social concepts. Japan: Osaka. 1983.   2076

Children of a Lesser God

Plays/librettos/scripts

Examination of plays adapted for movies. USA. 1974.   1345

Children of the Dead End

Tom Lannon discusses background of his play *Children of the Dead End*. UK-Scotland. 1983.   1339

Children's theatre

Audience

Audience development programs for young people. UK-England. USA: Santa Barbara, CA. 1980.   169

Characteristics of a typical children's audience. USA. 1983.   2034

Design/technology

Puppets and performance techniques used in Kennedy Center production of *The Tale of Peter Rabbit*. USA: Washington, DC. 1983.   2035

Institutions

History and concerns of Green Thumb Theatre. Canada. 1975-1983.   293

Formation of joint committee by amateur theatres and its Training Council. Finland. 1983.   300

Profile of theatres for young people. USA. 1983.   353

New awards — Distinguished Play Award and Campton Bell Award — honor those serving children's theatre. USA. 1983.   354

Review of Children's and Youth Theatre Festival. Germany, East: Halle. 1983.   600

State of school-theatre and theatre for young people. Germany, West. 1980-1983.   605

Edward Bond's *Saved* and Shakespeare's *Troilus and Cressida* at the Jugendclub Kritisches Theater. Germany, West: Stuttgart. 1981-1983.   608

Need for mythology in the repertory of children's theatre to cope with the modern world. Sweden. 1983.   620

History of Karamu Children's Theatre. USA: Cleveland, OH. 1915-1975.   647

Production of *Nightingale* by First All Children's Theatre, and Meridee Stein, the group's founder. USA: New York, NY. 1982.   650

Performance/production

Seven basic rules for writing songs for children's theatre. USA. 1983.   460

Rehearsal methods of director Finn Poulsen. Sweden: Göteborg, Gävleborg. 1969-1983.   839

Director of Polka Children's Theatre discusses children's attitude to plays and puppets. UK. 1983.   852

Enactment and narration as particularly appropriate methods of dramatization. USA. 1968-1980.   906

Children's Theatre Association of America standards for productions for young audiences. USA. 1983.   2056

Plays/librettos/scripts

Approaches to drama for young people. UK-England. 1970-1983.   1296

Peter Terson's work, especially his association with National Youth Theatre. UK-England. 1960-1983.   1299

Decrease in stereotypes of older adults in children's theatre. USA: New York, NY. 1980.   1351

Stereotypes of old age in children's plays, and some examples that break it. USA. 1983.   1369

Plays and productions at Young Playwrights Festival. USA: New York, NY. 1982.   1384

Reference materials

Bibliography of education resources on creativity and dramatic activities in elementary schools. USA. 1976-1982.   42

Relation to other fields

Documents available from Educational Resources Information Center related to educational theatre. USA. 1983.   73

Elementary teachers' attitudes toward creative drama in the classroom. USA. 1983.   75

Impact of the creative drama activities on language disordered children. USA. 1983.   77

Comparison of various methods, including creative drama, in teaching literature. USA. 1983.   1467

Description of Jane Addams' creative drama activities at Hull House. USA: Chicago, IL. 1889-1910.   1469

Effects of creative drama on development of language skills. USA. 1983.   1471

Senior citizens use puppets to teach handicapped children. USA: Akron, OH. 1983.   2068

Research/historiography

Categories devised to measure young people's responses to children's theatre productions. USA. 1983.   1474

Descriptive and empirical research in children's drama. USA. 1900-1983.   1475

Results of a study which measures acting and monitoring skills in children. USA. 1983.   1476

Training

Comparison of various training programs in children's theatre and creative dramatics. USA. 1950-1982.   509

Children's Theatre Association of America (CTAA)

Performance/production

Children's Theatre Association of America standards for productions for young audiences. USA. 1983.   2056

Performances by Ragabush Puppet Theatre and Lampoon Puppet theatre at Children's Theatre Association of America Showcase. USA: Syracuse, NY. 1983.   2058

Children's theatre SEE ALSO: Creative drama

Chin, Daryl

Performance/production

Daryl Chin's theories and analysis of his own work. USA. 1976.   1753

Chinese Cultural Revolution

Relation to other fields

Impressions of the Chinese intellectual reaction to Shakespeare, freedom of thought and Cultural Revolution. China, People's Republic of: Beijing, Shanghai. 1920-1982.   1445

Chinese Opera

Performance/production

Relationship between Bertolt Brecht and Asian theatre. Asia. Germany. 1925-1981.   665

Chips with Everything

Plays/librettos/scripts

Modern plays set in confining institutions. North America. Europe. 1900-1983.   1200

Chocrón, Isaac

Effects of national and international politics on playwrights of the 'generation of 1958'. Venezuela. 1945-1983.   1392

Choiński, Krysztof

Analysis of Krysztof Choiński's plays. Poland. 1961-1983.   1215

Chong, Ping

Performance/production

Description and analysis of Ping Chong's work. USA. 1972-1983.   1752

Career of performance artist Ping Chong. USA: New York, NY. 1972-1982.   1755

Choreographers SEE: Choreography

Choreography

Institutions

Dance training at Theatre Academy of Finland. Finland: Helsinki. 1910-1983.   516

Performance/production

Autobiographical survey by choreographer Lincoln Kirstein. USA. India: Marrakesh. Europe. 1916-1949.   514

Discussion of ballet in Monte Carlo. Monaco. 1948-1983.   519

Choreography — cont'd

Documentation on Judson Dance Theater and creation of post-modern dance. USA: New York, NY. 1962-1964.   527

View of man and recurring Greek symbolism in Martha Graham's choreography. USA. 1947.   528

Origins and evolution of the *Kuchipudi* dance drama. India. 200 B.C.-1983 A.D.   532

Stylized system of movements is used to convey a story and to portray character in the Indonesian theatre. Indonesia. 1977-1980.   533

Typical movement, music, costumes, performers and historic influences in *odori* and *mai* dance. Japan. 900-1900.   544

Career of performance artist Ping Chong. USA: New York, NY. 1972-1982.   1755

Production elements and choreography of *On Your Toes*. USA. 1982.   1782

George Balanchine's contribution to dance in musical theatre. USA: New York, NY. 1929-1962.   1787

Overview of Jack Cole's career as dancer, teacher and choreographer. USA. 1933-1974.   1788

Production, casts and review of musical *My One and Only*. USA: New York, NY. 1971-1983.   1791

Nine critics review George Abbott's production of the musical *On Your Toes*. USA: New York, NY. 1983.   1803

Work of the director/choreographer N.M. Forreger in the musical theatre. USSR. 1929-1939.   1930

Plays/librettos/scripts

Analysis of John Neumeier's production of *St. Matthew Passion*. Germany, West: Hamburg. USA: New York, NY. 1982-1983.   521

Shift in dramatic emphasis in Igor Strawinsky's *Apollon Musagete* due to sets, costumes and choreography. USA: Washington, DC, New York, NY. 1927-1979.   522

Tradition of warrior heroines in Chinese dance and myth. China. 500 B.C.-1978 A.D.   538

Characterization in classical Yogyanese dance. Java. 1755-1980.   541

Reference materials

Bibliography of performing arts periodicals. 1982.   11

Theory/criticism

Lack of socio-political engagement in contemporary performance. USA. 1983.   111

Training

Ballet work and training in opera houses in East Germany. Germany, East: Leipzig, Dresden, East Berlin. 1981-1983.   523

Christoff, Boris

Performance/production

Boris Christoff, bass, speaks of his career and art. USA: New York, NY. 1947-1983.   1924

Chudožestvennyj teat'r SEE: Moskovskij Chudožestvennyj Akademičeskij Teat'r

Church and Drama League of America

Institutions

Activities of church and theatre associations to promote 'decent' dramaturgy. USA: New York, NY, Chicago, IL. 1910-1940.   649

Churchill, Caryl

Performance/production

First German production of Caryl Churchill's *Cloud Nine* at Schlossparktheater directed by Harald Clemens. Germany, West: West Berlin. 1983.   775

Eight critics review Max Stafford-Clark's production of Caryl Churchill's play *Top Girls*. USA: New York, NY. 1983.   958

Six critics review Les Waters' production of Caryl Churchill's play *Fen*. USA: New York, NY. 1983.   964

Plays/librettos/scripts

Epic structure in contemporary drama. UK. 1968-1981.   1275

Ciarenz, Egische

Egische Ciarenz's plays, particularly *Kafkaz*, are placed between Futurism and agitprop theatre. Armenia. 1923.   1634

Ciceri, Pierre-Luc-Charles

Theme of monarchy in French Romantic opera and its effect on scenery. France: Paris. 1814-1850.   1939

Ciléa, Francesco

Performance/production

Photographs, cast lists, synopsis and discography of Metropolitan Opera production of *Adriana Lecouvreur*. USA: New York, NY. 1983.   1897

Cincinnati Summer Opera

Account of *Risurrezione*, to be performed by Cincinnati Summer Opera. USA: Cincinnati, OH. 1904-1983.   1923

Cinna

Plays/librettos/scripts

Aesthetic continuity in Pierre Corneille's movement from comedy to tragedy. France. 1606-1684.   1112

Circle in the Square (New York, NY)

Performance/production

Ten critics review Anthony Page's production of *Heartbreak House* presented at Circle in the Square. USA: New York, NY. 1983.   910

Seven critics review Arthur Sherman's production of Herman Wouk's play *The Caine Mutiny Court-Martial*. USA: New York, NY. 1983.   955

Circle of Waters Circus

Institutions

Description of *Circle of Waters Circus*, a travelling puppet pageant using 150 puppets and 30 performers. USA: Minneapolis, MN. 1983.   2048

Circle Repertory Company (New York, NY)

Performance/production

Seven critics review Sam Shepard's production of his play *Fool for Love* presented by Circle Repertory Company. USA: New York, NY. 1983.   963

Circus

Enactment and narration as particularly appropriate methods of dramatization. USA. 1968-1980.   906

Attitude of Western audiences to the performances of native Africans in various settings. USA. UK. 1800-1899.   1994

Documentation on André Heller's *Flic Flac, Theater des Feuers* and *Roncalli*. Austria. Germany, West. Portugal: Lisbon. 1975-1983.   2027

Reference materials

Reference guide to popular entertainments. USA. 1840.   1998

Relation to other fields

Circus as a staging device for a political satire. USSR. Germany. Italy. 1914-1930.   1668

Circus Gregory (Athens)

Performance/production

Circus life and performance based on the memoirs of acrobat Leonora Whiteley. Greece: Athens. 1880-1899.   2011

Circus Medrano

Story of a live horse and a marionette ballerina act at the Circus Medrano. France: Paris. 1980.   2010

Circus SEE ALSO: Classed Entries: POPULAR ENTERTAINMENT — Circus

Cité-Variétés

Relation to other fields

Relations between theatre and politics during the French Revolution. France: Paris, Tours. 1789-1794.   1451

Citizens' Theatre (Glasgow)

Performance/production

Fusion of visual and verbal elements creates a style of voluptuous theatricality at Citizens' Theatre. UK-Scotland: Glasgow. 1969-1979.   901

Conferences — cont'd

Study of sound technology at the 43rd Conference of Theatre Technology. Germany, West: Heilbronn. 1983.   204

Report of Nordisk TeaterTeknik 83 conference. Sweden: Stockholm. 1983.   223

Report on Lighting World II Conference. USA: New York, NY. 1983.   274

Institutions

Activities of the New York ATA convention program on Asian theatre. Asia. USA: New York, NY. 1983.   282

Overview of the German Shakespeare Society Conference. Germany, East: Weimar. 1982.   602

Performance spaces

Examples of theatre architecture as displayed at USITT conference. USA. Canada. 1972-1980.   393

Performance/production

Papers on Finnish-Soviet theatrical contacts. Finland. USSR. 1981.   423

Relation to other fields

Theatre in relation to other performing arts at the seminar of the International Centre of Aesthetic Studies. Italy. 1982.   64

Role of theatre in education. USA. 1983.   72

Inaugural address of American Theatre Association president Bernard S. Rosenblatt calling for support in creating public policy. USA: Minneapolis, MN. 1983.   76

Research/historiography

Recent publications, works in progress and coming events concerning 19th century theatre. Europe. North America. 1800-1899.   82

Confessions of an Actor

Performance/production

Italian translation of Laurence Olivier's autobiography *Confessions of an Actor*. UK-England. 1907-1983.   892

Connolly, Bill

Work of The Puppet People on Broadway production of *Alice in Wonderland*. USA: New York, NY. 1982.   2055

Conquest of Mexico, The

Plays/librettos/scripts

Contradiction in personal and artistic life of Antonin Artaud. France. 1921-1948.   1645

Conrad Schmitt Studios

Performance spaces

Process of theatre restoration by Conrad Schmitt Studios. USA. 1983.   397

Constant, Marius

Performance/production

Ten critics review Peter Brook's production of *La Tragédie de Carmen* at the Vivian Beaumont Theatre. USA: New York, NY. 1983.   1914

Construction

Design/technology

Fire-prevention equipment needed for theatres. Germany, West: West Berlin. 1973-1983.   210

Performance spaces

Building, restoration and revitalization of theatres. Canada: Toronto, ON. 1983.   360

Construction and technical equipment of a new theatre building. Germany, West: Heilbronn. 1961-1983.   372

Construction, renovation and technical equipment of historic theatre buildings. Italy: Modena, Reggio Emilia, Parma. 1588-1985.   382

Project for a new studio to optimize the audience/performer relationship. Germany, West: West Berlin. 1983.   1834

Constructivism

Design/technology

Comprehensive documented study of Russian Constructivism. USSR. 1917-1940.   278

Contes d'Hoffman, Les

Performance/production

Comparison of performances of tenor aria 'O Dieu de quelle ivresse' by Jacques Offenbach. France. USA. 1911-1983.   1857

Photographs, cast lists, synopsis and discography of Metropolitan Opera production of *Les Contes d'Hoffman*. USA: New York, NY. 1983.   1900

Plays/librettos/scripts

Identity and personality of the real E.T.A. Hoffman. Germany: Königsberg. 1776-1822.   1948

Contracts

Administration

Six payments to traveling entertainers from two hitherto unpublished documents in Warwick County Records Office. England: Warwick. 1601-1637.   121

Accounts of payment to assorted entertainers performing for Lord Berkeley. England: Coventry. 1593-1605.   122

Laws, provisions and contracts regulating conditions of employment in different fields of theatre. Italy. 1983.   139

Letters and documents concerning performances at local opera houses. USA: Grand Forks, ND, Crookston, MN. 1890-1899.   155

Institutions

Annual report of the Austrian Federal Theatres. Austria: Vienna. 1982-1983.   284

Controllo Totale

History and analysis of three productions by the avant-garde theatre group Falso Movimento. Italy. 1977-1983.   1607

Conventions SEE: Conferences

Cook, Will Marion

Performance/production

Account of a production of the musical *In Dahomey*. UK-England: London. 1903-1904.   1776

Cooper, Thomas Abthorpe

Shakespearean productions and festivals in the American South. USA. 1751-1980.   938

Copeau, Jacques

Institutions

Founding of periodical *Nouvelle Revue Française*. France: Paris. 1909-1914.   304

Performance/production

Artistic movements and critical thought that shaped modern directing. Europe. 1914-1940.   715

Son of actress Suzanne Bing recalls her memories of Jacques Copeau. France: Paris. 1913-1948.   724

Memories of Jacques Copeau by his son. France: Paris. USA: New York, NY. 1910-1949.   725

Actor-audience relationship in productions by Jacques Copeau, Bertolt Brecht and Russian directors. France. USSR. Germany. 1900-1956.   726

Jacques Copeau remembered by his granddaughter, actress Catherine Dasté. France: Pernand. 1940-1949.   727

Innovative production of Calderón de la Barca's *Life is a Dream*. France. 1922.   731

Plays/librettos/scripts

Comparison of two French translations of *Twelfth Night*, by Jacques Copeau/Théodore Lascarais and Suzanne Bing. France: Paris. 1914.   1567

Relation to other fields

Jacques Copeau's reading of his play *The Little Pauper* to the Cistercians during the Occupation. France: Pernand. 1940-1944.   1450

Training

Concept of school in Jacques Copeau's work. France: Paris. 1913-1930.   1523

Costuming — cont'd

David Ultz's career as scene and costume designer. UK-England: London. USA: New York, NY. 1983. 230

Unified approach to audiovisual design. USA. 1977. 241

Work of costume designer Tanya Moiseiwitsch. USA. UK. 1914-1982. 243

History and description of the Motley Theatre and Costume Arts Collection. Discussed at SIBMAS. USA: Urbana, IL. 1982. 247

New products for technical theatre use. USA. 1983. 254

Middle class morality reflected in nineteenth-century fashion. USA. 1830-1870. 258

Report of research among theatrical designers. USA. 1981-1983. 259

Costumes of 'La Belle Epoque' at the Metropolitan Museum of Art. USA: New York, NY. 1870-1910. 260

Guide to techniques of costume design. USA. 1983. 261

Suggestions regarding children's touring shows. USA. 1983. 262

Fashions for costuming. USA. 1915-1970. 266

How to construct women's garment sleeves. USA. 1930-1939. 268

Cutting and assembling an apron. USA. 1900-1983. 269

Theatre collection taxonomy based on an iconographic approach discussed at SIBMAS. USA: Columbus, OH. 1982. 276

Interview with Jane Greenwood on her experiences in costuming Ibsen, particularly *Hedda Gabler*. USA. 1980-1981. 581

Vincente Minnelli's pre-Hollywood years as Broadway designer. USA: Hollywood, CA, New York, NY. 1931-1939. 1769

Interviews with the designers of *Cats*. USA: New York, NY. UK-England: London. 1983. 1770

Technical aspects of Broadway production of *La Cage aux Folles*. USA: New York, NY. 1983. 1771

Costumes of Teatro alla Scala and chronology of its costumers. Italy: Milan. 1947-1982. 1819

Institutions

Summary of study about training costume designers. USA. 1979-1983. 346

Performance/production

Typical movement, music, costumes, performers and historic influences in *odori* and *mai* dance. Japan. 900-1900. 544

History of *Ru-howzi* improvisational theatre. Iran. 1780-1950. 792

Collection of photographs of Broadway productions and actors. USA: New York, NY. 1940-1967. 921

Richard Wagner's works, reception and influence. France. 1841-1983. 1859

Social status and role of minstrels. Europe. 1100-1500. 1986

Plays/librettos/scripts

Shift in dramatic emphasis in Igor Strawinsky's *Apollon Musagete* due to sets, costumes and choreography. USA: Washington, DC, New York, NY. 1927-1979. 522

Examination of semiotic elements in George Bernard Shaw's *Pygmalion*. UK. 1916. 1274

Relationship between costume changes and change in wearer's fate. Greece. 405 B.C. 1694

Reference materials

Models of scenery and costumes in the Bibliothèque Nationale. France: Paris. 1982. 24

Catalogue of the exhibition dealing with Leonardo da Vinci's activity as costume and scene designer and inventor of machinery for Sforza's festivals. Italy: Milan. 1484-1500. 28

Bibliography of flat pattern sources continued from *Theatre Design & Technology*, Winter 1983. USA. 1900-1983. 47

Description of archive holdings at Brigham Young University including personal papers of Howard Hawks and Dean Jagger. USA: Provo, UT. 1900-1983. 48

Description of David O. Selznick collection: '*Gone with the Wind*: A Legend Endures'. USA. 1939-1983. 1721

Relation to other fields

Dramatist Stanisław Wyspiański's painting of a Tartar costume, based on a folk tradition stock type — Lajkonik. Poland: Kraków. Austria. 1901-1907. 1461

COTR SEE: Commission of Theatre Research

Countess Cathleen, The

Plays/librettos/scripts

Images of the supernatural in William Butler Yeat's *The Countess Cathleen*. UK-Ireland. 1890. 1336

Country Roads Inc.

Performance spaces

Restoration of theatre chairs. USA. 1983. 409

Country Wife, The

Theory/criticism

Morality of Restoration comedy. England. 1670-1700. 1599

Court entertainment

Administration

Court entertainments during reign of Henry VII, from early records. England: London. 1485-1505. 1737

Design/technology

Cataloguing work done since 1975 at Drottningholm Theatre Museum. Sweden: Drottningholm, Gripsholm. 1766-1800. 222

Performance spaces

Location of the turret in Greenwich Park. England: London. 1500. 361

Performance/production

History of equestrian ballet with an emphasis on 17th century. Europe. 1559-1854. 1735

Plays/librettos/scripts

Pastoral as dramatic genre and its literary and scenic derivations. Italy. 1400-1599. 1185

Examination of Arthur Wing Pinero's court farces. UK-England. 1890-1899. 1591

Relationship between Jacobean tragedy and interpolated masque. England. 1600-1625. 1691

Reference materials

Catalogue of the exhibition dealing with Leonardo da Vinci's activity as costume and scene designer and inventor of machinery for Sforza's festivals. Italy: Milan. 1484-1500. 28

Court entertainment SEE ALSO: Classed Entries: MIXED PERFORMANCES - Court masque

Covent Garden Opera House SEE: Royal Opera House, Covent Garden

Coward, Noel

Institutions

Repertory and workings of Glasgow Citizens' Theatre. UK-Scotland: Glasgow. 1983. 642

Performance/production

Notes on three Broadway productions. USA: New York, NY. 1983. 911

Nine critics review Milton Katselas' production of Noel Coward's play *Private Lives*. USA: New York, NY. 1983. 1545

Plays/librettos/scripts

Biography of Noel Coward with analysis of his plays. UK-England. 1899-1973. 1298

Craig, Edward Gordon

Design/technology

Marionettes designed by Robert Edmond Jones for Metropolitan Opera production of *Oedipus Rex*, under the influence of Gordon Craig and *bunraku*. USA: New York, NY. 1931. 2079

Meyer Levin's marionettes as abstract visual images, influenced by Gordon Craig and Fernand Léger. USA. 1926-1930. 2081

Institutions

Background of Edward Gordon Craig's efforts to establish School for the Art of Theatre. Italy: Florence. UK-England: London. 1900-1917. 320

Craig, Edward Gordon — cont'd

Performance/production

History of directing. Europe. 1882-1982.   708

Polish director Bohden Korzeniewski reminisces about meeting Edward Gordon Craig. France: Vence. 1957.   733

Edward Gordon Craig's productions of and theories on Shakespeare. UK-England. Europe. 1872-1940.   862

Director Edward Gordon Craig's writings on theatre. UK-England. 1872-1966.   870

Study of director Edward Gordon Craig. UK-England. 1872-1966.   883

Reconstruction of Edward Gordon Craig's production of *Hamlet* at Moscow Art Theatre. Russia: Moscow. 1908-1912.   1682

Reference materials

Description of various documents, photographs, designs and engravings on display at Edward Gordon Craig exhibit. UK-England. 1900-1935.   36

Collection of Edward Gordon Craig materials available to researchers. UK-England. USA. 1872-1966.   1429

Theory/criticism

Writings of Edward Gordon Craig. UK-England. 1907-1957.   1513

Overview of early aesthetic theory of puppetry. Europe. 1907-1983.   2072

Crane, Hart

Plays/librettos/scripts

Hart Crane's influence on plays by Tennessee Williams. USA. 1938-1980.   1354

Crane, Richard

Administration

Interview with the new artistic director and literary advisor for the Iron Theatre (Glasgow). UK-Scotland. 1973-1983.   559

Crawford, Cheryl

Institutions

History of American Repertory Theatre. USA. 1945-1947.   652

Creation Production Company (New York, NY)

Performance/production

Analysis and critique of avant-garde trends in theatre. USA. 1970-1983.   470

Creative drama

Institutions

Formation of joint committee by amateur theatres and its Training Council. Finland. 1983.   300

Performance/production

Use of Inventory of Dramatic Behavior in actor training. USA. 1980-1983.   974

Reference materials

Bibliography of education resources on creativity and dramatic activities in elementary schools. USA. 1976-1982.   42

Relation to other fields

American Theatre Association statement of policy on theatre in elementary education. USA. 1983.   71

Elementary teachers' attitudes toward creative drama in the classroom. USA. 1983.   75

Impact of the creative drama activities on language disordered children. USA. 1983.   77

Comparison of various methods, including creative drama, in teaching literature. USA. 1983.   1467

Description of Jane Addams' creative drama activities at Hull House. USA: Chicago, IL. 1889-1910.   1469

Effects of creative drama on development of language skills. USA. 1983.   1471

Research/historiography

Discussion of the *Inventory of Dramatic Behavior Adapted for Group Observation.* USA. 1980.   91

Descriptive and empirical research in children's drama. USA. 1900-1983.   1475

Results of a study which measures acting and monitoring skills in children. USA. 1983.   1476

Training

Comparison of various training programs in children's theatre and creative dramatics. USA. 1950-1982.   509

Creative drama SEE ALSO: Children's theatre

Cricot 2 (Cracow)

Institutions

History of Tadeusz Kantor's alternative theatre, Cricot 2. Poland. 1955-1983.   1611

Performance/production

Comprehensive study of productions by Tadeusz Kantor's experimental theatre group Cricot 2 and Kantor's philosophy. Poland. 1975-1980.   1626

Interview with playwright-director Tadeusz Kantor about *Wielopole, Wielopole.* Poland: Wielopole. 1982.   1628

Tadeusz Kantor's theory of art and theatre, and productions of his company Cricot 2. Poland: Kraków. 1943-1975.   1629

Production styles of directors Peter Brook and Tadeusz Kantor. USA: New York, NY. France: Paris. Poland: Wielopole. 1982.   1632

Crimes and Crimes SEE: *Brott och brott*

Cristophe, Henri

Relation to other fields

Relationship between politics and the heroic tradition of Caribbean drama. Haiti. Trinidad and Tobago. Martinique. 1962-1979.   1456

Criticism SEE: Theory/criticism

Croatian Faust

Plays/librettos/scripts

Current state of drama and theatre seen through plays and playwrights. Yugoslavia. 1983.   1393

Cronyn, Tandy

Interview with director and cast of Yale Repertory's production of G.B. Shaw's *The Philanderer.* USA: New Haven, CT. 1982.   1389

Crouse-Hinds Concert Theatre (Syracuse, NY)

Performance spaces

Conversion of Crouse-Hinds Concert Theatre for use as convention hall. USA: Syracuse, NY. 1982-1983.   406

Crow, Brian

Relation to other fields

Workshop on the use of puppets in education and therapy. Nigeria: Zaria. 1983.   2067

Cruel Games SEE: *Žestokije igry*

Cruikshank

Basic theatrical documents

Revised edition of Punch and Judy script. UK-England. 1873-1983.   2017

CTAA SEE: Children's Theatre Association of America

Cuatrotablas

Institutions

Evolution and theories of Odin Teatret. Sweden. 1964-1979.   621

Plays/librettos/scripts

Collected materials on Eugenio Barba and Odin Teatret. Sweden. 1964-1979.   1258

Dance — cont'd

Design/technology

Introductory lighting textbook. USA. 1982. 270

Staging, masks and dance of the Odo Festival. Nigeria. 1982. 2104

Institutions

Documentation on Karlsplatz festival, part of Wiener Festwochen. Austria: Vienna. 1983. 288

Discussion of performance group Jack Helen Brut consisting of fifteen art students, artists and dancers. Finland: Helsinki. 1983. 1739

Performance/production

Legal record details early career of dancer John Dennison and an episode in life of David Garrick. England: London. 1747-1757. 417

Collection of essays on performing arts. India. 431

Autobiographical survey by choreographer Lincoln Kirstein. USA. India: Marrakesh. Europe. 1916-1949. 514

Debbie Allen discusses her struggle for success and her relationship with her family. USA. 1983. 515

Evelyn Hart's debut as Giselle with the Royal Winnipeg Ballet. Canada: Winnipeg, ON. 1966-1982. 517

Contributors to dance reform in French theatre. France: Paris. 1752-1781. 518

Sociological and psychological implications faced by dancers at end of their performing careers. USA. 1982. 520

Biography of Isadora Duncan. Europe. USA. 1878-1927. 525

Working practice of Laurie Booth in light of contemporary attitudes toward dance. UK. 1978-1983. 526

Typical movement, music, costumes, performers and historic influences in *odori* and *mai* dance. Japan. 900-1900. 544

John Marshall production of the Digby plays at Winchester Cathedral places particular emphasis on dance. UK-England: Winchester. 1983. 889

Intimate relationship with the audience in the work designed for performance video. USA. 1980. 1723

Production elements and choreography of *On Your Toes*. USA. 1982. 1782

Overview of Jack Cole's career as dancer, teacher and choreographer. USA. 1933-1974. 1788

History of Broadway musical theatre with an extensive annotated discography. USA: New York, NY. 1800-1983. 1789

Reference materials

Bibliography of performing arts periodicals. 1982. 11

Biographies of theatre personalities. England: London. 1660-1800. 19

Catalogue of the exhibition on scenery, architecture, dance, opera and public theatres during Pietro Metastasio's life. Italy: Rome. 1698-1782. 1968

Theory/criticism

Physical experience and aesthetic perception of body movement. France. 1889. 100

Phenomenological theory of performing arts. USA. 1982. 1514

Training

Training manual for performers. 1982. 492

Dance a Little Closer

Performance/production

Six critics review Alan Jay Lerner's production of the musical *Dance a Little Closer*. USA: New York, NY. 1983. 1793

Dance SEE ALSO: Choreography and Classed Entries: DANCE

Dancers SEE: Dance

Danias, Starr

Performance/production

Production elements and choreography of *On Your Toes*. USA. 1982. 1782

Daniel

Plays/librettos/scripts

Aspects of liturgical drama cause it to be both ritual and theatre. France. 1100-1200. 1101

Daniel, L.

Performance/production

Productions of Russian classics by Bulgarian directors. Bulgaria: Sofia. 1960-1970. 681

Daoust, Julien

Administration

Biography and legacy of dramaturg Julien Daoust. Canada. 1866-1943. 552

Dark Crystal, The

Performance/production

Contributions made to puppetry by Jim Henson's *Dark Crystal*. USA. 1980-1983. 2059

Darlo todo y no dar nada (To Give It All and Nothing)

Plays/librettos/scripts

Comparison between a painting by Diego Velázquez and a play by Calderón de la Barca. Spain. 1625-1651. 1229

DaSilva, Joan

Institutions

Development of DaSilva Puppets, and establishment of permanent base for performance. UK-England: Norwich, Godmancester. 1962-1983. 2044

DaSilva, Ray

Development of DaSilva Puppets, and establishment of permanent base for performance. UK-England: Norwich, Godmancester. 1962-1983. 2044

Dasté, Catherine

Performance/production

Jacques Copeau remembered by his granddaughter, actress Catherine Dasté. France: Pernand. 1940-1949. 727

Data banks

Research/historiography

Records of Early English Drama (REED) project uses new typesetting and editing systems. UK. 1983. 88

Advantages and methods of transcribing theatrical documents directly into a computer file. UK. 1983. 89

Datolux-System

Design/technology

Technical construction and areas of application of the lighting Datolux-system. Germany, West. 1983. 206

Davenant, William

Performance spaces

Dimensions, orientation and dates established for theatre at Gibbon's Tennis Court. England: London. 1636-1660. 363

Davis, Bill

Institutions

Center Stage wins top honor in Toyama International Amateur Theatre Festival with *Ain't Misbehavin'*. Japan: Toyama. USA: Omaha, NE. 1983. 1772

Davis, Carlos

Performance/production

Five critics review Tony Tanner's production of the musical *Preppies*. USA: New York, NY. 1983. 1779

Davis, Ron

Relation to other fields

History, motivations and methods of North American guerrilla theatre. USA. 1965-1966. 1667

Days of the Commune, The SEE: *Tage der Kommune, Die*

De Bosio, Gianfranco

Plays/librettos/scripts

Theatres, actors and drama of the Renaissance in the work of modern directors. Italy. 1845-1982.   1193

De Filippo, Eduardo

Performance/production

Study of productions by leading Italian directors. Italy. 1945-1975.   798

Biography of actor/playwright Eduardo De Filippo. Italy. 1900-1983.   801

Plays/librettos/scripts

Critical analysis of the most significant themes in Eduardo De Filippo's plays and phases in his acting career. Italy. 1900-1982.   1162

Biographical and cultural sources of Eduardo De Filippo's plays. Italy. 1926-1982.   1174

Criticism of Eduardo De Filippo's plays and influence of Luigi Pirandello. Italy. 1905-1981.   1175

De Francesco, Roberto

Institutions

State of theatre in Southern Italy. Italy. 1982.   319

de Jongh, James

Performance/production

Five critics review Regge Life's production of *Do Lord Remember Me*. USA: New York, NY. 1983.   931

De Luigi, Gianni

Gianni De Luigi's staging of *Ruzante Returns from the Wars*. Italy. 1983.   1529

De Muro Lomanto, Enzo

Reference materials

Catalogue of the exhibition on soprano Toti Dal Monte and tenor Enzo De Muro Lomanto. Italy: Trieste. 1893-1975.   1967

De Witt, Johannes

Performance spaces

Interpretation of Johannes De Witt's drawing of the Swan theatre. England. 1596.   365

De' Somi, Leone Ebreo SEE: **Sommi, Leone de'**

Dead Class, The SEE: *Umarla klasa*

Death of a Salesman

Performance/production

Chinese version of *Death of a Salesman* directed by the author. China, People's Republic of: Beijing. 1983.   690

Critical essays on interpretations of *Death of a Salesman*. USA. 1949-1983.   939

Death of the King's Horseman, The

Plays/librettos/scripts

Wole Soyinka's plays echo themes of Aeschylus, Euripides and Shakespeare. Nigeria. Greece: Athens. UK-England: London. 1980.   1700

Debussy, Claude

Performance/production

Photographs, cast lists, synopsis and discography of Metropolitan Opera production of *Pelléas et Mélisande*. USA: New York, NY. 1983.   1901

Plays/librettos/scripts

Comparison of symbolist drama by Maurice Maeterlinck and opera by Claude Debussy. Belgium. 1900-1983.   1012

Decentralization

Administration

Efforts of Jack Lang, Minister of Culture, to decentralize theatre. France. 1982-1983.   124

Deconstruction

Plays/librettos/scripts

Ibsen's creation of realistic characters displaying unconscious desires. Norway. 1892.   1207

Theory/criticism

Significance of gender in feminist criticism with reference to historical materialism, deconstruction and phenomenon of cross-dressing in theatre. USA. France. UK-England. 1983.   1520

Decroux, Etienne

Performance/production

Italian translation of Etienne Decroux's *Paroles sur le mime (Words on Mime)*. France. 1935.   1726

Plays/librettos/scripts

Use of body language in the theatre by Samuel Beckett, Antonin Artaud, Etienne Decroux and Jerzy Grotowski. Europe. 1930-1980.   1638

Dekker, Thomas

Performance/production

List of productions of plays from English Renaissance drama with brief reviews. North America. Europe. 1982-1983.   822

Plays/librettos/scripts

Useful aspects of Cyrus Hoy's commentaries on Thomas Dekker. England: London. 1597-1630.   1030

Authorship, censorship and thematic analysis of *Westward Ho!*. England. 1570-1637.   1067

Uses of Thomas Dekker materials in analytical bibliography. UK-England: London. 1808-1983.   1278

Relationship between Jacobean tragedy and interpolated masque. England. 1600-1625.   1691

Del Monaco, Mario

Performance/production

Autobiography of tenor Mario Del Monaco. Italy. 1915-1975.   1880

Deliverer, The

Plays/librettos/scripts

Patriot Charles Stewart Parnell's influence on Irish drama. UK-Ireland. 1891-1936.   1337

Della Valle, Federico

Analysis of three tragedies written between Mannerism and the Age of Arcadia. Italy. 1627-1713.   1698

Delsarte, François

Performance/production

Persistence of Delsartian methodology in modern acting technique. USA. 1871-1970.   917

Demarigny, Claude

Plays/librettos/scripts

Contradiction in personal and artistic life of Antonin Artaud. France. 1921-1948.   1645

DeMille, Cecil B.

Reference materials

Description of archive holdings at Brigham Young University including personal papers of Howard Hawks and Dean Jagger. USA: Provo, UT. 1900-1983.   48

Denkmal (Memorial)

Plays/librettos/scripts

Title character of *Mother Courage* is contrasted with similar figure in Jürgen Gross' drama *Memorial*. Germany, East. 1980.   1145

Dennison, John

Performance/production

Legal record details early career of dancer John Dennison and an episode in life of David Garrick. England: London. 1747-1757. 417

Depero, Fortunato

Design/technology

Survey of Fortunato Depero's activities as a designer. Italy. 1916-1924. 213

Derricks, Clevant

Performance/production

Interview with principal male stars of *Dreamgirls*. USA: New York, NY. 1983. 1778

Derrida, Jacques

Theory/criticism

Significance of gender in feminist criticism with reference to historical materialism, deconstruction and phenomenon of cross-dressing in theatre. USA. France. UK-England. 1983. 1520

Descartes, René

Bertolt Brecht's perception of the philosophy of the Enlightenment. Germany. 1848-1956. 1498

Descent of Orpheus, The

Design/technology

Settings and machines for *The Descent of Orpheus*. England: London. France: Paris. Belgium: Brussels. 1640-1661. 181

Descriptions of resources

Published materials for sound technicians. USA. 1983. 244

History and description of the Motley Theatre and Costume Arts Collection. Discussed at SIBMAS. USA: Urbana, IL. 1982. 247

Reference materials

Description of the Stage Design Collection of National Arts Center. Canada: Ottawa, ON. 1969-1982. 16

Description of various documents, photographs, designs and engravings on display at Edward Gordon Craig exhibit. UK-England. 1900-1935. 36

Description of archive holdings at Brigham Young University including personal papers of Howard Hawks and Dean Jagger. USA: Provo, UT. 1900-1983. 48

References to theatre preserved in the Archives de Paris. France: Paris. 1825-1845. 1407

Description of the Brander Matthews Collection of theatre materials. USA: New York, NY. 1891-1929. 1436

Letters and documents placed in archives concerning Verdi's operas at Teatro La Fenice. Italy: Venice. 1844-1852. 1970

Design training SEE: Training, design

Design/technology

Administration

Financial problems facing scene designers. Germany, West. 1983. 135

Audience

Testing undergraduates' reactions to set designs. USA: Athens, GA. 1974. 174

Design/technology

New products for technical theatre use. USA. 1983. 254

Technical aspects of Broadway production of *La Cage aux Folles*. USA: New York, NY. 1983. 1771

Institutions

Finnish theatre groups and artists performing abroad. Finland. Sweden. 1982-1983. 299

Summary of study about training costume designers. USA. 1979-1983. 346

Textual and pictorial documentation of Deutsches Theater Berlin. Germany, East: East Berlin. 1883-1983. 599

Collaborative production efforts of Bush Theatre. UK-England. 1983. 630

Performance spaces

Construction and technical equipment of a new theatre building. Germany, West: Heilbronn. 1961-1983. 372

Technical problems Deutsches Schauspielhaus encountered by performing in a former factory. Germany, West: Hamburg. 1980-1983. 377

Technical aspects of modifying and restoring historic theatres. USA. 1983. 405

Giuseppe Piermarini built Teatro alla Scala in accordance with architectural theories of his time. Italy: Milan. 1776-1830. 1835

Performance/production

Influence of Cubism on staging and scenery. Europe. 1900. 421

Aspects of the development of European and American theatre: critical thought, staging, acting and design. USA. Europe. 1800-1970. 454

Americans tour Soviet theatres. USSR: Moscow, Kiev. 1981. 487

Typical movement, music, costumes, performers and historic influences in *odori* and *mai* dance. Japan. 900-1900. 544

Historical survey of theatre. 660

Catalogue of exhibition on Max Reinhardt's use of genres and performance spaces. Austria. 1893-1943. 672

Medieval theatre practice applied in Elizabethan playhouses. England: London. 1560-1600. 695

Richard Wagner's influence on modern theatrical conceptions, including those of Adolphe Appia, Stanisław Wyspiański and Bertolt Brecht. Germany. Poland. Switzerland. 1813-1983. 742

History of *Ru-howzi* improvisational theatre. Iran. 1780-1950. 792

Pirandello as a director and theatre theorist. Italy. 1867-1936. 814

Analysis of production elements in the Catalan theatre. Spain: Barcelona. 1983. 838

Edward Gordon Craig's productions of and theories on Shakespeare. UK-England. Europe. 1872-1940. 862

Collection of photographs of Broadway productions and actors. USA: New York, NY. 1940-1967. 921

Production journal of *King Lear*. Canada: Stratford, ON. 1979. 1676

Reconstruction of Edward Gordon Craig's production of *Hamlet* at Moscow Art Theatre. Russia: Moscow. 1908-1912. 1682

Evolution of director Harold Prince's concept for the Broadway musical *Cabaret*. USA: New York, NY. 1966. 1804

Comprehensive illustrated production history of Wagnerian opera. Europe. USA. Canada. 1832-1983. 1851

History of opera staging and its aesthetics. Europe. 1597-1982. 1852

Richard Wagner's works, reception and influence. France. 1841-1983. 1859

History of opera performances at French court, including work of scene designer Carlo Vigarani. France: Versailles. 1671-1704. 1860

History and production history of Wagnerian opera. Germany. USA. 1832-1982. 1865

Photographs and personnel of Bayreuth Festival production of *Siegfried*. Germany, West: Bayreuth. 1980. 1866

Photographs and personnel of Bayreuth Festival production of *Götterdämmerung*. Germany, West: Bayreuth. 1980. 1867

Peter Hall's production of Richard Wagner's *Ring* at Bayreuth Festspielhaus. Germany, West: Bayreuth. 1983. 1870

Photographs, cast lists, synopsis and discography of Metropolitan Opera production of *Boris Godunov*. USA: New York, NY. 1983. 1891

Photographs, cast lists, synopsis and discography of Metropolitan Opera production of *Parsifal*. USA: New York, NY. 1983. 1892

Photographs, cast lists, synopsis and discography of Metropolitan Opera production of *Arabella*. USA: New York, NY. 1983. 1894

Photographs, cast lists, synopsis and discography of Metropolitan Opera production of *Il Trovatore*. USA: New York, NY. 1983. 1895

Photographs, cast lists, synopsis and discography of Metropolitan Opera production of *Adriana Lecouvreur*. USA: New York, NY. 1983. 1897

Photographs, cast lists, synopsis and discography of Metropolitan Opera production of *La Gioconda*. USA: New York, NY. 1983. 1898

Design/technology — cont'd

Photographs, cast lists, synopsis and discography of Metropolitan Opera production of *Un Ballo in Maschera*. USA: New York, NY. 1983.   1899

Photographs, cast lists, synopsis and discography of Metropolitan Opera production of *Les Contes d'Hoffman*. USA: New York, NY. 1983.   1900

Photographs, cast lists, synopsis and discography of Metropolitan Opera production of *Pelléas et Mélisande*. USA: New York, NY. 1983.   1901

Photographs, cast lists, synopsis and discography of Metropolitan Opera production of *The Barber of Seville*. USA: New York, NY. 1983.   1902

Photographs, cast lists, synopsis and discography of the Metropolitan Opera production of *Die Walküre*. USA: New York, NY. 1983.   1903

Photographs, cast lists, synopsis and discography of the Metropolitan Opera production of *Don Carlo*. USA: New York, NY. 1983.   1904

Photographs, cast lists, synopsis and discography of Metropolitan Opera production of *La Bohème*. USA: New York, NY. 1983.   1905

Photographs, cast lists, synopsis and discography of Metropolitan Opera production of *Der Rosenkavalier*. USA: New York, NY. 1983.   1906

Photographs, cast lists, synopsis and discography of Metropolitan Opera production of *Les Dialogues des Carmélites*. USA: New York, NY. 1983.   1907

Photographs, cast lists, synopsis and discography of Metropolitan Opera production of *Ernani*. USA: New York, NY. 1983.   1908

Photographs, cast lists, synopsis and discography of the Metropolitan Opera production of *Tristan und Isolde*. USA: New York, NY. 1983.   1909

Photographs, cast lists, synopsis and discography of Metropolitan Opera production of *Hänsel und Gretel*. USA: New York, NY. 1983.   1910

Backstage look at San Francisco Opera. USA: San Francisco, CA. 1970-1982.   1911

Relationship between the phonograph and the Metropolitan Opera. USA: New York, NY. 1902-1983.   1918

Photographs, cast lists, synopsis and discography of Metropolitan Opera production of *Idomeneo*. USA: New York, NY. 1983.   1920

Social status and role of minstrels. Europe. 1100-1500.   1986

History of puppets and puppet-masters. Italy: Bologna. 1800-1923.   2053

Application of holography to the Salzburger Marionettentheater production of *Le Nozze di Figaro*. Austria: Salzburg. 1983.   2083

Reissue of some passages and drawings from books on hand shadow puppets. Italy. Germany. UK-England. 1850-1899.   2090

Plays/librettos/scripts

Shift in dramatic emphasis in Igor Strawinsky's *Apollon Musagete* due to sets, costumes and choreography. USA: Washington, DC, New York, NY. 1927-1979.   522

Metaphorical nature of decor implied in playtexts. France. 1806-1827.   1103

Adaptation of the Angel Guimerà play *Maria Rosa*. Spain. 1894.   1230

Staging and scenic practices in the plays of Lope de Vega's forerunners and contemporaries. Spain: Valencia. 1500-1699.   1253

History of American drama. USA. 1900-1982.   1378

Realism in drama, acting, staging and design. Yugoslavia. 1920-1930.   1395

Theme of monarchy in French Romantic opera and its effect on scenery. France: Paris. 1814-1850.   1939

Reference materials

Bibliography of performing arts periodicals. 1982.   11

Description of the Stage Design Collection of National Arts Center. Canada: Ottawa, ON. 1969-1982.   16

Models of scenery and costumes in the Bibliothèque Nationale. France: Paris. 1982.   24

Catalogue of the exhibition of Maria Antonietta Gambaro's paintings and scene designs. Italy. 1951-1980.   27

Catalogue of the exhibition dealing with Leonardo da Vinci's activity as costume and scene designer and inventor of machinery for Sforza's festivals. Italy: Milan. 1484-1500.   28

Description of various documents, photographs, designs and engravings on display at Edward Gordon Craig exhibit. UK-England. 1900-1935.   36

Vocational guidance directed at young people for non-acting careers in theatre. USA. 1983.   43

Bibliography of flat pattern sources continued from *Theatre Design & Technology*, Winter 1983. USA. 1900-1983.   47

Description of archive holdings at Brigham Young University including personal papers of Howard Hawks and Dean Jagger. USA: Provo, UT. 1900-1983.   48

Chronological listing, including personnel, of productions of John Webster's plays. England. USA. 1614-1983.   1401

Short essays and a catalogue of an exhibit on fireworks. Italy: Rome. 1500-1899.   1736

Catalogue of the exhibition on scenery, architecture, dance, opera and public theatres during Pietro Metastasio's life. Italy: Rome. 1698-1782.   1968

Catalogue of Galliari's scene designs owned by Museo Teatrale alla Scala. Italy: Milan. 1778-1823.   1969

Catalogue for an exhibition of Venetian marionettes and puppets. Italy: Venice. 1700-1899.   2086

Relation to other fields

Painter Oskar Kokoschka's dramatic works. Austria. 1917.   1442

Dramatist Stanisław Wyspiański's painting of a Tartar costume, based on a folk tradition stock type — Lajkonik. Poland: Kraków. Austria. 1901-1907.   1461

Construction and use of a puppet to teach basic grammar. USA. 1983.   2070

Research/historiography

Concise version of a theatre textbook.   79

Theory/criticism

Comprehensive discussion of theatre performance. Spain. 1983.   107

Nature and history of *nō* theatre. Japan. 1300-1980.   549

Dramatic theories of the 20th century reflect a complex relationship between plays, designs, staging and acting. Europe. North America. 1900-1982.   1482

Writings of Edward Gordon Craig. UK-England. 1907-1957.   1513

Training

Information concerning internships through Theatre Design and Technology Internship Clearinghouse. USA: New York, NY. 1983.   504

Design/technology SEE ALSO: Classed Entries 175-280, 529, 530, 577-582, 1675, 1705, 1706, 1708, 1768-1771, 1817-1826, 1977, 2035-2042, 2077-2081, 2092-2097, 2103, 2104.

Deutsche Oper (West Berlin)

Administration

Life and career of opera manager Egon Seefehlner. Austria: Vienna. Germany, West: West Berlin. 1912-1983.   1812

Performance spaces

Project for a new studio to optimize the audience/performer relationship. Germany, West: West Berlin. 1983.   1834

Performance/production

Erich Wolfgang Korngold's *Die tote Stadt* at the Deutsche Oper Berlin. Germany, West: West Berlin. 1855. 1983.   1871

Deutsche Oper am Rhein (Düsseldorf)

Baritone David Holloway speaks of career with Deutsche Oper am Rhein. Germany, West: Düsseldorf, Duisburg. 1940-1983.   1877

Deutsche Theatertechnische Gesellschaft

Design/technology

Report on the 43rd Conference for Theatre Technology and its welcoming speech. Germany, West: Heilbronn. 1983.   198

Deutsches Schauspielhaus (Hamburg)

Institutions

Intentions and working methods of the Deutsches Schauspielhaus. Germany, West: Hamburg. 1893.   606

Deutsches Schauspielhaus (Hamburg) — cont'd

Performance spaces

Technical problems Deutsches Schauspielhaus encountered by performing in a former factory. Germany, West: Hamburg. 1980-1983. 377

Performance/production

Ernst Wendt's staging of Heinrich von Kleist's *The Broken Jug* at Deutsches Schauspielhaus in Hamburg. Germany, West: Hamburg. 1983. 1527

Deutsches Theater (East Berlin)

Institutions

History of Deutsches Theater Berlin. Germany: Berlin. 1883-1983. 598

Textual and pictorial documentation of Deutsches Theater Berlin. Germany, East: East Berlin. 1883-1983. 599

Bertolt Brecht's return to Deutsches Theater and production of *Mother Courage* with Berliner Ensemble. Germany, East: East Berlin. 1949. 601

Performance/production

Portrait of the actor Christian Grashof. Germany, East: East Berlin. 1975-1983. 752

Obituary portrait of actor Dieter Franke. Germany, East: East Berlin. 1964-1982. 755

Gotthold Ephraim Lessing's *Nathan the Wise* at Deutsches Theater Berlin, directed by Fritz Wisten. Germany, East: East Berlin. 1945. 756

Problems in acting Shakespeare. Germany, East. 1982. 758

Developmental Drama Scale

Research/historiography

Results of a study which measures acting and monitoring skills in children. USA. 1983. 1476

Devil's Disciple, The

Plays/librettos/scripts

Analysis of character and structure in G.B. Shaw's *The Devil's Disciple*. UK-England. USA. 1897-1983. 1293

Actors' influence on Shaw's theatrical ending of *The Devil's Disciple*. UK-England. 1897. 1315

Dexter, John

Performance/production

Ten critics review John Dexter's production of *The Glass Menagerie*, by Tennessee Williams. USA: New York, NY. 1983. 981

Diadia Vania (Uncle Vania)

Harald Clemens' production of Anton Čechov's *Uncle Vanya* at Nationaltheater. Germany, West: Mannheim. 1983. 777

Descriptive account of Theodore Komisarjevsky's productions of Anton Čechov's plays. UK-England: London. 1926-1936. 875

Six critics review Čechov's *Uncle Vanya* directed by Andre Serban at La Mama. USA: New York, NY. 1982. 967

Diaghilev, Sergei SEE: Diaghilew, Serge de

Dialect theatre

Plays/librettos/scripts

Problems leading to gradual disappearance of the dialect theatre. Italy. 1863-1980. 1181

Some lesser known facts about Luigi Pirandello's plays and other writings. Italy. 1884-1935. 1192

Reference materials

Illustrated catalogue of an exhibition on Sicilian dialect theatre. Italy. 1902-1937. 1416

Dialectics

Plays/librettos/scripts

Materialistic reading of Samuel Beckett's work. France. 1938. 1107

Dialectics of the actor rebellion against the stage director in Luigi Pirandello's *Tonight We Improvise*. Italy. 1930. 1179

Theory/criticism

Systematic, analytic examination of sociology of performing arts. Europe. North America. 1983. 97

Study of realism, naturalism, symbolism, surrealism, expressionism and epic theatre. Europe. North America. 1900-1980. 1484

Marxist philosophy in Bertolt Brecht's work. Germany. 1922-1956. 1496

Dialectic contradiction in Bertolt Brecht's theory of theatre. Germany. 1898-1956. 1501

Louis Althusser's Marxist philosophy is contrasted with his review of Carlo Bertolazzi's play staged by Giorgio Strehler. USA. France. Italy. 1962-1985. 1674

Dialoghi in materia di rappresentazioni sceniche (Dialogues on Stage Affairs)

Design/technology

Methodology for the interpretation of symbolism in Renaissance costume. Italy. 1539. 212

Dialogues des Carmélites, Les

Performance/production

Photographs, cast lists, synopsis and discography of Metropolitan Opera production of *Les Dialogues des Carmélites*. USA: New York, NY. 1983. 1907

Plays/librettos/scripts

Composition of the opera *Les Dialogues des Carmélites*. France. 1931-1983. 1943

Dialogues on Stage Affairs SEE: *Dialoghi in materia di rappresentazioni sceniche*

Dialogus miraculorum

Plays/librettos/scripts

Sources and analogues of a lost miracle play. England: Durham. 1200-1500. 1084

Diaz, Jorge

Some paths for realism in Latin American theatre. South America. North America. 1955-1983. 1224

Dickens, Charles

Relation to other fields

Theatre arts compared to painting and literature. UK-England. 1805-1902. 69

Dictionaries

Reference materials

Alphabetical list of Latin theatrical terms with Old English translations. England. 21

Compilation of entries on the concepts and techniques practiced at the International School of Theatre Anthropology. Italy. 1981. 30

Dictionary of international theatre terms in nine languages. North America. Europe. 1983. 31

Dictionary of actors and actresses based on recent views. UK. USA. 1837-1901. 35

Dictionary of Black theatre. USA: New York, NY. 1983. 50

Diderot, Denis

Performance/production

Contributors to dance reform in French theatre. France: Paris. 1752-1781. 518

Dido

Plays/librettos/scripts

Irony and metadrama in Christopher Marlowe's plays. England. 1564-1593. 1044

Difficult Man, The SEE: *Schwierege, Der*

Digby plays

Performance/production

Census, with brief reviews, of performances of medieval drama. Europe. 1982-1983. 710

John Marshall production of the Digby plays at Winchester Cathedral places particular emphasis on dance. UK-England: Winchester. 1983. 889

Dime museums

Reference materials

Reference guide to popular entertainments. USA. 1840.   1998

Dinesen, Isak

Theory/criticism

Hannah Arendt's theoretical work with reference to Gotthold Lessing, Bertolt Brecht, Franz Kafka and Isak Dinesen. USA. Europe. 1900-1983.   1518

Dinev, Christo Christov

Performance/production

Autobiography of actor Christo Dinev. Bulgaria. 1900-1977.   680

Dinner theatres

Institutions

Folies-Bergère contribution to the development of dinner theatres and night clubs. USA: New York, NY. 1911.   2026

Dionysian rites

Performance/production

Similarities of shaman tradition and Greek Dionysian rites. Korea. 1977.   2105

Diorama

Design/technology

Innovations in stage design by Louis-Jacques Daguerre, including a catalogue of his designs. France. 1709-1850.   193

Diot, André

Methods and materials of lighting design, and interviews with designers. France. 1978.   194

Directing SEE: Staging

Director training SEE: Training, director

Directories

Design/technology

Description and listing of sound systems for theatres to aid hearing impaired. USA. 1960-1983.   246

Directors SEE: Staging

Discographies

Performance/production

Biography and all-inclusive reference materials to Charlie Chaplin. USA. 1889-1977.   1714

History of Broadway musical theatre with an extensive annotated discography. USA: New York, NY. 1800-1983.   1789

Photographs, cast lists, synopsis and discography of Metropolitan Opera production of *Boris Godunov*. USA: New York, NY. 1983.   1891

Photographs, cast lists, synopsis and discography of Metropolitan Opera production of *Parsifal*. USA: New York, NY. 1983.   1892

Photographs, cast lists, synopsis and discography from the Metropolitan Opera's September 28, 1983 telecast of Gaetano Donizetti's *Lucia di Lammermoor*. USA: New York, NY. 1983. 1893

Photographs, cast lists, synopsis and discography of Metropolitan Opera production of *Arabella*. USA: New York, NY. 1983.   1894

Photographs, cast lists, synopsis and discography of Metropolitan Opera production of *Il Trovatore*. USA: New York, NY. 1983. 1895

Photographs, cast lists, synopsis and discography of Metropolitan Opera production of *Tannhäuser*. USA: New York, NY. 1983. 1896

Photographs, cast lists, synopsis and discography of Metropolitan Opera production of *Adriana Lecouvreur*. USA: New York, NY. 1983.   1897

Photographs, cast lists, synopsis and discography of Metropolitan Opera production of *La Gioconda*. USA: New York, NY. 1983.   1898

Photographs, cast lists, synopsis and discography of Metropolitan Opera production of *Un Ballo in Maschera*. USA: New York, NY. 1983.   1899

Photographs, cast lists, synopsis and discography of Metropolitan Opera production of *Les Contes d'Hoffman*. USA: New York, NY. 1983.   1900

Photographs, cast lists, synopsis and discography of Metropolitan Opera production of *Pelléas et Mélisande*. USA: New York, NY. 1983.   1901

Photographs, cast lists, synopsis and discography of the Metropolitan Opera production of *Don Carlo*. USA: New York, NY. 1983.   1904

Photographs, cast lists, synopsis and discography of Metropolitan Opera production of *La Bohème*. USA: New York, NY. 1983.   1905

Photographs, cast lists, synopsis and discography of Metropolitan Opera production of *Der Rosenkavalier*. USA: New York, NY. 1983.   1906

Photographs, cast lists, synopsis and discography of Metropolitan Opera production of *Les Dialogues des Carmélites*. USA: New York, NY. 1983.   1907

Photographs, cast lists, synopsis and discography of Metropolitan Opera production of *Ernani*. USA: New York, NY. 1983.   1908

Photographs, cast lists, synopsis and discography of the Metropolitan Opera production of *Tristan und Isolde*. USA: New York, NY. 1983.   1909

Photographs, cast lists, synopsis and discography of Metropolitan Opera production of *Hänsel und Gretel*. USA: New York, NY. 1983.   1910

Photographs, cast lists, synopsis and discography of Metropolitan Opera production of *Idomeneo*. USA: New York, NY. 1983.   1920

Reference materials

Alphabetized abstracts on composers and their operas. Europe. 1567-1983.   1965

Catalogue of the exhibition on soprano Toti Dal Monte and tenor Enzo De Muro Lomanto. Italy: Trieste. 1893-1975.   1967

Disputation, A

Plays/librettos/scripts

Discussion of playwright Robert Greene's pamphlet *A Disputation*. England. 1581-1592.   1054

Divertissements

Performance/production

Historical overview and English translation of ten divertissement-parades. France. 1700-1799.   1987

Do Lord Remember Me

Five critics review Regge Life's production of *Do Lord Remember Me*. USA: New York, NY. 1983.   931

Dobčeva, I.

Productions of Russian classics by Bulgarian directors. Bulgaria: Sofia. 1960-1970.   681

Döblin, Alfred

Plays/librettos/scripts

Linguistic analysis of *Lydia und Mäxchen* by Alfred Döblin. Germany. 1906.   1120

Dobrowolski, Marek

Design/technology

Lighting designer Marek Dobrowolski contrasts profession in Poland and U.S.A. USA: New York, NY. Poland. 1983.   234

Document conservation

Why collecting, maintaining and exhibiting designers' work is problematical. Discussed at SIBMAS. USA. 1982.   273

Documentary theatre SEE ALSO: *Dokumentarisches Theater*

Dödsdansen (Dance of Death, The)

Performance/production

Productions of August Strindberg's *Miss Julie* and *The Dance of Death*. Germany, West: Giessen, Wilhelmshaven, Memmingen. 1981-1982.   786

Dödsdansen (Dance of Death, The) — cont'd

Year's outstanding productions of plays by August Strindberg and
other playwrights. UK-England. 1982-1983. 890

Dodson, Edith

Plays/librettos/scripts

Tribute to playwright Owen Dodson. USA. 1983. 1363

Dodson, Owen

Tribute to playwright Owen Dodson. USA. 1983. 1363

Dogg's Hamlet

Influence of Shakespeare, Beckett and Wittgenstein on the plays of
Tom Stoppard. UK-England. 1963-1979. 1302

Dōjōji (Woman and a Bell, A)

History of the narrative theme of *Dōjōji (A Woman and a Bell)*.
Japan. 1041-1800. 545

Dokumentarisches Theater (Documentary theatre)

Period plays and documentary theatre of the cold war. Germany,
West. 1945-1966. 1152

Doll's House, A SEE: **Dukkehjem, Et**

Doll's Life, A

Plays/librettos/scripts

Musical adaptation of *A Doll's House*. USA: New York, NY. 1983.
1809

Dom Juan (Molière)

Performance/production

Ingmar Bergman directs Molière's *Dom Juan* at Salzburg Festival.
Austria: Salzburg. 1983. 673

Domingo, Placido

Making of the Franco Zeffirelli film of *La Traviata*. Italy: Rome.
1981-1983. 1885

Don Carlo

Photographs, cast lists, synopsis and discography of the Metropolitan
Opera production of *Don Carlo*. USA: New York, NY. 1983. 1904

Don Carlos

Theory/criticism

Schiller's philosophy of history. Germany: Jena. 1789-1791. 1499

Don Giovanni

Plays/librettos/scripts

Leporello as alter ego of protagonist in *Don Giovanni*. Italy. 1787.
1957

Don Juan (Molière) SEE: **Dom Juan**

Dönch, Karl

Performance/production

Career of Karl Dönch, opera singer and manager of Vienna's
Volksoper. Austria: Vienna. 1915-1983. 1761

Donizetti, Gaetano

Photographs, cast lists, synopsis and discography from the
Metropolitan Opera's September 28, 1983 telecast of Gaetano
Donizetti's *Lucia di Lammermoor*. USA: New York, NY. 1983. 1893

Donnelly, Donal

Five critics review Donal Donnelly's production of John B. Keane's
play *Big Maggie*. USA: New York, NY. 1983. 966

Donnybrook

Overview of Jack Cole's career as dancer, teacher and
choreographer. USA. 1933-1974. 1788

Doonesbury

Nine critics review Jacques Levy's production of the musical
Doonesbury. USA: New York, NY. 1983. 1799

Dostoevskij, Fëdor Michajlovič

Influence of Russian playwrights, directors and actors on American
theatre. USA. Russia. 1905-1979. 976

Dottori, Carlo

Plays/librettos/scripts

Analysis of three tragedies written between Mannerism and the Age
of Arcadia. Italy. 1627-1713. 1698

Dottori, Gerardo

Design/technology

Short notes written by Gerardo Dottori in 1930 on the Renaissance
of scene design. Italy. 1906-1930. 216

Douglass, Frederick

Performance/production

History of a production about nine Black leaders by the African
American Drama Company. USA. 1976-1983. 979

Drama League of America

Institutions

Activities of church and theatre associations to promote 'decent'
dramaturgy. USA: New York, NY, Chicago, IL. 1910-1940. 649

Drama Review, The

Research/historiography

Historical survey of theatre periodical *The Drama Review*. USA.
1955-1983. 90

Drama therapy

Relation to other fields

Workshop on the use of puppets in education and therapy. Nigeria:
Zaria. 1983. 2067

Dramatic structure

Performance/production

History of opera staging and its aesthetics. Europe. 1597-1982. 1852

Plays/librettos/scripts

Denunciation of collective violence reflected in the role of sacrifice
in Michel de Ghelderode's *Barabbas*. Belgium. 1929. 1010

Study of Thomas Otway's plays. England. 1652-1685. 1039

Study of recurring themes and dramatic structure of *Richard II*.
England. 1595-1596. 1062

Semiotic analysis of *Richard II*. England. 1595. 1077

Structural analysis of Gaunt's last speech in Shakespeare's *Richard
II*. England. 1595-1596. 1078

Influence of Eugène Scribe and the Well-Made Play on later drama.
France: Paris. 1830-1840. 1102

Play-within-a-play in Renaissance drama. France. 1500-1599. 1104

Brechtian play construction in contemporary theatrical practice.
Germany. UK. 1920-1983. 1127

Dramatic structure of Gotthold Ephraim Lessing's *Minna of
Barnhelm* represents cultural atmosphere of the time. Germany. 1767.
1138

Analysis of the early plays of Bertolt Brecht. Germany. 1925. 1140

Heiner Müller continues the Brechtian tradition in political drama.
Germany, East. 1960-1982. 1144

Paul Claudel as influenced by *nō* drama. Japan. France. 1921-1927.
1196

Experimentation with Enlish-language drama. Malaysia. 1957-1982.
1197

Analysis of Henrik Ibsen's *Ghosts*. Norway. 1881. 1202

Henrik Ibsen's retrospective technique. Norway. 1881. 1206

Continuity of technique throughout Anton Čechov's career. Russia.
1860-1904. 1220

Segmental analysis of Anton Čechov's plays. Russia. 1860-1904.
1222

Psychological analysis of Semiramis character from Calderón's
Daughter of the Air. Spain. 1600-1699. 1235

Discussion of Miguel de Cervantes' *The Farce of the Divorce Judge*
in view of Aristotelian *mimesis*. Spain. 1547-1616. 1248

Dramatic structure – cont'd

Work and life of the playwright and novelist Ramón María del Valle-Inclán. Spain: Galicia. 1866-1936.　1251

Lope de Vega's forty extant texts are examined to determine authorship of *The False Lackey*. Spain. 1609-1635.　1254

Cubism in art (space) related to cubism in drama (time). Sweden. Norway. 1828-1912.　1259

Fairy-tale elements in *Miss Julie* intensify the play's tragic impact. Sweden. 1870-1908.　1264

Epic structure in contemporary drama. UK. 1968-1981.　1275

Plot, structure and action in John Arden's *Serjeant Musgrave's Dance*. UK-England. 1959.　1288

Analysis of plays by John Osborne. UK-England. 1929-1982.　1291

Study of Bernard Pomerance's dramatic parable, *The Elephant Man*. UK-England. 1978.　1300

Shaw's manipulation of audience reaction in *Major Barbara*. UK-England. 1907.　1307

Similarities between the plays *The Dutchman* and *Zoo Story*. USA: New York, NY. 1964.　1350

Bertolt Brecht's theory of alienation applied to characters and situations in Tennessee Williams' *Camino Real*. USA. Germany, East. 1941-1953.　1352

Realistic structure of Eugene O'Neill's *The Iceman Cometh*. USA: New York, NY. 1940-1949.　1371

Handbook of textual analysis. USSR. 1983.　1390

Realism in drama, acting, staging and design. Yugoslavia. 1920-1930.　1395

Comparison of Greek and Roman comedy as reflected in works of Menander and Terence and in revivals by Italian humanists. Greece. Roman Empire. 343 B.C.-1400 A.D.　1582

Use of vernacular in Ariosto's, Machiavelli's and Ruzante's comedies, as compared with Roman drama. Italy. Roman Empire. 1508-1533.　1584

Comic mechanism in Plautus' *Amphitruo* and *Casina*. Roman Republic. 254-184 B.C.　1586

Farcical style in Michael Frayn's *Noises Off*. USA. 1983.　1597

Structural similarities between Jean Genet's *The Screens* and medieval dramaturgy. France. 1961.　1641

Incremental repetition and inter-relationship in the plays of Wole Soyinka. Nigeria. 1956-1982.　1652

Study of form, style and theme in John Webster's plays. England: London. 1603-1640.　1686

Linguistic analysis of *Macbeth*. England. 1605-1606.　1690

Semiotic analysis of popular radio comedy. Canada. 1939-1958.　1709

Relationship between dramatic structure and film writing. France. 1900-1983.　1718

Examination of Act III of *Die Walküre*. Germany. 1852.　1950

Theory/criticism

Critical analysis of dramatic methods from Sophocles to Harold Pinter. Europe. North America. 499 B.C.-1983 A.D.　1485

Freudian analysis is used to divide dramatic fantasy into three phases, from genital-masochism to anal-sadism. Germany, West. France. USA. 1974-1983.　1506

Dramatisches Zentrum (Vienna)

Institutions

Structure, aims and methods of animation by Dramatisches Zentrum (Vienna). Austria: Vienna. 1972-1983.　287

Performance/production

Documentation on Ruben Fraga's production of *The Tower of Babel* by the Dramatic Center Vienna. Austria: Vienna. 1980-1983.　670

Dramatists Guild

Plays/librettos/scripts

Plays and productions at Young Playwrights Festival. USA: New York, NY. 1982.　1384

Dramatizations

Dramatization of Remigio Zena's novel *The Wolf's Mouth* by Teatro Stabile di Genova. Italy: Genoa. 1980.　1186

Adaptation of Flannery O'Connor's stories to readers theatre. USA. 1982.　1381

Dramaturgs

Administration

Biography and legacy of dramaturg Julien Daoust. Canada. 1866-1943.　552

Andy Arnold on his work with Theatre Workshop in Edinburgh. UK-Scotland. 1983.　556

Interview with the new artistic director and literary advisor for the Iron Theatre (Glasgow). UK-Scotland. 1973-1983.　559

Definition and duties of literary managers in regional theatres. USA. 1980.　561

Institutions

Interview with Reinhold Auer, dramatic advisor of Jura Soyfer Theater am Spittelberg, Vienna. Austria: Vienna. 1980-1983.　583

Interview with Rod Graham, head of BBC Scotland's television drama department. UK-Scotland. 1946-1983.　1722

Performance/production

Memoirs of dramaturg Jan Kott. Poland. Austria: Vienna. 1957-1981.　440

Plays/librettos/scripts

Problems of contemporary dramatists, including formal productions and criticism. Sweden. 1983.　1261

Training

Examination of Ritva Holmberg's teaching methods for dramaturgs. Finland: Helsinki. 1965-1983.　1522

Dramaturgy

Institutions

Interviews with personnel of Freiburg theatres on obtaining subsidies and other aspects of administration. Germany, West: Freiburg. 1911-1983.　607

Plays/librettos/scripts

Assessment of dramaturgy in English-speaking theatre. USA. 1983.　1361

Reference materials

Encyclopedia of world historical and modern drama. 499 B.C.-1983 A.D.　1396

Draussen vor der Tür (Man Outside, The)

Performance/production

Productions of Wolfgang Borchert's play *The Man Outside* in Hamburg and Berlin. Germany, West: West Berlin, Hamburg. 1947-1948.　778

Dream Play, A SEE: *Drömspel, Ett*

Dreamgirls

Performance/production

Interview with principal male stars of *Dreamgirls*. USA: New York, NY. 1983.　1778

Dreaming Dust, The

Plays/librettos/scripts

Influences of Jonathan Swift's satire in plays by W.B. Yeats and Denis Johnston. Eire. 1928-1960.　1026

Dresdner Staatsoper SEE: Staatsoper (Dresden)

Dresen, Adolf

Plays/librettos/scripts

Compilation of comments by various artists on Tennessee Williams. USA. 1911-1983.　1342

Dresser, The

Ronald Harwood discusses his plays *The Dresser* and *After the Lions*, the latter play based on the life of Sarah Bernhardt. UK-England: London. 1983.　1286

Dutchman, The

Similarities between the plays *The Dutchman* and *Zoo Story*. USA: New York, NY. 1964.   1350

Two principal female archetypes of Imamu Amiri Baraka's drama. USA. 1964-1978.   1375

Theory/criticism

Imamu Amiri Baraka's aesthetics find their origins in Blues music. USA. 1963-1967.   1521

Dyer, Chris

Design/technology

Scenic practices of various designers. UK. 1960-1983.   227

Dýskolos (Grouch, The)

Plays/librettos/scripts

Comparison of the misanthrope in *Dýskolos, Timon of Athens* and *Le Misanthrope*. Greece. England. France. 317 B.C.-1666 A.D.   1155

Easter SEE: *Påsk*

Eastward Ho!

Plays/librettos/scripts

Authorship, censorship and thematic analysis of *Westward Ho!*. England. 1570-1637.   1067

Ebb, Fred

Performance/production

Nine critics review Michael Cacoyannis' production of the musical *Zorba*. USA: New York, NY. 1983.   1798

Ebreo, Leone SEE: Sommi, Leone De'

Eco Theatre (West Virginia)

Institutions

Origin and work of Eco Theatre in West Virginia. USA. 1975.   349

Economics

Plays/librettos/scripts

Sociological approach to Lope de Vega's drama. Spain. 1573-1635.   1256

Problems of contemporary dramatists, including formal productions and criticism. Sweden. 1983.   1261

Edgar, David

Epic structure in contemporary drama. UK. 1968-1981.   1275

Edinburgh Festival

Performance/production

Changes of directors and reviews of performances at the Edinburgh Festival and Lyceum Theatre. UK-Scotland: Edinburgh. 1983.   903

Editions

History of Wagnerian study and performance. Spain. 1878-1926.   1887

Plays/librettos/scripts

Shakespearean and editorial designation of locale. England: London. 1605-1606.   1069

Misquotation of Shakespeare in Edmond Malone's 1790 edition. England: London. 1790-1821.   1070

Authorship of *The Fatal Extravagance*. England: London. 1721-1760.   1082

Uses of Thomas Dekker materials in analytical bibliography. UK-England: London. 1808-1983.   1278

Analysis of Samuel Beckett's earliest typescript of *Eh Joe* to revision as *Ghost Trio*. UK-Ireland. France. 1958.   1323

Editorial problems in the first folio of *Hamlet, Othello* and *King Lear*. England: London. 1558-1621.   1692

Edmund Kean

Performance/production

Eight critics review Alison Sutcliffe's production of Raymund FitzSimons' play *Edmund Kean*. USA: New York, NY. 1983.   965

Education

Audience

Audience development programs for young people. UK-England. USA: Santa Barbara, CA. 1980.   169

Techniques and activities for educating the playgoer. USA. 1983.   172

Design/technology

Projects and materials for the education of theatre technicians. USA. 1900-1983.   272

Institutions

Formation of joint committee by amateur theatres and its Training Council. Finland. 1983.   300

Professional artists' continue training at Theatre Academy of Finland. Finland: Helsinki. 1973-1983.   301

Profile of theatres for young people. USA. 1983.   353

Dance training at Theatre Academy of Finland. Finland: Helsinki. 1910-1983.   516

Performance/production

Charles Burket Rittenhouse as actor, playwright, director, administrator and educator. Canada: Montreal, PQ. 1925-1976.   688

Tribute to Mordecai Gorelik, scenic designer, theorist, teacher, director and playwright. USA. 1899-1983.   936

Plays/librettos/scripts

Approaches to drama for young people. UK-England. 1970-1983.   1296

Reference materials

Bibliography of education resources on creativity and dramatic activities in elementary schools. USA. 1976-1982.   42

Relation to other fields

Karl Valentin's humorous proposal that theatre be mandatory for purposes of educating and improving society. Germany. 1882-1948.   55

Interview with Gardy Labad on education and theatre. Philippines. 1983.   66

American Theatre Association statement of policy on theatre in elementary education. USA. 1983.   71

Role of theatre in education. USA. 1983.   72

Documents available from Educational Resources Information Center related to educational theatre. USA. 1983.   73

Elementary teachers' attitudes toward creative drama in the classroom. USA. 1983.   75

Impact of the creative drama activities on language disordered children. USA. 1983.   77

Comparison of various methods, including creative drama, in teaching literature. USA. 1983.   1467

Use of improvisation in the teaching of foreign languages. USA. 1983.   1470

Effects of creative drama on development of language skills. USA. 1983.   1471

Videotapes created as instructional material on Elizabethan theatre. USA: Cortland, NY. 1973-1983.   1724

Brief introduction of *commedia dell'arte* for children of primary schools. Italy. 1550-1750.   2022

Workshop on the use of puppets in education and therapy. Nigeria: Zaria. 1983.   2067

Senior citizens use puppets to teach handicapped children. USA: Akron, OH. 1983.   2068

Using puppets in cross-cultural education. USA: Albuquerque, NM. 1983.   2069

Construction and use of a puppet to teach basic grammar. USA. 1983.   2070

Training

Examination of training program at Theatre Academy of Finland. Finland: Helsinki. 1983.   495

Improvisational theatre as a tool for special education teachers. USA. 1983.   500

Zelda Fichandler expresses her philosophy of theatre education. USA: New York, NY, Washington, DC. 1950-1983.   506

Description of Education Resources Information Center documents dealing with theatre instruction and research. USA. 1983.   508

Education — cont'd

Comparison of various training programs in children's theatre and creative dramatics. USA. 1950-1982.   509

Four basic questions a theatre curriculum should address. USA. 1983.   510

Examination of Ritva Holmberg's teaching methods for dramaturgs. Finland: Helsinki. 1965-1983.   1522

Education Resources Information Center (ERIC)

Reference materials

Bibliography of education resources on creativity and dramatic activities in elementary schools. USA. 1976-1982.   42

Relation to other fields

Documents available from Educational Resources Information Center related to educational theatre. USA. 1983.   73

Training

Description of Education Resources Information Center documents dealing with theatre instruction and research. USA. 1983.   508

Edward II

Plays/librettos/scripts

Irony and metadrama in Christopher Marlowe's plays. England. 1564-1593.   1044

Egk, Werner

Theatrical effect preserved in operatic adaptations of Werner Egk's *Peer Gynt* and Aribert Reimann's *King Lear* at the Münchener Festspiele. Germany, West: Munich. 1982.   1953

Egyptology

Performance/production

Notes on three Broadway productions. USA: New York, NY. 1983.   911

Eh Joe

Plays/librettos/scripts

Analysis of Samuel Beckett's earliest typescript of *Eh Joe* to revision as *Ghost Trio*. UK-Ireland. France. 1958.   1323

Eight Men Speak

Performance/production

Production of *Eight Men Speak* by Popular Projects Society. Canada: Halifax, NS. 1982.   683

Eighty-four Charing Cross Road

Extracts from journal of James Roose-Evans, director of *84 Charing Cross Road*. USA: New York, NY. 1982.   973

Eisenherz (Ironheart)

Plays/librettos/scripts

Interview with Gerlind Reinshagen and review of his play *Eisenherz (Ironheart)* produced in Bochum and Zürich. Switzerland: Zürich. Germany, West: Bochum. 1983.   1271

Eisenstein, Sergei Mikhailovich SEE: Ejzenštejn, Sergej Michailovič

Eisler, Hanns

Plays/librettos/scripts

The Measures Taken as Bertolt Brecht's first Marxist play. Germany. 1930.   1139

Ejzenštejn, Sergej Michailovič

Performance/production

Role experimental studios played in the formation of the Soviet theatre. USSR: Moscow, Leningrad. 1920-1939.   993

El Paso Festival

Repertory of the Golden Age of Spanish theatre at the El Paso Festival. Mexico. USA: El Paso, TX. Spain. 1983.   1681

Elements of Semiology

Theory/criticism

Spectator at the center of semiological network of theoretical approaches to theatre. France. 1982.   99

Elephant Man, The

Plays/librettos/scripts

Study of Bernard Pomerance's dramatic parable, *The Elephant Man*. UK-England. 1978.   1300

Elite theatre

Relation to other fields

Class-conscious approach to theatre. Germany, West. 1983.   56

Elizabethan theatre

Administration

Six payments to traveling entertainers from two hitherto unpublished documents in Warwick County Records Office. England: Warwick. 1601-1637.   121

Accounts of payment to assorted entertainers performing for Lord Berkeley. England: Coventry. 1593-1605.   122

Performance spaces

Location of the turret in Greenwich Park. England: London. 1500.   361

Interpretation of Johannes De Witt's drawing of the Swan theatre. England. 1596.   365

Reconstruction of a typical theatre of the Siglo de Oro period, with comparison to English playhouses. Spain: Madrid. 1583-1744.   388

Performance/production

Other trades plied by English actors. England: London. 1616-1640.   416

Medieval theatre practice applied in Elizabethan playhouses. England: London. 1560-1600.   695

Marxist theory applied in comparison of public theatres in England and Spain. England. Spain. 1576-1635.   696

Review article of *Theatre Production Series*, seeking to define theatre's strengths. England. Germany. 1500-1939.   706

Plays/librettos/scripts

Shakespeare's historical plays and the reaction of the Elizabethan audience. England. 1590-1613.   1031

Stage directions in Shakespeare are used to reconstruct Elizabethan staging practice. England. 1590-1612.   1073

Sources used by Shakespeare for his play *Richard III*, and changes made to cater to his sovereign's political beliefs. England. 1592-1593.   1076

Relation to other fields

Videotapes created as instructional material on Elizabethan theatre. USA: Cortland, NY. 1973-1983.   1724

Training

Conditions of apprenticeship in Elizabethan acting companies. England: Bridgewater. 1597-1599.   494

Elizabethan theatre SEE ALSO: Geographical-Chronological Index under England 1558-1603

Elocution

Theory/criticism

Vocal emission as a mode of theatricalization in experimental theatre. Canada. 1970-1979.   1669

Emilia-Romagna Teatro SEE: ATER (Associazione Teatri Emilia-Romagna)

Emperor Jones, The

Plays/librettos/scripts

Eugene O'Neill plays that have been made into films. USA. 1916.   1347

Empirical research SEE: Research/historiography

Employment

Administration

Unemployment among Black theatre professionals. UK-England: London. 1974-1979.   146

Employment — cont'd

Institutions

Summary of study about training costume designers. USA. 1979-1983.   346

Training

Information concerning internships through Theatre Design and Technology Internship Clearinghouse. USA: New York, NY. 1983.   504

Encina, Juan de la

Plays/librettos/scripts

New Vatican documents regarding the dramatist Juan de la Encina's political and ecclesiastical appointments. Spain: Salamanca. Vatican. 1469-1529.   1252

Encyclopedias

Treatment of Franz Grillparzer in Polish encyclopedias. Austria. Poland. 1800-1983.   1007

Reference materials

Generic guide to theatre terms, institutions and personalities.   12

Chronological guide to premieres, revivals, personalities and events. USA. UK. Canada. 1900-1979.   45

Encyclopedia of world historical and modern drama. 499 B.C.-1983 A.D.   1396

Ben Jonson encyclopedia. England. 1572-1637.   1400

Guide to operetta terms and personalities, organized chronologically by composer. Europe. USA. 1600-1983.   1976

Enemy of the People, An SEE: *Folkefiende, En*

English Players

Institutions

Letters signed by George Jolly concerning the visit of his troupe to Gdansk in August, 1650. Poland: Gdańsk. England. Germany. 1649-1650.   614

Enlightenment

Theory/criticism

Bertolt Brecht's perception of the philosophy of the Enlightenment. Germany. 1848-1956.   1498

Enquist, Per Olov

Plays/librettos/scripts

Critical notes on Enquist's play *Theatre-Truth* about August Strindberg. Sweden. 1974.   1260

Enrico Quarto (Henry IV)

Luigi Pirandello's earlier plays are considered prologues to *The Giants of the Mountain*. Italy. 1921-1937.   1189

Enters, Angna

Theory/criticism

Collected theory and criticism by women in theatre on women in theatre. USA. UK. 1850-1983.   114

Entrée Libre (Free Admission)

Plays/librettos/scripts

Variations on the bedroom farce form in the works of Eugène Labiche, Roger Vitrac and Samuel Beckett. France. 1870-1983.   1573

Entremés

Discussion of Miguel de Cervantes' *The Farce of the Divorce Judge* in view of Aristotelian *mimesis*. Spain. 1547-1616.   1248

Entremés del Juez de los divorcios (Farce of the Divorce Judge, The)

Discussion of Miguel de Cervantes' *The Farce of the Divorce Judge* in view of Aristotelian *mimesis*. Spain. 1547-1616.   1248

Enzensberger, Christian

Performance/production

Brief comments on and German translation of Edward Bond's *Summer*. Germany, West: Munich. 1983.   764

Epic theatre

Design/technology

Influence of the designers on staging styles. UK. 1958-1983.   226

Plays/librettos/scripts

Bertolt Brecht's theory of alienation applied to characters and situations in Tennessee Williams' *Camino Real*. USA. Germany, East. 1941-1953.   1352

Theory/criticism

Study of realism, naturalism, symbolism, surrealism, expressionism and epic theatre. Europe. North America. 1900-1980.   1484

Epicoene, or The Silent Women

Plays/librettos/scripts

Adaptation of Ben Jonson's *Epicoene* by Marcel Achard, directed by Charles Dullin. France: Paris. 1926.   1100

Epsom Downs

Epic structure in contemporary drama. UK. 1968-1981.   1275

Equestrian ballet

Performance/production

History of equestrian ballet with an emphasis on 17th century. Europe. 1559-1854.   1735

Equipment

Design/technology

Settings and machines for *The Descent of Orpheus*. England: London. France: Paris. Belgium: Brussels. 1640-1661.   181

Electro-technical systems of the Neues Gewandhaus. Germany, East: Leipzig. 1781-1983.   196

Description of new theatre building and technical equipment used in performances since 1981. Germany, West: West Berlin. 1962-1982.   201

Description and function of the lightboard designed by Rank Strand firm. Germany, West: Stuttgart. 1964-1983.   203

Fire-prevention equipment needed for theatres. Germany, West: West Berlin. 1973-1983.   210

Surviving upper-wing groove mechanisms in five provincial theatres. UK. 1850-1983.   225

New products of interest to designers and technicians. USA. 1900-1983.   236

Guidelines for use of loudspeakers. USA. 1945-1983.   245

Properties of and hints for the correct use of GOBOs in stage lighting. USA. 1900-1983.   249

New products for technical theatre use. USA. 1983.   254

Application of automatic microphone mixers in theatre. USA. 1945-1983.   255

Sound systems and techniques for controlling sound. USA: New York, NY. 1945-1983.   264

First live broadcast of a complete opera performance from the Metropolitan Opera House. USA: New York, NY. 1910.   1708

Technical realization of the main platform for the sets of *Der Ring des Nibelungen*. Germany, West: Bayreuth. 1983.   1817

Various safety requirements for the construction of the platform for the production of *Der Ring des Nibelungen*. Germany, West: Bayreuth. 1983.   1818

Performance spaces

Construction and technical equipment of a new theatre building. Germany, West: Heilbronn. 1961-1983.   372

Restoration of theatre chairs. USA. 1983.   409

Performance/production

Medieval theatre practice applied in Elizabethan playhouses. England: London. 1560-1600.   695

Reference materials

Catalogue of the exhibition dealing with Leonardo da Vinci's activity as costume and scene designer and inventor of machinery for Sforza's festivals. Italy: Milan. 1484-1500.   28

Equus

Plays/librettos/scripts

Examination of plays adapted for movies. USA. 1974.   1345

ERIC SEE: Education Resources Information Center

Ernani

Performance/production

Photographs, cast lists, synopsis and discography of Metropolitan Opera production of *Ernani*. USA: New York, NY. 1983.   1908

Plays/librettos/scripts

Victor Hugo and the original plot for the opera *Ernani* by Giuseppe Verdi. France. 1830.   1940

Italian tenor Luciano Pavarotti discusses the title role of *Ernani* by Giuseppe Verdi. Italy. 1983.   1958

Creation of the title role in *Ernani* for tenor Nicolai Ivanoff. Italy. Russia. 1844.   1959

Reference materials

Letters and documents placed in archives concerning Verdi's operas at Teatro La Fenice. Italy: Venice. 1844-1852.   1970

Erudite drama SEE: *Commedia erudita*

Escola d'Art Dramàtic Adrà Gual (Andria Gual School of Dramatic Art, Barcelona)

Institutions

Interview with the director of the Centre Dramàtic de la Generalitat. Spain. 1945-1982.   327

Estate romana

Performance/production

Review of Futurist theatrical and musical performances during Roman Summer festival. Italy: Rome. 1983.   1618

Ester

Plays/librettos/scripts

Analysis of three tragedies written between Mannerism and the Age of Arcadia. Italy. 1627-1713.   1698

Estes, Simon

Performance/production

Simon Estes, American baritone, speaks of his life and career as a Black artist. USA. Europe. 1939-1983.   1927

Esto sí que es negociar (This Is Business)

Plays/librettos/scripts

Authorship and dating of *The Melancholic* and *This Is Business*. Spain. 1623.   1241

Etherege, George

Performance/production

Activities of King's Company and their staging of George Etherege's *The Man of Mode*. UK-Scotland: Edinburgh. 1678-1680.   448

Ethics

Decisions needed in staging plays with inherent sexist or racist themes. USA. 1980-1983.   904

Plays/librettos/scripts

Moral and social themes in contemporary Finnish drama. Finland. 1981.   1097

Relation to other fields

Thematic study of work ethic in American drama. USA. 1920-1969.   1465

Theory/criticism

Morality of Restoration comedy. England. 1670-1700.   1599

Ethnic theatre

Design/technology

Description of Indian masks. Colombia. 1982.   2094

Assessment of Native American ritual masks. North America.   2097

Institutions

Activities of the New York ATA convention program on Asian theatre. Asia. USA: New York, NY. 1983.   282

Theatre-activities of Turkish immigrant workers. Germany, West: West Berlin. 1982.   306

History of Spanish-language repertory troupe activities in Texas. USA. Mexico. 1848-1900.   352

Swedish language theatre in southern Finland. Finland. 1983.   589

History of Teatr Zydowski (Warsaw Jewish Theatre). Poland: Warsaw. 1876-1983.   616

History of the Glasgow Jewish Institute Players. UK-Scotland: Glasgow. 1930-1963.   640

Activism, internationalism and preservation in minority theatre groups. USA. 1981-1983.   646

History and organization of the Irish Rebel Theatre. USA: New York, NY. 1973-1983.   648

Performance/production

History of German immigrants' theatre. USA. 1830-1939.   10

History of Italian immigrant theatre. USA: New York, NY. 1871-1970.   449

French theatre in New Orleans. USA: New Orleans, LA. 1764-1902.   450

History of Spanish language theatre in the southwestern United States. USA. 1845-1980.   452

History of Chicano theatre. USA. Mexico. 1965-1983.   453

History of Swedish language theatre in America. USA. 1860-1925.   462

Survey of Native American dramatists and their use of dramatic ritual. USA. 1850-1980.   463

History of Danish immigrant theatre in the American West and Midwest. USA. 1900-1961.   464

History of Byelorussian immigrant theatre. USA. 1920-1975.   467

History of Yiddish theatre. USA. Europe. 1876-1960.   469

History of Puerto Rican theatre on the American mainland. USA: New York, NY. 1800-1983.   471

History of the Irish immigrant theatre. USA. 1830-1974.   472

History of Ukrainian theatre in America since its inception. USA. 1900-1979.   473

History of Armenian immigrant theatre. USA: New York, NY. 1903-1979.   474

History of the Finnish immigrant theatre. USA. 1880-1939.   475

Essays on ethnic theatre. USA. 1983.   476

History of Black theatre with emphasis on actors and dramatists. USA. 1795-1975.   477

History of Latvian language theatre in America. USA. 1888-1976.   478

History of the Hungarian immigrants' theatre. USA. 1870-1979.   479

Slovak language theatre in Europe and America. USA. Slovakia. 1890-1919.   481

History of Lithuanian language theatre. USA. 1885-1970.   482

History of Polish language theatre in America. USA. 1850-1940.   483

Survey of Sicilian theatre institutions, repertory, actors and playwrights. Italy. 1800-1950.   794

Attitude of Western audiences to the performances of native Africans in various settings. USA. UK. 1800-1899.   1994

Composers whose songs were played at Irish variety performances, especially those of John McCormack. USA. UK. 1800-1899.   2029

Extensively illustrated study of popular form of Sicilian puppetry. Italy. 1800-1983.   2052

Plays/librettos/scripts

Jewish stereotypes in contemporary drama. Europe. North America. 1982.   1094

Pre-colonial material in modern Mexican drama. Mexico. 1910-1983.   1198

Interview with the playwright Joan Oliver about his work. Spain. 1899-1983.   1236

Essays on the trends of the Jewish-American theatre and its personalities. USA. 1900-1983.   1353

Collection of articles, interviews and scripts on Mexican American theatre. USA. Mexico. 1983.   1362

Reference materials

Bibliography of Black French theatre in Africa. Africa. 1977-1983.   1397

Ethnic theatre — cont'd

Theory/criticism

History and philosophy of Chicano theatre movement. USA. 1965-1982.   113

Étoile du Nord, L' (Sweden)

Institutions

History of dance group L'Étoile du Nord. Sweden. USA. 1636-1983.   524

Euripides

Plays/librettos/scripts

Relationship between costume changes and change in wearer's fate. Greece. 405 B.C.   1694

Mutes in Greek tragedy. Greece. 523-406 B.C.   1695

English translation of Albin Lesky's standard work on Greek tragedy. Greece. 499-400 B.C.   1696

Dramatic and military conflict in Greek tragedy. Greece. 484-415 B.C.   1697

Wole Soyinka's adaptation of Euripides' *The Bacchae*. Nigeria. 1973.   1699

Wole Soyinka's plays echo themes of Aeschylus, Euripides and Shakespeare. Nigeria. Greece: Athens. UK-England: London. 1980.   1700

Theory/criticism

Effect of social conditions on performance styles. USA. Greece. 499 B.C.-1983 A.D.   1517

Euryanthe

Plays/librettos/scripts

Carl Maria von Weber's influence on Richard Wagner. Europe. 1822-1844.   1935

Eveling, Stanley

Career of playwright Stanley Eveling. UK-Scotland. 1930-1983.   1341

Everding, August

Performance/production

History and production history of Wagnerian opera. Germany. USA. 1832-1982.   1865

Every Man Out of His Humour

Plays/librettos/scripts

Ironic satire in *Every Man Out of His Humour*. England. 1599.   1052

Everyman

Performance/production

Census, with brief reviews, of performances of medieval drama. Europe. 1982-1983.   710

Exhibitions

Design/technology

International exhibition of theatre architecture and scenery. Czechoslovakia: Prague. 1983.   179

Supplemental materials to costume exhibit. Europe. 1700-1800.   186

Exhibition of works and portrait of the scene and costume designer Emanuele Luzzati. Italy. 1921-1983.   214

Supplementary materials to exhibit of Baroque theatre and stage design. Italy. 1600.   219

Essays and supplemental materials to exhibition of David Hockney designs, with plates. UK-England. USA. 1937.   229

Articles on designer Oliver Messel. UK-England. 1904-1978.   231

Report of research among theatrical designers. USA. 1981-1983.   259

Costumes of 'La Belle Epoque' at the Metropolitan Museum of Art. USA: New York, NY. 1870-1910.   260

Choosing audio-visual materials for exhibits. Discussed at SIBMAS. France: Paris. 1982.   1705

Description of 'Four Centuries of Opera' exhibition. USA: New York, NY. 1583-1983.   1825

Exhibition of fifty puppets owned by Tom Maud. USA: Fort Worth, TX. 1983.   2036

Performance/production

Exhibition about the tendency toward the *Gesamtkunstwerk*. Switzerland: Zürich. Austria: Vienna. 1983.   444

Catalogue of exhibition on Max Reinhardt's use of genres and performance spaces. Austria. 1893-1943.   672

Plays/librettos/scripts

Catalogue of the exhibition on the copyright debate between playwright Paolo Giacometti and actress Adelaide Ristori. Italy. 1836-1882.   1191

Reference materials

Catalogue of the exhibition of Maria Antonietta Gambaro's paintings and scene designs. Italy. 1951-1980.   27

Description of various documents, photographs, designs and engravings on display at Edward Gordon Craig exhibit. UK-England. 1900-1935.   36

Catalogue of the exhibition on scenery, architecture, dance, opera and public theatres during Pietro Metastasio's life. Italy: Rome. 1698-1782.   1968

Catalogue of an exhibition dealing with Neapolitan comedians. Italy: Naples. 1799-1982.   1997

Catalogue of exhibition on *Commedia dell'arte* and erudite drama with a list of plays by Southern authors. Italy. 1550-1750.   2021

Catalogue for an exhibition of Venetian marionettes and puppets. Italy: Venice. 1700-1899.   2086

Existentialism

Plays/librettos/scripts

The themes of freedom, death and suicide in Albert Camus' *Caligula*. France. 1945.   1110

Jean Genet's *The Blacks* and his theory of ritual in context of Theatre of the Absurd and Total Theatre. France: Paris. 1948-1968.   1647

Experimental theatre

Audience

Political theatre for audiences of common age, economic and ethnic background. Germany, West. 1960-1983.   167

Institutions

Status report of the Århus Theatre Academy. Denmark: Århus. 1983.   297

Background of Edward Gordon Craig's efforts to establish School for the Art of Theatre. Italy: Florence. UK-England: London. 1900-1917.   320

Effect of women's movement on experimental theatre. Sweden: Stockholm. 1970-1983.   328

Multi-media methods employed by experimental theatre groups. Sweden: Stockholm. 1983.   329

Effects of political instability and materialism on Chilean theatre. Chile. 1970-1983.   587

History of Puerto Rican avant-garde theatre. Puerto Rico. 1811-1970.   617

Development of nationalistic and experimental theatre in Latin America. South America. North America. 1800-1983.   618

Steven Rumbelow and experimental work of Triple Action Theatre. Canada: Toronto, ON. 1980-1983.   1606

Free operating groups and institutionalized theatre. Netherlands. 1963-1983.   1609

Workshops of Latin American popular theatre. North America. South America. 1983.   1610

Growth of alternative theatre and its influence on traditional theatre productions. UK. 1983.   1612

Performance spaces

Design, construction and partitions of the Musiktheater im Revier. Germany, West: Gelsenkirchen. 1962-1983.   375

Design and history of the Nationaltheater Mannheim. Germany, West: Mannheim. 1777-1983.   376

Performance/production

Influence of Cubism on staging and scenery. Europe. 1900.   421

Analysis and critique of avant-garde trends in theatre. USA. 1970-1983.   470

Enactment and narration as particularly appropriate methods of dramatization. USA. 1968-1980.   906

Experimental theatre — cont'd

Role experimental studios played in the formation of the Soviet theatre. USSR: Moscow, Leningrad. 1920-1939. 993

Comprehensive study of productions by Tadeusz Kantor's experimental theatre group Cricot 2 and Kantor's philosophy. Poland. 1975-1980. 1626

Production styles of directors Peter Brook and Tadeusz Kantor. USA: New York, NY. France: Paris. Poland: Wielopole. 1982. 1632

Fifteen-hour pageant by Jean-Pierre Ronfard and Théâtrale Expérimental de Montréal. Canada: Montreal, PQ. 1982. 2025

Multi-media Biblical creation story presented with puppets by Esteban Fernandez Sanchez. USA: New York, NY. 1983. 2064

Plays/librettos/scripts

Experimentation with Enlish-language drama. Malaysia. 1957-1982. 1197

Problems of reconciling experimentation and acceptance are discussed by four new playwrights. USA. 1983. 1656

Survey of alternative theatre. USA. 1945. 1657

Theory/criticism

Expressionistic proposal for the future of theatre by a founding member of Squat Theatre. USA. 1983. 110

Vocal emission as a mode of theatricalization in experimental theatre. Canada. 1970-1979. 1669

Postscriptive performance text and experimental theatre groups. North America. 1983. 1672

Experimental theatre SEE ALSO: Classed Entries: DRAMA — Experimental forms

Expressionism

Design/technology

Lou Bunin memoirs of Meyer Levin's marionettes as ideally cast abstract visual images. USA: Chicago, IL. 1925-1930. 2080

Meyer Levin's marionettes as abstract visual images, influenced by Gordon Craig and Fernand Léger. USA. 1926-1930. 2081

Performance/production

Review article of *Theatre Production Series*, seeking to define theatre's strengths. England. Germany. 1500-1939. 706

Artistic movements and critical thought that shaped modern directing. Europe. 1914-1940. 715

Post-World War II forms of American theatre. USA. 1945-1983. 1633

Erich Wolfgang Korngold's *Die tote Stadt* at the Deutsche Oper Berlin. Germany, West: West Berlin. 1855. 1983. 1871

Plays/librettos/scripts

Playwrights and dramatic forms influencing Eugene O'Neill's *The Calms of Capricorn*. Europe. USA. 1953. 1088

Theme of war in German expressionist drama. Germany. 1914-1919. 1133

Expressionism in contemporary Spanish theatre. Spain. 1920-1980. 1257

Analysis of Oskar Kokoschka's theory through *Murderer Hope of Womankind*. Austria: Vienna. 1904-1912. 1635

Theory/criticism

Expressionistic proposal for the future of theatre by a founding member of Squat Theatre. USA. 1983. 110

Study of realism, naturalism, symbolism, surrealism, expressionism and epic theatre. Europe. North America. 1900-1980. 1484

Extremities

Performance/production

Seven critics review Robert Allan Ackerman's production of William Mastrosimone's play *Extremities*. USA: New York, NY. 1983. 980

Eysenck Personality Inventory

Audience

Testing undergraduates' reactions to set designs. USA: Athens, GA. 1974. 174

Fabbri, Marisa

Training

Research project in theatre heresy and Stanislavskij. Italy: Pontedera. 1981-1983. 1524

Fábula de Perseo, La (Fable of Perseus, The)

Plays/librettos/scripts

Dating of Lope de Vega's *The Fable of Perseus*. Spain. 1604-1635. 1244

Fachbibliothek für Theaterwissenschaft an der Universität Wien

Institutions

Problems and prospects of the theatre research library at the University of Vienna. Austria: Vienna. 1983. 286

Facio, Angel

Performance/production

Interview with director Angel Facio. Spain. 1966-1983. 835

Factory, The (Toronto, ON)

Institutions

Change in idealism among alternative theatres. Canada: Toronto, ON. 1973-1983. 295

Faculty SEE: Teaching methods, and Training, teacher

Fågel Blå (Stockholm)

Institutions

Effect of women's movement on experimental theatre. Sweden: Stockholm. 1970-1983. 328

Falconer, Edmund

Performance/production

Composers whose songs were played at Irish variety performances, especially those of John McCormack. USA. UK. 1800-1899. 2029

Falconi, Arturo

Critical summary of theatrical anecdotes as they are reported in four books. Italy. 1891-1965. 803

Fallon, Richard G.

Institutions

American Theatre Association President's address to 1983 annual business meeting. USA: Minneapolis, MN. 1983. 344

Falso Movimento (Italy)

History and analysis of three productions by the avant-garde theatre group Falso Movimento. Italy. 1977-1983. 1607

Falstaff

Performance/production

Bass Walter Berry's debut in *Falstaff* at the Vienna Staatsoper. Austria: Vienna. 1983. 1841

Fanon, Frantz

Plays/librettos/scripts

Jean Genet's *The Blacks* and his theory of ritual in context of Theatre of the Absurd and Total Theatre. France: Paris. 1948-1968. 1647

Fanshen

Epic structure in contemporary drama. UK. 1968-1981. 1275

Farce

Performance/production

Staging of Eugène Labiche's plays in Catalonia. Spain. France. 1967-1982. 1532

Plays/librettos/scripts

Playwrights and dramatic forms influencing Eugene O'Neill's *The Calms of Capricorn*. Europe. USA. 1953. 1088

Dario Fo's drama in Scandinavia. Italy. Sweden. Norway. 1983. 1184

Adaptation of a French farce into *Johan Johan*. England. France. 1520-1533. 1559

Farce — cont'd

Alfred Jarry's *Ubu* Cycle with an emphasis on its protagonist. France. 1896-1907.   1566

Analysis of farces by Eugène Labiche and Georges Feydeau. France. 1815-1921.   1575

Examination of Arthur Wing Pinero's court farces. UK-England. 1890-1899.   1591

Farcical style in Michael Frayn's *Noises Off*. USA. 1983.   1597

Theory/criticism

Nature and history of farce in theatre, film and media. Europe. USA. 425 B.C.-1982 A.D.   1600

Farce nouvelle très bonne et fort joyeuse du Pasté

Plays/librettos/scripts

Adaptation of a French farce into *Johan Johan*. England. France. 1520-1533.   1559

Farce of the Divorce Judge, The SEE: *Entremes del juez de los divorcios*

Farfalle, Le (Butterflies, The)

Basic theatrical documents

Annotated texts of Giovanni Verga's plays. Italy. 1865-1908.   573

Farrah, Abd'Elkader

Design/technology

Trends in scenic practices by British designers. UK. 1960-1983.   228

Fascism

Performance/production

Analysis of problems concerning the staging of Heinar Kipphardt's *Brother Eichmann*. Germany, West: Munich. 1983.   765

Plays/librettos/scripts

Brief comments on Heinar Kippardt's play *Brother Eichmann*. Germany, West. 1983.   1149

German Fascism as the main theme of Heinar Kipphardt's plays. Germany, West. 1982.   1153

Analysis of Giovacchino Forzano's play *Cesare*. Italy. 1939.   1173

Reference materials

Source materials on Richard Wagner's influence on theatre. Germany. Austria. USA. 1869-1976.   1966

Fassbinder, Rainer Werner

Performance/production

Portrait of the actor and director Rainer Werner Fassbinder. Germany, West. 1966-1981.   782

Plays/librettos/scripts

Cult of manhood in dramas of Yukio Mishima, Jean Genet and Rainer Werner Fassbinder. France. Japan. 1947-1983.   1099

Fatal Extravagance, The

Authorship of *The Fatal Extravagance*. England: London. 1721-1760.
                                                                                 1082

Father, The SEE: *Fadren*

Fathers and Sons SEE: *Ocy i dèti*

Faust

Basic theatrical documents

Catalan translation of *Ur-Faust* and articles on the play and its production by the Company Andrià Gual. Germany. Spain. 1887-1983.   571

Performance/production

Documents of Max Reinhardt's production of Goethe's *Faust*. Austria: Salzburg. 1933-1937.   667

List and short reviews of Shakespearean productions. Germany, East. 1981.   749

Interview with and influences on actor Bernhard Minetti, including production of *Faust*. Germany, East: East Berlin. 1982-1983.   751

Plays/librettos/scripts

Goethe's regard for Shakespeare and influences observed in *Faust*. Germany. 1770-1832.   1125

Composition and thematic analysis of Goethe's *Ur-Faust*. Germany. 1775-1832.   1137

Genesis of Goethe's *Faust* and changes introduced in the play thereafter. Germany. 1480-1832.   1141

Fay, William

Reference materials

Correspondence relating to administrative concerns at the Abbey Theatre between William Butler Yeats, Lady Gregory and John Millington Synge. UK-Ireland: Dublin. 1904-1909.   1432

Fear and Loathing in Gotham

Performance/production

Description and analysis of Ping Chong's work. USA. 1972-1983.
                                                                                 1752

Fearon, W.R.

Plays/librettos/scripts

Patriot Charles Stewart Parnell's influence on Irish drama. UK-Ireland. 1891-1936.   1337

Feasibility studies

Performance spaces

Steps involved in restoring historic theatres. USA. 1983.   396

Feast of Fools

Performance/production

Links between popular forms of medieval drama and theatrical presentations during the carnival period. France. 1200-1599.   2007

Feast of Unreason, The

Tribute to Mordecai Gorelik, scenic designer, theorist, teacher, director and playwright. USA. 1899-1983.   936

Federal Theatre Project

Federal Theatre Project's often innovative approach to staging Shakespeare's plays. USA. 1930-1939.   978

Federici, Mario

Plays/librettos/scripts

Unpublished writings, biographical notes, themes and political influence in Mario Federici's plays. Italy. 1900-1975.   1161

Fehling, Jürgen

Performance/production

Productions of *The Flies* at Düsseldorfer Schauspielhaus and Hebbeltheater Berlin. Germany, West: Düsseldorf, West Berlin. 1947-1948.   785

Félicité (Happiness)

Aspects of Jean Audureau's *Happiness* produced at the Comédie-Française. France: Paris. 1983.   739

Felipe, León

Plays/librettos/scripts

Report concerning poet León Felipe and his play *The Juggler*. Spain. Mexico. 1939-1983.   1227

Female Transport

Epic structure in contemporary drama. UK. 1968-1981.   1275

Feminism

Institutions

Effect of women's movement on experimental theatre. Sweden: Stockholm. 1970-1983.   328

Profile of the women's company Bloodgroup. UK. 1983.   1741

Performance/production

Jane Martin's *Talking With* at Manhattan Theatre Club, directed by Jon Jory. USA: New York, NY. 1982.   937

Interview with playwright Dario Fo and his actress-wife and collaborator Franca Rame. Italy: Milan. 1982.   1623

Festivals — cont'd

Reference materials

European music and theatre festivals in 1983: cities, productions and dates. Europe. 1983. 22

Cast listings and other information on 19 productions mounted at Charlottetown Festival. Canada: Charlottetown, PE. 1965-1982. 1399

Source materials on Richard Wagner's influence on theatre. Germany. Austria. USA. 1869-1976. 1966

Relation to other fields

Development of Teyyam, an Indian religious festival. India. 1982. 2108

Feydeau, Georges

Plays/librettos/scripts

Analysis of farces by Eugène Labiche and Georges Feydeau. France. 1815-1921. 1575

Fichandler, Zelda

Training

Zelda Fichandler expresses her philosophy of theatre education. USA: New York, NY, Washington, DC. 1950-1983. 506

Field Day Theatre Company (UK)

Performance/production

Career of actor Stephen Rea. UK-England. UK-Ireland. 1900-1983. 881

Field, Ron

Five critics review Ron Field's production of *Five-Six-Seven-Eight...Dance!*. USA: New York, NY. 1983. 1783

Fielding, Henry

Plays/librettos/scripts

Essays on Restoration theatre and drama, with devised criteria for evaluation. England. 1660-1800. 1046

Fierstein, Harvey

Performance/production

Notes on three Broadway productions. USA: New York, NY. 1983. 911

Six critics review Peter Pope's production of Harvey Fierstein's play *Torch Song Trilogy*. USA: New York, NY. 1983. 1536

Ten critics review *La Cage aux Folles*. USA: New York, NY. 1983. 1806

Plays/librettos/scripts

Examination of Harvey Fierstein's *Torch Song Trilogy*. USA: New York, NY. 1983. 1596

Figlia di Jorio, La (Jorio's Daughter)

Psychoanalysis of the protagonists in Gabriele D'Annunzio's *Jorio's Daughter*. Italy. 1904. 1188

Figurative arts

Administration

Impact of government funding on the arts. USA. 1965-1982. 159

Effect of different kinds of financial support on artists. USA. 1950-1982. 163

Audience

Sociological studies suggest that democratization of the arts has not taken place. USA. 1830-1982. 173

Design/technology

Methodology for the interpretation of symbolism in Renaissance costume. Italy. 1539. 212

Performance/production

Comprehensive theatre history presented within a cultural context. 499 B.C.-1983 A.D. 412

Influence of Cubism on staging and scenery. Europe. 1900. 421

Portrait of Ira Aldridge as Othello in painting by James Northcote. UK-England: Manchester. USA. 1826. 869

Comprehensive study of productions by Tadeusz Kantor's experimental theatre group Cricot 2 and Kantor's philosophy. Poland. 1975-1980. 1626

Richard Wagner's works, reception and influence. France. 1841-1983. 1859

Plays/librettos/scripts

Relationship of various arts to Shakespearean production. England. USA. 1590-1981. 1035

Conference on August Strindberg's relation to modern culture, painting, photography and theatrical productions. Italy: Bari. 1982. 1178

Cubism in art (space) related to cubism in drama (time). Sweden. Norway. 1828-1912. 1259

Revolutionary vision of collaborative effort between Oscar Wilde and illustrator Aubrey Beardsley. UK. 1894-1900. 1273

Relation to other fields

Essays on five main concerns of oral interpretation: language, culture, teaching, theory and entertainment. Europe. North America. 499 B.C.-1980 A.D. 53

Theatre in relation to other performing arts at the seminar of the International Centre of Aesthetic Studies. Italy. 1982. 64

Theatre arts compared to painting and literature. UK-England. 1805-1902. 69

Painter Oskar Kokoschka's dramatic works. Austria. 1917. 1442

Shakespeare's rhetoric in *Love's Labour's Lost* expresses commonplace figures also to be found in pictorial art of the period. England. 1594-1595. 1446

Imagery of *Hamlet* is linked to Medieval and Renaissance decorative art. England: Stratford-upon-Avon. 1600-1601. 1447

Comparison of the character of Herod in two Fleury plays. France. England. 1100-1200. 1452

Statue of playwright Henrik Ibsen. Norway: Oslo. 1828-1906. 1460

Dramatist Stanisław Wyspiański's painting of a Tartar costume, based on a folk tradition stock type — Lajkonik. Poland: Kraków. Austria. 1901-1907. 1461

Association between literature of J.M. Synge and pictorial art of Jack B. Yeats. UK-Ireland. 1896-1948. 1463

Theory/criticism

Semiotic study of the specific nature of theatre in relation to other arts and audience interaction with it. Spain. 1983. 108

Film

Plays/librettos/scripts

Analysis of Samuel Beckett's earliest typescript of *Eh Joe* to revision as *Ghost Trio*. UK-Ireland. France. 1958. 1323

Film

Administration

Autobiography of Broadway producer Irene Mayer Selznick. USA. 1910-1983. 161

Design/technology

Techniques for using film or still projection in live theatre performances. USA. 1983. 250

Use of film and theatrical techniques in rock concert. USA. 1983. 1706

Vincente Minnelli's pre-Hollywood years as Broadway designer. USA: Hollywood, CA, New York, NY. 1931-1939. 1769

Institutions

Teatro Escambray reflects developments in Cuban society. Cuba. Nicaragua: Managua. 1961-1983. 588

Performance spaces

Renovation of theatre now used for community theatre and film. USA: Chambersburg, PA. 1926-1983. 401

Performance/production

Americans tour Soviet theatres. USSR: Moscow, Kiev. 1981. 487

Rehearsal methods of director Finn Poulsen. Sweden: Göteburg, Gävleborg. 1969-1983. 839

Study of Ingmar Bergman's approach to directing, and the influences on it. Sweden. Germany. 1930-1983. 842

Biography of actress Katharine Hepburn. USA. 1909-1983. 915

Autobiography of actress Shirley MacLaine. USA. 1934-1983. 943

Authentic expression in Black theatre and film is contrasted with stereotypical Black portrayals by white authors and performers. USA: New York, NY. 1890-1930. 983

Film — cont'd

Interweaving of theatrical and cinematographic techniques in Mejerchol'd's staging. USSR. 1915-1927. 997

Comedian Harry Langdon as a stage director. USA. 1884-1944. 1539

Max Reinhardt's film adaptations of his theatre productions. Europe. North America. 1910-1943. 1711

Voice and movement for film acting. USA. 1983. 1717

Biography of singer-actress Julie Andrews. UK-England. USA. 1935-1983. 1777

Production history of *The Best Little Whorehouse in Texas*. USA: New York, NY. 1974-1982. 1784

Overview of Jack Cole's career as dancer, teacher and choreographer. USA. 1933-1974. 1788

Biography of Liza Minnelli. USA. 1946-1983. 1790

Making of the Franco Zeffirelli film of *La Traviata*. Italy: Rome. 1981-1983. 1885

Brief biography and interview with Cab Calloway. USA: White Plains, NY, Hollywood, CA. 1930-1983. 1993

Interaction of technology and popular entertainment. USA. 1900-1982. 1995

Contributions made to puppetry by Jim Henson's *Dark Crystal*. USA. 1980-1983. 2059

Plays/librettos/scripts

Comprehensive study of Neil Simon's plays, screenplays and musical comedies. USA. 1927-1981. 488

Treatment of violence and its aesthetics in theatre, film and literature. Europe. 1983. 1090

Biographical and cultural sources of Eduardo De Filippo's plays. Italy. 1926-1982. 1174

Playwright David Hare's career and interests in Fringe theatre, television and film. UK-England. 1947-1983. 1304

Examination of plays adapted for movies. USA. 1974. 1345

Eugene O'Neill plays that have been made into films. USA. 1916. 1347

Essays on the trends of the Jewish-American theatre and its personalities. USA. 1900-1983. 1353

The Long Voyage Home and *Long Day's Journey into Night* successfully transferred to film. USA. 1940-1962. 1383

Reference materials

Biographical entries on playwrights and screenwriters. 1983. 13

Yearbook of theatre, television and cinema, with brief critical notations. Italy. 1983. 29

Description of David O. Selznick collection: '*Gone with the Wind*: A Legend Endures'. USA. 1939-1983. 1721

Relation to other fields

Political reactions to anti-war plays and films. Germany. 1930. 1453

Circus as a staging device for a political satire. USSR. Germany. Italy. 1914-1930. 1668

Theory/criticism

Italian translation of *Theater-Schriften und Reden, Dramaturgisches und Kritisches, Der Mitmacher*. Europe. 1921. 94

Semiotic study of the specific nature of theatre in relation to other arts and audience interaction with it. Spain. 1983. 108

Significance of gender in feminist criticism with reference to historical materialism, deconstruction and phenomenon of cross-dressing in theatre. USA. France. UK-England. 1983. 1520

Film SEE ALSO: Classed Entries: MEDIA — Film

Filmographies

Performance/production

Biography and all-inclusive reference materials to Charlie Chaplin. USA. 1889-1977. 1714

Financial operations

Administration

Censorship of Brazilian theatre, causing only Broadway hits to be produced. Brazil. 1557-1983. 116

Six payments to traveling entertainers from two hitherto unpublished documents in Warwick County Records Office. England: Warwick. 1601-1637. 121

Accounts of payment to assorted entertainers performing for Lord Berkeley. England: Coventry. 1593-1605. 122

Success of French cultural policy in subsidizing theatre, reviews of some productions. France. 1900-1983. 125

Economical and financial problems facing today's theatres. Germany, West. 1983. 126

Private ownership — a solution for the economic crisis of the government-funded theatre. Germany, West. 1983. 127

Economic organization of and financial problems faced by today's theatres. Germany, West. 1983. 129

Political and cultural background of Würzburg theatres and their financial operations. Germany, West: Würzburg. 1945-1983. 131

Financial and political situation of theatre institutions. Germany, West. 1982. 132

Plans to overcome financial crisis in theatre. Germany, West. 1983. 133

Financial situation of municipal theatres. Germany, West. 1982. 134

Financial problems facing scene designers. Germany, West. 1983. 135

Effect of corporate sponsorship on freedom of expression in theatre. Sweden. 1983. 143

Resolution concerning billing guidelines of American Theatre Association. USA. 1983. 149

How to locate free or low-cost professional assistance in law, finance and management. USA. 1983. 156

Effects of arts administration on artistic objectives. USA. 1982. 158

Recent tax law changes. USA. 1983. 162

Sound financial practices of the productions mounted by the actor-manager Tate Wilkinson. England. 1781-1784. 554

Relationship between funding, repertoire and commissioning of new works. UK-Scotland. 1982. 558

Court entertainments during reign of Henry VII, from early records. England: London. 1485-1505. 1737

Management and fiscal administration at the Royal Academy of Music. England: London. 1719-1721. 1814

Institutions

State of theatre in Ruhr-District. Germany, West: Dortmund. 1972-1982. 307

Brief survey of productions and financial situation of a local theatre. Germany, West: Nürnberg. 1983. 314

History, financial situation and productions of the Schlosstheater. Germany, West: Moers. 1975-1983. 315

Economic and political aspects of several Black theatre groups. USA: New York, NY, Chicago, IL. 1982. 340

Financial situation of Städtische Bühnen Dortmund. Germany, West: Dortmund. 1970-1982. 604

Interviews with personnel of Freiburg theatres on obtaining subsidies and other aspects of administration. Germany, West: Freiburg. 1911-1983. 607

History of Royal Shakespeare Company with emphasis on financial and aesthetic aspects and internal politics. UK-England: London. 1864-1981. 624

Critical examination of lack of idealism among non-profit theatres. USA. 1960-1983. 654

Performance spaces

Great Hall at Gawthorpe and financial accounts provide information on the activities of Jacobean traveling companies. England. 1600-1618. 364

Steps involved in restoring historic theatres. USA. 1983. 396

Finke, Jochen

Design/technology

Recent scene designs by Jochen Finke and Sergei Barkhin. USSR. Germany, East. 1970-1983. 277

Finnish National Opera SEE: Suomen Kansallisooppera

Fire, The SEE: *Fuoco, Il*

Folkefiende, En (Enemy of the People, An) — cont'd

Plays/librettos/scripts

Examination of Stockmann's relationship to the community in *An Enemy of the People*. Norway. 1882.   1203

Folklore

Role of folklore in Irish Literary Revival. UK-Ireland. 1888-1920.   1322

Imagery of the apocalyptic symbol of the black pig in works by William Butler Yeats. UK-Ireland. 1880-1910.   1334

Ironic use of folklore in Sam Shepard's *Buried Child*. USA. 1978.   1373

Folkteatern (Gothenburg)

Performance/production

Rehearsal methods of director Finn Poulsen. Sweden: Göteburg, Gävleborg. 1969-1983.   839

Fontanesi, Francesco

Design/technology

Scene designers and scenery at Teatro alla Scala in Neoclassic period. Italy: Milan. 1778-1832.   1821

Fool for Love

Performance/production

Seven critics review Sam Shepard's production of his play *Fool for Love* presented by Circle Repertory Company. USA: New York, NY. 1983.   963

Plays/librettos/scripts

Review essay of Sam Shepard's *Fool for Love*. USA: San Francisco, CA. 1983.   1595

Fools

Administration

Accounts of payment to assorted entertainers performing for Lord Berkeley. England: Coventry. 1593-1605.   122

Footfalls

Plays/librettos/scripts

Sources of power in Samuel Beckett's *Footfalls*. UK-Ireland. France. 1957.   1335

Forces de l'Amour et de la Magie, Les (Powers of Love and Magic, The)

Institutions

History of Théâtre de la Foire. France: Paris. 1679-1721.   1979

Ford, John

Performance/production

List of productions of plays from English Renaissance drama with brief reviews. North America. Europe. 1982-1983.   822

Plays/librettos/scripts

The Long Voyage Home and *Long Day's Journey into Night* successfully transferred to film. USA. 1940-1962.   1383

Bunraku version of John Ford's *'Tis Pity She's a Whore* at University of California. USA: Los Angeles, CA. 1983.   2075

Foreman, Richard

Performance/production

Notes on three Broadway productions. USA: New York, NY. 1983.   911

Plays/librettos/scripts

Problems of play translations without caricature. Germany, West. USA. 1900-1983.   1148

Forreger, N.M.

Performance/production

Work of the director/choreographer N.M. Forreger in the musical theatre. USSR. 1929-1939.   1930

Forrest, Edwin

Shakespearean productions and festivals in the American South. USA. 1751-1980.   938

Forza del Destino, La

Career of soprano Leona Mitchell at the Metropolitan Opera. USA. 1983.   1912

Forzano, Giovacchino

Plays/librettos/scripts

Analysis of Giovacchino Forzano's play *Cesare*. Italy. 1939.   1173

Found spaces

Institutions

Street theatre production of Århus theater akademi in collaboration with Jordcirkus and Johnny Melville. Denmark: Århus. 1982.   298

Performance spaces

Technical problems Deutsches Schauspielhaus encountered by performing in a former factory. Germany, West: Hamburg. 1980-1983.   377

Use of urban areas to mount theatre spectacles. Italy: Palermo. 1500-1600.   381

Proposals and experiences by theatrical operators to utilize the urban space for performances. Italy. 1983.   384

Fourberies de Scapin, Les (Tricks of Scapin, The)

Plays/librettos/scripts

Discussion of Molière's *The Tricks of Scapin* addressed to teachers and children of primary schools. France. Italy: Turin. 1671-1983.   1562

Fowler, Charles

Institutions

History of Royal Shakespeare Company with emphasis on financial and aesthetic aspects and internal politics. UK-England: London. 1864-1981.   624

Foxy

Performance/production

Overview of Jack Cole's career as dancer, teacher and choreographer. USA. 1933-1974.   1788

Fraga, Ruben

Documentation on Ruben Fraga's production of *The Tower of Babel* by the Dramatic Center Vienna. Austria: Vienna. 1980-1983.   670

Francis, Henry

Plays/librettos/scripts

Possible authorship of a lost Chester Corpus Christi play. England: Chester. 1268-1375.   1037

Francovich, Guillermo

Development of social themes in Bolivian drama. Bolivia. 1944-1983.   1014

Frank, Doug

Performance/production

Seven critics review Kenny Ortega's production of the musical *Marilyn: An American Fable*. USA: New York, NY. 1983.   1792

Franke, Dieter

Obituary portrait of actor Dieter Franke. Germany, East: East Berlin. 1964-1982.   755

Frankel, Kenneth

Eight critics review Kenneth Frankel's production of Simon Gray's play *Quartermaine's Terms*. USA: New York, NY. 1983.   957

Frayn, Michael

Ten critics review Michael Blakemore's production of Michael Frayn's play *Noises Off*. USA: New York, NY. 1983.   1541

Plays/librettos/scripts

Farcical style in Michael Frayn's *Noises Off*. USA. 1983.   1597

Freie Volksbühne (West Berlin)

Performance/production

The Comedy of Errors at Freie Volksbühne, directed by Werner Schroeter. Germany, West: West Berlin. 1983.   774

Freischütz, Der

Plays/librettos/scripts

Carl Maria von Weber's influence on Richard Wagner. Europe. 1822-1844.   1935

Fremstad, Olive

Reference materials

Annotated selections of photographs taken by Herman Mishkin of Metropolitan Opera singers. USA: New York, NY. 1910-1932.   1971

French Classicism SEE: Neoclassicism

French Revolution

Performance/production

Contemporary events reflected in staging plays about Jean-Paul Marat's death. France. 1793-1797.   732

Freud, Sigmund

Plays/librettos/scripts

Freudian analysis of the character of Caterina Leher in *The Housekeeper* by Vitaliano Brancati. Italy. 1952.   1172

Ibsen's creation of realistic characters displaying unconscious desires. Norway. 1892.   1207

Relation to other fields

Santuzza Papa's transition from Freudian psychodrama to Jungian conception. Italy. 1960.   1663

Theory/criticism

Freudian analysis is used to divide dramatic fantasy into three phases, from genital-masochism to anal-sadism. Germany, West. France. USA. 1974-1983.   1506

Friedentheater (Århus)

Institutions

Street theatre production of Århus theater akademi in collaboration with Jordcirkus and Johnny Melville. Denmark: Århus. 1982.   298

Friedrich, Götz

Performance/production

History and production history of Wagnerian opera. Germany. USA. 1832-1982.   1865

Erich Wolfgang Korngold's *Die tote Stadt* at the Deutsche Oper Berlin. Germany, West: West Berlin. 1855. 1983.   1871

Discussion of centennial production of *Parsifal* directed by Götz Friedrich. Germany, West: Bayreuth. 1982.   1876

Friel, Brian

Five critics review Nye Heron's production of Brian Friel's play *Winners*. USA: New York, NY. 1983.   962

Fringe theatre

Institutions

Collaborative production efforts of Bush Theatre. UK-England. 1983.
630

Organization and productions of Black Theatre Co-operative. UK-England. 1979.   631

Artistic directors, policy, development and funding of The Traverse studio theatre. UK-England. 1963.   632

Development and funding of Foco Novo, Fringe theatre company. UK-England. 1972.   633

Joint Stock, a collective theatre company. UK-England. 1974.   635

Performance/production

Career of actor Stephen Rea. UK-England. UK-Ireland. 1900-1983.
881

Plays/librettos/scripts

Playwright David Hare's career and interests in Fringe theatre, television and film. UK-England. 1947-1983.   1304

Frisch, Max

Theory/criticism

Influence of Richard Wagner's *Gesamtkunstwerk* on modern theatre. Germany. 1849-1977.   1495

Froboess, Cornelia

Performance/production

Portrait and interview with the actress Cornelia Froboess. Germany, West: Munich. 1951-1983.   763

Fröken Julie (Miss Julie)

Productions of August Strindberg's *Miss Julie* and *The Dance of Death*. Germany, West: Giessen, Wilhelmshaven, Memmingen. 1981-1982.   786

Documentation of Ingmar Bergman's tripartite theatre project. Sweden. Germany, West: Munich. 1981.   844

August Strindberg productions in eleven countries. Sweden. Italy. USA. 1982.   847

Year's outstanding productions of plays by August Strindberg and other playwrights. UK-England. 1982-1983.   890

Plays/librettos/scripts

Fairy-tale elements in *Miss Julie* intensify the play's tragic impact. Sweden. 1870-1908.   1264

Examination of August Strindberg's attitude towards and use of impressionism. Sweden. 1874-1884.   1270

From the House of the Dead SEE: Z Mrtvého Domu

Fruchtmann, Karl

Performance/production

World premiere of Martin Walser's *In Goethe's Hand* at Vienna's Akademietheater, directed by Karl Fruchtmann. Austria: Vienna. 1983.   671

FTV (Uppsala)

Institutions

Limited success of staged readings. Sweden. Denmark. 1969-1983.
619

Fuchs, Georg

Theory/criticism

Reformers on their theories. Europe. 1870-1910.   98

Fuentes, Giorgio

Design/technology

Scene designers and scenery at Teatro alla Scala in Neoclassic period. Italy: Milan. 1778-1832.   1821

Fugard, Athol

Plays/librettos/scripts

Universal themes overshadow autobiographical references in two plays by Athol Fugard. South Africa, Republic of: Port Elizabeth. USA: New Haven, CT, New York, NY. 1979-1983.   1223

Relation to other fields

Athol Fugard's plays are compared to Bantustan agitprop and historical drama. South Africa, Republic of. 1955-1980.   1665

Fulton Theatre (New York, NY)

Institutions

Folies-Bergère contribution to the development of dinner theatres and night clubs. USA: New York, NY. 1911.   2026

Fundraising

Administration

Critique of recommendations made by Canadian Federal Cultural Policy Review Committee. Canada. 1976-1983.   118

Ministry of Education report on theatre funding. Finland. 1980-1983.
123

Efforts of Jack Lang, Minister of Culture, to decentralize theatre. France. 1982-1983.   124

Success of French cultural policy in subsidizing theatre, reviews of some productions. France. 1900-1983.   125

Private ownership — a solution for the economic crisis of the government-funded theatre. Germany, West. 1983.   127

Suggestions for government theatre funding policy. Italy. 1983.   137

Scottish Arts Council's policy of funding community theatre. UK-Scotland. 1980-1983.   147

Genres — cont'd

Song of Songs as medieval dramatic literature. Europe. 1400-1499.
1089

Aspects of liturgical drama cause it to be both ritual and theatre. France. 1100-1200.
1101

Typology and analysis of French sacred drama. France. 1550-1650.
1111

Aesthetic continuity in Pierre Corneille's movement from comedy to tragedy. France. 1606-1684.
1112

Comparison of two German adaptations of Molière's *The Misanthrope* to determine the genre of the play. Germany, West: Cologne. 1982.
1151

Period plays and documentary theatre of the cold war. Germany, West. 1945-1966.
1152

Pastoral as dramatic genre and its literary and scenic derivations. Italy. 1400-1599.
1185

Study of playwrights, forms and styles in the Spanish theatre. Spain. 1939-1980.
1247

Sociological approach to Lope de Vega's drama. Spain. 1573-1635.
1256

Fairy-tale elements in *Miss Julie* intensify the play's tragic impact. Sweden. 1870-1908.
1264

Debate on folk and literary theatre. Sweden.
1265

Representational and modernist comedic aspects of J.M. Synge's *The Playboy of the Western World*. UK-Ireland. 1907.
1326

Definiton of the new dramatic genre — hypernaturalism. USA. Europe. 1970-1983.
1386

Realism in drama, acting, staging and design. Yugoslavia. 1920-1930.
1395

Relation between couplet and parody as exemplified in Johann Nestroy' songs. Austria. 1833-1862.
1546

Parody on the stage of Viennese Popular Theatre before Johann Nestroy. Austria: Vienna. 1801-1861.
1547

Genre analysis and comparison of Johann Nestroy's play *Die verhängnisvolle Faschingsnacht* with Karl von Holtei's *Ein Trauerspiel in Berlin*. Austria. 1839.
1548

Genre classification of parody and related forms in Johann Nestroy's plays. Austria. 1833-1862.
1552

Genre reevaluation of the Restoration, sentimental, and cynical comedy. England: London. 1678-1693.
1558

Variations on the bedroom farce form in the works of Eugène Labiche, Roger Vitrac and Samuel Beckett. France. 1870-1983. 1573

Comic mechanism in Plautus' *Amphitruo* and *Casina*. Roman Republic. 254-184 B.C.
1586

Analysis of forms, styles, characters and influences in Valle-Inclán's *comedias bárbaras*. Spain: Galicia. 1866-1936.
1588

Comic techniques in Alan Ayckbourn's *The Norman Conquests*. UK-England. 1974.
1589

Examination of Arthur Wing Pinero's court farces. UK-England. 1890-1899.
1591

Farcical style in Michael Frayn's *Noises Off*. USA. 1983. 1597

Egische Ciarenz's plays, particularly *Kafkaz*, are placed between Futurism and agitprop theatre. Armenia. 1923.
1634

Study of Fernando Arrabal's playwriting technique. France. 1932.
1644

Study of form, style and theme in John Webster's plays. England: London. 1603-1640.
1686

Realism in *Arden of Faversham*. England: London. 1588-1593.
1689

Analysis of three tragedies written between Mannerism and the Age of Arcadia. Italy. 1627-1713.
1698

Composer Jean-Philippe Rameau's contribution to development of opera. France. 1683-1764.
1941

Phenomenon of Grand Opera is examined in view of its music, librettos and staging. France. 1828-1865.
1942

Naturalism in the works of Pietro Mascagni and Giacomo Puccini. Italy. 1879-1926.
1955

Relation to other fields

Current dramatic themes in relation to historical development. China. 1900-1983.
1444

Theory/criticism

Effect of social conditions on performance styles. USA. Greece. 499 B.C.-1983 A.D.
1517

Nature and history of farce in theatre, film and media. Europe. USA. 425 B.C.-1982 A.D.
1600

Theory and definition of the comedy genre. Europe. North America. 499 B.C.-1980 A.D.
1601

Calderón de la Barca's plays and theory of comedy advanced in essay by Robert Ter Horst. Spain. 1600-1681.
1602

Study of genesis, development, structural components and consequences of theatre-drama performed by the Black workers. South Africa, Republic of. 1981-1983.
1673

Gentry, Philippe

Performance/production

Recent production by the Philippe Gentry puppet company. France. 1980.
2050

German Shakespeare Society SEE: Deutsche Shakespeare Gesellschaft

Gershwin, George

Performance/production

Production, casts and review of musical *My One and Only*. USA: New York, NY. 1971-1983.
1791

Nine critics review Jack O'Brien's production of *Porgy and Bess*. USA: New York, NY. 1983.
1795

Ten critics review *My One and Only*, staged by Thommie Walsh and Tommy Tune. USA: New York, NY. 1983.
1808

Study of revue songs by Irving Berlin, George Gershwin and Cole Porter in their theatrical contexts. USA: New York, NY. 1910-1937.
2032

Gershwin, Ira

Production, casts and review of musical *My One and Only*. USA: New York, NY. 1971-1983.
1791

Nine critics review Jack O'Brien's production of *Porgy and Bess*. USA: New York, NY. 1983.
1795

Ten critics review *My One and Only*, staged by Thommie Walsh and Tommy Tune. USA: New York, NY. 1983.
1808

Gesamtkunstwerk

Exhibition about the tendency toward the *Gesamtkunstwerk*. Switzerland: Zürich. Austria: Vienna. 1983.
444

Theory/criticism

Influence of Richard Wagner's *Gesamtkunstwerk* on modern theatre. Germany. 1849-1977.
1495

Getting Out

Plays/librettos/scripts

The character of Arlene in Marsha Norman's play *Getting Out*, and her effect on the audience. USA. 1981.
1372

Ghelderode, Michel de

Poetry in the theatre of Ghelderode. Belgium. 1918-1962. 1009

Denunciation of collective violence reflected in the role of sacrifice in Michel de Ghelderode's *Barabbas*. Belgium. 1929.
1010

Influences on Michel de Ghelderode from his national culture and Bertolt Brecht. Belgium. 1919-1962.
1011

Translating works by Michel de Ghelderode into Polish. Belgium. 1918-1973.
1013

Lack of familiarity in Britain with the work of Michel de Ghelderode. UK-England. Belgium. 1957-1982.
1292

Ghost Sonata SEE: *Spöksonaten*

Ghost Trio

Plays/librettos/scripts

Analysis of Samuel Beckett's earliest typescript of *Eh Joe* to revision as *Ghost Trio*. UK-Ireland. France. 1958.
1323

Ghosts SEE: *Gengangere*

Giacometti, Paolo

Plays/librettos/scripts

Catalogue of the exhibition on the copyright debate between playwright Paolo Giacometti and actress Adelaide Ristori. Italy. 1836-1882.　　1191

Gibbon's Tennis Court (London)

Performance spaces

Dimensions, orientation and dates established for theatre at Gibbon's Tennis Court. England: London. 1636-1660.　　363

Gide, André

Institutions

Founding of periodical *Nouvelle Revue Française*. France: Paris. 1909-1914.　　304

Gielgud, John

Performance/production

John Gielgud discusses nervous tension in actors. UK-England. 1983.　　878

Giganti della montagna, I (Giants of the Mountain, The)

Plays/librettos/scripts

Luigi Pirandello's earlier plays are considered prologues to *The Giants of the Mountain*. Italy. 1921-1937.　　1189

Gilbert, Edward

Administration

Disappointments and mismanagement at Centre Stage. Canada: Toronto, ON. 1983.　　119

Gilbert, Gabriel

Plays/librettos/scripts

Representation of court manners in comedy. France: Paris. 1650-1715.　　1565

Gilbert, W.S.

Performance/production

Assorted material on Gilbert and Sullivan operas on stage and screen. UK-England. 1867-1983.　　1888

Plays/librettos/scripts

Examination of Samuel Johnson as a character in plays by William Brough and W.S. Gilbert. UK-England: London. 1862-1893.　　1313

Gill, Peter

Performance/production

Two examples of staging *Macbeth* in the 1970's. USA: Stratford, CT. Canada: Stratford, ON. 1971-1973.　　908

Gill, Richard

Director of Polka Children's Theatre discusses children's attitude to plays and puppets. UK. 1983.　　852

Gillette, William

Plays/librettos/scripts

Sixty-three year career of William Gillette as actor and playwright. USA. 1873-1936.　　1380

Gilman, Richard

Institutions

Reflections on the significance of The Open Theatre by several of its performers, writers and critical advisers. USA: New York, NY. 1963-1973.　　1613

Gioconda, La

Performance/production

Photographs, cast lists, synopsis and discography of Metropolitan Opera production of *La Gioconda*. USA: New York, NY. 1983.　　1898

Plays/librettos/scripts

Shakespeare's influence on Arrigo Boito's libretto for *La Gioconda*, based on Victor Hugo's play. Italy. 1862-1900.　　1956

Giselle

Performance/production

Evelyn Hart's debut as Giselle with the Royal Winnipeg Ballet. Canada: Winnipeg, ON. 1966-1982.　　517

Gisors, Comte de

Impressions of theatre and popular entertainment by a French visitor. England: London. 1754.　　419

Giuliani, Fulvia

Biographical notes on the actress Fulvia Giuliani. Italy. 1900-1983.　　815

Gladiatorial contests

Performance spaces

Naumachiae, gladiatorial contests, circus races and other acts in ancient Rome. Roman Republic. Roman Empire. 616 B.C.-523 A.D.　　387

Glasgow Citizens' Theatre

Institutions

Repertory and workings of Glasgow Citizens' Theatre. UK-Scotland: Glasgow. 1983.　　642

Glasgow Jewish Institute Players

History of the Glasgow Jewish Institute Players. UK-Scotland: Glasgow. 1930-1963.　　640

Glasgow Unity Theatre

Post-war years of the Glasgow Unity Theatre. UK-Scotland: Glasgow. 1945-1959.　　639

Glass Menagerie, The

Performance/production

Ten critics review John Dexter's production of *The Glass Menagerie*, by Tennessee Williams. USA: New York, NY. 1983.　　981

Plays/librettos/scripts

Hart Crane's influence on plays by Tennessee Williams. USA. 1938-1980.　　1354

Globe, The

Relation to other fields

Videotapes created as instructional material on Elizabethan theatre. USA: Cortland, NY. 1973-1983.　　1724

Globe, The (London)

Performance/production

Reconstruction of Richard Mansfield's production of *Richard III*. UK-England: London. USA. 1889.　　893

Globe, The (Regina, SK)

Administration

Four artistic directors discuss theatre relationship with community. Canada: Regina, SK, Vancouver, BC, Toronto, ON, Calgary, AB. 1983.　　553

Glossaries

Performance/production

Linguistic study of the letters written by the actor-manager Gustavo Modena. Italy. 1829-1861.　　811

Glups

Ten years in the life of Dagoll-Dagom Company and their new play *Glups*. Spain. 1973-1983.　　834

Gobert, Boy

Administration

Heribert Sasse succeeds Boy Gobert as manager at Staatliche Schauspielbühnen Berlin. Germany, West: West Berlin. 1983.　　128

Godínez, Felipe

Plays/librettos/scripts

Theological content of Felipe Godínez's play *The Queen Esther Play*, may have been responsible for his Inquisition trial. Spain. 1624.　　1240

Goebbels, Heiner

Performance/production

Portrait and interview with theatre composer Heiner Goebbels. Germany, West. 1983. 1763

Goertz, Heinrich

Karlheinz Stroux's production of *The Skin of Our Teeth* by Thornton Wilder at Hebbeltheater. Germany, West: West Berlin, Darmstadt. 1946. 779

Goethe, Johann Wolfgang von

Basic theatrical documents

Catalan translation of *Ur-Faust* and articles on the play and its production by the Company Andrià Gual. Germany. Spain. 1887-1983. 571

Institutions

Repertory and workings of Glasgow Citizens' Theatre. UK-Scotland: Glasgow. 1983. 642

Performance/production

Documents of Max Reinhardt's production of Goethe's *Faust*. Austria: Salzburg. 1933-1937. 667

Interview with and influences on actor Bernhard Minetti, including production of *Faust*. Germany, East: East Berlin. 1982-1983. 751

Plays/librettos/scripts

Bourgeois interests in *Wilhelm Meister's Theatrical Mission* by Goethe. Germany. 1777-1785. 1116

Goethe's regard for Shakespeare and influences observed in *Faust*. Germany. 1770-1832. 1125

Catholic interpretation of *Der 24 Februar* by Zacharias Werner. Germany. 1809-1814. 1134

Influence of Siglo de Oro on German pre-romantic theatre. Germany. Spain. 1765-1832. 1135

Composition and thematic analysis of Goethe's *Ur-Faust*. Germany. 1775-1832. 1137

Genesis of Goethe's *Faust* and changes introduced in the play thereafter. Germany. 1480-1832. 1141

Theory/criticism

Goethe's thought on German literature in relation to literature of other nations. Germany. 1766-1832. 1503

Gogol, Nikolai Vasiljevič

Performance/production

Production of Russian classical plays at Eastern European theatres. Bulgaria. Yugoslavia. Czechoslovakia. 1850-1914. 682

Golden Windows, The

Plays/librettos/scripts

Robert Wilson discusses current and forthcoming projects. USA: New York, NY. 1983. 1963

Goldenberg, Jorge

Latin American theatre and progressive social movements. Costa Rica. Argentina. Peru. 1588-1983. 1022

Goldman, Emma

Theory/criticism

Collected theory and criticism by women in theatre on women in theatre. USA. UK. 1850-1983. 114

Goldoni, Carlo

Plays/librettos/scripts

Relationship between mercantile society and playwright's creation in Carlo Goldoni's plays. Italy: Venice. 1734-1793. 1159

Goldsmith, Oliver

Essays on Restoration theatre and drama, with devised criteria for evaluation. England. 1660-1800. 1046

Golubnjača (Pigeon-cleft, The)

Current state of drama and theatre seen through plays and playwrights. Yugoslavia. 1983. 1393

Gombrowicz, Witold

Influences and theoretical views held by the playwright Witold Gombrowicz. Poland. 1904-1969. 1216

Director Jacques Rosner on meeting with playwright Witold Gombrowicz. Poland. France. 1969-1982. 1218

Gómez, Antonio Enrique

Indictment of Christian notion of honor, bigotry and injustice in Antonio Gómez' play *The Valiant Campuzano*. Spain. 1649. 1233

Gómez, José Luis

New José Luis Gómez version of Calderón de la Barca's tragedy, *Absalón*. Spain. 1983. 1701

Gone with the Wind

Reference materials

Description of archive holdings at Brigham Young University including personal papers of Howard Hawks and Dean Jagger. USA: Provo, UT. 1900-1983. 48

Description of David O. Selznick collection: '*Gone with the Wind*: A Legend Endures'. USA. 1939-1983. 1721

Gonzaga, Pietro

Design/technology

Scene designers and scenery at Teatro alla Scala in Neoclassic period. Italy: Milan. 1778-1832. 1821

Gooch, Steve

Plays/librettos/scripts

Epic structure in contemporary drama. UK. 1968-1981. 1275

Good

Performance/production

Cecil P. Taylor's *Good* at Kleines Haus, directed by Thomas Schulte-Michels. Germany, West: Düsseldorf. 1982. 776

Plays/librettos/scripts

Problems of play translations without caricature. Germany, West. USA. 1900-1983. 1148

Gorbačov, I.O.

Performance/production

Articles discussing the work of individual actors at the Academic Drama Theatre of A.S. Puškin. USSR: Leningrad. 1910-1970. 987

Gordějěv, Georgi Ivanovič

Autobiographical survey by choreographer Lincoln Kirstein. USA. India: Marrakesh. Europe. 1916-1949. 514

Gorelik, Mordecai

Mordecai Gorelik discusses stage fright and compares acting styles. USA. 1983. 461

Tribute to Mordecai Gorelik, scenic designer, theorist, teacher, director and playwright. USA. 1899-1983. 936

Gorky, Maxim

Design/technology

Interview with Yannis Kokkos, designer of Comédie-Française production of Maxim Gorky's *Summer Folk*. France. 1983. 577

Performance/production

Production of Russian classical plays at Eastern European theatres. Bulgaria. Yugoslavia. Czechoslovakia. 1850-1914. 682

Jacques Lassalle on staging Maxim Gorky's *Summer Folk* for Comédie-Française. France. Russia. 1904-1983. 738

Influence of Russian playwrights, directors and actors on American theatre. USA. Russia. 1905-1979. 976

Gosch, Jürgen

Jürgen Gosch production of *A Midsummer Night's Dream* at the Köln Schauspielhaus. Germany, West: Cologne. 1983. 780

Götterdämmerung

Photographs and personnel of Bayreuth Festival production of *Götterdämmerung*. Germany, West: Bayreuth. 1980. 1867

Green Thumb Theatre (Canada)

Institutions

History and concerns of Green Thumb Theatre. Canada. 1975-1983.
293

Green, John

Performance/production

English actors' work in Germany, with mention of stock comic characters. Germany. England: London. 1590-1620. 1525

Green, Paul

Institutions

Harlem Little Theatre movement started to produce plays by, with, for and about Blacks. USA: New York, NY. 1915-1934. 653

Greene, Robert

Plays/librettos/scripts

Discussion of playwright Robert Greene's pamphlet *A Disputation*. England. 1581-1592. 1054

Greenwood, Jane

Design/technology

Interview with Jane Greenwood on her experiences in costuming Ibsen, particularly *Hedda Gabler*. USA. 1980-1981. 581

Gregory, Isabella Augusta, Lady

Institutions

Rejection of O'Casey's play *The Silver Tassie* by the Abbey Theatre and the subsequent furor. UK-Ireland: Dublin. 1928. 637

Plays/librettos/scripts

Role of folklore in Irish Literary Revival. UK-Ireland. 1888-1920. 1322

Patriot Charles Stewart Parnell's influence on Irish drama. UK-Ireland. 1891-1936. 1337

Irreverent aspects of Irish comedy seen through the works of 14 playwrights. Eire. UK-Ireland. 1840-1965. 1555

Comic irony and anti-heroes in Irish comedy and influence on Harold Pinter, Samuel Beckett and Tom Stoppard. UK-Ireland. Eire. 1900-1940. 1593

Reference materials

Correspondence relating to administrative concerns at the Abbey Theatre between William Butler Yeats, Lady Gregory and John Millington Synge. UK-Ireland: Dublin. 1904-1909. 1432

Theory/criticism

Collected theory and criticism by women in theatre on women in theatre. USA. UK. 1850-1983. 114

Griffin, Hayden

Design/technology

Scenic practices of various designers. UK. 1960-1983. 227

Griffiths, Linda

Plays/librettos/scripts

Interview with actress-playwright Linda Griffiths. Canada: Saskatoon, SK. 1983. 1016

Grillparzer, Franz

Grégoire de Tours' influence on Franz Grillparzer's play *Thou Shalt Not Lie*. Austria. 1838. 1004

Treatment of justice and order in plays by Franz Grillparzer. Austria. 1791-1872. 1006

Treatment of Franz Grillparzer in Polish encyclopedias. Austria. Poland. 1800-1983. 1007

Grizzard, George

Institutions

Guthrie Theatre's architectural features and its directors, with emphasis on Liviu Ciulei's production of *Peer Gynt*. USA: Minneapolis, MN. 1963-1983. 655

Gros Mourn

Audience

Evolution of *Gros Mourn* by Newfoundland Mummers Troupe. Canada. 1973. 1604

Gross, Jürgen

Plays/librettos/scripts

Title character of *Mother Courage* is contrasted with similar figure in Jürgen Gross' drama *Memorial*. Germany, East. 1980. 1145

Grosser, Helmut

Design/technology

Report on the 43rd Conference for Theatre Technology and its welcoming speech. Germany, West: Heilbronn. 1983. 198

Grosz, George

Designer George Grosz's collaborations with Bertolt Brecht and Erwin Piscator. Germany. 1926. 578

Grotesque

Plays/librettos/scripts

Effects of foreign invasion and political instability on theatre. Argentina. 1900-1983. 999

Grotowski, Jerzy

Institutions

Evolution and theories of Odin Teatret. Sweden. 1964-1979. 621

Performance/production

Memoirs of dramaturg Jan Kott. Poland. Austria: Vienna. 1957-1981. 440

History of directing. Europe. 1882-1982. 708

Modern analyses of Konstantin Stanislavskij's acting theory. Russia. USSR. 1904-1983. 831

Richard Wagner's influence on modern theatrical conceptions, including those of Vsevolod Mejerchol'd, Evgeni Vachtangov and Jerzy Grotowski. USSR. Poland. Germany. 1813-1983. 991

Description of group that performs with and for remote and rural areas. Poland: Gardzienice. 1968-1983. 1627

Plays/librettos/scripts

Collected materials on Eugenio Barba and Odin Teatret. Sweden. 1964-1979. 1258

Use of body language in the theatre by Samuel Beckett, Antonin Artaud, Etienne Decroux and Jerzy Grotowski. Europe. 1930-1980. 1638

Reference materials

Compilation of entries on the concepts and techniques practiced at the International School of Theatre Anthropology. Italy. 1981. 30

Theory/criticism

Intermingling of Eastern and Western performance aesthetics. China. Japan. 1900-1983. 93

Effect of social conditions on performance styles. USA. Greece. 499 B.C.-1983 A.D. 1517

Grouch, The SEE: *Dýscolos*

Group Theatre (New York, NY)

Performance/production

Stanislavskij's system in the USA and the tour by the Moscow Art Theatre. USA. USSR. 1910-1959. 923

Grüber, Klaus Michael

Interview with and influences on actor Bernhard Minetti, including production of *Faust*. Germany, East: East Berlin. 1982-1983. 751

Six essays on the productions and artistic views held by leading European directors. Europe. 1960-1980. 1615

Klaus Michael Grüber directs Richard Wagner's *Tannhäuser* at Teatro Comunale, Florence. Italy: Florence. 1983. 1882

Grum, Slavko

Plays/librettos/scripts

Influence of European avant-garde on Slavko Grum's drama. Yugoslavia. 1920-1929. 1394

Gründgens, Gustaf

Performance/production

Productions of *The Flies* at Düsseldorfer Schauspielhaus and Hebbeltheater Berlin. Germany, West: Düsseldorf, West Berlin. 1947-1948.   785

Gruppe Baal (Netherlands)

Institutions

Free operating groups and institutionalized theatre. Netherlands. 1963-1983.   1609

Gruppe Bewth (Netherlands)

Free operating groups and institutionalized theatre. Netherlands. 1963-1983.   1609

Gruppe de Appel (Netherlands)

Free operating groups and institutionalized theatre. Netherlands. 1963-1983.   1609

Gruppo Abeliano (Italy)

Performance/production

August Strindberg productions in eleven countries. Sweden. Italy. USA. 1982.   847

Guelph Royal Opera House

Administration

Construction of Guelph Royal Opera House and management under Albert Tavernier. Canada: Guelph, ON. 1893-1895.   117

Guerrilla theatre

Relation to other fields

History, motivations and methods of North American guerrilla theatre. USA. 1965-1966.   1667

Guicciardini, Roberto

Plays/librettos/scripts

Theatres, actors and drama of the Renaissance in the work of modern directors. Italy. 1845-1982.   1193

Guides

Design/technology

Guide to costume design, including prevailing period fashions. 3000 B.C.-1983 A.D.   176

Guidelines for use of loudspeakers. USA. 1945-1983.   245

Reference materials

Biographical entries on playwrights and screenwriters. 1983.   13

Music guide for Austria with names, addresses and other information. Austria. 1983.   14

Biographies of theatre personalities. England: London. 1660-1800.   19

Guide to theatre organizations and professionals. Finland. 1983.   23

Pseudonym encyclopedia of entertainers. North America. Europe.   32

Directory of resources for presenters of performing arts. USA. 1983.   37

Directory of university theatre programs. USA. 1983.   38

Collection of theatre trivia. USA.   40

Vocational guidance directed at young people for non-acting careers in theatre. USA. 1983.   43

Guide to theatre training. USA: New York, NY, Los Angeles, CA. 1980-1983.   46

Bibliography of Black French theatre in Africa. Africa. 1977-1983.   1397

Brief biographies of Renaissance playwrights. Europe. 1400-1600.   1404

Chronological reference guide to works on and about Alfred de Musset. France. 1830-1980.   1408

Guide to work of 63 popular theatres. North America. South America. 1980-1983.   1417

Brief survey of post-war theatre with 25 play synopses. UK. 1945-1983.   1420

Survey of twentieth century British dramatists. UK. 1902-1975.   1422

Biographical guide to British playwrights. UK. 1945-1983.   1423

Reference guide to playwrights Peter and Anthony Shaffer. UK-England. USA. 1926-1982.   1426

Calendar of theatrical performances. UK-England: London. 1910-1919.   1428

Guide to shows that closed before coming to Broadway. USA. 1900-1982.   1438

Alphabetized abstracts on composers and their operas. Europe. 1567-1983.   1965

Reference guide to popular entertainments. USA. 1840.   1998

Guilfoyle, Molly

Institutions

Educational project of Intriplicate Mime Company using puppets. UK. 1977-1983.   2043

Guilpin, Edward

Plays/librettos/scripts

Ironic satire in *Every Man Out of His Humour*. England. 1599.   1052

Guimerà, Angel

Adaptation of the Angel Guimerà play *Maria Rosa*. Spain. 1894.   1230

Gunter, John

Design/technology

Scenic practices of various designers. UK. 1960-1983.   227

Gurney, A.R., Jr.

Administration

Round table discussion between playwrights and their agents. USA. 1983.   562

Performance/production

Seven critics review David Trainer's production of A.R. Gurney, Jr.'s play *The Middle Ages*. USA: New York, NY. 1983.   1542

Plays/librettos/scripts

World-wide response to A.R. Gurney Jr.'s dramas of New England life. USA. 1983.   1365

Gute Mensch von Sezuan, Der (Good Woman of Sezuan, The)

Contradiction between good and evil in capitalist society as reflected in Bertolt Brecht's *The Good Woman of Sezuan*. Germany. 1938-1941.   1122

Guthrie Theatre (Minneapolis, MN)

Institutions

Guthrie Theatre's architectural features and its directors, with emphasis on Liviu Ciulei's production of *Peer Gynt*. USA: Minneapolis, MN. 1963-1983.   655

Guthrie, Tyrone

Performance/production

Problems of antisemitism in staging *The Merchant of Venice*. Israel. 1936-1980.   663

Gutierrez, Gerald

Five critics review Gerald Gutierrez's production of *Isn't It Romantic*. USA: New York, NY. 1983.   926

Guys in the Truck, The

Three critics review Howard Reifsnyder's *The Guys in the Truck* directed by David Black. USA: New York, NY. 1983.   929

Gyges und sein Ring (Gyges and His Ring)

Ernst Wendt's staging of Friedrich Hebbel's *Gyges and His Ring*. Germany, West: Hamburg. 1983.   1679

HaBimah, Teatron (Tel Aviv)

Problems of antisemitism in staging *The Merchant of Venice*. Israel. 1936-1980.   663

Hagen, Uta

Memoirs of the noted actress and theorist Uta Hagen. USA. Germany. 1919-1983.   932

Hampton, Christopher

Critical account of Christopher Hampton's work. UK-England. 1900-1983.　　　　1316

Handel, George Frederic

Administration

Management and fiscal administration at the Royal Academy of Music. England: London. 1719-1721.　　　　1814

Performance/production

Conductor John Eliot Gardiner discusses baroque opera. England. 1597-1759.　　　　1849

Hands, Terry

Institutions

History of Royal Shakespeare Company with emphasis on financial and aesthetic aspects and internal politics. UK-England: London. 1864-1981.　　　　624

Hanl, Ilse

Structure, aims and methods of animation by Dramatisches Zentrum (Vienna). Austria: Vienna. 1972-1983.　　　　287

Hansberry, Lorraine

Plays/librettos/scripts

Critical examination of Lorraine Hansberry's influence on drama. USA. 1960-1979.　　　　1387

Theory/criticism

Collected theory and criticism by women in theatre on women in theatre. USA. UK. 1850-1983.　　　　114

Hänsel und Gretel

Performance/production

Photographs, cast lists, synopsis and discography of Metropolitan Opera production of *Hänsel und Gretel*. USA: New York, NY. 1983.　　　　1910

The life and career of Lina Abarbanell, the first Hänsel at the Metropolitan Opera House. USA: New York, NY. Germany: Berlin. 1905-1963.　　　　1917

Happiest of the Three, The SEE: *Plus heureux des trois, Le*

Happy Days

Performance/production

Samuel Beckett's *Happy Days* with Giulia Lazzarini at Piccolo Teatro di Milano, directed by Giorgio Strehler. Italy: Milan. 1983.　　　　807

Harden, Mary

Administration

Round table discussion between playwrights and their agents. USA. 1983.　　　　562

Hare, David

Performance/production

Eight critics review David Hare's production of his play *Plenty*. USA: New York, NY. 1983.　　　　953

Plays/librettos/scripts

Epic structure in contemporary drama. UK. 1968-1981.　　　　1275

Playwright David Hare's career and interests in Fringe theatre, television and film. UK-England. 1947-1983.　　　　1304

Harlem Experimental Theatre (New York, NY)

Institutions

Harlem Little Theatre movement started to produce plays by, with, for and about Blacks. USA: New York, NY. 1915-1934.　　　　653

Harlem Little Negro Theatre (New York, NY)

Harlem Little Theatre movement started to produce plays by, with, for and about Blacks. USA: New York, NY. 1915-1934.　　　　653

Harlem theatre

Performance/production

Authentic expression in Black theatre and film is contrasted with stereotypical Black portrayals by white authors and performers. USA: New York, NY. 1890-1930.　　　　983

Reference materials

Dictionary of Black theatre. USA: New York, NY. 1983.　　　　50

Harney, Ben

Performance/production

Interview with principal male stars of *Dreamgirls*. USA: New York, NY. 1983.　　　　1778

Harrigan Theatre (New York, NY)

Performance spaces

Construction and history of Edward Harrigan's Theatre, later renamed the Garrick. USA: New York, NY. 1890-1932.　　　　1773

Harrigan, Edward

Construction and history of Edward Harrigan's Theatre, later renamed the Garrick. USA: New York, NY. 1890-1932.　　　　1773

Harris, Margaret

Design/technology

History and description of the Motley Theatre and Costume Arts Collection. Discussed at SIBMAS. USA: Urbana, IL. 1982.　　　　247

Harris, Sophia

History and description of the Motley Theatre and Costume Arts Collection. Discussed at SIBMAS. USA: Urbana, IL. 1982.　　　　247

Hart, Evelyn

Performance/production

Evelyn Hart's debut as Giselle with the Royal Winnipeg Ballet. Canada: Winnipeg, ON. 1966-1982.　　　　517

Hart, Lorenz

Nine critics review George Abbott's production of the musical *On Your Toes*. USA: New York, NY. 1983.　　　　1803

Hart, Moss

Eight critics review Ellis Rabb's production of George S. Kaufman's and Moss Hart's play *You Can't Take It with You*. USA: New York, NY. 1983.　　　　972

Harwood, Ronald

Plays/librettos/scripts

Ronald Harwood discusses his plays *The Dresser* and *After the Lions*, the latter play based on the life of Sarah Bernhardt. UK-England: London. 1983.　　　　1286

Häuptling Abendwind

Role of censorship in Johann Nestroy's *Häuptling Abendwind* as an adaptation of Jacques Offenbach's *Vent de soir*. Austria. 1833.　　　　1549

Hauptmann, Gerhart

Performance/production

Topical production of Gerhart Hauptmann's *The Weavers* in working class neighborhood. Germany, West: Recklinghausen. 1979.　　　　768

Rudolph Noelte directs Gerhart Hauptmann's *Michael Kramer*. Germany, West: Hamburg. 1983.　　　　781

Plays/librettos/scripts

Italian translation of Bogdal's essay on Gerhart Hauptmann's *Florian Geyer*. Germany. 1896.　　　　1117

Haus, Heinz-Uwe

Examples of folklore and humanistic philosophy in *Pericles*. England. 1608-1609.　　　　1029

Hauser Orkater (Netherlands)

Institutions

History of the Hauser Orkater theatre company and two groups that emerged from it: De Mexicaanse Hond (The Mexican Hound) and De Horde (The Herd). Netherlands. 1971-1983.　　　　1608

Hauser, Dick

History of the Hauser Orkater theatre company and two groups that emerged from it: De Mexicaanse Hond (The Mexican Hound) and De Horde (The Herd). Netherlands. 1971-1983.　　　　1608

Hauser, Rob

History of the Hauser Orkater theatre company and two groups that emerged from it: De Mexicaanse Hond (The Mexican Hound) and De Horde (The Herd). Netherlands. 1971-1983.　1608

Haute Surveillance (Deathwatch)

Plays/librettos/scripts

Modern plays set in confining institutions. North America. Europe. 1900-1983.　1200

Havel, Vaclav

Performance/production

Five critics review Lee Grant's production of Vaclav Havel's play *A Private View* translated by Vera Blackwell. USA: New York, NY. 1983.　927

Havergal, Giles

Fusion of visual and verbal elements creates a style of voluptuous theatricality at Citizens' Theatre. UK-Scotland: Glasgow. 1969-1979.　901

Hawks, Howard

Reference materials

Description of archive holdings at Brigham Young University including personal papers of Howard Hawks and Dean Jagger. USA: Provo, UT. 1900-1983.　48

Hayesville Opera House (Hayesville, OH)

Performance spaces

Case-study of renovation of small-town opera house. USA: Hayesville, OH. 1886-1983.　1837

Haymarket Theatre (London)

Reference materials

Licensing papers related to managerial and repertorial changes at London theatres. England: London. 1706-1715.　20

He Who Says Yes SEE: *Jasager und der Neinsager, Der*

Health/safety

Design/technology

Risks involved in technical workshops. Germany, West. 1983.　208
Fire-prevention equipment needed for theatres. Germany, West: West Berlin. 1973-1983.　210
Safety and accident-prevention. Switzerland: St. Gallen. 1983.　224
Safety curtain at Covent Garden, designed by Christopher Le Brun. UK-England: London. 1983.　232
Description and listing of sound systems for theatres to aid hearing impaired. USA. 1960-1983.　246
Precautions for safe use of chemical substances. USA. 1983.　251
Various safety requirements for the construction of the platform for the production of *Der Ring des Nibelungen*. Germany, West: Bayreuth. 1983.　1818

Performance spaces

Problem of drafts in theatres. Germany, West. 1983.　373
Security measures and regulations in Italian theatres. Italy. 1983.　383

Hearing impaired

Design/technology

Description and listing of sound systems for theatres to aid hearing impaired. USA. 1960-1983.　246

Heart of the Beast Puppet and Mask Theatre (Minneapolis, MN)

Institutions

Description of *Circle of Waters Circus*, a travelling puppet pageant using 150 puppets and 30 performers. USA: Minneapolis, MN. 1983.　2048

Heartbreak House

Performance/production

Ten critics review Anthony Page's production of *Heartbreak House* presented at Circle in the Square. USA: New York, NY. 1983.　910

Hebbel, Friedrich

Ernst Wendt's staging of Friederich Hebbel's *Gyges and His Ring*. Germany, West: Hamburg. 1983.　1679

Reference materials

Illustrated documentation of Friedrich Hebbel's stay in Vienna. Austria: Vienna. 1845-1863.　1398

Hebbeltheater (West Berlin)

Performance/production

Karlheinz Stroux's production of *The Skin of Our Teeth* by Thornton Wilder at Hebbeltheater. Germany, West: West Berlin, Darmstadt. 1946.　779
Productions of *The Flies* at Düsseldorfer Schauspielhaus and Hebbeltheater Berlin. Germany, West: Düsseldorf, West Berlin. 1947-1948.　785

Hechos de Garcilaso, Los (Deeds of Garcilaso, The)

Plays/librettos/scripts

Dating and authorship of *Los hechos de Garcilaso*. Spain. 1573.　1231

Hecuba

Dramatic and military conflict in Greek tragedy. Greece. 484-415 B.C.　1697

Hedda Gabler

Design/technology

Edvard Munch's set designs for plays by Henrik Ibsen. Norway. 1892-1909.　580
Interview with Jane Greenwood on her experiences in costuming Ibsen, particularly *Hedda Gabler*. USA. 1980-1981.　581

Plays/librettos/scripts

Thematic analysis of Ibsen's *Hedda Gabler*. Norway. 1890.　1211

Hegel, Georg Wilhelm Friedrich

'Great Method' used by Bertolt Brecht in his plays, and influences from others. Germany. 1918-1956.　1130

Theory/criticism

History of theories of drama from George Wilhelm Hegel to Karl Marx. Germany. 1770-1883.　1491
Bertolt Brecht's perception of the philosophy of the Enlightenment. Germany. 1848-1956.　1498

Heinz, Gerd

Performance/production

Opening nights of productions directed by Arie Zinger and Gerd Heinz. Germany, West: Munich. Switzerland: Zürich. 1983.　771

Helen Hayes Theatre (New York, NY)

Institutions

Folies-Bergère contribution to the development of dinner theatres and night clubs. USA: New York, NY. 1911.　2026

Heller, André

Performance/production

Documentation on André Heller's *Flic Flac, Theater des Feuers* and *Roncalli*. Austria. Germany, West. Portugal: Lisbon. 1975-1983.　2027

Hellman, Lillian

Plays/librettos/scripts

Essays on the trends of the Jewish-American theatre and its personalities. USA. 1900-1983.　1353
Only three Tony-Award-winning plays reflect feminist ideology. USA: New York, NY. UK-England. 1960-1979.　1374

Heltau, Michael

Performance/production

Interview with actor Michael Heltau about his career and forthcoming roles at the Burgtheater. Austria: Vienna. 1983.　674

Heminges, William

List of productions of plays from English Renaissance drama with brief reviews. North America. Europe. 1982-1983.　822

Henley, Beth

Plays/librettos/scripts

Interview with playwright Beth Henley. USA. 1983. 1594

Henrich, Leopold

Composition and thematic analysis of Goethe's *Ur-Faust*. Germany. 1775-1832. 1137

Henry IV

Performance/production

Compagnia del Collettivo/Teatro Due productions of three plays by William Shakespeare. Italy: Parma. 1980-1983. 795

Shakespearean productions by Compagnia del Collettivo/Teatro Due, Theater an der Ruhr (Hamburg) and Schaubühne (West Berlin). Italy: Parma. Germany, West: West Berlin, Hamm. 1983. 810

Plays/librettos/scripts

Animal nature and eating habits of characters in Shakespeare's plays. England. 1590-1613. 1058

Struggle for power in Shakespeare's history plays. England. 1591-1595. 1059

Henry IV (Pirandello) SEE: *Enrico Quarto*

Henry VI

Plays/librettos/scripts

Animal nature and eating habits of characters in Shakespeare's plays. England. 1590-1613. 1058

Struggle for power in Shakespeare's history plays. England. 1591-1595. 1059

Henry VII

Administration

Court entertainments during reign of Henry VII, from early records. England: London. 1485-1505. 1737

Henson, Jim

Performance/production

Contributions made to puppetry by Jim Henson's *Dark Crystal*. USA. 1980-1983. 2059

Hepburn, Katharine

Biography of actress Katharine Hepburn. USA. 1909-1983. 915

Her Majesty's Theatre (Ottawa, ON)

Institutions

Prominence of Ottawa's theatres in South-Eastern Ontario touring circuit. Canada: Ottawa, ON. 1870-1879. 291

Herbert, Jocelyn

Design/technology

Influence of the designers on staging styles. UK. 1958-1983. 226

Scenic practices of various designers. UK. 1960-1983. 227

Herder, Johann Gottfried

Plays/librettos/scripts

Influence of Siglo de Oro on German pre-romantic theatre. Germany. Spain. 1765-1832. 1135

Herford, Beatrice

Performance/production

Careers of solo performers Beatrice Herford, Cissie Loftus and Dorothy Sands. USA. 1900-1920. 942

Herman, Jerry

Six critics review John Bowab's production of the musical *Mame*. USA: New York, NY. 1983. 1801

Ten critics review *La Cage aux Folles*. USA: New York, NY. 1983. 1806

Hermannschlacht (Battle of Arminius, The)

Plays/librettos/scripts

Study of Hermann's character in Heinrich von Kleist's *The Battle of Arminius*. Germany. 1808. 1143

Hernani

Victor Hugo and the original plot for the opera *Ernani* by Giuseppe Verdi. France. 1830. 1940

Heron, Nye

Performance/production

Five critics review Nye Heron's production of Brian Friel's play *Winners*. USA: New York, NY. 1983. 962

Hersey, David

Design/technology

Interviews with the designers of *Cats*. USA: New York, NY. UK-England: London. 1983. 1770

Hesitate and Demonstrate (Leeds)

Institutions

History and analysis of Hesitate and Demonstrate, an English group that creates surrealistic performances based on juxtapostion of images. UK-England: Leeds, London. Netherlands: Rotterdam. 1972-1983. 1743

Hessische Jugendbildungsanstalt (Dietzenbach)

Training

Workshops and theatre productions by and for apprentices. Germany, West: West Berlin. 1971-1983. 498

Heston, Charlton

Performance/production

Training and career of Charlton Heston. USA. 1956-1976. 451

Heyme, Hansgünther

Hansgünther Heyme's production of *The Persians*. Germany, West: Stuttgart. 1983. 1680

Heyward, DuBose

Nine critics review Jack O'Brien's production of *Porgy and Bess*. USA: New York, NY. 1983. 1795

Heywood, John

Plays/librettos/scripts

Adaptation of a French farce into *Johan Johan*. England. France. 1520-1533. 1559

Heywood, Thomas

Heywood's *A Woman Killed with Kindness* as a source for Shakespeare's *Othello*. England. 1604. 1066

Hija del aire, La (Daughter of the Air)

Psychological analysis of Semiramis character from Calderón's *Daughter of the Air*. Spain. 1600-1699. 1235

Hilanderas, Las (Spinners, The)

Comparison between a painting by Diego Velázquez and a play by Calderón de la Barca. Spain. 1625-1651. 1229

Hill, Aaron

Authorship of *The Fatal Extravagance*. England: London. 1721-1760. 1082

Hinduism

Epic texts form the thematic basis of Indian dance-drama. India. 800-1800. 539

Hiob, Hanne

Performance/production

Portrait of the actress (and daughter of Bertolt Brecht) Hanne Hiob. Germany, West. 1923-1983. 761

Hippodrome (Los Angeles, CA)

Performance spaces

Recollections of the Hippodrome, formerly the Adolphus Theatre. USA: Los Angeles, CA. 1911-1940. 1981

Hirsh, John

Institutions

Richard Ouzounian attempts to restore community interest in Manitoba Theatre Centre. Canada: Winnipeg, MB. 1958-1983. 292

Homans, Margaret — cont'd

historical materialism, deconstruction and phenomenon of cross-dressing in theatre. USA. France. UK-England. 1983.   1520

Hombre urbano, El (Urban Man, The)

Performance/production

Original vision of man in Albert Vidal's mime *El hombre urbano.* Spain: Sitges. 1983.   1727

Home

Plays/librettos/scripts

Modern plays set in confining institutions. North America. Europe. 1900-1983.   1200

Homecoming, The

Only three Tony-Award-winning plays reflect feminist ideology. USA: New York, NY. UK-England. 1960-1979.   1374

Honour, The SEE: *Onore, L'*

Hoover, Nan

Performance/production

Work of video performance artist Nan Hoover. UK-England. 1900-1983.   1746

Hoppe, Marianne

Plays/librettos/scripts

Compilation of comments by various artists on Tennessee Williams. USA. 1911-1983.   1342

Horde, De (Netherlands)

Institutions

History of the Hauser Orkater theatre company and two groups that emerged from it: De Mexicaanse Hond (The Mexican Hound) and De Horde (The Herd). Netherlands. 1971-1983.   1608

Horse and Bamboo (Lancashire)

Performance/production

Horse and Bamboo, a collaborative company that tours by horse and cart. UK-England: Lancashire. 1983.   1989

Horst, Robert Ter

Theory/criticism

Calderón de la Barca's plays and theory of comedy advanced in essay by Robert Ter Horst. Spain. 1600-1681.   1602

Horzyca, Wilam

Performance/production

Career of director and stage manager Wilam Horzyca. Poland: Warsaw, Lwów, Poznań. 1889-1959.   829

Hostage, The

Plays/librettos/scripts

Modern plays set in confining institutions. North America. Europe. 1900-1983.   1200

Hothouse, The

Modern plays set in confining institutions. North America. Europe. 1900-1983.   1200

House management SEE: **Management, house**

Houseman, John

Performance/production

Actor John Houseman comments on producers and directors. USA. 1983.   934

Howe, Tina

Five critics review Carole Rothman's production of *Painting Churches*, by Tina Howe. USA: New York, NY. 1983.   959

Howell, Jane

Six critics review Jane Howell's production of *Richard III* mounted by the Public Theater. USA: New York, NY. 1983.   1684

Hoy, Cyrus

Plays/librettos/scripts

Useful aspects of Cyrus Hoy's commentaries on Thomas Dekker. England: London. 1597-1630.   1030

Huang, Zuo-lin

Performance/production

Relationship between Bertolt Brecht and Asian theatre. Asia. Germany. 1925-1981.   665

Plays/librettos/scripts

Adaptation of *Galileo* for Chinese stage. China, People's Republic of: Peking. 1979.   1020

Hugo, Victor

Victor Hugo and the original plot for the opera *Ernani* by Giuseppe Verdi. France. 1830.   1940

Shakespeare's influence on Arrigo Boito's libretto for *La Gioconda*, based on Victor Hugo's play. Italy. 1862-1900.   1956

Theory/criticism

French romantic theories of drama. France. 1800-1850.   1487

Hulewicz, Jerzy

Plays/librettos/scripts

Censorship involving Jerzy Hulewicz' play *Aruna*, produced at Municipal Theatre of Cracow. Poland: Kraków. 1925.   1217

Hull House

Relation to other fields

Description of Jane Addams' creative drama activities at Hull House. USA: Chicago, IL. 1889-1910.   1469

Hult Center for the Performing Arts (Eugene, OR)

Performance spaces

History of the Hult Center for the Performing Arts. USA: Eugene, OR. 1982.   399

Humana Festival (Louisville, KY)

Performance/production

Description of plays presented at Humana Festival of New American Plays. USA: Louisville, KY. 1983.   940

Humanism

Plays/librettos/scripts

Examples of folklore and humanistic philosophy in *Pericles*. England. 1608-1609.   1029

Humanist examination of Samuel Beckett's plays. Europe. 1906-1983.   1637

Humanities Research Center, Univ. of Texas

Reference materials

Acquisition of Gloria Swanson's silent film archive by University of Texas, Austin. USA: Austin, TX. 1913-1983.   1720

Humboldt's Current

Performance/production

Description and analysis of Ping Chong's work. USA. 1972-1983.   1752

Humperdinck, Engelbert

Photographs, cast lists, synopsis and discography of Metropolitan Opera production of *Hänsel und Gretel*. USA: New York, NY. 1983.   1910

The life and career of Lina Abarbanell, the first Hänsel at the Metropolitan Opera House. USA: New York, NY. Germany: Berlin. 1905-1963.   1917

Hypernaturalism

Plays/librettos/scripts

Definiton of the new dramatic genre — hypernaturalism. USA. Europe. 1970-1983.   1386

Iconographies – cont'd

Photographs, cast lists, synopsis and discography of Metropolitan Opera production of *Un Ballo in Maschera*. USA: New York, NY. 1983.   1899

Photographs, cast lists, synopsis and discography of Metropolitan Opera production of *Les Contes d'Hoffman*. USA: New York, NY. 1983.   1900

Photographs, cast lists, synopsis and discography of Metropolitan Opera production of *Pelléas et Mélisande*. USA: New York, NY. 1983.   1901

Photographs, cast lists, synopsis and discography of Metropolitan Opera production of *The Barber of Seville*. USA: New York, NY. 1983.   1902

Photographs, cast lists, synopsis and discography of the Metropolitan Opera production of *Die Walküre*. USA: New York, NY. 1983.   1903

Photographs, cast lists, synopsis and discography of the Metropolitan Opera production of *Don Carlo*. USA: New York, NY. 1983.   1904

Photographs, cast lists, synopsis and discography of Metropolitan Opera production of *La Bohème*. USA: New York, NY. 1983.   1905

Photographs, cast lists, synopsis and discography of Metropolitan Opera production of *Der Rosenkavalier*. USA: New York, NY. 1983.   1906

Photographs, cast lists, synopsis and discography of Metropolitan Opera production of *Les Dialogues des Carmélites*. USA: New York, NY. 1983.   1907

Photographs, cast lists, synopsis and discography of Metropolitan Opera production of *Ernani*. USA: New York, NY. 1983.   1908

Photographs, cast lists, synopsis and discography of the Metropolitan Opera production of *Tristan und Isolde*. USA: New York, NY. 1983.   1909

Photographs, cast lists, synopsis and discography of Metropolitan Opera production of *Hänsel und Gretel*. USA: New York, NY. 1983.   1910

Backstage look at San Francisco Opera. USA: San Francisco, CA. 1970-1982.   1911

Photographs, cast lists, synopsis and discography of Metropolitan Opera production of *Idomeneo*. USA: New York, NY. 1983.   1920

Reference materials

Catalogue of photographic exhibition of the Teatro Comunale di Ferrara. Italy: Ferrara. 1982.   489

Annotated selections of photographs taken by Herman Mishkin of Metropolitan Opera singers. USA: New York, NY. 1910-1932.   1971

Ideal Husband, An

Plays/librettos/scripts

Oscar Wilde's stage directions in various editions of *An Ideal Husband* and other plays. UK-England. 1880-1900.   1295

Idomeneo

Performance/production

Photographs, cast lists, synopsis and discography of Metropolitan Opera production of *Idomeneo*. USA: New York, NY. 1983.   1920

Plays/librettos/scripts

Evaluation of Wolfgang Amadeus Mozart's opera *Idomeneo*. Austria: Munich. 1780-1781.   1933

Ilanga Le So Phonela Abasebenzi

Theory/criticism

Study of genesis, development, structural components and consequences of theatre-drama performed by the Black workers. South Africa, Republic of. 1981-1983.   1673

Illes flotants, Les (Floating Islands, The)

Institutions

Evolution and theories of Odin Teatret. Sweden. 1964-1979.   621

Illusion comique, L' (Comic Illusion, The)

Plays/librettos/scripts

Love, freedom and the emergence of the generous hero in Pierre Corneille's early plays. France. 1629-1640.   1105

Aesthetic continuity in Pierre Corneille's movement from comedy to tragedy. France. 1606-1684.   1112

Problems of theatricality and limits of illusion in Pierre Corneille's *The Comic Illusion*. France. 1606-1684.   1563

Essays on and a bibliographical guide to Pierre Corneille's comedies. France. 1606-1684.   1572

Im Dickicht der Städte (In the Jungle of Cities)

Relation to other fields

Circus as a staging device for a political satire. USSR. Germany. Italy. 1914-1930.   1668

Imaginary Invalid, The SEE: Malade imaginaire, Le

Imatran teatteri (Imatra)

Institutions

Imatra theatre's 1983-1984 season. Finland: Imatra. 1983.   593

Impact Theatre Co-operative (England)

Performance/production

Political profile of work by Impact Theatre Co-operative. UK-England. 1983.   1750

Impressionism

Plays/librettos/scripts

Examination of August Strindberg's attitude towards and use of impressionism. Sweden. 1874-1884.   1270

Improvisation

Institutions

Tschauner-Theatre: Vienna's only surviving improvisation company. Austria: Vienna. 1938-1983.   1978

Performance/production

History and forms of political improvisational theatre. Iran. 1600-1980.   432

History of *Ru-howzi* improvisational theatre. Iran. 1780-1950.   792

Theatrical spontaneity, role-playing and improvisation in Sicilian opera. Italy. 1907-1983.   1879

Plays/librettos/scripts

Approaches to drama for young people. UK-England. 1970-1983.   1296

Relation to other fields

Introduction of Luigi Pirandello's play *Tonight We Improvise*. Italy. 1930.   1458

Use of improvisation in the teaching of foreign languages. USA. 1983.   1470

Improvisation for the Theatre

Use of improvisation in the teaching of foreign languages. USA. 1983.   1470

In Dahomey

Performance/production

Account of a production of the musical *In Dahomey*. UK-England: London. 1903-1904.   1776

In Defence of Poetry

Theory/criticism

Wystan Hugh Auden's poetic meditation on art as related to Shakespeare's *The Tempest* and Kierkegaardian thought. UK-England. 1939-1962.   1511

In Goethe's Hand

Performance/production

World premiere of Martin Walser's *In Goethe's Hand* at Vienna's Akademietheater, directed by Karl Fruchtmann. Austria: Vienna. 1983.   671

In the Jungle of Cities SEE: Im Dickicht der Städte

Indexes

Plays/librettos/scripts

Index to Sean O'Casey's autobiography. UK-Ireland. 1880-1964.   1330

Institutions, associations — cont'd

Plays/librettos/scripts
Essays on Vitaliano Brancati's plays and motion picture scripts. Italy: Catania. 1924-1954.   1160

Reference materials
New officers of American Theatre Association. USA. 1983.   39

Relation to other fields
Inaugural address of American Theatre Association president Bernard S. Rosenblatt calling for support in creating public policy. USA: Minneapolis, MN. 1983.   76

Research/historiography
Method for using models of scenery as study documents. Discussed at SIBMAS. Europe. North America. 1982.   83

Institutions, performing SEE: Institutions, producing

Institutions, producing

Administration
Censorship of Brazilian theatre, causing only Broadway hits to be produced. Brazil. 1557-1983.   116

Economical and financial problems facing today's theatres. Germany, West. 1983.   126

Private ownership — a solution for the economic crisis of the government-funded theatre. Germany, West. 1983.   127

Heribert Sasse succeeds Boy Gobert as manager at Staatliche Schauspielbühnen Berlin. Germany, West: West Berlin. 1983.   128

Economic organization of and financial problems faced by today's theatres. Germany, West. 1983.   129

Political and cultural background of Würzburg theatres and their financial operations. Germany, West: Würzburg. 1945-1983.   131

Financial and political situation of theatre institutions. Germany, West. 1982.   132

Financial situation of municipal theatres. Germany, West. 1982.   134

Objections to the ad-hoc theatre company and temporary writer-in-residence phenomenon. UK. 1983.   145

Promotional campaigns for performing arts institutions. USA. 1983.   160

Four artistic directors discuss theatre relationship with community. Canada: Regina, SK, Vancouver, BC, Toronto, ON, Calgary, AB. 1983.   553

Network of subscription among several theatres. Italy. 1981.   555

Funding and theatre activity, particularly Mayfest. UK-Scotland. 1922-1983.   557

Interview with the new artistic director and literary advisor for the Iron Theatre (Glasgow). UK-Scotland. 1973-1983.   559

Peter Weck, new manager of Theater an der Wien plans to produce first German language production of Andrew Lloyd Webber's *Cats*. Austria: Vienna. 1983.   1767

Administration in the making of a production at Vienna's Staatsoper. Austria: Vienna. 1983.   1811

Evaluation of Glynn Ross's tenure as founding general director of Seattle Opera. USA: Seattle, WA. 1964-1983.   1815

Audience
Sign interpretation at the New York City Opera. USA: New York, NY. 1979.   1816

Basic theatrical documents
Catalan translation of *Ur-Faust* and articles on the play and its production by the Company Andrià Gual. Germany. Spain. 1887-1983.   571

Playtext and manifesto of the Teatro Visionico and their production of Pino Masnata's *Tocca a me*. Italy. 1920.   572

Playtext and accompanying materials from the Magazzini Criminali production of *On the Road*. Italy. 1982.   1605

Design/technology
Interview with Yannis Kokkos, designer of Comédie-Française production of Maxim Gorky's *Summer Folk*. France. 1983.   577

Mannerist elements in some set designs for *Hamlet*. UK-England: Stratford-upon-Avon, London. 1948-1976.   1675

First live broadcast of a complete opera performance from the Metropolitan Opera House. USA: New York, NY. 1910.   1708

Technical realization of the main platform for the sets of *Der Ring des Nibelungen*. Germany, West: Bayreuth. 1983.   1817

Various safety requirements for the construction of the platform for the production of *Der Ring des Nibelungen*. Germany, West: Bayreuth. 1983.   1818

Costumes of Teatro alla Scala and chronology of its costumers. Italy: Milan. 1947-1982.   1819

Career of Metropolitan Opera wigmaker Adolf Senz. USA: New York, NY. 1930-1983.   1826

Meyer Levin's marionettes as abstract visual images, influenced by Gordon Craig and Fernand Léger. USA. 1926-1930.   2081

Institutions
Broad social movement started by Teatro Abierto. Argentina: Buenos Aires. 1981-1983.   281

Program of the Carinthian Summer. Austria. 1983.   283

Annual report of the Austrian Federal Theatres. Austria: Vienna. 1982-1983.   284

Review of Austrian summer festivals. Austria. 1983.   285

Structure, aims and methods of animation by Dramatisches Zentrum (Vienna). Austria: Vienna. 1972-1983.   287

Documentation on Karlsplatz festival, part of Wiener Festwochen. Austria: Vienna. 1983.   288

Frederick Brown and Montreal's doomed Theatre Royal. Canada: Montreal, PQ. 1825-1826.   289

History of the Great Canadian Theatre Company. Canada: Ottawa, ON. 1976-1983.   290

Prominence of Ottawa's theatres in South-Eastern Ontario touring circuit. Canada: Ottawa, ON. 1870-1879.   291

Richard Ouzounian attempts to restore community interest in Manitoba Theatre Centre. Canada: Winnipeg, MB. 1958-1983.   292

History and concerns of Green Thumb Theatre. Canada. 1975-1983.   293

Change in idealism among alternative theatres. Canada: Toronto, ON. 1973-1983.   295

Survey of alternative theatres. Canada: Toronto, ON. 1979-1983. 296

Street theatre production of Århus theater akademi in collaboration with Jordcirkus and Johnny Melville. Denmark: Århus. 1982.   298

Finnish theatre groups and artists performing abroad. Finland. Sweden. 1982-1983.   299

Current manager Taisto-Bertil Orsmaa, and history of Turku Municipal Theatre. Finland: Turku. 1946-1983.   303

Theatre on the battle-front during the World Wars. Germany. 1914-1945.   305

Theatre-activities of Turkish immigrant workers. Germany, West: West Berlin. 1982.   306

State of theatre in Ruhr-District. Germany, West: Dortmund. 1972-1982.   307

Theatre in Ulm as an example for the conditions and problems of regional theatre. Germany, West: Ulm. 1983.   308

Report on Theatre Festival Munich, including brief survey of productions. Germany, West: Munich. 1983.   309

Drama critics and members of the *Theaterzeitschrift* editorial staff talk about regional theatre. Germany, West. 1983.   310

Theatrical conditions and cultural work in small towns. Germany, West. 1976-1982.   311

Motivation and goals of free theatre groups. Germany, West: West Berlin. 1982.   312

Brief survey of productions and financial situation of a local theatre. Germany, West: Nürnberg. 1983.   314

History, financial situation and productions of the Schlosstheater. Germany, West: Moers. 1975-1983.   315

Description of street theatre performances whose purpose is social change. India: Calcutta. 1983.   316

Efforts to establish 'modern' theatre. Netherlands. 1945-1983.   321

Polish theatre under Russian rule as reflected in György Spiró's novel *Az Ikszek*. Poland: Warsaw. Russia. Hungary. 1815-1829.   325

Diversity of Latin American theatre. South America. North America. 1950-1983.   326

Effect of women's movement on experimental theatre. Sweden: Stockholm. 1970-1983.   328

Institutions, producing — cont'd

Institutions, producing — cont'd

Performance spaces

Performance/production

Institutions, producing — cont'd

Institutions, producing — cont'd

Photographs and personnel of Bayreuth Festival production of *Siegfried*. Germany, West: Bayreuth. 1980.   1866

1983 Bayreuth *Der Ring des Nibelungen*, directed by Peter Hall, conducted by Georg Solti. Germany, West: Bayreuth. 1983.   1873

Baritone David Holloway speaks of career with Deutsche Oper am Rhein. Germany, West: Düsseldorf, Duisburg. 1940-1983.   1877

History of openings at Teatro alla Scala is conveyed through newspaper reviews. Italy: Milan. 1778-1977.   1884

Photographs of gala centennial concert at the Metropolitan Opera House. USA: New York, NY. 1983.   1890

Photographs, cast lists, synopsis and discography of Metropolitan Opera production of *Boris Godunov*. USA: New York, NY. 1983.   1891

Photographs, cast lists, synopsis and discography of Metropolitan Opera production of *Parsifal*. USA: New York, NY. 1983.   1892

Photographs, cast lists, synopsis and discography from the Metropolitan Opera's September 28, 1983 telecast of Gaetano Donizetti's *Lucia di Lammermoor*. USA: New York, NY. 1983.   1893

Photographs, cast lists, synopsis and discography of Metropolitan Opera production of *Arabella*. USA: New York, NY. 1983.   1894

Photographs, cast lists, synopsis and discography of Metropolitan Opera production of *Il Trovatore*. USA: New York, NY. 1983.   1895

Photographs, cast lists, synopsis and discography of Metropolitan Opera production of *Tannhäuser*. USA: New York, NY. 1983.   1896

Photographs, cast lists, synopsis and discography of Metropolitan Opera production of *Adriana Lecouvreur*. USA: New York, NY. 1983.   1897

Photographs, cast lists, synopsis and discography of Metropolitan Opera production of *La Gioconda*. USA: New York, NY. 1983.   1898

Photographs, cast lists, synopsis and discography of Metropolitan Opera production of *Un Ballo in Maschera*. USA: New York, NY. 1983.   1899

Photographs, cast lists, synopsis and discography of Metropolitan Opera production of *Les Contes d'Hoffman*. USA: New York, NY. 1983.   1900

Photographs, cast lists, synopsis and discography of Metropolitan Opera production of *Pelléas et Mélisande*. USA: New York, NY. 1983.   1901

Photographs, cast lists, synopsis and discography of Metropolitan Opera production of *The Barber of Seville*. USA: New York, NY. 1983.   1902

Photographs, cast lists, synopsis and discography of the Metropolitan Opera production of *Die Walküre*. USA: New York, NY. 1983.   1903

Photographs, cast lists, synopsis and discography of the Metropolitan Opera production of *Don Carlo*. USA: New York, NY. 1983.   1904

Photographs, cast lists, synopsis and discography of Metropolitan Opera production of *La Bohème*. USA: New York, NY. 1983.   1905

Photographs, cast lists, synopsis and discography of Metropolitan Opera production of *Der Rosenkavalier*. USA: New York, NY. 1983.   1906

Photographs, cast lists, synopsis and discography of Metropolitan Opera production of *Les Dialogues des Carmélites*. USA: New York, NY. 1983.   1907

Photographs, cast lists, synopsis and discography of Metropolitan Opera production of *Ernani*. USA: New York, NY. 1983.   1908

Photographs, cast lists, synopsis and discography of the Metropolitan Opera production of *Tristan und Isolde*. USA: New York, NY. 1983.   1909

Photographs, cast lists, synopsis and discography of Metropolitan Opera production of *Hänsel und Gretel*. USA: New York, NY. 1983.   1910

Backstage look at San Francisco Opera. USA: San Francisco, CA. 1970-1982.   1911

Life and career of Metropolitan Opera soprano Alwina Valleria. USA: New York, NY. 1848-1925.   1915

Photographs, cast lists, synopsis and discography of Metropolitan Opera production of *Idomeneo*. USA: New York, NY. 1983.   1920

Account of *Risurrezione*, to be performed by Cincinnati Summer Opera. USA: Cincinnati, OH. 1904-1983.   1923

Career of Metropolitan Opera stage manager Stanley Levine. USA: New York, NY. 1949-1982.   1925

Actors and companies entertaining Canadian troops during World War I. Canada. UK. France. 1914-1918.   1984

One hundred years of popular theatre. Czechoslovakia. 1883-1983.   1985

Reviews of performances at Teatro Sancarluccio. Italy: Naples. 1972-1982.   2003

History of *commedia dell'arte* and companies of comedians. Italy. 1550-1750.   2019

Fifteen-hour pageant by Jean-Pierre Ronfard and Théâtrale Expérimental de Montréal. Canada: Montreal, PQ. 1982.   2025

Recent production by the Philippe Gentry puppet company. France. 1980.   2050

Review of international puppet theatre festival. Sweden: Uppsala. 1983.   2054

Performances by Ragabush Puppet Theatre and Lampoon Puppet theatre at Children's Theatre Association of America Showcase. USA: Syracuse, NY. 1983.   2058

Use of puppets and puppetry techniques in Arena Stage production of *Candide*. USA: Washington, DC. 1983.   2061

Artistry of Burr Tillstrom and his Kuklapolitan Players. USA. 1983.   2065

Bunraku performances of the Osaka Bunraku Theatre at New York's Japan House. USA: New York, NY. 1983.   2074

Application of holography to the Salzburger Marionettentheater production of *Le Nozze di Figaro*. Austria: Salzburg. 1983.   2083

Life of writer and puppet theatre promoter Walter Wilkinson. UK-England. 1889-1970.   2084

Performances of shadow puppet theatres at 1979 French Festival of Traditional Arts. France. 1979.   2089

Plays/librettos/scripts

Excerpts from Betty Jane Wylie's journal during collective theatre venture. Canada. 1976.   1018

Essays on Vitaliano Brancati's plays and motion picture scripts. Italy: Catania. 1924-1954.   1160

Dramatization of Remigio Zena's novel *The Wolf's Mouth* by Teatro Stabile di Genova. Italy: Genoa. 1980.   1186

Censorship involving Jerzy Hulewicz' play *Aruna*, produced at Municipal Theatre of Cracow. Poland: Kraków. 1925.   1217

Problems of contemporary dramatists, including formal productions and criticism. Sweden. 1983.   1261

Assessment of dramaturgy in English-speaking theatre. USA. 1983.   1361

Effects of national and international politics on playwrights of the 'generation of 1958'. Venezuela. 1945-1983.   1392

Discussion of Molière's *The Tricks of Scapin* addressed to teachers and children of primary schools. France. Italy: Turin. 1671-1983.   1562

Traditional approaches to acting and staging as clarifying methods for complex Shakespeare scenes. UK-England: Stratford-upon-Avon. 1980.   1702

Reference materials

Advertised and reviewed performances of professional troupes. Canada: Ottawa, ON. 1870-1879.   15

Licensing papers related to managerial and repertorial changes at London theatres. England: London. 1706-1715.   20

European music and theatre festivals in 1983: cities, productions and dates. Europe. 1983.   22

Guide to theatre organizations and professionals. Finland. 1983.   23

Annals of theatre productions in Catalonia for the 1982-1983 season. Spain. 1982-1983.   34

Annual record of Broadway and Off Broadway season. USA: New York, NY. 1981-1982.   49

Cast listings and other information on 19 productions mounted at Charlottetown Festival. Canada: Charlottetown, PE. 1965-1982.   1399

Chronological listing, including personnel, of productions of John Webster's plays. England. USA. 1614-1983.   1401

Guide to work of 63 popular theatres. North America. South America. 1980-1983.   1417

Correspondence relating to administrative concerns at the Abbey Theatre between William Butler Yeats, Lady Gregory and John Millington Synge. UK-Ireland: Dublin. 1904-1909.   1432

Institutions, producing — cont'd

Script opportunities for the playwright. USA. 1983.   1434

Directory of Theatre Communications Group members. USA. 1983-1984.   1437

List of theatre companies, playwriting awards and grants. USA. 1983.   1439

Catalogue of Galliari's scene designs owned by Museo Teatrale alla Scala. Italy: Milan. 1778-1823.   1969

Letters and documents placed in archives concerning Verdi's operas at Teatro La Fenice. Italy: Venice. 1844-1852.   1970

Annotated selections of photographs taken by Herman Mishkin of Metropolitan Opera singers. USA: New York, NY. 1910-1932.   1971

Relation to other fields

German theatre in Cracow and its relationship to Polish people during the uprising against Russia. Austro-Hungarian Empire: Cracow. Poland. 1863-1865.   1443

Relations between theatre and politics during the French Revolution. France: Paris, Tours. 1789-1794.   1451

Bunraku is seen as Japanese miniaturization of social concepts. Japan: Osaka. 1983.   2076

Theory/criticism

Expressionistic proposal for the future of theatre by a founding member of Squat Theatre. USA. 1983.   110

Renzo Casali's theory of acting. Italy. 1983.   1671

Training

Conditions of apprenticeship in Elizabethan acting companies. England: Bridgewater. 1597-1599.   494

Institutions, research

Design/technology

Problems of collecting and preserving documents of African stage design. Africa. 1982.   177

Report on the 43rd Conference for Theatre Technology and its welcoming speech. Germany, West: Heilbronn. 1983.   198

Cataloguing work done since 1975 at Drottningholm Theatre Museum. Sweden: Drottningholm, Gripsholm. 1766-1800.   222

Report of Nordisk TeaterTeknik 83 conference. Sweden: Stockholm. 1983.   223

SIBMAS keynote address calling for accumulation of records to preserve theatre history. USA. 1982.   239

History and description of the Motley Theatre and Costume Arts Collection. Discussed at SIBMAS. USA: Urbana, IL. 1982.   247

Observations concerning the French-English translation of scenographic terms. Discussed at SIBMAS. USA. France. 1982.   257

Why collecting, maintaining and exhibiting designers' work is problematical. Discussed at SIBMAS. USA. 1982.   273

Theatre collection taxonomy based on an iconographic approach discussed at SIBMAS. USA: Columbus, OH. 1982.   276

Remarks by scientific advisor to Serbian Museum of Theatrical Art on document collection. Discussed at SIBMAS. Yugoslavia: Belgrade. 1982.   279

Institutions

Problems and prospects of the theatre research library at the University of Vienna. Austria: Vienna. 1983.   286

Founding of periodical *Nouvelle Revue Française*. France: Paris. 1909-1914.   304

First hundred years of the Società Italiana degli Autori ed Editori published in celebration of its centenary. Italy. 1882-1982.   318

Background of Edward Gordon Craig's efforts to establish School for the Art of Theatre. Italy: Florence. UK-England: London. 1900-1917.   320

How the International Theatre Institute (ITI) has expanded the universal character of theatre. Poland. 1900-1983.   323

History of the Polish International Theatre Institute Centre. Poland. 1958-1982.   324

Interview with the director of the Centre Dramàtic de la Generalitat. Spain. 1945-1982.   327

Organization, objectives and projects of the Institute for American Theatre Studies. USA: Bloomington, IN. 1983-1984.   351

Workshops of Latin American popular theatre. North America. South America. 1983.   1610

Support, information, publicity, study facilities, fundraising advice, etc., offered by the Puppet Centre Trust. UK-England: London. 1983.   2045

Plays/librettos/scripts

Essays on Vitaliano Brancati's plays and motion picture scripts. Italy: Catania. 1924-1954.   1160

Recently discovered documents on playwright Johann Nestroy. Austria. 1801-1862.   1550

Reference materials

Description of the Stage Design Collection of National Arts Center. Canada: Ottawa, ON. 1969-1982.   16

Relation to other fields

Theatre in relation to other performing arts at the seminar of the International Centre of Aesthetic Studies. Italy. 1982.   64

Research/historiography

Method for using models of scenery as study documents. Discussed at SIBMAS. Europe. North America. 1982.   83

Institutions, service

Institutions

Project to intensify cultural work in the village of Niederbrechen, subsidized by the Ministry for Youth, Health and Family. Germany, West: Niederbrechen. 1979-1982.   313

Institutions, training

Status report of the Århus Theatre Academy. Denmark: Århus. 1983.   297

Formation of joint committee by amateur theatres and its Training Council. Finland. 1983.   300

Professional artists' continue training at Theatre Academy of Finland. Finland: Helsinki. 1973-1983.   301

Founding and history of acting program at Tampere University. Finland: Tampere. 1967-1983.   302

State of theatre schools in Italy and suggestions for their improvement. Italy. 1982.   317

Popular theatre workshop for training theatre educators. Nigeria: Gboko. 1981-1982.   322

Interview with the director of the Centre Dramàtic de la Generalitat. Spain. 1945-1982.   327

Summary of study about training costume designers. USA. 1979-1983.   346

Dance training at Theatre Academy of Finland. Finland: Helsinki. 1910-1983.   516

Evolution and theories of Odin Teatret. Sweden. 1964-1979.   621

Performances and training at Academy of Vocal Arts. USA: Philadelphia, PA. 1934-1983.   1829

Account of the relationship between the Juilliard School and the Metropolitan Opera. USA: New York, NY. 1919-1983.   1831

Account of the Metropolitan Opera Company's Young Artist Development Program. USA: New York, NY. 1980-1983.   1832

Performance/production

Deficiencies of the Catalonian theatre during the Spanish Civil War, as compared to the contemporary theatrical activities in USSR and other European countries. USSR: Moscow. Spain. 1936-1937.   486

Interview with director and head of Theatre Academy of Finland Jouko Turkka on his views of art and society. Finland. 1983.   723

Role experimental studios played in the formation of the Soviet theatre. USSR: Moscow, Leningrad. 1920-1939.   993

String of wooden pearls as a means of nonverbal communication in a production of *Mandragola*. Germany, West: Munich. 1979-1980.   1528

Plays/librettos/scripts

Collected materials on Eugenio Barba and Odin Teatret. Sweden. 1964-1979.   1258

Reference materials

Compilation of entries on the concepts and techniques practiced at the International School of Theatre Anthropology. Italy. 1981.   30

Training

Examination of training program at Theatre Academy of Finland. Finland: Helsinki. 1983.   495

SUBJECT INDEX

Ion

Plays/librettos/scripts

English translation of Albin Lesky's standard work on Greek tragedy. Greece. 499-400 B.C. 1696

Ionesco, Eugène

Institutions

New season's productions at the Basel Stadttheater. Switzerland: Basel. 1983. 622

Plays/librettos/scripts

Linguistic problems in translating Eugène Ionesco's plays. France. 1950-1970. 1113

Iredyński, Ireneusz

Description and analysis of Ireneusz Iredyński's plays. Poland. 1962-1982. 1213

Irish Literary Revival

Role of folklore in Irish Literary Revival. UK-Ireland. 1888-1920. 1322

Irish Literary Society

Institutions

Rejection of O'Casey's play *The Silver Tassie* by the Abbey Theatre and the subsequent furor. UK-Ireland: Dublin. 1928. 637

Plays/librettos/scripts

Comic irony and anti-heroes in Irish comedy and influence on Harold Pinter, Samuel Beckett and Tom Stoppard. UK-Ireland. Eire. 1900-1940. 1593

Irish Rebel Theatre (New York, NY)

Institutions

History and organization of the Irish Rebel Theatre. USA: New York, NY. 1973-1983. 648

Iron Theatre (Glasgow)

Administration

Interview with the new artistic director and literary advisor for the Iron Theatre (Glasgow). UK-Scotland. 1973-1983. 559

Irving, Henry

Performance/production

Analysis of C.V. Stanford's incidental music for *Becket*. UK-England: London. 1893. 872

Reconstruction of Richard Mansfield's production of *Richard III*. UK-England: London. USA. 1889. 893

Relation to other fields

Theatre arts compared to painting and literature. UK-England. 1805-1902. 69

Irwin, Bill

Performance/production

New vaudevillians use established music hall forms for expression. USA: New York, NY. 1980. 2033

Isn't It Romantic

Five critics review Gerald Gutierrez's production of *Isn't It Romantic*. USA: New York, NY. 1983. 926

ITI SEE: International Theatre Institute

Ivanoff, Nicolai

Plays/librettos/scripts

Creation of the title role in *Ernani* for tenor Nicolai Ivanoff. Italy. Russia. 1844. 1959

Ivanov

Performance/production

Arie Zinger's production of Čechov's *Ivanov* at Züricher Schauspielhaus. Switzerland: Zürich. 1983. 849

Jack Helen Brut (Helsinki)

Institutions

Discussion of performance group Jack Helen Brut consisting of fifteen art students, artists and dancers. Finland: Helsinki. 1983. 1739

History and nature of performance group Jack Helen Brut. Finland: Helsinki. 1981-1983. 1740

Jack Juggler

Plays/librettos/scripts

Folly in Renaissance comedy. England. 1530-1555. 1560

Jackson, Glenda

Performance/production

Philip Prowse's production of Robert MacDonald's Nazi psychothriller *Summit Conference*. UK-England: London. 1982. 888

Jackson, Sir Barry

Institutions

History of the Malvern Festival. UK-England. 1929-1977. 629

Jacques ou La Soumission (Jack, or the Submission)

Plays/librettos/scripts

Linguistic problems in translating Eugène Ionesco's plays. France. 1950-1970. 1113

Jagger, Dean

Reference materials

Description of archive holdings at Brigham Young University including personal papers of Howard Hawks and Dean Jagger. USA: Provo, UT. 1900-1983. 48

Jamaica

Performance/production

Overview of Jack Cole's career as dancer, teacher and choreographer. USA. 1933-1974. 1788

James, Emrys

Actor Emrys James discusses his work, especially with the Royal Shakespeare Company. UK-England. 1900-1983. 879

Jameson, Molly

Interview with puppeteer Molly Jameson. USA. 1983. 2063

Janáček, Leos

Background of the U.S. premiere of Janáček's opera *From the House of the Dead*. USA: New York, NY. Czechoslovakia: Prague. 1930-1983. 1916

Japanese-American Toy Theatre (London)

Work of performance artist Kazuko Hohki with the Japanese-American Toy Theatre. Japan. UK-England: London. 1983. 1745

Jarry, Alfred

History of directing. Europe. 1882-1982. 708

Plays/librettos/scripts

Alfred Jarry's *Ubu* Cycle with an emphasis on its protagonist. France. 1896-1907. 1566

Reference materials

Catalogue of exhibition on pataphysics in figurative arts, theatre and cinema. France. 1873-1907. 1406

Jasager, Der (Yes-Man, The)

Performance/production

Relationship between Bertolt Brecht and Asian theatre. Asia. Germany. 1925-1981. 665

Jaspers, Karl

Theory/criticism

Karl Jaspers' philosophy is applied to a discussion of Luigi Pirandello. Italy. 1916-1936. 1703

Jeeves Takes Charge

Performance/production

Seven critics review Gillian Lynne's production of *Jeeves Takes Charge*. USA: New York, NY. 1983. 946

Jelliffe, Rowena

Institutions

History of Karamu Children's Theatre. USA: Cleveland, OH. 1915-1975. 647

Jessner, Leopold

Performance/production

Problems of antisemitism in staging *The Merchant of Venice*. Israel. 1936-1980. 663

Jesuit theatre

School theatre in the debate between Church and public theatre. France. 1600-1699. 737

Relation to other fields

History of Jesuit theatre to temporary suppression of the Order. Europe. Japan. 1550-1773. 1449

Jewess from Toledo, The SEE: *Jüdin von Toledo, Die*

Jewish Theatre (Warsaw) SEE: Teatr Zydowski

Jewish theatre SEE: Ethnic theatre

Joglars, Els

Performance/production

Semiotic analysis of Els Joglars' production of *Mary d'Ous*. Spain. 1972. 1729

Johan Johan

Plays/librettos/scripts

Adaptation of a French farce into *Johan Johan*. England. France. 1520-1533. 1559

Johnson, Philip

Performance spaces

Philip Johnson's design for Cleveland Playhouse. USA: Cleveland, OH. 1915-1983. 407

Johnson, Samuel

Plays/librettos/scripts

Examination of Samuel Johnson as a character in plays by William Brough and W.S. Gilbert. UK-England: London. 1862-1893. 1313

Krapp's Last Tape by Samuel Beckett as a parody of both performance and themes in poetry. UK-Ireland. 1957. 1321

Theory/criticism

Morality of Restoration comedy. England. 1670-1700. 1599

Johnston, Denis

Plays/librettos/scripts

Influences of Jonathan Swift's satire in plays by W.B. Yeats and Denis Johnston. Eire. 1928-1960. 1026

Irreverent aspects of Irish comedy seen through the works of 14 playwrights. Eire. UK-Ireland. 1840-1965. 1555

Joint Stock (England)

Institutions

Joint Stock, a collective theatre company. UK-England. 1974. 635

Jolly, George

Letters signed by George Jolly concerning the visit of his troupe to Gdansk in August, 1650. Poland: Gdańsk. England. Germany. 1649-1650. 614

Jones, LeRoi SEE: Baraka, Imamu Amiri

Jones, Margo

Performance/production

Biography of director Margo Jones. USA. 1913-1955. 941

Jones, Richard

English actors' work in Germany, with mention of stock comic characters. Germany. England: London. 1590-1620. 1525

Jones, Robert Edmond

Design/technology

Marionettes designed by Robert Edmond Jones for Metropolitan Opera production of *Oedipus Rex*, under the influence of Gordon Craig and *bunraku*. USA: New York, NY. 1931. 2079

Jones, Welton

Performance/production

Conversations with theatre critics from four newspapers. USA. 1983. 468

Jonson, Ben

List of productions of plays from English Renaissance drama with brief reviews. North America. Europe. 1982-1983. 822

Plays/librettos/scripts

Shakespearean influence on Ben Jonson's *Bartholomew Fair*. England. 1614. 1033

Plato's concept of androgyny in Jonson's *The New Inn*. England. 1629. 1036

Involvement of the audience in Ben Jonson's work as satirist and playwright, with some playtexts from the First Folio. England. 1598-1614. 1042

Ironic satire in *Every Man Out of His Humour*. England. 1599. 1052

Authorship, censorship and thematic analysis of *Westward Ho!*. England. 1570-1637. 1067

Essays on Renaissance drama. Europe. 1513-1616. 1085

Adaptation of Ben Jonson's *Epicoene* by Marcel Achard, directed by Charles Dullin. France: Paris. 1926. 1100

Reference materials

Ben Jonson encyclopedia. England. 1572-1637. 1400

Jordcirkus (Sweden)

Institutions

Street theatre production of Århus theater akademi in collaboration with Jordcirkus and Johnny Melville. Denmark: Århus. 1982. 298

Jorio's Daughter SEE: *Figlia di Jorio, La*

Jory, Jon

Performance/production

Jane Martin's *Talking With* at Manhattan Theatre Club, directed by Jon Jory. USA: New York, NY. 1982. 937

Joubert, Elsa

Eight critics review Hilary Blecher's production of *Poppie Nongena*. USA: New York, NY. 1983. 945

Joyce, James

Plays/librettos/scripts

Role of folklore in Irish Literary Revival. UK-Ireland. 1888-1920. 1322

Judson Dance Theater (New York, NY)

Performance/production

Documentation on Judson Dance Theater and creation of post-modern dance. USA: New York, NY. 1962-1964. 527

Jugendclub Kritisches Theater (Stuttgart)

Institutions

Edward Bond's *Saved* and Shakespeare's *Troilus and Cressida* at the Jugendclub Kritisches Theater. Germany, West: Stuttgart. 1981-1983. 608

Juglarón, El (Juggler, The)

Plays/librettos/scripts

Report concerning poet León Felipe and his play *The Juggler*. Spain. Mexico. 1939-1983. 1227

Juilliard School (New York)

Institutions

Account of the relationship between the Juilliard School and the Metropolitan Opera. USA: New York, NY. 1919-1983. 1831

Julie

Performance/production

Documentation of Ingmar Bergman's tripartite theatre project. Sweden. Germany, West: Munich. 1981. 844

Julius Caesar

Relationship between verbal and nonverbal communication in productions of *Macbeth, Othello* and *Julius Caesar*. UK-England. 1980. 868

Federal Theatre Project's often innovative approach to staging Shakespeare's plays. USA. 1930-1939. 978

Junction Avenue Theatre Group (Kwa Zulu)

Theory/criticism

Study of genesis, development, structural components and consequences of theatre-drama performed by the Black workers. South Africa, Republic of. 1981-1983. 1673

Jung, Carl Gustav

Plays/librettos/scripts

Jungian point of view on personality in Luigi Pirandello's work. Italy. 1916-1936. 1169

Psychological analysis of Semiramis character from Calderón's *Daughter of the Air*. Spain. 1600-1699. 1235

Relation to other fields

Argument against application of Jungian ideas to theatre. 490

Santuzza Papa's transition from Freudian psychodrama to Jungian conception. Italy. 1960. 1663

Juno and the Paycock

Plays/librettos/scripts

Influence on Brecht of Sean O'Casey's use of songs to overcome the boundaries of illusion in his drama. UK-Ireland: Dublin. 1923-1926. 1325

Theme of insurrection in Sean O'Casey's three Dublin plays. UK-Ireland: Dublin. 1923-1926. 1331

Junyent, Oleguer

Design/technology

Development of Wagnerian stage design and groups and movements involved in its production. Spain. 1882-1960. 1822

Jura Soyfer Theater am Spittelberg (Vienna)

Institutions

Interview with Reinhold Auer, dramatic advisor of Jura Soyfer Theater am Spittelberg, Vienna. Austria: Vienna. 1980-1983. 583

Jurjev, Juri Michailovič

Performance/production

Actor Juri Jurjev and director Vsevolod Mejerchol'd at the Aleksandrinskij Theatre (now Academic Drama Theatre of A.S. Pushkin). Russia: St. Petersburg. USSR: Leningrad. 1910-1938. 830

Jyväskylän kaupunginteatteri (Jyväskylä)

Institutions

Jyväskylä City Theatre's 1983-1984 season. Finland: Jyväskylä. 1983. 594

Kabuki

Performance/production

Comparison of Indian traditional theatre and *kabuki* in aspects of stylization, participation, and total theatre. India. Japan. 1600-1980. 430

History and development of *bunraku* as theatre, alongside *kabuki*. Japan. 1600-1983. 2073

Plays/librettos/scripts

History of the narrative theme of *Dōjōji (A Woman and a Bell)*. Japan. 1041-1800. 545

Japanese influence on American poetry and drama. Japan. USA. 1900-1980. 1195

Relation to other fields

Historical consideration of the many forms of Japanese drama in terms or religious origins and aspects. Japan. 1300-1800. 543

Theory/criticism

Intermingling of Eastern and Western performance aesthetics. China. Japan. 1900-1983. 93

Kabuki SEE ALSO: Classed Entries: DANCE-DRAMA — *Kabuki*

Kafka, Franz

Institutions

New season's productions at the Basel Stadttheater. Switzerland: Basel. 1983. 622

Theory/criticism

Hannah Arendt's theoretical work with reference to Gotthold Lessing, Bertolt Brecht, Franz Kafka and Isak Dinesen. USA. Europe. 1900-1983. 1518

Kafkaz

Plays/librettos/scripts

Egische Ciarenz's plays, particularly *Kafkaz*, are placed between Futurism and agitprop theatre. Armenia. 1923. 1634

Kähler, Otto

Design/technology

Portrait of scene designer Otto Kähler and his work. Germany, East. 1969-1983. 197

Kahn, Michael

Performance/production

Two examples of staging *Macbeth* in the 1970's. USA: Stratford, CT. Canada: Stratford, ON. 1971-1973. 908

Eight critics review Michael Kahn's production of *Show Boat*. USA: New York, NY. 1983. 1807

Kaiser, Georg

Portrait of and interview with Douglas Sirk, director of *Silverlake*. Germany. Switzerland. USA. 1933-1983. 426

Kajaanin kaupunginteatteri (Kajaani)

Institutions

Articles on Kajaani City Theatre. Finland: Kajaani. 1983. 590

Kajzar, Helmut

Performance/production

Dramatist and director Helmut Kajzar during the years of martial law. Poland: Warsaw. 1941-1982. 827

Plays/librettos/scripts

Description and analysis of Helmut Kajzar's plays. Poland. 1969-1981. 1214

Kalcheim, Lee

Performance/production

Six critics review Barnet Kellerman's production of Lee Kalcheim's play *Breakfast with Les and Bess*. USA: New York, NY. 1983. 1540

Kalldewey, Farce

Botho Strauss' *Kalldewey, Farce* played by the theatre group Baal at Theater Frascati. Netherlands: Amsterdam. 1983. 821

Plays/librettos/scripts

Analysis of Botho Strauss' *Kalldewey, Farce*. Europe. 1964. 1091

Kameri, Teatron (Tel Aviv)

Performance/production

Problems of antisemitism in staging *The Merchant of Venice*. Israel. 1936-1980. 663

Kamińska, Esther Rachel

Institutions

History of Teatr Zydowski (Warsaw Jewish Theatre). Poland: Warsaw. 1876-1983. 616

Kampnagelfabrik (Hamburg)

Performance spaces

Technical problems Deutsches Schauspielhaus encountered by performing in a former factory. Germany, West: Hamburg. 1980-1983. 377

Kamuf, Peggy

Theory/criticism

Significance of gender in feminist criticism with reference to historical materialism, deconstruction and phenomenon of cross-dressing in theatre. USA. France. UK-England. 1983. 1520

Kander, John

Performance/production

Nine critics review Michael Cacoyannis' production of the musical *Zorba*. USA: New York, NY. 1983. 1798

Kant, Immanuel

Theory/criticism

Schiller's philosophy of history. Germany: Jena. 1789-1791. 1499

Kantor, Tadeusz

Institutions

History of Tadeusz Kantor's alternative theatre, Cricot 2. Poland. 1955-1983. 1611

Performance/production

Comprehensive study of productions by Tadeusz Kantor's experimental theatre group Cricot 2 and Kantor's philosophy. Poland. 1975-1980. 1626

Interview with playwright-director Tadeusz Kantor about *Wielopole, Wielopole*. Poland: Wielopole. 1982. 1628

Tadeusz Kantor's theory of art and theatre, and productions of his company Cricot 2. Poland: Kraków. 1943-1975. 1629

Production styles of directors Peter Brook and Tadeusz Kantor. USA: New York, NY. France: Paris. Poland: Wielopole. 1982. 1632

Kapital, Das

Plays/librettos/scripts

Influence of Marxist and Leninist ideology on Bertolt Brecht's plays. Germany. 1926-1934. 1132

Karajan, Herbert von

Performance/production

Biography of conductor and director Herbert von Karajan. Austria. Germany. 1908-1982. 1838

History and production history of Wagnerian opera. Germany. USA. 1832-1982. 1865

Reference materials

Program of Easter Festival Salzburg, including essays on Richard Wagner and Johannes Brahms. Austria: Salzburg. France: Paris. 1983. 1964

Karamu Children's Theatre (Cleveland, OH)

Institutions

History of Karamu Children's Theatre. USA: Cleveland, OH. 1915-1975. 647

Kareda, Urjo

Administration

Four artistic directors discuss theatre relationship with community. Canada: Regina, SK, Vancouver, BC, Toronto, ON, Calgary, AB. 1983. 553

Karge, Manfred

Performance/production

Opening night review and playtext of Heiner Müller's *Wrecked Shore Medeamaterial Landscape with Argonauts*. Germany, West: Bochum. 1983. 767

Karlsplatz Festival (Vienna)

Institutions

Documentation on Karlsplatz festival, part of Wiener Festwochen. Austria: Vienna. 1983. 288

Karlsson, Sture

Plays/librettos/scripts

Arne Andersson, creator of local history plays. Sweden: Härnösand, Norberg, Sundsvall. 1970-1983. 1263

Kaska, Jan

Performance/production

Biography of Czech actor Jan Kaska. Czechoslovakia. 1810-1869. 694

Kathakali SEE ALSO: Classed Entries: DANCE-DRAMA — ***Kathakali***

Katselas, Milton

Performance/production

Nine critics review Milton Katselas' production of Noel Coward's play *Private Lives*. USA: New York, NY. 1983. 1545

Kaufman, George S.

Eight critics review Ellis Rabb's production of George S. Kaufman's and Moss Hart's play *You Can't Take It with You*. USA: New York, NY. 1983. 972

Plays/librettos/scripts

Memoir of meeting with playwright George S. Kaufman. USA. 1922-1961. 1359

Kaufman, Oskar

Theory/criticism

Reformers on their theories. Europe. 1870-1910. 98

Kaukasische Kreidekreis, Der (Caucasian Chalk Circle, The)

Relation to other fields

Reception of Bertolt Brecht in Argentina vis-à-vis political situation in the country. Argentina. 1980-1983. 1441

Kaverin, F.N.

Performance/production

Role experimental studios played in the formation of the Soviet theatre. USSR: Moscow, Leningrad. 1920-1939. 993

Kazan, Elia

Stanislavskij's system in the USA and the tour by the Moscow Art Theatre. USA. USSR. 1910-1959. 923

Playwright Robert Anderson and director Elia Kazan discuss the creation of *Tea and Sympathy*. USA. 1953. 944

Politics, psychology and director Elia Kazan's career. USA. 1909-1965. 949

Kean

Overview of Jack Cole's career as dancer, teacher and choreographer. USA. 1933-1974. 1788

Kean, Charles

Charles Kean's staging methods and the influences on them. UK-England: London. 1850-1859. 898

Shakespearean productions and festivals in the American South. USA. 1751-1980. 938

Kean, Edmund

Shakespearean productions and festivals in the American South. USA. 1751-1980. 938

Keane, John B.

Five critics review Donal Donnelly's production of John B. Keane's play *Big Maggie*. USA: New York, NY. 1983. 966

Keith Memorial Theatre (Boston, MA)

Performance spaces

History of the Keith Memorial Theatre. USA: Boston, MA. 1925-
1980.   1982

Kellerman, Barnet

Performance/production

Six critics review Barnet Kellerman's production of Lee Kalcheim's
play *Breakfast with Les and Bess*. USA: New York, NY. 1983. 1540

Kelling, Petra

Eight actors take positions on their political and social
responsibilities. Germany, East. 1983.   428

Kemble, Charles

Theory/criticism

Effect of social conditions on performance styles. USA. Greece. 499
B.C.-1983 A.D.   1517

Kemble, Fanny

Performance/production

Biography of actress Fanny Kemble. UK-England. USA. 1809-1893.
                                                                         877

Performances, editing and audience response to Fanny Kemble's first
American tour. USA: Boston, MA, New York, NY, Philadelphia,
PA. 1849-1850.   935

Theory/criticism

Collected theory and criticism by women in theatre on women in
theatre. USA. UK. 1850-1983.   114

Kemble, John Philip

Performance/production

Examination of John Philip Kemble's vocal technique. England.
1780-1817.   415

Kent State University

Institutions

Development of a community theatre under the auspices of Kent
State University. USA: Akron, OH. 1972-1983.   343

Kenyon C. Bolton Theatre (Cleveland, OH)

Performance spaces

Philip Johnson's design for Cleveland Playhouse. USA: Cleveland,
OH. 1915-1983.   407

Kern, Jerome

Performance/production

Eight critics review Michael Kahn's production of *Show Boat*. USA:
New York, NY. 1983.   1807

Kertész, André

Design/technology

André Kertész' photographic documentation for surrealist's
fascination with marionettes. Belgium: Liège. 1925-1929.   2077

Kidnapping, The SEE: *Sequestro, Il*

Kierkegaard, Sören

Theory/criticism

Wystan Hugh Auden's poetic meditation on art as related to
Shakespeare's *The Tempest* and Kierkegaardian thought. UK-
England. 1939-1962.   1511

Kilanyi, Edward

Performance/production

History of *tableaux vivants*, with emphasis on work of Edward
Kilanyi. USA: New York, NY. 1831-1899.   2030

Killigrew, Thomas

Performance spaces

Dimensions, orientation and dates established for theatre at Gibbon's
Tennis Court. England: London. 1636-1660.   363

Killing of the Children

Performance/production

Census, with brief reviews, of performances of medieval drama.
Europe. 1982-1983.   710

Killing the Calf

Plays/librettos/scripts

Origins of Hamlet's 'calf' reference. England: London. 1600-1601.
                                                                       1061

Kimball, Francis Hatch

Performance spaces

Construction and history of Edward Harrigan's Theatre, later
renamed the Garrick. USA: New York, NY. 1890-1932.   1773

King Lear

Performance/production

Theodore Komisarjevsky's productions of Shakespeare's plays at
Stratford-upon-Avon. UK-England: Stratford-upon-Avon. 1932-1939.
                                                                       864

Production journal of *King Lear*. Canada: Stratford, ON. 1979. 1676

Evolution of the text of *King Lear* through performance. England.
1605-1983.   1677

Plays/librettos/scripts

Animal nature and eating habits of characters in Shakespeare's
plays. England. 1590-1613.   1058

Shakespearean and editorial designation of locale. England: London.
1605-1606.   1069

Brecht's directorial approach to staging Shakespeare's *Coriolanus,
Macbeth* and *King Lear*. Germany. 1920-1930.   1136

Critical essays on *King Lear*. England. 1605.   1688

Editorial problems in the first folio of *Hamlet, Othello* and *King
Lear*. England: London. 1558-1621.   1692

Theatrical effect preserved in operatic adaptations of Werner Egk's
Peer Gynt and Aribert Reimann's *King Lear* at the Münchener
Festspiele. Germany, West: Munich. 1982.   1953

Relation to other fields

Theatre arts compared to painting and literature. UK-England. 1805-
1902.   69

King, Martin Luther, Jr.

Performance/production

History of a production about nine Black leaders by the African
American Drama Company. USA. 1976-1983.   979

King's Company (Edinburgh)

Activities of King's Company and their staging of George Etherege's
The Man of Mode. UK-Scotland: Edinburgh. 1678-1680.   448

Kinney, Terry

Six critics review Terry Kinney's production of C.P. Taylor's play
And a Nightingale Sang. USA: New York, NY. 1983.   961

Kipphardt, Heinar

Analysis of problems concerning the staging of Heinar Kipphardt's
Brother Eichmann. Germany, West: Munich. 1983.   765

Plays/librettos/scripts

Brief comments on Heinar Kippardt's play *Brother Eichmann*.
Germany, West. 1983.   1149

German Fascism as the main theme of Heinar Kipphardt's plays.
Germany, West. 1982.   1153

Kirchner, Alfred

Performance/production

Tendencies of Bertolt Brecht stage interpretations. Germany, East.
USSR. Italy. 1956-1983.   747

Kisatachie Playhouse

Institutions

Organization, people and theatres involved in the Army Theatre Arts
Association. USA: Fort Polk, LA. 1960-1983.   336

Labiche, Eugène

Performance/production

Staging of Eugène Labiche's plays in Catalonia. Spain. France. 1967-1982. 1532

Plays/librettos/scripts

Variations on the bedroom farce form in the works of Eugène Labiche, Roger Vitrac and Samuel Beckett. France. 1870-1983. 1573

Analysis of farces by Eugène Labiche and Georges Feydeau. France. 1815-1921. 1575

Labor relations

Administration

Round table discussion between playwrights and their agents. USA. 1983. 562

Lacan, Jacques

Theory/criticism

Significance of gender in feminist criticism with reference to historical materialism, deconstruction and phenomenon of cross-dressing in theatre. USA. France. UK-England. 1983. 1520

Lacayo fingido, El (False Lackey, The)

Plays/librettos/scripts

Lope de Vega's forty extant texts are examined to determine authorship of *The False Lackey*. Spain. 1609-1635. 1254

Ladies Visiting Day, The

Performance/production

Questionable chronology results from performances by English officers. Belgium: Maastricht. 1703. 679

Lady Windermere's Fan

Plays/librettos/scripts

Earlier date suggested for composition of *A Wife's Tragedy*. UK-England. 1882-1900. 1312

Laederach, Jürgen

Institutions

New season's productions at the Basel Stadttheater. Switzerland: Basel. 1983. 622

Lahden kaupunginteatteri (Lahti)

Building and performances at Lahti City Theatre. Finland: Lahti. 1983. 592

Lajkonik

Relation to other fields

Dramatist Stanisław Wyspiański's painting of a Tartar costume, based on a folk tradition stock type — Lajkonik. Poland: Kraków. Austria. 1901-1907. 1461

Lamb, Thomas W.

Performance spaces

History of the Keith Memorial Theatre. USA: Boston, MA. 1925-1980. 1982

Lampoon Puppet Theatre

Performance/production

Performances by Ragabush Puppet Theatre and Lampoon Puppet theatre at Children's Theatre Association of America Showcase. USA: Syracuse, NY. 1983. 2058

Lan-fang, Mei

Relationship between Bertolt Brecht and Asian theatre. Asia. Germany. 1925-1981. 665

Lanari, Alessandro

Research/historiography

Classification system of Biblioteca Nazionale Centrale used by Alessandro Lanari. Italy: Florence. 1815-1870. 1972

Lanchester, Elsa

Performance/production

Autobiography of actress Elsa Lanchester. UK. 1902-1983. 853

Lanchester, Waldo

Institutions

Foundation and history of the London Marionette Theatre. UK-England: London. 1927-1935. 2082

Land of Promise, The

Plays/librettos/scripts

Audience reaction and cancellation of tour of Somerset Maugham's *The Land of Promise*. Canada. USA. UK-England. 1914. 1015

Landriani, Paolo

Design/technology

Scene designers and scenery at Teatro alla Scala in Neoclassic period. Italy: Milan. 1778-1832. 1821

Lang, Alexander

Performance/production

Interview with director Alexander Lang on importance of ensemble productions. Germany, East. 1983. 753

Directors on Bertolt Brecht's dramas. Germany, East: Schwerin, Erfurt, East Berlin. 1983. 754

Lang, Jack

Administration

Efforts of Jack Lang, Minister of Culture, to decentralize theatre. France. 1982-1983. 124

Lang, Lotte

Performance/production

Career of actress Lotte Lang. Austria: Vienna. 1900-1983. 669

Lang, Tony

Five critics review David Holdgrive's production of the musical *Tallulah*. USA: New York, NY. 1983. 1796

Långbacka, Ralf

Institutions

Current manager Taisto-Bertil Orsmaa, and history of Turku Municipal Theatre. Finland: Turku. 1946-1983. 303

Performance spaces

Interview with director Ralf Långback about performance spaces. Finland. 1983. 368

Langdon, Harry

Performance/production

Comedian Harry Langdon as a stage director. USA. 1884-1944. 1539

Lange, Hartmut

Dramatists as directors of their own plays. Germany, West: Bonn, Lüneburg, Hamburg. 1983. 789

Language

Plays/librettos/scripts

Interpretations of locale of scenes in *As You Like It*. England. 1599-1600. 1038

Analysis of the fool's rhetorical technique of speech in Shakespeare's plays. England. 1592-1605. 1060

Placement of the caesura in Shakespearean texts. England. 1559-1603. 1083

Linguistic analysis of *Lydia und Mäxchen* by Alfred Döblin. Germany. 1906. 1120

Problems leading to gradual disappearance of the dialect theatre. Italy. 1863-1980. 1181

Analysis of Henrik Ibsen's *Ghosts*. Norway. 1881. 1202

Adaptation of the Angel Guimerà play *Maria Rosa*. Spain. 1894. 1230

Language in the plays of Harold Pinter. UK-England. 1930-1983. 1279

Graphic and linguistic structure of Antonin Artaud's last writings. France. 1938-1948. 1646

Techniques of dehumanization and linguistic usage in Futurist theatre. Italy. 1909-1931. 1651

Linguistic analysis of *Macbeth*. England. 1605-1606. 1690

Language — cont'd

Relation to other fields

Essays on five main concerns of oral interpretation: language, culture, teaching, theory and entertainment. Europe. North America. 499 B.C.-1980 A.D.   53

Theory/criticism

Dramatic language related to action. England. 1559-1603.   1480

Freudian analysis is used to divide dramatic fantasy into three phases, from genital-masochism to anal-sadism. Germany, West. France. USA. 1974-1983.   1506

Vocal emission as a mode of theatricalization in experimental theatre. Canada. 1970-1979.   1669

Language development

Relation to other fields

Impact of the creative drama activities on language disordered children. USA. 1983.   77

Effects of creative drama on development of language skills. USA. 1983.   1471

Lannon, Tom

Plays/librettos/scripts

Tom Lannon discusses background of his play *Children of the Dead End*. UK-Scotland. 1983.   1339

Larson, Gary

Administration

Debate on federal arts subsidies. USA. 1943-1965.   157

Lascarais, Théodore

Plays/librettos/scripts

Comparison of two French translations of *Twelfth Night*, by Jacques Copeau/Théodore Lascarais and Suzanne Bing. France: Paris. 1914.   1567

Lasers

Design/technology

Laser holography as an element of scene design. Austria: Salzburg. 1948-1985.   178

Lasky, Jesse L.

Institutions

Folies-Bergère contribution to the development of dinner theatres and night clubs. USA: New York, NY. 1911.   2026

Last Days of Pompeii

Plays/librettos/scripts

Louisa Medina's popular dramatic adaptations of the works of Edward Bulwer-Lytton, Ernest Maltravers and Robert Bird. USA. 1833-1838.   1346

Latin American Popular Theatre Festival (New York, NY)

Institutions

Cultural and political aspects of Latin American Popular Theatre Festival. USA: New York, NY. 1982.   1980

Lauda drammatica

Reference materials

List of 94 twentieth century works dealing with Italian sacred drama. Italy. 1300-1983.   1413

Laurence, Jerome

Performance/production

Six critics review John Bowab's production of the musical *Mame*. USA: New York, NY. 1983.   1801

Laurents, Arthur

Ten critics review *La Cage aux Folles*. USA: New York, NY. 1983.   1806

Lautenschläger, Karl

Theory/criticism

Reformers on their theories. Europe. 1870-1910.   98

Lawrence, Beth

Performance/production

Seven critics review Kenny Ortega's production of the musical *Marilyn: An American Fable*. USA: New York, NY. 1983.   1792

Lawrence, D.H.

Plays/librettos/scripts

D.H. Lawrence as dramatist. UK-England. 1885-1930.   1303

Analysis of D.H. Lawrence's plays. UK-England. 1885-1930.   1305

Lawson, John Howard

Relation to other fields

'Progressive' society's reactions to death of Eugene O'Neill. USA. 1954.   1472

Lazarenko, Vitali

Circus as a staging device for a political satire. USSR. Germany. Italy. 1914-1930.   1668

Lazarus

Performance/production

Description and analysis of Ping Chong's work. USA. 1972-1983.   1752

Career of performance artist Ping Chong. USA: New York, NY. 1972-1982.   1755

Lazzarini, Giulia

Samuel Beckett's *Happy Days* with Giulia Lazzarini at Piccolo Teatro di Milano, directed by Giorgio Strehler. Italy: Milan. 1983.   807

Lazzi

English translations of *commedia dell'arte* lazzi and two complete scenarios. Italy. 1734.   2018

Le Gallienne, Eva

Institutions

History of American Repertory Theatre. USA. 1945-1947.   652

Theory/criticism

Collected theory and criticism by women in theatre on women in theatre. USA. UK. 1850-1983.   114

League of Chicago Theatres

Institutions

History of League of Chicago Theatres. USA: Chicago, IL. 1970-1983.   651

Lear

Plays/librettos/scripts

Theatrical effect preserved in operatic adaptations of Werner Egk's *Peer Gynt* and Aribert Reimann's *King Lear* at the Münchener Festspiele. Germany, West: Munich. 1982.   1953

Learned Ladies, The SEE: *Femmes savantes, Le*

Leben des Galileo Galilei, Das (Life of Galileo, The)

Plays/librettos/scripts

Adaptation of *Galileo* for Chinese stage. China, People's Republic of: Peking. 1979.   1020

LeBrun, Christopher

Design/technology

Safety curtain at Covent Garden, designed by Christopher Le Brun. UK-England: London. 1983.   232

Leçon, La (Lesson, The)

Plays/librettos/scripts

Linguistic problems in translating Eugène Ionesco's plays. France. 1950-1970.   1113

Ledoux, Claude-Nicolas

Performance spaces

Relation between architectural structure and social function of theatre. France. 1736-1806.   369

Lee, Nathaniel

Plays/librettos/scripts

Essays on Restoration theatre and drama, with devised criteria for evaluation. England. 1660-1800.   1046

Lee, Peggy

Performance/production

Six critics review Robert Drivas' production of Peggy Lee's play *Peg*. USA: New York, NY. 1983.   1794

Lee, Richard Nelson

Reference materials

Biography of Richard Nelson Lee and list of 132 works. UK-England: London. 1830-1872.   1734

Lee, Robert E.

Performance/production

Six critics review John Bowab's production of the musical *Mame*. USA: New York, NY. 1983.   1801

Legal aspects

Administration

Censorship of Brazilian theatre, causing only Broadway hits to be produced. Brazil. 1557-1983.   116

Firearm laws as they relate to theatre. Germany, West. 1983.   130

History of censorship in journals, theatre, cinema, radio and television. Italy. 1944-1980.   136

New, augmented manual of copyright laws. Italy. 1983.   138

Laws, provisions and contracts regulating conditions of employment in different fields of theatre. Italy. 1983.   139

Intervention of censorship in cinema, radio and theatre. Italy. 1924-1982.   140

Legislation on theatre presented to the parliament by the Socialist Party of Catalonia. Spain. 1982.   141

Effect of corporate sponsorship on freedom of expression in theatre. Sweden. 1983.   143

Private prosecution of Michael Bogdanov's production of Howard Brenton's *The Romans in Britain*. UK. 1968-1986.   144

Proposed amendments to by-laws of the American Theatre Association. USA: Minneapolis, MN. 1983.   150

Two additional proposed changes in the by-laws of the American Theatre Association. USA. 1983.   151

Legislative planning, advocacy, audience development and support discussed by American Theatre Association officers. USA: New York, NY. 1983.   152

Letters and documents concerning performances at local opera houses. USA: Grand Forks, ND, Crookston, MN. 1890-1899.   155

How to locate free or low-cost professional assistance in law, finance and management. USA. 1983.   156

Effect of different kinds of financial support on artists. USA. 1950-1982.   163

Premiere of *Caste* contributed to passage of American Copyright Act. USA: New York, NY. UK-England: London. 1866-1891.   560

Copyrights for directors' contributions to the plays they stage. USA. 1983.   563

Censorship on the American stage, particularly of Bertolt Brecht. USA. 1941-1949.   564

Yearbook of the international society for copyright. Austria. Italy. North America. 1976-1981.   1704

Brief history of the organization and legislation of musical theatre. Italy. 1920-1981.   1759

Institutions

Annual report of the Austrian Federal Theatres. Austria: Vienna. 1982-1983.   284

First hundred years of the Società Italiana degli Autori ed Editori published in celebration of its centenary. Italy. 1882-1982.   318

Activities of church and theatre associations to promote 'decent' dramaturgy. USA: New York, NY, Chicago, IL. 1910-1940.   649

Performance/production

Evolution of *tableaux vivants* into displays of nudity which were eventually suppressed. USA: New York, NY. 1800-1899.   2031

Plays/librettos/scripts

Essays on Restoration theatre and drama, with devised criteria for evaluation. England. 1660-1800.   1046

Catalogue of the exhibition on the copyright debate between playwright Paolo Giacometti and actress Adelaide Ristori. Italy. 1836-1882.   1191

Censorship involving Jerzy Hulewicz' play *Aruna*, produced at Municipal Theatre of Cracow. Poland: Kraków. 1925.   1217

Léger, Fernand

Design/technology

Meyer Levin's marionettes as abstract visual images, influenced by Gordon Craig and Fernand Léger. USA. 1926-1930.   2081

Legislation

Relation to other fields

Legislative documents related to Byzantine mime, pantomime and masquerade. Byzantine Empire. Asia. 691-1200.   1731

Lehrstücke

Plays/librettos/scripts

Bertolt Brecht's experiments in audience education through his plays. Germany, East. 1954-1956.   1147

Leipziger Opernhaus

Training

Ballet work and training in opera houses in East Germany. Germany, East: Leipzig, Dresden, East Berlin. 1981-1983.   523

Lempert, Leon H.

Performance spaces

History of the Columbia Theatre. USA: Boston, MA. 1881-1957.   395

Lenin, Vladimir Iljič

Plays/librettos/scripts

Influence of Lenin's writings on Bertolt Brecht's plays. Germany. 1930.   1128

'Great Method' used by Bertolt Brecht in his plays, and influences from others. Germany. 1918-1956.   1130

Influence of Marxist and Leninist ideology on Bertolt Brecht's plays. Germany. 1926-1934.   1132

Leonardo da Vinci

Reference materials

Catalogue of the exhibition dealing with Leonardo da Vinci's activity as costume and scene designer and inventor of machinery for Sforza's festivals. Italy: Milan. 1484-1500.   28

Léotard, Philippe

Performance/production

Patrice Chéreau directs Bernard-Marie Koltès' *Fight of the Negro and the Dogs* at Théâtre des Amandiers. France: Nanterre. 1982.   736

Lerner, Alan Jay

Six critics review Alan Jay Lerner's production of the musical *Dance a Little Closer*. USA: New York, NY. 1983.   1793

Lessing, Gotthold Ephraim

Gotthold Ephraim Lessing's *Nathan the Wise* at Deutsches Theater Berlin, directed by Fritz Wisten. Germany, East: East Berlin. 1945.   756

Plays/librettos/scripts

Goethe's regard for Shakespeare and influences observed in *Faust*. Germany. 1770-1832.   1125

Study of plays and criticism of Gotthold Lessing. Germany. 1729-1781.   1131

Dramatic structure of Gotthold Ephraim Lessing's *Minna of Barnhelm* represents cultural atmosphere of the time. Germany. 1767.   1138

Theory/criticism

Gotthold Ephraim Lessing's 'Beyträge zur Historie und Aufnahme des Theaters' and contemporary German criticism of Plautus. Germany. 1747-1755.   1492

Ljubimov, Juri Petrovič

Performance/production

Tendencies of Bertolt Brecht stage interpretations. Germany, East. USSR. Italy. 1956-1983. 747

Interview with actor-director Tamás Major on staging plays by Bertolt Brecht. Hungary. 1962-1982. 791

Lo Strascino SEE: Campani, Niccolò

Loftus, Cissie

Performance/production

Careers of solo performers Beatrice Herford, Cissie Loftus and Dorothy Sands. USA. 1900-1920. 942

Lohengrin

First performance of Richard Wagner's *Lohengrin* and the debate generated with followers of Giuseppe Verdi. Spain. 1862-1901. 1886

London Cuckolds, The

Theory/criticism

Morality of Restoration comedy. England. 1670-1700. 1599

London Marionette Theatre

Institutions

Foundation and history of the London Marionette Theatre. UK-England: London. 1927-1935. 2082

Londré, Felicia

Plays/librettos/scripts

Assessment of dramaturgy in English-speaking theatre. USA. 1983. 1361

Long Day's Journey into Night

Philosophic examination of Eugene O'Neill's *Long Day's Journey into Night*. USA. 1940. 1360

The Long Voyage Home and *Long Day's Journey into Night* successfully transferred to film. USA. 1940-1962. 1383

Long Voyage Home, The

The Long Voyage Home and *Long Day's Journey into Night* successfully transferred to film. USA. 1940-1962. 1383

Loomis, Payson Walker

Performance/production

Autobiographical survey by choreographer Lincoln Kirstein. USA. India: Marrakesh. Europe. 1916-1949. 514

Lope de Vega SEE: Vega Carpio, Lope Félix de

Lorca, Federico GarcOia SEE: García Lorca, Federico

Lord Malquist and Mr. Moon

Plays/librettos/scripts

Playfulness in Tom Stoppard's plays. UK-England. 1937-1983. 1592

Lorick, Robert

Performance/production

Nine critics review Vivian Matalon's production of the musical *The Tap Dance Kid*. USA: New York, NY. 1983. 1781

Los Angeles Herald Examiner

Conversations with theatre critics from four newspapers. USA. 1983. 468

Los Angeles Times

Conversations with theatre critics from four newspapers. USA. 1983. 468

Lost Salt Gift of Blood, The

Regional theatre production of *The Lost Salt Gift of Blood* by Alistair MacLeod. Canada. 1981-1983. 685

Louis XIII

Relation to other fields

Political ramifications of the theatrical patronage of Louis XIII and Cardinal de Richelieu. France. 1610-1643. 54

Louis XIV

Performance/production

History of opera performances at French court, including work of scene designer Carlo Vigarani. France: Versailles. 1671-1704. 1860

Louisiana troupes

Chronology of Black entertainers associated with 'Louisiana troupes'. Europe. 1901-1916. 2028

Love's Labour's Lost

Relation to other fields

Shakespeare's rhetoric in *Love's Labour's Lost* expresses commonplace figures also to be found in pictorial art of the period. England. 1594-1595. 1446

Lovely to Look At SEE *Mojo zagliadénije* sh *Tales of Old Arbat* SEE: *Skazki starova Arbata*

Lover, The

Performance/production

Year's outstanding productions of plays by August Strindberg and other playwrights. UK-England. 1982-1983. 890

Lubicz-Sarnowska, Stanisława

Guest performance in Prague of eminent Polish actors Juliusz Osterwa and Stanisława Lubicz-Sarnowska from Warsaw. Czechoslovakia: Prague. Poland. 1920-1935. 693

Lucia di Lammermoor

Photographs, cast lists, synopsis and discography from the Metropolitan Opera's September 28, 1983 telecast of Gaetano Donizetti's *Lucia di Lammermoor*. USA: New York, NY. 1983. 1893

Luckham, Claire

Five critics review Chris Bond's production of Clair Luckham's play *Teaneck Tanzi: The Venus Flytrap*. USA: New York, NY. 1983. 954

Ludlam, Charles

Six critics review Charles Ludlam's production of his play *Galas*. USA: New York, NY. 1983. 1797

Lugné-Poë

Critical reaction to early productions of Oscar Wilde's *Salome*. Europe. USA: New York, NY. 1892-1917. 711

Lugné, Aurélien-François-Marie SEE: Lugné-Poë

Lukács, György (Georg)

Relation to other fields

Difference in dialectics and philosophy in writings by Karl Korsch, Bertolt Brecht and György Lukács. Germany. Hungary. 1898-1971. 1454

Theory/criticism

Bertolt Brecht's theatrical poetics and polemic with György Lukács on realism. Germany. Hungary. 1918-1956. 1493

Bertolt Brecht's and György Lukács' debate on realism. Germany. Hungary. 1900-1956. 1500

Lulli, Giambattista

Performance/production

History of opera performances at French court, including work of scene designer Carlo Vigarani. France: Versailles. 1671-1704. 1860

Lumet, Sidney

Plays/librettos/scripts

The Long Voyage Home and *Long Day's Journey into Night* successfully transferred to film. USA. 1940-1962. 1383

Lunačarskij, Anatoli Vasil'evič

Performance/production

Deficiencies of the Catalonian theatre during the Spanish Civil War, as compared to the contemporary theatrical activities in USSR and other European countries. USSR: Moscow. Spain. 1936-1937.   486

Luscombe, George

Theory and style of director George Luscombe. Canada: Toronto, ON. 1983.   1614

Luzzati, Emanuele

Design/technology

Exhibition of works and portrait of the scene and costume designer Emanuele Luzzati. Italy. 1921-1983.   214

Lyceum Theatre (Edinburgh)

Institutions

History of the Edinburgh Royal Lyceum Theatre. UK-Scotland: Edinburgh. 1883-1983.   333

Performance/production

Changes of directors and reviews of performances at the Edinburgh Festival and Lyceum Theatre. UK-Scotland: Edinburgh. 1983.   903

Relation to other fields

Theatre arts compared to painting and literature. UK-England. 1805-1902.   69

Lydia und Mäxchen

Plays/librettos/scripts

Linguistic analysis of *Lydia und Mäxchen* by Alfred Döblin. Germany. 1906.   1120

Lynne, Gillian

Performance/production

Seven critics review Gillian Lynne's production of *Jeeves Takes Charge*. USA: New York, NY. 1983.   946

Maazel, Lorin

Administration

Lorin Maazel's first season as intendant of Vienna Staatsoper. Austria: Vienna. USA. 1983.   1810

Performance/production

Harold Prince's production of Giacomo Puccini's *Turandot* at Vienna's Staatsoper. Austria: Vienna. 1983.   1839

Macbeth

Compagnia del Collettivo/Teatro Due productions of three plays by William Shakespeare. Italy: Parma. 1980-1983.   795

Shakespearean productions by Compagnia del Collettivo/Teatro Due, Theater an der Ruhr (Hamburg) and Schaubühne (West Berlin). Italy: Parma. Germany, West: West Berlin, Hamm. 1983.   810

Three productions of *Macbeth* by director Ingmar Bergman. Sweden: Stockholm, Hälsingborg, Göteburg. 1940-1948.   840

Beerbohm Tree's conceptual and directorial approach to staging Shakespeare. UK-England: London. 1905-1911.   863

Theodore Komisarjevsky's productions of Shakespeare's plays at Stratford-upon-Avon. UK-England: Stratford-upon-Avon. 1932-1939.   864

Relationship between verbal and nonverbal communication in productions of *Macbeth, Othello* and *Julius Caesar.* UK-England. 1980.   868

Federal Theatre Project's often innovative approach to staging Shakespeare's plays. USA. 1930-1939.   978

Dispute about Heiner Müller's production of *Macbeth.* Germany, East: East Berlin. 1971-1982.   1678

Plays/librettos/scripts

Appearance of Banquo's ghost in *Macbeth* clarifies the relation of the audience to the play. England. 1605-1606.   1034

Political prophecy in *Macbeth* IV.i. England: London. 1605-1606.   1048

Animal nature and eating habits of characters in Shakespeare's plays. England. 1590-1613.   1058

Textual analysis of the past in theatre productions to achieve a relationship with the present. Europe. 1605-1606.   1086

Brecht's directorial approach to staging Shakespeare's *Coriolanus, Macbeth* and *King Lear.* Germany. 1920-1930.   1136

Linguistic analysis of *Macbeth.* England. 1605-1606.   1690

Macbeth, Robert

Performance/production

Founder-director of New Lafayette Theatre discusses purpose and style of rituals. USA: New York, NY. 1969-1972.   2102

MacDonald, Robert Davis

Philip Prowse's production of Robert MacDonald's Nazi psychothriller *Summit Conference.* UK-England: London. 1982.   888

Machiavelli, Niccolò

String of wooden pearls as a means of nonverbal communication in a production of *Mandragola.* Germany, West: Munich. 1979-1980.   1528

Plays/librettos/scripts

Essays on Renaissance drama. Europe. 1513-1616.   1085

Views on Lucretia held by Titus Livius and Niccolò Machiavelli. Italy. 1513-1520.   1183

Use of vernacular in Ariosto's, Machiavelli's and Ruzante's comedies, as compared with Roman drama. Italy. Roman Empire. 1508-1533.   1584

Machines SEE: Equipment

MacLaine, Shirley

Performance/production

Autobiography of actress Shirley MacLaine. USA. 1934-1983.   943

MacLeod, Alistair

Regional theatre production of *The Lost Salt Gift of Blood* by Alistair MacLeod. Canada. 1981-1983.   685

MacNeil, Cornell

Making of the Franco Zeffirelli film of *La Traviata.* Italy: Rome. 1981-1983.   1885

Macready, William Charles

Edward Bulwer-Lytton's theory of the need for unified approach to productions, in response to John Calcraft's staging of *Richelieu.* UK-Ireland: Dublin. 1839.   900

Shakespearean productions and festivals in the American South. USA. 1751-1980.   938

Madama Butterfly

Career of soprano Leona Mitchell at the Metropolitan Opera. USA. 1983.   1912

Madame Bovary

Plays/librettos/scripts

Literary influences on Henrik Ibsen's *Vildanden (The Wild Duck).* Norway. 1884.   1205

Madame Vestris

Performance/production

Adverse reception of Madame Vestris and Charles Mathews on tour in USA. USA: New York, NY, Philadelphia, PA. UK-England: London. 1838.   933

Madang nori

Recent performances of *madang nori,* developed originally from religious festivals of ancient society. Korea. 1982.   536

Madheart

Plays/librettos/scripts

Two principal female archetypes of Imamu Amiri Baraka's drama. USA. 1964-1978.   1375

Maeterlinck, Maurice

Performance/production

Critical reaction to early productions of Oscar Wilde's *Salome.* Europe. USA: New York, NY. 1892-1917.   711

Maeterlinck, Maurice — cont'd

Plays/librettos/scripts

Comparison of symbolist drama by Maurice Maeterlinck and opera by Claude Debussy. Belgium. 1900-1983.   1012

Playwrights and dramatic forms influencing Eugene O'Neill's *The Calms of Capricorn*. Europe. USA. 1953.   1088

Maffei, Scipione

Performance spaces

History of Teatro Filarmonico in Verona and productions mounted there. Italy: Verona. 1732-1978.   378

Plays/librettos/scripts

Analysis of three tragedies written between Mannerism and the Age of Arcadia. Italy. 1627-1713.   1698

Magazzini Criminali (Italy)

Basic theatrical documents

Playtext and accompanying materials from the Magazzini Criminali production of *On the Road*. Italy. 1982.   1605

Magic

Performance/production

Eight critics review Ivan Reitman's production of the musical *Merlin*. USA: New York, NY. 1983.   1802

Reference materials

Reference guide to popular entertainments. USA. 1840.   1998

Magnanimous Cuckold, The SEE: *Cocu Magnifique, Le*

Magnificent Ambersons, The

Plays/librettos/scripts

Reasons for Deeley's calling himself Orson Welles in *Old Times* are based on film *The Magnificent Ambersons*. UK-England. USA. 1942-1971.   1289

Mahābhārata

Epic texts form the thematic basis of Indian dance-drama. India. 800-1800.   539

Mahler, Gustav

Performance/production

Erich Wolfgang Korngold's *Die tote Stadt* at the Deutsche Oper Berlin. Germany, West: West Berlin. 1855. 1983.   1871

Plays/librettos/scripts

Diary of Austrian dramatist Arthur Schnitzler. Austria. 1913-1916.   1005

Mai

Performance/production

Typical movement, music, costumes, performers and historic influences in *odori* and *mai* dance. Japan. 900-1900.   544

Maid's Tragedy, The

Plays/librettos/scripts

Relationship between Jacobean tragedy and interpolated masque. England. 1600-1625.   1691

Maids, The SEE: *Bonnes, Les*

Mairet, Jean de

Plays/librettos/scripts

Comparative sociological study of French theatre. France. 1610-1643.   1109

Maître Guérin

Émile Augier's *Maître Guérin* is seen as the most likely source for the ending of *A Doll's House*. Norway. France. 1864-1879.   1212

Majakovskij, Vladimir Vladimirovič

Italian translation of Walter Benjamin's articles, aphorisms and other notes on theatrical events. Europe. 1926-1927.   1087

Relation to other fields

Circus as a staging device for a political satire. USSR. Germany. Italy. 1914-1930.   1668

Major Barbara

Plays/librettos/scripts

Characterization and setting used to challenge audience views in George Bernard Shaw's *Major Barbara*. UK-England. 1907.   1287

Shaw's manipulation of audience reaction in *Major Barbara*. UK-England. 1907.   1307

Major, Leon

Administration

Disappointments and mismanagement at Centre Stage. Canada: Toronto, ON. 1983.   119

Major, Tamás

Performance/production

Interview with actor-director Tamás Major on staging plays by Bertolt Brecht. Hungary. 1962-1982.   791

Makarova, Natalia

Production elements and choreography of *On Your Toes*. USA. 1982.   1782

Make-up

Design/technology

Practical and theoretical hand-book for aspiring make-up artists. Italy. 1982.   215

Use of color theory in designing make-up. USA. 1983.   235

Techniques of three dimensional make-up. USA. 1982.   240

Unified approach to audiovisual design. USA. 1977.   241

Suggestions regarding children's touring shows. USA. 1983.   262

Technical aspects of Broadway production of *La Cage aux Folles*. USA: New York, NY. 1983.   1771

Performance/production

Collection of photographs of Broadway productions and actors. USA: New York, NY. 1940-1967.   921

Backstage look at San Francisco Opera. USA: San Francisco, CA. 1970-1982.   1911

Malade Imaginaire, Le (Imaginary Invalid, The)

Actor Branko Samarovski as Argan in Alfred Kirchner's production of *The Imaginary Invalid*. Germany, West: Bochum. 1983.   760

Malina, Judith

Institutions

Reflections on the significance of The Open Theatre by several of its performers, writers and critical advisers. USA: New York, NY. 1963-1973.   1613

Performance/production

Writings by the founders of the Living Theatre. USA. Europe. 1952-1962.   1631

Theory/criticism

Collected theory and criticism by women in theatre on women in theatre. USA. UK. 1850-1983.   114

Mallam Company

Performance/production

Shakespearean productions and festivals in the American South. USA. 1751-1980.   938

Mallarmé, Stéphane

Plays/librettos/scripts

Memoirs of journalist Stephen McKenna on John Millington Synge's apprenticeship years in Paris. UK-Ireland. France: Paris. 1895-1902.   1324

Malone, Edmond

Misquotation of Shakespeare in Edmond Malone's 1790 edition. England: London. 1790-1821.   1070

Malone, Mike

Performance/production

Debbie Allen discusses her struggle for success and her relationship with her family. USA. 1983. 515

Maltby, Richard, Jr.

Ten critics review Richard Maltby's production of *Baby*. USA: New York, NY. 1983. 1805

Maltravers, Ernest

Plays/librettos/scripts

Louisa Medina's popular dramatic adaptations of the works of Edward Bulwer-Lytton, Ernest Maltravers and Robert Bird. USA. 1833-1838. 1346

Malvern Festival

Institutions

History of the Malvern Festival. UK-England. 1929-1977. 629

Malyj Teat'r (Moscow)

Performance/production

Role experimental studios played in the formation of the Soviet theatre. USSR: Moscow, Leningrad. 1920-1939. 993

Mame

Six critics review John Bowab's production of the musical *Mame*. USA: New York, NY. 1983. 1801

Mamet, David

Six critics review Arvin Brown's production of David Mamet's play *American Buffalo*. USA: New York, NY. 1983. 960

Plays/librettos/scripts

Study of David Mamet's *American Buffalo*. USA. 1977. 1379

Man and Superman

Performance/production

Survey of stage history of G.B. Shaw's *Man and Superman*. UK-England. 1903-1982. 876

Director Stephen Porter comments on George Bernard Shaw. USA: New York, NY. 1964-1982. 947

Plays/librettos/scripts

Function of props and settings in plays by George Bernard Shaw. UK-England. 1894-1907. 1281

Man of La Mancha

Performance/production

Overview of Jack Cole's career as dancer, teacher and choreographer. USA. 1933-1974. 1788

Man of Mode, The

Activities of King's Company and their staging of George Etherege's *The Man of Mode*. UK-Scotland: Edinburgh. 1678-1680. 448

Man Outside, The SEE: *Draussen vor der Tür*

Man Who Had Three Arms, The

Performance/production

Eight critics review Edward Albee's production of his play *The Man Who Had Three Arms*. USA: New York, NY. 1983. 956

Management

Administration

Construction of Guelph Royal Opera House and management under Albert Tavernier. Canada: Guelph, ON. 1893-1895. 117

Legislative planning, advocacy, audience development and support discussed by American Theatre Association officers. USA: New York, NY. 1983. 152

Purdue University study on modern uses of historic theatres and guidelines for management. USA. 1981-1983. 154

How to locate free or low-cost professional assistance in law, finance and management. USA. 1983. 156

Four artistic directors discuss theatre relationship with community. Canada: Regina, SK, Vancouver, BC, Toronto, ON, Calgary, AB. 1983. 553

Lorin Maazel's first season as intendant of Vienna Staatsoper. Austria: Vienna. USA. 1983. 1810

Life and career of opera manager Egon Seefehlner. Austria: Vienna. Germany, West: West Berlin. 1912-1983. 1812

Management and fiscal administration at the Royal Academy of Music. England: London. 1719-1721. 1814

Evaluation of Glynn Ross's tenure as founding general director of Seattle Opera. USA: Seattle, WA. 1964-1983. 1815

Institutions

Frederick Brown and Montreal's doomed Theatre Royal. Canada: Montreal, PQ. 1825-1826. 289

Richard Ouzounian attempts to restore community interest in Manitoba Theatre Centre. Canada: Winnipeg, MB. 1958-1983. 292

Economic and political aspects of several Black theatre groups. USA: New York, NY, Chicago, IL. 1982. 340

Actor-managers with self-serving interests at Shakespeare Memorial National Theatre. UK. 1905-1915. 623

Aspects of the National Theatre and the Royal Shakespeare Company are compared. UK-England. 1960. 627

Artistic directors, policy, development and funding of The Traverse studio theatre. UK-England. 1963. 632

Administration and repertory of Finnish National Opera. Finland: Helsinki. 1983. 1828

Performance spaces

Steps involved in restoring historic theatres. USA. 1983. 396

Career of Oscar Hammerstein I and the theatres he built. USA: New York, NY. 1889-1904. 1760

Performance/production

Charles Burket Rittenhouse as actor, playwright, director, administrator and educator. Canada: Montreal, PQ. 1925-1976. 688

Career of Karl Dönch, opera singer and manager of Vienna's Volksoper. Austria: Vienna. 1915-1983. 1761

Reference materials

Music guide for Austria with names, addresses and other information. Austria. 1983. 14

Licensing papers related to managerial and repertorial changes at London theatres. England: London. 1706-1715. 20

Vocational guidance directed at young people for non-acting careers in theatre. USA. 1983. 43

List of theatre companies, playwriting awards and grants. USA. 1983. 1439

Management SEE ALSO: Administration

Management, stage

Design/technology

Notation of sound effects in relationship to other cues. North America. 1983. 220

Performance/production

Career of director and stage manager Wilam Horzyca. Poland: Warsaw, Lwów, Poznań. 1889-1959. 829

Career of Metropolitan Opera stage manager Stanley Levine. USA: New York, NY. 1949-1982. 1925

Management, top

Administration

Heribert Sasse succeeds Boy Gobert as manager at Staatliche Schauspielbühnen Berlin. Germany, West: West Berlin. 1983. 128

Autobiography of Broadway producer Irene Mayer Selznick. USA. 1910-1983. 161

Interview with the new artistic director and literary advisor for the Iron Theatre (Glasgow). UK-Scotland. 1973-1983. 559

Portrait of Rolf Kutschera, manager of Theater an der Wien. Austria: Vienna. 1961-1983. 1766

Peter Weck, new manager of Theater an der Wien plans to produce first German language production of Andrew Lloyd Webber's *Cats*. Austria: Vienna. 1983. 1767

Interview with Terry McEwen, general director of War Memorial Opera House. Canada: Montreal, PQ. USA: San Francisco, CA. 1983. 1813

Management, top — cont'd

Institutions

Peter Hall's role as artistic director of the National Theatre, including devising the repertory and obtaining funds. UK-England: London. 1973-1983.   636

History of League of Chicago Theatres. USA: Chicago, IL. 1970-1983.   651

Performance/production

Vienna's English Theatre's 20th anniversary production of G.B. Shaw's *Candida*. Austria: Vienna. 1963.   668

25 interviews with Wilam Horzyca as manager of Municipal Theatre in Lwów, published in various periodicals. Poland: Lvov. 1931-1936.
                                                                826

Changes of directors and reviews of performances at the Edinburgh Festival and Lyceum Theatre. UK-Scotland: Edinburgh. 1983.   903

Interview with Steven Thomas, artistic director of Opera Hamilton. Canada: Hamilton, ON. 1983.   1844

Bass Martti Talvela produces Finnish opera at the Opera-festival at Savonlinna Castle. Finland: Savonlinna. 1983.   1856

Manchester City Art Gallery

Portrait of Ira Aldridge as Othello in painting by James Northcote. UK-England: Manchester. USA. 1826.   869

Mandragola, La (Mandrake, The)

String of wooden pearls as a means of nonverbal communication in a production of *Mandragola*. Germany, West: Munich. 1979-1980.
                                                                1528

Plays/librettos/scripts

Views on Lucretia held by Titus Livius and Niccolò Machiavelli. Italy. 1513-1520.   1183

Mandrake, The SEE: Mandragola, La

Manfred

Performance/production

Theories of acting and theatre by controversial director Carmelo Bene. Italy. 1960-1982.   1621

Manhattan Theatre Club (New York, NY)

Jane Martin's *Talking With* at Manhattan Theatre Club, directed by Jon Jory. USA: New York, NY. 1982.   937

Manitoba Theatre Centre (Winnipeg, MB)

Institutions

Richard Ouzounian attempts to restore community interest in Manitoba Theatre Centre. Canada: Winnipeg, MB. 1958-1983.   292

Mann, Emily

Performance/production

Five critics review Emily Mann's production of Kathleen Tolan's play *A Weekend Near Madison*. USA: New York, NY. 1983.   977

Mannerism

Design/technology

Mannerist elements in some set designs for *Hamlet*. UK-England: Stratford-upon-Avon, London. 1948-1976.   1675

Plays/librettos/scripts

Relationship of various arts to Shakespearean production. England. USA. 1590-1981.   1035

Analysis of three tragedies written between Mannerism and the Age of Arcadia. Italy. 1627-1713.   1698

Mannheimer Nationaltheater

Performance/production

Harald Clemens' production of Anton Čechov's *Uncle Vanya* at Nationaltheater. Germany, West: Mannheim. 1983.   777

Mansfield, Richard

Reconstruction of Richard Mansfield's production of *Richard III*. UK-England: London. USA. 1889.   893

Mantegna, Andrea

Design/technology

Methodology for the interpretation of symbolism in Renaissance costume. Italy. 1539.   212

Manuscripts

Performance/production

Opera production textbook. Italy. 1597-1699.   1881

Plays/librettos/scripts

Recently discovered manuscript of Johann Nestroy's *Prinz Friedrich*. Austria. 1833.   1551

Mao, Tse-tung

Performance/production

Theatre before and after Mao Tse-tung. China, People's Republic of. 1949-1956.   414

Maraino, Innocente

Design/technology

Career of Italian designer and architect Innocente Maraino. Poland: Warsaw, Lvov, Slonim. 1767-1799.   221

Marat/Sade

Plays/librettos/scripts

Modern plays set in confining institutions. North America. Europe. 1900-1983.   1200

Marat, Jean-Paul

Performance/production

Contemporary events reflected in staging plays about Jean-Paul Marat's death. France. 1793-1797.   732

Marceau, Marcel

Seven critics review *Marcel Marceau on Broadway*. USA: New York, NY. 1983.   1730

Marcel Marceau on Broadway

Seven critics review *Marcel Marceau on Broadway*. USA: New York, NY. 1983.   1730

Marga, Iris

Autobiography of actress Iris Marga. Argentina. 1945.   664

Maria Rosa

Plays/librettos/scripts

Adaptation of the Angel Guimerà play *Maria Rosa*. Spain. 1894.
                                                                1230

Maria Stuart (Mary Stuart)

Performance/production

Aspects of Friedrich von Schiller's *Mary Stuart* produced at Comédie-Française. France. 1800.   734

Marilyn: An American Fable

Seven critics review Kenny Ortega's production of the musical *Marilyn: An American Fable*. USA: New York, NY. 1983.   1792

Marinetti, Filippo Tommaso

Artistic movements and critical thought that shaped modern directing. Europe. 1914-1940.   715

Plays/librettos/scripts

Luigi Pirandello's earlier plays are considered prologues to *The Giants of the Mountain*. Italy. 1921-1937.   1189

Marionette Studio, The (Chicago, IL)

Design/technology

Lou Bunin memoirs of Meyer Levin's marionettes as ideally cast abstract visual images. USA: Chicago, IL. 1925-1930.   2080

Meyer Levin's marionettes as abstract visual images, influenced by Gordon Craig and Fernand Léger. USA. 1926-1930.   2081

Marionettes SEE ALSO: Classed Entries: PUPPETRY — Marionettes

Medieval theatre — cont'd

Plays/librettos/scripts

List of 94 twentieth century works dealing with Italian sacred drama. Italy. 1300-1983. 1413

Relation to other fields

Comparison of the character of Herod in two Fleury plays. France. England. 1100-1200. 1452

Research/historiography

Advantages and methods of transcribing theatrical documents directly into a computer file. UK. 1983. 89

Medina, Carlos

Performance/production

Tendencies of Bertolt Brecht stage interpretations. Germany, East. USSR. Italy. 1956-1983. 747

Medina, Louisa

Plays/librettos/scripts

Louisa Medina's popular dramatic adaptations of the works of Edward Bulwer-Lytton, Ernest Maltravers and Robert Bird. USA. 1833-1838. 1346

Mei, Lang-fang

Performance/production

Theatre before and after Mao Tse-tung. China, People's Republic of. 1949-1956. 414

Meidal, Björn

Plays/librettos/scripts

Interpretation of August Strindberg's *The Ghost Sonata* in light of contemporary problems. Sweden. 1907-1983. 1269

Mein Leben (My Life)

Italian translation of Kokoschka's autobiography *Mein Leben*, with editorial essay. Austria. 1886-1970. 1636

Meinert, Sylvester

Performance/production

Biography of blind entertainer Sylvester Meinert. USA. 1914-1983. 1996

Meiningen, Saxe SEE: Sachsen-Meiningen, Georg II von

Meinrad, Josef

Performance/production

Portrait of actor Josef Meinrad. Austria: Vienna. 1983. 676

Meistersinger von Nürnberg, Die

Design/technology

Josef Svoboda's scenography of Wagnerian opera. Switzerland. UK-England: London. Czechoslovakia: Prague. 1948-1983. 1823

Plays/librettos/scripts

Pertinence of human characterizations in Wagner's operas. Germany. 1845-1951. 1946

Mejerchol'd, Vsevolod Emil'evič

Design/technology

Comprehensive documented study of Russian Constructivism. USSR. 1917-1940. 278

Institutions

Evolution and theories of Odin Teatret. Sweden. 1964-1979. 621

Performance/production

History of directing. Europe. 1882-1982. 708

Actor Juri Jurjev and director Vsevolod Mejerchol'd at the Aleksandrinskij Theatre (now Academic Drama Theatre of A.S. Pushkin). Russia: St. Petersburg. USSR: Leningrad. 1910-1938. 830

Richard Wagner's influence on modern theatrical conceptions, including those of Vsevolod Mejerchol'd, Evgeni Vachtangov and Jerzy Grotowski. USSR. Poland. Germany. 1813-1983. 991

Role experimental studios played in the formation of the Soviet theatre. USSR: Moscow, Leningrad. 1920-1939. 993

Interweaving of theatrical and cinematographic techniques in Mejerchol'd's staging. USSR. 1915-1927. 997

Plays/librettos/scripts

Collected materials on Eugenio Barba and Odin Teatret. Sweden. 1964-1979. 1258

Relation to other fields

Circus as a staging device for a political satire. USSR. Germany. Italy. 1914-1930. 1668

Theory/criticism

Reformers on their theories. Europe. 1870-1910. 98

Melancólico, El (Melancholic, The)

Plays/librettos/scripts

Authorship and dating of *The Melancholic* and *This Is Business*. Spain. 1623. 1241

Melendres, Jaume

Performance/production

Staging of Eugène Labiche's plays in Catalonia. Spain. France. 1967-1982. 1532

Mélite

Plays/librettos/scripts

Love, freedom and the emergence of the generous hero in Pierre Corneille's early plays. France. 1629-1640. 1105

Aesthetic continuity in Pierre Corneille's movement from comedy to tragedy. France. 1606-1684. 1112

Psychological foundations of Pierre Corneille's dramatic *oeuvre* in *Mélite*. France. 1606-1684. 1564

Unhappy rival in Pierre Corneille's early comedies. France. 1606-1684. 1568

Pierre Corneille's early comedies as variations in comic form. France. 1606-1684. 1570

Essays on and a bibliographical guide to Pierre Corneille's comedies. France. 1606-1684. 1572

Mellors, Arthur

Performance/production

Circus life and performance based on the memoirs of acrobat Leonora Whiteley. Greece: Athens. 1880-1899. 2011

Melodrama

Collection of illustrations of melodramas in performance. France: Paris. 1800-1900. 735

Plays/librettos/scripts

Playwrights and dramatic forms influencing Eugene O'Neill's *The Calms of Capricorn*. Europe. USA. 1953. 1088

Analysis of character and structure in G.B. Shaw's *The Devil's Disciple*. UK-England. USA. 1897-1983. 1293

Developments of Irish melodrama and its influence on later writers. UK-Ireland: Dublin. 1860-1905. 1338

Louisa Medina's popular dramatic adaptations of the works of Edward Bulwer-Lytton, Ernest Maltravers and Robert Bird. USA. 1833-1838. 1346

Stage incarnations of the characters in Aleksej Nikolajevič Arbuzov's plays. USSR. 1930-1970. 1391

Melville, Herman

American influence of Melville's short story *Cock-A-Doodle Doo!* on O'Casey's play. UK-Ireland. USA. 1949. 1333

Melville, Johnny

Institutions

Street theatre production of Århus theater akademi in collaboration with Jordcirkus and Johnny Melville. Denmark: Århus. 1982. 298

Memories of Circus, Variety, etc. as I Knew it

Performance/production

Circus life and performance based on the memoirs of acrobat Leonora Whiteley. Greece: Athens. 1880-1899. 2011

Menander

Plays/librettos/scripts

Comparison of the misanthrope in *Dýskolos, Timon of Athens* and *Le Misanthrope*. Greece. England. France. 317 B.C.-1666 A.D. 1155

Menander — cont'd

Comparison of Greek and Roman comedy as reflected in works of Menander and Terence and in revivals by Italian humanists. Greece. Roman Empire. 343 B.C.-1400 A.D.　　　　1582

Menéndez y Pelayo, Marcelino

Dating and authorship of *Los hechos de Garcilaso*. Spain. 1573. 1231

Mennicken, Rainer

Institutions

Interviews with personnel of Freiburg theatres on obtaining subsidies and other aspects of administration. Germany, West: Freiburg. 1911-1983.　　　　607

Menteur, Le (Liar, The)

Plays/librettos/scripts

Discursive authority in Pierre Corneille's *Le Menteur*. France. 1606-1684.　　　　1571

Essays on and a bibliographical guide to Pierre Corneille's comedies. France. 1606-1684.　　　　1572

Merchant of Venice, The

Performance/production

Problems of antisemitism in staging *The Merchant of Venice*. Israel. 1936-1980.　　　　663

Questionable chronology results from performances by English officers. Belgium: Maastricht. 1703.　　　　679

Review of four Shakespeare productions. Germany, East: Meiningen, Zwickau, Leipzig. 1983.　　　　746

Theodore Komisarjevsky's productions of Shakespeare's plays at Stratford-upon-Avon. UK-England: Stratford-upon-Avon. 1932-1939.　　　　864

Decisions needed in staging plays with inherent sexist or racist themes. USA. 1980-1983.　　　　904

Federal Theatre Project's often innovative approach to staging Shakespeare's plays. USA. 1930-1939.　　　　978

Plays/librettos/scripts

Animal nature and eating habits of characters in Shakespeare's plays. England. 1590-1613.　　　　1058

Mercury Theatre (Toronto, ON)

Institutions

Survey of alternative theatres. Canada: Toronto, ON. 1979-1983. 296

Meredith, Sylvia

Performance/production

Sylvia Meredith discusses her work as actress and puppeteer. USA. 1938-1983.　　　　2062

Mérida Roman Theatre (Mérida)

Exhibit to commemorate Margarita Xirgu's debut as Medea. Spain: Mérida. 1932-1933.　　　　1683

Merkurjev, V.V.

Articles discussing the work of individual actors at the Academic Drama Theatre of A.S. Puškin. USSR: Leningrad. 1910-1970.　　　987

Merlin

Eight critics review Ivan Reitman's production of the musical *Merlin*. USA: New York, NY. 1983.　　　　1802

Merope

Plays/librettos/scripts

Analysis of three tragedies written between Mannerism and the Age of Arcadia. Italy. 1627-1713.　　　　1698

Merry Wives of Windsor, The

Performance/production

Theodore Komisarjevsky's productions of Shakespeare's plays at Stratford-upon-Avon. UK-England: Stratford-upon-Avon. 1932-1939.　　　　864

Messel, Oliver

Design/technology

Articles on designer Oliver Messel. UK-England. 1904-1978.　　　231

Mestske Divadlo

Performance/production

Guest performance in Prague of eminent Polish actors Juliusz Osterwa and Stanisława Lubicz-Sarnowska from Warsaw. Czechoslovakia: Prague. Poland. 1920-1935.　　　　693

Metacriticism

Plays/librettos/scripts

Metacritical analysis of Calderón's plays applying criteria devised for Lope de Vega. Spain. 1608-1681.　　　　1238

Metadrama

Performance/production

Self-reflexivity of Helsinki avant-garde theatre. Finland: Helsinki. 1978-1983.　　　　1616

Plays/librettos/scripts

Irony and metadrama in Christopher Marlowe's plays. England. 1564-1593.　　　　1044

Metadramatic analysis of *Hamlet*. England. 1600-1601.　　　1687

Metamorphoses

Use of and variations on Ovidian metamorphosis in *The Taming of the Shrew*. England. 1592-1603.　　　　1065

Metaphysical theatre

Relation to other fields

Revival of religious and metaphysical theatre, church operas and mystery plays. Austria. 1983.　　　　52

Metastasio, Pietro

Plays/librettos/scripts

Stage notations in Metastasio's libretti. Italy. 1698-1782.　　　1960

Reference materials

Catalogue of the exhibition on scenery, architecture, dance, opera and public theatres during Pietro Metastasio's life. Italy: Rome. 1698-1782.　　　　1968

Methodology

Performance spaces

Interpretation of Johannes De Witt's drawing of the Swan theatre. England. 1596.　　　　365

Performance/production

Study of the Italian actor Luigi Vestri applying Mario Apollonio's historiographic methodology. Italy. 1781-1841.　　　　802

Relation to other fields

Introduction to essay collection *The Sociology of Theatre*. Europe. North America. 1983.　　　　1448

Research/historiography

Method for using models of scenery as study documents. Discussed at SIBMAS. Europe. North America. 1982.　　　　83

Records of Early English Drama (REED) project uses new type-setting and editing systems. UK. 1983.　　　　88

Advantages and methods of transcribing theatrical documents directly into a computer file. UK. 1983.　　　　89

Discussion of the *Inventory of Dramatic Behavior Adapted for Group Observation*. USA. 1980.　　　　91

Categories devised to measure young people's responses to children's theatre productions. USA. 1983.　　　　1474

Metonymy

Theory/criticism

Study of genesis, development, structural components and consequences of theatre-drama performed by the Black workers. South Africa, Republic of. 1981-1983.　　　　1673

Metropol Theater (East Berlin)

Performance/production

Two productions of *A Midsummer Night's Dream*. Germany, East: East Berlin. 1975-1982.　　　　1526

Midbøes, Hans

Performance/production

Productions of Henrik Ibsen's *Peer Gynt* by Hans Midbøes. Norway. 1976-1980. 823

Middle Ages, The

Seven critics review David Trainer's production of A.R. Gurney, Jr.'s play *The Middle Ages*. USA: New York, NY. 1983. 1542

Middleton, Thomas

List of productions of plays from English Renaissance drama with brief reviews. North America. Europe. 1982-1983. 822

Plays/librettos/scripts

Relationship between Jacobean tragedy and interpolated masque. England. 1600-1625. 1691

Midsummer Night's Dream, A

Performance/production

List and short reviews of Shakespearean productions. Germany, East. 1981. 749

Jürgen Gosch production of *A Midsummer Night's Dream* at the Köln Schauspielhaus. Germany, West: Cologne. 1983. 780

Shakespearean productions by Compagnia del Collettivo/Teatro Due, Theater an der Ruhr (Hamburg) and Schaubühne (West Berlin). Italy: Parma. Germany, West: West Berlin, Hamm. 1983. 810

Two productions of *A Midsummer Night's Dream*. Germany, East: East Berlin. 1975-1982. 1526

Plays/librettos/scripts

History of criticism and interpretation of Shakespeare's *A Midsummer Night's Dream*. Germany. 1700-1982. 1142

A Midsummer Night's Dream as a parody of Edmund Spenser's *The Teares of the Muses*. England. 1595. 1556

Mielziner, Jo

Design/technology

Supplementary materials to exhibit of Jo Mielziner's works. USA. 1928-1960. 233

Migliara, Giovanni

Scene designers and scenery at Teatro alla Scala in Neoclassic period. Italy: Milan. 1778-1832. 1821

Military theatre

Institutions

Organization, people and theatres involved in the Army Theatre Arts Association. USA: Fort Polk, LA. 1960-1983. 336

Performance/production

Actors and companies entertaining Canadian troops during World War I. Canada. UK. France. 1914-1918. 1984

Miller, Arthur

Chinese version of *Death of a Salesman* directed by the author. China, People's Republic of: Beijing. 1983. 690

Critical essays on interpretations of *Death of a Salesman*. USA. 1949-1983. 939

Nine critics review Arvin Brown's production of Arthur Miller's play *A View from the Bridge*. USA: New York, NY. 1983. 969

Plays/librettos/scripts

Compilation of comments by various artists on Tennessee Williams. USA. 1911-1983. 1342

Essays on the trends of the Jewish-American theatre and its personalities. USA. 1900-1983. 1353

Relation to other fields

Thematic study of work ethic in American drama. USA. 1920-1969. 1465

Miller, Nancy

Theory/criticism

Significance of gender in feminist criticism with reference to historical materialism, deconstruction and phenomenon of cross-dressing in theatre. USA. France. UK-England. 1983. 1520

Millerd, Bill

Administration

Four artistic directors discuss theatre relationship with community. Canada: Regina, SK, Vancouver, BC, Toronto, ON, Calgary, AB. 1983. 553

Mime

Institutions

Educational project of Intriplicate Mime Company using puppets. UK. 1977-1983. 2043

Performance/production

Analysis of production elements in the Catalan theatre. Spain: Barcelona. 1983. 838

Enactment and narration as particularly appropriate methods of dramatization. USA. 1968-1980. 906

Training

Training manual for performers. 1982. 492

Mime SEE ALSO: Classed Entries: MIME

Mimesis

Plays/librettos/scripts

Discussion of Miguel de Cervantes' *The Farce of the Divorce Judge* in view of Aristotelian *mimesis*. Spain. 1547-1616. 1248

Minetti, Bernhard

Performance/production

Interview with and influences on actor Bernhard Minetti, including production of *Faust*. Germany, East: East Berlin. 1982-1983. 751

Minna von Barnhelm (Minna of Barnhelm)

Plays/librettos/scripts

Dramatic structure of Gotthold Ephraim Lessing's *Minna of Barnhelm* represents cultural atmosphere of the time. Germany. 1767. 1138

Minnelli, Liza

Performance/production

Biography of Liza Minnelli. USA. 1946-1983. 1790

Minnelli, Vincente

Design/technology

Vincente Minnelli's pre-Hollywood years as Broadway designer. USA: Hollywood, CA, New York, NY. 1931-1939. 1769

Minstrels

Performance/production

Social status and role of minstrels. Europe. 1100-1500. 1986

Minstrelsy

Authentic expression in Black theatre and film is contrasted with stereotypical Black portrayals by white authors and performers. USA: New York, NY. 1890-1930. 983

Reference materials

Reference guide to popular entertainments. USA. 1840. 1998

Miracle du pain doré, Le (Miracle of the Glazed Bread, The)

Performance/production

Jacques Copeau remembered by his granddaughter, actress Catherine Dasté. France: Pernand. 1940-1949. 727

Miracle plays

Plays/librettos/scripts

Sources and analogues of a lost miracle play. England: Durham. 1200-1500. 1084

Religious rites and ideology of medieval urban societies as seen in Corpus Christi plays. England. 1300-1499. 2106

Misanthrope, Le

Institutions

Productions of the Théâtre National of Strasbourg. France: Strasbourg. 1975-1980. 595

Molière — cont'd

Satire addressed against both sexes in Molière's comedies. France. 1642-1673.   1576

Molière's intended meaning in *The Learned Ladies*. France. 1672.   1577

Molina, Tirso de

Authorship and dating of *The Melancholic* and *This Is Business*. Spain. 1623.   1241

Moll, Kurt

Performance/production

Bass Kurt Moll speaks about his career and role in *Der Rosenkavalier*. Germany, West. 1950-1983.   1874

Mon Ismen (My Ismenia)

Staging of Eugène Labiche's plays in Catalonia. Spain. France. 1967-1982.   1532

Monk, Meredith

Description and analysis of Ping Chong's work. USA. 1972-1983.   1752

Monodrama

Careers of solo performers Beatrice Herford, Cissie Loftus and Dorothy Sands. USA. 1900-1920.   942

History and problems of monodrama. USA. 1982.   950

Plays/librettos/scripts

Description of *thullal*, a form of comedy, created by Kunchan Nambiar, and performed by a single actor. India: Kerala. 1700-1799.   1583

Relation to other fields

Essays on five main concerns of oral interpretation: language, culture, teaching, theory and entertainment. Europe. North America. 499 B.C.-1980 A.D.   53

Montgomery, Elizabeth

Design/technology

History and description of the Motley Theatre and Costume Arts Collection. Discussed at SIBMAS. USA: Urbana, IL. 1982.   247

Moore, Tom

Performance/production

Interview with director Tom Moore. USA. 1983.   924

Eight critics review Tom Moore's production of Marsha Norman's play *'Night Mother*. USA: New York, NY. 1983.   971

Moose Murders

Six critics review John Roach's production of Arthur Bicknell's play *Moose Murders*. USA: New York, NY. 1983.   968

Morality plays

Plays/librettos/scripts

Determining factor of the demonstrative mode of Morality play characters. England. 1300-1550.   1032

The condemnation of pleasure dominated by lust and gluttony in morality plays. France. 1400-1499.   1106

Moratín, Leandro Fernández de

Development of older, comic woman as character type. Spain: Madrid. 1780-1825.   1234

Moreno, Zerka

Relation to other fields

Zerka Moreno's work explains dialectics of human interaction. USA. 1917-1983.   1464

Technique of 'symbolical mediation' applied by Zerka Moreno can be found in Luigi Pirandello's drama. USA. Italy. 1916-1983. 1468

Experience of neurotic conflict in staging of psychodrama. Italy. 1980.   1659

Zerka Moreno's psychodrama in Italy. USA: New York, NY. Italy: Rome. 1960-1983.   1666

Morgan Library (New York, NY)

Design/technology

Description of 'Four Centuries of Opera' exhibition. USA: New York, NY. 1583-1983.   1825

Morir del todo (To Die Totally)

Plays/librettos/scripts

Two reports about playwright Paco Ignacio Taibo and his play *Morir del todo*. Spain. Mexico. 1958-1973.   1226

Morris dancing

Administration

Accounts of payment to assorted entertainers performing for Lord Berkeley. England: Coventry. 1593-1605.   122

Morsa, La (Morse, The)

Plays/librettos/scripts

Productions of Luigi Pirandello's early work contrasted with later ones. Italy. 1898-1917.   1180

Moscow Art Theatre SEE: Moskovskij Chudožestvennyj Akedemičeskij Teat'r

Moscow is Burning SEE: Moskva gorit

Mosheim, Grete

Plays/librettos/scripts

Compilation of comments by various artists on Tennessee Williams. USA. 1911-1983.   1342

Moskovskij Chudožestvennyj Akademičeskij Teat'r (Moscow Art Theatre)

Performance/production

Stanislavskij's system in the USA and the tour by the Moscow Art Theatre. USA. USSR. 1910-1959.   923

Overview of the Konstantin Stanislavskij system. USSR. Russia. 1863-1938.   988

Role experimental studios played in the formation of the Soviet theatre. USSR: Moscow, Leningrad. 1920-1939.   993

Political censorship and Soviet productions of *Hamlet*. USSR. 1930.   995

Reconstruction of Edward Gordon Craig's production of *Hamlet* at Moscow Art Theatre. Russia: Moscow. 1908-1912.   1682

Konstantin Stanislavskij's stage adaptation of Shakespeare's *Othello* for the Moscow Art Theatre. USSR: Moscow. 1929-1930. 1685

Theory/criticism

Effect of social conditions on performance styles. USA. Greece. 499 B.C.-1983 A.D.   1517

Moskva gorit (Moscow is Burning)

Relation to other fields

Circus as a staging device for a political satire. USSR. Germany. Italy. 1914-1930.   1668

Motley designers

Design/technology

SIBMAS papers on collections of designs and scenography. Europe. North America. 1982.   183

History and description of the Motley Theatre and Costume Arts Collection. Discussed at SIBMAS. USA: Urbana, IL. 1982.   247

Mouches, Les (Flies, The)

Performance/production

Productions of *The Flies* at Düsseldorfer Schauspielhaus and Hebbeltheater Berlin. Germany, West: Düsseldorf, West Berlin. 1947-1948.   785

Moussorgsky, Modeste SEE: Mussorgskij, Modest Pavlovič

Mozart, Wolfgang Amadeus

Performance spaces

History and architecture of Teatro Scientifico and Palazzo Accademico. Italy: Mantua. 1767-1982.   379

Performance/production

Originators of female roles in operas by Wolfgang Amadeus Mozart. Austria. 1777-1791.   1843

Photographs, cast lists, synopsis and discography of Metropolitan Opera production of *Idomeneo*. USA: New York, NY. 1983.   1920

Plays/librettos/scripts

Peter Shaffer's revision of *Amadeus*. UK-England: London. USA: New York, NY. 1979-1980.   1290

Evaluation of Wolfgang Amadeus Mozart's opera *Idomeneo*. Austria: Munich. 1780-1781.   1933

Leporello as alter ego of protagonist in *Don Giovanni*. Italy. 1787.   1957

Mrs. Warren's Profession

Performance/production

Director's analysis of Shaw's *Mrs. Warren's Profession*. UK-England. 1923.   871

Much Ado About Nothing

Beerbohm Tree's conceptual and directorial approach to staging Shakespeare. UK-England: London. 1905-1911.   863

Mulgrave Road Co-op Theatre (Nova Scotia)

Regional theatre production of *The Lost Salt Gift of Blood* by Alistair MacLeod. Canada. 1981-1983.   685

Müller, Heiner

Opening night review and playtext of Heiner Müller's *Wrecked Shore Medeamaterial Landscape with Argonauts*. Germany, West: Bochum. 1983.   767

Dispute about Heiner Müller's production of *Macbeth*. Germany, East: East Berlin. 1971-1982.   1678

Plays/librettos/scripts

Heiner Müller continues the Brechtian tradition in political drama. Germany, East. 1960-1982.   1144

Treatment of power by German playwrights and Volker Braun's *Dmitri*. Germany, West: Karlsruhe. 1983.   1154

Theory/criticism

Influence of Bertolt Brecht's methods on playwright Heiner Müller and concept of today's theatre. Germany, East. 1983.   1504

Mummers' plays

Plays/librettos/scripts

Plot, structure and action in John Arden's *Serjeant Musgrave's Dance*. UK-England. 1959.   1288

Munch, Edvard

Design/technology

Edvard Munch's set designs for plays by Henrik Ibsen. Norway. 1892-1909.   580

Münchener Festspiele

Plays/librettos/scripts

Theatrical effect preserved in operatic adaptations of Werner Egk's *Peer Gynt* and Aribert Reimann's *King Lear* at the Münchener Festspiele. Germany, West: Munich. 1982.   1953

Münchener Kammerspiele

Performance/production

Brief comments on and German translation of Edward Bond's *Summer*. Germany, West: Munich. 1983.   764

Peter Zadek's production of *The Master Builder* at the Residenztheater. Germany, West: Munich. 1983.   772

Munich Opera Festival SEE: Münchener Festspieler

Municipal Theatre of Cracow SEE: Teatru Miejskiego (Cracow)

Municipal Theatre of Lwów SEE: Teatru Miejskiego (Lwów)

Municipal theatres

Administration

Financial situation of municipal theatres. Germany, West. 1982.   134

Institutions

Current manager Taisto-Bertil Orsmaa, and history of Turku Municipal Theatre. Finland: Turku. 1946-1983.   303

Articles on Kajaani City Theatre. Finland: Kajaani. 1983.   590

Vaasa City Theatre's season in review. Finland: Vaasa. 1983.   591

Building and performances at Lahti City Theatre. Finland: Lahti. 1983.   592

Imatra theatre's 1983-1984 season. Finland: Imatra. 1983.   593

Jyväskylä City Theatre's 1983-1984 season. Finland: Jyväskylä. 1983.   594

Financial situation of Städtische Bühnen Dortmund. Germany, West: Dortmund. 1970-1982.   604

New season's productions at the Basel Stadttheater. Switzerland: Basel. 1983.   622

Performance spaces

Architecture of Municipal Theatre at Forlimpopoli. Italy: Forlimpopoli. 1600-1982.   380

Construction, renovation and technical equipment of historic theatre buildings. Italy: Modena, Reggio Emilia, Parma. 1588-1985.   382

Engravings of the Municipal Theatre of Girona. Spain: Girona. 1769-1860.   390

Cultural history and architectural design of Europe's oldest municipal theatre. Yugoslavia: Hvar. 1612-1983.   411

Performance/production

25 interviews with Wilam Horzyca as manager of Municipal Theatre in Lwów, published in various periodicals. Poland: Lvov. 1931-1936.   826

Plays/librettos/scripts

Censorship involving Jerzy Hulewicz' play *Aruna*, produced at Municipal Theatre of Cracow. Poland: Kraków. 1925.   1217

Munn, Tom

Design/technology

Tom Munn, lighting director of San Francisco Opera Company. USA: San Francisco, CA. 1975-1983.   1824

Murderer Hope of Womankind

Plays/librettos/scripts

Analysis of Oskar Kokoschka's theory through *Murderer Hope of Womankind*. Austria: Vienna. 1904-1912.   1635

Muriccioli, un fico, un uccellino, I (Low Walls, a Fig-tree, a Birdie, The)

Some lesser known facts about Luigi Pirandello's plays and other writings. Italy. 1884-1935.   1192

Musatti, Cesare

Relation to other fields

Cesare Musatti's work with psychodrama. Italy. 1960.   1457

Museo Teatrale alla Scala SEE: Teatro alla Scala

Museums

Design/technology

Cataloguing work done since 1975 at Drottningholm Theatre Museum. Sweden: Drottningholm, Gripsholm. 1766-1800.   222

Costumes of 'La Belle Epoque' at the Metropolitan Museum of Art. USA: New York, NY. 1870-1910.   260

Remarks by scientific advisor to Serbian Museum of Theatrical Art on document collection. Discussed at SIBMAS. Yugoslavia: Belgrade. 1982.   279

Reference materials

Catalogue of Galliari's scene designs owned by Museo Teatrale alla Scala. Italy: Milan. 1778-1823.   1969

Music

Administration

Accounts of payment to assorted entertainers performing for Lord Berkeley. England: Coventry. 1593-1605. 122

Impact of government funding on the arts. USA. 1965-1982. 159

Promotional campaigns for performing arts institutions. USA. 1983. 160

Effect of different kinds of financial support on artists. USA. 1950-1982. 163

Audience

Audience development survey. USA: Atlanta, GA, Baton Rouge, LA, Columbia, SC, Memphis, TN. 1983. 170

Sociological studies suggest that democratization of the arts has not taken place. USA. 1830-1982. 173

Design/technology

Lighting design for touring concerts. USA. 1979-1983. 248

Model for musical design training. USA. 1982. 256

Use of film and theatrical techniques in rock concert. USA. 1983. 1706

Institutions

Documentation on Karlsplatz festival, part of Wiener Festwochen. Austria: Vienna. 1983. 288

Performance/production

Collection of essays on performing arts. India. 431

Seven basic rules for writing songs for children's theatre. USA. 1983. 460

Typical movement, music, costumes, performers and historic influences in *odori* and *mai* dance. Japan. 900-1900. 544

Henry Carey's missing music for *tableaux vivant* in the production of *Hamlet* inspired by funeral services for the Duke of Buckingham. England: London. 1736. 698

Analysis of C.V. Stanford's incidental music for *Becket*. UK-England: London. 1893. 872

Review of *Shaw's Music: The Complete Musical Criticism* (1981) discusses Shaw's career as critic. UK-England. 1876-1897. 897

Production journal of *King Lear*. Canada: Stratford, ON. 1979. 1676

Mixing popular entertaining, particularly rock music, with performance art. UK-England. 1970-1980. 1749

Critical assessment of Kurt Weill's music and his biography. Germany. USA. 1900-1950. 1762

Portrait and interview with theatre composer Heiner Goebbels. Germany, West. 1983. 1763

Composer Sylvano Bussotti's memoirs and essays on musical theatre. Italy. 1978-1981. 1764

Interview with and influences on postmodern composer Mestres Quaderny. Spain. 1945-1955. 1775

Biography of Broadway and film songwriter Vincent Youmans. USA. 1898-1946. 1780

History of Broadway musical theatre with an extensive annotated discography. USA: New York, NY. 1800-1983. 1789

Harold Prince's production of Giacomo Puccini's *Turandot* at Vienna's Staatsoper. Austria: Vienna. 1983. 1839

Recent productions of operas by Alexander von Zemlinsky. Austria: Vienna. 1983. 1842

Conductor John Eliot Gardiner discusses baroque opera. England. 1597-1759. 1849

Illustrated biographical survey of 37 major opera personalities. Europe. North America. 1945-1983. 1853

Richard Wagner's works, reception and influence. France. 1841-1983. 1859

Social status and role of minstrels. Europe. 1100-1500. 1986

Study of revue songs by Irving Berlin, George Gershwin and Cole Porter in their theatrical contexts. USA: New York, NY. 1910-1937. 2032

Plays/librettos/scripts

Relationship of various arts to Shakespearean production. England. USA. 1590-1981. 1035

Anti-war themes in Sean O'Casey's ballads. UK-Ireland: Dublin. 1916-1918. 1319

Influence on Brecht of Sean O'Casey's use of songs to overcome the boundaries of illusion in his drama. UK-Ireland: Dublin. 1923-1926. 1325

Relation between couplet and parody as exemplified in Johann Nestroy' songs. Austria. 1833-1862. 1546

Characterization through music in Richard Strauss' *Arabella*. Austria: Vienna. 1927-1929. 1932

Personal and professional relationship of Georges Bizet and Charles Gounod. France: Paris. 1856-1875. 1937

Reference materials

Bibliography of performing arts periodicals. 1982. 11

Music guide for Austria with names, addresses and other information. Austria. 1983. 14

Biographies of theatre personalities. England: London. 1660-1800. 19

Vocational guidance directed at young people for non-acting careers in theatre. USA. 1983. 43

Catalogue of exhibition on Giuseppe Sarti, composer and man of the theatre. Italy. 1729-1802. 1765

Theory/criticism

Systematic, analytic examination of sociology of performing arts. Europe. North America. 1983. 97

Nature and history of *nō* theatre. Japan. 1300-1980. 549

Phenomenological theory of performing arts. USA. 1982. 1514

Music Box Theatre (New York, NY)

Performance/production

Seven critics review Carroll O'Connor's production of George Sibbald's play *Brothers*. USA: New York, NY. 1983. 985

Music hall

Interview with theatre and music hall actress Esperanza Roy. Spain. 1936-1983. 442

Chronology of Black entertainers associated with 'Louisiana troupes'. Europe. 1901-1916. 2028

History of *tableaux vivants*, with emphasis on work of Edward Kilanyi. USA: New York, NY. 1831-1899. 2030

New vaudevillians use established music hall forms for expression. USA: New York, NY. 1980. 2033

Music hall SEE ALSO: Classed Entries: POPULAR ENTERTAINMENT — Variety acts

Music SEE: *Musik*

Music-drama

Design/technology

Influence of stage design on music-drama. Yugoslavia: Belgrade. 1980. 280

Plays/librettos/scripts

Aspects of liturgical drama cause it to be both ritual and theatre. France. 1100-1200. 1101

Music-drama SEE ALSO: Classed Entries: MUSIC-DRAMA

Musical theatre

Audience

Audience development survey. USA: Atlanta, GA, Baton Rouge, LA, Columbia, SC, Memphis, TN. 1983. 170

Design/technology

Vincente Minnelli's pre-Hollywood years as Broadway designer. USA: Hollywood, CA, New York, NY. 1931-1939. 1769

Performance spaces

History of West 42nd Street theatres. USA: New York, NY. 1893-1944. 400

Performance/production

Actress Shelley Bruce's struggle with childhood leukemia. USA. 1964. 914

Autobiography of actress Shirley MacLaine. USA. 1934-1983. 943

Musical theatre – cont'd

Authentic expression in Black theatre and film is contrasted with stereotypical Black portrayals by white authors and performers. USA: New York, NY. 1890-1930.   983

Composer Sylvano Bussotti's memoirs and essays on musical theatre. Italy. 1978-1981.   1764

Account of a production of the musical *In Dahomey*. UK-England: London. 1903-1904.   1776

Five critics review Tony Tanner's production of the musical *Preppies*. USA: New York, NY. 1983.   1779

George Balanchine's contribution to dance in musical theatre. USA: New York, NY. 1929-1962.   1787

Six critics review Robert Drivas' production of Peggy Lee's play *Peg*. USA: New York, NY. 1983.   1794

Eight critics review Ivan Reitman's production of the musical *Merlin*. USA: New York, NY. 1983.   1802

Brief biography and interview with Cab Calloway. USA: White Plains, NY, Hollywood, CA. 1930-1983.   1993

Interaction of technology and popular entertainment. USA. 1900-1982.   1995

Chronology of Black entertainers associated with 'Louisiana troupes'. Europe. 1901-1916.   2028

Study of revue songs by Irving Berlin, George Gershwin and Cole Porter in their theatrical contexts. USA: New York, NY. 1910-1937.   2032

Plays/librettos/scripts

Comprehensive study of Neil Simon's plays, screenplays and musical comedies. USA. 1927-1981.   488

Reference materials

Cast listings and other information on 19 productions mounted at Charlottetown Festival. Canada: Charlottetown, PE. 1965-1982.   1399

Guide to shows that closed before coming to Broadway. USA. 1900-1982.   1438

Relation to other fields

Revival of religious and metaphysical theatre, church operas and mystery plays. Austria. 1983.   52

Musical theatre SEE ALSO: Classed Entries: MUSIC DRAMA – Musical theatre

Musicians SEE: Music

Musik (Music)

Performance/production

Analysis of Mario Missiroli's productions of Jean Genet's *The Maids* and Frank Wedekind's *Music*. Italy. 1980.   796

Musiktheater im Revier (Gelsenkirchen)

Performance spaces

Design, construction and partitions of the Musiktheater im Revier. Germany, West: Gelsenkirchen. 1962-1983.   375

Musorsky, Modeste SEE: Mussorgskij, Modest Pavlovič

Musset, Alfred de

Reference materials

Chronological reference guide to works on and about Alfred de Musset. France. 1830-1980.   1408

Mussolini, Benito

Plays/librettos/scripts

Analysis of Giovacchino Forzano's play *Cesare*. Italy. 1939.   1173

Mussorgskij, Modest Pavlovič

Performance/production

Photographs, cast lists, synopsis and discography of Metropolitan Opera production of *Boris Godunov*. USA: New York, NY. 1983.   1891

Boris Christoff, bass, speaks of his career and art. USA: New York, NY. 1947-1983.   1924

Konstantin Stanislavskij's training of opera singers. USSR. 1918-1935.   1929

Muto di Saint Malo, Il (Mute of Saint Malo, The)

History of puppets and puppet-masters. Italy: Bologna. 1800-1923.   2053

Mutran, Khali

Plays/librettos/scripts

Shakespeare's knowledge of Arab world and influence on later regional writers. England. Arabia. 1606-1981.   1075

Mutter Courage (Mother Courage)

Institutions

Bertolt Brecht's return to Deutsches Theater and production of *Mother Courage* with Berliner Ensemble. Germany, East: East Berlin. 1949.   601

Plays/librettos/scripts

Title character of *Mother Courage* is contrasted with similar figure in Jürgen Gross' drama *Memorial*. Germany, East. 1980.   1145

Mutter Courage und ihre Kinder (Mother Courage and Her Children)

Performance/production

Relationship between Bertolt Brecht and Asian theatre. Asia. Germany. 1925-1981.   665

Muzej pozorišne umetnosti (Serbian Museum of Theatrical Art, Belgrade)

Design/technology

Remarks by scientific advisor to Serbian Museum of Theatrical Art on document collection. Discussed at SIBMAS. Yugoslavia: Belgrade. 1982.   279

Muzio, Claudia

Reference materials

Annotated selections of photographs taken by Herman Mishkin of Metropolitan Opera singers. USA: New York, NY. 1910-1932.   1971

My One and Only

Administration

Difficulties of getting some plays on Broadway. USA: New York, NY. 1982-1983.   565

Performance/production

Production, casts and review of musical *My One and Only*. USA: New York, NY. 1971-1983.   1791

Ten critics review *My One and Only*, staged by Thommie Walsh and Tommy Tune. USA: New York, NY. 1983.   1808

Mystery Bouffe (by Dario Fo) SEE: *Mistero Buffo*

Mystery Bouffe (by Majakovskij) SEE: *Misterija Buff*

Mystery plays

Design/technology

Puppets and design concept for production of *The Second Shepherds Play*. USA: Lincoln, NE. 1983.   2039

Performance/production

Review of contemporary three-day performance of the Chester plays. Canada: Toronto, ON. 1983.   684

Review of the Chester cycle performed in Toronto, May 1983. Canada: Toronto, ON. 1983.   687

Men acting in women's roles, particularly in the Chester cycle's *Purification*. England: Chester. 1300-1550.   702

Review of the Chester plays performed in Chester, June 1983. England: Chester. 1983.   703

Review of the Chester cycle performed in a 1550's design. UK: Leeds. England: Chester. 1550-1983.   851

Plays/librettos/scripts

Possible authorship of a lost Chester Corpus Christi play. England: Chester. 1268-1375.   1037

Mystery plays — cont'd

Possible meanings of characterization in the Mystery plays. England. 1200-1550. 1057

York Creed plays may not have been confiscated by the ecclesiastical authorities. England: York. 1420-1580. 1081

Relation to other fields

Revival of religious and metaphysical theatre, church operas and mystery plays. Austria. 1983. 52

Mystery, The SEE: *Mistero, Il*

Nakano, Jack

Audience

Audience development programs for young people. UK-England. USA: Santa Barbara, CA. 1980. 169

Nambiar, Kunchan

Plays/librettos/scripts

Description of *thullal*, a form of comedy, created by Kunchan Nambiar, and performed by a single actor. India: Kerala. 1700-1799. 1583

Nang Yai

Performance/production

State of puppetry in Thailand from perspective of Swedish cultural delegation. Thailand. 1983. 2091

Nannie's Night Out

Plays/librettos/scripts

Influence on Brecht of Sean O'Casey's use of songs to overcome the boundaries of illusion in his drama. UK-Ireland: Dublin. 1923-1926. 1325

Napier, John

Design/technology

Influence of the designers on staging styles. UK. 1958-1983. 226

Scenic practices of various designers. UK. 1960-1983. 227

Interviews with the designers of *Cats*. USA: New York, NY. UK-England: London. 1983. 1770

Napoli, Jeanne

Performance/production

Seven critics review Kenny Ortega's production of the musical *Marilyn: An American Fable*. USA: New York, NY. 1983. 1792

Nathan der Weise (Nathan the Wise)

Gotthold Ephraim Lessing's *Nathan the Wise* at Deutsches Theater Berlin, directed by Fritz Wisten. Germany, East: East Berlin. 1945. 756

Nathan, George Jean

Theory/criticism

Approach and impact of George Jean Nathan's criticism. USA: New York, NY. 1909-1922. 115

National Arts Center (Ottawa, ON)

Reference materials

Description of the Stage Design Collection of National Arts Center. Canada: Ottawa, ON. 1969-1982. 16

National Endowment for the Arts (NEA)

Administration

Debate on federal arts subsidies. USA. 1943-1965. 157

Relation to other fields

American Theatre Association statement of policy on theatre in elementary education. USA. 1983. 71

National Ethiopian Art Theatre (and School) (New York, NY)

Institutions

Harlem Little Theatre movement started to produce plays by, with, for and about Blacks. USA: New York, NY. 1915-1934. 653

National Health, The

Plays/librettos/scripts

Modern plays set in confining institutions. North America. Europe. 1900-1983. 1200

National Players

Relation to other fields

Role of theatre in education. USA. 1983. 72

National theatre

Institutions

Influential producers outline two different plans for a national theatre. USA. 1983. 339

National Theatre (London)

Design/technology

Mannerist elements in some set designs for *Hamlet*. UK-England: Stratford-upon-Avon, London. 1948-1976. 1675

Institutions

Company members review successes of Cottesloe Company. UK-England: London. 1900-1983. 625

Balance of classic plays against modern plays at the National Theatre and the Royal Shakespeare Company. UK-England. 1900-1983. 626

Aspects of the National Theatre and the Royal Shakespeare Company are compared. UK-England. 1960. 627

Peter Hall's role as artistic director of the National Theatre, including devising the repertory and obtaining funds. UK-England: London. 1973-1983. 636

Performance/production

Career of National Theatre actress Geraldine McEwan. UK-England. 1900-1983. 882

Peter Wood's productions of Tom Stoppard's *The Real Thing* and Harold Pinter's *Other Places*. UK-England: London. 1983. 887

Actor Laurence Olivier's autobiography. UK-England. 1907-1983. 891

Italian translation of Laurence Olivier's autobiography *Confessions of an Actor*. UK-England. 1907-1983. 892

National Theatre's production of Richard Brinsley Sheridan's *The Rivals*. UK-England: London. 1983. 1533

Plays/librettos/scripts

Wole Soyinka's plays echo themes of Aeschylus, Euripides and Shakespeare. Nigeria. Greece: Athens. UK-England: London. 1980. 1700

Reference materials

Bibliography of Laurence Olivier. UK-England. 1907-1983. 1427

National Youth Theatre (London)

Audience

Audience development programs for young people. UK-England. USA: Santa Barbara, CA. 1980. 169

Institutions

History of the National Youth Theatre. UK-England. 1956. 628

Plays/librettos/scripts

Peter Terson's work, especially his association with National Youth Theatre. UK-England. 1960-1983. 1299

Nationaltheater (Mannheim)

Performance spaces

Design and history of the Nationaltheater Mannheim. Germany, West: Mannheim. 1777-1983. 376

Nationaltheater (Munich)

Design/technology

Construction and operating procedures of new sound systems at the München Nationaltheater. Germany, West: Munich. 1983. 199

Native American theatre

Performance/production

Survey of Native American dramatists and their use of dramatic ritual. USA. 1850-1980. 463

Native American theatre — cont'd

Relation to other fields

Dramatic religious rituals of pre-Hispanic Latin America. North America. South America. 1200-1533.   2109

Naturalism

Design/technology

Development of Wagnerian stage design and groups and movements involved in its production. Spain. 1882-1960.   1822

Performance/production

Overview of modern theatre from realism and naturalism onward. 1850-1982.   659

Plays/librettos/scripts

Italian translation of Bogdal's essay on Gerhart Hauptmann's *Florian Geyer*. Germany. 1896.   1117

Fairy-tale elements in *Miss Julie* intensify the play's tragic impact. Sweden. 1870-1908.   1264

Philosophic examination of Eugene O'Neill's *Long Day's Journey into Night*. USA. 1940.   1360

Naturalism in the works of Pietro Mascagni and Giacomo Puccini. Italy. 1879-1926.   1955

Theory/criticism

Study of realism, naturalism, symbolism, surrealism, expressionism and epic theatre. Europe. North America. 1900-1980.   1484

Effect of social conditions on performance styles. USA. Greece. 499 B.C.-1983 A.D.   1517

Naumachiae

Performance spaces

Naumachiae, gladiatorial contests, circus races and other acts in ancient Rome. Roman Republic. Roman Empire. 616 B.C.-523 A.D.   387

Nazaire et Barnabé

Plays/librettos/scripts

Semiotic analysis of popular radio comedy. Canada. 1939-1958.   1709

NEA SEE: National Endowment for the Arts

Nederlander Theatre

Performance/production

Eight critics review Philip Rose's production of the musical *Amen Corner*. USA: New York, NY. 1983.   1800

Nederlands Opernstichting, De

Institutions

Free operating groups and institutionalized theatre. Netherlands. 1963-1983.   1609

Nègres, Les (Blacks, The)

Plays/librettos/scripts

Jean Genet's *The Blacks* and his theory of ritual in context of Theatre of the Absurd and Total Theatre. France: Paris. 1948-1968.   1647

Négritude

Bernard Dadié's plays intended for African audiences, bewilder Europeans. Ivory Coast. 1933-1973.   1194

Jean Genet's *The Blacks* and his theory of ritual in context of Theatre of the Absurd and Total Theatre. France: Paris. 1948-1968.   1647

Negro Ensemble Theatre (New York, NY)

Institutions

Activism, internationalism and preservation in minority theatre groups. USA. 1981-1983.   646

Neo-realism

Performance/production

Post-World War II forms of American theatre. USA. 1945-1983.   1633

Neoclassicism

Design/technology

Relation of perspective scenery to social structures. France. 1500-1750.   191

Scene designers and scenery at Teatro alla Scala in Neoclassic period. Italy: Milan. 1778-1832.   1821

Performance spaces

Giuseppe Piermarini built Teatro alla Scala in accordance with architectural theories of his time. Italy: Milan. 1776-1830.   1835

Neoclassicism SEE ALSO: Geographical-Chronological Index under Europe 1540-1660, France 1629-1660, Italy 1540-1576

Nestroy, Johann

Plays/librettos/scripts

Relation between couplet and parody as exemplified in Johann Nestroy' songs. Austria. 1833-1862.   1546

Parody on the stage of Viennese Popular Theatre before Johann Nestroy. Austria: Vienna. 1801-1861.   1547

Genre analysis and comparison of Johann Nestroy's play *Die verhängnisvolle Faschingsnacht* with Karl von Holtei's *Ein Trauerspiel in Berlin*. Austria. 1839.   1548

Role of censorship in Johann Nestroy's *Häuptling Abendwind* as an adaptation of Jacques Offenbach's *Vent de soir*. Austria. 1833.   1549

Recently discovered documents on playwright Johann Nestroy. Austria. 1801-1862.   1550

Recently discovered manuscript of Johann Nestroy's *Prinz Friedrich*. Austria. 1833.   1551

Genre classification of parody and related forms in Johann Nestroy's plays. Austria. 1833-1862.   1552

Critical reception of performances of Johann Nestroy's plays. Austria. 1837-1838.   1553

Neuenfels, Hans

Performance/production

Jean Genet's *The Balcony* at Schillertheater Berlin, directed by Hans Neuenfels. Germany, West: West Berlin. 1983.   773

Neues Gewandhaus (Leipzig)

Design/technology

Electro-technical systems of the Neues Gewandhaus. Germany, East: Leipzig. 1781-1983.   196

Neues Kammertheater (Stuttgart)

Performance/production

Hansgünther Heyme's production of *The Persians*. Germany, West: Stuttgart. 1983.   1680

Neuhaus, Dieter

Institutions

Interviews with personnel of Freiburg theatres on obtaining subsidies and other aspects of administration. Germany, West: Freiburg. 1911-1983.   607

Neumeier, John

Plays/librettos/scripts

Analysis of John Neumeier's production of *St. Matthew Passion*. Germany, West: Hamburg. USA: New York, NY. 1982-1983.   521

New Inn, The

Plato's concept of androgyny in Jonson's *The New Inn*. England. 1629.   1036

New Lafayette Theatre (New York, NY)

Performance/production

Founder-director of New Lafayette Theatre discusses purpose and style of rituals. USA: New York, NY. 1969-1972.   2102

New Negro Art Theatre (New York, NY)

Institutions

Harlem Little Theatre movement started to produce plays by, with, for and about Blacks. USA: New York, NY. 1915-1934.   653

Noccioli, Guido

Performance/production

Playwright Guido Noccioli's account of Eleonora Duse's tour. Italy. 1906-1907.   809

Noelte, Rudolf

Productions of Wolfgang Borchert's play *The Man Outside* in Hamburg and Berlin. Germany, West: West Berlin, Hamburg. 1947-1948.   778

Rudolph Noelte directs Gerhart Hauptmann's *Michael Kramer*. Germany, West: Hamburg. 1983.   781

Noguchi, Isamu

View of man and recurring Greek symbolism in Martha Graham's choreography. USA. 1947.   528

Noises Off

Ten critics review Michael Blakemore's production of Michael Frayn's play *Noises Off*. USA: New York, NY. 1983.   1541

Plays/librettos/scripts

Farcical style in Michael Frayn's *Noises Off*. USA. 1983.   1597

Nora

Performance/production

Documentation of Ingmar Bergman's tripartite theatre project. Sweden. Germany, West: Munich. 1981.   844

Nordisk TeaterTeknik

Design/technology

Report of Nordisk TeaterTeknik 83 conference. Sweden: Stockholm. 1983.   223

Norman Conquests, The

Plays/librettos/scripts

Comic techniques in Alan Ayckbourn's *The Norman Conquests*. UK-England. 1974.   1589

Norman, Marsha

Administration

Difficulties of getting some plays on Broadway. USA: New York, NY. 1982-1983.   565

Performance/production

Eight critics review Tom Moore's production of Marsha Norman's play *'Night Mother*. USA: New York, NY. 1983.   971

Plays/librettos/scripts

The character of Arlene in Marsha Norman's play *Getting Out*, and her effect on the audience. USA. 1981.   1372

Northcote, James

Performance/production

Portrait of Ira Aldridge as Othello in painting by James Northcote. UK-England: Manchester. USA. 1826.   869

Norton, Harold

Career of dancer Margot Webb. USA. 1933-1947.   1991

Norwich Puppet Theatre

Institutions

Development of DaSilva Puppets, and establishment of permanent base for performance. UK-England: Norwich, Godmancester. 1962-1983.   2044

Nost Milan, El (Our Milan)

Theory/criticism

Louis Althusser's Marxist philosophy is contrasted with his review of Carlo Bertolazzi's play staged by Giorgio Strehler. USA. France. Italy. 1962-1985.   1674

Not I

Plays/librettos/scripts

Analysis of Samuel Beckett's *Not I*. UK-Ireland. France. 1971.   1329

Nouvelle Revue Française

Institutions

Founding of periodical *Nouvelle Revue Française*. France: Paris. 1909-1914.   304

Noverre, Jean Georges

Performance/production

Contributors to dance reform in French theatre. France: Paris. 1752-1781.   518

Nozze di Figaro, Le

Application of holography to the Salzburger Marionettentheater production of *Le Nozze di Figaro*. Austria: Salzburg. 1983.   2083

Nuit Blanche

Description and analysis of Ping Chong's work. USA. 1972-1983.   1752

Nunn, Trevor

Institutions

History of Royal Shakespeare Company with emphasis on financial and aesthetic aspects and internal politics. UK-England: London. 1864-1981.   624

Performance/production

Nine critics review Trevor Nunn's production of *All's Well That Ends Well*. USA: New York, NY. 1983.   1538

O'Brien, Jack

Nine critics review Jack O'Brien's production of *Porgy and Bess*. USA: New York, NY. 1983.   1795

O'Brien, Timothy

Design/technology

Trends in scenic practices by British designers. UK. 1960-1983.   228

O'Casey, Sean

Institutions

Rejection of O'Casey's play *The Silver Tassie* by the Abbey Theatre and the subsequent furor. UK-Ireland: Dublin. 1928.   637

Plays/librettos/scripts

Influence of Percy Bysshe Shelley's poetry on Sean O'Casey. UK-Ireland: Dublin. 1923-1946.   1318

Anti-war themes in Sean O'Casey's ballads. UK-Ireland: Dublin. 1916-1918.   1319

Influence on Brecht of Sean O'Casey's use of songs to overcome the boundaries of illusion in his drama. UK-Ireland: Dublin. 1923-1926.   1325

Changes made in the three different versions of the play *Red Roses for Me* by Sean O'Casey. UK-Ireland. 1942-1956.   1328

Index to Sean O'Casey's autobiography. UK-Ireland. 1880-1964.   1330

Theme of insurrection in Sean O'Casey's three Dublin plays. UK-Ireland: Dublin. 1923-1926.   1331

Influence of Shakespeare and Percy Bysshe Shelley on Sean O'Casey's *The Shadow of a Gunman*. UK-Ireland: Dublin. 1923.   1332

American influence of Melville's short story *Cock-A-Doodle Doo!* on O'Casey's play. UK-Ireland. USA. 1949.   1333

Developments of Irish melodrama and its influence on later writers. UK-Ireland: Dublin. 1860-1905.   1338

Irreverent aspects of Irish comedy seen through the works of 14 playwrights. Eire. UK-Ireland. 1840-1965.   1555

Comic irony and anti-heroes in Irish comedy and influence on Harold Pinter, Samuel Beckett and Tom Stoppard. UK-Ireland. Eire. 1900-1940.   1593

Reference materials

Sean O'Casey bibliography. UK-Ireland. 1923-1982.   1430

O'Connor, Carroll

Performance/production

Seven critics review Carroll O'Connor's production of George Sibbald's play *Brothers*. USA: New York, NY. 1983.   985

Off Broadway theatre — cont'd

Five critics review Carole Rothman's production of *Painting Churches*, by Tina Howe. USA: New York, NY. 1983.   959

Five critics review Nye Heron's production of Brian Friel's play *Winners*. USA: New York, NY. 1983.   962

Seven critics review Sam Shepard's production of his play *Fool for Love* presented by Circle Repertory Company. USA: New York, NY. 1983.   963

Six critics review Les Waters' production of Caryl Churchill's play *Fen*. USA: New York, NY. 1983.   964

Five critics review Donal Donnelly's production of John B. Keane's play *Big Maggie*. USA: New York, NY. 1983.   966

Six critics review Čechov's *Uncle Vanya* directed by Andre Serban at La Mama. USA: New York, NY. 1982.   967

Five critics review Emily Mann's production of Kathleen Tolan's play *A Weekend Near Madison*. USA: New York, NY. 1983.   977

Seven critics review Robert Allan Ackerman's production of William Mastrosimone's play *Extremities*. USA: New York, NY. 1983.   980

Five critics review Joseph Papp's production of Thomas Babe's play *Buried Inside Extra*. USA: New York, NY. 1983.   982

Seven critics review David Trainer's production of A.R. Gurney, Jr.'s play *The Middle Ages*. USA: New York, NY. 1983.   1542

Five critics review Jerry Zak's production of Christopher Durang's play *Baby with the Bathwater*. USA: New York, NY. 1983.   1544

Arthur Kopit's and Sam Shepard's plays on and off Broadway. USA: New York, NY. 1957-1983.   1630

Five critics review Tony Tanner's production of the musical *Preppies*. USA: New York, NY. 1983.   1779

Shift of public interest from Broadway to Off Broadway. USA: New York, NY. 1983.   1786

Five critics review David Holdgrive's production of the musical *Tallulah*. USA: New York, NY. 1983.   1796

Six critics review Charles Ludlam's production of his play *Galas*. USA: New York, NY. 1983.   1797

Reference materials

Annual record of Broadway and Off Broadway season. USA: New York, NY. 1981-1982.   49

Dictionary of Black theatre. USA: New York, NY. 1983.   50

Offenbach, Jacques

Performance/production

Comparison of performances of tenor aria 'O Dieu de quelle ivresse' by Jacques Offenbach. France. USA. 1911-1983.   1857

Photographs, cast lists, synopsis and discography of Metropolitan Opera production of *Les Contes d'Hoffman*. USA: New York, NY. 1983.   1900

Plays/librettos/scripts

Role of censorship in Johann Nestroy's *Häuptling Abendwind* as an adaptation of Jacques Offenbach's *Vent de soir*. Austria. 1833.   1549

Identity and personality of the real E.T.A. Hoffman. Germany: Königsberg. 1776-1822.   1948

Officium Pastorum

Aspects of liturgical drama cause it to be both ritual and theatre. France. 1100-1200.   1101

Ohio Impromptu

Performance/production

Four critics review Alan Schneider's production of three Samuel Beckett plays. USA: New York, NY. 1983.   928

Old Times

Plays/librettos/scripts

Reasons for Deeley's calling himself Orson Welles in *Old Times* are based on film *The Magnificent Ambersons*. UK-England. USA. 1942-1971.   1289

Oliver, Joan

Interview with the playwright Joan Oliver about his work. Spain. 1899-1983.   1236

Olivier, Laurence

Performance/production

Actor Laurence Olivier's autobiography. UK-England. 1907-1983.   891

Italian translation of Laurence Olivier's autobiography *Confessions of an Actor*. UK-England. 1907-1983.   892

Plays/librettos/scripts

Examination of the preproduction script for Laurence Olivier's film *Hamlet*. UK-England. 1948.   1719

Reference materials

Bibliography of Laurence Olivier. UK-England. 1907-1983.   1427

Olsztyn Mime of the Deaf

Institutions

History of the Olsztyn Mime of the Deaf theatre company. Poland: Olsztyn. 1958-1983.   1725

Omnibus

Performance/production

Survey of theatrical activity in Rome, based on criticism by Alberto Savinio. Italy: Rome. France. 1937-1939.   812

On Baile's Strand

Plays/librettos/scripts

Patriot Charles Stewart Parnell's influence on Irish drama. UK-Ireland. 1891-1936.   1337

On Despising Death

Fusion of Stoicism and Christianity in *Hamlet*. England: London. 1600-1601.   1041

On Golden Pond

Examination of plays adapted for movies. USA. 1974.   1345

On the Razzle

Problems of play translations without caricature. Germany, West. USA. 1900-1983.   1148

On Your Toes

Performance/production

Production elements and choreography of *On Your Toes*. USA. 1982.   1782

Nine critics review George Abbott's production of the musical *On Your Toes*. USA: New York, NY. 1983.   1803

Onore, L' (Honour, The)

Basic theatrical documents

Annotated texts of Giovanni Verga's plays. Italy. 1865-1908.   573

Open Theatre, The (New York, NY)

Institutions

Reflections on the significance of The Open Theatre by several of its performers, writers and critical advisers. USA: New York, NY. 1963-1973.   1613

Theory/criticism

Postscriptive performance text and experimental theatre groups. North America. 1983.   1672

Opera

Administration

Impact of government funding on the arts. USA. 1965-1982.   159

Promotional campaigns for performing arts institutions. USA. 1983.   160

Effect of different kinds of financial support on artists. USA. 1950-1982.   163

Audience

Audience development survey. USA: Atlanta, GA, Baton Rouge, LA, Columbia, SC, Memphis, TN. 1983.   170

Sociological studies suggest that democratization of the arts has not taken place. USA. 1830-1982.   173

Design/technology

Supplementary materials to exhibit of Baroque theatre and stage design. Italy. 1600.   219

Influence of the designers on staging styles. UK. 1958-1983.   226

Safety curtain at Covent Garden, designed by Christopher Le Brun. UK-England: London. 1983.   232

Pantomime SEE ALSO: Classed Entries: MIME – Pantomime

Papa, Santuzza
   Relation to other fields
      Santuzza Papa's transition from Freudian psychodrama to Jungian
      conception. Italy. 1960.   1663

Paper Mill Playhouse (Millburn, NJ)
   Performance spaces
      History and reconstruction of Paper Mill Playhouse. USA: Millburn,
      NJ. 1980-1982.   394

Papp, Joseph
   Institutions
      Influential producers outline two different plans for a national
      theatre. USA. 1983.   339
   Performance/production
      Five critics review Joseph Papp's production of Thomas Babe's play
      Buried Inside Extra. USA: New York, NY. 1983.   982

Parade Rest Cabaret
   Institutions
      Organization, people and theatres involved in the Army Theatre Arts
      Association. USA: Fort Polk, LA. 1960-1983.   336

**Parades SEE ALSO: Classed Entries: POPULAR
ENTERTAINMENT – Pageants/parades**

Paratheatrical forms
   Performance/production
      Description of group that performs with and for remote and rural
      areas. Poland: Gardzienice. 1968-1983.   1627

Paravents, Les (Screens, The)
   Plays/librettos/scripts
      Structural similarities between Jean Genet's *The Screens* and
      medieval dramaturgy. France. 1961.   1641

Paris Opera SEE: Opéra de Paris

Park Theatre (New York, NY)
   Performance/production
      Adverse reception of Madame Vestris and Charles Mathews on tour
      in USA. USA: New York, NY, Philadelphia, PA. UK-England:
      London. 1838.   933

Parker, Gilbert
   Administration
      Round table discussion between playwrights and their agents. USA.
      1983.   562

Parker, Stanley
   Performance/production
      Review of international puppet theatre festival. Sweden: Uppsala.
      1983.   2054

Parker, Stewart
   Plays/librettos/scripts
      Interview with playwright Stewart Parker. UK. 1941-1983.   1276

Parnell of Avondale
      Patriot Charles Stewart Parnell's influence on Irish drama. UK-
      Ireland. 1891-1936.   1337

Parnell, Charles Stewart
      Patriot Charles Stewart Parnell's influence on Irish drama. UK-
      Ireland. 1891-1936.   1337

Parody
      Krapp's Last Tape by Samuel Beckett as a parody of both
      performance and themes in poetry. UK-Ireland. 1957.   1321
      Relation between couplet and parody as exemplified in Johann
      Nestroy' songs. Austria. 1833-1862.   1546

      Parody on the stage of Viennese Popular Theatre before Johann
      Nestroy. Austria: Vienna. 1801-1861.   1547
      Genre analysis and comparison of Johann Nestroy's play *Die
      verhängnisvolle Faschingsnacht* with Karl von Holtei's *Ein
      Trauerspiel in Berlin*. Austria. 1839.   1548
      Genre classification of parody and related forms in Johann Nestroy's
      plays. Austria. 1833-1862.   1552

Paroles sur le Mime (Words on Mime)
   Performance/production
      Italian translation of Etienne Decroux's *Paroles sur le mime (Words
      on Mime)*. France. 1935.   1726

Parsifal
      One hundred years of recordings and Bayreuth Festival performances
      of Wagner's *Parsifal*. Germany: Bayreuth. 1882-1982.   1864
      Discussion of centennial production of *Parsifal* directed by Götz
      Friedrich. Germany, West: Bayreuth. 1982.   1876
      Photographs, cast lists, synopsis and discography of Metropolitan
      Opera production of *Parsifal*. USA: New York, NY. 1983.   1892
   Plays/librettos/scripts
      Pertinence of human characterizations in Wagner's operas. Germany.
      1845-1951.   1946
      Discussion of character development of Wotan in *Parsifal* by
      Richard Wagner. Germany. 1870-1900.   1952

Partit Socialista Unificat de Catalunya (PSUC)
   Administration
      Legislation on theatre presented to the parliament by the Socialist
      Party of Catalonia. Spain. 1982.   141

Pasolini, Pier Paolo
   Institutions
      New season's productions at the Basel Stadttheater. Switzerland:
      Basel. 1983.   622

Passe Muraille (Toronto, ON)
      Change in idealism among alternative theatres. Canada: Toronto,
      ON. 1973-1983.   295
      Survey of alternative theatres. Canada: Toronto, ON. 1979-1983.   296
      Steven Rumbelow and experimental work of Triple Action Theatre.
      Canada: Toronto, ON. 1980-1983.   1606
   Plays/librettos/scripts
      Excerpts from Betty Jane Wylie's journal during collective theatre
      venture. Canada. 1976.   1018

Passion
   Performance/production
      Ten critics review Marshall Mason's production of Peter Nichols'
      play *Passion*. USA: New York, NY. 1983.   919

Pastoral scenes
   Plays/librettos/scripts
      Interpretations of locale of scenes in *As You Like It*. England. 1599-
      1600.   1038

Pastorals
      Pastoral as dramatic genre and its literary and scenic derivations.
      Italy. 1400-1599.   1185

Pathé
   Relation to other fields
      Circus as a staging device for a political satire. USSR. Germany.
      Italy. 1914-1930.   1668

Patronage
   Performance/production
      Marxist theory applied in comparison of public theatres in England
      and Spain. England. Spain. 1576-1635.   696
   Relation to other fields
      Political ramifications of the theatrical patronage of Louis XIII and
      Cardinal de Richelieu. France. 1610-1643.   54

Paul Thompson Forever

Performance/production

Tribute to Mordecai Gorelik, scenic designer, theorist, teacher, director and playwright. USA. 1899-1983. 936

Paul, Kegan

Review article of *Theatre Production Series*, seeking to define theatre's strengths. England. Germany. 1500-1939. 706

Paul, Routledge

Review article of *Theatre Production Series*, seeking to define theatre's strengths. England. Germany. 1500-1939. 706

Pavarotti, Luciano

Interview with tenor Luciano Pavarotti about his career and forthcoming roles. Europe. North America. 1983. 1855

Plays/librettos/scripts

Italian tenor Luciano Pavarotti discusses the title role of *Ernani* by Giuseppe Verdi. Italy. 1983. 1958

Payró, Roberto Jorge

Latin American theatre and progressive social movements. Costa Rica. Argentina. Peru. 1588-1983. 1022

Pearson, Sybille

Performance/production

Ten critics review Richard Maltby's production of *Baby*. USA: New York, NY. 1983. 1805

Pedrell, Felip

First performance of Richard Wagner's *Lohengrin* and the debate generated with followers of Giuseppe Verdi. Spain. 1862-1901. 1886

Pedroni, Giovanni

Design/technology

Scene designers and scenery at Teatro alla Scala in Neoclassic period. Italy: Milan. 1778-1832. 1821

Peer Gynt

Institutions

Guthrie Theatre's architectural features and its directors, with emphasis on Liviu Ciulei's production of *Peer Gynt*. USA: Minneapolis, MN. 1963-1983. 655

Performance/production

Productions of Henrik Ibsen's *Peer Gynt* by Hans Midbøes. Norway. 1976-1980. 823

Plays/librettos/scripts

Lee Strasberg on Ibsen and *Peer Gynt*. USA: New York, NY. 1906-1982. 1385

Theatrical effect preserved in operatic adaptations of Werner Egk's *Peer Gynt* and Aribert Reimann's *King Lear* at the Münchener Festspiele. Germany, West: Munich. 1982. 1953

Peg

Performance/production

Six critics review Robert Drivas' production of Peggy Lee's play *Peg*. USA: New York, NY. 1983. 1794

Pelican, The SEE: *Pelikanen*

Pelikanen (Pelican, The)

Performance/production

August Strindberg productions in eleven countries. Sweden. Italy. USA. 1982. 847

Pelléas et Mélisande

Photographs, cast lists, synopsis and discography of Metropolitan Opera production of *Pelléas et Mélisande*. USA: New York, NY. 1983. 1901

Plays/librettos/scripts

Comparison of symbolist drama by Maurice Maeterlinck and opera by Claude Debussy. Belgium. 1900-1983. 1012

Percedes, Jorge Acuna

Latin American theatre and progressive social movements. Costa Rica. Argentina. Peru. 1588-1983. 1022

Perego, Giovanni

Design/technology

Scene designers and scenery at Teatro alla Scala in Neoclassic period. Italy: Milan. 1778-1832. 1821

Peregrinus

Performance/production

Census, with brief reviews, of performances of medieval drama. Europe. 1982-1983. 710

Plays/librettos/scripts

Aspects of liturgical drama cause it to be both ritual and theatre. France. 1100-1200. 1101

Pérez Galdós, Benito

Study of Benito Pérez Galdós' plays. Spain. 1843-1920. 1237

Performance art

Performance/production

Career of performance artist Ping Chong. USA: New York, NY. 1972-1982. 1755

Performance art SEE ALSO: Classed Entries: MIXED PERFORMANCES — Performance art

Performance spaces

Administration

Purdue University study on modern uses of historic theatres and guidelines for management. USA. 1981-1983. 154

Design/technology

International exhibition of theatre architecture and scenery. Czechoslovakia: Prague. 1983. 179

Performance spaces and effect of scenery on the audience. Europe. 1970-1983. 184

Relation of perspective scenery to social structures. France. 1500-1750. 191

Electro-technical systems of the Neues Gewandhaus. Germany, East: Leipzig. 1781-1983. 196

Description of new theatre building and technical equipment used in performances since 1981. Germany, West: West Berlin. 1962-1982. 201

Career of Italian designer and architect Innocente Maraino. Poland: Warsaw, Lvov, Slonim. 1767-1799. 221

Surviving upper-wing groove mechanisms in five provincial theatres. UK. 1850-1983. 225

Institutions

Street theatre production of Århus theater akademi in collaboration with Jordcirkus and Johnny Melville. Denmark: Århus. 1982. 298

History of Spanish-language repertory troupe activities in Texas. USA. Mexico. 1848-1900. 352

Building and performances at Lahti City Theatre. Finland: Lahti. 1983. 592

Development of DaSilva Puppets, and establishment of permanent base for performance. UK-England: Norwich, Godmancester. 1962-1983. 2044

Performance spaces

Security measures and regulations in Italian theatres. Italy. 1983. 383

Performance/production

Present situation of theater in Ghana, including plays, performers, promoters and spaces. Ghana. 1983. 429

Current state of Syrian theatre. Syria: Damascus, Aleppo, Basra. 1983. 445

Catalogue of exhibition on Max Reinhardt's use of genres and performance spaces. Austria. 1893-1943. 672

New evidence suggests that Castle Ashby plays were performed at Canonbury House. England: London. 1637-1659. 707

Social status and role of minstrels. Europe. 1100-1500. 1986

Performance spaces — cont'd

Plays/librettos/scripts

Essays on Restoration theatre and drama, with devised criteria for evaluation. England. 1660-1800. 1046

Comparison between a painting by Diego Velázquez and a play by Calderón de la Barca. Spain. 1625-1651. 1229

Reference materials

Music guide for Austria with names, addresses and other information. Austria. 1983. 14

Relation to other fields

Theatre as a social mirror of the town. Italy: Reggio Emilia. 1851. 65

Research/historiography

Concise version of a theatre textbook. 79

Theory/criticism

Trend toward mobility and profanation in contemporary theatre. Europe. 1970-1980. 96

Performance spaces SEE ALSO: Classed Entries 356-411, 1760, 1773, 1774, 1833-1837, 1981-1983.

Performance/production

Comparative study of Australian and Canadian theatre. Australia. Canada. 1970-1983. 8

Articles on various aspects of Chinese theatre from early plays to contemporary practice. China. 206 B.C.-1983 A.D. 9

Administration

Sound financial practices of the productions mounted by the actor-manager Tate Wilkinson. England. 1781-1784. 554

Censorship on the American stage, particularly of Bertolt Brecht. USA. 1941-1949. 564

Interview with Terry McEwen, general director of War Memorial Opera House. Canada: Montreal, PQ. USA: San Francisco, CA. 1983. 1813

Audience

Performance artist and audience relationship in night clubs. UK-England: London. 1983. 1738

Basic theatrical documents

Texts and descriptions of all aspects of the production of medieval religious plays. Europe. 1300-1600. 570

Catalan translation of *Ur-Faust* and articles on the play and its production by the Company Andrià Gual. Germany. Spain. 1887-1983. 571

Playtext and manifesto of the Teatro Visionico and their production of Pino Masnata's *Tocca a me*. Italy. 1920. 572

Design/technology

Model for musical design training. USA. 1982. 256

Introductory lighting textbook. USA. 1982. 270

First live broadcast of a complete opera performance from the Metropolitan Opera House. USA: New York, NY. 1910. 1708

Puppets and performance techniques used in Kennedy Center production of *The Tale of Peter Rabbit*. USA: Washington, DC. 1983. 2035

Institutions

Review of Austrian summer festivals. Austria. 1983. 285

Current manager Taisto-Bertil Orsmaa, and history of Turku Municipal Theatre. Finland: Turku. 1946-1983. 303

Brief survey of productions and financial situation of a local theatre. Germany, West: Nürnberg. 1983. 314

History, financial situation and productions of the Schlosstheater. Germany, West: Moers. 1975-1983. 315

Diversity of Latin American theatre. South America. North America. 1950-1983. 326

Multi-media methods employed by experimental theatre groups. Sweden: Stockholm. 1983. 329

Theoretical and theatrical foundations of the Squat Theatre. USA: New York, NY. Hungary: Budapest. 1975-1977. 342

Concepts of and preparations for Théâtre de l'Europe, managed by Giorgio Strehler. France: Paris. 1983. 596

Textual and pictorial documentation of Deutsches Theater Berlin. Germany, East: East Berlin. 1883-1983. 599

Bertolt Brecht's return to Deutsches Theater and production of *Mother Courage* with Berliner Ensemble. Germany, East: East Berlin. 1949. 601

Edward Bond's *Saved* and Shakespeare's *Troilus and Cressida* at the Jugendclub Kritisches Theater. Germany, West: Stuttgart. 1981-1983. 608

New season's productions at the Basel Stadttheater. Switzerland: Basel. 1983. 622

Organization and productions of Black Theatre Co-operative. UK-England. 1979. 631

Joint Stock, a collective theatre company. UK-England. 1974. 635

Workshops of Latin American popular theatre. North America. South America. 1983. 1610

Growth of alternative theatre and its influence on traditional theatre productions. UK. 1983. 1612

Innovative projects of Welfare State Company, and community benefits. UK-England. 1983. 1742

Tschauner-Theatre: Vienna's only surviving improvisation company. Austria: Vienna. 1938-1983. 1978

Performance spaces

Use of urban areas to mount theatre spectacles. Italy: Palermo. 1500-1600. 381

Plays/librettos/scripts

Shift in dramatic emphasis in Igor Strawinsky's *Apollon Musagete* due to sets, costumes and choreography. USA: Washington, DC, New York, NY. 1927-1979. 522

Terukkuttu, a street theatre piece developed from traditional dance-drama. India: Tamil Nadu. 1980. 540

Audience reaction and cancellation of tour of Somerset Maugham's *The Land of Promise*. Canada. USA. UK-England. 1914. 1015

Adaptation of *Galileo* for Chinese stage. China, People's Republic of: Peking. 1979. 1020

Composition and thematic analysis of Goethe's *Ur-Faust*. Germany. 1775-1832. 1137

History of criticism and interpretation of Shakespeare's *A Midsummer Night's Dream*. Germany. 1700-1982. 1142

Treatment of power by German playwrights and Volker Braun's *Dmitri*. Germany, West: Karlsruhe. 1983. 1154

Biographical note, chronology and a brief analysis of Dario Fo's plays in performance. Italy. 1926-1982. 1167

Conference on August Strindberg's relation to modern culture, painting, photography and theatrical productions. Italy: Bari. 1982. 1178

Productions of Luigi Pirandello's early work contrasted with later ones. Italy. 1898-1917. 1180

Dramatization of Remigio Zena's novel *The Wolf's Mouth* by Teatro Stabile di Genova. Italy: Genoa. 1980. 1186

Some lesser known facts about Luigi Pirandello's plays and other writings. Italy. 1884-1935. 1192

Theatres, actors and drama of the Renaissance in the work of modern directors. Italy. 1845-1982. 1193

Censorship involving Jerzy Hulewicz' play *Aruna*, produced at Municipal Theatre of Cracow. Poland: Kraków. 1925. 1217

Staging and scenic practices in the plays of Lope de Vega's forerunners and contemporaries. Spain: Valencia. 1500-1699. 1253

Interview with Gerlind Reinshagen and review of his play *Eisenherz (Ironheart)* produced in Bochum and Zürich. Switzerland: Zürich. Germany, West: Bochum. 1983. 1271

Index to Sean O'Casey's autobiography. UK-Ireland. 1880-1964. 1330

Critical reception of performances of Johann Nestroy's plays. Austria. 1837-1838. 1553

Study of Ludvig Holberg's plays. Denmark. 1684-1754. 1554

Comparison and contrast of radio and stage presentations of Arthur Kopit's play *Wings*. USA. 1978-1979. 1655

Composer Jean-Philippe Rameau's contribution to development of opera. France. 1683-1764. 1941

Richard Wagner's life and work in Paris. France: Paris. 1830-1897. 1944

Performance/production — cont'd

Reference materials

Guide to theatre organizations and professionals. Finland. 1983.   23

List of dramatic, cinematographic and television productions with short critical notes on the most important ones. Italy. 1982.   26

Annals of theatre productions in Catalonia for the 1982-1983 season. Spain. 1982-1983.   34

Cast listings and other information on 19 productions mounted at Charlottetown Festival. Canada: Charlottetown, PE. 1965-1982.   1399

Comprehensive listing of the dramatic repertory, with a note on important productions. Europe. North America. 672 B.C.-1982 A.D.   1403

Chronological reference guide to works on and about Alfred de Musset. France. 1830-1980.   1408

Bibliography of research on Shakespearean productions in German-speaking countries. German-speaking countries. 1981-1982.   1410

Calendar of theatrical performances. UK-England: London. 1910-1919.   1428

Guide to shows that closed before coming to Broadway. USA. 1900-1982.   1438

Relation to other fields

Interview with Fritz Bennewitz on theatre work in the Third World. India. Venezuela. Sri Lanka. 1970-1983.   59

Reception of Bertolt Brecht in Argentina vis-à-vis political situation in the country. Argentina. 1980-1983.   1441

Painter Oskar Kokoschka's dramatic works. Austria. 1917.   1442

Zerka Moreno's psychodrama in Italy. USA: New York, NY. Italy: Rome. 1960-1983.   1666

Theory/criticism

Systematic, analytic examination of sociology of performing arts. Europe. North America. 1983.   97

Comprehensive discussion of theatre performance. Spain. 1983.   107

Semiotic study of the specific nature of theatre in relation to other arts and audience interaction with it. Spain. 1983.   108

Articles on performance theory and practice. 1976-1983.   1477

Dramatic theories of the 20th century reflect a complex relationship between plays, designs, staging and acting. Europe. North America. 1900-1982.   1482

Anthology of theory and criticism regarding the relationship of playtext and production. Europe. 384 B.C.-1983 A.D.   1483

Study of realism, naturalism, symbolism, surrealism, expressionism and epic theatre. Europe. North America. 1900-1980.   1484

Phenomenological theory of performing arts. USA. 1982.   1514

Effect of social conditions on performance styles. USA. Greece. 499 B.C.-1983 A.D.   1517

Training

Training manual for performers. 1982.   492

Workshops and theatre productions by and for apprentices. Germany, West: West Berlin. 1971-1983.   498

Performance/production SEE ALSO: Classed Entries 412-487, 511-515, 517-520, 525-528, 531-536, 544, 547, 658-998, 1525-1545, 1614-1633, 1676-1685, 1711-1717, 1723, 1726-1630, 1732, 1733, 1735, 1744-1757, 1761-1764, 1775-1808, 1838-1931, 1984-1996, 2000-2004, 2006, 2007, 2009-2015, 2018-2020, 2025, 2027-2033, 2049-2065, 2073, 2074, 2083-2085, 2088-2091, 2098, 2101, 2102, 2105.

Performing Arts Libraries and Museums of the World

Design/technology

Observations concerning the French-English translation of scenographic terms. Discussed at SIBMAS. USA. France. 1982.   257

Research/historiography

Method for using models of scenery as study documents. Discussed at SIBMAS. Europe. North America. 1982.   83

Performing institutions SEE: Institutions, producing

Peribáñez

Plays/librettos/scripts

Comparative analysis of miscellaneous adaptations of Lope de Vega's *Peribáñez*. Spain. 1607.   1250

Pericles

Examples of folklore and humanistic philosophy in *Pericles*. England. 1608-1609.   1029

Period plays SEE: *Zeitstücke*

Persians, The

Performance/production

Hansgünther Heyme's production of *The Persians*. Germany, West: Stuttgart. 1983.   1680

Plays/librettos/scripts

Dramatic and military conflict in Greek tragedy. Greece. 484-415 B.C.   1697

Personnel

Administration

Disappointments and mismanagement at Centre Stage. Canada: Toronto, ON. 1983.   119

Unemployment among Black theatre professionals. UK-England: London. 1974-1979.   146

How to locate free or low-cost professional assistance in law, finance and management. USA. 1983.   156

Biography and legacy of dramaturg Julien Daoust. Canada. 1866-1943.   552

Interview with the new artistic director and literary advisor for the Iron Theatre (Glasgow). UK-Scotland. 1973-1983.   559

Definition and duties of literary managers in regional theatres. USA. 1980.   561

Round table discussion between playwrights and their agents. USA. 1983.   562

Management and fiscal administration at the Royal Academy of Music. England: London. 1719-1721.   1814

Institutions

Annual report of the Austrian Federal Theatres. Austria: Vienna. 1982-1983.   284

Interview with Reinhold Auer, dramatic advisor of Jura Soyfer Theater am Spittelberg, Vienna. Austria: Vienna. 1980-1983.   583

Interviews with personnel of Freiburg theatres on obtaining subsidies and other aspects of administration. Germany, West: Freiburg. 1911-1983.   607

Perspective scenery

Design/technology

Relation of perspective scenery to social structures. France. 1500-1750.   191

Peškov, Aleksey Maksimovič SEE: Gorky, Maxim

PETA SEE: Phillipine Educational Theatre Association

Peter Pan

Performance/production

Importance of boy actor playing the title role in *Peter Pan*. UK-England. 1902-1983.   867

Petit pauvre, Le (Little Pauper, The)

Relation to other fields

Jacques Copeau's reading of his play *The Little Pauper* to the Cistercians during the Occupation. France: Pernand. 1940-1944.   1450

Petrolini, Ettore

Reference materials

Illustrated catalogue of the exposition at the Palazzo Braschi in Rome — dedicated to the actor Ettore Petrolini. Italy. 1982.   1412

Peymann, Claus

Performance/production

Claus Peymann's production of Shakespeare's *A Winter's Tale*. Germany, West: Bochum. 1983.   784

Phèdre

Design/technology

Three costume and two set designs by Leon Bakst for ballet. 1911-1923.   175

Phenomenology

Theory/criticism

Trend toward mobility and profanation in contemporary theatre. Europe. 1970-1980.   96

Spectator at the center of semiological network of theoretical approaches to theatre. France. 1982.   99

Application of Frank Pierce's phenomenology and semiotics to theory of drama. France. Italy. 1980.   1488

Bertolt Brecht's theatrical poetics and polemic with György Lukács on realism. Germany. Hungary. 1918-1956.   1493

Phenomenological theory of performing arts. USA. 1982.   1514

Philanderer, The

Plays/librettos/scripts

Interview with director and cast of Yale Repertory's production of G.B. Shaw's *The Philanderer*. USA: New Haven, CT. 1982.   1389

Philippe, Gérard

Performance/production

Biography of actor Gérard Philippe. France. 1922-1959.   729

Philippine Educational Theatre Association (PETA)

Relation to other fields

Interview with Gardy Labad on education and theatre. Philippines. 1983.   66

Phillips, Robin

Performance/production

Production journal of *King Lear*. Canada: Stratford, ON. 1979. 1676

Philosophy

Comparative study of Peter Oskarsson's production of August Strindberg's *A Dream Play* with that of Ingmar Bergman. USA: Seattle, WA. 1982.   907

Comprehensive study of productions by Tadeusz Kantor's experimental theatre group Cricot 2 and Kantor's philosophy. Poland. 1975-1980.   1626

Plays/librettos/scripts

Examples of folklore and humanistic philosophy in *Pericles*. England. 1608-1609.   1029

Fusion of Stoicism and Christianity in *Hamlet*. England: London. 1600-1601.   1041

Jungian point of view on personality in Luigi Pirandello's work. Italy. 1916-1936.   1169

Catholicism and Oriental philosophy in plays of Eugene O'Neill. USA. 1888-1953.   1377

Epistemological paradox in Samuel Beckett's plays. Europe. 1906-1983.   1640

Relation to other fields

Argument against application of Jungian ideas to theatre.   490

Difference in dialectics and philosophy in writings by Karl Korsch, Bertolt Brecht and György Lukács. Germany. Hungary. 1898-1971.   1454

Santuzza Papa's transition from Freudian psychodrama to Jungian conception. Italy. 1960.   1663

Theory/criticism

History and criticism of theatre. Bulgaria. 1900-1983.   1478

History of theories of drama from George Wilhelm Hegel to Karl Marx. Germany. 1770-1883.   1491

Marxist philosophy in Bertolt Brecht's work. Germany. 1922-1956.   1496

Bertolt Brecht's perception of the philosophy of the Enlightenment. Germany. 1848-1956.   1498

Schiller's philosophy of history. Germany: Jena. 1789-1791.   1499

Wystan Hugh Auden's poetic meditation on art as related to Shakespeare's *The Tempest* and Kierkegaardian thought. UK-England. 1939-1962.   1511

Karl Jaspers' philosophy is applied to a discussion of Luigi Pirandello. Italy. 1916-1936.   1703

Phonography

Performance/production

Laurence Witten's collection of historic sound recordings at Yale University. USA: New Haven, CT. 1983.   1913

Physiker, Die (Physicists, The)

Plays/librettos/scripts

Modern plays set in confining institutions. North America. Europe. 1900-1983.   1200

Piccoli, Michel

Performance/production

Patrice Chéreau directs Bernard-Marie Koltès' *Fight of the Negro and the Dogs* at Théâtre des Amandiers. France: Nanterre. 1982.   736

Piccolo Teatro di Milano

Samuel Beckett's *Happy Days* with Giulia Lazzarini at Piccolo Teatro di Milano, directed by Giorgio Strehler. Italy: Milan. 1983.   807

Pickleherring

English actors' work in Germany, with mention of stock comic characters. Germany. England: London. 1590-1620.   1525

Picnic on the Battlefield SEE: *Piquenique en Campagne*

Pierce, Frank

Theory/criticism

Application of Frank Pierce's phenomenology and semiotics to theory of drama. France. Italy. 1980.   1488

Piermarini, Giuseppe

Performance spaces

History and architecture of Teatro Scientifico and Palazzo Accademico. Italy: Mantua. 1767-1982.   379

Giuseppe Piermarini built Teatro alla Scala in accordance with architectural theories of his time. Italy: Milan. 1776-1830. 1835

Pilgrim, Geraldine

Institutions

History and analysis of Hesitate and Demonstrate, an English group that creates surrealistic performances based on juxtaposition of images. UK-England: Leeds, London. Netherlands: Rotterdam. 1972-1983.   1743

Pinero, Arthur Wing

Plays/librettos/scripts

Examination of Arthur Wing Pinero's court farces. UK-England. 1890-1899.   1591

Pinocchio

Performance/production

Analysis of Carmelo Bene's avant-garde adaptation and staging of *Pinocchio*. Italy. 1981.   1625

Pinter, Harold

Peter Wood's productions of Tom Stoppard's *The Real Thing* and Harold Pinter's *Other Places*. UK-England: London. 1983.   887

Year's outstanding productions of plays by August Strindberg and other playwrights. UK-England. 1982-1983.   890

Plays/librettos/scripts

Modern plays set in confining institutions. North America. Europe. 1900-1983.   1200

Plays/librettos/scripts — cont'd

Brief survey of post-war theatre with 25 play synopses. UK. 1945-1983. 1420

Survey of twentieth century British dramatists. UK. 1902-1975. 1422

Revision of T.W. Robertson's playlist in *History of English Drama 1660-1900, V*. UK-England: London. 1849-1866. 1424

Calendar of theatrical performances. UK-England: London. 1910-1919. 1428

Letters of playwright John Millington Synge. UK-Ireland. 1871-1909. 1431

Guide to shows that closed before coming to Broadway. USA. 1900-1982. 1438

Bibliography of Pierre Corneille criticism. France. 1633-1980. 1598

Relation to other fields

Painter Oskar Kokoschka's dramatic works. Austria. 1917. 1442

Comparison of the character of Herod in two Fleury plays. France. England. 1100-1200. 1452

Political reactions to anti-war plays and films. Germany. 1930. 1453

Wole Soyinka's journalism related to his poems and plays. Nigeria. 1962-1982. 1459

Athol Fugard's plays are compared to Bantustan agitprop and historical drama. South Africa, Republic of. 1955-1980. 1665

Circus as a staging device for a political satire. USSR. Germany. Italy. 1914-1930. 1668

Bunraku is seen as Japanese miniaturization of social concepts. Japan: Osaka. 1983. 2076

Research/historiography

Descriptive and empirical research in children's drama. USA. 1900-1983. 1475

Theory/criticism

Spectator at the center of semiological network of theoretical approaches to theatre. France. 1982. 99

Dramatic language related to action. England. 1559-1603. 1480

Dramatic theories of the 20th century reflect a complex relationship between plays, designs, staging and acting. Europe. North America. 1900-1982. 1482

Anthology of theory and criticism regarding the relationship of playtext and production. Europe. 384 B.C.-1983 A.D. 1483

Study of realism, naturalism, symbolism, surrealism, expressionism and epic theatre. Europe. North America. 1900-1980. 1484

Critical analysis of dramatic methods from Sophocles to Harold Pinter. Europe. North America. 499 B.C.-1983 A.D. 1485

Bertolt Brecht's didactic plays function in the development of Socialism. Germany. 1922-1956. 1497

Theatre as text and performance. Spain. 1983. 1510

Semiotic comparison of dramatic theory, philosophy and performance. USA. Europe. 1850-1956. 1515

Imamu Amiri Baraka's aesthetics find their origins in Blues music. USA. 1963-1967. 1521

Morality of Restoration comedy. England. 1670-1700. 1599

Theory of ritual is used to clarify the relationship between ritual and drama. USA. Africa. 1983. 2110

Plays/librettos/scripts SEE ALSO: Playwriting and Classed Entries 488, 521, 522, 537-541, 545, 546, 999-1395, 1546-1597, 1634-1657, 1686-1702, 1709, 1710, 1718, 1719, 1809, 1932-1963, 1975, 2005, 2066, 2075, 2106.

Playtexts

Basic theatrical documents

Catalan translation of *Ur-Faust* and articles on the play and its production by the Company Andrià Gual. Germany. Spain. 1887-1983. 571

Playtext and manifesto of the Teatro Visionico and their production of Pino Masnata's *Tocca a me*. Italy. 1920. 572

Annotated texts of Giovanni Verga's plays. Italy. 1865-1908. 573

Discussion of prints and translation of the *fragmenten verzameling* 3-8 found in Zutphen Archive. Netherlands. 1400-1499. 574

Publication of *The Princess and the Jester*, a lost play by Pádraic Colum. UK-Ireland. 1900. 575

Playtext and accompanying materials from the Magazzini Criminali production of *On the Road*. Italy. 1982. 1605

Revised edition of Punch and Judy script. UK-England. 1873-1983. 2017

Performance/production

Aspects of Korean mask-dance theatre, including an annotated translation of *Pongsan T'alch'um*. Korea. 1700-1983. 535

Brief comments on and German translation of Edward Bond's *Summer*. Germany, West: Munich. 1983. 764

Documentation of Ingmar Bergman's tripartite theatre project. Sweden. Germany, West: Munich. 1981. 844

English translations of *commedia dell'arte* lazzi and two complete scenarios. Italy. 1734. 2018

Plays/librettos/scripts

Turkish siege and the relief of Vienna as a subject of drama and theatre. Austria: Vienna. 1683-1983. 1001

Involvement of the audience in Ben Jonson's work as satirist and playwright, with some playtexts from the First Folio. England. 1598-1614. 1042

Collection of articles, interviews and scripts on Mexican American theatre. USA. Mexico. 1983. 1362

Unpublished scene from Richard Cumberland's *The Wheel of Fortune*. England: London. 1795. 1557

Playwrights Horizons (New York, NY)

Performance/production

Albert Innaurato directs production of his revision of *Benno Blimpie*. USA: New York, NY. 1973-1983. 1537

Five critics review Jerry Zak's production of Christopher Durang's play *Baby with the Bathwater*. USA: New York, NY. 1983. 1544

Playwrights SEE: Playwriting, and Plays/librettos/scripts

Playwriting

Administration

Efforts of Jack Lang, Minister of Culture, to decentralize theatre. France. 1982-1983. 124

Unemployment among Black theatre professionals. UK-England: London. 1974-1979. 146

Relationship between funding, repertoire and commissioning of new works. UK-Scotland. 1982. 558

Round table discussion between playwrights and their agents. USA. 1983. 562

Copyrights for directors' contributions to the plays they stage. USA. 1983. 563

Censorship on the American stage, particularly of Bertolt Brecht. USA. 1941-1949. 564

Audience

Interaction needed among playwright, audience and actors. USA. 1983. 171

Institutions

Annual report of the Austrian Federal Theatres. Austria: Vienna. 1982-1983. 284

Classical and anti-classical traditions in contemporary theatre. Canada. 1960-1979. 586

Balance of classic plays against modern plays at the National Theatre and the Royal Shakespeare Company. UK-England. 1900-1983. 626

Collaborative production efforts of Bush Theatre. UK-England. 1983. 630

Organization and productions of Black Theatre Co-operative. UK-England. 1979. 631

Performance/production

Comprehensive theatre history presented within a cultural context. 499 B.C.-1983 A.D. 412

Survey of Native American dramatists and their use of dramatic ritual. USA. 1850-1980. 463

History of Black theatre with emphasis on actors and dramatists. USA. 1795-1975. 477

Relationship between Bertolt Brecht and Asian theatre. Asia. Germany. 1925-1981. 665

Playwriting — cont'd

Plays/librettos/scripts

Playwriting — cont'd

Segmental analysis of Anton Čechov's plays. Russia. 1860-1904.
1222

Two reports about playwright Paco Ignacio Taibo and his play *Morir del todo*. Spain. Mexico. 1958-1973.
1226

Development of older, comic woman as character type. Spain: Madrid. 1780-1825.
1234

Study of Benito Pérez Galdós' plays. Spain. 1843-1920.
1237

Theatre as lie and reality as truth in García Lorca's plays. Spain. English-speaking countries. North America. 1930-1978.
1243

Interview with playwright José Bergamín. Spain. 1925-1980.
1245

Work and life of the playwright and novelist Ramón María del Valle-Inclán. Spain: Galicia. 1866-1936.
1251

Lope de Vega's forty extant texts are examined to determine authorship of *The False Lackey*. Spain. 1609-1635.
1254

Expressionism in contemporary Spanish theatre. Spain. 1920-1980.
1257

Problems of contemporary dramatists, including formal productions and criticism. Sweden. 1983.
1261

August Strindberg's life and plays. Sweden. 1849-1912.
1267

Analysis of August Strindberg's plays. Sweden. 1849-1912.
1268

Interview with Gerlind Reinshagen and review of his play *Eisenherz (Ironheart)* produced in Bochum and Zürich. Switzerland: Zürich. Germany, West: Bochum. 1983.
1271

Epic structure in contemporary drama. UK. 1968-1981.
1275

Interview with playwright Stewart Parker. UK. 1941-1983.
1276

Essays on George Bernard Shaw's life and works. UK. 1856-1950.
1277

Description of a letter by playwright T.W. Robertson. UK-England: London. 1862.
1280

Study of George Bernard Shaw's 'Unreasonable Man'. UK-England. 1885-1950.
1282

Willy Russell's work as a playwright with discussion of his social and political commitment. UK-England. 1970-1983.
1283

George Bernard Shaw as director-playwright. UK-England. 1914.
1284

Plot, structure and action in John Arden's *Serjeant Musgrave's Dance*. UK-England. 1959.
1288

Peter Shaffer's revision of *Amadeus*. UK-England: London. USA: New York, NY. 1979-1980.
1290

Analysis of plays by John Osborne. UK-England. 1929-1982.
1291

Analysis of character and structure in G.B. Shaw's *The Devil's Disciple*. UK-England. USA. 1897-1983.
1293

Analysis of playwright Peter Nichols' work, and his reasons for retiring from playwriting. UK-England. 1967-1983.
1297

Biography of Noel Coward with analysis of his plays. UK-England. 1899-1973.
1298

Peter Terson's work, especially his association with National Youth Theatre. UK-England. 1960-1983.
1299

Influence of Shakespeare, Beckett and Wittgenstein on the plays of Tom Stoppard. UK-England. 1963-1979.
1302

D.H. Lawrence as dramatist. UK-England. 1885-1930.
1303

Playwright David Hare's career and interests in Fringe theatre, television and film. UK-England. 1947-1983.
1304

Evolution of Edward Bond's *Summer*. UK-England. 1980-1983. 1308

Character analysis of Carr in *Travesties*, by Tom Stoppard. UK-England. 1974.
1309

Analysis of Tom Stoppard's plays. UK-England. 1967-1983. 1311

Actors' influence on Shaw's theatrical ending of *The Devil's Disciple*. UK-England. 1897.
1315

Critical account of Christopher Hampton's work. UK-England. 1900-1983.
1316

Memoirs of journalist Stephen McKenna on John Millington Synge's apprenticeship years in Paris. UK-Ireland. France: Paris. 1895-1902.
1324

Representational and modernist comedic aspects of J.M. Synge's *The Playboy of the Western World*. UK-Ireland. 1907.
1326

William Butler Yeats as visionary dramatist. UK-Ireland. 1865-1939.
1327

Analysis of Samuel Beckett's *Not I*. UK-Ireland. France. 1971. 1329

Influence of Shakespeare and Percy Bysshe Shelley on Sean O'Casey's *The Shadow of a Gunman*. UK-Ireland: Dublin. 1923.
1332

Tom Lannon discusses background of his play *Children of the Dead End*. UK-Scotland. 1983.
1339

Life and works of playwright Joe Corrie. UK-Scotland. 1894-1968.
1340

Career of playwright Stanley Eveling. UK-Scotland. 1930-1983. 1341

Louisa Medina's popular dramatic adaptations of the works of Edward Bulwer-Lytton, Ernest Maltravers and Robert Bird. USA. 1833-1838.
1346

Eugene O'Neill's life and work. USA. 1888-1953. 1349

Similarities between the plays *The Dutchman* and *Zoo Story*. USA: New York, NY. 1964.
1350

Memoir of meeting with playwright George S. Kaufman. USA. 1922-1961.
1359

Eugene O'Neill's mysticism linked to *Light on the Path* by Mabel Collins. USA. Japan. 1915-1956.
1364

World-wide response to A.R. Gurney Jr.'s dramas of New England life. USA. 1983.
1365

Tennessee Williams' life and analysis of his plays. USA. 1914-1983.
1366

Assessment of the apparent artistic decline in Tennessee Williams' later writings. USA. 1965-1983.
1367

Plea that plays be considered serious literature. USA. 1900-1983.
1368

Realistic structure of Eugene O'Neill's *The Iceman Cometh*. USA: New York, NY. 1940-1949.
1371

Implications of Black and non-Black theatre segregation, noting that Black playwrights are expected to write about life. USA. 1980. 1376

History of American drama. USA. 1900-1982. 1378

Sixty-three year career of William Gillette as actor and playwright. USA. 1873-1936.
1380

Errors in various Eugene O'Neill biographies. USA. 1888-1953. 1382

Plays and productions at Young Playwrights Festival. USA: New York, NY. 1982.
1384

Critical examination of Lorraine Hansberry's influence on drama. USA. 1960-1979.
1387

Effects of national and international politics on playwrights of the 'generation of 1958'. Venezuela. 1945-1983.
1392

Irreverent aspects of Irish comedy seen through the works of 14 playwrights. Eire. UK-Ireland. 1840-1965.
1555

Unpublished scene from Richard Cumberland's *The Wheel of Fortune*. England: London. 1795.
1557

Plays of Plautus and Terence related to Roman society. Roman Republic. 254-159 B.C.
1587

Comic techniques in Alan Ayckbourn's *The Norman Conquests*. UK-England. 1974.
1589

Comic irony and anti-heroes in Irish comedy and influence on Harold Pinter, Samuel Beckett and Tom Stoppard. UK-Ireland. Eire. 1900-1940.
1593

Review essay of Sam Shepard's *Fool for Love*. USA: San Francisco, CA. 1983.
1595

Analysis of Oskar Kokoschka's theory through *Murderer Hope of Womankind*. Austria: Vienna. 1904-1912.
1635

New forms of realism. Europe. North America. 1970. 1639

Study of Fernando Arrabal's playwriting technique. France. 1932.
1644

Contradiction in personal and artistic life of Antonin Artaud. France. 1921-1948.
1645

Text of a speech by playwright Dario Fo. Italy. 1974. 1650

Change in style of Arthur Kopit's playwriting after *Wings*. USA. 1965-1982.
1654

Problems of reconciling experimentation and acceptance are discussed by four new playwrights. USA. 1983.
1656

Survey of alternative theatre. USA. 1945. 1657

Realism in *Arden of Faversham*. England: London. 1588-1593. 1689

Relationship between costume changes and change in wearer's fate. Greece. 405 B.C.
1694

Playwriting — cont'd

Wole Soyinka's plays echo themes of Aeschylus, Euripides and Shakespeare. Nigeria. Greece: Athens. UK-England: London. 1980.
1700

Theatrical effect preserved in operatic adaptations of Werner Egk's *Peer Gynt* and Aribert Reimann's *King Lear* at the Münchener Festspiele. Germany, West: Munich. 1982.
1953

Review of puppet plays for adults by Eric Bass presented at the Uppsala Festival. USA: New York, NY. Sweden: Uppsala. 1970-1983.
2066

Reference materials

Biographical entries on playwrights and screenwriters. 1983.
13

Encyclopedia of world historical and modern drama. 499 B.C.-1983 A.D.
1396

Illustrated documentation of Friedrich Hebbel's stay in Vienna. Austria: Vienna. 1845-1863.
1398

Ben Jonson encyclopedia. England. 1572-1637.
1400

Brief biographies of Renaissance playwrights. Europe. 1400-1600.
1404

Chronological reference guide to works on and about Alfred de Musset. France. 1830-1980.
1408

Bibliography of Jean Genet criticism. France. 1943-1980.
1409

Playwright Dario Niccodemi's letters to actress Niobe Sanguinetti. Italy. 1921-1927.
1415

Brief survey of post-war theatre with 25 play synopses. UK. 1945-1983.
1420

Survey of twentieth century British dramatists. UK. 1902-1975. 1422

Biographical guide to British playwrights. UK. 1945-1983. 1423

Revision of T.W. Robertson's playlist in *History of English Drama 1660-1900, V.* UK-England: London. 1849-1866.
1424

Letters of playwright John Millington Synge. UK-Ireland. 1871-1909.
1431

Career opportunities for playwrights. USA. 1983.
1433

List of theatre companies, playwriting awards and grants. USA. 1983.
1439

Biography of Richard Nelson Lee and list of 132 works. UK-England: London. 1830-1872.
1734

Relation to other fields

Introduction to essay collection *The Sociology of Theatre*. Europe. North America. 1983.
1448

History of Jesuit theatre to temporary suppression of the Order. Europe. Japan. 1550-1773.
1449

Jacques Copeau's reading of his play *The Little Pauper* to the Cistercians during the Occupation. France: Pernand. 1940-1944. 1450

Wole Soyinka's journalism related to his poems and plays. Nigeria. 1962-1982.
1459

Statue of playwright Henrik Ibsen. Norway: Oslo. 1828-1906. 1460

Dramatist Stanisław Wyspiański's painting of a Tartar costume, based on a folk tradition stock type — Lajkonik. Poland: Kraków. Austria. 1901-1907.
1461

First hand experience of performing mythical plays in country fields. Italy. 1983.
1664

Athol Fugard's plays are compared to Bantustan agitprop and historical drama. South Africa, Republic of. 1955-1980.
1665

Theory/criticism

Collected theory and criticism by women in theatre on women in theatre. USA. UK. 1850-1983.
114

Dramatic language related to action. England. 1559-1603. 1480

Critical analysis of dramatic methods from Sophocles to Harold Pinter. Europe. North America. 499 B.C.-1983 A.D.
1485

Rapport between social setting and dramatic text. France: Paris. 1971-1980.
1489

Influence of Bertolt Brecht's methods on playwright Heiner Müller and concept of today's theatre. Germany, East. 1983.
1504

Imamu Amiri Baraka's links to aesthetically white culture. USA. 1969.
1516

Effect of social conditions on performance styles. USA. Greece. 499 B.C.-1983 A.D.
1517

Hannah Arendt's theoretical work with reference to Gotthold Lessing, Bertolt Brecht, Franz Kafka and Isak Dinesen. USA. Europe. 1900-1983.
1518

Imamu Amiri Baraka's aesthetics find their origins in Blues music. USA. 1963-1967.
1521

Postscriptive performance text and experimental theatre groups. North America. 1983.
1672

Training

Examination of Ritva Holmberg's teaching methods for dramaturgs. Finland: Helsinki. 1965-1983.
1522

Playwriting SEE ALSO: Plays/librettos/scripts

Plebejer proben den Aufstand, Die (Plebeians Test the Revolt, The)

Plays/librettos/scripts

Two versions of *Coriolanus* by Bertolt Brecht and Günter Grass in view of events of June 17, 1953. Germany, East: East Berlin. Germany, West. 1953.
1146

Plenty

Performance/production

Eight critics review David Hare's production of his play *Plenty*. USA: New York, NY. 1983.
953

Plot/subject/theme

Institutions

History of Puerto Rican avant-garde theatre. Puerto Rico. 1811-1970.
617

Need for mythology in the repertory of children's theatre to cope with the modern world. Sweden. 1983.
620

Performance/production

Origins and evolution of the *Kuchipudi* dance drama. India. 200 B.C.-1983 A.D.
532

Problems of antisemitism in staging *The Merchant of Venice*. Israel. 1936-1980.
663

Production of *Wiespätissn*, a peace play, and audience reactions. Germany, West: West Berlin. 1982.
783

Karl Kraus' and Jehoshua Sobol's plays devoted to Vienna of 1900 and produced at Edinburgh Festival. UK-Scotland: Edinburgh. 1983.
902

Plays/librettos/scripts

Comprehensive study of Neil Simon's plays, screenplays and musical comedies. USA. 1927-1981.
488

Shift in dramatic emphasis in Igor Strawinsky's *Apollon Musagete* due to sets, costumes and choreography. USA: Washington, DC, New York, NY. 1927-1979.
522

References to dance in the *Shih Ching* and other early Chinese texts. China. 1099-600 B.C.
537

Epic texts form the thematic basis of Indian dance-drama. India. 800-1800.
539

History of the narrative theme of *Dōjōji (A Woman and a Bell)*. Japan. 1041-1800.
545

Bhāva (mood) as expressed through the presentational techniques of *kathakali*. India. 1600-1983.
546

Effects of foreign invasion and political instability on theatre. Argentina. 1900-1983.
999

History of contemporary Australian drama with emphasis on popular playwright David Williamson. Australia. 1969-1980.
1000

Turkish siege and the relief of Vienna as a subject of drama and theatre. Austria: Vienna. 1683-1983.
1001

Playwright Thomas Bernhard's affinity with philosophy of Ludwig Josef Johan Wittgenstein. Austria. 1970-1982.
1002

Grégoire de Tours' influence on Franz Grillparzer's play *Thou Shalt Not Lie*. Austria. 1838.
1004

Treatment of justice and order in plays by Franz Grillparzer. Austria. 1791-1872.
1006

Critical analysis of three of Elias Canetti's plays. Austria. 1932-1964.
1008

Denunciation of collective violence reflected in the role of sacrifice in Michel de Ghelderode's *Barabbas*. Belgium. 1929.
1010

Influences on Michel de Ghelderode from his national culture and Bertolt Brecht. Belgium. 1919-1962.
1011

Plot/subject/theme — cont'd

Comparison of symbolist drama by Maurice Maeterlinck and opera by Claude Debussy. Belgium. 1900-1983.   1012

Development of social themes in Bolivian drama. Bolivia. 1944-1983.   1014

Audience reaction and cancellation of tour of Somerset Maugham's *The Land of Promise*. Canada. USA. UK-England. 1914.   1015

Canadian theatre and history as subject in Canadian drama. Canada. 1867-1982.   1017

Research, writing and first performance of historical drama by Yan Haiping on the subject of Chinese Emperor Li Shimin. China, People's Republic of. 1979-1982.   1021

Latin American theatre and progressive social movements. Costa Rica. Argentina. Peru. 1588-1983.   1022

Modern Cuban theatre, influenced by Bertolt Brecht, reflects the revolutionary process. Cuba. 1850-1983.   1023

Profile of bilingual playwright Antoine O'Flatharta. Eire. 1981.   1025

Influences of Jonathan Swift's satire in plays by W.B. Yeats and Denis Johnston. Eire. 1928-1960.   1026

Examination of *Hamlet*, I.iv. 13-38 applying Aristotelian criteria. England: London. 1600-1601.   1027

Feminist analysis of sex roles in Shakespeare. England. 1595-1615.   1028

Examples of folklore and humanistic philosophy in *Pericles*. England. 1608-1609.   1029

Useful aspects of Cyrus Hoy's commentaries on Thomas Dekker. England: London. 1597-1630.   1030

Shakespearean influence on Ben Jonson's *Bartholomew Fair*. England. 1614.   1033

Appearance of Banquo's ghost in *Macbeth* clarifies the relation of the audience to the play. England. 1605-1606.   1034

Relationship of various arts to Shakespearean production. England. USA. 1590-1981.   1035

Plato's concept of androgyny in Jonson's *The New Inn*. England. 1629.   1036

Study of Thomas Otway's plays. England. 1652-1685.   1039

Fusion of Stoicism and Christianity in *Hamlet*. England: London. 1600-1601.   1041

Involvement of the audience in Ben Jonson's work as satirist and playwright, with some playtexts from the First Folio. England. 1598-1614.   1042

Irony and metadrama in Christopher Marlowe's plays. England. 1564-1593.   1044

Essays on Restoration theatre and drama, with devised criteria for evaluation. England. 1660-1800.   1046

Political prophecy in *Macbeth* IV.i. England: London. 1605-1606.   1048

Art of rule and rule of art in Shakespeare's histories. England. 1590-1599.   1050

Ironic satire in *Every Man Out of His Humour*. England. 1599.   1052

Imitation and creation in *Measure for Measure*. England. 1604-1605.   1053

Discussion of playwright Robert Greene's pamphlet *A Disputation*. England. 1581-1592.   1054

Hidden topicality of 'Saracen' drama. England: London. 1580-1642.   1056

Struggle for power in Shakespeare's history plays. England. 1591-1595.   1059

Origins of Hamlet's 'calf' reference. England: London. 1600-1601.   1061

Study of recurring themes and dramatic structure of *Richard II*. England. 1595-1596.   1062

Themes of repentance and retribution in Renaissance drama. England. 1500-1600.   1063

Heywood's *A Woman Killed with Kindness* as a source for Shakespeare's *Othello*. England. 1604.   1066

Authorship, censorship and thematic analysis of *Westward Ho!*. England. 1570-1637.   1067

John Webster's visual drama. England. 1580-1634.   1068

Ironic parallels between *The Tempest* and the political activities of the time. England. North America. South America. 1611-1612.   1072

Metadramatic elements in Shakespeare's *Troilus and Cressida*. England. 1601-1602.   1074

Shakespeare's knowledge of Arab world and influence on later regional writers. England. Arabia. 1606-1981.   1075

Paternal authority and sex roles in Shakespeare's plays. England. 1595-1615.   1079

Sources and analogues of a lost miracle play. England: Durham. 1200-1500.   1084

Textual analysis of the past in theatre productions to achieve a relationship with the present. Europe. 1605-1606.   1086

Treatment of violence and its aesthetics in theatre, film and literature. Europe. 1983.   1090

Analysis of Botho Strauss' *Kalldewey, Farce*. Europe. 1964.   1091

Bourgeois life as seen through children's plays. Europe. 1770-1800.   1092

Theme of madness in theatre. Europe. 1664-1936.   1093

Critical examination of playwright Ilpo Tuomarila. Finland. 1972-1983.   1096

Moral and social themes in contemporary Finnish drama. Finland. 1981.   1097

Cult of manhood in dramas of Yukio Mishima, Jean Genet and Rainer Werner Fassbinder. France. Japan. 1947-1983.   1099

Metaphorical nature of decor implied in playtexts. France. 1806-1827.   1103

Love, freedom and the emergence of the generous hero in Pierre Corneille's early plays. France. 1629-1640.   1105

The condemnation of pleasure dominated by lust and gluttony in morality plays. France. 1400-1499.   1106

Materialistic reading of Samuel Beckett's work. France. 1938.   1107

The themes of freedom, death and suicide in Albert Camus' *Caligula*. France. 1945.   1110

Typology and analysis of French sacred drama. France. 1550-1650.   1111

Aesthetic continuity in Pierre Corneille's movement from comedy to tragedy. France. 1606-1684.   1112

Michel Vinaver's plays and their production histories. France. 1954-1980.   1114

Folklore spectacles and 'safe' subjects have replaced political drama in French Black African theatre. French-speaking countries. 1937-1980.   1115

Bourgeois interests in *Wilhelm Meister's Theatrical Mission* by Goethe. Germany. 1777-1785.   1116

Attitude towards war in Ernst Toller's plays. Germany. 1918-1927.   1118

Divergence of theoretical and practical concerns in Bertolt Brecht's plays. Germany. 1918-1956.   1121

Contradiction between good and evil in capitalist society as reflected in Bertolt Brecht's *The Good Woman of Sezuan*. Germany. 1938-1941.   1122

Elusive meaning and non-verbal communication in Hofmannsthal's *The Difficult Man*. Germany. 1921.   1124

Goethe's regard for Shakespeare and influences observed in *Faust*. Germany. 1770-1832.   1125

Anti-war plays by Bertolt Brecht and Johannes R. Becher on German invasion of the Soviet Union. Germany. 1942-1943.   1126

Bertolt Brecht's theory of social basis of personal contradictions. Germany. 1918-1956.   1129

Theme of war in German expressionist drama. Germany. 1914-1919.   1133

Catholic interpretation of *Der 24 Februar* by Zacharias Werner. Germany. 1809-1814.   1134

Composition and thematic analysis of Goethe's *Ur-Faust*. Germany. 1775-1832.   1137

Dramatic structure of Gotthold Ephraim Lessing's *Minna of Barnhelm* represents cultural atmosphere of the time. Germany. 1767.   1138

The Measures Taken as Bertolt Brecht's first Marxist play. Germany. 1930.   1139

Analysis of the early plays of Bertolt Brecht. Germany. 1925.   1140

History of criticism and interpretation of Shakespeare's *A Midsummer Night's Dream*. Germany. 1700-1982.   1142

Heiner Müller continues the Brechtian tradition in political drama. Germany, East. 1960-1982.   1144

SUBJECT INDEX

SUBJECT INDEX

Plot/subject/theme — cont'd

Function of props and settings in plays by George Bernard Shaw. UK-England. 1894-1907. 1281

Willy Russell's work as a playwright with discussion of his social and political commitment. UK-England. 1970-1983. 1283

George Bernard Shaw as director-playwright. UK-England. 1914. 1284

Tragic value of *Hamlet* changed by 20th century criticism. UK-England: London. USA. 1864-1983. 1285

Ronald Harwood discusses his plays *The Dresser* and *After the Lions*, the latter play based on the life of Sarah Bernhardt. UK-England: London. 1983. 1286

Characterization and setting used to challenge audience views in George Bernard Shaw's *Major Barbara*. UK-England. 1907. 1287

Reasons for Deeley's calling himself Orson Welles in *Old Times* are based on film *The Magnificent Ambersons*. UK-England. USA. 1942-1971. 1289

Peter Shaffer's revision of *Amadeus*. UK-England: London. USA: New York, NY. 1979-1980. 1290

Analysis of plays by John Osborne. UK-England. 1929-1982. 1291

Analysis of playwright Peter Nichols' work, and his reasons for retiring from playwriting. UK-England. 1967-1983. 1297

Study of Bernard Pomerance's dramatic parable, *The Elephant Man*. UK-England. 1978. 1300

Universal myths in *Pygmalion* as encouragement for the audience to break from settled beliefs. UK-England. 1914. 1301

Influence of Shakespeare, Beckett and Wittgenstein on the plays of Tom Stoppard. UK-England. 1963-1979. 1302

D.H. Lawrence as dramatist. UK-England. 1885-1930. 1303

Alan Ayckbourn's plays: their seriousness. UK-England. 1970-1979. 1306

Shaw's manipulation of audience reaction in *Major Barbara*. UK-England. 1907. 1307

Evolution of Edward Bond's *Summer*. UK-England. 1980-1983. 1308

Political aspects of London-based plays. UK-England: London. 1983. 1310

Analysis of Tom Stoppard's plays. UK-England. 1967-1983. 1311

Actors' influence on Shaw's theatrical ending of *The Devil's Disciple*. UK-England. 1897. 1315

Analysis of Tom Stoppard's *The Real Thing*. UK-England. 1982. 1317

Influence of Percy Bysshe Shelley's poetry on Sean O'Casey. UK-Ireland: Dublin. 1923-1946. 1318

Anti-war themes in Sean O'Casey's ballads. UK-Ireland: Dublin. 1916-1918. 1319

Comparison of experiential writing of J.M. Synge and Henry David Thoreau. UK-Ireland. USA. 1898-1907. 1320

Krapp's Last Tape by Samuel Beckett as a parody of both performance and themes in poetry. UK-Ireland. 1957. 1321

Role of folklore in Irish Literary Revival. UK-Ireland. 1888-1920. 1322

Influence on Brecht of Sean O'Casey's use of songs to overcome the boundaries of illusion in his drama. UK-Ireland: Dublin. 1923-1926. 1325

Representational and modernist comedic aspects of J.M. Synge's *The Playboy of the Western World*. UK-Ireland. 1907. 1326

William Butler Yeats as visionary dramatist. UK-Ireland. 1865-1939. 1327

Changes made in the three different versions of the play *Red Roses for Me* by Sean O'Casey. UK-Ireland. 1942-1956. 1328

Analysis of Samuel Beckett's *Not I*. UK-Ireland. France. 1971. 1329

Theme of insurrection in Sean O'Casey's three Dublin plays. UK-Ireland: Dublin. 1923-1926. 1331

Influence of Shakespeare and Percy Bysshe Shelley on Sean O'Casey's *The Shadow of a Gunman*. UK-Ireland: Dublin. 1923. 1332

American influence of Melville's short story *Cock-A-Doodle Doo!* on O'Casey's play. UK-Ireland. USA. 1949. 1333

Imagery of the apocalyptic symbol of the black pig in works by William Butler Yeats. UK-Ireland. 1880-1910. 1334

Sources of power in Samuel Beckett's *Footfalls*. UK-Ireland. France. 1957. 1335

Images of the supernatural in William Butler Yeat's *The Countess Cathleen*. UK-Ireland. 1890. 1336

Tom Lannon discusses background of his play *Children of the Dead End*. UK-Scotland. 1983. 1339

Life and works of playwright Joe Corrie. UK-Scotland. 1894-1968. 1340

Career of playwright Stanley Eveling. UK-Scotland. 1930-1983. 1341

Themes of and influences on Sam Shepard's plays. USA. 1943-1983. 1343

Similarities between the plays *The Dutchman* and *Zoo Story*. USA: New York, NY. 1964. 1350

Hart Crane's influence on plays by Tennessee Williams. USA. 1938-1980. 1354

Treatment of the war in American dramaturgy. USA. 1936-1943. 1356

Memoir of meeting with playwright George S. Kaufman. USA. 1922-1961. 1359

Philosophic examination of Eugene O'Neill's *Long Day's Journey into Night*. USA. 1940. 1360

World-wide response to A.R. Gurney Jr.'s dramas of New England life. USA. 1983. 1365

Study of Hamlin Garland's regional social drama *Under the Wheel*. USA. 1890. 1370

The character of Arlene in Marsha Norman's play *Getting Out*, and her effect on the audience. USA. 1981. 1372

Ironic use of folklore in Sam Shepard's *Buried Child*. USA. 1978. 1373

Only three Tony-Award-winning plays reflect feminist ideology. USA: New York, NY. UK-England. 1960-1979. 1374

Implications of Black and non-Black theatre segregation, noting that Black playwrights are expected to write about life. USA. 1980. 1376

Catholicism and Oriental philosophy in plays of Eugene O'Neill. USA. 1888-1953. 1377

Study of David Mamet's *American Buffalo*. USA. 1977. 1379

Adaptation of Flannery O'Connor's stories to readers theatre. USA. 1982. 1381

Lee Strasberg on Ibsen and *Peer Gynt*. USA: New York, NY. 1906-1982. 1385

Critical examination of Lorraine Hansberry's influence on drama. USA. 1960-1979. 1387

Interview with director and cast of Yale Repertory's production of G.B. Shaw's *The Philanderer*. USA: New Haven, CT. 1982. 1389

Handbook of textual analysis. USSR. 1983. 1390

Effects of national and international politics on playwrights of the 'generation of 1958'. Venezuela. 1945-1983. 1392

Influence of European avant-garde on Slavko Grum's drama. Yugoslavia. 1920-1929. 1394

Realism in drama, acting, staging and design. Yugoslavia. 1920-1930. 1395

Irreverent aspects of Irish comedy seen through the works of 14 playwrights. Eire. UK-Ireland. 1840-1965. 1555

A Midsummer Night's Dream as a parody of Edmund Spenser's *The Teares of the Muses*. England. 1595. 1556

Folly in Renaissance comedy. England. 1530-1555. 1560

Comparison of family relationships in Shakespeare and Restoration comedy of manners. England. 1595-1699. 1561

Problems of theatricality and limits of illusion in Pierre Corneille's *The Comic Illusion*. France. 1606-1684. 1563

Psychological foundations of Pierre Corneille's dramatic *oeuvre* in *Mélite*. France. 1606-1684. 1564

Representation of court manners in comedy. France: Paris. 1650-1715. 1565

Alfred Jarry's *Ubu* Cycle with an emphasis on its protagonist. France. 1896-1907. 1566

Affinities between Pierre Corneille's *The Royal Square* and Molière's *The Misanthrope*. France. 1606-1684. 1569

Pierre Corneille's early comedies as variations in comic form. France. 1606-1684. 1570

Discursive authority in Pierre Corneille's *Le Menteur*. France. 1606-1684. 1571

International Bibliography of Theatre: 1983   249

Plot/subject/theme — cont'd

Essays on and a bibliographical guide to Pierre Corneille's comedies. France. 1606-1684. 1572

Reasons for different responses to the Amphitryon myth between the 17th and 20th century audiences. France. 1668-1980. 1574

Molière's intended meaning in *The Learned Ladies*. France. 1672. 1577

Aesthetic imbalance resulting from Pierre Corneille's concern for propriety in *Théodore*. France. 1606-1684. 1578

Themes of gift-giving and women in Pierre Corneille's works. France. 1606-1684. 1579

Political meaning of Caspar Stieler's comedies places them within the mainstream of other contemporary European plays. Germany. 1600-1699. 1580

Examination of Baroque themes and writers. Germany. 1618-1685. 1581

Description of *thullal*, a form of comedy, created by Kunchan Nambiar, and performed by a single actor. India: Kerala. 1700-1799. 1583

Comparison of *kyōgen* and early English comedy. Japan. England. 1400. 1585

Plays of Plautus and Terence related to Roman society. Roman Republic. 254-159 B.C. 1587

Analysis of forms, styles, characters and influences in Valle-Inclán's *comedias bárbaras*. Spain: Galicia. 1866-1936. 1588

Playfulness in Tom Stoppard's plays. UK-England. 1937-1983. 1592

Comic irony and anti-heroes in Irish comedy and influence on Harold Pinter, Samuel Beckett and Tom Stoppard. UK-Ireland. Eire. 1900-1940. 1593

Interview with playwright Beth Henley. USA. 1983. 1594

Review essay of Sam Shepard's *Fool for Love*. USA: San Francisco, CA. 1983. 1595

Examination of Harvey Fierstein's *Torch Song Trilogy*. USA: New York, NY. 1983. 1596

Egische Ciarenz's plays, particularly *Kafkaz*, are placed between Futurism and agitprop theatre. Armenia. 1923. 1634

Analysis of Oskar Kokoschka's theory through *Murderer Hope of Womankind*. Austria: Vienna. 1904-1912. 1635

Humanist examination of Samuel Beckett's plays. Europe. 1906-1983. 1637

New forms of realism. Europe. North America. 1970. 1639

Epistemological paradox in Samuel Beckett's plays. Europe. 1906-1983. 1640

Study of Jean Tardieu's plays. France. 1947-1980. 1642

Negation of the theatre by Samuel Beckett, Antonin Artaud and Carmelo Bene. France. Italy. 1925-1960. 1643

Study of Fernando Arrabal's playwriting technique. France. 1932. 1644

Contradiction in personal and artistic life of Antonin Artaud. France. 1921-1948. 1645

Jean Genet's *The Blacks* and his theory of ritual in context of Theatre of the Absurd and Total Theatre. France: Paris. 1948-1968. 1647

Part one of an essay on Ruggero Vasari's *macchinismo* as a theme of the Futurist theatre. Italy. 1923-1932. 1648

Part two of an essay on Ruggero Vasari's plays and machinery as a theme of the Futurist theatre. Italy. 1923-1932. 1649

Text of a speech by playwright Dario Fo. Italy. 1974. 1650

Incremental repetition and inter-relationship in the plays of Wole Soyinka. Nigeria. 1956-1982. 1652

Miron Bialaszewski's experiments in producing his own work. Poland. 1955-1983. 1653

Change in style of Arthur Kopit's playwriting after *Wings*. USA. 1965-1982. 1654

Study of form, style and theme in John Webster's plays. England: London. 1603-1640. 1686

Metadramatic analysis of *Hamlet*. England. 1600-1601. 1687

Critical essays on *King Lear*. England. 1605. 1688

Realism in *Arden of Faversham*. England: London. 1588-1593. 1689

Relationship between Jacobean tragedy and interpolated masque. England. 1600-1625. 1691

Principle of 'poetic justice' in the major works of Corneille. France: Paris. 1630-1639. 1693

Dramatic and military conflict in Greek tragedy. Greece. 484-415 B.C. 1697

Wole Soyinka's plays echo themes of Aeschylus, Euripides and Shakespeare. Nigeria. Greece: Athens. UK-England: London. 1980. 1700

Traditional approaches to acting and staging as clarifying methods for complex Shakespeare scenes. UK-England: Stratford-upon-Avon. 1980. 1702

Themes of British Broadcasting Corporation radio drama. UK-England: London. 1970-1980. 1710

Examination of the preproduction script for Laurence Olivier's film *Hamlet*. UK-England. 1948. 1719

Evaluation of Wolfgang Amadeus Mozart's opera *Idomeneo*. Austria: Munich. 1780-1781. 1933

Collaboration of Hugo von Hofmannsthal and Richard Strauss on *Arabella*. Austria: Vienna. 1920-1929. 1934

Carl Maria von Weber's influence on Richard Wagner. Europe. 1822-1844. 1935

Theme of war in European opera. Europe. 1597-1983. 1936

Historical subjects of the lyric repertory. France: Paris. 1850-1900. 1938

Theme of monarchy in French Romantic opera and its effect on scenery. France: Paris. 1814-1850. 1939

Victor Hugo and the original plot for the opera *Ernani* by Giuseppe Verdi. France. 1830. 1940

Analysis of Richard Wagner's *Der Ring des Nibelungen*. Germany. 1840-1860. 1945

Source material for Richard Wagner's *Tannhäuser*. Germany: Dresden. 1842-1845. 1947

In *Tristan und Isolde*, Wagner explores the world of darkness outside reality. Germany. 1854-1983. 1951

Shakespeare's influence on Arrigo Boito's libretto for *La Gioconda*, based on Victor Hugo's play. Italy. 1862-1900. 1956

Leporello as alter ego of protagonist in *Don Giovanni*. Italy. 1787. 1957

Interview with Giacomo Puccini. Italy: Milan. 1913. 1961

Robert Wilson discusses current and forthcoming projects. USA: New York, NY. 1983. 1963

Manners and customs of old Madrid in the Spanish light opera *Zarzuela*. Spain: Madrid. 1850-1935. 1975

Review of puppet plays for adults by Eric Bass presented at the Uppsala Festival. USA: New York, NY. Sweden: Uppsala. 1970-1983. 2066

Religious rites and ideology of medieval urban societies as seen in Corpus Christi plays. England. 1300-1499. 2106

Relation to other fields

Political reactions to anti-war plays and films. Germany. 1930. 1453

Theory/criticism

Imamu Amiri Baraka's aesthetics find their origins in Blues music. USA. 1963-1967. 1521

Morality of Restoration comedy. England. 1670-1700. 1599

Plough and the Stars, The

Plays/librettos/scripts

Theme of insurrection in Sean O'Casey's three Dublin plays. UK-Ireland: Dublin. 1923-1926. 1331

Plus heureux des trois, Le (Happiest of the Three, The)

Performance/production

Staging of Eugène Labiche's plays in Catalonia. Spain. France. 1967-1982. 1532

Plays/librettos/scripts

Variations on the bedroom farce form in the works of Eugène Labiche, Roger Vitrac and Samuel Beckett. France. 1870-1983. 1573

Pobreza estimada, La

Concern for the Christian minority in Lope de Vega's plays. Spain. 1600. 1239

Political theatre — cont'd

Study of genesis, development, structural components and consequences of theatre-drama performed by the Black workers. South Africa, Republic of. 1981-1983. 1673

Politics

Administration

Censorship of Brazilian theatre, causing only Broadway hits to be produced. Brazil. 1557-1983. 116

Political and cultural background of Würzburg theatres and their financial operations. Germany, West: Würzburg. 1945-1983. 131

Debate on federal arts subsidies. USA. 1943-1965. 157

Impact of government funding on the arts. USA. 1965-1982. 159

Effect of different kinds of financial support on artists. USA. 1950-1982. 163

Institutions

Broad social movement started by Teatro Abierto. Argentina: Buenos Aires. 1981-1983. 281

Theatre on the battle-front during the World Wars. Germany. 1914-1945. 305

State of theatre in Ruhr-District. Germany, West: Dortmund. 1972-1982. 307

Polish theatre under Russian rule as reflected in György Spiró's novel *Az Ikszek*. Poland: Warsaw. Russia. Hungary. 1815-1829. 325

Diversity of Latin American theatre. South America. North America. 1950-1983. 326

Effects of political instability and materialism on Chilean theatre. Chile. 1970-1983. 587

History of Puerto Rican avant-garde theatre. Puerto Rico. 1811-1970. 617

Development of nationalistic and experimental theatre in Latin America. South America. North America. 1800-1983. 618

History of Royal Shakespeare Company with emphasis on financial and aesthetic aspects and internal politics. UK-England: London. 1864-1981. 624

Collaborative effort in Welsh community results in play *All's Fair*. UK-Wales: Mid Glamorgan. 1983. 645

Cultural and political aspects of Latin American Popular Theatre Festival. USA: New York, NY. 1982. 1980

Performance/production

Comprehensive theatre history presented within a cultural context. 499 B.C.-1983 A.D. 412

Eight actors take positions on their political and social responsibilities. Germany, East. 1983. 428

History and present state of Central American theatre. Panama. Costa Rica. Guatemala. 1954-1983. 439

Memoirs of dramaturg Jan Kott. Poland. Austria: Vienna. 1957-1981. 440

History of Chicano theatre. USA. Mexico. 1965-1983. 453

Relationship between Bertolt Brecht and Asian theatre. Asia. Germany. 1925-1981. 665

Politics and theatre. Canada. 1930-1939. 689

Chinese version of *Death of a Salesman* directed by the author. China, People's Republic of: Beijing. 1983. 690

Contemporary events reflected in staging plays about Jean-Paul Marat's death. France. 1793-1797. 732

History of Agitprop theatre. Germany. USSR. 1848-1930. 743

Politics, psychology and director Elia Kazan's career. USA. 1909-1965. 949

Political censorship and Soviet productions of *Hamlet*. USSR. 1930. 995

State of political cabaret. Germany, West: Hamburg. 1982. 2002

Plays/librettos/scripts

Effects of foreign invasion and political instability on theatre. Argentina. 1900-1983. 999

Development of social themes in Bolivian drama. Bolivia. 1944-1983. 1014

Latin American theatre and progressive social movements. Costa Rica. Argentina. Peru. 1588-1983. 1022

Shakespeare's historical plays and the reaction of the Elizabethan audience. England. 1590-1613. 1031

Shakespeare's use of sources. England. 1590-1616. 1043

Political prophecy in *Macbeth* IV.i. England: London. 1605-1606. 1048

Hidden topicality of 'Saracen' drama. England: London. 1580-1642. 1056

Ironic parallels between *The Tempest* and the political activities of the time. England. North America. South America. 1611-1612. 1072

Sources used by Shakespeare for his play *Richard III*, and changes made to cater to his sovereign's political beliefs. England. 1592-1593. 1076

Textual analysis of the past in theatre productions to achieve a relationship with the present. Europe. 1605-1606. 1086

Jewish stereotypes in contemporary drama. Europe. North America. 1982. 1094

Influence of Lenin's writings on Bertolt Brecht's plays. Germany. 1930. 1128

Two versions of *Coriolanus* by Bertolt Brecht and Günter Grass in view of events of June 17, 1953. Germany, East: East Berlin. Germany, West. 1953. 1146

Dario Fo's drama in Scandinavia. Italy. Sweden. Norway. 1983. 1184

Revolutionary theatre in Nicaragua. Nicaragua. 1980-1983. 1199

Some paths for realism in Latin American theatre. South America. North America. 1955-1983. 1224

Study of Benito Pérez Galdós' plays. Spain. 1843-1920. 1237

New Vatican documents regarding the dramatist Juan de la Encina's political and ecclesiastical appointments. Spain: Salamanca. Vatican. 1469-1529. 1252

Interpretation of August Strindberg's *The Ghost Sonata* in light of contemporary problems. Sweden. 1907-1983. 1269

Epic structure in contemporary drama. UK. 1968-1981. 1275

Willy Russell's work as a playwright with discussion of his social and political commitment. UK-England. 1970-1983. 1283

Political aspects of London-based plays. UK-England: London. 1983. 1310

Effects of national and international politics on playwrights of the 'generation of 1958'. Venezuela. 1945-1983. 1392

Alfred Jarry's *Ubu* Cycle with an emphasis on its protagonist. France. 1896-1907. 1566

Plays of Plautus and Terence related to Roman society. Roman Republic. 254-159 B.C. 1587

Historical subjects of the lyric repertory. France: Paris. 1850-1900. 1938

Relation to other fields

Political ramifications of the theatrical patronage of Louis XIII and Cardinal de Richelieu. France. 1610-1643. 54

Interrelationship of Bengali political theatre with historical events. India: Bengal. 1757-1983. 58

Survival of theatre under martial law. Poland. 1981-1982. 67

Danger of using theatrical metaphors to discuss nuclear arms race. Sweden. 1982. 68

Inaugural address of American Theatre Association president Bernard S. Rosenblatt calling for support in creating public policy. USA: Minneapolis, MN. 1983. 76

History, function and methods of Soviet agitprop theatre. USSR. 1919-1934. 78

Occasions on which cultural policy issues were debated. USA. 1800-1983. 491

Reception of Bertolt Brecht in Argentina vis-à-vis political situation in the country. Argentina. 1980-1983. 1441

German theatre in Cracow and its relationship to Polish people during the uprising against Russia. Austro-Hungarian Empire: Cracow. Poland. 1863-1865. 1443

Political reactions to anti-war plays and films. Germany. 1930. 1453

Relationship between politics and the heroic tradition of Caribbean drama. Haiti. Trinidad and Tobago. Martinique. 1962-1979. 1456

Renewed interest in Bertolt Brecht stimulated by political situations. UK. 1980-1983. 1462

Athol Fugard's plays are compared to Bantustan agitprop and historical drama. South Africa, Republic of. 1955-1980. 1665

Princess Theatre (London)

Charles Kean's staging methods and the influences on them. UK-England: London. 1850-1859. 898

Principal de València

Performance spaces

One hundred fifty years of Principal de València Theatre. Spain: Valencia. 1823-1979. 391

Prinz Friedrich (Prince Friedrich)

Plays/librettos/scripts

Recently discovered manuscript of Johann Nestroy's *Prinz Friedrich*. Austria. 1833. 1551

Private Lives

Performance/production

Notes on three Broadway productions. USA: New York, NY. 1983. 911

Nine critics review Milton Katselas' production of Noel Coward's play *Private Lives*. USA: New York, NY. 1983. 1545

Private View, A

Five critics review Lee Grant's production of Vaclav Havel's play *A Private View* translated by Vera Blackwell. USA: New York, NY. 1983. 927

Processional theatre

Design/technology

Scenery for the first performance of *Representation of Saint Ursula*. Italy. 1400-1599. 579

Performance/production

Review of contemporary three-day performance of the Chester plays. Canada: Toronto, ON. 1983. 684

Men acting in women's roles, particularly in the Chester cycle's *Purification*. England: Chester. 1300-1550. 702

New information from York about problems with the Girdlers' pageant wagon and their play, *The Slaughter of the Innocents*. England: York. 1548-1554. 705

Plays/librettos/scripts

Sympathetic portrayals of splendid monarchs are rare in the Corpus Christi cycles. England. 1264-1560. 1055

Reference materials

List of 94 twentieth century works dealing with Italian sacred drama. Italy. 1300-1983. 1413

Processional theatre SEE ALSO: Pageants/parades and Classed Entries: POPULAR ENTERTAINMENT — Pageants/parades

Producing

Administration

Autobiography of Broadway producer Irene Mayer Selznick. USA. 1910-1983. 161

Difficulties of getting some plays on Broadway. USA: New York, NY. 1982-1983. 565

Design/technology

Suggestions for puppet construction, producing and marketing puppet shows. USA. 1983. 2041

Performance spaces

Proposals and experiences by theatrical operators to utilize the urban space for performances. Italy. 1983. 384

Reference materials

Letters of circus entrepreneur P.T. Barnum. USA. 1832-1891. 2016

Producing institutions SEE: Institutions, producing

Production histories

Audience

Evolution of *Gros Mourn* by Newfoundland Mummers Troupe. Canada. 1973. 1604

Design/technology

Interviews with the designers of *Cats*. USA: New York, NY. UK-England: London. 1983. 1770

Performance/production

Productions of Henrik Ibsen's *Peer Gynt* by Hans Midbøes. Norway. 1976-1980. 823

Survey of stage history of G.B. Shaw's *Man and Superman*. UK-England. 1903-1982. 876

History of a production about nine Black leaders by the African American Drama Company. USA. 1976-1983. 979

Production history of *The Best Little Whorehouse in Texas*. USA: New York, NY. 1974-1982. 1784

Comprehensive illustrated production history of Wagnerian opera. Europe. USA. Canada. 1832-1983. 1851

History and production history of Wagnerian opera. Germany. USA. 1832-1982. 1865

Plays/librettos/scripts

Michel Vinaver's plays and their production histories. France. 1954-1980. 1114

George Bernard Shaw as director-playwright. UK-England. 1914. 1284

Composition and production of George Bernard Shaw's *Saint Joan*. UK-England. 1923. 1314

Production histories SEE ALSO: Staging, and Performance/production

Professional Association of Canadian Theatres (PACT)

Institutions

Curtis Barlow as director of Professional Association of Canadian Theatres. Canada. 1983. 294

Profilo di Gustavo Modena (Profile of Gustavo Modena, A)

Performance/production

Critical re-examination of the monograph on the actor Gustavo Modena. Italy. 1832-1861. 793

Programs SEE: Collected materials

Projection SEE: Camera work/projection

Proletarian theatre

Performance/production

Topical production of Gerhart Hauptmann's *The Weavers* in working class neighborhood. Germany, West: Recklinghausen. 1979. 768

Relation to other fields

Class-conscious approach to theatre. Germany, West. 1983. 56

Circus as a staging device for a political satire. USSR. Germany. Italy. 1914-1930. 1668

Theory/criticism

Study of genesis, development, structural components and consequences of theatre-drama performed by the Black workers. South Africa, Republic of. 1981-1983. 1673

Prometheus porte-feu

Institutions

Productions of the Théâtre National of Strasbourg. France: Strasbourg. 1975-1980. 595

Promise, The SEE: *Moj bednyj Marat*

Promptbooks

Performance/production

Activities of King's Company and their staging of George Etherege's *The Man of Mode*. UK-Scotland: Edinburgh. 1678-1680. 448

Documentation on Ruben Fraga's production of *The Tower of Babel* by the Dramatic Center Vienna. Austria: Vienna. 1980-1983. 670

Production journal of *King Lear*. Canada: Stratford, ON. 1979. 1676

Psychology — cont'd

Experience of neurotic conflict in staging of psychodrama. Italy. 1980.   1659

Genesis of mnemodrama by its founder. Italy. 1983.   1660

Description of psychodrama sessions with a young boy. Italy. 1983.   1661

Special difficulties faced by a psychodrama group with paranoid patient. Italy. 1983.   1662

Santuzza Papa's transition from Freudian psychodrama to Jungian conception. Italy. 1960.   1663

First hand experience of performing mythical plays in country fields. Italy. 1983.   1664

Zerka Moreno's psychodrama in Italy. USA: New York, NY. Italy: Rome. 1960-1983.   1666

Workshop on the use of puppets in education and therapy. Nigeria: Zaria. 1983.   2067

Research/historiography

Results of a study which measures acting and monitoring skills in children. USA. 1983.   1476

Theory/criticism

Physical experience and aesthetic perception of body movement. France. 1889.   100

Issues of role playing and identity in theatre. Europe. North America. 1982.   1486

Karl Jaspers' philosophy is applied to a discussion of Luigi Pirandello. Italy. 1916-1936.   1703

Training

Psychodrama as a method of actor training within academic structure. Italy. 1960.   499

Public relations

Administration

Activities of the Audience Development Committee. USA: New York, NY. 1983.   153

Promotional campaigns for performing arts institutions. USA. 1983.   160

Four artistic directors discuss theatre relationship with community. Canada: Regina, SK, Vancouver, BC, Toronto, ON, Calgary, AB. 1983.   553

Audience

Techniques and activities for educating the playgoer. USA. 1983. 172

Sign interpretation at the New York City Opera. USA: New York, NY. 1979.   1816

Institutions

Support, information, publicity, study facilities, fundraising advice, etc., offered by the Puppet Centre Trust. UK-England: London. 1983.   2045

Reference materials

Vocational guidance directed at young people for non-acting careers in theatre. USA. 1983.   43

Public Theater (New York, NY)

Institutions

Cultural and political aspects of Latin American Popular Theatre Festival. USA: New York, NY. 1982.   1980

Performance/production

Five critics review Lee Grant's production of Vaclav Havel's play *A Private View* translated by Vera Blackwell. USA: New York, NY. 1983.   927

Six critics review Les Waters' production of Caryl Churchill's play *Fen*. USA: New York, NY. 1983.   964

Five critics review Joseph Papp's production of Thomas Babe's play *Buried Inside Extra*. USA: New York, NY. 1983.   982

Six critics review Jane Howell's production of *Richard III* mounted by the Public Theater. USA: New York, NY. 1983.   1684

Publico, El (Public, The)

Plays/librettos/scripts

Theatre as lie and reality as truth in García Lorca's plays. Spain. English-speaking countries. North America. 1930-1978.   1243

Publiekstheater (Netherlands)

Institutions

Free operating groups and institutionalized theatre. Netherlands. 1963-1983.   1609

Puccini, Giacomo

Performance/production

Harold Prince's production of Giacomo Puccini's *Turandot* at Vienna's Staatsoper. Austria: Vienna. 1983.   1839

Photographs, cast lists, synopsis and discography of Metropolitan Opera production of *La Bohème*. USA: New York, NY. 1983.   1905

Career of soprano Leona Mitchell at the Metropolitan Opera. USA. 1983.   1912

Konstantin Stanislavskij's training of opera singers. USSR. 1918-1935.   1929

Plays/librettos/scripts

Naturalism in the works of Pietro Mascagni and Giacomo Puccini. Italy. 1879-1926.   1955

Interview with Giacomo Puccini. Italy: Milan. 1913.   1961

Pulcinella

Performance/production

English translations of *commedia dell'arte* lazzi and two complete scenarios. Italy. 1734.   2018

Punch and Judy

Basic theatrical documents

Revised edition of Punch and Judy script. UK-England. 1873-1983.   2017

Puppet Centre Trust (England)

Institutions

Support, information, publicity, study facilities, fundraising advice, etc., offered by the Puppet Centre Trust. UK-England: London. 1983.   2045

Puppet People, The (New York, NY)

Performance/production

Work of The Puppet People on Broadway production of *Alice in Wonderland*. USA: New York, NY. 1982.   2055

Puppeteers

Institutions

Highlights of the festival of the Puppeteers of America. USA: Ames, IA. 1983.   2046

Performance/production

Autobiography of puppeteer Gianni Colla. Italy. 1946-1981.   2051

History of puppets and puppet-masters. Italy: Bologna. 1800-1923.   2053

Review of international puppet theatre festival. Sweden: Uppsala. 1983.   2054

Interview with puppeteer Bruce D. Schwartz. USA. 1983.   2060

Use of puppets and puppetry techniques in Arena Stage production of *Candide*. USA: Washington, DC. 1983.   2061

Sylvia Meredith discusses her work as actress and puppeteer. USA. 1938-1983.   2062

Interview with puppeteer Molly Jameson. USA. 1983.   2063

Artistry of Burr Tillstrom and his Kuklapolitan Players. USA. 1983.   2065

Interview with puppeteer Rod Young. USA: New York, NY. 1937-1983.   2085

Brief history of shadow puppetry. Europe. Asia. North America. 1500-1982.   2088

Research/historiography

Ways that library research can help puppeteers. USA. 1983.   2071

Puppeteers of America

Institutions

Highlights of the festival of the Puppeteers of America. USA: Ames, IA. 1983.   2046

Puppeteers of America — cont'd

Performance/production

Events and exhibits of Puppeteers of America Festival. USA: Ames, IA. 1983. 2057

Puppetry

Basic theatrical documents

Revised edition of Punch and Judy script. UK-England. 1873-1983. 2017

Design/technology

Laser holography as an element of scene design. Austria: Salzburg. 1948-1985. 178

Performance/production

Story of a live horse and a marionette ballerina act at the Circus Medrano. France: Paris. 1980. 2010

Theory/criticism

Semiotic study of the specific nature of theatre in relation to other arts and audience interaction with it. Spain. 1983. 108

Puppetry SEE ALSO: Classed Entries: PUPPETRY

Puppets

Design/technology

Puppets and performance techniques used in Kennedy Center production of *The Tale of Peter Rabbit*. USA: Washington, DC. 1983. 2035

Exhibition of fifty puppets owned by Tom Maud. USA: Fort Worth, TX. 1983. 2036

Technique for creating a self-contained balloon-blowing puppet. USA. 1983. 2037

Construction and use of monster puppets for teaching spelling. USA. 1980. 2038

Puppets and design concept for production of *The Second Shepherds Play*. USA: Lincoln, NE. 1983. 2039

Hints on construction of puppets and properties and lighting techniques. USA. 1983. 2040

Suggestions for puppet construction, producing and marketing puppet shows. USA. 1983. 2041

André Kertész' photographic documentation for surrealist's fascination with marionettes. Belgium: Liège. 1925-1929. 2077

All-string-controlled marionettes introduced by Samuel Seward. UK-England. 1796-1852. 2078

Marionettes designed by Robert Edmond Jones for Metropolitan Opera production of *Oedipus Rex*, under the influence of Gordon Craig and *bunraku*. USA: New York, NY. 1931. 2079

Lou Bunin memoirs of Meyer Levin's marionettes as ideally cast abstract visual images. USA: Chicago, IL. 1925-1930. 2080

Meyer Levin's marionettes as abstract visual images, influenced by Gordon Craig and Fernand Léger. USA. 1926-1930. 2081

Performance/production

Director of Polka Children's Theatre discusses children's attitude to plays and puppets. UK. 1983. 852

History of puppets and puppet-masters. Italy: Bologna. 1800-1923. 2053

Reissue of some passages and drawings from books on hand shadow puppets. Italy. Germany. UK-England. 1850-1899. 2090

Reference materials

Catalogue for an exhibition of Venetian marionettes and puppets. Italy: Venice. 1700-1899. 2086

Purdue University

Administration

Purdue University study on modern uses of historic theatres and guidelines for management. USA. 1981-1983. 154

Purification

Performance/production

Men acting in women's roles, particularly in the Chester cycle's *Purification*. England: Chester. 1300-1550. 702

Pygmalion

Plays/librettos/scripts

Examination of semiotic elements in George Bernard Shaw's *Pygmalion*. UK. 1916. 1274

George Bernard Shaw as director-playwright. UK-England. 1914. 1284

Universal myths in *Pygmalion* as encouragement for the audience to break from settled beliefs. UK-England. 1914. 1301

Quadreny, Mestres

Performance/production

Interview with and influences on postmodern composer Mestres Quaderny. Spain. 1945-1955. 1775

¿Quál es mayor perfección? (Which is Greater perfection?)

Plays/librettos/scripts

Metacritical analysis of Calderón's plays applying criteria devised for Lope de Vega. Spain. 1608-1681. 1238

Quare Fellow, The

Modern plays set in confining institutions. North America. Europe. 1900-1983. 1200

Quartermaine's Terms

Performance/production

Eight critics review Kenneth Frankel's production of Simon Gray's play *Quartermaine's Terms*. USA: New York, NY. 1983. 957

Queen Henrietta's Men (London)

New evidence suggests that Castle Ashby plays were performed at Canonbury House. England: London. 1637-1659. 707

Queen's Royal Theatre (Dublin)

Plays/librettos/scripts

Developments of Irish melodrama and its influence on later writers. UK-Ireland: Dublin. 1860-1905. 1338

Questa sera si recita a soggetto (Tonight We Improvise)

Dialectics of the actor rebellion against the stage director in Luigi Pirandello's *Tonight We Improvise*. Italy. 1930. 1179

Luigi Pirandello's earlier plays are considered prologues to *The Giants of the Mountain*. Italy. 1921-1937. 1189

Relation to other fields

Introduction of Luigi Pirandello's play *Tonight We Improvise*. Italy. 1930. 1458

Experience of neurotic conflict in staging of psychodrama. Italy. 1980. 1659

Quilico, Gino

Performance/production

Careers of father-son baritones Louis and Gino Quilico. USA: New York, NY. Canada. 1960-1983. 1922

Quilico, Louis

Performance/production

Interview with Metropolitan Opera baritone Louis Quilico. Canada: Montreal, PQ. USA: New York, NY. 1983. 1848

Careers of father-son baritones Louis and Gino Quilico. USA: New York, NY. Canada. 1960-1983. 1922

Rabb, Ellis

Eight critics review Ellis Rabb's production of George S. Kaufman's and Moss Hart's play *You Can't Take It with You*. USA: New York, NY. 1983. 972

Rabe, David

Plays/librettos/scripts

Modern plays set in confining institutions. North America. Europe. 1900-1983. 1200

Rachel, Élisa Félix

Relation to other fields

Theatrical vision and the portrait of the great French actress Rachel in Charlotte Brontë's *Villette*. UK-England. France. 1853. 70

Racine, Jean

Plays/librettos/scripts

Theme of madness in theatre. Europe. 1664-1936.
1093

Radio City Music Hall (New York, NY)

Performance/production

Holdings of the Radio City Music Hall Archives. USA: New York, NY. 1933-1979.
459

Radio drama

Plays/librettos/scripts

Comparison and contrast of radio and stage presentations of Arthur Kopit's play *Wings*. USA. 1978-1979.
1655

Semiotic analysis of popular radio comedy. Canada. 1939-1958. 1709

Themes of British Broadcasting Corporation radio drama. UK-England: London. 1970-1980.
1710

Radio SEE: Audio forms

Radlov, Sergej Ernestovič

Performance/production

Role experimental studios played in the formation of the Soviet theatre. USSR: Moscow, Leningrad. 1920-1939.
993

Radulović, Jovan

Plays/librettos/scripts

Current state of drama and theatre seen through plays and playwrights. Yugoslavia. 1983.
1393

Ragabush Puppet Theatre

Performance/production

Performances by Ragabush Puppet Theatre and Lampoon Puppet theatre at Children's Theatre Association of America Showcase. USA: Syracuse, NY. 1983.
2058

Ragionamento ingenuo, Il (Naive Reasoning, The)

Theory/criticism

Gozzi's theories of drama. Italy. 1772-1773.
1508

Raimundtheater (Vienna)

Institutions

Brief history of Raimundtheater. Austria: Vienna. 1893-1983. 1974

Rainbow Terrace

Performance/production

Tribute to Mordecai Gorelik, scenic designer, theorist, teacher, director and playwright. USA. 1899-1983.
936

Rainer and the Knife

Description and analysis of Ping Chong's work. USA. 1972-1983.
1752

Rajatabla

Plays/librettos/scripts

Effects of national and international politics on playwrights of the 'generation of 1958'. Venezuela. 1945-1983.
1392

Ralph Roister Doister

Folly in Renaissance comedy. England. 1530-1555.
1560

Rāmāyana

Epic texts form the thematic basis of Indian dance-drama. India. 800-1800.
539

Rame, Franca

Performance/production

Interview with playwright Dario Fo and his actress-wife and collaborator Franca Rame. Italy: Milan. 1982.
1623

Rameau, Jean-Philippe

Plays/librettos/scripts

Composer Jean-Philippe Rameau's contribution to development of opera. France. 1683-1764.
1941

Ramila

Theory/criticism

Articles on performance theory and practice. 1976-1983.
1477

Randolph, Thomas

Plays/librettos/scripts

Works of academic playwright Thomas Randolph. England. 1605-1635.
1064

Rank Strand

Design/technology

Description and function of the lightboard designed by Rank Strand firm. Germany, West: Stuttgart. 1964-1983.
203

Ranulf, Higden

Plays/librettos/scripts

Possible authorship of a lost Chester Corpus Christi play. England: Chester. 1268-1375.
1037

Rapp, C.W.

Performance spaces

History and restoration of Rialto Square Theatre. USA: Joliet, IL. 1926-1983.
403

Rapp, George L.

History and restoration of Rialto Square Theatre. USA: Joliet, IL. 1926-1983.
403

Rappresentazione di Sant'Orsola, La (Representation of Saint Ursula, The)

Design/technology

Scenery for the first performance of *Representation of Saint Ursula*. Italy. 1400-1599.
579

Rasi, Luigi

Performance/production

Critical summary of theatrical anecdotes as they are reported in four books. Italy. 1891-1965.
803

Review of Eleonora Duse's first biography. Italy. 1859-1901. 813

Rasselas, Prince of Abyssinia

Plays/librettos/scripts

Examination of Samuel Johnson as a character in plays by William Brough and W.S. Gilbert. UK-England: London. 1862-1893.
1313

Rational Foundation of Music, The

Theory/criticism

Phenomenological theory of performing arts. USA. 1982.
1514

Rational Theatre (Edinburgh)

Performance/production

Philosophy and intentions of Rational Theatre and ABDC Workshop's Edinburgh project. UK-England. UK-Scotland: Edinburgh. 1983.
1747

Raum

Plays/librettos/scripts

Part one of an essay on Ruggero Vasari's *macchinismo* as a theme of the Futurist theatre. Italy. 1923-1932.
1648

Part two of an essay on Ruggero Vasari's plays and machinery as a theme of the Futurist theatre. Italy. 1923-1932.
1649

Ravenscroft, Edward

Theory/criticism

Morality of Restoration comedy. England. 1670-1700.
1599

Raymond, Bill

Performance/production

Five critics review Bill Raymond and Dale Worsley's production of *Cold Harbor*. USA: New York, NY. 1983.
925

Rea, Stephen

Career of actor Stephen Rea. UK-England. UK-Ireland. 1900-1983.
881

Readers theatre

Plays/librettos/scripts

Adaptation of Flannery O'Connor's stories to readers theatre. USA. 1982.				1381

Real Thing, The

Performance/production

Peter Wood's productions of Tom Stoppard's *The Real Thing* and Harold Pinter's *Other Places*. UK-England: London. 1983.				887

Plays/librettos/scripts

Political aspects of London-based plays. UK-England: London. 1983.				1310

Analysis of Tom Stoppard's *The Real Thing*. UK-England. 1982.				1317

Realism

Institutions

Development of nationalistic and experimental theatre in Latin America. South America. North America. 1800-1983.				618

Performance/production

Overview of modern theatre from realism and naturalism onward. 1850-1982.				659

References to acting in works of Restif de la Bretonne. France: Paris. 1700-1799.				728

Edward Bulwer-Lytton's theory of the need for unified approach to productions, in response to John Calcraft's staging of *Richelieu*. UK-Ireland: Dublin. 1839.				900

Konstantin Stanislavskij's stage adaptation of Shakespeare's *Othello* for the Moscow Art Theatre. USSR: Moscow. 1929-1930.				1685

Plays/librettos/scripts

Ibsen's creation of realistic characters displaying unconscious desires. Norway. 1892.				1207

Some paths for realism in Latin American theatre. South America. North America. 1955-1983.				1224

Interview with the playwright Joan Oliver about his work. Spain. 1899-1983.				1236

Study of Hamlin Garland's regional social drama *Under the Wheel*. USA. 1890.				1370

Realistic structure of Eugene O'Neill's *The Iceman Cometh*. USA: New York, NY. 1940-1949.				1371

Realism in drama, acting, staging and design. Yugoslavia. 1920-1930.				1395

New forms of realism. Europe. North America. 1970.				1639

Naturalism in the works of Pietro Mascagni and Giacomo Puccini. Italy. 1879-1926.				1955

Theory/criticism

Study of realism, naturalism, symbolism, surrealism, expressionism and epic theatre. Europe. North America. 1900-1980.				1484

Bertolt Brecht's theatrical poetics and polemic with György Lukács on realism. Germany. Hungary. 1918-1956.				1493

Bertolt Brecht's and György Lukács' debate on realism. Germany. Hungary. 1900-1956.				1500

Nature and history of farce in theatre, film and media. Europe. USA. 425 B.C.-1982 A.D.				1600

Reconstruction

Performance spaces

Town-planning and reconstruction of Roman amphitheatre in Málaga. Spain: Málaga. Roman Empire. 200.				389

Records of Early English Drama

Performance spaces

Index to the contents of *Records of Early English Drama*, the first eight volumes. UK. 1976-1983.				7

Red River Valley Circuit

Administration

Letters and documents concerning performances at local opera houses. USA: Grand Forks, ND, Crookston, MN. 1890-1899.				155

Red Room, The SEE: Roda rummet

Red Roses for Me

Plays/librettos/scripts

Influence of Percy Bysshe Shelley's poetry on Sean O'Casey. UK-Ireland: Dublin. 1923-1946.				1318

Changes made in the three different versions of the play *Red Roses for Me* by Sean O'Casey. UK-Ireland. 1942-1956.				1328

Red Shoes, The

Performance/production

Discussion of ballet in Monte Carlo. Monaco. 1948-1983.				519

Redford, John

List of productions of plays from English Renaissance drama with brief reviews. North America. Europe. 1982-1983.				822

Redgrave, Michael

Autobiography of actor Michael Redgrave. UK. 1908-1983.				855

Reduce, Il (Ruzante Returns from the Wars)

Gianni De Luigi's staging of *Ruzante Returns from the Wars*. Italy. 1983.				1529

Reference materials

Basic theatrical documents

Discussion of prints and translation of the *fragmenten verzameling* 3-8 found in Zutphen Archive. Netherlands. 1400-1499.				574

Design/technology

Guide to costume design, including prevailing period fashions. 3000 B.C.-1983 A.D.				176

Illustrated costume history. Europe. 1500-1599.				182

Supplemental materials to costume exhibit. Europe. 1700-1800.				186

Illustrated costume history. Europe. 1700-1799.				188

Innovations in stage design by Louis-Jacques Daguerre, including a catalogue of his designs. France. 1709-1850.				193

Illustrated catalogue of work of designer Duilio Cambellotti. Italy. 1876-1960.				218

Supplementary materials to exhibit of Baroque theatre and stage design. Italy. 1600.				219

Essays and supplemental materials to exhibition of David Hockney designs, with plates. UK-England. USA. 1937.				229

Articles on designer Oliver Messel. UK-England. 1904-1978.				231

Supplementary materials to exhibit of Jo Mielziner's works. USA. 1928-1960.				233

New products of interest to designers and technicians. USA. 1900-1983.				236

Published materials for sound technicians. USA. 1983.				244

Description and listing of sound systems for theatres to aid hearing impaired. USA. 1960-1983.				246

History and description of the Motley Theatre and Costume Arts Collection. Discussed at SIBMAS. USA: Urbana, IL. 1982.				247

New products for technical theatre use. USA. 1983.				254

Comprehensive documented study of Russian Constructivism. USSR. 1917-1940.				278

André Kertész' photographic documentation for surrealist's fascination with marionettes. Belgium: Liège. 1925-1929.				2077

Institutions

Annual symposium of Mid-America Theatre Conference. USA: Iowa City, IA. 1983.				334

Document concerning foundation of Polish theatre. Poland: Kraków. 1781.				612

Letters signed by George Jolly concerning the visit of his troupe to Gdansk in August, 1650. Poland: Gdańsk. England. Germany. 1649-1650.				614

History of Teatro Colón in essays and photographs. Argentina: Buenos Aires. 1857-1983.				1827

Performance spaces

Engravings of the Municipal Theatre of Girona. Spain: Girona. 1769-1860.				390

Performance/production

Reference materials — cont'd

Plays/librettos/scripts

Relation to other fields

Reference materials SEE ALSO: Classed Entries 11-51, 489, 1396-1440, 1598, 1720, 1721, 1734, 1736, 1765, 1964-1971, 1976, 1997, 1998, 2016, 2021, 2086.

Regional theatre

Administration

Audience

Design/technology

Institutions

Repertory — cont'd

Productions of the Théâtre National of Strasbourg. France: Strasbourg. 1975-1980. 595

Brief survey of productions at German theatres in January 1983. Germany, West. 1983. 603

Presentations by Polish theatre companies at Théâtre des Nations. Poland. France: Paris. 1954-1982. 611

Need for mythology in the repertory of children's theatre to cope with the modern world. Sweden. 1983. 620

New season's productions at the Basel Stadttheater. Switzerland: Basel. 1983. 622

Balance of classic plays against modern plays at the National Theatre and the Royal Shakespeare Company. UK-England. 1900-1983. 626

Aspects of the National Theatre and the Royal Shakespeare Company are compared. UK-England. 1960. 627

Peter Hall's role as artistic director of the National Theatre, including devising the repertory and obtaining funds. UK-England: London. 1973-1983. 636

Repertory and workings of Glasgow Citizens' Theatre. UK-Scotland: Glasgow. 1983. 642

History and organization of the Irish Rebel Theatre. USA: New York, NY. 1973-1983. 648

Interview with Rod Graham, head of BBC Scotland's television drama department. UK-Scotland. 1946-1983. 1722

Administration and repertory of Finnish National Opera. Finland: Helsinki. 1983. 1828

Performance/production

Review of year's theatrical activity. Korea. 1982. 437

Monthly report about main productions at Viennese theatres. Austria: Vienna. 1983. 666

Production of Russian classical plays at Eastern European theatres. Bulgaria. Yugoslavia. Czechoslovakia. 1850-1914. 682

Survey of Sicilian theatre institutions, repertory, actors and playwrights. Italy. 1800-1950. 794

Director Stephen Porter comments on George Bernard Shaw. USA: New York, NY. 1964-1982. 947

Success of bourgeois comedy over *commedia dell'arte*. Italy: Venice. 1770-1797. 1530

Repertory of the Golden Age of Spanish theatre at the El Paso Festival. Mexico. USA: El Paso, TX. Spain. 1983. 1681

Plays/librettos/scripts

Essays on Restoration theatre and drama, with devised criteria for evaluation. England. 1660-1800. 1046

Playwrights and dramatic forms influencing Eugene O'Neill's *The Calms of Capricorn*. Europe. USA. 1953. 1088

Folklore spectacles and 'safe' subjects have replaced political drama in French Black African theatre. French-speaking countries. 1937-1980. 1115

Critical report on new plays in Spanish theatre. Spain. 1983. 1228

Problems of contemporary dramatists, including formal productions and criticism. Sweden. 1983. 1261

Historical subjects of the lyric repertory. France: Paris. 1850-1900. 1938

Evaluation of the place of Richard Wagner in opera today. Germany. 1833-1983. 1949

Reference materials

Licensing papers related to managerial and repertorial changes at London theatres. England: London. 1706-1715. 20

Annual record of Broadway and Off Broadway season. USA: New York, NY. 1981-1982. 49

Comprehensive listing of the dramatic repertory, with a note on important productions. Europe. North America. 672 B.C.-1982 A.D. 1403

Representation of Saint Ursula, The SEE: *Rappresentazione di Sant'Orsola, La*

Requeno, Vincenzo

Performance/production

Instructional material on the art of pantomimic gesture. Italy. 1982. 1733

Research institutions SEE: Institutions, research

Research/historiography

Design/technology

SIBMAS keynote address calling for accumulation of records to preserve theatre history. USA. 1982. 239

Report of research among theatrical designers. USA. 1981-1983. 259

Institutions

Organization, objectives and projects of the Institute for American Theatre Studies. USA: Bloomington, IN. 1983-1984. 351

Performance spaces

Interpretation of Johannes De Witt's drawing of the Swan theatre. England. 1596. 365

Performance/production

Study of the Italian actor Luigi Vestri applying Mario Apollonio's historiographic methodology. Italy. 1781-1841. 802

Theatre scholars said to focus too narrowly on directors. Sweden. 1983. 846

Use of cognitive complexity questionnaire in selecting and training cast. USA: Denton, TX. 1981. 918

Use of Inventory of Dramatic Behavior in actor training. USA. 1980-1983. 974

Relation to other fields

Impact of the creative drama activities on language disordered children. USA. 1983. 77

Introduction to essay collection *The Sociology of Theatre*. Europe. North America. 1983. 1448

Effects of creative drama on development of language skills. USA. 1983. 1471

Training

Description of Education Resources Information Center documents dealing with theatre instruction and research. USA. 1983. 508

Research/historiography SEE ALSO: Classed Entries 79-91, 1473-1476, 1972, 2071.

Residenztheater (Munich)

Performance/production

Peter Zadek's production of *The Master Builder* at the Residenztheater. Germany, West: Munich. 1983. 772

Documentation of Ingmar Bergman's tripartite theatre project. Sweden. Germany, West: Munich. 1981. 844

Restif de la Bretonne, Nicolas-Edme

References to acting in works of Restif de la Bretonne. France: Paris. 1700-1799. 728

Restoration

Design/technology

Procedures for collecting and preserving costumes. Europe. North America. 1750-1983. 190

Performance spaces

Building, restoration and revitalization of theatres. Canada: Toronto, ON. 1983. 360

Architecture and restorations of Teatro Quirino in Rome. Italy: Rome. 1870-1954. 385

Steps involved in restoring historic theatres. USA. 1983. 396

Process of theatre restoration by Conrad Schmitt Studios. USA. 1983. 397

History and restoration of Rialto Square Theatre. USA: Joliet, IL. 1926-1983. 403

Restoration of theatre chairs. USA. 1983. 409

Reference materials

List of books related to the restoration of historic theatres. USA. 1935-1983. 44

Restoration theatre

Plays/librettos/scripts

Essays on Restoration theatre and drama, with devised criteria for evaluation. England. 1660-1800.   1046

Genre reevaluation of the Restoration, sentimental, and cynical comedy. England: London. 1678-1693.   1558

Restoration theatre SEE ALSO: Geographical-Chronological Index under England 1660-1685

Revenger's Tragedy, The

Plays/librettos/scripts

Relationship between Jacobean tragedy and interpolated masque. England. 1600-1625.   1691

Revolution Theatre SEE Teat'r imeni Majakovskova

Reynolds, Burt

Performance/production

Biography of actor Burt Reynolds. USA. 1936-1983.   1716

Reynolds, Robert

English actors' work in Germany, with mention of stock comic characters. Germany. England: London. 1590-1620.   1525

Reynolds, W.B.

Institutions

Ulster Literary Theatre and relationship of critic Forrest Reid to the literary magazine *Uladh*. UK-Ireland: Belfast, Ulster. 1902-1905.   332

Rialto Square Theatre (Joliet, IL)

Performance spaces

History and restoration of Rialto Square Theatre. USA: Joliet, IL. 1926-1983.   403

Riberia, Maria

Plays/librettos/scripts

Development of older, comic woman as character type. Spain: Madrid. 1780-1825.   1234

Ricchi, Renzo

Critical notes on Renzo Ricchi's *Proposte di teatro*. Italy. 1973-1983.   1176

Ricci, Luigi

Training

Biographical sketch of Italian voice coach Luigi Ricci. Italy: Rome. 1920-1983.   1973

Rice, Dan

Performance/production

Career of Dan Rice, circus clown, whose act included political and cultural debates. USA. 1823-1900.   2013

Rice, Elmer

Plays/librettos/scripts

Essays on the trends of the Jewish-American theatre and its personalities. USA. 1900-1983.   1353

Relation to other fields

Thematic study of work ethic in American drama. USA. 1920-1969.   1465

Richard II

Plays/librettos/scripts

Struggle for power in Shakespeare's history plays. England. 1591-1595.   1059

Study of recurring themes and dramatic structure of *Richard II*. England. 1595-1596.   1062

Semiotic analysis of *Richard II*. England. 1595.   1077

Structural analysis of Gaunt's last speech in Shakespeare's *Richard II*. England. 1595-1596.   1078

Richard III

Performance/production

Role of Richmond in Shakespeare's *Richard III* on West German stage. Germany, West. UK-England. 1945.   788

Reconstruction of Richard Mansfield's production of *Richard III*. UK-England: London. USA. 1889.   893

Six critics review Jane Howell's production of *Richard III* mounted by the Public Theater. USA: New York, NY. 1983.   1684

Plays/librettos/scripts

Animal nature and eating habits of characters in Shakespeare's plays. England. 1590-1613.   1058

Struggle for power in Shakespeare's history plays. England. 1591-1595.   1059

Sources used by Shakespeare for his play *Richard III*, and changes made to cater to his sovereign's political beliefs. England. 1592-1593.   1076

Richard, Mae

Performance/production

Five critics review David Holdgrive's production of the musical *Tallulah*. USA: New York, NY. 1983.   1796

Richelieu

Edward Bulwer-Lytton's theory of the need for unified approach to productions, in response to John Calcraft's staging of *Richelieu*. UK-Ireland: Dublin. 1839.   900

Richelieu, Cardinal de

Relation to other fields

Political ramifications of the theatrical patronage of Louis XIII and Cardinal de Richelieu. France. 1610-1643.   54

Richter, Friedrich

Performance/production

Eight actors take positions on their political and social responsibilities. Germany, East. 1983.   428

Ricketts, Charles

Critical reaction to early productions of Oscar Wilde's *Salome*. Europe. USA: New York, NY. 1892-1917.   711

Right You Are if You Think You Are SEE: *Così è (se vi pare)*

Righter, Anne

Performance/production

John Barton's staging of *Hamlet* influenced by Anne Righter. UK-England. 1961-1980.   860

Rigoletto

Reference materials

Letters and documents placed in archives concerning Verdi's operas at Teatro La Fenice. Italy: Venice. 1844-1852.   1970

Rimskij-Korsakov, Nikolai Andreevič

Performance/production

Konstantin Stanislavskij's training of opera singers. USSR. 1918-1935.   1929

Ring des Nibelungen, Der

Design/technology

Technical realization of the main platform for the sets of *Der Ring des Nibelungen*. Germany, West: Bayreuth. 1983.   1817

Various safety requirements for the construction of the platform for the production of *Der Ring des Nibelungen*. Germany, West: Bayreuth. 1983.   1818

Josef Svoboda's scenography of Wagnerian opera. Switzerland. UK-England: London. Czechoslovakia: Prague. 1948-1983.   1823

Performance/production

History and production history of Wagnerian opera. Germany. USA. 1832-1982.   1865

Photographs and personnel of Bayreuth Festival production of *Siegfried*. Germany, West: Bayreuth. 1980.   1866

Ring des Nibelungen, Der — cont'd

Photographs and personnel of Bayreuth Festival production of *Götterdämmerung*. Germany, West: Bayreuth. 1980. 1867

Photographs and personnel of Bayreuth Festival production of *Die Walküre*. Germany, West: Bayreuth. 1980. 1869

Peter Hall's production of Richard Wagner's *Ring* at Bayreuth Festspielhaus. Germany, West: Bayreuth. 1983. 1870

1983 Bayreuth *Der Ring des Nibelungen*, directed by Peter Hall, conducted by Georg Solti. Germany, West: Bayreuth. 1983. 1873

Patrice Chéreau talks about his production of Richard Wagner's *Der Ring des Nibelungen*. Germany, West: Bayreuth. 1976. 1875

Photographs, cast lists, synopsis and discography of the Metropolitan Opera production of *Die Walküre*. USA: New York, NY. 1983. 1903

Plays/librettos/scripts

Analysis of Richard Wagner's *Der Ring des Nibelungen*. Germany. 1840-1860. 1945

Pertinence of human characterizations in Wagner's operas. Germany. 1845-1951. 1946

Examination of Act III of *Die Walküre*. Germany. 1852. 1950

Analysis and interpretation of Richard Wagner's librettos for the Ring Tetralogy. Germany, West: Bayreuth. 1853-1874. 1954

Ringtheater (Vienna)

Performance spaces

Concise history of theatre buildings in Vienna. Austria: Vienna. 1300-1983. 358

Rink Music Hall (Ottawa, ON)

Institutions

Prominence of Ottawa's theatres in South-Eastern Ontario touring circuit. Canada: Ottawa, ON. 1870-1879. 291

Rise and Fall of the City of Mahagonny SEE: *Aufstieg und Fall der Stadt Mahagonny*

Risorgimento SEE: Geographical-Chronological Index under Italy 1815-1876

Ristori, Adelaide

Plays/librettos/scripts

Catalogue of the exhibition on the copyright debate between playwright Paolo Giacometti and actress Adelaide Ristori. Italy. 1836-1882. 1191

Risurrezione

Performance/production

Account of *Risurrezione*, to be performed by Cincinnati Summer Opera. USA: Cincinnati, OH. 1904-1983. 1923

Rites SEE ALSO: Ritual and Classed Entries: RITUAL-CEREMONY

Rittenhouse, Charles Burket

Performance/production

Charles Burket Rittenhouse as actor, playwright, director, administrator and educator. Canada: Montreal, PQ. 1925-1976. 688

Ritual

Design/technology

Design and use of masks for ritual dances. Korea. 1600-1899. 529

Designs and uses of masks for sacred dances. Tibet. Sri Lanka. India. 530

Performance/production

Ritual and theatre in Ivory Coast. Ivory Coast. 1800-1983. 435

Ritual, masks and metaphors of Black theatre. USA. 1983. 458

Survey of Native American dramatists and their use of dramatic ritual. USA. 1850-1980. 463

Recent performances of *madang nori*, developed originally from religious festivals of ancient society. Korea. 1982. 536

Inculcation of national values through civic ritual. Chile: Santiago. 1938-1980. 2101

Plays/librettos/scripts

Denunciation of collective violence reflected in the role of sacrifice in Michel de Ghelderode's *Barabbas*. Belgium. 1929. 1010

Aspects of liturgical drama cause it to be both ritual and theatre. France. 1100-1200. 1101

Comparison of *kyōgen* and early English comedy. Japan. England. 1400. 1585

Jean Genet's *The Blacks* and his theory of ritual in context of Theatre of the Absurd and Total Theatre. France: Paris. 1948-1968. 1647

Relation to other fields

Papal cultural policy and organization of various public festivities. Italy: Rome. Vatican. 1450-1550. 62

Description of *Bandia Woli*, a traditional folk drama. Senegal. USA. 1976. 2100

Religious belief and ritual performance as related to astronomy and architecture. Egypt. 1000-500 B.C. 2107

Ritual SEE ALSO: Classed Entries: RITUAL-CEREMONY

Rivals, The

Performance/production

National Theatre's production of Richard Brinsley Sheridan's *The Rivals*. UK-England: London. 1983. 1533

Rivel, Charlie

Biography of the clown Charlie Rivel and influence of Charlie Chaplin. Spain. 1896-1983. 2012

Rižskij Teat'r Russkoj Dramy (Riga)

Institutions

History of Russian Drama Theatre of Riga. USSR: Riga. 1940-1983. 657

Roach, John

Performance/production

Six critics review John Roach's production of Arthur Bicknell's play *Moose Murders*. USA: New York, NY. 1983. 968

Road to Damascus, The SEE: *Till Damaskus*

Robertson, Patrick

Design/technology

Trends in scenic practices by British designers. UK. 1960-1983. 228

Robertson, T.W.

Plays/librettos/scripts

Description of a letter by playwright T.W. Robertson. UK-England: London. 1862. 1280

Reference materials

Revision of T.W. Robertson's playlist in *History of English Drama 1660-1900, V*. UK-England: London. 1849-1866. 1424

Robeson, Paul

Institutions

Harlem Little Theatre movement started to produce plays by, with, for and about Blacks. USA: New York, NY. 1915-1934. 653

Robinson, Lennox

Plays/librettos/scripts

Patriot Charles Stewart Parnell's influence on Irish drama. UK-Ireland. 1891-1936. 1337

Irreverent aspects of Irish comedy seen through the works of 14 playwrights. Eire. UK-Ireland. 1840-1965. 1555

Rödel, Fritz

Performance/production

Dispute about Heiner Müller's production of *Macbeth*. Germany, East: East Berlin. 1971-1982. 1678

Rodero, José María

Interview with actor José María Rodero. Spain. 1943-1983. 833

Rodgers, Richard

Production elements and choreography of *On Your Toes*. USA. 1982.
1782

Nine critics review George Abbott's production of the musical *On Your Toes*. USA: New York, NY. 1983.
1803

Rodriguez, Lucas

Plays/librettos/scripts

Dating and authorship of *Los hechos de Garcilaso*. Spain. 1573. 1231

Rogoff, Gordon

Institutions

Reflections on the significance of The Open Theatre by several of its performers, writers and critical advisers. USA: New York, NY. 1963-1973.
1613

Rohmer, Rolf

History of Deutsches Theater Berlin. Germany: Berlin. 1883-1983.
598

Roles SEE: Characters/roles

Roller, Alfred

Performance/production

Comprehensive illustrated production history of Wagnerian opera. Europe. USA. Canada. 1832-1983.
1851

Theory/criticism

Reformers on their theories. Europe. 1870-1910.
98

Rolodny, Annette

Significance of gender in feminist criticism with reference to historical materialism, deconstruction and phenomenon of cross-dressing in theatre. USA. France. UK-England. 1983.
1520

Roman theatre

Performance/production

Actor's role in theatre and social status in ancient Greece and Rome. Greece. Roman Empire. 600-1 B.C.
790

Plays/librettos/scripts

Comic mechanism in Plautus' *Amphitruo* and *Casina*. Roman Republic. 254-184 B.C.
1586

Plays of Plautus and Terence related to Roman society. Roman Republic. 254-159 B.C.
1587

Relation to other fields

Different social functions of the dramatic theatre in Greece and Rome and their modifications. Greece. Roman Empire. 600-1 B.C.
1455

Roman theatre SEE ALSO: Geographical-Chronological Index under Roman Republic 509-27 BC, Roman Empire 27 BC-476 AD

Romans in Britain, The

Administration

Private prosecution of Michael Bogdanov's production of Howard Brenton's *The Romans in Britain*. UK. 1968-1986.
144

Romanticism

Plays/librettos/scripts

Henrick Ibsen as a romantic playwright. Norway. 1828-1906. 1204

Literary influences on Henrik Ibsen's *Vildanden (The Wild Duck)*. Norway. 1884.
1205

Theme of monarchy in French Romantic opera and its effect on scenery. France: Paris. 1814-1850.
1939

Shakespeare's influence on Arrigo Boito's libretto for *La Gioconda*, based on Victor Hugo's play. Italy. 1862-1900.
1956

Reference materials

References to theatre preserved in the Archives de Paris. France: Paris. 1825-1845.
1407

Theory/criticism

French romantic theories of drama. France. 1800-1850. 1487

Romanticism SEE ALSO: Geographical-Chronological Index under Europe 1800-1850, France 1810-1857, Germany 1798-1830, Italy 1815-1876, Russia 1820-1850, UK 1801-1850

Romeo and Juliet

Performance/production

List and short reviews of Shakespearean productions. Germany, East. 1981.
749

Summer productions of Shakespeare and Molière involving professional and amateur actors. Sweden: Södertälje. 1981-1983. 841

Roncalli

Documentation on André Heller's *Flic Flac, Theater des Feuers* and *Roncalli*. Austria. Germany, West. Portugal: Lisbon. 1975-1983. 2027

Ronconi, Luca

Six essays on the productions and artistic views held by leading European directors. Europe. 1960-1980.
1615

Ronfard, Jean-Pierre

Fifteen-hour pageant by Jean-Pierre Ronfard and Théâtrale Expérimental de Montréal. Canada: Montreal, PQ. 1982.
2025

Rood, Arnold

Reference materials

Collection of Edward Gordon Craig materials available to researchers. UK-England. USA. 1872-1966.
1429

Roose-Evans, James

Performance/production

Extracts from journal of James Roose-Evans, director of *84 Charing Cross Road*. USA: New York, NY. 1982.
973

Rosamond

Questionable chronology results from performances by English officers. Belgium: Maastricht. 1703.
679

Rose, Philip

Eight critics review Philip Rose's production of the musical *Amen Corner*. USA: New York, NY. 1983.
1800

Rosenblatt, Bernard S.

Relation to other fields

Inaugural address of American Theatre Association president Bernard S. Rosenblatt calling for support in creating public policy. USA: Minneapolis, MN. 1983.
76

Rosencrantz and Guildenstern Are Dead

Plays/librettos/scripts

Influence of Shakespeare, Beckett and Wittgenstein on the plays of Tom Stoppard. UK-England. 1963-1979.
1302

Playfulness in Tom Stoppard's plays. UK-England. 1937-1983. 1592

Rosenkavalier, Der

Performance/production

Bass Kurt Moll speaks about his career and role in *Der Rosenkavalier*. Germany, West. 1950-1983.
1874

Photographs, cast lists, synopsis and discography of Metropolitan Opera production of *Der Rosenkavalier*. USA: New York, NY. 1983.
1906

Rosner, Jacques

Plays/librettos/scripts

Director Jacques Rosner on meeting with playwright Witold Gombrowicz. Poland. France. 1969-1982.
1218

Ross, Glynn

Administration

Evaluation of Glynn Ross's tenure as founding general director of Seattle Opera. USA: Seattle, WA. 1964-1983.
1815

Rossini, Gioacchino

Performance/production

Photographs, cast lists, synopsis and discography of Metropolitan Opera production of *The Barber of Seville*. USA: New York, NY. 1983.
1902

Rothman, Carole

Five critics review Carole Rothman's production of *Painting Churches*, by Tina Howe. USA: New York, NY. 1983.   959

Rotrou, Jean de

Plays/librettos/scripts

Comparative sociological study of French theatre. France. 1610-1643.   1109

Rotrou, Pierre de

Typology and analysis of French sacred drama. France. 1550-1650.   1111

Roundheads and Pinheads SEE: *Rundköpfe und die Spitzköpfe, Die*

Rousseau, Jean-Jacques

Theory/criticism

Schiller's philosophy of history. Germany: Jena. 1789-1791.   1499

Roy, Esperanza

Performance/production

Interview with theatre and music hall actress Esperanza Roy. Spain. 1936-1983.   442

Royal Academy of Music (London)

Administration

Management and fiscal administration at the Royal Academy of Music. England: London. 1719-1721.   1814

Royal Hunt of the Sun, The

Plays/librettos/scripts

Contradiction in personal and artistic life of Antonin Artaud. France. 1921-1948.   1645

Royal Opera House, Covent Garden (London)

Design/technology

Safety curtain at Covent Garden, designed by Christopher Le Brun. UK-England: London. 1983.   232

Performance spaces

History of the Royal Opera House, Covent Garden. UK-England: London. 1732-1983.   1836

Royal Shakespeare Company (London)

Administration

Difficulties of getting some plays on Broadway. USA: New York, NY. 1982-1983.   565

Design/technology

Mannerist elements in some set designs for *Hamlet*. UK-England: Stratford-upon-Avon, London. 1948-1976.   1675

Institutions

History of Royal Shakespeare Company with emphasis on financial and aesthetic aspects and internal politics. UK-England: London. 1864-1981.   624

Balance of classic plays against modern plays at the National Theatre and the Royal Shakespeare Company. UK-England. 1900-1983.   626

Aspects of the National Theatre and the Royal Shakespeare Company are compared. UK-England. 1960.   627

Performance/production

John Barton's staging of *Hamlet* influenced by Anne Righter. UK-England. 1961-1980.   860

Actor Miles Anderson, his wife Lesley Duff, and their work with the Royal Shakespeare Company. UK-England. 1900-1983.   861

Importance of boy actor playing the title role in *Peter Pan*. UK-England. 1902-1983.   867

Actor Emrys James discusses his work, especially with the Royal Shakespeare Company. UK-England. 1900-1983.   879

Nine critics review Trevor Nunn's production of *All's Well That Ends Well*. USA: New York, NY. 1983.   1538

Plays/librettos/scripts

Traditional approaches to acting and staging as clarifying methods for complex Shakespeare scenes. UK-England: Stratford-upon-Avon. 1980.   1702

Royal Square, The SEE: *Place Royale, La*

Royal Winnipeg Ballet (Winnipeg, ON)

Performance/production

Evelyn Hart's debut as Giselle with the Royal Winnipeg Ballet. Canada: Winnipeg, ON. 1966-1982.   517

Ru-howzi

History of *Ru-howzi* improvisational theatre. Iran. 1780-1950.   792

Rudkin, David

Plays/librettos/scripts

Epic structure in contemporary drama. UK. 1968-1981.   1275

Rudolf, Niels-Peter

Institutions

Intentions and working methods of the Deutsches Schauspielhaus. Germany, West: Hamburg. 1893.   606

Rudolph, Hermann

Training

Ballet work and training in opera houses in East Germany. Germany, East: Leipzig, Dresden, East Berlin. 1981-1983.   523

Rumbelow, Steven

Institutions

Steven Rumbelow and experimental work of Triple Action Theatre. Canada: Toronto, ON. 1980-1983.   1606

Rundköpfe und die Spitzköpfe, Die (Roundheads and Pinheads)

Performance/production

Directors on Bertolt Brecht's dramas. Germany, East: Schwerin, Erfurt, East Berlin. 1983.   754

Russell, Anna

Interview with concert singer and comedienne Anna Russell. Canada: Toronto, ON. 1912-1983.   1847

Russell, Willy

Plays/librettos/scripts

Willy Russell's work as a playwright with discussion of his social and political commitment. UK-England. 1970-1983.   1283

Russian Revolution SEE: **October Socialist Revolution**

Rutherford, Margaret

Performance/production

Biography of actress Margaret Rutherford. UK. 1892-1972.   858

Ruyters, André

Institutions

Founding of periodical *Nouvelle Revue Française*. France: Paris. 1909-1914.   304

Ruzante

Performance/production

Gianni De Luigi's staging of *Ruzante Returns from the Wars*. Italy. 1983.   1529

Plays/librettos/scripts

Use of vernacular in Ariosto's, Machiavelli's and Ruzante's comedies, as compared with Roman drama. Italy. Roman Empire. 1508-1533.   1584

Ruzante Returns from the Wars SEE: *Reduce, Il*

Saber del mal y del bien (Knowledge of Good and Evil)

Plays/librettos/scripts

Metacritical analysis of Calderón's plays applying criteria devised for Lope de Vega. Spain. 1608-1681.   1238

Sachsen-Meiningen, Georg II von

Performance/production

History of directing. Europe. 1882-1982. 708

Charles Kean's staging methods and the influences on them. UK-England: London. 1850-1859. 898

Sacre rappresentazioni

Design/technology

Scenery for the first performance of *Representation of Saint Ursula*. Italy. 1400-1599. 579

Reference materials

List of 94 twentieth century works dealing with Italian sacred drama. Italy. 1300-1983. 1413

Sadler Wells Royal Ballet (London)

Performance/production

Evelyn Hart's debut as Giselle with the Royal Winnipeg Ballet. Canada: Winnipeg, ON. 1966-1982. 517

Sadler, Harley

Tent show performances in a rural Christian fundamentalist area. USA. 1912-1950. 1990

Safety SEE: Health/safety

Saint Genet

Plays/librettos/scripts

Typology and analysis of French sacred drama. France. 1550-1650. 1111

Saint Joan

Performance/production

Production elements used to render *Saint Joan* a symbol of imagination. UK-England. 1923. 865

Importance of vocal techniques for Shavian drama. UK-England. 1945-1981. 896

Plays/librettos/scripts

Composition and production of George Bernard Shaw's *Saint Joan*. UK-England. 1923. 1314

Saint-Denis, Michel

Training

Theory and practice of actor training by director, Michel Saint-Denis. USA. 1897-1971. 507

Saks, Gene

Performance/production

Ten critics review Gene Saks' production of Neil Simon's play *Brighton Beach Memoirs*. USA: New York, NY. 1983. 1535

Salieri, Antonio

Plays/librettos/scripts

Peter Shaffer's revision of *Amadeus*. UK-England: London. USA: New York, NY. 1979-1980. 1290

Šaljapin, Fëdor Ivanovič SEE: Chaliapin, Feodor

Salmelainen, Eino

Institutions

Founding and history of acting program at Tampere University. Finland: Tampere. 1967-1983. 302

Salmón, Raúl

Plays/librettos/scripts

Development of social themes in Bolivian drama. Bolivia. 1944-1983. 1014

Salome

Performance/production

Critical reaction to early productions of Oscar Wilde's *Salome*. Europe. USA: New York, NY. 1892-1917. 711

Plays/librettos/scripts

Revolutionary vision of collaborative effort between Oscar Wilde and illustrator Aubrey Beardsley. UK. 1894-1900. 1273

Saltz, Amy

Performance/production

Five critics review Amy Saltz's production of *Win/Lose/Draw* at the Provincetown Playhouse. USA: New York, NY. 1983. 909

Salzburger Festspiele

Ingmar Bergman directs Molière's *Dom Juan* at Salzburg Festival. Austria: Salzburg. 1983. 673

Salzburger Marionettentheater

Design/technology

Laser holography as an element of scene design. Austria: Salzburg. 1948-1985. 178

Performance/production

Application of holography to the Salzburger Marionettentheater production of *Le Nozze di Figaro*. Austria: Salzburg. 1983. 2083

Samaritani, Pier Luigi

Design/technology

Discussion of Pier Luigi Samaritani and his work in scene design. Italy. USA: New York, NY. 1954-1983. 1820

Performance/production

Photographs, cast lists, synopsis and discography of Metropolitan Opera production of *Ernani*. USA: New York, NY. 1983. 1908

Samarovski, Branko

Actor Branko Samarovski as Argan in Alfred Kirchner's production of *The Imaginary Invalid*. Germany, West: Bochum. 1983. 760

San Diego Union

Conversations with theatre critics from four newspapers. USA. 1983. 468

San Francisco Chronicle

Conversations with theatre critics from four newspapers. USA. 1983. 468

San Francisco Opera

Administration

Interview with Terry McEwen, general director of War Memorial Opera House. Canada: Montreal, PQ. USA: San Francisco, CA. 1983. 1813

Design/technology

Tom Munn, lighting director of San Francisco Opera Company. USA: San Francisco, CA. 1975-1983. 1824

Performance/production

Backstage look at San Francisco Opera. USA: San Francisco, CA. 1970-1982. 1911

Sanchez, Esteban Fernandez

Multi-media Biblical creation story presented with puppets by Esteban Fernandez Sanchez. USA: New York, NY. 1983. 2064

Sands, Dorothy

Careers of solo performers Beatrice Herford, Cissie Loftus and Dorothy Sands. USA. 1900-1920. 942

Sanguinetti, Niobe

Reference materials

Playwright Dario Niccodemi's letters to actress Niobe Sanguinetti. Italy. 1921-1927. 1415

Sanquirico, Alessandro

Design/technology

Scene designers and scenery at Teatro alla Scala in Neoclassic period. Italy: Milan. 1778-1832. 1821

Sanskrit drama

Performance/production

Origins and evolution of the *Kuchipudi* dance drama. India. 200 B.C.-1983 A.D. 532

Scenery — cont'd

Institutions

Performance spaces

Performance/production

Plays/librettos/scripts

Reference materials

Scenery — cont'd

Description of various documents, photographs, designs and engravings on display at Edward Gordon Craig exhibit. UK-England. 1900-1935.   36

Description of archive holdings at Brigham Young University including personal papers of Howard Hawks and Dean Jagger. USA: Provo, UT. 1900-1983.   48

Collection of Edward Gordon Craig materials available to researchers. UK-England. USA. 1872-1966.   1429

Description of the Brander Matthews Collection of theatre materials. USA: New York, NY. 1891-1929.   1436

Catalogue of the exhibition on scenery, architecture, dance, opera and public theatres during Pietro Metastasio's life. Italy: Rome. 1698-1782.   1968

Catalogue of Galliari's scene designs owned by Museo Teatrale alla Scala. Italy: Milan. 1778-1823.   1969

Research/historiography

Method for using models of scenery as study documents. Discussed at SIBMAS. Europe. North America. 1982.   83

Theory/criticism

Writings of Edward Gordon Craig. UK-England. 1907-1957.   1513

Scenes from a Marriage

Performance/production

Documentation of Ingmar Bergman's tripartite theatre project. Sweden. Germany, West: Munich. 1981.   844

Schafranek, Franz

Vienna's English Theatre's 20th anniversary production of G.B. Shaw's *Candida*. Austria: Vienna. 1963.   668

Schaubühne (West Berlin)

Shakespearean productions by Compagnia del Collettivo/Teatro Due, Theater an der Ruhr (Hamburg) and Schaubühne (West Berlin). Italy: Parma. Germany, West: West Berlin, Hamm. 1983.   810

Schaubühne am Halleschen Ufer (West Berlin)

Performance spaces

New aesthetic forms of staging. Germany, West: Bremen, Bochum, Hanover. 1962-1980.   374

Schaubühne am Lehniner Platz (West Berlin)

Design/technology

Description of new theatre building and technical equipment used in performances since 1981. Germany, West: West Berlin. 1962-1982.
                                                                 201

Schauspielhaus (Cologne)

Performance/production

Jürgen Gosch production of *A Midsummer Night's Dream* at the Köln Schauspielhaus. Germany, West: Cologne. 1983.   780

Schauspielhaus (Düsseldorf)

Productions of *The Flies* at Düsseldorfer Schauspielhaus and Hebbeltheater Berlin. Germany, West: Düsseldorf, West Berlin. 1947-1948.   785

Schelling, Friedrich Wilhelm Joseph von

Theory/criticism

History of theories of drama from George Wilhelm Hegel to Karl Marx. Germany. 1770-1883.   1491

Schiller, Friedrich von

Institutions

New season's productions at the Basel Stadttheater. Switzerland: Basel. 1983.   622

Performance/production

Aspects of Friedrich von Schiller's *Mary Stuart* produced at Comédie-Française. France. 1800.   734

Plays/librettos/scripts

Influence of Siglo de Oro on German pre-romantic theatre. Germany. Spain. 1765-1832.   1135

Theory/criticism

Bertolt Brecht's perception of the philosophy of the Enlightenment. Germany. 1848-1956.   1498

Schiller's philosophy of history. Germany: Jena. 1789-1791.   1499

Schiller, Leon

Performance/production

Tribute to the leading Polish director Leon Schiller. Poland. 1918-1954.   825

Leon Schiller's directing career at the Reduta Theatre. Poland: Warsaw. 1922-1923.   828

Schillertheater (West Berlin)

Jean Genet's *The Balcony* at Schillertheater Berlin, directed by Hans Neuenfels. Germany, West: West Berlin. 1983.   773

Schilling, Tom

Training

Ballet work and training in opera houses in East Germany. Germany, East: Leipzig, Dresden, East Berlin. 1981-1983.   523

Schlacht um Moskau (Battle for Moscow)

Plays/librettos/scripts

Anti-war plays by Bertolt Brecht and Johannes R. Becher on German invasion of the Soviet Union. Germany. 1942-1943.   1126

Schlossparktheater (West Berlin)

Performance/production

First German production of Caryl Churchill's *Cloud Nine* at Schlossparktheater directed by Harald Clemens. Germany, West: West Berlin. 1983.   775

Schlosstheater (Moers)

Institutions

History, financial situation and productions of the Schlosstheater. Germany, West: Moers. 1975-1983.   315

Schlumberger, Jean

Founding of periodical *Nouvelle Revue Française*. France: Paris. 1909-1914.   304

Schmidt, Douglas

Design/technology

Douglas Schmidt discusses his career, particularly designing Ibsen plays. USA. 1964-1982.   582

Schmidt, Heinrich

Performance/production

Portrait of actor Heinrich Schmidt. Germany, East. 1922-1983.   427

Schneider-Siemessen, Günter

History and production history of Wagnerian opera. Germany. USA. 1832-1982.   1865

Photographs, cast lists, synopsis and discography of Metropolitan Opera production of *Arabella*. USA: New York, NY. 1983.   1894

Schneider, Alan

Four critics review Alan Schneider's production of three Samuel Beckett plays. USA: New York, NY. 1983.   928

Schnitzler, Arthur

Plays/librettos/scripts

Diary of Austrian dramatist Arthur Schnitzler. Austria. 1913-1916.
                                                                 1005

School for Scandal, The

Performance/production

Changes in acting and audiences at Theatre Royal. Canada: Montreal, PQ. 1829-1839.   686

School for the Art of Theatre

Institutions

Background of Edward Gordon Craig's efforts to establish School for the Art of Theatre. Italy: Florence. UK-England: London. 1900-1917.   320

Schopenhauer, Arthur

Theory/criticism

History of theories of drama from George Wilhelm Hegel to Karl
Marx. Germany. 1770-1883.   1491

Schroeter, Werner

Performance/production

The Comedy of Errors at Freie Volksbühne, directed by Werner
Schroeter. Germany, West: West Berlin. 1983.   774

Schroth, Christoph

Directors on Bertolt Brecht's dramas. Germany, East: Schwerin,
Erfurt, East Berlin. 1983.   754

Schulte-Michels, Thomas

Cecil P. Taylor's *Good* at Kleines Haus, directed by Thomas Schulte-
Michels. Germany, West: Düsseldorf. 1982.   776

Schwartz, Bruce D.

Interview with puppeteer Bruce D. Schwartz. USA. 1983.   2060

Schweyk im Zweiten Weltkrieg (Schweik in World War II)

Plays/librettos/scripts

Anti-war plays by Bertolt Brecht and Johannes R. Becher on
German invasion of the Soviet Union. Germany. 1942-1943.   1126

Schwierige, Der (Difficult Man, The)

Elusive meaning and non-verbal communication in Hofmannsthal's
The Difficult Man. Germany. 1921.   1124

Schwitters, Kurt

Performance/production

Exhibition about the tendency toward the *Gesamtkunstwerk.*
Switzerland: Zürich. Austria: Vienna. 1983.   444

Scores

Design/technology

Description of 'Four Centuries of Opera' exhibition. USA: New
York, NY. 1583-1983.   1825

Reference materials

Description of archive holdings at Brigham Young University
including personal papers of Howard Hawks and Dean Jagger. USA:
Provo, UT. 1900-1983.   48

Scottish Arts Council

Administration

Scottish Arts Council's policy of funding community theatre. UK-
Scotland. 1980-1983.   147
Funding policy of Scottish Arts Council. UK-Scotland. 1983.   148

Institutions

Interview with Rod Graham, head of BBC Scotland's television
drama department. UK-Scotland. 1946-1983.   1722

Scowrers, The

Performance/production

Questionable chronology results from performances by English
officers. Belgium: Maastricht. 1703.   679

Screamers, The

Theory/criticism

Imamu Amiri Baraka's aesthetics find their origins in Blues music.
USA. 1963-1967.   1521

Scribe, Eugène

Plays/librettos/scripts

Influence of Eugène Scribe and the Well-Made Play on later drama.
France: Paris. 1830-1840.   1102

Ščukin, Boris Vasil'evič

Performance/production

Political censorship and Soviet productions of *Hamlet.* USSR. 1930.
                                                                   995

Sea and the Mirror, The

Theory/criticism

Wystan Hugh Auden's poetic meditation on art as related to
Shakespeare's *The Tempest* and Kierkegaardian thought. UK-
England. 1939-1962.   1511

Seagull, The SEE: *Čajka*

Seasons

Institutions

Vaasa City Theatre's season in review. Finland: Vaasa. 1983.   591
Imatra theatre's 1983-1984 season. Finland: Imatra. 1983.   593
Jyväskylä City Theatre's 1983-1984 season. Finland: Jyväskylä. 1983.
                                                                   594

Performance/production

Review of year's theatrical activity. Korea. 1982.   437

Seattle Opera (Seattle, WA)

Administration

Evaluation of Glynn Ross's tenure as founding general director of
Seattle Opera. USA: Seattle, WA. 1964-1983.   1815

Seattle-Intiman (Seattle, WA)

Performance/production

Comparative study of Peter Oskarsson's production of August
Strindberg's *A Dream Play* with that of Ingmar Bergman. USA:
Seattle, WA. 1982.   907

Second Shepherds Play, The

Design/technology

Puppets and design concept for production of *The Second Shepherds
Play.* USA: Lincoln, NE. 1983.   2039

Second Surprise of Love, The SEE: *Seconde surprise de l'amour,
La*

Secondary School Theatre Association (SSTA)

Institutions

Three awards presented by American Theatre Association. USA.
1983.   347

Security

Performance spaces

Security measures and regulations in Italian theatres. Italy. 1983. 383

Seefehlner, Egon

Administration

Life and career of opera manager Egon Seefehlner. Austria: Vienna.
Germany, West: West Berlin. 1912-1983.   1812

Segawa, Kikunojō

Plays/librettos/scripts

History of the narrative theme of *Dōjōji (A Woman and a Bell).*
Japan. 1041-1800.   545

Segerström, Michael

Institutions

Effect of women's movement on experimental theatre. Sweden:
Stockholm. 1970-1983.   328

**Sei personaggi in cerca d'autore (Six Characters in Search of an
Author)**

Plays/librettos/scripts

Luigi Pirandello's earlier plays are considered prologues to *The
Giants of the Mountain.* Italy. 1921-1937.   1189

Selznick, David O.

Reference materials

Description of David O. Selznick collection: '*Gone with the Wind: A
Legend Endures*'. USA. 1939-1983.   1721

Semantics

Theory/criticism

Linguistic and semantic analysis of theatrical dream phenomenon in terms of a 'play within a play'. Italy. 1983.   1509

Semiotics

Audience

Process by which audience assigns meaning to a performance. Italy. 1983.   168

Performance spaces

Socio-semiotic analysis of performance spaces. USA: New York, NY. France: Paris. 1967.   398

Performance/production

Semiotic analysis of Els Joglars' production of *Mary d'Ous*. Spain. 1972.   1729

Plays/librettos/scripts

Semiotic analysis of *Richard II*. England. 1595.   1077

Examination of semiotic elements in George Bernard Shaw's *Pygmalion*. UK. 1916.   1274

Semiotic analysis of popular radio comedy. Canada. 1939-1958. 1709

Theory/criticism

Performance and communication: problems of semiotic approach. Europe. 1983.   95

Spectator at the center of semiological network of theoretical approaches to theatre. France. 1982.   99

Semiotics of theatre. Germany, West. 1983.   102

Semiotic study of the specific nature of theatre in relation to other arts and audience interaction with it. Spain. 1983.   108

Application of Frank Pierce's phenomenology and semiotics to theory of drama. France. Italy. 1980.   1488

Playtext as an interlacing of different expressive theatrical components. Italy. 1982.   1507

Semiotic comparison of dramatic theory, philosophy and performance. USA. Europe. 1850-1956.   1515

Vocal emission as a mode of theatricalization in experimental theatre. Canada. 1970-1979.   1669

Study of genesis, development, structural components and consequences of theatre-drama performed by the Black workers. South Africa, Republic of. 1981-1983.   1673

Seneca

Plays/librettos/scripts

Fusion of Stoicism and Christianity in *Hamlet*. England: London. 1600-1601.   1041

Senghor, Léopold

Jean Genet's *The Blacks* and his theory of ritual in context of Theatre of the Absurd and Total Theatre. France: Paris. 1948-1968.   1647

Sentimental comedy

Genre reevaluation of the Restoration, sentimental, and cynical comedy. England: London. 1678-1693.   1558

Senz, Adolf

Design/technology

Career of Metropolitan Opera wigmaker Adolf Senz. USA: New York, NY. 1930-1983.   1826

Sequestro, Il (Kidnapping, The)

Plays/librettos/scripts

Dario Fo's drama in Scandinavia. Italy. Sweden. Norway. 1983.   1184

Serapionstheater (Vienna)

Performance/production

Guest production of Japanese Butō-company Ariadone at Serapionstheater, Vienna. Japan. Austria: Vienna. 1983.   534

Serban, Andre

Six critics review Čechov's *Uncle Vanya* directed by Andre Serban at La Mama. USA: New York, NY. 1982.   967

Serbian Museum of Theatrical Art SEE: Muzej pozorišne umetnosti

Serjeant Musgrave's Dance

Plays/librettos/scripts

Plot, structure and action in John Arden's *Serjeant Musgrave's Dance*. UK-England. 1959.   1288

Service institutions SEE: Institutions, service

Set design SEE: Scenery

Seven: Eighty-Four Theatre Company (Scotland)

Institutions

Touring accounts of Actors Touring Company, 7:84 Theatre Company and Cardiff Laboratory Theatre. UK-England. UK-Wales. UK-Scotland. USSR. 1983.   634

Tour of the USSR by the Scottish 7:84 Theatre Company. UK-Scotland. USSR. 1982.   643

Seward, Samuel

Design/technology

All-string-controlled marionettes introduced by Samuel Seward. UK-England. 1796-1852.   2078

Seyffert, Dietmar

Training

Ballet work and training in opera houses in East Germany. Germany, East: Leipzig, Dresden, East Berlin. 1981-1983.   523

Sforza, Lodovico

Reference materials

Catalogue of the exhibition dealing with Leonardo da Vinci's activity as costume and scene designer and inventor of machinery for Sforza's festivals. Italy: Milan. 1484-1500.   28

Shadow of a Gunman, The

Plays/librettos/scripts

Influence of Percy Bysshe Shelley's poetry on Sean O'Casey. UK-Ireland: Dublin. 1923-1946.   1318

Influence on Brecht of Sean O'Casey's use of songs to overcome the boundaries of illusion in his drama. UK-Ireland: Dublin. 1923-1926.   1325

Theme of insurrection in Sean O'Casey's three Dublin plays. UK-Ireland: Dublin. 1923-1926.   1331

Influence of Shakespeare and Percy Bysshe Shelley on Sean O'Casey's *The Shadow of a Gunman*. UK-Ireland: Dublin. 1923.   1332

Shadow puppets SEE ALSO: Classed Entries: PUPPETRY — Shadow puppets

Shadwell, Thomas

Performance/production

Questionable chronology results from performances by English officers. Belgium: Maastricht. 1703.   679

Theory/criticism

Morality of Restoration comedy. England. 1670-1700.   1599

Shaffer, Anthony

Reference materials

Reference guide to playwrights Peter and Anthony Shaffer. UK-England. USA. 1926-1982.   1426

Shaffer, Peter

Plays/librettos/scripts

Peter Shaffer's revision of *Amadeus*. UK-England: London. USA: New York, NY. 1979-1980.   1290

Contradiction in personal and artistic life of Antonin Artaud. France. 1921-1948.   1645

Shaffer, Peter — cont'd

Reference materials

Reference guide to playwrights Peter and Anthony Shaffer. UK-England. USA. 1926-1982. 1426

Shaffytheater (Netherlands)

Institutions

Free operating groups and institutionalized theatre. Netherlands. 1963-1983. 1609

Shakespeare Memorial National Theatre (SMNT, Stratford-upon-Avon)

Actor-managers with self-serving interests at Shakespeare Memorial National Theatre. UK. 1905-1915. 623

Shakespeare, William

Design/technology

Mannerist elements in some set designs for *Hamlet*. UK-England: Stratford-upon-Avon, London. 1948-1976. 1675

Institutions

Overview of the German Shakespeare Society Conference. Germany, East: Weimar. 1982. 602

Edward Bond's *Saved* and Shakespeare's *Troilus and Cressida* at the Jugendclub Kritisches Theater. Germany, West: Stuttgart. 1981-1983. 608

History of Royal Shakespeare Company with emphasis on financial and aesthetic aspects and internal politics. UK-England: London. 1864-1981. 624

Repertory and workings of Glasgow Citizens' Theatre. UK-Scotland: Glasgow. 1983. 642

Performance/production

Problems of antisemitism in staging *The Merchant of Venice*. Israel. 1936-1980. 663

Survey of director Max Reinhardt's career. Austria. 1873-1943. 677

Questionable chronology results from performances by English officers. Belgium: Maastricht. 1703. 679

Career of director Otomar Krejča, and his interpretations of major playwrights. Czechoslovakia. 1898-1983. 692

Marxist theory applied in comparison of public theatres in England and Spain. England. Spain. 1576-1635. 696

Henry Carey's missing music for *tableaux vivant* in the production of *Hamlet* inspired by funeral services for the Duke of Buckingham. England: London. 1736. 698

Biography of Harley Granville-Barker. England. 1877-1946. 701

Statistical history of acting editions of Shakespeare. Europe. North America. 1590. 713

Shakespearean productions of the 1981-1982 season. German-speaking countries. 1977-1982. 740

Purposes, goals and rewards of performing Shakespeare on socialist amateur stages. Germany, East. 1982. 744

Review of four Shakespeare productions. Germany, East: Meiningen, Zwickau, Leipzig. 1983. 746

Marxist orientation in Shakespearean plays on German stage. Germany, East. 1982. 748

List and short reviews of Shakespearean productions. Germany, East. 1981. 749

Staging Shakespeare with amateur actors. Germany, East. 1981. 750

Problems in acting Shakespeare. Germany, East. 1982. 758

The Comedy of Errors at Freie Volksbühne, directed by Werner Schroeter. Germany, West: West Berlin. 1983. 774

Jürgen Gosch production of *A Midsummer Night's Dream* at the Köln Schauspielhaus. Germany, West: Cologne. 1983. 780

Claus Peymann's production of Shakespeare's *A Winter's Tale*. Germany, West: Bochum. 1983. 784

Role of Richmond in Shakespeare's *Richard III* on West German stage. Germany, West. UK-England. 1945. 788

Compagnia del Collettivo/Teatro Due productions of three plays by William Shakespeare. Italy: Parma. 1980-1983. 795

Andrzej Wajda's staging of *Hamlet* at Teatro Argentina. Italy. Poland: Rome. 1982. 797

Eleonora Duse's portrayal of Cleopatra in the Boito/D'Annunzio production. Italy. 1873-1924. 804

Shakespearean productions by Compagnia del Collettivo/Teatro Due, Theater an der Ruhr (Hamburg) and Schaubühne (West Berlin). Italy: Parma. Germany, West: West Berlin, Hamm. 1983. 810

Three productions of *Macbeth* by director Ingmar Bergman. Sweden: Stockholm, Hälsingborg, Göteburg. 1940-1948. 840

Summer productions of Shakespeare and Molière involving professional and amateur actors. Sweden: Södertälje. 1981-1983. 841

John Barton's staging of *Hamlet* influenced by Anne Righter. UK-England. 1961-1980. 860

Edward Gordon Craig's productions of and theories on Shakespeare. UK-England. Europe. 1872-1940. 862

Beerbohm Tree's conceptual and directorial approach to staging Shakespeare. UK-England: London. 1905-1911. 863

Theodore Komisarjevsky's productions of Shakespeare's plays at Stratford-upon-Avon. UK-England: Stratford-upon-Avon. 1932-1939. 864

Relationship between verbal and nonverbal communication in productions of *Macbeth, Othello* and *Julius Caesar*. UK-England. 1980. 868

Portrait of Ira Aldridge as Othello in painting by James Northcote. UK-England: Manchester. USA. 1826. 869

Critical examination of modern interpretations of Shakespeare's plays. UK-England: London. USA. Canada: Stratford, ON. 1975-1982. 873

Various treatments of the induction scene with Christopher Sly in *The Taming of the Shrew*, including lists. UK-England. USA. 1844-1978. 874

Reconstruction of Richard Mansfield's production of *Richard III*. UK-England: London. USA. 1889. 893

Director Harley Granville-Barker's career. UK-England. 1877-1946. 895

Decisions needed in staging plays with inherent sexist or racist themes. USA. 1980-1983. 904

Two examples of staging *Macbeth* in the 1970's. USA: Stratford, CT. Canada: Stratford, ON. 1971-1973. 908

Performances, editing and audience response to Fanny Kemble's first American tour. USA: Boston, MA, New York, NY, Philadelphia, PA. 1849-1850. 935

Shakespearean productions and festivals in the American South. USA. 1751-1980. 938

Career of actor-manager John Wilkes Booth. USA. 1855-1865. 975

Federal Theatre Project's often innovative approach to staging Shakespeare's plays. USA. 1930-1939. 978

Political censorship and Soviet productions of *Hamlet*. USSR. 1930. 995

Two productions of *A Midsummer Night's Dream*. Germany, East: East Berlin. 1975-1982. 1526

Catalan version of Shakespeare's *As You Like It* by Teatre Lliure. Spain. 1983. 1531

Critical analysis of Carmelo Bene's rewritten version of *Hamlet*. Italy. 1961-1975. 1619

Production journal of *King Lear*. Canada: Stratford, ON. 1979. 1676

Evolution of the text of *King Lear* through performance. England. 1605-1983. 1677

Dispute about Heiner Müller's production of *Macbeth*. Germany, East: East Berlin. 1971-1982. 1678

Reconstruction of Edward Gordon Craig's production of *Hamlet* at Moscow Art Theatre. Russia: Moscow. 1908-1912. 1682

Six critics review Jane Howell's production of *Richard III* mounted by the Public Theater. USA: New York, NY. 1983. 1684

Konstantin Stanislavskij's stage adaptation of Shakespeare's *Othello* for the Moscow Art Theatre. USSR: Moscow. 1929-1930. 1685

Plays/librettos/scripts

Reception of *Hamlet* in China and problems in production. China. 1903-1983. 1019

Examination of *Hamlet*, I.iv. 13-38 applying Aristotelian criteria. England: London. 1600-1601. 1027

Feminist analysis of sex roles in Shakespeare. England. 1595-1615. 1028

Examples of folklore and humanistic philosophy in *Pericles*. England. 1608-1609. 1029

Shakespeare, William — cont'd

Shakespeare's historical plays and the reaction of the Elizabethan audience. England. 1590-1613.　　1031

Shakespearean influence on Ben Jonson's *Bartholomew Fair*. England. 1614.　　1033

Appearance of Banquo's ghost in *Macbeth* clarifies the relation of the audience to the play. England. 1605-1606.　　1034

Relationship of various arts to Shakespearean production. England. USA. 1590-1981.　　1035

Interpretations of locale of scenes in *As You Like It*. England. 1599-1600.　　1038

Fusion of Stoicism and Christianity in *Hamlet*. England: London. 1600-1601.　　1041

Shakespeare's use of sources. England. 1590-1616.　　1043

Contrast between public and private life in Shakespeare's history plays. England. 1590-1612.　　1045

Analysis of clowns and fools in plays by Shakespeare. England. 1590-1613.　　1047

Political prophecy in *Macbeth* IV.i. England: London. 1605-1606.　　1048

Status of women in Elizabethan society as reflected in Shakespeare's plays. England. 1590-1613.　　1049

Art of rule and rule of art in Shakespeare's histories. England. 1590-1599.　　1050

Psychological examination of title character in *Othello*. England: London. 1604-1605.　　1051

Imitation and creation in *Measure for Measure*. England. 1604-1605.　　1053

Struggle for power in Shakespeare's history plays. England. 1591-1595.　　1059

Analysis of the fool's rhetorical technique of speech in Shakespeare's plays. England. 1592-1605.　　1060

Origins of Hamlet's 'calf' reference. England: London. 1600-1601.　　1061

Study of recurring themes and dramatic structure of *Richard II*. England. 1595-1596.　　1062

Use of and variations on Ovidian metamorphosis in *The Taming of the Shrew*. England. 1592-1603.　　1065

Heywood's *A Woman Killed with Kindness* as a source for Shakespeare's *Othello*. England. 1604.　　1066

Shakespearean and editorial designation of locale. England: London. 1605-1606.　　1069

Misquotation of Shakespeare in Edmond Malone's 1790 edition. England: London. 1790-1821.　　1070

Ironic parallels between *The Tempest* and the political activities of the time. England. North America. South America. 1611-1612.　　1072

Stage directions in Shakespeare are used to reconstruct Elizabethan staging practice. England. 1590-1612.　　1073

Metadramatic elements in Shakespeare's *Troilus and Cressida*. England. 1601-1602.　　1074

Shakespeare's knowledge of Arab world and influence on later regional writers. England. Arabia. 1606-1981.　　1075

Sources used by Shakespeare for his play *Richard III*, and changes made to cater to his sovereign's political beliefs. England. 1592-1593.　　1076

Semiotic analysis of *Richard II*. England. 1595.　　1077

Structural analysis of Gaunt's last speech in Shakespeare's *Richard II*. England. 1595-1596.　　1078

Paternal authority and sex roles in Shakespeare's plays. England. 1595-1615.　　1079

Caesar's Revenge as a source for *Antony and Cleopatra*. England. 1606-1607.　　1080

Placement of the caesura in Shakespearean texts. England. 1559-1603.　　1083

Essays on Renaissance drama. Europe. 1513-1616.　　1085

Textual analysis of the past in theatre productions to achieve a relationship with the present. Europe. 1605-1606.　　1086

Playwrights and dramatic forms influencing Eugene O'Neill's *The Calms of Capricorn*. Europe. USA. 1953.　　1088

Goethe's regard for Shakespeare and influences observed in *Faust*. Germany. 1770-1832.　　1125

Brecht's directorial approach to staging Shakespeare's *Coriolanus*, *Macbeth* and *King Lear*. Germany. 1920-1930.　　1136

Composition and thematic analysis of Goethe's *Ur-Faust*. Germany. 1775-1832.　　1137

History of criticism and interpretation of Shakespeare's *A Midsummer Night's Dream*. Germany. 1700-1982.　　1142

Comparison of the misanthrope in *Dýskolos*, *Timon of Athens* and *Le Misanthrope*. Greece. England. France. 317 B.C.-1666 A.D.　　1155

Shakespearean and Platonic conceptions of wisdom. Greece. England. 400 B.C.-1613 A.D.　　1156

Influences and theoretical views held by the playwright Witold Gombrowicz. Poland. 1904-1969.　　1216

Tragic value of *Hamlet* changed by 20th century criticism. UK-England: London. USA. 1864-1983.　　1285

Influence of Shakespeare, Beckett and Wittgenstein on the plays of Tom Stoppard. UK-England. 1963-1979.　　1302

Influence of Shakespeare and Percy Bysshe Shelley on Sean O'Casey's *The Shadow of a Gunman*. UK-Ireland: Dublin. 1923.　　1332

A Midsummer Night's Dream as a parody of Edmund Spenser's *The Teares of the Muses*. England. 1595.　　1556

Comparison of family relationships in Shakespeare and Restoration comedy of manners. England. 1595-1699.　　1561

Comparison of two French translations of *Twelfth Night*, by Jacques Copeau/Théodore Lascarais and Suzanne Bing. France: Paris. 1914.　　1567

Review essay of *Hamlet* burlesques from a collection of Shakespeare parodies. UK-England. USA. 1810-1888.　　1590

Metadramatic analysis of *Hamlet*. England. 1600-1601.　　1687

Critical essays on *King Lear*. England. 1605.　　1688

Linguistic analysis of *Macbeth*. England. 1605-1606.　　1690

Editorial problems in the first folio of *Hamlet*, *Othello* and *King Lear*. England: London. 1558-1621.　　1692

Wole Soyinka's plays echo themes of Aeschylus, Euripides and Shakespeare. Nigeria. Greece: Athens. UK-England: London. 1980.　　1700

Traditional approaches to acting and staging as clarifying methods for complex Shakespeare scenes. UK-England: Stratford-upon-Avon. 1980.　　1702

Examination of the preproduction script for Laurence Olivier's film *Hamlet*. UK-England. 1948.　　1719

Theatrical effect preserved in operatic adaptations of Werner Egk's *Peer Gynt* and Aribert Reimann's *King Lear* at the Münchener Festspiele. Germany, West: Munich. 1982.　　1953

Shakespeare's influence on Arrigo Boito's libretto for *La Gioconda*, based on Victor Hugo's play. Italy. 1862-1900.　　1956

Reference materials

Annotated Shakespearean bibliography. Europe. North America. France. 1980.　　1405

Bibliography of research on Shakespearean productions in German-speaking countries. German-speaking countries. 1981-1982.　　1410

Relation to other fields

Theatre arts compared to painting and literature. UK-England. 1805-1902.　　69

Impressions of the Chinese intellectual reaction to Shakespeare, freedom of thought and Cultural Revolution. China, People's Republic of: Beijing, Shanghai. 1920-1982.　　1445

Shakespeare's rhetoric in *Love's Labour's Lost* expresses commonplace figures also to be found in pictorial art of the period. England. 1594-1595.　　1446

Imagery of *Hamlet* is linked to Medieval and Renaissance decorative art. England: Stratford-upon-Avon. 1600-1601.　　1447

Videotapes created as instructional material on Elizabethan theatre. USA: Cortland, NY. 1973-1983.　　1724

Theory/criticism

Dramatic language related to action. England. 1559-1603.　　1480

Wystan Hugh Auden's poetic meditation on art as related to Shakespeare's *The Tempest* and Kierkegaardian thought. UK-England. 1939-1962.　　1511

Writings of Edward Gordon Craig. UK-England. 1907-1957.　　1513

Shamanism

Performance/production

Similarities of shaman tradition and Greek Dionysian rites. Korea. 1977. 2105

Theory/criticism

Spirituality for the dancer-actor in Zeami's and Zenchiku's writings on the *nō*. Japan. 1363-1470. 550

Shanghai Youth Modern Drama Troupe

Plays/librettos/scripts

Research, writing and first performance of historical drama by Yan Haiping on the subject of Chinese Emperor Li Shimin. China, People's Republic of. 1979-1982. 1021

Shaqui, Ahmad

Shakespeare's knowledge of Arab world and influence on later regional writers. England. Arabia. 1606-1981. 1075

Shaw, Ann

Institutions

Four new members inducted into American Theatre Association's College of Fellows. USA. 1983. 335

Shaw, George Bernard

History of the Malvern Festival. UK-England. 1929-1977. 629

Performance/production

Vienna's English Theatre's 20th anniversary production of G.B. Shaw's *Candida*. Austria: Vienna. 1963. 668

George Bernard Shaw's remarks on multiple staging. UK. 1909. 856

Production elements used to render *Saint Joan* a symbol of imagination. UK-England. 1923. 865

Director's analysis of Shaw's *Mrs. Warren's Profession*. UK-England. 1923. 871

Survey of stage history of G.B. Shaw's *Man and Superman*. UK-England. 1903-1982. 876

Collection of Shaw's addresses and essays concerning his plays in performance. UK-England: London. 1856-1950. 884

Collection of materials dealing with directing and acting Shavian drama. UK-England. 1892. 885

Reprint of Lillah McCarthy's interview with George Bernard Shaw. UK-England. 1927. 886

Importance of vocal techniques for Shavian drama. UK-England. 1945-1981. 896

Review of *Shaw's Music: The Complete Musical Criticism* (1981) discusses Shaw's career as critic. UK-England. 1876-1897. 897

Ten critics review Anthony Page's production of *Heartbreak House* presented at Circle in the Square. USA: New York, NY. 1983. 910

Director Stephen Porter comments on George Bernard Shaw. USA: New York, NY. 1964-1982. 947

Plays/librettos/scripts

Playwrights and dramatic forms influencing Eugene O'Neill's *The Calms of Capricorn*. Europe. USA. 1953. 1088

Criticism of George Bernard Shaw's plays from the standpoint of twentieth century critical methodology. UK. 1856-1950. 1272

Examination of semiotic elements in George Bernard Shaw's *Pygmalion*. UK. 1916. 1274

Essays on George Bernard Shaw's life and works. UK. 1856-1950. 1277

Function of props and settings in plays by George Bernard Shaw. UK-England. 1894-1907. 1281

Study of George Bernard Shaw's 'Unreasonable Man'. UK-England. 1885-1950. 1282

George Bernard Shaw as director-playwright. UK-England. 1914. 1284

Characterization and setting used to challenge audience views in George Bernard Shaw's *Major Barbara*. UK-England. 1907. 1287

Analysis of character and structure in G.B. Shaw's *The Devil's Disciple*. UK-England. USA. 1897-1983. 1293

Universal myths in *Pygmalion* as encouragement for the audience to break from settled beliefs. UK-England. 1914. 1301

Shaw's manipulation of audience reaction in *Major Barbara*. UK-England. 1907. 1307

Composition and production of George Bernard Shaw's *Saint Joan*. UK-England. 1923. 1314

Actors' influence on Shaw's theatrical ending of *The Devil's Disciple*. UK-England. 1897. 1315

Developments of Irish melodrama and its influence on later writers. UK-Ireland: Dublin. 1860-1905. 1338

Interview with director and cast of Yale Repertory's production of G.B. Shaw's *The Philanderer*. USA: New Haven, CT. 1982. 1389

Irreverent aspects of Irish comedy seen through the works of 14 playwrights. Eire. UK-Ireland. 1840-1965. 1555

Reference materials

George Bernard Shaw bibliography. UK. 1856-1983. 1421

Theory/criticism

George Bernard Shaw as theatre critic. UK-England. 1880-1950. 1512

Shelley, Percy Bysshe

Plays/librettos/scripts

Influence of Percy Bysshe Shelley's poetry on Sean O'Casey. UK-Ireland: Dublin. 1923-1946. 1318

Krapp's Last Tape by Samuel Beckett as a parody of both performance and themes in poetry. UK-Ireland. 1957. 1321

Influence of Shakespeare and Percy Bysshe Shelley on Sean O'Casey's *The Shadow of a Gunman*. UK-Ireland: Dublin. 1923. 1332

Shepard, Sam

Performance/production

Seven critics review Sam Shepard's production of his play *Fool for Love* presented by Circle Repertory Company. USA: New York, NY. 1983. 963

Arthur Kopit's and Sam Shepard's plays on and off Broadway. USA: New York, NY. 1957-1983. 1630

Plays/librettos/scripts

Themes of and influences on Sam Shepard's plays. USA. 1943-1983. 1343

Ironic use of folklore in Sam Shepard's *Buried Child*. USA. 1978. 1373

Review essay of Sam Shepard's *Fool for Love*. USA: San Francisco, CA. 1983. 1595

Theory/criticism

Phenomenology of audience reception of Sam Shepard's *Curse of the Starving Class*. USA: New York, NY, Buffalo, NY, Tempe, AZ. 1982. 1519

Sheridan, Richard Brinsley

Performance/production

National Theatre's production of Richard Brinsley Sheridan's *The Rivals*. UK-England: London. 1983. 1533

Plays/librettos/scripts

Essays on Restoration theatre and drama, with devised criteria for evaluation. England. 1660-1800. 1046

Sheridan, Thomas

Performance/production

Examination of John Philip Kemble's vocal technique. England. 1780-1817. 415

Sherman, Arthur

Seven critics review Arthur Sherman's production of Herman Wouk's play *The Caine Mutiny Court-Martial*. USA: New York, NY. 1983. 955

Sherman, Garry

Eight critics review Philip Rose's production of the musical *Amen Corner*. USA: New York, NY. 1983. 1800

Sherrin, Ned

Memoirs of director Ned Sherrin. UK. 1931-1983. 857

Singing — cont'd

Career of Karl Dönch, opera singer and manager of Vienna's Volksoper. Austria: Vienna. 1915-1983. 1761

Biography of singer-actress Julie Andrews. UK-England. USA. 1935-1983. 1777

History of Broadway musical theatre with an extensive annotated discography. USA: New York, NY. 1800-1983. 1789

Bass Walter Berry's debut in *Falstaff* at the Vienna Staatsoper. Austria: Vienna. 1983. 1841

Originators of female roles in operas by Wolfgang Amadeus Mozart. Austria. 1777-1791. 1843

Interview with soprano Lynn Blaser. Canada. 1983. 1845

Profile of tenor Ermanno Mauro. Canada. USA: New York, NY. 1958-1983. 1846

Interview with concert singer and comedienne Anna Russell. Canada: Toronto, ON. 1912-1983. 1847

Interview with Metropolitan Opera baritone Louis Quilico. Canada: Montreal, PQ. USA: New York, NY. 1983. 1848

Pianist Claudio Arrau recalls operas and singers he has heard. Europe. USA. 1903-1983. 1850

Illustrated biographical survey of 37 major opera personalities. Europe. North America. 1945-1983. 1853

Mezzosoprano Fiorenza Cossotto speaks about her career and art. Europe. 1957-1983. 1854

Interview with tenor Luciano Pavarotti about his career and forthcoming roles. Europe. North America. 1983. 1855

Comparison of performances of tenor aria 'O Dieu de quelle ivresse' by Jacques Offenbach. France. USA. 1911-1983. 1857

Richard Wagner's works, reception and influence. France. 1841-1983. 1859

Contribution to opera vocal technique by Gilbert-Louis Duprez. France: Paris. 1806-1896. 1863

One hundred years of recordings and Bayreuth Festival performances of Wagner's *Parsifal*. Germany: Bayreuth. 1882-1982. 1864

German tenor Peter Hofman speaks of his career and art. Germany, West. 1983. 1868

Bass Kurt Moll speaks about his career and role in *Der Rosenkavalier*. Germany, West. 1950-1983. 1874

Baritone David Holloway speaks of career with Deutsche Oper am Rhein. Germany, West: Düsseldorf, Duisburg. 1940-1983. 1877

Eva Marton, Hungarian dramatic soprano, speaks of her art and career. Hungary. USA. 1968-1983. 1878

Autobiography of tenor Mario Del Monaco. Italy. 1915-1975. 1880

Opera production textbook. Italy. 1597-1699. 1881

Collection of materials on the most famous opera singers and directors. Italy: Milan. 1958-1982. 1883

Interview with soprano Kiri Te Kanawa. UK-England. USA. New Zealand. 1945-1983. 1889

Photographs of gala centennial concert at the Metropolitan Opera House. USA: New York, NY. 1983. 1890

Backstage look at San Francisco Opera. USA: San Francisco, CA. 1970-1982. 1911

Career of soprano Leona Mitchell at the Metropolitan Opera. USA. 1983. 1912

Laurence Witten's collection of historic sound recordings at Yale University. USA: New Haven, CT. 1983. 1913

Life and career of Metropolitan Opera soprano Alwina Valleria. USA: New York, NY. 1848-1925. 1915

The life and career of Lina Abarbanell, the first Hänsel at the Metropolitan Opera House. USA: New York, NY. Germany: Berlin. 1905-1963. 1917

Relationship between the phonograph and the Metropolitan Opera. USA: New York, NY. 1902-1983. 1918

American baritone Thomas Stewart speaks of his career and art. USA: Houston, TX. 1925-1983. 1919

American mezzo-soprano Blanche Thebom reminisces about her career and art. USA: New York, NY. 1944-1983. 1921

Careers of father-son baritones Louis and Gino Quilico. USA: New York, NY. Canada. 1960-1983. 1922

Boris Christoff, bass, speaks of his career and art. USA: New York, NY. 1947-1983. 1924

Interview with lyric mezzo soprano Frederica von Stade. USA: New York, NY. 1945-1983. 1926

Simon Estes, American baritone, speaks of his life and career as a Black artist. USA. Europe. 1939-1983. 1927

James Beard, American cooking expert, recalls opera performances he has seen. USA: New York, NY. 1983. 1928

Konstantin Stanislavskij's training of opera singers. USSR. 1918-1935. 1929

Artistic career of the cabaret performer Giorgio Gaber. Italy. 1959-1981. 2004

Chronology of Black entertainers associated with 'Louisiana troupes'. Europe. 1901-1916. 2028

Composers whose songs were played at Irish variety performances, especially those of John McCormack. USA. UK. 1800-1899. 2029

Plays/librettos/scripts

Italian tenor Luciano Pavarotti discusses the title role of *Ernani* by Giuseppe Verdi. Italy. 1983. 1958

Reference materials

Bibliography of performing arts periodicals. 1982. 11

Catalogue of the exhibition on soprano Toti Dal Monte and tenor Enzo De Muro Lomanto. Italy: Trieste. 1893-1975. 1967

Annotated selections of photographs taken by Herman Mishkin of Metropolitan Opera singers. USA: New York, NY. 1910-1932. 1971

Theory/criticism

Phenomenological theory of performing arts. USA. 1982. 1514

Training

Training manual for performers. 1982. 492

Vocal training manual. USA. 1982. 503

Biographical sketch of Italian voice coach Luigi Ricci. Italy: Rome. 1920-1983. 1973

Singspiel

Plays/librettos/scripts

Genre classification of parody and related forms in Johann Nestroy's plays. Austria. 1833-1862. 1552

Sirk, Douglas (Sierck, Detlef)

Performance/production

Portrait of and interview with Douglas Sirk, director of *Silverlake*. Germany. Switzerland. USA. 1933-1983. 426

Plays/librettos/scripts

Compilation of comments by various artists on Tennessee Williams. USA. 1911-1983. 1342

Six Characters in Search of an Author SEE: *Sei personaggi in cerca d'autore*

Sjöberg, Alf

Performance/production

Study of Ingmar Bergman's approach to directing, and the influences on it. Sweden. Germany. 1930-1983. 842

Sjögren, Henrik

Theory/criticism

Political stagnation and bureaucratization of theatre critics. Sweden. 1960-1983. 109

Sjöman, Vilgot

Performance/production

August Strindberg productions in eleven countries. Sweden. Italy. USA. 1982. 847

Skin of Our Teeth, The

Karlheinz Stroux's production of *The Skin of Our Teeth* by Thornton Wilder at Hebbeltheater. Germany, West: West Berlin, Darmstadt. 1946. 779

Slab Boys

Six critics review Robert Allan Ackerman's production of John Byrne's play *Slab Boys*. USA: New York, NY. 1983. 970

Slaughter of the Innocents, The

New information from York about problems with the Girdlers'

Slaughter of the Innocents, The — cont'd

pageant wagon and their play, *The Slaughter of the Innocents.* England: York. 1548-1554.   705

Sleeping Beauty

Design/technology

Three costume and two set designs by Leon Bakst for ballet. 1911-1923.   175

Smiley, Sam M.

Institutions

Four new members inducted into American Theatre Association's College of Fellows. USA. 1983.   335

Šnajder, Slobodan

Plays/librettos/scripts

Current state of drama and theatre seen through plays and playwrights. Yugoslavia. 1983.   1393

SNMT SEE: Shakespeare National Memorial Theatre

Sobol, Jehoshua

Performance/production

Karl Kraus' and Jehoshua Sobol's plays devoted to Vienna of 1900 and produced at Edinburgh Festival. UK-Scotland: Edinburgh. 1983.   902

Social institutions SEE: Institutions, social

Social realism

Design/technology

Comprehensive documented study of Russian Constructivism. USSR. 1917-1940.   278

Performance/production

Purposes, goals and rewards of performing Shakespeare on socialist amateur stages. Germany, East. 1982.   744

Emergence and development of social criticism in Uzbek drama and performance. USSR. 1917-1930.   994

Two productions of *A Midsummer Night's Dream.* Germany, East: East Berlin. 1975-1982.   1526

Dispute about Heiner Müller's production of *Macbeth.* Germany, East: East Berlin. 1971-1982.   1678

Theory/criticism

Marxist philosophy in Bertolt Brecht's work. Germany. 1922-1956.   1496

Social/community relations

Administration

Activities of the Audience Development Committee. USA: New York, NY. 1983.   153

Socialist Revolution SEE: October Socialist Revolution

Sociedad Wagneriana (Wagnerian Society)

Performance/production

First performance of Richard Wagner's *Lohengrin* and the debate generated with followers of Giuseppe Verdi. Spain. 1862-1901. 1886

Società Italiana degli Autori ed Editori (SIAE)

Institutions

First hundred years of the Società Italiana degli Autori ed Editori published in celebration of its centenary. Italy. 1882-1982. 318

Société Internationale des Bibliothèques et Musées des Arts du Spectacle (SIBMAS)

Design/technology

Problems of collecting and preserving documents of African stage design. Africa. 1982.   177

SIBMAS papers on collections of designs and scenography. Europe. North America. 1982.   183

Cataloguing work done since 1975 at Drottningholm Theatre Museum. Sweden: Drottningholm, Gripsholm. 1766-1800.   222

SIBMAS keynote address calling for accumulation of records to preserve theatre history. USA. 1982.   239

History and description of the Motley Theatre and Costume Arts Collection. Discussed at SIBMAS. USA: Urbana, IL. 1982.   247

Observations concerning the French-English translation of scenographic terms. Discussed at SIBMAS. USA. France. 1982.   257

Why collecting, maintaining and exhibiting designers' work is problematical. Discussed at SIBMAS. USA. 1982.   273

Theatre collection taxonomy based on an iconographic approach discussed at SIBMAS. USA: Columbus, OH. 1982.   276

Remarks by scientific advisor to Serbian Museum of Theatrical Art on document collection. Discussed at SIBMAS. Yugoslavia: Belgrade. 1982.   279

Influence of stage design on music-drama. Yugoslavia: Belgrade. 1980.   280

Choosing audio-visual materials for exhibits. Discussed at SIBMAS. France: Paris. 1982.   1705

Reference materials

Description of the Stage Design Collection of National Arts Center. Canada: Ottawa, ON. 1969-1982.   16

Models of scenery and costumes in the Bibliothèque Nationale. France: Paris. 1982.   24

Research/historiography

Method for using models of scenery as study documents. Discussed at SIBMAS. Europe. North America. 1982.   83

Society for the Suppression of Vice

Institutions

Activities of church and theatre associations to promote 'decent' dramaturgy. USA: New York, NY, Chicago, IL. 1910-1940.   649

Sociology

Administration

Impact of government funding on the arts. USA. 1965-1982.   159

Effect of different kinds of financial support on artists. USA. 1950-1982.   163

Audience

Study of public perception of theatrical performances. 1982. 164

Poll on characteristics of audience attending Theater in der Josefstadt in Vienna. Austria: Vienna. 1982.   165

Sociological studies suggest that democratization of the arts has not taken place. USA. 1830-1982.   173

Effects of theatre on suburban audience. Finland. 1979-1981. 567

Design/technology

Concise history of costuming. Europe. North America. 999 B.C.-1969 A.D.   185

Middle class morality reflected in nineteenth-century fashion. USA. 1830-1870.   258

Institutions

Description of street theatre performances whose purpose is social change. India: Calcutta. 1983.   316

Classical and anti-classical traditions in contemporary theatre. Canada. 1960-1979.   586

Performance spaces

Relation between architectural structure and social function of theatre. France. 1736-1806.   369

Performance/production

Theatre before and after Mao Tse-tung. China, People's Republic of. 1949-1956.   414

Eight actors take positions on their political and social responsibilities. Germany, East. 1983.   428

Sociological and psychological implications faced by dancers at end of their performing careers. USA. 1982.   520

Status and work of actors since beginning of professional theatre in Finland. Finland. 1872-1980.   721

Actor's role in theatre and social status in ancient Greece and Rome. Greece. Roman Empire. 600-1 B.C.   790

History of *Ru-howzi* improvisational theatre. Iran. 1780-1950. 792

Sociology — cont'd

Politics, psychology and director Elia Kazan's career. USA. 1909-1965. 949

Work of performance artist Kazuko Hohki with the Japanese-American Toy Theatre. Japan. UK-England: London. 1983. 1745

Social status and role of minstrels. Europe. 1100-1500. 1986

Plays/librettos/scripts

Latin American theatre and progressive social movements. Costa Rica. Argentina. Peru. 1588-1983. 1022

Status of women in Elizabethan society as reflected in Shakespeare's plays. England. 1590-1613. 1049

Paternal authority and sex roles in Shakespeare's plays. England. 1595-1615. 1079

Jewish stereotypes in contemporary drama. Europe. North America. 1982. 1094

Moral and social themes in contemporary Finnish drama. Finland. 1981. 1097

Necessity of an urban middle class to the development of drama in the Middle Ages. France. 1200. 1108

Comparative sociological study of French theatre. France. 1610-1643. 1109

Tendency of Bertolt Brecht's plays to promote social change as barrier to their universal value. Germany. 1918-1956. 1119

Divergence of theoretical and practical concerns in Bertolt Brecht's plays. Germany. 1918-1956. 1121

Influence of Lenin's writings on Bertolt Brecht's plays. Germany. 1930. 1128

Bertolt Brecht's theory of social basis of personal contradictions. Germany. 1918-1956. 1129

'Great Method' used by Bertolt Brecht in his plays, and influences from others. Germany. 1918-1956. 1130

Influence of Marxist and Leninist ideology on Bertolt Brecht's plays. Germany. 1926-1934. 1132

Bertolt Brecht's experiments in audience education through his plays. Germany, East. 1954-1956. 1147

Relationship between mercantile society and playwright's creation in Carlo Goldoni's plays. Italy: Venice. 1734-1793. 1159

Luigi Pirandello's concept of the relationships of character, society and reality. Italy. 1916-1936. 1182

Study of Benito Pérez Galdós' plays. Spain. 1843-1920. 1237

Sociological approach to Lope de Vega's drama. Spain. 1573-1635. 1256

Willy Russell's work as a playwright with discussion of his social and political commitment. UK-England. 1970-1983. 1283

Stereotypes of old age in children's plays, and some examples that break it. USA. 1983. 1369

Study of Hamlin Garland's regional social drama *Under the Wheel.* USA. 1890. 1370

Comparison of family relationships in Shakespeare and Restoration comedy of manners. England. 1595-1699. 1561

Alfred Jarry's *Ubu* Cycle with an emphasis on its protagonist. France. 1896-1907. 1566

Essays on and a bibliographical guide to Pierre Corneille's comedies. France. 1606-1684. 1572

Description of *thullal,* a form of comedy, created by Kunchan Nambiar, and performed by a single actor. India: Kerala. 1700-1799. 1583

Plays of Plautus and Terence related to Roman society. Roman Republic. 254-159 B.C. 1587

Religious rites and ideology of medieval urban societies as seen in Corpus Christi plays. England. 1300-1499. 2106

Relation to other fields

Karl Valentin's humorous proposal that theatre be mandatory for purposes of educating and improving society. Germany. 1882-1948. 55

Class-conscious approach to theatre. Germany, West. 1983. 56

Interview with Fritz Bennewitz on theatre work in the Third World. India. Venezuela. Sri Lanka. 1970-1983. 59

Theatre as a social mirror of the town. Italy: Reggio Emilia. 1851. 65

Argument against application of Jungian ideas to theatre. 490

Current dramatic themes in relation to historical development. China. 1900-1983. 1444

Impressions of the Chinese intellectual reaction to Shakespeare, freedom of thought and Cultural Revolution. China, People's Republic of: Beijing, Shanghai. 1920-1982. 1445

Introduction to essay collection *The Sociology of Theatre.* Europe. North America. 1983. 1448

Different social functions of the dramatic theatre in Greece and Rome and their modifications. Greece. Roman Empire. 600-1 B.C. 1455

Racial stereotypes in American theatre. USA. 1983. 1466

Description of Jane Addams' creative drama activities at Hull House. USA: Chicago, IL. 1889-1910. 1469

'Progressive' society's reactions to death of Eugene O'Neill. USA. 1954. 1472

Bunraku is seen as Japanese miniaturization of social concepts. Japan: Osaka. 1983. 2076

Theory/criticism

Systematic, analytic examination of sociology of performing arts. Europe. North America. 1983. 97

Communist approach to theatrical tradition. Germany, East: East Berlin. 1982. 101

Political stagnation and bureaucratization of theatre critics. Sweden. 1960-1983. 109

Rapport between social setting and dramatic text. France: Paris. 1971-1980. 1489

Bertolt Brecht's didactic plays function in the development of Socialism. Germany. 1922-1956. 1497

Bertolt Brecht's view that all wars stem from social conflict. Germany. 1898-1956. 1502

Phenomenological theory of performing arts. USA. 1982. 1514

Effect of social conditions on performance styles. USA. Greece. 499 B.C.-1983 A.D. 1517

Sociology of Theater, The

Relation to other fields

Introduction to essay collection *The Sociology of Theatre.* Europe. North America. 1983. 1448

Socrates

Theory/criticism

Bertolt Brecht's perception of the philosophy of the Enlightenment. Germany. 1848-1956. 1498

Soldiers Fortune, The

Morality of Restoration comedy. England. 1670-1700. 1599

Soler i Rovirosa

Design/technology

Development of Wagnerian stage design and groups and movements involved in its production. Spain. 1882-1960. 1822

Solidarność (Solidarity)

Relation to other fields

Survival of theatre under martial law. Poland. 1981-1982. 67

Solís y Rivandeneyra, Antonio de

Plays/librettos/scripts

Notes and bibliographic descriptions of the Vatican copy of Antonio de Solís y Rivadeneyra's *Triumph of Love and Fortune.* Spain. Vatican. 1658. 1242

Solter, Friedo

Performance/production

Solter's concept for staging Bertolt Brecht's *Baal.* Germany, East. 1983. 745

Tendencies of Bertolt Brecht stage interpretations. Germany, East. USSR. Italy. 1956-1983. 747

Directors on Bertolt Brecht's dramas. Germany, East: Schwerin, Erfurt, East Berlin. 1983. 754

Solti, Georg

Peter Hall's production of Richard Wagner's *Ring* at Bayreuth Festspielhaus. Germany, West: Bayreuth. 1983. 1870

Solti, Georg — cont'd

1983 Bayreuth *Der Ring des Nibelungen*, directed by Peter Hall, conducted by Georg Solti. Germany, West: Bayreuth. 1983.   1873

Sommi, Leone de'

Design/technology

Methodology for the interpretation of symbolism in Renaissance costume. Italy. 1539.   212

Song of Songs

Plays/librettos/scripts

Song of Songs as medieval dramatic literature. Europe. 1400-1499.   1089

Sophocles

Performance/production

Japanese adaptations and productions of Sophocles' *Oedipus*. Japan. 1922-1978.   818

Plays/librettos/scripts

Mutes in Greek tragedy. Greece. 523-406 B.C.   1695

English translation of Albin Lesky's standard work on Greek tragedy. Greece. 499-400 B.C.   1696

Sotties

Performance/production

Links between popular forms of medieval drama and theatrical presentations during the carnival period. France. 1200-1599.   2007

Soul of a Jew, The

Karl Kraus' and Jehoshua Sobol's plays devoted to Vienna of 1900 and produced at Edinburgh Festival. UK-Scotland: Edinburgh. 1983.   902

Sound

Design/technology

Construction and operating procedures of new sound systems at the München Nationaltheater. Germany, West: Munich. 1983.   199

Study of sound technology at the 43rd Conference of Theatre Technology. Germany, West: Heilbronn. 1983.   204

Notation of sound effects in relationship to other cues. North America. 1983.   220

New products of interest to designers and technicians. USA. 1900-1983.   236

Unified approach to audiovisual design. USA. 1977.   241

Published materials for sound technicians. USA. 1983.   244

Guidelines for use of loudspeakers. USA. 1945-1983.   245

Description and listing of sound systems for theatres to aid hearing impaired. USA. 1960-1983.   246

New products for technical theatre use. USA. 1983.   254

Application of automatic microphone mixers in theatre. USA. 1945-1983.   255

Model for musical design training. USA. 1982.   256

Sound systems and techniques for controlling sound. USA: New York, NY. 1945-1983.   264

Master sheet format for sound plots. USA: New York, NY. 1983.   265

Performance spaces

Technical aspects of modifying and restoring historic theatres. USA. 1983.   405

Acoustical problems encountered in theatre renovation. USA. 1983.   408

Acoustical modifications at the Orpheum Theatre made to accommodate Broadway musicals. USA: San Francisco, CA. 1981-1983.   1774

Performance/production

Relationship between the phonograph and the Metropolitan Opera. USA: New York, NY. 1902-1983.   1918

Southey, Robert

Documentation of the performance of Robert Southey's play *Wat Tyler* (1794) at Whittington Theatre. England: Whittington. 1817.   699

Soviet Army Theatre SEE: Centralnyj Teat'r Soveckoj Armii

Soviet Revolution SEE: October Socialist Revolution

Soyfer, Jura

Institutions

Interview with Reinhold Auer, dramatic advisor of Jura Soyfer Theater am Spittelberg, Vienna. Austria: Vienna. 1980-1983.   583

Soyinka, Wole

Plays/librettos/scripts

Incremental repetition and inter-relationship in the plays of Wole Soyinka. Nigeria. 1956-1982.   1652

Wole Soyinka's adaptation of Euripides' *The Bacchae*. Nigeria. 1973.   1699

Wole Soyinka's plays echo themes of Aeschylus, Euripides and Shakespeare. Nigeria. Greece: Athens. UK-England: London. 1980.   1700

Relation to other fields

Wole Soyinka's journalism related to his poems and plays. Nigeria. 1962-1982.   1459

Space at City Center (New York, NY)

Performance/production

Seven critics review Gillian Lynne's production of *Jeeves Takes Charge*. USA: New York, NY. 1983.   946

Spanish Tragedy, The

Plays/librettos/scripts

Relationship between Jacobean tragedy and interpolated masque. England. 1600-1625.   1691

Special institutions SEE: Institutions, special

Spectacle Theatre (Wales)

Institutions

Collaborative effort in Welsh community results in play *All's Fair*. UK-Wales: Mid Glamorgan. 1983.   645

Spenser, Edmund

Plays/librettos/scripts

A Midsummer Night's Dream as a parody of Edmund Spenser's *The Teares of the Muses*. England. 1595.   1556

Spira, Steffi

Performance/production

Eight actors take positions on their political and social responsibilities. Germany, East. 1983.   428

Spiró, György

Institutions

Polish theatre under Russian rule as reflected in György Spiró's novel *Az Ikszek*. Poland: Warsaw. Russia. Hungary. 1815-1829.   325

Spivak, Gayatri

Theory/criticism

Significance of gender in feminist criticism with reference to historical materialism, deconstruction and phenomenon of cross-dressing in theatre. USA. France. UK-England. 1983.   1520

Spöksonaten (Ghost Sonata, The)

Plays/librettos/scripts

Interpretation of August Strindberg's *The Ghost Sonata* in light of contemporary problems. Sweden. 1907-1983.   1269

Spolin, Viola

Relation to other fields

Use of improvisation in the teaching of foreign languages. USA. 1983.   1470

Squat Theatre (New York, NY)

Institutions
Theoretical and theatrical foundations of the Squat Theatre. USA: New York, NY. Hungary: Budapest. 1975-1977.　342

Theory/criticism
Expressionistic proposal for the future of theatre by a founding member of Squat Theatre. USA. 1983.　110

Squire of Alsantia, The
Morality of Restoration comedy. England. 1670-1700.　1599

SSTA SEE: Secondary School Theatre Association

St. Lawrence Centre (Toronto, ON)

Administration
Disappointments and mismanagement at Centre Stage. Canada: Toronto, ON. 1983.　119

Staatliche Schauspielbühnen (West Berlin)
Heribert Sasse succeeds Boy Gobert as manager at Staatliche Schauspielbühnen Berlin. Germany, West: West Berlin. 1983.　128

Staatsoper (Dresden)

Training
Ballet work and training in opera houses in East Germany. Germany, East: Leipzig, Dresden, East Berlin. 1981-1983.　523

Staatsoper (East Berlin)
Ballet work and training in opera houses in East Germany. Germany, East: Leipzig, Dresden, East Berlin. 1981-1983.　523

Staatsoper (Vienna)

Administration
Lorin Maazel's first season as intendant of Vienna Staatsoper. Austria: Vienna. USA. 1983.　1810

Administration in the making of a production at Vienna's Staatsoper. Austria: Vienna. 1983.　1811

Life and career of opera manager Egon Seefehlner. Austria: Vienna. Germany, West: West Berlin. 1912-1983.　1812

Institutions
Annual report of the Austrian Federal Theatres. Austria: Vienna. 1982-1983.　284

Performance/production
Harold Prince's production of Giacomo Puccini's *Turandot* at Vienna's Staatsoper. Austria: Vienna. 1983.　1839

Making of a production at Vienna's Staatsoper: rehearsals. Austria: Vienna. 1983.　1840

Bass Walter Berry's debut in *Falstaff* at the Vienna Staatsoper. Austria: Vienna. 1983.　1841

Stade, Frederica von
Interview with lyric mezzo soprano Frederica von Stade. USA: New York, NY. 1945-1983.　1926

Städtische Bühnen (Dortmund)

Institutions
Financial situation of Städtische Bühnen Dortmund. Germany, West: Dortmund. 1970-1982.　604

Stafford-Clark, Max

Performance/production
Eight critics review Max Stafford-Clark's production of Caryl Churchill's play *Top Girls*. USA: New York, NY. 1983.　958

Stage combat
Manual of stage combat. USA. 1983.　466

Stage management SEE: Management, stage

Stage modifications

Performance spaces
Technical aspects of modifying and restoring historic theatres. USA. 1983.　405

Staged readings

Institutions
Limited success of staged readings. Sweden. Denmark. 1969-1983.　619

Staging

Administration
Unemployment among Black theatre professionals. UK-England: London. 1974-1979.　146

Interview with the new artistic director and literary advisor for the Iron Theatre (Glasgow). UK-Scotland. 1973-1983.　559

Copyrights for directors' contributions to the plays they stage. USA. 1983.　563

Interview with Terry McEwen, general director of War Memorial Opera House. Canada: Montreal, PQ. USA: San Francisco, CA. 1983.　1813

Audience
Modern productions of Renaissance drama. Europe. 1982.　566

Basic theatrical documents
Texts and descriptions of all aspects of the production of medieval religious plays. Europe. 1300-1600.　570

Design/technology
Influence of the designers on staging styles. UK. 1958-1983.　226

Techniques for using film or still projection in live theatre performances. USA. 1983.　250

Model for musical design training. USA. 1982.　256

Introductory lighting textbook. USA. 1982.　270

Use of projections to enforce subtexts. USA. 1945-1983.　271

Comprehensive documented study of Russian Constructivism. USSR. 1917-1940.　278

Close collaboration between director and lighting designer in *Cats*. USA: New York, NY. 1982.　1768

Interviews with the designers of *Cats*. USA: New York, NY. UK-England: London. 1983.　1770

Josef Svoboda's scenography of Wagnerian opera. Switzerland. UK-England: London. Czechoslovakia: Prague. 1948-1983.　1823

Staging, masks and dance of the Odo Festival. Nigeria. 1982.　2104

Institutions
Finnish theatre groups and artists performing abroad. Finland. Sweden. 1982-1983.　299

Background of Edward Gordon Craig's efforts to establish School for the Art of Theatre. Italy: Florence. UK-England: London. 1900-1917.　320

History of dance group L'Étoile du Nord. Sweden. USA. 1636-1983.　524

Events leading to Roger Hodgman's resignation as Artistic Director of Vancouver Playhouse. Canada: Vancouver, BC. 1973-1983.　585

Concepts of and preparations for Théâtre de l'Europe, managed by Giorgio Strehler. France: Paris. 1983.　596

History of Deutsches Theater Berlin. Germany: Berlin. 1883-1983.　598

Bertolt Brecht's return to Deutsches Theater and production of *Mother Courage* with Berliner Ensemble. Germany, East: East Berlin. 1949.　601

Edward Bond's *Saved* and Shakespeare's *Troilus and Cressida* at the Jugendclub Kritisches Theater. Germany, West: Stuttgart. 1981-1983.　608

History of Royal Shakespeare Company with emphasis on financial and aesthetic aspects and internal politics. UK-England: London. 1864-1981.　624

Aspects of the National Theatre and the Royal Shakespeare Company are compared. UK-England. 1960.　627

Collaborative production efforts of Bush Theatre. UK-England. 1983.　630

Artistic directors, policy, development and funding of The Traverse studio theatre. UK-England. 1963.　632

Production of *Nightingale* by First All Children's Theatre, and Meridee Stein, the group's founder. USA: New York, NY. 1982.　650

Staging — cont'd

Performance spaces

Performance/production

Staging – cont'd

Rehearsal methods of director Finn Poulsen. Sweden: Göteburg, Gävleborg. 1969-1983.   839

Three productions of *Macbeth* by director Ingmar Bergman. Sweden: Stockholm, Hälsingborg, Göteburg. 1940-1948.   840

Summer productions of Shakespeare and Molière involving professional and amateur actors. Sweden: Södertälje. 1981-1983.   841

Study of Ingmar Bergman's approach to directing, and the influences on it. Sweden. Germany. 1930-1983.   842

Analysis of Ingmar Bergman's stage and film direction. Sweden. 1918-1982.   843

Documentation of Ingmar Bergman's tripartite theatre project. Sweden. Germany, West: Munich. 1981.   844

Ingmar Bergman's use of text, stage and audience. Sweden. Germany, West. 1944.   845

Theatre scholars said to focus too narrowly on directors. Sweden. 1983.   846

August Strindberg productions in eleven countries. Sweden. Italy. USA. 1982.   847

Arie Zinger's production of Čechov's *Ivanov* at Züricher Schauspielhaus. Switzerland: Zürich. 1983.   849

Review of the Chester cycle performed in a 1550's design. UK: Leeds. England: Chester. 1550-1983.   851

Director of Polka Children's Theatre discusses children's attitude to plays and puppets. UK. 1983.   852

George Bernard Shaw's remarks on multiple staging. UK. 1909.   856

Memoirs of director Ned Sherrin. UK. 1931-1983.   857

John Barton's staging of *Hamlet* influenced by Anne Righter. UK-England. 1961-1980.   860

Edward Gordon Craig's productions of and theories on Shakespeare. UK-England. Europe. 1872-1940.   862

Beerbohm Tree's conceptual and directorial approach to staging Shakespeare. UK-England: London. 1905-1911.   863

Theodore Komisarjevsky's productions of Shakespeare's plays at Stratford-upon-Avon. UK-England: Stratford-upon-Avon. 1932-1939.   864

Production elements used to render *Saint Joan* a symbol of imagination. UK-England. 1923.   865

Relationship between verbal and nonverbal communication in productions of *Macbeth, Othello* and *Julius Caesar*. UK-England. 1980.   868

Director Edward Gordon Craig's writings on theatre. UK-England. 1872-1966.   870

Director's analysis of Shaw's *Mrs. Warren's Profession*. UK-England. 1923.   871

Analysis of C.V. Stanford's incidental music for *Becket*. UK-England: London. 1893.   872

Critical examination of modern interpretations of Shakespeare's plays. UK-England: London. USA. Canada: Stratford, ON. 1975-1982.   873

Various treatments of the induction scene with Christopher Sly in *The Taming of the Shrew*, including lists. UK-England. USA. 1844-1978.   874

Descriptive account of Theodore Komisarjevsky's productions of Anton Čechov's plays. UK-England: London. 1926-1936.   875

Survey of stage history of G.B. Shaw's *Man and Superman*. UK-England. 1903-1982.   876

Peter Hall's diaries regarding his productions. UK-England. 1930.   880

Study of director Edward Gordon Craig. UK-England. 1872-1966.   883

Collection of materials dealing with directing and acting Shavian drama. UK-England. 1892.   885

Reprint of Lillah McCarthy's interview with George Bernard Shaw. UK-England. 1927.   886

Peter Wood's productions of Tom Stoppard's *The Real Thing* and Harold Pinter's *Other Places*. UK-England: London. 1983.   887

Philip Prowse's production of Robert MacDonald's Nazi psychothriller *Summit Conference*. UK-England: London. 1982.   888

John Marshall production of the Digby plays at Winchester Cathedral places particular emphasis on dance. UK-England: Winchester. 1983.   889

Year's outstanding productions of plays by August Strindberg and other playwrights. UK-England. 1982-1983.   890

Actor Laurence Olivier's autobiography. UK-England. 1907-1983.   891

Italian translation of Laurence Olivier's autobiography *Confessions of an Actor*. UK-England. 1907-1983.   892

Reconstruction of Richard Mansfield's production of *Richard III*. UK-England: London. USA. 1889.   893

Discussion of political theatre. UK-England. 1970-1979.   894

Director Harley Granville-Barker's career. UK-England. 1877-1946.   895

Charles Kean's staging methods and the influences on them. UK-England: London. 1850-1859.   898

Edward Bulwer-Lytton's theory of the need for unified approach to productions, in response to John Calcraft's staging of *Richelieu*. UK-Ireland: Dublin. 1839.   900

Fusion of visual and verbal elements creates a style of voluptuous theatricality at Citizens' Theatre. UK-Scotland: Glasgow. 1969-1979.   901

Karl Kraus' and Jehoshua Sobol's plays devoted to Vienna of 1900 and produced at Edinburgh Festival. UK-Scotland: Edinburgh. 1983.   902

Changes of directors and reviews of performances at the Edinburgh Festival and Lyceum Theatre. UK-Scotland: Edinburgh. 1983.   903

Decisions needed in staging plays with inherent sexist or racist themes. USA. 1980-1983.   904

Guide to play production. USA. 1982.   905

Enactment and narration as particularly appropriate methods of dramatization. USA. 1968-1980.   906

Comparative study of Peter Oskarsson's production of August Strindberg's *A Dream Play* with that of Ingmar Bergman. USA: Seattle, WA. 1982.   907

Two examples of staging *Macbeth* in the 1970's. USA: Stratford, CT. Canada: Stratford, ON. 1971-1973.   908

Five critics review Amy Saltz's production of *Win/Lose/Draw* at the Provincetown Playhouse. USA: New York, NY. 1983.   909

Ten critics review Anthony Page's production of *Heartbreak House* presented at Circle in the Square. USA: New York, NY. 1983.   910

Ten critics review Marshall Mason's production of Peter Nichols' play *Passion*. USA: New York, NY. 1983.   919

Textbook for introductory directing course. USA. 1982.   920

Francis Fergusson talks about his involvement with Ibsen productions. USA. 1945-1982.   922

Stanislavskij's system in the USA and the tour by the Moscow Art Theatre. USA. USSR. 1910-1959.   923

Interview with director Tom Moore. USA. 1983.   924

Five critics review Bill Raymond and Dale Worsley's production of *Cold Harbor*. USA: New York, NY. 1983.   925

Five critics review Gerald Gutierrez's production of *Isn't It Romantic*. USA: New York, NY. 1983.   926

Five critics review Lee Grant's production of Vaclav Havel's play *A Private View* translated by Vera Blackwell. USA: New York, NY. 1983.   927

Four critics review Alan Schneider's production of three Samuel Beckett plays. USA: New York, NY. 1983.   928

Three critics review Howard Reifsnyder's *The Guys in the Truck* directed by David Black. USA: New York, NY. 1983.   929

Seven critics review *The Corn Is Green*. USA: New York, NY. 1983.   930

Five critics review Regge Life's production of *Do Lord Remember Me*. USA: New York, NY. 1983.   931

Actor John Houseman comments on producers and directors. USA. 1983.   934

Tribute to Mordecai Gorelik, scenic designer, theorist, teacher, director and playwright. USA. 1899-1983.   936

Jane Martin's *Talking With* at Manhattan Theatre Club, directed by Jon Jory. USA: New York, NY. 1982.   937

Shakespearean productions and festivals in the American South. USA. 1751-1980.   938

Critical essays on interpretations of *Death of a Salesman*. USA. 1949-1983.   939

Biography of director Margo Jones. USA. 1913-1955.   941

SUBJECT INDEX

Staging – cont'd

Director, actor and playwright Carmelo Bene's autobiography. Italy. 1959-1983. 1620

Theories of acting and theatre by controversial director Carmelo Bene. Italy. 1960-1982. 1621

Role of the actor in experimental theatre. Italy. 1968-1977. 1622

Interview with playwright Dario Fo and his actress-wife and collaborator Franca Rame. Italy: Milan. 1982. 1623

Ezio Maria Caserta's theories and practice of theatre. Italy. 1983-1975. 1624

Analysis of Carmelo Bene's avant-garde adaptation and staging of *Pinocchio*. Italy. 1981. 1625

Comprehensive study of productions by Tadeusz Kantor's experimental theatre group Cricot 2 and Kantor's philosophy. Poland. 1975-1980. 1626

Interview with playwright-director Tadeusz Kantor about *Wielopole, Wielopole*. Poland: Wielopole. 1982. 1628

Tadeusz Kantor's theory of art and theatre, and productions of his company Cricot 2. Poland: Kraków. 1943-1975. 1629

Arthur Kopit's and Sam Shepard's plays on and off Broadway. USA: New York, NY. 1957-1983. 1630

Writings by the founders of the Living Theatre. USA. Europe. 1952-1962. 1631

Production styles of directors Peter Brook and Tadeusz Kantor. USA: New York, NY. France: Paris. Poland: Wielopole. 1982. 1632

Production journal of *King Lear*. Canada: Stratford, ON. 1979. 1676

Evolution of the text of *King Lear* through performance. England. 1605-1983. 1677

Dispute about Heiner Müller's production of *Macbeth*. Germany, East: East Berlin. 1971-1982. 1678

Ernst Wendt's staging of Friederich Hebbel's *Gyges and His Ring*. Germany, West: Hamburg. 1983. 1679

Hansgünther Heyme's production of *The Persians*. Germany, West: Stuttgart. 1983. 1680

Reconstruction of Edward Gordon Craig's production of *Hamlet* at Moscow Art Theatre. Russia: Moscow. 1908-1912. 1682

Six critics review Jane Howell's production of *Richard III* mounted by the Public Theater. USA: New York, NY. 1983. 1684

Konstantin Stanislavskij's stage adaptation of Shakespeare's *Othello* for the Moscow Art Theatre. USSR: Moscow. 1929-1930. 1685

Max Reinhardt's film adaptations of his theatre productions. Europe. North America. 1910-1943. 1711

Semiotic analysis of Els Joglars' production of *Mary d'Ous*. Spain. 1972. 1729

Seven critics review *Marcel Marceau on Broadway*. USA: New York, NY. 1983. 1730

Philosophy and intentions of Rational Theatre and ABDC Workshop's Edinburgh project. UK-England. UK-Scotland: Edinburgh. 1983. 1747

Performance art and organization of events staged by The Basement Group. UK-England: Newcastle upon Tyne. 1983. 1748

Mixing popular entertaining, particularly rock music, with performance art. UK-England. 1970-1980. 1749

Account of a production of the musical *In Dahomey*. UK-England: London. 1903-1904. 1776

Five critics review Tony Tanner's production of the musical *Preppies*. USA: New York, NY. 1983. 1779

Nine critics review Vivian Matalon's production of the musical *The Tap Dance Kid*. USA: New York, NY. 1983. 1781

Production elements and choreography of *On Your Toes*. USA. 1982. 1782

Five critics review Ron Field's production of *Five-Six-Seven-Eight...Dance!*. USA: New York, NY. 1983. 1783

Production history of *The Best Little Whorehouse in Texas*. USA: New York, NY. 1974-1982. 1784

Changes needed in production and direction of musical theatre. USA. 1982. 1785

History of Broadway musical theatre with an extensive annotated discography. USA: New York, NY. 1800-1983. 1789

Production, casts and review of musical *My One and Only*. USA: New York, NY. 1971-1983. 1791

Seven critics review Kenny Ortega's production of the musical *Marilyn: An American Fable*. USA: New York, NY. 1983. 1792

Six critics review Alan Jay Lerner's production of the musical *Dance a Little Closer*. USA: New York, NY. 1983. 1793

Six critics review Robert Drivas' production of Peggy Lee's play *Peg*. USA: New York, NY. 1983. 1794

Nine critics review Jack O'Brien's production of *Porgy and Bess*. USA: New York, NY. 1983. 1795

Five critics review David Holdgrive's production of the musical *Tallulah*. USA: New York, NY. 1983. 1796

Six critics review Charles Ludlam's production of his play *Galas*. USA: New York, NY. 1983. 1797

Nine critics review Michael Cacoyannis' production of the musical *Zorba*. USA: New York, NY. 1983. 1798

Nine critics review Jacques Levy's production of the musical *Doonesbury*. USA: New York, NY. 1983. 1799

Eight critics review Philip Rose's production of the musical *Amen Corner*. USA: New York, NY. 1983. 1800

Six critics review John Bowab's production of the musical *Mame*. USA: New York, NY. 1983. 1801

Eight critics review Ivan Reitman's production of the musical *Merlin*. USA: New York, NY. 1983. 1802

Nine critics review George Abbott's production of the musical *On Your Toes*. USA: New York, NY. 1983. 1803

Evolution of director Harold Prince's concept for the Broadway musical *Cabaret*. USA: New York, NY. 1966. 1804

Ten critics review Richard Maltby's production of *Baby*. USA: New York, NY. 1983. 1805

Ten critics review *La Cage aux Folles*. USA: New York, NY. 1983. 1806

Eight critics review Michael Kahn's production of *Show Boat*. USA: New York, NY. 1983. 1807

Ten critics review *My One and Only*, staged by Thommie Walsh and Tommy Tune. USA: New York, NY. 1983. 1808

Biography of conductor and director Herbert von Karajan. Austria. Germany. 1908-1982. 1838

Harold Prince's production of Giacomo Puccini's *Turandot* at Vienna's Staatsoper. Austria: Vienna. 1983. 1839

Interview with Steven Thomas, artistic director of Opera Hamilton. Canada: Hamilton, ON. 1983. 1844

Comprehensive illustrated production history of Wagnerian opera. Europe. USA. Canada. 1832-1983. 1851

History of opera staging and its aesthetics. Europe. 1597-1982. 1852

Bass Martti Talvela produces Finnish opera at the Opera-festival at Savonlinna Castle. Finland: Savonlinna. 1983. 1856

Correspondence between two figures of seventeenth century Parisian opera. France: Paris. 1694-1696. 1858

The Paris Opera production of Peter Brook's *La Tragédie de Carmen*. France: Paris. 1981. 1861

One hundred years of recordings and Bayreuth Festival performances of Wagner's *Parsifal*. Germany: Bayreuth. 1882-1982. 1864

History and production history of Wagnerian opera. Germany. USA. 1832-1982. 1865

Photographs and personnel of Bayreuth Festival production of *Siegfried*. Germany, West: Bayreuth. 1980. 1866

Photographs and personnel of Bayreuth Festival production of *Götterdämmerung*. Germany, West: Bayreuth. 1980. 1867

Photographs and personnel of Bayreuth Festival production of *Die Walküre*. Germany, West: Bayreuth. 1980. 1869

Peter Hall's production of Richard Wagner's *Ring* at Bayreuth Festspielhaus. Germany, West: Bayreuth. 1983. 1870

Erich Wolfgang Korngold's *Die tote Stadt* at the Deutsche Oper Berlin. Germany, West: West Berlin. 1855. 1983. 1871

Discussion of Leonard Bernstein's production of Wagner's *Tristan und Isolde*. Germany, West: Munich. 1981. 1872

1983 Bayreuth *Der Ring des Nibelungen*, directed by Peter Hall, conducted by Georg Solti. Germany, West: Bayreuth. 1983. 1873

Patrice Chéreau talks about his production of Richard Wagner's *Der Ring des Nibelungen*. Germany, West: Bayreuth. 1976. 1875

Discussion of centennial production of *Parsifal* directed by Götz Friedrich. Germany, West: Bayreuth. 1982. 1876

Opera production textbook. Italy. 1597-1699. 1881

Klaus Michael Grüber directs Richard Wagner's *Tannhäuser* at Teatro Comunale, Florence. Italy: Florence. 1983. 1882

Staging — cont'd

Collection of materials on the most famous opera singers and directors. Italy: Milan. 1958-1982.   1883

Making of the Franco Zeffirelli film of *La Traviata*. Italy: Rome. 1981-1983.   1885

Ten critics review Peter Brook's production of *La Tragédie de Carmen* at the Vivian Beaumont Theatre. USA: New York, NY. 1983.   1914

Account of *Risurrezione*, to be performed by Cincinnati Summer Opera. USA: Cincinnati, OH. 1904-1983.   1923

Konstantin Stanislavskij's training of opera singers. USSR. 1918-1935.   1929

Work of the director/choreographer N.M. Forreger in the musical theatre. USSR. 1929-1939.   1930

Current state of Bolshoi opera performance. USSR: Moscow. 1982-1983.   1931

Tent show performances in a rural Christian fundamentalist area. USA. 1912-1950.   1990

Fifteen-hour pageant by Jean-Pierre Ronfard and Théâtrale Expérimental de Montréal. Canada: Montreal, PQ. 1982.   2025

Documentation on André Heller's *Flic Flac, Theater des Feuers* and *Roncalli*. Austria. Germany, West. Portugal: Lisbon. 1975-1983.   2027

History of *tableaux vivants*, with emphasis on work of Edward Kilanyi. USA: New York, NY. 1831-1899.   2030

Study of revue songs by Irving Berlin, George Gershwin and Cole Porter in their theatrical contexts. USA: New York, NY. 1910-1937.   2032

Recent production by the Philippe Gentry puppet company. France. 1980.   2050

Use of puppets and puppetry techniques in Arena Stage production of *Candide*. USA: Washington, DC. 1983.   2061

Application of holography to the Salzburger Marionettentheater production of *Le Nozze di Figaro*. Austria: Salzburg. 1983.   2083

Inculcation of national values through civic ritual. Chile: Santiago. 1938-1980.   2101

Founder-director of New Lafayette Theatre discusses purpose and style of rituals. USA: New York, NY. 1969-1972.   2102

Plays/librettos/scripts

Adaptation of *Galileo* for Chinese stage. China, People's Republic of: Peking. 1979.   1020

Profile of bilingual playwright Antoine O'Flatharta. Eire. 1981.   1025

John Webster's visual drama. England. 1580-1634.   1068

Stage directions in Shakespeare are used to reconstruct Elizabethan staging practice. England. 1590-1612.   1073

Adaptation of Ben Jonson's *Epicoene* by Marcel Achard, directed by Charles Dullin. France: Paris. 1926.   1100

Michel Vinaver's plays and their production histories. France. 1954-1980.   1114

Biography of playwright Bertolt Brecht. Germany. 1898-1956.   1123

Brecht's directorial approach to staging Shakespeare's *Coriolanus, Macbeth* and *King Lear*. Germany. 1920-1930.   1136

Composition and thematic analysis of Goethe's *Ur-Faust*. Germany. 1775-1832.   1137

Problems in stage adaptation of Elias Canetti's *The Limited*. Germany, West: Stuttgart. 1983.   1150

General biography of Gabriele D'Annunzio. Italy. 1863-1938.   1158

Critical analysis of the most significant themes in Eduardo De Filippo's plays and phases in his acting career. Italy. 1900-1982.   1162

Biographical note, chronology and a brief analysis of Dario Fo's plays in performance. Italy. 1926-1982.   1167

Catalogue of the exhibition on the copyright debate between playwright Paolo Giacometti and actress Adelaide Ristori. Italy. 1836-1882.   1191

Theatres, actors and drama of the Renaissance in the work of modern directors. Italy. 1845-1982.   1193

Director Jacques Rosner on meeting with playwright Witold Gombrowicz. Poland. France. 1969-1982.   1218

Comparison between a painting by Diego Velázquez and a play by Calderón de la Barca. Spain. 1625-1651.   1229

Adaptation of the Angel Guimerà play *Maria Rosa*. Spain. 1894.   1230

Staging and scenic practices in the plays of Lope de Vega's forerunners and contemporaries. Spain: Valencia. 1500-1699.   1253

George Bernard Shaw as director-playwright. UK-England. 1914.   1284

Oscar Wilde's stage directions in various editions of *An Ideal Husband* and other plays. UK-England. 1880-1900.   1295

Approaches to drama for young people. UK-England. 1970-1983.   1296

Playwright David Hare's career and interests in Fringe theatre, television and film. UK-England. 1947-1983.   1304

History of American drama. USA. 1900-1982.   1378

Interview with director and cast of Yale Repertory's production of G.B. Shaw's *The Philanderer*. USA: New Haven, CT. 1982.   1389

Stage incarnations of the characters in Aleksej Nikolajevič Arbuzov's plays. USSR. 1930-1970.   1391

Realism in drama, acting, staging and design. Yugoslavia. 1920-1930.   1395

Use of body language in the theatre by Samuel Beckett, Antonin Artaud, Etienne Decroux and Jerzy Grotowski. Europe. 1930-1980.   1638

Negation of the theatre by Samuel Beckett, Antonin Artaud and Carmelo Bene. France. Italy. 1925-1960.   1643

Contradiction in personal and artistic life of Antonin Artaud. France. 1921-1948.   1645

Graphic and linguistic structure of Antonin Artaud's last writings. France. 1938-1948.   1646

Text of a speech by playwright Dario Fo. Italy. 1974.   1650

Traditional approaches to acting and staging as clarifying methods for complex Shakespeare scenes. UK-England: Stratford-upon-Avon. 1980.   1702

Examination of the preproduction script for Laurence Olivier's film *Hamlet*. UK-England. 1948.   1719

Phenomenon of Grand Opera is examined in view of its music, librettos and staging. France. 1828-1865.   1942

Robert Wilson discusses current and forthcoming projects. USA: New York, NY. 1983.   1963

Bunraku version of John Ford's *'Tis Pity She's a Whore* at University of California. USA: Los Angeles, CA. 1983.   2075

Reference materials

Bibliography of performing arts periodicals. 1982.   11

Guide to theatre organizations and professionals. Finland. 1983.   23

Cast listings and other information on 19 productions mounted at Charlottetown Festival. Canada: Charlottetown, PE. 1965-1982.   1399

Chronological listing, including personnel, of productions of John Webster's plays. England. USA. 1614-1983.   1401

Bibliography of research on Shakespearean productions in German-speaking countries. German-speaking countries. 1981-1982.   1410

Relation to other fields

Survival of theatre under martial law. Poland. 1981-1982.   67

Jacques Copeau's reading of his play *The Little Pauper* to the Cistercians during the Occupation. France: Pernand. 1940-1944.   1450

Zerka Moreno's work explains dialectics of human interaction. USA. 1917-1983.   1464

Experience of neurotic conflict in staging of psychodrama. Italy. 1980.   1659

Circus as a staging device for a political satire. USSR. Germany. Italy. 1914-1930.   1668

Research/historiography

Concise version of a theatre textbook.   79

Theory/criticism

Intermingling of Eastern and Western performance aesthetics. China. Japan. 1900-1983.   93

Reformers on their theories. Europe. 1870-1910.   98

Spectator at the center of semiological network of theoretical approaches to theatre. France. 1982.   99

Comprehensive discussion of theatre performance. Spain. 1983.   107

Articles on performance theory and practice. 1976-1983.   1477

Dramatic theories of the 20th century reflect a complex relationship between plays, designs, staging and acting. Europe. North America. 1900-1982.   1482

Staging — cont'd

Writings of Edward Gordon Craig. UK-England. 1907-1957. 1513

Semiotic comparison of dramatic theory, philosophy and performance. USA. Europe. 1850-1956. 1515

Effect of social conditions on performance styles. USA. Greece. 499 B.C.-1983 A.D. 1517

Vocal emission as a mode of theatricalization in experimental theatre. Canada. 1970-1979. 1669

Renzo Casali's theory of acting. Italy. 1983. 1671

Study of genesis, development, structural components and consequences of theatre-drama performed by the Black workers. South Africa, Republic of. 1981-1983. 1673

Training

Examination of training program at Theatre Academy of Finland. Finland: Helsinki. 1983. 495

Theory and practice of actor training by director, Michel Saint-Denis. USA. 1897-1971. 507

Stalin, Joseph

Performance/production

Political censorship and Soviet productions of *Hamlet*. USSR. 1930. 995

Stanford, C.V.

Analysis of C.V. Stanford's incidental music for *Becket*. UK-England: London. 1893. 872

Stanislavskij, Konstantin Sergeevič

Audience

Speculative argument for adopting a rationalist account for spectator knowledge, based on Konstantin Stanislavskij's treatment of the question. USA. 1982. 569

Institutions

Evolution and theories of Odin Teatret. Sweden. 1964-1979. 621

History of Masterworks Laboratory Theatre. USA. 1965-1980. 656

Performance/production

Acting of medieval plays in a simulated session using Stanislavskij's methods of acting. England. 1900-1983. 704

History of directing. Europe. 1882-1982. 708

Influence of the Russian drama and Stanislavskij's system on European and American theatre. Europe. USA. 1850-1979. 714

Interview with and influences on actor Bernhard Minetti, including production of *Faust*. Germany, East: East Berlin. 1982-1983. 751

Development of acting from declamatory style to physical expressiveness. Peru. 1950-1983. 824

Modern analyses of Konstantin Stanislavskij's acting theory. Russia. USSR. 1904-1983. 831

Stanislavskij's system in the USA and the tour by the Moscow Art Theatre. USA. USSR. 1910-1959. 923

Influence of Russian playwrights, directors and actors on American theatre. USA. Russia. 1905-1979. 976

Overview of the Konstantin Stanislavskij system. USSR. Russia. 1863-1938. 988

Political censorship and Soviet productions of *Hamlet*. USSR. 1930. 995

Reconstruction of Edward Gordon Craig's production of *Hamlet* at Moscow Art Theatre. Russia: Moscow. 1908-1912. 1682

Konstantin Stanislavskij's stage adaptation of Shakespeare's *Othello* for the Moscow Art Theatre. USSR: Moscow. 1929-1930. 1685

Konstantin Stanislavskij's training of opera singers. USSR. 1918-1935. 1929

Plays/librettos/scripts

Possible meanings of characterization in the Mystery plays. England. 1200-1550. 1057

Collected materials on Eugenio Barba and Odin Teatret. Sweden. 1964-1979. 1258

Debate on folk and literary theatre. Sweden. 1265

Theory/criticism

Renzo Casali's theory of acting. Italy. 1983. 1671

Training

Research project in theatre heresy and Stanislavskij. Italy: Pontedera. 1981-1983. 1524

Stankovski, Vojo

Performance/production

Review of international puppet theatre festival. Sweden: Uppsala. 1983. 2054

Statistics

Institutions

Annual report of the Austrian Federal Theatres. Austria: Vienna. 1982-1983. 284

Summary of study about training costume designers. USA. 1979-1983. 346

Performance/production

Statistical history of acting editions of Shakespeare. Europe. North America. 1590. 713

Stein, Gertrude

Theory/criticism

Collected theory and criticism by women in theatre on women in theatre. USA. UK. 1850-1983. 114

Stein, Joseph

Performance/production

Nine critics review Michael Cacoyannis' production of the musical *Zorba*. USA: New York, NY. 1983. 1798

Stein, Meridee

Institutions

Production of *Nightingale* by First All Children's Theatre, and Meridee Stein, the group's founder. USA: New York, NY. 1982. 650

Stein, Peter

Performance/production

Six essays on the productions and artistic views held by leading European directors. Europe. 1960-1980. 1615

Steiner, Max

Reference materials

Description of archive holdings at Brigham Young University including personal papers of Howard Hawks and Dean Jagger. USA: Provo, UT. 1900-1983. 48

Steirischer Herbst (Austria)

Institutions

Review of Austrian summer festivals. Austria. 1983. 285

Steps Must Be Gentle: A Dramatic Reading for Two Performers

Plays/librettos/scripts

Hart Crane's influence on plays by Tennessee Williams. USA. 1938-1980. 1354

Stevens, Roger

Institutions

Influential producers outline two different plans for a national theatre. USA. 1983. 339

Stewart, Thomas

Performance/production

American baritone Thomas Stewart speaks of his career and art. USA: Houston, TX. 1925-1983. 1919

Sthur, Jeray

Training

Research project in theatre heresy and Stanislavskij. Italy: Pontedera. 1981-1983. 1524

Stieler, Caspar

Plays/librettos/scripts

Political meaning of Caspar Stieler's comedies places them within the mainstream of other contemporary European plays. Germany. 1600-1699. 1580

Stock-types

Performance/production

English actors' work in Germany, with mention of stock comic characters. Germany. England: London. 1590-1620.   1525

Plays/librettos/scripts

Calderón's departure from the stock types in the character of the fool, or *gracioso*. Spain. 1626-1681.   1255

Stockfish

Performance/production

English actors' work in Germany, with mention of stock comic characters. Germany. England: London. 1590-1620.   1525

Stohr, Peter B.

Productions of August Strindberg's *Miss Julie* and *The Dance of Death*. Germany, West: Giessen, Wilhelmshaven, Memmingen. 1981-1982.   786

Stoicism

Plays/librettos/scripts

Fusion of Stoicism and Christianity in *Hamlet*. England: London. 1600-1601.   1041

Stone, Peter

Performance/production

Ten critics review *My One and Only*, staged by Thommie Walsh and Tommy Tune. USA: New York, NY. 1983.   1808

Stoppard, Tom

Peter Wood's productions of Tom Stoppard's *The Real Thing* and Harold Pinter's *Other Places*. UK-England: London. 1983.   887

Plays/librettos/scripts

Problems of play translations without caricature. Germany, West. USA. 1900-1983.   1148

Study of Tom Stoppard's plays. UK-England. 1937-1982.   1294

Influence of Shakespeare, Beckett and Wittgenstein on the plays of Tom Stoppard. UK-England. 1963-1979.   1302

Character analysis of Carr in *Travesties*, by Tom Stoppard. UK-England. 1974.   1309

Analysis of Tom Stoppard's plays. UK-England. 1967-1983.   1311

Analysis of Tom Stoppard's *The Real Thing*. UK-England. 1982.   1317

Playfulness in Tom Stoppard's plays. UK-England. 1937-1983.   1592

Comic irony and anti-heroes in Irish comedy and influence on Harold Pinter, Samuel Beckett and Tom Stoppard. UK-Ireland. Eire. 1900-1940.   1593

Reference materials

Biographical guide to British playwrights. UK. 1945-1983.   1423

Storey, David

Plays/librettos/scripts

Modern plays set in confining institutions. North America. Europe. 1900-1983.   1200

Storie di palcoscenico (Stories of the Stage)

Performance/production

Critical summary of theatrical anecdotes as they are reported in four books. Italy. 1891-1965.   803

Storm, The SEE: *Ováder*

Storytelling

Institutions

History of Karamu Children's Theatre. USA: Cleveland, OH. 1915-1975.   647

Performance/production

Rehearsal methods of director Finn Poulsen. Sweden: Göteburg, Gävleborg. 1969-1983.   839

Enactment and narration as particularly appropriate methods of dramatization. USA. 1968-1980.   906

Study of storytelling techniques. USA. 1983.   913

Plays/librettos/scripts

Effects of foreign invasion and political instability on theatre. Argentina. 1900-1983.   999

Strand Theatre (London)

Performance/production

Peter Wood's productions of Tom Stoppard's *The Real Thing* and Harold Pinter's *Other Places*. UK-England: London. 1983.   887

Strasberg, Lee

Stanislavskij's system in the USA and the tour by the Moscow Art Theatre. USA. USSR. 1910-1959.   923

Plays/librettos/scripts

Lee Strasberg on Ibsen and *Peer Gynt*. USA: New York, NY. 1906-1982.   1385

Stratas, Teresa

Performance/production

Making of the Franco Zeffirelli film of *La Traviata*. Italy: Rome. 1981-1983.   1885

Stratford Festival Company (Stratford, ON)

Two examples of staging *Macbeth* in the 1970's. USA: Stratford, CT. Canada: Stratford, ON. 1971-1973.   908

Production journal of *King Lear*. Canada: Stratford, ON. 1979.   1676

Strauss, Botho

Botho Strauss' *Kalldewey, Farce* played by the theatre group Baal at Theater Frascati. Netherlands: Amsterdam. 1983.   821

Plays/librettos/scripts

Analysis of Botho Strauss' *Kalldewey, Farce*. Europe. 1964.   1091

Strauss, Richard

Performance/production

Erich Wolfgang Korngold's *Die tote Stadt* at the Deutsche Oper Berlin. Germany, West: West Berlin. 1855. 1983.   1871

Bass Kurt Moll speaks about his career and role in *Der Rosenkavalier*. Germany, West. 1950-1983.   1874

Photographs, cast lists, synopsis and discography of Metropolitan Opera production of *Arabella*. USA: New York, NY. 1983.   1894

Photographs, cast lists, synopsis and discography of Metropolitan Opera production of *Der Rosenkavalier*. USA: New York, NY. 1983.   1906

Plays/librettos/scripts

Characterization through music in Richard Strauss' *Arabella*. Austria: Vienna. 1927-1929.   1932

Collaboration of Hugo von Hofmannsthal and Richard Strauss on *Arabella*. Austria: Vienna. 1920-1929.   1934

Strawinsky, Igor

Performance/production

Autobiographical survey by choreographer Lincoln Kirstein. USA. India: Marrakesh. Europe. 1916-1949.   514

Plays/librettos/scripts

Shift in dramatic emphasis in Igor Strawinsky's *Apollon Musagete* due to sets, costumes and choreography. USA: Washington, DC, New York, NY. 1927-1979.   522

Streamers

Modern plays set in confining institutions. North America. Europe. 1900-1983.   1200

Street theatre

Institutions

Documentation on Karlsplatz festival, part of Wiener Festwochen. Austria: Vienna. 1983.   288

Street theatre production of Århus theater akademi in collaboration with Jordcirkus and Johnny Melville. Denmark: Århus. 1982.   298

Description of street theatre performances whose purpose is social change. India: Calcutta. 1983.   316

Plays/librettos/scripts

Terukkuttu, a street theatre piece developed from traditional dance-drama. India: Tamil Nadu. 1980.   540

Street-vendor, The SEE: *Strascino, Lo*

Strehler, Giorgio

Institutions

Concepts of and preparations for Théâtre de l'Europe, managed by
Giorgio Strehler. France: Paris. 1983.   596

Performance/production

Memoirs of dramaturg Jan Kott. Poland. Austria: Vienna. 1957-1981.
                                                                          440
Tendencies of Bertolt Brecht stage interpretations. Germany, East.
USSR. Italy. 1956-1983.   747
Interview with actor-director Tamás Major on staging plays by
Bertolt Brecht. Hungary. 1962-1982.   791
Study of productions by leading Italian directors. Italy. 1945-1975.
                                                                          798
Samuel Beckett's *Happy Days* with Giulia Lazzarini at Piccolo
Teatro di Milano, directed by Giorgio Strehler. Italy: Milan. 1983.
                                                                          807

Theory/criticism

Louis Althusser's Marxist philosophy is contrasted with his review of
Carlo Bertolazzi's play staged by Giorgio Strehler. USA. France.
Italy. 1962-1985.   1674

Strindberg, August

Performance/production

Survey of director Max Reinhardt's career. Austria. 1873-1943.   677
Productions of August Strindberg's *Miss Julie* and *The Dance of
Death*. Germany, West: Giessen, Wilhelmshaven, Memmingen. 1981-
1982.   786
Documentation of Ingmar Bergman's tripartite theatre project.
Sweden. Germany, West: Munich. 1981.   844
August Strindberg productions in eleven countries. Sweden. Italy.
USA. 1982.   847
August Strindberg's advice for the actors of Intima Theatre. Sweden.
1907-1920.   848
Year's outstanding productions of plays by August Strindberg and
other playwrights. UK-England. 1982-1983.   890
Comparative study of Peter Oskarsson's production of August
Strindberg's *A Dream Play* with that of Ingmar Bergman. USA:
Seattle, WA. 1982.   907

Plays/librettos/scripts

Playwrights and dramatic forms influencing Eugene O'Neill's *The
Calms of Capricorn*. Europe. USA. 1953.   1088
Unpublished writings, biographical notes, themes and political
influence in Mario Federici's plays. Italy. 1900-1975.   1161
Conference on August Strindberg's relation to modern culture,
painting, photography and theatrical productions. Italy: Bari. 1982.
                                                                         1178
Cubism in art (space) related to cubism in drama (time). Sweden.
Norway. 1828-1912.   1259
Critical notes on Enquist's play *Theatre-Truth* about August
Strindberg. Sweden. 1974.   1260
Autobiographical aspects of August Strindberg's *To Damascus*.
Sweden. 1898.   1262
Fairy-tale elements in *Miss Julie* intensify the play's tragic impact.
Sweden. 1870-1908.   1264
Different phases of August Strindberg's ideology seen in his plays.
Sweden. 1849-1912.   1266
August Strindberg's life and plays. Sweden. 1849-1912.   1267
Analysis of August Strindberg's plays. Sweden. 1849-1912.   1268
Interpretation of August Strindberg's *The Ghost Sonata* in light of
contemporary problems. Sweden. 1907-1983.   1269
Examination of August Strindberg's attitude towards and use of
impressionism. Sweden. 1874-1884.   1270

Strong Breed, The

Wole Soyinka's plays echo themes of Aeschylus, Euripides and
Shakespeare. Nigeria. Greece: Athens. UK-England: London. 1980.
                                                                         1700

Stronger, The SEE: *Starkare, Den*

Strouse, Charles

Performance/production

Six critics review Alan Jay Lerner's production of the musical *Dance
a Little Closer*. USA: New York, NY. 1983.   1793

Stroux, Karlheinz

Karlheinz Stroux's production of *The Skin of Our Teeth* by
Thornton Wilder at Hebbeltheater. Germany, West: West Berlin,
Darmstadt. 1946.   779

Structure SEE: Dramatic structure

Studies in Honor of Everette W. Hesse

Theory/criticism

Calderón de la Barca's plays and theory of comedy advanced in
essay by Robert Ter Horst. Spain. 1600-1681.   1602

Studio and Forum of Stage Design

Design/technology

Lighting designer Marek Dobrowolski contrasts profession in Poland
and U.S.A. USA: New York, NY. Poland. 1983.   234

Studio theatre

Performance/production

Role experimental studios played in the formation of the Soviet
theatre. USSR: Moscow, Leningrad. 1920-1939.   993

Sturm und Drang

Plays/librettos/scripts

Influence of Siglo de Oro on German pre-romantic theatre.
Germany. Spain. 1765-1832.   1135
Composition and thematic analysis of Goethe's *Ur-Faust*. Germany.
1775-1832.   1137
Genesis of Goethe's *Faust* and changes introduced in the play
thereafter. Germany. 1480-1832.   1141

Sturm und Drang SEE ALSO: Geographical-Chronological Index under
Germany 1767-1787

Subject SEE: Plot/subject/theme

Subscriptions

Administration

Network of subscription among several theatres. Italy. 1981.   555

Subsidies SEE: Government funding

Suddenly Last Summer

Plays/librettos/scripts

Hart Crane's influence on plays by Tennessee Williams. USA. 1938-
1980.   1354

Suhovo-Kobilin

Performance/production

Productions of Russian classics by Bulgarian directors. Bulgaria:
Sofia. 1960-1970.   681

Sukowa, Barbara

Peter Zadek's production of *The Master Builder* at the
Residenztheater. Germany, West: Munich. 1983.   772

Sulla strada (On the Road)

Basic theatrical documents

Playtext and accompanying materials from the Magazzini Criminali
production of *On the Road*. Italy. 1982.   1605

Sullivan, Arthur

Performance/production

Assorted material on Gilbert and Sullivan operas on stage and screen. UK-England. 1867-1983. 1888

Sullivan, Dan

Conversations with theatre critics from four newspapers. USA. 1983. 468

Summer

Brief comments on and German translation of Edward Bond's *Summer*. Germany, West: Munich. 1983. 764

Plays/librettos/scripts

Evolution of Edward Bond's *Summer*. UK-England. 1980-1983. 1308

Summer Folk SEE: *Dačniki*

Summit Conference

Performance/production

Philip Prowse's production of Robert MacDonald's Nazi psychothriller *Summit Conference*. UK-England: London. 1982. 888

Suomen Kansallisooppera (Finnish National Opera)

Institutions

Administration and repertory of Finnish National Opera. Finland: Helsinki. 1983. 1828

Surrealism

Design/technology

André Kertész' photographic documentation for surrealist's fascination with marionettes. Belgium: Liège. 1925-1929. 2077

Institutions

History and analysis of Hesitate and Demonstrate, an English group that creates surrealistic performances based on juxtapostion of images. UK-England: Leeds, London. Netherlands: Rotterdam. 1972-1983. 1743

Theory/criticism

Study of realism, naturalism, symbolism, surrealism, expressionism and epic theatre. Europe. North America. 1900-1980. 1484

Susan Bloch Theatre (New York, NY)

Performance/production

Five critics review Nye Heron's production of Brian Friel's play *Winners*. USA: New York, NY. 1983. 962

Sushkevica, B.N.

Role experimental studios played in the formation of the Soviet theatre. USSR: Moscow, Leningrad. 1920-1939. 993

Sutcliffe, Alison

Eight critics review Alison Sutcliffe's production of Raymund FitzSimons' play *Edmund Kean*. USA: New York, NY. 1983. 965

Svevo, Italo

Reference materials

Chronological listing of Italo Svevo's plays. Italy. 1885-1928. 1414

Svoboda, Josef

Design/technology

Techniques for using film or still projection in live theatre performances. USA. 1983. 250

Josef Svoboda's scenography of Wagnerian opera. Switzerland. UK-England: London. Czechoslovakia: Prague. 1948-1983. 1823

Performance/production

History and production history of Wagnerian opera. Germany. USA. 1832-1982. 1865

Swados, Elizabeth

Nine critics review Jacques Levy's production of the musical *Doonesbury*. USA: New York, NY. 1983. 1799

Swan theatre (London)

Performance spaces

Interpretation of Johannes De Witt's drawing of the Swan theatre. England. 1596. 365

Swanson, Gloria

Reference materials

Acquisition of Gloria Swanson's silent film archive by University of Texas, Austin. USA: Austin, TX. 1913-1983. 1720

Swift, Jonathan

Plays/librettos/scripts

Influences of Jonathan Swift's satire in plays by W.B. Yeats and Denis Johnston. Eire. 1928-1960. 1026

Syberberg, Jürgen

Reference materials

Source materials on Richard Wagner's influence on theatre. Germany. Austria. USA. 1869-1976. 1966

Symbolism

Design/technology

Development of Wagnerian stage design and groups and movements involved in its production. Spain. 1882-1960. 1822

Performance/production

View of man and recurring Greek symbolism in Martha Graham's choreography. USA. 1947. 528

History of directing. Europe. 1882-1982. 708

Plays/librettos/scripts

Comparison of symbolist drama by Maurice Maeterlinck and opera by Claude Debussy. Belgium. 1900-1983. 1012

Playwrights and dramatic forms influencing Eugene O'Neill's *The Calms of Capricorn*. Europe. USA. 1953. 1088

Theory/criticism

Study of realism, naturalism, symbolism, surrealism, expressionism and epic theatre. Europe. North America. 1900-1980. 1484

Synge, John Millington

Plays/librettos/scripts

Comparison of experiential writing of J.M. Synge and Henry David Thoreau. UK-Ireland. USA. 1898-1907. 1320

Memoirs of journalist Stephen McKenna on John Millington Synge's apprenticeship years in Paris. UK-Ireland. France: Paris. 1895-1902. 1324

Representational and modernist comedic aspects of J.M. Synge's *The Playboy of the Western World*. UK-Ireland. 1907. 1326

Irreverent aspects of Irish comedy seen through the works of 14 playwrights. Eire. UK-Ireland. 1840-1965. 1555

Comic irony and anti-heroes in Irish comedy and influence on Harold Pinter, Samuel Beckett and Tom Stoppard. UK-Ireland. Eire. 1900-1940. 1593

Reference materials

Letters of playwright John Millington Synge. UK-Ireland. 1871-1909. 1431

Correspondence relating to administrative concerns at the Abbey Theatre between William Butler Yeats, Lady Gregory and John Millington Synge. UK-Ireland: Dublin. 1904-1909. 1432

Relation to other fields

Association between literature of J.M. Synge and pictorial art of Jack B. Yeats. UK-Ireland. 1896-1948. 1463

Szyfman, Arnold

Institutions

Career of Arnold Szyfman and establishment of the Teatr Polski. Poland: Warsaw. 1882-1967. 613

Tableaux vivants

Performance/production

Henry Carey's missing music for *tableaux vivant* in the production of *Hamlet* inspired by funeral services for the Duke of Buckingham. England: London. 1736. 698

Teatro alla Scala (Milan)

Design/technology

Costumes of Teatro alla Scala and chronology of its costumers. Italy: Milan. 1947-1982.　　　1819

Performance spaces

Giuseppe Piermarini built Teatro alla Scala in accordance with architectural theories of his time. Italy: Milan. 1776-1830.　　　1835

Performance/production

History of openings at Teatro alla Scala is conveyed through newspaper reviews. Italy: Milan. 1778-1977.　　　1884

Reference materials

Catalogue of Galliari's scene designs owned by Museo Teatrale alla Scala. Italy: Milan. 1778-1823.　　　1969

Teatro Argentina (Rome)

Performance/production

Andrzej Wajda's staging of *Hamlet* at Teatro Argentina. Italy. Poland: Rome. 1982.　　　797

Teatro Ariosto (Reggio Emilia)

Performance spaces

Construction, renovation and technical equipment of historic theatre buildings. Italy: Modena, Reggio Emilia, Parma. 1588-1985.　　　382

Teatro Campesino

Performance/production

History of Chicano theatre. USA. Mexico. 1965-1983.　　　453

Theory/criticism

History and philosophy of Chicano theatre movement. USA. 1965-1982.　　　113

Teatro Colón (Buenos Aires)

Institutions

History of Teatro Colón in essays and photographs. Argentina: Buenos Aires. 1857-1983.　　　1827

Teatro Comunale di Ferrara

Reference materials

Catalogue of photographic exhibition of the Teatro Comunale di Ferrara. Italy: Ferrara. 1982.　　　489

Teatro Comunale di Firenze

Performance/production

Klaus Michael Grüber directs Richard Wagner's *Tannhäuser* at Teatro Comunale, Florence. Italy: Florence. 1983.　　　1882

Teatro Comunale di Forlimpopoli

Performance spaces

Architecture of Municipal Theatre at Forlimpopoli. Italy: Forlimpopoli. 1600-1982.　　　380

Teatro Comunale di Modena

Construction, renovation and technical equipment of historic theatre buildings. Italy: Modena, Reggio Emilia, Parma. 1588-1985.　　　382

Teatro de la Esperanza

Theory/criticism

History and philosophy of Chicano theatre movement. USA. 1965-1982.　　　113

Teatro degli Indipendenti (Rome)

Performance/production

Biographical notes on the actress Fulvia Giuliani. Italy. 1900-1983.　　　815

Teatro dell'Arte (Rome)

Pirandello as a director and theatre theorist. Italy. 1867-1936.　　　814

Plays/librettos/scripts

Luigi Pirandello's earlier plays are considered prologues to *The Giants of the Mountain*. Italy. 1921-1937.　　　1189

Teatro di Cittadella (Reggio Emilia)

Relation to other fields

Theatre as a social mirror of the town. Italy: Reggio Emilia. 1851.　　　65

Teatro di Gianni e Cosetta Colla (Italy)

Performance/production

Autobiography of puppeteer Gianni Colla. Italy. 1946-1981.　　　2051

Teatro e la sua gente, Il (Theatre and Its People)

Critical summary of theatrical anecdotes as they are reported in four books. Italy. 1891-1965.　　　803

Teatro Eliseo (Rome)

Collection of writings by actor Romolo Valli, founder/director of Compagnia dei Giovani del Teatro Eliseo. Italy. 1942-1980.　　　817

Teatro Escambray (Managua)

Institutions

Teatro Escambray reflects developments in Cuban society. Cuba. Nicaragua: Managua. 1961-1983.　　　588

Teatro Español (Madrid)

Performance/production

Review of the production of *Life Is a Dream* at Teatro Español. Spain: Madrid. 1636. 1981.　　　836

Teatro Farnese (Parma)

Performance spaces

Construction, renovation and technical equipment of historic theatre buildings. Italy: Modena, Reggio Emilia, Parma. 1588-1985.　　　382

Teatro Filarmonico (Verona)

History of Teatro Filarmonico in Verona and productions mounted there. Italy: Verona. 1732-1978.　　　378

Teatro Flaiano (Rome)

Relation to other fields

Zerka Moreno's psychodrama in Italy. USA: New York, NY. Italy: Rome. 1960-1983.　　　1666

Teatro La Fenice (Venice)

Reference materials

Letters and documents placed in archives concerning Verdi's operas at Teatro La Fenice. Italy: Venice. 1844-1852.　　　1970

Teatro Metastasio (Prato)

Plays/librettos/scripts

Theatres, actors and drama of the Renaissance in the work of modern directors. Italy. 1845-1982.　　　1193

Teatro Municipale (Reggio Emilia)

Performance spaces

Construction, renovation and technical equipment of historic theatre buildings. Italy: Modena, Reggio Emilia, Parma. 1588-1985.　　　382

Teatro Nacional de Aztlán

Institutions

Activism, internationalism and preservation in minority theatre groups. USA. 1981-1983.　　　646

Performance/production

History of Chicano theatre. USA. Mexico. 1965-1983.　　　453

Teatro Olimpico (Sabionetta)

Performance spaces

Construction, renovation and technical equipment of historic theatre buildings. Italy: Modena, Reggio Emilia, Parma. 1588-1985.　　　382

Teatro Quirino (Rome)

Architecture and restorations of Teatro Quirino in Rome. Italy: Rome. 1870-1954.　　　385

Teatro Regio (Parma)

Construction, renovation and technical equipment of historic theatre buildings. Italy: Modena, Reggio Emilia, Parma. 1588-1985.　　　382

Teatro Rodante

Institutions

Activism, internationalism and preservation in minority theatre groups. USA. 1981-1983.   646

Teatro Sancarlucccio (Naples)

Performance/production

Reviews of performances at Teatro Sancarluccio. Italy: Naples. 1972-1982.   2003

Teatro Scientifico (Mantua)

Performance spaces

History and architecture of Teatro Scientifico and Palazzo Accademico. Italy: Mantua. 1767-1982.   379

Teatro Stabile di Catania

Plays/librettos/scripts

Essays on Vitaliano Brancati's plays and motion picture scripts. Italy: Catania. 1924-1954.   1160

Teatro Stabile di Genova

Dramatization of Remigio Zena's novel *The Wolf's Mouth* by Teatro Stabile di Genova. Italy: Genoa. 1980.   1186

Teatro Stabile di Torino

Discussion of Molière's *The Tricks of Scapin* addressed to teachers and children of primary schools. France. Italy: Turin. 1671-1983.
1562

Teatro Storchi (Emilia Romagna)

Performance spaces

Construction, renovation and technical equipment of historic theatre buildings. Italy: Modena, Reggio Emilia, Parma. 1588-1985.   382

Teatro Visionico (Italy)

Basic theatrical documents

Playtext and manifesto of the Teatro Visionico and their production of Pino Masnata's *Tocca a me*. Italy. 1920.   572

Teatru Miejskiego (Cracow)

Institutions

Reading-room of the Municipal theatre of Cracow, where the professional and educational association of Polish actors was founded. Poland: Kraków. Austro-Hungarian Empire. 1902-1912. 615

Plays/librettos/scripts

Censorship involving Jerzy Hulewicz' play *Aruna*, produced at Municipal Theatre of Cracow. Poland: Kraków. 1925.   1217

Teatru Miejskiego (Lwów)

Performance/production

25 interviews with Wilam Horzyca as manager of Municipal Theatre in Lwów, published in various periodicals. Poland: Lvov. 1931-1936.
826

Teatru Reduta (Warsaw)

Leon Schiller's directing career at the Reduta Theatre. Poland: Warsaw. 1922-1923.   828

Technicians/crews

Design/technology

Training of the non-artistic technical staff. Germany, West. 1983.
202

Projects and materials for the education of theatre technicians. USA. 1900-1983.   272

Technology SEE: Design/technology

Teendreams

Plays/librettos/scripts

Epic structure in contemporary drama. UK. 1968-1981.   1275

Tejedora de sueños, La (Knitter of Dreams, The)

Role constraints versus self identity in plays by Antonio Gala and Antonio Buero Vallejo. Spain. 1949.   1249

Television SEE: Video forms

Tempest, The

Performance/production

List and short reviews of Shakespearean productions. Germany, East. 1981.   749

Summer productions of Shakespeare and Molière involving professional and amateur actors. Sweden: Södertälje. 1981-1983. 841

Plays/librettos/scripts

Ironic parallels between *The Tempest* and the political activities of the time. England. North America. South America. 1611-1612. 1072

Shakespearean and Platonic conceptions of wisdom. Greece. England. 400 B.C.-1613 A.D.   1156

Theory/criticism

Wystan Hugh Auden's poetic meditation on art as related to Shakespeare's *The Tempest* and Kierkegaardian thought. UK-England. 1939-1962.   1511

Ten Commandments, The

Reference materials

Description of archive holdings at Brigham Young University including personal papers of Howard Hawks and Dean Jagger. USA: Provo, UT. 1900-1983.   48

Tennyson, Alfred, Lord

Performance/production

Analysis of C.V. Stanford's incidental music for *Becket*. UK-England: London. 1893.   872

Tent shows

Tent show performances in a rural Christian fundamentalist area. USA. 1912-1950.   1990

Reference materials

Reference guide to popular entertainments. USA. 1840.   1998

Terentius Afer, Publius

Plays/librettos/scripts

Comparison of Greek and Roman comedy as reflected in works of Menander and Terence and in revivals by Italian humanists. Greece. Roman Empire. 343 B.C.-1400 A.D.   1582

Plays of Plautus and Terence related to Roman society. Roman Republic. 254-159 B.C.   1587

Teresa Carreño Arts Center (Caracas)

Performance spaces

Opening of the Teresa Carreño Arts Center in Caracas. Venezuela: Caracas. 1983.   410

Terminology

Design/technology

Observations concerning the French-English translation of scenographic terms. Discussed at SIBMAS. USA. France. 1982.   257

Performance/production

Linguistic study of the letters written by the actor-manager Gustavo Modena. Italy. 1829-1861.   811

Reference materials

Dictionary of international theatre terms in nine languages. North America. Europe. 1983.   31

Terry, Ellen

Performance/production

Charles Kean's staging methods and the influences on them. UK-England: London. 1850-1859.   898

Theory/criticism

Collected theory and criticism by women in theatre on women in theatre. USA. UK. 1850-1983.   114

Terson, Peter

Plays/librettos/scripts

Peter Terson's work, especially his association with National Youth Theatre. UK-England. 1960-1983.   1299

Theatres — cont'd

Construction, renovation and technical equipment of historic theatre buildings. Italy: Modena, Reggio Emilia, Parma. 1588-1985. 382

Security measures and regulations in Italian theatres. Italy. 1983. 383

Architecture and restorations of Teatro Quirino in Rome. Italy: Rome. 1870-1954. 385

History and design of Teatr Wielki. Poland: Warsaw. 1779-1983. 386

Reconstruction of a typical theatre of the Siglo de Oro period, with comparison to English playhouses. Spain: Madrid. 1583-1744. 388

Engravings of the Municipal Theatre of Girona. Spain: Girona. 1769-1860. 390

One hundred fifty years of Principal de València Theatre. Spain: Valencia. 1823-1979. 391

Placement of the prompter's and royal boxes at Drury Lane by David Garrick. UK-England: London. 1747-1776. 392

Examples of theatre architecture as displayed at USITT conference. USA. Canada. 1972-1980. 393

History and reconstruction of Paper Mill Playhouse. USA: Millburn, NJ. 1980-1982. 394

History of the Columbia Theatre. USA: Boston, MA. 1881-1957. 395

Steps involved in restoring historic theatres. USA. 1983. 396

Process of theatre restoration by Conrad Schmitt Studios. USA. 1983. 397

Socio-semiotic analysis of performance spaces. USA: New York, NY. France: Paris. 1967. 398

History of the Hult Center for the Performing Arts. USA: Eugene, OR. 1982. 399

History of West 42nd Street theatres. USA: New York, NY. 1893-1944. 400

Renovation of theatre now used for community theatre and film. USA: Chambersburg, PA. 1926-1983. 401

Design for the Wortham Theatre Center. USA: Houston, TX. 1983. 402

History and restoration of Rialto Square Theatre. USA: Joliet, IL. 1926-1983. 403

Successful example of how to save historic theatres. USA: Washington, DC. 1980-1983. 404

Technical aspects of modifying and restoring historic theatres. USA. 1983. 405

Conversion of Crouse-Hinds Concert Theatre for use as convention hall. USA: Syracuse, NY. 1982-1983. 406

Philip Johnson's design for Cleveland Playhouse. USA: Cleveland, OH. 1915-1983. 407

Acoustical problems encountered in theatre renovation. USA. 1983. 408

Opening of the Teresa Carreño Arts Center in Caracas. Venezuela: Caracas. 1983. 410

Cultural history and architectural design of Europe's oldest municipal theatre. Yugoslavia: Hvar. 1612-1983. 411

Career of Oscar Hammerstein I and the theatres he built. USA: New York, NY. 1889-1904. 1760

Construction and history of Edward Harrigan's Theatre, later renamed the Garrick. USA: New York, NY. 1890-1932. 1773

Acoustical modifications at the Orpheum Theatre made to accommodate Broadway musicals. USA: San Francisco, CA. 1981-1983. 1774

Influence of Bayreuth Festival on architecture of Kitchener-Waterloo Symphony Hall. Canada: Kitchener, ON. 1983. 1833

Project for a new studio to optimize the audience/performer relationship. Germany, West: West Berlin. 1983. 1834

Giuseppe Piermarini built Teatro alla Scala in accordance with architectural theories of his time. Italy: Milan. 1776-1830. 1835

History of the Royal Opera House, Covent Garden. UK-England: London. 1732-1983. 1836

Case-study of renovation of small-town opera house. USA: Hayesville, OH. 1886-1983. 1837

Performance/production

Present situation of theater in Ghana, including plays, performers, promoters and spaces. Ghana. 1983. 429

Marxist theory applied in comparison of public theatres in England and Spain. England. Spain. 1576-1635. 696

Charles Kean's staging methods and the influences on them. UK-England: London. 1850-1859. 898

Reviews of performances at Teatro Sancarluccio. Italy: Naples. 1972-1982. 2003

Reference materials

List of books related to the restoration of historic theatres. USA. 1935-1983. 44

Catalogue of photographic exhibition of the Teatro Comunale di Ferrara. Italy: Ferrara. 1982. 489

Relation to other fields

Theatre as a social mirror of the town. Italy: Reggio Emilia. 1851. 65

Theatres, historic

Administration

Purdue University study on modern uses of historic theatres and guidelines for management. USA. 1981-1983. 154

Performance spaces

Successful example of how to save historic theatres. USA: Washington, DC. 1980-1983. 404

Theatricalism

Theory/criticism

Nature and history of farce in theatre, film and media. Europe. USA. 425 B.C.-1982 A.D. 1600

Thebom, Blanche

Performance/production

American mezzo-soprano Blanche Thebom reminisces about her career and art. USA: New York, NY. 1944-1983. 1921

Theme SEE: Plot/subject/theme

Théodore

Plays/librettos/scripts

Essays on and a bibliographical guide to Pierre Corneille's comedies. France. 1606-1684. 1572

Aesthetic imbalance resulting from Pierre Corneille's concern for propriety in *Théodore*. France. 1606-1684. 1578

Theory/criticism

History of European theatre, drama and criticism. Europe. 2

Audience

Process by which audience assigns meaning to a performance. Italy. 1983. 168

Design/technology

Performance spaces and effect of scenery on the audience. Europe. 1970-1983. 184

Theatre critics and their problems in discussing design. Germany, West. 1980-1982. 207

Work of costume designer Tanya Moiseiwitsch. USA. UK. 1914-1982. 243

Institutions

Theoretical and theatrical foundations of the Squat Theatre. USA: New York, NY. Hungary: Budapest. 1975-1977. 342

Evolution and theories of Odin Teatret. Sweden. 1964-1979. 621

Performance/production

Comprehensive theatre history presented within a cultural context. 499 B.C.-1983 A.D. 412

Examination of John Philip Kemble's vocal technique. England. 1780-1817. 415

Attitudes toward psychological involvement and emotionalism in acting. Germany. 1700-1800. 425

Aspects of the development of European and American theatre: critical thought, staging, acting and design. USA. Europe. 1800-1970. 454

Mordecai Gorelik discusses stage fright and compares acting styles. USA. 1983. 461

Conversations with theatre critics from four newspapers. USA. 1983. 468

Theory/criticism — cont'd

Study of genesis, development, structural components and consequences of theatre-drama performed by the Black workers. South Africa, Republic of. 1981-1983.   1673

Training

Theory and practice of actor training by director, Michel Saint-Denis. USA. 1897-1971.   507

Theory/criticism SEE ALSO: Classed Entries 92-115, 548-551, 1477-1521, 1599-1602, 1669-1674, 1703, 1707, 2072, 2087, 2110.

Thespis

Plays/librettos/scripts

English translation of Albin Lesky's standard work on Greek tragedy. Greece. 499-400 B.C.   1696

Third Theatre

Institutions

Evolution and theories of Odin Teatret. Sweden. 1964-1979.   621

Plays/librettos/scripts

Collected materials on Eugenio Barba and Odin Teatret. Sweden. 1964-1979.   1258

Thomas, Steven

Performance/production

Interview with Steven Thomas, artistic director of Opera Hamilton. Canada: Hamilton, ON. 1983.   1844

Thoreau, Henry David

Plays/librettos/scripts

Comparison of experiential writing of J.M. Synge and Henry David Thoreau. UK-Ireland. USA. 1898-1907.   1320

Thou Shalt Not Lie SEE: *Weh' dem, der lügt*

Thourneur, Cyril

Performance/production

List of productions of plays from English Renaissance drama with brief reviews. North America. Europe. 1982-1983.   822

Three Acts of Recognition

Plays/librettos/scripts

Problems of play translations without caricature. Germany, West. USA. 1900-1983.   1148

Three Muskateers, The

Reference materials

Description of archive holdings at Brigham Young University including personal papers of Howard Hawks and Dean Jagger. USA: Provo, UT. 1900-1983.   48

Three Sisters SEE: *Tri Sestry*

Thullal

Plays/librettos/scripts

Description of *thullal*, a form of comedy, created by Kunchan Nambiar, and performed by a single actor. India: Kerala. 1700-1799.   1583

Till Damaskus (To Damascus)

Autobiographical aspects of August Strindberg's *To Damascus*. Sweden. 1898.   1262

Tillstrom, Burr

Performance/production

Artistry of Burr Tillstrom and his Kuklapolitan Players. USA. 1983.   2065

Tillyard, E.M.W.

Role of Richmond in Shakespeare's *Richard III* on West German stage. Germany, West. UK-England. 1945.   788

Timon of Athens

Plays/librettos/scripts

Comparison of the misanthrope in *Dýskolos*, *Timon of Athens* and *Le Misanthrope*. Greece. England. France. 317 B.C.-1666 A.D.   1155

Tis Pity She's a Whore

Bunraku version of John Ford's *'Tis Pity She's a Whore* at University of California. USA: Los Angeles, CA. 1983.   2075

Tivoli Theatre (Washington, DC)

Performance spaces

Successful example of how to save historic theatres. USA: Washington, DC. 1980-1983.   404

To Damascus SEE: *Till Damaskus*

To Give It All and Nothing SEE: *Darlo toda y no dar nada*

Tocca a me (It's My Turn)

Basic theatrical documents

Playtext and manifesto of the Teatro Visionico and their production of Pino Masnata's *Tocca a me*. Italy. 1920.   572

Tocqueville, Alexis de

Audience

Sociological studies suggest that democratization of the arts has not taken place. USA. 1830-1982.   173

Todd, Edgar

Plays/librettos/scripts

Epic structure in contemporary drama. UK. 1968-1981.   1275

Todd, Susan

Epic structure in contemporary drama. UK. 1968-1981.   1275

Tofano, Sergio

Performance/production

Critical summary of theatrical anecdotes as they are reported in four books. Italy. 1891-1965.   803

Tolan, Kathleen

Five critics review Emily Mann's production of Kathleen Tolan's play *A Weekend Near Madison*. USA: New York, NY. 1983.   977

Toller, Ernst

Plays/librettos/scripts

Attitude towards war in Ernst Toller's plays. Germany. 1918-1927.   1118

Theory/criticism

Influence of Richard Wagner's *Gesamtkunstwerk* on modern theatre. Germany. 1849-1977.   1495

Tolubjev, U.V.

Performance/production

Articles discussing the work of individual actors at the Academic Drama Theatre of A.S. Puškin. USSR: Leningrad. 1910-1970.   987

Tonight We Improvise SEE: *Questa sera si recita a soggetto*

Tony Awards SEE: Awards, Tony

Tootsie

Theory/criticism

Significance of gender in feminist criticism with reference to historical materialism, deconstruction and phenomenon of cross-dressing in theatre. USA. France. UK-England. 1983.   1520

Top Girls

Performance/production

Eight critics review Max Stafford-Clark's production of Caryl Churchill's play *Top Girls*. USA: New York, NY. 1983.   958

Triunfos de amor y fortuna (Triumph of Love and Fortune)

Notes and bibliographic descriptions of the Vatican copy of Antonio de Solís y Rivadeneyra's *Triumph of Love and Fortune*. Spain. Vatican. 1658. 1242

Troilus and Cressida

Institutions

Edward Bond's *Saved* and Shakespeare's *Troilus and Cressida* at the Jugendclub Kritisches Theater. Germany, West: Stuttgart. 1981-1983. 608

Plays/librettos/scripts

Metadramatic elements in Shakespeare's *Troilus and Cressida*. England. 1601-1602. 1074

Trojan Women, The

Dramatic and military conflict in Greek tragedy. Greece. 484-415 B.C. 1697

Trommeln in der Nacht (Drums in the Night)

Performance/production

Directors on Bertolt Brecht's dramas. Germany, East: Schwerin, Erfurt, East Berlin. 1983. 754

Trottier, Pierre

Design/technology

Methods and materials of lighting design, and interviews with designers. France. 1978. 194

Trovatore, Il

Performance/production

Photographs, cast lists, synopsis and discography of Metropolitan Opera production of *Il Trovatore*. USA: New York, NY. 1983. 1895

Trudeau, Garry

Nine critics review Jacques Levy's production of the musical *Doonesbury*. USA: New York, NY. 1983. 1799

True West

Plays/librettos/scripts

Themes of and influences on Sam Shepard's plays. USA. 1943-1983. 1343

Tsariov, Mikhail SEE: Carëv, Michail Ivanovič

Tschauner-Theatre (Vienna)

Institutions

Tschauner-Theatre: Vienna's only surviving improvisation company. Austria: Vienna. 1938-1983. 1978

Tscholakowa, Ginka

Performance/production

Dispute about Heiner Müller's production of *Macbeth*. Germany, East: East Berlin. 1971-1982. 1678

Tumanišvili, M.

Autobiography of Georgian director M. Tumanišvili. USSR. 1905-1983. 996

Tumor Brainiowicz

Comprehensive study of productions by Tadeusz Kantor's experimental theatre group Cricot 2 and Kantor's philosophy. Poland. 1975-1980. 1626

Tune, Tommy

Administration

Difficulties of getting some plays on Broadway. USA: New York, NY. 1982-1983. 565

Performance/production

Production, casts and review of musical *My One and Only*. USA: New York, NY. 1971-1983. 1791

Ten critics review *My One and Only*, staged by Thommie Walsh and Tommy Tune. USA: New York, NY. 1983. 1808

Tuomarila, Ilpo

Plays/librettos/scripts

Critical examination of playwright Ilpo Tuomarila. Finland. 1972-1983. 1096

Turandot

Performance/production

Harold Prince's production of Giacomo Puccini's *Turandot* at Vienna's Staatsoper. Austria: Vienna. 1983. 1839

Turgenjev, Ivan Sergejevič

Production of Russian classical plays at Eastern European theatres. Bulgaria. Yugoslavia. Czechoslovakia. 1850-1914. 682

Plays/librettos/scripts

Literary influences on Henrik Ibsen's *Vildanden (The Wild Duck)*. Norway. 1884. 1205

Turia, Ricardo de

Staging and scenic practices in the plays of Lope de Vega's forerunners and contemporaries. Spain: Valencia. 1500-1699. 1253

Turkka, Jouko

Performance/production

Interview with director and head of Theatre Academy of Finland Jouko Turkka on his views of art and society. Finland. 1983. 723

Training

Physical training as part of the curriculum at Theatre Academy of Finland. Finland: Helsinki. 1982-1983. 496

Teaching methods and acting theory of Jouko Turkka of Theatre Academy of Finland. Finland: Helsinki. 1983. 497

Turku Municipal Theatre (Turku)

Institutions

Current manager Taisto-Bertil Orsmaa, and history of Turku Municipal Theatre. Finland: Turku. 1946-1983. 303

Turmbau von Babel, Der (Tower of Babel, The)

Performance/production

Documentation on Ruben Fraga's production of *The Tower of Babel* by the Dramatic Center Vienna. Austria: Vienna. 1980-1983. 670

Turrets

Performance spaces

Location of the turret in Greenwich Park. England: London. 1500. 361

Twelfth Hour, The SEE: *Dvenacatyj čas*

Twelfth Night

Plays/librettos/scripts

Comparison of two French translations of *Twelfth Night*, by Jacques Copeau/Théodore Lascarais and Suzanne Bing. France: Paris. 1914. 1567

Twenty-fourth of February, The SEE: *Vierundzwanzigste Februar, Der*

Twiggy

Performance/production

Production, casts and review of musical *My One and Only*. USA: New York, NY. 1971-1983. 1791

Two Angry Women of Abingdon, The

Plays/librettos/scripts

Folly in Renaissance comedy. England. 1530-1555. 1560

Two Executioners, The SEE: *Deux Bourreaux, Les*

Tzariov, Mikhail SEE: Carëv, Michail Ivanovič

Vaudeville

Performance spaces

History of the Columbia Theatre. USA: Boston, MA. 1881-1957. 395

History of West 42nd Street theatres. USA: New York, NY. 1893-1944. 400

Career of Oscar Hammerstein I and the theatres he built. USA: New York, NY. 1889-1904. 1760

Recollections of the Hippodrome, formerly the Adolphus Theatre. USA: Los Angeles, CA. 1911-1940. 1981

History of the Keith Memorial Theatre. USA: Boston, MA. 1925-1980. 1982

Survey of vaudeville houses in the Fourteenth Street area. USA: New York, NY. 1881-1940. 1983

Performance/production

History and problems of monodrama. USA. 1982. 950

Authentic expression in Black theatre and film is contrasted with stereotypical Black portrayals by white authors and performers. USA: New York, NY. 1890-1930. 983

Staging of Eugène Labiche's plays in Catalonia. Spain. France. 1967-1982. 1532

Career of dancer Margot Webb. USA. 1933-1947. 1991

Brief biography and interview with Cab Calloway. USA: White Plains, NY, Hollywood, CA. 1930-1983. 1993

Chronology of Black entertainers associated with 'Louisiana troupes'. Europe. 1901-1916. 2028

New vaudevillians use established music hall forms for expression. USA: New York, NY. 1980. 2033

Plays/librettos/scripts

Conventions of vaudeville in Anton Čechov's one-act plays. Russia. 1884-1892. 1221

Collection of articles, interviews and scripts on Mexican American theatre. USA. Mexico. 1983. 1362

Reference materials

Reference guide to popular entertainments. USA. 1840. 1998

Vaudeville SEE ALSO: Classed Entries: POPULAR ENTERTAINMENT – Variety acts

Veblen, Thorstein

Audience

Sociological studies suggest that democratization of the arts has not taken place. USA. 1830-1982. 173

Vedantam Satyam

Performance/production

Origins and evolution of the *Kuchipudi* dance drama. India. 200 B.C.-1983 A.D. 532

Vega Carpio, Lope Félix de

Performance spaces

Reconstruction of a typical theatre of the Siglo de Oro period, with comparison to English playhouses. Spain: Madrid. 1583-1744. 388

Performance/production

Marxist theory applied in comparison of public theatres in England and Spain. England. Spain. 1576-1635. 696

Plays/librettos/scripts

Influence of Siglo de Oro on German pre-romantic theatre. Germany. Spain. 1765-1832. 1135

Dating and authorship of *Los hechos de Garcilaso*. Spain. 1573. 1231

Metacritical analysis of Calderón's plays applying criteria devised for Lope de Vega. Spain. 1608-1681. 1238

Concern for the Christian minority in Lope de Vega's plays. Spain. 1600. 1239

Dating of Lope de Vega's *The Fable of Perseus*. Spain. 1604-1635. 1244

Comparative analysis of miscellaneous adaptations of Lope de Vega's *Peribáñez*. Spain. 1607. 1250

Staging and scenic practices in the plays of Lope de Vega's forerunners and contemporaries. Spain: Valencia. 1500-1699. 1253

Lope de Vega's forty extant texts are examined to determine authorship of *The False Lackey*. Spain. 1609-1635. 1254

Sociological approach to Lope de Vega's drama. Spain. 1573-1635. 1256

Vega, Lope de SEE: Vega Carpio, Lope Félix de

Velázquez, Diego

Plays/librettos/scripts

Comparison between a painting by Diego Velázquez and a play by Calderón de la Barca. Spain. 1625-1651. 1229

Vent de soir

Role of censorship in Johann Nestroy's *Häuptling Abendwind* as an adaptation of Jacques Offenbach's *Vent de soir*. Austria. 1833. 1549

Verdi, Giuseppe

Performance/production

Bass Walter Berry's debut in *Falstaff* at the Vienna Staatsoper. Austria: Vienna. 1983. 1841

Making of the Franco Zeffirelli film of *La Traviata*. Italy: Rome. 1981-1983. 1885

First performance of Richard Wagner's *Lohengrin* and the debate generated with followers of Giuseppe Verdi. Spain. 1862-1901. 1886

Photographs, cast lists, synopsis and discography of Metropolitan Opera production of *Il Trovatore*. USA: New York, NY. 1983. 1895

Photographs, cast lists, synopsis and discography of Metropolitan Opera production of *Un Ballo in Maschera*. USA: New York, NY. 1983. 1899

Photographs, cast lists, synopsis and discography of the Metropolitan Opera production of *Don Carlo*. USA: New York, NY. 1983. 1904

Photographs, cast lists, synopsis and discography of Metropolitan Opera production of *Ernani*. USA: New York, NY. 1983. 1908

Career of soprano Leona Mitchell at the Metropolitan Opera. USA. 1983. 1912

Plays/librettos/scripts

Victor Hugo and the original plot for the opera *Ernani* by Giuseppe Verdi. France. 1830. 1940

Italian tenor Luciano Pavarotti discusses the title role of *Ernani* by Giuseppe Verdi. Italy. 1983. 1958

Creation of the title role in *Ernani* for tenor Nicolai Ivanoff. Italy. Russia. 1844. 1959

Reference materials

Letters and documents placed in archives concerning Verdi's operas at Teatro La Fenice. Italy: Venice. 1844-1852. 1970

Verfremdungseffekt (Alienation Effect)

Performance/production

Relationship between Bertolt Brecht and Asian theatre. Asia. Germany. 1925-1981. 665

Plays/librettos/scripts

Bertolt Brecht's theory of alienation applied to characters and situations in Tennessee Williams' *Camino Real*. USA. Germany, East. 1941-1953. 1352

Verga, Giovanni

Basic theatrical documents

Annotated texts of Giovanni Verga's plays. Italy. 1865-1908. 573

Plays/librettos/scripts

Analysis of Giovanni Verga's life, plays and views on art and other matters. Italy. 1840-1922. 1165

Verhängnisvolle Faschingsnacht, Die (Fateful Carnival Night, The)

Genre analysis and comparison of Johann Nestroy's play *Die verhängnisvolle Faschingsnacht* with Karl von Holtei's *Ein Trauerspiel in Berlin*. Austria. 1839. 1548

Verisimilitude

Performance/production

Edward Bulwer-Lytton's theory of the need for unified approach to productions, in response to John Calcraft's staging of *Richelieu*. UK-Ireland: Dublin. 1839. 900

Verismo

Plays/librettos/scripts

Naturalism in the works of Pietro Mascagni and Giacomo Puccini. Italy. 1879-1926. 1955

Verkommenes Ufer Medeamaterial Landschaft Mit Argonauter (Wrecked Shore Medeamaterial Landscape with Argonauts)

Performance/production

Opening night review and playtext of Heiner Müller's *Wrecked Shore Medeamaterial Landscape with Argonauts*. Germany, West: Bochum. 1983. 767

Vermeinte Printz, Der (Imaginary Prince, The)

Plays/librettos/scripts

Political meaning of Caspar Stieler's comedies places them within the mainstream of other contemporary European plays. Germany. 1600-1699. 1580

Verting, William

Performance/production

Shakespearean productions and festivals in the American South. USA. 1751-1980. 938

Veuve, La (Widow, The)

Plays/librettos/scripts

Unhappy rival in Pierre Corneille's early comedies. France. 1606-1684. 1568

Pierre Corneille's early comedies as variations in comic form. France. 1606-1684. 1570

Viagem, A (Journey, The)

Analysis of Helda Costa's plays about Portuguese Renaissance navigators. Portugal. 1981-1982. 1219

Vichy-Fictions Kafka-Theatre Complet

Institutions

Productions of the Théâtre National of Strasbourg. France: Strasbourg. 1975-1980. 595

Victor/Victoria

Theory/criticism

Significance of gender in feminist criticism with reference to historical materialism, deconstruction and phenomenon of cross-dressing in theatre. USA. France. UK-England. 1983. 1520

Victor, Winni

Performance/production

Productions of August Strindberg's *Miss Julie* and *The Dance of Death*. Germany, West: Giessen, Wilhelmshaven, Memmingen. 1981-1982. 786

Victorian theatre

Review article of *Theatre Production Series*, seeking to define theatre's strengths. England. Germany. 1500-1939. 706

Plays/librettos/scripts

Examination of Samuel Johnson as a character in plays by William Brough and W.S. Gilbert. UK-England: London. 1862-1893. 1313

Reference materials

Biography of Richard Nelson Lee and list of 132 works. UK-England: London. 1830-1872. 1734

Victorian theatre SEE ALSO: Geographical-Chronological Index under England 1837-1901

Victory over the Sun SEE: Pobeda nad solncem

Vida es sueño, La (Life Is a Dream)

Performance/production

Innovative production of Calderón de la Barca's *Life is a Dream*. France. 1922. 731

Review of the production of *Life Is a Dream* at Teatro Español. Spain: Madrid. 1636. 1981. 836

Vidal, Albert

Original vision of man in Albert Vidal's mime *El hombre urbano*. Spain: Sitges. 1983. 1727

Interview with the mime Albert Vidal. Spain: Catalonia. 1983. 1728

Video forms

Design/technology

Practical and theoretical hand-book for aspiring make-up artists. Italy. 1982. 215

Performance/production

Biography of actor and television personality Dick Cavett. USA. 1936-1983. 916

Work of video performance artist Nan Hoover. UK-England. 1900-1983. 1746

Interaction of technology and popular entertainment. USA. 1900-1982. 1995

Plays/librettos/scripts

Playwright David Hare's career and interests in Fringe theatre, television and film. UK-England. 1947-1983. 1304

Reference materials

Yearbook of theatre, television and cinema, with brief critical notations. Italy. 1983. 29

Theory/criticism

Semiotic study of the specific nature of theatre in relation to other arts and audience interaction with it. Spain. 1983. 108

Video forms SEE ALSO: Classed Entries: MEDIA — Video forms

Vie et mort du Roi Boiteux (Life and Death of King Boiteux)

Performance/production

Fifteen-hour pageant by Jean-Pierre Ronfard and Théâtrale Expérimental de Montréal. Canada: Montreal, PQ. 1982. 2025

Vienna's English Theatre

Vienna's English Theatre's 20th anniversary production of G.B. Shaw's *Candida*. Austria: Vienna. 1963. 668

Viertel, Jack

Conversations with theatre critics from four newspapers. USA. 1983. 468

Vierundzwanzigste Februar, Der (Twenty-fourth of February, The)

Plays/librettos/scripts

Catholic interpretation of *Der 24 Februar* by Zacharias Werner. Germany. 1809-1814. 1134

Vieux Carré Music Center (Fort Polk, LA)

Institutions

Organization, people and theatres involved in the Army Theatre Arts Association. USA: Fort Polk, LA. 1960-1983. 336

Vieux Colombier SEE: Théâtre du Vieux Colombier

View from the Bridge, A

Performance/production

Nine critics review Arvin Brown's production of Arthur Miller's play *A View from the Bridge*. USA: New York, NY. 1983. 969

Vigarani, Carlo

History of opera performances at French court, including work of scene designer Carlo Vigarani. France: Versailles. 1671-1704. 1860

Vildanden (Wild Duck, The)

Plays/librettos/scripts

Literary influences on Henrik Ibsen's *Vildanden (The Wild Duck)*. Norway. 1884. 1205

Villette

Relation to other fields

Theatrical vision and the portrait of the great French actress Rachel in Charlotte Brontë's *Villette*. UK-England. France. 1853. 70

Vinaver, Michel

Performance/production

Opening nights of productions directed by Arie Zinger and Gerd Heinz. Germany, West: Munich. Switzerland: Zürich. 1983. 771

Plays/librettos/scripts

Michel Vinaver's plays and their production histories. France. 1954-1980. 1114

Vincent, George

Performance/production

English actors' work in Germany, with mention of stock comic characters. Germany. England: London. 1590-1620. 1525

Vincent, Jean-Pierre

Institutions

Productions of the Théâtre National of Strasbourg. France: Strasbourg. 1975-1980. 595

Virginia

Performance/production

Interview with English actress Sandra Duncan. South Africa, Republic of: Johannesburg. 1983. 832

Virués, Cristóbal

Plays/librettos/scripts

Staging and scenic practices in the plays of Lope de Vega's forerunners and contemporaries. Spain: Valencia. 1500-1699. 1253

Visconti, Luchino

Performance/production

Study of productions by leading Italian directors. Italy. 1945-1975. 798

Višněvy Sad (Cherry Orchard, The)

Descriptive account of Theodore Komisarjevsky's productions of Anton Čechov's plays. UK-England: London. 1926-1936. 875

Visual arts

Administration

Critique of recommendations made by Canadian Federal Cultural Policy Review Committee. Canada. 1976-1983. 118

Vitrac, Roger

Plays/librettos/scripts

Variations on the bedroom farce form in the works of Eugène Labiche, Roger Vitrac and Samuel Beckett. France. 1870-1983. 1573

Vivian Beaumont Theatre (New York, NY)

Performance/production

Ten critics review Peter Brook's production of _La Tragédie de Carmen_ at the Vivian Beaumont Theatre. USA: New York, NY. 1983. 1914

Voice

Importance of vocal techniques for Shavian drama. UK-England. 1945-1981. 896

Training

Manual on voice and respiration, with exercises. Austria. 1983. 493

Vol dans les Andes (Flight in the Andes)

Performance/production

Opening nights of productions directed by Arie Zinger and Gerd Heinz. Germany, West: Munich. Switzerland: Zürich. 1983. 771

Volksbühne (East Berlin)

Interview with and influences on actor Bernhard Minetti, including production of _Faust_. Germany, East: East Berlin. 1982-1983. 751

Dispute about Heiner Müller's production of _Macbeth_. Germany, East: East Berlin. 1971-1982. 1678

Volksoper (Vienna)

Institutions

Annual report of the Austrian Federal Theatres. Austria: Vienna. 1982-1983. 284

Performance/production

Career of Karl Dönch, opera singer and manager of Vienna's Volksoper. Austria: Vienna. 1915-1983. 1761

Von der Wahreit (Of the Truth)

Theory/criticism

Karl Jaspers' philosophy is applied to a discussion of Luigi Pirandello. Italy. 1916-1936. 1703

Vormärz

Plays/librettos/scripts

Grégoire de Tours' influence on Franz Grillparzer's play _Thou Shalt Not Lie_. Austria. 1838. 1004

Vultures, The SEE: _Corbeaux, Les_

Vychodil, Ladislav

Design/technology

Current trends in Czechoslovakian scene design. Czechoslovakia. 1983. 180

Wachowiak, Jutta

Performance/production

Eight actors take positions on their political and social responsibilities. Germany, East. 1983. 428

Wagner, Cosima

Comprehensive illustrated production history of Wagnerian opera. Europe. USA. Canada. 1832-1983. 1851

Wagner, Richard

Design/technology

Technical realization of the main platform for the sets of _Der Ring des Nibelungen_. Germany, West: Bayreuth. 1983. 1817

Various safety requirements for the construction of the platform for the production of _Der Ring des Nibelungen_. Germany, West: Bayreuth. 1983. 1818

Development of Wagnerian stage design and groups and movements involved in its production. Spain. 1882-1960. 1822

Josef Svoboda's scenography of Wagnerian opera. Switzerland. UK-England: London. Czechoslovakia: Prague. 1948-1983. 1823

Performance/production

Exhibition about the tendency toward the _Gesamtkunstwerk_. Switzerland: Zürich. Austria: Vienna. 1983. 444

Richard Wagner's influence on modern theatrical conceptions, including those of Adolphe Appia, Stanisław Wyspiański and Bertolt Brecht. Germany. Poland. Switzerland. 1813-1983. 742

Comprehensive illustrated production history of Wagnerian opera. Europe. USA. Canada. 1832-1983. 1851

Richard Wagner's works, reception and influence. France. 1841-1983. 1859

One hundred years of recordings and Bayreuth Festival performances of Wagner's _Parsifal_. Germany: Bayreuth. 1882-1982. 1864

History and production history of Wagnerian opera. Germany. USA. 1832-1982. 1865

Photographs and personnel of Bayreuth Festival production of _Siegfried_. Germany, West: Bayreuth. 1980. 1866

Photographs and personnel of Bayreuth Festival production of _Götterdämmerung_. Germany, West: Bayreuth. 1980. 1867

German tenor Peter Hofman speaks of his career and art. Germany, West. 1983. 1868

Photographs and personnel of Bayreuth Festival production of _Die Walküre_. Germany, West: Bayreuth. 1980. 1869

Peter Hall's production of Richard Wagner's _Ring_ at Bayreuth Festspielhaus. Germany, West: Bayreuth. 1983. 1870

Discussion of Leonard Bernstein's production of Wagner's _Tristan und Isolde_. Germany, West: Munich. 1981. 1872

1983 Bayreuth _Der Ring des Nibelungen_, directed by Peter Hall, conducted by Georg Solti. Germany, West: Bayreuth. 1983. 1873

Patrice Chéreau talks about his production of Richard Wagner's _Der Ring des Nibelungen_. Germany, West: Bayreuth. 1976. 1875

Wagner, Richard — cont'd

Discussion of centennial production of *Parsifal* directed by Götz
Friedrich. Germany, West: Bayreuth. 1982.   1876

Klaus Michael Grüber directs Richard Wagner's *Tannhäuser* at
Teatro Comunale, Florence. Italy: Florence. 1983.   1882

First performance of Richard Wagner's *Lohengrin* and the debate
generated with followers of Giuseppe Verdi. Spain. 1862-1901. 1886

History of Wagnerian study and performance. Spain. 1878-1926.
                                                             1887

Photographs, cast lists, synopsis and discography of Metropolitan
Opera production of *Parsifal*. USA: New York, NY. 1983.   1892

Photographs, cast lists, synopsis and discography of Metropolitan
Opera production of *Tannhäuser*. USA: New York, NY. 1983.   1896

Photographs, cast lists, synopsis and discography of the Metropolitan
Opera production of *Die Walküre*. USA: New York, NY. 1983.
                                                             1903

Photographs, cast lists, synopsis and discography of the Metropolitan
Opera production of *Tristan und Isolde*. USA: New York, NY. 1983.
                                                             1909

Plays/librettos/scripts

Composition and thematic analysis of Goethe's *Ur-Faust*. Germany.
1775-1832.   1137

Carl Maria von Weber's influence on Richard Wagner. Europe.
1822-1844.   1935

Richard Wagner's life and work in Paris. France: Paris. 1830-1897.
                                                             1944

Analysis of Richard Wagner's *Der Ring des Nibelungen*. Germany.
1840-1860.   1945

Pertinence of human characterizations in Wagner's operas. Germany.
1845-1951.   1946

Source material for Richard Wagner's *Tannhäuser*. Germany:
Dresden. 1842-1845.   1947

Evaluation of the place of Richard Wagner in opera today.
Germany. 1833-1983.   1949

Examination of Act III of *Die Walküre*. Germany. 1852.   1950

In *Tristan und Isolde*, Wagner explores the world of darkness
outside reality. Germany. 1854-1983.   1951

Discussion of character development of Wotan in *Parsifal* by
Richard Wagner. Germany. 1870-1900.   1952

Analysis and interpretation of Richard Wagner's librettos for the
Ring Tetralogy. Germany, West: Bayreuth. 1853-1874.   1954

Essays on Richard Wagner's influence on Catalonian culture. Spain.
1868-1983.   1962

Reference materials

Program of Easter Festival Salzburg, including essays on Richard
Wagner and Johannes Brahms. Austria: Salzburg. France: Paris.
1983.   1964

Source materials on Richard Wagner's influence on theatre.
Germany. Austria. USA. 1869-1976.   1966

Theory/criticism

Influence of Richard Wagner's *Gesamtkunstwerk* on modern theatre.
Germany. 1849-1977.   1495

Wagner, Robin

Design/technology

Biography, views and production chronology of scene designer Robin
Wagner. USA. 1957-1983.   252

Wagner, Wieland

Performance/production

Comprehensive illustrated production history of Wagnerian opera.
Europe. USA. Canada. 1832-1983.   1851

History and production history of Wagnerian opera. Germany. USA.
1832-1982.   1865

Wagner, Wolfgang

Comprehensive illustrated production history of Wagnerian opera.
Europe. USA. Canada. 1832-1983.   1851

Waiting for Godot

Plays/librettos/scripts

Influence of Shakespeare, Beckett and Wittgenstein on the plays of
Tom Stoppard. UK-England. 1963-1979.   1302

Wajda, Andrzej

Performance/production

Andrzej Wajda's staging of *Hamlet* at Teatro Argentina. Italy.
Poland: Rome. 1982.   797

Walken, Christopher

Plays/librettos/scripts

Interview with director and cast of Yale Repertory's production of
G.B. Shaw's *The Philanderer*. USA: New Haven, CT. 1982.   1389

Walker, George

Performance/production

Account of a production of the musical *In Dahomey*. UK-England:
London. 1903-1904.   1776

Walker, John

Examination of John Philip Kemble's vocal technique. England.
1780-1817.   415

Walküre, Die

Photographs and personnel of Bayreuth Festival production of *Die
Walküre*. Germany, West: Bayreuth. 1980.   1869

Photographs, cast lists, synopsis and discography of the Metropolitan
Opera production of *Die Walküre*. USA: New York, NY. 1983.
                                                             1903

Plays/librettos/scripts

Examination of Act III of *Die Walküre*. Germany. 1852.   1950

Waller, Fats

Institutions

Center Stage wins top honor in Toyama International Amateur
Theatre Festival with *Ain't Misbehavin'*. Japan: Toyama. USA:
Omaha, NE. 1983.   1772

Walser, Martin

Performance/production

World premiere of Martin Walser's *In Goethe's Hand* at Vienna's
Akademietheater, directed by Karl Fruchtmann. Austria: Vienna.
1983.   671

Dramatists as directors of their own plays. Germany, West: Bonn,
Lüneburg, Hamburg. 1983.   789

Walsh, Thommie

Production, casts and review of musical *My One and Only*. USA:
New York, NY. 1971-1983.   1791

Ten critics review *My One and Only*, staged by Thommie Walsh and
Tommy Tune. USA: New York, NY. 1983.   1808

Wandtke, Harald

Training

Ballet work and training in opera houses in East Germany.
Germany, East: Leipzig, Dresden, East Berlin. 1981-1983.   523

Wannseeheim für Jugendarbeit (West Berlin)

Workshops and theatre productions by and for apprentices.
Germany, West: West Berlin. 1971-1983.   498

Want, Te-k'un

Performance/production

Theatre before and after Mao Tse-tung. China, People's Republic of.
1949-1956.   414

War Memorial Opera House SEE: San Francisco Opera

Wasserstein, Wendy

Performance/production

Five critics review Gerald Gutierrez's production of *Isn't It
Romantic*. USA: New York, NY. 1983.   926

Wat Tyler

Documentation of the performance of Robert Southey's play *Wat
Tyler* (1794) at Whittington Theatre. England: Whittington. 1817.
                                                             699

Waterloo Community Playhouse (Waterloo, IA)

Institutions

Distinguished Service award presented to Waterloo Community Playhouse. USA: Waterloo, IA. 1983.   337

Waters, Les

Performance/production

Six critics review Les Waters' production of Caryl Churchill's play *Fen*. USA: New York, NY. 1983.   964

Wayang Wong

Plays/librettos/scripts

Characterization in classical Yogyanese dance. Java. 1755-1980.   541

Weavers, The SEE: *Weber, Die*

Webb, Margot

Performance/production

Career of dancer Margot Webb. USA. 1933-1947.   1991

Webber, Andrew Lloyd

Administration

Peter Weck, new manager of Theater an der Wien plans to produce first German language production of Andrew Lloyd Webber's *Cats*. Austria: Vienna. 1983.   1767

Weber, Carl Maria von

Plays/librettos/scripts

Carl Maria von Weber's influence on Richard Wagner. Europe. 1822-1844.   1935

Reference materials

Program of Easter Festival Salzburg, including essays on Richard Wagner and Johannes Brahms. Austria: Salzburg. France: Paris. 1983.   1964

Weber, Die (Weavers, The)

Performance/production

Topical production of Gerhart Hauptmann's *The Weavers* in working class neighborhood. Germany, West: Recklinghausen. 1979.   768

Weber, Frieder

Institutions

Interviews with personnel of Freiburg theatres on obtaining subsidies and other aspects of administration. Germany, West: Freiburg. 1911-1983.   607

Weber, Max

Theory/criticism

Phenomenological theory of performing arts. USA. 1982.   1514

Webern, Anton

Performance/production

Interview with and influences on postmodern composer Mestres Quaderny. Spain. 1945-1955.   1775

Webster, John

List of productions of plays from English Renaissance drama with brief reviews. North America. Europe. 1982-1983.   822

Plays/librettos/scripts

John Webster's visual drama. England. 1580-1634.   1068

Study of form, style and theme in John Webster's plays. England: London. 1603-1640.   1686

Relationship between Jacobean tragedy and interpolated masque. England. 1600-1625.   1691

Reference materials

Chronological listing, including personnel, of productions of John Webster's plays. England. USA. 1614-1983.   1401

Webster, Margaret

Institutions

History of American Repertory Theatre. USA. 1945-1947.   652

Weck, Peter

Administration

Peter Weck, new manager of Theater an der Wien plans to produce first German language production of Andrew Lloyd Webber's *Cats*. Austria: Vienna. 1983.   1767

Wedekind, Frank

Performance/production

Analysis of Mario Missiroli's productions of Jean Genet's *The Maids* and Frank Wedekind's *Music*. Italy. 1980.   796

Plays/librettos/scripts

Luigi Pirandello's earlier plays are considered prologues to *The Giants of the Mountain*. Italy. 1921-1937.   1189

Weekend Near Madison, A

Performance/production

Five critics review Emily Mann's production of Kathleen Tolan's play *A Weekend Near Madison*. USA: New York, NY. 1983.   977

Weh' dem, der lügt! (Though Shalt Not Lie)

Plays/librettos/scripts

Grégoire de Tours' influence on Franz Grillparzer's play *Thou Shalt Not Lie*. Austria. 1838.   1004

Weigel, Helene

Performance/production

Notes on Helene Weigel's letters as resources for theatre history. Germany. 1900-1971.   741

Weill, Kurt

Portrait of and interview with Douglas Sirk, director of *Silverlake*. Germany. Switzerland. USA. 1933-1983.   426

Critical assessment of Kurt Weill's music and his biography. Germany. USA. 1900-1950.   1762

Weiner, Bernard

Conversations with theatre critics from four newspapers. USA. 1983.   468

Weininger, Otto

Karl Kraus' and Jehoshua Sobol's plays devoted to Vienna of 1900 and produced at Edinburgh Festival. UK-Scotland: Edinburgh. 1983.   902

Weise, Christian Felix

Plays/librettos/scripts

Examination of Baroque themes and writers. Germany. 1618-1685.   1581

Weiss, Peter

Modern plays set in confining institutions. North America. Europe. 1900-1983.   1200

Wekwerth, Manfred

Performance/production

Tendencies of Bertolt Brecht stage interpretations. Germany, East. USSR. Italy. 1956-1983.   747

Welfare State Company (England)

Institutions

Innovative projects of Welfare State Company, and community benefits. UK-England. 1983.   1742

Well-made Play

Plays/librettos/scripts

Influence of Eugène Scribe and the Well-Made Play on later drama. France: Paris. 1830-1840.   1102

Theory/criticism

Nature and history of farce in theatre, film and media. Europe. USA. 425 B.C.-1982 A.D.   1600

Welles, Orson

Plays/librettos/scripts

Reasons for Deeley's calling himself Orson Welles in *Old Times* are

Welles, Orson — cont'd

based on film *The Magnificent Ambersons*. UK-England. USA. 1942-1971.   1289

Wells, Stanley

Review essay of *Hamlet* burlesques from a collection of Shakespeare parodies. UK-England. USA. 1810-1888.   1590

Wendt, Ernst

Performance/production

Ernst Wendt's staging of Heinrich von Kleist's *The Broken Jug* at Deutsches Schauspielhaus in Hamburg. Germany, West: Hamburg. 1983.   1527

Ernst Wendt's staging of Friederich Hebbel's *Gyges and His Ring*. Germany, West: Hamburg. 1983.   1679

Werkteater (Amsterdam)

Institutions

Free operating groups and institutionalized theatre. Netherlands. 1963-1983.   1609

Werner, Zacharias

Plays/librettos/scripts

Catholic interpretation of *Der 24 Februar* by Zacharias Werner. Germany. 1809-1814.   1134

Wesker, Arnold

Modern plays set in confining institutions. North America. Europe. 1900-1983.   1200

West End theatre

Administration

Private prosecution of Michael Bogdanov's production of Howard Brenton's *The Romans in Britain*. UK. 1968-1986.   144

Institutions

Failing popularity of West End theatre. UK-England: London. 1942-1960.   331

Performance/production

Philip Prowse's production of Robert MacDonald's Nazi psychothriller *Summit Conference*. UK-England: London. 1982.   888

Reference materials

Chronological guide to premieres, revivals, personalities and events. USA. UK. Canada. 1900-1979.   45

West, Thomas Wade

Performance/production

Shakespearean productions and festivals in the American South. USA. 1751-1980.   938

Westward Ho!

Plays/librettos/scripts

Authorship, censorship and thematic analysis of *Westward Ho!*. England. 1570-1637.   1067

Whanslaw, H.W.

Institutions

Foundation and history of the London Marionette Theatre. UK-England: London. 1927-1935.   2082

What Where

Performance/production

Four critics review Alan Schneider's production of three Samuel Beckett plays. USA: New York, NY. 1983.   928

Wheel of Fortune, The

Plays/librettos/scripts

Unpublished scene from Richard Cumberland's *The Wheel of Fortune*. England: London. 1795.   1557

When You Coming Back, Red Ryder?

Performance/production

Use of cognitive complexity questionnaire in selecting and training cast. USA: Denton, TX. 1981.   918

Plays/librettos/scripts

Examination of plays adapted for movies. USA. 1974.   1345

Whitbread, J.W.

Developments of Irish melodrama and its influence on later writers. UK-Ireland: Dublin. 1860-1905.   1338

White Snake-Women Tales

Tradition of warrior heroines in Chinese dance and myth. China. 500 B.C.-1978 A.D.   538

Whiteley, Henry Allen Alexander

Performance/production

Circus life and performance based on the memoirs of acrobat Leonora Whiteley. Greece: Athens. 1880-1899.   2011

Whiteley, Leonora

Circus life and performance based on the memoirs of acrobat Leonora Whiteley. Greece: Athens. 1880-1899.   2011

Whittington Theatre

Documentation of the performance of Robert Southey's play *Wat Tyler* (1794) at Whittington Theatre. England: Whittington. 1817.   699

Widow, The SEE: Veuve, La

Wielopole, Wielopole

Performance/production

Comprehensive study of productions by Tadeusz Kantor's experimental theatre group Cricot 2 and Kantor's philosophy. Poland. 1975-1980.   1626

Interview with playwright-director Tadeusz Kantor about *Wielopole, Wielopole*. Poland: Wielopole. 1982.   1628

Production styles of directors Peter Brook and Tadeusz Kantor. USA: New York, NY. France: Paris. Poland: Wielopole. 1982.   1632

Wiener Festwochen

Institutions

Documentation on Karlsplatz festival, part of Wiener Festwochen. Austria: Vienna. 1983.   288

Wiespätissn

Performance/production

Production of *Wiespätissn*, a peace play, and audience reactions. Germany, West: West Berlin. 1982.   783

Wife's Tragedy, A

Plays/librettos/scripts

Earlier date suggested for composition of *A Wife's Tragedy*. UK-England. 1882-1900.   1312

Wigs

Design/technology

Career of Metropolitan Opera wigmaker Adolf Senz. USA: New York, NY. 1930-1983.   1826

Wilbur, Richard

Performance/production

Seven critics review Stephen Porter's production of Molière's *The Misanthrope*. USA: New York, NY. 1983.   1543

Wild Duck, The SEE: Vildanden

Wild West exhibitions

Reference materials

Reference guide to popular entertainments. USA. 1840.   1998

Wilde, Oscar

Performance/production

Critical reaction to early productions of Oscar Wilde's *Salome*. Europe. USA: New York, NY. 1892-1917.   711

Plays/librettos/scripts

Playwrights and dramatic forms influencing Eugene O'Neill's *The Calms of Capricorn*. Europe. USA. 1953.   1088

Wilde, Oscar — cont'd

Revolutionary vision of collaborative effort between Oscar Wilde and illustrator Aubrey Beardsley. UK. 1894-1900.   1273

Oscar Wilde's stage directions in various editions of *An Ideal Husband* and other plays. UK-England. 1880-1900.   1295

Earlier date suggested for composition of *A Wife's Tragedy*. UK-England. 1882-1900.   1312

Wilder, Thornton

Performance/production

Karlheinz Stroux's production of *The Skin of Our Teeth* by Thornton Wilder at Hebbeltheater. Germany, West: West Berlin, Darmstadt. 1946.   779

Theory/criticism

Effect of social conditions on performance styles. USA. Greece. 499 B.C.-1983 A.D.   1517

Wilhelm Meisters theatralische Sendung (Wilhelm Meister's Theatrical Mission)

Plays/librettos/scripts

Bourgeois interests in *Wilhelm Meister's Theatrical Mission* by Goethe. Germany. 1777-1785.   1116

Wilkinson, Tate

Administration

Sound financial practices of the productions mounted by the actor-manager Tate Wilkinson. England. 1781-1784.   554

Wilkinson, Walter

Performance/production

Life of writer and puppet theatre promoter Walter Wilkinson. UK-England. 1889-1970.   2084

Willet, John

Relationship between Bertolt Brecht and Asian theatre. Asia. Germany. 1925-1981.   665

Williams, Addis

Work of The Puppet People on Broadway production of *Alice in Wonderland*. USA: New York, NY. 1982.   2055

Williams, Aubrey

Theory/criticism

Morality of Restoration comedy. England. 1670-1700.   1599

Williams, Bert

Performance/production

Account of a production of the musical *In Dahomey*. UK-England: London. 1903-1904.   1776

Williams, Emlyn

Seven critics review *The Corn Is Green*. USA: New York, NY. 1983.   930

Williams, Faynia

Administration

Interview with the new artistic director and literary advisor for the Iron Theatre (Glasgow). UK-Scotland. 1973-1983.   559

Williams, Robert

Institutions

Educational project of Intriplicate Mime Company using puppets. UK. 1977-1983.   2043

Williams, Tennessee

Performance/production

Ten critics review John Dexter's production of *The Glass Menagerie*, by Tennessee Williams. USA: New York, NY. 1983.   981

Plays/librettos/scripts

Compilation of comments by various artists on Tennessee Williams. USA. 1911-1983.   1342

Tennessee Williams collection at the University of Texas at Austin. USA: Austin, TX. 1962-1971.   1344

Bertolt Brecht's theory of alienation applied to characters and situations in Tennessee Williams' *Camino Real*. USA. Germany, East. 1941-1953.   1352

Hart Crane's influence on plays by Tennessee Williams. USA. 1938-1980.   1354

Tennessee Williams' life and analysis of his plays. USA. 1914-1983.   1366

Assessment of the apparent artistic decline in Tennessee Williams' later writings. USA. 1965-1983.   1367

Only three Tony-Award-winning plays reflect feminist ideology. USA: New York, NY. UK-England. 1960-1979.   1374

Biography of Tennessee Williams. USA. 1911-1983.   1388

Williams, Wheeler

Administration

Debate on federal arts subsidies. USA. 1943-1965.   157

Williamson, David

Plays/librettos/scripts

History of contemporary Australian drama with emphasis on popular playwright David Williamson. Australia. 1969-1980.   1000

Wilson, Lanford

Performance/production

Eight critics review Marshall Mason's production of Lanford Wilson's play *Angels Fall*. USA: New York, NY. 1983.   952

Wilson, Robert

Plays/librettos/scripts

Robert Wilson discusses current and forthcoming projects. USA: New York, NY. 1983.   1963

Win/Lose/Draw

Performance/production

Five critics review Amy Saltz's production of *Win/Lose/Draw* at the Provincetown Playhouse. USA: New York, NY. 1983.   909

Winestreet Playhouse (Bristol)

Performance spaces

Location and dating of the Winestreet Playhouse operations. England: Bristol. 1580-1630.   366

Wings

Plays/librettos/scripts

Modern plays set in confining institutions. North America. Europe. 1900-1983.   1200

Change in style of Arthur Kopit's playwriting after *Wings*. USA. 1965-1982.   1654

Comparison and contrast of radio and stage presentations of Arthur Kopit's play *Wings*. USA. 1978-1979.   1655

Winners

Performance/production

Five critics review Nye Heron's production of Brian Friel's play *Winners*. USA: New York, NY. 1983.   962

Winter's Tale, A

Claus Peymann's production of Shakespeare's *A Winter's Tale*. Germany, West: Bochum. 1983.   784

Wisten, Fritz

Gotthold Ephraim Lessing's *Nathan the Wise* at Deutsches Theater Berlin, directed by Fritz Wisten. Germany, East: East Berlin. 1945.   756

Witcover, Walt

Institutions

History of Masterworks Laboratory Theatre. USA. 1965-1980.   656

With Yellow Gloves SEE: Con i guanti gialli

Witkacy SEE: Witkiewicz, Stanisław Ignacy

Witkiewicz, Stanisław Ignacy

Performance/production

Comprehensive study of productions by Tadeusz Kantor's

Witkiewicz, Stanisław Ignacy — cont'd

experimental theatre group Cricot 2 and Kantor's philosophy.
Poland. 1975-1980.   1626

Tadeusz Kantor's theory of art and theatre, and productions of his
company Cricot 2. Poland: Kraków. 1943-1975.   1629

Witten, Laurence

Laurence Witten's collection of historic sound recordings at Yale
University. USA: New Haven, CT. 1983.   1913

Wittgenstein, Ludwig Josef Johan

Plays/librettos/scripts

Playwright Thomas Bernhard's affinity with philosophy of Ludwig
Josef Johan Wittgenstein. Austria. 1970-1982.   1002

Influence of Shakespeare, Beckett and Wittgenstein on the plays of
Tom Stoppard. UK-England. 1963-1979.   1302

Wodehouse, P.G.

Performance/production

Seven critics review Gillian Lynne's production of *Jeeves Takes
Charge*. USA: New York, NY. 1983.   946

Wolf, Georg Jakob

Theory/criticism

Reformers on their theories. Europe. 1870-1910.   98

Wolf's Mouth, The SEE: *Bocca del Lupo, La*

WOMAD Festival

Institutions

Study of the nature and the international scope of theatre festivals.
UK-England: London. 1983.   330

Woman and a Bell, A SEE: *Dōjōji*

Woman Killed with Kindness, A

Plays/librettos/scripts

Heywood's *A Woman Killed with Kindness* as a source for
Shakespeare's *Othello*. England. 1604.   1066

Women Beware Women

Relationship between Jacobean tragedy and interpolated masque.
England. 1600-1625.   1691

Women in theatre

Institutions

Effect of women's movement on experimental theatre. Sweden:
Stockholm. 1970-1983.   328

Collaborative effort in Welsh community results in play *All's Fair*.
UK-Wales: Mid Glamorgan. 1983.   645

Profile of the women's company Bloodgroup. UK. 1983.   1741

Performance/production

Directing objectives and career of Kaisa Korhonen. Finland:
Helsinki. 1965-1983.   719

Biography of director Margo Jones. USA. 1913-1955.   941

Interview with playwright Dario Fo and his actress-wife and
collaborator Franca Rame. Italy: Milan. 1982.   1623

Work of video performance artist Nan Hoover. UK-England. 1900-
1983.   1746

Women's involvement in performance art in the context of feminism.
USA. 1970-1980.   1757

Plays/librettos/scripts

Status of women in Elizabethan society as reflected in Shakespeare's
plays. England. 1590-1613.   1049

Louisa Medina's popular dramatic adaptations of the works of
Edward Bulwer-Lytton, Ernest Maltravers and Robert Bird. USA.
1833-1838.   1346

Two principal female archetypes of Imamu Amiri Baraka's drama.
USA. 1964-1978.   1375

Relation to other fields

Argument against application of Jungian ideas to theatre.   490

Theory/criticism

Collected theory and criticism by women in theatre on women in
theatre. USA. UK. 1850-1983.   114

Wood, Peter

Performance/production

Peter Wood's productions of Tom Stoppard's *The Real Thing* and
Harold Pinter's *Other Places*. UK-England: London. 1983.   887

Words upon the Window-pane, The

Plays/librettos/scripts

Influences of Jonathan Swift's satire in plays by W.B. Yeats and
Denis Johnston. Eire. 1928-1960.   1026

Workshops

Institutions

Popular theatre workshop for training theatre educators. Nigeria:
Gboko. 1981-1982.   322

Workshops of Latin American popular theatre. North America. South
America. 1983.   1610

Performance/production

Theory and style of director George Luscombe. Canada: Toronto,
ON. 1983.   1614

Worsley, Dale

Five critics review Bill Raymond and Dale Worsley's production of
Cold Harbor. USA: New York, NY. 1983.   925

Wortham Theatre Center (Houston, TX)

Performance spaces

Design for the Wortham Theatre Center. USA: Houston, TX. 1983.
    402

Wouk, Herman

Performance/production

Seven critics review Arthur Sherman's production of Herman Wouk's
play *The Caine Mutiny Court-Martial*. USA: New York, NY. 1983.
    955

WPA Arts Projects

Administration

Debate on federal arts subsidies. USA. 1943-1965.   157

Württembergisches Staatstheater (Stuttgart)

Performance/production

Productions on the occasion of 'Peace Offensive at Theatre' and
political reactions. Germany, West: Stuttgart. 1982.   770

Wycherley, William

Theory/criticism

Morality of Restoration comedy. England. 1670-1700.   1599

Wylie, Betty Jane

Plays/librettos/scripts

Excerpts from Betty Jane Wylie's journal during collective theatre
venture. Canada. 1976.   1018

Wyspiański, Stanisław

Performance/production

Richard Wagner's influence on modern theatrical conceptions,
including those of Adolphe Appia, Stanisław Wyspiański and Bertolt
Brecht. Germany. Poland. Switzerland. 1813-1983.   742

Relation to other fields

Dramatist Stanisław Wyspiański's painting of a Tartar costume,
based on a folk tradition stock type — Lajkonik. Poland: Kraków.
Austria. 1901-1907.   1461

Xirgu, Margarita

Performance/production

Exhibit to commemorate Margarita Xirgu's debut as Medea. Spain:
Mérida. 1932-1933.   1683

Yale Repertory (New Haven, CT)

Plays/librettos/scripts

Interview with director and cast of Yale Repertory's production of G.B. Shaw's *The Philanderer*. USA: New Haven, CT. 1982.   1389

Yale University

Performance/production

Laurence Witten's collection of historic sound recordings at Yale University. USA: New Haven, CT. 1983.   1913

Yankowitz, Susan

Institutions

Reflections on the significance of The Open Theatre by several of its performers, writers and critical advisers. USA: New York, NY. 1963-1973.   1613

Yearbooks

Administration

Yearbook of the international society for copyright. Austria. Italy. North America. 1976-1981.   1704

Reference materials

List of dramatic, cinematographic and television productions with short critical notes on the most important ones. Italy. 1982.   26

Yearbook of theatre, television and cinema, with brief critical notations. Italy. 1983.   29

Annals of theatre productions in Catalonia for the 1982-1983 season. Spain. 1982-1983.   34

Yeats, Jack B.

Relation to other fields

Association between literature of J.M. Synge and pictorial art of Jack B. Yeats. UK-Ireland. 1896-1948.   1463

Yeats, William Butler

Institutions

Rejection of O'Casey's play *The Silver Tassie* by the Abbey Theatre and the subsequent furor. UK-Ireland: Dublin. 1928.   637

Performance/production

Yeats's theories on acting and the Abbey Theatre. UK-Ireland: Dublin. 1904-1939.   899

Plays/librettos/scripts

Influences of Jonathan Swift's satire in plays by W.B. Yeats and Denis Johnston. Eire. 1928-1960.   1026

Playwrights and dramatic forms influencing Eugene O'Neill's *The Calms of Capricorn*. Europe. USA. 1953.   1088

Role of folklore in Irish Literary Revival. UK-Ireland. 1888-1920.   1322

Memoirs of journalist Stephen McKenna on John Millington Synge's apprenticeship years in Paris. UK-Ireland. France: Paris. 1895-1902.   1324

William Butler Yeats as visionary dramatist. UK-Ireland. 1865-1939.   1327

Imagery of the apocalyptic symbol of the black pig in works by William Butler Yeats. UK-Ireland. 1880-1910.   1334

Images of the supernatural in William Butler Yeat's *The Countess Cathleen*. UK-Ireland. 1890.   1336

Patriot Charles Stewart Parnell's influence on Irish drama. UK-Ireland. 1891-1936.   1337

Irreverent aspects of Irish comedy seen through the works of 14 playwrights. Eire. UK-Ireland. 1840-1965.   1555

Comic irony and anti-heroes in Irish comedy and influence on Harold Pinter, Samuel Beckett and Tom Stoppard. Eire. 1900-1940.   1593

Reference materials

Correspondence relating to administrative concerns at the Abbey Theatre between William Butler Yeats, Lady Gregory and John Millington Synge. UK-Ireland: Dublin. 1904-1909.   1432

Yes and No

Performance/production

Tribute to Mordecai Gorelik, scenic designer, theorist, teacher, director and playwright. USA. 1899-1983.   936

Yes Man and the No Man, The SEE: Jasager und der Neinsager, Der

Yes, Giorgio

Performance/production

Career of soprano Leona Mitchell at the Metropolitan Opera. USA. 1983.   1912

Yiddish theatre

Plays/librettos/scripts

Essays on the trends of the Jewish-American theatre and its personalities. USA. 1900-1983.   1353

Yiddish theatre SEE ALSO: Ethnic theatre

York cycle

Performance/production

New information from York about problems with the Girdlers' pageant wagon and their play, *The Slaughter of the Innocents*. England: York. 1548-1554.   705

Plays/librettos/scripts

York Creed plays may not have been confiscated by the ecclesiastical authorities. England: York. 1420-1580.   1081

Yorkshire Tragedy, A

Performance/production

List of productions of plays from English Renaissance drama with brief reviews. North America. Europe. 1982-1983.   822

You Can't Take It with You

Eight critics review Ellis Rabb's production of George S. Kaufman's and Moss Hart's play *You Can't Take It with You*. USA: New York, NY. 1983.   972

Youmans, Vincent

Biography of Broadway and film songwriter Vincent Youmans. USA. 1898-1946.   1780

Young Artist Development Program

Institutions

Account of the Metropolitan Opera Company's Young Artist Development Program. USA: New York, NY. 1980-1983.   1832

Young Playwrights Festival

Plays/librettos/scripts

Plays and productions at Young Playwrights Festival. USA: New York, NY. 1982.   1384

Young, Rod

Performance/production

Interview with puppeteer Rod Young. USA: New York, NY. 1937-1983.   2085

Youth theatre SEE: Children's theatre

Yvonne, Princesse de Bourgogne

Plays/librettos/scripts

Director Jacques Rosner on meeting with playwright Witold Gombrowicz. Poland. France. 1969-1982.   1218

Yzraeli, Yossi

Performance/production

Problems of antisemitism in staging *The Merchant of Venice*. Israel. 1936-1980.   663

Z Mrtvého Domu (From the House of the Dead)

Background of the U.S. premiere of Janáček's opera *From the House of the Dead*. USA: New York, NY. Czechoslovakia: Prague. 1930-1983.   1916

Zadek, Peter

Peter Zadek's production of *The Master Builder* at the Residenztheater. Germany, West: Munich. 1983.   772

Zahova, Boris Evgenjevič
Role experimental studios played in the formation of the Soviet theatre. USSR: Moscow, Leningrad. 1920-1939. 993

Zaks, Jerry
Five critics review Jerry Zak's production of Christopher Durang's play *Baby with the Bathwater*. USA: New York, NY. 1983. 1544

Zan Pollo Theater (West Berlin)
Production of *Wiespätissn*, a peace play, and audience reactions. Germany, West: West Berlin. 1982. 783

Zanni
Relation to other fields
Research on the origin and meaning of Zanni's names and masks. Italy. Germany. 1300-1599. 2023

Zappulla Muscarà, Sarah
Plays/librettos/scripts
Some lesser known facts about Luigi Pirandello's plays and other writings. Italy. 1884-1935. 1192

Zariov, Mikhail SEE: Carëv, Michail Ivanovič

Zarzuela
Plays/librettos/scripts
Manners and customs of old Madrid in the Spanish light opera *Zarzuela*. Spain: Madrid. 1850-1935. 1975

Zeami Motokiyo
Theory/criticism
Principal themes in Zeami's treatises on *nō* performance. Japan. 1363-1443. 548
Nature and history of *nō* theatre. Japan. 1300-1980. 549
Spirituality for the dancer-actor in Zeami's and Zenchiku's writings on the *nō*. Japan. 1363-1470. 550
Zeami's dramatic theory of *nō*. Japan. 1402-1430. 551

Zeffirelli, Franco
Performance/production
Study of productions by leading Italian directors. Italy. 1945-1975. 798
Making of the Franco Zeffirelli film of *La Traviata*. Italy: Rome. 1981-1983. 1885
Photographs, cast lists, synopsis and discography of Metropolitan Opera production of *La Bohème*. USA: New York, NY. 1983. 1905

Zeitstücke (Period plays)
Plays/librettos/scripts
Period plays and documentary theatre of the cold war. Germany, West. 1945-1966. 1152

Zemlinsky, Alexander von
Performance/production
Recent productions of operas by Alexander von Zemlinsky. Austria: Vienna. 1983. 1842

Zen
Theory/criticism
Spirituality for the dancer-actor in Zeami's and Zenchiku's writings on the *nō*. Japan. 1363-1470. 550

Zena, Remigio
Plays/librettos/scripts
Dramatization of Remigio Zena's novel *The Wolf's Mouth* by Teatro Stabile di Genova. Italy: Genoa. 1980. 1186

Zenchiku SEE: Komparu Zenchiku

Zenda
Performance/production
Overview of Jack Cole's career as dancer, teacher and choreographer. USA. 1933-1974. 1788

Zerbrochene Krug, Der (Broken Jug, The)
Ernst Wendt's staging of Heinrich von Kleist's *The Broken Jug* at Deutsches Schauspielhaus in Hamburg. Germany, West: Hamburg. 1983. 1527

Zglinicki, Simone von
Eight actors take positions on their political and social responsibilities. Germany, East. 1983. 428

Ziegfield Follies
Study of revue songs by Irving Berlin, George Gershwin and Cole Porter in their theatrical contexts. USA: New York, NY. 1910-1937. 2032

Ziegfield Follies (New York, NY)
Overview of Jack Cole's career as dancer, teacher and choreographer. USA. 1933-1974. 1788

Zimet, Paul
Institutions
Reflections on the significance of The Open Theatre by several of its performers, writers and critical advisers. USA: New York, NY. 1963-1973. 1613

Zinger, Arie
Performance/production
Opening nights of productions directed by Arie Zinger and Gerd Heinz. Germany, West: Munich. Switzerland: Zürich. 1983. 771
Arie Zinger's production of Čechov's *Ivanov* at Züricher Schauspielhaus. Switzerland: Zürich. 1983. 849

Zip
Importation of African Blacks for exhibition as 'exotics' and evolution of this practice into a circus side-show. USA. 1810-1926. 2014

Zola, Emile
Institutions
Development of nationalistic and experimental theatre in Latin America. South America. North America. 1800-1983. 618

Zoo Story
Plays/librettos/scripts
Similarities between the plays *The Dutchman* and *Zoo Story*. USA: New York, NY. 1964. 1350

Zorba
Performance/production
Nine critics review Michael Cacoyannis' production of the musical *Zorba*. USA: New York, NY. 1983. 1798

Züricher Schauspielhaus
Arie Zinger's production of Čechov's *Ivanov* at Züricher Schauspielhaus. Switzerland: Zürich. 1983. 849

Zutphen Archive
Basic theatrical documents
Discussion of prints and translation of the *fragmenten verzameling* 3-8 found in Zutphen Archive. Netherlands. 1400-1499. 574

GEOGRAPHICAL - CHRONOLOGICAL INDEX

Denmark — cont'd

Need for new cultural policy and cooperation between amateur and professional theatre.   142

1982.   Institutions.
Street theatre production of Århus theater akademi in collaboration with Jordcirkus and Johnny Melville.   298

1983.   Institutions.
Status report of the Århus Theatre Academy.   297

Egypt

1000-500 B.C.   Relation to other fields.
Religious belief and ritual performance as related to astronomy and architecture.   2107

1900-1930.   Reference materials.
Bibliography of Arabic theatre.   18

Eire

1840-1965.   Plays/librettos/scripts.
Irreverent aspects of Irish comedy seen through the works of 14 playwrights.   1555

1900-1940.   Plays/librettos/scripts.
Comic irony and anti-heroes in Irish comedy and influence on Harold Pinter, Samuel Beckett and Tom Stoppard.   1593

1928-1960.   Plays/librettos/scripts.
Influences of Jonathan Swift's satire in plays by W.B. Yeats and Denis Johnston.   1026

1981.   Plays/librettos/scripts.
Profile of bilingual playwright Antoine O'Flatharta.   1025

England

Reference materials.
Alphabetical list of Latin theatrical terms with Old English translations.   21

400 B.C.-1613 A.D.   Plays/librettos/scripts.
Shakespearean and Platonic conceptions of wisdom.   1156

317 B.C.-1666 A.D.   Plays/librettos/scripts.
Comparison of the misanthrope in *Dýskolos*, *Timon of Athens* and *Le Misanthrope*.   1155

1100-1200.   Relation to other fields.
Comparison of the character of Herod in two Fleury plays.   1452

1200.   Performance/production.
Possible dramatic convention used in the medieval performance of the *Adoration of the Magi* plays.   700

1200.   Plays/librettos/scripts.
Six recently discovered allusions to the medieval drama.   1040

1200-1500.   Plays/librettos/scripts.
Sources and analogues of a lost miracle play.   1084

1200-1550.   Plays/librettos/scripts.
Possible meanings of characterization in the Mystery plays.   1057

1264-1560.   Plays/librettos/scripts.
Sympathetic portrayals of splendid monarchs are rare in the Corpus Christi cycles.   1055

1268-1375.   Plays/librettos/scripts.
Possible authorship of a lost Chester Corpus Christi play.   1037

1300-1499.   Plays/librettos/scripts.
Religious rites and ideology of medieval urban societies as seen in Corpus Christi plays.   2106

1300-1550.   Performance/production.
Men acting in women's roles, particularly in the Chester cycle's *Purification*.   702

1300-1550.   Plays/librettos/scripts.
Determining factor of the demonstrative mode of Morality play characters.   1032

1400.   Plays/librettos/scripts.
Comparison of *kyōgen* and early English comedy.   1585

1420-1580.   Plays/librettos/scripts.
York Creed plays may not have been confiscated by the ecclesiastical authorities.   1081

1485-1505.   Administration.
Court entertainments during reign of Henry VII, from early records.   1737

1500.   Performance spaces.
Location of the turret in Greenwich Park.   361

1500-1600.   Plays/librettos/scripts.
Themes of repentance and retribution in Renaissance drama.   1063

1500-1939.   Performance/production.
Review article of *Theatre Production Series*, seeking to define theatre's strengths.   706

1520-1533.   Plays/librettos/scripts.
Adaptation of a French farce into *Johan Johan*.   1559

1530-1555.   Plays/librettos/scripts.
Folly in Renaissance comedy.   1560

1548-1554.   Performance/production.
New information from York about problems with the Girdlers' pageant wagon and their play, *The Slaughter of the Innocents*.   705

1550-1983.   Performance/production.
Review of the Chester cycle performed in a 1550's design.   851

1558-1621.   Plays/librettos/scripts.
Editorial problems in the first folio of *Hamlet*, *Othello* and *King Lear*.   1692

1559-1603.   Plays/librettos/scripts.
Placement of the caesura in Shakespearean texts.   1083

1559-1603.   Theory/criticism.
Dramatic language related to action.   1480

1560-1600.   Performance/production.
Medieval theatre practice applied in Elizabethan playhouses.   695

1564-1593.   Plays/librettos/scripts.
Irony and metadrama in Christopher Marlowe's plays.   1044

1570-1637.   Plays/librettos/scripts.
Authorship, censorship and thematic analysis of *Westward Ho!*.   1067

1572-1637.   Reference materials.
Ben Jonson encyclopedia.   1400

1576-1635.   Performance/production.
Marxist theory applied in comparison of public theatres in England and Spain.   696

1580-1630.   Performance spaces.
Location and dating of the Winestreet Playhouse operations.   366

1580-1634.   Plays/librettos/scripts.
John Webster's visual drama.   1068

1580-1642.   Plays/librettos/scripts.
Hidden topicality of 'Saracen' drama.   1056

1581-1592.   Plays/librettos/scripts.
Discussion of playwright Robert Greene's pamphlet *A Disputation*.   1054

1588-1593.   Plays/librettos/scripts.
Realism in *Arden of Faversham*.   1689

1590-1599.   Plays/librettos/scripts.
Art of rule and rule of art in Shakespeare's histories.   1050

1590-1612.   Plays/librettos/scripts.

GEOGRAPHICAL - CHRONOLOGICAL INDEX

France — cont'd

1830.   Plays/librettos/scripts.
Victor Hugo and the original plot for the opera *Ernani* by Giuseppe Verdi.   1940

1830-1840.   Plays/librettos/scripts.
Influence of Eugène Scribe and the Well-Made Play on later drama.   1102

1830-1897.   Plays/librettos/scripts.
Richard Wagner's life and work in Paris.   1944

1830-1980.   Reference materials.
Chronological reference guide to works on and about Alfred de Musset.   1408

1841-1983.   Performance/production.
Richard Wagner's works, reception and influence.   1859

1850-1900.   Plays/librettos/scripts.
Historical subjects of the lyric repertory.   1938

1853.   Relation to other fields.
Theatrical vision and the portrait of the great French actress Rachel in Charlotte Brontë's *Villette*.   70

1856-1875.   Plays/librettos/scripts.
Personal and professional relationship of Georges Bizet and Charles Gounod.   1937

1864-1879.   Plays/librettos/scripts.
Émile Augier's *Maître Guérin* is seen as the most likely source for the ending of *A Doll's House*.   1212

1870-1983.   Plays/librettos/scripts.
Variations on the bedroom farce form in the works of Eugène Labiche, Roger Vitrac and Samuel Beckett.   1573

1873-1907.   Reference materials.
Catalogue of exhibition on pataphysics in figurative arts, theatre and cinema.   1406

1880-1950.   Theory/criticism.
Theoretical approach to modern drama.   1490

1889.   Theory/criticism.
Physical experience and aesthetic perception of body movement.   100

1895-1902.   Plays/librettos/scripts.
Memoirs of journalist Stephen McKenna on John Millington Synge's apprenticeship years in Paris.   1324

1896-1907.   Plays/librettos/scripts.
Alfred Jarry's *Ubu* Cycle with an emphasis on its protagonist.   1566

1899-1978.   Performance/production.
Biography of actor Charles Boyer, including filmography of his work.   1712

1900-1956.   Performance/production.
Actor-audience relationship in productions by Jacques Copeau, Bertolt Brecht and Russian directors.   726

1900-1983.   Administration.
Success of French cultural policy in subsidizing theatre, reviews of some productions.   125

1900-1983.   Plays/librettos/scripts.
Relationship between dramatic structure and film writing.   1718

1904-1983.   Performance/production.
Jacques Lassalle on staging Maxim Gorky's *Summer Folk* for Comédie-Française.   738

1909-1914.   Institutions.
Founding of periodical *Nouvelle Revue Française*.   304

1910-1949.   Performance/production.
Memories of Jacques Copeau by his son.   725

1911-1983.   Performance/production.
Comparison of performances of tenor aria 'O Dieu de quelle ivresse' by Jacques Offenbach.   1857

1913-1930.   Training.
Concept of school in Jacques Copeau's work.   1523

1913-1948.   Performance/production.
Son of actress Suzanne Bing recalls her memories of Jacques Copeau.   724

1914.   Plays/librettos/scripts.
Comparison of two French translations of *Twelfth Night*, by Jacques Copeau/Théodore Lascarais and Suzanne Bing.   1567

1914-1918.   Performance/production.
Actors and companies entertaining Canadian troops during World War I.   1984

1920-1929.   Performance/production.
Development of theatre from circus acts.   2009

1921-1927.   Plays/librettos/scripts.
Paul Claudel as influenced by *nō* drama.   1196

1921-1948.   Plays/librettos/scripts.
Contradiction in personal and artistic life of Antonin Artaud.   1645

1922.   Performance/production.
Innovative production of Calderón de la Barca's *Life is a Dream*.   731

1922-1926.   Design/technology.
Georges Valmier's designs for Théâtre de l'Art et Action.   195

1922-1959.   Performance/production.
Biography of actor Gérard Philippe.   729

1925-1960.   Plays/librettos/scripts.
Negation of the theatre by Samuel Beckett, Antonin Artaud and Carmelo Bene.   1643

1926.   Plays/librettos/scripts.
Adaptation of Ben Jonson's *Epicoene* by Marcel Achard, directed by Charles Dullin.   1100

1931-1983.   Plays/librettos/scripts.
Composition of the opera *Les Dialogues des Carmélites*.   1943

1932.   Plays/librettos/scripts.
Study of Fernando Arrabal's playwriting technique.   1644

1935.   Performance/production.
Eastern and Western techniques in productions by Jean-Louis Barrault.   730

1935.   Performance/production.
Italian translation of Etienne Decroux's *Paroles sur le mime (Words on Mime)*.   1726

1937-1939.   Performance/production.
Survey of theatrical activity in Rome, based on criticism by Alberto Savinio.   812

1938.   Plays/librettos/scripts.
Materialistic reading of Samuel Beckett's work.   1107

1938-1948.   Plays/librettos/scripts.
Graphic and linguistic structure of Antonin Artaud's last writings.   1646

1940-1944.   Relation to other fields.
Jacques Copeau's reading of his play *The Little Pauper* to the Cistercians during the Occupation.   1450

1940-1949.   Performance/production.
Jacques Copeau remembered by his granddaughter, actress Catherine Dasté.   727

1943-1980.   Reference materials.
Bibliography of Jean Genet criticism.   1409

1945.   Plays/librettos/scripts.
The themes of freedom, death and suicide in Albert Camus' *Caligula*.   1110

1947-1980.   Plays/librettos/scripts.
Study of Jean Tardieu's plays.   1642

Germany — cont'd

Germany, West — cont'd

Ernst Wendt's staging of Heinrich von Kleist's *The Broken Jug* at Deutsches Schauspielhaus in Hamburg.   1527

1983.   Performance/production.
Ernst Wendt's staging of Friederich Hebbel's *Gyges and His Ring.*   1679

1983.   Performance/production.
Hansgünther Heyme's production of *The Persians.*   1680

1983.   Performance/production.
Portrait and interview with theatre composer Heiner Goebbels.   1763

1983.   Performance/production.
German tenor Peter Hofman speaks of his career and art.   1868

1983.   Performance/production.
Peter Hall's production of Richard Wagner's *Ring* at Bayreuth Festspielhaus.   1870

1983.   Performance/production.
1983 Bayreuth *Der Ring des Nibelungen*, directed by Peter Hall, conducted by Georg Solti.   1873

1983.   Plays/librettos/scripts.
Brief comments on Heinar Kippardt's play *Brother Eichmann.*   1149

1983.   Plays/librettos/scripts.
Problems in stage adaptation of Elias Canetti's *The Limited.*   1150

1983.   Plays/librettos/scripts.
Treatment of power by German playwrights and Volker Braun's *Dmitri.*   1154

1983.   Plays/librettos/scripts.
Interview with Gerlind Reinshagen and review of his play *Eisenherz (Ironheart)* produced in Bochum and Zürich.   1271

1983.   Relation to other fields.
Class-conscious approach to theatre.   56

1983.   Theory/criticism.
Semiotics of theatre.   102

1983.   Theory/criticism.
Development and function of theatre in our time.   104

Ghana

1983.   Performance/production.
Present situation of theater in Ghana, including plays, performers, promoters and spaces.   429

Greece

999-560 B.C.   Design/technology.
Terracotta masks from the sanctuary of Artemis Orthia.   211

600-1 B.C.   Performance/production.
Actor's role in theatre and social status in ancient Greece and Rome.   790

600-1 B.C.   Relation to other fields.
Different social functions of the dramatic theatre in Greece and Rome and their modifications.   1455

523-406 B.C.   Plays/librettos/scripts.
Mutes in Greek tragedy.   1695

499-400 B.C.   Plays/librettos/scripts.
English translation of Albin Lesky's standard work on Greek tragedy.   1696

499 B.C.-1983 A.D.   Theory/criticism.
Effect of social conditions on performance styles.   1517

484-415 B.C.   Plays/librettos/scripts.
Dramatic and military conflict in Greek tragedy.   1697

405 B.C.   Plays/librettos/scripts.
Relationship between costume changes and change in wearer's fate.   1694

400 B.C.-1613 A.D.   Plays/librettos/scripts.
Shakespearean and Platonic conceptions of wisdom.   1156

343 B.C.-1400 A.D.   Plays/librettos/scripts.
Comparison of Greek and Roman comedy as reflected in works of Menander and Terence and in revivals by Italian humanists.   1582

317 B.C.-1666 A.D.   Plays/librettos/scripts.
Comparison of the misanthrope in *Dýskolos, Timon of Athens* and *Le Misanthrope.*   1155

1880-1899.   Performance/production.
Circus life and performance based on the memoirs of acrobat Leonora Whiteley.   2011

1980.   Plays/librettos/scripts.
Wole Soyinka's plays echo themes of Aeschylus, Euripides and Shakespeare.   1700

Guatemala

1954-1983.   Performance/production.
History and present state of Central American theatre.   439

Haiti

1956-1976.   Relation to other fields.
Relationship of theatre methods to forms of folk performance.   57

1962-1979.   Relation to other fields.
Relationship between politics and the heroic tradition of Caribbean drama.   1456

Holland SEE: Netherlands

Hong Kong

1950-1982.   Plays/librettos/scripts.
Themes and techniques employed by dramatists and performing groups.   1157

Hungary

1815-1829.   Institutions.
Polish theatre under Russian rule as reflected in György Spirò's novel *Az Ikszek.*   325

1898-1971.   Relation to other fields.
Difference in dialectics and philosophy in writings by Karl Korsch, Bertolt Brecht and György Lukács.   1454

1900-1956.   Theory/criticism.
Bertolt Brecht's and György Lukács' debate on realism. 1500

1918-1956.   Theory/criticism.
Bertolt Brecht's theatrical poetics and polemic with György Lukács on realism.   1493

1962-1982.   Performance/production.
Interview with actor-director Tamás Major on staging plays by Bertolt Brecht.   791

1968-1983.   Performance/production.
Eva Marton, Hungarian dramatic soprano, speaks of her art and career.   1878

1975-1977.   Institutions.
Theoretical and theatrical foundations of the Squat Theatre.   342

India

Design/technology.
Designs and uses of masks for sacred dances.   530

Performance/production.
Collection of essays on performing arts.   431

200 B.C.-1983 A.D.   Performance/production.
Origins and evolution of the *Kuchipudi* dance drama.   532

800-1800.   Plays/librettos/scripts.
Epic texts form the thematic basis of Indian dance-drama. 539

DOCUMENT AUTHORS INDEX

MASTER LIST OF PERIODICALS IN ACRONYM ORDER

Asterisks follow the names of publications that are represented in this bibliography. A plus sign (+) identifies the publication as dedicated to theatre subjects.

A&A	Art and Artists (Croydon, Surrey, England)		BlC	Black Collegian The (New Orleans, LA) *
A&AR	Art and Artists (New York, NY)		BM	Burlington Magazine (London, England) *
A&L	Art and the Law (New York, NY)		BPAN	British Performing Arts Newsletter (London, England)
ABNPPA	Annotated Bibliography of New Publications in Performing Arts (New York, NY)		BPM	Black Perspectives in Music (Cambria Heights, NY) *
AbqJ	Arabesque (Johannesburg, Republic of South Africa)		BPTV	Bühne und Parkett: Theater Journal Volksbühnen-Spiegel (Berlin, West Germany) +
AbqN	Arabesque (New York, NY)		BR	Ballet Review (New York, NY)
ACom	Art Com: Contemporary Arts Communication (San Francisco, CA)		BrechtJ	Brecht Jahrbuch (Frankfurt a.M., West Germany) +
Act	Act (Wellington, New Zealand) +		Brs	Broadside (New York, NY) + *
AdP	Atti dello Psicodramma (Rome, Italy) *		BSOAS	Bulletin of the School of Oriental & African Studies (London, England)
ADS	Australian Drama Studies (University of Queensland, Australia) +		BSSJ	Bernard Shaw Society Journal (Dagenahm, Essex, England)
AG	An Gael: Irish Traditional Culture Alive in America Today (New York, NY) *		BTD	British Theatre Directory (Eastbourne, East Sussex, England) +
AL	American Literature (Durham, NC)		BtR	Bühnentechnische Rundschau (Zürich, Switzerland) * +
Alfold	Alford (Debrecen, Hungary)		Buhne	Die Bühne (Vienna, Austria) * +
Alive	Alive (New York, NY) +		CAM	City Arts Monthly (San Francisco, CA)
AltT	Alternatives Théâtrales (Brussels, Belgium) +		CanL	Canadian Literature/Littérature Canadienne (Vancouver, BC)
AmAr	American Arts (New York, NY) - becomes Vantage Point in 1984		CB	Call Board (San Francisco, CA) +
AMN	Arts Management Newsletter (New York, NY)		CDO	Courrier Dramatique de l'Ouest (Rennes, France) +
AmTh	American Theatre (New York, NY) - Theatre Communications until fall 1984 +		CDr	Canadian Drama (University of Waterloo, ON) * +
Anim	Animations (London, England) *		CDT	Contributions in Drama & Theatre (Westport, CT) +
AnSt	Another Standard (Manchester, England)		CE	College English (Urbana, IL)
AnT	L'Annuaire Théâtral (Montréal, PQ) +		CF	Comédie-Francaise (Paris, France) * +
Apollo	Apollo (London, England) *		Cfl	Confluent (Rennes, France)
AQ	American Quarterly (Philadelphia, PA)		CFT	Contemporary French Civilization (Mobile, AL)
AReview	Arts Review (Washington, DC)		ChinL	Chinese Literature (Peking, China) *
Ark	Arkkitehti: The Finnish Architectural Review (Helsinki, Finland)		ChTR	Children's Theatre Review (Washington, DC) * +
ArNy	Arte Nyt (Copenhagen, Denmark)		CIQ	Callahan's Irish Quarterly (Berkeley, CA)
ASTRN	ASTR Newsletter (New York, NY) * +		CityL	City Limits (London, England)
ATJ	Asian Theatre Journal (Honolulu, HI) +		CJC	Cahiers Jean Cocteau (Paris, France) +
Atr	Acteurs (Marseilles, France) +		CJG	Cahiers Jean Giraudoux (Paris, France) +
BaI	Ballett International (Cologne, West Germany)		Cjo	Conjunto: Revista de Teatro Latinamericano (Habana, Cuba) +
BALF	Black American Literature Forum (Indiana State University, IN) *		CLAJ	College Language Association Journal (Atlanta, GA)*
BaNe	Ballet News (New York, NY) *		CO	Comédie de l'Ouest (Rennes, France) +
BAQ	Black Art Quarterly (Los Angeles, CA)		CompD	Comparative Drama (Kalamazoo, MI) * +
BATD	British Alternative Theatre Directory (Eastbourne, East Sussex, England) +		Con	Connoisseur (New York, NY) *
BCl	The Beckett Circle (Lima, OH) +		Confes	Confessio (Budapest, Hungary)
BCom	Bulletin of the Commediantes (University of California, Los Angeles, CA) *		CORD	CORD Dance Research Annual (New York, NY) *
BGs	Bühnengenossenschaft (Hamburg, West Germany) * +		COS	Central Opera Service Bulletin (New York, NY) +
BiT	Biblioteca Teatrale (Rome, Italy) +		Costume	Costume: The Journal of the Costume Society (London, England)
BK	Bauten der Kultur (Berlin, East Germany) *			

CrAr	Critical Arts (Garhamstown, Republic of South Africa)	E	Essence (New York, NY)
CRB	Cahiers de la Compagnie Madeleine Renaud-Jean Louis Barrault (Paris, France) * +	E&AM	Entertainment and Arts Management (East Sussex, England) *
Crisis	Crisis (New York, NY)	Ebony	Ebony (Chicago, IL) *
CritQ	Critical Quarterly (Manchester, England)	ECrit	Essays in Criticism (Oxford, England)
CRT	La Cabra: Revista de Teatro (Mexico City, Mexico) +	EE	Estudis Escenics (Barcelona, Spain) *
		Egk	Engekikai (Tokyo, Japan) +
CS	Canada on Stage (Downsview, ON) +	EHR	Economic History Review (Birmingham, England)
CSAN	Costume Society of America Newsletter (Englishtown, NJ)	Eire	Eire-Ireland (St. Paul, MN) *
CTA	California Theatre Annual (Beverly Hills, CA) +	EIT	Escena: Informativo Teatral (San José, Costa Rica) +
CTL	Cahiers Théâtre Louvain (Louvain-la-Neuve, Belgium) +	Elet	Eletunk (Szombathely, Hungary)
		Ell	Elet es Irodalom (Budapest, Hungary)
CTR	Canadian Theatre Review (Downsview, ON) * +	ElPu	El Público (Madrid, Spain) *
CU	Le Cirque dans l'Univers (Paris, France)	ELR	English Literary Renaissance Journal (University of Massachusetts, MA)
Cue	Cue (Oxfordshire, England)		
CueM	Cue, The (Montclair State College, NJ) * +	EN	Equity News (New York, NY) +
CuPo	Cultural Post (Washington, DC)	Enact	Enact (Delhi, India) +
D	Dialogue: Canadian Philosophical Review/Revue Canadienne de Philosophie (Montréal, PQ)	Encore	Encore (New York, NY) +
		Entre	Entré (Solna, Sweden) * +
DA	Dance Australia (Keysborough, Australia)	EON	The Eugene O'Neill Newsletter (Boston, MA) * +
D&D	Dance and Dancers (Croyden, Surrey, England)	EquityJ	Equity Journal (London, England)
DB	Die Deutsche Bühne (Cologne, West Germany) +	ERT	Empirical Research in Theatre (Bowling Green, OH) * +
DBj	Deutsches Bühnenjahrbuch (Hamburg, West Germany) +		
		Estreno	Estreno (University of Cincinnati, OH)
DC	Dance in Canada (Toronto, ON)	ET	Essays in Theatre (Guelph, ON) * +
DCD	Documents del Centre Dramatic (Barcelona, Spain)	Fanf	Fanfare (Stratford, ON)
DGQ	Dramatists Guild Quarterly (New York, NY) * +	FDi	Film a Divadlo (Bratislava, Czechoslovakia)
DHS	Dix-huitième Siècle (Paris, France)	Fds	Freedomways (New York, NY) *
DialogW	Dialog (Warsaw, Poland)	FemR	Feminist Review (London, England)
DiN	Divadelni Noviny (Prague, Czechoslovakia) +	FiloK	Filologiai Kozlony (Budapest, Hungary)
Dm	Dancemagazine (New York, NY) *	FMa	The Fight Master (New York, NY)
DMC	Dramatics (Cincinnati, OH)	FO	Federal One (Fairfax, VA)
DnC	Dance Chronicle (New York, NY) +	Forras	Forras (Kecskemet, Hungary)
Dockt	Dockteater-eko (Grodinge, Sweden) +	FR	The French Review (Champaign, IL) *
Drama	Drama (London, England) * +	FrF	French Forum (Lexington, KY) *
DrammaR	Dramma (Rome, Italy) +	FS	French Studies (Cambridge, England)
DrammaT	Dramma: Il Mensile dello Spettacolo (Turin, Italy) +	FSM	Film, Szinház, Muzsika (Budapest, Hungary)
		Ftr	Figurentheater (Bochum, West Germany) +
Dress	Dress (Englishtown, NJ)	Gambit	Gambit (London, England) +
DRJ	Dance Research Journal (New York, NY)	Gap	The Gap (Washington, DC)
DRs	Dance Research (London, England)	GaR	Georgia Review (University of Georgia, GA)
DSGM	Dokumenti Slovenskega Gledaliskega Muzeja (Yugoslavia) +	GdBA	Gazette des Beaux Arts (Paris, France) *
		GerSR	German Studies Review (Arizona State University, AZ) *
DSo	Dramatists Sourcebook (New York, NY) +		
DSS	Dix-septième Siècle (Paris, France) *	GQ	German Quarterly (Cherry Hill, NJ) *
DTh	Divadlo Theater (Czechoslovakia) +	GSTB	George Spelvin's Theatre Book (Newark, DE) +
Dtherapy	Dramatherapy (St. Albans, Hertfordshire, England)	HArts	Hispanic Arts (New York, NY)
DTi	Dancing Times (London, England)	Helik	Helikon (Budapest, Hungary)
DTJ	Dance Theatre Journal (London, England)	HgK	Higeki kigeki (Tokyo, Japan) +
DTN	Drama and Theatre Newsletter (London, England) +	HisSt	Historical Studies (University of Melbourne, Australia)

HJFTR	Historical Journal of Film, TV, Radio (Abingdon, Oxfordshire, England)	JSH	Journal of Social History (Pittsburgh, PA)
HP	High Performance (Los Angeles, CA)	JSSB	Journal of the Siam Society (Bangkok, Thailand)
Horis	Horisont (Tammerfors, Finland) *	JTV	Journal du Théâtre de la Ville (Paris, France) +
HSt	Hamlet Studies (New Delhi, India) +	JWCI	Journal of the Warburg & Courtauld Institutes (London, England) *
HTHD	Hungarian Theatre/Hungarian Drama (Budapest, Hungary) +	JWGT	Jahrbuch der Wiener Gesellschaft für Theaterforschung (Vienna, Austria)
HW	History Workshop (Henley-on-Thames, Oxon, England)	Kabuki	Kabuki (Tokyo, Japan) +
I	Indonesia (Ithaca, NY)	Kanava	Kanava (Helsinki, Finland) *
IÅ	Contemporary Approaches to Ibsen: Ibsenårboken/ Ibsen Yearbook (Oslo, Norway) * +	KAPM	Kassette: Almanach für Bühne, Podium und Manege (Berlin, East Germany)
IAS	Interscena/Acta Scaenographica (Prague, Czechoslovakia) +	KingP	King Pole: The U.K. Circus Journal (Harlow, Essex, England)
IdS	L'Information du Spectacle (Paris, France) +	KK	Kultura es Kozosseg (Budapest, Hungary)
IHoL	Irodalomtortenet: History of Literature (Budapest, Hungary)	KoJ	Korea Journal (Seoul, Korea) *
IHS	Irish Historical Studies (Dublin, Ireland)	Kortars	Kortars (Budapest, Hungary)
IK	Irodalomtudomany Kozlemenyek (Budapest Hungary)	Krit	Kritika (Budapest, Hungary)
		KSF	Korean Studies Forum (Seoul, Korea)
INC	Ibsen News & Comments (New York, NY) * +	KSGT	Kleine Schriften der Gesellschaft für Theatergeschichte (Berlin, West Germany) +
ITY	International Theatre Yearbook (Warsaw, Poland) +	KWN	Kurt Weill Newsletter (New York, NY)
IUR	Irish University Review (Dublin, Ireland) *	KZ	Kultura i Žyzn (Moscow, USSR)
IW	Ireland of the Welcomes (Dublin, Ireland) *	L&H	Literature and History (London, England) *
JAAS	Journal of the Association for Asian Studies (University of Michigan, MI)	LAQ	Livres et Auteurs Québecois (Montréal, PQ)
JAC	The Journal of American Culture (Bowling Green, OH) *	LATR	Latin American Theatre Review (University of Kansas, KS) +
JAML	Journal of Arts Management and Law (Washington, DC)	LDA	Lighting Design & Application (New York, NY) +
		LDM	Lighting Dimensions Magazine (New York, NY) * +
JASt	Journal of Asian Studies (Ann Arbor, MI)	LDrama	London Drama (London, England)
JBeckS	Journal of Beckett Studies (London, England) +	LDT	Letture Drammatiche (Turin, Italy)
JCSt	Journal of Caribbean Studies (Coral Gables, FL) *	LFQ	Literature/Film Quarterly (Salisbury, MD)
JCT	Jeu: Cahiers de Théâtre (Montréal, PQ) +	Library	Library (Oxford, England)
JdPC	Journal du Palais de Chaillot (Paris, France) +	Literatura	Literatura (Budapest, Hungary)
JDSh	Jahrbuch der Deutschen Shakespeare-Gesellschaft (Bochum, West Germany) * +	Live	Live (New York, NY)
		LPer	Literature in Performance (Lousiana State University, LA) * +
JDt	Journal of Dramatherapy (York, England)	LST	L'Avant Scène Théâtre (Paris, France) +
Jelenkor	Jelenkor (Pecs, Hungary)	LTI	London Theatre Index (London, England) +
JGG	Jahrbuch der Grillparzer-Gesellschaft (Vienna, Austria) *	LTR	London Theatre Record (London, England) +
		M	Marquee (Chicago, IL) * +
JGT	Journal du Grenier de Toulouse (Toulouse, France) +	Maksla	Maksla (Riga, Latvian SSR)
		MAL	Modern Austrian Literature (University of California, Riverside, CA)
JJIT	Journal of the Japanese Institute for Theatre Technology (Tokyo, Japan) +	MC&S	Media, Culture and Society (London, England)
JJS	Journal of Japanese Studies (Seattle, WA)	MD	Modern Drama (Toronto, ON) * +
JMH	Journal of Magic History (Toledo, OH)	MdVÖ	Mitteilungen der Vereinigung Österreichischer Bibliothekare (Vienna, Austria) *
JNZL	Journal of New Zealand Literature (Wellington, New Zealand)	MET	Medieval English Theatre (University of Lancaster, England) * +
JPC	Journal of Popular Culture (Bowling Green, OH) *	MfS	Meddelanden från Strindbergssällskapet (Stockholm, Sweden) * +
JRASM	Journal of the Royal Asiatic Society of Malaysia (Malaysia)	MHall	Music Hall (London, England) +

MHRADS	Modern Humanities Research Association Dissertation Series (London, England)
MimeJ	Mime Journal (Claremont, CA) * +
MLet	Music & Letters (Oxford, England)
MLR	Modern Language Review (London, England)
MMDN	Medieval Music-Drama News (Staunton, VA)
MN	Monumenta Nipponica (Tokyo, Japan)
MoD	Monthly Diary (Sydney, Australia) +
MP	Modern Philology (Chicago, IL)
MPI	Manadens Premiarer och Information (Sweden)
MRenD	Medieval and Renaissance Drama (New York, NY) +
MT	Material zum Theater (East Berlin, East Germany) +
Mud	Musikdramatik (Stockholm, Sweden) +
Muhely	Muhely (Gyor, Hungary)
MuK	Maske und Kothurn (Vienna, Austria) * +
MuQ	Musical Quarterly (New York, NY)
MV	Mozgo Vilag (Budapest, Hungary)
Napj	Napjaink (Miskolc, Hungary)
NCM	Nineteenth Century Music (University of California, Berkeley, CA)
NConL	Notes on Contemporary Literature (Carrollton, GA) *
NCPA	National Center for the Performing Arts Journal (Bombay, India)
NCTR	Nineteenth Century Theatre Research (University of Arizona, AZ) * +
NFT	News form the Finnish Theatre (Helsinki, Finland) * +
NIMBZ	Notate: Informations-und-Mitteilungsblatt des Brecht-Zentrums der DDR (Berlin, East Germany) + *
Nk	Nakopiiri (Helsinki, Finland)
NO	New Observations (New York, NY)
Ns	Nestroyana (Vienna, Austria) * +
NSEEDT	Newsnotes on Soviet & East European Drama & Theatre (New York, NY) +
NT	Nya Teatertidningen (Johanneshov, Sweden)
NTQ	New Theatre Quarterly (Cambridge, England) +
NTTJ	Nederlands Theatre-en-Televisie Jaarboek (Amsterdam, Netherlands)
Nvilag	Nagyvilag (Budapest, Hungary)
NWR	NeWest Review (Saskatoon, SK) +
NYO	New York Onstage (New York, NY) +
NYTCR	New York Theatre Critic's Review (New York, NY) * +
Ob	Obliques (Lyons, France)
OC	Opera Canada (Toronto, ON) * +
OCA	O'Casey Annual (London, England) * +
OJ	Opera Journal (University of Mississippi, MS) +
Oper	Oper (Zürich, Switzerland) +
Opera	Opera (London, England) * +
OperH	Oper heute (East Berlin, East Germany) +

OpN	Opera News (New York, NY) * +
Opw	Opernwelt (Seelze, West Germany) +
OQ	Opera Quarterly (University of North Carolina, NC) +
OSS	On-Stage Studies (Boulder, CO) +
OvA	Overture (New York, NY) +
Ovs	Overtures (Middlesex, England) +
PA	Présence Africaine (Paris, France) *
Pa&Pr	Past and Present (Oxford, England) *
PAC	Performing Arts in Canada (Toronto, ON) +
PAR	Performing Arts Resources (New York, NY) +
Part	Partenaires (Paris, France)
PArts	Performing Arts (Los Angeles, CA) * +
PaT	Pamietnik Teatralny (Wroclaw, Poland) +
PaV	Paraules al Vent (Barcelona, Spain) *
Pb	Playbill (New York, NY) +
Pe	Performance (South Croydon, England)
PeM	Pesti Musor (Budapest, Hungary)
PerAJ	Performing Arts Journal (New York, NY) * +
Pf	Platform (London, England) +
PFr	Présence Francophone (Quebéc, PQ)
PiP	Plays in Process (New York, NY) +
Pja	Pipirijaina (Madrid, Spain) +
Pl	Plays (London, England) +
Plays	Plays (Peking, China) +
PlPl	Plays and Players (Croydon, England) +
PM	Performance Magazine (London, England) *
PMLA	PMLA (New York, NY) *
Pnpa	Peuples noirs, peuples africains (Washington, DC) *
Podium	Podium (Rijswijk, Netherlands)
PQ	Philological Quarterly (University of Iowa, IA)
PQCS	Philippine Quarterly of Culture and Society (Cebu City, Philippines)
PrAc	Primer Acto (Madrid, Spain) *
Prof	Profile: The Newsletter of the New Zealand Association of Theatre Technicians (Ponsonby, Auckland, New Zealaeand)
Prolog	Prolog (Yugoslavia) +
PrTh	Pratiques Théâtrales (Montréal, PQ) +
PS	Passing Show (New York, NY) +
PTh	People's Theatre (Peking, China) +
PuJ	Puppetry Journal (Alexandria, VA) *
Pusp	Puppenspiel und Puppenspieler (Riehen, Switzerland) +
Pz	Proszenium (Zürich, Switzerland) +
PZBT	Podium: Zeitschrift für Bühnenbildner und Theatertechnik (Berlin, East Germany) +
QT	Quaderni di Teatro (Florence, Italy) * +
QTST	Quaderni del Teatro Stabile di Torino (Turin, Italy) +
Radius	Radius (Kent, England)
RAL	Research in African Literatures (Austin, TX) *
Raritan	Raritan (Rutgers University, NJ) *

RdA	La Revue de l'Art (Paris, France)
REEDN	Records of Early English Drama Newsletter (University of Toronto, ON) * +
RenD	Renaissance Drama (Northwestern University, Evanston, IL) +
REsT	Revista de Estudios de Teatro (Buenos Aires, Argentina) +
RHSTMC	Revue Roumaine d'Histoire de l'Art: Série Théâtre, Musique, Cinéma (Bucharest, Romania)
RHT	Revue d'Histoire du Théâtre (Paris, France) * +
RLC	Revue de Littérature Comparée (Paris, France)
RLtrs	Red Letters (London, England) *
RN	Rouge et Noir (Grenoble, France)
RORD	Research Opportunities in Renaissance Drama (University of Kansas, KS) * +
RRMT	Ridotto: Rassegna Mensile di Teatro (Rome, Italy) +
RSCNews	RSC Newsletter (Stratford-upon-Avon, Warwickshire, England)
RT	Revista de Teatro (Rio de Janiero, Brazil) +
S	Segismundo (Madrid, Spain) +
SAADYT	SAADYT Journal (Pretoria, Republic of South Africa) +
SAITT	SAITT Focus (Pretoria, Republic of South Africa) +
ScenaB	Scena (East Berlin, East Germany) +
ScenaM	Scena (Milan, Italy) +
ScenaN	Scena (Novisad, Yugoslavia) +
Scenaria	Scenaria (Johannesburg, Republic of South Africa) * +
Scenarium	Scenarium (Amsterdam, Netherlands) +
ScenaW	Scena (Warsaw, Poland) +
ScenoS	Scen och Salong (Stockholm, Sweden)
SchwT	Schweizer Theaterjahrbuch (Bonstetten, Switzerland)
Screen	Screen (London, England)
SCYPT	SCYPT Journal (London, England) *
SD	Simon's Directory (New York, NY)
SDi	Slovenské Divadlo (Bratislava, Czechoslovakia) +
SdO	Serra d'Or (Barcelona, Spain) *
SDS	Slovenské Divadlo V Sezone (Czechoslovakia) +
SEEA	Slavic & East European Arts (Stony Brook, NY)
SFN	Shakespeare on Film Newsletter (Garden City, NY) *
SFC	Samuel French Catalog (New York, NY) +
SFo	Szinháztechnikai Forum (Budapest, Hungary) +
Sg	Shingeki (Tokyo, Japan) +
SGT	Schriften der Gesellschaft für Theatergeschichte (Berlin, West Germany)
ShakS	Shakespeare Studies (New York, NY) +
ShakSN	Shakespeare Studies (Nashville, TN) +
Shavian	The Shavian (Essex, England) +
ShawR	Shaw: The Annual of Bernard Shaw Studies (Pennsylvania State University, PA) +

ShN	Shakespeare Newsletter (Evanston, IL) +
ShS	Shakespeare Survey (Cambridge, England) * +
Si	Sipario (Milan, Italy) +
SIBMAS	SIBMAS Congress Papers (London, England)
Sin	Sightline (London, England) +
Sis	Sightlines (New York, NY) *
SiSo	Sight and Sound (London, England)
SJW	Shakespeare Jahrbuch (Weimar, East Germany) * +
SMR	SourceMonthly: The Resource for Mimes, Clowns, Jugglers, and Puppeteers (New York, NY) +
SNJPA	Sangeet Natak: Journal of the Performing Arts (New Delhi, India) *
SobCh	Sobcota Chelovneta (Tbilisi, Georgian SSR) +
SocH	Social History (London, England)
Somo	Somogy (Kaposvar, Hungary)
SORev	The Sean O'Casey Review (New York, NY) +
SoTh	Southern Theatre (Greensboro, NC) +
SovBal	Soveckij Balet (Moscow, USSR) +
SovD	Sovremennaja Dramaturgija (Moscow, USSR) +
SovEC	Soveckaja Estrada i Cirk (Moscow, USSR) +
Spa	Shilpakala (Dacca, Bangladesh)
Spl	Der Spielplan (Braunschweig, West Germany) +
SQ	Shakespeare Quarterly (Washington, DC) * +
SSSS	Szene Schweiz/Scène Suisse/Scena Svizzera (Bonstetten, Switzerland) +
SSTJ	Secondary School Theater Journal (Washington, DC)
Staff	Staffrider (Johannesburg, Republic of South Africa)
Stage	The Stage (London, England) +
STD	Summer Theater Directory (Dorset, VT) +
STILB	STILB (Rome, Italy) +
STN	Scottish Theater News (Glasgow, Scotland) * +
StPh	Studies in Philology (Chapel Hill, NC)
STT	Sceničeskaja Technica i Technologija (Moscow, USSR) +
SuK	Suomen Kuvalehti (Helsinki, Finland) *
SwTS	Swedish Theater/Théâtre Suédois (Stockholm, Sweden) +
Sz	Szinház: Theatre, the Journal of the Institute of Theatrical Arts (Budapest, Hungary) +
Szene	Szene (Vienna, Austria) +
SzeneAT	Szene: Fachzeitschrift der DDR für Amateur-theater, -kabarett, -puppenspiel und -pantomime (Leipzig, East Germany) +
SzSz	Szinháztudomanyi Szemle (Budapest, Hungary)
TA	Theatre Annual (Akron, OH) +
Tabs	Tabs (Middlesex, England) +
Talent	Talent (New York, NY)
TArch	Teatro Archivio (Genoa, Italy) +
TArsb	Teaterårsboken (Solna, Sweden)
TAT	Theatre Annual (Tokyo, Japan) +
Tbuch	Theaterbuch (Munich, West Germany) +
TC	Theory/crit (University of Richmond, VA)
TCom	Theatre Communications (New York, NY) +

TD	Teaching Drama (Edinburgh, Scotland) +		TJ	Theatre Journal (Baltimore, MD) * +
TD&T	Theatre Design and Technology (New York, NY) * +		TJV	Teater Jaarboek voor Vlaanderen (Antwerp, Belgium) +
TDR	The Drama Review (Cambridge, MA) * +		Tk	Theaterwork (Mankato, MN) * +
TDS	Theater & Dramatic Studies (Ann Arbor, MI) +		Tka	Theatrika (Athens, Greece) +
Teat	Teatteri (Helsinki, Finland) * +		TkR	TamKang Review: A Quarterly of Comparative Studies between Chinese and Foreign Literatures (Taipei, Taiwan)
Teaterf	Teaterforum (Fagersta, Sweden) +			
TeatL	Teatr Lalek (Prague, Czechoslovakia) +			
TeatM	Teatraluri Moambe (Tbilisi, Georgian SSR) +		TMK	Teater, Musika, Kyno (Talin, Estonian SSR) +
Teatoro	Teatoro (Tokyo, Japan) +		TN	Theatre Notebook (London, England) * +
Teatras	Teatras (Vilnius, Lithuanian SSR) +		TNS	TNS Actualité (Théâtre National de Strasbourg, France) +
TeatrC	Teatro Contemporaneo (Rome, Italy) * +			
TeatrE	Teatro en España (Madrid, Spain) +		TO	Time Out (London, England)
TeatrM	Teatr (Moscow, USSR) +		Toneel	Toneel Teatral (Amsterdam, Netherlands) +
Teatro	Teatro (Athens, Greece) +		TP	Théâtre en Pologne (Warsaw, Poland) * +
TeatrS	Teatr (Sofia, Bulgaria) +		TQ	Theatre Quarterly (London, England) +
Teatrul	Teatrul (Bucharest,Romania) +		Tret	Treteaux (University of Pennsylvania, PA) +
TeatrW	Teatr (Warsaw, Poland) +		TT	Theatre Times (New York, NY) +
TeatZ	Teatralnaja Žyzn (Moscow, USSR)		TTT	Tenaz Talks Teatro (University of California, La Jolla, CA) +
TechB	Technical Briefs (New Haven, CT)			
TF	Teaterforum (University of Potchefstroom, Republic of South Africa) +		TU	Théâtre et Université (Nancy, France) +
			Tv	Teatervetenskap (Stockholm, Sweden) +
TGDR	Theatre in the GDR (Berlin, East Germany) +		TWNew	Tennessee Williams Review (Boston, MA) +
Tgoer	The Theatergoer (New York, NY) +		TY	Theatre Yearbook (Tokyo, Japan) +
TH	Theater Heute (Zürich, Switzerland) * +		TZ	Theater der Zeit (East Berlin, East Germany) * +
Th	Théâtre (Québec, PQ) +		Tzs	Theaterzeitschrift (West Berlin, West Germany) * +
THC	Theatre History in Canada (University of Toronto, ON) * +		UCrow	Upstart Crow (Martin, TN) +
ThCr	Theatre Crafts (New York, NY) * +		Ufa	Ufahamu: Journal of the African Activist Association (Los Angeles, CA) *
ThD	Theatre in Denmark (Copenhagen, Denmark) +			
TheatreS	Theatre Studies (Columbus, OH) * +		UjIras	Uj Iras (Budapest, Hungary)
Theatro	Theatro (Athens, Greece) +		USITT	USITT Newsletter (New York, NY) * +
Theatron	Theatron (Rome, Italy) +		UTeatr	Ukrainskij Teat'r (Kiev, Ukranian SSR)
ThIn	Theaterwissenschaftlicher Informationsdienst (Leipzig, East Germany) +		UZ	Unterhaltungskunst: Zeitschrift für Bühne, Podium und Manege (Berlin, East Germany)
			V	Valiverho (Finland) +
ThIr	Theatre Ireland (Queens, NY) +		Valo	Valosag (Budapest, Hungary)
ThM	Theater Magazine (New Haven, CT) * +		Vig	Vigilia (Budapest, Hungary)
ThNe	Theatre News (Washington, DC) * +		Vilag	Vilagszinház (Budapest, Hungary)
ThPa	Theatre Papers (Devon, England) +		VS	Victorian Studies (Bloomington, IN) *
ThPh	Theatrephile (London, England) +		VSov	V soveckom teat're (Moscow, USSR) +
ThPr	Theatre Profiles (New York, NY) +		VV	The Village Voice (New York, NY) *
ThPu	Theatre Public (Gennevilliers, France) +		WB	Weimarer Beiträge (Weimar, East Germany)
ThR	Theatre Research International (Oxford, England) * +		WCP	West Coast Plays (Berkeley, CA) +
			WIAL	Washington International Arts Letter (Washington, DC)
ThS	Theatre Survey (Albany, NY) * +			
THSt	Theatre History Studies (University of North Dakota, ND) * +		WJBS	Western Journal of Black Studies (Pullman, WA) *
			WLT	World Literature Today (University of Oklahoma) *
TI	Théâtre International (Paris, France) +		WPerf	Women & Performance (New York, NY)
TIB	Theatre Information Bulletin (New York, NY) +		YCT	Young Cinema & Theatre (Prague, Czechoslovakia) +
TID	Themes in Drama (New York, NY) * +			
Tisz	Tiszataj (Szeged, Hungary)		ZDi	Zahranicni Divadlo (Prague, Czechoslovakia) +

Photocomposition and printing services for this volume
of the International Bibliography of Theatre were
provided by Volt Information Sciences Inc.,
Garden City, New York.

Cover Design by Irving Brown